T0211776

Lecture Notes in Computer Science 11953

Tom Gedeon · Kok Wai Wong ·
Minho Lee (Eds.)

Neural Information Processing

26th International Conference, ICONIP 2019
Sydney, NSW, Australia, December 12–15, 2019
Proceedings, Part I

Editors
Tom Gedeon ⓘ
Australian National University
Canberra, ACT, Australia

Kok Wai Wong ⓘ
Murdoch University
Murdoch, WA, Australia

Minho Lee ⓘ
Kyungpook National University
Daegu, Korea (Republic of)

ISSN 0302-9743   ISSN 1611-3349   (electronic)
Lecture Notes in Computer Science
ISBN 978-3-030-36707-7   ISBN 978-3-030-36708-4   (eBook)
https://doi.org/10.1007/978-3-030-36708-4

LNCS Sublibrary: SL1 – Theoretical Computer Science and General Issues

This Springer imprint is published by the registered company Springer Nature Switzerland AG
The registered company address is: Gewerbestrasse 11, 6330 Cham, Switzerland

Preface

Welcome to the proceedings of the 26th International Conference on Neural Information Processing of the Asia-Pacific Neural Network Society (APNNS 2019), held in Sydney during December 12–15, 2019.

The mission of the Asia-Pacific Neural Network Society is to promote active interactions among researchers, scientists, and industry professionals who are working in Neural Networks and related fields in the Asia-Pacific region. APNNS had Governing Board Members from 13 countries/regions – Australia, China, Hong Kong, India, Japan, Malaysia, New Zealand, Singapore, South Korea, Qatar, Taiwan, Thailand, and Turkey. The society's flagship annual conference is the International Conference of Neural Information Processing (ICONIP).

The three-volume set of LNCS 11953–11955 includes 177 papers from 645 submission, and represents an acceptance rate of 27.4%, reflecting the increasingly high quality of research in Neural Networks and related areas in the Asia-Pacific.

The conference had three main themes, "Theory and Algorithms," "Computational and Cognitive Neurosciences," and "Human Centred Computing and Applications." The three volumes are organized in topical sections which were also the names of the 20-minute presentation sessions at the conference. The topics were Adversarial Networks and Learning; Convolutional Neural Networks; Deep Neural Networks; Feature Learning and Representation; Human Centred Computing; Hybrid Models; Artificial Intelligence and Cybersecurity; Image Processing by Neural Techniques; Learning from Incomplete Data; Model Compression and Optimisation; Neural Learning Models; Neural Network Applications; Social Network Computing; Semantic and Graph Based Approaches; Spiking Neuron and Related Models; Text Computing Using Neural Techniques; Time-Series and Related Models; and Unsupervised Neural Models.

Thanks very much in particular to the reviewers who devoted their time to our rigorous peer-review process. Their insightful reviews and timely feedback ensured the high quality of the papers accepted for publication. Finally, thank you to all the authors of papers, presenters, and participants at the conference. Your support and engagement made it all worthwhile.

October 2019

Tom Gedeon
Kok Wai Wong
Minho Lee

Organization

Program Chairs

Tom Gedeon   The Australian National University, Australia
Kok Wai Wong   Murdoch University, Australia
Minho Lee   Kyungpook National University, South Korea

Program Committee

Hussein Abbass	UNSW Canberra, Australia
Hosni Adil Imad Eddine	Beijing Institute of Technology, China
Shotaro Akaho	AIST, Japan
Alaa Al-Kaysi	University of Technology, Iraq
Bradley Alexander	The University of Adelaide, Australia
Georgios Alexandridis	National Technical University of Athens, Greece
Usman Ali	Shanghai Jiao Tong University, China
Ahmad Ali	Shanghai Jiao Tong University, China
Abdulrahman Altahhan	Leeds Beckett University, UK
Muhamad Erza Aminanto	NICT, Japan
Ali Anaissi	The University of Sydney, Australia
Khairul Anam	University of Jember, Indonesia
Emel Arslan	Istanbul University, Turkey
Sunil Aryal	Deakin University, Australia
Arnulfo Azcarraga	De La Salle University, Philippines
Donglin Bai	Shanghai Jiao Tong University, China
Hongliang Bai	Beijing Faceall Technology Co., Ltd., China
Mehala Balamurali	The University of Sydney, Australia
Mohamad Hardyman Barawi	Universiti Malaysia Sarawak, Malaysia
Younès Bennani	Université Paris 13 and Université Sorbonne-Paris-Cité, France
Christoph Bergmeir	Monash University, Australia
Gui-Bin Bian	Chinese Academy of Sciences, China
Larbi Boubchir	University of Paris 8, France
Amel Bouzeghoub	Télécom SudParis, France
Congbo Cai	Xiamen University, China
Jian Cao	Shanghai Jiaotong University, China
Xiaocong Chen	University of New South Wales, Australia
Junsha Chen	UCAS, China
Junjie Chen	Inner Mongolia University, China
Qingcai Chen	Harbin Institute of Technology, Shenzhen, China

Gang Chen	Victoria University of Wellington, New Zealand
Junya Chen	Fudan University, USA
Dong Chen	Wuhan University, China
Weiyang Chen	Qilu University of Technology, China
Jianhui Chen	Institute of Neuroscience, Chinese Academy of Science, China
Girija Chetty	University of Canberra, Australia
Sung-Bae Cho	Yonsei University, South Korea
Chaikesh Chouragade	Indian Institute of Science, India
Tan Chuanqi	Tsinghua University, China
Yuk Chung	The University of Sydney, Australia
Younjin Chung	The Australian National University, Australia
Tao Dai	Tsinghua University, China
Yong Dai	Hunan University, China
Popescu Dan	UPB, Romania
V. Susheela Devi	Indian Institute of Science, India
Bettebghor Dimitri	Expleo Group, France
Hai Dong	RMIT University, Australia
Anan Du	University of Technology Sydney, Australia
Piotr Duda	Czestochowa University of Technology, Poland
Pratik Dutta	IIT Patna, India
Asif Ekbal	IIT Patna, India
Mounim El Yacoubi	Télécom SudParis, France
Haytham Elghazel	LIRIS Lab, France
Zhijie Fang	Chinese Academy of Sciences, China
Yuchun Fang	Shanghai University, China
Yong Feng	Chongqing University, China
Raul Fernandez Rojas	UNSW Canberra, Australia
Junjie Fu	Southeast University, China
Bogdan Gabrys	University of Technology Sydney, Australia
Junbin Gao	The University of Sydney, Australia
Guangwei Gao	Nanjing University of Posts and Telecommunications, China
Tom Gedeon	The Australian National University, Australia
Ashish Ghosh	Indian Statistical Institute, India
Heitor Murilo Gomes	The University of Waikato, New Zealand
Iqbal Gondal	Federation University, Australia
Yuri Gordienko	National Technical University of Ukraine, Ukraine
Raju Gottumukkala	University of Louisiana at Lafayette, USA
Jianping Gou	Jiangsu University, China
Xiaodong Gu	Fudan University, China
Joachim Gudmundsson	The University of Sydney, Australia
Xian Guo	Nankai University, China
Jun Guo	East China Normal University, China
Katsuyuki Hagiwara	Mie University, Japan
Sangchul Hahn	Handong Global University, South Korea

Ali Haidar   University of New South Wales, Australia
Rim Haidar   The University of Sydney, Australia
Fayçal Hamdi   CEDRIC-CNAM Paris, France
Maissa Hamouda   SETIT, Tunisia
Jiqing Han   Harbin Institute of Technology, China
Chansu Han   National Institute of Information and Communications
                                Technology, Japan
Tao Han   Hubei Normal University, China
Jean Benoit Heroux   IBM Research - Tokyo, Japan
Hansika Hewamalage   Monash University, Australia
Md. Zakir Hossain   Murdoch University, Australia
Zexi Hu   The University of Sydney, Australia
Shaohan Hu   Tsinghua University, China
Xiyuan Hu   Chinese Academy of Sciences, China
Gang Hu   Ant Financial Services Group, China
Xinyi Hu   State Key Laboratory of Mathematical Engineering
                                and Advanced Computing, China
Han Hu   Tsinghua University, China
Yue Huang   Xiamen University, China
Shudong Huang   University of Electronic Science and Technology of China,
                                China
Kaizhu Huang   Xi'an Jiaotong-Liverpool University, China
Yanhong Huang   East China Normal University, China
Xiaolin Huang   Shanghai Jiao Tong University, China
Chaoran Huang   University of New South Wales, Australia
Shin-Ying Huang   Institute for Information Industry, Taiwan
Mohamed Ibm Khedher   IRT SystemX, France
Loretta Ichim   UPB, Romania
David Andrei Iclanzan   Sapientia University, Romania
Keiichiro Inagaki   Chubu University, Japan
Radu Ionescu   University of Bucharest, Romania
Masatoshi Ishii   IBM Research - Tokyo, Japan
Masumi Ishikawa   Kyushu Institute of Technology, Japan
Megumi Ito   IBM Research - Tokyo, Japan
Yi Ji   Soochow University, China
Sun Jinguang   Liaoning Technical University, China
Francois Jacquenet   University of Lyon, France
Seyed Mohammad Jafar   Deakin University, Australia
  Jalali
Zohaib Muhammad Jan   Central Queensland University, Australia
Yasir Jan   Murdoch University, Australia
Norbert Jankowski   Nicolaus Copernicus University, Poland
Sungmoon Jeong   Kyungpook National University, South Korea
Xiaoyan Jiang   Shanghai University of Engineering Science, China
Fei Jiang   Shanghai Jiao Tong University, China
Houda Jmila   Télécom SudParis, France

Mingyong Li	Donghua University, China
Chengcheng Li	Tianjin University, China
Xia Liang	University of Science and Technology, China
Alan Wee-Chung Liew	Griffith University, Australia
Chin-Teng Lin	UTS, Australia
Zheng Lin	Chinese Academy of Sciences, China
Yang Lin	The University of Sydney, Australia
Wei Liu	University of Technology Sydney, Australia
Jiayang Liu	Tsinghua University, China
Yunlong Liu	Xiamen University, China
Yi Liu	Zhejiang University of Technology, China
Ye Liu	Nanjing University of Posts and Telecommunications, China
Zhilei Liu	Tianjin University, China
Zheng Liu	Nanjing University of Posts and Telecommunications, China
Cheng Liu	City University of Hong Kong, Hong Kong, China
Linfeng Liu	Nanjing University of Posts and Telecommunications, China
Baoping Liu	IIE, China
Guiping Liu	Hetao College, China
Huan Liu	Xi'an Jiaotong University, China
Gongshen Liu	Shanghai Jiao Tong University, China
Zhi-Yong Liu	Institute of Automation, Chinese Academy of Science, China
Fan Liu	Beijing Ant Financial Services Information Service Co., Ltd., China
Zhi-Wei Liu	Huazhong University of Science and Technology, China
Chu Kiong Loo	University of Malaya, Malaysia
Xuequan Lu	Deakin University, Australia
Huimin Lu	Kyushu Institute of Technology, Japan
Biao Lu	Nankai University, China
Qun Lu	Yancheng Institute of Technology, China
Bao-Liang Lu	Shanghai Jiao Tong University, China
Shen Lu	The University of Sydney, Australia
Junyu Lu	University of Electronic Science and Technology of China, China
Zhengding Luo	Peking University, China
Yun Luo	Shanghai Jiao Tong University, China
Xiaoqing Lyu	Peking University, China
Kavitha MS	Hiroshima University, Japan
Wanli Ma	University of Canberra, Australia
Jinwen Ma	Peking University, China
Supriyo Mandal	Indian Institute of Technology Patna, India
Sukanya Manna	Santa Clara University, USA
Basarab Matei	University of Paris 13, France

Jimson Mathew	IIT Patna, India
Toshihiko Matsuka	Chiba University, Japan
Timothy McIntosh	La Trobe University, Australia
Philip Mehrgardt	The University of Sydney, Australia
Jingjie Mo	Chinese Academy of Sciences, China
Seyed Sahand Mohammadi Ziabari	Vrije Universiteit Amsterdam, The Netherlands
Rafiq Mohammed	Murdoch University, Australia
Bonaventure Molokwu	University of Windsor, Canada
Maram Monshi	The University of Sydney, Australia
Ajit Narayanan	Auckland University of Technology, New Zealand
Mehdi Neshat	The University of Adelaide, Australia
Aneta Neumann	The University of Adelaide, Australia
Frank Neumann	The University of Adelaide, Australia
Dang Nguyen	University of Canberra, Australia
Thanh Nguyen	Robert Gordon University, UK
Tien Dung Nguyen	University of Technology Sydney, Australia
Thi Thu Thuy Nguyen	Griffith University, Australia
Boda Ning	RMIT University, Australia
Roger Nkambou	UQAM, Canada
Akiyo Nomura	IBM Research - Tokyo, Japan
Anupiya Nugaliyadde	Murdoch University, Australia
Atsuya Okazaki	IBM Research, Japan
Jonathan Oliver	Trend Micro, Australia
Toshiaki Omori	Kobe University, Japan
Takashi Omori	Tamagawa University, Japan
Shih Yin Ooi	Multimedia University, Malaysia
Seiichi Ozawa	Kobe University, Japan
Huan Pan	Ningxia University, China
Paul Pang	Unitec Institute of Technology, New Zealand
Shuchao Pang	Macquarie University, Australia
Kitsuchart Pasupa	King Mongkut's Institute of Technology Ladkrabang, Thailand
Jagdish Patra	Swinburne University of Technology, Australia
Cuong Pham	Griffith University, Australia
Mukesh Prasad	University of Technology Sydney, Australia
Yu Qiao	Shanghai Jiao Tong University
Feno Heriniaina Rabevohitra	Chongqing University, China
Sutharshan Rajasegarar	Deakin University, Australia
Md Mashud Rana	CSIRO, Australia
Md Mamunur Rashid	Central Queensland University, Australia
Pengju Ren	Xi'an Jiaotong University, China
Rim Romdhane	Devoteam, France
Yi Rong	Wuhan University of Technology, China
Leszek Rutkowski	Częstochowa University of Technology, Poland

Xiaolian Wang	University of Chinese Academy of Sciences, China
Zeyuan Wang	The University of Sydney, Australia
Dong Wang	Hunan University, China
Qiufeng Wang	Xi'an Jiaotong-Liverpool University, China
Chen Wang	Institute of Automation, Chinese Academy of Sciences, China
Jue Wang	BIT, China
Xiaokang Wang	Beihang University, China
Zhenhua Wang	Zhejiang University of Technology, China
Zexian Wang	Shanghai Jiao Tong University, China
Lijie Wang	University of Macau, Macau, China
Ding Wang	Chinese Academy of Sciences, China
Peijun Wang	Anhui Normal University, China
Yaqing Wang	HKUST, China
Zheng Wang	Southwest University, China
Shuo Wang	Monash University and CSIRO, Australia
Shi-Lin Wang	Shanghai Jiaotong University, China
Yu-Kai Wang	University of Technology Sydney, Australia
Weiqun Wang	Institute of Automation, Chinese Academy of Sciences, China
Yoshikazu Washizawa	University of Electro-Communications, Japan
Chihiro Watanabe	NTT Communication Science Laboratories, Japan
Michael Watts	Auckland Institute of Studies, New Zealand
Yanling Wei	University of Leuven, Belgium
Hongxi Wei	Inner Mongolia University, China
Kok-Wai Wong	Murdoch University, Australia
Marcin Woüniak	Silesian University of Technology, Poland
Dongrui Wu	Huazhong University of Science and Technology, China
Huijun Wu	University of New South Wales, Australia
Fei Wu	Nanjing University of Posts and Telecommunications, China
Wei Wu	Inner Mongolia University, China
Weibin Wu	Chinese University of Hong Kong, Hong Kong, China
Guoqiang Xiao	Shanghai Jiao Tong University, China
Shi Xiaohua	Shanghai Jiao Tong University, China
Zhenchang Xing	The Australian National University, Australia
Jianhua Xu	Nanjing Normal University, China
Huali Xu	Inner Mongolia University, China
Peng Xu	Jiangnan University, China
Guoxia Xu	Hohai University, China
Jiaming Xu	Institute of Automation, Chinese Academy of Sciences, China
Qing Xu	Tianjin University, China
Li Xuewei	Tianjin University, China
Toshiyuki Yamane	IBM, Japan
Haiqin Yang	Hang Seng University of Hong Kong, Hong Kong, China

Bo Yang	University of Electronic Science and Technology of China, China
Wei Yang	University of Science and Technology of China, China
Xi Yang	Xi'an Jiaotong-Liverpool University, China
Chun Yang	University of Science and Technology Beijing, China
Deyin Yao	Guangdong University of Technology, China
Yinghua Yao	Southern University of Science and Technology, China
Yuan Yao	Tsinghua University, China
Lina Yao	University of New South Wales, Australia
Wenbin Yao	Beijing Key Laboratory of Intelligent Telecommunications Software and Multimedia, China
Xu-Cheng Yin	University of Science and Technology Beijing, China
Xiaohan Yu	Griffith University, Australia
Yong Yuan	Chinese Academy of Science, China
Ye Yuan	Southwest University, China
Yun-Hao Yuan	Yangzhou University, China
Xiaodong Yue	Shanghai University, China
Seid Miad Zandavi	The University of Sydney, Australia
Daren Zha	Chinese Academy of Sciences, China
Yan Zhang	Tianjin University, China
Xiao Zhang	Huazhong University of Science and Technology, China
Yifan Zhang	CSIRO, Australia
Wei Zhang	The University of Adelaide, Australia
Lin Zhang	Beijing Institute of Technology, China
Yifei Zhang	University of Chinese Academy of Sciences, China
Huisheng Zhang	Dalian Maritime University, China
Gaoyan Zhang	Tianjin University, China
Liming Zhang	University of Macau, Macau, China
Xiang Zhang	University of New South Wales, Australia
Yuren Zhang	ByteDance Ltd., China
Jianhua Zhang	Zhejiang University of Technology, China
Dalin Zhang	University of New South Wales, Australia
Bo Zhao	Beijing Normal University, China
Jing Zhao	East China Normal University, China
Baojiang Zhong	Soochow University, China
Guoqiang Zhong	Ocean University, China
Caiming Zhong	Ningbo University, China
Jinghui Zhong	South China University of Technology, China
Mingyang Zhong	Central Queensland University, Australia
Xinyu Zhou	Jiangxi Normal University, China
Jie Zhou	Shenzhen University, China
Yuanping Zhu	Tianjin Normal University, China
Lei Zhu	Lingnan Normal University, China
Chao Zhu	University of Science and Technology Beijing, China

Contents – Part I

Convolutional Neural Networks

Deep Neural Networks

Feature Learning and Representation

Human Centred Computing

Hybrid Models

Artificial Intelligence and Cybersecurity

Adversarial Networks and Learning

FH-GAN: Face Hallucination and Recognition Using Generative Adversarial Network

Bayram Bayramli[✉], Usman Ali, Te Qi, and Hongtao Lu

Shanghai Jiao Tong University, Shanghai, China
{bayram_bai,usmanali,qite1030,htlu}@sjtu.edu.cn

Abstract. There are many factors affecting visual face recognition, such as low resolution images, aging, illumination and pose variance, etc. One of the most important problem is low resolution face images which can result in bad performance on face recognition. The modern face hallucination models demonstrate reasonable performance to reconstruct high-resolution images from its corresponding low resolution images. However, they do not consider identity level information during hallucination which directly affects results of the recognition of low resolution faces. To address this issue, we propose a Face Hallucination Generative Adversarial Network (FH-GAN) which improves the quality of low resolution face images and accurately recognize those low quality images. Concretely, we make the following contributions: (1) we propose FH-GAN network, an end-to-end system, that improves both face hallucination and face recognition simultaneously. The novelty of this proposed network depends on incorporating identity information in a GAN-based face hallucination algorithm via combining a face recognition network for identity preserving. (2) We also propose a new face hallucination network, namely Dense Sparse Network (DSNet), which improves upon the state-of-art in face hallucination. (3) We demonstrate benefits of training the face recognition and GAN-based DSNet jointly by reporting good result on face hallucination and recognition.

Keywords: Low level vision · Super-resolution · Convolutional neural networks

1 Introduction

In recent years, super-resolution models [4,21] which produce high-resolution (HR) images from low-resolution (LR) images has progressed tremendously thanks to the deep learning techniques. Since it is an ill posed problem, LR input may correspond to many HR candidate images which may lead to losing identity information. Many existing works do not consider identity information while hallucinating LR face images, as a result they cannot produce HR faces similar to the real identity. On the other hand, the extensive use of surveillance systems and security cameras makes a challenging use case for face recognition in an environment where detected faces will be in low resolution. Although some face recognition methods [10,27] achieved satisfactory results, these algorithms cannot perform well on the low resolution images. Since LR face images may match with many HR candidates, this uncertainty may lead to distorted

© Springer Nature Switzerland AG 2019
T. Gedeon et al. (Eds.): ICONIP 2019, LNCS 11953, pp. 3–15, 2019.
https://doi.org/10.1007/978-3-030-36708-4_1

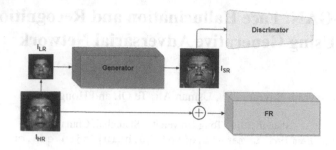

Fig. 1. The architecture of our proposed FH-GAN

identity information. Based on these facts, we can see that recovering identity information can improve low resolution face recognition systems and as well as performance
of face hallucination.

To address this issue, we aim to answer how to hallucinate low resolution face
images which can also improve face recognition performance. The goal of the proposed method, FH-GAN, is to enhance upon the visual quality and recognizability of
low resolution facial images by considering the identity information recovery during
super-resolution process. The architecture of FH-GAN is illustrated in Fig. 1.

Specifically, we propose an end-to-end FH-GAN network to hallucinate low resolution faces and preserve the identity information which is qualified for face recognition.
To achieve it, we introduce:

- a novel generator architecture for GAN which is sparsely aggregating the output
  of previous layers at any given depth. It offers fewer parameters, improves flow of
  information through the network and alleviates gradient vanishing problem.
- our GAN-based face hallucination utilizes both pixel level and feature level information as the supervisory signal to preserve the identity information.
- identity loss which measures identity difference between hallucinated HR image and
  ground truth HR images by using the face recognition.

2   Related Work

Single Image Super Resolution (SISR). SISR aims to reconstruct HR image from its
corresponding LR input. Many super resolution methods have been developed including
classical approaches [2,24] and deep learning based approaches [4,21]. In recent years,
huge improvements in deep learning methods have also resulted in significant enhancements in image super resolution techniques. The first work that utilized convolutional
networks for super-resolution purposes was SRCNN by Dogn et al. [3] to predict mapping between interpolated LR and HR pair images using three layers of convolutional
networks. This benchmark was further enhanced by expanding network depth. To further
improve the reconstruction accuracy [15] used more convolutional deep neural networks.
They both used interpolation of original LR images as an input which causes an increase
in computation and information loss. Later on, [21] used sub-pixel convolutional layer
to learn effective upscaling. Notably, we also use sub-pixel layer in our network. Later,
[5] exploited advantage of residual learning by using sub-pixel layer. However, all these

methods ignore to take advantages of information from each convolutional layer. Consequently, these methods lose useful hierarchical features from LR image. [23] introduced the basic dense block from DenseNet [6] to learn hierarchical features but the problem with this method is that feature maps aggregated by dense skip connections are not fully exploited. To solve these issues, we propose sparsely aggregated skip connection blocks in our generator network (DSNet) to concatenate features at different levels.

Face Hallucination. Image SR methods can be applied to all kind of images which do not incorporate face-specific information. Generally, face hallucination is a type of class-specific image SR. [31] introduced bichannel convolutional networks to hallucinate face images in the wild. [26] introduced two-step auto-encoder architecture to hallucinate unaligned, noisy low resolution face images. [12] also introduced identity information recovery in their proposed method. [25] proposed GAN-based method to super resolve very low resolution image without using perceptual loss. Except from [12] which is not using GAN-based generator, above mentioned methods do not consider identity information in hallucination process which is vital for recognition and visual quality. In our method, we used perceptual loss to achieve more realistic results and identity loss to incorporate with face recognition model to facilitate identity space by utilizing advanced GAN method. Our experiments demonstrate indistinguishable visual quality images and improve the performance of low resolution face recognition.

Face Recognition. The low-resolution face recognition task is a subset of the face recognition. There are many useful application scenarios for this task such as security cameras and surveillance systems. In this scenario, face images are captured in the wild from cameras with a large standoff. Some state-of-art techniques [10, 27] has already achieved an accuracy over 99%. However, those algorithms can only deal effectively on faces with large region of interest. Therefore, when resolution drops, the performance of these algorithms drops respectively. [32] proposed a relationship-learning-based SR between the high-resolution image space and the LR image space. [30] showed the problem of very low resolution recognition cases through deep learning based architecture.

This is one of the main motivations in our work. We employed the face recognition model of [10]. ArcFace model provides excellent performance on face verification on high resolution images as shown in [10]. In our paper, ArcFace is trained specifically to preserve identity of low resolution face image as well as to enhance the face image quality while hallucinating. As a result, one of our contributions is to demonstrate that a face recognition model when incorporated and trained end-to-end with a super resolution network can still give high accuracy on low resolution face images.

3 Method

In this section, we will first describe the proposed architecture including three connected networks and their loss functions: the first network is a super-resolution network which is also used as a generator, Densely connected Sparse Blocks network (DSNet), used to super-resolve LR face images to HR face images. The second one is an adversarial network used to distinguish super-resolved images from HR correspond. The third

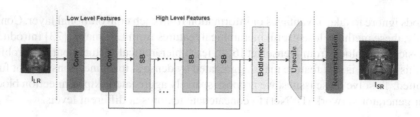

Fig. 2. The architecture of our proposed super-resolution network, DSNet.

network is Face Recognition for identity preserving on the hallucinated facial images. In the end we will describe our identity loss. During evaluation time, the discriminator is not used. In general, we call our algorithm FH-GAN, shown in Fig. 1

3.1 Face Hallucination Network

Notably, we propose an architecture that aims to learn end-to-end mapping function between low-resolution facial image I_{LR} and it's corresponding high-resolution facial images I_{HR}. As shown in Fig. 2, Dense Sparse network (DSNet) is mainly composed of four parts: low level feature extractor (LLFE), sparely aggregated CNN blocks for learning high level features (SparseBlock - SpB), upscaling layer for increasing the resolution size and a reconstruction layer for generating the HR output.

LLFE. We denote I_{LR} and I_{SR} as the input and output of DSNet. Specifically, we use two convolutional layers, from now on we call Conv, to extract shallow level features. The first Conv layer extracts features from LR input

$$y_0 = F_{LLFE_0}(I_{LR}), \tag{1}$$

where $F_{LLFE_0}(\cdot)$ denotes the convolution operation and y_0 is the output of first low level feature extractor. The output of (1) will be the input of second Conv layer

$$y_1 = F_{LLFE_1}(y_0), \tag{2}$$

where $F_{LLFE_1}(\cdot)$ denotes the second low level feature extractor convolution operation and y_1 is the output of respective layer.

Sparse Blocks (SpB). After applying LLFE layers to learn low level features, (2) is used as input to Sparse Blocks for learning high-level features. The sparse block structure is inspired by sparse aggregation in convolutional networks, first proposed in [17]. In the structure of SparseNet [17] feature maps from previous layers are sparsely concatenated together rather than directly summed as in ResNets [13]. As shown in Fig. 3, each sparse block in our network consists of multiple layers, where each layer is a composition of a convolution followed by PReLu activation function. Within a sparse block, rather than concatenating features from all previous layers, the number of incoming links to a layer are reduced by aggregating the state of preceding layers at an exponential offsets; for example $i - 1, i - 2, i - 4, i - 8...$ layers will be concatenated as input for i-th layer. The output of l-th convolutional layer in SpB is computed as:

$$y_l = \sigma(W_l[y_{l-c^0}, y_{l-c^1}, y_{l-c^2}, ..., y_{l-c^k}]) \qquad (3)$$

where $[y_{l-c^0}, y_{l-c^1}, y_{l-c^2}, ..., y_{l-c^k}]$ refers to the concatenation of feature maps, W_l is the weights of the $l - th$ Conv layer and σ denotes the PReLU activation function. Bias term is omitted for simplicity. c is a positive integer and k is the largest non-negative integer such that $c^k \leq l$.

The main difference of SparseNet from DenseNet and ResNet is that the input to a particular layer is formed by aggregation of a subset of previous outputs. The power of short gradient paths is maintained in the Sparse Blocks. The importance of short paths is to enhance the flow of information thence alleviating the vanishing gradient problem. Moreover, altering the number of incoming links to be logarithmic, the sparse block architecture drastically reduce the number of parameters, thereby require less memory and computation cost to achieve high performance.

Multiple sparse blocks are joined together to constitute a high-level feature learner component. Each sparse block receives a concatenation of low-level features from (2) and all preceding sparse blocks as input via skip connections. This enables each sparse block to directly see low-level as well as high-level feature information for better reconstruction performance.

Bottleneck Layer. As described above, features from the previous SpB are introduced directly to the next SpB in a concatenation way. This yields a large sized input for the subsequent up-sampling layer, so it is essential to reduce the features size. It has been studied in [28] that a convolutinonal layer size of 1×1 kernel can be utilized as a bottleneck layer to diminish the size features map. To enhance model computational efficiency, we utilize bottleneck layer to diminish number of features before feeding them to upsampling layer. The number of feature maps is reduced to 128.

UpSampling and Reconstruction Layer. We use sub-pixel [21] to upscale the LR feature maps to HR feature maps. The ultimate Conv layer in the DSNet which has 3×3 kernel size and 3 channels is used for reconstruction.

Pixel and Perceptual Loss. Given a set of low resolution images I_{LR} and its corresponding high resolution images I_{HR} we minimize the Mean Squared Error (MSE) in image space which is named Pixel-wise loss:

$$l_{pixel} = \frac{1}{N} \sum_{i=1}^{N} ||I_{HR}^i - G(I_{LR})^i||^2 \qquad (4)$$

where $G(\cdot)$ represents the output of generator network and N is the batch size. Although, MSE loss achieves high PSNR values, it usually results in blurry and unrealistic images. To handle this, perceptual loss is proposed in [11] to achieve visually

good and sharper images. In perceptual loss, MSE is used in feature space of hallucinated image and its corresponding HR image. We extracted features of HR image and
hallucinated image from VGG-19 [22] to calculate the following loss:

$$l_{perceptual} = \frac{1}{N} \sum_{i=1}^{N} ||\phi(I_{HR}^i) - \phi(G(I_{LR})^i)||^2 \tag{5}$$

where ϕ denotes the feature maps obtained from the last convolutional layer of VGG-19
[22] and $G(I_{LR})^i$ is the $i-th$ super-resolved face image.

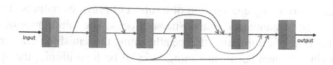

Fig. 3. The architecture of our Sparse Block.

3.2 Adversarial Network

In this subsection, we define adversarial loss to produce realistic super resolved face
images. The idea of using GAN [8] is straightforward: the goal of discriminator D is to
distinguish super-resolved images generated by generator G from the original images.
The generator G aims to generate realistic face images to fool D. In DSNet, we use
Wasserstein GAN (WGAN) [18] which is then improved in WGAN-GP [9]. The reason to use WGAN-GP is not to enhance the quality of hallucinated face images but to
stabilize and reduce the overall training time. As the generator of WGAN-GP we use
our super-resolution network and for the discriminator network we utilize the discriminator of DCGAN [1] without using batch normalization.

Adversarial Loss. We employ the WGAN-GP loss in our face hallucination network:

$$l_{WGAN} = \mathbb{E}_{\hat{I} \sim \mathbb{P}_g}[D(\hat{I})] - \mathbb{E}_{I \sim \mathbb{P}_r}[D(I^{HR})]$$
$$+ \lambda \mathbb{E}_{\hat{I} \sim \mathbb{P}_{\hat{I}}}[(||\nabla_{\hat{I}} D(\hat{I})||_2 - 1)^2], \tag{6}$$

where $\mathbb{P}_r$ is the input data distribution and $\mathbb{P}_g$ is the generator G distribution defined
by $\hat{I} = G(I_{LR})$ is obtained by uniformly sampling along straight lines between pairs of
samples from $\mathbb{P}_r$ and $\mathbb{P}_g$. λ is a penalty coefficient which we set to 10 in our experiments.

3.3 Face Recognition Network

Herein, we employ ArcFace as our face recognition model due to it is state-of-the-art
performance on identity representation. ArcFace is Resnet-like [13] CNN model and it
is trained by Additive Angular Margin Loss (ArcFace) which can effectively enhance

the discriminative power of feature embeddings. ArcFace loss function is modified traditional Softmax loss. The keypoint in ArcFace is that the classification boundary is maximized directly in the angular space. More details about ArcFace can be found here [10]. The loss function of ArcFace on a training image sample is represented as:

$$l_{ArcFace}(y_i) = -\frac{1}{N}\sum_{i=1}^{N} \log \frac{e^{s(cos(\theta_{y_i}+m))}}{e^{s(cos(\theta_{y_i}+m))}+\sum_{j=1,j\neq y_i}^{n} e^{scos\theta_j}} \tag{7}$$

where y_i is the i-th sample, N is a batch size. m is the hyperparameter of angular margin and s is the feature scale. Given a mini-batch, we compute the $l_{ArcFace}$ on concatenation of non-paired I_{HR} and $I_S R$ face images. We train ArcFace using the following loss:

$$l_{FR} = l_{ArcFace}(\{I_{HR}^i, I_{SR}^i\}) \tag{8}$$

where, { } denotes concatenation.

Identity Loss. Equations (4), (5), (6) have been used in general purpose super-resolution. Although, they do provide decent results for facial super-resolution, during the super-resolution process identity information is easy to be lost as these losses are not incorporating information related to face identity information. We have examined that when these losses are used alone identity details may be missing and the performance of the face recognition decreasing (see Table 3.)

To alleviate this issue, we propose to enforce facial identity consistency between the low and the high resolution face images via integrating face recognition network. Simply, we further use a constrain on the identity level. Therefore, for better preservation of human face identity of the super-resolved images, identity-wise feature representation with face recognition network used as supervisory signal. The identity loss described as follows:

$$l_{identity} = \frac{1}{N}\sum_{i=1}^{N} ||FR(I_{HR}^i) - FR(G(I_{LR})^i)||^2 \tag{9}$$

where $FR(I_{HR}^i)$ and $FR(G(I_{LR})^i)$ are the identity features extracted from the fully connected layer of our face recognition model. $G(I_{LR})^i$ represents i-th generated facial images.

3.4 Overall Training Loss

In summary, the overall losses used for training FH-GAN is weighted sum of the above loss functions:

$$l_{total} = \lambda_1 l_{pixel} + \lambda_2 l_{perceptual} + \lambda_3 l_{WGAN} + \lambda_4 l_{id} \tag{10}$$

where λ_1, λ_2, λ_3, λ_4 are the corresponding loss weights.

4   Experiments

In this section, we will describe our experimental results including datasets, implementation details and comparison with state-of-the-art!

4.1 Dataset and Preprocessing

To train our network, we randomly select 1.2M images from VGGFACE2 [19] dataset. We use two different datasets for for testing purposes. The first one is LFW [7] dataset used for testing both face verification and face hallucination performance in the wild. We use CFP [20] dataset to evaluate face verification. These two dataset are considered in unconstrained settings. Several state-of-the-art models such as, SRGAN [5], SRDenseNet [23], RDN [29] have been used to compare our approach. In order to conduct a fair comparison with other methods, training data is detected by MTCNN [14] and aligned to a canonical view of size 112×112.

4.2 Implementation Details

HR image size is cropped and aligned to 112×112 and LR input image was obtained by downsampling the HR images using bilinear kernel with a scale factor of $4\times$.

To train ArcFace, we employed ResNet34 [13] and set the embedding features to 512. We follow [13] to set the feature scale s to 64 and choose the angular margin m of ArcFace at 0.5 We set the batch size to 256 and the learning rate is started from 0.01 and divided by 10 after 15, 18 epochs. The training process has finished at 20 epoch.

To train GAN-based DSNet, we used 6 Sparse Blocks while each Sparse Block has 6 convolutional layers. In total, depth of face hallucination network size is 41 layers including, sparse blocks, low level feature extractors, bottleneck, upsampling and reconstitution layers. Within each Sparse Block, we used growth rate of 32. Low level feature extractors have filter size of 64 and size of all convolutional layers were set to 3×3 except bottleneck layer, where size is 1×1. The parametric rectified linear units (PReLu) was used as the activation function. All the networks were optimized using Adam. We used the mini batch size of 128. The learning rate is set to 1e-3 and gradually decreased to 1e-5. Training has finished at 56k iterations.

For end-to-end training of the FH-GAN, all networks (DSNet, discriminator and ArcFace) were training jointly for 4 epochs and learning rate of 1e-4. Face Hallucination model and ArchFace were trained using Adam [16] and SGD respectively. All models are implemented in PyTorch.

4.3 Discussions

Difference to SRDenseNet. First and foremost, SRDenseNet uses local dense connections from DenseNet [6] which concatenates all the outputs of previous layers thus results in over-burdening the model. However, concatenation allows every subsequent layer a clean view of all previous features but densely concatenation of features mean that a primary portion of the model is dedicated to process previously seen features. Consequently, it is hard for the model to make full use of dense skip connections and all the parameters. But, we exploit the local sparse connections into our proposed network inspired from SparseNets [17] which concatenated the features in an logarithmic manner rather than a linear manner. This property allows to utilize larger growth rate, which is filter size, and enlarge our model by using more layers. By using sparse aggregation topolopy in our proposed method, we reduce parameters size to half and achieve faster convergence compare to SRDenseNet. Another difference is that SRDenseNet only uses MSE loss but we use multiple losses to make the model robust to get better hallucinated face images. As a result, our method achieves better performance and generate visually pleasing face images.

Table 1. Effectiveness of identity loss on face verification performance.

Method	Identity loss	Accuracy
FH-GAN	x	99.00%
FH-GAN	✓	**99.14%**

Difference to SRGAN and RDN. In terms different choice of loss function, we mainly summarize differences of our method compared with SRGAN and RDN. RDN only uses L_1 loss function but in contrast we do not only use pixel level information but we also incorporate feature level information in our method. Using only pixel-wise loss will result in blurry images and lose identity information which is very crucial for face recognition. However, SRGAN utilizes feature level loss (perceptual loss) to make super-resolved images sharper but sometimes super-resolved images have some artifacts, such as white and red spots on the face. Additionally, SRGAN does not consider to preserve identity information in metric space which will lead to miss identity information and generate additional artifacts in super-resolved images. In our method, we use perceptual loss as well as identity loss to impose identity level constraint by jointly training face hallucination model with face recognition model.

4.4   Effectiveness of Identity Loss

Identity Loss. Table 1 shows the ablation investigation on the effects of identity loss. We find that, face recognition performance decreases when we do not include identity loss in our propose method. As we said earlier, because of ill-posed behavior of face hallucination methods it is easier to lose identity information during hallucination.

As shown in Table 1, we get better accuracy when we train FH-GAN jointly with face recognition network. We constrain identity level information by adding face recognition loss. The Identity level difference can be measured by robust face recognition model. The face recognition model with the identity-wise feature representation is used as supervisory signal which helps to preserve identity information and increase the performance of face verification.

4.5   Super Resolution Results

We compared the PSNR and SSIM results using the proposed method and using other networks and losses, including bilinear interpolation. As we discussed, because of robustness of our model, it achieves better results as compared to others. According to [5] the result of PSNR and SSIM are not indicative of visual quality. As it is shown

Fig. 4. From top to bottom: LR image, Bilinear interpolation, SRGAN [5], [29], [23], our results (×4 upscaling) and HR. Best viewed in color and zoomed in. (Color figure online)

in the Table 2, in terms of PSNR and SSIM best results are achived by Ours-pixel and FH-GAN respectively. As it also can be seen in Table 2, the PSNR value of RDN is better then our FH-GAN but Fig. 4 shows the sharper and more detailed facial images are obtained by our FH-GAN. Although bilinear method is fast and very light in super resolving but as shown in Fig. 4, the face images generated by this method are blurry and have artifacts. Face images generated by RDN and SRDenseNet result in over-smoothed images because of learning only pixel-wise information. Consequently, over-smoothed images do not contain face features completely. SRGAN faces contains white dots arti-facts in hallucinated face images. Because of effectiveness of our generator network and identity loss we comparatively obtain visually good images.

Table 2. PSNR and SSIM based Face Hallucination performance on LFW. Our-pixel: DSNet (Subsect. 3.1) trained with pixel loss of Eq. (4). Our-pixel-perceptual: DSNet (Subsect. 3.1) trained with pixel loss of Eq. (4) and perceptual loss of Eq. (5). The results are not indicative of visual quality.

Method	Bilinear	SR-GAN	SrDenseNet	RDN	Our-pixel	Our-pixel-feature	FH-GAN
PSNR	20.3	20.78	20.26	21.26	**21.35**	20.75	20.17
SSIM	0.76	0.77	0.79	0.81	0.79	0.80	**0.83**

4.6   Face Recognition Results

The proposed FH-GAN aims to recognize low resolution human faces. Therefore, for verifying the identity preserving capacity of different super-resoution models, face recognition on two benchmark datasets is studied by using the ArcFace extracted features of hallucinated face images.

Face Verification on Low Resolution LFW and CFP. As it can be seen on Table 3, the performance of RDN and SRDenseNet are flawed because of their weak specificity to identity preservation. Even though SRGAN has utilized perceptual loss but still their face verification accuracy is not good because they do not consider identity preservation in identity metric space. Our model achieves best results of face verification on two datasets which are very close to face verification results on HR face images. This is indicative of superiority of our face hallucination method.

Table 3. Face verification results on LFW and CFP dataset. FR stands for Face Recognition model. The results in this case, are indicative of visual quality. FR-Bilinear means this method super-resolved the face image using bilinear interpolation and run Face Recognition model on that and similarly other methods.

Method	FR-Bilinear	FR-SRGAN	FR-RDN	FR-SrDenseNet	FH-GAN	FR-HR images
LFW ACC	98.62%	99.03%	98.92%	98.87%	**99.16%**	99.47%
CFP ACC	92.3%	93.08%	92.6%	92.16%	**93.36%**	95.05%

5   Conclusion

This paper has answered how to hallucinate and recognize the faces simultaneously if the face image resolution is not sufficient enough. Specifically, we proposed FH-GAN: an end-to-end system for super-resolving face images and recognizing those images. Our method incorporates facial identity information in a newly proposed generator architecture using WGAN for face hallucination. The face recognition model aims to improve identity preservation and quality of hallucinated images. We show improvements on both face hallucination and low resolution face recognition.

Acknowledgements. This paper is supported by NSFC (No. 61772330, 61533012, 61876109), the pre-research project (no.61403120201), Shanghai authentication Key Lab. (2017XCWZK01), and Technology Committee the interdisciplinary Program of Shanghai Jiao Tong University (YG2019QNA09).

References

1. Radford, A., Luke Metz, S.C.: Unsupervised representation learning with deep convolutional generative adversarial networks. arXiv:1511.06434 (2015)
2. Chang, H., Yeung, D.Y., Xiong, Y.: Super-resolution through neighbor embedding. In: CVPR (2004)

3. Dong, C., Loy, C.C., He, K., Tang, X.: Learning a deep convolutional network for image super-resolution. In: Fleet, D., Pajdla, T., Schiele, B., Tuytelaars, T. (eds.) ECCV 2014, Part IV. LNCS, vol. 8692, pp. 184–199. Springer, Cham (2014). https://doi.org/10.1007/978-3-319-10593-2_13

4. Dong, C., Loy, C.C., He, K., Tang, X.: Image super-resolution using deep convolutional networks. IEEE Trans. Pattern Anal. Mach. Intell. (TPAMI) **38**, 295–307 (2016)

5. Christian, L., et al.: Photo-realistic single image super-resolution using a generative adversarial network. arXiv (2016)

6. Huang, G., Liu, Z., Weinberger, K.Q., van der Maaten, L.: Densely connected convolutional networks. In: ICCV (2017)

7. Huang, G.B., Ramesh, M., Berg, T., Learned-Miller, E.: Labeled faces in the wild: A database for studying face recognition in unconstrained environments. Technical report 07–49, University of Massachusetts, Amherst, October 2007

8. Goodfellow, I.J., et al.: Generative adversarial networks. In: NIPS (2014)

9. Gulrajani, I., Ahmed, F., Arjovsky, M., Dumoulin, V., Courville, A.C.: Improved training of wasserstein gans. CoRR, abs/1704.00028 (2017)

10. Deng, J., Guo, J., Xue, N., Zafeiriou, S.: Arcface: Additive angular margin loss for deep face recognition. arXiv preprint arXiv:1801.07698, (2018)

11. Johnson, J., Alahi, A., Fei-Fei, L.: Perceptual losses for real-time style transfer and super-resolution. In: Leibe, B., Matas, J., Sebe, N., Welling, M. (eds.) ECCV 2016, Part II. LNCS, vol. 9906, pp. 694–711. Springer, Cham (2016). https://doi.org/10.1007/978-3-319-46475-6_43

12. Zhang, K., et al.: Super-identity convolutional neural network for face hallucination. In: Ferrari, V., Hebert, M., Sminchisescu, C., Weiss, Y. (eds.) ECCV 2018, Part XI. LNCS, vol. 11215, pp. 196–211. Springer, Cham (2018). https://doi.org/10.1007/978-3-030-01252-6_12

13. He, K., Zhang, X., Ren, S., Sun, J.: Deep residual learning for image recognition. In: ICCV (2017)

14. Zhang, K., Zhang, Z., Li, Z., Qiao, Y.: Joint face detection and alignment using multitask cascaded convolutional networks. SPL **23**, 1499–1503 (2016)

15. Kim, J., Kwon Lee, J., Mu Lee, K.: Accurate image super-resolution using very deep convolutional networks. In: CVPR (2016)

16. Kingma, D., Ba., J.: Adam: a method for stochastic optimization. In: ICLR (2014)

17. Zhu, L., Deng, R., Maire, M., Deng, Z., Mori, G., Tan, P.: Sparsely aggregated convolutional networks. In: Ferrari, V., Hebert, M., Sminchisescu, C., Weiss, Y. (eds.) ECCV 2018, Part XII. LNCS, vol. 11216, pp. 192–208. Springer, Cham (2018). https://doi.org/10.1007/978-3-030-01258-8_12

18. Arjovsky, M., Soumith Chintala, L.B.: Wasserstein gan. arXiv:1701.07875 (2017)

19. Cao, Q., Shen, L., Xie, W., Parkhi, O.M., Zisserman, A.: Vggface2: a dataset for recognising faces across pose and age. In: FG (2018)

20. Sengupta, S., Chen, J.C., Castillo, C., Patel, V.M., Chellappa, R., Jacobs, D.W.: Frontal to profile face verification in the wild. In: WACV (2016)

21. Shi, W., et al.: Real-time single image and video super-resolution using an efficient sub-pixel convolutional neural network. In: CVPR (2016)

22. Simonyan, K., Zisserman, A.: Very deep convolutional networks for large-scale image recognition. arXiv (2014)

23. Tong, T., Li, G., Liu, X., Gao, Q.: Image super-resolution using dense skip connections. In: ICCV (2017)

24. Dong, W., Zhang, L., Shi, G., Wu, X.: Image deblurring and super-resolution by adaptive sparse domain selection and adaptive regularization. TIP **20**, 1838–1857 (2011)

25. Yu, X., Porikli, F.: Ultra-resolving face images by discriminative generative networks. In: Leibe, B., Matas, J., Sebe, N., Welling, M. (eds.) ECCV 2016, Part V. LNCS, vol. 9909, pp. 318–333. Springer, Cham (2016). https://doi.org/10.1007/978-3-319-46454-1_20
26. Xin Yu, F.P.: Hallucinating very low-resolution unaligned and noisy face images by transformative discriminative autoencoders. In: CVPR (2017)
27. Sun, Y., Wang, X., Tang, X.: Deep learning face representation from predicting 10,000 classes. In: CVPR (2014)
28. Tai, Y., Yang, J., Liu, X., Xu, C.: Memnet: a persistent memory network for image restoration. In: CVPR (2016)
29. Zhang, Y., Tian, Y., Kong, Y., Zhong, B., Fu, Y.: Residual dense network for image super-resolution. In: CVPR (2018)
30. Wang, Z., Chang, S., Yang, Y., Liu, D., Huang, T.S.: Studying very low resolution recognition using deep networks. In: IEEE CVPR (2016)
31. Zhou, E., Fan, H., Cao, Z., Jiang, Y., Yin, Q.: Learning face hallucination in the wild. In: AAAI (2015)
32. Zou, W., Yuen, P.C.: Very low resolution face recognition in parallel environment. IEEE Trans. Image Process. **3**, 4408–4410 (2012)

Adversarial Learning for Cross-Modal Retrieval with Wasserstein Distance

Qingrong Cheng, Youcai Zhang, and Xiaodong Gu$^{(\boxtimes)}$

Department of Electronic Engineering, Fudan University, Shanghai 200433, China
xdgu@fudan.edu.cn

Abstract. This paper presents a novel approach for cross-modal retrieval in an *Adversarial Learning* with *Wasserstein Distance* (ALWD) manner, which aims at learning aligned representation for various modalities in a GAN framework. The generator projects the image and the text features into an aligned representation space, while the discriminator ensures that the image and text features are not too far from each other, in a way which would maintain the semantic relation between the input samples. That is, ALWD reformulates the cross-modal retrieval as an image-text domain adaptation problem aiming at reducing domain discrepancy. To learn domain invariant representations, a domain critic network is adopted to estimate Wasserstein distance between different modal distributions and the feature extractor network is optimized to minimize the Wasserstein distance under an adversarial manner. Meanwhile, ALWD introduces additive margin softmax function to make sure the learned representations should also be discriminative in label prediction. Furthermore, a structure preservation constraint is imposed to keep local structure consistent during the learning process. Extensive comparison experiments on three widely used datasets demonstrate that ALWD outperforms the state-of-the-art cross-modal retrieval methods.

Keywords: Adversarial learning · Cross-modal retrieval · Wasserstein distance · Domain adaptation

1 Introduction

With the rapid development of the multi-media device, multi-modal data is produced in a shocked speed, especially in social network such as Facebook, Flickr and WeChat. Therefore, cross-modal analysis has become a focused research topic with the exponential explosion of multimedia data. The common application of cross-modal analysis is cross-modal retrieval, which aims to search the relevant instances among different modalities with a query. Beyond that, this technology can also be applied to many other applications. For example, cross-modal analysis techniques have made remarkable improvements in image caption [1] and text-to-image generation [2].

The main problem behind cross-modal retrieval is how to bridge the modal gap between image and text, and compute the similarities of instances across different modalities. Therefore, accomplishing cross-modal retrieval need map the different modal data to aligned representation space where the similarity can be calculated by

© Springer Nature Switzerland AG 2019
T. Gedeon et al. (Eds.): ICONIP 2019, LNCS 11953, pp. 16–29, 2019.
https://doi.org/10.1007/978-3-030-36708-4_2

Euclidean distance or other metrics. Many methods are proposed to learn aligned representations for cross modalities, such as traditional methods CCA [3], CFA [4]; DNN-based methods deep-SM [5], CMDN [6]; and adversarial learning based method, ACMR [7], MHTN [8].

Traditional methods [3, 4, 9, 10] in the literature aim at forming a shared representation space by optimizing projection matrices for different modal data. For example, Canonical Correlation Analysis (CCA) [3] and Cross-modal Factor Analysis (CFA) [4] try to maximize the correlation between different modalities by using linear projection. Zhai et al. propose Joint Representation Learning [9] that jointly embeds pairwise relations and semantic features in a graph based model. Wang et al. [10] propose a Joint Feature Selection and Subspace Learning (JFSSL) framework for cross-modal retrieval, which combines common subspace learning and coupled feature selection. However, these methods are unable to bridge the modal gap between multimodal data by using linear projection.

Deep neural networks (DNNs) show powerful ability in learning feature representation in many real applications, such as image classification [11], face recognition [12], object detection [13]. Therefore, another strand of cross-modal analysis methods convert different modalities to a shared representation space non-linearly by deep neural networks [5, 6, 14, 15]. Specifically, He et al. [14] construct a deep convolutional neural network to exploit the relations between image and text for fine-grained classification. Wei et al. [5] fulfill cross-modal retrieval by using deep visual features that are extracted from pretrained CNN model on large-scale dataset. Peng et al. [6] solve cross-modal retrieval problem by using stack strategy, which consists of two stages, the first stage learns the cross-media correlation and the second stage learns the shared representation. Huang et al. propose a transfer learning based Cross-modal Hybrid Transfer Network (CHTN) [15], which utilizes large-scale available dataset to promote cross-modal performance.

Recently, Generative Adversarial Networks (GANs) [16], proposed by Ian Goodfellow, have shown remarkable performance in generative tasks. The GANs consist of a discriminator and a generator that cooperate and compete in a minimax game until them achieve zero-sum game. Inspired by his work, employing adversarial learning mechanism becomes a competitive solution for domain adaption [17, 18]. Those methods formulate an adversarial objective to reduce domain discrepancy by introducing a domain discriminative network. For example, Xu et al. introduce adversarial metric learning mechanism [19] as additional regularization in cross-modal retrieval. However, the difficulties of training GAN also occurred in those methods, such as gradient vanishing or gradient explosion. In this situation, Wasserstein distance [20] is a reasonable way to stabilize training process, which can provide useful gradient to reduce the domain discrepancy. This distance measurement shows outstanding performance in representation learning for domain adaption [21].

Inspired by previous work, we propose a novel cross-domain retrieval approach by introducing Adversarial Learning with Wasserstein Distance (ALWD) in this paper. The key mechanism of the proposed method is adversarial learning, as illustrated in Fig. 1. We use neural network as a generator to map the extracted text features and image features to an aligned representation space, and introduce a critic network as a modality classifier to estimate the Wasserstein distance between embedded image features and text features.

Firstly, image and text feature are extracted by the widely used feature extraction model, such as CNN model and SIFT for image, and BoW and LDA for text. Then, the aligned representation is produced by a generator consisting of multi fully-connected layers. During adversarial learning process, the critic network with Wasserstein distance can provide effective gradient information to generator for optimizing. In training process, updating weight parameters of the generator and critic network is executed alternately until the network converges. In addition to this, we adopt two constraints 'Pair Similarity' and 'Category Distribution' to ensure structure preserved and label prediction consistent during adversarial leaning. In testing step, the retrieval results are returned by ranking the dot-product similarity of normalized aligned representations between query and gallery instances.

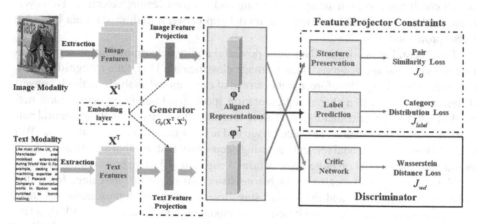

Fig. 1. The overall framework of the proposed adversarial learning method with Wasserstein Distance. The left blue block is the generator that project the image and text feature to aligned representation space, and the green block is the discriminator with Wasserstein distance that discriminate whether the projected image-text feature is close. The 'Pair Similarity' and 'Category Distribution' are two constraints for structure preservation and label prediction. (Color figure online)

Compared to existing work, the main contributions of our work are as follows.

(1) Wasserstein distance is adopted to guide cross-modal aligned representations learning under an adversarial manner.
(2) Additive margin softmax (AMSoftmax) [22] is introduced into cross-modal retrieval to learn more discriminative feature in label prediction.
(3) An efficient sampling based structure preservation constraint is utilized to keep the original inner structure relations.

The structure of this paper is organized as follows. The main details of the proposed method are shown in the next section. Empirical results shown in the third section verifies the effectiveness of our proposed approach. An overall conclusion are drawn in the last section.

2 The Proposed Method

2.1 Problem Formulation

Suppose text features and image features are extracted in a N pairs document corpus $(\mathbf{X^I}, \mathbf{X^T})$, where $\mathbf{X^I}$ denotes extracted feature set of images, and $\mathbf{X^T}$ is text feature vectors. The detail of encoding the text and image into feature vectors presents in the implement details section. More specifically, for the i-th text-image pair (x_i^P, x_i^P), $p \in \{I, T\}$, we use one-hot encoded feature vector $\mathbf{y} \in \mathbb{R}^{1 \times C}$ to represent the label information, where C is the number of categories. In order to measure similarity, we adopt neural networks to learn aligned representation as follows.

$$G_\theta : \left(x_i^I, x_j^T \right) \rightarrow \left(\varphi_i^I, \varphi_j^T \right), \tag{1}$$

where φ_i^P denotes the shared aligned feature space with the target dimension of d. Therefore, randomly given a specific aligned representation instance $\varphi(x_i^P) \in \mathbb{R}^{1 \times d}$, the top-k retrieval results are returned by computing the distance between neighboring instances directly.

2.2 Adversarial Learning with Wasserstein Distance

In our proposed adversarial learning approach, neural networks map the source domain data to the target domain. However, the evaluation whether the two different domains are matched or not is a challengeable problem. In order to solve this problem, we use empirical Wasserstein distance to measure the difference of two-domain feature representations by adversarial learning. Randomly given an original image-text instance pair (x_i^I, x_j^T), a new d-dimensional representation $(\varphi_i^I, \varphi_j^T)$ is generated by a generator. While the generator over all the image-text pairs, we obtain two new distributions φ^I and φ^T of image feature and text feature. For purpose of reducing the discrepancy between the generated image feature and text feature, we use a critic network to measure the Wasserstein distance of the mentioned two distributions (φ^I, φ^T).

Before introducing the adversarial learning mechanism of the proposed method, we introduce Wasserstein distance briefly. The Wasserstein Distance [20], also named Earth-Mover distance, is a kind of distance metric that measures the difference of two probability distribution. The widely used representation of the first Wasserstein distance between two probability distributions is written as follows.

$$W(P, Q) = \sup_{\|f\|_L \leq K} E_{x \sim P}[f(x)] - E_{x \sim Q}[f(x)], \tag{2}$$

where P, Q are two probability distributions and $\|f\|_L \leq K$ is K-Lipschitz constraint.

The Wasserstein distance between image-text aligned feature representations can be calculate as follows.

$$W(\varphi^I, \varphi^T) = \frac{1}{K} \sup_{\|f\|_L \leq K} E_{h \sim \varphi^I}[f(h)] - E_{h \sim \varphi^T}[f(h)], \tag{3}$$

where supremum is over all the K-Lipschitz functions. Considering a w-parameterized family of functions that are all obey K-Lipschitz constraint, we can approximate the empirical Wasserstein distance by maximizing the domain critic loss J_{wd} as following,

$$J_{wd} = W(\varphi^I, \varphi^T) = \max_{w \in W} E_{h \sim \varphi^I}[f_w(h)] - E_{h \sim \varphi^T}[f_w(h)]. \qquad (4)$$

Arjovsky et al. [20] propose a way of clipping the weighs of critic network in $[-c, c]$ to enforce the Lipschitz constraint. However, Gulrajani et al. [23] indicate that weight clipping cannot make the best use of fitting capacity of deep neural network. In practical situation, Gradient Penalty [23] is adopted in discriminator to satisfy K-Lipschitz constraint as follows.

$$J_{grad} = E[(\left\| \nabla_{\hat{h}} f_w(\hat{h}) \right\|_2 - 1)^2], \qquad (5)$$

where $\hat{h}$ are random points sampled from the straight line between the image-text feature pairs (φ^I, φ^T),

$$\hat{h} = \lambda \cdot \varphi^I + (1 - \lambda) \cdot \varphi^T. \qquad (6)$$

Finally, the Wasserstein distance satisfied with K-Lipschitz constraint can be estimated by solving the following problem.

$$max_{\theta_w}\{J_{wd} - \gamma \cdot J_{grad}\}, \qquad (7)$$

where γ is a balancing factor.

Because critic network is satisfied with K-Lipschitz constraint, the estimated Wasserstein distance is continuous and differentiable everywhere [20]. We train the critic network firstly and then optimize the generative network with fixed parameters of critic network. By minimizing the estimated Wasserstein distance, the generator can learn the aligned representation with discrepancy between image and text reduced. Therefore, the adversarial learning process for aligned representations can be presented by solving the minimax game

$$min_{\theta_g} max_{\theta_w}\{J_{wd} - \gamma \cdot J_{grad}\}, \qquad (8)$$

where γ is set 0 when updating the generator since the gradient penalty does not contribute to the optimization of generator. By iteratively optimizing, the objective of adversarial learning can finally learn the aligned representations when it reaches lowest Wasserstein distance.

Label Prediction with AMSoftmax. In the supervised learning process, the class distribution between the original data and the embedded feature should be consistent. To be specific, the original class-label distribution is definite, while the class label of latent vector generated from the generator need predict. In detail, we derive the class distribution prediction by formulating a logistic regression that adopts cross-entropy loss function. The formulation is defined as follows.

$$J_{label} = E\left[\sum_{k=1}^{C} \mathbf{y}_k \log(\hat{\mathbf{y}}_k)\right], \tag{9}$$

$$\hat{\mathbf{y}}_k = p(c = k|z) = AMSoftmax(\mathbf{Z}) = \frac{e^{s \cdot (\mathbf{z}_{y_i} - m_0)}}{e^{s \cdot (\mathbf{z}_{y_i} - m_0)} + \sum_{j=1, j \neq y_i}^{C} e^{s \cdot \mathbf{z}_j}}, \tag{10}$$

where, s denotes a scale factor setting as 30, m_0 is a constant setting as 0.35, and

$$\mathbf{z}_i = \cos \theta_i = \frac{W_i^T \varphi(\mathbf{x}_i^P)}{\|W_i\| \|\varphi(\mathbf{x}_i^P)\|} = W_i^T \varphi(\mathbf{x}_i^P) \in \Re^{1 \times C}, \tag{11}$$

is cosine similarity between weights and embedded feature representations, which is normalized. Besides, $\varphi(\mathbf{x}_i^P)$ is the representation generated from $\mathbf{x}_i^P$, W denotes the learnable parameters of the fully-connected layer. Compared to original softmax function

$$\tilde{\mathbf{y}}_k = p(c = k|z) = softmax(\mathbf{Z}) = \frac{e^{\mathbf{z}_k}}{\sum_{j=1}^{C} e^{\mathbf{z}_j}}, \tag{12}$$

the AMSoftmax [22] has fixed width decision margin which can both reduce the intra-class variation and separate different classes, while the original softmax function is typically good at optimizing the inter-class difference but not good at reducing the intra-class variation.

As mentioned above, we use one fully-connected layer with AMSoftmax function to get the categorical probability distribution in the prediction process. Finally, we need minimize the cross-entropy loss function among the entire input instances to optimize the parameters θ_c of the fully-connected layer.

Structure Preservation. The generator contributes to convert the two aforementioned image and text feature vector into aligned representations. In the original data, the inter-connection between two instances indicates the semantic information relationship among different texts and images. This assume that the embedded text and image aligned representations with similar semantic information are also clustered closely. Intuitively, we hope that the embedded representations produced by the generator should maintain close if they are close in original data. Therefore, the Pair Similarity constraint is proposed to ensure the embedded feature structure information keep consistent with original data feature.

Specifically, we consider a pair of instances (x_i^q, x_j^P) of m-size batch that are mini-batch data of k-nearest neighbor instances sampled from the original dataset. The generator maps the original data to embedded feature $(\varphi_i^I, \varphi_j^T)$. As the feature vector in our method is normalized, we use the dot-product distance to measure the similarity between the embedded feature vectors of the two instances, as defined following.

$$\langle \varphi(\mathbf{x}_i^P), \varphi(\mathbf{x}_j^q) \rangle = \varphi(\mathbf{x}_i^P)^T \varphi(\mathbf{x}_j^q), \tag{13}$$

where $\varphi(\mathbf{x}_i^p) \in \mathbb{R}^{1 \times d}$ is embedded representation generated by the generator. The pair similarity constraint is conducted by a logistic loss of pair similarity penalty as follows.

$$J_G = \mathrm{E}_{\left(\mathbf{x}_i^p, \mathbf{x}_j^q\right)}\left[\log\left(1 + e^{-\left\langle\varphi(\mathbf{x}_i^p), \varphi(\mathbf{x}_j^q)\right\rangle}\right)\right]. \tag{14}$$

2.3 Joint Multi-task Adversarial Learning Process

With weighted combination the three loss functions, eventually, we attain the objective function

$$min_{\theta_g, \theta_c}\{\lambda_1 J_G + \lambda_2 J_{label} + \lambda_3 max_{\theta_w}\{J_{wd} - \gamma \cdot J_{grad}\}\}, \tag{15}$$

where $\lambda_1, \lambda_2, \lambda_3$ are trade-off factors for different losses. The hyper-parameters $\lambda_1, \lambda_2, \lambda_3$ set as 0.1, 0.5, and 0.2, which are determined by experiments.

According to the training process of Generative Adversarial Networks (GAN), the parameters of generator, critic network and label prediction layer in our proposed method are updated alternatively. The details of adversarial learning process is presented in Algorithm 1.

Algorithm 1: Adversarial Learning with Wasserstein distance

Input: m : mini-batch size; α_1 : critic network learning rate; α_2 : learning rate for generative network and class prediction layer; $\lambda_1, \lambda_2, \lambda_3$: trade-off factors for different losses;

Output: weight parameters $\theta_g, \theta_w, \theta_c$ of generator network, critic network and prediction layer.

---

begin

Initialize each layers with random weights $\theta_g, \theta_w, \theta_c$.

  repeat

    Sample mini-batch size m pairs $\{x_i^I, x_j^T\}$ from dataset

    for each step t , fine-tuning the overall model

      • $\varphi_i^I \leftarrow G_\theta(x_i^I), \varphi_j^T \leftarrow G_\theta(x_j^T)$

      • Sample h as random points along straight lines between $(\varphi_i^I, \varphi_j^T)$ pairs

      • $\hat{h} \leftarrow \{\varphi_i^I, \varphi_j^T, h\}$

      • $\theta_w \leftarrow \theta_w + \alpha_1 \nabla_{\theta_w}[J_{wd}(\varphi_i^I, \varphi_j^T) - \gamma J_{grad}(\hat{h})]$

    end for

    $\theta_c \leftarrow \theta_c - \alpha_2 \nabla_{\theta_c} J_{label}(\varphi_i^I, \varphi_j^T)$

    $\theta_g \leftarrow \theta_g - \alpha_2 \nabla_{\theta_g}[\lambda_1 J_G(\varphi_i^I, \varphi_j^T) + \lambda_2 J_{label}(\varphi_i^I, \varphi_j^T) + \lambda_3 J_{wd}(\varphi_i^I, \varphi_j^T)]$

  end until $\theta_g, \theta_w, \theta_c$ converge

end

---

3 Experimental Results and Evaluation

3.1 Datasets and Features

In our work, we conduct extensive experiments on three well-known benchmark datasets, Wiki [24] datasets, NUS-WIDE [25] datasets and Pascal VOC 2007 [26] datasets, to evaluate the proposed method. Here we give a brief introduction for the three datasets. General statistic information of the three datasets in our experiments are illustrated in Table 1.

For a fair comparison, the dataset partition and feature extraction method of Wiki and Pascal VOC 2007 are same as [24, 27]. We apply the latent Dirichlet allocation model to convert the text into 10-dimensional feature vector for Wiki. The image features are extracted from the last fully connected layer of the VGG-19 model pretrained on the ImageNet datasets for both Wikipedia and Pascal VOC 2007. For NUS-WIDE dataset, shallow features are extracted by adopting SIFT-based bag of visual words for image and BoW for text. According to [28], we choose the 10 largest classes as the experiment dataset for NUS-WIDE dataset.

Table 1. Details of evaluated datasets.

Dataset	Category	Train/Test	Image feature	Text feature
Wikipedia	10	2,173/693	4,096d VGG	10d LDA
Pascal VOC 2007	20	2,808/2,841	4,096d VGG	399d Word Frequency
NUS-WIDE-top10	10	36,256/24,020	500d SIFT	1,000d BoW
MSCOCO	80	82,783/40,470	4,096d VGG19	500d BoW

3.2 Evaluation Metric

We adopt Mean Average Precision (MAP) [24] to evaluate the cross-modal retrieval task, which is computed as

$$AP = \frac{1}{R} \sum_{j=1}^{N} \frac{R_j}{j} \times rel_j, \tag{16}$$

where rel_j is denoted by $\{Good = 1; Bad = 0\}$ and R_j represents the number of the relevant results among the top-j results. Then, we calculate the average value of the AP on all the queries to obtain the qualitative MAP results. It is worth to be mentioned that we compute the Average Precision (AP) on all the results rather than top-50 results to calculate MAP.

3.3 Experimental Results and Comparison

In experiments, we conduct extensive experimental comparison with the state-of-the-art methods to evaluate the performance of our proposed method. The compared methods includes traditional models, CCA [3] and CFA [4], JFSSL [10], SCM [29], CMOMKS [30], CVH [31], STMH [32]; state-of-the-art DNN-based methods, Corr-AE [33], CMDN [6], deep-SM [5], ACMR [7], DCMH [34], MNiL [35].

Overall Comparison on Various Datasets. In the experiment of cross-modal retrieval on three datasets, Table 2 shows the details of comparison of the mentioned methods above. As we can see, our proposed method achieves the highest score in both image-text retrieval accuracy and text-image retrieval accuracy. Apart from considering all the retrieval results, some methods adopt top 50 retrieval results to calculate MAP score, such as ACMR [7] and Corr-AE [31]. Although the experimental details is different, we also compute the MAP score of top-50 results as presented in Table 3. It is shown that our proposed method also achieves competitive performance on the two datasets.

Next, we should make a concrete analysis of experimental difference. On Wiki dataset, we use shallow 10d LDA text feature rather than large-size feature, such as 3,000d BoW for both ACMR and MHTN. Meanwhile, we use shallow SIFT-based bag of visual words as image feature not 4,096d VGG deep feature and adopt 1000 dimensional BoW text feature for NUS-WIDE-top10 dataset. Except adopting different feature, our proposed method chooses the 10 largest categories about 58,276 text-image pairs as the experimental dataset rather than use NUS-WIDE-10k that just contains 10,000 pairs for experiment, such as ACMR and CHTN. Therefore, some methods outperform our proposed method in MAP score, such as MHTN [8], which adopts merely 1k image-text pairs as testing dataset. In addition, MHTN adopts transfer learning to relieve the problem of insufficient training, which introduces extra information from ImageNet dataset. Therefore, MHTN outperforms the results of ACMR and our proposed method.

Table 2. MAP (@all) scores of cross-modal retrieval performance compared with state-of-the-art methods.

Dataset	Methods	Image2txt	Txt2image	Avg.
Wiki	CFA	39.6	37.3	38.4
	JFSSL	42.8	39.6	41.2
	CMOMKS	43.4	38.8	41.1
	CCA	38.4	36.7	37.5
	Corr-AE	37.3	35.7	36.5
	CMDN	40.9	36.4	38.7
	Deep-SM	39.8	35.4	37.6
	ACMR	43.9	36.1	40.0
	ALWD	46.9	43.3	45.1

(continued)

Table 2. (*continued*)

Dataset	Methods	Image2txt	Txt2image	Avg.
PASCAL VOC 2007	CFA	65.0	66.0	65.5
	CCA	66.6	67.2	66.9
	CMOMKS	70.9	70.7	70.8
	SCM	73.3	73.7	73.5
	ALWD	80.3	81.2	80.7
NUS-WIDE-top10	CCA	28.9	28.5	28.7
	JFSSL	40.4	37.5	39.0
	Corr-AE	30.6	34.0	32.3
	Deep-SM	38.9	49.6	44.3
	ACMR	44.5	47.3	45.9
	CMDN	41.0	45.0	43.0
	ALWD	48.5	44.0	46.2

Nonetheless, our proposed method is also competitive and validated among up to 20 k gallery instances.

ACMR is the first attempt that introduces the adversarial learning mechanism in cross-modal retrieval task. Compared with ACMR, ACMR adopts traditional cross-entropy loss with softmax function for label prediction, while ALWD use AMSoftmax function for label prediction, which can improve the MAP score about one percentage point. ACMR projects the image and text feature to aligned representation by multi fully connected layers, the proposed method only adopts one embedding layer for common space learning. In addition, adversarial learning mechanism in ALWD contains Wasserstein distance for reducing domain discrepancy while traditional adversarial learning in applied in ACMR. Therefore, ALWD can achieve competitive experimental results on MAP@50 and outperforms ACMR on MAP(@all) metric.

Table 3. MAP (@50) scores on Wiki and NUS-WIDE-top10 datasets.

Dataset	Method	Image2txt	Txt2image	Avg.
Wiki	CFA	39.6	37.3	38.4
	ACMR	61.9	48.9	54.6
	ALWD	49.7	58.4	54.1
NUS-WIDE-top10	Corr-AE	36.6	41.7	39.2
	ACMR	54.4	53.8	54.1
	ALWD	49.7	58.9	54.3

In order to evaluate the effectiveness of the proposed method, we conduct experiment on the large-scale dataset MSCOCO, which contains 120,000 images and 5 sentences per image. Compared with other datasets, MSCOCO is more difficult for cross-modal retrieval because of massive amounts of image-text pairs and various kinds of categories. CVH, STMH, DCMH are hash-based method for cross-modal retrieval and MNiL is DNN-based method which combines LSTM and ResNet. The results in Table 4 indicates that ALWD can obtain competitive results on the large-scale dataset.

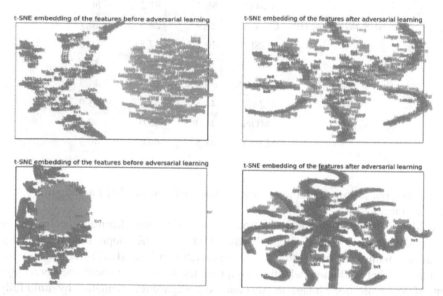

Fig. 2. Feature visualization using t-SNE on the Wikipedia dataset and Pascal VOC dataset. The first row is t-SNE embedding on Wikipedia dataset and the second row is t-SNE for Pascal VOC dataset. (Color figure online)

Table 4. MAP (@all) scores on large-scale MSCOCO dataset.

Dataset	Methods	Image2txt	Txt2image	Avg.
MSCOCO	CVH	40.2	38.8	39.5
	STMH	50.2	50.6	50.4
	SCM	49.8	49.2	49.6
	DCMH	51.1	52.7	51.9
	MNiL	35.6	35.0	37.1
	ALWD	52.4	52.2	52.3

Feature Visualization. For better Visualization, we draw the t-SNE visualization to visualize original feature distribution and the learned aligned representations distribution. Visualized results as shown in Fig. 2. The yellow points indicates the text instances, while the gray points denotes the image instances. The first row is visualization of Wikipedia dataset and the second row is visualization of Pascal VOC dataset. The left column is feature visualization before adversarial learning, the right column is learned feature representation after adversarial. The comparison of adversarial learning indicates the feature structure is well preserved, different categories are divided more clearly, and image-text features are in aligned representation rather than in two different domains.

4 Conclusion

This paper presents a novel adversarial learning with Wasserstein distance approach for cross-modal retrieval by mapping the text and image to aligned representations. Compared with the state-of-the-art cross-modal retrieval methods, MAP evaluation metric of our method indicates that the proposed method achieve competitive and validated performance on various datasets.

Acknowledgments. The first two authors contributed equally to this work. This work is supported by National Natural Science Foundation of China under grant 61771145 and grant 61371148.

References

1. Li, L., Tang, S., Deng, L., Zhang, Y., Tian, Q.: Image caption with global-local attention. In: AAAI, pp. 4133–4139, San Francisco (2017)
2. Zhang, H., et al.: Stackgan ++: realistic image synthesis with stacked generative adversarial networks. arXiv preprint arXiv:1710.10916 (2017)
3. Hardoon, D., Szedmak, S., Shawe-Taylor, J.: Canonical correlation analysis: an overview with application to learning methods. Neural Comput. 16(12), 2639–2664 (2004)
4. Li, D., Dimitrova, N., Li, M., Sethi, I.K.: Multimedia content processing through cross-modal association. In: Proceedings of ACM Multimedia, pp. 604–611 (2003)
5. Wei, Y., et al.: Cross-modal retrieval with CNN visual features: a new baseline. IEEE Trans. Cybern. 47(2), 449–460 (2017)
6. Peng, Y., Huang X., Qi J.: Cross-media shared representation by hierarchical learning with multiple deep networks. In: Proceedings of International Joint Conference on Artificial Intelligence, pp. 3846–3853, New York (2016)
7. Wang, B., Yang, Y., Xu, X., Hanjalic, A., Shen, H.T.: Adversarial cross-modal retrieval. In: Proceedings of ACM Multimedia, pp. 154–162 (2017)
8. Huang, X., Peng, Y., Yuan, M.: MHTN: modal-adversarial hybrid transfer network for cross-modal retrieval. IEEE Trans. Cybern. (2018)
9. Zhai, X., Peng, Y., Xiao, J.: Learning cross-media joint representation with sparse and semi-supervised regularization. IEEE Trans. Circuits Syst. Video Technol. 24(6), 965–978 (2014)
10. Wang, K., He, R., Wang, L., Wang, W., Tan, T.: Joint feature selection and subspace learning for cross-modal retrieval. IEEE Trans. Pattern Anal. Mach. Intell. 38(10), 2010–2023 (2015)

11. Ciresan, D.C., Meier, U., Masci, J., Maria Gambardella, L., Schmidhuber, J.: Flexible, high performance convolutional neural networks for image classification. In: Proceedings of International Joint Conference on Artificial Intelligence, vol.22, issue 1, p. 1237, (2011)

12. Zheng, L., Yang, Y., Hauptmann A.G.: Person re-identification: past, present and future. arXiv preprint arXiv:1610.02984 (2016)

13. Ren, S., He, K., Girshick, R., Sun, J.: Faster R-CNN: towards real-time object detection with region proposal networks. In: Advances in Neural Information Processing Systems, pp. 91–99 (2015)

14. He, X., Peng, Y.: Fine-grained image classification via combining vision. and language. In: Proceedings of IEEE Conference on Computer Vision and Pattern Recognition, pp. 5994–6022 (2017)

15. Huang, X., Peng, Y., Yuan, M.: Cross-modal Common Representation Learning by Hybrid Transfer Network. arXiv preprint arXiv:1706.00153 (2017)

16. Goodfellow, I., Pouget-Abadie, J., Mirza, M., et al.: Generative adversarial nets. In Advances in neural information processing systems, pp. 2672–2680 (2014)

17. Tzeng, E., Hoffman, J., Saenko, K., Darrell, T.: Adversarial discriminative domain adaptation. In: Proceedings of the IEEE Conference on Computer Vision and Pattern Recognition, pp. 7167–7176 (2017)

18. Ganin, Y., et al.: Domain-adversarial training of neural networks. J. Mach. Learn. Res. **17**(1), 2096–2030 (2016)

19. Xu, X., He, L., Lu, H., Gao, L., Ji, Y.: Deep adversarial metric learning for cross-modal retrieval. World Wide Web, pp. 1–16, (2018)

20. Arjovsky, M., Chintala, S., Bottou, L.: Wasserstein gan. arXiv preprint arXiv:1701.07875 (2017)

21. Shen, J., Qu, Y., Zhang, W., Yu, Y.: Wasserstein Distance Guided Representation Learning for Domain Adaptation. arXiv preprint arXiv:1707.01217 (2017)

22. Wang, F., Cheng, J., Liu, W., Liu, H.: Additive margin softmax for face verification. IEEE Signal Process. Lett. **25**(7), 926–930 (2018)

23. Gulrajani, I., Ahmed, F., Arjovsky, M., Dumoulin, V., Courville, A.C.: Improved training of Wasserstein GANs. In: Advances in Neural Information Processing Systems, pp. 5767–5777 (2017)

24. Rasiwasia, N., Costa Pereira, J., Coviello, E., Doyle, G., Lanckriet, G.R.G., Levy, R., et al.: A new approach to cross-modal multimedia. In: Proceeding of ACM International Conference on Multimedia, pp. 251–260 (2010)

25. Chua, T.-S., Tang, J., Hong, R., Li, H., Luo, Z., Zheng, Y.: NUS-WIDE: a real-world web image database from National University of Singapore. In: Proceedings of ACM International Conference on image and video retrieval, p. 48 (2009)

26. Hwang, S.J., Grauman, K.: Reading between the lines: object localization using implicit cues from image tags. IEEE Trans. Pattern Anal. Mach. Intell. **34**(6), 1145–1158 (2012)

27. Sharma, A., Kumar, A., Daume, H., Jacobs, D.W.: Generalized multiview analysis: a discriminative latent space. In: Proceeding of IEEE Conference on Computer Vision and Pattern Recognition, pp. 2160–2167 (2012)

28. Peng, Y., Huang, X., Zhao, Y.: An overview of cross-media retrieval: concepts, methodologies, benchmarks and challenges. IEEE Trans. Circuits Syst. Video Technol. **28**(9), 2372–2385 (2018)

29. Pereira, C., Coviello, E., Doyle, G., Rasiwasia, N., Lanckriet, G.R., Levy, R., et al.: On the role of correlation and abstraction in cross-modal multimedia retrieval. IEEE Trans. Pattern Anal. Mach. Intell. **36**(3), 521–535 (2013)

30. Wu, Y., Wang, S., Huang, Q.: Online asymmetric similarity learning for cross-modal retrieval. In Proceeding of IEEE Conference on Computer Vision and Pattern Recognition, pp. 4269–4278, (2017)

31. Kumar, S., Udupa, R.: Learning hash functions for cross-view similarity search. In: Twenty-Second International Joint Conference on Artificial Intelligence (2011)
32. Wang, D., Gao, X., Wang, X., He, L.. Semantic topic multimodal hashing for cross-media retrieval. In: Twenty-Fourth International Joint Conference on Artificial Intelligence (2015)
33. Feng, F., Wang, X., Li, R.: Cross-modal retrieval with correspondence auto-encoder. In: Proceeding on ACM International Conference on Multimedia, pp. 7–16 (2014)
34. Jiang, Q.Y., Li, W.J.: Deep cross-modal hashing. In: Proceedings of the IEEE Conference on Computer Vision and Pattern Recognition. pp. 3232–3240 (2017)
35. Zhang, L., Ma, B., Li, G., Huang, Q., Tian, Q.: Multi-networks joint learning for large-scale cross-modal retrieval. In: Proceedings of the 25th ACM International Conference on Multimedia, pp. 907–915 (2017)

Reducing the Subject Variability of EEG Signals with Adversarial Domain Generalization

Bo-Qun Ma[1], He Li[1], Wei-Long Zheng[2], and Bao-Liang Lu[1,3,4(✉)]

[1] Center for Brain-Like Computing and Machine Intelligence,
Department of Computer Science and Engineering, Shanghai Jiao Tong University,
800 Dong Chuan Road, Shanghai 200240, China
boqun.ma@hotmail.com, bllu@sjtu.edu.cn
[2] Department of Neurology, Massachusetts General Hospital,
Harvard Medical School, Boston, MA 02114, USA
[3] Key Laboratory of Shanghai Education Commission for Intelligent Interaction
and Cognition Engineering, Shanghai Jiao Tong University, Shanghai, China
[4] Brain Science and Technology Research Center, Shanghai Jiao Tong University,
800 Dong Chuan Road, Shanghai 200240, China

Abstract. A major obstacle in generalizing brain-computer interface (BCI) systems to previously unseen subjects is the subject variability of electroencephalography (EEG) signals. To deal with this problem, the existing methods focus on domain adaptation with subject-specific EEG data, which are expensive and time consuming to collect. In this paper, domain generalization methods are introduced to reduce the influence of subject variability in BCI systems without requiring any information from unseen subjects. We first modify a deep adversarial network for domain generalization and then propose a novel adversarial domain generalization framework, DResNet, in which domain information is utilized to learn two components of weights: unbiased weights that are common across subjects and biased weights that are subject-specific. Experimental results on two public EEG datasets indicate that our proposed methods can achieve a performance comparable to and more stable than that of the state-of-the-art domain adaptation method. In contrast to existing domain adaptation methods, our proposed domain generalization approach does not require any data from test subjects and can simultaneously generalize well to multiple test subjects.

Keywords: Brain-computer interface · EEG subject variability · Domain adaptation · Domain generalization · Domain residual network · Emotion recognition · Vigilance estimation

1 Introduction

Brain-Computer Interface (BCI) systems focus on establishing a direct pathway between a human brain and an external device. As a reliable indicator of the human brain state, electroencephalography (EEG) has become a widely used modality in BCI systems [11]. In the past decades, EEG-based BCI systems have attracted researchers' interest and have been successfully applied in many applications [2]. However, the individual differences across subjects in the functional and anatomical connectivity of the

© Springer Nature Switzerland AG 2019
T. Gedeon et al. (Eds.): ICONIP 2019, LNCS 11953, pp. 30–42, 2019.
https://doi.org/10.1007/978-3-030-36708-4_3

brain, head shapes, mental states, etc., have become a major obstacle for BCI applications in real-life scenarios [15]. Conventional models trained with data recorded from one subject often fail to perform robustly on other subjects. Consequently, to obtain an effective model for a new subject, data recollecting and model retraining are required; unfortunately, such efforts are rather time consuming and expensive in practice.

Previous studies tackling the issue of subject variability can be classified into two categories: subject-dependent models with calibration and subject-independent models with features that are robust across subjects, according to the available information from new subjects. Several researchers have explored subject-dependent approaches in which the pretrained models are tuned with a small amount of calibration data recorded from test subjects [12]. The calibration phase needs to be repeated whenever the models are extended to new subjects; thus, good performance is achieved, but at a high cost. On the other hand, subject-independent approaches focus on extracting features that are robust across subjects for model training, thus achieving the necessary generalization ability to provide accurate predictions for new subjects [19]. However, if the calibration phase is removed, the models usually suffer compromised performance.

In recent years, efforts have been made to deal with the subject variability problem in BCI systems using transfer learning methods [7]. In traditional machine learning methods, it is assumed that the training data and test data are sampled from the same distribution; however, this assumption usually cannot be satisfied for cross-subject BCI systems. In contrast, transfer learning methods consider domain differences [18], thus allowing models trained on source-domain data to generalize well to the target domain. From the perspective of transfer learning, subject variability can be regarded as a kind of domain shift, i.e., distribution differences across several related domains.

Two of the main branches of transfer learning, domain adaptation (DA) and domain generalization (DG), are capable of reducing the influence of subject variability. DA methods enhance the performance of a model on the target domain by eliminating the domain shift between the source and target domains. Thus, these methods require acquaintance with the target-domain data in the training phase in order to measure the discrepancy between the source and target domains. Researchers have successfully applied DA methods in BCI systems [23]. In particular, deep adversarial models such as Domain-Adversarial Neural Network (DANNs) have achieved significant performance improvements [3,9]. However, since each individual is regarded as an independent domain in EEG-based BCI systems, DA methods, which require data collection and model training for each target domain (subject), are high in cost and low in efficiency. In particular, information from target subjects is usually unavailable in real-world cross-subject EEG-based BCI applications. One solution to these problems is to apply DG methods in EEG-based BCI systems. DG methods can extract domain-invariant features by exploiting domain differences across multiple source subjects without the need to acquire any data from the target subjects [1]. Therefore, systems based on DG models can perform robustly when applied to previously unseen domains.

In this paper, we aim to reduce subject variability in BCI systems without requiring any information from target subjects through two kinds of DG approaches. As the first approach, we adopt the Domain-Invariant Component Analysis (DICA) and Scatter Component Analysis (SCA) methods, proposed in [16] and [5], respectively.

We further apply deep adversarial networks to this problem by extending Domain-Adversarial Neural Network (DANN) to the DG condition (DG-DANN). These methods can project features from different domains into a domain-invariant feature space in which the dissimilarity among the domains can be reduced. Thus, the models can achieve a better generalization ability on new subjects. As the second approach, we exploit the information from the training domains to learn a set of regulated model weights. Inspired by [8], we propose a novel framework called the Domain Residual Network (DResNet) in which the network weights are explicitly divided into biased weights that are exclusive to each individual domain and unbiased weights that are shared by all domains. In this way, we can obtain a robust model that achieves a better generalization ability for unknown domains by means of the unbiased weights. In experiments, we evaluated the performance of these approaches on two different BCI tasks. We chose SEED, a public emotion recognition EEG dataset, for the classification evaluation and SEED-VIG, a public multimodal vigilance estimation dataset, for the regression evaluation.

2   Methods

2.1   Domain Generalization Problem

Given the input space $\mathcal{X}$ and the output space $\mathcal{Y}$, $\mathbb{P}_{XY}$ is the set of all joint distributions on $\mathcal{X} \times \mathcal{Y}$. We assume that the $P_{XY}^i \in \mathbb{P}_{XY}$ is observed from a distribution P. A domain is denoted by $D_i = \{X_i, Y_i\}$, where the $\{X_i, Y_i\} = \{(x_1, y_1), (x_2, y_2), ..., (x_{n_i}, y_{n_i})\}$ are n_i samples from the joint distribution P_{XY}^i. Thus, we can obtain the marginal probability distribution P_X^i and the conditional probability distribution $P_{Y|X}^i$ of domain D_i. For k domains $D_1, D_2, ..., D_k$, we assume that the marginal distributions are different while the conditional distributions remain stable, i.e., $P_X^i \neq P_X^j, P_{Y|X}^i \approx P_{Y|X}^j$ when $i \neq j$. In the domain generalization problem, we aim to find a function $f : \mathcal{X} \rightarrow \mathcal{Y}$, which is insensitive to changes in P_X, to represent the conditional distribution $P_{Y|X}$. This f can be generalized to any previously unseen domain $D_t = \{X_t\}$, where the X_t are sampled from the unknown distribution P_X^t [1].

2.2   Domain-Invariant Component Analysis (DICA)

The goal of DICA is to find a low-dimensional feature subspace to minimize the discrepancy across domains [16]. Specifically, distributions can be represented as points in a reproducing kernel Hilbert space (RKHS) using the mean map function:

$$\mu : \mathbb{P}_x \rightarrow \mathcal{H} : P \mapsto \int_{\mathcal{X}} k(x, \cdot) dP(x) =: \mu_P. \tag{1}$$

Suppose that we have data samples $\mathcal{S} = \{S^i\}_{i=1}^k = \{(x_m^i, y_m^i)_{m=1}^{n_i}\}_{i=1}^k$ sampled from k domains. DICA can be applied to learn an orthogonal transformation $\mathcal{B}$ that minimizes the distributional variance across the different domains in a domain-invariant

m-dimensional feature subspace. The empirical distributional variance of $\mathcal{S}$ after the transformation can be calculated as:

$$\hat{\mathbb{V}}_{\mathcal{H}}(\mathcal{B}\mathcal{S}) = tr(B^T KLKB). \tag{2}$$

where K is the block kernel matrix, B is the coefficient matrix for transformation $\mathcal{B}$, and L is a coefficient matrix.

On the other hand, DICA also preserves the functional relationship P_{XY}^i. Given $\Phi_y = [\varphi(y_1), ..., \varphi(y_n)]$ and $U = \Phi_y^T \Phi_y$, the final objective function of DICA is

$$\max_{B \in \mathbb{R}^{n \times m}} \frac{\frac{1}{n} tr(B^T U(U + n\epsilon I_n)^{-1} K^2 B)}{tr(B^T KLKB + BKB)}, \tag{3}$$

where ϵ is a kernel regularizer. For further details, readers are referred to [16].

2.3 Scatter Component Analysis (SCA)

The goal of SCA is to find a projection B into an m-dimensional space where (1) the training domains are similar, (2) samples with the same label are similar, (3) samples with different labels are separated, and (4) the variance of the whole training set is maximized [5]. These constraints are quantified by means of a new concept called *scatter*:

$$\Psi_\phi(P) := \mathbb{E}_{x \sim P} \left[\|\mu_P - \phi(x)\|_{\mathcal{H}}^2 \right], \tag{4}$$

where $\| \cdot \|_{\mathcal{H}}$ is the norm on $\mathcal{H}$. The four constraints mentioned above are quantified in terms of the following four scatters.

Domain Scatter. Given N samples $\{x_1, ..., x_N\}$ from a k-domain distribution set $\{P_X^i\}_{i=1}^k$ on $\mathcal{X}$, the domain scatter is defined with $\overline{\mu} = \frac{1}{k} \sum_{i=1}^k \mu_{P_X^i}$ as

$$\Psi(\{\mu_{P_X^i}\}_{i=1}^k) = \frac{1}{k} \sum_{i=1}^k \|\overline{\mu} - \mu_{P_X^i}\|^2, \tag{5}$$

Class Scatter. Assuming the label set is $\{1, ..., C\}$, we denote the conditional distribution on $\mathcal{X}$ by $P_{X|t}^l = \frac{1}{k} \sum_{i=1}^k P_{XY}^i$, for $Y = t$. Therefore, the within-class scatter is defined as

$$\sum_{t=1}^C \Psi_{B \circ \phi}(\hat{P}_{X|y_t}^s) = Tr(B^T Q_s B) \tag{6}$$

and the between-class scatter is defined as

$$\Psi_B(\{\mu_{\hat{P}_{X|y_t}^l}\}_{t=1}^C) = Tr(B^T P_s B), \tag{7}$$

where $P_s = \sum_{t=1}^C n_t(m_t - \overline{m})(m_t - \overline{m})^T$ and $Q_s = \sum_{t=1}^C K_t H_t K_t^T$, with $m_k = \frac{1}{n_t} \sum_{n_t}^i k(\cdot, x_{it})$, $\overline{m} = \frac{1}{N} \sum_{i=1}^N k(\cdot, x_i)$, $[K_t]_{ij} = [k(x_{it}, x_{jt})]$, and $H_t = I_{n_t} - \frac{1}{n_t} 1_{n_t} 1_{n_t}^T$.

Total Scatter. Given the total domain as calculated from the mean of the k domain distributions, namely, $P_X = \frac{1}{k}\sum_{i=1}^{k} P_X^i$, the total scatter can be derived by using B and K as follows:

$$\Psi_{B \circ \phi}(\hat{P}_X) = Tr(\frac{1}{N} B^T KKB). \tag{8}$$

The objective function of SCA for the DG problem is expressed as

$$\underset{B \in \mathbb{R}^{N \times m}}{argmax} \frac{\Psi_{B \circ \phi}(\hat{P}_X) + \Psi(\{\mu_{P_{X|t=k}^l}\}_{k=1}^C)}{\Psi(\{\mu_{P_X^i}\}_{i=1}^k) + \sum_{t=1}^C \Psi_{B \circ \phi}(P_{X|t}^l)}, \tag{9}$$

where $\beta, \delta > 0$ are hyperparameters. The objective function can be further rewritten as

$$(\frac{(1-\beta)}{N} KK + \beta P)B^* = (\delta KLK + K + Q)B^* \Lambda, \tag{10}$$

where $B^* = [b_1, ..., b_m]$ represents the first m eigenvectors and $\Lambda = diag(\lambda_1, ..., \lambda_m)$ represents the corresponding eigenvalues. According to [5], the solution to Eq. (9) consists of the m leading eigenvectors in Eq. (10).

2.4 Domain Generalization in Domain-Adversarial Neural Network

DANN is a deep adversarial domain adaptation model [3]. In this paper, we extend the DANN concept to the case of domain generalization (DG-DANN).

Specifically, there are three components in DG-DANN. Initially, the feature extractor G_f learns a feature mapping $G_f(x; \theta_f) = f(W_f x + b_f)$, where features are projected with an activation function f and parameters $\theta_f = \{W_f, b_f\} \in \mathbb{R}^{d \times p} \times \mathbb{R}^d$. Secondly, the label predictor G_y predicts the labels of the inputs by means of a function $G_y(G_f(X); \theta_y)$. The prediction loss on a sample (x_i, y_i) for a prediction $\hat{y}_i$ is denoted by $L_y(\hat{y}_i, y_i)$. Finally, the domain classifier $G_d(G_f(X); \theta_d)$ judges the source domain of each input feature.

In DA problems, the inputs are sampled from one source domain and one target domain. Thus, the domain classifier G_d is a binary classifier. According to [3], the loss of a binary G_d is defined as

$$L_d(G_d(G_f(x_i)), d_i) = d_i \log \frac{1}{G_d(G_f(x_i))} + (1 - d_i) \log \frac{1}{1 - G_d(G_f(x_i))} \tag{11}$$

for a sample (x_i, y_i, d_i), where d_i is the binary domain label of sample x_i.

In DG problems, the training data consist of N samples (x_i, y_i, d_i) from k different known domains. Following the idea of finding a domain-invariant feature space, we generalize the domain classifier G_d to a k-class domain classifier. Therefore, the loss of G_d can be modified as follows:

$$L_d(G_d(G_f(x_i)), d_i) = \log \frac{1}{G_d(G_f(x_i))_{d_i}}. \tag{12}$$

For brevity, we denote the loss of G_d by $L_d(\hat{d}_i, d_i)$, where $\hat{d}_i$ is the domain prediction for x_i. Therefore, the loss function of the DG-DANN is formulated as

$$E(\theta_f, \theta_y, \theta_d) = \frac{1}{N} \sum_{i=1}^{N} L_y(\hat{y}_i, y_i) - \lambda \frac{1}{N} \sum_{i=1}^{N} L_d(\hat{d}_i, d_i). \tag{13}$$

During optimization, the DANN is trained through a special layer called Gradient Reversal Layer (GRL), which connects G_f and G_d. The GRL can be ignored during forward propagation and reverses the gradient passed backward from G_d to G_f [3]. The optimization can be integrated as follows:

$$
\begin{aligned}
(\hat{\theta}_f, \hat{\theta}_y) &= arg \min_{\theta_f, \theta_y} E(\theta_f, \theta_y, \hat{\theta}_d), \\
(\hat{\theta}_d) &= arg \max_{\theta_d} E(\hat{\theta}_f, \hat{\theta}_y, \theta_d).
\end{aligned}
\tag{14}
$$

2.5 Domain Residual Network (DResNet)

Another option for adversarial domain generalization is to utilize the domain information of the training domains to regulate the model parameters. We assume that each $P_{XY}^i \in \mathbb{P}_{XY}$ is a sample from a distribution $\boldsymbol{P}$. Thus, the domain shift can be regarded as the bias affecting observations of the true common space $\boldsymbol{P}$. According to [8], we can explicitly define the bias for each known training domain and approximate the parameters of the common space by undoing these biases. The common unbiased weights and the individual biased weights for each domain can be jointly trained to improve the generalization ability of the model. Based on the DG-DANN concept, we propose a novel model called the Domain Residual Network (DResNet) model.

In the DResNet model, the feature extractor G_f of the DG-DANN model is extended. The unbiased weights in D_f, which are shared by all domains, are denoted by θ_f^c. In contrast, the domain biases are explicitly described by biased weights $\theta_f^{\delta_i}$, which are unique for each known training domain D_i. Therefore, the parameters in each layer of G_f are formulated as follows:

$$\theta_f^i = \theta_f^c + \theta_f^{\delta_i} = \{W_f^c + W_f^{\delta_i}, b_f^c + b_f^{\delta_i}\}. \tag{15}$$

Hence, given an input x from domain i, each layer of the feature extractor G_f in DResNet is organized as follows:

$$G_f(x; \theta_f^i) = f\left((W_f^c x + b_f^c) + (W_f^{\delta_i} x + b_f^{\delta_i})\right). \tag{16}$$

During backward propagation, for a sample (x_i, y_i, d_i) from domain D_i, the gradient in G_f simultaneously updates only the domain-specific $\theta_f^{\delta_i}$ and the common θ_f^c. After optimization, only the label predictor G_y and the common part of the feature extractor G_f are activated. The DResNet architecture is described in Fig. 1.

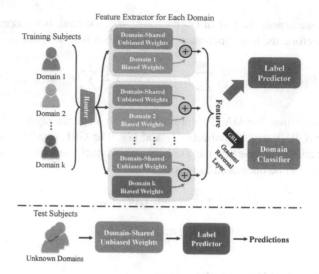

Fig. 1. The DResNet architecture. The colors for each domain in the training set indicate different domain shifts. For the test subjects, the domain shifts are unknown, and only the unbiased weights are activated. (Color figure online)

3 Experimental Setup

3.1 The SEED Dataset

The SEED[1] dataset is a public affective EEG dataset for emotion recognition. For SEED, 15 healthy subjects were recruited to be the participants in 3 sessions of experiments. Each experiment consisted of 15 trials of Chinese emotional film clips, which were selected in a preliminary study to induce 3 kinds of emotional states: positive, negative and neutral. The subjects were requested to exhibit their own corresponding emotions while watching the affective film clips. During the experiment, 62-electrode EEG signals were recorded in accordance with the international 10–20 system using an ESI Neuroscan system. The EEG signals were first downsampled to 200 Hz and then processed with a bandpass filter of 1–75 Hz. Finally, differential entropy (DE) features were extracted with nonoverlapping 1 s time windows in the five frequency bands (δ: 1–3 Hz, θ: 4–7 Hz, α: 8–13 Hz, β: 14–30 Hz, and γ: 31–50 Hz) [22]. For each subject, 3394 samples of 310-dimensional features were collected.

3.2 The SEED-VIG Dataset

The SEED-VIG[2] dataset is a public multimodal vigilance estimation dataset including EEG and electrooculography (EOG) signals [24]. Using SMI eye tracking glasses, the

---

[1] http://bcmi.sjtu.edu.cn/~seed/seed.html.

[2] http://bcmi.sjtu.edu.cn/~seed/seed-vig.html.

data were labeled with the percentage of eye closure (PERCLOS) [4], which is a continuous number varying from 0 (drowsy) to 1 (alert). For SEED-VIG, 23 subjects participated in the driving experiment, which was conducted in a simulation system consisting of a large screen, a real car and a corresponding software system. Forehead EEG and EOG signals were collected during the experiment with 4 electrodes using a ESI Neuroscan system. The data were first downsampled to 125 Hz and then segmented with nonoverlapping 8 s time windows. To separate the EEG and EOG components from the mixed signals, we applied the independent component analysis method. We extracted DE features from the EEG components in adjacent nonoverlapping 2 Hz bands within the range from 1 Hz to 50 Hz, thus obtaining 100-dimensional EEG features. On the other hand, the EOG components were processed with the Mexican hat wavelet transform to extract 36 eye movement features, including blinks, saccades and fixation. By concatenating the EEG and EOG features, 885 samples of 136-dimensional features were extracted for each subject.

3.3 Evaluation Details

To compare the DG and DA methods in terms of prediction accuracy, we adopted leave-one-subject-out cross-validation. In each iteration, for the DG methods, we selected one subject as the test domain and the others as the training domains, while for the DA methods, all training subjects were considered as one source domain and the test subject as the target domain. According to the total numbers of subjects, 15 and 23 iterations were performed for SEED and SEED-VIG, respectively.

For comparison in terms of generalization ability, we designed another setting called leave-multiple-random-subjects-out cross-validation, which also consisted of several iterations. In each iteration, one-third of the subjects were randomly selected as the test domains and the others as the training domains. To maintain the granularity of the evaluation, the numbers of iterations in this setting were the same as in the first setting.

For the kernel-based conventional methods, we adopted a linear kernel function. A subset of the samples in SEED (1000 samples for each subject) was randomly selected as the training data because of the practical infeasibility of loading all the training data due to the limited available memory and computation time. For dimensional reduction, the number of subspace dimensions was selected from the range of $\{10, 20, ..., 120\}$. For the shallow models, the parameters were randomly sought in the range $\{2^n | n \in \{-10, ..., 10\}\}$. For the deep models, we applied the Adam optimizer and a random search strategy. The search spaces for the learning rate and the hyperparameter λ for GRL were set to $\{2^n \times 10^{-4} | n \in [-10, 10]\}$ and $\{10^n | n \in [-5, -1]\}$, respectively.

4 Results and Discussion

4.1 Leave-one-subject-out Evaluation

Emotion Recognition. The performance of the DG methods for the classification task was evaluated on the SEED dataset. We adopted the leave-one-subject-out evaluation scheme and compared the DG methods with several conventional DA methods, such as

TCA [17] and TPT [20], as well as deep DA methods, such as DANN [3], DAN [10] and WGANDA [13]. Table 1 presents the mean accuracies (Avg) and standard deviations (Std). The baseline SVM method shows relatively poor performance due to the subject variability between the training subjects and the test subject. Among the shallow methods, TPT outperforms the other methods with an accuracy of 75.17% [23], while SCA and DICA achieve lower accuracy but more stable performance. Among the deep methods, WGANDA achieves the best performance with a mean accuracy of 87.07% [13]. In addition, the deep DG methods are also effective, exhibiting comparable performance, with DResNet being slightly better than DG-DANN. In general, the DA methods perform the best due to the additional information from the test subject. However, the DA methods require a large amount of unlabeled data from the test subjects to measure the discrepancy between the source and target domains. By comparison, the DG methods are capable of achieving the same level of prediction accuracy as the DA methods while requiring no data from the test subjects.

Table 1. Leave-one-subject-out evaluation results for classification on SEED

	Baseline	Domain adaptation methods					Domain generalization methods			
	SVM	TCA	TPT	DANN	DAN	WGAN-DA	DICA	SCA	DG-DANN	DResNet
Avg	0.5818	0.6400	0.7517	0.7919	0.8381	**0.8707**	0.6941	0.6633	0.8430	0.8530
Std	0.1385	0.1466	0.1283	0.1314	0.0856	**0.0714**	0.0779	0.1060	0.0832	0.0797

Vigilance Estimation. We also investigated the effectiveness of the proposed DG methods for the regression task on the SEED-VIG dataset. The Pearson correlation coefficient (PCC) and the root-mean-square error (RMSE) were calculated for the evaluation. Support vector regression (SVR) with a linear kernel was chosen as the baseline method for vigilance estimation. We compared the DG methods with two shallow DA methods, TCA [17] and GFK [6], as well as the latest deep DA methods, DANN [3] and ADDA [21]. As shown in Table 2, the DG models achieve stable performance that is comparable to that of the DA models; ADDA shows the best accuracy, with a PCC of 0.8442 and an RMSE of 0.1405 [9]. The performance of DResNet (PCC: 0.8440, RMSE: 0.1420) is quite similar to that of the state-of-the-art methods on the same task, even without additional data from the test subjects. In terms of performance stability, DResNet and DG-DANN outperform the other methods. These results are consistent with the conclusions summarized for the emotion recognition task.

Table 2. Leave-one-subject-out evaluation results for regression on SEED-VIG

		Baseline	Domain adaptation methods				Domain generalization methods		
		SVR	TCA	GFK	DANN	ADDA	DICA	DG-DANN	DResNet
PCC	Avg	0.7606	0.7786	0.7907	0.8402	**0.8442**	0.7733	0.8320	0.8440
	Std	0.2314	0.2152	0.1260	0.1535	0.1336	0.1382	0.1000	**0.0935**
RMSE	Avg	0.1689	0.1596	0.1910	0.1427	**0.1405**	0.2007	0.1470	0.1420
	Std	0.0673	0.0544	0.0636	0.0588	0.0514	0.0674	0.0444	**0.0402**

4.2 Leave-multiple-random-subjects-out Evaluation

As mentioned above, for practical BCI applications, DA methods become ineffective when extended to multiple unknown test subjects with only one well-trained model. To evaluate the generalization ability of the DG models under these circumstances, we adopted the leave-multiple-random-subjects-out cross-validation scheme. The experimental results of the baseline SVM method and all DG methods on SEED and SEED-VIG are shown in Tables 3 and 4, respectively. The performance drops slightly due to the decreased size of the training set. Here, DResNet outperforms the other methods on both datasets, achieving an accuracy improvement of 27.57% compared to the SVM model on SEED and a PCC improvement of 0.0887 compared to the baseline SVR model on SEED-VIG.

Table 3. Leave-multiple-random-subjects-out evaluation results on SEED

	SVM	DICA	SCA	DG-DANN	DResNet
Avg	0.5413	0.6435	0.6083	0.8146	**0.8170**
Std	0.1348	0.0896	**0.0505**	0.0788	0.0737

Table 4. Leave-multiple-random-subjects-out evaluation results on SEED-VIG

		SVR	DICA	DG-DANN	DResNet
PCC	Avg	0.7499	0.7719	0.8294	**0.8386**
	Std	0.1980	0.1841	0.1541	**0.1532**
RMSE	Avg	0.2068	0.1735	0.1604	**0.1569**
	Std	0.0587	**0.0468**	0.0782	0.0735

4.3 Discussion

To further investigate the effectiveness of the DG models on features extracted from different domains, we visualized the features from the leave-one-subject-out evaluation using the t-SNE algorithm [14]. The visualization results are depicted in Fig. 2. The first row shows the raw features from the datasets, while the second row shows the features extracted by the DResNet feature extractor. In the first column, the features are colored in accordance with their source subjects. In the second column, the blue points represent the training data, and the red points represent the test data. Finally, we visualize all features in accordance with their labels in the third column. The features from SEED are colored with red, blue and green, which represent positive, negative and neutral emotions, respectively. The features from SEED-VIG are colored in accordance with their PERCLOS labels, where the red points denote lower vigilance levels.

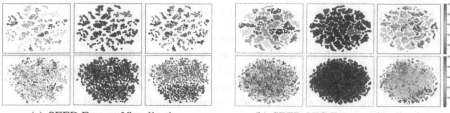

(a) SEED Feature Visualization   (b) SEED-VIG Feature Visualization

Fig. 2. Domain generalization feature visualization.

Firstly, the phenomenon of subject variability is clearly evident in the raw features in the first colume. After DResNet processing, the subject variability is significantly reduced since the data from different domains are evenly mixed together. In addition, the figures in the second colume demonstrate the reason for the remarkable performance of the DG models, since the training data and test data are aligned with similar distributions. Furthermore, it can be observed that the DResNet features vary smoothly with their labels in the third column and thus can be more easily predicted by the label predictor.

5   Conclusion

In this paper, we focused on reducing the influence of EEG subject variability on BCI systems for unknown subjects. DG methods were introduced to address this problem without needing to collect additional information from the test subjects. Following two different approaches to DG, we generalized the DANN concept and then proposed a novel framework called DResNet. In evaluations on classification and regression tasks, we compared our methods with other DA and DG methods on two public datasets related to different topics. We applied two different schemes for evaluation in terms of prediction accuracy and generalization ability. The experimental results show that the proposed methods are effective for solving the subject variability problem in cross-subject BCI systems for unknown users.

Acknowledgments. This work was supported in part by the grants from the National Key Research and Development Program of China (Grant No. 2017YFB1002501), the National Natural Science Foundation of China (Grant No. 61673266), and the Fundamental Research Funds for the Central Universities.

References

1. Blanchard, G., Lee, G., Scott, C.: Generalizing from several related classification tasks to a new unlabeled sample. In: Advances in Neural Information Processing Systems, pp. 2178–2186 (2011)
2. Brunner, C., et al.: BNCI horizon 2020: towards a roadmap for the BCI community. Brain-Comput. Interfaces **2**(1), 1–10 (2015)

3. Ganin, Y., et al.: Domain-adversarial training of neural networks. J. Mach. Learn. Res. **17**(1), 2030–2096 (2016)
4. Gao, X.Y., Zhang, Y.F., Zheng, W.L., Lu, B.L.: Evaluating driving fatigue detection algorithms using eye tracking glasses. In: 2015 7th International IEEE/EMBS Conference on Neural Engineering (NER), pp. 767–770. IEEE (2015)
5. Ghifary, M., Balduzzi, D., Kleijn, W.B., Zhang, M.: Scatter component analysis: a unified framework for domain adaptation and domain generalization. IEEE Trans. Pattern Anal. Mach. Intell. **39**(7), 1414–1430 (2017)
6. Gong, B., Shi, Y., Sha, F., Grauman, K.: Geodesic flow kernel for unsupervised domain adaptation. In: 2012 IEEE Conference on Computer Vision and Pattern Recognition (CVPR), pp. 2066–2073. IEEE (2012)
7. Jayaram, V., Alamgir, M., Altun, Y., Scholkopf, B., Grosse-Wentrup, M.: Transfer learning in brain-computer interfaces. IEEE Comput. Intell. Mag. **11**(1), 20–31 (2016)
8. Khosla, A., Zhou, T., Malisiewicz, T., Efros, A.A., Torralba, A.: Undoing the damage of dataset bias. In: Fitzgibbon, A., Lazebnik, S., Perona, P., Sato, Y., Schmid, C. (eds.) ECCV 2012, Part I. LNCS, vol. 7572, pp. 158–171. Springer, Heidelberg (2012). https://doi.org/10.1007/978-3-642-33718-5_12
9. Li, H., Zheng, W.L., Lu, B.L.: Multimodal vigilance estimation with adversarial domain adaptation networks. In: 2018 International Joint Conference on Neural Networks (IJCNN), pp. 1–6. IEEE (2018)
10. Long, M., Cao, Y., Wang, J., Jordan, M.: Learning transferable features with deep adaptation networks. In: the 32nd International Conference on Machine Learning, vol. 37, pp. 97–105. PMLR (2015)
11. Lotte, F., Congedo, M., Lécuyer, A., Lamarche, F., Arnaldi, B.: A review of classification algorithms for EEG-based brain-computer interfaces. J. Neural Eng. **4**(2), R1 (2007)
12. Lotte, F., Guan, C.: Learning from other subjects helps reducing brain-computer interface calibration time. In: IEEE International Conference on Acoustics Speech and Signal Processing (ICASSP), pp. 614–617 (2010)
13. Luo, Y., Zhang, S.-Y., Zheng, W.-L., Lu, B.-L.: WGAN domain adaptation for EEG-based emotion recognition. In: Cheng, L., Leung, A.C.S., Ozawa, S. (eds.) ICONIP 2018, Part V. LNCS, vol. 11305, pp. 275–286. Springer, Cham (2018). https://doi.org/10.1007/978-3-030-04221-9_25
14. Maaten, L.V.D., Hinton, G.: Visualizing data using t-SNE. J. Mach. Learn. Res. **9**, 2579–2605 (2008)
15. Morioka, H., et al.: Learning a common dictionary for subject-transfer decoding with resting calibration. NeuroImage **111**, 167–178 (2015)
16. Muandet, K., Balduzzi, D., Schölkopf, B.: Domain generalization via invariant feature representation. In: International Conference on Machine Learning, pp. 10–18 (2013)
17. Pan, S.J., Tsang, I.W., Kwok, J.T., Yang, Q.: Domain adaptation via transfer component analysis. IEEE Trans. Neural Netw. **22**(2), 199–210 (2011)
18. Pan, S.J., Yang, Q.: A survey on transfer learning. IEEE Trans. Knowl. Data Eng. **22**(10), 1345–1359 (2010)
19. Samek, W., Kawanabe, M., Müller, K.R.: Divergence-based framework for common spatial patterns algorithms. IEEE Rev. Biomed. Eng. **7**, 50–72 (2014)
20. Sanvineto, E., Zen, G., Ricci, E., Sebe, N.: We are not all equal: personalizing models for facial expression analysis with transductive parameter transfer. In: the 22nd ACM International Conference on Multimedia, pp. 357–366. ACM (2014)
21. Tzeng, E., Hoffman, J., Saenko, K., Darrell, T.: Adversarial discriminative domain adaptation. In: Proceedings of the IEEE Conference on Computer Vision and Pattern Recognition, pp. 7167–7176 (2017)

22. Zheng, W.L., Lu, B.L.: Investigating critical frequency bands and channels for EEG-based emotion recognition with deep neural networks. IEEE Trans. Auton. Mental Dev. **7**(3), 162–175 (2015)
23. Zheng, W.L., Lu, B.L.: Personalizing EEG-based affective models with transfer learning. In: The Twenty-Fifth International Joint Conference on Artificial Intelligence, pp. 2732–2738. AAAI Press (2016)
24. Zheng, W.L., Lu, B.L.: A multimodal approach to estimating vigilance using EEG and forehead EOG. J. Neural Eng. **14**(2), 026017 (2017)

Multi-view Image Generation by Cycle CVAE-GAN Networks

Zhichen Lai, Chenwei Tang, and Jiancheng Lv[✉]

College of Computer Science, Sichuan University,
Chengdu 610065, Sichuan, People's Republic of China
lvjiancheng@scu.edu.cn

Abstract. In this paper, we address the problem of multi-view image generation from a single view. To this end, we investigate Variational Auto-Encoder (VAE) and Generative Adversarial Network (GAN) as effective solutions to this problem. Inspired by CycleGAN playing an important role in image-to-image translation applications, we utilize the idea of cycle consistency to generate images in multi-view. With VAE and GAN as the basic components, we propose Cycle Conditional-VAE-GAN (Cycle CVAE-GAN) to tackle the problem within four steps. First, the source image with target-view condition and the target image are both mapped to the shared latent variable space by two encoders. Second, we sample a variable from the shared variable space as the input of a designed decoder for the low-resolution target image generation. Third, we repeat the previous two steps. It is worth mentioning that the inputs of those two encoders are the generated low-resolution target image with source-view condition and the source image. Then the reconstructed source image can contribute to the cycle consistency loss. Finally, a GAN framework with a dual-input U-Net generator and a patch discriminator are proposed to generate high-resolution and realistic target images. Experiments on the Multi-View Clothing (MVC) dataset demonstrate that the proposed method achieves better results than the state-of-the-art models.

Keywords: Multi-view image generation · Generative adversarial network · Variational auto-encoder · Cycle consistency loss

1 Introduction

In e-commerce websites, products are displayed in multiple views, e.g., front, back, left side and right side. Consumers can get comprehensive information of products from images in these views. Multi-view image generation from a single view gains interest in the research community, but it is far from being solved. Many existing approaches generate target images by constructing the latent 3D structure of the objects, which are only effective on rigid objects with simple textures [2,6,16]. Fortunately, the task of multi-view image generation from a single view belongs to the image translation applications [24]. And there are many deep learning based methods achieve significant performances in image translation tasks [5,26].

Recently, multi-view image generation from a single view has achieved tremendous improvements due to the prosperous progress of deep learning and the availability

© Springer Nature Switzerland AG 2019
T. Gedeon et al. (Eds.): ICONIP 2019, LNCS 11953, pp. 43–54, 2019.
https://doi.org/10.1007/978-3-030-36708-4_4

of generative models [14,23–25]. Variational Auto-Encoder (VAE) [7] and Generative Adversarial Network (GAN) [3], two generative models have become the mainstream models to generate multi-view images. VAE adopts variational inference and representation learning to learn a generative model [7]. However, VAE tends to generate blurry images with few details. Benefiting from the reactions of discriminator, GAN can generate images with richer details, but the diversity of generated samples is poor [1].

In this paper, we propose a deep learning based model, called Cycle CVAE-GAN, to generate multi-view images from a single view. We propose Cycle CVAE to generate the low-resolution multi-view images. It offers the ability to generate images with rich diversity. In addition, we propose the GAN of high-resolution multi-view generation, which fills the low-resolution multi-view images with richer details and correct textures. In general, the Cycle CVAE-GAN achieves the rich diversity, details, and correct textures at the same time. The proposed Cycle CVAE-GAN method includes four steps: (1) inputting the source image with target-view condition and the target image into the encoders respectively, and enforcing the outputs of the two encoders to obey the same distribution, (2) sampling variable from the shared latent variable space as the input of the decoder of the low-resolution multi-view generation, (3) using the generated low-resolution target image with source-view condition and the source image as the inputs and repeating the previous two steps, (4) generating the high-resolution target image by the proposed GAN framework with a dual-input U-Net generator and a patch discriminator.

The main contributions of our work can be summarized as follows:

– By introducing cycle consistency loss, we design a Cycle CVAE network for generating the low-resolution target image with rich diversity.
– We adopt a dual-input U-Net generator and a patch discriminator for the high-resolution multi-view generation from the low-resolution image, which is proved to be effective in image generation with rich details and correct textures.

2 Related Work

2.1 Image Generation

Image generation is one of the most fundamental problems in computer vision, which has been widely researched for decades. By the powerful capabilities of extracting image features, Convolution Neural Networks (CNNs) [9] have achieved great success in quality improvement of image generation. Moreover, recent advances on representation learning using deep neural networks nourish a series of deep generative models that enjoy joint generative modeling and representation learning through bayesian inference or adversarial training.

Yan et al. proposed a conditional image generation model called Attribute2Image, which models an image as a composite of foreground and background and extends the VAE with disentangled latent variables [22]. The proposal of Deep Recurrent Attentive Writer (DRAW) introduced the attention mechanism to VAE [4]. Since GAN was proposed by Goodfellow et al. [3], researchers have studied it vigorously. Pix2Pix, a conditional GAN, was proposed for image translation problems [5], which has been extended for generating high-resolution images [19]. The trainable loss function of discriminator makes GAN automatically adapt to the differences between the generated image and the real image in the target domain. After that, most image generation approaches are based on variant GANs.

2.2 View Synthesizing

Many efforts have been made to explicitly model the latent 3D structure of objects [2,6, 16]. However, the appealing results are guaranteed only when source images with multiple views are available. When the source images only have single view, the modeling work can hardly be accomplished due to the sparse input.

To this end, approaches based on mapping source pixels to corresponding pixels are proposed [14,23,25]. Zhou et al. proposed to synthesize novel views of the same object by learning appearance flows [25]. Yvain et al. explicitly utilized learned dense correspondences to predict the image in the middle view of a pair of source images [15]. Recently, inspired by [1], Zhao et al. proposed a cVAE-GAN model to generate multi-view images of clothing from a single-view image [24]. As we know, the products displayed in e-commerce websites should be with rich details. However, the above-mentioned methods are only effective on objects with simple textures and the images generated are blurry.

3   Model

Figures 1 and 2 show the overall architectures of the proposed low-resolution multi-view generation and the high-resolution multi-view generation. Here, we first introduce some notations and the problem definition. Let T and S denote the target image and the source image. C_{ST} and C_{TS} denote the target-view condition and the source-view condition. In addition, let g denote the low-resolution multi-view generation function. The formulation of the multi-view image generation from a single view is:

$$T = g(S, C_{ST}) \tag{1}$$

In order to generate high-quality multi-view images, the proposed Cycle CVAE-GAN consists of two generative phases. First, the Cycle CVAE is designed for generating the low-resolution target image T_{LR} from the source image S with target-view condition C_{ST}. The proposed Cycle CVAE learns two mapping $T = g(S, C_{ST})$ and $S = g(T, C_{TS})$, as well as enforces $S = g(g(S, C_{ST}), C_{TS})$ by introducing the cycle consistency loss. We also adopt a novel constraint loss to enforce the source image S with target-view condition C_{ST} and the target image T to be consistent in feature representation. Second, a GAN framework, composed of a dual-input U-Net generator and a patch discriminator, is proposed to generate the high-resolution target-view image T_{HR} from T_{LR}.

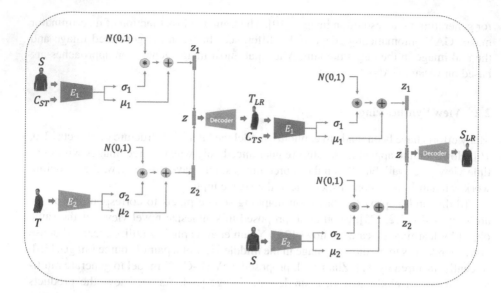

Fig. 1. The framework of the proposed low-resolution multi-view generation.

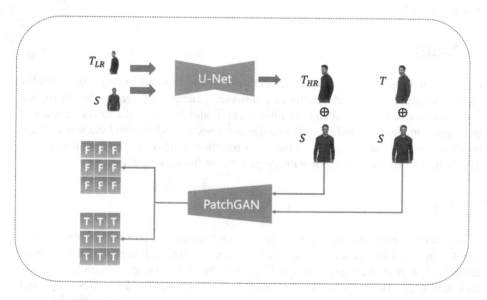

Fig. 2. The framework of the proposed high-resolution multi-view generation.

3.1 Low-Resolution Multi-view Generation

As shown in Fig. 1, the model of the low-resolution multi-view generation consists of two VAE networks with dual-encoder. The source image S with target-view condition C_{ST} and the target image T are passed through two encoders, respectively. Their fea-

---

Algorithm 1. Training the low-resolution multi-view generation

---
Input:
    The source image, S;
    The target image, T;
    The source view, C_{TS};
    The target view, C_{ST};
    The weights of losses, α, β and γ.
Output:
    The generated low-resolution target image, T_{LR};
    The generated low-resolution source image, S_{LR}.
1: $\mu_1, \sigma_1 \leftarrow E_1(S, C_{ST})$;
2: Sample a random vector $z_1 = \mu_1 + \sigma_1 \odot \mathcal{N}(0, 1)$;
3: $\mu_2, \sigma_2 \leftarrow E_2(T)$;
4: Sample a random vector $z_2 = \mu_2 + \sigma_2 \odot \mathcal{N}(0, 1)$;
5: $z = \frac{1}{2}(z_1 + z_2)$;
6: $T_{LR} \leftarrow Decoder(z)$;
7: $\mu_1', \sigma_1' \leftarrow E_1(T_{LR}, C_{TS})$;
8: Sample a random vector $z_1' = \mu_1' + \sigma_1' \odot \mathcal{N}(0, 1)$;
9: $\mu_2', \sigma_2' \leftarrow E_2(S)$;
10: Sample a random vector $z_2' = \mu_2' + \sigma_2' \odot \mathcal{N}(0, 1)$;
11: $z' = \frac{1}{2}(z_1' + z_2')$;
12: $S_{LR} \leftarrow Decoder(z')$;
13: Compute losses $\mathcal{L}_{recon}^{LR}$, $\mathcal{L}_{KL}$, $\mathcal{L}_{idt}^{LR}$ and $\mathcal{L}_{cyc}^{LR}$ by Eq. 2, Eq. 3, Eq. 4 and Eq. 5;
14: $\mathcal{L}^{LR} = \mathcal{L}_{recon}^{LR} + \alpha\mathcal{L}_{KL} + \beta\mathcal{L}_{idt}^{LR} + \gamma\mathcal{L}_{cyc}^{LR}$;
15: Perform a backpropagation.

---

ture representations are enforced to be consistent. The encoders E_1 and E_2 output the standard deviations σ_1 and σ_2, and means μ_1 and μ_2 of the latent variables z_1 and z_2, respectively. Then, we regard $\frac{1}{2}(z_1 + z_2)$ as the latent variable z. Finally, the decoder G generates the low-resolution target image T_{LR} from the latent variable z.

To reconstruct the target image and stabilize the training procedure, we introduce the L1 reconstruction loss $\mathcal{L}_{recon}^{LR}$:

$$\mathcal{L}_{recon}^{LR} = \|T_{LR} - T\|_1 = \|g(S, C_{ST}) - T\|_1, \tag{2}$$

where g denotes the low-resolution multi-view generation function.

In addition to minimizing the L1 reconstruction loss, the VAE regularizes the encoder by imposing a prior over the latent distribution $p(z)$ where $z \sim \mathcal{N}(0, 1)$. Thus, we introduce the KL regularized loss $\mathcal{L}_{KL}$:

$$\mathcal{L}_{KL} = KL(q(z|S, C_{ST}; T) \| \mathcal{N}(0, 1)) = \frac{1}{2}(1 + log(\sigma^2) - \mu^2 - \sigma^2), \tag{3}$$

where z, σ and μ denote $\frac{1}{2}(z_1 + z_2)$, $\frac{1}{2}(\sigma_1 + \sigma_2)$ and $\frac{1}{2}(\mu_1 + \mu_2)$, respectively.

To enforce the outputs of two encoders to obey the same distribution, we also introduce the identity constraint loss $\mathcal{L}_{idt}^{LR}$:

$$\mathcal{L}_{idt}^{LR} = \|z_1 - z_2\|_2 + \|\sigma_1 - \sigma_2\|_2 + \|\mu_1 - \mu_2\|_2. \tag{4}$$

Finally, to maintain the cycle consistency among different views, we clone the left VAE network and enforce $S = g(g(S, C_{ST}), C_{TS})$, where C_{TS} denotes the source-view condition. Hence, we introduce the cycle consistency loss $\mathcal{L}_{cyc}^{LR}$:

$$\mathcal{L}_{cyc}^{LR} = \|S_{LR} - S\|_1 = \|g(g(S, C_{ST}), C_{TS}) - S\|_1, \qquad (5)$$

where S_{LR} denotes the generated low-resolution source image.

The complete learning objective for the low-resolution multi-view generation is given by:

$$\min \mathcal{L}^{LR} = \mathcal{L}_{recon}^{LR} + \alpha \mathcal{L}_{KL} + \beta \mathcal{L}_{idt}^{LR} + \gamma \mathcal{L}_{cyc}^{LR}, \qquad (6)$$

where α, β and γ denote the weights of different losses.

Algorithm 1 shows the details of training the low-resolution multi-view generation.

3.2 High-Resolution Multi-view Generation

In this subsection, we investigate how to deblur the intermediate low-resolution target image T_{LR} to be more accurate and appealing with richer details. Inspired by U-Net [17], we adopt a dual-input U-Net generator to enrich the details and improve the textures. We also adopt a patch discriminator which is proved to be effective in multi-view image generation. In particular, we introduce the L1 reconstruction loss to the total loss of the generator $\mathcal{L}_{gen}$. Finally, the GAN of high-resolution multi-view generation trains the discriminator D and the generator F alternatively by maximizing $\mathcal{L}_{dis}$ and minimizing $\mathcal{L}_{gen}$:

$$\max \mathcal{L}_{dis} = \mathbb{E}[log(D(S, T))] + \mathbb{E}[log(1 - D(S, T_{HR}))], \qquad (7)$$

$$\min \mathcal{L}_{gen} = \mathbb{E}[log(1 - D(S, T_{HR}))] + \lambda \mathbb{E}[\|T - T_{HR}\|_1], \qquad (8)$$

where $T_{HR} = F(T_{LR}, S)$ denotes the generated high-resolution target image, S and T are sampled from the true data distribution, λ denotes the weight of L1 loss.

Algorithm 2 shows the details of training the high-resolution multi-view generation.

Algorithm 2. Training the high-resolution multi-view generation
___
Input:
    The source image, S;
    The target image, T;
    The generated low-resolution target image, T_{LR};
    The weight of L1 loss, λ.
Output:
    The generated high-resolution target image, T_{HR}.
1: $T_{HR} \leftarrow F(S, T_{LR})$;
2: Update D by ascending its gradient: $\nabla_{\theta_d} [\mathbb{E}[log\, D(S, T)] + \mathbb{E}[log\, (1 - D(S, T_{HR}))]]$;
3: Update F by descending its gradient: $\nabla_{\theta_f} [\mathbb{E}[log\, (1 - D(S, T_{HR}))] + \lambda \mathbb{E}[\|T - T_{HR}\|_1]]$;
4: Perform a backpropagation.

3.3 Implementation Details

For the low-resolution multi-view generation, the encoders E_1 and E_2 both contain six convolution layers followed by two fully-connected layers (convolution layers have 64, 128, 256, 256, 256 and 1024 channels with filter size of 5×5, 5×5, 5×5, 3×3, 3×3 and 4×4, respectively; the fully-connected layers both have 1024 neurons). Output size is set as 1024. The representations of the source image and the target-view condition are concatenated at the first layer of the encoder E_1. The decoder G consists of a fully-connected layer with 256 neurons, followed by six de-convolutional layers with 2×2 upsampling (with 256, 256, 256, 128, 64 and 3 channels with filter size of 3×3, 5×5, 5×5, 5×5, 5×5 and 5×5).

For the high-resolution multi-view generation, the two encoders of the generator both contain eight convolution layers (with 32, 32, 64, 64, 128, 128, 256 and 256 channels with filter size of 4×4 and stride 2). The decoder of the generator consists of seven de-convolutional layers with 512, 512, 512, 256, 128, 64 and 3 channels with filter size 4×4 and stride 2. The discriminator contains five convolution layers (with 64, 128, 256, 512, 1 channel(s) with filter size of 4×4 and stride 2, 2, 2, 1). Thus, the receptive field is set as 70×70.

For the training phase of the low-resolution multi-view generation, there are five steps. First, the target view is embedded into a 64×64 vector C_{ST}. Second, the source image S and the target-view condition C_{ST} are concatenated as input to generate the 1024-d latent variable z_1 by the encoder E_1. Third, the target image T is passed through another encoder E_2 to generate the 1024-d latent variable z_2. Then, the decoder G generates the 64×64 low-resolution target image T_{LR}. Finally, we clone the left VAE network. The low-resolution target image T_{LR} with source-view condition C_{TS} and the source image S are as the inputs of the clone VAE to generate the reconstructed source image S_{LR}.

For the training phase of the high-resolution multi-view generation, there are three steps. First, the source image S and the generated low-resolution target image T_{LR} are passed through the encoder. Then, the decoder generates the 128×128 high-resolution target image T_{HR}. Finally, the generated target image T_{HR} and the ground-truth target image T are concatenated with the source image S by channels to form the negative sample and positive sample, respectively.

For the whole training phase, we first train the low-resolution multi-view generator for 500 epochs. Then, We train the high-resolution multi-view generator and discriminator for another 500 epochs. All networks are trained with ADAM optimizers [8] with a batch size of 32 and a learning rate of 0.0001. For the setting of the hyper parameters, we set $\alpha = 0.005$, $\beta = \gamma = 1$, and $\lambda = 100$.

For the testing phase, we input the source image S with target-view condition C_{ST} into the encoder E_1 to obtain the latent variable z without the encoder E_2. Then, the decoder generates the low-resolution target image T_{LR} from the latent variable z. Finally, the dual-input U-Net generator generates the high-resolution target image T_{HR} from T_{LR} and S.

4 Experiments

To demonstrate the effectiveness and efficiency of the proposed method, we conduct extensive experiments on the most widely used benchmark dataset for multi-view image generation. First, we introduce the experimental settings, mainly including the dataset and evaluation metrics. Then, we compare the proposed method with existing state-of-the-art methods. Finally, we analyze the qualitative results of the proposed method.

4.1 Experimental Settings

Dataset. Multi-View Clothing (MVC) dataset [11] contains 36,323 groups of clothing items including shirts & tops, sweaters, jeans, pants, etc., which are collected from several online shopping websites, such as Amazon.com, Zappos.com and Shopbop.com. Figure 3 shows some examples of MVC dataset. Most samples of MVC dataset have four views, i.e., front, back, left side and right side. To simplify the problem, we only consider three generation tasks in this work: (1) generating the left-side image conditioned on the front image and the back image, respectively; (2) generating the front image conditioned on the left-side image and the back image, respectively; (3) generating the back image conditioned on the left-side image and the front image, respectively. After data cleaning, we remove some incorrect or inappropriate samples. Finally, We split the dataset into the training set with 30,000 groups of samples and the testing set with 2,000 groups of samples.

Fig. 3. Some sample multi-view clothing images from MVC dataset.

Evaluation Metrics. To measure the similarity between the generated image and the Ground Truth image (GT), we adopt Peak Signal to Noise Ratio (PSNR) [21] and Structural Similarity Index Measure (SSIM) [20] as the evaluation metrics.

PSNR is the ratio between the maximum possible power of a signal and the power of corrupting noise that affects the fidelity of its representation. PSNR is commonly used for measuring the quality of image reconstruction. The signal in this case is the original image data, and the noise is the error introduced by reconstruction. The higher the PSNR, the better the image quality [21]. PSNR value between the generated image X and the GT image Y of the same size is defined as:

$$PSNR(X, Y) = 10 \cdot log_{10}(\frac{N^2}{\frac{1}{mn} \sum\limits_{i=0}^{m-1} \sum\limits_{j=0}^{n-1} [X(i,j) - Y(i,j)]^2}), \qquad (9)$$

where N denotes the maximum possible pixel value of the image, e.g., the pixels are represented using 8 bits per sample, N is 255, and the value of PSNR typically ranges from 30 dB to 50 dB. m and n denote the length and the width of images X and Y. $X(i,j)$ and $Y(i,j)$ denote the pixel value at the coordinate point (i,j) of X and Y.

We also adopt which is a method for predicting the perceived quality of pictures, since we focus on the visual quality of generated images.

SSIM is widely adopted by many other image generation problems [10, 12, 24]. It evaluates the similarity of two images in the structural information without being influenced by the light or small pose variance. Its value ranges from 0 to 1. The higher the SSIM, the better the image quality. SSIM between the generated image X and the GT image Y of the same size is defined as:

$$SSIM(X, Y) = \frac{(2\mu_x\mu_y + c_1)(2\sigma_x\sigma_y + c_2)}{(\mu_x^2 + \mu_y^2 + c_1)(\sigma_x^2 + \sigma_y^2 + c_2)}, \qquad (10)$$

where μ_x and μ_y denote the average pixel value, σ_x and σ_y denote the variance of pixel values, c_1 and c_2 are two variables to stabilize the division, which are determined by the dynamic range of the images.

4.2 Comparison with State-of-The-Art Methods

We compare the performance of our model with several state-of-the-art multi-view generation methods: cVAE [18], cGAN [13] and cVAE-GAN [24] on MVC dataset. Table 1 shows the average SSIM and PSNR values of the results of these models. We can see that the cVAE model has the lowest SSIM and PSNR values among these models on MVC dataset. The cGAN model shows a great improvement, which has 5% promotion than cVAE model. Meanwhile, cVAE-GAN model shows better result than cVAE and cGAN models. Our model shows the greatest performance among these models on MVC dataset, which indicates that our model has a better ability to generate realistic multi-view images from a single view.

We also compare some representative samples of state-of-the-art models with our model in Fig. 4. The cVAE model can only generate a blurry result with a left-side shadow, and even the color of the T-shirt is incorrect. The cGAN model shows a clearer result than cVAE and the generated image presents richer details, moreover, the color of T-shirt is correct. However, it can be seen that the generated image looks much unrealistic. The image generated by cVAE-GAN model shows a more realistic result than cVAE and cGAN, however, the result is still unrealistic, especially for the face part. Benefiting from the cycle consistency, our Cycle CVAE generates a blurry result T_{LR} with the correct color of the T-shirt and the general shape of the person with correct view, which shows better performance than cVAE. Based on the generated low-resolution target image T_{LR}, the image T_{HR} generated by the proposed high-resolution multi-view generator fill much richer details and correct textures among all methods.

Table 1. SSIM and PSNR values of the state-of-art models and our model on MVC dataset.

Model	SSIM	PSNR(dB)
cVAE [18]	0.66	35.46
cGAN [13]	0.69	37.47
cVAE-GAN [24]	0.70	38.28
Ours	**0.75**	**41.22**

(a) Input   (b) cVAE   (c) cGAN   (d) cVAE-GAN   (e) Ours   (f) GT

Fig. 4. Comparison in multi-view image generation with several state-of-the-art methods.

4.3 Qualitative Results

Figure 5 shows several example results generated by our model. (a) and (d) are the source images from the MVC dataset, (b) and (e) are the generated target images by our model, (c) and (f) are the GT target images. The first row is the multi-view image generation from front view to left-side view. The second row is the multi-view image generation from left-side view to front view. The third row is the multi-view image generation from back view to left-side view. Compared with the GT images, our model shows a great ability to restore details and textures of target images. Moreover, the colors of clothes and poses of models of our results are the same as the GT images. It is worth mentioning that our model can generate realistic faces with clear eyes, noses, mouths, etc. In addition, the hair colors of our results are almost correct. All the results demonstrate that our model is able to generate realistic multi-view images with rich details and correct textures.

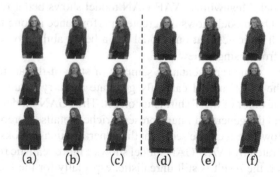

(a)   (b)   (c)   (d)   (e)   (f)

Fig. 5. Several example results generated by our model.

5 Conclusion and Future Work

In this work, we propose the Cycle CVAE-GAN to generate multi-view images from a single view. We introduce cycle consistency in our Cycle CVAE network. To deblur the generated low-resolution image, we present the high-resolution multi-view generator with a dual-input U-Net. In order to model richer details, we introduce a patch discriminator. Experimental results on MVC dataset support that our model is able to generate more realistic results than other state-of-the-art methods. In the future, we will further optimize our model and explore the adaptability and the generalization ability of our model in other scenes. The practical applications are to be developed not only restricted in the clothing generation domain, but also in other multi-view image generation tasks.

Acknowledgments. This work is supported by National Natural Science Fund for Distinguished Young Scholars (Grant No. 61625204) and partially supported by the State Key Program of the National Science Foundation of China (Grant Nos. 61836006 and 61432014).

References

1. Bao, J., Chen, D., Wen, F., Li, H., Hua, G.: CVAE-GAN: fine-grained image generation through asymmetric training. In: Proceedings of the IEEE International Conference on Computer Vision, pp. 2745–2754 (2017)
2. Chen, T., Zhu, Z., Shamir, A., Hu, S.M., Cohen-Or, D.: 3-sweep: extracting editable objects from a single photo. ACM Trans. Graph. (TOG) **32**(6), 195 (2013)
3. Goodfellow, I., et al.: Generative adversarial nets. In: Advances in Neural Information Processing Systems, pp. 2672–2680 (2014)
4. Gregor, K., Danihelka, I., Graves, A., Rezende, D.J., Wierstra, D.: Draw: a recurrent neural network for image generation. arXiv preprint arXiv:1502.04623 (2015)
5. Isola, P., Zhu, J.Y., Zhou, T., Efros, A.A.: Image-to-image translation with conditional adversarial networks. In: Proceedings of the IEEE Conference on Computer Vision and Pattern Recognition, pp. 1125–1134 (2017)
6. Kholgade, N., Simon, T., Efros, A., Sheikh, Y.: 3D object manipulation in a single photograph using stock 3D models. ACM Trans. Graph. (TOG) **33**(4), 127 (2014)
7. Kingma, D.P., Welling, M.: Auto-encoding variational bayes. arXiv preprint arXiv:1312.6114 (2013)
8. Kingma, D.P., Ba, J.: Adam: a method for stochastic optimization. arXiv preprint arXiv:1412.6980 (2014)
9. LeCun, Y., Bengio, Y., et al.: Convolutional networks for images, speech, and time series. Handb. Brain Theory Neural Netw. **3361**(10), 1995 (1995)
10. Ledig, C., et al.: Photo-realistic single image super-resolution using a generative adversarial network. In: Proceedings of the IEEE Conference on Computer Vision and Pattern Recognition, pp. 4681–4690 (2017)
11. Liu, K.H., Chen, T.Y., Chen, C.S.: MVC: a dataset for view-invariant clothing retrieval and attribute prediction. In: Proceedings of the 2016 ACM on International Conference on Multimedia Retrieval, pp. 313–316. ACM (2016)
12. Ma, L., Jia, X., Sun, Q., Schiele, B., Tuytelaars, T., Van Gool, L.: Pose guided person image generation. In: Advances in Neural Information Processing Systems, pp. 406–416 (2017)

13. Mirza, M., Osindero, S.: Conditional generative adversarial nets. arXiv preprint arXiv:1411.1784 (2014)
14. Park, E., Yang, J., Yumer, E., Ceylan, D., Berg, A.C.: Transformation-grounded image generation network for novel 3D view synthesis. In: Proceedings of the IEEE Conference on Computer Vision and Pattern Recognition, pp. 3500–3509 (2017)
15. Quéau, Y., Mélou, J., Durou, J.D., Cremers, D.: Dense multi-view 3D-reconstruction without dense correspondences. arXiv preprint arXiv:1704.00337 (2017)
16. Rock, J., Gupta, T., Thorsen, J., Gwak, J., Shin, D., Hoiem, D.: Completing 3D object shape from one depth image. In: Proceedings of the IEEE Conference on Computer Vision and Pattern Recognition, pp. 2484–2493 (2015)
17. Ronneberger, O., Fischer, P., Brox, T.: U-Net: convolutional networks for biomedical image segmentation. In: Navab, N., Hornegger, J., Wells, W.M., Frangi, A.F. (eds.) MICCAI 2015, Part III. LNCS, vol. 9351, pp. 234–241. Springer, Cham (2015). https://doi.org/10.1007/978-3-319-24574-4_28
18. Sohn, K., Lee, H., Yan, X.: Learning structured output representation using deep conditional generative models. In: Advances in Neural Information Processing Systems, pp. 3483–3491 (2015)
19. Wang, T.C., Liu, M.Y., Zhu, J.Y., Tao, A., Kautz, J., Catanzaro, B.: High-resolution image synthesis and semantic manipulation with conditional gans. In: Proceedings of the IEEE Conference on Computer Vision and Pattern Recognition, pp. 8798–8807 (2018)
20. Wang, Z., Bovik, A.C., Sheikh, H.R., Simoncelli, E.P., et al.: Image quality assessment: from error visibility to structural similarity. IEEE Trans. Image Process. **13**(4), 600–612 (2004)
21. Welstead, S.T.: Fractal and wavelet image compression techniques. SPIE Optical Engineering Press, Bellingham (1999)
22. Yan, X., Yang, J., Sohn, K., Lee, H.: Attribute2Image: conditional image generation from visual attributes. In: Leibe, B., Matas, J., Sebe, N., Welling, M. (eds.) ECCV 2016, Part IV. LNCS, vol. 9908, pp. 776–791. Springer, Cham (2016). https://doi.org/10.1007/978-3-319-46493-0_47
23. Yan, X., Yang, J., Yumer, E., Guo, Y., Lee, H.: Perspective transformer nets: learning single-view 3D object reconstruction without 3D supervision. In: Advances in Neural Information Processing Systems, pp. 1696–1704 (2016)
24. Zhao, B., Wu, X., Cheng, Z.Q., Liu, H., Jie, Z., Feng, J.: Multi-view image generation from a single-view. In: 2018 ACM Multimedia Conference on Multimedia Conference, pp. 383–391. ACM (2018)
25. Zhou, T., Tulsiani, S., Sun, W., Malik, J., Efros, A.A.: View synthesis by appearance flow. In: Leibe, B., Matas, J., Sebe, N., Welling, M. (eds.) ECCV 2016, Part IV. LNCS, vol. 9908, pp. 286–301. Springer, Cham (2016). https://doi.org/10.1007/978-3-319-46493-0_18
26. Zhu, J.Y., Park, T., Isola, P., Efros, A.A.: Unpaired image-to-image translation using cycle-consistent adversarial networks. In: Proceedings of the IEEE International Conference on Computer Vision, pp. 2223–2232 (2017)

B-DCGAN: Evaluation of Binarized DCGAN for FPGA

Hideo Terada[1]([⊠]) and Hayaru Shouno[2]

[1] Open Stream, Inc., 2-7-1 Nishi-Shinjuku, Shinjuku, Tokyo 163-0709, Japan
terada.h@opst.co.jp
[2] Graduate School of Informatics and Engineering,
University of Electro-Communications,
Chofugaoka 1-5-1, Chofu, Tokyo 182-8585, Japan
shouno@uec.ac.jp

Abstract. In this work, we demonstrate an implementation of Deep Convolution Generative Adversarial Network (DCGAN), into a Field Programmable Gate Array (FPGA). In order to implement the DCGAN, we modified the DCGAN model with binary weights and activations, and with using integer-valued operations in the forwarding path (train-time and run-time). We call the modified one as Binary-DCGAN (B-DCGAN). Using the B-DCGAN, we do a feasibility study of FPGA's characteristics and performance for Deep Learning. Because the binarization and using integer-valued operation reduce the memory capacity and the number of the circuit gates, it is very effective for FPGA implementation. On the other hand, these reductions in the model might decrease the quality of the generated data. So we investigate the influence of these reductions.

1 Introduction

We try to implement a deep neural network in the edge computing environment for real-world applications such as the IoT (Internet of Things), the FinTech, to utilize the significant achievement of Deep Learning in recent years. Especially, we now focus on algorithm implementation on FPGA, because it is one of the promising devices for low-cost and low-power implementation in edge computing.

A well-known fact, Graphics Processing Unit (GPU) is now the most common computing resources for Deep Neural Networks (DNNs). GPU is one of the most useful devices to execute massive scale numerical operations such as DNNs. Furthermore, thanks to the effort of world-wide researchers and developers, now there are many software tools, libraries, and frameworks suitable for GPU, so it is easy to write the DNNs software for GPU. However, GPU has very high power consumption, so that it needs an abundant power supply and cooling equipment. Thus, it is hard to apply GPUs in the small edge machines for IoT.

As a way for low-power and low-cost dedicated computation, Field Programmable Gate Array (FPGA) is gathering attention recently again, since its cost performance has improved and the prices of related software tools have also declined.

© Springer Nature Switzerland AG 2019
T. Gedeon et al. (Eds.): ICONIP 2019, LNCS 11953, pp. 55–64, 2019.
https://doi.org/10.1007/978-3-030-36708-4_5

While FPGA is user-programmable hardware, its development in the early times was pretty tricky and complicated, because the program requires 'low-level' notations such as Hardware Description Language (HDL) or schematic circuit diagrams, so the developers had to have these kinds of special skills.

However, nowadays, owing to the High-Level Synthesis (HLS) technique has been evolving, the developer programs the FPGA using a high-level programming language such as C/C++. It is a much easier way for the developer who is not an expert of hardware.

1.1   The Problem of Using FPGA for DNN

The algorithm development using FPGA has the following problems: First, the number of gates and the capacity of fast memory is much smaller than that of the GPU. While it is available to use either multi FPGAs, or FPGA with external memories, however, the processing speed will drop considerably because of the communication overheads. Second, the more the algorithm uses multiplication, division, or floating-point value of those operations, the much larger gates it will consume. Third, if the circuit is not optimized appropriately in the hardware-specific way, such as parallelizing or pipelining, the FPGA could get slower speed than a CPU with the same clock range.

As the solution for these problems, various researches make the circuit scale smaller for DNNs: Courbariaux et al. showed that image classification using the neural networks with binary weights and activations (BNN) is enough possible [4]. Moreover, they showed the method to train the BNN. Umuroglu et al. presented the FINN [9], a framework for building fast and flexible FPGA accelerators that enable efficient mapping of binarized neural networks to hardware. Adelouahab et al. published a good survey [1], which reports various types of implementation techniques of CNN on FPGA. Cheng et al. also published another good survey [3], in which they discussed the recent techniques for compacting and accelerating CNNs in detail.

1.2   Contributions

This work makes the following contributions:

- We introduce binarized & integer-valued deep convolutional conditional generative adversarial networks. Hereafter we call it as B-DCGAN.
- We show the quality change of output from B-DCGAN Generator when the extent of binarization was changed.

2   B-DCGAN: DCGAN with Binarized Generator

Binary Deep Convolutional & Conditional Generative Adversarial Networks (B-DCGAN) is a modified version of DCGAN [8]. In the B-DCGAN, the Discriminator network is a vanilla network as the normal DCGAN; that is, it uses real-valued operation. However, the Generator network adopts the binary weights, binary activations, and integer-valued operations.

2.1   Network Structure

Figure 1 is a schematic diagram of the network structure of B-DCGAN Generator. The first half of the Generator is consist of full connection layers, which is called Encoder. The last half is named Decoder, is consist of deconvolution layers.

We show the details of these layers in the following sections.

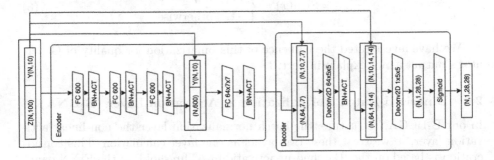

Fig. 1. Schematic diagram of B-DCGAN Generator

2.2   Integer-Valued Inputs

The Generator's inputs are z and y. In vanilla GAN, z is 1D-vector of random floating point values in range $[-1.0 \sim +1.0]$. In B-DCGAN, we use integer value z^i for input as follows:

$$z = (z_1, z_2, \cdots, z_n) \tag{1}$$

$$z^i = (z_1^i, z_2^i, \cdots, z_n^i) \tag{2}$$

$$z_k^i = \mathrm{round}(A \cdot z_k) \quad (k = 1, 2, \cdots, n) \tag{3}$$

$$A = 2^{h-1} - 1 \qquad (h = 2, 3, 4, \cdots). \tag{4}$$

The B-DCGAN treats the conditional input method like as CGAN [7]. The y is one-hot vector representation of class label to be generated. It is also converted into integer value y^i:

$$y^i = A \cdot y = (y_1^i, y_2^i, \cdots, y_l^i, \cdots, y_c^i) \ (l = 1, 2, \cdots, c), \tag{5}$$

where the constant A is a hyper-parameter of B-DCGAN. z_k^i and y_l^i is integer values represented by signed k bits. The integer value is very advantageous from a hardware perspective because the number of circuit logics of integer process is much smaller than those of floating point in FPGA. We have investigated the influence of the value A setting for quality of Generator's output as we explain in Sect. 3.

2.3 Binarized Full Connection Layer (B-FC)

Implementation of Full Connection layer in B-DCGAN is based on those of BNN [4]. During the backward path (at train-time), its weight value is real-valued variable the same as the usual full connection. During the forward path calculation (both at run-time and train-time), we treat the weight as binary, that is, the value is constrained to either $+1$ or -1 as follows:

$$x^b = \text{Sign}(x) = \begin{cases} +1, & \text{if } x >= 0 \\ -1, & \text{otherwise} \end{cases} \tag{6}$$

We have investigated the influence of this binarization for quality of Generator's output as we explain in Sect. 3.

2.4 Binarized Batch Normalization + Activation Layer (B-BNA)

In our B-DCGAN structure, the batch normalization layer the non-linear activation layer, so we treat these two layers as one layer calculation. This consideration is based on the 'Batchnorm-activation as Threshold' in the FINN paper (Umuroglu et al. [9]); that is, we have modified it as integer-valued version.

Let a_j is the output of jth neuron in the previous layer, and $\Theta_j = (\gamma_j, \mu_j, i_j, B_j)$ is the batch normalization parameter set learned during the training phase. The output of this layer a_j^b in computed as:

$$a_j^b = \begin{cases} +1, & \text{if } a_j >= \tau_j^b \\ -1, & \text{otherwise} \end{cases} \tag{7}$$

The threshold τ_j^b is computed by solving $BatchNorm(\tau_j, \Theta_j) = 0$ and rounding:

$$\text{BatchNorm}(\tau_j, \Theta_j) = \gamma_j \cdot (\tau_j - \mu_j) \cdot i_j + B_j = 0 \tag{8}$$

$$\therefore \tau_j = \mu_j - (B_j/(\gamma_j \cdot i_j)) \tag{9}$$

$$\tau_j^b = \text{round}(\tau_j) \tag{10}$$

During the training phase, τ_j^b value is always modified according to the change of $BatchNorm$ parameters; however, in the run-time phase, the value can be treated as a fixed value.

2.5 Binarized Deconvolution Layer (B-Deconv)

The behavior of the binarized deconvolution layer (B-Deconv) is similar to those of the B-FC layer described at Sect. 2.3. That is, during the backward path calculation at the train-time, the weight values of filters are real-valued variable same as the normal deconvolution. However, in the forward path calculation both at the run-time and train-time, we treat the weight values as binarized to either $+1$ or -1 according to the Eq. (6).

We have also investigated the influence of using B-Deconv for output quality of the Generator (see Sect. 3.2).

3   Evaluation

3.1   Experimental Setup

Scenario. To exam B-BDCGAN, we arranged several configurations of network binarization. We present a configuration as a set of flags and hyper-parameters described in Table 1. We call it '**Scenario.**' The 'Input as integer' flag represents whether the input is integer-valued (Y) or real-valued (n). Other flags correspond with whether each layer is binarized (Y) or not (n). The 'A value' is input scale value that is only effective when the 'Input as integer' is positive (Y), had explained in Sect. 2.2.

Table 1. Setup scenario. 'Y' is positive, 'n' is negative.

	Scenario #						
	S0	S1-1	S1-2	S2-1	S2-2	S3-1	S3-2
Encoder							
Input as integer	n	Y	Y	Y	Y	Y	Y
A value	–	1	1	127	4095	1	1
B-FC	n	Y	Y	Y	Y	Y	Y
B-BNA-1	n	n	Y	Y	Y	Y	Y
Decoder							
B-Deconv-1	n	n	n	n	n	Y	Y
B-BNA-2	n	n	n	n	n	Y	Y
B-Deconv-2	n	n	n	n	n	n	Y

Constant of Hyper-parameters. We adopt the following constant as the hyper-parameters for the network: The number of units in Full Connection layer is 600. The Kernel sizes in Deconvolution layer-1, and -2 is 5×5. The number of filters of Deconvolution layer-1 is 64. Also, the number of filters of Deconvolution layer-2 is 1.

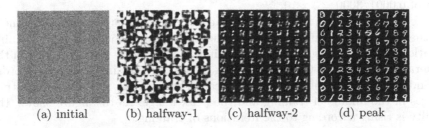

(a) initial   (b) halfway-1   (c) halfway-2   (d) peak

Fig. 2. Generator's output images in the middle of training

Fig. 3. Peak image of S0 (baseline)

Fig. 4. Peak image of S1-1   **Fig. 5.** Peak image of S1-2

Training. We apply the MNIST [6] dataset for training. We make the training program by python using Theano [2] library and Lasagne [5] library, and partially using BinaryNet [4] code and DCGAN [8] code. We run the program on Ubuntu Linux with NVIDIA Titan-X GPU. Our program code is available on-line[1].

We adopt a stochastic gradient descent (SGD) method as the training method, in which we set the number of mini-batches as 128, and the initial learning rate as 0.0001 that was linearly decreased down to 0 with the decay step of $0.0001/3000 = 3 \times 10^{-8}$.

We judge the finish of training of each Scenario through visual assessment for the quality of output images from the Generator. That is, at each training iteration, the program generates output image and current parameters from the Generator at that time to individual files, so we can examine these files in order to find when the quality reaches its peak. For example, Fig. 2 shows output images in the middle of training and the peak image. As this figure shows, the quality is rising according to the iterations of training.

---

[1] https://github.com/hterada/b-dcgan.

Fig. 6. Peak image of S2-1

Fig. 7. Peak image of S2-2

FPGA Implementation. After the training of the DCGAN network model, we extracted the set of model parameters of the peak quality. These parameters were written in python pickle formatted files with filename extension '.jl'. We made a dedicated python program called 'model_to_ch.py', which converts '.jl' file to C++ header files, where the model parameters are expressed as C++ constant variables. The building of the B-DCGAN Generator in Xilinx Vivado HLS for FPGA requires these header files.

A binarized parameter represented by +1 or −1 in training model should be represented by 1 or 0 (1-bit value) in FPGA, so the 'model_to_ch.py' is converted ±1 parameters into such bit-mapped expression.

3.2   Training Results in Scenarios

S0: Not Binarized (Vanilla) DCGAN. The Scenario S0 is the baseline of image quality. Figure 3 shows output image of peak quality (we call it '**peak image**') from the trained model configured in S0.

S1-1 vs S1-2: Encoder only Binarization. The Scenario S1-1 and S1-2 are experiments to examine the influence of binarization of Encoder.

- The S1-1 makes input as integer and binarize only FC layer (see Sect. 2.3).
- The S1-2 makes input as integer and binarize FC and BNA layer (see Sect. 2.4).

Figure 4 shows peak of S1-1, and Fig. 5 shows peak of S1-2.

S2-1 vs S2-2: A Value Change. The Scenario S2-1 and the S2-2 are experiments to examine the influence of 'A' value of Encoder.

- In the S2-1, we set A value as 127.
- In the S2-2, we set A value to 4095.

Figures 6 and 7 show the peak generations of the S2-1 and S2-2, respectively.

S3-1 vs S3-2: Encoder and Decoder Binarization. The Scenario S3-1 and S3-2 are experiments to examine influence of Decoder binarization.

- The S3-1 adopts the binarize Encoder, B-Deconv-1 and B-BNA-2 in Decoder

- The S3-2 adopts the binarize Encoder, B-Deconv-1, B-BNA-2 and B-Deconv-2 in Decoder; that is all layers in Decoder

Figure 8 shows the peak of the S3-1. Figure 9 shows the results of candidates for peak of the S3-2. According to the training results, in the S3-2 Scenario, the quality of the output image looks very unstable. So we could not decide a single peak in clear. Therefore, we picked up some candidates for the peak.

Fig. 8. Peak image of S3-1

Fig. 9. Peak candidates of S3-2

4   Conclusion and Discussion

We have introduced B-DCGAN; that is DCGAN with binary weights and activations, and integer-valued input. We have conducted several scenarios of experiments on the Theano/Lasagne libraries, which show that it is possible to binarize

DCGAN model, moreover, show what extent is the binarization available with keeping output quality acceptable.

According to the results of these experiments, the last layer B-Deconv-2 mainly have the initiative for output image quality. So the last layer has to operate in the real-valued process. Except for the last layer, other layers can be fully binarized.

According to the results in each Scenario above, we conduct the following speculations:

1. The output quality is affected very few by only binarization of the Encoder (cf. S0, S1-1, S1-2).
2. No influence for quality appears when the A value has changed (cf. S2-1, S2-2).
3. The output quality is somewhat degraded by binarization both the Encoder and partially of the Decoder (cf. S3-1)
4. The output quality is degraded seriously by full binarization of both the Encoder and the Decoder (cf. S3-2)
5. The output quality chiefly depends on the Deconv-2 layer because of the quality difference between S3-1 and S3-2.

At least on the MNIST dataset, we can select the S3-1 as the best Scenario for the B-DCGAN.

Acknowledgements. We would like to thank the UEC Shouno lab (http://daemon. inf.uec.ac.jp/ja/) members: Satoshi Suzuki and Aiga Suzuki for theoretical and technical discussion; Seigo Kawamura, Kurosaka Mamoru, Yoshihiro Kusano, Toya Teramoto and Akihiro Endo for kind technical assistance and humor. We thank Kazuhiko Yoshihara and all the members of Open Stream, Inc. We also thank the developers of Theano, Lasagne, and Python environment. This work is supported under the funds of Open Stream, Inc. (https://www.opst.co.jp/).

References

1. Abdelouahab, K., Pelcat, M., Berry, F., Sérot, J.: Accelerating CNN inference on FPGAs: a survey. Research report, Université Clermont Auvergne; Institut Pascal, Clermont Ferrand; IETR/INSA Rennes, January 2018. https://hal.archives-ouvertes.fr/hal-01695375
2. Al-Rfou, R., et al.: Theano: a Python framework for fast computation of mathematical expressions. arXiv e-prints abs/1605.02688, May 2016. http://arxiv.org/abs/1605.02688
3. Cheng, Y., Wang, D., Zhou, P., Zhang, T.: A survey of model compression and acceleration for deep neural networks. arXiv e-prints, October 2017
4. Courbariaux, M., Hubara, I., Soudry, D., El-Yaniv, R., Bengio, Y.: Binarized neural networks: training deep neural networks with weights and activations constrained to +1 or −1. arXiv e-prints, February 2016
5. Dieleman, S., et al.: Lasagne: first release, August 2015. https://doi.org/10.5281/zenodo.27878

6. LeCun, Y., Bottou, L., Bengio, Y., Haffner, P.: Gradient-based learning applied to document recognition. Proc. IEEE **86**(11), 2278–2324 (1998)
7. Mirza, M., Osindero, S.: Conditional generative adversarial nets. arXiv e-prints, November 2014
8. Radford, A., Metz, L., Chintala, S.: Unsupervised representation learning with deep convolutional generative adversarial networks. arXiv e-prints, November 2015
9. Umuroglu, Y., et al.: FINN: a framework for fast, scalable binarized neural network inference. arXiv e-prints, December 2016

A Natural Scene Text Extraction Approach Based on Generative Adversarial Learning

Huali Xu, Xiangdong Su[✉], Tongyang Liu, Pengcheng Guo, Guanglai Gao, and Feilong Bao

College of Computer Science, Inner Mongolia University, Hohhot, China
xuhuali.purple@gmail.com, sxddxs5747@sina.com

Abstract. Extracting textual information embodied in natural scenes is a very challenge task, and has a great influence on the performance of the following text recognition and understanding. It can be seen as an image-to-image conversion task, in which we transform the front text in each natural image into a specified color and the background into black. After that, we use the connected component algorithm to extract text from the two-color image. Based on such motivation, we proposed an approach based on generative adversarial learning to deal with the image-to-image conversion. The neural network in our approach consists of a generator sub-network and a discriminator sub-network, which are trained with paired images (scene images and their corresponding two-color images) in an adversarial way. After the training stage, the generator network is used to perform image conversion. Experiments on standard datasets including KAIST scene text database and MSRA text detection 500 database demonstrate that the proposed algorithm achieves a very competitive performance.

Keywords: Text extraction · Image-to-image · Generative adversarial network · Loss function

1 Introduction

Recently, extracting and understanding textual information in natural scenes have become increasingly important and popular. Text extraction prepares the text image for recognition and understanding in the following stage. Previous text extraction approaches [1–5] have already obtained promising performances on public benchmarks. Most of these approaches rely on manually designed features to capture the properties of scene text. With the development of deep learning, some methods [2,3,6–9] use the features learned from training data to facilitate text detection and extraction. However, existing methods usually takes multiple sequential steps, making the systems highly complicated and errors accumulated in the later steps. It is necessary to propose a fast and accurate scene text extraction approach.

© Springer Nature Switzerland AG 2019
T. Gedeon et al. (Eds.): ICONIP 2019, LNCS 11953, pp. 65–73, 2019.
https://doi.org/10.1007/978-3-030-36708-4_6

From the perspective of image processing, text extraction is to distinguish text from backgrounds. It can be seen as an image-to-image conversion problem, in which we transform the text and background of the natural scene into two different colors. Here, we named the resulting image as two-color image. After that, we use the connected component algorithm to extract text. Inspired by the pix2pix work [10], we proposed an approach based on generative adversarial learning as a fast solution to the image-to-image conversion task. The neural network in our approach consists of a generator sub-network and a discriminator sub-network, which are trained in an adversarial way. After the training stage, the generator network is used to perform image conversion.

As a deep learning model, generative adversarial network (GAN) was first proposed by Goodfellow in 2014 [11]. It cast generative modeling as a game between two networks: a generator network produces synthetic data given some noise source and a discriminator network discriminates between the generator's output and true data. After training, the generator can produce fairly good output. When adding a condition to the generator in GAN, we can control the output of the generator more closer to our expectation. This allows the condition GAN is quite suitable for image-to-image problems. To optimize the generator network, two strategies are used, including skip connection and patch segmentation.

There are three main advantages of the proposed approach. First, we formulate the text extraction from natural scenes as an image-to-image problem and take conditional GAN to solve it. Second, our approach is free of feature design and acting in an end-to-end fashion. Third, the generated text image can be recognized directly without additional processing, such as binarization.

This paper is organized as follows. Section 2 presents related works. Section 3 describes the proposed approach. Section 4 reports the evaluation experiment. We conclude in Sect. 5.

2   Related Work

Scene text extraction is a subtask of scene text understanding, which generates the text images to be recognized from natural scenes. Several works on scene text detection use hand-crafted features [4,7,12,13] to detect characters or text components from images. They take multiple steps and sequentially group text-related pixels into characters. These approaches are complicated, and identification of text using low-level features is neither robust nor reliable. Sliding window based methods [8,14–18] belong to a kind of representative methods, which shifts a window in each position with multiple scales on a natural image to detect text. Although these methods can effectively recall text, they often affected by the window size and position, and carry various background noise.

Recently, Convolutional Neural Networks [19–23] have been proved powerful enough to capture the latent features in images, which advances the researches on scene text detection. Huang et al. [24] integrated Maximally Stable Extremal Regions (MSER) and CNN to significantly enhance performance over conventional methods. Zhang et al. [25] utilized Fully Convolutional Network (FCN) to efficiently generate a pixel-wise text/nontext salient map, resulting in a text detector able to explore rich regional information. It is worth mentioning that the common ground of these successful methods is to utilized textual intrinsic information for training the CNN. However, these pixel-based text detectors are difficult to provide sufficient localization accuracy. Accurate segmentation of text from a predicted heat map is complicated, and often requires a number of heuristic post-processing steps.

This paper employs a GAN-based approach to achieve text extraction. The networks in GAN can learn the mapping from the input image to the output image. It is free of feature design when transforming the natural images to their two-color images, Previous works have proved that GAN is effective in many image transformation problems, such as style transferring [10,26], image restoration [27,28], colorization, and segmentation [29].

3   Approach

3.1   Module Architecture

To transform the natural scene to the two-value images, our approach takes a conditional GAN-based architecture, as shown in Fig. 1. It consists of two components, a discriminator network and a generator network, who play a min-max game against each other. The discriminator network D maps from an input image to a probability that the image is from the real data distribution: $D(x) \to (0,1)$. In contrast, the generator network G maps from random noise vector z and observed condition x (natural image) to target two-color image y: $G(z,x) \to y$. The objective of the conditional GAN can be expressed as Eq. (1):

$$\mathcal{L}_{conditionalGAN}(G,D) = \mathbb{E}_{x,y}[logD(x,y)]$$
$$+ \mathbb{E}_{x,z}[log(1 - D(x,G(x,z)))] \qquad (1)$$

Where G tries to minimize this objective against an adversarial D that tries to maximize it.

The generator is an encoder-decoder structure with 14 layers, as shown in Fig. 1(a). The input (including the noise variables z and the color image y) is first compressed into a higher level representation through a series of encoders (convolution + activation function) including 7 blocks. Then, the compressed representation is converted into the target image through a series of decoders (deconvolution + activation function) including 7 blocks. Batch normalization is used in each convolutional layer to ensure network performance and stability [30, 31]. Each of the blocks here take the form convolution-BatchNorm-ReLu [30]. The discriminator also uses an encoder-like structure, as shown in Fig. 1(b). The inputs of the discriminator are the two-color images from the generator and the ground truth, which are concatenated together when input into the discriminator.

The training process takes several epochs. For each epoch, we alternate training the generator and discriminator. We first train the discriminator and freeze the parameters of the generator. The discriminator is trained on the classified samples as in traditional supervised learning. Then, we train the generator and freeze the discriminator. After training, the generator has a good mapping from natural image to its corresponding two-color image.

The previous study has proved that it is beneficial to mix the GAN objective with a L1 loss function. The discriminator's job remains unchanged, but the generator is tasked with not only fooling the discriminator but also being near the ground truth output through decrease the L1 loss. The L1 loss function can be written as Eq. (2):

$$\mathcal{L}_{L1}(G) = \mathbb{E}_{x,y,z}[y - G(x, z)] \tag{2}$$

Thus, the final objective is Eq. (3):

$$G^* = \arg \min_G \max_D (\mathcal{L}_{conditionalGAN}(G, D) + \lambda \mathcal{L}_{L_1}(G)) \tag{3}$$

3.2 Optimization

Since the natural scene images and its corresponding two-color images represent the same text content, they are the renderings of the same underlying structure. To integrate such limitation, we directly give an output of each ith convolution layer to the $(n - i)$th deconvolution layer by adding a skip connection between them, where n is the total number of layers. Each skip connection simply concatenates all channels at ith layer with those at $(n-i)$th layer. Such a strategy can be viewed as low-level information sharing to control the generated two-color image. Previous study proved that PatchGAN can sufficiently model high-frequency structure of those images. This paper also used this strategy in the discriminator D, which tries to classify if each $N \times N$ patch in an output image is real or fake, averaging all responses to generate the ultimate output of discriminator D.

4   Experiments

4.1 Data

In this section, we quantitatively evaluate our method on the public dataset: KAIST scene text dataset [32] and MSRA text detection 500 dataset [12]. Both of them are collected from different environments, including outdoors and indoors under different lighting condition. They released publicly as a benchmark to evaluate text extraction algorithms in natural images of arbitrary orientations. Text extraction on them is challenging due to both the diversity of the texts and the complexity of the background in the images.

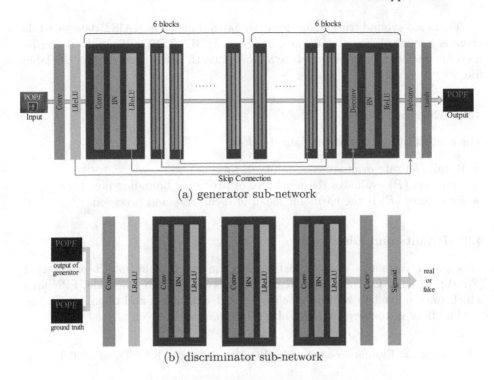

(a) generator sub-network

(b) discriminator sub-network

Fig. 1. The generator and discriminator sub-networks

The KAIST scene text dataset comprises 2,483 images. All images have been resized to 640 × 480. It is categorized according to the language of the scene text captured: Korean, English, and Mixed (Korean + English). The scene text in the images is representative of common text in Korean streets or shops.

The MSRA text detection 500 database (MSRA-TD500) contains 500 natural images. The resolutions of the images vary from 1296 × 864 to 1920 × 1280. The indoor images are mainly signs, doorplates and caution plates while the outdoor images are mostly guide boards and billboards in complex background. All the images in this dataset are fully annotated. The text is in Chinese, English and mixture of both.

The training dataset consists of 1600 images from KAIST and 400 images from MSRA-TD500. The testing dataset consists of 400 images from KAIST and 100 images from MSRA-TD500, which are different from the training dataset. To make the model more robust, we augmented the training dataset to 10000 images through four kinds of operation, including translation, rotation, scaling, and RGB channel translation.

There is a ground truth image for each natural image in KAIST dataset while there is a label file for each natural image in MSRA-TD500. To make it can be used for model training, we produce a ground truth image according to the label file.

4.2 Metrics

The evaluation metrics are explained below:

- Recall (R) rate evaluates the ability of finding text.
- Precision (P) evaluates the reliability of predicted bounding box.
- F-measure (F) is the harmonic mean of recall rate and precision.

4.3 Results and Discussion

This paper compares our approach with the single shot multibox detector (SSD) [17], Fully-Convolutional Regression Network FCRN [33] and CTPN [34], which have proved to be very efficient in text extraction and often be used as the baselines in text extraction. Table 1 summarizes the results.

Table 1. Evaluation on the mixed testing dataset of KAIST and MSRA

Model	R (%)	P (%)	F (%)
SSD [17]	28.56	57.41	38.15
FCRN [33]	**44.21**	63.58	52.15
CTPN [34]	39.27	64.92	48.94
Our approach	42.60	**68.92**	**52.65**

Our approach achieves a recall of 42.60%, a precision of 68.92%, and an F-measure 52.65%. Although the recall rate of our approach is not the highest, the precision has increased prominently than SSD, FCRN and CTPN, owing to the well-defined network architecture and loss function described in Sect. 3. The F-measure of our approach is the highest among these four models, indicating that our approach is very competitive. Comparing with the traditional methods, our approach is free of feature design.

Figure 2 shows several extracted results taken from the test set. It is clear that the output images of our approach are close to the ground truth. However, due to the complexity of the natural scene, our method may fail to recall some inconspicuous text. The resulting images from our approach are two-color ones, which can be used directly for text recognition without binarization.

(a) Original image   (b) Out of Generator   (c) Ground truth

Fig. 2. Illustration of our approach. (a) original image, (b) output of our approach, (c) ground truth

5 Conclusion

This paper treats scene text extraction as an image-to-image problem and proposes a conditional GAN based approach to deal with it. The two sub-networks (the generator and the discriminator) are trained in an adversarial learning way. The trained generator is used to perform the scene image to the two-color image transformation. Experiments on standard datasets including KAIST scene text database and MSRA text detection 500 database demonstrate that the proposed algorithm achieves a very competitive performance. The merits of our approach that it requires no feature design and the resulting two-color images can be used directly for text recognition without binarization.

Acknowledgement. This work was funded by National Natural Science Foundation of China (Grant No. 61563040, 61773224, 61762069, 61866029), Natural Science Foundation of Inner Mongolia Autonomous Region (Grant No. 2017BS0601, 2016ZD06), and program of higher-level talents of Inner Mongolia University (Grant No. 21500-5165161).

References

1. Busta, M., Neumann, L., Matas, J.: FASText: efficient unconstrained scene text detector. In: Proceedings of the IEEE International Conference on Computer Vision, pp. 1206–1214 (2015)
2. Gupta, A., Vedaldi, A., Zisserman, A.: Synthetic data for text localisation in natural images. In: Proceedings of the IEEE Conference on Computer Vision and Pattern Recognition, pp. 2315–2324 (2016)
3. Jaderberg, M., Simonyan, K., Vedaldi, A., Zisserman, A.: Reading text in the wild with convolutional neural networks. Int. J. Comput. Vision **116**(1), 1–20 (2016)
4. Tian, S., Pan, Y., Huang, C., Lu, S., Yu, K., Lim Tan, C.: Text flow: a unified text detection system in natural scene images. In: Proceedings of the IEEE International Conference on Computer Vision, pp. 4651–4659 (2015)
5. Zhang, Z., Zhang, C., Shen, W., Yao, C., Liu, W., Bai, X.: Multi-oriented text detection with fully convolutional networks. In: Proceedings of the IEEE Conference on Computer Vision and Pattern Recognition, pp. 4159–4167 (2016)
6. Coates, A., et al.: Text detection and character recognition in scene images with unsupervised feature learning. In: 2011 International Conference on Document Analysis and Recognition. IEEE, pp. 440–445 (2011)
7. Huang, W., Qiao, Y., Tang, X.: Robust scene text detection with convolution neural network induced MSER trees. In: Fleet, D., Pajdla, T., Schiele, B., Tuytelaars, T. (eds.) ECCV 2014. LNCS, vol. 8692, pp. 497–511. Springer, Cham (2014). https://doi.org/10.1007/978-3-319-10593-2_33
8. Jaderberg, M., Vedaldi, A., Zisserman, A.: Deep features for text spotting. In: Fleet, D., Pajdla, T., Schiele, B., Tuytelaars, T. (eds.) ECCV 2014. LNCS, vol. 8692, pp. 512–528. Springer, Cham (2014). https://doi.org/10.1007/978-3-319-10593-2_34
9. Zhang, Z., Zhang, C., Shen, W., Yao, C., Liu, W., Bai, X.: Multi-oriented text detection with fully convolutional networks. CoRR, vol. abs/1604.04018 (2016)
10. Isola, P., Zhu, J.-Y., Zhou, T., Efros, A.A.: Image-to-image translation with conditional adversarial networks. In: The IEEE Conference on Computer Vision and Pattern Recognition (CVPR), July 2017
11. Goodfellow, I., et al.: Generative adversarial nets. In: Ghahramani, Z., Welling, M., Cortes, C., Lawrence, N.D., Weinberger, K.Q. (eds.) Advances in Neural Information Processing Systems 27, pp. 2672–2680. Curran Associates Inc., Red Hook (2014)
12. Yao, C., Bai, X., Liu, W., Ma, Y., Tu, Z.: Detecting texts of arbitrary orientations in natural images. In: CVPR, pp. 1083–1090, June 2012
13. Yin, X., Yin, X., Huang, K.: Robust text detection in natural scene images. CoRR, vol. abs/1301.2628 (2013)
14. Cho, H., Sung, M., Jun, B.: Canny text detector: fast and robust scene text localization algorithm. In: The IEEE Conference on Computer Vision and Pattern Recognition (CVPR), June 2016
15. Tong, H., Huang, W., Qiao, Y., Yao, J.: Text-attentional convolutional neural network for scene text detection, October 2015
16. Karatzas, D., et al.: ICDAR 2015 competition on robust reading. In: Proceedings of the 2015 13th International Conference on Document Analysis and Recognition (ICDAR), Ser. ICDAR 2015, pp. 1156–1160. IEEE Computer Society, Washington, D.C. (2015)

17. Liu, W., et al.: SSD: single shot multibox detector. CoRR, vol. abs/1512.02325 (2015)
18. Wang, T., Wu, D.J., Coates, A., Ng, A.Y.: End-to-end text recognition with convolutional neural networks. In: Proceedings of the 21st International Conference on Pattern Recognition (ICPR 2012), pp. 3304–3308 (2012)
19. Girshick, R.: Fast R-CNN. In: The IEEE International Conference on Computer Vision (ICCV), December 2015
20. Liu, W., et al.: SSD: single shot multibox detector. In: Leibe, B., Matas, J., Sebe, N., Welling, M. (eds.) ECCV 2016. LNCS, vol. 9905, pp. 21–37. Springer, Cham (2016). https://doi.org/10.1007/978-3-319-46448-0_2
21. Redmon, J., Divvala, S., Girshick, R., Farhadi, A.: You only look once: unified, real-time object detection. In: The IEEE Conference on Computer Vision and Pattern Recognition (CVPR), June 2016
22. Ren, S., He, K., Girshick, R., Sun, J.: Faster R-CNN: towards real-time object detection with region proposal networks. In: Cortes, C., Lawrence, N.D., Lee, D.D., Sugiyama, M., Garnett, R. (eds.) Advances in Neural Information Processing Systems 28, pp. 91–99. Curran Associates Inc., Red Hook (2015)
23. Simonyan, K., Zisserman, A.: Very deep convolutional networks for large-scale image recognition. CoRR, vol. abs/1409.1556 (2014)
24. Huang, W., Lin, Z., Yang, J., Wang, J.: Text localization in natural images using stroke feature transform and text covariance descriptors. In: The IEEE International Conference on Computer Vision (ICCV), December 2013
25. Zhang, Z., Zhang, C., Shen, W., Yao, C., Liu, W., Bai, X.: Multi-oriented text detection with fully convolutional networks. arXiv:1604.04018 (2016)
26. Zhu, J.-Y., Park, T., Isola, P., Efros, A.A.: Unpaired image-to-image translation using cycle-consistent adversarial networks. In: The IEEE International Conference on Computer Vision (ICCV), October 2017
27. Liu, G., Reda, F.A., Shih, K.J., Wang, T.-C., Tao, A., Catanzaro, B.: Image inpainting for irregular holes using partial convolutions. In: Ferrari, V., Hebert, M., Sminchisescu, C., Weiss, Y. (eds.) ECCV 2018. LNCS, vol. 11215, pp. 89–105. Springer, Cham (2018). https://doi.org/10.1007/978-3-030-01252-6_6
28. Pathak, D., Krahenbuhl, P., Donahue, J., Darrell, T., Efros, A.A.: Context encoders: feature learning by inpainting. In: The IEEE Conference on Computer Vision and Pattern Recognition (CVPR), June 2016
29. Luc, P., Couprie, C., Chintala, S., Verbeek, J.: Semantic segmentation using adversarial networks. CoRR, vol. abs/1611.08408 (2016)
30. Ioffe, S., Szegedy, C.: Batch normalization: accelerating deep network training by reducing internal covariate shift. CoRR, vol. abs/1502.03167 (2015)
31. Collis, J.: Glossary of deep learning: batch normalisation (2017)
32. Jung, J., Lee, S., Cho, M.S., Kim, J.H.: Touch TT: scene text extractor using touch screen interface. ETRI J. **33**(1), 78–88 (2011)
33. Gupta, A., Vedaldi, A., Zisserman, A.: Synthetic data for text localization in natural images. In: CVPR (2016)
34. Tian, Z., Huang, W., He, T., He, P., Qiao, Y.: Detecting text in natural image with connectionist text proposal network. In: Leibe, B., Matas, J., Sebe, N., Welling, M. (eds.) ECCV 2016. LNCS, vol. 9912, pp. 56–72. Springer, Cham (2016). https://doi.org/10.1007/978-3-319-46484-8_4

Weakly Supervised Fine-Grained Visual Recognition via Adversarial Complementary Attentions and Hierarchical Bilinear Pooling

Xiaofei Li, Jianming Liu[✉], and Mingwen Wang

School of Computer and Information Engineering, Jiangxi Normal University,
Nanchang 330022, China
liujianming@jxnu.edu.cn

Abstract. Learning subtle and distinctive features is the key to fine-grained object recognition. Previous approaches use attention mechanisms to localize discriminatory regions and learn fine-grained details, which often treat each object part attention independently while neglecting the correlations among them and may lead them attentive to the same distinctive features. In this paper, we proposed a novel fine-grained visual recognition method to solve this problem by adversarial complementary attention (ACA) strategy and hierarchical bilinear pooling. Our method learns an attention-based classification branch through an attention module, and then train a counterpart classifier branch with adversarial complementary attention parts by erasing attentive regions in the first network branch from the feature maps. To capture different attention features interactions, a hierarchical bilinear pooling framework is used. Our method can be trained end-to-end without any bounding box/part annotations. Extensive experiments indicate that our approach is efficient and achieves the state-of-the-art performance on widely used fine-grained classification datasets, including CUB-200-2011, Stanford Cars, and FGVC-Aircraft datasets.

Keywords: Weakly supervised · Fine-grained visual recognition · Adversarial complementary attentions · Bilinear Pooling

1 Introduction

Fine-grained visual recognition (FGVC) is to recognize hundreds of subcategories belonging to the same basic-level category, such as hundreds of subcategories of birds [1], cars [2, 3], dogs [4], flowers [5] and aircraft [6]. It is easier to identify basic categories of objects (e.g. tables, bicycles, mineral water bottles, etc.), but it is extremely difficult to judge more refined object categories.

Existing FGVC methods can be roughly divided into strong supervised learning-based models [11, 12] and weakly-supervised learning-based models [14–17]. Although these models based on strong supervised information, which requires bounding box/part annotations, have achieved satisfactory recognition accuracy, the practical applications of such algorithms are limited to a certain extent due to the high cost of manual tagging

© Springer Nature Switzerland AG 2019
T. Gedeon et al. (Eds.): ICONIP 2019, LNCS 11953, pp. 74–85, 2019.
https://doi.org/10.1007/978-3-030-36708-4_7

information acquisition. Therefore, an obvious trend for fine-grained visual recognition is to use only image-level annotation information in model training, instead of using additional part annotation information.

Although huge successes in visual recognition [7–10] have been achieved with the development of Neural Networks, Fine-grained visual recognition is still challenging task, where discriminative details are too subtle to be well located and represented by traditional CNN. Existing FGVC methods try to solve this problem by attention models which learn part detectors to localize discriminatory regions and learn fine-grained details. However, there are several problems for these methods: (1) Most of them focus on the most discriminatory parts while missing other object parts. If some of these parts are obscured, the recognition rate will be limited. For instance, the beak, wings, or tail of the birds may be invisible or covered, once this happens, the discriminative object regions will be missing and fine-grained features will be lacked, recognition rate will be affected to some extent. (2) most of the approach treat each object part attention independently while neglecting the correlations among them and may lead them attentive to the same distinctive features. (3) Some methods are multi-models or multi-stages cooperation, which is not efficient enough or need some complex initialization, without a doubt it's a heavy workload.

In this paper, we propose a novel weakly supervised fine-grained recognition framework to address the above problems. It contains three branches: one trunk branch to obtain middle-level features and two sub-branches to learn discriminative regions complementarily, using Convolutional Block Attention Module (CBAM) [32] to get attention maps. To avoid missing any discriminative regions, the adversarial complementary attention (ACA) strategy is proposed, which contains two adversarial complementary attention branches. These two adversarial complementary branches apply attention supervision severally to extract local fine-grained features. At last, a hierarchical bilinear pooling framework is used to capture different attention features interactions.

2 Related Work

2.1 Fine-Grained Recognition

The biggest challenge of fine-grained recognition is that visual differences between different subcategories are minimal in the same super-category (e.g., birds [20], cars [22] and aircraft [23]). In order to solve this challenge, previous straightforward works usually use expensive manual object bounding box/part annotations [11, 21, 22], which is very expensive and difficult to be promoted and applied in practice. Focus on this defect, some unsupervised methods [1, 10, 23, 24] are employed. Though these unsupervised ways are more cost-saving, it can't locate to discriminative regions precisely, it's accuracy is also relatively lower.

With the development of the deep neural network, more and more approaches are proposed to learn fine-grained without any human annotations. Mask-CNN [28] not only use the fully connected network (FCN) to locate targets and parts in fine-grained images but also regard the predicted segmentation as a mask of targets and parts. Spatial Transformer Network (ST-CNN) [29] learns a spatial transformation model to locate accurate discriminative regions. Pose normalized CNN [12] extracts the local information of different levels firstly, then use pose alignment operation to improve FGVC performance. The ensemble networks based approaches [26, 27] divide fine-grained data sets into several similar subsets or directly using multiple neural networks can improve the performance of fine-grained recognition. The scheme of constellations [25] uses convolutional network features to generate some key points, and then uses these key points to extract local region information. Fu et al. proposed a recurrent attention convolutional neural network (RA-CNN) [7] which consists of an attention proposal network and region-based classifier network representation at multiple scales in a mutually reinforced way. In order to achieve better detection of key parts, Zhou et al. proposed Multi-Attention Multi-Class Constraint Network (MAMC) [8] to regulate multiple object parts between different input images.

2.2 Adversarial Complementary Learning

Adversarial Erasing (AE) method has been proposed in [33] to gradually acquire and expand the target regions, the top 20% pixels of the generated location maps are erased. The specific erasure method is to set the value of the corresponding pixels to the average value of the pixels of all training set pictures. Similar with AE, Adversarial Complementary Learning (ACoL) [19] also uses the same strategy, which automatically locates integrated regions of interest through a weak supervisory approach, and selects class-specific feature maps directly from the final convolution layer. The whole network consists of two classifiers, one of which is used to locate discriminatory regions, and the other is used to define regions of interest that A does not locate, thus forming a complementarity. In this paper, we draw lessons from above adversarial complementary learning strategies and combine with an attention mechanism to improve fine-grained image recognition performance.

2.3 Visual Attention

Visual attention module simulates the recognition process of the human visual system that has been used in many visual recognition tasks, the two-level attention [14] combines three types of attention: bottom-up attention to generating candidate image blocks, top-down attention to select relevant blocks to form specific objects, and bottom-up attention to locating discriminant components. By integrating these types of attention mechanisms to specific DCNN which is trained to extract foreground objects and components with strong features. Zhao et al. proposed Diversified Visual Attention Network (DVAN) [24] to explicitly pursue the diversity of attention and better gather discriminative information. Fully Convolutional Attention Localization Network [9], a visual attention model based on reinforcement learning is used to simulate learning to locate part of an object and classify objects in a scene. In order to make the part generation and feature learning in a mutually reinforcing way, Fu et al. proposed Recurrent Attention CNN (RA-CNN) [7] consists of a classification sub-network and an attention proposal sub-network (APN). Similar with RA-CNN, Zheng et al. proposed Learning Multi-Attention Convolutional Neural Network (MA-CNN) [10] to generate several attention discriminative regions and channel grouping loss to make intra-class similarity and inter-class separability as far as possible.

3 Approach

In this section, we will introduce the proposed weakly supervised fine-grained visual recognition via adversarial complementary attention strategy and hierarchical bilinear pooling (ACAHBP), which enable the learning of rich adversarial complementary interaction fine-grained features. As shown in Fig. 1, given an input image X, we first take it through several convolution layers of ResNet-50 which were pre-trained on ImageNet classification dataset [35] to extract mid-level features. Then the backbone network is divided into three modules: an attention module to locate the most discriminative region, an adversarial complementary attention module to find other discriminative parts by erasing the most discriminative region, and a hierarchical bilinear pooling module used to exact interaction features.

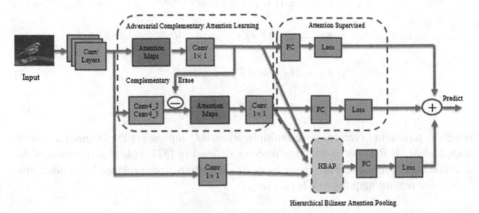

Fig. 1. Overview of our network architecture (ACAHBP), which consists of: (a) an attention module to find discriminative regions in a weakly supervised way. (b) an adversarial complementary attention module to constraint the two adversarial complementary attention branches to learn different discriminative regions. (c) a hierarchical bilinear attention pooling module to obtain interaction features.

3.1 Adversarial Complementary Attention Strategy

The idea of adversarial complementary learning strategy has improved great performance in weakly supervised semantic segmentation [33] and weakly supervised object localization [19]. Inspired by these, we propose an adversarial complementary attention strategy which discovering as many discriminant regions as possible through an adversarial learning manner.

Given an input image I, we first generate deep features by feeding the images into the pre-trained ImageNet convolutional neural network backbone which includes a set of convolutional, batch normalization, ReLU, and pooling layers, such as VGG-16 [34], ResNet-50 [35] and so on. Assume the output of the deep convolutional feature maps are denoted as $F \in \mathbb{R}^{C \times H \times W}$. Then we fed the feature maps F extracting from the backbone into two adversarial complementary attention learning branches. In each adversarial complementary branch, we use Convolutional Block Attention Module (CBAM) [32] to discover discriminative regions for the input image in an adversarial complementary way. Firstly, the attention map M_A and attentive feature F_A are obtained by the first branch $Classifier_A$, and then the corresponding regions within the input feature maps F for the second branch $Classifier_B$ are erased in an adversarial manner via replacing the values by zeros. Such an operation encourages second branch to discover other discriminative regions. For $Classifier_B$, we can get a different attention map M_B and attentive feature F_B. The overall adversarial complementary attention process can be summarized as:

$$M_A = M_s(M_c(F) \circ F) \in \mathbb{R}^{H \times W} \tag{1}$$

$$\widetilde{F} = F \circ 1(M_A < \sigma) \in \mathbb{R}^{C \times H \times W} \tag{2}$$

$$M_B = M_s(M_c(\widetilde{F}) \circ \widetilde{F}) \in \mathbb{R}^{H \times W} \tag{3}$$

$$F_A = M_A \circ M_c(F) \circ F \mathbb{R}^{C \times H \times W} \tag{4}$$

$$F_B = M_B \circ M_c(\widetilde{F}) \circ \widetilde{F} \mathbb{R}^{C \times H \times W} \tag{5}$$

Where $\circ$ represents element-wise multiplication, M_c represents the channel attention map, and M_s is the spatial attention map, as defined in [32]. $1(M_A < \sigma)$ denotes the threshold operation where the elements of M_A less than σ are replaced by 1, otherwise 0. $\widetilde{F}$ is the feature map fed to $Classifier_B$.

3.2 Hierarchical Bilinear Pooling

A method of combining feature maps of two CNNs (A and B) with matrix outer product has been proposed as Bilinear CNN [15], which can captures the pair-wise feature relations to improve the classification effect of the fine-grained image. The bilinear model consists of a quadruple

$$B = (f_A, f_B, P, C) \tag{6}$$

where f_A and f_B are feature functions, P is a pooling function and C is a classification function.

The bilinear feature combination of f_A and f_B at a location l is given by bilinear

$$(l, I, f_A, f_B) = f_A(l, I)^{\mathrm{T}} f_B(l, I) \tag{7}$$

As bilinear pooling produces a high dimensional features of quadratic expansion, factorized bilinear pooling using Hadamard product is proposed in [13]. In this section, we introduce our Hierarchical Bilinear Attention Pooling. Except for the two adversarial complementary attention learning branches $Classifier_1$, $Classifier_2$, we also use the primary mid-level feature $F_M \in \mathbb{R}^{C \times H \times W}$ to bilinear pooling with the other two adversarial complementary attention learning branches individually, and then, we get three bilinear pooling features

$$f_1 = P_1^T \left(U_1^T f_{A,l} \circ V_1^T f_{B,l} \right) \tag{8}$$

$$f_2 = P_2^T \left(U_2^T f_{A,l} \circ V_2^T f_{M,l} \right) \tag{9}$$

$$f_3 = P_3^T \left(U_3^T f_{B,l} \circ V_3^T f_{M,l} \right) \tag{10}$$

where $\circ$ represents element-wise multiplication, $f_{A,l}$, $f_{B,l}$, and $f_{M,l}$ represent local descriptors from different feature maps at the same spatial location l. we expect that f_1 represent the interaction characteristics between these two adversarial complementary attention branches, f_2, f_3 represent the interaction features between different cross layers. P_i^T, U_i^T, V_i^T are the parameters learned by projection matrices. Then, we use the Global Average Pooling (GAP) to further extract discriminative local features S_i by another feature extraction function $\varphi(\cdot)$

$$S_i = \varphi(F_i) \ (i = 1, 2, 3) \tag{11}$$

In order to get more hierarchical interaction features, we concatenate these hierarchical bilinear attention pooling discriminative local features $S_i (i = 1, 2, 3)$ (Fig. 2).

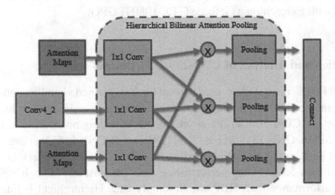

Fig. 2. An illustration of the hierarchical bilinear attention pooling. We apply a 1×1 Conv projection matrix to these three branches to obtain representations of object regions, then the interaction features between different layers are obtained by element-wise multiplication. After that, each branch through an average pooling to get the main features individually.

4 Experiments

4.1 Datasets and Implementation Details

Datasets: We comprehensive experiments on three publicly available datasets, including Caltech-CUB-200-2011 [32], Stanford Cars [3] and FGVC Aircraft [6], which are the widely used benchmark for fine-grained visual recognition. Table 1 showing the statistics of the three datasets.

Table 1. The statistic for three fine-grained datasets used in this paper.

Datasets	#Category	#Training	#Testing
CUB-200-2011 [32]	200	5994	5794
Stanford Cars [3]	196	8144	8041
FGVC-Aircraft [6]	100	6667	3333

Implementation Details: In all of our following experiments, the input images are resized to 448 × 448 for both training and testing, which is standard in the literature. We use ResNet-50 [35] as the backbone network pre-trained on ImageNet classification dataset [35] without any part or human bounding box annotations, and use Batch Normalization as regular. Based on empirical knowledge, we train our framework using Stochastic Gradient Descent (SGD) with the momentum of 0.9, weight decay of 0.00001, a batch size of 16, and the initial learning rate is set to 0.001. All of our experiments are implemented with Pytorch on a Geforce GTX 1080Ti GPU.

4.2 Evaluation and Analysis of CUB-200-2011 Dataset

CUB-200-2011 is the most widely-used dataset for fine-grained visual recognition. From Table 2 we can see that our framework is very competitive. For example, we obtain 87.4% accuracy on CUB-200-2011 test set without bounding box during testing, which is better than SPDA-CNN [31], Mask-CNN [28], and B-CNN [15] that even use strong supervision of both human-defined bounding box and ground truth parts. Our proposed ACAHBP achieves 5.8% better performance than the baseline with ResNet-50, and 0.4% better performance than HBP which simply uses Hierarchical Bilinear Pooling operations. At the same time, it indicates that adding attention mechanism to Bilinear Pooling model's performance is very competitive.

Table 2. Comparison of our approach (ACAHBP) to recent results on CUB-200-2011 dataset. Anno. Represents using bounding box in training.

Method	Anno.	Accuracy
ResNet-50 [35]		81.7%
SPDA-CNN [31]	√	85.1%
Mask-CNN [28]	√	85.45%
B-CNN (250 k-dims) [15]	√	85.1%
Bilinear CNN [15]		84.1%
Boost-CNN [30]		85.6%
CBP [5]		84.0%
RA-CNN [6]		85.3%
MA-CNN [9]		86.5%
MAMC [7]		86.5%
PC [15]		86.9%
HBP [17]		87.1%
ACAHBP		**87.4%**

4.3 Evaluation and Analysis on Stanford Cars Dataset

The recognition accuracy on Stanford Cars dataset is summarized in Table 3. Because the front and back of most cars are designed differently, and the foregrounds are larger, the recognition accuracy of different cars is difficult to be improved a lot. Relaying on adversarial complementary attentions for cross-layer feature interaction learning, our approach achieves 5.4%, 2.5%, and 1.2% improvement than R-CNN [14], FCAN [11] and PA-CNN [2] which use human-defined bounding box. We can find that we also obtain better recognition accuracy than the methods that exploiting multi-scale information such as RA-CNN [6].

4.4 Evaluation and Analysis of FGVC-Aircraft Dataset

The recognition accuracy on FGVC-Aircraft dataset is further summarized in Table 3. Because of the clear spatial structures, we can find that our proposed ACAHBP approach enables to achieve the highest performance among all the approaches. Note that our proposed ACAHBP significantly boosts the performance to 91.0%, which also obtains better results than the human annotation-based approach MDTP [23], and better than learning a filter bank-based approach DFL-CNN. This good performance once again demonstrates that our proposed ACAHBP can learn better feature representation.

Table 3. Comparison of our approach (ACAHBP) to recent results on Stanford Cars dataset and FGVC-Aircraft, respectively. Anno. Represents using the bounding box in training.

Method	Anno.	Accuracy on Stanford Cars	Anno.	Accuracy on FGVC-Aircraft
R-CNN [1]	√	88.4%		–
FCAN [11]	√	91.3%		–
PA-CNN [1]	√	92.6%		–
B-CNN [14]		91.3%		84.1%
MG-CNN [10]		–	√	86.6%
MDTP [23]		–	√	88.4%
Boost-CNN [32]		92.1%		88.5%
RA-CNN [6]		92.5%		88.2%
MA-CNN [9]		92.8%		89.9%
MAMC [7]		93.0%		–
PC [15]		93.4%		89.2%
HBP [17]		93.7%		90.3%
ACAHBP		**93.8%**		**91.0%**

4.5 Ablation Analysis

In order to understand the influence of different components of our framework, we remove different part of our framework on CUB-200-2011 dataset and research the contribution of each module. We report the results in Table 4.

Table 4. Contribution of our approach (ACAHBP) on CUB-200-2011 dataset.

Adversarial complementary mechanism	Attention mechanism	Attention supervision	Accuracy
	√	√	86.8%
√		√	86.3%
√	√		86.9%
√	√	√	**87.4%**

Importance of Adversarial Complementary Mechanism. We investigate the contribution of the adversarial complementary mechanism by training the ACAHBP, we just use two ordinary convolution layers include attention mechanism without adversarial complementary mechanism and comparing with the full ACAHBP framework. Table 4 shown the result, we can see a significant performance improvement when we use adversarial complementary mechanism intuitively. The recognition accuracy improves 1% from 86.8% to 87.4%. This result illustrates that adversarial complementary attention module can promote the improvement of classification accuracy.

Contribution of Attention Mechanism. The attention mechanism is very important for attending discriminative regions. In order to analyze the contribution of attention mechanism for attending more discriminative regions, we conduct ablation studies to understand the effectiveness of our approach. Table 4 shown the recognition accuracy whether we use attention mechanism. When we apply attention mechanisms to our framework, the recognition accuracy is 87.26%, once we don't apply any attention mechanisms, the recognition accuracy decreases to 86.3%, from which we find that applying attention mechanism we can get better performance. This indicates the importance of attention mechanism.

Effect of Complementary Attention Supervision. In order to verify complementary attention supervision is necessary. We remove the complementary attention supervision module to perform the experiment and compared with the full ACAHBP framework. From the classification accuracy of Table 4 we can notice that once we cut down the complementary attention supervision, the experimental result dropped from 87.4% to 86.9%.

5 Conclusions

In this paper, we propose a weakly supervised fine-grained visual recognition via adversarial complimentary attentions and hierarchical bilinear pooling, which can learn more discriminative features. Our proposed network can be trained end-to-end without any bounding box or part annotations. Extensive experiments in CUB-200-2011, Stanford Cars, and FGVC-Aircraft dataset show superior performances. In the future, we will further research how to learn more object regions correctly and reducing irrelevant background noise.

Acknowledgments. This work was financially supported by the Natural Science Foundation of China (No. 61662034), the Natural Science Foundation of China (No. 61876074), the Natural Science Foundation of China (No. 61562031), the Science Foundation of Education Department of Jiangxi Province (No. 150353), and the Project Funding of Graduate Innovation Fund of Jiangxi Education Department (No. YC2018-S186).

References

1. Zhang, X., Xiong, H., Zhou, W., Lin, W., Tian, Q.: Picking deep filter responses for fine-grained image recognition. In: CVPR, pp. 1134–1142, June 2016
2. Krause, J., Jin, H., Yang, J., et al.: Fine-grained recognition without part annotations. In: Proceedings of the IEEE Conference on Computer Vision and Pattern Recognition, pp. 5546–5555 (2015)

3. Krause, J., Stark, M., Deng, J., Fei-Fei, L.: 3D object representations for fine-grained categorization. In: Proceedings of the IEEE International Conference on Computer Vision Workshops, pp. 554–561 (2013)
4. Khosla, A., Jayadevaprakash, N., Yao, B., Li, F.-F.: Novel dataset for fine-grained image categorization: stanford dogs. In: Proceedings of the CVPR Workshop on Fine-Grained Visual Categorization (FGVC), vol. 2 (2011)
5. Nilsback, M.E., Zisserman, A.: Automated flower classification over a large number of classes. In: Sixth Indian Conference on Computer Vision, Graphics & Image Processing, pp. 722–729 (2008)
6. Maji, S., Rahtu, E., Kannala, J., Blaschko, M., Vedaldi, A.: Fine-grained visual classification of aircraft. arXiv preprint arXiv:1306.5151 (2013)
7. Fu, J., Zheng, H., Mei, T.: Look closer to see better: recurrent attention convolutional neural network for fine-grained image recognition. In: 2017 IEEE Conference on Computer Vision and Pattern Recognition, CVPR 2017, Honolulu, HI, USA, 21–26 July 2017, pp. 4476–4484 (2017)
8. Sun, M., Yuan, Y., Zhou, F., Ding, E.: Multi-attention multi-class constraint for fine-grained image recognition. In: Ferrari, V., Hebert, M., Sminchisescu, C., Weiss, Y. (eds.) ECCV 2018. LNCS, vol. 11220, pp. 834–850. Springer, Cham (2018). https://doi.org/10.1007/978-3-030-01270-0_49
9. Liu, X., Xia, T., Wang, J., Lin, Y.: Fully convolutional attention localization networks: efficient attention localization for fine-grained recognition. CoRR, abs/1603.06765 (2016)
10. Zheng, H., Fu, J., Mei, T., Luo, J.: Learning multi-attention convolutional neural network for fine-grained image recognition. In: ICCV, October 2017
11. Zhang, N., Donahue, J., Girshick, R., Darrell, T.: Part-based R-CNNs for fine-grained category detection. In: Fleet, D., Pajdla, T., Schiele, B., Tuytelaars, T. (eds.) ECCV 2014. LNCS, vol. 8689, pp. 834–849. Springer, Cham (2014). https://doi.org/10.1007/978-3-319-10590-1_54
12. Branson, S., Van Horn, G., Belongie, S., Perona, P.: Bird species categorization using pose normalized deep convolutional nets (2014). https://arxiv.org/abs/1406.2952
13. Kim, J.H., On, K.W., Lim, W., et al.: Hadamard product for low-rank bilinear pooling. arXiv preprint arXiv:1610.04325 (2016)
14. Xiao, T., Xu, Y., Yang, K., Zhang, J., Peng, Y., Zhang, Z.: The application of two-level attention models in deep convolutional neural network for fine-grained image classification. In: CVPR (2014)
15. Lin, T.Y., Roy-Chowdhury, A., Maji, S.: Bilinear CNN models for fine-grained visual recognition. In: Proceedings of the IEEE International Conference on Computer Vision, pp. 1449–1457 (2015)
16. Dubey, A., Gupta, O., Guo, P., Raskar, R., Farrell, R., Naik, N.: Pairwise confusion for fine-grained visual classification. In: Ferrari, V., Hebert, M., Sminchisescu, C., Weiss, Y. (eds.) ECCV 2018. LNCS, vol. 11216, pp. 71–88. Springer, Cham (2018). https://doi.org/10.1007/978-3-030-01258-8_5
17. Yang, Z., Luo, T., Wang, D., Hu, Z., Gao, J., Wang, L.: Learning to navigate for fine-grained classification. In: Ferrari, V., Hebert, M., Sminchisescu, C., Weiss, Y. (eds.) Computer Vision – ECCV 2018. LNCS, vol. 11218, pp. 438–454. Springer, Cham (2018). https://doi.org/10.1007/978-3-030-01264-9_26
18. Yu, C., Zhao, X., Zheng, Q., Zhang, P., You, X.: Hierarchical bilinear pooling for fine-grained visual recognition. In: Ferrari, V., Hebert, M., Sminchisescu, C., Weiss, Y. (eds.) ECCV 2018. LNCS, vol. 11220, pp. 595–610. Springer, Cham (2018). https://doi.org/10.1007/978-3-030-01270-0_35
19. Zhang, X., Wei, Y., Feng, J., Yang, Y., Huang, T.S.: Adversarial complementary learning for weakly supervised object localization. In: The IEEE Conference on Computer Vision and Pattern Recognition (CVPR), June 2018

20. Wah, C., Branson, S., Welinder, P., Perona, P., Belongie, S.: The Caltech-UCSD birds 200–2011 dataset. In: Technical Report CNS-TR-2011-001, Caltech (2011)
21. Berg, T., Belhumeur, P.N.: POOF: part-based one-vs.-one features for fine-grained categorization, face verification, and attribute estimation. In: CVPR (2013)
22. Yao, B., Bradski, G.R., Fei-Fei, L.: A codebook-free and annotation-free approach for fine-grained image categorization. In: CVPR (2012)
23. Wang, D., Shen, Z., Shao, J., Zhang, W., Xue, X., Zhang, Z.: Multiple granularity descriptors for fine-grained categorization. In: ICCV, pp. 2399–2406 (2015)
24. Zhao, B., Wu, X., Feng, J., Peng, Q., Yan, S.: Diversified visual attention networks for fine-grained object classification. Trans. Multi. **19**(6), 1245–1256 (2017)
25. Simon, M., Rodner, E.: Neural activation constellations: unsupervised part model discovery with convolutional networks. In: Proceedings of the IEEE International Conference on Computer Vision, pp. 1143–1151 (2015)
26. Ge, Z.Y., Bewley, A., McCool, C., et al.: Fine-grained classification via mixture of deep convolutional neural networks. In: 2016 IEEE Winter Conference on Applications of Computer Vision (WACV), pp. 1–6. IEEE (2016)
27. Wang, Z., Wang, X., Wang, G.: Learning fine-grained features via a CNN tree for large-scale classification. Neurocomputing **275**, 1231–1240 (2018)
28. Wei, X.S., Xie, C.W., Wu, J.: Mask-CNN: localizing parts and selecting descriptors for fine-grained image recognition. arXiv preprint arXiv:1605.06878 (2016)
29. Jaderberg, M., Simonyan, K., Zisserman, A.: Spatial transformer networks. In: Advances in Neural Information Processing Systems, pp. 2017–2025 (2015)
30. Moghimi, M., Belongie, S.J., Saberian, M.J., et al.: Boosted convolutional neural networks. In: BMVC, pp. 24.1–24.13 (2016)
31. Zhang, H., Xu, T., Elhoseiny, M., et al.: SPDA-CNN: unifying semantic part detection and abstraction for fine-grained recognition. In: Proceedings of the IEEE Conference on Computer Vision and Pattern Recognition, pp. 1143–1152 (2016)
32. Woo, S., Park, J., Lee, J.-Y., Kweon, I.S.: CBAM: convolutional block attention module. In: Ferrari, V., Hebert, M., Sminchisescu, C., Weiss, Y. (eds.) ECCV 2018. LNCS, vol. 11211, pp. 3–19. Springer, Cham (2018). https://doi.org/10.1007/978-3-030-01234-2_1
33. Wei, Y., Feng, J., Liang, X., et al.: Object region mining with adversarial erasing: a simple classification to semantic segmentation approach. In: Proceedings of the IEEE Conference on Computer Vision and Pattern Recognition, pp. 1568–1576 (2017)
34. Simonyan, K., Zisserman, A.: Very deep convolutional networks for large-scale image recognition. arXiv preprint arXiv:1409.1556 (2014)
35. He, K., Zhang, X., Ren, S., et al.: Deep residual learning for image recognition. In: Proceedings of the IEEE Conference on Computer Vision and Pattern Recognition, pp. 770–778 (2016)

Learning an Adversarial Network for Speech Enhancement Under Extremely Low Signal-to-Noise Ratio Condition

Xiangdong Su, Xiang Hao$^{(\boxtimes)}$, Zhiyu Wang, Yun Liu, Huali Xu, Tongyang Liu, Guanglai Gao, and Feilong

Inner Mongolia Key Laboratory of Mongolian Information Processing Technology, College of Computer Science, Inner Mongolia Univeristy, Hohhot, China
haoxiangsnr@gmail.com

Abstract. Speech enhancement under low Signal-to-noise ratio (SNR) condition is a challenging task. This paper formulates the speech enhancement as a spectrogram mapping problem that converts the noisy speech spectrogram to the clean speech spectrogram. On such basis, we propose a robust speech enhancement approach based on deep adversarial learning for extremely low SNR Condition. The deep adversarial network is trained on a few paired spectrograms of the noisy and the clean speeches, and several strategies are applied to optimize it, skip connection, patchGAN and spectral normalization. Our approach is evaluated under extremely low SNR conditions (the lowest SNR is $-20\,\mathrm{dB}$), and the result demonstrates that our approach significantly improves the speech quality and substantially outperforms the representative deep learning models, including DNN, SEGAN and Bidirectional LSTM using phase-sensitive spectrum approximation cost function (PSA-BLSTM) regarding Short-Time Objective Intelligibility (STOI) and Perceptual evaluation of speech quality (PESQ).

Keywords: Speech enhancement · Low SNR · Spectrogram · Adversarial learning

1 Introduction

Speech enhancement is a hot topic in speech signal processing. It intends to recover the clean speech from the noisy speech [12]. Such technologies are widely used in related processing systems, e.g., hearing prosthesis [23], mobile telecommunication [7], and automatic speech recognition [29], and so on. With the emergence of deep learning, a large number of methods were established [26,28]. However, these methods may not adequate for speech enhancement under low Signal-to-noise ratio (SNR) condition, which is more challenge than that under high SNR condition. There are many communication scenarios under extremely low SNR condition. For examples, workers communicating with the walkie-talkie in a metal cutting factory, mechanics communication with the wireless headset

© Springer Nature Switzerland AG 2019
T. Gedeon et al. (Eds.): ICONIP 2019, LNCS 11953, pp. 86–97, 2019.
https://doi.org/10.1007/978-3-030-36708-4_8

when testing a helicopter, and so on. Even in some noisy environments, people can only use gestures to communicate, because the sound collected by the microphone has serious noise, which makes the other party unable to hear clearly. Therefore, it is necessary to develop a more robust speech enhancement method for extremely low SNR condition.

From the perspective of signal processing, speech enhancement is a mapping problem from the noisy spectrogram (magnitude spectrogram) to their clean counterparts. Previous works [27, 28] have shown that the human ear is relatively insensitive to phase. Therefore, the core of speech enhancement is spectrogram transformation, which is a special case of image conversion. Motivated by the promising results of generative adversarial networks (GANs) [6] in a variety of image processing tasks [9, 15], we put forward an adversarial learning-based approach to solve the problem of speech enhancement under low SNR condition. Our approach consists of a generative model G and a discriminative model D. These two models are trained with paired spectrograms of noise speeches and clean speeches in an adversarial fashion. After that, we send the spectrograms of the noisy speech to the generator to obtain the target spectrograms, which is used to reconstruct the clean speech. To optimize our network, three strategies are used, including skip connection [22], PatchGAN [9], spectral normalization [16]. To select the suitable spectrogram, this paper compares the four most popular spectrograms in details, including magnitude spectrogram, log-power spectrogram (LPS), mel-scaled spectrogram, log mel-scaled spectrogram.

The proposed approach is evaluated under extremely low SNR conditions, including 0 dB, -3 dB, -5 dB, -7 dB, -10 dB, -12 dB, -15 dB, -17 dB and -20 dB. Comparison is also made between the proposed approach and other representative speech enhancement approaches, including DNN [31], SEGAN [19], and Bidirectional LSTM using phase-sensitive spectrum approximation cost function (PSA-BLSTM) [3]. Experiment results demonstrate that our approach significantly improves the speech quality and substantially outperforms other approaches regarding Short-Time Objective Intelligibility (STOI) [24] and Perceptual evaluation of speech quality (PESQ) [21].

Although SEGAN first used GAN for speech enhancement, there are two critical differences between SEGAN and our approach. First, the network structure in our approach is different from that in SEGAN. Second, our approach operates in the frequency domain while SEGAN operates in the time domain and employs a high-frequency preemphasis filter to the input data. There is another GAN-based speech enhancement approach is proposed by Michelsanti et al. [14]. Except for the difference in network structure, our approach explores four kinds of spectrograms.

There are two main advantages of the proposed approach. First and foremost, our approach significantly improves the speech quality and achieves state-of-the-art performance in speech enhancement under extremely low SNR conditions. Second, our approach only needs a small dataset, and the network can be trained very fast.

2   Related Work

Over the past years, speech enhancement has been widely studied, and many methods have been proposed, including spectral subtraction [25], Wiener filtering [5], statistical model-based method [2] and subspace algorithm [32], etc. Recently, neural network based approaches have been proved more effective in such task, for instance, denoising autoencoder [13], deep neural networks (DNNs) [31], convolutional neural networks (CNNs) [17], recurrent neural networks [18], and GAN based network [14,19]. The recurrent neural networks have shown significant performance exploiting the temporal context information in embedded signals. SEGAN [19] is operating at the waveform level to train an end-to-end enhancement model.

In our approach, the key challenge is converting the source spectrogram of the noisy speech to the target spectrogram of the clean speech. It is similar to the image-to-image problem. We tackle spectrogram-to-spectrogram mapping with conditional GAN [15], which was proved to be suitable for the image-to-image task [9]. Denton et al. in [1] introduce a generative model capable of producing high-quality samples of natural images. Gauthier in [4] applies a conditional GAN to generate faces with specific attributes. Karacan et al. in [10] propose a deep conditional generative adversarial network architecture to generate outdoor scenes, which takes the strength from the semantic layout and scene attributes integrated as conditioning variables. Reed et al. in [20] develop a deep architecture and GAN formulation to effectively bridge the advances of recurrent neural networks and convolution networks in text and image modeling, translating visual concepts from characters to pixels.

3   Approach

The computational objective of spectrogram-based speech enhancement is to estimate the clean spectrogram from the noisy spectrogram, and use the clean spectrogram to reconstruct the enhanced speech. It is worth noting that the resulted spectrogram of STFT is a complex-valued matrix and can be decomposed into a magnitude spectrogram and a phase spectrogram. It is traditionally believed that the magnitude spectrogram plays a dominant role for shorter windows (20–30 ms) in speech signal processing, while the phase is less important [27,31]. Therefore, we only focus on the magnitude spectrogram estimation rather than phase estimation in this paper and use the enhanced magnitude spectrogram and the noisy phase spectrogram to reconstruct the enhanced speech. The next Subsect. 3.1 will describe our conditional GAN model for mapping noisy magnitude spectrogram to clean magnitude spectrogram in details.

3.1   Module Architecture

The conditional GAN in our approach consists of two components, a generator and a discriminator. The generator network G maps from noise spectrogram to enhanced counterpart. In contrast, the discriminator network D maps from a spectrogram to a probability that the spectrogram is from the real data distribution: $D(x) \to (0, 1)$. These two networks are trained in an adversarial way. For a fixed generator G, the discriminator D is trained to classify the output spectrogram as either being from the training data (close to 1) or a fixed generator (close to 0). When the discriminator is optimal, it can be frozen, and the generator G can continue to be trained to lower the accuracy of the discriminator. This process repeated several times and the generator is improved gradually. Once trained, the generator can be used to do spectrogram mapping.

The generator (shown in Fig. 1) possesses an encoder-decoder structure. The mixture spectrogram is first compressed into a higher level representation through a series of encoders (Convolution + Batch Normalization [8] + Leaky ReLU [30]). Then, the compressed representation is converted into the enhanced spectrogram through a series of decoders (Deconvolution + Batch Normalization + ReLU). Batch Normalization [8] is used in each convolutional layer to ensure network performance and stability. The discriminator (shown in Fig. 2) uses an encoder-like structure, in which the inputs are the mixture spectrum together with the enhanced spectrum from the generator or the clean counterpart. They are concatenated together and passed through the processing modules in sequence.

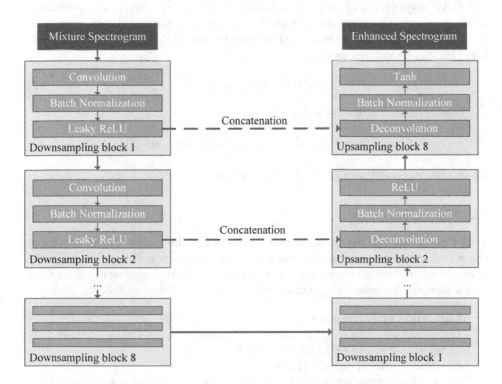

Fig. 1. The generator in our approach.

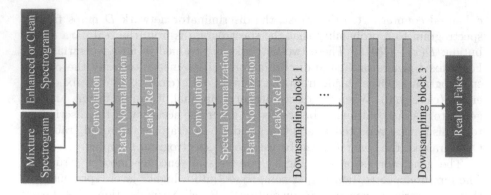

Fig. 2. The discriminator in our approach.

The objective of the conditional GAN can be expressed as Eq. 1:

$$\mathcal{L}_{conditionalGAN}(G, D) = \mathbb{E}_{x,y}[logD(x,y)] + \mathbb{E}_x[log(1 - D(x, G(x)))] \quad (1)$$

where G tries to minimize this objective against an adversarial D that tries to maximize it. The previous study [9] has proved that it is beneficial to mix the GAN objective with a $L1$ loss function. The discriminator's job remains unchanged, but the generator is tasked with not only fooling the discriminator but also being near the ground truth output from a $L1$ perspective. The $L1$ loss function can be written as Eq. 2:

$$\mathcal{L}_{L1}(G) = \mathbb{E}_{x,y}|y - G(x)| \quad (2)$$

Thus, the final objective is Eq. 3:

$$G^* = \arg\min_G \max_D(\mathcal{L}_{conditionalGAN}(G, D) + \lambda\mathcal{L}_{L_1}(G)) \quad (3)$$

which λ is the coefficient of the $L1$ loss function.

3.2   Spectrogram

There are many spectrograms have been proposed in earlier works. To select the suitable one, we compare the magnitude spectrogram and its variants in the experiment, including log-power spectrogram, mel-scaled spectrogram and log mel-scaled spectrogram. These four spectrograms are listed as follows:

– **Magnitude spectrogram**
  The magnitude spectrogram can be obtained by performing a short-time Fourier transform (STFT) on the speech.
– **Log-power spectrogram (LPS)**
  Log-power spectrogram is the Logarithmic result of the power of the magnitude spectrogram.

- **Mel-scaled spectrogram**
  As a kind of improved magnitude spectrogram, the mel-scaled spectrogram is obtained by multiplying mel filter bank on the magnitude spectrogram. It is equally spaced on the mel scale. Mel frequency bands approximate the human auditory system's response more closely than the linearly-spaced frequency bands.
- **Log mel-scaled spectrogram (Log-Mel)**
  According to our observation, most of the values in the mel-scaled spectrogram approximates to zero. We performed a non-linear scaling (Logarithmic operation) on the mel-scaled spectrogram, used the resulting data as the network input.

3.3 Optimization

Skip Connection. Since the noisy speech and its enhanced counterpart represent the same content, their spectrograms are the renderings of the same underlying structure. To integrate such limitation, we follow the literature [9] to design the generator in conditional GAN. We directly give an output of each ith convolution layer to the $(n - i)$th deconvolution layer by adding a skip connection between them, where n is the total number of layers. Each skip connection simply concatenates all channels at ith layer with those at $(n - i)$th layer. Such a strategy can be viewed as low-level information sharing to control the enhanced spectrogram.

PatchGAN. PatchGAN can sufficiently model high-frequency structure of those images. In our approach, we treated spectrograms as a kind of special images which represent speech. Therefore, the PatchGAN used in image-to-image tasks also adopted in our approach. This discriminator D tries to classify if each $N \times N$ patch in a spectrogram is real or fake, averaging all responses to provide the ultimate output of discriminator D.

Spectral Normalization. Spectral normalization [16] controls the Lipschitz constant of the discriminator function by literally constraining the spectral normalization of each layer. It imposes sample data independent regularization on the cost function, just like $L2$ regularization and Lasso. It can stabilize the training of the discriminator. More details can be found in the work [16].

4 Experiments

4.1 Dataset and Metrics

To evaluate the proposed approach, the TIMIT and NOISEX-92 corpus are used in the experiment. The TIMIT corpus is used as the clean database and the NOISEX-92 corpus are used as interference, respectively. We randomly selected

400 utterances from the TIMIT and divided them into three parts: the training part (280 utterances), the validation part (60 utterances) and the test part (60 utterances). We employ babble, factoryfloor1, destroyerengine and destroyerops from NOISEX-92 corpus for training. We mix the 280 utterances and 60 utterances with these noise at 0 dB, −5 dB, −10 dB and −15 dB SNR to create the training dataset and validation dataset, respectively. Beside these noises, we use factoryfloor2 to evaluate generalization performance. We mix all five noises with the 60 testing utterances at 0 dB, −3 dB, −5 dB, −7 dB, −10 dB, −12 dB, −15 dB and −20 dB SNR to create the testing dataset, where −3 dB, −7 dB, −12 dB, −17 dB and −20 dB are unseen SNR conditions. We use STOI and PESQ score to measure the intelligibility and speech quality, respectively. The range of STOI is 0–1, and the range of PESQ is −0.5–4.5. The higher the STOI and PESQ, the better.

4.2 Training

To training our networks, we use the Adam optimizer [11] with leaning rate = 0.0002, decay rates $\beta_1 = 0.5$, $\beta_2 = 0.999$. We set batch size to 150 and negative slope of Leaky ReLU to 0.1. We perform gradient descent on the generator G and the discriminator D alternatively to optimize both of them. Once we reached the inference phase, we ran the generator in the same manner as we had during the training phase. The λ in Eq. 2 is set according to the validation experiment, which equals 120 in the best model.

4.3 Comparison of Different Spectrograms

As mentioned, there are four typical spectrograms, including magnitude spectrogram, log-power spectrogram, mel-scaled spectrogram and log mel-scaled spectrogram. In this section, experiments are conducted to select the best spectrogram. Each spectrogram is used individually in the training and the testing section. Table 1 lists the results on 9 different SNR conditions in terms of STOI and PESQ. The "Mixture" line represents the unprocessed speech.

From Table 1, we can see that no matter at any SNR condition, our approach obtains the best performance when using log mel-scaled spectrogram as input. Mel-scaled spectrogram is better than the magnitude spectrogram in our approach due to the mel filter bank. Compared to the linearly-spaced frequency bands in magnitude spectrogram and LPS, the mel frequency bands are closer to the human auditory system. Log mel-scaled spectrogram is the variant of mel-scaled spectrogram. The log operation makes the value distribution more dispersed and further improved the STOI and PESQ. Also, the LPS is better than magnitude spectrogram on STOI while worse than it on PESQ.

4.4 Comparison with Baseline Models

This paper compares our approach with the following approaches, including DNN [31], SEGAN [19], and PSA-BLSTM [3]. DNN is a typical approach used in

Table 1. Comparison of different spectrograms.

	Target	0 dB	−3 dB	−5 dB	−7 dB	−10 dB	−12 dB	−15 dB	−17 dB	−20 dB	Mean
STOI	Mixture	0.666	0.609	0.571	0.534	0.482	0.451	0.412	0.392	0.368	0.498
	Magnitude	0.786	0.757	0.733	0.706	0.661	0.629	0.576	0.539	0.483	0.652
	LPS	0.785	0.757	0.735	0.712	0.672	0.643	0.597	**0.564**	0.512	0.664
	Mel	0.786	0.757	0.733	0.706	0.661	0.629	0.576	0.539	0.483	0.652
	Log-Mel	**0.792**	**0.764**	**0.742**	**0.718**	**0.677**	**0.647**	**0.598**	**0.564**	**0.513**	**0.668**
PESQ	Mixture	1.762	1.554	1.421	1.298	1.112	1.075	1.107	0.976	1.010	1.257
	Magnitude	2.405	2.286	2.192	2.084	1.912	1.795	1.617	1.479	1.282	1.894
	LPS	2.382	2.232	2.138	2.031	1.857	1.738	1.544	1.410	1.231	1.840
	Mel	2.405	2.286	2.192	2.084	1.912	1.795	1.617	1.479	1.282	1.894
	Log-Mel	**2.455**	**2.342**	**2.260**	**2.171**	**2.029**	**1.928**	**1.763**	**1.639**	**1.453**	**2.004**

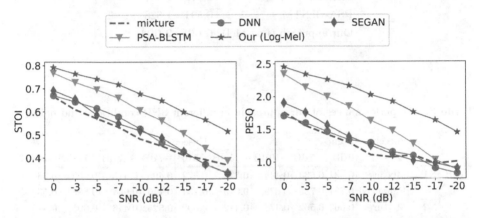

Fig. 3. Illustration of the average performances of our approach and the baseline approaches at different SNRs.

speech enhancement. It provides substantial speech intelligibility improvements in background noise. SEGAN is a GAN-based approach which operates in the time domain. PSA-BLSTM is a bidirectional LSTM for speech enhancement, in which phase-sensitive spectrum approximation (PSA) is used as a cost function. All hyperparameters in these approaches were set according to the description in the above works. To fine-tuning the BiLSTM, we used an augmented dataset resulting from the training dataset to train PSA-BLSTM. According to the Sect. 4.3, the most suitable spectrogram is the log mel-scaled spectrogram for our approach. Therefore, we compare our approach of log mel-scaled spectrogram with the other three approaches.

As shown in Fig. 3, our approach achieves the best performance at each SNR condition. The improvement is very significant than the mixture before processing. With the decrease of SNR, our approach keep a very obvious improvement on STOI and PESQ while the other three approaches only get little or almost no improvement. PSA-BLSM is the best among the baseline approaches.

Table 2 shows the average performance of our approach and the baseline models on the test dataset. Compared with unprocessed speech, our approach produced a 34.14% improvement on STOI and a 59.43% improvement on PESQ. It is worth noting that, compared with PSA-BLSTM, our approach obtains a better performance with rather less training data.

Table 2. The average performances of our approach and the baseline approaches on the test set.

Method	STOI	PESQ
Mixture	0.498	1.257
DNN	0.514	1.266
SEGAN	0.516	1.321
PSA-BLSTM	0.594	1.628
Our approach (Log-Mel)	**0.668**	**2.004**

Table 3. The performances of our approach on different SNR conditions and noises.

	Noise	Speech	Seen				Unseen				
			0 dB	−5 dB	−10 dB	−15 dB	−3 dB	−7 dB	−12 dB	−17 dB	−20 dB
STOI	N1	Mixture	0.631	0.533	0.444	0.378	0.572	0.495	0.415	0.359	0.338
		Enhanced	0.781	0.735	0.679	0.613	0.754	0.715	0.654	0.583	0.539
	N2	Mixture	0.663	0.562	0.474	0.412	0.602	0.525	0.446	0.395	0.376
		Enhanced	0.807	0.759	0.698	0.625	0.780	0.736	0.669	0.595	0.548
	N3	Mixture	0.670	0.578	0.488	0.415	0.616	0.542	0.456	0.393	0.368
		Enhanced	0.793	0.749	0.694	0.628	0.768	0.728	0.669	0.599	0.554
	N4	Mixture	0.619	0.517	0.432	0.375	0.557	0.480	0.405	0.360	0.344
		Enhanced	0.772	0.721	0.658	0.586	0.743	0.697	0.631	0.556	0.511
	N5	Mixture	0.750	0.667	0.574	0.484	0.702	0.630	0.536	0.453	0.414
		Enhanced	0.806	0.749	0.657	0.537	0.775	0.716	0.612	0.484	0.410
PESQ	N1	Mixture	1.700	1.369	0.892	0.702	1.493	1.264	0.767	0.644	0.590
		Enhanced	2.423	2.246	2.045	1.830	2.316	2.173	1.960	1.725	1.554
	N2	Mixture	1.663	1.402	1.202	1.118	1.496	1.316	1.121	1.014	0.960
		Enhanced	2.456	2.276	2.064	1.823	2.351	2.199	1.972	1.716	1.528
	N3	Mixture	1.786	1.389	1.104	1.189	1.552	1.238	1.059	0.945	1.176
		Enhanced	2.482	2.306	2.116	1.885	2.379	2.225	2.030	1.769	1.584
	N4	Mixture	1.576	1.234	1.014	1.465	1.366	1.111	1.211	1.324	1.400
		Enhanced	2.376	2.183	1.972	1.735	2.269	2.095	1.881	1.623	1.448
	N5	Mixture	2.090	1.712	1.352	1.071	1.864	1.563	1.224	0.961	0.932
		Enhanced	2.538	2.289	1.945	1.534	2.396	2.162	1.789	1.354	1.142

4.5   Comparison on Different SNR Conditions and Noises

To better understand our approach, Table 3 shows test result at different SNR conditions and noises. The noises N1, N2, N3, N4 and N5 are babble, destroyerengine, destroyerops, factoryfloor1 and factoryfloor2, respectively. For each noise, the "Mixture" line represents the unprocessed speech, and the "Enhanced" line represents the result after speech enhancement.

For each noise, the improvements after speech enhancement are significant, indicating that our approach is effective. The huge improvement is obtained at $-20\,\mathrm{dB}$ SNR, proving that our approach can perform well at extremely low SNR. For the unseen SNR conditions and noise, the improvement is distinguished, showing that our approach has a good generalization ability. Also, the best performance of our network is obtained at the 120th epoch, which manifests our approach can be trained very fast. Furthermore, the strategies used in the experiment are quite important for network training.

5   Conclusion

This paper proposes a robust speech enhancement approach based on deep adversarial learning for extremely low SNR condition. We formulate speech enhancement as a mapping problem of spectrogram and proposes a conditional GAN based approach to solve it. The network is trained in an adversarial learning way, which integrates several strategies to optimize it, including skip connection, PatchGAN and spectral normalization. Our approach outperforms DNN, SEGAN and PSA-BLSTM on low SNR conditions and achieves very significant improvement than the mixture before processing. For the unseen SNR conditions and noise, the improvement is distinguished, showing that our approach has a good generalization ability. Besides, our approach is efficient and straightforward, which needs rather small training data and can be trained very fast.

Acknowledgement. This work was funded by National Natural Science Foundation of China (Grant No. 61563040, 61773224, 61762069), Natural Science Foundation of Inner Mongolia Autonomous Region (Grant No. 2017BS0601, 2016ZD06, 2018MS06006), Inner Mongolia University Research and Innovation Project: (Grant No. 10000-15010109), and program of higher-level talents of Inner Mongolia University (Grant No. 21500-5165161).

References

1. Denton, E.L., Chintala, S., Szlam, A., Fergus, R.: Deep generative image models using a Laplacian pyramid of adversarial networks. In: NIPS (2015)
2. Ephraim, Y.: Statistical-model-based speech enhancement systems. Proc. IEEE **80**(10), 1526–1555 (1992). https://doi.org/10.1109/5.168664
3. Erdogan, H., Hershey, J.R., Watanabe, S., Le Roux, J.: Phase-sensitive and recognition-boosted speech separation using deep recurrent neural networks. In: 2015 IEEE International Conference on Acoustics, Speech and Signal Processing (ICASSP), pp. 708–712, April 2015. https://doi.org/10.1109/ICASSP.2015.7178061

4. Gauthier, J.: Conditional generative adversarial nets for convolutional face generation (2014)
5. Ghael, S., Sayeed, A.M., Baraniuk, R.G.: Improved wavelet denoising via empirical Wiener filtering. In: SPIE Technical Conference on Wavelet Applications in Signal Processing (1997)
6. Goodfellow, I.J., et al.: Generative adversarial nets. In: International Conference on Neural Information Processing Systems, pp. 2672–2680 (2014)
7. Granovetter, R.P., Sinclair, M.J., Zhang, Z., Liu, Z.: Method and apparatus for multi-sensory speech enhancement on a mobile device. US Patent 7,283,850, 16 October 2007
8. Ioffe, S., Szegedy, C.: Batch normalization: accelerating deep network training by reducing internal covariate shift. In: Proceedings of the 32nd International Conference on International Conference on Machine Learning - Volume 37, ICML 2015, pp. 448–456. JMLR.org (2015)
9. Isola, P., Zhu, J.Y., Zhou, T., Efros, A.A.: Image-to-image translation with conditional adversarial networks. In: 2017 IEEE Conference on Computer Vision and Pattern Recognition (CVPR) (2017)
10. Karacan, L., Akata, Z., Erdem, A., Erdem, E.: Learning to generate images of outdoor scenes from attributes and semantic layouts. arXiv preprint arXiv:1612.00215 (2016)
11. Kingma, D., Ba, J.: Adam: a method for stochastic optimization. In: International Conference on Learning Representations, December 2014
12. Loizou, P.C.: Speech Enhancement: Theory and Practice, 2nd edn. CRC Press Inc., Boca Raton (2013)
13. Lu, X., Tsao, Y., Matsuda, S., Hori, C.: Speech enhancement based on deep denoising autoencoder (2013)
14. Michelsanti, D., Tan, Z.H.: Conditional generative adversarial networks for speech enhancement and noise-robust speaker verification. In: Proceedings of the Interspeech 2017, pp. 2008–2012. ISCA (2017). https://doi.org/10.21437/Interspeech.2017-1620
15. Mirza, M., Osindero, S.: Conditional generative adversarial nets. arXiv:1411.1784, November 2014
16. Miyato, T., Kataoka, T., Koyama, M., Yoshida, Y.: Spectral normalization for generative adversarial networks. arXiv preprint arXiv:1802.05957 (2018)
17. Park, S.R., Lee, J.: A fully convolutional neural network for speech enhancement. In: INTERSPEECH (2017)
18. Parveen, S., Green, P.: Speech enhancement with missing data techniques using recurrent neural networks. In: Proceedings of the IEEE International Conference on Acoustics, Speech, and Signal Processing, vol. 1, p. I-733-6 (2004)
19. Pascual, S., Bonafonte, A., Serrà, J.: SEGAN: speech enhancement generative adversarial network. In: Proceedings of the Interspeech 2017, pp. 3642–3646 (2017). https://doi.org/10.21437/Interspeech.2017-1428
20. Reed, S., Akata, Z., Yan, X., Logeswaran, L., Schiele, B., Lee, H.: Generative adversarial text to image synthesis. arXiv preprint arXiv:1605.05396 (2016)
21. Rix, A.W., Beerends, J.G., Hollier, M.P., Hekstra, A.P.: Perceptual evaluation of speech quality (PESQ)-a new method for speech quality assessment of telephone networks and codecs. In: Proceedings of the IEEE International Conference on Acoustics, Speech, and Signal Processing, vol. 2, pp. 749–752 (2001)

22. Ronneberger, O., Fischer, P., Brox, T.: U-Net: convolutional networks for biomedical image segmentation. In: Navab, N., Hornegger, J., Wells, W.M., Frangi, A.F. (eds.) MICCAI 2015. LNCS, vol. 9351, pp. 234–241. Springer, Cham (2015). https://doi.org/10.1007/978-3-319-24574-4_28

23. Saunders, G.H., Kates, J.M.: Speech intelligibility enhancement using hearing-aid array processing. J. Acoust. Soc. Am. **102**(3), 1827–1837 (1997)

24. Taal, C.H., Hendriks, R.C., Heusdens, R., Jensen, J.: A short-time objective intelligibility measure for time-frequency weighted noisy speech. In: 2010 IEEE International Conference on Acoustics, Speech and Signal Processing, pp. 4214–4217. IEEE (2010)

25. Vaseghi, S.V.: Advanced Digital Signal Processing and Noise Reduction. Wiley, Hoboken (2008)

26. Vincent, E., Virtanen, T., Gannot, S.: Audio Source Separation and Speech Enhancement. Wiley, Hoboken (2018)

27. Wang, D., Lim, J.: The unimportance of phase in speech enhancement. IEEE Trans. Acoust. Speech Signal Process. **30**(4), 679–681 (1982). https://doi.org/10.1109/TASSP.1982.1163920

28. Wang, D., Chen, J.: Supervised speech separation based on deep learning: an overview. IEEE/ACM Trans. Audio Speech Lang. Process. **26**(10), 1702–1726 (2018)

29. Weninger, F., et al.: Speech enhancement with LSTM recurrent neural networks and its application to noise-robust ASR. In: Vincent, E., Yeredor, A., Koldovský, Z., Tichavský, P. (eds.) LVA/ICA 2015. LNCS, vol. 9237, pp. 91–99. Springer, Cham (2015). https://doi.org/10.1007/978-3-319-22482-4_11

30. Xu, B., Wang, N., Chen, T., Li, M.: Empirical evaluation of rectified activations in convolutional network. arXiv preprint arXiv:1505.00853 (2015)

31. Xu, Y., Du, J., Dai, L., Lee, C.: A regression approach to speech enhancement based on deep neural networks. IEEE/ACM Trans. Audio Speech Lang. Process. **23**(1), 7–19 (2015). https://doi.org/10.1109/TASLP.2014.2364452

32. Wang, Y., Brookes, M.: A subspace method for speech enhancement in the modulation domain. In: 21st European Signal Processing Conference (EUSIPCO 2013), pp. 1–5, September 2013

HaGAN: Hierarchical Attentive Adversarial Learning for Task-Oriented Dialogue System

Ting Fang, Tingting Qiao, and Duanqing Xu[⌐]

College of Computer Science and Technology, Zhejiang University, Hangzhou, China
{fang-ting,qiaott,xdq}@zju.edu.cn

Abstract. Task-oriented dialogue system is commonly formulated as a reinforcement learning problem. A reward served as a learning objective is offered at the end of the generated dialogue to help optimize the system. As fulfilling a specific task often takes many turns between the system and the user, a scalar reward signal after this long process can be delayed and sparse. To address the above problems in the reinforcement learning (RL) based task-completion system, we propose a novel hierarchical attentive adversarial network HaGAN which features a cascaded attentive generator CAG that explores a state-action space to generate a dialogue and global-local attentive discriminators GLAD to give a relevant reward at multi-scale dialogue states. Specifically, after every turn of the dialogue generation, the turn-based discriminator tests the current turn and give a local reward representing the generator's current generating ability. When the dialogue finishes, the dialogue-based discriminator gives a global reward concerns the whole dialog. Finally, a synthesized reward computed by combining global and local reward is returned to the generator. By doing so, the generator is able to generate globally and locally fluent and informative dialogues. Through experiments on two public benchmark datasets demonstrate the superiority of our HaGAN over other representative state-of-the-art methods.

Keywords: Task-oriented dialogue · Dialogue policy · Adversarial learning

1 Introduction

Exploiting reinforcement learning (RL) [1,2] for policy learning in task-oriented dialogue systems has attracted increasing interest recently [3–7]. In contrast to the chit-chat system which mainly focuses on the next single turn, task-oriented system [3,8] involves the multi-turns reasoning and the final task completion, leading to a long trajectory.

Typical approaches usually used real dialogue data, training an RNN-based network to maximize the reward related to slot-values and actions. Williams et al. [6] proposed a hybrid end-to-end dialogue network which combined supervised and reinforcement learning together. Dhingra et al. [7] proposed an RL-based model which learned online by interacting with users. Lipton et al. [9] proposed

© Springer Nature Switzerland AG 2019
T. Gedeon et al. (Eds.): ICONIP 2019, LNCS 11953, pp. 98–109, 2019.
https://doi.org/10.1007/978-3-030-36708-4_9

BBQ-Networks which designed a new policy algorithm to explore action space for dialogue policy learning. However, these methods all needed to have access to a reward signal, either a continuous score or binary feedback from a user, which may lead to the problem that these rewards may be inconsistent [10] with true dialogue successes. Also, the reward signals were acquired at the end of the long dialogue process, which may bring about the problem that these signals are delayed and insufficient. Additionally, the guiding reward signals were sparse due to the complexity of long action sequences chosen from large action spaces. All of these drawbacks led to the results that model optimization could be very slow and the generated dialogues are not fluent and natural enough.

In light of the above, Some researchers started to use GANs in the dialogue generation system, trying to use judgments from a discriminator as rewards. Liu et al. [11] first proposed to use GANs for this task-oriented dialogue generation problem, in which a generator produced task-oriented dialogue by interacting with the environment. Then a discriminator took the whole dialogue as input and output 1 or 0 as a reward for the generator. Peng et al. [12] explored this task using task completion plus adversarial loss as the final reward for the agent to update its parameters. They both borrowed adversarial learning thoughts to the definition of more reliable and precise reward functions, accelerating the training of dialogue agent. However, the problem that binary reward signal from the discriminator is delayed and sparse remained unsolved as it is only available when the whole dialogue task is done. In addition, the problem of dialogues being unnatural and finishing the relevant task still exists.

To address the above-discussed challenges, we investigate the effectiveness of modeling task-oriented dialogue frameworks into hierarchical structures. We propose a new hierarchical attentive adversarial learning network (HaGAN) which contains two modules, a Cascaded Attentive Generator (CAG) that explores a state-action space to generate a dialogue, and Global-Local Attentive Discriminators (GLAD) to give a relevant reward at multi-scale dialogue states. Different from common dialogue agents that output an action word as the final answer. The CAG is an end-to-end RNN network that outputs a complete sentence answer at every turn, all of which form a whole dialogue. The corresponding GLAD contains two parts, turn-based discriminator, and dialogue-based discriminator. The former keeps watching over each single turn testing whether the current answer is human-generated or machine-generated and give a local turn-based reward. The latter one attends to the whole dialogue to distinguish machine-generated dialogues from human-generated ones when the task ends, giving a global whole-dialogue-based reward. Next, the generator updates its policy parameters based on the sum of turn-based rewards and whole-dialogue-based reward, learning to generate indistinguishable answers. As the reward contains rich and timely information about the performance of the generator, our model can learn to generate human-like dialogues which fulfill the given task much easier and faster. Our experimental results in two large public datasets show that dialogue agents optimized with the proposed HaGAN achieve advanced task success rate comparing to start-of-the-art baseline methods.

2   Related Work

2.1   Task-Oriented Dialogue System

Task-oriented dialogue system is usually framed as a partially-observable Markov decision process (POMDP) in which reinforcement learning techniques are used to learn policy by designed reward [13]. Recent efforts have been made to design the task-oriented dialogue model both in end-to-end and modularized approaches. In most of the modularized approaches, four modules form a typical pipeline network [14–17]. A limitation is that errors made by latter modules may disturb the former components' training. On the other hand, end-to-end methods have also shown some promising results. A few works consider the task as a next utterance retrieval problem. Wu et al. [18] and Liu et al. [19] both applied memory networks to perform multi-hop design to strengthen reasoning ability. Also, some approaches viewed the task as a sequence generation problem. Dhingra et al. [7] proposed an RL dialogue agent for information access. Lei et al. [8] designed an RL-based network that built explicit dialogue states tracking into delexicalized sequence generation to simplify the whole network training. In most of the above models, a reward was expected at the end of dialogue generation to help the agent optimizing its parameters. However, as a dialogue needs several turns to finish the task completely, a scalar reward acquired after this long trajectory can be sparse and delayed. In this work, we tackle this problem by incorporate adversarial learning thought into the seq2seq model.

2.2   Adversarial Dialogue Reward

Reward design is an important part of the task-oriented dialogue system. Traditional networks took user rating or binary success judgments as a reward. However, both man-made scalar rewards may be inconsistent with the true performance of the dialogue agent [10]. Generative adversarial networks (GANs) have been introduced into dialogue generation by Li firstly [20] to address the unsuitable evaluating metric problem in which the dialogue generation was measured by a discriminator. Similarly, Liu et al. [11] also applied the thought of GANs into the task-oriented dialogue system for the first time. Peng et al. [12] proposed to add adversarial loss as a supplementary reward besides the traditional reward function based on task completion. While the above adversarial learning method helped solving dependency on the man-made reward, the reward given by the discriminator is only accessible when the whole dialogue is generated and thus the guiding reward signal is still sparse during the training of the generator, which may lead to the problem that the generated dialogues are not human-like enough. In our cascaded network, the generator can receive rewards from both a turn-based discriminator and a dialogue-based discriminator. Thus, the reward contains rich information about the performance of the generator, both local and global. So the generator (dialogue agent) can update its policy network more precisely and efficiently, and the generate dialogues can be more globally and locally informative and fluent.

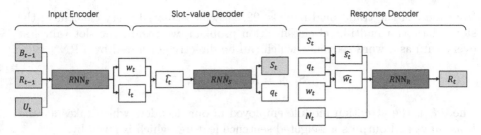

Fig. 1. Design of the cascaded attentive generator which generates a response sentence through multi-stage processing.

3   Methodology

In this section, we describe the structures of our proposed HaGAN which embodies a hierarchical attentive adversarial learning structure and consists of a local cascaded attentive generator (CAG) and global-local attentive discriminators (GLAD). The generator interacts with the user to fulfill a complete dialogue. The corresponding discriminators examine the generated dialogue at both the local-turn-level and the global-dialog-level, giving a well-informed reward to help the generator produce globally and locally informative dialogues. The details of each module are described in the following sections.

3.1   CAG: Cascaded Attentive Generator

First, we propose a cascaded attentive generator which generate a response sentence through multi-stage processing. The model architecture is shown in Fig. 1. Mathematically, we use $\{(S_{t-1}, R_{t-1}, U_t; S_t, R_t), t = 1, \ldots, T\}$ to denote the dialogue utterances, where S_{t-1} and R_{t-1} are the key slot values and the response of the agent at the last turn, respectively, U_t, S_t and R_t are utterance of the user, the key slot values and the response of the agent at current turn, respectively. As in [8], we consider that the dialogue history is represented by (S_{t-1}, R_{t-1}, U_t) which is fed into the generator to output the key slot values S_t and the response R_t at current turn.

Input Encoder: At turn t, we first fuse the current user utterances with the previous information in dialogue to obtain a rich joint representations of the known utterances. Specifically, S_{t-1}, R_{t-1} and U_t are first concatenated and then embedded as continuous representations by a bi-RNN [21] resulting in a word feature w_t and a sentence feature l_t.

$$w_t, l_t = RNN_E\left([S_{t-1}, R_{t-1}, U_t]\right), \tag{1}$$

where $[\cdot]$ denotes the concatenate operation, $w_t \in \mathbb{R}^{L \times D}$ is a concatenation of the L hidden states while $l_t \in \mathbb{R}^D$ is the last hidden state in the RNN network.

Slot and Response Decoders: In the decoding process, we generate the slot value S_t and the response R_t in two separated serial stages. To be specific, S_t is first generated based on the results of the previous encoder network. Different from most of the traditional models [22,23] which treated every element of the slot values as a multi-label classification problem, we regard the slot values at every turn as a word sequence which can be directly generated by a RNN [8]:

$$S_t, q_t = RNN_S\left(\hat{l}_t\right),\tag{2}$$

where $\hat{l}_t$ is the attention module employed in our decoders which takes w_t and l_t as input and outputs a weighted sentence feature, which is given by:

$$\hat{w}_t = \sum_{i=1}^{L}\frac{e^{u_i}}{\sum_i e^{u_i}}w_t^i;\; u_i = \sigma(W_1[w_t^i, l_t]),\tag{3}$$

$$\hat{l}_t = softmax(W_2[\hat{w}_t, l_t]),\tag{4}$$

where W_1 and W_2 are the parameters and σ is a sigmoid function.

Then, the decoding process pauses to perform a knowledge base search using the decoded S_t to get the number of eligible results of the search N_t. Finally, we generate the response R_t with the additional help of N_t.

$$R_t = RNN_R\left([\hat{w}_t, \hat{s}_t, Nt]\right),\tag{5}$$

where $\hat{w}_t$ and $\hat{s}_t$ are attentive textual features calculated by the same attention mechanism as described in Eqs. 3 and 4. $\hat{w}_t$ is obtained by fusing w_t and q_t. $\hat{s}_t$ is calculated by combining S_t and q_t.

3.2   GLAD: Global-Local Attentive Discriminators

In this section, we introduce the proposed global-local attentive discriminators. Specifically, we employ a turn-based discriminator to judge whether the response in a single turn generated by the generator is successful or not, and a dialogue-based discriminator which is employed to distinguish whether the whole dialogue is human- or machine-generated. The design of the discriminators is shown in Fig. 2.

Turn-Based Discriminator. After a turn is finished, the turn-based discriminator takes in the utterance of the user and the generated response at current turn and output a number indicating whether the response generated by dialogue agent successful one or not. Mathematically, we first use two bi-RNNs to encode the utterance of the user U_t, i.e.,

$$h_{u_t} = RNN_{T_1}(U_t);\; h_t = RNN_{T_2}(R_t, h_{u_t}),\tag{6}$$

where h_{u_t} represents the last hidden vector of the RNN_{T_1}.

The final representation of current turn h_t is a concatenation of the last forward output $\overrightarrow{h_t}$ and the last backward output $\overleftarrow{h_t}$ of RNN_{T_2}, i.e., $h_t = [\overrightarrow{h_t}, \overleftarrow{h_t}]$. h_t is then fed into a softmax function, returning the probability p_t of the current turn being machine-generated or human-generated:

$$p_t = \sigma(W_3(tanh(h_t))),\tag{7}$$

where W_3 is the parameter and σ is a sigmoid function.

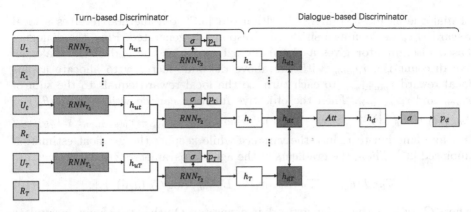

Fig. 2. Design of the Global-Local Attentive Discriminators which employ a turn-based discriminator and a dialogue-based discriminator to give a relevant reward at multi-scale dialogue states.

Dialogue-Based Discriminator. When the whole dialogue is finished, the dialogue-based discriminator encodes the whole dialogue using all the turn representation vectors generated above. Then we put the obtained dialogue representation into a softmax function to obtain the probability of the entire dialogue p_d being machine-generated one or human-generated. Mathematically, we first use a bi-RNN to encode the representations of all turns [24].

$$h_d = RNN_{D_d}(h_{turns}); h_{dialog} = Att(h_d), \tag{8}$$

where $h_{turns} = \{h_i | i = 1, 2, \dots, T\}$ obtained from the turn-based discriminator. $Att(h_d) = h_d(W_4 h_d)^T$ is a global attention module to embed the dialogue representation comprehensively, in which W_4 is the parameter. Then, the 2-class softmax function is designed as below:

$$p_d = \sigma(W_5(tanh(h_{dialog}))), \tag{9}$$

where W_5 is the parameter and σ is a sigmoid function.

The probabilities from all turns $\{p_1, p_2, \dots, p_T\}$ is considered as locally turn-based rewards $\{r_0, r_1, \dots, r_{T-1}\}$ while the probability p_d given by the dialogue-based discriminator is counted as the globally dialogue-based reward r_{dialog}. All of these rewards are delivered to the generator to help optimizing the parameters of the dialogue agent.

3.3   Efficient Adversarial Training

The final objective of this dialogue generating process is training a policy that maximizes the cumulative reward R. The expected cumulative reward is defined as $R = \sum_{t=0}^{T-1} \gamma^t r_t$ where T is the dialogue length, r_t is the reward at turn t, and γ is the discount factor. Different from receiving the reward at the end of dialogue as most training algorithm did [6,7], our method receives a local reward r_{turn} as soon as a single turn response is generated. Plus, the dialogue-based discriminator gives a global reward r_{dialog} at the end of the dialogue. We discount the r_{dialog} with the above discount factor γ to allocate a plus local reward r_{plus_turn} to each turn, so the local reward equals to the sum of r_{turn} and r_{plus_turn}. Then the objective function can be written as $J(\theta_G) = E_{\theta_G}(R) = E_{\theta_G}\left[\sum_{t=0}^{T-1} \gamma^t r_t - V(s_k)\right]$, where $r_t = r_{turn} + r_{plus\_turn}$. $V(s_k)$ is a baseline function to reduce the variance while keeping the gradient estimation unbiased [25]. Then, the gradients of the agent's parameters can be derived as:

$$\nabla_{\theta_G} J(\theta_G) = \nabla_{\theta_G} E_{\theta_G}[r_t] = E[\nabla_{\theta_G}(\log G_\theta(a_t|\cdot)) r_t], \qquad (10)$$

where $G_\theta(a_t|\cdot)$ is the policy network in generator. On the other hand, we update the parameters of the global-local attentive discriminators as below:

$$\nabla D_{turn}[E_{machine}[\log(D_{turn}(turn))] + E_{demo}[\log(D_{turn}(turn))]], \qquad (11)$$

where we maximize the probability of turn-based discriminator assigning the correct labels to the successful response from human demonstration and the dialogue conducted by the machine agent.

$$\nabla D_{dialog}[E_{machine}[\log(D_{dialog}(dialog))] + E_{demo}[\log(D_{dialog}(dialog))]], \qquad (12)$$

where we maximize the probability of dialogue-based discriminator assigning the correct labels to the successful dialogue from human demonstration and the dialog conducted by the machine agent.

Based on the above formulas, we update both the generator (dialogue agent) and the discriminators alternatively. A brief review of the training of the generator and the discriminators of HaGAN is shown in Algorithm 1.

4   Experiments

4.1   Datasets

Our method is evaluated on two benchmark datasets, which are CamRes676 [26] and KVRET [27]. CamRes676's dialogues focus on one single domain while KVRET includes three domains. Table 1 shows more details about the slot information and the data splits of the two datasets.

4.2   Evaluation Metrics

We adopt three quantitative evaluating metrics in our experiment: (1) BLEU [28], which is used to evaluate language quality; (2) entity match rate [8], which evaluates task completion. If the generated response includes all the indicated entities of the user, the task is judged as well done; (3) success F1, which is proposed in [8] to measure how a system responds to the user's requests at dialogue level. Traditional Success rate only measures whether the machine answers

Algorithm 1. HaGAN Training for Task-oriented Dialogue.

---

for number of training iterations **do**
  for $i = 1, G_{steps}$ **do**
    for *turns* in *dialog* **do**
      Simulate turn between U and G
      Compute reward r_{turn} with D_{turn}
    end for
    Compute reward r_{dialog} with D_{dialog}
    Get cumulative reward R for dialog. Update G with R
  end for
  for $i = 1, D_{steps}$ **do**
    for *turns* in *dialog* **do**
      Simulate turn between U and G
      Compute reward r_{turn} with D_{turn}
    end for
    Compute reward r_{dialog} with D_{turn}
    Update D_{turn} with $\sum r_{turn}$. Update D_{dialog} with r_{dialog}
  end for
end for

---

all the requested information. However, the machine may give information about some request slots that are irrelevant to the current dialogue. So success F1 is introduced to better evaluate dialogue agent performance. Success F1 is defined as the F1 score of required slots answered in the current dialogue.

4.3   Training Settings

We pretrain CAG with supervised learning (*i.e.*, MLE) before performing the adversarial learning of HaGAN. The MLE training gives the dialogue agent basic ability to generate coherent responses and complete the dialogue. We train the dialogue agent to minimize the cross-entropy loss on slot value prediction and response. Then the turn-based discriminator and dialogue-based discriminator are trained respectively. The machine-generated dialogues are labeled as zero and human-generated dialogues are labeled as one. The embedding size and the hidden size are set to 50. All RNNs in our model adopt the GRU structure. The model uses Adam optimizer [29], with learning rate of 0.003 for supervised training and 0.00008 for adversarial learning. Inspired by [30], we use temperature control during the training. We select a higher temperature when pretraining the model and lower temperature when training HaGAN.

4.4   Baselines for Comparison

We compare our model with four state-of-the-art baselines as follow:

- NDM [22]: This model adopts pipeline designs in which belief tracker is depended on delexicalization.

Table 1. Statistics of CamRes676 and KVRET.

Datasets	CamRes676	KVRET		
Size	Train: 408/Test: 136/Dev: 136	Train: 2425/Test: 302/Dev: 302		
Domains	Restaurant reservation	Calendar	Weather info.	POI
Slot types	Food types, prices etc.	Date	Location	poi
Distinct slot values	99	79	65	140

– LIDM [26]: This model is based on NDM which adopts neural variational inference and reinforcement learning.
– TSCP [8]: This model employs a two-stage seq2seq framework. It first generates dialogue states then produces system responses. They perform supervised training and them fine-tune the model using RL algorithm.
– TSCP\RL [8]: TSCP without reinforce learning.

We also performed two ablation experiments to observe the effectiveness of each component in our HaGAN model.

– HaGAN\D_{turn}: Our model without the turn-based discriminator.
– HaGAN\D_{dialog}: Our model without the dialogue-based discriminator.

5   Experiment Results

As shown in Table 2, HaGAN outperforms most of other models in success F1 and entity rate and BLEU. While the BLEU score of TSCP is the highest, we observe that TSCP tends to over-finetune and generate repeated and unmeaningful words. From the Table 2, we can see that HaGAN has better performance than HaGAN\$D_{turn}$ and HaGAN\$D_{dialog}$, validating our idea that the global-local attentive discriminators help the dialogue agent generate more meaningful and informative task-oriented dialogues. In addition, from the Table 2, we can see

Table 2. Model performance on CamRes676 and KVRET datasets.

	CamRes676			KVRET		
	Mat.	BLEU	SuccF1	Mat.	BLEU	SuccF1
(1) NDM [22]	0.904	0.212	0.832	0.724	0.186	0.741
(2) LIDM [26]	0.912	0.246	0.840	0.721	0.173	0.762
(3) TSCP\RL [8]	0.927	0.234	0.834	0.845	0.191	0.774
(4) TSCP [8]	0.927	**0.253**	0.854	0.845	0.219	0.811
(5) HaGAN\D_{turn}	0.925	0.237	0.859	0.846	0.210	0.819
(6) HaGAN\D_{dialog}	0.924	0.233	0.849	0.843	0.209	0.808
(7) HaGAN	**0.931**	0.247	**0.868**	**0.848**	**0.213**	**0.826**

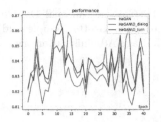

Fig. 3. Ablation experiment results on CamRes676 datasets.

Table 3. Generated examples

User	Is there a cheap place in the north part of town?
Agent	There are two restaurants that meet your specification One is Indian and the other is Italian
User	Indian, thanks. Can you give me the address?
Agent	Royal spice is in the north part of town. Their address is Victoria Avenue Chesterton
User	What is the phone number please?
Agent	Royal spice's phone number is 01733 55335 Is there anything that I can help you?
User	No, thanks
Agent	Thanks, goodbye

the difference of performance by our model on the CamRes676 and the KVRET, which may be due to the scale of the two datasets, *i.e.*, the CamRes676 is a relatively small dataset where the network is easy to train while KVRET is a large dataset varying in lexical diversity, leading to the harder training (Table 3).

Figure 3 shows that HaGAN can yield better dialogue policies than both GAN models with only a dialogue-based discriminator or with only a turn-based discriminator. The horizontal axises are training epochs. The vertical axises are the success F1 score introduced above. As is shown in Fig. 3, all of the three types of methods performed advanced results. However, HaGAN\$D_{turn}$ falls behind HaGAN method which proves that turn-based discriminator can help training the generator, indicating the effectiveness of the employment of the turn-based discriminator. Also, the learning curve of HaGAN shows a better result than HaGAN\$D_{dialog}$ because that the dialog-based discriminator offers extra rewards to the generator, showing the validness of the employment of the dialogue-based discriminator. It is noticed that the model arrives at a peak periodically. We consider the reason may be that the balance between the generator and the discriminators is hard to maintain, leading to the instability of the training, which is one of the nature inside the GAN.

6   Conclusion and Future Work

We propose HaGAN, a novel adversarial learning model to address task-oriented dialogue problem. Our model adopts a compact end2end generator which generates sentences sequentially to compose dialogues. The hierarchical discriminators give a feedback about the performance of the dialogue agent on multi-scale states enabling the agent to generate more human-like dialogues and have better performance on the given task. Experiment results on two datasets demonstrate the superiority and efficiency of our model, outperforming the state-of-the-art approaches. For our future work, we consider several further directions: (1) try other novel architectures [31–33] for the hierarchical discriminators, making the model more efficient and easier to train. (2) apply the model to other dialogue tasks, for example, chit-chat type and knowledge base question answering problems.

Acknowledgements. This work is supported in part by Chinese National Double First-rate Project about digital protection of cultural relics in Grotto Temple and equipment upgrading of the Chinese National Cultural Heritage Administration scientific research institutes.

References

1. Mnih, V., et al.: Playing atari with deep reinforcement learning. arXiv preprint arXiv:1312.5602 (2013)
2. Mnih, V., et al.: Human-level control through deep reinforcement learning. Nature **518**(7540), 529 (2015)
3. Young, S., Gašić, M., Thomson, B., Williams, J.D.: POMDP-based statistical spoken dialog systems: a review. Proc. IEEE **101**(5), 1160–1179 (2013)
4. Fatemi, M., Asri, L.E., Schulz, H., He, J., Suleman, K.: Policy networks with two-stage training for dialogue systems. arXiv preprint arXiv:1606.03152 (2016)
5. Su, P.H., et al.: Continuously learning neural dialogue management. arXiv preprint arXiv:1606.02689 (2016)
6. Williams, J.D., Asadi, K., Zweig, G.: Hybrid code networks: practical and efficient end-to-end dialog control with supervised and reinforcement learning. arXiv preprint arXiv:1702.03274 (2017)
7. Dhingra, B., et al.: Towards end-to-end reinforcement learning of dialogue agents for information access. arXiv preprint arXiv:1609.00777 (2016)
8. Lei, W., Jin, X., Kan, M.Y., Ren, Z., He, X., Yin, D.: Sequicity: simplifying task-oriented dialogue systems with single sequence-to-sequence architectures. In: Proceedings of the 56th Annual Meeting of the Association for Computational Linguistics (Volume 1: Long Papers), pp. 1437–1447 (2018)
9. Lipton, Z., Li, X., Gao, J., Li, L., Ahmed, F., Deng, L.: BBQ-networks: efficient exploration in deep reinforcement learning for task-oriented dialogue systems. In: Thirty-Second AAAI Conference on Artificial Intelligence (2018)
10. Su, P.H., et al.: On-line active reward learning for policy optimisation in spoken dialogue systems. arXiv preprint arXiv:1605.07669 (2016)
11. Liu, B., Lane, I.: Adversarial learning of task-oriented neural dialog models. arXiv preprint arXiv:1805.11762 (2018)
12. Peng, B., Li, X., Gao, J., Liu, J., Chen, Y.N., Wong, K.F.: Adversarial advantage actor-critic model for task-completion dialogue policy learning. In: 2018 IEEE International Conference on Acoustics, Speech and Signal Processing (ICASSP), pp. 6149–6153. IEEE (2018)
13. Sutton, R.S., Barto, A.G., et al.: Introduction to Reinforcement Learning, vol. 135. MIT Press, Cambridge (1998)
14. Williams, J.D., Young, S.: Partially observable markov decision processes for spoken dialog systems. Comput. Speech Lang. **21**(2), 393–422 (2007)
15. Silva, J., Coheur, L., Mendes, A.C., Wichert, A.: From symbolic to sub-symbolic information in question classification. Artif. Intell. Rev. **35**(2), 137–154 (2011)
16. Liu, B., Lane, I.: Iterative policy learning in end-to-end trainable task-oriented neural dialog models. In: 2017 IEEE Automatic Speech Recognition and Understanding Workshop (ASRU), pp. 482–489. IEEE (2017)
17. Sharma, S., He, J., Suleman, K., Schulz, H., Bachman, P.: Natural language generation in dialogue using lexicalized and delexicalized data. arXiv preprint arXiv:1606.03632 (2016)

18. Wu, C.S., Madotto, A., Winata, G.I., Fung, P.: End-to-end dynamic query memory network for entity-value independent task-oriented dialog. In: 2018 IEEE International Conference on Acoustics, Speech and Signal Processing (ICASSP), pp. 6154–6158. IEEE (2018)

19. Liu, F., Perez, J.: Gated end-to-end memory networks. In: Proceedings of the 15th Conference of the European Chapter of the Association for Computational Linguistics: Volume 1, Long Papers, pp. 1–10 (2017)

20. Li, J., Monroe, W., Shi, T., Jean, S., Ritter, A., Jurafsky, D.: Adversarial learning for neural dialogue generation. arXiv preprint arXiv:1701.06547 (2017)

21. Schuster, M., Paliwal, K.K.: Bidirectional recurrent neural networks. IEEE Trans. Signal Process. **45**(11), 2673–2681 (1997)

22. Wen, T.H., et al.: A network-based end-to-end trainable task-oriented dialogue system. arXiv preprint arXiv:1604.04562 (2016)

23. Henderson, M., Thomson, B., Young, S.: Deep neural network approach for the dialog state tracking challenge. In: Proceedings of the SIGDIAL 2013 Conference, pp. 467–471 (2013)

24. Vaswani, A., et al.: Attention is all you need. In: Advances in Neural Information Processing Systems, pp. 5998–6008 (2017)

25. Mnih, V., et al.: Asynchronous methods for deep reinforcement learning. In: International Conference on Machine Learning, pp. 1928–1937 (2016)

26. Wen, T.H., Miao, Y., Blunsom, P., Young, S.: Latent intention dialogue models. In: Proceedings of the 34th International Conference on Machine Learning-Volume 70, pp. 3732–3741. JMLR. org (2017)

27. Eric, M., Manning, C.D.: Key-value retrieval networks for task-oriented dialogue. arXiv preprint arXiv:1705.05414 (2017)

28. Papineni, K., Roukos, S., Ward, T., Zhu, W.J.: BLEU: a method for automatic evaluation of machine translation. In: Proceedings of the 40th Annual Meeting on Association for Computational Linguistics, pp. 311–318. Association for Computational Linguistics (2002)

29. Kingma, D.P., Ba, J.: Adam: a method for stochastic optimization. arXiv preprint arXiv:1412.6980 (2014)

30. Guo, J., Lu, S., Cai, H., Zhang, W., Yu, Y., Wang, J.: Long text generation via adversarial training with leaked information. In: Thirty-Second AAAI Conference on Artificial Intelligence (2018)

31. Donahue, D., Rumshisky, A.: Adversarial text generation without reinforcement learning. arXiv preprint arXiv:1810.06640 (2018)

32. Subramanian, S., Mudumba, S.R., Sordoni, A., Trischler, A., Courville, A.C., Pal, C.: Towards text generation with adversarially learned neural outlines. In: Advances in Neural Information Processing Systems, pp. 7551–7563 (2018)

33. Bau, D., et al.: GAN dissection: visualizing and understanding generative adversarial networks. arXiv preprint arXiv:1811.10597 (2018)

Learning to Generate Ambiguous Sequences

David Iclanzan[✉] and László Szilágyi

Sapientia University, Târgu-Mureş, Romania
david.iclanzan@gmail.com

Abstract. In this paper, we experiment with methods for obtaining binary sequences with a random probability mass function and with low autocorrelation and use it to generate ambiguous outcomes.

Outputs from a neural network are mixed and shuffled, resulting in binary sequences whose probability mass function is non-convergent, constantly moving and changing.

Empirical comparison with algorithms that generate ambiguity shows that the sequences generated by the proposed method have a significantly lower serial dependence. Therefore, the method is useful in scenarios where observes can see and record the outcome of each draw sequentially, by hindering the ability to make useful statistical inferences.

Keywords: Neural networks · Generative adversarial networks · Objective ambiguity · Knightian uncertainty

1 Introduction

Many real world processes involve a high degree of uncertainty and modelling them is an important and challenging aspect of the analysis of complex systems. Typically it is assumed that uncertainty should be modelled in the form of risk, where the uncertainty can be described with a probability distribution. However, uncertainty is a complex concept that goes beyond risk; there are also unpredictable events where probabilities cannot be assigned to the possible outcomes. [9] explicitly distinguishes risk from so called Knightian uncertainty, on the basis of whether (objectively or subjectively derived) probabilistic information about the possible outcomes is present or not.

For example, if urn A contains n red and blue balls in equal proportion while urn B contains n total red and blue balls but the number of each is unknown: (i) the probability of drawing a red ball from urn A is $1/2$; (ii) no such probability can be assigned in the case of urn B.

Looking at the sources of unpredictability, we can distinguish between ignorance, where probabilistic information about the external events that affect the outcomes are withheld or hidden; and true ambiguity, where there is a lack of any quantifiable knowledge about the possible occurrences [6].

© Springer Nature Switzerland AG 2019
T. Gedeon et al. (Eds.): ICONIP 2019, LNCS 11953, pp. 110–121, 2019.
https://doi.org/10.1007/978-3-030-36708-4_10

Typically, experiments that need to convey uncertainty [3] have chosen to achieve this by withholding information; here an objective probability exists, but the subjects are placed in a state of unawareness, they lack the sufficient information to infer a probabilistic.

Withholding information can become difficult in experiments involving repetition as experience can reduce subjects ignorance. Therefore, there are also efforts to generate so called objective ambiguity in the laboratory [13] where true probabilities are incognizable to the subjects, even with arbitrarily large numbers of repetitions. In the devised process, even the experimenter, with full knowledge of the operations involved does not have a way to assess the probability distribution of the outcomes.

Extensive evidence corroborate that subjects behave differently under Knightian uncertainty and risk. Specifically, most subjects are ambiguity averse, as exemplified in the Ellsberg Paradox [3]. Other results show that Knightian uncertainty can be used in games strategically to gain an advantage [11], given that the other players are ambiguity averse.

Ambiguity averse behaviour can be explained by the maxmin expected utility model [4], where one maximizes the minimum utility across different probability distributions. Here, players focus on worst-case scenarios to determine their optimal decisions. However, even if ambiguity aversion may usually prevail among players, there are also other behaviours and choices that occur in situations that feature ambiguity [8,12]. Focusing exclusively on worst-case scenarios may place an excessive and unrealistic limitation on the domain of admissible individual preferences in the presence of ambiguity [7]. This is especially true in the case of objective ambiguity devices, whose properties can be freely studied. In the case of these devices, a subject could learn form experience, that the setup is not adversarial, and assuming the worst case scenario is not the most appropriate.

If subjects are not averted by the fact that the precise probability of outcomes stay unknown, there still remains quantifiable and exploitable knowledge about the possible occurrences. By definition, if the outcomes do not follow the uniform probability distribution, the entropy is not maximal, there might be useful information that could be used to gain an advantage. For example, in the objective ambiguity generation process described in [13] there is a strong serial dependence between realizations. In experiments where one can observe each realization as it is made, a savvy agent could infer which outcomes have a higher probability than others; that is an exploitable edge even if the true exact probabilities remain unknowable.

In order to induce ambiguity aversion in a larger spectrum of subjects, data coming from an objective ambiguity generation processes should (i) have a divergent cumulative distribution function; (ii) be non-predictable not just in the sense that the exact probability of outcomes are impossible to known taking into account past data, but also in a stronger sense, where it is hard to identify outcomes more likely to occur in the short term than the others.

To achieve the above desiderates, in this paper we fuse a neural network's outputs for ambiguity generation. We train a neural network as generative model, to transform noise into binary sequences with low autocorrelation. The outputs of the network are combined to obtain binary sequences with a divergent cumulative distribution function and low serial dependence.

2 Background

2.1 Compound Lotteries

The simplest way to induce ambiguity, is to generate a distributions of balls in an Ellsberg-type urn using a uniform distribution over possible ratios of the balls [1]. For example, if $rand()$ is a function to generate a number according to a uniform distribution, then an ambiguous bit can be generated with the $b = rand()<rand()$ expression.

This method is suitable just for one-shot experiments. It is not suitable for repeated outcomes as the cumulative distribution function of the generated series is not divergent.

2.2 Objective Ambiguity

[13] introduces a data generating process in which the cumulative distribution function is divergent, and for which it is not possible to infer any quantile or moment of the underlying distribution.

The method is centred around three building blocks:

1. A process with a unit root, that leads to divergence as the number of draws becomes large.
2. A Cauchy distribution for individual draws, which is a distribution without any integer moments.
3. Controlling the scale of the Cauchy distribution, to prevent the process from diverging too quickly.

The Cauchy distribution is defined as

$$F(x) = \frac{1}{\pi} arctan(\frac{x - x_0}{\gamma}) + \frac{1}{2} \tag{1}$$

where x_0 is called the location of the distribution, and γ is the scale.

The parametrized distribution is denoted by $C[x_0, \gamma]$.

The trick is that the realized draws are used to shift the location and scale of the distribution, making the process non-stationary (giving the process a unit root). When γ is small the location is usually shifted slowly, but large draws also materialize, that induce a larger jumps.

Let capital letters denote random variables, lower case letters realizations and ϕ, $\psi \in (0, 1)$ two parameters, both small. Formally, the procedure described in [13] works as follows:

1. Draw $Z_0 \sim C[0, 1]$
2. Draw $Z_1 \sim C[z_0, 1]$
3. For $t \geq 2$ draw $Z_t \sim C[z_{t-1}, \phi|z_{t-1}| + \psi]$

Binary outcomes are generated, by checking if the greatest integer no larger than z_t is even or odd: $b_t = \lfloor z_t \rfloor \bmod 2$.

The procedure alternates between stable and volatile phases. When γ is small, the generated values tend to stay close together (stable period). When an extreme realization arrives that is far from x_0, it is embedded into the scale parameter two draws later. This increases the chance that subsequent draws are also far from the location, causing the process to shift to an unstable period, until a draw with a small absolute value arrives again, causing the scale to be reduced again. The period lengths are unpredictable.

The cumulative sums of some sample runs, containing 10e4 binary outcomes generated according to the above described process, are shown in Fig. 1. Zero values have been replaced with -1 to make the ratio of the two possible outcomes more easily assessable visually. The $0X$ axis is depicted with a red line. We can observe that the cumulative sums do not converge and the stable and extreme periods alternate randomly.

We can also observe that the data is serially dependent, there are long periods when the process only generates one kind of output. Figure 2 shows the sample autocorrelation function (ACF) of the runs, with lag $k = 20$. Autocorrelation is very high, close to 1 for all lags, in almost every run.

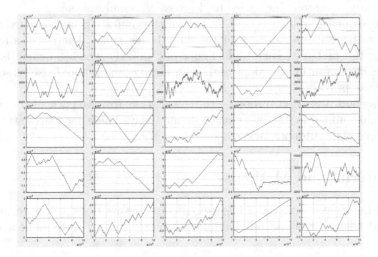

Fig. 1. Cumulative sums of sample runs. Stable and extreme periods alternate randomly. (Color figure online)

To hinder the ability to exploit the serial dependence, resulting from whether the process is in a calm or unstable period, the authors in [13] propose to remedies.

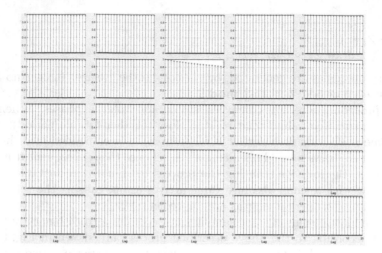

Fig. 2. Sample ACF of the example runs from Fig. 1. Values are close to 1 for all lags, in almost every run.

The first one requires to randomly permute the original sequence, and present the data in the randomly garbled order. While this approach destroys the auto-correlation it also introduces a look ahead bias as depicted in Fig. 3. With the random shuffle the amount of divergence at time-step t is "smoothed out", resulting in mostly monotone increasing or decreasing cumulative sums.

If the sequence is long enough, a random permutation makes it extremely unlikely to have mean reversals of the cumulative sums. Therefore, a subject observing the first outcomes could figure out quickly which outcome is more probable; by computing the slope of the cumulative sum it could also reasonably estimate the probabilities.

The second approach, proposes the generation from a path of ambiguous length, and shuffled in an ambiguously defined way. These sequences still suffer from a very high autocorrelation.

3   Material and Methods

To provide reduced serial dependence and also strong divergence, we propose a method where the basic building-blocks are the binary outputs of a neural network.

3.1   Generative Adversarial Networks

Recently, generative adversarial networks (GAN) [5] have gained a lot of attention due to their capability to generate complex data without explicitly modelling the probability density function. GAN models proved their power and flexibility by achieving state-of-the-art performance in multiple hard generation tasks,

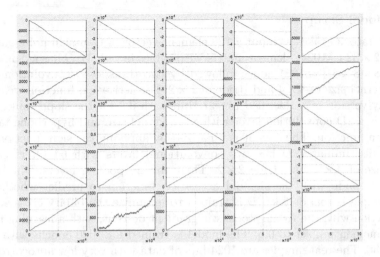

Fig. 3. Cumulative sums of the randomly shuffled sample runs from Fig. 1.

like plausible sample generation for datasets [15], realistic photograph generation [2], text-to-image synthesis [14], image-to-image translation [16], super-resolution [10] and many more.

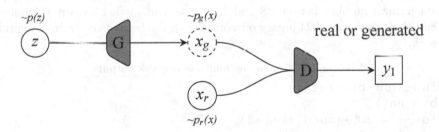

Fig. 4. GAN schematic view. Generator G transforms a sample z from $p(z)$ into a generated sample x_g. Discriminator D is a binary classifier that differentiates the generated and real samples formed by x_g and x_r respectively.

As depicted in Fig. 4, in the GAN model two networks are trained simultaneously, the generator G focused on data generation from pure noise z and network D centered on discrimination. The output of the generator G, x_g is expected to be similar to the samples x_r. D is a simple binary classifier; it takes as input a real or a generated sample and outputs y_1, the probability of the input being real. G receives a feedback signal from D, by the back propagated gradient information. G adapts its weights in order to produce samples that can pass the discriminator.

3.2   Model Setup

The generator G takes as input a 128 element vector of Gaussian noise and outputs a 32×32 (=1024) element matrix with values in $[-1, 1]$. G has a dense layer with $128 \times 8 \times 8$ (=8192) nodes followed by two transposed convolution layers with a kernel size of 4×4 and stride of 2×2. For activation function we choose the leaky version of a Rectified Linear Unit with 0.2 for the slope value. Coming last is a 2D convolution layer with 8×8 kernel size and hyperbolic tangent activation function. The output is binarized by applying the sign function.

The discriminator D has two convolutional layers with 64 filters each, a kernel size of 4×4 and stride 2×2. There are no pooling layers. The output is a single node with the sigmoid activation function to predict whether the input sample is real or fake. D is trained to minimize the binary cross entropy loss function with the Adam stochastic gradient descent, with a learning rate of 0.0001, momentum set to 0.5. The model is trained for 1000 epochs with batch size of 256. The real samples are 1024 bits of data with very low autocorrelation and random probability mass.

3.3   Using the Output

After training, the network output can be used to obtain 1 KB of data with low autocorrelation. However, we found that the probability distribution stays close to uniform. Therefore, to obtain one sample we combine a number of m networks outputs by randomly applying binary **and** or **or**, where m is randomly chosen natural number between 8 and 16, as seen in Listing 1.1. $nn()$ denotes the call that generates 1024 binary outcomes with the help of the trained neural network.

Listing 1.1. Combining multiple network outputs

```
1  function b = bseq()
2  b = nn();
3  for i = 2:8+round(rand*8)
4      if rand < 0.5
5          b = and(b, nn());
6      else
7          b = or(b, nn());
8  end
```

Now, to obtain a sequence of desired length, one just have to concatenate outputs until the length threshold is reached. The disadvantage of this basic concatenation procedure is that the series has a fixed period, after every 1024 outcomes is given that the distribution changes.

3.4   Mixing and Overlapping

To avoid the hardcoded period and further reduce autocorrelation, we devise a sequence generating protocol based on mixing and overlapping the outputs obtained from the network.

In our experiments, at each step we use two binary samples b_1 and b_2, each obtained by combining multiple network outputs as detailed in the previous section. The samples are mixed, then a randomly chosen fraction of the result is overlapped and mixed again with the sequence's end.

The mixing function is outlined in Listing 1.2. It takes two binary vectors of length n, $b1$, $b2$ and produces a third one b, where the ith element of b is set to either $b1[i]$, $b2[i]$ or the two values combined with either *and* or the *or* operator. All four possible outcomes have the same probability to be chosen.

Listing 1.2. Function for mixing two binary vectors

```
 1  function  b = mix(b1, b2, n)
 2  for  i = 1:n
 3      r = floor(1+rand()*4);
 4      switch r
 5          case 1
 6              v = b1[i];
 7          case 2
 8              v = b2[i];
 9          case 3
10              v = b1[i] and b2[i];
11          case 4
12              v = b1[i] or b2[i];
13      end
14      b[i] = v;
15  end
```

To break up the fixed period resulting from simple concatenations of $bseq()$ calls, the described sequence generation admits random overlaps between outputs. The entire generation process is presented in Listing 1.3.

The sequence is initialized with the mixed result of two $bseq()$ calls. Then, inside a loop a new mixed sequence b is generated. In line 4 it is randomly decided what is the maximum percentage (25%, 50%, 75% or 100%) of the last 1024 outcomes that will potentially overlap and mix with b. In line 5 the overlap index is randomly chosen, and line 6 and 7 perform the overlap, mix and concatenation. The loop repeats until the desired sequence length is achieved.

Listing 1.3. Mixing and overlapping

```
 1  s = mix(bseq(), bseq(), 1024);
 2  while length(s) < limit
 3      b = mix(bseq(), bseq(), 1024);
 4      max_overlap = floor(1+rand()*4);
 5      overlap = floor(rand()*1024/max_overlap);
 6      b[1:overlap] = mix(b[1:overlap],s[end−overlap+1:
            end], 1024);
 7      s = concatenate(s[1:end−overlap], b[1:end]);
 8  end
```

4   Results

Figure 5 presents the cumulative sums of some sample sequences obtained (a) by just simply concatenating the outputs of the network; (b) also applying the proposed mix and overlap steps. The runs obtained in (b) show a more pronounced zigzag patterns. Again, the zeros have been replaced by −1 for better visualization of the proportion of the two outputs.

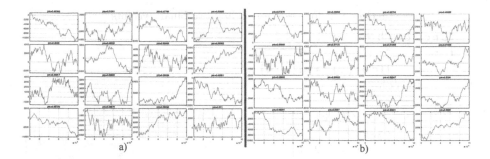

Fig. 5. Cumulative sum of sample runs obtained (a) simple concatenation of network outputs; (b) outputs obtained by also applying the mix and overlap steps.

Analyzing the autocorrelation of the runs, presented in Fig. 6, we can observe that in case of simple concatenation, the coefficients are around 0.4; applying the mix and overlap steps more than half this value, reducing it to bellow 0.2. We can observe that with the reduced autocorrelation, it seems that the divergence of the cumulative sum from 0 also decreases.

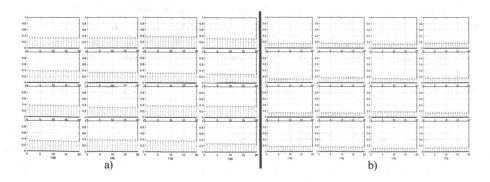

Fig. 6. Autocorrelation coefficients of the runs from Fig. 5

To statistically analyze the properties of the proposed methods, we generated 1000 sequences, each of length 10e4 for both the simple concatenation and mix and overlap. For comparison, we consider the objective ambiguity method presented in [13] as the baseline. We used the implementation[1] of the ambiguity generator provided by the authors to obtain 1000 samples of length 10e4.

Figure 7 depicts the average of the autocorrelation coefficients at each lag index over the 1000 runs, for the 3 methods. The results confirm that the mix and overlap steps are highly beneficial in reducing the autocorrelation to 0.17.

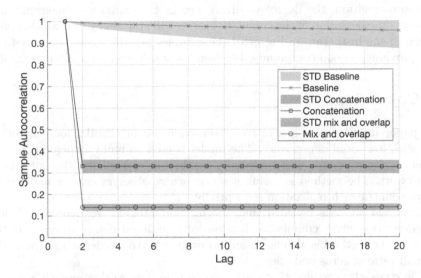

Fig. 7. Comparison of the autocorrelation coefficients for the tree methods.

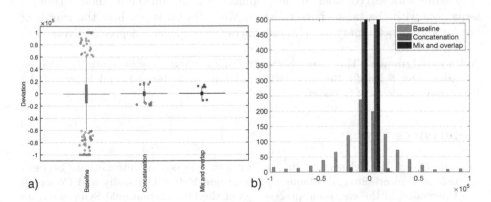

Fig. 8. Cumulative sums at the end of sequences for the three methods: (a) boxplot; (b) histogram.

---

[1] https://github.com/HaskellAmbiguity/AmbiguityGenerator.

We analyzed the divergence of the methods by measuring how far is the cumulative sum from 0 at the end of sequences. The results are presented in Fig. 8.

We can observe in Fig. 8(a) too the baseline method presents many outliers, with some of the values very close to the length of the sequence, meaning that that in these runs mostly the output was all ones or all zeros.

As the proposed methods shorten these monotone runs, in order to decrease the autocorrelation, the degree of divergence in the examined timeframe also decreases, the deviation of the cumulative sums will stay closer to zero. However, as seen in the histogram in Fig. 8(b), these values are still quite far away from zero, providing a good compromise between low autocorrelation and divergence.

5   Conclusions

The paper introduced a generative adversarial network model for generating data with low serial dependence. The model is used to build ambiguous binary sequences, by randomly and repeatedly combining and mixing the outputs of the network. The method is useful in setups where observes can see and record the outcome of each realization sequentially.

Empirical analysis revealed that the method provides sequences with low autocorrelation whose cumulative distribution function is non-convergent. In the long run, the method is also less likely to produce extreme departures from the half-half ratio of zeros and ones.

The study also revealed that the proposed neural network approach is not an efficient building-block for generating ambiguous sequences. In order to obtain satisfactory results, many network outputs must be combined and mixed, making the method needlessly computationally expensive.

Future work will consider the development of more efficient methods to obtain sequences with the same characteristics. We will also study how the length of the building-block binary samples influences the sequence's degree of divergence.

Acknowledgments. This research was partially supported by Sapientia Foundation – Institute for Scientific Research (KPI). L. Szilágyi is János Bolyai Fellow of the Hungarian Academy of Sciences.

References

1. Arló-Costa, H., Helzner, J.: Iterated random selection as intermediate between risk and uncertainty. In: Manuscript, Carnegie Mellon University and Columbia University. In the electronic proceedings of the 6th International Symposium on Imprecise Probability: Theories and Applications. Citeseer (2009)
2. Brock, A., Donahue, J., Simonyan, K.: Large scale GAN training for high fidelity natural image synthesis. arXiv preprint arXiv:1809.11096 (2018)
3. Ellsberg, D.: Risk, ambiguity, and the savage axioms. Q. J. Econ. **75**, 643–669 (1961)

4. Gilboa, I., Schmeidler, D.: Maxmin expected utility with non-unique prior. In: Uncertainty in Economic Theory, pp. 141–151. Routledge (2004)
5. Goodfellow, I., et al.: Generative adversarial nets. In: Advances in Neural Information Processing Systems, pp. 2672–2680 (2014)
6. Guidolin, M., Rinaldi, F.: Ambiguity in asset pricing and portfolio choice: a review of the literature. Theory Decis. **74**(2), 183–217 (2013)
7. Kast, R., Lapied, A., Roubaud, D.: Modelling under ambiguity with dynamically consistent Choquet random walks and Choquet-Brownian motions. Econ. Model. **38**, 495–503 (2014)
8. Kim, K., Kwak, M., Choi, U.J.: Investment under ambiguity and regime-switching environment. Available at SSRN 1424604 (2009)
9. Knight, F.: Risk, Uncertainty and Profit. Kelley and Millman Inc., New York (1921)
10. Ledig, C., et al.: Photo-realistic single image super-resolution using a generative adversarial network. In: Proceedings of the IEEE Conference on Computer Vision and Pattern Recognition, pp. 4681–4690 (2017)
11. Riedel, F., Sass, L.: Ellsberg games. Theory Decis. **76**(4), 469–509 (2014)
12. Schröder, D.: Investment under ambiguity with the best and worst in mind. Math. Financ. Econ. **4**(2), 107–133 (2011)
13. Stecher, J., Shields, T., Dickhaut, J.: Generating ambiguity in the laboratory. Manag. Sci. **57**(4), 705–712 (2011)
14. Xu, T., et al.: AttnGAN: fine-grained text to image generation with attentional generative adversarial networks. In: Proceedings of the IEEE Conference on Computer Vision and Pattern Recognition, pp. 1316–1324 (2018)
15. Yu, Y., Gong, Z., Zhong, P., Shan, J.: Unsupervised representation learning with deep convolutional neural network for remote sensing images. In: Zhao, Y., Kong, X., Taubman, D. (eds.) ICIG 2017, LNCS, vol. 10667, pp. 97–108. Springer, Cham (2017). https://doi.org/10.1007/978-3-319-71589-6_9
16. Zhu, J.Y., Park, T., Isola, P., Efros, A.A.: Unpaired image-to-image translation using cycle-consistent adversarial networks. In: Proceedings of the IEEE International Conference on Computer Vision, pp. 2223–2232 (2017)

Convolutional Neural Networks

Deep Learning for Combo Object Detection

Jing Zhao$^{(\boxtimes)}$, Iman Tabatabaei Ardekani, and Shaoning Pang

Unitec Institute of Technology, Auckland, New Zealand
{jzhao,iardekani,ppang}@unitec.ac.nz

Abstract. Convolutional neural networks (CNNs) have become the most vigorous technique for a variety of different tasks in computer vision, due to their proficiency in automatically learning high-level visual representations for images. In this paper, we investigate the effect of deep neural networks on the accuracy in combo object detection setting. The insufficiency of labeled data, coupled with the uncertainty of spacial distribution and dynamic changes in luminance, creates situations where combo object detection is far more challenging. Using transfer learning, we present a system for combo object detection based on a deep CNN called ComboNN. The proposed ComboNN is pre-trained on a huge auxiliary dataset ImageNet and fine-tuned on our small dataset. The use of data augmentation and regularization technique significantly reduces overfitting and improves the robustness of the ComboNN. Experimental results demonstrate that our system is capable of making reliable prediction on combo object detection in the real-world images, and achieves much better accuracy than the state-of-the-art CNNs.

Keywords: Convolutional neural network (CNN) · Transfer learning · Combo object detection · Pre-training · Fine-tuning

1 Introduction

Substantial domain knowledge and cautious manual engineering are needed to develop a representation descriptor for building a conventional pattern-recognition system, since the traditional machine-learning technologies are restricted in their capability to manipulate natural data in their raw structure. In contrast, deep-learning techniques are representation-learning techniques, which enable a learner to accept raw data and to automatically extract the features required for classification or object recognition [1].

Deep learning is producing considerable improvements in solving a variety of problems, such as visual image understanding, speech classification, answering questions and natural language translation. Training deep CNNs became feasible primarily due to the availability of large-scale labelled image repositories, such as ImageNet [2], as well as the computing devices with high-capacity, such as distributed and parallel clusters and GPUs.

© Springer Nature Switzerland AG 2019
T. Gedeon et al. (Eds.): ICONIP 2019, LNCS 11953, pp. 125–137, 2019.
https://doi.org/10.1007/978-3-030-36708-4_11

Tremendous progress has been achieved in computer vision since Krizhevsky et al. [3] relighted the interests in deep convolutional neural networks (CNNs) on the ImageNet Large Scale Visual Recognition Challenge (ILSVRC) 2012 [4]. One example is object classification, where our aim is to categorize a given image dataset into a set of predefined classes. Girshick et al. [5] demonstrated how the CNNs could be employed to object detection as well as object segmentation. Zhou et al. [6] used deep neural networks to tackle the task of scene understanding. The CNNs have been studied for a range of face analysis problems, such as face detection, face recognition and face clustering [7]. A typical usage for deep neural networks is to apply them in tracking single or multiple objects. Research on deep learning has drawn more and more attention from medical image understanding, such as nodule detection, pathologies identification in chest x-rays and interstitial lung disease classification [8].

Fig. 1. Example cat-flower combo images from our dataset.

This paper considers the application of deep convolutional neural networks for combo object (i.e., the combination of flowers and cats) detection on the real-world images. Figure 1 gives the examples of combo object images which our research is based on. As seen in this figure, the spacial distribution of combo object changes over time with the movement of cats. Moreover, the appearance of objects seen in these scenes can be substantially dynamic because of the changes in levels of luminance throughout the day. As a consequence, combo object detection in this context is especially difficult. Another challenge in this research is the scarcity of the labeled data and the number of currently usable examples is inadequate for training the deep convolutional neural networks from scratch. The deep CNN models trained on a small dataset can easily suffer from overfitting.

In this paper, we propose a combo object detection system which is based on a new deep neural network (ComboNN) to cope with the challenges addressed above. Transfer learning [5] is used to address the issue of data insufficiency, in which the proposed ComboNN is pre-trained on a huge auxiliary dataset ImageNet [4] and fine-tuned on our small dataset. In particular, the use of data augmentation [9] and regularization technique [10] significantly decreases overfitting and improves the accuracy of the ComboNN. Moreover, the low computing cost and high level of training efficiency maximizes the potential utility of the ComboNN.

We compare the ComboNN with the state-of-the-art convolutional neural networks on combo object detection, the empirical results show higher performance of the proposed ComboNN.

2 Related Work

2.1 Combo Object Modelling

Pellegrini et al. [11] designed an effective dynamic model for detecting multiple persons in the crowded scenarios. They took into account the interactions between different targets as well as scene information in the form of desired directions. Their model gives better predictions and consistently improves the performance compared to other dynamic models which ignore social interactions. Baumgartner et al. [12] developed a probabilistic algorithm for classifying such person-object interactions. They associated objects to persons, and predicted how the interaction would most likely continue in challenging real-world scenarios. Yamaguchi et al. [13] proposed an agent-based behavioral model of the pedestrians to improve the performance in realistic scenarios. In their model, the pedestrians are viewed as the decision-making agents, who use a variety of personal, social, and environmental factors to decide where to go next. The estimation of pedestrian behavior is formulated as an energy minimization on this model. Pellegrini et al. [14] designed a third-order graphical model which can jointly estimate the correct trajectories and group memberships over a short time window. The proposed model attempts to improve data association in semi-crowded environment, where the people are distinguished as individually moving entities undergoing many interactions with other people in their direct surrounding. Zhao et al. [15] addressed the issue of combo object modelling for maritime boat ramps traffic monitoring. In this scenario, the retrieving boat is always pulled by the vehicle when they leave the boat ramp, and the launching boat is always pushed by the vehicle and they move backwards to the shoreline. Instead of tracking the trailer boat as a single object, they proposed a boat-vehicle combo object model, by which each boat is tracked as a combination of a trailered boat and a towing vehicle. The relationship of these two components is measured in terms of the distance estimation between two single objects within the combination.

2.2 Transfer Learning

Girshick et al. [5] first addressed transfer learning in CNNs by employing AlexNet [3] pre-trained on ImageNet [4] to PASCAL dataset [16]. ImageNet is a large dataset collected for classification tasks, which has the image-level annotations without the bounding box labels. PASCAL is a canonical dataset for the evaluation of object detection performance. This work attempted to generalize the categorization capabilities on ImageNet to object detection on PASCAL. The remarkably increased performance on 20-class object detection and object segmentation demonstrates the effectiveness of supervised pre-training and fine-tuning when training data is insufficient. Based on [5], Agrawal et al. [17] conducted experiments to further analyze the efficiency of transfer learning. Their results show that supervised pre-training is still beneficial and leads to a large improvement in detection performance when training data is not scarce. They also obtained the similar results for image classification. Razavian et al. [18] pre-trained the OverFeat [19] neural network on ILSVRC13 [2]. They utilized the extracted features to deal with a set of image identification tasks, such as fine-grained detection, attribute analysis, scene recognition, and retrieving visual images. Zhou et al. [6] applied convolutional neural networks to scene understanding. They visualized the feedbacks from the neural layers to demonstrate the dissimilarities of features between scene-centric and object-centric networks. Transfer learning also saw heavy uses in medical image analysis. Bar et al. [8] investigated the capacity of CNNs trained on a non-medical dataset to classify a group of different pathologies on chest x-rays. This is the first experiment in such domain and reveals that generic medical image analysis may be tackled by deep neural networks with ImageNet rather than domain specific features. Van Ginneken et al. [20] used the features from the OverFeat [19] network, which was trained for identifying objects on natural images, for distinguishing nodules in tomography scans.

3 Combo Object Detection with ComboNN

In this section, we describe the design considerations for the core components of our combo object detection system, detail the network architecture of the proposed deep convolutional neural network for combo object detection (ComboNN), and present how to learn the parameters for ComboNN.

3.1 Network Architecture of Proposed ComboNN

We start with VGG19 [21] and use this model as the backbone network for our ComboNN. The overall architecture of the ComboNN is depicted in Fig. 2. The network consists of sixteen convolutional layers followed by two fully-connected (FC) layers. The first FC contains 512 channels. The second FC conducts binary classification and thus has two channels (one for each category).

All hidden layers are provided with the rectified linear unit (ReLU) [22]. Currently, the ReLU is the most common non-linear function that is straight-forwardly the half-wave rectifier

$$f(z) = max(z, 0). \tag{1}$$

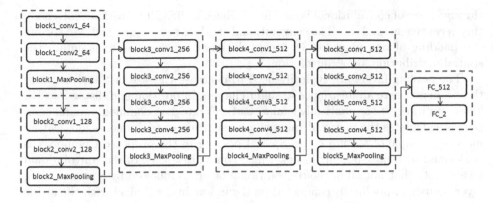

Fig. 2. An illustration of the overall architecture for the proposed ComboNN.

Neural networks previously employed smoother non-linearities, such as

$$f(z) = tanh(z) \tag{2}$$

or

$$f(z) = 1/(1 + exp(-z)), \tag{3}$$

but the ReLU usually learns much more rapidly in neural nets with many layers, which allows training of the deep supervised neural networks in the absence of unsupervised pre-training. The ReLU has the desirable attribute that it does not need input normalizations to prevent it from saturation. If only some training instances provide a positive feedback to the ReLU, learning will be performed in that neuron.

Krizhevsky et al. [3] used Local Response Normalization (LRN) after the ReLU to improve generalization. The response-normalized operation $c_{x,y}^i$ can be formulated as

$$c_{x,y}^i = d_{x,y}^i / \left(n + \beta \sum_{j=max(0,i-k/2)}^{min(K-1,i+k/2)} (d_{x,y}^j)^2 \right)^\alpha, \tag{4}$$

where $d_{x,y}^i$ denotes the action of a neuron calculated by utilizing kernel i at point (x, y), α, β, n and k represent hyper-parameters whose quantities are decided by a verification set, K stands for the number of kernels in this layer, and the sum is performed over k neighboring kernel maps in the same place.

Our ComboNN does not include LRN, since such normalization cannot increase the performance on ILSVRC2012 dataset, but raises computational time as well as memory utilization [21].

The number of channels contained in each convolutional layer is quite small, beginning from 64 in the first one and then enlarging by a factor of two succeeding each layer for max-pooling, until it arrives at 512. During training, the input to our ComboNN is one RGB image in the size of 224×224. The image is moved through a set of convolutional layers, in which we utilize filters with an extremely tiny receptive field: 3×3. The convolutional stride is set as one pixel. We specify the padding of one pixel for 3×3 convolutional layers so as to maintain the spatial distribution after convolution.

The pooling layers are typically used to decrease the size of the representations and generate an invariance to slight changes in position and distortions [1]. They can integrate semantically similar features into 1. A common pooling component calculates the maximal value of a local group of components in a feature map or a couple of feature maps. Spatial pooling in the proposed ComboNN is performed by 5 max-pooling layers, which come after some of the convolutional layers, note that not all of the convolutional layers is followed by a max-pooling layer. Our max-pooling is conducted on a window in 2×2 pixel with the stride of two.

3.2   Training

Pre-training for ComboNN. We discriminatively pre-train the proposed ComboNN on a huge visual dataset ImageNet [4], which is currently the largest image dataset for visual recognition. ImageNet contains around 1000 images in each of 1000 classes. In total number, there are about 1,200,000, 50,000 and 150,000 images for training, validation and testing, respectively. Pre-training is conducted using the open source Keras [23] implementation of the CNN presented by Simonyan et al. [21].

Fine-Tuning for ComboNN. To adapt our ComboNN to the new task (combo object detection), we continue Stochastic Gradient Descent (SGD) [24] training of the ComboNN parameters using our small dataset. When learning the deep neural network models, we usually specify the loss function as the addition to the set of functions:

$$\mathcal{L}(x) = \frac{1}{k} \sum_{j=1}^{k} \mathcal{L}_j(x), \tag{5}$$

where $\mathcal{L}_j(x)$ denotes an objective function relevant with the training example indicated by j, and k is the size of training dataset. Apparently, the expense for per-iteration computing gradient descent is huge if k becomes very large.

SGD provides a lighter-weight method to cope with this issue. It stochastically takes sample j at uniform and calculates $\nabla \mathcal{L}_j(\mathbf{x})$ in each iteration, rather than calculating the gradient $\nabla \mathcal{L}(\mathbf{x})$. SGD employs $\nabla \mathcal{L}_j(\mathbf{x})$ as an unbiased approximation of $\nabla \mathcal{L}(\mathbf{x})$ since

$$\mathbb{E}_j \nabla \mathcal{L}_j(\mathbf{x}) = \frac{1}{k} \sum_{j=1}^{k} \nabla \mathcal{L}_j(\mathbf{x}) = \nabla \mathcal{L}(\mathbf{x}). \tag{6}$$

Given a training instance, SGD searches the direction in which the lost function should be decreased fastest in each iteration. This straightforward process often discovers a good group of parameters unexpectedly rapidly, when in comparison with more complicated optimization approaches. If the dataset for training is big enough, SGD only needs much less cycles to search desirable results, thus the whole computing expense is much smaller than that of gradient descent.

We perform SGD at a learning rate of 0.0001 which is 1/100th of the early learning rate for pre-training. This small value enables the fine-tuning to achieve improvement while not wrecking the initialization. The learning rate is identical for each layer. The parameters for every layer are initialized as a Gaussian distribution of zero-mean with 0.01 for standard deviation. The ComboNN model is learned utilizing SGD with 16 instances in a mini-batch as well as 0.9 for momentum [25]. We train the ComboNN for around 50 epochs through the training dataset of 2360 images, which take about 1.5 h on one NVIDIA GeForce GTX 1070 8 GB GPU.

The two principal methods used by us to prevent overfitting are data augmentation and a regularization technique called dropout [10]. The most popular approach to decreasing overfitting on images is to artificially expand the imagery datasets utilizing label-preserving conversions [9], which enable translated imagery data to be generated from the initial images in very low computing cost.

We apply dropout technique to the first fully connected layer in Fig. 2 for reducing overfitting. Each layer would excessively rely on the particular patterns on the previous layer, if the deep neural nets overfit severely on the training examples. To deal with this issue, Srivastava et al. [10] suggested to drop out the neurons in hidden layers at random with a certain chance. The nodes that are dropped out in such technique cannot make contributions to forward propagation or take part in backward propagation. This technology minimizes complicated co-adaptations of neural nodes and approximately doubles the number of cycles needed for converging.

4   Experimental Results

In this section, we evaluate the performance of the proposed ComboNN and compare it with the state-of-art convolutional neural networks on the combo object detection.

4.1   Datasets

We report the experimental results in this paper using one standard dataset as well as our own small dataset, which we summarize here.

Dataset for Pre-training. The proposed ComboNN is pre-trained on Large Scale Annotated Natural Image Dataset (ImageNet) [4]. ImageNet has more than 1.2 million 256×256 images categorized under 1000 object class categories. There are more than 1000 training images per class. The database is organized according to the WordNet [26] hierarchy, which currently contains only nouns in 1000 object categories. The image object labels are obtained largely through crowd-sourcing, such as Amazon Mechanical Turk, and human inspection.

Due to the large number (1000+) of object classes, the objects belonging to each ImageNet class category can be occluded, partial and small, relative to those in the previous public image datasets. This significant intra-class variation poses greater challenges to any data-driven learning system that builds a classifier to fit given data and generalize to unseen data.

ImageNet is currently the largest image dataset among other standard datasets for visual recognition. The ImageNet dataset is publicly available, and the ImageNet Large Scale Visual Recognition Challenge (ILSVRC) has become the standard benchmark for large-scale object recognition.

Table 1. Experimental image dataset

Image no	Train	Validation	Test
Combo	1180	509	333
Not-combo	1180	500	320
Total	4022		

Dataset for Fine-Tuning and Performance Evaluation. The proposed ComboNN is fine-tuned and evaluated on our small dataset which was collected from the Internet. The overview of the dataset is illustrated in Table 1. As seen in this table, there are total of 4022 images in our dataset, which contains 2022 and 2000 examples for combo and not-combo, respectively. We randomly choose 59% (i.e., 2360) images for training and 25% (i.e., 1009) images for validation, and use the remaining (i.e., 653) for testing.

4.2 Experimental Setting

Our implementation is based on the open source Keras [23] (using TensorFlow backend), which is tied with the NVIDIA CuDNN libraries to speed up the training of deep neural network. All of our experiments are conducted on one NVIDIA GeForce GTX 1070 GPU with 8 GB of onboard memory. This is crucial due to the huge memory requirement for the deep convolutional neural nets.

At test time, we warp a given testing image to a 224×224 RGB image which is required by the proposed ComboNN. We forward propagate the resized image through the trained ComboNN in order to read off features from the desired layer and make the prediction on the task label.

4.3 Performance on Testing Dataset

The combo object detection performance of the proposed ComboNN model is evaluated on our testing dataset. We achieve an accuracy of 96.87% on

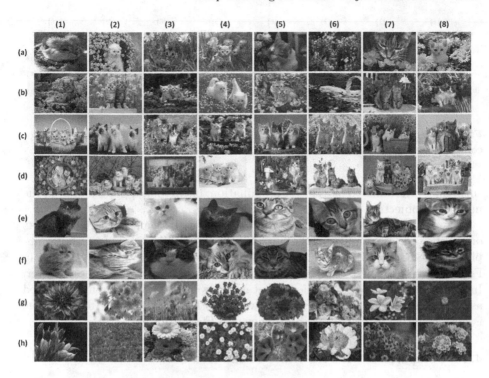

Fig. 3. Some examples of successful combo/not-combo detection on our testing dataset. (a)–(d) for combo examples, and (e)–(h) for not-combo examples

not-combo examples, an accuracy of 94.59% on combo examples, and an overall accuracy of 95.71% on the whole testing dataset.

Figure 3 demonstrates some successful cases of combo/not-combo detection on our testing dataset, in which rows (a)–(d) show combo examples, whereas rows (e)–(h) for not-combo examples. We use Fig. 3(a) and (a)(1) to denote the images in row(a) and the first image in row(a), respectively. This is similar for other images.

The selected cases cover a wide variety of real-world circumstances. In Fig. 3(a), one cat can be observed to play with the flowers in different poses. Two cats surrounded by the flowers interact with each other as shown in Fig. 3(b). Three and more than three cats can be found together with the flowers in Fig. 3(c) and (d), respectively. The cats without the company of flowers show in Fig. 3(e)–(f), while Fig. 3(g)–(h) display the bunch of flowers with the absence of cats.

As seen in Fig. 3, the spacial appearance of combo object changes over time with the motion of cats. Moreover, the scene contains the dynamic variation on luminance level which raises the unpredictability of the background. Figure 3 shows that our model can readily account for such uncertainties and generate the reliable prediction for testing data. It provides an apparent showcase of the

Fig. 4. Examples of failed combo/not-combo detection on our testing dataset. (a) for combo examples, and (b) for not-combo examples

surprising invariance to movement, illumination, background, poses and even the number of objects.

Figure 4 gives an illustration of the failed cases. It displays the false rejects on combo object examples at the top, and the false rejects on not-combo examples at the bottom. Note that our model only fails on a few cases. As seen in Fig. 4(a), most of these cases contain a couple of flowers or even only one flower. In such scenario, the combination of cat and flower could be easily misidentified as cat rather than combo object. It is worth noting that only one flower image is misrecognized as combo object as shown in Fig. 4(b)(8).

4.4   Comparison with the State-of-the-Art CNNs

The combo object detection performance of the proposed ComboNN was evaluated and compared against five state-of-the-art CNNs: the InceptionV3 [27], the ResNet50 [28], the VGG16 [21], the Xception [29], and the VGG19 [21]. These five CNNs are pre-trained on dataset ILSVRC2012 [4] using the implementations provided by the open source Keras [23] neural network library.

We further fine-tune the ResNet50, VGG16, Xception, VGG19 and InceptionV3 on our small dataset to adapt them to combo/not-combo detection. The fine-tuning for these five CNNs follows the same procedure. We take away the classification layer of the CNNs, which is particularly designed for the pre-training objective (i.e., the 1000-way classification on ILSVRC2012) and is not applicable for our task. Instead, we attach a brand new classification layer, which is initialized at random and has the appropriate number (i.e., two) of outputs for the new goal. Finally, we conduct SGD [24] training of the neural network weights with a learning rate of 0.0001.

Table 2. Comparison of validation accuracy

CNN	InceptionV3	ResNet50	VGG16	Xception	VGG19	Proposed
Accuracy (%)	50.03	50.08	50.03	49.95	50.09	**95.83**

The results after fine-tuning for all CNN models are presented in Table 2, which are measured in terms of the validation accuracy on our validation dataset.

As seen from the table, the validation accuracy for the Xception is less than 50%, with only 49.95%. The InceptionV3, VGG16, ResNet50 and VGG19 give a better accuracy of 50.03%, 50.03%, 50.08% and 50.09%, respectively. Since the VGG19 is a little bit better than others, we choose it as the starting point for the proposed ComboNN. Among the six neural networks in comparison, our ComboNN is seen achieving constantly the best validation accuracy of 95.83% for all conditions, which indicates that the ComboNN has the ability to resolve the overfitting problems, and can adapt to surveillance images taken from dynamic environments of different situations.

5   Conclusion

In this paper, we propose a deep CNN (ComboNN) based combo object detection system which is intended to be used for the real-world images. The identification of combo object in this context is especially challenging, due to the inadequacy of labeled data and the dynamic changes in spacial construction of combo object caused by the motion of cats and varying levels of illumination. Transfer learning is employed to cope with the issue of data scarcity, where the proposed ComboNN is pre-trained on a huge dataset ImageNet and fine-tuned on our small dataset. We make use of data augmentation and regularization technique to prevent overfitting and improve the generalization of the ComboNN. The highly effective training procedure and low computational expense maximizes the prospective usages of the ComboNN. Experimental tests and quantitative performance evaluations on the real-world dataset show the benefits of the proposed system. The ComboNN obtains much better accuracy on combo object detection when compared with the state-of-the-art convolutional neural networks.

References

1. LeCun, Y., Bengio, Y., Hinton, G.: Deep learning. Nature **521**(7553), 436 (2015)
2. Deng, J., Dong, W., Socher, R., Li, L., Li, K., Li, F.: ImageNet: a large-scale hierarchical image database. In: Computer Vision and Pattern Recognition, pp. 248–255. IEEE (2009)
3. Krizhevsky, A., Sutskever, I., Hinton, G.: ImageNet classification with deep convolutional neural networks. In: Advances in Neural Information Processing Systems, pp. 1097–1105 (2012)
4. Deng, J., Berg, A., Satheesh, S., Su, H., Khosla, A., Li, F: ImageNet large scale visual recognition competition 2012 (ILSVRC2012). In: net.org/challenges/LSVRC (2012)
5. Girshick, R., Donahue, J., Darrell, T., Malik, J.: Rich feature hierarchies for accurate object detection and semantic segmentation. In: Proceedings of the IEEE Conference on Computer Vision and Pattern Recognition, pp. 580–587. IEEE (2014)
6. Zhou, B., Lapedriza, A., Xiao, J., Torralba, A., Oliva, A.: Learning deep features for scene recognition using places database. In Advances in Neural Information Processing Systems, pp. 487–495 (2014)

7. Schroff, F., Kalenichenko, D., Philbin, J.: FaceNet: a unified embedding for face recognition and clustering. In Proceedings of the IEEE Conference on Computer Vision and Pattern Recognition, pp. 815–823 (2015)
8. Bar, Y., Diamant, I., Wolf, L., Lieberman, S., Konen, E., Greenspan, H.: Chest pathology detection using deep learning with non-medical training. In: 2015 IEEE 12th International Symposium on Biomedical Imaging (ISBI), pp. 294–297. IEEE (2015)
9. Ciregan, D., Meier, U., Schmidhuber, J.: Multi-column deep neural networks for image classification. In: Computer Vision and Pattern Recognition (CVPR), pp. 3642–3649 (2012)
10. Srivastava, N., Hinton, G., Krizhevsky, A., Sutskever, I., Salakhutdinov, R.: Dropout: a simple way to prevent neural networks from overfitting. J. Mach. Learn. Res. **15**(1), 1929–1958 (2014)
11. Pellegrini, S., Ess, A., Schindler, K., Van, L.: You'll never walk alone: modeling social behavior for multi-target tracking. In: IEEE International Conference on Computer Vision (ICCV), pp. 261–268 (2009)
12. Baumgartner, T., Mitzel, D., Leibe, B.: Tracking people and their objects. In: IEEE Conference on Computer Vision and Pattern Recognition (CVPR), pp. 3658–3665 (2013)
13. Yamaguchi, K., Berg, A., Ortiz, L., Berg, T.: Who are you with and where are you going. In: IEEE Conference on Computer Vision and Pattern Recognition (CVPR), pp. 1345–1352 (2011)
14. Pellegrini, S., Ess, A., Van Gool, L.: Improving data association by joint modeling of pedestrian trajectories and groupings. In: Daniilidis, K., Maragos, P., Paragios, N. (eds.) ECCV 2010. LNCS, vol. 6311, pp. 452–465. Springer, Heidelberg (2010). https://doi.org/10.1007/978-3-642-15549-9_33
15. Zhao, J., Pang, S., Hartill, B., Sarrafzadeh, A.: A combo object model for maritime boat ramps traffic monitoring. In: Hirose, A., Ozawa, S., Doya, K., Ikeda, K., Lee, M., Liu, D. (eds.) ICONIP 2016. LNCS, vol. 9947, pp. 623–630. Springer, Cham (2016). https://doi.org/10.1007/978-3-319-46687-3_69
16. Everingham, M., Eslami, A., Van, L., Williams, K., Winn, J., Zisserman, A.: The Pascal visual object classes challenge: a retrospective. Int. J. Comput. Vis. **111**(1), 98–136 (2015)
17. Agrawal, P., Girshick, R., Malik, J.: Analyzing the performance of multilayer neural networks for object recognition. In: Fleet, D., Pajdla, T., Schiele, B., Tuytelaars, T. (eds.) ECCV 2014. LNCS, vol. 8695, pp. 329–344. Springer, Cham (2014). https://doi.org/10.1007/978-3-319-10584-0_22
18. Razavian, A., Azizpour, H., Sullivan, J., Carlsson, S.: CNN features off-the-shelf: an astounding baseline for recognition. In: Computer Vision and Pattern Recognition Workshops (CVPRW), pp. 512–519 (2014)
19. Sermanet, P., Eigen, D., Zhang, X., Mathieu, M.F., LeCun, Y.: OverFeat: integrated recognition, localization and detection using convolutional networks. arXiv:1312.6229 (2013)
20. Van, G., Setio, A., Jacobs, C., Ciompi, F.: On-the-shelf convolutional neural network features for pulmonary nodule detection in computed tomography scans. In: Biomedical Imaging (ISBI), pp. 286–289 (2015)
21. Simonyan, K., Zisserman, A.: Very deep convolutional networks for large-scale image recognition. arXiv:1409.1556 (2014)
22. Glorot, X., Bordes, A., Bengio, Y.: Deep sparse rectifier neural networks. In: Proceedings of the Fourteenth International Conference on Artificial Intelligence and Statistics, pp. 315–323 (2011)

23. Chollet, F., et al.: Keras. https://keras.io (2015)
24. Bottou, L.: Large-scale machine learning with stochastic gradient descent. In: Lechevallier, Y., Saporta, G. (eds.) Proceedings of COMPSTAT, pp. 177–186. Springer, Heidelberg (2010). https://doi.org/10.1007/978-3-7908-2604-3_16
25. Sutskever, I., Martens, J., Dahl, G., Hinton, G.: On the importance of initialization and momentum in deep learning. In: International Conference on Machine Learning, pp. 1139–1147 (2013)
26. Miller, G.: WordNet: a lexical database for english. Commun. ACM **38**(11), 39–41 (1995)
27. Szegedy, C., Vanhoucke, V., Ioffe, S., Shlens, J., Wojna, Z.: Rethinking the inception architecture for computer vision. In: Proceedings of the IEEE Conference on Computer Vision and Pattern Recognition, pp. 2818–2826 (2016)
28. He, K., Zhang, X., Ren, S., Sun, J.: Deep residual learning for image recognition. In: Proceedings of the IEEE Conference on Computer Vision and Pattern Recognition, pp. 770–778 (2016)
29. Chollet, F.: Xception: deep learning with depthwise separable convolutions. arXiv preprint (2016)

DasNet: Dynamic Adaptive Structure for Accelerating Multi-task Convolutional Neural Network

Yinan Ma, Jing Wu, and Chengnian Long[(✉)]

Department of Automation, School of Electronic Information and Electrical Engineering, Shanghai Jiao Tong University and Key Laboratory of System Control and Information Processing, Ministry of China, Shanghai, China
{yinanma,jingwu,longcn}@sjtu.edu.cn

Abstract. Multi-task learning solves a collection of different tasks by sharing a large encoder (common network). However, due to high computational demand for large common network, deploying multi-task learning on resource constrained devices is a challenging task. To guarantee overall accuracy with less computation, we introduce DasNet, which (1) automatically searches the adaptive common network sub-structure for each task; (2) fine-tunes corresponding decoders to adapt to the common network sub-structure. Our method can accelerate the real time inference procedure by dynamically building adaptive structure according to specific task requirements in actual scenarios. Notably, all extra memory and calculations we need for our method can be negligible. Experiments conducted on four public datasets (i.e., ILSCRC-2012, Birds200, CatVsDog, MIT67) demonstrate that our proposed method performs effectively compared with general multi-task network architecture and present related state of the art (SOTA) methods.

Keywords: Multi-task learning · Common network · Less computation · Adaptive sub-structure

1 Introduction

Multi-task learning in Convolutional Neural Networks (CNNs) has displayed remarkable success in the field of computer vision in recent years. Multi-task learning aims to improve the overall prediction quality by processing the tasks jointly and sharing information between them. Specifically, their approaches share a common network over different tasks and have different branches, each implementing a decoder for a given task. Usually a common network is much larger than a single decoder in design. In this way, it's efficient to solve many tasks with a limited memory budget on training stage.

Some methods implement multi-task learning for the same input source [1–3]. Others have different input sources [4–6]. To some extent, the former can be seen as a special case of the latter. This paper focuses on the latter that requires

© Springer Nature Switzerland AG 2019
T. Gedeon et al. (Eds.): ICONIP 2019, LNCS 11953, pp. 138–150, 2019.
https://doi.org/10.1007/978-3-030-36708-4_12

higher calculations. The left dashed box in Fig. 1 shows the general framework of multi-task learning with different input sources. Generally, all existing multi-task learning approaches hold the same view that certain level of common network redundancy is necessary to guarantee enough capacity [5]. Therefore, there is a high demand to deploy such cumbersome model with millions of parameters on computing resource constrained device.

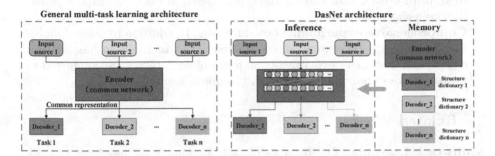

Fig. 1. General Multi-task Learning *v.s.* **DasNet**. We mark encoder and decoder networks as box, while adjustment unit as circle. For general multi-task learning, each task shares same large common network. For DasNet, memory needs to record the corresponding common network optimal sub-architecture in structure dictionary for each task. In inference phase, DasNet adjusts structure units according to structure dictionaries.

Present popular works on accelerating CNNs can be roughly divided into two categories, namely, pruning and lightweight network. Nevertheless, all these works optimized the network structure for a specific task rather than multiple tasks. They still suffer from the problems of (1) *the necessary model capacity reduction* and (2) *destruction of the common network*. Specifically, lightweight network is often designed to contain model capacity that exactly matches one task due to its compact architecture, so it is not suitable for handling multiple tasks. For pruning methods, the common network can not be directly fine-tuned for a specific task after removing parameters. This is because the common network can not be optimized on one single task but ignores the impact on other tasks.

To address the above mentioned two problems, we propose a novel DasNet architecture. The DasNet automatically searches for the optimal common network sub-structure for each task. On the storage, the complete common network is stored in memory to ensure the necessary model redundancy. In real time inference phase, the common network structure is dynamically adjusted according to the specific task requirements. The right dashed box in Fig. 1 shows the DasNet architecture. It can accelerate multi-task CNNs in a very efficient way. We demonstrate the effectiveness of our approach in 4 challenging tasks. In summary, we highlight three contributions:

- **Effective acceleration strategy.** We propose DasNet, which performs a common network structure optimization for each specific task and only fine-tunes corresponding decoders to remedy the performance. It can effectively reduce calculation by directly skipping unnecessary network structure units in inference phase.
- **Negligible extra memory and calculations.** We choose both block and path structure as the adjustment unit. Only 528 binary parameters are used to record for each task and all these parameters do not participate in the floating point operation.
- **Comprehensive experimental evaluations.** In addition to general multi-task learning, we also extend recent related SOTA methods to baselines for comparison. Extensive experiments on four public datasets are conducted to measure both parameter efficiency and computational efficiency.

2 Related Works

Multi-task Learning. The term multi-task learning itself has been broadly used as an umbrella term to include computer vision [1,2,4,5], and representation learning [6–8], transfer learning [1,7,9] etc. Most researchers perform experiments using versions of VGG16 [10] or ResNet [11] as a common network [1–4]. [5] believes with an increasing number of tasks, the capacity of common networks should increase. The latest work [8] combined 6 source networks into a common network. It can be seen that the common network tends to become larger. This is because of the highly non-convex optimization nature in model training and certain level of model redundancy is necessary to guarantee enough capacity during training. Most multi-task learning methods focus on solving more kinds of tasks in a joint way. However, such a cumbersome model will slow down the running speed of model inference. In real-world applications, the common network scale is also too large when performing on only one small task. Hence, there is a great need to remove the redundancy.

Pruning Methods. Pruning methods aim to remove the unnecessary parameters and are first studied by [12] and [13]. They select parameters to prune according to a second-order Taylor expansion to improve generalization during the training. Some works prune a CNN after fully training. [14] directly prunes the parameters under a pre-set threshold. In recent years, an increasingly popular method using the backpropagation algorithm to self-train the search for the optimal structure of the network [9,15,16] is proposed. The advantage of this method is to reduce algorithmic computational complexity based on traditional statistical methods. And it can integrate the network structure search process into the training phase. Other research focuses on selection of pruning unit because non-structured connection pruning can lead to an irregular convolution, which needs a special algorithm or dedicated hardware for efficient inference, thus is hard to harvest actual computational savings. To address the weakness of non-structured random pruning, structured sparsity learning algorithms are proposed [17]. In these works, only groups of structured neurons, such as whole filter [18] can be pruned. However, overall parameters' fine-tuning and optimized structure make it suitable for only one specific task. Different from the previous work, DasNet searches for the optimal common network sub-structure and only fine-tunes decoder for each task.

Lightweight Network. In addition to pruning, lightweight network is another optimization method. SqueezeNet [19] implemented the same accuracy as AlexNet on ImageNet, but only used 1/50 of the parameters. Recent work MobileNet [20] uses depth-wise separable convolution, which is divided into deep convolution and 1×1 convolution. These works greatly improve parameter efficiency. However, it is difficult to design a suitable compact network structure for multi-task learning due to their limited network capacity.

3   Methodology

In this section, we explain the details of the proposed DasNet and implement on ResNeXt-50 [21] which is a new variant of ResNet for multi-task learning. Our method consists of three main parts: block structure units search, path structure units search and decoder fine-tuning. Next, we go deep into details about DasNet and give comprehensive introductions to above three parts.

3.1   Block Structure Units Search

ResNeXt contains a shortcut connection between any two adjacent block structures. As shown in Fig. 2. Formally, the block output is defined as:

$$y_j = A_j(x) + x. \tag{1}$$

where $j \in Block$ and $Block = \{j|j = 1, 2, \cdots, n\}$ denotes the block serial number of ResNeXt. $A_j(x)$ represents a transformation with parameters of block j and input x before shortcut connection. Now, we introduce extra trainable block connection coefficient $BC_j \in BC$ where $BC = \{BC_j|\forall j \in Block\}$ to evaluate the importance of every block structure unit. So we redefine y_j as:

$$y_j = BC_j \cdot A_j(x) + x. \tag{2}$$

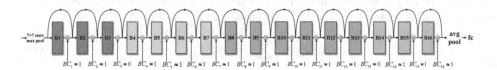

Fig. 2. Block structure units search in ResNeXt-50. We mark residual block as box. Different colors represent different filter sizes and filters in the block. The set BC comes from one of our experiments. (Color figure online)

If the value of BC_j is close to 0 and accuracy drops very little, we can directly skip the calculations in block j in forward propagation process. Like the set BC shown in Fig. 2, block 3 and 13 can be skipped in inference phase. Then block structure units search problem can be translated into how to find accurate evaluation set BC. So, we exploit the backpropagation training method to train the block connection coefficients separately. After training, several blocks whose corresponding connection coefficients are not close to zero are chosen to form the final optimal structure. Since our goal is to make the size of the sub-structure as compact as possible. The next question is, how to control the sparsity of all block connection coefficients. Compared with previous sparsity regularization methods [9], we propose a new soft sparsity control loss function without any clear model compression indicators. We formulate our loss function L_{total} as follow:

$$p_j = \frac{BC_j}{\sum_{j \in Block} BC_j}, \tag{3}$$

$$L_{spa} = \frac{1}{|Block|} \sum_{j \in Block} p_j \cdot log\frac{1}{p_j}, \tag{4}$$

$$\alpha = gc \cdot step, \tag{5}$$

$$L_{total} = L_{ori} + \alpha \cdot L_{spa}. \tag{6}$$

where $|\ |$ denotes a function to find the number of collection elements and L_{ori} is a standard classification loss (i.e., cross entropy loss). $step$ denotes the current iteration step and gc denotes growth coefficient which is set to constant. Equation (3) normalizes all block connection coefficients. Equation (4) uses the form of information entropy to construct the sparse loss. This is because we assume that each connection coefficient reflects the importance of the corresponding block for all samples and the importance of each block is different. Equation (6) adds sparse loss to the original loss function, and α is an acceleration factor that can help to speed up the search process by increasing the value. By minimizing Eq. (6) with backpropagation training algorithm, we can obtain the final indicator set BC.

3.2   Path Structure Units Search

In addition to the block structure, ResNeXt also contains path structures. So we can extend the strategy in Sect. 3.1 to path structure units search. Formally, the aggregated transformations in one block can be presented as:

$$A_j(x) = \sum_{i \in Path} T_j^i(x, W_j^i), \tag{7}$$

where $Path = \{i | i = 1, 2, \cdots, m\}$ denotes the path serial number set. $T_j^i(x, W_j^i)$ represents a transformation with parameters W_j^i and input x. $PC_j^i \in PC$ where

$PC = \{PC_j^i | \forall i \in Path, \forall j \in Block\}$ is introduced to evaluate the importance of each path structure unit. So we formulate a weighted $A_j(x)$ as:

$$A_j(x) = \sum_{i \in Path} PC_j^i \cdot T_j^i(x, W_j^i), \tag{8}$$

Similar to the methods in Sect. 3.1, we construct the loss function for the path structures search phase as:

$$p_j^i = \frac{PC_j^i}{\sum_{j \in Block} \sum_{i \in Path} PC_j^i}, \tag{9}$$

$$L_{spa} = \frac{1}{|Block| \cdot |Path|} \sum_{j \in Block} \sum_{i \in Path} p_j^i \cdot log\frac{1}{p_j^i}, \tag{10}$$

$$L_{total} = L_{ori} + \beta \cdot L_{spa}. \tag{11}$$

Figure 3 shows path structure units search implementation in one block. By gradually forcing the sparsity of the all path connection coefficients with back-propagation algorithm, some paths' outputs gradually become all zero. And convolution operations on these paths can be skipped directly during real-time inference, like gray path in Fig. 3.

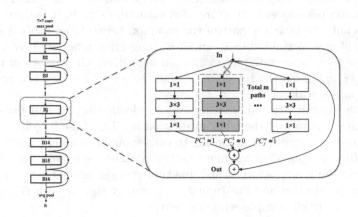

Fig. 3. Path structure units search in one block.

After block and path structure units search, the elements in BC and PC will be binarized to 0 or 1 according to the preset threshold. Finally, these binaries form the structure dictionary which represents 512 path structures and 16 block structures for each task.

Algorithm 1. Block selection and fine-tuning

Input: Training set $\{(\hat{x}_k, \hat{y}_k)\}_{train}$; Maximum iteration of fine-tuning S_{ft} and block selection S_{bs}; Growth coefficient gc

Output: Block connection coefficients: BC; Weights of decoder: W_{de}; Accuracy set: AC

1: Initialize BC;
2: **while** *Iteration* **do**
3:    $\alpha = gc \cdot step$;
4:    Train BC with backpropagation algorithm;
5:    **if** *step* mod $S_{bs} = 0$ **then**
6:       $\alpha = 0$; $step_{fine-tune} = 1$;
7:       **while** $step_{fine-tune} < S_{ft}$ **do**
8:          Train W_{de} with backpropagation algorithm;
9:          $step_{fine-tune} = step_{fine-tune} + 1$;
10:       **end while**
11:       $AC = AC \cup$accuracy on training set;
12:    **end if**
13:    $step = step + 1$
14: **end while**

3.3 Decoder Fine-Tuning

Similar to present pruning methods, the decoders need to be fine-tuned to adapt to the common network sub-structure after structure search. It is worth noting that we do not fine-tune any part of the common network, and this is because fine-tuning of any specialized task can affect the performance of other tasks.

Now, we give the overall implementation algorithm. Given a set of training samples $\{(\hat{x}_k, \hat{y}_k)\}_{train}$, the key steps of block selection and fine-tuning can be illustrated in Algorithm 1.

It mainly contains two alternating stages: block selection and fine-tuning. Line 3 to line 4 is to find the block evaluation set BC. Line 5 to line 12 is to fine-tune decoder parameters according to corresponding common network sub-structure. By changing α, we can more easily switch between two stages. In addition to Algorithm 1, path selection and fine-tuning is also needed to evaluate each path. As path selection and fine-tuning is extremely similar with Algorithm 1, we don't give a detailed implementation here.

4 Experiment

In this section, we first describe the datasets for experiments and give implementation details in our experiments including the data preprocessing, the setting of hyperparameters and some useful tricks. Then we demonstrate the improvement brought about by DasNet in both parameter and computational efficiency by comparing to the baselines. All the experiments are completed using tensorflow on 1 Nvidia 1080 GPU.

4.1   Datasets and Experimental Setup

In order to provide comprehensive results, our method is comparatively evaluated on four datasets: the ImageNet ILSVRC-12 [22], Birds200 [23], CatVsDog [24], MIT67 [25], which represent multiple classification tasks in computer vision. These datasets are among the most common benchmarks employed by the recent related work.

The ImageNet ILSVRC-2012 dataset is a 1000 classes classification task with 1.2M training examples and 50k validation examples. The CatVsDog dataset has 12,500 training data and 12,500 test data, and we use 10% of the original test data as validation examples. Birds200 dataset has 6000 training images and 5700 test images of 200 bird species. MIT67 has 80 training images and 20 test images per indoor scene class.

Common network is pre-trained on ImageNet and decoder network has only one fully-connected layer in terms of classification problems. To augment the training images, we employed random jittering and subtle scaling and rotation perturbations to the training images. A 224×224 crop of all involved datasets is randomly sampled. During test phase, we adopted only one center crop instead of the standard 10-crop training for classification tasks. In training phase, we used a batch size of 20 and a momentum of 0.9 on all the datasets, which is helpful to achieve stable convergence. In fine-tuning phase, the learning rate of all involved datasets start from 0.01 and is multiplied by 0.55 when the error plateaus, while in sub-structure selection phase the learning rate has always been 0.005. The threshold for binarizing the elements in BC and PC is 0.02.

We also study the effect of growth coefficient gc on accuracy drop. Figure 4 shows effect of different growth coefficients gc on accuracy drop. As we can see, smaller gc can make accuracy drop more slowly. However, smaller gc also slow down structure search process. To balance two factors, the value of gc we set is 0.01. In addition to gc, the initial value of the connection coefficients BC and

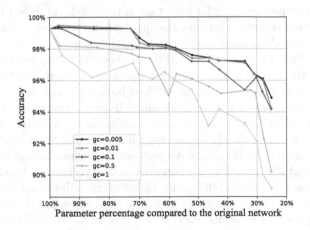

Fig. 4. Effect of growth coefficient gc on accuracy drop. The result comes from one of our experiments with CatVsDog dataset.

PC also have the same impact on accuracy. Through experiment tests, we finally set the initial value of the connect coefficients as 0.3.

4.2 Parameter Efficiency

For fair comparison, ResNeXt-50 is used to be the common network for all methods. In order to have a comprehensive comparison, we also extend Taylor Prune [26], AutoPruner [16] and Data-driven [15] to baseline methods. To keep the same amount of parameters between these methods, we first build the original DasNet architecture as stated in Sects. 3.1, 3.2 and 3.3. Since the actual common network sub-structure is determined by approach itself, we can not predict the size of the final sub-structure. So according to DasNet architecture, the same number of parameters are removed by using other methods. Notice that for pruning methods, we only fine-tune the decoder parameters. For all above methods, we use the best performing parameters on the validation or test set. Table 1 shows parameter efficiency comparison using different algorithms.

Table 1. Parameter efficiency comparison using different algorithms. In "Size" column, the value represents the size of the network in real-time inference. The "Ac" is the accuracy of each task on test or validation datasets.

Methods	ImageNet		Birds200		CatVsDog		MIT67		Average results	
	Size	Ac	Size	Ac	Size	Ac	Size	Ac	Size	Ac
Standard	25M	74.2%	25M	68.6%	25M	99.3%	25M	68.0%	25M	77.5%
Taylor Prune	20.87M	73.1%	16.92M	64.3%	8.53M	95.8%	18.34M	62.3%	16.17M	73.9%
AutoPruner	20.71M	74.5%	16.73M	63.5%	8.75M	95.6%	18.17M	63.8%	16.09M	74.35%
Data-driven	21.02M	71.08%	15.5M	61.2%	8.81M	92.1%	18.27M	61.2%	15.9M	71.39%
DasNet	**21.24M**	**72.8%**	**16.73M**	**65.6%**	**7.76M**	**97.4%**	**18.23M**	**64.5%**	**15.99M**	**75.1%**

In Table 1, the network size for each task is recorded. As shown in the table, DasNet can further compress network size involved in the actual calculation compared with the standard multi-task learning architecture. The average network model size is reduced by nearly 40% while the accuracy dropped by only 2.4%. Compare with the recent popular pruning methods, we can see that DasNet is slightly better. Although Data-driven method holds the same view about structure selection, our approach has no absolute limit on the model compression ratio, making DasNet have no major impact on accuracy loss. It's worth noting that original common network is too large for subtasks like CatVsDog. Even for multi-task learning, it is not always possible to perform all subtasks in real-world scenarios at the same time. Therefore, it is necessary to build a targeted multi-task learning network architecture based on real-time task requirements.

For memory, we also make some optimizations. First, if one structure unit (block or path structure) is not selected for any task, we will remove it from the whole network. Second, we only use 1bit byte units to record the binary structure dictionary. Table 2 shows our memory strategy results compared to standard multi-task learning. DasNet storage is smaller and extra memory for structure dictionary can be negligible. If we use other baselines like Taylor Prune, structure dictionary needs to record 4.98×10^5 filters for each task. And The extra memory required is 1000 times that of DasNet. Next, we go deep into computation complexity analysis and device response time.

Table 2. Parameter memory.

Methods	Data Type	Network size	Extra memory
Standard	32bit	102 MB	0 MB
DasNet	32bit & 1bit	98.4 MB	2.64×10^{-4} MB

4.3   Computational Complexity Analysis

In addition to inference parameter efficiency, another direct evaluation criterion is the amount of floating point operations, which is a popular metric to evaluate the complexity of CNN models. Figure 5 shows the floating point calculations of DasNet and other baselines while using different sized network in inference procedure. The dataset used is CatVsDog. As shown in Fig. 5, when the network has the same size, DasNet is better at reducing floating point operations. There are two main reasons for this. One is that the common network still retains numerous 3×3 filters with a large number of floating point calculations after using these baselines, the other is that extra zero-padding operation affects the performance of reducing floating point operations.

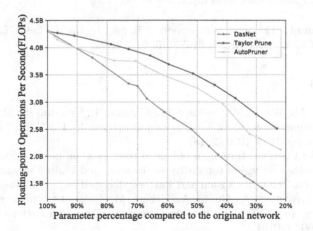

Fig. 5. FLOPs reduction efficiency comparison.

We also give actual computational complexity analysis of DasNet and other baselines when performing 4 tasks simultaneously. Table 3 shows the FLOPs and speed up comparison using different algorithms. In Table 3(a) DasNet achieves ×1.6559 acceleration and achieves the SOTA method compared to other baselines. In Table 3(b) we can find that DasNet is more prominent on small tasks like CatVsDog.

Table 3. FLOPs and speed up comparison using different algorithms

(a) Total FlOPs and Speed up

Methods	Total FlOPs	Speed up
Standard	17.2B	×1
Taylor Prune	13.91B	×1.2365
AutoPruner	13.47B	×1.2762
DasNet	**10.38B**	**×1.6559**

(b) Speed up for each task

Dataset	AutoPruner	**DasNet**
ImageNet	×1.0845	**×1.1275**
Birds200	×1.1644	**×1.4379**
CatVsDog	×1.7174	**×2.6425**
MIT67	×1.1386	**×1.4157**

5   Conclusions

In this paper, we propose DasNet that dynamically adjusts common structure according to specific task requirements. Remarkably, DasNet can ensure the necessary redundancy by dividing the traditional multi-task learning architecture into two phases: storage and real-time inference. All extra memory and calculations we need for our method can be negligible. We demonstrate that the proposed method can significantly speed up inference procedure under the existing general multi-task learning framework.

Acknowledgment. This work was supported in part by the National Nature Science Foundation of China under Grants 61673275, 61873166.

References

1. Teichmann, M., Weber, M., Zoellner, M., Cipolla, R., Urtasun, R.: MultiNet: real-time joint semantic reasoning for autonomous driving. In: IEEE Intelligent Vehicles Symposium, pp. 1013–1020 (2018)
2. Kokkinos, I.: UberNet: training a universal convolutional neural network for low-, mid-, and high-level vision using diverse datasets and limited memory. In: IEEE Conference on Computer Vision and Pattern Recognition, pp. 5454–5463 (2017)
3. Misra, I., Shrivastava, A., Gupta, A., Hebert, M.: Cross-stitch networks for multi-task learning. In: IEEE Conference on Computer Vision and Pattern Recognition, pp. 3994–4003 (2016)
4. Jou, B., Chang, S.-F.: Deep cross residual learning for multitask visual recognition. In: Proceedings of the 24th ACM International Conference on Multimedia, Amsterdam, pp. 998–1007 (2016)

5. Aljundi, R., Chakravarty, P., Tuytelaars, T.: Expert gate: lifelong learning with a network of experts. In: The IEEE Conference on Computer Vision and Pattern Recognition, pp. 3366–3375 (2017)
6. Doersch, C., Zisserman, A.: Multi-task self-supervised visual learning. In: The IEEE International Conference on Computer Vision, pp. 2051–2060 (2017)
7. Zhong, Y., Li, V., Okada, R., Maki, A.: Target aware network adaptation for efficient representation learning. In: Leal-Taixé, L., Roth, S. (eds.) ECCV 2018. LNCS, vol. 11132, pp. 450–467. Springer, Cham (2019). https://doi.org/10.1007/978-3-030-11018-5_38
8. Zamir, A.R., Sax, A., Shen, W., Guibas, L.J., Malik, J., Savarese, S.: Taskonomy: disentangling task transfer learning. In: Proceedings of the IEEE Conference on Computer Vision and Pattern Recognition, pp. 3712–3722 (2018)
9. Luo, J.H., Wu, J.: AutoPruner: an end-to-end trainable filter pruning method for efficient deep model inference (2018)
10. Zeiler, M.D., Fergus, R.: Visualizing and understanding convolutional networks. In: Fleet, D., Pajdla, T., Schiele, B., Tuytelaars, T. (eds.) ECCV 2014. LNCS, vol. 8689, pp. 818–833. Springer, Cham (2014). https://doi.org/10.1007/978-3-319-10590-1_53
11. He, K., Zhang, X., Ren, S., Sun, J.: Deep residual learning for image recognition. In: Proceedings of the IEEE Conference on Computer Vision and Pattern Recognition, pp. 770–778. IEEE Press, New York (2016)
12. LeCun, Y., Denker, J.S., Solla, S.A.: Optimal brain damage. In: Advances in Neural Information Processing Systems, pp. 598–605 (1990)
13. Hassibi, B., Stork, D.G.: Second order derivatives for network pruning: optimal brain surgeon. In: Advances in Neural Information Processing Systems, San Mateo, pp. 164–171 (1993)
14. Han, S., Pool, J., Tran, J., Dally, W.: Learning both weights and connections for efficient neural network. In: Advances in Neural Information Processing Systems, vol. 28, pp. 1135–1143 (2015)
15. Huang, Z., Wang, N.: Data-driven sparse structure selection for deep neural networks. In: The European Conference on Computer Vision, pp. 304–320 (2018)
16. Manessi, F., Rozza, A., Bianco, S., Napoletano, P., Schettini, R.: Automated pruning for deep neural network compression. In: 24th International Conference on Pattern Recognition, pp. 657–664 (2018)
17. Wen, W., Wu, C., Wang, Y., Chen, Y., Li, H.: Learning structured sparsity in deep neural networks. In: Advances in Neural Information Processing Systems, vol. 29, pp. 2074–2082 (2016)
18. Luo, J.H., Wu, J., Lin, W.: ThiNet: a filter level pruning method for deep neural network compression. In: IEEE International Conference on Computer Vision, pp. 5068–5076 (2017)
19. Iandola, F.N., Han, S., Moskewicz, M.W., Ashraf, K., Dally, W.J., Keutzer, K.: SqueezeNet: AlexNet-level accuracy with 50x fewer parameters and <1MB model size. In: CoRR (2016)
20. Howard, A.G., et al.: MobileNets: efficient convolutional neural networks for mobile vision applications. In: CoRR (2017)
21. Xie, S., Girshick, R., Dollár, P., Tu, Z., He, K.: Aggregated residual transformations for deep neural networks. In: Proceedings of the IEEE Conference on Computer Vision and Pattern Recognition, pp. 5987–5995. IEEE Press, New York (2017)
22. Russakovsky, O., et al.: ImageNet large scale visual recognition challenge. Int. J. Comput. Vis. **115**(3), 211–252 (2015)

23. Wah, C., Branson, S., Welinder, P., Perona, P., Belongie, S.: The Caltech-UCSD Birds-200-2011 Dataset (2011)
24. Elson, J., Douceur, J.J., Howell, J., Saul, J.: A CAPTCHA that exploits interest-aligned manual image categorization. In: Proceedings of 14th ACM Conference on Computer and Communications Security (2007)
25. Quattoni, A., Torralba, A.: Recognizing indoor scenes. In: IEEE Conference on Computer Vision and Pattern Recognition, pp. 413–420 (2009)
26. Molchanov, P., Tyree, S., Karras, T., Aila, T., Kautz, J.: Pruning convolutional neural networks for resource efficient transfer learning. In: International Conference of Learning Representation (2016)

Confusion-Aware Convolutional Neural Network for Image Classification

Liguang Yan[1], Baojiang Zhong[1(✉)], and Kai-Kuang Ma[2]

[1] School of Computer Science and Technology, Soochow University, Suzhou, China
lgyan@stu.suda.edu.cn, bjzhong@suda.edu.cn
[2] School of Electrical and Electronic Engineering, Nanyang Technological University,
Singapore, Singapore
ekkma@ntu.edu.sg

Abstract. In image classification, it is often encountered that the decision boundaries of some image categories are ambiguous and easy to confuse with each other, thus yielding inferior accuracy on image classification. In this paper, a novel *confusion-aware* convolutional neural network (CNN) is proposed to address this issue. Different from the *coarse-to-fine* strategy that has been practiced in existing hierarchical classifiers, our proposed method performs *predict-then-correct* strategy. At the training stage, a conventional classifier (referred to as the *prediction* classifier) is trained, and its confusion matrix is estimated by exploiting a cross validation process conducted on the training set. Based on this estimated confusion matrix, a *confusion-aware model* is then established, and it is used as a decision maker to train a set of *correction* classifiers for those confusing categories. At the classifying stage, the prediction and correction classifiers collaboratively work together via a hierarchical structure, and the confusion-aware model is used again as a decision maker to select a proper prediction classifier for each confusing category. Experimental results conducted on the Mnist and CIFAR-10 datasets show that the proposed confusion-aware network outperforms the existing CNN classifiers on image classification.

Keywords: Image classification · Convolutional neural networks ·
Confusion matrix · Cross-validation · Confusion-aware model

1 Introduction

Most of the existing convolutional neural network (CNN) classifiers for conducting image classification task have a 'flat' structure [1], which treat all classes as independent ones and ignore their visual separability. However, some categories could be substantially more difficult to be differentiated than others and hence more sophisticated classifiers are needed. For example, in the CIFAR-10 dataset [2] it is easy to distinguish a 'cat' from a 'truck', but could be very difficult to distinguish a 'cat' from a 'dog' due to an ambiguous decision boundary between this two categories. A CNN classifier, LeNet-5 [12], can achieve an accuracy of

© Springer Nature Switzerland AG 2019
T. Gedeon et al. (Eds.): ICONIP 2019, LNCS 11953, pp. 151–161, 2019.
https://doi.org/10.1007/978-3-030-36708-4_13

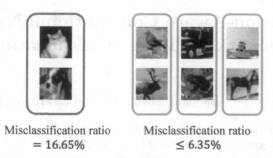

Misclassification ratio   Misclassification ratio
= 16.65%   ≤ 6.35%

Fig. 1. An example of confusing categories. By using the LeNet-5 [12] method to the dataset, the ratio of misclassifications between 'cats' and 'dogs' categories reaches 16.65%, while the highest ratio of misclassifications between any other two categories is only 6.35%.

76.92% on this dataset; however, the ratio of misclassifications between 'cats' and 'dogs' reaches 16.65%, which is much higher than that of any other two categories with less ambiguous decision boundary or confusion (as demonstrated in Fig. 1).

In this paper, a *confusion-aware* CNN is proposed with incorporation of a confusion-aware model in our developed *predictor-corrector* hierarchical framework. The proposed method is much more capable on distinguishing those image categories that have ambiguous decision boundaries, and it comprises two stages as follows. First, we train a conventional CNN (called the *prediction* classifier) using a training set to conduct a cross validation on the set for computing its confusion matrix. Based on this estimated confusion matrix, a confusion-aware model is then established. Second, by using the confusion-aware model as a decision-making system, a set of *correction* classifiers are trained for yielding a more discriminated decision boundary for each pair of ambiguous categories. Finally, the prediction and correction classifiers as obtained above are collaboratively used via a hierarchical structure for delivering much improved image classification.

The remainder of the paper is organized as follows. In Sect. 2, related works are briefly reviewed, and the relationship between our proposed method and the existing ones are clarified. In Sect. 3, the proposed confusion-aware CNN is described in detail. In Sect. 4, we present the experimental results of the confusion-aware CNN on the Mnist and CIFAR-10 datasets. Finally, Sect. 5 concludes this paper.

2 Backgrounds

2.1 Convolutional Neural Networks

Many CNN-based algorithms have shown their capability on delivering state-of-the-art performance in various computer-vision tasks, including image classification [4,17], object detection [7,16], semantic segmentation [8,15], and so

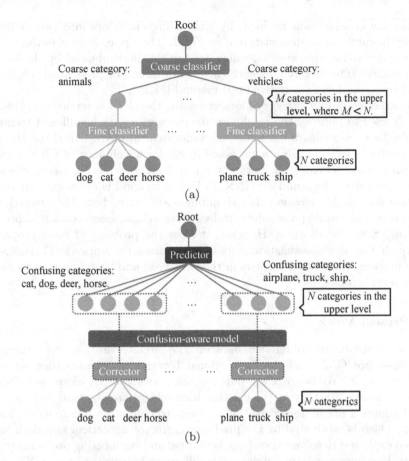

Fig. 2. A comparison of the architectures of the conventional hierarchical classification as shown in (a) and our proposed confusion-aware CNN as presented in (b).

on. Previous investigations mainly focus on enhancing the CNN's components, such as its pooling layers [5], nonlinear layers [21], or activation units [9]. In this work, there is no attempt to modify any of these components. Instead, a new and generalized CNN architecture (i.e., the *predictor-corrector* hierarchical framework) is proposed, in which any CNN classifier can be used. In other words, any superior CNN classifier developed in the future can be simply substituted into our proposed framework for yielding better performance.

2.2 Hierarchical Classification

For image classification, most of the existing deep CNNs are trained as an N-way 'flat' classifier. Since certain hierarchical relationships might be existing among some categories, *hierarchical* classification has been considered as an effective approach for conducting large-scaled visual recognition task [10,11,20,22].

It solves the classification problem by embedding classifiers into two or more category hierarchies, as demonstrated in Fig. 2. The upper-level classifiers produce coarse classification results, which are further discriminated by the lower-level classifiers. The hierarchy of such classifications can be predefined [10,20] or learned by a top-down (or bottom-up) method [11,22].

An earlier work of a category hierarchy using the CNN is reported in [18]. It is mainly used to improve the results for the categories with insufficient training examples by transfer learning. Later on, a hierarchical CNN, called the Hierarchical Deep CNN (HD-CNN), is proposed in [6], for which a set of CNN models based on a two-level category hierarchy are trained to achieve superior classification results over the standard CNN. In [19], a method is developed for regularization and model selection that simultaneously learns both the hierarchical architecture and model parameters. Indeed, hierarchical classification improves the accuracy of classification. However, it faces the problem of error propagation [1]; that is, the classification errors yielded from the upper-level classifiers will be propagated to the classifiers in the next level and therefore lead to more classification errors.

2.3   Present Work

There is a significant difference between the architecture of our proposed confusion-aware CNN and the conventional hierarchical classification as presented in Fig. 2. To be precise, our confusion-aware CNN does *not* follow the coarse-to-fine strategy of the existing hierarchical architecture [6,17,19]. It instead adopts a prediction-correction strategy to conduct a hierarchical classification, which is motivated by the predictor-corrector numerical approach that has been exploited to solve various mathematical and engineering problems (e.g., [23–25]). In other words, the fundamental difference between existing CNNs and our proposed lies in *coarse-to-fine* versus *predict-then-correct*.

3   Confusion-Aware Convolutional Neural Network

3.1   Outline

Components of our proposed confusion-aware CNN include one prediction classifier and a set of correction classifiers. A confusion-aware model is generated with the estimated confusion matrix of the prediction classifier, and the outputs of the prediction classifier and correction classifier are integrated by a probabilistic averaging layer, as demonstrated in Fig. 3 and described in detail as follows.

3.2   Prediction Classifier

The prediction classifier is a 'flat' classifier trained on the training set with all categories. At the classifying stage, it is employed to produce a prediction category of the input image. This prediction is usually not accurate enough

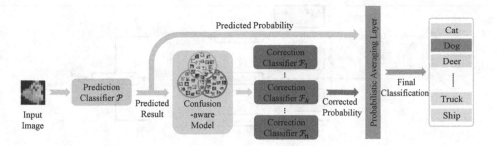

Fig. 3. A full picture of the proposed confusion-aware convolutional neural networks.

and hence need to be corrected. Let a_{ij} be the number of misclassified images between the ith and the jth categories; that is, the number of those images that belong to the ith category but have been misclassified into the jth category by using the predictor. Further define r_{ij} as the ratio of a_{ij} to the total number of misclassified images over every pair of categories; i.e.,

$$r_{ij} = \frac{a_{ij}}{\sum_{i \neq j} a_{ij}}, \qquad \text{for } i, j = 1, ..., K. \tag{1}$$

Based on the set of $\{r_{ij}\}$, those more confusing categories can be recognized from the others by simply applying a threshold to $\{r_{ij}\}$ which will be exploited as a prior to establish our confusion-aware model.

3.3 Confusion-Aware Model

Our confusion-aware model plays an important role in the proposed method. It serves as a decision maker both in the training stage (for training a set of correction classifiers) and in the classifying stage (for selecting a proper correction classifier). The confusion-aware model is constructed on the estimated confusion matrix of the prediction classifier, which is a specific table layout that represents the distribution of those easily confused categories. In detail, each column of the confusion matrix marks the instances in a predicted category while each row marks the instances in an actual category. The confusion matrix F is defined as:

$$F = (a_{ij}), \qquad \text{for } i, j = 1, ..., K. \tag{2}$$

A cross-validation process is used to estimate the confusion matrix of the prediction classifier. For that, we first divide the training set into N clusters and thus apply an N-fold cross-validation process to perform classification. In detail, $N - 1$ clusters of the training set are selected in turns to train the model, followed by testing the trained model on the remaining cluster to yield a misclassification result. Then, after every cluster has been selected for testing, all the misclassification results are integrated to produce the confusion matrix (as demonstrated in Fig. 4). Compared with the existing validation approach that

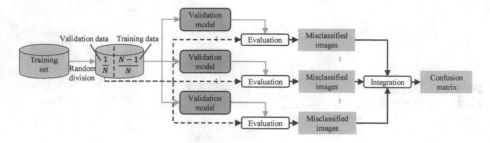

Fig. 4. A N-fold cross-validation step is adopted to estimate the confusion matrix of the prediction classifier.

only uses *one* randomly-sampled image cluster to generate the confusion matrix [6], our cross validation can maximize the use of the training set and obtain a more reliable confusion matrix. The prediction classifier could yield many confusing categories with ambiguous decision boundaries. As shown in Fig. 5, images in the overlapping areas of adjacent categories are easily misclassified. With the estimated confusion matrix, those easily-confusing categories can be recognized. To be specific, a proper threshold T which is less than 30% of the elements in the confusion matrix is used to select the top 30% ambiguous categories based on a ranking of a_{ij}, and then a set of correction classifiers can be trained to generate their clear decision boundaries.

3.4 Correction Classifiers

The confusion-aware model is established as a decision-making system to guide the training of correction classifiers. To be precise, for a predicted category (say, the kth), if $a_{ik} \geq T$ and $a_{jk} \geq T$ in the confusion matrix, a correction classifier $\mathcal{F}_k$ with the ith, jth, and the kth categories (a union of these three categories is denoted as $\mathbb{C}_k$) is trained. At the stage of classifying, if the prediction classifier $\mathcal{P}$ classifies the query image into the kth category, then the correction classifier $\mathcal{F}_k$ will again be selected by the confusion-aware model to conduct a correction classification. The final classification result is generated with a probabilistic averaging layer, where the results of the prediction classifier and the selected correction classifier will be integrated.

3.5 Probabilistic Averaging Layer

As mentioned in Sect. 2.2, error propagation could occur if the classification result is produced by using one classifier *only*. To overcome the difficulty, a probabilistic averaging layer is used to integrate the results of the prediction and the correction classifiers. For that, individual output of each classifier should be normalized with a softmax function, which is defined as

$$\sigma(z_j) = \frac{\exp(z_j)}{\sum_{i=1}^{K} \exp(z_i)}, \qquad \text{for } j = 1, ..., K, \tag{3}$$

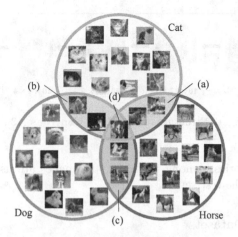

Fig. 5. An exemplary demonstration of the confusion yielded by the prediction classifier among three image classes—*Cat*, *Dog*, and *Horse*; upon which, our confusion-aware model is established. The images commonly shared by adjacent classes denote the confusion yielded between: (a) *Cat* and *Horse*; (b) *Cat* and *Dog*; (c) *Dog* and *Horse*; and (d) *Cat*, *Dog*, and *Horse*.

where z is a K-dimensional vector and its j-th element z_j is mapped onto the interval $(0, 1)$ as a probability $\sigma(z_j)$. Then, the probabilistic averaging layer is applied to average the two probabilities with different dimensions; that is,

$$p(y = j|X) = \begin{cases} \frac{1}{2}(B_j + p_c^k(y = j|X)), & j \in \mathbb{C}_k; \\ B_j, & j \notin \mathbb{C}_k, \end{cases} \quad (4)$$

where X is the input image and y is its category label. The probabilities predicted by the prediction classifier $\mathcal{P}$, and the correction classifier for category j are denoted as B_j and $p_c^k(y = j|X)$, respectively. Note that the $\mathcal{F}_k$ is trained on the union category $\mathbb{C}_k$. The category with the highest probability in p is the final classification of confusion-aware CNN.

4   Experiments

The proposed confusion-aware convolutional neural network is evaluated on the Mnist [12] and the CIFAR-10 [2] datasets. Experiments are implemented in PyTorch [13] and on a single NVIDIA Titan X card. The network is trained with back propagation [4]. The Mnist is a handwritten digital image dataset, with a size of 28×28 in each image. There are 10 categories, corresponding to numbers 0 to 9, respectively. In total, it contains 70,000 gray-scaled images of handwritten digits, of which 60,000 are used as the training data and the remaining 10,000 are the test data. The CIFAR-10 is a commonly-used computer vision dataset, containing a total of 60,000 images, with a size of 32×32 in each image.

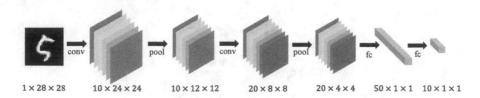

$1 \times 28 \times 28$ $10 \times 24 \times 24$ $10 \times 12 \times 12$ $20 \times 8 \times 8$ $20 \times 4 \times 4$ $50 \times 1 \times 1$ $10 \times 1 \times 1$

Fig. 6. Structure of the Mnist ConvNets [13].

It also has 10 categories. Among them, 50,000 images are used as the training set and the rest as the test set.

4.1   The Mnist Dataset

The Mnist ConvNets [13] is employed as the base model in our confusion-aware CNN framework; that is, it is exploited as the prediction classifier and also used to construct the correction classifiers. The Mnist ConvNets consists of two convolution layers and two fully-connected layers, as shown in Fig. 6. On the basis of the Mnist ConvNets, a confusion-aware CNN and a hierarchical CNN called HD-CNN [6] are trained. At the training stage of the confusion-aware CNN, the prediction classifier is iterated 500 epochs on the training set with learning rate 0.01 and momentum 0.9. The training set is divided into six sub-training sets and each set has 10,000 images. With these sub-training sets the six-fold cross-validation method is adopted to arrive at the confusion matrix. The correction classifiers are trained with confusing categories selected from the confusion matrix. The confusion-aware CNN is then tested on the test set, and the experimental results are shown in Table 1.

Table 1. Performance evaluation of different CNN models conducted on the Mnist dataset (without data augmentation).

Networks	Layers	Parameters	Accuracy
Mnist ConvNets [13]	4	22K	99.05%
ResNet-32 [3]	32	460K	99.18%
HD-CNN [6]	4	216K	99.21%
Confusion-Aware (Ours)	4	238K	99.31%

Experimental results as documented in Table 1 have shown that the accuracy of the Mnist ConvNets [13] is 99.05%. When one layer is replaced by our proposed confusion-aware CNN, the accuracy of the network is increased to 99.31%. The error rate of the confusion-aware CNN is about 25% lower than that of the single CNN. The number of parameters used in the confusion-aware CNN is 238,000, which are about 10 times more than that of Mnist ConvNets. Compared with

Fig. 7. Structure of the first two networks incorporated in our proposed method.

the ResNet-32 [3] (460,000 parameters) and the HD-CNN (216,000 parameters), the confusion-aware CNN is able to maintain high accuracy with a small amount of parameters, as documented in Table 1.

4.2 The CIFAR-10 Dataset

Three different CNNs are employed as the base model to further incorporate our developed confusion-aware model for evaluating the resulted performance. The depth and total parameters of these networks are increased gradually. The first network is structurally the same as that of LeNet-5 [12]. The only difference is that the size of the input image is changed from $28 \times 28 \times 1$ to $32 \times 32 \times 3$. The second network also has the same structure, however, the number of convolution kernels and the number of hidden nodes of the first network have been increased. The structure of the first two networks is shown in Fig. 7. Classifiers are trained with a learning rate of 0.1, which is decreased by a factor of 10 for every 100 epochs. These are iterated for 500 epochs over the training set with momentum 0.9 and weight decay 0.0005 [14]. The last one uses a residual network of 18 layers, called as the ResNet-18 [3], which includes 17 convolution layers and a fully-connected layer. Each classifier is iterated for 200 epochs. Initial learning rate is set to be 0.01 and is decreased by a factor of 10 for every 50 epochs. Randomly cropped and flipped strategies are used in the training.

Table 2. Performance comparison of three state-of-the-art CNNs (the second column) and the corresponding ones after incorporating our proposed confusion-aware model into these CNNs (the third column), respectively.

Networks	Conventional classifier	Confusion-aware CNN
LeNet-5 [12]	76.92%	80.99%
LeNet-5 (enhanced)	85.23%	86.97%
ResNet-18 [3]	94.63%	94.84%

As observed, and expected, from Table 2, the gain of accuracy decreases from 4.07% to 0.21% as the complexity of the base model increases. Therefore, it is considered that the simpler the base CNN is, the more gain of our confusion-aware CNN can achieve. For the exemplary experiment presented in Fig. 1, The ratio of the misclassified images between 'cats' and 'dogs' in our proposed confusion-aware CNN significantly drops, as shown in Fig. 8.

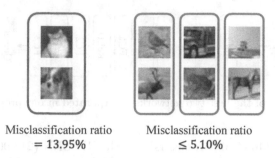

Misclassification ratio   Misclassification ratio
        = 13.95%   ≤ 5.10%

Fig. 8. The ratio of the misclassified images between 'cats' and 'dogs' shows a appreciable decrease with the use of confusion-aware CNN.

5   Conclusion

A novel CNN framework, called the confusion-aware CNN, is proposed in this paper and have clearly shown that it is able to improve the accuracy of image classification. By incorporating the confusion-aware model into a prediction-correction hierarchical structure, our proposed method is able to distinguish those image categories with ambiguous boundaries. Experiments conducted on the Mnist and CIFAR-10 datasets clearly show that the confusion-aware CNN can deliver the superior classification performance over the existing CNN models.

Acknowledgments. This work was supported by the National Natural Science Foundation of China (NSFC No. 61572341) and a Project Funded by the Priority Academic Program Development of Jiangsu Higher Education Institutions.

References

1. Silla, N., Freitas, A.: A survey of hierarchical classification across different application domains. Data Min. Knowl. Disc. **22**(1), 31–72 (2011)
2. Krizhevsky, A., Hinton, G.: Learning multiple layers of features from tiny images. Technical report (2011)
3. He, K., Zhang, X., Ren, S., Sun, J.: Deep residual learning for image recognition. In: IEEE Conference on Computer Vision and Pattern Recognition, pp. 770–778 (2016)
4. Krizhevsky, A., Sutskever, I., Hinton, G.: ImageNet classification with deep convolutional neural networks. In: Advances in Neural Information Processing Systems, pp. 1097–1105 (2012)
5. Zeiler, M.D., Fergus, R.: Stochastic pooling for regularization of deep convolutional neural networks. In: Proceedings of the International Conference on Learning Representation (2018)
6. Yan, Z., et al.: HD-CNN: hierarchical deep convolutional neural networks for large scale visual recognition. In: IEEE Conference on Computer Vision and Pattern Recognition, pp. 2740–2748 (2015)
7. Dai, D., Li, Y., He, K.M., Sun, J.: R-FCN: object detection via region-based fully convolutional networks. In: Advances in Neural Information Processing Systems, pp. 379–387 (2016)

8. Long, J., Shelhamer, E., Darrell, T.: Fully convolutional networks for semantic segmentation. In: IEEE Conference on Computer Vision and Pattern Recognition, pp. 3431–3440 (2015)
9. Goodfellow, I., Warde-Farley, D., Mirza, M., Courville, A., Bengio, Y.: Maxout networks. In: Proceedings of International Conference on Machine Learning, pp. 1319–1327 (2013)
10. Marszalek, M., Schmid, C.: Semantic hierarchies for visual object recognition. In: IEEE Conference on Computer Vision and Pattern Recognition, pp. 1–7 (2007)
11. Salakhutdinov, R., Torralba, A., Tenenbaum, J.: Learning to share visual appearance for multiclass object detection. In: IEEE Conference on Computer Vision and Pattern Recognition, pp. 1481–1488 (2011)
12. Lecun, Y., Bottou, L., Bengio, Y., Haffner, P.: Gradient-based learning applied to document recognition. Proc. IEEE **86**(11), 2278–2324 (1998)
13. Paszke, A., et al.: Automatic differentiation in PyTorch. In: Conference on Neural Information Processing Systems (2017)
14. Krogh, A., Hertz, J.: A simple weight decay can improve generalization. In: Proceedings of the Conference on Neural Information Processing Systems, pp. 950–957 (1991)
15. Chen, L., Papandreou, G., Kokkinos, I., Murphy, K., Yuille, A.L.: DeepLab: semantic image segmentation with deep convolutional nets, atrous convolution, and fully connected CRFs. IEEE Trans. Pattern Anal. Mach. Intell. **40**(4), 834–848 (2018)
16. Lin, T., Goyal, P., Girshick, R., He, K., Dollar, P.: Focal loss for dense object detection. IEEE Trans. Pattern Anal. Mach. Intell. **99**, 1 (2018)
17. Zoph, B., Vasudevan, V., Shlens, J., Le, Q.: Learning transferable architectures for scalable image recognition. In: IEEE Conference on Computer Vision and Pattern Recognition, pp. 8697–7710 (2018)
18. Srivastava, N., Salakhutdinov, R.: Discriminative transfer learning with tree-based priors. In: Advances in Neural Information Processing Systems, pp. 2094–2102 (2013)
19. Murdock, C., Li, Z., Zhou, H., Duerig, T.: Blockout: dynamic model selection for hierarchical deep networks. In: IEEE Conference on Computer Vision and Pattern Recognition, pp. 2583–2591 (2016)
20. Liu, B., Sadeghi, F., Tappen, M.F., Shamir, O., Liu, C.: Probabilistic label trees for efficient large scale image classification. In: IEEE Conference on Computer Vision and Pattern Recognition, pp. 843–850 (2013)
21. Lin, M., Chen, Q., Yan, S.: Network in network. In: International Conference on Learning Representations (2014)
22. Marszałek, M., Schmid, C.: Constructing category hierarchies for visual recognition. In: Forsyth, D., Torr, P., Zisserman, A. (eds.) ECCV 2008. LNCS, vol. 5305, pp. 479–491. Springer, Heidelberg (2008). https://doi.org/10.1007/978-3-540-88693-8_35
23. Butcher, J.C.: Numerical Methods for Ordinary Differential Equations. Wiley, Chichester (2016)
24. Chaudhuri, N.R., Chakraborty, D., Chaudhuri, B.: Damping control in power systems under constrained communication bandwidth: a predictor corrector strategy. IEEE Trans. Control Syst. Technol. **20**(1), 223–231 (2012)
25. Simonetto, A., DallAnese, E.: Prediction-correction algorithms for time- varying constrained optimization. IEEE Trans. Signal Process. **65**(20), 5481–5494 (2017)

Feature Learning and Data Compression of Biosignals Using Convolutional Autoencoders for Sleep Apnea Detection

Rim Haidar[(✉)], Irena Koprinska, and Bryn Jeffries

School of Computer Science, University of Sydney, Sydney, Australia
{rhai6781,irena.koprinska,bryn.jeffries}@sydney.edu.au

Abstract. Sleep apnea is a medical condition that can be diagnosed from events in respiratory biosignals, and many supervised machine learning techniques can readily be applied to automate this task. Opportunities to use unsupervised techniques to identify different variants (phenotypes) of sleep apnea from such data require feature reduction techniques that capture essential details, ideally without requiring expert knowledge that might be biased to expected outcomes. Convolutional neural networks have shown successful results in detecting apnea events using raw respiratory data. In this work, we propose the use of convolutional autoencoders to compress and learn features from biosignals for sleep apnea analysis. We test reducing the original signals into latent space representations of a range of sizes, that are then used in conjunction with convolutional neural network classifiers. We compare their performance to down-sampling and principle component analysis feature reduction methods. We demonstrate that apnea and hypopnea events can be accurately detected even when the signals are reduced to a latent space representation 2–3% of the original size. We show that with a simple classifier architecture and very short training time, the reduced features from the convolutional autoencoders can give high performance in detecting apnea events. Our results are useful for the design of low-cost and portable devices for sleep monitoring.

Keywords: Convolutional autoencoder · Dimensionality reduction · Sleep apnea detection · Biosignals · Polysomnography

1 Introduction

Sleep disorders affect the ability of a person to sleep well. One of the most common types of sleep disorders is *sleep apnea respiratory disorder*, affecting 2–4% of the adult population. It is characterised by *hypopnea* (partial reduction in breathing), and *obstructive apnea* (complete or almost complete cessation in breathing) events during sleep. If left untreated, sleep apnea could lead to serious problems such as heart attack, stroke, diabetes, and even early death.

Sleep apnea is detected by monitoring patients overnight, with multiple sensors attached to their bodies, to collect biological signals such as respiratory,

© Springer Nature Switzerland AG 2019
T. Gedeon et al. (Eds.): ICONIP 2019, LNCS 11953, pp. 162–174, 2019.
https://doi.org/10.1007/978-3-030-36708-4_14

EEG, ECG and EMG, collectively known as polysomnography (PSG) signals. The PSG recordings are then manually analysed by trained sleep experts to detect the obstructive apnea and hypopnea events. The severity of sleep apnea is determined by the number of these abnormal events during the night. Manual inspection of PSG recordings is labor intensive, slow, subjective and expensive.

Several machine learning approaches for automatic detection of sleep apnea events have been developed, e.g. based on neural networks (NNs)[13], support vector machines (SVMs) [10], and decision trees [7]. The most common approach involves feature extraction and selection, then building a classifier. Recently, deep learning techniques have been successfully applied for automatic feature learning from raw data in various domains, including for apnea detection [5,12].

We have previously demonstrated the efficacy of convolutional neural network (CNN) models to automatically classify the presence of apnea or hypopnea events within sleep PSG recordings [5], with an accuracy of 77.6% using just the nasal flow signal, and achieving 79.8% when the nasal signal was first processed to generate a wavelet spectrogram. We subsequently increased the performance of the raw-signal CNN approach to 83.5% by incorporating abdominal and thoracic movement signals that provide further information on respiratory effort [6].

Clinicians use the hourly rate of apnea and hypopnea events, known as the apnea-hypopnea index (AHI), to determine the severity of a subject's sleep apnea condition before considering appropriate treatment. As well as the severity of the condition, it is believed that several forms (phenotypes) of sleep apnea exist [3], and it would be desireable to identify which form is present based upon the PSG data. To that end, we are exploring unsupervised approaches that may provide insights into objective differences in breathing activity. A crucial first step towards this is to reduce the dimensionality of the respiratory signals while preserving the salient features. A powerful deep learning tool for this is the autoencoder [1], which learns an efficient latent space representation of the input data whilst being able to reconstruct the orignal signal with high fidelity. A variant of autoencoders, convolutional autoencoder (CAE), uses CNN elements to process complex high-dimensional data such as images [9].

In the work reported here we explore the use of autoencoders, built around the CNN architectures developed previously, to generate low-dimension representations of respiratory PSG data that could be used in a data-driven approach to phenotyping sleep apnea. The main contributions of this work are as follows.

1. We conduct a systematic investigation of CAEs as unsupervised feature reduction technique for PSG data, with architectures across a range of latent-space sizes, to identify the relationship between the latent space size and the ability to correctly classify respiratory events from the decompressed data.
2. We compare the classification performance of our CAE approach to approaches using principle component analysis (PCA) and simple down-sampling. Importantly, we found that using reduced feature sizes of only 2–3% of the original input, CAE was still able to achieve high classification accuracy (close to or above 80%), significantly outperforming the other approaches.

3. We identify upper limits to sampling frequencies required for accurate classification of sleep apnea events. Importantly, we found the effective frequency can be reduced to 1/4 or even 1/8 of the original sampling frequency with little reduction in classifier accuracy. This is a significant finding that is instructive for future portable device design.

2   Related Work

Detection of apneic events (i.e., events containing an instance of apnea or hypopnea), and the related task of predicting sleep apnea condition in a subject, is an appealing machine learning task. By convention PSG data is usually scored in contiguous subsequences (epochs) of 30 s or 1 min duration, and analysis typically involves using all the samples collected in an epoch.

Since apneic events involve an interruption to the airflow, a common target biosignal is the nasal flow. In [4] the single-channel airflow (10 Hz) signal was used to derive a respiratory rate variability signal, and statistical, spectral and nonlinear features from both signals were used in logistic regression (LR) models to classify individuals as having sleep apnea. In a cohort of 148 subjects, the best LR model achieved 82% accuracy against physician diagnoses.

Some work has also investigated alternatives to analysis of disjoint epochs. For instance, in [8], several statistical and frequency domain features were extracted from (200 Hz) oronasal airflow signal, then a SVM was used for feature selection and classification of apnea and hypopnea events, to derive the AHI for a sliding time window. A correlation of 0.982 with clinical expert AHI was obtained for a cohort of 56 subjects. This work is notable for making a distinction between apnea and hypopnea events, in line with the recommendations of the American Academy of Sleep Medicine, which is more challenging than simple classification of apnic events, and tends to yield lower overall accuracy.

Since nasal flow does not capture the effort being made to breathe, additional information may usefully be drawn from other signals including the thoracic and abdominal movements. In [10], statistical features from Haar wavelet decomposition of nasal, thoracic, and abdominal respiratory signals (10 Hz) were fed to a SVM model to classify 1-minute epochs as normal or apneic. An accuracy of 89% was reported for 7500 epochs from a cohort of 12 subjects.

Other studies have investigated alternatives to respiratory signals, especially electrocardiography (ECG). In [13], heart rate variability and the ECG-derived respiration features were fed to a feed-forward NN to classify 1 min epochs into apneic and non-apneic. The approach achieved a 10-fold cross-validation accuracy of 82% for 17,041 records from 35 subjects.

In recent years, the interest in using deep learning algorithms to automatically classify raw data of PSG signals has increased. Algorithms such as CNN, long short-term memory (LSTM) and recurrent neural network (RNN) have showed impressive classification results and ability to automatically learn informative features from raw data. In our previous work [5,6], we showed that CNN models were able to classify obstructive apnea and hypopnea events using raw data from nasal, abdominal, and thoracic signals with an accuracy of up to 83.5%. In [14], a CNN model was used to automatically detect obstructive sleep apnea events from ECG signals, achieving accuracy of 96%. In [15], an LSTM model trained on respiratory signals was used to classify epochs into different apnea events, and was able to outperform LR, non-deep feed-forward NN and random forest.

CAEs have achieved impressive results especially in computer vision tasks, demonstrating ability to learn informative features and to provide a compressed data representation in an unsupervised way [9]. In this paper, we explore their potential for feature learning and data compression of respiratory PSG biosignals for sleep apnea detection.

3   Proposed Approach

We propose the use of a CAE to reduce the dimensionality of the respiratory PSG signals. As illustrated in Fig. 1, the three main respiratory signals (flow, abdominal, thoracic) are used as input and output to the CAE, to learn a reduced representation of the signals for subsequent analysis.

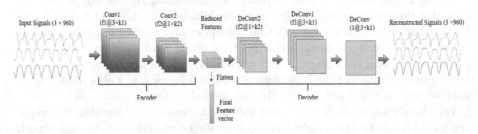

Fig. 1. Structure of the autoencoder. It includes 2 convolutions layers in the encoder and 3 deconvolutional in the decoder; f is the number of filters and k is the kernel size.

Autoencoders aim to learn a lower-dimensional representation of high dimensional data, in unsupervised manner, by reducing the reconstruction loss between the input and output, where the output is set to be the same as the input. They consist of an encoder and decoder. Given a dataset S, the encoder maps the input s_i to a reduced representation z_i, while the decoder reconstructs z_i to s_i' where s_i' has the same dimension as s_i. The reduction and reconstruction depend on several parameters such as the structure of the encoder and decoder, the activation functions used and the type of the loss function.

CNNs are state-of-the-art deep NNs, initially developed for image data. A CNN includes convolutional and max-pooling hidden layers, repeated several times, and a fully connected output layer. The combination of a convolutional and max-pooling layer allows to extract informative and shift-invariant features from the input, which is vital for respiratory data as the phasing of breathing within an epoch is uncontrolled.

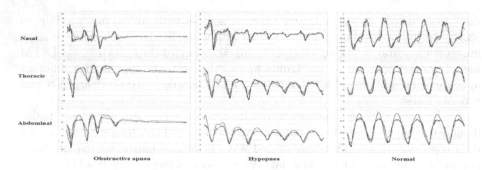

Fig. 2. Comparison of respiratory signals for 30 s epochs of different events, before and after feature reduction. Black - original 32 Hz signals; green - the same signals down-sampled by 1/32 to 1 Hz; red - the reconstructed signals from the CAE representation of 90 features. (Color figure online)

CAEs combine the properties of autoencoders and CNNs by using convolutional and/or max-pooling layers in the encoder, mirrored by de-convolutional and/or upsampling layers in the decoder [11].

In Fig. 2, the original nasal, thoracic and abdominal signals are plotted (in black) for three representative 30 s epochs exhibiting the different major forms of breathing activity. It can be seen that hypopnea and normal breathing exhibit a mostly repeated motif in each channel that might lend itself to compression. It also can be seen that thoracic and abdominal signals are often very similar, suggesting that much of the information captured by each signal is redundantly captured and so could also be readily compressed.

For these reasons, it is reasonable to expect that a deep learning technique such as CAE will be able to identify the breathing characteristics in each signal, learning a compact representation. An example of the reconstructed output from our approach, described in more detail below, is shown in Fig. 2 (in red), along with a down-sampled version of the same level of compression (green). It can be seen that the CAE approach manages to retain high-frequency features that are discarded in the down-sampled version. We explore whether CAE preserve the essential features of respiration biosignals below.

4   Experiments

Figure 3 presents an overview of our approach. To evaluate how well the relevant features of the signals are preserved in the latent space representation from a CAE, we built CNN classifiers for each reduced representation for a range of sizes. The classifiers identify the presence of normal, apnea and hypopnea events as in [6]. For comparison, we performed an assessment using the popular PCA feature reduction, as well as a simple down-sampling of the input signals.

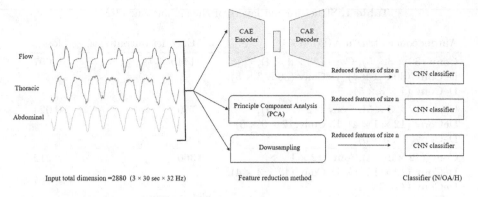

Fig. 3. Experimental process to compare the performance of CAE feature reduction to the PCA and down-sampling methods.

4.1 Data

As in our earlier work [6], we use the Multi-Ethnic Study of Atherosclerosis (MESA) dataset [2]. The data was collected between 2010 and 2011, through a sleep study of 2,056 participants. It includes a full night PSG recording for each participant. Each recording (32 Hz) is divided into sub-sequences (epochs) of 30 s which were manually classified by experts as instances of normal breathing, apnea or hypopnea. Consistent with our earlier work, we selected a balanced dataset of 69,264 epochs, composed of 23,088 epochs from each of the three classes. The data was normalized based on the mean and standard deviation of the normal samples for each subject.

4.2 Convolutional Autoencoder Structure and Parameters

We reduce the input features to 6 representations of different sizes: 1440, 720, 360, 180, 90, 45. For each targeted size, we want to select the best possible architecture - the one with the minimal reconstruction loss. As shown in Fig. 1, the input to the CAE is a 30-s epoch consisting of three PSG signals (nasal, abdominal, thoracic). The original sampling rate of the PSG signals is 32 Hz (i.e., 32 features per second). Therefore, the total number of input features is 2880 (3 signals $\times$ 32 Hz $\times$ 30 s).

The main CAE parameters that require optimization are: number of and type of layers; type of activation function, loss function and optimizer; number of filters and strides; kernel size and number of training epochs. For each targeted reduced representation, different parameter combinations were evaluated and the best one was selected based on the minimal reconstruction loss between the input and the output. To do this, the dataset was divided into two stratified subsets: 75% for training and 25% for hold-out testing. For every parameter combination, the CAE performance was evaluated using 10-fold cross validation on the 75% dataset; the CAE with the minimum reconstruction error over the 10 folds was selected, evaluated on the hold-out test set (Table 1) and used with the CNN.

Table 1. Structure and layers of the six autoencoders

Autoencoder Structure (layers)	Encoder output size	loss
Conv ($30 \times 3 \times 5$), Conv ($30 \times 1 \times 4$), DeConv ($30 \times 1 \times 4$), DeConv ($30 \times 3 \times 5$), DeConv ($1 \times 3 \times 5$)	1440	0.007
Conv ($12 \times 3 \times 5$), Conv ($12 \times 1 \times 4$), DeConv ($12 \times 1 \times 4$), DeConv($12 \times 3 \times 5$), DeConv($1 \times 3 \times 5$)	720	0.024
Conv ($12 \times 3 \times 4$),Conv ($12 \times 1 \times 8$), DeConv ($12 \times 1 \times 8$), DeConv ($12 \times 3 \times 4$), DeConv ($1 \times 3 \times 4$)	360	0.212
Conv ($9 \times 3 \times 16$), Conv ($9 \times 1 \times 3$), DeConv ($9 \times 1 \times 3$), DeConv ($9 \times 3 \times 16$), DeConv ($1 \times 3 \times 16$)	180	0.176
Conv ($15 \times 3 \times 32$), Conv ($15 \times 1 \times 5$), DeConv ($15 \times 1 \times 5$), DeConv ($15 \times 3 \times 32$), DeConv ($1 \times 3 \times 32$)	90	0.455
Conv ($15 \times 3 \times 32$), Conv ($15 \times 1 \times 10$), DeConv ($15 \times 1 \times 10$), DeConv ($15 \times 3 \times 32$), DeConv ($1 \times 3 \times 32$)	45	1.090

The most commonly used layers in CAEs are convolutional and max-pooling in the encoder, and de-convolutional and up-sampling in the decoder. Hence, for each targeted dimension, we searched different CAE architectures using these four types of layers. We set the maximum number of layers to 4, hence we searched for encoders and decoders with 2, 3 and 4 layers. We found that architectures including max-pooling and up-sampling layers tended to have a larger reconstruction loss compared to only using convolutional and de-convolutional layers. We also found that increasing the number of layers didn't improve the reconstruction loss, and therefore fixed the number of layers in the encoder to 2 convolutional and the number of layers in the decoder to 2 de-convolutional, with an extra de-convolutional layer in the decoder (with a filter size of 1) to produce the final reconstructed output. Then for each targeted reduced dimension, we tested different numbers of filters, kernel sizes and strides for each layer, and also different activation functions and optimisers.

The final selected CAE architecture for each targeted reduced dimension is shown in Table 1, with its reconstruction loss on the test set. For all architectures, the convolutional and de-convolutional layers use linear activation function. During training, the RMSprop optimizer was employed to minimize the mean squared error. The maximum number of training epochs was 50. The autoencoders were implemented using Python with Keras and Tensorflow.

4.3   PCA and Down-Sampling

In order to evaluate the relative effectiveness of the features extracted from CAE, we applied two other feature reduction techniques to the original PSG signals, PCA and down-sampling, selecting the same reduced dimensions as CAE (1440, 720, 360, 180, 90, 45). We used Matlab to implement and apply both methods.

Table 2. Structure of the selected CNN classifiers for the reduced datasets by CAE, PCA and Down-Sampling (DS)

Input size	Method	Classifier Structure
1440	CAE	Conv $(60 \times 1 \times 180)$, Conv $(60 \times 1 \times 8)$
	PCA	Conv $(60 \times 3 \times 40)$, Maxpool(1×2), Conv $(60 \times 1 \times 6)$
	DS	Conv $(60 \times 3 \times 60)$, Maxpool(1×2), Conv $(60 \times 1 \times 4)$
720	CAE	Conv $(60 \times 1 \times 45)$, Conv $(60 \times 1 \times 16)$
	PCA	Conv $(60 \times 3 \times 30)$, Maxpool(1×2), Conv $(60 \times 1 \times 4)$
	DS	Conv $(60 \times 3 \times 40)$, Maxpool(1×2), Conv $(60 \times 1 \times 3)$
360	CAE	Conv $(60 \times 1 \times 60)$, Conv $(60 \times 1 \times 6)$
	PCA	Conv $(60 \times 3 \times 24)$, Maxpool(1×2), Conv $(60 \times 1 \times 2)$
	DS	Conv $(60 \times 3 \times 60)$, Maxpool(1×2), Conv $(60 \times 1 \times 2)$
180	CAE	Conv $(60 \times 1 \times 18)$, Conv $(60 \times 1 \times 10)$
	PCA	Conv $(60 \times 3 \times 30)$, Maxpool(1×2), Conv $(60 \times 1 \times 10)$
	DS	Conv $(60 \times 3 \times 20)$, Maxpool(1×2), Conv $(60 \times 1 \times 5)$
90	CAE	Conv $(60 \times 1 \times 15)$, Conv $(60 \times 1 \times 12)$
	PCA	Conv $(60 \times 3 \times 25)$, Maxpool(1×2), Conv $(60 \times 1 \times 6)$
	DS	Conv $(60 \times 3 \times 5)$, Maxpool(1×2), Conv $(60 \times 1 \times 3)$
45	CAE	Conv $(60 \times 1 \times 15)$, Conv $(60 \times 1 \times 12)$
	PCA	Conv $(60 \times 3 \times 15)$, Conv $(60 \times 1 \times 2)$
	DS	Conv $(60 \times 3 \times 15)$, Conv $(60 \times 1 \times 2)$

PCA is a popular unsupervised dimensionality reduction method. It constructs a lower dimensional feature subspace that maximizes the captured data variance. The new axes (principal components) are linear combinations of the original features and are ordered based on the captured data variance. To achieve the desired size of n features, only the top n principle components are selected.

In down-sampling, n evenly-spaced samples are retained from the original signal. As the original sampling rate of the PSG signals was 32 Hz, down-sampling each signal to the desired sizes yielded effective sampling rates of 16 Hz, 8 Hz, 4 Hz, 2 Hz, 1 Hz, and 0.5 Hz.

4.4   CNN Classifiers

We have previously found CNNs to be effective in detecting apnea and hypopnea events, outperforming state-of-the-art methods such as SVMs[5]. Therefore, we used a CNN classifier to evaluate and compare the performance of the three feature reduction methods.

Since the produced feature sets are different, it is necessary to optimise the parameters of the CNN classifiers separately, to select the best CNN classifier for each feature set and dimensionality size.

We followed the same procedure as for CAE but using the reduced feature sets. For the same 75% training and 25% hold-out testing split as in CAE, we obtained the reduced feature sets and used 10-fold cross validation on the 75% set to evaluate different combinations of CNN architectures and parameters (different number of convolutional and maxpooling layers, kernel and stride sizes). The parameter combination with the best average accuracy over the 10 folds was considered as the best model, and selected for evaluation on the holdout 25% dataset.

The selected best CNNs are shown in Table 2. They have different structures and parameters but most often, for the same feature reduction method, have the same number of layers, while the kernel size and number of strides are different. In all classifiers, the convolutional layers have the same number of filters (60) and use ReLu activation function. The last CNN layer is a fully connected layer of 3 nodes, with softmax activation function. Each node outputs the probability for one of the three classes (normal, obstructive apnea, hypopnea).

The training was done using the Adam optimization algorithm, minimizing the categorical cross entropy loss function. The maximum number of training epochs was set to 50 and a dropout rate of 50% was used to reduce overfitting.

5   Results and Discussion

To evaluate the effectiveness of the feature reduction methods, we used the following evaluation measures: recall, precision, F1 score and accuracy. Table 3 shows the classification results for each feature reduction method, when used in conjunction with the selected CNN classifier, on the hold-out test dataset. It also shows the classification results on the original dataset with 2880 features (without feature reduction), for the best performing classifier on this dataset from our previous work [6] - a CNN with 9 layers.

Figure 4 illustrates how the accuracy is affected by the reduction of the feature set, for each of the three methods. Recall that the original feature size is 2880. At feature size 1440 (50% feature reduction), the down-sampling and CAE features achieved accuracy of 80–81%, only 2% lower than using the original, unreduced feature set, while the accuracy of the PCA features is 7% lower. As the feature size further decreases to 360 features (which is 12.5% of the original feature size), there is very little change in the accuracy of all methods, with CAE and down-sampling maintaining accuracy of about 80%. Further feature reduction decreases the accuracy of the down-sampling method to about 71%

Table 3. Classification performance on the hold-out test set (N - Normal, H - Hypopnea, O - Obstructive apnea; p - precision, r - Recall, f_1 - F1 score, Acc. - accuracy); best values for each latent feature size f shown in bold.

f	M	p^N	r^N	f_1^N	p^O	r^O	f_1^O	p^H	r^H	f_1^H	$\bar{p}$	$\bar{r}$	$\bar{f_1}$	Acc.
2880	none	80.1	83.8	81.9	92.5	92.8	92.7	76.5	72.7	74.6	83.1	83.1	83.1	83.1
	CAE	76.9	81.1	**78.9**	90.0	90.1	90.1	71.7	67.7	69.6	79.5	79.6	79.5	79.6
1440	PCA	72.3	**81.4**	76.6	83.4	81.7	82.6	62.7	56.0	59.2	72.8	73.1	72.8	73.1
	DS	**78.7**	79.1	**78.9**	**92.0**	**90.5**	**91.2**	**71.9**	**72.7**	**72.3**	**80.9**	**80.8**	**80.8**	**80.8**
	CAE	75.1	**83.8**	79.2	90.1	89.9	90.0	**72.8**	64.6	68.5	79.3	79.4	79.2	79.4
720	PCA	72.5	80.8	76.5	83.2	83.5	83.3	63.6	56.1	59.7	73.1	73.4	73.1	73.4
	DS	**79.4**	80.0	**79.7**	**90.2**	**90.5**	90.4	72.3	**71.5**	**71.9**	**80.7**	**80.7**	**80.6**	**80.6**
	CAE	**76.6**	83.4	79.9	89.0	**90.3**	**90.1**	**73.2**	66.4	69.6	79.9	**80.0**	**79.9**	**80.0**
360	PCA	71.7	81.9	76.5	80.9	80.9	82.6	64.3	52.2	57.6	72.9	72.9	72.9	72.9
	DS	75.7	**85.1**	**80.1**	**91.4**	87.9	89.6	72.9	**66.7**	**69.7**	**80.0**	79.9	79.8	79.9
	CAE	**76.9**	**83.1**	**79.9**	89.4	**91.5**	90.4	**74.1**	**66.5**	**70.1**	**80.2**	**80.3**	**80.1**	**80.3**
180	PCA	72.8	81.6	76.9	83.2	80.9	82.1	62.6	56.8	59.6	73.1	73.1	73.1	73.1
	DS	74.5	80.6	77.4	88.5	84.9	86.7	66.9	64.1	65.5	76.6	76.6	76.5	76.5
	CAE	**78.2**	81.9	**80.0**	**88.3**	**91.7**	**89.9**	**73.7**	67.2	**70.3**	**80.0**	**80.3**	**80.1**	**80.3**
90	PCA	73.9	79.1	76.4	81.5	84.7	83.1	62.8	56.0	59.2	73.3	73.3	73.3	73.3
	DS	73.5	78.1	75.8	87.5	85.7	86.5	64.8	62.1	63.4	75.2	75.3	75.2	75.3
	CAE	**75.5**	**85.1**	**80.0**	**88.2**	87.9	**88.1**	**72.3**	**63.3**	**67.5**	**78.8**	**78.8**	**78.5**	**78.8**
45	PCA	70.5	82.4	75.9	81.8	81.1	81.5	61.8	51.9	56.4	71.8	71.8	71.8	71.8
	DS	69.4	72.8	71.1	82.7	83.7	83.2	58.6	55.1	56.7	70.3	70.5	70.4	70.5

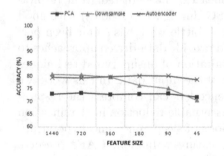

Fig. 4. Accuracy of the CNN classifiers on the reduced feature sets

Fig. 5. Training time of the CNN classifiers using the CAE features (1440, 720, 360, 180, 90, 45) and the original data (2880)

for 45 features (2% of the original feature size), while the accuracy of PCA and CAE is almost unaffected.

Overall, CAE is the most accurate method for all feature sizes, followed by down-sampling and PCA. CAE and PCA are almost not affected by the feature reduction. One of the best results is achieved by CAE with only 90 features (3% of the original feature set) - accuracy of 80.3% compared to 83.1% when using the original 2880 features. Another important observation is that the CNN structure for the reduced datasets is much simpler than the structure used for the original dataset - 2 hidden layers (convolutional) compared to 9. Hence, using this simpler CNN structure and only 2–3% of the original 2880 features, we were able to achieve high accuracy results, that were only 2–2.5% lower than the results of the original high-dimensional data.

The simplest method, down-sampling, produced highly accurate results for feature sizes from 1440 to 360 features (50%–12.5% of the original feature size), on-par with the more sophisticated CAE. These results suggest that the respiratory signals could be sampled at a frequency of 8 Hz instead of 32 Hz and still be able to capture the salient features. This is an important finding for the design of low-cost devices for sleep monitoring.

Figure 2 compares the original signal, the down-sampled signal to 1 Hz (90 features) and the reconstructed signal from the reduced CAE representation with 90 features. It shows that the reduced features are able to capture and retain the shape of the signals and the patterns important for the detection of all three types of respiratory events (obstractive apnea, hypopnea and normal).

Figure 5 shows the training time of the CNN classifiers for the CAE feature sets, for a single cross validation fold. As expected, the training time decreases as the feature size decreases. It takes 15 min to train (1 fold) the 9-layer CNN classifier for the original dataset with 2880 features and 1 min to train a 2-layer CNN classifier for dataset with 45 features.

6   Conclusion

The respiratory events relating to sleep apnea can be detected from respiratory biosignals (as commonly collected in PSG during sleep studies) with good accuracy using supervised learning techniques. Little work has so far been performed on unsupervised techniques that could provide data-driven approaches to identify phenotypes of sleep apnea. A key limitation of unsupervised techniques such as clustering is the high dimensionality of the input data. In this work, we have demonstrated that convolutional autoencoders can compress the respiratory data with high efficiency and with no discernable reduction in classification accuracy for the purposes of identifying periods of sleep apnea and hypopnea.

In contrast to down-sampling or PCA feature reduction, CAEs preserve salient details required for classifying sleep apnea even when the resulting feature vector is reduced to 2–3% of the original input size. Compression of the respiratory signals also has the extra benefit of reducing the complexity and training time of CNN classifiers. Using the compressed representation, it is also easier to incorporate on-board analysis of sleep apnea within portable devices.

Another important finding is that a simple 1/4 or even 1/8 down-sampling of the respiratory signals impacted very little the classification accuracy (a decrease from 80.81 to 79.92 and 76.59, respectively), suggesting that these signals could be sampled at a frequency of 8 Hz whilst still capturing salient features. This finding may have useful application in the design of low-cost or portable devices for monitoring sleep.

Having demonstrated that respiratory data can be very efficiently compressed without significant loss of classification accuracy, we plan in future work to explore clustering in these low-dimensionality representations, in order to determine whether distinct sleep apnea phenotypes can be identified.

Acknowledgement. This research was supported by the high performance computing services provided by the Sydney University Informatics Hub. MESA is supported by contracts N01-HC-95159 - N01-HC-95169 from the National Heart, Lung, and Blood Institute (NHLBI). MESA Sleep was supported by NHLBI R01 L098433.

References

1. Baldi, P.: Autoencoders, unsupervised learning, and deep architectures. In: Proceedings ICML Workshop on Unsupervised and Transfer Learning, pp. 37–49 (2012)
2. Dean, D.A., et al.: Scaling up scientific discovery in sleep medicine: the national sleep research resource. Sleep **39**(5), 1151–1164 (2016)
3. Eckert, D.J., White, D.P., Jordan, A.S., Malhotra, A., Wellman, A.: Defining phenotypic causes of obstructive sleep apnea identification of novel therapeutic targets. Am. J. Respir. Crit. Care Med. **188**(8), 996–1004 (2013)
4. Gutiérrez-Tobal, G.C., Hornero, R., Álvarez, D., Marcos, J.V., del Campo, F.: Linear and nonlinear analysis of airflow recordings to help in sleep apnoea-hypopnoea syndrome diagnosis. Physiol. Measur. **33**(7), 1261 (2012)
5. Haidar, R., Koprinska, I., Jeffries, B.: Sleep apnea event detection from nasal airflow using convolutional neural networks. In: Liu, D., Xie, S., Li, Y., Zhao, D., El-Alfy, E.-S.M. (eds.) ICONIP 2017. LNCS, vol. 10638, pp. 819–827. Springer, Cham (2017). https://doi.org/10.1007/978-3-319-70139-4_83
6. Haidar, R., McCloskey, S., Koprinska, I., Jeffries, B.: Convolutional neural networks on multiple respiratory channels to detect hypopnea and obstructive apnea events. In: Proceedings of International Joint Conference on Neural Networks (IJCNN), pp. 1–7. IEEE (2018)
7. Kaimakamis, E., Tsara, V., Bratsas, C., Sichletidis, L., Karvounis, C., Maglaveras, N.: Evaluation of a decision support system for obstructive sleep apnea with nonlinear analysis of respiratory signals. PloS one **11**(3), e0150163 (2016)
8. Koley, B.L., Dey, D.: Automatic detection of sleep apnea and hypopnea events from single channel measurement of respiration signal employing ensemble binary SVM classifiers. Measurement **46**(7), 2082–2092 (2013)
9. Luo, W., Li, J., Yang, J., Xu, W., Zhang, J.: Convolutional sparse autoencoders for image classification. IEEE Trans. Neural Networks Learn. Syst. **29**(7), 3289–3294 (2018)
10. Maali, Y., Al-Jumaily, A.: Automated detecting sleep apnea syndrome: A novel system based on genetic SVM. In: Proceedings of 11th International Conference on Hybrid Intelligent Systems (HIS), pp. 590–594. IEEE (2011)
11. Noh, H., Hong, S., Han, B.: Learning deconvolution network for semantic segmentation. In: Proceedings of the IEEE International Conference on Computer Vision (ICCV), pp. 1520–1528 (2015)
12. Novák, D., Mucha, K., Al-Ani, T.: Long short-term memory for apnea detection based on heart rate variability. In: 30th Annual International Conference of the IEEE Engineering in Medicine and Biology Society (EMBS), pp. 5234–5237. IEEE (2008)

13. da Silva Pinho, A.M., Pombo, N., Garcia, N.M.: Sleep apnea detection using a feed-forward neural network on ECG signal. In: Proceedings of 18th International Conference on e-Health Networking, Applications and Services (Healthcom), pp. 1–6. IEEE (2016)
14. Urtnasan, E., Park, J.U., Joo, E.Y., Lee, K.J.: Automated detection of obstructive sleep apnea events from a single-lead electrocardiogram using a convolutional neural network. J. Med. Syst. **42**, 1–8 (2018)
15. Van Steenkiste, T., Groenendaal, W., Deschrijver, D., Dhaene, T.: Automated sleep apnea detection in raw respiratory signals using long short-term memory neural networks. J. Biomed. Health Inform. **23**(6), 2354–2364 (2018)

Self-Adaptive Network Pruning

Jinting Chen[1], Zhaocheng Zhu[2], Cheng Li[1], and Yuming Zhao[1(✉)]

[1] Department of Automation, Shanghai Jiao Tong University, Shanghai, China
arola_zym@sjtu.edu.cn
[2] Mila - Québec AI Institute, Montreal, Canada

Abstract. Deep convolutional neural networks have been proved successful on a wide range of tasks, yet they are still hindered by their large computation cost in many industrial scenarios. In this paper, we propose to reduce such cost for CNNs through a self-adaptive network pruning method ($SANP$). Our method introduces a general Saliency-and-Pruning Module (SPM) for each convolutional layer, which learns to predict saliency scores and applies pruning for each channel. Given a total computation budget, $SANP$ adaptively determines the pruning strategy with respect to each layer and each sample, such that the average computation cost meets the budget. This design allows $SANP$ to be more efficient in computation, as well as more robust to datasets and backbones. Extensive experiments on 2 datasets and 3 backbones show that $SANP$ surpasses state-of-the-art methods in both classification accuracy and pruning rate.

Keywords: Convolutional Neural Networks · Channel pruning · Saliency prediction · Multi-task learning

1 Introduction

Recently, convolutional neural networks (CNNs) have become a dominant approach in a wide range of visual tasks. Typical applications of CNNs include image classification [14], object detection [5] and semantic segmentation [19]. Despite their success, it is still a challenge to deploy CNNs in industrial scenarios. This is mainly because CNNs are designed to be over-parameterized [3], and require much computation during inference. For example, ResNet-18, the smallest version of ResNet [7], requires 2 GFLOPs for a single prediction, which is unaffordable for most smartphones or embedded systems.

To reduce the computation demand of CNNs, many methods have been proposed from several perspectives. A bunch of methods [1,21,24] propose to build efficient architectures with depthwise separable convolutions. Some methods [2,22,26] learn models for low-precision inference. However, these methods require careful design of models or quantization functions, which can hardly generalize to other tasks without heavy engineering. Most recently, there are a number of methods [6,15,18] that try to prune the connections in networks.

© Springer Nature Switzerland AG 2019
T. Gedeon et al. (Eds.): ICONIP 2019, LNCS 11953, pp. 175–186, 2019.
https://doi.org/10.1007/978-3-030-36708-4_15

These methods drop parameters or channels according to some saliency scores, such as L_1-norm values of parameters or channels. As the scores are adaptively computed with regard to the model as well as the task, these methods can be easily applied to different scenarios. Therefore, we also follow this stream in this paper, and propose a novel self-adaptive pruning method.

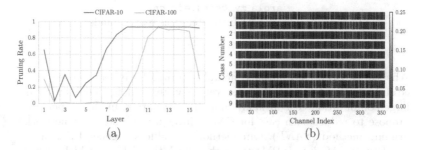

Fig. 1. Visualization of channel activations in a pruned VGGNet. (a) Pruning rate w.r.t. layers. The pruning rate varies from layer to layer on both datasets. (b) Average activation of each channel in the last convolutional layer w.r.t. categories in *CIFAR-100*. Only a small subset of channels is activated for each category.

Typically, a network pruning recipe at channel level consists of 2 ingredients, a saliency estimation module and a pruning module. Given a budget, the pruning algorithms [15,18] first learn saliency scores for each channel, and then prune channels that have low scores. However, we argue this formulation is not enough for a good pruning. Take VGGNet [23] pruned by Network Slimming (NS) [18] as an example, we observe two phenomena:

1. For different layers, the optimal pruning rates are very different.
2. For each category, it only activates a small subset of remaining channels.

Figure 1 illustrates these phenomena. The first phenomenon shows that there does not exist a constant pruning rate for every layer. In other words, layers would be either over-pruned or under-pruned by any global pruning rate. This is because most CNN architectures are designed for *ImageNet*, and the capacity of layers does not necessarily fit *CIFAR-10*, *CIFAR-100* and other datasets. Hence, a good pruning strategy should set different pruning rates for each layer. The second phenomenon indicates that a static pruning strategy is sub-optimal, since only a small set of channels is required for each category. To get better pruning performance, the pruning strategy needs to be conditioned on the input images. Ideally, we would like to have a pruning method that has both properties.

In this paper, we propose a self-adaptive method (*SANP*) for network pruning. Our method satisfies the above two properties through a layer-adaptive and sample-adaptive design. Specifically, the layer adaptiveness is achieved by a cost estimation step for each layer, with only budget constraints on the total computation cost. The sample adaptiveness is achieved by a saliency prediction step over the current input sample. Both steps utilize differentiable modules and thereby can be jointly trained with classification objective using a multi-task loss. Our method adaptively determines the computation routine for each layer and each sample, and improves the pruning rate over state-of-the-art methods, without sacrifice on performance. The contribution of this paper is three folds:

1. We propose a novel method *SANP* for network pruning, which adaptively learns the pruning rate for each layer and each sample.
2. We instantiate *SANP* with differentiable modules, and enable joint training with classification and cost objectives.
3. We empirically evaluate our method on 2 datasets and 3 backbones and it achieves state-of-the-art performance in all settings.

2 Related Works

2.1 Static Network Pruning

Static pruning methods generate a fixed network for all novel images. They can be divided into weight pruning methods and channel pruning methods. Weight pruning methods work on pruning fine-grained weights of the filters, resulting in unstructured sparsity. For example, Han et al. [6] iteratively prune near-zero weights to obtain a pruned network without loss of precision. Channel pruning methods reduce model size at channel level and can achieve a sparse structure. [15] iteratively prunes filters whose L_1-norm values are relatively small and retrains the remaining network. NS [18] introduces sparsity on the scaling parameters of Batch Normalization (BN) layers and proposes an iterative two-step algorithm to prune the network. AutoPruner [20] integrates channel pruning and model fine-tuning into a single end-to-end trainable framework. Filter Clustering and Pruning (FCP) [27] adds an extra cluster loss to the loss function, which forces the filters in each cluster to be similar and thereby prunes redundant channels. NS, AutoPruner and FCP could adaptively determine pruning rate for each layer, but their pruning strategies are invariant with regard to different samples.

2.2 Dynamic Path Network

Instead of using the entire feed forward graph of the network, dynamic path networks [4,9,16,17] selectively execute a subset of modules at inference time based on input samples. Runtime Neural Pruning [16] uses an agent to judge channel importance and prunes unimportant channels according to different samples with reinforcement learning. Liu et al. [17] propose a dynamic deep neural network to execute a subset of neurons and use deep Q-learning to train the controller modules. The above dynamic networks train their strategies through reinforcement learning because the binary decisions cannot be represented by differentiable functions. Therefore these methods are hard to generalize on multiple datasets and networks. Recently, several methods overcome this limitation. Channel Gating (CG) [9] splits channels in each layer into two groups and the proportion of the first group is uniform for all layers. Then it identifies ineffectual receptive fields based on the first group of channels and skips computation on the second group in these fields. It uses continuous functions to approximate the gradient of non-differentiable binary functions. Feature Boosting and Suppression (FBS) [4] sets a constant pruning rate for each layer and amplifies salient channels based on the current input sample. It utilizes a k-winners-take-all function which is partially differentiable. Though both CG and FBS are sample-adaptive methods, they lack layer-adaptiveness to regulate pruning rate for different layers.

3   Our Method

Figure 2 shows the main pipeline of *SANP*. Firstly, Saliency-and-Pruning Module is embedded in each convolutional layer of backbone network. It predicts saliency scores for channels based on input features and then generates pruning decision for each channel. The convolution operation would be skipped for these channels whose corresponding pruning decision is 0, as indicated by the dashed arrow. Then we jointly train the backbone network and SPMs with both classification objective and cost objective. We estimate computation cost dependent on the pruning decisions in each layer. The estimation adjusts importance of two objectives so that network could adaptively determine pruning rate per layer with a total computation budget. Since input features and output features are both sparse, the expensive convolution operation can be accelerated from both sides. Then we will go into details about the proposed method.

3.1   Saliency-and-Pruning Module

To prune channels layer-by-layer, some modules or separate networks are required. And the pruning strategy must be decided before each layer is activated. We propose a Saliency-and-Pruning Module, a lightweight network module for this purpose.

Since we observe that only a subset of channels is actually activated for different categories, we decide to determine channel pruning strategy dependent on each input image to get better performance. And in order to adaptively find the most important channels for each sample, we generate saliency scores for kernels based on the input features from previous layer $x^{l-1} \in \mathbb{R}^{C_{l-1} \times H_{l-1} \times W_{l-1}}$. Saliency prediction can be defined as

$$s^l(x^{l-1}) = SaliencyPrediction(x^{l-1}, W) \tag{1}$$

where $SaliencyPrediction(\cdot)$ denotes saliency function. In Sect. 3.2, we would introduce this function specifically.

Then the channels with low saliency scores could be pruned so as to accelerate backbone network. We need to adopt 0/1 binary valued function to decide

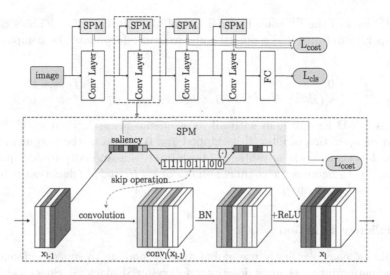

Fig. 2. The overall pipeline and layer pipeline of *SANP*. Colors of channels indicate their saliency scores, where white denotes zero saliency. First, the input features are down-sampled and passed into SPM to get saliency scores and pruning decisions for channels. Then channel pruning decisions are used to estimate current computation cost. The estimation automatically adjusts importance of classification loss and cost loss so that the network adaptively determines pruning rate for each layer with regard to the computation budget.

whether the calculation of each channel is skipped or not. However, binary functions are not differentiable and thereby these problems are usually approached with reinforcement learning. Unlike previous work, we utilize a discretization technique called Improved Semantic Hashing [11], which enables classification loss back-propagate to SPMs. Hence, the backbone network and SPMs could be jointly trained in an end-to-end manner. The pruning decisions could be formulated as:

$$b^l(x^{l-1}) = Binarize(s^{l-1}) \tag{2}$$

where $Binarize(\cdot)$ denotes binarization function. In Sect. 3.3, we would introduce this function specifically.

Further, channels with higher saliency scores are naturally the more significant channels, therefore we propose to rescale the output features with saliency scores to make these channels more decisive. Since modern deep neural networks [7,10,24] apply BN layers after convolutional layers, we leverage the rescaling operation directly after each BN layer. Here, we propose to define the calculation of a batch-normalized convolutional layer with SPM. The ith channel of output features $x^l \in \mathbb{R}^{C_l \times H_l \times W_l}$ is formulated as:

$$x_i^l = s_i^l(x^{l-1}) \cdot b_i^l(x^{l-1}) \cdot BatchNorm(f_i^l * x^{l-1}) \tag{3}$$

where f_i^l denotes the ith convolutional kernel of lth layer and $*$ denotes convolution operation. Since b^l is a binary code, we can reformulate the computation of x_i^l:

$$x_i^l = \begin{cases} \mathbf{0}, & if \quad b_i^l = 0 \\ s_i^l(x^{l-1}) \cdot b_i^l(x^{l-1}) \cdot BatchNorm(f_i^l * x^{l-1}), & if \quad b_i^l \neq 0 \end{cases} \quad (4)$$

Here $\mathbf{0}$ is a 2-D feature map with all its elements being 0. That is, if $b_i^l = 0$, convolution operation of filter f_i^l is skipped and $\mathbf{0}$ is used as the output instead. All convolutions can take advantage of both input-side and output-side sparsity. Additionally, C_l denotes the channel number of x^l, H_l and W_l denotes the height and width of feature map.

3.2 Saliency Function

To obtain saliency, we firstly use global average pooling to squeeze global spatial information into a channel descriptor following SEblock [8]. Specifically, the channel descriptor $d \in \mathbb{R}^{C_{l-1}}$ is calculated by the following formula:

$$d = \frac{1}{H_{l-1} \times W_{l-1}} \sum_{i=1}^{H_{l-1}} \sum_{j=1}^{W_{l-1}} x^{l-1}(i,j) \quad (5)$$

Then we consider using fully-connected layers to map channel-wise statics to predict saliency scores for kernels in l^{th} layer. In order to reduce computation, we use a reduction rate r like SEblock [18]. The saliency scores $s \in \mathbb{R}^{C_l}$ can be defined as:

$$s^l(x^{l-1}) = SaliencyPrediction(x^{l-1}, W) = W_2 \delta(W_1 d) \quad (6)$$

where δ refers to the ReLU function, $W_1 \in \mathbb{R}^{\frac{C_l}{r} \times C_{l-1}}$, $W_2 \in \mathbb{R}^{C_l \times \frac{C_l}{r}}$.

3.3 Binarization Function

We adopt a recently proposed discretization technique namely Improved Semantic Hashing [11] to generate channel pruning strategy from saliency scores $s^l(x^{l-1})$.

During training, a Gaussian noise $\xi \sim N(0,1)^{C_l}$ is add to $s^l(x^{l-1})$. As with all of the operations below, the sum operation is element-wise. Then we compute the vector through a saturating sigmoid function [12]:

$$s_1 = \max(0, \min(1, a \cdot \sigma(s^l(x^{l-1}) + \xi) - b)) \quad (7)$$

where σ denotes the original sigmoid function, a and b denote hyperparameters.

The binary code is then constructed via rounding:

$$s_2 = \mathbb{1}(s_1 > 0.5) \quad (8)$$

In the forward propagation, we use s_1 half of the time and s_2 the other half. s_2 is computed from non-differentiable function. Therefore in the backward propagation, we let gradients always flow to s_1, even if s_2 is used in the forward propagation.

During evaluation and inference, s_2 is used all the time. Note that the Gaussian noise is only used for training and we set ξ to $\mathbf{0}$ during evaluation and inference.

3.4   Multi-task Training

Until now, one question remains that how to control sparsity of the network, so that it reaches a computation budget. We observe that the optimal pruning rate varies with different layers and thereby the pruning method should adaptively learn pruning rate for each layer. To solve this problem, we propose a multi-task training with both classification objective and cost objective. We induce network sparsity with L_1-norm on saliency scores and estimate the current computation cost with pruning decisions generated by SPMs in each layer. The cost estimation adjusts importance of two objectives so that network could adaptively determine pruning rate for each layer with a total computation budget. The multi-task loss could be formulated as:

$$\mathcal{L}_{multi} = \mathcal{L}_{cls} + \lambda \frac{1}{N_c} \sum_{l=1}^{L} \|s^l\|_1 \tag{9}$$

where the first term is a classification loss (e.g., cross entropy loss), and the second term is the cost loss $\mathcal{L}_{cost}$. N_c denotes total filter number of backbone network, L denotes total layers of backbone network.

The value of λ is automatically adjusted according to the estimation of current computation cost:

$$\lambda = \lambda_0 \cdot \frac{(p_t - p)}{p_0} \tag{10}$$

where p_t is the estimation of current computation cost, calculated from binary code b^l of each layer. In practice, we collect several estimated values during training, and then calculate p_t based on these data. p is the given budget, p_0 is computation cost of the total network. λ_0 is a constant, and the range of λ is $[-\lambda_0, \lambda_0]$ according to Eq. 10.

If current computation cost is far from expectation, then λ is relatively large and thus the training could pay more attention to cost loss. In more detail, if $p_t > p$, then λ is positive and the network becomes more sparse so that p_t would decline. Otherwise, λ is negative and the network becomes less sparse so that p_t would increase. Once p_t is rather close to the budget, λ is relatively low, which means the network can focus on classification task. The actual obtained computation cost can be close to the budget, but not necessarily equal to it.

4   Experiments

4.1   Experiment Setup

Datasets and Evaluation Metrics. We evaluate our method on *CIFAR-10* and *CIFAR-100* [13]. Both datasets contain 60,000 32×32 colored images, with 50,000 images for training and 10,000 for testing. They are labeled for 10 and 100 classes in *CIFAR-10* and *CIFAR-100* respectively.

Classification performance is measured by top-1 accuracy and computation cost is evaluated by the floating-point operations (FLOPs). The FLOPs of lth convolutional layer in inference is calculated as $FLOPs = HW(C_{in}k^2 + 1)C_{out}$. H, W, C_{out} is the height, width and channel number of output features, k is the kernel size, C_{in} is channel number of input features and 1 refers to bias.

Implementation Details. We use M-CifarNet [25], VGGNet [23], ResNet-18 [7] as backbone networks in our experiments. The additional computation required for SPMs in inference is approximately 0.01% of the total network. We adopt PyTorch for implementation and utilize Momentum SGD as the optimizer. We use a batch size of 256 for *CIFAR-10* and *CIFAR-100*. We set the initial learning rate to 0.1 and decrease it by a factor of 10 every 100 epochs. λ_0 is set to 0.01 in our experiments. The backbone network is firstly trained to match state-of-the-art performance on those datasets. Then we replace all batch-normalized convolutional layer calculations with Eq. 4 and initialize the convolution kernels with the pre-trained weights. Afterwards, we warm up the SPMs using the classification loss, with fixed parameters of convolutional kernels. Finally, we jointly fine-tune backbone and SPMs with multi-task loss to meet the computation budget, as well as maximize the accuracy.

4.2   Experiment Results

We compare our method with several state-of-the-art network pruning methods on *CIFAR-10* and *CIFAR-100*: (1) FBS [4], (2) NS [18], (3) FCP [27], and (4) CG [9]. NS and FCP are layer-adaptive pruning methods while FBS and CG are sample-adaptive pruning methods. Tables 1 and 2 present results on *CIFAR-10* and *CIFAR-100* respectively. We observe that our method would perform better compared with these methods. With almost the same accuracy, our model uses less computational cost.

5   Ablation Study

In this section, we design several ablation studies to give a comprehensive understanding of the two adaptiveness in *SANP*. For convenience, all experiments in this section are conducted on *CIFAR-10* and ResNet-18.

Table 1. Comparison of different methods on *CIFAR-10*. The best results from pruning methods are emphasized. 'L-a' and 'S-a' denote layer adaptiveness and sample adaptiveness respectively.

Backbone	Model	L-a	S-a	Test error (%)	FLOPs (M/image)	Pruned rate (%)
M-CifarNet	Unpruned			8.63	174.3	
	FBS [4]		✓	9.41	44.3	74.6
	SANP	✓	✓	9.41	**39.3**	**77.5**
VGGNet	Unpruned			6.34	398.5	
	NS [18]	✓		6.20	195.5	51.0
	FCP [27]	✓		6.24	143.9	63.9
	SANP	✓	✓	**6.18**	**133.9**	**66.4**
ResNet-18	Unpruned			5.40	501	
	CG [9]		✓	**5.62**	172	65.6
	SANP	✓	✓	5.64	**163**	**67.5**

Table 2. Comparison of different methods on *CIFAR-100*. The best results from pruning methods are emphasized. 'L-a' and 'S-a' denote layer adaptiveness and sample adaptiveness respectively. Note that M-CifarNet does not have unpruned baseline on *CIFAR-100*, and is ignored in this table.

Backbone	Model	L-a	S-a	Test error (%)	FLOPs (M/image)	Pruned rate (%)
VGGNet	Unpruned			26.74	398.5	
	NS [18]	✓		26.52	250.5	37.1
	FCP [27]	✓		**26.45**	196.3	50.7
	SANP	✓	✓	26.47	**170.6**	**57.2**
ResNet-18	Unpruned			24.95	501	
	CG [9]		✓	25.24	200	59.9
	SANP	✓	✓	**25.20**	**189**	**62.3**

5.1 Are Layer-Adaptiveness and Sample-Adaptiveness Necessary?

In *SANP*, we propose to prune channels adaptively for each layer and each input sample. To see whether such a design is necessary, we compare our method with two variants.

1. FIXED K. This variant removes the binarization function of *SANP* and always selects fixed k percentage of channels with highest saliency scores for each layer. k is predefined and we choose k to match the expected computational cost. Therefore, the rate of activated channels is invariant across layers.
2. STATIC. This variant generates saliency scores from the same static vector and thereby the channel pruning strategy is invariant for all input samples.

Table 3 shows the results of *SANP* and its variants. It is observed that under similar computation budget, *SANP* achieves the best performance among all methods, indicating that both layer-adaptiveness and sample-adaptiveness are necessary for good pruning.

Table 3. Results of test error and computation cost by different designs. *SANP* with layer-adaptiveness and sample-adaptiveness gets the best performance.

Model	L-a	S-a	Test error (%)	FLOPs (M/image)	Pruned rate (%)
FIXED K		✓	5.62	331	33.9
STATIC	✓		5.48	337	32.8
SANP	✓	✓	**5.41**	333	33.5

5.2   What Is the Distribution of Pruned Channels?

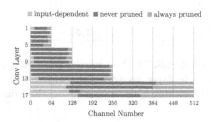

Fig. 3. Distribution of channel types across different layers. The ratio of pruned channels in 16th layer is much larger than those in other layers.

Fig. 4. Distribution of unpruned channels in the last block of ResNet-18 w.r.t. samples. It is noticed that the number of unpruned channels varies much among samples.

Though *SANP* outperforms its variants, it is still wondered that how the distribution of pruned channels look like. It is possible that the pruning rates are same for different layers and it is also possible that the pruned channels are same for all input samples. To answer the above questions, we investigate the pruning strategies generated by *SANP*. We conduct forward propagation of ResNet-18 in Table 3 and collect the channel pruning decisions generated by SPMs for all samples in *CIFAR-10* test set. Then we divide channels into three categories: channels that are never pruned, channels that are pruned dependent on input sample, channels that are always pruned.

Figure 3 shows the distribution of three types of channels. It could be clearly seen that the pruning rate varies across layers and many channels are pruned dependent on input samples, especially channels in deep layers. We also investigate how many channels are utilized with regard to input samples. Figure 4 illustrates the distribution, which indicates that the channel pruning varies much based on input samples.

6   Conclusion

We propose a novel method *SANP* for channel pruning. Our method adaptively adjusts pruning strategy for each layer according to the input samples, which enables better pruning rate and classification performance. With a differentiable design, our adaptive method can be jointly trained by classification and cost objectives, and thus maximize performance under the computational cost budget. Experiments on *CIFAR-10* and *CIFAR-100* show that our method achieves state-of-the-art performance over existing methods.

References

1. Chollet, F.: Xception: deep learning with depthwise separable convolutions. In: Proceedings of the IEEE Conference on Computer Vision and Pattern Recognition, pp. 1251–1258 (2017)
2. Courbariaux, M., Hubara, I., Soudry, D., El-Yaniv, R., Bengio, Y.: Binarized neural networks: training deep neural networks with weights and activations constrained to +1 or −1. arXiv preprint arXiv:1602.02830 (2016)
3. Du, S.S., Zhai, X., Poczos, B., Singh, A.: Gradient descent provably optimizes over-parameterized neural networks. In: International Conference on Learning Representations (2019)
4. Gao, X., Zhao, Y., Dudziak, L., Mullins, R., Xu, C.-z.: Dynamic channel pruning: feature boosting and suppression. In: International Conference on Learning Representations (2019)
5. Girshick, R., Donahue, J., Darrell, T., Malik, J.: Rich feature hierarchies for accurate object detection and semantic segmentation. In: Proceedings of the IEEE Conference on Computer Vision and Pattern Recognition, pp. 580–587 (2014)
6. Han, S., Mao, H., Dally, W.J.: Deep compression: compressing deep neural networks with pruning, trained quantization and huffman coding. In: International Conference on Learning Representations (2016)
7. He, K., Zhang, X., Ren, S., Sun, J.: Deep residual learning for image recognition. In: Proceedings of the IEEE Conference on Computer Vision and Pattern Recognition, pp. 770–778 (2016)
8. Hu, J., Shen, L., Sun, G.: Squeeze-and-excitation networks. In: Proceedings of the IEEE Conference on Computer Vision and Pattern Recognition, pp. 7132–7141 (2018)
9. Hua, W., De Sa, C., Zhang, Z., Suh, G.E.: Channel gating neural networks. In: Proceedings of the 55th Annual Design Automation Conference (2018)
10. Huang, G., Liu, Z., Van Der Maaten, L., Weinberger, K.Q.: Densely connected convolutional networks. In: Proceedings of the IEEE Conference on Computer Vision and Pattern Recognition, pp. 4700–4708 (2017)
11. Kaiser, Ł., Bengio, S.: Discrete autoencoders for sequence models. arXiv preprint arXiv:1801.09797 (2018)
12. Kaiser, Ł., Sutskever, I.: Neural gpus learn algorithms. arXiv preprint arXiv:1511.08228 (2015)
13. Krizhevsky, A., Hinton, G.: Learning multiple layers of features from tiny images. Technical report, Citeseer (2009)
14. Krizhevsky, A., Sutskever, I., Hinton, G.E.: Imagenet classification with deep convolutional neural networks. In: Advances in Neural Information Processing Systems, pp. 1097–1105 (2012)
15. Li, H., Kadav, A., Durdanovic, I., Samet, H., Graf, H.P.: Pruning filters for efficient convnets. In: International Conference on Learning Representations (2017)

16. Lin, J., Rao, Y., Lu, J., Zhou, J.: Runtime neural pruning. In: Advances in Neural Information Processing Systems, pp. 2181–2191 (2017)
17. Liu, L., Deng, J.: Dynamic deep neural networks: optimizing accuracy-efficiency trade-offs by selective execution. In: Thirty-Second AAAI Conference on Artificial Intelligence (2018)
18. Liu, Z., Li, J., Shen, Z., Huang, G., Yan, S., Zhang, C.: Learning efficient convolutional networks through network slimming. In: Proceedings of the IEEE International Conference on Computer Vision, pp. 2736–2744 (2017)
19. Long, J., Shelhamer, E., Darrell, T.: Fully convolutional networks for semantic segmentation. In: Proceedings of the IEEE Conference on Computer Vision and Pattern Recognition, pp. 3431–3440 (2015)
20. Luo, J.H., Wu, J.: Autopruner: An end-to-end trainable filter pruning method for efficient deep model inference. arXiv preprint arXiv:1805.08941 (2018)
21. Ma, N., Zhang, X., Zheng, H.T., Sun, J.: Shufflenet v2: practical guidelines for efficient CNN architecture design. In: Proceedings of the European Conference on Computer Vision (ECCV), pp. 116–131 (2018)
22. Micikevicius, P., et al.: Mixed precision training. In: International Conference on Learning Representations (2018)
23. Simonyan, K., Zisserman, A.: Very deep convolutional networks for large-scale image recognition. arXiv preprint arXiv:1409.1556 (2014)
24. Zhang, X., Zhou, X., Lin, M., Sun, J.: Shufflenet: an extremely efficient convolutional neural network for mobile devices. In: Proceedings of the IEEE Conference on Computer Vision and Pattern Recognition, pp. 6848–6856 (2018)
25. Zhao, Y., Gao, X., Mullins, R., Xu, C.: Mayo: a framework for auto-generating hardware friendly deep neural networks. In: Proceedings of the 2nd International Workshop on Embedded and Mobile Deep Learning, pp. 25–30. ACM (2018)
26. Zhou, S., Wu, Y., Ni, Z., Zhou, X., Wen, H., Zou, Y.: Dorefa-net: training low bitwidth convolutional neural networks with low bitwidth gradients. arXiv preprint arXiv:1606.06160 (2016)
27. Zhou, Z., Zhou, W., Li, H., Hong, R.: Online filter clustering and pruning for efficient convnets. In: 2018 25th IEEE International Conference on Image Processing (ICIP), pp. 11–15. IEEE (2018)

Text-Augmented Knowledge Representation Learning Based on Convolutional Network

Chunfeng Liu[1,3,4], Yan Zhang[1,3,4], Mei Yu[1,3,4], Ruiguo Yu[1,3,4], Xuewei Li[1,3,4], Mankun Zhao[1,3,4], Tianyi Xu[1,3,4], Hongwei Liu[2], and Jian Yu[1,3,4]([✉])

[1] College of Intelligence and Computing, Tianjin University, Tianjin, China
{cfliu,yanz,yumei,rgyu,lixuewei,zmk,tianyi.xu,yujian}@tju.edu.cn
[2] Foreign Language, Literature, and Culture Studies Center, Tianjin Foreign Studies University, Tianjin, China
liuhongwei@tjfsu.edu.cn
[3] Tianjin Key Laboratory of Advanced Networking (TANK Lab), Tianjin, China
[4] Tianjin Key Laboratory of Cognitive Computing and Application, Tianjin, China

Abstract. Knowledge graphs describe concepts, entities in the objective world and relations in a structured form, thus providing a better way to manage and understand the infinite information on the Internet. Although there are various knowledge embedding models, most of them only focus on factual triples. In fact, there are usually concise descriptions for entities, which cannot be well employed by these existing models. For instance, a knowledge embedding model based on convolutional networks (ConvKB [9]), has shown remarkable results in the knowledge link prediction, which have not fully utilized the complementary texts of entities. Therefore, we propose a text-augmented embedding model based on ConvKB, which firstly uses bidirectional short and long term memory network with attention (A-BiLSTM) to encode the descriptions of the entities, then combines the structure of the symbol triples embeddings and text embeddings with novel gate mechanism (in the form of the LSTM gates). In this way, structural representations and textual representations can all be learned. The experiments have shown that our method is superior to the previous ConvKB in tasks like link prediction.

Keywords: Knowledge representation · Text-augmented · Convolutional networks · Entity descriptions

1 Introduction

Knowledge graphs (KGs) have brought vitality to Internet information retrieval, and also show great power in intelligent question answering. It has become the infrastructure of intelligent application driven by Internet knowledge. Some well-known KGs are DBpedia, Freebase, YAGO and the Google Knowledge Graph. KGs containing relationship triples (subject, relation, object), denoted as (h,r,t),

© Springer Nature Switzerland AG 2019
T. Gedeon et al. (Eds.): ICONIP 2019, LNCS 11953, pp. 187–198, 2019.
https://doi.org/10.1007/978-3-030-36708-4_16

are the useful resources for many information retrieval applications. However, these large knowledge graphs, even containing billions of triples, are still incomplete, (i.e., missing a lot of valid triples). Therefore, much research efforts have focused on the knowledge graph completion or link prediction task which aims to predict missing triples in KGs.

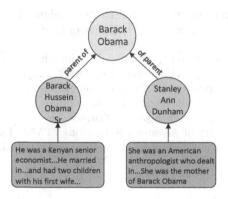

Fig. 1. Example of entities descriptions in Freebase.

Rescal [11] model uses matrix decomposition for knowledge representation learning. Later DistMult [18] model sets relation matrix as diagonal matrix, which uses "circular correlation" of the head and tail entity vectors to represent the entity pair. Bordes has put forward the TransE [4] model, which is inspired by the the interesting translation invariance between lexical semantics and syntactic relations in the word vector space. In order to solve the limitations of the TransE model in dealing with complex relations, the TransH [14] model is proposed to allow an entity to have different forms under different relations. The TransD [16] constructs a dynamic mapping matrix for each entity-relation pair by considering the diversity of entities and relations simultaneously. In addition, ConvE [6] is the first model applying convolutional neural network for the knowledge graph completion task. ConvKB [9] applies a convolutional neural network to calculate the fraction of the input triples.

There is a large amount of text descriptions in the knowledge base as is shown in Fig. 1. Although the traditional KGs embedding models have been successful, they still need text descriptions. The semantic expression between entities can identify true triples. For example, we want get the triple (Barack Hussein Obama Sr, parent of, Barack Obama), which indicates "Barack Hussein Obama Sr" is the parent of "Barack Obama". However, the relation "parent of" may refer to two different meanings of "father" and "mother". So it is quite difficult to get true facts only from symbolic triples. In contrast, in the text description of the true entity, the keywords are "he" and "his wife", and the false entity text description has "she" and "mother". So it is easy to infer the true triple facts. If we can effectively use the description information, we can improve task performance such as link prediction.

However, the latest ConvKB model based on convolutional neural network only learn factual triples from knowledge graph but failed to fully utilize the rich semantic information about entities descriptions in the knowledge base as shown in the Fig. 1. To address this problem, we propose a text augmented method based on ConvKB (TA-ConvKB), which can effectively combine the structural information of the factual triples and the descriptions of the enti- ties, thus enhancing the accuracy of knowledge graphs link prediction. We at first extract a multiple of keywords after pretraining the entities descriptions and use fastText [3] to encode those words into vectors. Then, we input word embeddings into the A-BiLSTM encoder [20] to extract distinctive features and finally acquire a text vector that best expresses the entity information. The next key issue is how to better integrate structural embeddings obtained by training StransE model [10] and textual embeddings, we use the gate mechanism originat- ing from LSTM gate units, so that our model can learn structural representations and text representations at the same time.

Our contributions in this paper are as follows:

- We introduce the TA-ConvKB model to deal with that ConvKB only focus on the structural information of triples. We use A-BiLSTM to encode entities descriptions, which enriches entities textual representations.
- We put forward a brand-new gate mechanism originating from LSTM gate units to learn and build the interaction between knowledge embeddings and text embeddings by point multiplication.
- Using text-augmented method in ConvKB when analyzing FB15k-237 and WN18RR data bases in link prediction, and the results are better than Con- vKB Model. Moreover, the same pre-trained method and gate mechanism applies to other knowledge embedding models such as TransH [14], the exper- imental results are also significantly improved.

2   Related Work

The most widely used embedding model is TransE [4], which views relations as transformations from the heads to tails on the same low-dimensional plane. The scoring function of TransE is defined as

$$E(h, r, t) = \|h + r - t\|_{L_n} \tag{1}$$

It measures the L_n distance between the converted head entity $h + r$ and a certain tail entity t.

Its extensions like TransH [14], TransD [16]. STransE [10] is a simple com- bination of the SE and TransE model, which uses two projection matrices and one translation vector to represent each relation. [7] exploit information about relation paths into KG.

ConvKB [9] uses a convolution neural network to improve the latest model so that it captures the overall relations and transformation characteristics of entities and relations in the knowledge base. In ConvKB, each triple (head, relation, tail) is represented as a three-column matrix, where each column vector represents a triple.

In order to enhance the representation learning of KG, utilizing text information in knowledge base is now considered. There are several methods using entity textual information to help KG representation learning. [1] attempts to align the knowledge graph with corpus and then jointly operates knowledge embeddings and word embeddings. However, the necessity of aligning information limits the method in terms of performance and practical applicability.

Therefore, [19] proposes a "joint" approach that aligns only the freebase entity with the corresponding wiki page. DKRL [15] extends the translation-based embedding method from a specific triple method to a "text-augmented" model. More importantly, DKRL uses the convolutional neural network structure to represent words, which enhances the expressiveness of words. However, these models divide the objective function into two kinds of energy functions: structure-based representation and description-based representation. In order to learn these two representations, they need to further estimate the optimal weight coefficients in a specific task.

In addition, [17] proposes a novel deep architecture to utilize both structural and textual information of entities, which combines the triples-embeddings and text-embeddings first using a weighted sum and then calculates the L_n distance between the translated head entity and tail entity. In general, text-augmented embedding models achieve state-of-the-art performance through integrating knowledge and text.

3   Text-Augmented Knowledge Graph Representation

We define a knowledge graph as $G = (E, R, T)$, where E is the set of entities, R is the set of relation types, and T is the set of factual triples. For each knowledge triple $(h, r, t) \in T$, it indicates a relation $r \in R$ between $h \in E$ and $t \in E$. In order to utilize the knowledge triples' structural information and the entities descriptions at the same time, we give two kinds of entity representation types: structure representation e_s and text representation e_d. For a given knowledge triple $(h, r, t) \in T$, $h_s \in e_s$ and $t_s \in e_s$ represent head and tail structure representation respectively, which are typically derived from existing translation-based models (such as TransE [4]). $h_d \in e_d$ and $t_d \in e_d$ represent the representation derived from the description text coding of the head and tail respectively. For entities, relations, and descriptions, we use R^d representing their corresponding low-dimensional vectors. For example, embedding $h, t \in E$ and $r \in R$ are equal to $h, t, r \in R^d$ respectively in the d−dimension (Fig. 2).

3.1   Neural Network Text Encoding

In pre-process, we first remove all stop words from the original text, then mark all the phrases in the descriptions (we simply select all the entity names in the training set as phrases) and treat those phrases as words. Then, we extract

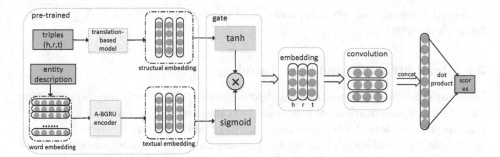

Fig. 2. Framework of TA-ConvKB model. $\otimes$ is point multiplication. tanh and sigmoid are activation functions. Each column in structural embedding or text embedding represents head entity, relation, and tail entity.

multi-themed words for each entity as description. In order to accurately express textual information, in our experiments, we use fastText [3] to encode the subject words into word vectors as input to the A-BiLSTM encoder. We define each entity as a series of words $X = x_i \ldots x_n$, where $x_i \in R^d$ is the word embedding of each word at position i.

BiLSTM Encoder. The basic idea of bidirectional [8] is to apply a forward and backward LSTM network to each training sequence, and the two are connected to the same output layer. Such a network structure can provide the complete contextual information of each sequence point to the output layer.

Forward LSTM network receives a first time input x_1 sequentially to x_t and calculates the forward hidden state $\overrightarrow{h_1}, \overrightarrow{h_2}, \cdots, \overrightarrow{h_t}$ in turn, while backward LSTM network receiving a last time input x_t sequentially to x_1 and calculating the backward hidden state $\overleftarrow{h_1}, \overleftarrow{h_2}, \cdots, \overleftarrow{h_t}$ in turn. So that we reach the bidirectional feature at each time, and combine the features in the two directions to obtain a bidirectional expression: $h_i = \overrightarrow{h_i} \oplus \overleftarrow{h_i}$, where $\oplus$ is the joint symbol.

Self Attentive BiLSTM Encoder. Self-attention is exceptionally useful in sequence learning tasks [20]. We lead an attention mechanism into BiLSTM to encode depending on the different relations of the context in order to improve the text representations. For each position i of the text description, the attention to a given word embedding h_i is defined as a_i.

$$a_i = \frac{exp(v_a^T tanh(W_a h_i + b_a))}{\sum_{j=1} exp(v_a^T tanh(W_a h_j + b_a))} \tag{2}$$

where $h_i \in R^d$ is the output of BiLSTM at position i, $v_a \in R^{d \times d}$ is a parameter vector, $W_a, b_a \in R^d$ are parameter matrixs.

The attention a_i is interpreted as the concern degree of the neural network. The contextual text encoding of the entity description can be formed by a weighted sum of the attention codes, and the final output is $e_i = \sum_{i=1}^{n} a_i \cdot h_i$ for each description.

3.2   Joint Structure and Text Encoding

Because structural information and textual descriptions both are valuable for an entity's representation, it is necessary to integrate all of information into a joint representation. To balance two sources of information, we need to define the whole representation of an entity. For an entity e, the main concern is how to combine e_s and e_d.

[2] and [17] combine the structural embeddings and textual embeddings as follows:

$$e = \alpha \cdot e_s + (1 - \alpha) \cdot (e_d) \tag{3}$$

where $0 < \alpha < 1$ and α is uncertain. It only learns first-order linear combination features from descriptions and triples.

To make semantics of descriptions more senses, textual descriptions must interact with triples for better embedding. For the above example of "parent", the textual descriptions imply two candidate answers "mother" and "father". Thus, by considering both triples and texts, we can obtain the true answer. To learn the second-order interaction between textual descriptions and triples, referring to the gated mechanism in LSTM gate units, which also help it to control the flow of information, we can extract important features from textual embeddings and structure embeddings as follows:

$$e = tanh(e_s) \otimes sigmoid(e_d) \tag{4}$$

where $sigmoid$ and $tanh$ are activation functions. $\otimes$ is point multiplication.

In this way, we get the final entity representation e. Because the relations have not descriptions, we use the structural embeddings as the textual embeddings for relation. A triple embedding consisting of entity representation and relation representation which can be fed to convolutional networks to extract features for link prediction.

3.3   Training and Socre Function

Let κ and τ denote the set of filters and the number of filters, respectively, i.e. $\tau = |\kappa|$, resulting in τ feature maps. These τ feature maps are concatenated into a single vector $\in R^{\tau d \times 1}$ which is then computed with a weight vector $w \in R^{\tau d \times 1}$ via a dot product to give a score for the triple (h, r, t). The score function of TA-ConvKB is as follows:

$$f(h, r, t) = concat(g(tanh([h_s, r, t_s]) \otimes \sigma([h_d, r, t_d])) * \kappa) \cdot w \tag{5}$$

where g, $tanh$ and σ are respectively $Relu$, $Tanh$, $Sigmoid$ activation functions; $\otimes$ is point multiplication between matrixs; κ is the number of filters and w

is shared parameters; $*$ denotes a convolution operator; and *concat* denotes a concatenation operator.

We use the Adam optimizer to train TA-ConvKB by minimizing the loss function L with L_2 regularization on the weight vector w of the model:

$$L = \Sigma_{(h,r,t)} log(1 + exp((l_{(h,r,t)}) \cdot f(h, r, t))) + \frac{\lambda}{2} \|w\|_2^2 \qquad (6)$$

where $(h, r, t) \in G \cup G'$, $l_{(h,r,t)} = 1$ when $(h, r, t) \in G$, $l_{(h,r,t)} = -1$ when $(h, r, t) \in G'$, here G' is a collection of invalid triples generated by corrupting valid triples in G.

4   Experiments

4.1   Data Set

We evaluate TA-ConvKB on two reference data sets: WN18RR [6] and FB15k-237 [12]. WN18RR and FB15k-237 are correspondingly a subset of two common data sets WN18 and FB15k. WN18 and FB15k [4] are very easy, because they contain a number of reversible relations. So, knowing the reversibility of relationships allows us to easily predict most test triples. For example, the latest results for WN18 and FB15k are through the use of a simple inversion rule. Therefore, it is necessary to create WN18RR and FB15k-237 in order not to suffer from the problem of reversible relations in WN18 and FB15k. It is more suitable to complete the task of entity link in WN18RR and FB15k-237. Table 1 gives the statistics of WN18RR and FB15K-237.

There are 14515 entities in FB15K-237 with descriptions. To ensure the integrity of the training set and test set data, the text vectors of the remaining 36 entities are randomly generated without using fastText [3]. In the WN18RR data set, each entity has a description text.

4.2   Assessment Strategy

In the KG link prediction task, the purpose is to predict a missing entity given a relation and another entity, (i.e., inferring h given (r, t) or inferring t given (h, r)). The results are calculated based on ranking the scores produced by the score function on test triples. For each valid test triple (h, r, t), we replace either h or t by each of other entities in E to create a set of corrupted triples. We use the "Filtered" setting protocol, not taking any corrupted triples that appear in the KG into accounts.

We rank the valid test triples and corrupted triples in ascending order of their scores. We employ three common evaluation metrics: mean rank (MR), mean reciprocal rank (MRR), and H@10 (i.e., the proportion of the valid test triples ranking in top 10 predictions). Lower MR, higher MRR or higher H@10 indicate better performance.

Table 1. Statistics of the experimental dataset

Dataset	$|\varepsilon|$	$|R|$	#Triples in train/valid/test		
WN18RR	40,943	11	86,835	3,034	3,134
FB15k-237	14,541	237	272,115	17,535	20,466

4.3   Training Strategy

When processing the entities descriptions in FB15k-237, 10 keywords are extracted for each entity description, and fastText [3] is used to encode a 100-dimensional word vector. In the A-BiLSTM encoder, we set the embedding dimension to 100, the sequence length to 10, and the number of hidden layer units to 50. The encoder will output a 100-dimensional text vector. Similarly, in the WN18RR data set, because the words in each entity description are fewer, we extract 3 keywords for each entity description and encode them into 100-dimensional word vectors with fastText [3]. We will also get a 100-dimensional vector through A-BiLSTM encoder for each entity.

We train STransE [10] for 3,000 epochs to get structural embeddings. We run TA-ConvKB up to 200 epochs and use outputs from the last epoch for evaluation and use Adam as optimizer. We use ReLU as the activation function. We fix the batch size at 256 and set the $L2$-regularizer λ at 0.005 in our objective function. The highest H@10 scores on the validation set are obtained when using $k = 100$, $\tau = 200$, the truncated normal distribution for filter ω initialization, and the initial learning rate at 1^{1e-4} on WN18RR, and $k = 100$, $\tau = 40$, $[0.1, 0.1, -0.1]$ for filter ω initialization, and the initial learning rate at 5^{e-6} on FB15k-237.

4.4   Main Experimental Results

Table 2. Experimental results on link prediction

Method	WN18RR			FB15k-237		
	MR	MRR	H@10	MR	MRR	H@10
Complex [13]	5261	0.440	51.0	644	0.247	42.8
ConvE [6]	5277	**0.460**	48.0	246	0.316	49.1
TransE [4]	3390	0.220	49.2	350	0.284	45.4
KBGAN [5]	–	0.213	49.1	–	0.278	45.8
DISTMULT [18]	5110	0.43	49	254	0.241	41.9
ConvKB [*](Baseline) [9]	1754	0.248	52.0	257	0.406	51.7
KB$_{LRN}$ [7]	–	–	–	**209**	0.309	49.3
Node+LinkFeat [12]	–	–	–	–	0.293	46.2
DKRL(CNN)[*] [15]	**286**	–	22.4	360	–	37.0
TA-ConvKB	1360	0.274	**56.8**	248	**0.426**	**53.9**

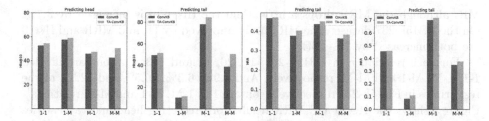

Fig. 3. H@10 (in %) and MRR on the FB15k-237 test set w.r.t each relation category.

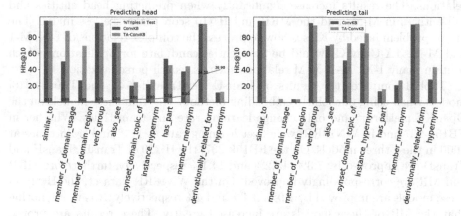

Fig. 4. H@10 on the WN18RR test set w.r.t each relation.

Table 3. Experimental results in other models using our text-augmented method on link prediction

Method	WN18RR				FB15k-237			
	MR	MRR	H@10	H@10 Improv.	MR	MRR	H@10	H@10 Improv.
TransE [4]	3390	0.220	49.2	–	350	0.284	45.4	–
TransE+TA	678	0.239	56.5	+7.3%	278	0.293	47.3	+1.9%
TransH [14]	5646	0.176	43.3	–	399	0.132	33.6	–
TransH+TA	695	0.236	56.1	+13.2%	312	0.158	37.0	+3.4%
TransD [16]	4955	0.178	42.2	–	411	0.147	35.7	–
TransD+TA	688	0.235	56.3	+14.1%	298	0.182	39.7	+4%

Table 2 compares the experimental results of our TA-ConvKB model with previous published results. [*] indicate the results of our experiments. Other results are taken from [9]. The best score is in bold. Table 2 shows that TA-ConvKB obtains the best MR and second-best H@10 scores on WN18RR and also the highest MRR, second-best MR and H@10 scores on FB15k-237. It can be seen that MR, H@10 are significantly improved compared to ConvKB results. On WN18RR, our model gains significant improvements of $1774 - 647 = 1127$ in

MR, although the MRR drops a little. And the Hist@10 is increased by 3.7%. On the FB15k-237 dataset, the MR is only improved by 11, and MRR and H@10 are both increased by 2%−3%.

For each relation r in FB15k-237, 17, 26, 81 and 113 relations are labeled 1-1, 1-M, M-1 and M-M, respectively. And 0.9%, 6.3%, 20.5% and 72.3% of the test triples in FB15k-237 respectively contain 1-1, 1-M, M-1 and M-M relations[1]. Figure 3 shows the H@10 and MRR results for predicting head and tail entities w.r.t each relation category on FB15k-237. TA-ConvKB works better than ConvKB whenever predicting head entities and tail entities in 1-M, M-M, M-1, 1-1 relations. The results increase significantly when predicting head entities and tail entities in M-M, and the MRR and H@10 scores increase less in 1-1. The major problem faced by KGs is how to process the complex relations of 1-M, M-1 and M-M. TA-ConvKB would be a potential candidate for applications which contain many 1-M, M-1, M-M relations such as search personalization.

Table 3 compares the results of TransE [4], TransH [14], and TransD [16] models when using our jointly embedding method. We train these models on the OpenKE platform[2] and only change learning rate and train_times. Whether in FB15k-237 and in WN18RR, we all set learning rate at 1^{e-5} and train_times at 4000 in these three models. On the FB15k-237, the H@10 of TransE, TransH and TransD are improved by 7.3%, 13.2% and 14.1% respectively, furthermore MRR and MR are correspondingly improved. On the WN18RR dataset, the H@10 of these models are improved by 1.9%, 3.4% and 4% respectively. It is worth noting that the MR of these models are increased greatly. These results are proved that our gate mechanism applied to the combination of textual embeddings and structural embeddings is effective. Figure 4 shows the H@10 scores w.r.t each relation on WN18RR. Our TA-ConvKB also performs better than ConvKB on these four types of relations in general, except when predicting tail entities in verb_group and head entities in has_part.

5   Conclusion

In this paper, we put forward a new model TA-ConvKB, which uses A-BiLSTM for entities descriptions encoding and novel gate mechanism originating from LSTM gate units to combine text embeddings and structural embeddings. Experimental results show that our model TA-ConvKB outperforms ConvKB model on two benchmark datasets WN18RR and FB15k-237. This text-augmented method can also be used on other models, the assessment results have also been greatly improved. To conclude, our proposed jointly representation learning with gate mechanism is effective, which benefits modeling the representation of an entity.

---

[1] We calculate the averaged number η_s of head entities per tail entity and the averaged number η_o of tail entities per head entity. If $\eta_s < 1.5$ and $\eta_o < 1.5$, r is categorized one-to-one (1-1). If $\eta_s < 1.5$ and $\eta_o > 1.5$, r is categorized one-to-many (1-M). If $\eta_s > 1.5$ and $\eta_o < 1.5$, r is categorized many-to-one (M-1). If $\eta_s > 1.5$ and $\eta_o > 1.5$, r is categorized many-to-many (M-M).

[2] https://github.com/thunlp/OpenKE.

In future work, we will consider to use more accurate word vector representations, such as using the Elmo model to generate word vectors. It is possible to explore kinds of combinations between structural embeddings and textual embeddings. We also consider to integrate the image information of the entities to enhance the representations of entities to better accomplish the task of link prediction.

Acknowledgment. This work was partially funded by National Natural Science Foundation of China (No.61877043 and 61877044).

References

1. Predicting rich drug-drug interactions via biomedical knowledge graphs and text jointly embedding. CoRR, abs/1712.08875 (2017). Withdrawn
2. An, B., Chen, B., Han, X., Sun, L.: Accurate text-enhanced knowledge graph representation learning. In: Proceedings of the 2018 Conference of the North American Chapter of the Association for Computational Linguistics: Human Language Technologies, vol. 1 (Long Papers) (2018)
3. Bojanowski, P., Grave, E., Joulin, A., Mikolov, T.: Enriching word vectors with subword information. TACL **5**, 135–146 (2017)
4. Bordes, A., Usunier, N., García-Durán, A., Weston, J., Yakhnenko, O.: Translating embeddings for modeling multi-relational data. In: Advances in Neural Information Processing Systems 26: 27th Annual Conference on Neural Information Processing Systems 2013. Proceedings of a meeting held 5–8 December 2013, Lake Tahoe, Nevada, United States, pp. 2787–2795 (2013)
5. Cai, L., Wang, W.Y.: KBGAN: adversarial learning for knowledge graph embeddings. In: Proceedings of the 2018 Conference of the North American Chapter of the Association for Computational Linguistics: Human Language Technologies, NAACL-HLT 2018, New Orleans, Louisiana, USA, 1–6 June 2018, vol. 1 (Long Papers), pp. 1470–1480 (2018)
6. Dettmers, T., Minervini, P., Stenetorp, P., Riedel, S.: Convolutional 2D knowledge graph embeddings. In: Proceedings of the Thirty-Second AAAI Conference on Artificial Intelligence, (AAAI-18), the 30th innovative Applications of Artificial Intelligence (IAAI-18), and the 8th AAAI Symposium on Educational Advances in Artificial Intelligence (EAAI-18), New Orleans, Louisiana, USA, 2–7 February 2018, pp. 1811–1818 (2018)
7. García-Durán, A., Niepert, M.: Kblrn: end-to-end learning of knowledge base representations with latent, relational, and numerical features. In Proceedings of the Thirty-Fourth Conference on Uncertainty in Artificial Intelligence, UAI 2018, Monterey, California, USA, 6–10 August 2018, pp. 372–381 (2018)
8. Heck, J., Salem, F.M.: Simplified minimal gated unit variations for recurrent neural networks. CoRR, abs/1701.03452 (2017)
9. Nguyen, D.Q., Nguyen, T.D., Nguyen, D.Q., Phung, D.Q.: A novel embedding model for knowledge base completion based on convolutional neural network. In: Proceedings of the 2018 Conference of the North American Chapter of the Association for Computational Linguistics: Human Language Technologies, NAACL-HLT, New Orleans, Louisiana, USA, 1–6 June 2018, vol. 2 (Short Papers), pp. 327–333 (2018)

10. Nguyen, D.Q., Sirts, K., Qu, L., Johnson, M.: Stranse: a novel embedding model of entities and relationships in knowledge bases. In: NAACL HLT 2016, The 2016 Conference of the North American Chapter of the Association for Computational Linguistics: Human Language Technologies, San Diego California, USA, 12–17 June 2016, pp. 460–466 (2016)
11. Nickel, M., Tresp, V., Kriegel, H.-P.: A three-way model for collective learning on multi-relational data. In: Proceedings of the 28th International Conference on Machine Learning, ICML 2011, Bellevue, Washington, USA, June 28 – July 2, 2011, pp. 809–816 (2011)
12. Toutanova, K., Chen, D.: Observed versus latent features for knowledge base and text inference. In: Workshop on Continuous Vector Space Models & Their Compositionality (2015)
13. Trouillon, T., Welbl, J., Riedel, S., Gaussier, É., Bouchard, G.: Complex embeddings for simple link prediction. In: Proceedings of the 33nd International Conference on Machine Learning, ICML 2016, New York City, NY, USA, 19–24 June 2016, pp. 2071–2080 (2016)
14. Wang, Z., Zhang, J., Feng, J., Chen, Z.: Knowledge graph embedding by translating on hyperplanes. In: Proceedings of the Twenty-Eighth AAAI Conference on Artificial Intelligence, 27–31 July 2014, Québec City, Québec, Canada, pp. 1112–1119 (2014)
15. Xie, R., Liu, Z., Jia, J., Luan, H., TransEun, M.: Representation learning of knowledge graphs with entity descriptions. In: AAAI, pp. 2659–2665 (2016)
16. Xiong, S., Huang, W., Duan, P.: Knowledge graph embedding via relation paths and dynamic mapping matrix. In: Woo, C., Lu, J., Li, Z., Ling, T.W., Li, G., Lee, M.L. (eds.) ER 2018. LNCS, vol. 11158, pp. 106–118. Springer, Cham (2018). https://doi.org/10.1007/978-3-030-01391-2_18
17. Xu, J., Qiu, X., Chen, K., Huang, X.: Knowledge graph representation with jointly structural and textual encoding. In: Proceedings of the Twenty-Sixth International Joint Conference on Artificial Intelligence, IJCAI 2017, Melbourne, Australia, 19–25 August 2017, pp. 1318–1324 (2017)
18. Yang, B., Yih, W., He, X., Gao, J., Deng, L.: Embedding entities and relations for learning and inference in knowledge bases. In: 3rd International Conference on Learning Representations, ICLR 2015, San Diego, CA, USA, 7–9 May 2015, Conference Track Proceedings (2015)
19. Zhong, H., Zhang, J., Wang, Z., Wan, H., Chen, Z.: Aligning knowledge and text embeddings by entity descriptions. In: Proceedings of the 2015 Conference on Empirical Methods in Natural Language Processing, EMNLP 2015, Lisbon, Portugal, 17–21 September 2015, pp 267–272 (2015)
20. Zhou, P., et al.: Attention-based bidirectional long short-term memory networks for relation classification. In: Proceedings of the 54th Annual Meeting of the Association for Computational Linguistics, ACL 2016, 7–12 August 2016, Berlin, Germany, vol. 2: Short Papers (2016)

A Novel Online Ensemble Convolutional Neural Networks for Streaming Data

Xuan Cuong Pham[✉], Thi Thu Thuy Nguyen, and Alan Wee-Chung Liew

School of Information and Communication Technology,
Griffith University, Gold Coast, QLD 4215, Australia
cuong.pham2@griffithuni.edu.au

Abstract. In this study, we introduce an online ensemble method based on convolutional neural networks (CNNs) for streaming data. Recent work has shown that a convolution operation has been an effective way to extract features. In particular, we proposed a CNN working in an online manner as a base classifier. Then, an ensemble approach is devised to boost the performance of all base classifiers. We also propose two loss terms which can adapt to the imbalanced data stream as well as handling the forgetting issue of deep networks. The experiments conducted on a number of datasets chosen from different sources demonstrate that the proposed ensemble approach performs significantly better than a single network and some well-known online learning algorithms including additive models and Online Bagging.

Keywords: Online learning · Ensemble method · Multi-classifier system · Convolutional neural networks · Deep learning

1 Introduction

Deep learning techniques such as a convolutional neural network (CNN) have been shown to provide significant advantages in the offline learning setting. However, little work has been done exploring these methods in the online setting. Offline algorithms require re-training when new data are available, so re-training CNN usually take a lot of resources and time even when train on GPU cards. Therefore, the online learning framework that deals with data streams has become increasingly popular [19].

In this paper, we focus on supervised online learning, where the training data arrive sequentially. Online learning is performed in a sequence of consecutive rounds, where at each round the learner is given an instance and is required to provide prediction to this instance. After predicting, the correct label of the instance is revealed and the learner suffers a loss if there is a discrepancy between its prediction and the correct label.

Many approaches have been proposed to solve the supervised online learning problems. The most popular approach in online learning is the additive model in which given a misclassified instance $(\mathbf{x}_t, y_t)$, the prediction model is updated

© Springer Nature Switzerland AG 2019
T. Gedeon et al. (Eds.): ICONIP 2019, LNCS 11953, pp. 199–210, 2019.
https://doi.org/10.1007/978-3-030-36708-4_17

by shifting along the direction of $\mathbf{w} + \alpha_t y_t \mathbf{x}_t$ where $\mathbf{w}$ is the weight vector, $y_t \in \{-1, 1\}$ is the class label of $\mathbf{x}_t$ and α_t is the weight of the misclassified instance. The additive model can be categorized into first-order or second-order models depending on the assumption put on the weight vector. There are some well-known first-order additive models including Perceptron [24], Online Gradient Descent (OGD) [27], Passive Aggressive learning (PA) [5], and second-order methods such as Soft Confident Weighted (SCW) [26], and Adaptive Regularization of Weights (AROW) [6].

Ensemble-based methods are among the most widely used techniques for data stream classification as they can obtain better performance than single classifiers [11]. Online Bagging and Online Boosting [20] are two well-known online ensemble algorithms. RP Hoeffding tree was recently proposed in [21] in which random projection technique have been used to generate lower-dimension data from the original data. Then, base classifiers operate on these transformed data and their results are combined into an ensemble hypothesis. Besides, several offline classifers are modified to adapt to the online learning problem, for example the Naïve Bayes online classifier and Hoeffding tree induction [4,8]. Nguyen et al. [19] proposed a Bayesian online learning method in which the likelihood is approximated and updated via Variational Inference using Gaussian distribution.

In this study, we propose an ensemble method based on convolutional neural networks to solve the online learning problem. First, we initialize a number of CNNs to form the ensemble. These CNNs are different in their settings of the first convolution layer. Second, we derive a new loss function which can handle the imbalanced data issue in stream learning and the forgetting issue of deep models. Finally, a combining algorithm is then used to combine the outputs of the base classifiers for the final prediction. The ensemble system has better accuracy than a single classifier system [16–18]. In addition, as each base CNN classifier can easily be trained on GPU, our approach can take this advantage to make the learning process faster.

Our main contributions can be summarized as follows:

- We propose an online classifier based on CNN (denoted as OCNN).
- We also propose a new loss function which helps the OCNN method to tackle the imbalanced data problem.
- A forgetting penalty term is introduced to handle the forgetting problem of online CNN classifiers.
- We define a novel ensemble system called OECNN, using OCNNs as the base classifiers.
- Comprehensive study is carried out to empirically evaluate the proposed OECNN.

The paper is organized as follows. In Sect. 2, we introduce our OCNN approach with the new loss function which can handle the imbalanced data and the forgetting issues. Moreover, an ensemble system using OCNNs as the base classifiers is also propose in Sect. 2. Experimental results are presented in Sect. 3. Finally, Sect. 4 concludes our work.

2   Proposed Method

2.1   Online CNN Classifier

In this study, we introduce an online CNN acting as the base classifier in our
ensemble system. Our CNN, shown in Fig. 1, can take a data point $\mathbf{x}_t$ which is
a vector of size p or a mini-batch of data points as input from a data stream.
The proposed CNN architecture comprises three convolution blocks, following by
two fully-connected layers. The first layer is a 1D convolution layer with k filters,
the kernel size is set to 3 and stride number is 1. The second layer is also a 1D
convolution layer with a stride of 2, which means that the data dimension will be
reduced by a factor of 2. Between the second and the third convolution layers, we
employ a stacking layer to form a matrix, which is the input for the third layer
(2D convolution layer). The purpose of the 2D convolution layer is that it helps
to extract representative features across all channels of the output from the 1D
convolution layer and further reduce the number of dimensions of an observation.
Then, the output of the third layer is flattened and passed through the fully-
connected layer. The last layer in the proposed CNN has the same number of
hidden units as the number of class labels in the training set. We apply softmax
function at the end of the network to obtain the posterior probabilities p_t of
observation $\mathbf{x}_t$ belong to each class m with $m \in \{0, 1, \ldots, M-1\}$. To avoid overfitting, Instance Normalization and PReLU activation are applied after every
convolution layer. We also apply PReLU activation in the fully-connected layer
except the last one.

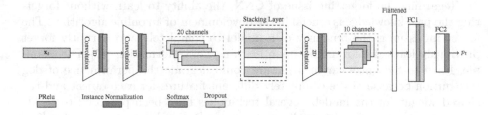

Fig. 1. Our OCNN architecture

There are two main issues that an online learning algorithm needs to be concerned with, which are imbalanced data and forgetting in the learning process.
The most common way to address imbalanced data is by using cost-sensitive
learning. Specifically, we reduce the loss of majority class while increase that of
the other classes by applying a corresponding weight to each class. Focal loss
[13] is one of the loss functions invented to deal with the data imbalance problem in CNN. In detail, the focal loss is built by multiplying a modulating factor
$(1-p_t)^\gamma$ to the convention loss function, i.e. Cross entropy loss function, where p_t
is the probability of the prediction vector with respect to the input $\mathbf{x}_t$ and $\gamma \geq 0$
is a tunable *focusing* parameter. However, the focal loss faces several issues.

First, the weights of the networks are usually initialized according to some distributions so that the output from each layer will be normally distributed. If so, the value of the output layer will also be normally distributed. Therefore, the initial probability distributions of all the classes, regardless of positive or negative instances, will follow some distributions centered at 0.5. This makes the minor positive instances less important in the initial training stage. Second, the focal loss is unstable and leads to the exploding gradient problem where the model loss goes to NaN during training in some cases. Eventually, the model can not learn from confident data points where $p_{t,y_t} = 1$.

In our work, we adopt a modified focal loss to address these issues. In the online setting, the ratio of the arriving data points for each class could help us detect the imbalanced problem in the data stream. Here, we combine it with the focal loss to reduce the contribution of well-classified data points. In this way, the model can learn from the harder but rare data points. Intuitively, the modulating factor reduces the loss contribution from easy instances while increase the loss for instances that belong to rare classes. In practice, we use the ratio of the arriving data points instead of a fixed α as in the original focal loss since it yields improved accuracy. The loss function for each data point is defined as follow:

$$\mathcal{L}_{imb}(p_t, y_t) = -\frac{c_{y_t}}{t}(1 - \frac{c_{y_t}}{t}p_{t,y_t})^\gamma (p_{t,y_t} - \log \sum_{m=0}^{M-1} \exp(p_{t,m})) \tag{1}$$

where c_{y_t} is the number of past data points belong to class $y_t \in \{0, 1, \ldots, M-1\}$ and t is the total number of past data points.

Regarding the forgetting issue of CNN, the ability to learn without forgetting the past knowledge is crucial in the development of an online algorithm. The forgetting issue is the tendency of a model to completely and abruptly forget previously learned information upon learning new information [15]. For example, learn to recognize car in a picture could degrade the performance of dog recognition because of the completely different features for each object and the shared weights of the model. Several techniques have been proposed to tackle this issue such as influence gradient alignment [14] and experience replay [23]. In this work, we propose an addition penalty to the loss function to address the forgetting issue. Our penalty is based on the *Transfer-Interference Trade-off* [22], but we only focus on the current arriving data points instead of penalize between the current instances and the past instances which are kept in a memory buffer. Assuming that our model works on a mini-batch of the arriving data points. Clearly, the instance which has the minimum loss value (denoted as $(\mathbf{x}_{min}, y_{min})$) is the most likely correct one in the training mini-batch. Therefore, we choose $(\mathbf{x}_{min}, y_{min}) \in B_t$ as a pivot instance to penalize the other instances in the mini-batch. The penalty is calculated by the dot product of gradient with respect to $\mathbf{x}_{min} \in B_t$ and the other instances, as follow:

$$\mathcal{L}_{forget} = \mathbb{E}_{(\mathbf{x}_i, y_i) \in B_t}[-\alpha \frac{\partial \mathcal{L}(\mathbf{x}_i, y_i)}{\partial \theta} \cdot \frac{\partial \mathcal{L}(\mathbf{x}_{min}, y_{min})}{\partial \theta}] \tag{2}$$

where B_t is the mini-batch of instances arriving at time step t, $\frac{\partial \mathcal{L}(\mathbf{x}_i, y_i)}{\partial \theta}$ and $\frac{\partial \mathcal{L}(\mathbf{x}_{min}, y_{min})}{\partial \theta}$ is the gradient of loss function with respect to data point $(\mathbf{x}_i, y_i)$ and $(\mathbf{x}_{min}, y_{min})$, respectively.

Overall, the objective function for training of our online CNN architecture is defined as follow:

$$\mathcal{L} = \mathbb{E}_{(\mathbf{x}_i, y_i) \in B_t}[\mathcal{L}_{imb}(\mathbf{x}_i, y_i)] + \mathcal{L}_{forget} \tag{3}$$

In the training process, the network was trained with the number of epochs on an arriving datapoint which is set to 50 for all experiments. An initial learning rate of 0.0002 and Adam optimization [10] with a momentum of 0.5 were used. The α and γ are set to 0.25 and the batch size is 6 in all experiments. The detail of our online CNN approach is provided in Table 1.

Table 1. Detail of our OCNN structure

Layers	Type	Stride	Kernel size	Padding size	# Filters	Output size
Input						$(1, 1, p)$
C1	1D Convolution	1	$(1, 3)$	1	20	$(1, 20, a)$
N1	Instance Norm					$(1, 1, 20, a)$
L1	PReLU					$(1, 1, 20, a)$
C2	1D Convolution	2	$(1, 3)$	1	20	$(1, 20, 1, b)$
N2	Instance Norm					$(1, 20, 1, b)$
L2	PReLU					$(1, 20, 1, b)$
S	Stacking layer					$(1, 1, 20, b)$
C3	2D Convolution	2	$(3, 3)$	1	10	$(1, 10, c, d)$
N3	Instance Norm					$(1, 10, c, d)$
L3	PReLU					$(1, 10, c, d)$
FC1	Fully-connected					$(1, 40)$
L4	PReLU					$(1, 40)$
D1	Dropout					$(1, 40)$
FC2	Fully-connected					$(1, M)$
Output	Softmax					$(1, M)$

p is dimension of input data, $a = \lfloor \frac{p-3+2}{1} \rfloor + 1$, $b = \lfloor \frac{a-3+2}{2} \rfloor + 1$, $c = \lfloor \frac{20-3+2}{2} \rfloor + 1$, $d = \lfloor \frac{b-3+2}{2} \rfloor + 1$ and M is the number of classes

2.2 Online Ensemble CNN Method

We propose here a heterogeneous ensemble method using the proposed OCNNs as the base classifiers to handle the online learning problem. In an ensemble system, there are two phases to be considered, namely generation and combination. Heterogeneous ensemble methods focus on the combination phase to develop combining algorithms that combine the output of base classifiers generated by different learning algorithms on the same training set [17].

In this work, the arriving data point is first passed to the K base classifiers which are OCNNs with different settings of parameters such as the kernel size. Each data point is then classified by the associated base classifier to output the class membership hypothesis in the form of probabilities. The final hypothesis is obtained by a combining method that combines the class membership hypotheses. Finally, these base classifiers are updated by computing the loss between its hypothesis and the true hypothesis through backpropagation.

In detail, the learning process begins with the initialization of K OCNN classifiers H_k, $k = 1, \ldots, K$. At the tth step of the online learning process, the arrived instance $\mathbf{x}_t$ will be predicted by the associated classifier H_k to output the posterior probabilities $p_{t_k} = \{P_k(y_m|\mathbf{x}_t)\}$ that $\mathbf{x}_t$ belongs to the mth class ($m = 0, \ldots, M - 1$). In this paper, we use the output in the form of *soft label* that $P_k(y_m|\mathbf{x}_t) \in [0,1]$ and $\sum_{m=1}^{M} P_k(y_m|\mathbf{x}_t) = 1$ [17]. The output of all K base classifiers are given in the form of:

$$
\begin{bmatrix}
P_1(y_0|\mathbf{x}_t) & \cdots & P_1(y_{M-1}|\mathbf{x}_t) \\
\vdots & \ddots & \vdots \\
P_K(y_0|\mathbf{x}_t) & \cdots & P_K(y_{M-1}|\mathbf{x}_t)
\end{bmatrix}
\tag{4}
$$

The outputs from the K base classifiers given in (3) are combined to obtain the final hypothesis. Several popular fixed combining methods, namely Sum, Product, Majority Vote, Max, Min, and Median can be used as the combiner [17,18]. Among these, Vote and Sum are the most popular rules and have been successfully applied to many combining classifier situations [17,18]. In this work, we use Sum rule to combine the outputs of K classifiers, which is defined as follows:

$$
\mathbf{x}_t \in y_s \text{ if } s = \text{argmax}_{m=0,\ldots,M-1} \sum_{k=1}^{K} P_k(y_m|\mathbf{x}_t)
\tag{5}
$$

The overall structure of our proposed method is illustrated in Algorithm 1.

3   Experiment Studies

3.1   Datasets

We conducted extensive experiments to evaluate the proposed methods on 24 datasets from UCI [3], LibSVM [1], MOA [2]. These datasets were chosen from different sources with a varying number of features, classes, and samples to ensure a fair comparison. Information about the datasets is shown in Table 2.

3.2   Benchmark Selection and Experimental Settings

We evaluated the effectiveness of our method with several state-of-the-art algorithms. These including several well-known additive model i.e. PA [5], SCW [26], OGD [27], AROW [6] (these algorithms were implemented in LIBOL library [9],

---

Algorithm 1. Online ensemble convolution neural networks (OECNN) algorithm

---

Input: Ensemble size K, the number of filter size for each OCNN classifier $F = \{f_1, \ldots, f_K\}$
1: **for** $k = 1 \ldots K$ **do**
2:    Initialize OCNN H_k with the number of filter size f_k for the first 1D convolution layer
3: **end for**
4: **repeat**
5:    Get new example $(\mathbf{x}_t, y_t)$ from the stream
6:    **for** $k = 1 \ldots K$ **do**
7:       **for** $e = 1 \ldots E$ (Epochs) **do**
8:          Applying H_k on $\mathbf{x}_t$ to output soft label $p_{t_k} = \{P_k(y_m|\mathbf{x}_t)\}$, $m = 0, \ldots, M-1$
9:          Computing the loss using (3)
10:          Update H_k by using backpropagation
11:       **end for**
12:    **end for**
13:    Predict label of $\mathbf{x}_t$ using combining rule (5)
14: **until** (exist data from stream)

Table 2. Information of datasets in evaluation

Dataset	# of sample	# of features	# of classes	Imbalanced ratio	Dataset	# of sample	# of features	# of classes	Imbalanced ratio
Breast Cancer	683	9	2	1.86/1	Optdigits	5620	64	10	Balanced
Contraceptive	1473	9	3	1.89/1/1.53	Optical	3823	64	10	Balanced
Dermatology	358	34	6	5.55/3/3.55/2.40/2.40/1	Page Blocks	5472	10	5	175.46/11.75/1/3.11/4.11
Fertility	100	9	2	7.33/1	Penbased	10992	16	10	Balanced
Hepatitis	80	19	2	1/5.15	Segment	2310	19	7	Balanced
Hill valley	2424	100	2	Balanced	Sonar	208	60	2	1/1.14
Ionosphere	351	34	2	1.79/1	Spambase	4601	57	2	1.54/1
Isolet	7797	617	26	Balanced	SPECTF Heart	267	44	2	1/3.85
Letter	20000	16	26	Balanced	Texture	5500	40	10	1/1/1/2/1 1/1/1/1/1
Madelon	2000	500	2	Balanced	Thyroid	7200	21	3	1/2.22/40.16
Musk1	476	166	2	1.3/1	Tic-tac-toe	958	9	2	1.80/1
Musk2	6598	166	2	5.49/1	Zoo	101	16	7	10.25/5/1.25 3.25/1/2/2.50

*The value of balanced in imbalanced ratio column means that the different in the number of instances belong to each class label is less than 10% and the number 1 represents the most minor class while the biggest number represents the most major class.

default parameter were used if available) and Online Bagging [20] (we used the implementation in MOA library [4], where the learner is the Hoeffding tree). AROW, OGD and SCW are algorithms published in top machine learning venues like NIPS, KDD and ICML and Online Bagging is a high performance ensemble online learning method. For the proposed method, we tested our ensemble system with 4 OCNNs as the base classifiers. Each of these network has the same number of filters (20-20-10 for the first, second and third convolution layer in all experiments). Meanwhile, these networks are different in the kernel sizes, which are set to 1, 3, 5 and 7, respectively. The number of epochs is set to 50 in all experiments. The number of learners in Online Bagging was set to 200 as in [17].

We first compared our method to the benchmark algorithms on the classification error rate and F1 score (which is the harmonic mean of Precision and Recall) [25]. To evaluate the performance of our proposed method on imbalanced data, we used Gmean [12] as an evaluation metric because the error rate is not suitable to measure the performance for imbalanced data as it is dominated by the majority classes. Gmean balances accuracy among classes without depending on the size of each class. We drew S random permutations from each dataset to obtain the sequences of arriving data (i.e. Permutation i, $i = 1, \ldots, S$), then run the proposed method on these permutations to output the S classification error rates, F1 score, and Gmean and finally computed the average and variance of these values. In this paper, the number of permutations S was set to 10. An arriving instance is first used to test then train afterward.

We conducted Wilcoxon signed rank test [7] (level of significance α is set to 0.05) to compare algorithms pairwise, i.e. a benchmark algorithm and the proposed algorithm. Here we tested the null hypothesis that "two methods perform equally". Based on the value of the statistics in the Wilcoxon procedure, we can obtain the P-Value of the test. The performance scores of two methods are treated as significantly different if the P-Value of the test is smaller than 0.05. When the test indicated that the performance of two algorithms is different, we then use the classification error rate or F1 score to decide which algorithm wins on a particular dataset and count the number of wins and losses on the set of datasets.

3.3   Experimental Results and Comparison

We first compare the effectiveness of our proposed methods with the benchmark algorithms on the classification error rate and F1 scores. The statistical test results displayed in Fig. 2 show that the proposed OECNN method is significantly better than all first-order benchmark algorithms on the experimental datasets. In detail, OECNN clearly outperforms all first-order additive models, for example it wins PA and OGD on 22 and 21 datasets in terms of error rate, respectively. Our OECNN approach also achieves better results than the Online Bagging (16 wins vs 4 losses) and a single OCNN (15 wins vs 0 losses).

Concerning F1 score, a similar pattern can be observed in the statistical test results displayed in Fig. 3 in which the proposed method continues to outperform all benchmark algorithms. For instance, it wins PA on 19 datasets and OGD on 18 datasets. In comparison with second-order methods, our approach wins AROW on 14 datasets and achieves competitive results with SCW (9 wins vs 8 losses). Moreover, our OECNN method also performs better than Online Bagging on 17 datasets. This demonstrates that the proposed method has superior performance in supervised online learning over the benchmark algorithms. In

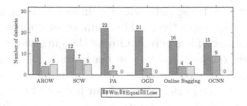

Fig. 2. Statistical test result comparing classifier error rate of the OECNN proposed method to the benchmark algorithms

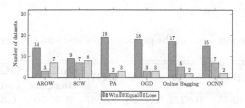

Fig. 3. Statistical test Result comparing F1 score of the OECNN proposed method to the benchmark algorithms

comparison of Gmean, our approaches show significant improvement on not only imbalanced datasets but also balanced datasets. Table 3 describes the Gmean result of our approaches and benchmarks algorithms. It is clear from Table 3 that our approaches achieve the best performance in terms of Gmean on 17 datasets. Interestingly, there are 4 datasets in which the benchmark algorithms such as AROW, SCW, PA and OGD make completely wrong prediction for the minor class (Gmean equals zero). This demonstrates that our proposed loss function helps the network handle the imbalanced data issue and improve the prediction for the minority class.

It is noted that although we have more classifiers to train, the base classifiers can be trained independently, making them easily parallelizable. Moreover, in the proposed OCNN method, the convolutional layers acting as feature extraction modules help to reduce the dimension of the input data. The reduction of dimensionality will boost the training process to be much faster compared to using the original data like in Online Bagging, especially for high dimensional datasets. On Isolet dataset, for example, the total running times (test and train) on a permutation of OECNN method (run on CPU) is faster than that of Online Bagging, 1966.52 s vs. 3142.033 s, respectively. Besides, our approach can take advantage of using GPU for improving the running time. For example, the running time for a permutation on Isolet is improved to 1376.10 s (around 30.02% faster).

The number of epochs for training OCNN is an important hyperparameter in our approach. Theoretically, the more the number of training iteration, the better the model is. Thus, we validate this by conduct experiment on different number of epochs. As shown in Fig. 4, the error rate of OCNN on Dermatology dataset reduce by increasing the number of epochs. In contrast, the running time increase significantly. Therefore, we set the number of epochs to 50 in our experiments.

Table 3. Means of Gmean score of the proposed method and the benchmark algorithms

Dataset	AROW	SCW	PA	OGD	Online Bagging	OCNN (ours)	OECNN (ours)
Breast Cancer	0.8345	0.8322	0.7205	0.8087	**0.9566**	0.8368	0.9129
Contraceptive	0.4266	0.4425	0.3333	0.3694	0.3925	**0.5375**	0.5354
Dermatology	0.9078	0.8983	0.4134	0.4032	0.5198	0.8975	**0.9196**
Fertility	0.1109	0.2850	0.3141	0.0765	0.0567	**0.5057**	0.4987
Hepatitis	**0.6225**	0.4939	0.3992	0.3570	0.0856	0.5001	0.4778
Hill Valley	0.0000	0.0000	0.0000	0.0000	0.1311	0.9880	**0.9889**
Ionosphere	0.0000	0.0000	0.0000	0.0000	0.8225	0.8471	**0.8690**
Isolet	0.8517	0.9201	0.8175	0.8247	0.2036	0.8990	**0.9445**
Letter	0.4837	0.4720	0.4332	0.5405	0.1156	0.7948	**0.8425**
Madelon	0.5204	0.5285	0.4980	0.5222	0.0484	0.5520	**0.5747**
Musk1	0.6862	**0.7547**	0.6598	0.6813	0.3893	0.6902	0.7126
Musk2	0.0000	0.0000	0.0000	0.0000	0.1221	0.5117	**0.5231**
Optdigits	0.8733	0.9362	0.9046	0.9009	0.6125	0.9001	**0.9645**
Optical	0.8625	0.9347	0.8940	0.8918	0.6371	0.8987	**0.9670**
Page Blocks	0.5362	**0.6239**	0.3454	0.0983	0.1874	0.4144	0.4245
Penbased	0.8099	0.8549	0.8160	0.8510	0.5813	0.9270	**0.9596**
Segment	0.7561	0.8334	0.5239	0.5926	0.4847	0.8612	**0.9044**
Sonar	**0.7228**	0.7046	0.5672	0.5762	0.6650	0.6766	0.6888
Spambase	**0.9044**	0.8895	0.6246	0.5656	0.8369	0.8278	0.8749
SPECTF Heart	0.5279	**0.5426**	0.4029	0.4277	0.3994	0.5082	0.5033
Texture	0.9667	0.9667	0.7084	0.7681	0.4065	0.9383	**0.9843**
Thyroid	0.0111	0.4495	0.3433	0.0000	0.2507	0.4718	**0.7014**
Tic-tac-toe	0.0000	0.0000	0.0000	0.0000	0.3299	**0.5944**	0.5782
Zoo	0.6503	0.5262	0.0000	0.1385	0.0782	0.6242	**0.8355**

*Bold value indicates the highest Gmean score

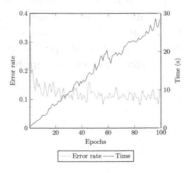

Fig. 4. Trade-off between time and error rate for varying the number of epoch in OCNN method on Dermatology dataset

4   Conclusion

In this paper, we introduced OECNN which is an ensemble of online convolutional neural networks (OCNNs). In our OCNN, three convolution layers are designed to reduce data dimension and extract features from the input. Then, two fully-connected layers are used to make classification from the output of the convolution layers. In addition, we propose a new loss function which helps the network deals with imbalanced data and the forgetting issues. Extensive experimental results demonstrated the superior performance of our OECNN approach compared to several well-known benchmark algorithms with respect to classification error rate, F1 score and Gmean.

Acknowledgment. This research was supported by the Griffith University International Postgraduate Research Scholarship (GUIPRS).

References

1. Libsvm. https://www.csie.ntu.edu.tw/~cjlin/libsvmtools/datasets/
2. Moa dataset. http://moa.cms.waikato.ac.nz/datasets/
3. The UCI dataset website. http://archive.ics.uci.edu/ml/datasets.html
4. Bifet, A., et al.: MOA: massive online analysis, a framework for stream classification and clustering. In: Proceedings of the First Workshop on Applications of Pattern Analysis. Proceedings of Machine Learning Research, vol. 11, pp. 44–50 (2010)
5. Crammer, K., Dekel, O., Keshet, J., Shalev-Shwartz, S., Singer, Y.: Online passive-aggressive algorithms. J. Mach. Learn. Res. **7**, 551–585 (2006)
6. Crammer, K., Kulesza, A., Dredze, M.: Adaptive regularization of weight vectors. In: Proceedings of the 22nd International Conference on Neural Information Processing Systems, pp. 414–422 (2009)
7. Demsar, J.: Statistical comparisons of classifiers over multiple datasets. J. Mach. Learn. Res. **7**, 1–30 (2006)
8. Domingos, P., Hulten, G.: Mining high-speed data streams. In: Proceedings of the KDD Conference, pp. 71–80 (2000)
9. Hoi, S.C.H., Wang, J., Zhao, P.: LIBOL: a library for online learning algorithms. J. Mach. Learn. Res. **15**, 495–499 (2014)
10. Kingma, D.P., Ba, J.: Adam: a method for stochastic optimization. In: International Conference on Learning Representations (2014)
11. Krawczyk, B., Minku, L.L., Gama, J., Stefanowski, S.J., Woźniak, M.: Ensemble learning for data stream analysis: a survey. Inf. Fusion **37**, 132–156 (2017)
12. Kubat, M., Matwin, S.: Addressing the curse of imbalanced training sets: one-sided selection. In: Proceedings of the Fourteenth International Conference on Machine Learning, pp. 179–186 (1997)
13. Lin, T., Goyal, P., Girshick, R., He, K., Dollár, P.: Focal loss for dense object detection. In: 2017 IEEE International Conference on Computer Vision (ICCV), pp. 2999–3007 (2017)
14. Lopez-Paz, D., Ranzato, M.A.: Gradient episodic memory for continual learning. In: Advances in Neural Information Processing Systems 30, pp. 6467–6476 (2017)
15. McCloskey, M., Cohen, N.J.: Catastrophic interference in connectionist networks: the sequential learning problem. Psychol. Learn. Motiv. **24**, 109–165 (1989)

16. Nguyen, T.T., Liew, A.W.C., Tran, M.T., Pham, X.C., Nguyen, M.P.: A novel genetic algorithm approach for simultaneous feature and classifier selection in multi classifier system. In: IEEE Congress on Evolutionary Computation (CEC), pp. 1698–1705 (2014)

17. Nguyen, T.T., Nguyen, T.T.T., Pham, X.C., Liew, A.W.C.: A novel combining classifier method based on variational inference. Pattern Recogn. **49**, 198–212 (2016)

18. Nguyen, T.T., Pham, X.C., Liew, A.W.C., Pedrycz, W.: Aggregation of classifiers: a justifiable information granularity approach. IEEE Trans. Cybern. **49**(6), 2168–2177 (2019)

19. Nguyen, T.T.T., et al.: A novel online bayes classifier. In: 2016 International Conference on Digital Image Computing: Techniques and Applications (DICTA), pp. 1–6 (2016)

20. Oza, N., Russell, S.: Online bagging and boosting. In: Proceedings of the International Conference on Systems, Man and Cybernetics, pp. 2340–2345 (2005)

21. Pham, X.C., Dang, M.T., Dinh, V.S., Hoang, S., Nguyen, T.T., Liew, A.W.C.: Learning from data stream based on random projection and hoeffding tree classifier. In: 2017 International Conference on Digital Image Computing: Techniques and Applications, DICTA 2017, Sydney, Australia, pp. 1–8 (2017)

22. Riemer, M., et al.: Learning to learn without forgetting by maximizing transfer and minimizing interference. In: International Conference on Learning Representations (ICLR) (2019)

23. Riemer, M., Franceschini, M., Klinger, T.: Generation and consolidation of recollections for efficient deep lifelong learning (2017). http://arxiv.org/abs/1711.06761

24. Rosenblatt, F.: The perceptron: a probabilistic model for information storage and organization in the brain. Psychol. Rev. **65**(6), 386–408 (1958)

25. Sokolova, M., Lapalme, G.: A systematic analysis of performance measures for classification tasks. Inf. Process. Manag. **45**, 427–437 (2009)

26. Wang, J., Zhao, P., Hoi, S.C.H.: Exact soft confidence-weighted learning. In: Proceedings of ICML (2012)

27. Zinkevich, M.: Online convex programming and generalized infinitesimal gradient ascent. In: Proceedings of the ICML, pp. 928–936 (2003)

Cross-media Image-Text Retrieval
Based on Two-Level Network

Zhixin Li[⊠], Feng Ling, Fengqi Zhang, and Canlong Zhang

Guangxi Key Lab of Multi-source Information Mining and Security,
Guangxi Normal University, Guilin 541004, China
lizx@gxnu.edu.cn

Abstract. Cross-media retrieval is to find the relationship between different modal samples, and to use some modal samples to search for other modal samples of approximate semantics. The existing cross-media retrieval method only utilizes the information of the image and part of the text, that is, the whole image and the whole sentence are matched, or some image areas and some words are matched. In order to make better use of the integrated features of image and text, this paper proposes a cross-media image-text retrieval method that integrates two-level similarity to explore better matching between image and text semantics. Specifically, in this method, the image is divided into the whole picture and some image areas, the text is divided into the whole sentences and some words, to study respectively, to explore the full potential alignment of images and text, and then a two-level alignment framework is used to promote each other, fusion of two kinds of similarity can learn to complete representation of cross-media retrieval. Experimental results on the Flickr30K and MS-COCO datasets show that this model has a better recall rate than many of the current internationally advanced cross-media retrieval models.

Keywords: Convolutional neural network · Two-level network ·
Self-attention network · Attention mechanism · Cross-media image-text
retrieval

1 Introduction

Cross-media not only represent that coexistence of complex media objects such as web text, images, audio, video, etc. It is also manifested in the complex relation and organization structure formed by various media objects, as well as media objects with different modalities across media or the platform is highly interactive.

Since the characteristics of different modalities usually have inconsistent distributions and representations, a simple way to learn is to create a common subspace and then project all the data into that space. For example, in the early canonical correlation analysis (CCA) [6] method. The topic model is another commonly representation, such as the classic latent dirichlet allocation (LDA) [2] model. There is also a graph-based approach, constructing one or more graphs,

© Springer Nature Switzerland AG 2019
T. Gedeon et al. (Eds.): ICONIP 2019, LNCS 11953, pp. 211–222, 2019.
https://doi.org/10.1007/978-3-030-36708-4_18

and indicates cross-media correlation at the media instance. The rise of deep neural networks (DNN) has also quickly spread to the field of cross-media information expression. DNN can be used to handle the relevance of different media types. However, for a project in a modality, there may be multiple semantically different items with the same modality. It is not enough to simply match the representation by sharing the subspace, and a better model is needed. To match this semantic representation.

We propose a DNN-based cross-media retrieval method. Our method is based on global and local similarity. We refer to our model as GALR. For global features, we introduce a self-attention network to obtain a macro representation of the global image. For local text features, we use attention mechanisms, which are essentially similar to human selective visual attention mechanisms. The core goal is to remove redundant information from a wide range of information and select information that is more critical to the current mission objectives. Using two levels of similarity, the two methods can be combined in cross-media retrieval applications, and achieved good results.

2   Related Work

A large number of studies [3,4,11,18,25–27] explored mapping image and complete sentences into a common semantic vector space for image-text matching. Kiros et al. [15] used a deep convolutional neural network (CNN) [16] to encode images and used recursive neural networks (RNN) [29] to encode sentences with significant improvements. Feng et al. [4] used text and image features to map to a common subspace through the encoder, and then used L2 to measure the similarity between the text and the image, and then obtained the correlation loss, and then used the decoder to separate the common subspace. This framework is very classic, and many models [3,17,20,24,26] have used it since then. The idea of Wang et al. [27] is similar to Order-embeddings [24]. The biggest highlight is the introduction of hard triplet loss [9] and the addition of structure retention (hard triplet loss between texts). The main idea of Nam et al. [20] is to add attention to both sides of text and images, and then use triplet loss to measure the similarity between text and image in a common subspace. Wang et al. [25] used GAN in domain adaptation to draw on cross-media retrieval. Faghri et al. [3] used the hard of the triplet loss to the extreme and implemented end-to-end training. Huang et al. [11] obtained a better image representation by learning the rank loss of the image-text and the loss generated by the text. The main idea of Lee et al. [17] is to use the attention mechanism on the text and image side to learn better text and image representation, and then use hard triplet loss to measure the similarity between text and image in the common subspace, this approach uses the attention mechanism to better obtain potential semantic alignment.

Compared with previous work, how to combine image and text information is a problem that has not been well studied. The image is divided into a whole image and an image area. The text is divided into sentences and words, which should be studied separately in order to explore the complete potential alignment of the image and the text. This paper combines two levels of similarity to provide a more comprehensive semantic description of images and text. On the one hand, we were borrowed from the use of the common subspace, different media data are mapped from their independent representation spaces to a third party's common subspace, so that they can measure the similarity with each other. In this way you can get a better semantic space, and you can reduce the distance of the same semantics of different media modes. On the other hand, we were inspired by the ideas proposed in some ranking-based methods, the loss function based on triplet loss can be used to increase the distance representation of different semantics of different media modes. The result is a better modal matching representation of the image and text.

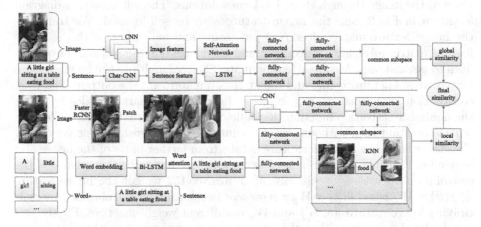

Fig. 1. Schematic diagram of the model. The input is an image/text pair dataset and the output is the final similarity score.

3   Cross-media Two-Level Model

The method of this paper is shown in Fig. 1. A cross-media attention network is constructed to explore a two-level model, which contains two subnets for global representation and local representation. Specifically, we not only use the self-attention network to get the global macro representation of the image, but also use local fine-grained patches. The two kinds of similarity can promote each other and provide a more comprehensive representation for cross-media retrieval.

We introduce the formal definition of cross-media datasets as $O = \{o_i\}_{i=1}^{N_0} = \{I, T\}$, where images $I = \{i_m\}_{m=1}^{N}$ and text $T = \{t_k\}_{k=1}^{N}$ have a total of N instances in each media type. That is N image/text pairs. i_m and t_k are the m_{th} and k_{th} instances of images and text, respectively. Finally, if given a modal and query another modal, we can get a global similarity $sim1$ and a local similarity $sim2$, the goal of cross-media retrieval is to measure cross-media final similarity $sim(i_m, t_k)$, and retrieve related instances of another media type.

3.1   Global Representation Processing

This paper extracts global and local representations from the proposed visual language attention model, which provides rich and comprehensive semantic information for cross-media retrieval.

For the global representation of the image, each input image is adjusted to 256×256 and is fed to a convolutional neural network to take advantage of the high level global semantic information. In particular, the convolutional neural network (CNN) has the same configuration as the pre-trained ResNet-152 [7] convolutional neural network, which is pre-trained on large-scale ImageNet datasets. We obtain the global image feature by taking a mean-pooling over the last spatial image features, expressed as x. Where $x = (x_1, x_2, ..., x_j, ..., x_i, ..., x_n)$.

Then we use the image self-attention mechanism [30] to pass the global features of the image through three 1×1 convolutions. The self-attention diagram is shown in Fig. 2, and the image features can be self-focused. We transpose the image feature matrix after $f(x)$ processing and multiply it with the image feature matrix after $y(x)$ processing, and then take out the softmax on all the lines to get an image feature attention map. Then we multiply the image feature matrix after $k(x)$ processing and the attention map to get the output. The 1×1 convolution kernel can greatly improve the nonlinear characteristics by using the nonlinear activation function that follows the premise that the image feature scale is constant (i.e., without loss of resolution), the network is done very deep. This layer helps the network capture details from farther parts of the image and remember that it does not replace the convolution, but rather complements the convolution operation. Specifically, after ResNet-152 we got the image feature x, $f(x) = W_f x$ and $y(x) = W_y x$ represent two feature spaces obtained by multiplying image features by W_f and W_y of different weight matrices. Firstly, $\alpha_{j,i}$ is calculated to indicate that the image content of region j synthesized by the model is the participation degree of region i, that is, the correlation:

$$\alpha_{j,i} = \frac{\exp(b_{ij})}{\sum_{i=1}^{n} \exp(b_{ij})}, where\ b_{ij} = f(x_i)^T y(x_j) \tag{1}$$

$\alpha_{j,i}$ is the result of softmax, then we calculate the output of the self-attention network c_j:

$$c_j = \sum_{i=1}^{N} \alpha_{j,i} k(x_i), where\ k(x_i) = W_k x_i \tag{2}$$

where $C = (c_1, c_2, ..., c_j, ..., c_i, ..., c_n)$, W_k is the weight parameter. This way we can integrate all the information together. Combining the original features of the image with the features of the attention layer, the final output is $g_i = \lambda c_i + x_i$ as a global feature of the image, where λ is initialized to 0.1.

Then, each input text t_k being composed of a sequence of characters, each of these characters is represented by a single thermal code. Based on experience, we built a Char-CNN [31] to handle the global text representation, to generate a representation sequence from the last activation layer and feed them into the recurrent neural network. Text classification from the character level, extracting

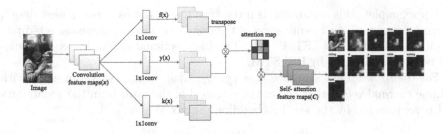

Fig. 2. Self-attention image convolution feature.

high-level abstract concepts. The advantage of this is that you do not need to use information such as pre-trained word vectors and grammatical syntax structures. In addition, there is an advantage that it can be easily extended to all languages. For each input text t_k, the text sequence output through Char-CNN is P.

For a global representation of text, the output of Char-CNN is used as the input to the long-term short-term memory (LSTM [8]). Specifically, we use LSTM networks to learn global representation. For the LSTM, P is the input text sequence, the output of the hidden unit is $H_i = \{h_1^i, ..., h_m^i\}$. So the output of the LSTM is $g_t = \frac{1}{m} \sum_{k=1}^{m} h_k^i$.

We add two fully-connected networks to transform the image and text global feature vector dimensions into 1024-dimensional vectors, which are mapped as cross-media semantic alignments into common subspaces to compute cross-media similarity between images and text.

3.2 Local Representation Processing

In order to process the local representation of the image, we use Faster R-CNN [22] to generate candidate image regions of visual objects with higher probability (such as "person" or "plane"). To generate an image region, all candidate image regions are detected from a Faster R-CNN and sorted by their score. Pick the first 5 candidate image areas. We use the method of Anderson et al. [1]. We used a Faster R-CNN model in combination with the pre-trained ResNet-152 in the ImageNet dataset. Specifically, each image i_m is fed to a Faster R-CNN implemented with a ResNet-152 network that is pre-trained on the MS-COCO detection dataset. We can get a few bounding boxes, and then we obtain the image feature by taking a mean-pooling over the last spatial image features. They represent n different regions within an image and then form an image local representation $\{l_i^1, ..., l_i^n\}$, where i represents the i_{th} image.

Then, in order to learn local representation of text, there is a problem if we only use LSTM to model sentences: we cannot encode back-to-front information. In the finer-grained classification, such as the strong degree of commendation, weak degree of commendation, neutral, weak degree of derogatory, strong degree of derogatory five classification tasks need to pay attention to the interaction between emotional words, degree words, negative words.

For example, "this restaurant is dirty very much, not as good as next door", where "very much" is a modification of the degree of "dirty", so we use a bidirectional LSTM called "Bi-LSTM" [12]. The bi-directional semantic dependencies can be better captured by Bi-LSTM.

For the i_{th} word in a sentence $Y = \{y_1, y_2, ..., y_i, ..., y_m\}$, we represent it with a single thermal vector that shows the retrieval of the word from the vocabulary and is represented by the word embedding matrix W_E as:

$$W_E \cdot y_i = W_E \omega_i, i \in [1, m] \tag{3}$$

Embedding words into a 300-dimensional vector, then we use Bi-LSTM to summarize the information in two directions in a sentence. The Bi-LSTM contains the forward LSTM, which reads the sentence Y from ω_1 to ω_m:

$$\overrightarrow{h_i} = \overrightarrow{LSTM}(y_i), i \in [1, m] \tag{4}$$

And using backward LSTM to read sentence Y from ω_m to ω_1:

$$\overleftarrow{h_i} = \overleftarrow{LSTM}(y_i), i \in [1, m] \tag{5}$$

The last word e_m is characterized by an average forward hidden state $\overrightarrow{h_i}$ and a backward hidden state $\overleftarrow{h_i}$, which summarizes the information of the sentence centered on ω_i.

$$e_m = \frac{(\overrightarrow{h_i} + \overleftarrow{h_i})}{2}, i \in [1, m] \tag{6}$$

Word embedding extracts the output of a word by Bi-LSTM network. Its output dimension is 2048. We can obtain a series of outputs from the hidden unit of the Bi-LSTM, denoted by $E = \{e_1, ...e_i, ...e_m\}$ as m different text segments in a sentence, as the final feature of the context in which the sentence is interpreted.

In addition, our goal is to focus the model on the necessary fine-grained patches, so we apply the attention mechanism [19] to capture useful text fragments. The elements in each set represent the input information in a spatial position in the input information, the output e_m^t is the current spatial position t, a certain context respectively represents the corresponding attention, and the m_{th} text segment is finally scored after passing softmax.

$$e_m^t = f_{ATT}(z_{t-1}, e_m, \{\alpha_j^{t-1}\}_{j=1}^m) \tag{7}$$

z_{t-1} means to select $(t-1)_{th}$ input information from Bi-LSTM hidden state. We normalize by softmax, and finally the corresponding weight (i.e. score) of each input context representation is 1:

$$\alpha_m^t = \frac{\exp(e_m^t)}{\sum_{j=1}^m \exp(e_j^t)} \tag{8}$$

The extent to which the decoder indicates attention to different contextual information in the segment E of a sentence can be reflected by this score. Where α_m^t denotes the attention weight of the generation of the text segment.

A piece of text with greater attention is more likely to contain keywords that describe the corresponding visual object. Therefore, after processing through the Bi-LSTM and attention mechanism, we can obtain a local representation of $\frac{1}{m}\sum_{k=1}^{m}\alpha_k^t e_k$ in a sentence.

Assuming there are n texts, we can get a series of outputs from the hidden unit of the Bi-LSTM, denoted as $E' = \{e_1^n, ...e_i^n, ..., e_m^n\}$, representing n sentences, each sentence has m different text segments. After processing through the Bi-LSTM and attention mechanism, we can obtain a text local representation of $l_t = \frac{1}{m}\sum_{k=1}^{m}\sum_{j=1}^{n}\alpha_k^t e_k^j$ in a sentence, as the final text local representation.

We add two fully-connected networks to transform the image and text local feature vector dimensions into 1024-dimensional vectors, which are mapped as cross-media semantic alignments into common subspaces to compute cross-media similarity between images and text.

3.3 Cross-media Two-Level Alignment

The loss function we use for global and local representations is based on triplet loss [9]. The core of triplet loss is the anchor example, the positive example, and the negative example shared model. Through the model, the anchor example is clustered with the positive example, away from the negative example. What triplet loss learned is a good embedding. Similar image/text pairs are similar in the common subspace, denoted as $Loss_{triplet} = max(d(a, p) - d(a, n) + margin, 0)$, where a is an anchor, p is a positive example, and n is a negative example. Triplet loss should make the difference between the similarity of matched image/text pairs and the similarity of mismatched pairs as large as possible. Therefore, using triplet loss, the objective function we designed is defined as follows:

$$L_{global} = \frac{1}{N}\sum_{n=1}^{N} L_1(i_+^n, t_+^n, t_-^n) + L_2(t_+^n, i_+^n, i_-^n)$$
$$L_1(i_+^n, t_+^n, t_-^n) = \max(0, \alpha - d(g_{i+}^n, g_{t+}^n) + d(g_{i+}^n, g_{t-}^n))$$
$$L_2(t_+^n, i_+^n, i_-^n) = \max(0, \alpha - d(g_{i+}^n, g_{t+}^n) + d(g_{i-}^n, g_{t+}^n))$$

$$(9)$$

Where L_1 and L_2 represent the similarity of the global image/text pair matched during model training, and the difference between the similarity of the mismatched pairs is as large as possible. $d(.)$ represents the dot product between the image/text pairs. We use the dot product of the projections to calculate the similarity in the common subspace. It shows their similarity (the bigger this value, the better). (g_{i+}^n, g_{t+}^n) denotes a matching image/text pair, (g_{i+}^n, g_{t-}^n) and (g_{i-}^n, g_{t+}^n) are pairs that do not match. n represents n image/text pairs. α represents the marginal parameter. N is the number of triple tuples sampled from the training set. Thus, cross-media global alignment can be leveraged from matched and unmatched image/text pairs. In previous work, Karpathy and FeiFei [13] defined region-word similarity as the dot product of regions and words, and we have extended this practice.

For local alignment, our goal is to find the best match between the text local representation l_t and the multiple image local representations $\{l_i^1, ..., l_i^n\}$ in a pair of images and text. Specifically, for each text local representation, we select k nearest neighbors (KNN) from multiple image local representations [23], if given a with n local image represents a picture, we assume that there is a particular visual features such as "Food". After extracting its feature vector, we can calculate the given distance between the feature vectors by the simple KNN tool, that is, L1 or L2 distance, it is found that k nearest neighbors are found from the n image local representations. This makes it possible to better match the image local representation and the text local representation, and gives the following objective function:

$$L_{local} = \max(0, \alpha - \frac{1}{K}\sum_{k=1}^{K} d(l_{t+}, l_{i+}^k) + \frac{1}{K}\sum_{k=1}^{K} d(l_{t+}, l_{i-}^k)) \qquad (10)$$

The K value of the k-nearest neighbor is usually set to 3. Finally, we designed a cross-media synthesis similarity between image i_m and text t_k, we calculate the similarity in the 1024-dimensional common subspace, which combines two levels of alignment. θ is a parameter defined between 0.3 and 0.7, which will be explained in detail in the experimental part later (mentioned in Subsect. 4.2).

$$sim1 = d(g_i, g_t)$$
$$sim2 = \frac{1}{K}\sum_{k=1}^{K} d(l_i^k, l_t) \qquad (11)$$
$$sim(i_m, t_k) = \theta * sim1 + (1 - \theta) * sim2$$

4   Analysis of Experimental Results

Our approach achieved good results on the MS-COCO and Flickr30K datasets, generally higher than other popular methods. On Flickr30K, our method performs 2.3% higher in image retrieval based on image query than current methods, and 12.7% higher in image retrieval based on text query (based on Recall@1). On MS-COCO, our method has improved sentence retrieval by 1.7% and image retrieval by 1.2% (based on Recall@5, using the 1 K test set).

4.1   Data Sets and Evaluation Indicators

We evaluate our method on the Flickr30K dataset and the Microsoft COCO dataset. Flickr30K has a standard 31,000 images for training. Following the split in [13], we use 1,000 images for validation and 1,000 images for testing and the rest for training. Each image comes with 5 captions. In MS-COCO dataset, the training set contains 82,783 images, 5,000 validation and 5,000 test images. Following the split in [13], we use 1,000 images for validation and 1,000 images for testing and the rest for training. Each image comes with 5 captions. The experimental results are shown in Tables 1 and 2. In the beginning, we only used global similarity to predict the results of the experiment, that is, "GALR(only global)". In addition, we only used local similarity to predict experimental results, namely "GALR(only local)". Finally, the results of the experiment are predicted by the combination of global similarity and local similarity, that is, "GALR".

Table 1. Results on the Flickr30K dataset.

Method	Text to image			Image to text		
	R@1	R@5	R@10	R@1	R@5	R@10
DCCA [28]	26.8	52.9	66.9	27.9	56.9	68.2
VSE++[3]	39.6	70.1	79.5	52.9	80.5	87.2
DAN [20]	39.4	69.2	79.1	55.0	81.8	89.0
SPE [27]	29.7	60.1	72.1	40.3	68.9	79.9
SCO [11]	41.1	70.5	80.1	55.5	82.0	89.3
SM-LSTM [10]	30.2	60.4	72.3	42.5	71.9	81.5
Embedding Net [26]	29.2	59.6	71.7	40.7	69.7	79.2
GALR(only global)	24.2	49.5	59.8	31.7	58.2	68.2
GALR(only local)	40.9	69.8	79.5	64.0	87.8	93.6
GALR	**43.4**	**73.5**	**82.5**	**68.2**	**89.1**	**94.5**

We use Recall@K (R@K, K = 1, 5, 10) to represent the percentage of queries that retrieved at least one ground-truth in the top K results. The higher the score of Recall@K, the better the model performance.

4.2 Experimental Parameter Settings

The method we proposed is implemented by pytorch. For global text features, there are three convolutional layers in Char-CNN, with parameter combinations (256, 4), (512, 4) and (2048, 4). The first parameter represents the number of cores and the second parameter represents the kernel width. The output of Char-CNN is the 2048 dimension. The number of dimensions embedded in the word input to the Bi-LSTM is set to 300. We use two fully-connected network in each subnet to generate a global and local representation with 1024 dimensions. Although the training speed of using two fully-connected networks was slower than that using one fully-connected network, the recall rate of experimental results was higher than that using one full connection network. In addition, all margins α in the loss function are set to 1. We use the Adam optimizer [14] to train our model. For the Flickr30K and MS-COCO datasets, we trained at a learning rate of 0.0002 in 15 iterations and then reduced the learning rate to 0.00002 in another 15 iterations. We designed θ to rearrange two levels of similarity.

Selection of θ: in the verification stage of the experiment, for the given global similarity $sim1$ and local similarity $sim2$, we can add them in a certain proportion to determine the optimal proportion of the two similarity.

Table 2. Results on the MS-COCO dataset.

Method	Text to image			Image to text		
	R@1	R@5	R@10	R@1	R@5	R@10
DCCA [28]	6.6	20.9	32.2	6.9	21.1	31.8
VSE++[3]	52.0	–	92.0	64.6	–	95.7
SCO [11]	56.7	87.5	94.8	**69.9**	92.9	97.5
GXN [5]	56.6	–	94.5	68.5	–	97.9
SM-LSTM [10]	40.7	75.8	87.4	53.2	83.1	91.5
HM-LSTM [21]	36.1	–	86.7	43.9	–	87.8
order-embeddings [24]	39.6	75.3	86.7	48.5	80.9	90.3
GALR(only global)	34.9	69.7	82.8	41.3	75.0	85.7
GALR(only local)	57.5	88.0	94.6	67.5	93.3	97.9
GALR	**58.6**	**88.2**	**94.9**	68.9	**94.1**	**98.0**

First, we use random numbers to iterate for 100 times in the minimum batch of each verification to determine the approximate range of θ. Then, according to the experiment in the verification phase, reorder based on the similarity of θ participation. If the result of the experiment is better than the result of the direct addition of the original global and local similarity, then θ will be output. On the contrary, the result of the experiment is still the addition of the original two similarity. Through many small batches of verification, we found that θ between 0.3 and 0.7 can obtain the best experimental results. In the test phase of the experiment, it is the same process, but not in small batches, but in full test data. Since the scope of θ has been determined before, we only need to iterate the θ value between 0.3 and 0.7 for 41 times in the test phase to get the best experimental results. In this way, we use fewer iterations to optimize the speed and improve the experimental results.

5   Conclusion

In this paper, we have proposed a two-level alignment framework for cross-media image-text retrieval. Firstly, we focus on the different characteristics of images and sentences and conduct a step-by-step study of them. Secondly, cross-media two-level alignment is proposed to model global, local alignment, which can promote each other to learn more accurate cross-media associations. We conducted experiments to verify the effectiveness of our approach. In future work, we will combine the deep learning method and knowledge reasoning to study the field of cross-media retrieval.

Acknowledgments. This work is supported by the National Natural Science Foundation of China (Nos. 61966004, 61663004, 61762078, 61866004), the Guangxi Natural Science Foundation (Nos. 2016GXNSFAA380146, 2017GXNSFAA198365,

2018GXNSFDA281009), the Research Fund of Guangxi Key Lab of Multi-source Information Mining and Security (16-A-03-02, MIMS18-08), the Guangxi Special Project of Science and Technology Base and Talents (AD16380008), Innovation Project of Guangxi Graduate Education (XYCSZ2019068), the Guangxi Bagui Scholar Teams for Innovation and Research Project, Guangxi Collaborative Innovation Center of Multi-source Information Integration and Intelligent Processing.

References

1. Anderson, P., et al.: Bottom-up and top-down attention for image captioning and visual question answering. In: Proceedings of the IEEE Conference on Computer Vision and Pattern Recognition, pp. 6077–6086 (2018)

2. Blei, D.M., Ng, A.Y., Jordan, M.I.: Latent Dirichlet allocation. J. Mach. Learn. Res. **3**, 993–1022 (2003)

3. Faghri, F., Fleet, D.J., Kiros, J.R., Fidler, S.: VSE++: improving visual-semantic embeddings with hard negatives. arXiv preprint arXiv:1707.05612 (2017)

4. Feng, F., Wang, X., Li, R.: Cross-modal retrieval with correspondence autoencoder. In: Proceedings of the 22nd ACM International Conference on Multimedia, pp. 7–16. ACM (2014)

5. Gu, J., Cai, J., Joty, S.R., Niu, L., Wang, G.: Look, imagine and match: improving textual-visual cross-modal retrieval with generative models. In: Proceedings of the IEEE Conference on Computer Vision and Pattern Recognition, pp. 7181–7189 (2018)

6. Hardoon, D.R., Szedmak, S., Shawe-Taylor, J.: Canonical correlation analysis: an overview with application to learning methods. Neural Comput. **16**(12), 2639–2664 (2004)

7. He, K., Zhang, X., Ren, S., Sun, J.: Deep residual learning for image recognition. In: Proceedings of the IEEE Conference on Computer Vision and Pattern Recognition, pp. 770–778 (2016)

8. Hochreiter, S., Schmidhuber, J.: Long short-term memory. Neural Comput. **9**(8), 1735–1780 (1997)

9. Hoffer, E., Ailon, N.: Deep metric learning using triplet network. In: Feragen, A., Pelillo, M., Loog, M. (eds.) SIMBAD 2015. LNCS, vol. 9370, pp. 84–92. Springer, Cham (2015). https://doi.org/10.1007/978-3-319-24261-3_7

10. Huang, Y., Wang, W., Wang, L.: Instance-aware image and sentence matching with selective multimodal LSTM. In: Proceedings of the IEEE Conference on Computer Vision and Pattern Recognition, pp. 2310–2318 (2017)

11. Huang, Y., Wu, Q., Song, C., Wang, L.: Learning semantic concepts and order for image and sentence matching. In: Proceedings of the IEEE Conference on Computer Vision and Pattern Recognition, pp. 6163–6171 (2018)

12. Huang, Z., Xu, W., Yu, K.: Bidirectional LSTM-CRF models for sequence tagging. arXiv preprint arXiv:1508.01991 (2015)

13. Karpathy, A., Fei-Fei, L.: Deep visual-semantic alignments for generating image descriptions. In: Proceedings of the IEEE Conference on Computer Vision and Pattern Recognition, pp. 3128–3137 (2015)

14. Kingma, D.P., Ba, J.: Adam: a method for stochastic optimization. arXiv preprint arXiv:1412.6980 (2014)

15. Kiros, R., Salakhutdinov, R., Zemel, R.S.: Unifying visual-semantic embeddings with multimodal neural language models. arXiv preprint arXiv:1411.2539 (2014)

16. Krizhevsky, A., Sutskever, I., Hinton, G.E.: Imagenet classification with deep convolutional neural networks. In: Advances in Neural Information Processing Systems, pp. 1097–1105 (2012)
17. Lee, K.-H., Chen, X., Hua, G., Hu, H., He, X.: Stacked cross attention for image-text matching. In: Ferrari, V., Hebert, M., Sminchisescu, C., Weiss, Y. (eds.) ECCV 2018. LNCS, vol. 11208, pp. 212–228. Springer, Cham (2018). https://doi.org/10.1007/978-3-030-01225-0_13
18. Liu, Y., Guo, Y., Bakker, E.M., Lew, M.S.: Learning a recurrent residual fusion network for multimodal matching. In: Proceedings of the IEEE International Conference on Computer Vision, pp. 4107–4116 (2017)
19. Mnih, V., Heess, N., Graves, A., et al.: Recurrent models of visual attention. In: Advances in Neural Information Processing Systems, pp. 2204–2212 (2014)
20. Nam, H., Ha, J.W., Kim, J.: Dual attention networks for multimodal reasoning and matching. In: Proceedings of the IEEE Conference on Computer Vision and Pattern Recognition, pp. 299–307 (2017)
21. Niu, Z., Zhou, M., Wang, L., Gao, X., Hua, G.: Hierarchical multimodal LSTM for dense visual-semantic embedding. In: Proceedings of the IEEE International Conference on Computer Vision, pp. 1881–1889 (2017)
22. Ren, S., He, K., Girshick, R., Sun, J.: Faster R-CNN: towards real-time object detection with region proposal networks. In: Advances in Neural Information Processing Systems, pp. 91–99 (2015)
23. Tibshirani, T.H.R.: Discriminant adaptive nearest neighbor classification and regression. In: Advances in Neural Information Processing Systems 8: Proceedings of the 1995 Conference, vol. 8, p. 409. MIT Press (1996)
24. Vendrov, I., Kiros, R., Fidler, S., Urtasun, R.: Order-embeddings of images and language. arXiv preprint arXiv:1511.06361 (2015)
25. Wang, B., Yang, Y., Xu, X., Hanjalic, A., Shen, H.T.: Adversarial cross-modal retrieval. In: Proceedings of the 25th ACM International Conference on Multimedia, pp. 154–162. ACM (2017)
26. Wang, L., Li, Y., Huang, J., Lazebnik, S.: Learning two-branch neural networks for image-text matching tasks. IEEE Trans. Pattern Anal. Mach. Intell. **41**(2), 394–407 (2019)
27. Wang, L., Li, Y., Lazebnik, S.: Learning deep structure-preserving image-text embeddings. In: Proceedings of the IEEE Conference on Computer Vision and Pattern Recognition, pp. 5005–5013 (2016)
28. Yan, F., Mikolajczyk, K.: Deep correlation for matching images and text. In: Proceedings of the IEEE Conference on Computer Vision and Pattern Recognition, pp. 3441–3450 (2015)
29. Zaremba, W., Sutskever, I., Vinyals, O.: Recurrent neural network regularization. arXiv preprint arXiv:1409.2329 (2014)
30. Zhang, H., Goodfellow, I., Metaxas, D., Odena, A.: Self-attention generative adversarial networks. arXiv preprint arXiv:1805.08318 (2018)
31. Zhang, X., Zhao, J., LeCun, Y.: Character-level convolutional networks for text classification. In: Advances in Neural Information Processing Systems, pp. 649–657 (2015)

Fusion Convolutional Attention Network for Opinion Spam Detection

Jiacheng Li[1,2], Qianwen Ma[1,2], Chunyuan Yuan[1,2], Wei Zhou[1,2(✉)],
Jizhong Han[1], and Songlin Hu[1,2]

[1] Institute of Information Engineering, Chinese Academy of Sciences, Beijing, China
{lijiacheng,maqianwen,yuanchunyuan,zhouwei,hanjizhong,
husonglin}@iie.ac.cn
[2] School of Cyber Security, University of Chinese Academy of Sciences,
Beijing, China

Abstract. Opinion spam detection is a critical task in opinion mining. Current researches mainly focus on manually designing the text or discrete user features, or concatenating the review text and user features as the representation of the review. However, these methods ignore the impact of user's preferences on review texts. Because of their different purposes, spammers and non-spammers usually show different preferences. These user-level differences are hard to be captured from the single review level by previous methods.

In this paper, we propose a novel Fusion Convolutional Attention Network (FCAN) to embed the user-level information into a continuous vector space, the representations of which capture essential clues such as user profiles or preferences. Such user representation, in turn, facilitates learning better user-aware textual representation at word and sentence level. Experimental results on four real-world datasets from different platforms demonstrate that our method significantly outperforms the state-of-the-art methods and can be easily expanded to different datasets and platforms.

Keywords: Opinion spam detection · Fusion convolutional attention network · User-aware textual representation · User preference

1 Introduction

Nowadays, more and more people tend to share their opinions about products or services on web platforms. These opinions are essential references when other people make purchase decisions. Both positive and negative opinions will lead to a significant influence on brand fame and financial profits. Some researches on Yelp.com have shown that an extra half-star rating causes restaurants to sell out 19% more products [1]. Because of the enormous benefits, deceptive reviews have been posted on the website such as Yelp. Such deceptive reviews could mislead consumers and damage the online review websites' reputations. Therefore, it is urgent to propose some methods to detect spam reviews automatically.

© Springer Nature Switzerland AG 2019
T. Gedeon et al. (Eds.): ICONIP 2019, LNCS 11953, pp. 223–235, 2019.
https://doi.org/10.1007/978-3-030-36708-4_19

Over the past decade, many methods have been proposed to facilitate spam review detection. This problem is firstly broached in [8]. Subsequent works paid attention to design elaborate features, such as psychological and linguistic clues [19], n-grams [6], and behavioral features like maximum number of reviews [18], rating deviation [17,20], temporal dynamics [2,25] are applied in many works. However, these features are designed for particular datasets or platforms, thus lack generalization.

Motivated by the great success of deep learning in the natural language process, recent methods [9,14,24,27] tackle this problem based on the deep learning models. Though these neural network based approaches have been quite useful for spam detection, they only focus on the review content while ignoring the crucial influences of the user preferences on the text information. Spammers and non-spammers usually show different preferences because of their different purposes. The intuitive insight behind this idea is that fake opinions are generated for the purpose to promote particular targets or denounce their competitors [3], while legitimate users share their experiences. The two different purposes would make a significant effect on the emotional intensity of the reviews. Because these user-level differences are hard to be captured from the single review level by the model, it is beneficial to incorporate the user information to learn a better user-aware textual representation of reviews.

In this paper, we propose a novel framework to encode review and user information automatically. Firstly, we apply two individual neural networks to learn the representations of reviews and users, respectively. Then, we design two fusion attention modules to fuse the user representation and reviews at word and sentence level, which enable the model to learn the user-aware review representation. The experimental results show that our model significantly outperforms other state-of-the-art methods on Mobile01 and Yelp datasets.

The contributions of this paper can be summarized as follows:

- We design a hierarchical network to automatically extract semantic representation for raw review content and embed the user information into the continuous vector space, which does not need manually designed features and overcomes the limitation of platforms.
- We propose two fusion attention modules to fuse the user representation with a review at word and sentence level to learn better user-aware textual representation for spam detection.
- Experimental results on four open datasets achieve significant improvement, which shows that FCAN outperforms the state-of-the-art models. The source code of this paper will be released for further research in the future.

2   Related Work

2.1   Feature-Based Methods

Jindal and Liu [8] firstly studied opinion spam in reviews and made a detailed study on opinion spam. After that, opinion spam detection problem have been paid attention by more and more researchers. Ott et al. [19] integrated work from psychology and computational linguistics to detect deceptive opinion spam. Feng et al. [5] investigated syntactic stylometry for deception detection and encoded syntactic information. Li et al. [13] extended a bayesian generative approach to obtain a deeper understanding of the general nature of deceptive opinion spam. Sandulescu and Ester [22] extended the semantic similarity based on the reviews level and reviews topic distributions. Wang et al. [23] learned the representation of reviews directly from the data without human ingenuity cost, experts' knowledge or any spammer-like assumption.

Beside the textual based features, some works apply behavioral based features [17] to detect spam reviews. Rayana and Akoglu [20] utilized clues from various metadata (text, timestamp, rating) as well as relational data, and harnessed them collectively under a unified framework to spot suspicious users and reviews, as well as products targeted by spam. Li et al. [12] proposed Hidden Markov Model to capture both reviewer posting behaviors and co-bursting signals.

Feature-based methods designed various hand-crafted features, which are relied on expert knowledge and time-consuming. Those features can capture linguistic and psychological cues but fail to encode the semantic meaning of a document from the discourse perspective [21]. In this paper, to detection deceptive opinion spam, we propose a model to learn global semantic representations.

2.2 Deep Learning Methods

Recently, deep neural network [7] and word embeddings [4,16] provide a better choice to learn the semantic representation of reviews. Ren and Zhang [21] designed a gated recurrent neural network to capture the complex semantic information that was difficult to express using traditional discrete bag-of-words feature. Li et al. [14] proposed a sentence weighted neural network model to learn the document-level representation of the spam review. Spam2Vec [15] was proposed to learn the spam representations of the node in the social network by leveraging biased random walks.

Although these neural network based methods achieve good performances for spam detection, these models ignore the important influences of users level information on learning the review semantic representation and the user-review relationship. These model mainly utilize textual based and behavioral based features.

3   Model

In this section, we introduce FCAN in detail. The overall structure of FCAN is demonstrated in Fig. 1. It contains several parts: user representation layer, text representation layer, user fusion attention layers and fully-connected layers. We take the reviews set $\mathbf{D}$ and the user's metadata $\mathbf{U}$ as the inputs. The outputs of our model are probabilities of each class and we use $p(c|\mathbf{D}, \mathbf{U}, \theta)$ to represent the probability of the sample being class c, where θ represents all the parameters in the network.

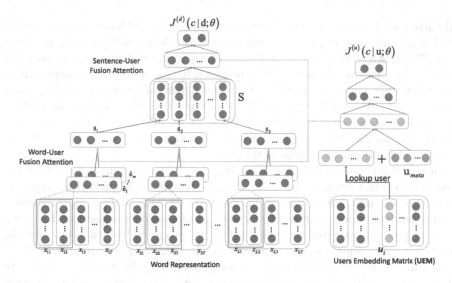

Fig. 1. The structure of the fusion attention network model.

3.1 User Representation

To capture important clues such as user profiles or preferences, the user information is embedded into a continuous vector space. Firstly, we apply user's id u_i to look up the user vector from the Users Embedding Matrix ($\mathbf{UEM} \in \mathbb{R}^{|U| \times d}$). Then, the user's metadata is adopted to model the user from different aspects.

$$\mathbf{u}_i = Lookup(u_i),$$
$$\mathbf{u} = \mathbf{u}_i + \mathbf{W}_m \mathbf{u}_{meta}, \tag{1}$$

where $\mathbf{u}_i \in \mathbb{R}^{d \times 1}$, $\mathbf{W}_m \in \mathbb{R}^{d \times l}$ and $\mathbf{u}_{meta} \in \mathbb{R}^{l \times 1}$. The metadata includes the registration time, the number of reviews, review length, etc., which is easily obtained from every website. This part also can be replaced by human-crafted features.

3.2 Text Representation

To learn fine-grained textual representation, we split every document to L sentences, and every sentence contains T words. Firstly, convolutional layers are applied to capture semantic representation of the sentence and document. A convolution kernel can be represented as $\mathbf{W} \in \mathbb{R}^{h \times d}$, which is applied to a window of h words to produce a new feature:

$$e_i = \mathbf{ReLU}(\mathbf{W} * \mathbf{X}_{i:i+h-1} + b), \tag{2}$$

where $\mathbf{X}$ is word embeddings of review, $b \in \mathbb{R}$ is a bias term, and $\mathbf{ReLU}(\cdot) = \max(0, \cdot)$. The filter is applied to each window of words in the sentence and generates a new feature map:

$$\hat{\mathbf{e}} = [e_1, e_2, \ldots, e_{T-h+1}], \tag{3}$$

with $\hat{e} \in \mathbb{R}^{T-h+1}$. The model uses m filters to obtain multiple feature vectors which constitute $\mathbf{E} = [\hat{e}_1, \hat{e}_2, \ldots, \hat{e}_m] \in \mathbb{R}^{(T-h+1) \times m}$.

3.3   Word-User Fusion Attention Layer

To learn the user-aware textual representation at word level, we propose to use word-user fusion attention to incorporate the user representation into the word-level textual vector:

$$
\begin{aligned}
\mathbf{F} &= \sigma \left(\mathbf{EW}_e + \mathbf{UW}_u + b \right), \\
\mathbf{Z} &= \mathbf{F} \odot \mathbf{E} + (1 - \mathbf{F}) \odot (\mathbf{UW}_u),
\end{aligned}
\tag{4}
$$

where $\sigma(\cdot)$ is sigmoid activation function. $\mathbf{U} = [\mathbf{u}, \mathbf{u}, \ldots, \mathbf{u}] \in \mathbb{R}^{(T-h+1) \times d}$ is the $T - h + 1$ copies of the user representation $\mathbf{u}$. $\mathbf{W}_e \in \mathbb{R}^{m \times m}$, $\mathbf{W}_u \in \mathbb{R}^{d \times m}$ are weight matrix. We obtain user-aware word representation $\mathbf{Z} \in \mathbb{R}^{(T-h+1) \times m}$.

From the user's point of view, not all words equally reflect the user's preferences. In order to address the issue, an attention layer is applied to extract such words that are important to the user's preferences and aggregate the word representations to form the sentence representation:

$$
\begin{aligned}
\mathbf{V} &= \tanh \left(\mathbf{ZW}_z + \mathbf{b}_z \right), \\
\alpha_t &= \frac{\exp \left(V_t^T v_w \right)}{\sum_{i=1}^{k} \exp \left(V_i^T v_w \right)}, \\
\mathbf{s}^{(\mathbf{h})} &= \sum_{t=1}^{T-h+1} \alpha_t \mathbf{E}_t,
\end{aligned}
\tag{5}
$$

where $\mathbf{W}_z \in \mathbb{R}^{m \times n}$, $\mathbf{V} \in \mathbb{R}^{(T-h+1) \times n}$ is learnt parameters, and $\mathbf{v_w} \in \mathbb{R}^{n \times 1}$ is a context vector. The word context vector $\mathbf{v_w}$ is randomly initialized and jointly learned during the training process. We compute the sentence vector $\mathbf{s}^{(\mathbf{h})} \in \mathbb{R}^m$ as a weighted sum of the word representation based on the weights α_t.

Following the settings of CNN [10], the convolutional kernel size is set to $h \in \{3, 4, 5\}$. Then, we concatenate every filter's outputs to form $\mathbf{s} = \mathbf{s}^{(\mathbf{2})} \oplus \mathbf{s}^{(\mathbf{3})} \oplus \mathbf{s}^{(\mathbf{4})}$ as the sentence representation, where $\mathbf{s} \in \mathbb{R}^{3m}$.

3.4   Sentence-User Fusion Attention Layer

After the sentence encoding process, the document matrix can be represented as $\mathbf{S} = [\mathbf{s}_1, \mathbf{s}_2, \ldots, \mathbf{s}_L] \in \mathbb{R}^{L \times 3m}$. To strengthen the influence of the user information, sentence-user fusion attention mechanism is applied to extract user-aware sentences that are critical to the meaning of the document and aggregate all sentence vectors to form a document representation.

Formally, the document representation is a weighted sum of important feature vectors from user's view as:

$$
\mathbf{d} = \sum_{t=1}^{L} \beta_t \mathbf{S}_t,
\tag{6}
$$

where β_t is the attention weight of $\mathbf{S_t}$ and measures the importance of sentences for the document representation. Specifically, the attention weight β_t for each feature map can be defined as follows:

$$\mathbf{M} = (\mathbf{SW}_z + \mathbf{b}_z) \odot \sigma\,(\mathbf{UW}_u + \mathbf{b}_u)\,,$$

$$\beta_t = \frac{\exp\,(\mathbf{M}_t \mathbf{v})}{\sum_{n=1}^{L} \exp\,(\mathbf{M}_n \mathbf{v})}, \tag{7}$$

where $\mathbf{b_z}, \mathbf{b_u} \in \mathbb{R}^k$, $\mathbf{W_z} \in \mathbb{R}^{3m \times m}$ and $\mathbf{W_u} \in \mathbb{R}^{d \times m}$ are weight matrices. $\mathbf{M} \in \mathbb{R}^{L \times m}$ is a hidden representation of $\mathbf{S}$, and $\mathbf{v} \in \mathbb{R}^{m \times 1}$ is the context vector and is randomly initialized and jointly learned during the training process.

3.5   Spam Classification

After above procedures, we get the review representation $\mathbf{d}$ and the user representation $\mathbf{u}$. In order to make full use of them, two different fully-connected layers are respectively connected to them, which will simultaneously train both vectors:

$$\begin{aligned} \mathbf{y}^{(u)} &= \mathbf{softmax}\,(\mathbf{W}_1 \mathbf{u} + \mathbf{b}_1)\,, \\ \mathbf{y}^{(d)} &= \mathbf{softmax}\,(\mathbf{W}_2 \mathbf{d} + \mathbf{b}_2)\,, \end{aligned} \tag{8}$$

where $\mathbf{W}_1, \mathbf{W}_2$ are weight matrices and $\mathbf{b}_1, \mathbf{b}_2$ are bias terms. Finally, the $\mathbf{softmax}(\mathbf{y}) = \frac{\mathbf{y}_i}{\sum_j \mathbf{y}_j}$ function is used to convert the $\mathbf{y}^{(u)}$ and $\mathbf{y}^{(d)}$ into probability distribution.

To make the review $\mathbf{d}$ and the user representation $\mathbf{u}$ both have predictive capability and further improve performance for spam reviews, we add a loss function respectively to $\mathbf{d}$ and $\mathbf{u}$, which we call review loss and user loss. The corresponding losses are defined as follows:

$$\begin{aligned} J^{(u)}\,(c|\mathbf{u}; \theta) &= -\sum_i \log p_i^{(u)}\,(c|\mathbf{u}; \theta)\,, \\ J^{(d)}\,(c|\mathbf{d}; \theta) &= -\sum_i \log p_i^{(d)}\,(c|\mathbf{d}; \theta)\,. \end{aligned} \tag{9}$$

The overall loss of our model is the summation of the review and user loss:

$$J\,(c|\mathbf{u}, \mathbf{d}; \theta) = J^{(u)}\,(c|\mathbf{u}; \theta) + J^{(d)}\,(c|\mathbf{d}; \theta)\,. \tag{10}$$

The training target of the network is to minimize the overall loss with all parameters. It is worth noting that we predict the review label according to the probability distribution $p_i^{(d)}\,(c|\mathbf{d}; \theta)$, because it contains both review and user information.

4   Experiments

In this section, we conduct a series of experiments on two real-world datasets to validate the effectiveness of our model and do some experiment analyses.

4.1   Datasets

In order to validate the effectiveness of our model, we conduct some experiments on two commonly used spam classification datasets. The statistics of the datasets are shown in Table 1.

Table 1. Data statistics.

Dataset	Train/test split	Average #words	#Spam	#Non-spam	#Users
Mobile01 FirstPost	Training set	691	546	10,405	5,130
	Test set	595	208	5,662	3,520
Mobile01 Reply	Training set	204	1,337	147,504	16,272
	Test set	188	1,020	66,005	12,310
YelpChi	Training set	165	7,135	46,780	32,475
	Test set	166	1,784	11,696	10,856
YelpNYC	Training set	138	29,508	257,733	138,185
	Test set	138	7,377	64,434	49,355
YelpZip	Training set	137	64,372	422,505	224,548
	Test set	137	16,094	105,627	81,855

Mobile01 Corpus[1] dataset is obtained from Mobile01 web forum [3]. This dataset is collected from a set of internal records of spam reviews leaked from a shady marketing campaign. In this campaign, Samsung has hired spammers to post negative comments about phones made by Taiwan's HTC.[2] This dataset contains two subsets: first post subset and reply subset.

YelpChi, YelpNYC and **YelpZip**[3] datasets are obtained from paper [20,28], which are three public spam detection datasets crawled from the Yelp website. Yelp has its spam filtering system. The filtered reviews are also made public.[4] The Yelp datasets contain both recommended and filtered reviews. The recommended and filtered reviews are considered as genuine and fake, respectively.

4.2   Baselines

We compare the FCAN with several baseline methods of opinion spam detection, including traditional approaches such as SVMs, graph-based methods, tensor decomposition methods, and some recent proposed deep learning models.

Feature-Based Methods
   SVM + Bag of Words (BoW)/n-grams + BF [3,17] mainly use unigram, bigram, trigram, or some manually designed features to do spam review detection. **Behavior Features (BF)** are obtained from papers [3,17].

---

[1] http://nlg3.csie.ntu.edu.tw/m01-corpus.
[2] http://www.bbc.com/news/technology-22166606.
[3] http://shebuti.com/collective-opinion-spam-detection.
[4] https://www.yelp.com/not_recommended_reviews/restaurant_name.

SPEAGLE[+] [20] is a kind of graph-based method, which utilizes clues from all metadata and relational data. The representations of reviews in [20] are combined with linguistic, behavioral, and review graph structure features.

TDSD [23] is a tensor decomposition model to learn the review representation and users' behavior information automatically. They extended 11 interactive relations to embed the reviewers and products jointly. The relation embeddings are concatenated with the review representation for spam detection.

CHMM [12] is the Coupled Hidden Markov Model (HMM) model with two parallel HMMs that incorporate both the reviewers' posting behavior and co-bursting behaviors from other reviewers.

Spam2Vec [15] is a framework to use both content and network information for spam detection collectively. The model learns the spam representations of the node in the review network by leveraging biased random walks.

Deep Learning Methods

CNN-GRNN [21] is the first model designed for spam detection. Convolutional neural network and gated recurrent network are applied on word level and sentence level, respectively to learn the discourse information of reviews.

SWNN [14] consists of two convolutional layers to extract local semantic features from the word and sentence level of reviews. The SWNN utilizes semantic and syntactic features to compute the importance weights of each sentence and incorporate them into the composition of document representation.

ABNN [24] is an attention-based neural network by jointly embedding linguistic and behavioral features for spam detection. The model can learn to distinguish whether each of the review spam is linguistically suspicious or behaviorally suspicious or both.

AEDA [26] is a CNN-based model for incorporating entities and their inherent attributes from various domains into a unified framework.

4.3   Experiment Settings

For fair comparison, we employed the same evaluation metrics and preprocessing procedures used in previous works [3, 20] in the experiments. Specifically, for the Mobile01 dataset, precision (P), recall (R), and F-measure (F_1) are used as evaluation metrics. For YelpChi, YelpNYC and YelpZip dataset, average precision (AP) and area under the curve (AUC) are used as evaluation metrics.

Hyper-parameter Settings. We use all review corpora to train domain specific pre-trained word vectors. The Skip-gram [16] architecture is used and its word dimension is set to 300. The hyperparameters of the FCAN are tuned by grid search on the validation dataset. In our experiments, the size of the convolutional kernel is set to $(3, 4, 5)$ with 100 feature map for each kernel. The dropout rate is set to 0.5. The hyperparameters of the baseline models are set to their default setting. The Adam [11] algorithm is applied to optimize training loss.

4.4 Results and Analysis

The experimental results are given in Tables 2 and 3. And we have the following observations:

Table 2. Experimental results on Mobile01 dataset. The state-of-the-art results have been highlighted by the underline.

Models	Mobile01_FirstPost			Mobile01_Reply		
	P	R	F_1	P	R	F_1
SVM + BoW + BF [3]	70.97	52.88	60.61	25.59	29.61	27.45
TDSD [23]	73.12	54.45	62.42	26.31	30.38	28.20
CHMM [12]	68.51	54.58	60.76	21.14	31.44	25.28
Spam2Vec [15]	68.64	55.35	61.28	26.35	30.59	28.31
CNN-GRNN [21]	63.21	64.42	63.81	23.42	33.43	27.54
SWNN [14]	65.57	57.69	61.38	22.53	35.78	27.65
ABNN [24]	61.21	68.27	64.55	27.13	35.00	30.57
AEDA [26]	68.54	62.39	65.32	28.37	37.11	32.16
FCAN	**78.65**	67.31	**72.54**	**54.22**	**38.43**	**44.98**

(1) Majority of neural network methods have an advantage over SVM-based methods. Compared with tensor decomposition and graph-based methods, neural network methods still show better performances. It demonstrates that the neural network based methods are more useful to capture textual features compared with conventional methods, which is a crucial factor to opinion spam reviews classification.

(2) The way of encoding and utilizing user information in our model is more effective than the way of manually designing behavioral features. Referring to Tables 2 and 3, the performances of spam classification get significant improvement over the state-of-the-art results. In detail, the FCAN outperforms the best baseline models by 7.22%, 12.82% respectively in f1 on the Mobile01 dataset and 3.48%, 6.08%, 6.04% respectively in AUC on the Yelp dataset. This significant improvement shows that fusing the user and text information does help to learn a better user-aware textual representation of reviews.

In conclusion, the experimental results demonstrate that our proposed model with user fusion attention achieves the best performance on all datasets. Moreover, it is easy to extend our approach to different datasets and platforms.

4.5 Ablation Study

To figure out the influence of every module to the performance, we perform a series of ablation studies over the different parts of the model. Specifically, the complete FCAN is treated as the baseline and every component is removed as the following orders:

Table 3. Experimental results on YelpChi, YelpNYC and YelpZip datasets. The state-of-the-art results have been highlighted by the underline.

Models	YelpChi		YelpNYC		YelpZip	
	AP	AUC	AP	AUC	AP	AUC
SpEagle[+]	32.36	78.87	27.57	78.29	35.45	80.40
TDSD [23]	34.68	78.82	36.62	78.86	45.15	81.63
CHMM [12]	35.14	78.68	35.13	78.71	49.56	82.64
Spam2Vec [15]	34.25	78.61	35.04	78.35	46.33	81.21
CNN-GRNN [21]	35.02	78.68	35.47	79.04	48.57	81.87
SWNN [14]	34.13	78.57	34.79	78.57	46.79	81.25
ABNN [24]	34.48	78.53	35.80	78.83	48.19	80.82
AEDA [26]	36.76	79.14	35.13	78.92	48.52	81.32
FCAN	**38.28**	**82.62**	**44.09**	**85.12**	**54.39**	**87.91**

- w/o SUF: The sentence-user fusion module is removed, but the attention module is reserved for aggregating the sentence representation to form the document representation.
- w/o WUF: The word-user fusion module is removed, but the attention module is reserved.
- w/o SUF & WUF: Both the sentence-user and word-user fusion module are removed, and the metadata (u_{meta} in formulation 1) are simply concatenated with the text representation.

Table 4. Ablation study results on the Mobile01 and Yelp datasets.

Model	Mobile01_FirstPost (F_1)	Mobile01_Reply (F_1)	YelpChi (AUC)	YelpNYC (AUC)	YelpZip (AUC)
$FCAN_{base}$	72.54	44.98	82.62	85.12	87.91
w/o SUF	64.25	36.43	79.54	81.26	84.31
w/o WUF	68.44	30.12	80.38	82.38	82.67
w/o SUF & WUF	53.66	24.26	72.74	72.46	74.25

The experimental results are shown in Table 4. Referring to the Table 4, we can observe that both word-user fusion module and sentence-user fusion module contribute to the model performance. Furthermore, removing all fusion modules will significantly affect the classification performance, which shows that the fusion of user information and textual information can help to learn a better user-aware representation of every review.

5   Case Study for Visualization of Fusion Attention

To obtain an intuitive insight into the features selected by the model, we visualize the attention layer to see which features get higher attention weights. Table 5 demonstrates experimental results. The important words and sentences have been colored according to their weights. The deeper the color is, the more important the word bears.

Table 5. Experiment results to explore the features that the FCAN model chosen from reviews. These samples are randomly selected from Yelp Hotel dataset.

Class	Word-User Fusion Attention	Sentence-User Fusion Attention
spam	Nice rooms, good staff, outstanding locations. Within easy walk of several site and shopping. And bus stop right outside for using public transportation to get to those places not so close. Hotel bar and restaurant are slightly above average, prices are typical. Only con is parking. Parking is tight and expensive. ...	Nice rooms, good staff, outstanding locations. Within easy walk of several site and shopping. And bus stop right outside for using public transportation tc get to those places not so close. Hotel bar and restaurant are slightly above average, prices are typical. Only con is parking. Parking is tight and expensive ...
non-spam	Rooms are what you come to expect from a Sheraton. Nothing fancy, but they work. The location was just ok, not really close to anything. View of the river was awesome ...	Rooms are what you come to expect from a Sheraton. Nothing fancy, but they work. The location was just ok, not really close to anything. View of the river was awesome ...

From the table, we can observe that some words or sentences that express extreme emotions have been highlighted. For example, the words, "nice", "outstanding", "absolutely", "one of the best", obtain very high attention scores compared with other words. These words express the users' preferences. At the sentence level, some key sentences that express the reviewers' opinions have been given higher scores, such as "Nice rooms, good staff, outstanding locations.", and "Nothing fancy, but they work". Spam reviews usually contain personal preferences because the spammers want to promote or demote a product. From this aspect, we can intuitively see that the model does learn some features to distinguish spam and non-spam reviews.

6   Conclusion

In this paper, we have presented a novel fusion convolutional attention network for opinion spam detection. The FCAN can learn the representation of reviews and users without manually designed features. Furthermore, we have proposed word-user and sentence-user fusion attention layers to encode user characteristics into review representation at word and sentence level to learn the user-aware review representation. The experiments are conducted on four real-world datasets. Our model have achieved significant improvement over the state-of-the-art models, which demonstrates that the proposed model is effective and promising.

Acknowledgement. We gratefully thank the anonymous reviewers for their insightful comments. This research is supported in part by the Beijing Municipal Science and Technology Project under Grant Z191100007119008 and Z181100002718004, the National Key Research and Development Program of China under Grant 2018YFC0806900 and 2017YFB1010000.

References

1. Anderson, M., Magruder, J.: Learning from the crowd: regression discontinuity estimates of the effects of an online review database. Econ. J. **122**(563), 957–989 (2012)
2. Santosh, K.C., Mukherjee, A.: On the temporal dynamics of opinion spamming: case studies on yelp. In: WWW 2016, pp. 369–379 (2016)
3. Chen, Y., Chen, H.: Opinion spam detection in web forum: a real case study. In: WWW 2015, pp. 173–183 (2015)
4. Collobert, R., Weston, J., Bottou, L., Karlen, M., Kavukcuoglu, K., Kuksa, P.P.: Natural language processing (almost) from scratch. J. Mach. Learn. Res. **12**, 2493–2537 (2011)
5. Feng, S., Banerjee, R., Choi, Y.: Syntactic stylometry for deception detection. In: ACL 2012, pp. 171–175 (2012)
6. Fornaciari, T., Poesio, M.: Identifying fake Amazon reviews as learning from crowds. In: EACL 2014, pp. 279–287 (2014)
7. Hinton, G., Salakhutdinov, R.: Reducing the dimensionality of data with neural networks. Science **313**(5786), 504–507 (2006)
8. Jindal, N., Liu, B.: Opinion spam and analysis. In: WSDM 2008, pp. 219–230 (2008)
9. Kennedy, S., Walsh, N., Sloka, K., McCarren, A., Foster, J.: Fact or factitious? Contextualized opinion spam detection. In: ACL 2019, pp. 344–350 (2019)
10. Kim, Y.: Convolutional neural networks for sentence classification. In: EMNLP 2014, pp. 1746–1751 (2014)
11. Kingma, D.P., Ba, J.: Adam: a method for stochastic optimization (2015)
12. Li, H., et al.: Bimodal distribution and co-bursting in review spam detection. In: WWW 2017, pp. 1063–1072 (2017)
13. Li, J., Ott, M., Cardie, C., Hovy, E.H.: Towards a general rule for identifying deceptive opinion spam. In: ACL 2014, pp. 1566–1576 (2014)
14. Li, L., Qin, B., Ren, W., Liu, T.: Document representation and feature combination for deceptive spam review detection. Neurocomputing **254**, 33–41 (2017)
15. Maity, S.K., Santosh, K.C., Mukherjee, A.: Spam2Vec: learning biased embeddings for spam detection in twitter. In: WWW 2018, pp. 63–64 (2018)
16. Mikolov, T., Sutskever, I., Chen, K., Corrado, G.S., Dean, J.: Distributed representations of words and phrases and their compositionality. In: NeurIPS 2013, pp. 3111–3119 (2013)
17. Mukherjee, A., Venkataraman, V., Liu, B., Glance, N.S.: What yelp fake review filter might be doing? In: ICWSM 2013 (2013)
18. Mukherjee, A., Venkataraman, V.V., Liu, B., Glance, N.S.: Fake review detection: classification and analysis of real and pseudo reviews. Technical report UIC-CS-2013-03, University of Illinois at Chicago (2013)
19. Ott, M., Choi, Y., Cardie, C., Hancock, J.T.: Finding deceptive opinion spam by any stretch of the imagination. In: ACL 2011, pp. 309–319 (2011)

20. Rayana, S., Akoglu, L.: Collective opinion spam detection: bridging review networks and metadata. In: SIGKDD 2015, pp. 985–994 (2015)
21. Ren, Y., Zhang, Y.: Deceptive opinion spam detection using neural network. In: COLING 2016, pp. 140–150 (2016)
22. Sandulescu, V., Ester, M.: Detecting singleton review spammers using semantic similarity. In: WWW 2015, pp. 971–976 (2015)
23. Wang, X., Liu, K., He, S., Zhao, J.: Learning to represent review with tensor decomposition for spam detection. In: EMNLP 2016, pp. 866–875 (2016)
24. Wang, X., Liu, K., Zhao, J.: Detecting deceptive review spam via attention-based neural networks. In: NLPCC 2017, pp. 866–876 (2017)
25. Ye, J., Kumar, S., Akoglu, L.: Temporal opinion spam detection by multivariate indicative signals. In: ICWSM 2016, pp. 743–746 (2016)
26. You, Z., Qian, T., Liu, B.: An attribute enhanced domain adaptive model for cold-start spam review detection. In: COLING 2018, pp. 1884–1895 (2018)
27. Yuan, C., Ma, Q., Zhou, W., Han, J., Hu, S.: Jointly embedding the local and global relations of heterogeneous graph for rumor detection. In: IEEE ICDM 2019 (2019)
28. Yuan, C., Zhou, W., Ma, Q., Lv, S., Han, J., Hu, S.: Learning review representations from user and product level information for spam detection. In: IEEE ICDM 2019 (2019)

Deep CNN Based System for Detection and Evaluation of RoIs in Flooded Areas

Dan Popescu(✉), Loretta Ichim, and George Cioroiu

Faculty of Automatic Control and Computers,
University Politehnica of Bucharest, Bucharest, Romania
{dan.popescu,loretta.ichim}@upb.ro, gcioroiu94@gmail.com

Abstract. The flood detection and damage evaluation in precision agriculture are of great interest nowadays. The paper proposes the simultaneously detection and evaluation of small regions affected by non-severe flooding and, also, small regions with vegetation in county areas. The images are taken by a UAV team in a photogrammetry mission. As novelty, the paper proposes and compares four cheap, real time, and accurate methods based on convolutional neural networks (Full LeNet, Half LeNet, Pixel YOLO, and Decision YOLO) to segment these regions of interest. These methods are compared with classical methods of region segmentation based on extracting and comparing features from images. The real masks are manually created by operators using information of the color components R, G, B, H. A set of 2000 images were used for the learning phase and another set of 1400 image were used for method validation. The method presents the advantages of accuracy and time processing (especially in the testing phase).

Keywords: Aerial images · Flood segmentation · Vegetation segmentation · Convolutional neural network · Comparing networks

1 Introduction

Natural disasters, especially the flooding generate important damages in agriculture. Even if the flooding is not severe, the agriculture production can be affected. In the case of moderate flooding, there are several ways, based on image processing, to detect and evaluate separately the mixed flooding and vegetation (crop) areas: satellite [1], aircraft, ground cameras [2], and UAVs (unmanned aerial vehicles) [3]. The cheapest and most accurate solution to obtain such information concerning the affected areas is the UAV surveillance [4, 5]. To this end, one or more UAVs having corresponding designed trajectories acquire successive and partial overlapped images for creating an ortophotoplan. Then, this is decomposed in images of dimension M × N pixels to be evaluated for regions' segmentation. Depending of high flight and camera performances, a UAV provides large area coverage over a relatively short period (120 ha/hour), with a ground resolution of centimetres [4]. For image processing, although there were numerous approaches, the artificial neural networks offer very good results concerning the accuracy and time in image classification [5].

© Springer Nature Switzerland AG 2019
T. Gedeon et al. (Eds.): ICONIP 2019, LNCS 11953, pp. 236–248, 2019.
https://doi.org/10.1007/978-3-030-36708-4_20

In parallel with the development of image classification by features, image classification by convolutional neural networks was used. The first such a network consisting of two convolution layers, followed by three completely connected layers, is introduced in [6]. This network was called LeNet and supported all classic convolution networks. Next, starting from LeNet and increasing the number of convolutional and fully connected layers, AlexNet [7] was obtained. Then, adding more convolutional routes to GoogLeNet was developed [8], and, also, adding connections from the lower to the upper layers (the process named skip connections) ResNet was obtained [9].

The first fully convoluted network used to detect objects in images is YOLO [10]. In its fast version, the network used only 5 layers of MaxPooling, making predictions at 150 frames per second for patches of 32×32 pixels, compared to 30 frames per second as far as the real-time networks were at that moment and, also, having better accuracy than these. The higher results are because the YOLO network has more parameters. This neural network was recently developed (YOLOv3) [11] adding UpSample layers to make predictions at other scales (32×32, 16×16, 8×8 pixels).

As mentioned above, the paper goal is addressed by the detection of floods and vegetation in aerial images captured by UAV. According to [12], monitoring of flooded areas is important to assess damages and make appropriate post-disaster decisions. Thus, to address this issue, three important classes were chosen: the flood (F), the vegetation (V), and the rest (R) classes (non-flood and non-vegetation). The authors searched for multiple simple solutions of building neural networks based on LeNet and YOLO. The experimental results on agriculture in flooded zone show that the neural network architectures combined with UAV surveillance offer the best results.

2 Methodology

In a previous authors work [13] a back propagation neural network (NN) having a single neuron (perceptron) is presented (Fig. 1).

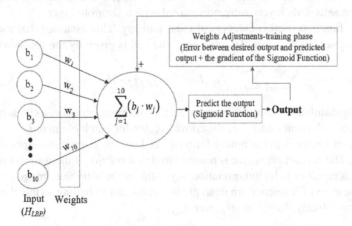

Fig. 1. General architecture of the perceptron type NN [13].

The input is bins of the LBP histogram on H component (HSV color space) of each analyzed patch (1). The output layer is dot product between the histogram vector H_{LBP} and the weight vector w (2).

$$H_{LBP} = [b_1, \ldots, b_{10}] \tag{1}$$

$$w = [w_1, \ldots, w_{10}] \tag{2}$$

The weight adjustment (learning phase) is a back-propagation process. To classify the region of interest from UAV images these are first decomposed in non-overlapped patches and second the LBP histograms on H component are calculated.

Although the method is simple and gives good results of accuracy, the classification time in the testing phase is still high. This is because the evaluation of the LBP histogram is necessary for each patch.

In this paper four CNNs were proposed. The first two derived from the classical ones (LeNet [6]) and the last two come from the new ones (YOLO [10]). The first LeNet, named Full LeNet (Fig. 2a), has 31×31 pixels neighborhoods as input and uses 5 Convolutional/MaxPooling layer combinations. Finally, the layer becomes 1×1. The second LeNet, named Half LeNet (Fig. 2b), has also 31×31 pixels neighborhoods as input and uses only 3 Convolutional/MaxPooling layer combinations. Finally, the layer becomes 4×4. The neurons number was doubled from a layer to the next.

Derived from YOLO concept two such architectures are proposed: Pixel YOLO (Fig. 3) and Decision YOLO (Fig. 4). The first operate are pixel level and the second operates at global level.

Regardless of the type of network, convolutional layers have been normalized by a BatchNorm layer (batch normalization). This was chosen because in [14] it is showed that the MaxNorm restriction applied in convolutional layers leads to better training results, but less test results than BatchNorm. In the feature extraction part, all convolutional layers were enabled with ReLU. The layers from decision part were activated with LeakyReLU, whether they were fully connected or convolutional layers. When the decision network was fully connected, its layers were normalized with a Dropout layer.

The cost function used is categorical cross-entropy. This assumed that each object in the training set belongs to a class and only one and is given by the formula (3):

$$Loss = -\frac{1}{N} \sum_{i=1}^{N} \sum_{j=1}^{C} y_{i,j} log(Nis\hat{y}_{i,j}) + (1 - y_{i,j})log(1 - \hat{y}_{i,j}) \tag{3}$$

where N is the number of examples from batch, C is the number of classes, y_i is prediction vector for batch element i and $\hat{y}_i$ is the correct vector for batch element i.

The correct vector is in the binary form (it has 1 for the correct class position and 0 for the rest). The prediction vector is passed through a softmax function, so that its sum of elements is equal to 1. Its interpretation is $y_{i,j}$ the probability that image i belongs to class j. In the case of inference, an example is considered to belong to the class against which it is most likely: $label_i = argmax \ y_{i,j}$.

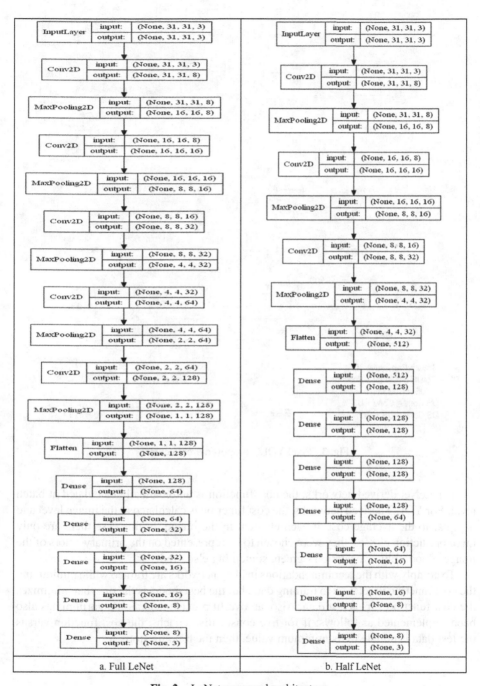

Fig. 2. LeNet proposed architecture.

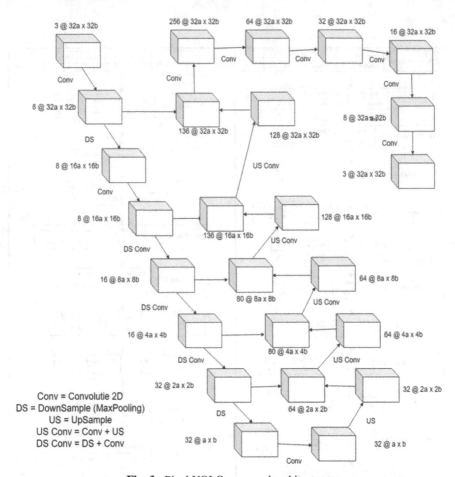

Fig. 3. Pixel YOLO proposed architecture.

For LeNet derived networks, the cost function is automatically calculated at batch level. For YOLO derived networks, the cost function is calculated at the image level and is equal to the average cost of each element in the image. In this case there are only three prediction classes, they were chosen to be represented on the primary colors of the image: flood - blue, vegetation - green, something else - red.

To comply with the recommendations in [15], networks are trained while minimizing the cost function in relation to training data, but the best model is the one that minimizes the cost function versus test data. Also, an overfit process detection algorithm has also been implemented as follows: if for five consecutive epochs, the cost function versus the test data is double to its minimum value, then the training stops.

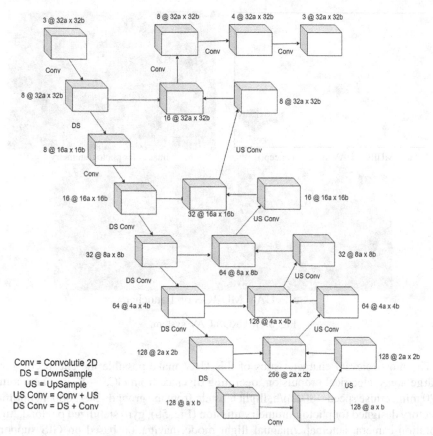

Fig. 4. Decision YOLO proposed architecture.

3   Experimental Results

The images for the experimental results were taken with a regular camera (24 megapixels, 5 images/s) which was mounted in the payload of a fixed-wing type UAV [16], MUROS (Fig. 5). The MUROS system consists in a series of modules connected to a common control bus. Each module is equipped with a Central Processor Unit, a Power Supply Unit and a Controller Area Network Adaptor. There are four basic modules (Fig. 5a): aerial platform (UAV), ground control station (GCS), ground data terminal (GDT) and Launcher (Fig. 5c).

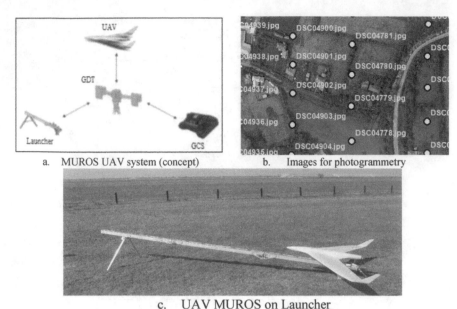

| a. MUROS UAV system (concept) | b. Images for photogrammetry |

c. UAV MUROS on Launcher

Fig. 5. MUROS UAV system.

The most relevant characteristics of this UAV make possible the cheap coverage of large areas: electrical propulsion, operating distance from GCS – 15 km, autonomy – 120 min., cruise speed – 80 km/h, flight altitude from the ground - 50–2000 m, optimal trajectory designed for photogrammetry mission (Fig. 5b), gyro stabilized payload, high resolution camera, automatic/manual flight mode, navigation based on GIS support, local and remote (via internet) control, and starting/landing with launcher/parachute.

From the ortophotoplan 4096 × 4096 pixels images are cropped, for example, Im 1, . . . , Im 15 (Fig. 6). Two approaches were used: global image analysis (Fig. 6) and patch analysis (Fig. 7).

For the testing phase, in the case of LeNet-derived networks, the same procedure as the learning phase is used. The resulting image thus has 30 pixels less for each dimension (required for borders). For YOLO-derived networks, the inference is made on discrete patches of 128 × 128 pixels, 256 × 256 or across the image.

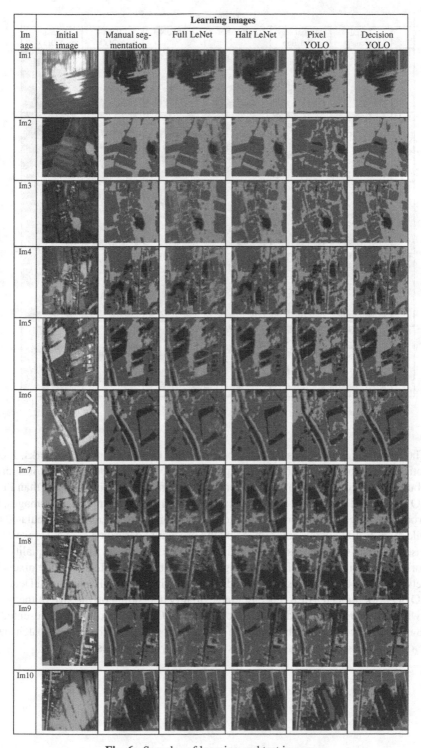

Fig. 6. Samples of learning and test images.

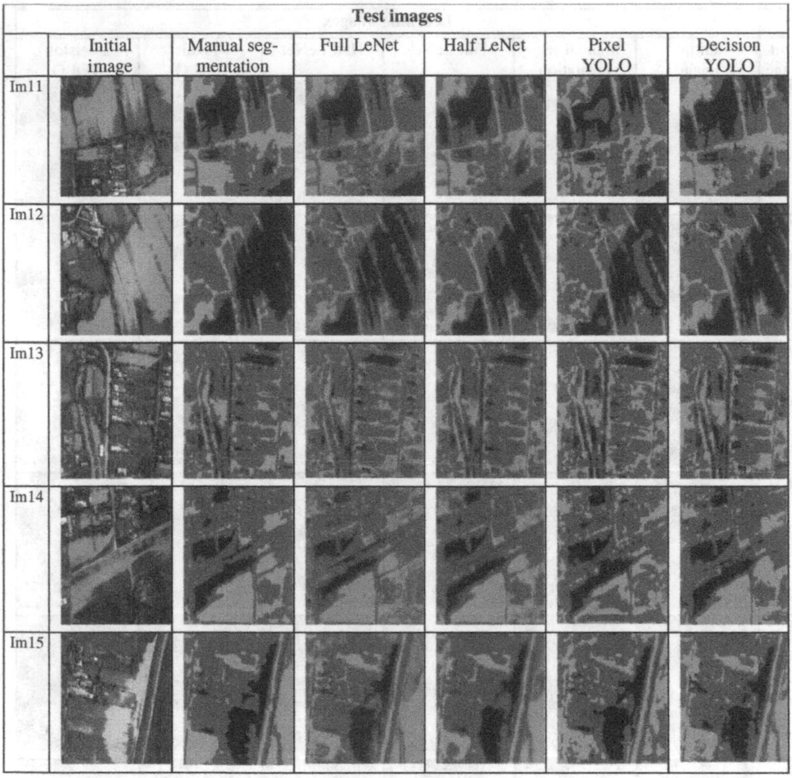

Fig. 6. continued

The following table shows the main performance indicators of the networks. It can be noticed that not only the number of parameters contributes to the drive/inference time but also the complexity of the networks (Decision YOLO being simpler than Pixel YOLO). The length of a drive time is calculated for all the above-mentioned images, by the procedure specific to each network, and the duration of the inference is calculated for a single 4096×4096 pixels color image by the procedure described above. However, in the case of Pixel YOLO, it was observed that the patch size affects the image quality, the network still missing the pixels on the edge. This is due to the affecting edge pixels by the network convolution layers which tend to keep the image size. Even though Decision YOLO network noticed a difference in image quality depending on the size of the patch with which inference was made, this is not as strong. One such example is presented in Fig. 8 in which a comparison between the segmentation made with different patch sizes (128×128, 256×256 pixels, and respectively, the whole images).

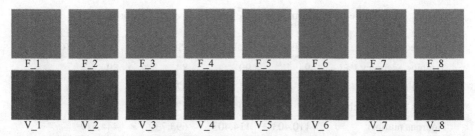

Fig. 7. Representative flood patches (F-up) and vegetation patches (V-down) for training phase.

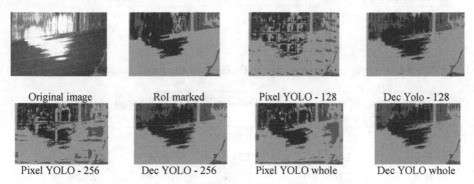

Fig. 8. The influence of the patch size in the segmentation results.

According to the proposed neural networks for flooded and vegetation detection in agriculture areas, the accuracy is the most useful indicator for performance evaluation (4):

$$ACC = \frac{T_p + T_n}{T_p + T_n + F_n + F_p} \tag{4}$$

where T_p, T_n, F_p, and F_n represent true positive, true negative, false positive, and, respectively, false negative cases.

In Table 1 some performances (accuracy, inference time, training epoch time) and some parameters (epoch overfit number and neurons number) are presented for the analyzed CNNs. In this case, Decision YOLO and Half LeNet give the best results for the classification accuracy. Also, the Decision YOLO and Pixel YOLO gives the best results for the training and operating time. Considering the flood (Table 2) and vegetation (Table 3) occupancy rates (comparing with the manual segmentation), the best results are given by Decision YOLO.

Table 1. Performances of the proposed neural networks

Architecture	Full LeNet	Half LeNet	Pixel YOLO	Decision YOLO
Training accuracy [%]	94	90	84	89
Testing accuracy [%]	89	88	82	89
Epochs overfit number	80	60	120	380
Neurons number	110,403	114,403	693,739	444,619
Training epoch time [s]	900	900	90	30
Inference time [s]	145	135	6	2

Table 2. Comparison between the flood occupancy rate for different CNNs used

Tested image	Manual segmentation	Decision YOLO	Half LeNet	Percepton
Im1	22.71%	19.16%	15.29%	14.02%
Im2	2.4%	2.34%	1.52%	2.42%
Im3	2.16%	2.13%	1.4%	2.12%
Im4	9.51%	8.99%	4.76%	3.77%
Im5	16.68%	15.29%	7.65%	8.24%
Im6	13.96%	12.86%	5.94%	6.38%
Im7	23.7%	20.84%	13.66%	13.36%
Im8	48.2%	42.63%	6.61%	32.58%
Im9	23.35%	19.87%	25.35%	14.17%
Im10	38.17%	36.2%	14.38%	30.69%
Im11	24.94%	25.9%	24.39%	17.39%
Im12	38.52%	35.6%	24.39%	28.47%
Im13	6.5%	7.54%	0.96%	4.18%
Im14	10.29%	10.68%	3.85%	3.12%
Im15	11.99%	11.34%	7.98%	5.48%

Table 3. Comparison between the vegetation occupancy rate for different CNNs used

Tested image	Manual segmentation	Decision YOLO	Half LeNet	Percepton
Im1	57.97%	54.53%	49.82%	61.73%
Im2	45.27%	47.16%	36.31%	88.06%
Im3	33.7%	35.62%	24.76%	91.01%
Im4	20.29%	24.62%	11.47%	80.4%
Im5	16.65%	18.64%	13.81%	67.75%
Im6	9.22%	9.92%	4.55%	67.55%
Im7	13.75%	16.48%	8.59%	69.12%
Im8	10%	12.42%	4.38%	48.45%
Im9	5.18%	7.35%	3.18%	71.34%
Im10	7.61%	9.32%	3.07%	53.07%
Im11	19.09%	19.72%	10.71%	61.74%
Im12	8.71%	10.05%	4.74%	53.32%
Im13	14.92%	17.82%	7.14%	86.96%
Im14	22.08%	23.76%	13.14%	85.72%
Im15	33.04%	31.19%	22.69%	78.33%

4 Conclusion

The proposed method differentiates the flooded vegetation areas from aerial images taken by UAV. The paper contribution is a proposal of some CNNs for multiple class image recognition and the comparison with other methods with the same tasks. The conclusions based on performances evaluation like accuracy and time are the Decision YOLO proposed CNN offers the best results.

Acknowledgements. The work has been funded by project MUWI 1224/2018 (NETIO).

References

1. Yulianto, F., Sofan, P., Zubaidah, A., Sukowati, K.A.D., Pasaribu, J.M., Khomarudin, M.R.: Detecting areas affected by flood using multi-temporal ALOS PALSAR remotely sensed data in Karawang, West Java, Indonesia. Nat. Hazards **77**, 959–985 (2015)
2. Pentari, A., Moirogiorgou, K., Livanos, G., Iliopoulou, D., Zervakis, M.: Feature analysis on river flow video data for floating tracers detection. In: Proceedings of the IEEE International Conference on Imaging Systems and Techniques (IST), Santorini Island, Greece, 14–17 October, pp. 287–292 (2014)
3. Lee, J.N., Kwak, K.C.: A trends analysis of image processing in unmanned aerial vehicle. Int. J. Comput. Inf. Sci. Eng. **8**, 261–264 (2014)

4. Popescu, D., Ichim, L., Stoican, F.: Unmanned aerial vehicle systems for remote estimation of flooded areas based on complex image processing. Sensors **17**(3), 446 (2017)
5. Ju, C., Bibaut, A., Laan, M.V.D.: The relative performance of ensemble methods with deep convolutional neural networks for image classification. J. Appl. Stat. **45**(15), 1–20 (2018)
6. Lecun, Y., Bottou, L., Bengio, Y., Haffner, P.: Gradient-based learning applied to document recognition. Proc. IEEE **86**(11), 2278–2324 (1998)
7. Krizhevsky, A., Sutskever, I., Hinton, G.E.: ImageNet classification with deep convolutional neural networks. Commun. ACM **60**(6), 84–90 (2017)
8. Szegedy, C., et al.: Going deeper with convolutions. In: IEEE Conference on Computer Vision and Pattern Recognition (CVPR), Boston, MA, USA, 7–12 June, pp. 1–9 (2015)
9. He, K., Zhang, X., Ren, S., Sun, J.: Deep residual learning for image recognition. In: IEEE Conference on Computer Vision and Pattern Recognition (CVPR), Las Vegas, NV, USA, 27–30 June, pp. 770–778 (2016)
10. Redmon, J., Divvala, S., Girshick, R., Farhadi, A.: You only look once: unified, real-time object detection. In: IEEE Conference on Computer Vision and Pattern Recognition (CVPR), Las Vegas, NV, USA, 27–30 June, pp. 779–788 (2016)
11. Redmon, J., Farhadi, A.: Yolov3: an incremental improvement. arXiv:1804.02767, pp. 1–6 (2018)
12. Popescu, D., Ichim, L., Caramihale, T.: Flood areas detection based on UAV surveillance system. In: 19th International Conference on System Theory, Control and Computing (ICSTCC), pp. 753–758 (2015)
13. Cirneanu, A.L., Popescu, D., Ichim L.: CNN based on LBP for evaluating natural disasters. In: 15th International Conference on Control, Automation, Robotics and Vision (ICARCV), Marina Bay Sands Expo and Convention Centre, Singapore, 18–21 November, pp. 568–573 (2018)
14. Gitman, I., Ginsburg, B.: Comparison of batch normalization and weight normalization algorithms for the large-scale image classification. arXiv:1709.08145, pp. 1–9 (2017)
15. Dehghani, M., Severyn, A., Rothe, S., Kamps, J.: Avoiding your teacher's mistakes: training neural networks with controlled weak supervision. arXiv:1711.00313, pp. 1–13 (2017)
16. MUROS. https://trimis.ec.europa.eu/project/multisensory-robotic-system-aerial-monitoring-critical-infrastructure-systems

Deep Neural Networks

Improving Deep Learning by Regularized Scale-Free MSE of Representations

Xufang Luo[1], Mingyang Yi[2,3], and Yunhong Wang[1]($\boxtimes$)

[1] Beijing Advanced Innovation Center for Big Data and Brain Computing,
Beihang University, Beijing, China
{luoxufang,yhwang}@buaa.edu.cn
[2] University of Chinese Academy of Sciences, Beijing, China
yimingyang17@mails.ucas.edu.cn
[3] Academy of Mathematics and Systems Science, Beijing, China

Abstract. Nowadays, the research for learning representations with deep neural networks (DNNs) is attracting more and more attentions. In general, most of studies focus on designing principles for learning representations when the learning model is stochastic, which is not widely used for all kinds of machine learning tasks. In this paper, we try to seek a principle to learn efficient representations for deterministic DNNs. Considering that the last DNN layer is often a linear mapping, we utilize the generalized linear model (GLM) theory to design a principle for learning representations. First, via choosing proper link functions, we build a connection between representation learning and the optimization of the last linear layer. Next, we propose a representation learning principle, *scale-free mean square error* (scale-free MSE), by leveraging the MSE analysis in the GLM. Here, we find that representations with a smaller scale-free MSE can lead to a better estimation of the parameters. Then, we further propose an algorithm to learn representations with a small scale-free MSE. Here, a regularization term is employed to make the scale-free MSE get small. Finally, we test our algorithm with typical DNN models in both supervised and unsupervised learning tasks. The experiment results show that our proposed algorithm is suitable to learn efficient representations over various of experiment settings.

Keywords: Representation learning · Deep neural networks · Generalized linear model

1 Introduction

Learning representations for raw signals always plays a crucial role in machine learning algorithms, and efficient representation learning methods can capture explanatory factors behind the raw data in downstream tasks. Nowadays, although deep neural networks (DNNs) are successfully applied in many fields, such as computer vision and nature language processing, representation learning methods still serve as the core of DNNs [1].

© Springer Nature Switzerland AG 2019
T. Gedeon et al. (Eds.): ICONIP 2019, LNCS 11953, pp. 251–263, 2019.
https://doi.org/10.1007/978-3-030-36708-4_21

Generally, there are two lines of work for learning representations. One is based on designing principles for more informative representations. For example, disentanglement and Infomax are two widely used principles. In such cases, the principles are mostly designed via Bayesian settings, and here the feature extractors are mostly stochastic functions [2–4]. The other is based on analyzing and explaining the learned representations. For example, Li *et al.* studied whether different neural networks could learn the same representations [5]. In [6], a method called Vector Canonical Correlation Analysis (SVCCA) was proposed to compare two representations. However, such works are always lack of efficient analysis-based algorithms. In this paper, we aim to seek a principle for learning representations using deterministic DNNs, which can improve the performance for many machine learning tasks.

Intuitively, DNNs can be regarded as a representation extractor followed by a linear model. For example, in many DNN models, such as VGG, PlainNet and ResNet [7,8], the last DNN layer is always a linear mapping [8]. Thus, we can leverage the statistical theory for linear models or generalized linear models (GLM), to design a principle for learning representations.

To make the intuition concrete, first, we prove that learning the last linear DNN layer with a mean square loss or a cross entropy (CE) loss, can be modeled with GLM. Hence, the optimal point for optimizing the last linear DNN layer, can be equivalent to a maximum likelihood estimation (MLE) for a GLM. Next, we analyze the mean square error (MSE) of the parameter in the last DNN layer and derive the explicit formulation of the MSE. The formulation shows that the MSE is related to the representation matrix. Then, based on the scale-invariant property of linear mapping, we propose a novel criterion called *scale-free MSE*, to evaluate the representation matrix. Meanwhile, we further propose a novel representation learning algorithm based on the proposed criterion. Specifically, we employ a regularization term which can make the *scale-free MSE* get small gradually during the iterative process. Finally, we conduct experiments on both supervised and unsupervised learning tasks on CIFAR-10 dataset and CIFAR-100 dataset, and we utilize the proposed regularizer to train DNN models. As a result, the improvements on accuracy demonstrate that the learned representations are efficiently enhanced by adding the proposed regularizer.

2   Background

We firstly introduce some notations used in this paper. We use a capital letter in bold to denote a random vector, and the corresponding lowercase letter to represent the vector sampled from the distribution of the random vector. For example, y is a vector sampled from the distribution of Y.

We will then briefly introduce the GLM theory in this section, we present the definition of exponential dispersion distribution [9] in Definition 1.

Definition 1 (Exponential Dispersion Distribution). *We say that Y has an exponential dispersion distribution, if it has a density function as*

$$f_Y(y|\theta) = \exp\left(\frac{\theta^T y - b(\theta)}{\phi} + c(y, \phi)\right), \tag{1}$$

where $b(\cdot)$ and $c(\cdot, \cdot)$ are deterministic functions, and θ and ϕ represent the natural parameter vector and the dispersion parameter, respectively.

In the GLM theory, since that many general distributions belong to exponential family, such as normal distribution and polynomial distribution, we can assume that the response variable Y is an exponential dispersion variable. Thus, according to Definition 1, we can obtain the mean and the variance of a random vector Y as follows:

$$E(Y|\theta) = \nabla b(\theta), \; Var(Y|\theta) = \phi \cdot H(\theta), \tag{2}$$

where $H(\cdot)$ is the Hessian matrix of function $b(\cdot)$.

The GLM theory can connect the response variable Y and the explanatory variable X, via a smooth enough and strictly monotonic function $h : \mathbb{R}^M \to \mathbb{R}^M$ (M is the dimension of y). Then we assume that

$$E(Y_i|X = x) = h(x^T \beta_i^*), \qquad i = 1, \cdots M,$$

where β^* is the ground-truth parameter.

According to the smooth and monotonic properties of function h, there is an inverse function $g(\cdot) : \mathbb{R}^M \to \mathbb{R}^M$, called *link function*, and thus, we can see that the connection between the explanatory variable and the response variable can be built by

$$X\beta^* = g(\mathbf{E}(Y|X = x)) = g(\nabla b(\theta)), \tag{3}$$

where X is $\text{diag}(x^T, \cdots, x^T)$, and $\mu(\theta)$ is used to denote $\nabla b(\theta)$. Note that there is a special case that $\mu(\theta) = \nabla b(\theta)$ may have an inverse function, i.e., $g = \mu^{-1}$, and we can see $X\beta^* = \mu^{-1}(\mu(\theta)) = \theta$. Here, we call such $g(\cdot)$ as a *canonical link function*.

According to Eqs. (1), (2) and (3), we can calculate the MLE of β^* as follows:

$$\hat{\beta}_N = \arg\max_\beta \sum_{i=1}^N y_i^T \mu^{-1}(h(X_i\beta)) - b(\mu^{-1}(h(X_i\beta)) \tag{4}$$

Here, $\{X_i, y_i\}_{i=1}^N$ are observations. Specifically, y_i and X_i ($i = 1, \cdots, N$) represent the response variable and its corresponding explanatory variable, respectively, and N is the number of observations. For example, in the classical least square regression problem, when the response variable Y is with only one dimension, $\hat{\beta}_N = (X^T X)^{-1} X y$. Thus, we can derive the MLE of β^* for the given observations.

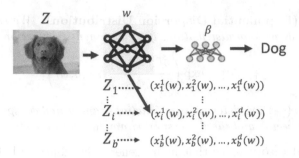

Fig. 1. A neural network extract representations $X(w)$ with last linear layer.

3   A Representation Learning Framework via GLM

In this section, we will build the connection between representation learning and GLM. First, we prove that the learning problem of the last linear DNN layer is a *β-optimization problem*, and such problem can be modeled into a GLM framework. Then, we propose a criterion of representations, i.e., scale-free MSE, under the GLM theory. Finally, we deliver an explicit formulation for the scale-free MSE.

3.1   A Model for β-Optimization Problem

A deep learning model can be divided into two main parts, in which the previous DNN layers are used to extract information from raw signals, and the last DNN layer is often a linear mapping. Hence, we can treat them as learning representations and generalized linear regression (GLR), respectively.

Learning Representations. For a DNN, we can define its representations in Definition 2.

Definition 2 (Representation). *Given an L-layered DNN whose last layer is a linear mapping, the input of the last layer can be called as the representation of input data z.*

As shown in Fig. 1, suppose that we have training samples $\{z_i, y_i\}_{i=1}^N$, where z_i is the raw input and y_i is the label. For an L-layered DNN, the first $L-1$ layer can be regarded as an extractor $h(\cdot; w)$ parameterized by w. Here, $h(\cdot; w)$ maps the raw input z_i to its representation $h(z_i; w)$. For simplicity, we use $x_i(w)$ to denote the representation of z_i, and $x_i(w)$ is fed into the last layer parameterized by β. Thus, the deep learning problem can be written as

$$\min_{w,\beta} \sum_{i=1}^N l(x_i(w), y_i; \beta),$$

where l stands for the loss function. So given the representations $x_i(w)$, the forementioned problem can degenerate into an optimization problem object to β, and such problem is so-called as a β-optimization problem.

GLR. For given representations $\{x_i(w)\}$, a β-optimization problem is equivalent to a GLR problem, and the optimal object has the same formulation with Eq. (4). We next show that a family of β-optimization problem can be concluded into the framework of GLM.

Proposition 1. *A β-optimization problem with a mean square loss or a CE loss, can be concluded into a framework of GLM.*

Proof: On the one hand, for a mean square loss, the $b(\theta)$ of a response variable y can be set by $b(\theta) = \frac{1}{2}\|\theta\|^2$, and the link function can be set as a canonical function. Thus, the β-optimization problem has the same formulation with Eq. (4). On the other hand, for a the CE loss, the $b(\theta)$ of a response variable Y can be set by $b(\theta) = \log \sum_{j=1}^{M} \exp(\theta(j))$, and we can get the conclusion again via setting the canonical function.

3.2   Scale-Free MSE of Representations

MSE. In general, the error between estimation $\hat{\beta}_N$ (i.e., the solution of the β-optimization problem) and ground truth β^*, can influence the performance of a DNN model. Meanwhile, MSE $E(\|\hat{\beta}_N - \beta^*\|^2)$ is a criterion to estimation $\hat{\beta}_N$, and the connection between the β-optimization problem and the GLR can give an explicit formulation for MSE. We next discuss how to estimate $E(\|\hat{\beta}_N - \beta^*\|^2)$ in Lemma 1, which can be derived from Theorem 4.18 in [10].

Lemma 1. *In some standard regularity conditions (described in Theorem 4.18 in [10]) of the density function, i.e., Eq. (1), we have*

$$E(\|\hat{\beta}_N - \beta^*\|^2) = \|E(\hat{\beta}_N - \beta^*)\|^2 + tr(Var(\hat{\beta}_N)) \to tr\left(F(\beta^*)^{-1}\right),$$

where $F(\beta^*)$ is the Fisher matrix of ground truth β^*.

Scale-Free MSE. For a β-optimization problem, ground truth β^* is varied corresponding to the representation distribution in the training process. For example, as for representations X and aX $(a \neq 0)$ corresponding to ground truth β^* and $\frac{1}{a}\beta^*$, respectively, they have exactly same performance, but the MSE corresponding to aX is $\frac{1}{a}$ of the one corresponding to X. Such example implies that the MSE can be altered while the final performance does not change. Thus, such variation of representations promote us to come up with a standardized error as a criterion for representations. We can then give a definition for such standardized error (i.e., scale-free MSE) in Definition 3.

Definition 3 (Scale-free MSE). *For the specific ground truth β^* in a GLM, $\frac{tr\left(F(\beta^*(X(w)))^{-1}\right)}{\|\beta^*(X(w))\|}$ is defined as a scale-free MSE of the estimation $\hat{\beta}_N$.*

From Definition 3, we can standardize an MSE by dividing norm $\|\beta^*(X(w))\|$. For simplicity, we omit $X(w)$ in the following context. And then, the scale-free MSE can be decided by the following Fisher matrix:

$$F(\beta)_{i,j} = -E\left(\frac{\partial^2 l(x(w), y; \beta)}{\partial\beta_i\partial\beta_j}\right) = E\left[\left(\frac{\partial l(x(w), y; \beta)}{\partial\beta_i} \cdot \frac{\partial l(x(w), y; \beta)}{\partial\beta_j}\right)\right]$$

Here, $l(\cdot)$ is a log-likelihood function. Now, we can deliver an explicit expression of Fisher matrix $F(\beta)$ for a GLM, and a similar result can refer to Section 4.2 in [9].

Proposition 2. *Fisher matrix $F(\beta)$ of β in Lemma 1 is*

$$\sum_{i=1}^{N} X_i^T W_i(\beta) X_i,$$

where $W_i = \frac{\partial h(X_i\beta)}{\partial X_i\beta} Var(y_i|X_i)^{-1}\frac{\partial h(X_i\beta)^T}{\partial X_i\beta}$.

Corollary 1. *For mean square loss, we have*

$$F(\beta) = \phi \cdot diag\left(\sum_{i=1}^{N} x_i x_i^T, \cdots, \sum_{i=1}^{N} x_i x_i^T\right)^{-1}$$

where the diag operator represents that the N matrices are listed diagonally in a large matrix, and other elements are 0.

For CE loss, we have $F(\beta)$ consists of $M \times M$ blocks of size $P \times P$ (P is the dimension of x_i), and each block perform as

$$\frac{\partial^2}{\partial\beta_u\partial\beta_v^T} \sum_{i=1}^{N} \log f(\boldsymbol{y}_i|x_i, \beta)$$

$$= \sum_{i=1}^{N} x_i \frac{\exp x_i^T \beta_u}{\sum_{j=1}^{N} \exp(x_i^T\beta_j)} \frac{\exp x_i^T \beta_v}{\sum_{j=1}^{N} \exp(x_i^T\beta_j)} x_i^T \quad if \ u \neq v,$$

$$\frac{\partial^2}{\partial\beta_u\partial\beta_u^T} \sum_{i=1}^{N} \log f(\boldsymbol{y}_i|x_i, \beta)$$

$$= \sum_{i=1}^{N} x_i \frac{\exp x_i^T \beta_u}{\sum_{j=1}^{N} \exp(x_i^T\beta_j)}\left(1 - \frac{\exp x_i^T \beta_u}{\sum_{j=1}^{N} \exp(x_i^T\beta_j)}\right) x_i^T \quad if \ u = v.$$

Here, β_i is the i-th block of parameter β.

This corollary ensure that we can compute the Fisher matrix for a β-optimization problem with a mean square loss or a CE loss, and it is also convenient to calculate the scale-free MSE using Fisher matrix.

3.3 Intuitively Explanation of Scale-Free MSE

As forementioned, the scale-free MSE under GLM framework can be decided by $F(\beta)$. Due to Proposition 2, we see that $F(\beta)$ can be rewritten into a matrix form as

$$
\begin{aligned}
X^T W X &= (X_1, \cdots, X_N) \cdot \mathrm{diag}(W_1, \cdots, W_N) \cdot (X_1, \cdots, X_N)^T \\
&= \left(W^{\frac{1}{2}} X \right)^T \cdot \left(W^{\frac{1}{2}} X \right)
\end{aligned}
$$

Here, we use a relation defined as

$$
W^{\frac{1}{2}} = \mathrm{diag}\left(Var(y_1)^{-\frac{1}{2}}, \cdots, Var(y_N)^{-\frac{1}{2}} \right) \cdot \mathrm{diag}\left(\frac{\partial h^T(X_1\beta)}{\partial X_1\beta}, \cdots, \frac{\partial h^T(X_N\beta)}{\partial X_N\beta} \right)
$$

Then, we have

$$
\mathrm{tr}(F(\beta)^{-1}) = \sum_{j=1}^{M \cdot P} \frac{1}{\sigma_j}, \tag{5}
$$

where σ_j is the j-th eigenvalue of matrix $X^T W X$. Specifically, if matrix $X^T W X$ has some small eigenvalue σ_j, scale-free MSE $\mathrm{tr}(F(\beta)^{-1})$ will be a large value according to Eq. (5). Hence, for the corresponded eigenvector ξ, we have $(W^{\frac{1}{2}} X \xi)^T (W^{\frac{1}{2}} X \xi) \approx 0$, which implies

$$
\sum_{u=1}^{M \cdot P} z_j(u)\xi(u) \approx 0 \tag{6}
$$

Here, $z_j(u)$ is a column vector of $W^{\frac{1}{2}} X$.

Besides, Eq. (6) also indicates that a series of effective representations should be linear-independent with each other after being rescaled by matrix $W^{\frac{1}{2}}$. As for the simplest least square regression, $W^{\frac{1}{2}}$ is an identity matrix. Then, if a series of representations are well performed, they are linearly independent with each other.

Overall, our conclusion can give a discussion on representations under the perspective of GLM based on the scale-free MSE.

4 Algorithm

Since we have shown that representations with a smaller scale-free MSE can help to learn a better estimation under the framework of GLM, we next consider to utilize the scale-free MSE as a penalization in deep learning algorithms.

Mostly, in the real circumstances, the cost of calculating the exact inverse of matrix $F(\beta)$ is highly expensive. According to Eq. (5), a small $\mathrm{tr}(F(\beta)^{-1})$ means that $F(\beta)$ has no eigenvalues close to zero. Thus, we consider to solve a substitute optimization problem regularized by the negative trace of $F(\beta, X(w))$ as follows:

$$\min_{\beta, w} L(\beta, w, \lambda) = \sum_{i=1}^{n} l(x_i(w), y_i; \beta) - \lambda \cdot \frac{\mathrm{tr}(F(\beta, X(w)))}{\|\beta(X(w))\|} \tag{7}$$

Here, the regularized direction of $-\lambda \cdot \frac{\mathrm{tr}(F(\beta, X(w)))}{\|\beta(X(w))\|}$ is the same as the one of $\lambda \cdot \frac{\mathrm{tr}(F(\beta, X(w))^{-1})}{\|\beta(X(w))\|}$, because a matrix without eigenvalues close to zero means that the eigenvalues of its inverse matrix will be relatively large. Hence, to simplify the calculation, we can choose the summation of eigenvalues over $F(\beta, X(w))$ as the regularization term.

Now, as shown in Algorithm 1, we can describe the proposed scale-free MSE regularized algorithm, to solve Eq. (7). Here, the algorithm consists of two loops, i.e., the outer loop and the inner loop. At each iteration of the outer loop, it firstly implements the forward propagation, and it next starts the inner loop to optimize the last layer by K_1 times, to solve the β-optimization problem. After the inner loop, it then implements the backward propagation to update w and then starts the following outer loop.

Algorithm 1. Scale-free MSE Regularized Algorithm

Input $\lambda > 0$, initialize parameter β, w, iterations K_1, K_2 and learning rate η.
$k_1, k_2 = 0$
while $k_2 \leq K_2$ **do**
  Implement the forward propagation
  Iterate K_1 times to solve the β-optimization problem
  while $k_1 \leq K_1$ **do**
    Update β using loss gradients: $\beta_{k_1+1} = \beta_{k_1} - \eta \cdot \nabla_{\beta_{k_1}} L(\beta_{k_1}, w_{k_2}, \lambda)$
    $k_1 = k_1 + 1$
  end while
  Update ω using loss gradients: $w_{k_2+1} = w_{k_2} - \eta \cdot \nabla_{w_{k_2}} L(\beta_{k_1}, w_{k_2}, \lambda)$
  $k_2 = k_2 + 1$
end while
return β_{K_1}, w_{K_2}

Besides, we next deliver some extra explanations about the inner loop in Algorithm 1. In fact, the motivation of designing the inner loop is to solve the β-optimization problem, because in the practical calculating process, the required ground truth β^* is always unavailable. Since we already know that $\hat{\beta}_N \xrightarrow{P} \beta^*$ referring to Theorem 4.18 in [10], then we can run the inner loop for K_1 times to estimate $\beta^*(X(w))$ in order to achieve a more accurate estimation for scale-free MSE. Meanwhile, the β-optimization problem is convex for L_2 loss and CE loss, which is easy to solve. Therefore, practically, we can choose a smaller K_1, and it will not lead to much extra computational cost.

5 Experiments

5.1 Experiment on Supervised Learning Tasks

For the experiment on supervised learning task, we apply our proposed algorithm (denoted using the suffix "+MSE") to classification and regression task, respectively. For each task, we use CIFAR-10 and CIFAR-100 [11] to evaluate the performance. CIFAR-10 and CIFAR-100 are two labeled datasets with 10 and 100 classes, respectively, and each of them include 60k 32×32 images. These two datasets have different class numbers, which can be utilized to figure out the relationship between the algorithm efficiency and the class number.

We use two different DNNs in our experiments. One is ResNet34 [8], the other is LeNet [12]. ResNet34 is a deeper DNN with residual blocks, and it is trained for 200 epochs with learning rate decay. Here, the learning rate is 0.1 at the beginning, and it is changed to 0.01 and 0.001 at epoch 80 and 120, respectively. LeNet is a basic DNN, and it is trained for 500 epochs with a fixed learning rate 0.01. The unit number of the last hidden layer in ResNet34 and LeNet, is set to 512 and 84, respectively. We also use stochastic gradient descent as optimizer and set the momentum coefficient and the weight decay to be 0.9 and 0.0005, respectively.

As for the computational cost, in our method, the size of representation matrix $X(w)$ is $B \times H$. Here, B and H stands for the batch size and the unit number of the last hidden layer, respectively. The costliest operation in our method is $X(w)^T X(w)$. Since that B and H are both small, our method has little extra computational cost. Specifically, for example, it both costs 2.5 h to train ResNet34 for CIFAR-10 and CE, with or without the the regularizer.

Besides, we use different loss functions for different learning tasks and investigate how the regularizer can influence the learning representation process. Here, the only hyper-parameter need to be tuned is the coefficient λ of the proposed regularizer, chosen from $\{10^{-6}, 10^{-7}, ..., 10^{-10}\}$.

Classification Task. The testing accuracy result of ResNet34, LeNet and these two with the proposed regularizer on CIFAR-10 and CIFAR-100, is listed in Table 1, and the curves tracking the testing accuracy during the training process, are plotted in Fig. 2. These results show that the testing accuracy can be improved by our proposed algorithm, and the improvement on CIFAR-100 is larger than which on CIFAR-10, indicating that our proposed regularizer can provide more benefit to the downstream task with a larger class number, because such task need more information to guide the direction of representation learning.

Regression Task. The testing accuracy of ResNet34, LeNet and these two with the proposed regularizer on CIFAR-10 and CIFAR-100, is listed in Table 1, and the curves tracking the testing accuracy during the training process, are plotted in Fig. 3. It can be observed that with our proposed regularizer, the performance

Table 1. Test accuracy result using CE loss and MSE loss for classification task and regression task, respectively.

Loss	CE		MSE	
Dataset	CIFAR-10	CIFAR-100	CIFAR-10	CIFAR-100
ResNet34	94.71%	75.93%	93.55%	14.60%
ResNet34+MSE	**94.97%**	**76.45%**	**93.81%**	**22.93%**
LeNet	73.20%	36.60%	71.56%	NA
LeNet+MSE	**73.71%**	**38.55%**	**71.66%**	NA

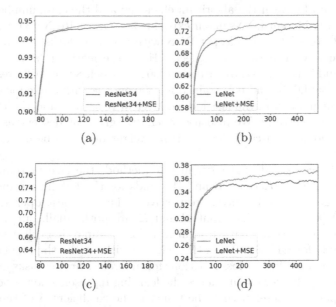

(a)   (b)

(c)   (d)

Fig. 2. Curves tracking the testing accuracy using CE loss. Curves related to CIFAR-10 are plotted in Figure (a) and (b), and curves related with CIFAR-100 to plotted in Figure (c) and (d). X-axis denotes the epoch number.

of ResNet34 on CIFAR-100 can be improved significantly. In particular, the result of LeNet on CIFAR-100 is not available, because LeNet with the MSE can not learn anything useful, and all testing accuracy values are 0.01.

5.2   Experiment on Unsupervised Learning Tasks

We next test our proposed regularizer under unsupervised learning settings. Here, we utilize an auto-encoder (AE) to evaluate the performance. We follow the settings in [13]. We use an encoder and a decoder, similar to a deep convolutional GAN discriminator and generator [14], respectively. We use the regularizer under an MSE loss which is simplified by omitting some β-related terms, because β is unavailable while training an AE. Thus, the regularizer can be denoted as

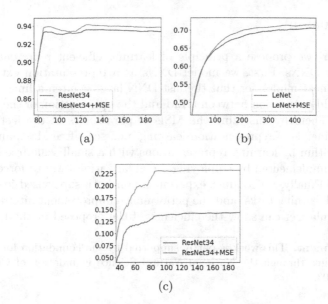

Fig. 3. Curves tracking the testing accuracy using the MSE loss. Curves related to CIFAR-10 are plotted in Figure (a) and (b), and curves related to CIFAR-100 are plotted in Figure (c). X-axis denotes the epoch number.

$$\lambda \cdot \mathrm{tr}\left[\left(\sum_{i=1}^{N} X_i X_i^T\right)^{-1}\right]$$

First, we train two AE models using reconstruction loss and regularized reconstruction loss, respectively. Next, we freeze the weights of AEs [13,15], and the outputs of the encoder are treated as representations. Then, the representations are applied to train an upper classifier, i.e., a two-layer MLP. When the classifier performs best on the validation dataset, the classification accuracy on the testing set is taken as the performance of the current AE, which can reveal the quality of learning representations. In Table 2, we list the classification accuracy result on CIFAR-10 and CIFAR-100, respectively. The result shows that the testing accuracy can be enhanced by adding the proposed regularizer.

Table 2. Classification accuracy (top 1) result for the unsupervised learning task.

Dataset	CIFAR-10	CIFAR-100
AE	57.35%	30.12%
AE+MSE	**59.61%**	**32.10%**

6 Conclusion

In this paper, we propose a principle of learning efficient representations for deterministic DNNs. First, we model DNNs as a representation extractor followed by a linear model, for that the last DNN layer is often a linear mapping. Next, we build connection between GLM and the optimization of the last linear DNN layer. Then, by analyzing the MSE of parameters in the last layer, we propose a principle of representation learning, i.e., scale-free MSE, and propose a novel algorithm by learning representations with a small scale-free MSE. The algorithm is implemented by employing a regularization term to force the error to get small. Finally, we conduct experiments on both supervised learning and unsupervised learning tasks, and the performance improvement after adding our proposed regularizer can show the efficiency of the proposed method.

Acknowledgment. This work is partly supported by the Foundation for Innovative Research Groups through the National Natural Science Foundation of China under Grant 61421003.

References

1. Bengio, Y., Courville, A., Vincent, P.: Representation learning: a review and new perspectives. IEEE Trans. Pattern Anal. Mach. Intell. **35**(8), 1798–1828 (2013)
2. Chen, X., Duan, Y., Houthooft, R., Schulman, J., Sutskever, I., Abbeel, P.: InfoGAN: interpretable representation learning by information maximizing generative adversarial nets. In: NeurIPS, pp. 2172–2180 (2016)
3. Kumar, A., Sattigeri, P., Balakrishnan, A.: Variational inference of disentangled latent concepts from unlabeled observations. arXiv:1711.00848 (2017)
4. Chen, T.Q., Li, X., Grosse, R., Duvenaud, D.: Isolating sources of disentanglement in variational autoencoders. arXiv:1802.04942 (2018)
5. Li, Y., Yosinski, J., Clune, J., Lipson, H., Hopcroft, J.E.: Convergent learning: do different neural networks learn the same representations? In: NeurIPS, pp. 196–212 (2015)
6. Raghu, M., Gilmer, J., Yosinski, J., Sohl-Dickstein, J.: SVCCA: singular vector canonical correlation analysis for deep learning dynamics and interpretability. In: NeurIPS, pp. 6076–6085 (2017)
7. Simonyan, K., Zisserman, A.: Very deep convolutional networks for large-scale image recognition. arXiv preprint arXiv:1409.1556 (2014)
8. He, K., Zhang, X., Ren, S., Sun, J.: Deep residual learning for image recognition. In: CVPR, pp. 770–778 (2016)
9. Agresti, A.: Foundations of Linear and Generalized Linear Models. Wiley, Hoboken (2015)
10. Shao, J.: Mathematical Statistics. Springer Texts in Statistics. Springer-Verlag, New York (2003). https://doi.org/10.1007/b97553
11. Krizhevsky, A., Hinton, G.: Learning multiple layers of features from tiny images. Citeseer, Technical report (2009)
12. LeCun, Y., Bottou, L., Bengio, Y., Haffner, P.: Gradient-based learning applied to document recognition. Proc. IEEE **86**, 2278–2324 (1998)

13. Hjelm, R.D., Fedorov, A., Lavoie-Marchildon, S., Grewal, K., Trischler, A., Bengio, Y.: Learning deep representations by mutual information estimation and maximization. arXiv:1808.06670 (2018)
14. Radford, A., Metz, L., Chintala, S.: Unsupervised representation learning with deep convolutional generative adversarial networks. arXiv:1511.06434 (2015)
15. Bojanowski, P., Joulin, A.: Unsupervised learning by predicting noise. arXiv:1704.05310 (2017)

Training Behavior of Deep Neural Network in Frequency Domain

Zhi-Qin John Xu[1]([✉]), Yaoyu Zhang[2], and Yanyang Xiao[3]

[1] School of Mathematical Sciences and Institute of Natural Sciences,
Shanghai Jiao Tong University, Shanghai, China
xuzhiqin@sjtu.edu.cn
[2] School of Mathematics, Institute for Advanced Study, Princeton, NJ 08540, USA
yaoyu@ias.edu
[3] The Brain Cognition and Brain Disease Institute, Shenzhen Institutes
of Advanced Technology, Chinese Academy of Sciences, Shenzhen, China
xyy82148@gmail.com

Abstract. Why deep neural networks (DNNs) capable of overfitting often generalize well in practice is a mystery [24]. To find a potential mechanism, we focus on the study of implicit biases underlying the training process of DNNs. In this work, for both real and synthetic datasets, we empirically find that a DNN with common settings first quickly captures the dominant low-frequency components, and then relatively slowly captures the high-frequency ones. We call this phenomenon Frequency Principle (F-Principle). The F-Principle can be observed over DNNs of various structures, activation functions, and training algorithms in our experiments. We also illustrate how the F-Principle helps understand the effect of early-stopping as well as the generalization of DNNs. This F-Principle potentially provides insight into a general principle underlying DNN optimization and generalization.

Keywords: Deep Neural Network · Deep learning · Fourier analysis · Generalization

1 Introduction

Although Deep Neural Networks (DNNs) are totally transparent, i.e., the value of each node and each parameter can be easily obtained, it is difficult to interpret how information is processed through DNNs. We can easily record the trajectories of the parameters of DNNs during the training. However, it remains unclear what is the general principle underlying the highly non-convex problem of DNN optimization [9]. Therefore, DNN is often criticized for being a "black box" [1,18]. Even for the simple problem of fitting one-dimensional (1-d) functions, the training process of DNN is still not well understood [16,19]. For example, Wu et al. [19] use DNNs of different depth to fit a few data points sampled from a 1-d target function of third-order polynomial. They find that, even when a

© Springer Nature Switzerland AG 2019
T. Gedeon et al. (Eds.): ICONIP 2019, LNCS 11953, pp. 264–274, 2019.
https://doi.org/10.1007/978-3-030-36708-4_22

DNN is capable of over-fitting, i.e., the number of its parameters is much larger than the size of the training dataset, it often generalizes well (i.e., no overfitting) after training. In practice, the same phenomenon is also observed for much more complicated datasets [7,10,11,19,24,28]. Intuitively, for a wide DNN, its solutions of zero training error lies in a huge space where well-generalized ones only occupy a small subset. Therefore, it is mysterious that DNN optimization often ignores a huge set of over-fitting solutions. To find an underlying mechanism, in this work, we characterize the behavior of the DNN optimization process in the frequency domain using 1-d functions as well as real datasets of image classification problems (MNIST and CIFAR10). Our work provides insight into an implicitly bias underlying the training process of DNNs.

We empirically find that, for real datasets or synthetic functions, a DNN with common settings first quickly captures their dominant low-frequency components while keeping its own high-frequency ones small, and then relatively slowly capture their high-frequency components. We call this phenomenon *Frequency Principle* (F-Principle). From our numerical experiments, this F-Principle can be widely observed for DNNs of different width (tens to thousands of neurons in each layer), depth (one to tens of hidden layers), training algorithms (gradient descent, stochastic gradient descent, Adam) and activation functions (tanh and ReLU). Remark that this strategy of the F-Principle, i.e., fitting the target function progressively in ascending frequency order, is also adopted explicitly in some numerical algorithms to achieve remarkable efficiency. These numerical algorithms include, for example, the Multigrid method for solving large-scale partial differential equations [5] and a recent numerical scheme that efficiently fits the three-dimensional structure of proteins and protein complexes from noisy two-dimensional images [3].

The F-Principle provides a potential mechanism of why DNNs often generalize well empirically albeit its ability of over-fitting [24]. For a finite training set, there exists an effective frequency range [12,17,23] beyond which the information of the signal is lost. By the F-Principle, with no constraint on the high-frequency components beyond the effective frequency range, DNNs tend to keep them small. For a wide class of low-frequency dominant natural signals (e.g., image and sound), this tendency coincides with their behavior of decaying power at high frequencies. Thus, DNNs often generalize well in practice. When the training data is noisy, the small-amplitude high-frequency components are easier to be contaminated. By the F-Principle, DNNs first capture the less noisy low-frequency components of the training data and keep higher-frequency components small. At this stage, although the loss function is not best optimized for the training data, DNNs could generalize better for not fitting the noise dominating the higher-frequencies. Therefore, as widely observed, early-stopping often helps generalization.

Our key contribution in this work is the discovery of an F-Principle underlying the training of DNNs for both synthetic and real datasets. In addition, we demonstrate how the F-Principle provides insight into the effectiveness of early stopping and the good generalization of DNNs in general.

2   Related Works

Consistent with other studies [2, 19], our analysis shows that over-parameterized DNNs tend to fit training data with low-frequency functions, which are naturally of lower complexity. Intuitively, lower-frequency functions also possess smaller Lipschitz constants. According to the study in Hardt et al. [6], which focuses on the relation between stability and generalization, smaller Lipschitz constants can lead to smaller generalization error.

The F-Principle proposed in this work initiates a series of works [4, 14, 20–22, 25, 27]. A stronger verification of the F-Principle for the high dimensional datasets can be found in Xu et al., [21]. Theoretical studies on the F-Principle can be found in Xu et al., Xu et al., and Zhang et al., [21, 22, 25]. The F-Principle is also used as an important phenomenon to pursue fundamentally different learning trajectories of meta-learning [14]. The theoretical framework [21, 22] of analyzing the F-Principle is used to analyze a nonlinear collaborative scheme for deep network training [27]. Based on the F-Principle, a fast algorithm by shifting high frequencies to lower ones is developed for fitting high frequency functions [4]. These subsequent works show the importance of the F-Principle.

3   Experimental Setup

We summarize the setups for each figure as follows. All DNNs are trained by the Adam optimizer, whose parameters are set to their default values [8]. The loss function is the mean-squared error. The parameters of DNNs are initialized by a Gaussian distribution with mean 0.

In Fig. 1, the setting of the fully-connected tanh-DNN is as follows. Width of hidden layers: 200-100-100; Batch size: 100; Learning rate: 10^{-5} for CIFAR10 and 10^{-6} for MNIST; Standard deviation of Gaussian initialization: 10^{-4}. The setting of the ReLU-CNN is as follows: two layers of 32 features with 3×3 convolutional kernel and 2×2 max-pooling, followed by 128-64 densely connected layers; Batch size: 128; Standard deviation of Gaussian initialization: 0.05. We select 10000 samples from each dataset for the training.

In Figs. 2, 3, 4 and 5, we use a fully-connected tanh-DNN of 4 hidden layers of width 200-200-200-100, standard deviation of Gaussian initialization 0.1, learning rate 2×10^{-5} and full-batch size training.

In addition, $\mathcal{F}[\cdot]$ indicates the Fourier transform, which is experimentally estimated on discrete training or test data points.

4   F-Principle

In this section, we study the training process of DNNs in the frequency domain. We empirically find that, for a general class of functions dominated by low-frequencies, the training process of DNNs follows the F-Principle by which low-frequency components are first captured, followed by high-frequency ones.

4.1 MNIST/CIFAR10

Since the computation of high-dimensional Fourier transform suffers from the curse of dimensionality, to verify the F-Principle in the image classification problems (MNIST and CIFAR10), we perform the Fourier analysis along the first principle component of the training inputs.

The training set is a list of labeled images denoted by $\{x_k; y_k\}_{k=0}^{n-1}$, where each image $x_k \in [0,1]^{N_{in}}$, N_{in} is the number of pixels of an image, each label $y_k \in \{0,1,2,\cdots 9\}$. We use DNNs of two structures to learn this training set, that is, a fully-connected DNN and a CNN. Denote $x_k = x_k \cdot v_{PC}$, which is the projection of image x_k along the direction of the first principle component of $\{x_k\}_{k=0}^{n-1}$ denoted by a unit vector v_{PC}. Using non-uniform Fourier transform, we obtain

$$\mathcal{F}_{PC}^n[y](\gamma) = \frac{1}{n} \sum_{j=0}^{n-1} y_j \exp\left(-2\pi i x_j \gamma\right),$$

where $\gamma \in \mathbb{Z}$ is the *frequency index*. For the DNN output $T(x_k)$, similarly, $\mathcal{F}_{PC}^n[T](\gamma) = \frac{1}{n} \sum_{j=0}^{n-1} T(x_j) \exp\left(-2\pi i x_j \gamma\right)$. To examine the convergence behavior of different frequency components during the training of a DNN, we compute the relative difference of $\mathcal{F}_{PC}^n[T][\gamma]$ and $\mathcal{F}_{PC}^n[y][\gamma]$ at each recording step, i.e.,

$$\Delta_F(\gamma) = \frac{|\mathcal{F}_{PC}^n[y](\gamma) - \mathcal{F}_{PC}^n[T](\gamma)|}{|\mathcal{F}_{PC}^n[y](\gamma)|}, \tag{1}$$

where $|\cdot|$ denotes the absolute value. As shown in the first column in Fig. 1, both datasets are dominated by low-frequency components along the first principle direction. Theoretically, frequency components other than the peaks are susceptible to the artificial periodic boundary condition implicitly applied in the Fourier transform, thereby are not essential to our frequency domain analysis [13]. In the following, we only focus on the convergence behavior of the frequency peaks during the training. By examining the relative error of certain selected key frequency components (marked by black squares), one can clearly observe that DNNs of both structures for both datasets tend to capture the training data in an order from low to high frequencies as stated by the F-Principle[1] (second and third column in Fig. 1).

4.2 Synthetic Data

In this section, we demonstrate the F-Principle by using synthetic data sampled from a target function of known intrinsic frequencies. We design a target function by discretizing a smooth function $f_0(x)$ as follows,

$$y = f(x) = \alpha \times \text{Round}(f_0(x)/\alpha), \quad \alpha \in (0, \infty), \tag{2}$$

---

[1] Almost at the same time, another research [15] finds a similar result. However, they add noise to MNIST, which contaminates the labels.

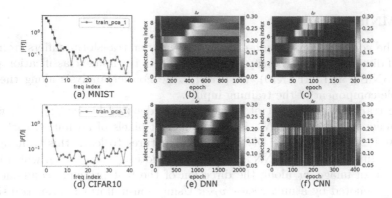

Fig. 1. Frequency analysis of DNN output function along the first principle component during the training. The training datasets for the first and the second row are from MNIST and CIFAR10, respectively. The neural networks for the second column and the third column are fully-connected DNN and CNN, respectively. (a,d) $|\mathcal{F}_{PC}^n[y](\gamma)|$. The selected frequencies are marked by black dots. (b, c, e, f) Δ_F at different recording epochs for different selected frequencies. Δ_F larger than 0.3 (or smaller than 0.05) is represented by blue (or red). (Color figure online)

where Round($\cdot$) takes the nearest integer value. We define $y = f_0(x)$ for $\alpha = 0$. We consider $f_0(x) = \sin(x) + 2\sin(3x) + 3\sin(5x)$ with $\alpha = 2$ as shown in Fig. 2a. As shown in Fig. 2b, for the discrete Fourier transform (DFT) of $f(x)$, i.e., $\mathcal{F}[f]$, there are three most important frequency components and some small peaks due to the discretization. In this case, we can observe a precise convergence order from low- to high-frequency for frequency peaks as shown in Fig. 2c.

We have performed the same frequency domain analysis for various low-frequency dominant functions, such as $f_0(x) = |x|$, $f_0(x) = x^2$ and $f_0(x) = \sin(x)$ with different α's (results are not shown), for both ReLU and tanh activation functions, and both gradient descent and Adam [8] optimizers. We find that F-Principle always holds during the training of DNNs. Therefore, the F-Principle seems to be an intrinsic character of DNN optimization.

5   Understanding the Training Behavior of DNNs by the F-Principle

In this section, we provide an explanation based on the F-Principle of why DNNs capable of over-fitting often generalize well in practice [7,10,11,19,24,28]. For a class of functions dominated by low frequencies, with finite training data points, there is an *effective frequency range* for this training set, which is defined as the range in frequency domain bounded by Nyquist-Shannon sampling theorem [17] when the sampling is evenly spaced, or its extensions [12,23] otherwise. When the number of parameters of a DNN is greater than the size of the training set, the DNN can overfit these sampling data points (i.e., training set) with different amount of powers outside the effective frequency range. However, by

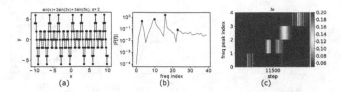

Fig. 2. Frequency domain analysis of the training process of a DNN for $f_0(x) = \sin(x) + 2\sin(3x) + 3\sin(5x)$ with $\alpha = 2$ in Eq. (2). (a) The target function. (b) $|\mathcal{F}[f]|$ at different frequency indexes. First four frequency peaks are marked by black dots. (c) Δ_F at different recording steps for different frequency peaks. The training data is evenly sampled in $[-10, 10]$ with sample size 600.

the F-Principle, the training process will implicitly bias the DNN towards a solution with a low power at the high-frequencies outside the effective frequency range. For functions dominated by low frequencies, this bias coincides with their intrinsic feature of low power at high frequencies, thus naturally leading to a well-generalized solution after training. By the above analysis, we can predict that, in the case of insufficient training data, when the higher-frequency components are not negligible, e.g., there exists a significant frequency peak above the effective frequency range, the DNN cannot generalize well after training.

In another case where the training data is contaminated by noise, early-stopping method is usually applied to avoid overfitting in practice [10]. By the F-Principle, early-stopping can help avoid fitting the noisy high-frequency components. Thus, it naturally leads to a well-generalized solution. We use the following example for illustration.

As shown in Fig. 3a, we consider $f_0(x) = \sin(x)$ with $\alpha = 0.5$ in Eq. (2). For each sample x, we add a noise ϵ on $f_0(x)$, where ϵ follows a Gaussian distribution with mean 0 and standard deviation 0.1. The DNN can well fit the sampled training set as the loss function of the training set decreases to a very small value (green stars in Fig. 3b). However, the loss function of the test set first decreases and then increases (red dots in Fig. 3b). That is, the generalization performance of the DNN gets worse during the training after a certain step. In Fig. 3c, $|\mathcal{F}[f]|$ for the training data (red) and the test data (black) only overlap around the dominant low-frequency components. Clearly, the high-frequency components of the training set are severely contaminated by noise. Around the turning step—where the best generalization performance is achieved, indicated by the green dashed line in Fig. 3b—the DNN well captures the dominant peak as shown in Fig. 3c. After that, clearly, the loss function of the test set increases as DNN start to capture the higher-frequency noise (red dots in Fig. 3b). These phenomena conform with our analysis that early-stopping can lead to a better generalization performance of DNNs as it helps prevent fitting the noisy high-frequency components of the training set.

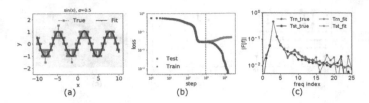

Fig. 3. Effect of Early-stopping on contaminated data. The training set and the test set consist of 300 and 6000 data points evenly sampled in $[-10, 10]$, respectively. (a) The sampled values of the test set (red square dashed line) and DNN outputs (blue solid line) at the turning step. (b) Loss functions for training set (green stars) and test set (red dots) at different recording steps. The green dashed line is drawn at the turning step, where the best generalization performance is achieved. (c) $|\mathcal{F}[f]|$ for the training set (red) and test set (black), and $|\mathcal{F}[T]|$ for the training set (green), and test set (magenta) at the turning step. (Color figure online)

6   Conclusions and Discussion

In this work, we empirically discover an F-Principle underlying the optimization process of DNNs. Specifically, for functions with dominant low-frequency components, a DNN with common settings first capture their low-frequency components while keeping its own high-frequency ones small. In our experiments, this phenomenon can be widely observed for DNNs of different width (tens to thousands in each layer), depth (one to tens), training algorithms (GD, SGD, Adam), and activation functions (tanh and ReLU). The F-Principle provides insights into the good generalization performance of DNNs often observed in experiments. In Appendix 7, we also discuss how the F-Principle helps understand the training behavior of DNNs in the information plane [18].

Note that initial parameters with large values could complicate the phenomenon of the F-Principle. In previous experiments, the training behavior of DNNs initialized by Gaussian distribution with mean 0 and small standard deviation follows the F-Principle. However, with large initialization, i.e., parameters initialized by a Gaussian distribution of large standard deviation, it is difficult to observe a clear phenomenon of the F-Principle. More importantly, these two initialization strategies could result in very different generalization performances. When the standard deviation for initialization is large[2], say, 10 (see Fig. 4a), the initial DNN output fluctuates strongly. In contrast, when the parameters of the DNN are initialized with small values, say, Gaussian distribution with standard deviation 0.1, the initial DNN output is flat (see Fig. 4d). For both initializations, DNNs can well fit the training data (see Fig. 4b and e). However, for test data, the DNN with small initialization generalizes well (Fig. 4f) whereas the DNN with large initialization clearly overfits (Fig. 4c). Intuitively, the above phenomenon can be understood as follows. Without explicit constraints on the high-frequency components beyond the effective frequency range of the training

---

[2] The bias terms are always initialized by standard deviation 0.1.

data, the DNN output after training tends to inherit these high-frequency components from the initial output. Therefore, with large initialization, the DNN output can easily overfit the training data with fluctuating high-frequency components. In practice, the parameters of DNNs are often randomly initialized with standard deviations close to zero. As suggested by our analysis, the small-initialization strategy may implicitly lead to a more efficient and well-generalized optimization process of DNNs as characterized by the F-Principle. Note that a quantitative study of how initialization affects the generalization of DNN can be found in a subsequent work [26].

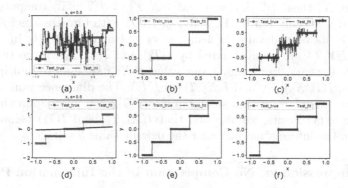

Fig. 4. DNN outputs with different initializations for fitting function $f(x)$ of $f_0(x) = x$ with $\alpha = 0.5$ in Eq. (2). The training data and the test data are evenly sampled in $[-1, 1]$ with sample size 600 and 1200, respectively. The parameters of DNNs are initialized by a Gaussian distribution with mean 0 and standard deviation either 10 (first row) or 0.1 (second row). (a, d): $f(x)$ (red dashed line) and initial DNN outputs (blue solid line) for the test data. (b, e): $f(x)$ (red dashed line) and DNN outputs (blue solid line) for the training data at the end of training. (c, f): $f(x)$ (red dashed line) and DNN outputs (blue solid line) for the test data at the end of training. (Color figure online)

Acknowledgments. The authors want to thank David W. McLaughlin for helpful discussions and thank Qiu Yang (NYU), Zheng Ma (Purdue University), and Tao Luo (Purdue University), Shixiao Jiang (Penn State), Kai Chen (SJTU) for critically reading the manuscript. Part of this work was done when ZX, YZ, YX are postdocs at New York University Abu Dhabi and visiting members at Courant Institute supported by the NYU Abu Dhabi Institute G1301. The authors declare no conflict of interest.

7   Appendix

Through the empirical exploration of the training behavior of DNNs in the information plane, regarding information compression phase, Schwartz-Ziv and Tishby [18] claimed that (i) information compression is a general process; (ii) information compression is induced by SGD. In this section, we demonstrate how the F-Principle can be used to understand the compression phase.

7.1   Computation of Information

For any random variables U and V with a joint distribution $P(u, v)$: the entropy of U is defined as $I(U) = -\sum_u P(u) \log P(u)$; their mutual information is defined as $I(U, V) = \sum_{u,v} P(u, v) \log \frac{P(u,v)}{P(u)P(v)}$; the conditional entropy of U on V is defined as

$$I(U|V) = \sum_{u,v} P(u, v) \log \frac{P(v)}{P(u,v)} = I(U) - I(U, V).$$

By the construction of the DNN, its output T is a deterministic function of its input X, thus, $I(T|X) = 0$ and $I(X, T) = I(T)$. To compute entropy numerically, we evenly bin X, Y, T to X_b, Y_b, T_b with bin size b as follows. For any value v, its binned value is define as $v_b = \text{Round}(v/b) \times b$. In our work, $I(T)$ and $I(Y, T)$ are approximated by $I(T_b)$ and $I(Y_b, T_b)$, respectively, with $b = 0.05$. Note that, after binning, one value of X_b may map to multiple values of T_b. Thus, $I(T_b|X_b) \neq 0$ and $I(X_b, T_b) \neq I(T_b)$. The difference vanishes as bin size shrinks. Therefore, with a small bin size, $I(T_b)$ is a good approximation of $I(X, T)$. In experiments, we also find that $I(X_b, T_b)$ and $I(T_b)$ behave almost the same in the information plane for the default value $b = 0.05$.

7.2   Compression vs. No Compression in the Information Plane

We demonstrate how compression can appear or disappear by tuning the parameter α in Eq. (2) with $f_0(x) = x$ for $x \in [-1, 1]$ using full batch gradient descent (GD) without stochasticity. In our simulations, the DNN well fits $f(x)$ for both α equal to 0 and 0.5 after training (see Fig. 5a and c). In the information plane, there is no compression phase for $I(T)$ for $\alpha = 0$ (see Fig. 5b). By increasing α in Eq. (2) we can observe that: (i) the fitted function is discretized with only few possible outputs (see Fig. 5c); (ii) the compression of $I(T)$ appears (see Fig. 5d). For $\alpha > 0$, behaviors of information plane are similar to previous results [18]. To understand why compression happens for $\alpha > 0$, we next focus on the training courses for different α in the frequency domain.

A key feature of the class of functions described by Eq. (2) is that the dominant low-frequency components for $f(x)$ with different α are the same. By the F-Principle, the DNN first captures those dominant low-frequency components, thus, the training courses for different α at the beginning are similar, i.e., (i) the DNN output is close to $f_0(x)$ at certain training epochs (blue lines in Fig. 5a and c); (ii) $I(T)$ in the information plane increases rapidly until it reaches a value close to the entropy of $f_0(x)$, i.e., $I(f_0(x))$ (see Fig. 5b and d). For $\alpha = 0$, the target function is $f_0(x)$, therefore, $I(T)$ will be closer and closer to $I(f_0(x))$ during the training. For $\alpha > 0$, the entropy of the target function, $I(f(x))$, is much less than $I(f_0(x))$. In the latter stage of capturing high-frequency components, the DNN output T would converge to the discretized function $f(x)$. Therefore, $I(T)$ would decrease from $I(f_0(x))$ to $I(f(x))$.

This analysis is also applicable to other functions. As the discretization is in general inevitable for classification problems with discrete labels, we can often observe information compression in practice as described in the previous study [18].

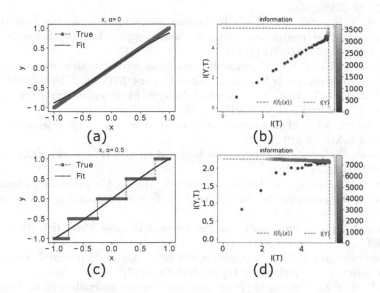

Fig. 5. Analysis of compression phase in the information plane. α is 0 for (a, b) and 0.5 for (c, d). (a, c) $f(x)$ (red square) with $f_0(x) = x$ in Eq. (2) and the DNN output (blue solid line) at a certain training step. (b, d) Trajectories of the training process of the DNN in the information plane. Color of each dot indicates its recording step. The green dashed vertical line and the red dashed horizontal line indicate constant values of $I(f_0(x))$ and $I(Y)$, respectively. (Color figure online)

References

1. Alain, G., Bengio, Y.: Understanding intermediate layers using linear classifier probes. arXiv preprint arXiv:1610.01644 (2016)
2. Arpit, D., et al.: A closer look at memorization in deep networks. arXiv preprint arXiv:1706.05394 (2017)
3. Barnett, A., Greengard, L., Pataki, A., Spivak, M.: Rapid solution of the cryo-EM reconstruction problem by frequency marching. SIAM J. Imaging Sci. **10**(3), 1170–1195 (2017)
4. Cai, W., Li, X., Liu, L.: Phasednn-a parallel phase shift deep neural network for adaptive wideband learning. arXiv preprint arXiv:1905.01389 (2019)
5. Hackbusch, W.: Multi-grid Methods and Applications, vol. 4. Springer Science & Business Media (2013)
6. Hardt, M., Recht, B., Singer, Y.: Train faster, generalize better: stability of stochastic gradient descent. arXiv preprint arXiv:1509.01240 (2015)
7. Kawaguchi, K., Kaelbling, L.P., Bengio, Y.: Generalization in deep learning. arXiv preprint arXiv:1710.05468 (2017)
8. Kingma, D.P., Ba, J.: Adam: a method for stochastic optimization. arXiv preprint arXiv:1412.6980 (2014)

9. LeCun, Y., Bengio, Y., Hinton, G.: Deep learning. Nature **521**(7553), 436 (2015)
10. Lin, J., Camoriano, R., Rosasco, L.: Generalization properties and implicit regularization for multiple passes SGM. In: International Conference on Machine Learning, pp. 2340–2348 (2016)
11. Martin, C.H., Mahoney, M.W.: Rethinking generalization requires revisiting old ideas: statistical mechanics approaches and complex learning behavior. arXiv preprint arXiv:1710.09553 (2017)
12. Mishali, M., Eldar, Y.C.: Blind multiband signal reconstruction: compressed sensing for analog signals. IEEE Trans. Signal Process. **57**(3), 993–1009 (2009)
13. Percival, D.B., Walden, A.T.: Spectral Analysis for Physical Applications. Cambridge University Press, Cambridge (1993)
14. Rabinowitz, N.C.: Meta-learners' learning dynamics are unlike learners'. arXiv preprint arXiv:1905.01320 (2019)
15. Rahaman, N., et al.: On the spectral bias of deep neural networks. arXiv preprint arXiv:1806.08734 (2018)
16. Saxe, A.M., Bansal, Y., Dapello, J., Advani, M.: On the information bottleneck theory of deep learning. In: International Conference on Learning Representations (2018)
17. Shannon, C.E.: Communication in the presence of noise. Proc. IRE **37**(1), 10–21 (1949)
18. Shwartz-Ziv, R., Tishby, N.: Opening the black box of deep neural networks via information. arXiv preprint arXiv:1703.00810 (2017)
19. Wu, L., Zhu, Z., Weinan, E.: Towards understanding generalization of deep learning: perspective of loss landscapes. arXiv preprint arXiv:1706.10239 (2017)
20. Xu, Z.Q.J.: Frequency principle in deep learning with general loss functions and its potential application. arXiv preprint arXiv:1811.10146 (2018)
21. Xu, Z.Q.J., Zhang, Y., Luo, T., Xiao, Y., Ma, Z.: Frequency principle: Fourier analysis sheds light on deep neural networks. arXiv preprint arXiv:1901.06523 (2019)
22. Xu, Z.J.: Understanding training and generalization in deep learning by Fourier analysis. arXiv preprint arXiv:1808.04295 (2018)
23. Yen, J.: On nonuniform sampling of bandwidth-limited signals. IRE Trans. Circuit Theory **3**(4), 251–257 (1956)
24. Zhang, C., Bengio, S., Hardt, M., Recht, B., Vinyals, O.: Understanding deep learning requires rethinking generalization. arXiv preprint arXiv:1611.03530 (2016)
25. Zhang, Y., Xu, Z.Q.J., Luo, T., Ma, Z.: Explicitizing an implicit bias of the frequency principle in two-layer neural networks. arXiv:1905.10264 [cs, stat], May 2019
26. Zhang, Y., Xu, Z.Q.J., Luo, T., Ma, Z.: A type of generalization error induced by initialization in deep neural networks. arXiv:1905.07777 [cs, stat], May 2019
27. Zhen, H.L., Lin, X., Tang, A.Z., Li, Z., Zhang, Q., Kwong, S.: Nonlinear collaborative scheme for deep neural networks. arXiv preprint arXiv:1811.01316 (2018)
28. Zheng, G., Sang, J., Xu, C.: Understanding deep learning generalization by maximum entropy. arXiv preprint arXiv:1711.07758 (2017)

On the Initialization of Long Short-Term Memory Networks

Mostafa Mehdipour Ghazi[1,2,3,4(✉)], Mads Nielsen[1,2,3], Akshay Pai[1,2,3],
Marc Modat[4,5], M. Jorge Cardoso[4,5], Sébastien Ourselin[4,5],
and Lauge Sørensen[1,2,3]

[1] Biomediq A/S, Copenhagen, Denmark
mehdipour@biomediq.com
[2] Cerebriu A/S, Copenhagen, Denmark
[3] Department of Computer Science, University of Copenhagen,
Copenhagen, Denmark
[4] Department of Medical Physics and Biomedical Engineering,
University College London, London, UK
[5] School of Biomedical Engineering and Imaging Sciences, King's College London,
London, UK

Abstract. Weight initialization is important for faster convergence and
stability of deep neural networks training. In this paper, a robust initialization
method is developed to address the training instability in
long short-term memory (LSTM) networks. It is based on a normalized
random initialization of the network weights that aims at preserving
the variance of the network input and output in the same range. The
method is applied to standard LSTMs for univariate time series regression
and to LSTMs robust to missing values for multivariate disease
progression modeling. The results show that in all cases, the proposed
initialization method outperforms the state-of-the-art initialization techniques
in terms of training convergence and generalization performance
of the obtained solution.

Keywords: Deep neural networks · Long short-term memory · Time
series regression · Initialization · Disease progression modeling

1 Introduction

Recurrent neural networks (RNNs) are the state-of-the-art nonparametric methods
for sequence learning that map an input sequence to an output sequence by
predicting the next time steps. RNN training using the backpropagation through
time algorithm is challenging due to vanishing and exploding gradients where
the norm of the backpropagated error gradient can increase or decrease exponentially,
hindering the network in capturing long-term dependencies [1].

Three main solutions have been proposed in the literature to improve RNN
training; modifications of the training algorithm, modifications of the network

© Springer Nature Switzerland AG 2019
T. Gedeon et al. (Eds.): ICONIP 2019, LNCS 11953, pp. 275–286, 2019.
https://doi.org/10.1007/978-3-030-36708-4_23

architecture, or different weight initialization schemes. In the first approach, advanced optimization techniques such as the Hessian-Free method [2] or regularized loss functions [3] are applied to improve the backpropagation through time algorithm for learning long sequences. The second approach is to properly initialize the RNN weight matrices, for example, to be identity [4] or orthogonal [5], to find solution to the long-term dependency problem. The third approach is to employ nonlinear reset units in the RNN architecture to store information for a long time, for instance, using long short-term memory (LSTM) networks [6] or gated recurrent units (GRUs) [7].

LSTM networks, the most successful type of RNNs, use a gated architecture to replace the hidden unit with a memory cell to efficiently capture long-term temporal dependencies by storing and retrieving sequence information over time. The memory cell is used as a feedback along with three nonlinear (multiplicative) reset units to keep the backpropagated error signal constant. The input and output gates of the cell learn their weights to incorporate the stored information or to control the output values. There is also a forget gate that learns to remember or forget the memory information over time by scaling the cell content. Therefore, in contrast to vanilla RNNs, LSTM units by design allow gradients to flow unchanged, but they can still suffer from instabilities (exploding gradient problem) when trained on long sequences [8].

In this paper, a simple, yet robust initialization method is proposed to tackle the training instabilities in LSTM networks. The idea is based on normalized random initialization of the network weights with the property that the input and output signals have the same variance. The proposed method is applied to standard LSTMs [1,9] for univariate time series regression using data from the UCR Time Series Archive [10] and to LSTMs robust to missing values [11] for multivariate disease progression modeling in the Alzheimer's Disease Neuroimaging Initiative (ADNI) cohort [12] using volumetric magnetic resonance imaging (MRI) measurements.

2   Related Work

Since deep neural network training is achieved by solving a nonconvex optimization problem, mostly in a stochastic way, a random weight initialization scheme is important for faster convergence and stability. Otherwise, the magnitudes of the input signal and error gradients at different layers can exponentially decrease or increase, leading to an ill-conditioned problem. Standard initialization of weights with zero-mean uniform/Gaussian distributions and heuristic variances ranging from 0.001 to 0.01 or an input layer size (N) dependent variance of $1/(3N)$ have been widely used in previous studies [13]. But, studies on the initialization, for instance, using unsupervised pre-training [14], showed its importance as a regularizer for the optimization procedure to robustly reach a local minimum and to improve generalization.

Accordingly, training difficulties have been investigated based on the variance of the responses in each layer, when the singular values of the Jacobian are not unit, and a normalized initialization of uniform weights with a variance of $1/N$ is suggested assuming that the activation functions are identity and/or hyperbolic tangent [13]. Likewise, a scaled initialization method has been developed to train deep rectified models from scratch using zero-mean Gaussian weights whose variances are $2/N$ [15].

To resolve the long-term temporal dependencies problem in RNNs, which can be seen as deep networks when unfolded through time, the (scaled) identity matrix has been applied to initialize the hidden (recurrent) weights matrix to output the previous hidden state in the absence of the current inputs in RNNs composed of rectified linear units (ReLU) [4]. Alternatively, (nearly) orthogonal matrices [5] and scaled positive-definite weight matrices [16] have been used to address vanishing and exploding gradients in RNNs by preserving the gradient norm during backpropagation.

As it can be seen, different initialization methods have been proposed to deal with the training convergence problem in deep neural networks including RNNs, assuming that LSTMs by design can handle the issue. Hence, the above-mentioned initialization methods, e.g., orthogonal recurrent weight matrices and current input weight matrices, both drawn i.i.d. from zero-mean Gaussian distributions with variances of $1/N$, have also been applied to LSTMs. However, as noted before, LSTMs can still suffer from instability with improper initialization due to the stochastic nature of the optimization and using multiplicative gates and feedback signals.

3   The Proposed Initialization

To address training instability and slow convergence in LSTMs, we propose a scaled random weights initialization method that aims to keep the variance of the network input and output in the same range. Let's $\boldsymbol{x}_j^t \in \mathbb{R}^{N \times 1}$ be the j-th observation of an N-dimensional input vector at time t. The feedforward pass of an LSTM network can be expressed as

$$\boldsymbol{f}_j^t = \sigma_g(W_f \boldsymbol{x}_j^t + U_f \boldsymbol{h}_j^{t-1} + \boldsymbol{b}_f),$$
$$\boldsymbol{i}_j^t = \sigma_g(W_i \boldsymbol{x}_j^t + U_i \boldsymbol{h}_j^{t-1} + \boldsymbol{b}_i),$$
$$\boldsymbol{z}_j^t = \sigma_c(W_c \boldsymbol{x}_j^t + U_c \boldsymbol{h}_j^{t-1} + \boldsymbol{b}_c),$$
$$\boldsymbol{c}_j^t = \boldsymbol{f}_j^t \odot \boldsymbol{c}_j^{t-1} + \boldsymbol{i}_j^t \odot \boldsymbol{z}_j^t,$$
$$\boldsymbol{o}_j^t = \sigma_g(W_o \boldsymbol{x}_j^t + U_o \boldsymbol{h}_j^{t-1} + \boldsymbol{b}_o),$$
$$\boldsymbol{h}_j^t = \boldsymbol{o}_j^t \odot \sigma_h(\boldsymbol{c}_j^t),$$

where $\{\boldsymbol{f}_j^t, \boldsymbol{i}_j^t, \boldsymbol{z}_j^t, \boldsymbol{c}_j^t, \boldsymbol{o}_j^t, \boldsymbol{h}_j^t\} \in \mathbb{R}^{M \times 1}$ are the j-th observation of forget gate, input gate, modulation gate, cell state, output gate, and hidden output at time t, respectively, and M is the number of output units. Also, $\{W_f, W_i, W_c, W_o\} \in \mathbb{R}^{M \times N}$ are weight matrices containing the connecting weights from input $\boldsymbol{x}_j^t$ to the gates and cell, $\{U_f, U_i, U_c, U_o\} \in \mathbb{R}^{M \times M}$ are weight matrices containing the connecting weights from recurrent input $\boldsymbol{h}_j^{t-1}$ to the gates and cell,

$\{b_f, b_i, b_c, b_o\} \in \mathbb{R}^{M \times 1}$ denote the corresponding biases of neurons, and $\odot$ is the Hadamard product. Finally, σ_g, σ_c, and σ_h are nonlinear activation functions allocated to the gates, input modulation, and hidden output, respectively. Note that, in a regression problem, $M = N$, and h_j^{t-1} is an estimation of x_j^t. The regression assumptions can still be applied to sequence-to-sequence or sequence-to-label learning problems simply by adding a fully-connected layer with N input nodes and a desired number of output units.

Assume that all of the weight matrices are independently initialized with zero-mean i.i.d. random values obtained from a symmetric distribution. The goal is to derive the condition(s) on the initialization of the weights to achieve $\mathrm{Var}(h_j^t) = \mathrm{Var}(x_j^t)$. Since the weights are independent from the input, assuming an exact estimation for the recurrent value, i.e., $h_j^{t-1} = x_j^t$, and mutually independent zero-mean input features – sharing the same distribution, the variance of the forget gate can be calculated as

$$
\begin{aligned}
\mathrm{Var}(f_j^t) &= \mathrm{Var}(\sigma_g(W_f x_j^t + U_f h_j^{t-1} + b_f)), \\
&= \mathrm{Var}(W_f x_j^t + U_f h_j^{t-1} + b_f), \\
&= \mathrm{Var}((W_f + U_f) x_j^t), \\
&= N\left(\mathrm{Var}(w_f) + \mathrm{Var}(u_f)\right) \mathrm{Var}(x_j^t),
\end{aligned}
$$

where w_f and u_f are the elements of W_f and U_f, respectively. The bias in the variance calculation is canceled out as it is an independent constant initialized to zero. Moreover, the second equality holds under the assumption that σ_g is an identity function. We will discuss other commonly used functions in LSTM units in Sect. 3.2.

Variance calculations for the input, modulation, and output gates can be performed in a similar way to the forget gate. That is to say,

$$
\begin{aligned}
\mathrm{Var}(i_j^t) &= N\left(\mathrm{Var}(w_i) + \mathrm{Var}(u_i)\right) \mathrm{Var}(x_j^t), \\
\mathrm{Var}(z_j^t) &= N\left(\mathrm{Var}(w_c) + \mathrm{Var}(u_c)\right) \mathrm{Var}(x_j^t), \\
\mathrm{Var}(o_j^t) &= N\left(\mathrm{Var}(w_o) + \mathrm{Var}(u_o)\right) \mathrm{Var}(x_j^t),
\end{aligned}
$$

where w_i, u_i, w_c, u_c, w_o, and u_o are the elements of W_i, U_i, W_c, U_c, W_o, and U_o, respectively.

The cell state formula is a form of the stochastic recurrence equation [17], also known as growing perpetuity, in which the moments of the cell state are time varying. Therefore, one tractable way to stabilize the network training is to set $\mathrm{Var}(c_j^t) = \mathrm{Var}(c_j^{t-1})$. Accordingly,

$$
\begin{aligned}
\mathrm{Var}(c_j^t) &= \mathrm{Var}(f_j^t \odot c_j^{t-1} + i_j^t \odot z_j^t), \\
&= \mathrm{Var}(f_j^t)\mathrm{Var}(c_j^{t-1}) + \mathrm{Var}(i_j^t)\mathrm{Var}(z_j^t), \\
&= \mathrm{Var}(i_j^t)\mathrm{Var}(z_j^t)/(1 - \mathrm{Var}(f_j^t)),
\end{aligned}
$$

where the above equation is obtained based on the zero-mean assumption and independence assumption between all of the gates and the cell state to avoid terms containing covariance matrices in the last expression. Also, note that $0 < \mathrm{Var}(f_j^t) < 1$.

Finally, the variance of the network output is computed as

$$\mathrm{Var}(h_j^t) = \mathrm{Var}(o_j^t \odot \sigma_h(c_j^t)),$$
$$= \mathrm{Var}(o_j^t)\mathrm{Var}(c_j^t),$$

where the last equality is obtained assuming that there is an identity activation function and independence between the output gate and the cell state. Considering all of the calculated variances and setting $\mathrm{Var}(h_j^t) = \mathrm{Var}(x_j^t) = 1$, the required condition can be summarized as

$$0 < \mathrm{Var}(w_f) + \mathrm{Var}(u_f) < 1/N,$$
$$1 - N\left(\mathrm{Var}(w_f) + \mathrm{Var}(u_f)\right) = \prod_{k \neq f} N\left(\mathrm{Var}(w_k) + \mathrm{Var}(u_k)\right), \tag{1}$$

where the right hand side of the above equation is the multiplication of the weights connected to the input, modulation, and output gates.

Similar to the feedforward pass, some initialization conditions can be derived to ensure that the variance of the backpropagated gradient remains unchanged, i.e., $\mathrm{Var}(\partial \mathcal{L}_j^t / \partial h_j^t) = \mathrm{Var}(\partial \mathcal{L}_j^t / \partial x_j^t)$ where $\mathcal{L} \in \mathbb{R}^{N \times 1}$ is the loss function defined based on the actual target and network output. However, as shown in [13] and [15], initialization with properly scaling the forward signal is equivalent to initialization with properly scaling the backward signal, and since the number of units in the input and output of the LSTM network are the same, similar conditions for weight initialization using backpropagation will be obtained.

3.1 Peephole Connections

In general, LSTMs can be extended to augment their internal cell state to the multiplicative gates using the so-called peephole connections. These cell-to-gate connections allow the gates to inspect the current cell state even if the output gate is closed, and consequently help improving the performance, especially when the task involves a precise duration of intervals [9]. The feedforward pass of the peephole LSTM can be formulated as

$$f_j^t = \sigma_g(W_f x_j^t + U_f h_j^{t-1} + V_f c_j^{t-1} + b_f),$$
$$i_j^t = \sigma_g(W_i x_j^t + U_i h_j^{t-1} + V_i c_j^{t-1} + b_i),$$
$$z_j^t = \sigma_c(W_c x_j^t + U_c h_j^{t-1} + b_c),$$
$$c_j^t = f_j^t \odot c_j^{t-1} + i_j^t \odot z_j^t,$$
$$o_j^t = \sigma_g(W_o x_j^t + U_o h_j^{t-1} + V_o c_j^t + b_o),$$
$$h_j^t = o_j^t \odot \sigma_h(c_j^t),$$

where $\{V_f, V_i, V_o\} \in \mathbb{R}^{M \times M}$ are diagonal peephole weight matrices. Hence, each gate will only look at its corresponding cell state. To achieve $\mathrm{Var}(h_j^t) = \mathrm{Var}(x_j^t)$, all the assumptions applied to the traditional LSTM are used for the peephole LSTM. Assuming that the peephole matrices are independent from the input and the cell state and are independently initialized with zero-mean i.i.d. random values obtained from a symmetric distribution, the variances can be calculated as

$$\mathrm{Var}(f_j^t) = N\left(\mathrm{Var}(w_f) + \mathrm{Var}(u_f)\right)\mathrm{Var}(x_j^t) + \mathrm{Var}(v_f)\mathrm{Var}(c_j^{t-1}), \tag{2}$$

$$\mathrm{Var}(i_j^t) = N\left(\mathrm{Var}(w_i) + \mathrm{Var}(u_i)\right)\mathrm{Var}(x_j^t) + \mathrm{Var}(v_i)\mathrm{Var}(c_j^{t-1}), \tag{3}$$

$$\mathrm{Var}(z_j^t) = N\left(\mathrm{Var}(w_c) + \mathrm{Var}(u_c)\right)\mathrm{Var}(x_j^t), \tag{4}$$

$$\mathrm{Var}(o_j^t) = N\left(\mathrm{Var}(w_o) + \mathrm{Var}(u_o)\right)\mathrm{Var}(x_j^t) + \mathrm{Var}(v_o)\mathrm{Var}(c_j^t), \tag{5}$$

$$\mathrm{Var}(c_j^t) = \mathrm{Var}(c_j^{t-1}) = \mathrm{Var}(i_j^t)\mathrm{Var}(z_j^t)/(1 - \mathrm{Var}(f_j^t)), \tag{6}$$

$$\mathrm{Var}(h_j^t) = \mathrm{Var}(o_j^t)\mathrm{Var}(c_j^t), \tag{7}$$

where v_f, v_i, and v_o are the diagonal elements of V_f, V_i, and V_o, respectively. Merging Eqs. (5) and (7) under the assumption that $\mathrm{Var}(h_j^t) = \mathrm{Var}(x_j^t) = 1$ results in a quadratic equation that can be expressed as

$$\beta_{01} + \beta_{11}\mathrm{Var}(c_j^t) + \beta_{21}\mathrm{Var}^2(c_j^t) = 0, \tag{8}$$

where $\beta_{01} = -1$, $\beta_{11} = N\left(\mathrm{Var}(w_o) + \mathrm{Var}(u_o)\right)$, and $\beta_{21} = \mathrm{Var}(v_o)$. Since the discriminant $\Delta_1 = \beta_{11}^2 - 4\beta_{21}\beta_{01}$ is always positive considering nonzero variances, there are two possible solutions for Eq. (8): $\mathrm{Var}(c_j^t) = (-\beta_{11} \pm \sqrt{\Delta_1})/(2\beta_{21})$. However, since $\beta_{21} > 0$ and $\beta_{01} < 0$, with a positive discriminant and based on the sign of the product of the roots (β_{01}/β_{21}), one of the real solutions would be negative, which cannot be accepted as $\mathrm{Var}(c_j^t) > 0$. Therefore, the desired solution to Eq. (8) will be obtained as

$$\mathrm{Var}(c_j^t) = \frac{-\beta_{11} + \sqrt{\Delta_1}}{2\beta_{21}}. \tag{9}$$

Likewise, combining Eqs. (2) to (4) and (6) using the same assumptions leads to another quadratic equation that can be written as

$$\beta_{02} + \beta_{12}\mathrm{Var}(c_j^t) + \beta_{22}\mathrm{Var}^2(c_j^t) = 0, \tag{10}$$

where $\beta_{02} = N^2\left(\mathrm{Var}(w_i) + \mathrm{Var}(u_i)\right)\left(\mathrm{Var}(w_c) + \mathrm{Var}(u_c)\right)$, $\beta_{22} = \mathrm{Var}(v_f)$, and $\beta_{12} = N\mathrm{Var}(v_i)\left(\mathrm{Var}(w_c) + \mathrm{Var}(u_c)\right) + N\left(\mathrm{Var}(w_f) + \mathrm{Var}(u_f)\right) - 1$. The two possible solutions for Eq. (10) will be obtained as $\mathrm{Var}(c_j^t) = (-\beta_{12} \pm \sqrt{\Delta_2})/(2\beta_{22})$, where $\Delta_2 = \beta_{12}^2 - 4\beta_{22}\beta_{02}$ is the discriminant of the equation. Here, since $\beta_{02}, \beta_{22} > 0$, assuming a nonnegative discriminant and based on the sign of the sum and product of the roots $(-\beta_{12}/\beta_{22}$ and $\beta_{02}/\beta_{22})$, both real solutions could be positive and acceptable provided that $\beta_{12} < 0$. However, to achieve a simple solution for initialization, one can set $\Delta_2 = 0$ and $\beta_{12} < 0$ which produces repeated real positive roots for the problem. Therefore, the real solution to Eq. (10) can be obtained as

$$\text{Var}(c_j^t) = \frac{-\beta_{12}}{2\beta_{22}}. \tag{11}$$

Finally, conditions for the existence of a common solution to Eqs. (8) and (10) can be obtained using Eqs. (9) and (11) as follows

$$0 < \text{Var}(v_i)\left(\text{Var}(w_c) + \text{Var}(u_c)\right) + \left(\text{Var}(w_f) + \text{Var}(u_f)\right) < 1/N,$$

$$\frac{\text{Var}(v_o)}{\text{Var}(v_f)}\sqrt{4N^2\text{Var}(v_f)\left(\text{Var}(w_i) + \text{Var}(u_i)\right)\left(\text{Var}(w_c) + \text{Var}(u_c)\right)} \tag{12}$$

$$= \sqrt{N^2\left(\text{Var}(w_o) + \text{Var}(u_o)\right)^2 + 4\text{Var}(v_o)} - N\left(\text{Var}(w_o) + \text{Var}(u_o)\right).$$

3.2 Nonlinear Activation Functions

All the abovementioned equations are obtained based on the assumption that the activation functions are identity functions. In general, symmetric functions with zero-intercepts such as the identity and hyperbolic tangent are suggested for σ_h and σ_c, respectively, and logistic sigmoid is suggested for σ_g [9]. Both the hyperbolic tangent and logistic sigmoid are nonlinear symmetric functions that can be linearly approximated using a Taylor series expansion. The former has a zero intercept and its expansion about zero leads to an identity function ($\sigma_c(x) \approx x$). The latter, however, has a nonzero intercept and its Taylor series about zero is approximated as $\sigma_g(x) \approx 0.5 + 0.25x$. Therefore, the sigmoid function approximately increases the input signal mean by $1/2$ and scales its variance by $1/16$. Note that the nonzero mean value of the sigmoid can induce important singular values in the Hessian matrix, resulting in saturation of the top layers and prohibition of gradients to flow backward to learn useful features in the lower layers [13]. Using the suggested activation functions in the gates, the variance calculations for the traditional LSTM network are updated as follows based on the aforementioned Taylor series expansion

$$\text{Var}(f_j^t) = N\left(\text{Var}(w_f) + \text{Var}(u_f)\right)\text{Var}(x_j^t)/16,$$

$$\text{Var}(i_j^t) = N\left(\text{Var}(w_i) + \text{Var}(u_i)\right)\text{Var}(x_j^t)/16,$$

$$\text{Var}(z_j^t) = N\left(\text{Var}(w_c) + \text{Var}(u_c)\right)\text{Var}(x_j^t),$$

$$\text{Var}(o_j^t) = N\left(\text{Var}(w_o) + \text{Var}(u_o)\right)\text{Var}(x_j^t)/16,$$

$$\text{Var}(c_j^t) = \text{Var}(c_j^{t-1}) = (\text{Var}(i_j^t) + 0.25)\text{Var}(z_j^t)/(0.75 - \text{Var}(f_j^t)),$$

where the last equation is obtained bearing in mind that $\text{Var}(xy) = \text{Var}(x)\text{Var}(y) + \mathbb{E}^2(x)\text{Var}(y) + \mathbb{E}^2(y)\text{Var}(x)$ for two independent random variables x and y, and considering $\mathbb{E}(z_j^t) = 0$, $\mathbb{E}(f_j^t) = \mathbb{E}(i_j^t) = 0.5$, and, hence, $\mathbb{E}(c_j^t) = \mathbb{E}(c_j^{t-1}) = 0$. Finally, the updated rule for initialization of a traditional LSTM network using Eq. (7) can be written as

$$0 < \text{Var}(w_f) + \text{Var}(u_f) < 12/N, \tag{13}$$

$$\frac{12 - N\left(\text{Var}(w_f) + \text{Var}(u_f)\right)}{N\left(\text{Var}(w_i) + \text{Var}(u_i)\right) + 4} = N^2\left(\text{Var}(w_o) + \text{Var}(u_o)\right)\left(\text{Var}(w_c) + \text{Var}(u_c)\right)/16.$$

Applying the same suggested functions in the peephole LSTM network generalizes the variance calculations as follows

$$\text{Var}(\boldsymbol{f}_j^t) = N\left(\text{Var}(w_f) + \text{Var}(u_f)\right)\text{Var}(\boldsymbol{x}_j^t)/16 + \text{Var}(v_f)\text{Var}(\boldsymbol{c}_j^{t-1})/16,$$

$$\text{Var}(\boldsymbol{i}_j^t) = N\left(\text{Var}(w_i) + \text{Var}(u_i)\right)\text{Var}(\boldsymbol{x}_j^t)/16 + \text{Var}(v_i)\text{Var}(\boldsymbol{c}_j^{t-1})/16,$$

$$\text{Var}(\boldsymbol{z}_j^t) = N\left(\text{Var}(w_c) + \text{Var}(u_c)\right)\text{Var}(\boldsymbol{x}_j^t),$$

$$\text{Var}(\boldsymbol{o}_j^t) = N\left(\text{Var}(w_o) + \text{Var}(u_o)\right)\text{Var}(\boldsymbol{x}_j^t)/16 + \text{Var}(v_o)\text{Var}(\boldsymbol{c}_j^t)/16,$$

$$\text{Var}(\boldsymbol{c}_j^t) = \text{Var}(\boldsymbol{c}_j^{t-1}) = (\text{Var}(\boldsymbol{i}_j^t) + 0.25)\text{Var}(\boldsymbol{z}_j^t)/(0.75 - \text{Var}(\boldsymbol{f}_j^t)),$$

Here also using Eq. (7), two quadratic equations can be obtained similar to Eqs. (8) and (10), where $\beta_{01} = -16$, $\beta_{11} = N\left(\text{Var}(w_o) + \text{Var}(u_o)\right)$, $\beta_{21} = \text{Var}(v_o)$, $\beta_{02} = N\left(\text{Var}(w_c) + \text{Var}(u_c)\right)\left(N\left(\text{Var}(w_i) + \text{Var}(u_i)\right) + 4\right)$, $\beta_{22} = \text{Var}(v_f)$, and $\beta_{12} = N\text{Var}(v_i)\left(\text{Var}(w_c) + \text{Var}(u_c)\right) + N\left(\text{Var}(w_f) + \text{Var}(u_f)\right) - 12$. Likewise, conditions for the existence of a common solution to Eqs. (8) and (10) can be obtained using Eqs. (9) and (11) as follows

$$0 < \text{Var}(v_i)\left(\text{Var}(w_c) + \text{Var}(u_c)\right) + \left(\text{Var}(w_f) + \text{Var}(u_f)\right) < 12/N,$$

$$\frac{\text{Var}(v_o)}{\text{Var}(v_f)}\sqrt{4N\text{Var}(v_f)\left(\text{Var}(w_c) + \text{Var}(u_c)\right)\left(N\left(\text{Var}(w_i) + \text{Var}(u_i)\right) + 4\right)} \quad (14)$$

$$= \sqrt{N^2\left(\text{Var}(w_o) + \text{Var}(u_o)\right)^2 + 64\text{Var}(v_o)} - N\left(\text{Var}(w_o) + \text{Var}(u_o)\right).$$

3.3 Initialization Summary

The proposed initialization rule can be summarized as follows:

- Standardize the input data to have a zero-mean and unit variance per feature, and initialize the LSTM network biases to zero.
- Initialize the weights in the weight matrices randomly using zero-mean i.i.d. Gaussian distributions with variances satisfying one of the following equations:
  - Equation (1), if using the traditional LSTM network based on identity or hyperbolic tangent functions.
  - Equation (12), if using the peephole LSTM network based on identity or hyperbolic tangent functions.
  - Equation (13), if using the traditional LSTM network based on identity or hyperbolic tangent for input modulation and cell activation, and logistic sigmoid functions in the gates.
  - Equation (14), if using the peephole LSTM network based on identity or hyperbolic tangent for input modulation and cell activation, and logistic sigmoid functions in the gates.

Note that the variances need to be selected subject to the specified conditions in the selected equation. For example, when using a peephole LSTM, and, correspondingly, Eq. (12) or (14), there are eleven variances to fix, $\text{Var}(v_f)$, $\text{Var}(v_i)$, $\text{Var}(v_o)$, $\text{Var}(w_f)$, $\text{Var}(u_f)$, $\text{Var}(w_i)$, $\text{Var}(u_i)$, $\text{Var}(w_o)$, $\text{Var}(u_o)$, $\text{Var}(w_c)$, and $\text{Var}(u_c)$.

4   Experiments and Results

4.1   Data

Both univariate and multivariate data are used to study the effect of initialization on LSTM training.

The following three univariate datasets are obtained from the UCR Time Series Archive [10] due to having the largest training samples size: *ElectricDevices* with 16,637 samples (8,926 for training and 7,711 for test) of sequence length 96; *FordA* with 4,921 samples (3,601 for training and 1,320 for test) of sequence length 500; and *Crop* with 24,000 samples (7,200 for training and 16,800 for test) of sequence length 46.

The multivariate dataset, *ADNI*, focuses on disease progression modeling and is obtained from the ADNI cohort [12]. It constitutes yearly measurements for 383 subjects (332 for training and 51 for test) of sequence length 3 to 10 with normal cognition, mild cognition impairment, or Alzheimer's disease. The multivariate feature set consists of T1-weighted MRI volumetric measurements of ventricles, hippocampus, whole brain, fusiform, middle temporal gyrus, and entorhinal cortex, all normalized for intracranial volume.

4.2   Experimental Setup

The proposed initialization method is assessed using a peephole LSTM [9] applied to the univariate data ($N = 1$) for time series regression and a peephole LSTM robust to missing values [11] applied to the multivariate data ($N = 6$) for disease progression modeling. In both cases, an identity function and a hyperbolic tangent are used in σ_h and σ_c, respectively, a logistic sigmoid is used in σ_g, and the network biases are initialized to zero. Therefore, the variance selection for weight matrices is performed using Eq. (14), and weight values are drawn from the zero-mean i.i.d. Gaussian distributions. Four different configurations of the variances are inspected as illustrated in Table 1.

Table 1. The utilized configurations of the variances satisfying Eq. (14).

Method	Var(v_f)	Var(v_i)	Var(v_o)	Var(w_f)	Var(u_f)	Var(w_i)	Var(u_i)	Var(w_o)	Var(u_o)	Var(w_c)	Var(u_c)
Proposed 1	1	1	1	$1/N$	$1/N$	$2/N$	$2/N$	$3/N$	$3/N$	$1/(4N)$	$1/(4N)$
Proposed 2	1/2	1/2	1/2	$1/N$	$1/N$	$2/N$	$2/N$	$1/N$	$1/N$	$1/(2N)$	$1/(2N)$
Proposed 3	1	1	1	$3/(4N)$	$1/(4N)$	$3/N$	$1/N$	$4/N$	$2/N$	$1/(4N)$	$1/(4N)$
Proposed 4	1	1	1	$1/(4N)$	$3/(4N)$	$1/N$	$3/N$	$2/N$	$4/N$	$1/(4N)$	$1/(4N)$

The input data is standardized to have a zero-mean and unit variance per feature dimension. Moreover, the batch size is set to 85% of training samples (15% used for validation to tune the optimization hyperparameters), and the first to penultimate time point is used to estimate the second to last time point per observation. The L2-norm is used as loss function and momentum batch gradient descent is applied to optimize the network parameters using L2 regularization. The optimization hyperparameters, i.e., the learning rate, momentum weight, and weight decay are set to 0.1, 0.9, and 0.0001, respectively. These values were selected according to the validation set error across the different experiments.

The proposed approach is compared with two state-of-the-art initialization techniques applied to the same LSTM networks assuming zero biases and using the same optimization setup: *normalized* [13], all weight matrices drawn i.i.d. from zero-mean Gaussian distributions with a scaled variance of $1/N$; *orthogonal* [5], same as normalized, but with orthogonal recurrent weight matrices drawn i.i.d. from zero-mean Gaussian distributions with a variance of $1/N$.

4.3   Results

Figure 1 compares the training loss of the proposed and state-of-the-art initialization methods applied to the univariate and multivariate datasets. As can be seen, the proposed method with any configuration outperforms the prevalent initialization techniques in all experiments, either by achieving a lower loss (ElectricDevices and FordA) or by faster convergence to the same loss (Crop and ADNI).

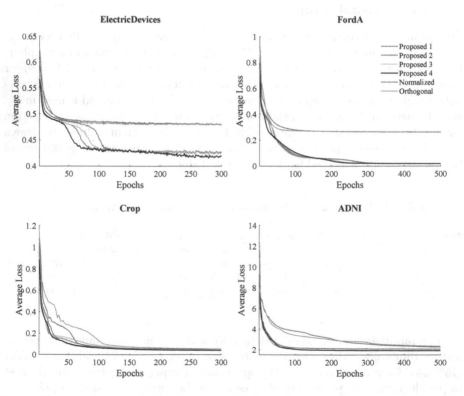

Fig. 1. The training loss of the different methods applied to the univariate and multivariate datasets.

To further investigate the influence of initialization on the performance, we also evaluate the generalization error in the test set. Table 2 reports the test mean square error (MSE) in predicting the feature values per dataset for the utilized initialization methods. As it can be deduced, the proposed initialization method with any configuration achieves superior results to the prevalent initialization approaches, which illustrates the generalizability of the proposed method.

Table 2. The generalization error (MSE) in predicting the feature values for the utilized test sets using the different initialization techniques.

Method	ElectricDevices	FordA	Crop	ADNI
Proposed 1	0.935	0.038	0.086	0.465
Proposed 2	0.942	0.037	0.088	0.468
Proposed 3	0.946	0.037	0.086	0.453
Proposed 4	0.895	0.038	0.082	0.449
Normalized	1.012	0.523	0.109	0.473
Orthogonal	0.998	0.526	0.110	0.471

More interestingly, the fourth configuration of the proposed method in which the recurrent weights receive more variance than the current input weights outperforms all the other methods in almost all of the experiments.

5   Conclusion

In this paper, a robust initialization method was proposed for LSTM networks to address training instability and slow convergence. The proposed method was based on scaled random weights initialization aiming to keep the variance of the network input and output signals in the same range subjected to a number of assumptions simplifying the initialization conditions. The proposed method was applied to univariate and multivariate time series regression datasets and outperformed two state-of-the-art initialization methods in all cases.

The obtained conditions can be optimized for eight or eleven unknowns using a traditional LSTM or peephole LSTM, respectively. In this work, different configurations of the variances were inspected to confirm the proposed assumption for initializing the network weights. Moreover, the proposed method can be used for sequence-to-sequence and sequence-to-label learning paradigms by connecting a fully-connected layer with a desired output size to the LSTM network output. It should also be noted that the initialization conditions need to be properly modified in case of using activation functions other than a hyperbolic tangent, identity function, or logistic sigmoid in the gates.

Acknowledgments. This project has received funding from the European Union's Horizon 2020 research and innovation programme under the Marie Skłodowska-Curie grant agreement No 721820.

References

1. Hochreiter, S., Bengio, Y., Frasconi, P., Schmidhuber, J.: Gradient flow in recurrent nets: the difficulty of learning long-term dependencies. In: A Field Guide to Dynamical Recurrent Neural Networks. IEEE Press (2001)
2. Martens, J., Sutskever, I.: Learning recurrent neural networks with Hessian-free optimization. In: Proceedings of the International Conference on Machine Learning, pp. 1033–1040 (2011)
3. Trinh, T.H., Dai, A.M., Luong, M.T., Le, Q.V.: Learning longer-term dependencies in RNNs with auxiliary losses. CoRR abs/1803.00144 (2018)
4. Le, Q.V., Jaitly, N., Hinton, G.E.: A simple way to initialize recurrent networks of rectified linear units. CoRR abs/1504.00941 (2015)
5. Vorontsov, E., Trabelsi, C., Kadoury, S., Pal, C.: On orthogonality and learning recurrent networks with long term dependencies. CoRR abs/1702.00071 (2017)
6. Hochreiter, S., Schmidhuber, J.: Long short-term memory. Neural Comput. **9**(8), 1735–1780 (1997)
7. Cho, K., et al.: Learning phrase representations using RNN encoder-decoder for statistical machine translation. In: Proceedings of the 2014 Conference on Empirical Methods in Natural Language Processing, pp. 1724–1734 (2014)
8. Sutskever, I., Vinyals, O., Le, Q.V.: Sequence to sequence learning with neural networks. In: Advances in Neural Information Processing Systems, pp. 3104–3112 (2014)
9. Gers, F.A., Schraudolph, N.N., Schmidhuber, J.: Learning precise timing with LSTM recurrent networks. J. Mach. Learn. Res. **3**, 115–143 (2002)
10. Dau, H.A., et al.: The UCR Time Series Archive. CoRR abs/1810.07758 (2018)
11. Ghazi, M.M., et al.: Training recurrent neural networks robust to incomplete data: application to Alzheimer's disease progression modeling. Med. Image Anal. **53**, 39–46 (2019)
12. Petersen, R.C., et al.: Alzheimer's Disease Neuroimaging Initiative (ADNI): clinical characterization. Neurology **74**, 201–209 (2010)
13. Glorot, X., Bengio, Y.: Understanding the difficulty of training deep feedforward neural networks. In: Proceedings of the International Conference on Artificial Intelligence and Statistics, pp. 249–256 (2010)
14. Erhan, D., Manzagol, P.A., Bengio, Y., Bengio, S., Vincent, P.: The difficulty of training deep architectures and the effect of unsupervised pre-training. In: Proceedings of the International Conference on Artificial Intelligence and Statistics, pp. 153–160 (2009)
15. He, K., Zhang, X., Ren, S., Sun, J.: Delving deep into rectifiers: surpassing human-level performance on ImageNet classification. In: Proceedings of the 2015 IEEE International Conference on Computer Vision, pp. 1026–1034 (2015)
16. Talathi, S.S., Vartak, A.: Improving performance of recurrent neural network with ReLU nonlinearity. CoRR abs/1511.03771 (2015)
17. Buraczewski, D., Damek, E., Mikosch, T., et al.: Stochastic Models with Power-Law Tails. Springer, Cham (2016). https://doi.org/10.1007/978-3-319-29679-1

A Multi-cascaded Deep Model
for Bilingual SMS Classification

Muhammad Haroon Shakeel(✉) (iD), Asim Karim(iD), and Imdadullah Khan(iD)

Department of Computer Science, Syed Babar Ali School of Science and Engineering,
Lahore University of Management Sciences (LUMS), Lahore, Pakistan
{15030040,akarim,imdad.khan}@lums.edu.pk

Abstract. Most studies on text classification are focused on the English language. However, short texts such as SMS are influenced by regional languages. This makes the automatic text classification task challenging due to the multilingual, informal, and noisy nature of language in the text. In this work, we propose a novel multi-cascaded deep learning model called *McM* for bilingual SMS classification. McM exploits n-gram level information as well as long-term dependencies of text for learning. Our approach aims to learn a model without any code-switching indication, lexical normalization, language translation, or language transliteration. The model relies entirely upon the text as no external knowledge base is utilized for learning. For this purpose, a 12 class bilingual text dataset is developed from SMS feedbacks of citizens on public services containing mixed Roman Urdu and English languages. Our model achieves high accuracy for classification on this dataset and outperforms the previous model for multilingual text classification, highlighting language independence of McM.

Keywords: Deep learning · Roman Urdu · SMS classification · Code-switching

1 Introduction

Social media such as Facebook, Twitter, and Short Text Messaging Service (SMS) are popular channels for getting feedback from consumers on products and services. In Pakistan, with the emergence of e-government practices, SMS is being used for getting feedback from the citizens on different public services with the aim to reduce petty corruption and deficient delivery in services. Automatic classification of these SMS into predefined categories can greatly decrease the response time on complaints and consequently improve the public services rendered to the citizens. While Urdu is the national language of Pakistan, English is treated as the official language of the country. This leads to the development of a distinct dialect of communication known as Roman Urdu, which utilizes English alphabets to write Urdu. Hence, the SMS texts contain multilingual text written in the non-native script and informal diction. The utilization of

© Springer Nature Switzerland AG 2019
T. Gedeon et al. (Eds.): ICONIP 2019, LNCS 11953, pp. 287–298, 2019.
https://doi.org/10.1007/978-3-030-36708-4_24

two or more languages simultaneously is known as multilingualism [2]. Consequently, alternation of two languages in a single conversation, a phenomenon known as code-switching, is inevitable for a multilingual speaker [15]. Factors like informal verbiage, improper grammar, variation in spellings, code-switching, and short text length make the problem of automatic bilingual SMS classification highly challenging.

In Natural Language Processing (NLP), deep learning has revolutionized the modeling and understanding of human languages. The richness, expressiveness, ambiguities, and complexity of the natural language can be addressed by deep neural networks without the need to produce complex engineered features [1]. Deep learning models have been successfully used in many NLP tasks involving multilingual text. A Convolutional Neural Network (CNN) based model for sentiment classification of a multilingual dataset was proposed in [4]. However, a particular record in the dataset belonged to one language only. In our case, a record can have either one or two languages. There is very little published work on this specific setting. One way to classify bilingual text is to normalize the different variations of a word to a standard spelling before training the model [8]. However, such normalization requires external resources such as lexical database, and Roman Urdu is under-resourced in this context. Another approach for an under-resourced language is to adapt the resources from resource-rich language [16]. However, such an approach is not generalizable in the case of Roman Urdu text as it is an informal language with no proper grammatical rules and dictionary. More recent approach utilizes code-switching annotations to improve the predictive performance of the model, where each word is annotated with its respective language label. Such an approach is not scalable for large data as annotation task becomes tedious.

In this paper, we propose a multi-cascaded deep learning network, called as *McM* for multi-class classification of bilingual short text. Our goal is to achieve this without any prior knowledge of the language, code-switching indication, language translation, normalizing lexical variations, or language transliteration. In multilingual text classification, previous approaches employ a single deep learning architecture, such as CNN or Long Short Term Memory (LSTM) for feature learning and classification. McM, on the other hand, employs three cascades (aka feature learners) to learn rich textual representations from three perspectives. These representations are then forwarded to a small discriminator network for final prediction. We compare the performance of the proposed model with existing CNN-based model for multilingual text classification [4]. We report a series of experiments using 3 kinds of embedding initialization approaches as well as the effect of attention mechanism [14].

The English language is well studied under the umbrella of NLP, hence many resources and datasets for the different problems are available. However, research on English-Roman Urdu bilingual text lags behind because of non-availability of gold standard datasets. Our second contribution is that we present a large scale annotated dataset in Roman Urdu and English language with code-switching, for

Table 1. Description of class label along with distribution of each class (in %) in the acquired dataset

Class label	Description	Class %
Appreciation	Citizen provided appreciative feedback	43.1%
Satisfied	Citizen satisfied with the service	31.1%
Peripheral complaint	Complains about peripheral service like non-availability of parking or complexity of the procedure	8.2%
Demanded inquiry	More inquiry is required on the complaint	5.7%
Corruption	Citizen reported bribery	3.5%
Lagged response	Department responded with delay	2.1%
Unresponsive	No response received by the citizen from the department	2.0%
Medicine payment	Complainant was asked to buy basic medicine on his expense	1.8%
Adverse behavior	Aggressive/intolerant behavior of the staff towards the citizen	1.5%
Resource nonexistence	Department lacks necessary resources	0.6%
Grievance ascribed	Malfeasance/Abuse of powers/official misconduct/sexual harassment to the complainant	0.3%
Obnoxious/irrelevant	The SMS was irrelevant to public services	0.2%

multi-class classification. The dataset consists of more than 0.3 million records and has been made available for future research.

The rest of the paper is organized as follows. Section 2 defines the dataset acquiring process and provides an explanation of the class labels. In Sect. 3, the architecture of the proposed model, its hyperparameters, and the experimental setup is discussed. We discuss the results in Sect. 4 and finally, concluding remarks are presented in Sect. 5.

2 Dataset Acquisition and Description

The dataset consists of SMS feedbacks of the citizens of Pakistan on different public services availed by them. The objective of collecting these responses is to measure the performance of government departments rendering different public services. Preprocessing of the data is kept minimal. All records having only single word in SMS were removed as cleaning step. To construct the "gold standard", 313, 813 samples are manually annotated into 12 predefined categories by

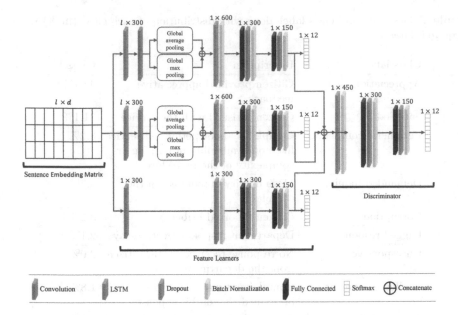

Fig. 1. Multi-cascaded model (McM) for bilingual short text classification (figure best seen in color) (Color figure online)

two annotators in supervision of a domain-expert. Involvement of the domain-expert was to ensure the practicality and quality of the "gold standard". Finally, stratified sampling method was opted for splitting the data into train and test partitions with $80 - 20$ ratio (i.e., 80% records for training and 20% records for testing). This way, training split has $251,050$ records while testing split has $62,763$ records. The rationale behind stratified sampling was to maintain the ratio of every class in both splits. The preprocessed and annotated data along with train and test split is made available[1]. Note that the department names and service availed by the citizens is mapped to an integer identifier for anonymity.

Class label ratios, corresponding labels, and it's description are presented in Table 1.

3   Proposed Model and Experimentation

The proposed model, named *McM*, is mainly inspired by the findings by Reimers and Gurevych (2017), who concluded that deeper model have minimal effect on the predictive performance of the model [9]. McM manifests a wider model, which employ three feature learners (cascades) that are trained for classification independently (in parallel).

---

[1] https://github.com/haroonshakeel/bilingual_sms_classification.

The input text is first mapped to embedding matrix of size $l \times d$ where l denotes the number of words in the text while d is dimensions of the embedding vector for each of these words. More formally, let $\mathcal{T} \in \{w_1, w_2, ..., w_l\}$ be the input text with l words, embedding matrix is defined by $X \in \mathbb{R}^{l \times d}$. This representation is then fed to three feature learners, which are trained with local supervision. The learned features are then forwarded to discriminator network for final prediction as shown in Fig. 1. Each of these components are discussed in subsequent subsections.

3.1 Stacked-CNN Learner

CNN learner is employed to learn n-gram features for identification of relationships between words. A 1-d convolution filter is used with a sliding window (kernel) of size k (number of n-grams) in order to extract the features. A filter W is defined as $W \in \mathbb{R}^{k \times d}$ for the convolution function. The word vectors starting from the position j to the position $j + k - 1$ are processed by the filter W at a time. The window h_j is expressed as:

$$h_j = [X_j \oplus X_{j+1} \oplus, ..., \oplus X_{j+k-1}] \tag{1}$$

Where, the $\oplus$ represents the concatenation of word vectors. The number of filters are usually decided empirically. Each filter convolves with one window at a time to generate a feature map f_j for that specific window as:

$$f_j = \sigma(h_j \odot W + b) \tag{2}$$

Where, the $\odot$ represents convolution operation, b is a bias term, and σ is a nonlinear transformation function $ReLU$, which is defined as $\sigma(x) = max(x, 0)$. The feature maps of each window are concatenated across all filters to get a high level vector representation and fed as input to next CNN layer. Output of second CNN layer is followed by (i) global max-pooling to remove low activation information from feature maps of all filters, and (ii) global average-pooling to get average activation across all the n-grams.

These two outputs are then concatenated and forwarded to a small feed-forward network having two fully-connected layers, followed by a *softmax* layer for prediction of this particular learner. Dropout and batch-normalization layers are repeatedly used between both fully-connected layers to avoid features co-adaptation [3,11].

3.2 Stacked-LSTM Learner

The traditional methods in deep learning do not account for previous information while processing current input. LSTM, however, is able to memorize past information and correlate it with current information [13]. LSTM structure has memory cells (aka LSTM cells) that store the information selectively. Each word is treated as one time step and is fed to LSTM in a sequential manner. While processing the input at current time step X_t, LSTM also takes into account the previous hidden state h_{t-1}. The LSTM represents each time step with an input, a memory, and an output gate, denoted as i_t, f_t and o_t respectively. The hidden state h_t of input X_t for each time step t is given by:

$$i_t = \sigma(W_i X_t + U_i h_{t-1} + b_i), \tag{3}$$

$$f_t = \sigma(W_f X_t + U_f h_{t-1} + b_f), \tag{4}$$

$$o_t = \sigma(W_o X_t + U_o h_{t-1} + b_o), \tag{5}$$

$$u_t = tanh(W_u + U_u h_{t-1} + b_u), \tag{6}$$

$$c_t = i_t * u_t + f_t * c_{t-1}, \tag{7}$$

$$h_t = o_t * tanh(c_t). \tag{8}$$

Where, the $*$ is element-wise multiplication and σ is sigmoid activation function.

Stacked-LSTM learner is comprised of two LSTM layers. Let H_1 be a matrix consisting of output vectors $\{h_1, h_2, ..., h_l\}$ that the first LSTM layer produced, denoting output at each time steps. This matrix is fed to second LSTM layer. Similarly, second layer produces another output matrix H_2 which is used to apply global max-pooling and global-average pooling. These two outputs are concatenated and forwarded to a two layered feedforward network for intermediate supervision (prediction), identical to previously described stacked-CNN learner.

3.3 LSTM Learner

LSTM learner is employed to learn long-term dependencies of the text as described in [13]. This learner encodes complete input text recursively. It takes one word vector at a time as input and outputs a single vector. The dimensions of the output vector are equal to the number of LSTM units deployed. This encoded text representation is then forwarded to a small feedforward network, identical to aforementioned two learners, for intermediate supervision in order to learn features. This learner differs from stacked-LSTM learner as it learns sentence features, and not average and max features of all time steps (input words).

3.4 Discriminator Network

The objective of discriminator network is to aggregate features learned by each of above described three learners and squash them into a small network for final prediction. The discriminator employs two fully-connected layers with batch-normalization and dropout layer along with *ReLU* activation function for non-linearity. The *softmax* activation function with categorical cross-entropy loss is used on the final prediction layer to get probabilities of each class. The class label is assigned based on maximum probability. This is treated as final prediction of the proposed model. The complete architecture, along with dimensions of each output is shown in Fig. 1.

3.5   Experimental Setup

Pre-trained word embeddings on massive data, such as GloVe [6], give boost to predictive performance for multi-class classification [12]. However, such embeddings are limited to English language only with no equivalence for Roman Urdu. Therefore, in this study, we avoid using any *word-based* pre-trained embeddings to give equal treatment to words of each language. We perform three kinds of experiments. (1) Embedding matrix is constructed using ELMo embeddings [7], which utilizes characters to form word vectors and produces a word vector with $d = 1024$. We call this variation of the model McM_E. (2) Embedding matrix is initialized randomly for each word with word vector of size $d = 300$. We refer this particular model as McM_R. (3) We train domain specific embeddings[2] using word2vec with word vector of size $d = 300$ as suggested in original study [5]. We refer to this particular model as McM_D.

Furthermore, we also introduce soft-attention [14] between two layers of CNN and LSTM (in respective feature learner) to evaluate effect of attention on bilingual text classification. Attention mechanism "highlights" (assigns more weight) a particular word that contributes more towards correct classification. We refer to attention based experiments with subscript A for all three embedding initializations. This way, a total of 6 experiments are performed with different variations of the proposed model. To mitigate effect of random initialization of network weights, we fix the random seed across all experiments. We train each model for 20 epochs and create a checkpoint at epoch with best predictive performance on test split.

We re-implement the model proposed in [4], and use it as a baseline for our problem. The rationale behind choosing this particular model as a baseline is it's proven good predictive performance on multilingual text classification. For McM, the choices of number of convolutional filters, number of hidden units in first dense layer, number of hidden units in second dense layer, and recurrent units for LSTM are made empirically. Rest of the hyperparameters were selected by performing grid search using 20% stratified validation set from training set on McM_R. Available choices and final selected parameters are mentioned in Table 2. These choices remained same for all experiments and the validation set was merged back into training set.

Table 2. Hyperparameter tuning, the selection range, and final choice

Hyperparameter	Possible values	Chosen value
First CNN layer kernel size (k)	1, 2, 3, 4, 5	1
Second CNN layer kernel size (k)	1, 2, 3, 4, 5	2
Dropout rate	0.1, 0.2, 0.3, 0.4, 0.5	0.2
Optimizer	Adam, Adadelta, SGD	Adam
Learning rate	0.001, 0.002, 0.003, 0.004, 0.005	0.002

---

[2] These embeddings are also made available along with dataset.

3.6 Evaluation Metrics

We employed the standard metrics that are widely adapted in the literature for measuring multi-class classification performance. These metrics are *accuracy, precision, recall,* and *F1-score*, where latter three can be computed using micro-average or macro-average strategies [10]. In micro-average strategy, each instance holds equal weight and outcomes are aggregated across all classes to compute a particular metric. This essentially means that the outcome would be influenced by the frequent class, if class distribution is skewed. In macro-average however, metrics for each class are calculated separately and then averaged, irrespective of their class label occurrence ratio. This gives each class equal weight instead of each instance, consequently favoring the under-represented classes.

In our particular dataset, it is more plausible to favor smaller classes (i.e., other than "Appreciation" and "Satisfied") to detect potential complaints. Therefore, we choose to report macro-average values for precision, recall, and F1-score which are defined by (9), (10), and (11) respectively.

$$Precision = \frac{\sum_{i=1}^{C} \frac{TP_i}{TP_i+FP_i}}{C}, \tag{9}$$

$$Recall = \frac{\sum_{i=1}^{C} \frac{TP_i}{TP_i+FN_i}}{C}, \tag{10}$$

$$F1 - score = \frac{\sum_{i=1}^{C} \frac{2 \times Precision_i \times Recall_i}{Precision_i+Recall_i}}{C}. \tag{11}$$

4 Results and Discussion

Before evaluating the McM, we first tested the baseline model on our dataset. Table 3 presents results of baseline and all variations of our experiments. We focus our discussion on F1-score as accuracy is often misleading for dataset with unbalanced class distribution. However, for completeness sake, all measures are reported.

It is observed from the results that baseline model performs worst among all the experiments. The reason behind this degradation in performance can be traced back to the nature of the texts in the datasets (i.e., datasets used in original paper of baseline model [4] and in our study). The approach in base model measure the performance of the model on multilingual dataset in which there is no code-switching involved. The complete text belongs to either one language or the other. However, in our case, the SMS text can have code-switching between two language, variation of spelling, or non-standard grammar. Baseline model is simple 1 layered CNN model that is unable to tackle such challenges. On the other hand, McM learns the features from multiple perspectives, hence feature representations are richer, which consequently leads to a superior predictive performance. As every learner in McM is also supervised, all 4 components of the proposed model (i.e., stacked-CNN learner, stacked-LSTM learner, LSTM-learner, and discriminator) can also be compared with each other.

Table 3. Performance evaluation of variations of the proposed model and baseline. Showing highest scores in boldface.

Model	Component	Accuracy	Precision	Recall	F1-score
Baseline [4]	–	0.68	0.52	0.37	0.39
McM$_E$	Stacked-CNN learner	0.83	0.66	0.62	0.63
	Stacked-LSTM learner	0.84	0.70	0.60	0.64
	LSTM learner	0.80	0.69	0.48	0.51
	Discriminator	0.84	0.68	0.63	0.66
McM$_{EA}$	Stacked-CNN learner	0.82	0.65	0.57	0.60
	Stacked-LSTM learner	0.82	0.65	0.57	0.60
	LSTM learner	0.80	0.62	0.49	0.51
	Discriminator	0.83	0.66	0.60	0.62
McM$_R$	Stacked-CNN learner	0.82	0.66	0.59	0.62
	Stacked-LSTM learner	0.82	0.66	0.58	0.61
	LSTM learner	0.81	0.62	0.59	0.59
	Discriminator	0.83	0.64	0.61	0.62
McM$_{RA}$	Stacked-CNN learner	0.80	0.65	0.52	0.53
	Stacked-LSTM learner	0.81	0.65	0.55	0.58
	LSTM learner	0.81	0.64	0.55	0.58
	Discriminator	0.81	0.64	0.58	0.59
McM$_D$	Stacked-CNN learner	0.84	0.71	0.63	0.66
	Stacked-LSTM learner	0.85	0.71	0.67	0.69
	LSTM learner	0.83	0.68	0.60	0.63
	Discriminator	**0.86**	**0.72**	**0.68**	**0.69**
McM$_{DA}$	Stacked-CNN learner	0.82	0.66	0.59	0.62
	Stacked-LSTM learner	0.84	0.69	0.64	0.66
	LSTM learner	0.83	0.67	0.61	0.63
	Discriminator	0.85	0.70	0.66	0.67

In our experiments, the best performing variation of the proposed model is McM$_D$. On this particular setting, discriminator is able to achieve an F1-score of 0.69 with precision and recall values of 0.72 and 0.68 respectively. Other components of McM also show the highest stats for all performance measures. However, for McM$_{DA}$, a significant reduction in performance is observed, although, attention-based models have been proven to show improvement in performance [14]. Investigating the reason behind this drop in performance is beyond the scope of this study. The model variations trained on ELMo embedding have second highest performance. Discriminator of McM$_E$ achieves an F1-score of 0.66, beating other learners in this experiment. However, reduction in performance is persistent when attention is used for McM$_{EA}$.

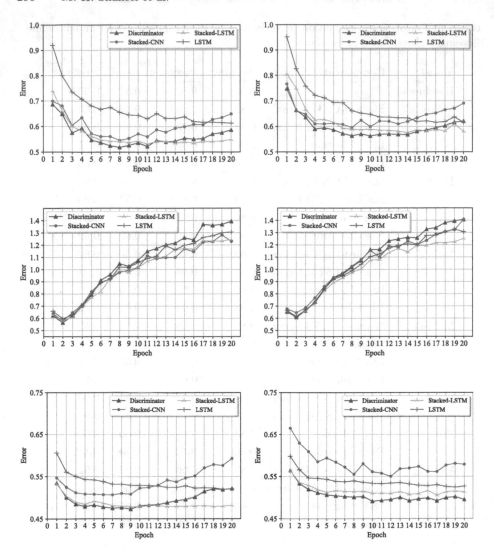

Fig. 2. Test error for all three feature learners and discriminator network over the epochs for all 4 variations of the model, showing lowest error for domain specific embeddings while highest for random embedding initialization.

Regarding the experiments with random embedding initialization, McM_R shows similar performance to McM_{EA}, while McM_{RA} performs the worst. It is worth noting that in each experiment, discriminator network stays on top or performs equally as compared to other components in terms of F1-score. This is indication that discriminator network is able to learn richer representations of text as compared to methods where only single feature learner is deployed.

Furthermore, the results for testing error for each component (i.e., 3 learners and a discriminator network) for all 4 variations of the proposed model are presented in Fig. 2. It is evident that the least error across all components is achieved by McM_D model. Turning now to individual component performance, in ELMo embeddings based two models, lowest error is achieved by discriminator network, closely followed by stacked LSTM learner and stacked-CNN learner, while LSTM learner has the highest error. As far as model variations with random embeddings initializations are concerned, most interesting results are observed. As shown in subplot (c) and (d) in Fig. 2, McM_R and McM_{RA} tend to overfit. After second epoch, the error rate for all components of these two variations tend to increase drastically. However, it shows minimum error for discriminator in both variations, again proving that the features learned through multiple cascades are more robust and hold greater discriminative power. Note that in all 6 variations of experiments, the error of discriminator network is the lowest as compared to other components of McM. Hence it can be deduced that learning features through multiple perspectives and aggregating them for final prediction is more fruitful as compared to single method of learning.

5   Concluding Remarks

In this work, a new large-scale dataset and a novel deep learning architecture for multi-class classification of bilingual (English-Roman Urdu) text with code-switching is presented. The dataset is intended for enhancement of petty corruption detection in public offices and provides grounds for future research in this direction. While deep learning architecture is proposed for multi class classification of bilingual SMS without utilizing any external resource. Three word embedding initialization techniques and soft-attention mechanism is also investigated. The observations from extensive experimentation led us to conclude that: (1) word embeddings vectors generated through characters tend to favor bilingual text classification as compared to random embedding initialization, (2) the attention mechanism tend to decrease the predictive performance of the model, irrespective of embedding types used, (3) using features learned through single perspective yield poor performance for bilingual text with code-switching, (4) training domain specific embeddings on a large corpus and using them to train the model achieves the highest performance.

With regards to future work, we intend to investigate the reason behind degradation of model performance with soft-attention.

References

1. Denecke, K.: Using SentiWordNet for multilingual sentiment analysis. In: International Conference on Data Engineering Workshop, pp. 507–512 (2008)
2. Fatima, M., et al.: Multilingual SMS-based author profiling: data and methods. Nat. Lang. Eng. (NLE) **24**(5), 695–724 (2018)

3. Ioffe, S., Szegedy, C.: Batch normalization: accelerating deep network training by reducing internal covariate shift. In: International Conference on Machine Learning (ICML), pp. 448–456 (2015)

4. Medrouk, L., Pappa, A.: Deep learning model for sentiment analysis in multilingual corpus. In: Liu, D., Xie, S., Li, Y., Zhao, D., El-Alfy, E.S. (eds.) ICONIP 2017. LNCS, vol. 10634, pp. 205–212. Springer, Cham (2017). https://doi.org/10.1007/978-3-319-70087-8_22

5. Mikolov, T., Sutskever, I., Chen, K., Corrado, G.S., Dean, J.: Distributed representations of words and phrases and their compositionality. In: Advances in Neural Information Processing Systems (NIPS), pp. 3111–3119 (2013)

6. Pennington, J., Socher, R., Manning, C.: GloVe: global vectors for word representation. In: Conference on Empirical Methods in Natural Language Processing (EMNLP), pp. 1532–1543 (2014)

7. Peters, M., et al.: Deep contextualized word representations. In: Conference of the North American Chapter of the Association for Computational Linguistics (ACACL): Human Language Technologies, Volume 1 (Long Papers), pp. 2227–2237 (2018)

8. Rafae, A., Qayyum, A., Moeenuddin, M., Karim, A., Sajjad, H., Kamiran, F.: An unsupervised method for discovering lexical variations in Roman Urdu informal text. In: Conference on Empirical Methods in Natural Language Processing (EMNLP), pp. 823–828 (2015)

9. Reimers, N., Gurevych, I.: Reporting score distributions makes a difference: performance study of lstm-networks for sequence tagging. In: Conference on Empirical Methods in Natural Language Processing (EMNLP), pp. 338–348 (2017)

10. Sokolova, M., Lapalme, G.: A systematic analysis of performance measures for classification tasks. Inf. Process. Manag. (IPM) **45**(4), 427–437 (2009)

11. Srivastava, N., Hinton, G., Krizhevsky, A., Sutskever, I., Salakhutdinov, R.: Dropout: a simple way to prevent neural networks from overfitting. J. Mach. Learn. Res. (JMLR) **15**(1), 1929–1958 (2014)

12. Subramani, S., Michalska, S., Wang, H., Du, J., Zhang, Y., Shakeel, H.: Deep learning for multi-class identification from domestic violence online posts. IEEE Access **7**, 46210–46224 (2019)

13. Wang, X., Jiang, W., Luo, Z.: Combination of convolutional and recurrent neural network for sentiment analysis of short texts. In: International Conference on Computational Linguistics (COLING): Technical Papers, pp. 2428–2437 (2016)

14. Wang, Z., Zhang, Y., Lee, S., Li, S., Zhou, G.: A bilingual attention network for code-switched emotion prediction. In: International Conference on Computational Linguistics (COLING): Technical Papers, pp. 1624–1634 (2016)

15. Williams, A., Srinivasan, M., Liu, C., Lee, P., Zhou, Q.: Why do bilinguals code-switch when emotional? Insights from immigrant parent-child interactions. Emotion (Washington, DC) (2019)

16. Zhou, X., Wan, X., Xiao, J.: Attention-based LSTM network for cross-lingual sentiment classification. In: Conference on Empirical Methods in Natural Language Processing (EMNLP), pp. 247–256 (2016)

Low Resource Named Entity Recognition Using Contextual Word Representation and Neural Cross-Lingual Knowledge Transfer

Soyeon Caren Han[1], Yingru Lin[2], Siqu Long[1(✉)], and Josiah Poon[1]

[1] 1 Cleveland Street School of Information Technologies Building J12,
University of Sydney, Sydney, NSW 2006, Australia
{caren.han,siqu.long,josiah.poon}@sydney.edu.au
[2] Ping An Technology (Shen Zhen) Co., Ltd.,
4/f, Pingan's Mansion, Bagualing Ind, Shenzhen 518028, China
LINYINGRU513@pingan.com.cn

Abstract. Low resource Named Entity Recognition can be solved by transferring knowledge from a high to a low-resource language with shared multilingual embedding spaces. In this paper, we focus on the extreme low-resource NER scenario of unsupervised cross-lingual knowledge transfer, where no labelled training data or parallel corpus is available. We apply word-alignment with the contextualised word embedding and propose an efficient cross-lingual centroid-based space translation mechanism for contextual embedding. We found that the proposed alignment mechanism works well between different languages, compared to current state-of-the-art models. Moreover, word order differences is another problem to be resolved in cross-lingual NER. We alleviate this issue by incorporating a transformer, which relies entirely on an attention mechanism to draw global dependency between input and output. Our method was evaluated against state-of-the-art results, and it indicate that our approach was better in terms of the performance and the amount of resources.

Keywords: Low resource NER · Cross-lingual knowledge transfer

1 Introduction

The introduction of deep learning architecture has demonstrated great success in state-of-the-art Named Entity Recognition (NER) models [15]. The biggest problem of such neural-based NER models is a high dependency on the large amount of annotated data. For low-resource languages, it is almost impossible for such models to provide higher performance because of the limited amount of labelled training data and supporting material [32]. Researchers have applied cross-lingual knowledge transfer approaches, which focus on transferring knowledge from a high-resource source language to a low-resource target language [23].

© Springer Nature Switzerland AG 2019
T. Gedeon et al. (Eds.): ICONIP 2019, LNCS 11953, pp. 299–311, 2019.
https://doi.org/10.1007/978-3-030-36708-4_25

Table 1. The word 'Washington' with different context and its named entity.

ID	Sentence	Entity
1	George *Washington* was an political leader	Person
2	*Washington*, DC, the U.S. capital, is a compact city	Location

High-resource language, like English, includes a plentiful supply of entity labels, but low-resources languages tend to have only few or no labels. Cross-lingual knowledge transfer approaches provide a reasonable proxy of training annotated data for the target languages to give higher performance but those still require abundant parallel corpora or bilingual dictionary of the low-resource language to project annotations between languages through word alignment [10]. As an alternative solution to cross-lingual NER, many researchers leveraged shared bi/multilingual embedding spaces, and demonstrated promising achievement by enriching models with lexical information, such as in [21]. However, it is difficult to find extensive bilingual dictionaries, specially in low-resource scenarios.

In this paper, we aim to focus on the extreme low-resource NER scenario of unsupervised cross-lingual knowledge transfer, where there is no labelled training data or parallel corpus or abundant dictionary in the target language. We explore methods to reduce the dependency on training data, parallel resources, and dictionary. To minimise the dependence of resources, attention is paid to context-independent word embeddings, like Word2Vec [20]. The fundamental issue of such embeddings is that it generates the same embedding for the same word in different contexts. For example, Table 1 shows two different sentences that include the word *'Washington'*. Using context-independent word embeddings, the word representation is always the same regardless of the context. We apply word-alignment using contextualised word embedding with different vectors corresponding to various specific content [24].

For the cross-lingual alignment of context-independent embeddings, it learns the alignment directly from the original shared embedding space, and it sometimes integrates with a dictionary to translate words [30]. Since contextual space is a rather complex with both the context and the word, it is not sufficient to apply the same cross-lingual alignment approaches used in the context-independent word embeddings. In this paper, we propose a cross-lingual space construction mechanism for contextual embedding. After the contextual embedding space is factorised into context-independent and dependent clusters, the centroid of each cluster is calculated. Then, we conduct discrete word translations by looking for the centroid of the nearest cluster in the projected space, and this mechanism improves the transfer by context-aware embeddings.

In addition to word alignment problem, word order differences is another important problem to solve in cross-lingual NER. [30] try to deal with the word order difference by combining Bi-LSTM-CRF with self attention. However, the fundamental issue of recurrent neural models, vanishing gradient, cannot be fully resolved, especially in longer time step scenarios. Hence, we alleviate this issue by incorporating a transformer, which rely entirely on an attention mechanism, to draw global dependencies between input and output.

In this paper, we introduce a cross-lingual NER by using contextual word embeddings and the transformer. Main contributions are summarised as follows:

- To propose an efficient method to build a shared cross-lingual space of contextual embeddings.
- To the best of our knowledge, this is the first attempt to deal with the extreme low-resource NER by incorporating with contextual embeddings.
- To handle word order difference in unsupervised cross-lingual transfer for NER by integrating the attention approach alone without using any recurrent layer, which is the first of its kind.

2   Related Work

2.1   Monolingual NER

NER is widely accepted as a problem of sequence labeling; so several research focus on building a name tagger with feature-based classification approaches, including hidden markov models (HMMs) [7] or conditional random fields (CRFs) [11]. However, most studies have relied on time-consuming feature engineering process; and they are still unable to discover or extract meaningful and understandable knowledge from data. Recent studies [3,14,18,31] have promoted to address this problem by adopting neural network methods to capture the orthographic and morphological context. Several neural network methods, such as LSTM-CRF [14], LSTM-CNN-CRF [18], CNN-CRF [31], BiLSTM-CNN [3] have been carried out to perform on NER.

2.2   Cross-Lingual NER

It is a prevailing approach to apply multilingual resources in improving monolingual name tagging tasks in literature. [13] proposed a linear-chain CRF model with the use of loopy belief propagation method to perform approximate inference. Despite the effectiveness of their feature-rich CRF formulation, this approach suffers from manually annotating bilingual corpora. Several methods [10] are presented in the literature to address this issue. In terms of low resource NER, [22,23] focused on improving the performances of multilingual name tagging and prescribed the use of multilingual Wikipedia entity type mappings. [32] extracted language-based features to encode linguistic knowledge from native speakers to build an expectation-driven model. Most of the previously mentioned methods suffer from error propagation or labor-intensive feature extraction.

2.3   Multilingual Embeddings

More recent attention has focused on the provision of cross-lingual embedding alignment. [4] presented approaches of multilingual unsupervised and supervised embeddings (MUSE), which align monolingual embedding spaces to create a multilingual space with supervised learning methods. Several recent studies have been carried out to improve the performance on context-independent representations for both the supervised [9] and unsupervised [8] ways. For contextual embedding alignments, several monolingual approaches [6,24] have shown their advantages. In recent years, many attempts have been made in order to improve embeddings by utilising bilingual dictionaries, such as in [1].

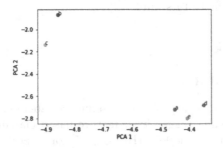

Fig. 1. ELMo Embeddings of the token 'Washington' in different context/sentences. (**a** = Washington is the only state to be named after a president, **b** = Washington was born at his father's plantation on Popes Creek, **c** = Washington was an American military general, **d** = Washington is the 18th largest state in America, **e** = Washington is the second most populous state on the West Coast.) **a**, **d**, **e** represents the state in U.S., while **b**, **c** shows the first president of the U.S.

3   Method

In this paper, we focus on the extreme low-resource scenario, and assume that it has the following characteristics: (1) No annotated NE dataset for low resource target language, (2) No parallel corpus between source and target language, and (3) Few or no bilingual dictionary/lexicon for target language. We also limit ourselves to a setting where we have the following resources: (1) Monolingual corpora in both source and target language and (2) Annotated NE training dataset in the high-resource source language. This would make us comparable to other state-of-the-art models [19,22,28,30].

3.1   Monolingual Contextual Word Embedding

We always assume that we have monolingual corpora in both source s and target language t so that we independently train two sets of contextual word embedding matrices S and T in the source and target language. For contextual word

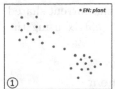
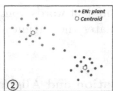
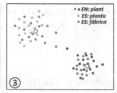
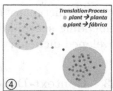

Fig. 2. Toy illustration of the proposed centroid-based alignment **(1)** Assume that there is contextual embeddings for the English word "plant", and assume there is two (2) definitions in the English dictionary (plant and factory) **(2)** Based on the number of the meaning in the dictionary, conduct k-means clustering (k is the number of definitions in the dictionary. In this example, k = 2), and calculate the centroid. **(3)** Add Spanish contextual embeddings in the shared space. Two possible Spanish Translation - "planta" (plant) in yellow and "fabrica" (factory) in orange. **(4)** Translate with the nearest centroid in the projected space. (Color figure online)

embedding, assume we are given a context c and a token w, the embedding of w will be denoted as $e_{w,c}$. In other words, $e_{w,*}$ represents the word embeddings for all context. We then define the word embedding of s as $e^s_{w,c}$ and t as $e^t_{w,c}$. The contextual word embeddings can be learned on monolingual text corpora in both languages with ELMo (Embeddings from Language Model), which learns both word and linguistic context using bidirectional LM (language model) [24]. Figure 1 represents the projection results of ELMo embedding using PCA, and each colour point represents the vector of the token 'Washington' in its specific context. The following contextual word embeddings can be divided into 2 clusters. The embeddings of 'Washington' in the bottom right cluster represents the state in U.S., while the upper left cluster shows the first U.S. president. By using contextual embeddings, the token has different word vectors depending on different contexts, and the words with the same sense will be close to each other.

3.2   Bilingual Context-Independent Alignment

In the cross-lingual setup, we first focus on the alignment of bilingual context-independent of S and T in this section, and then generalise it to the contextual case in the section 'Context-Dependent Alignment' (Sect. 3.3). For the cross-lingual embedding alignment, assume we are given an embedding of s $e^s_{w,c}$, the embedding in t space would be generated as $e^{s \to t}_{w,c}$, with the linear mapping $W^{s \to t}$.

As mentioned in the hypothesis, we assume that there is no dictionary/lexicon. For this type of unsupervised case, [21] trained a linear transformation, where e^t_w is estimated by using We^s_w with the learned matrix W. According to linear alignment, [5] proposed MUSE (Multilingual Unsupervised and Supervised Embeddings), which learns the context-independent alignment via adversarial training. The adversarial training is conducted by training a discriminator to distinguish between the aligned source embeddings and the target embeddings, and then conduct an iterative refinement procedure to develop a synthetic dictionary retaining only high confident words from the current shared embedding space. MUSE [5] then recalculates the alignment matrix using the developed dictionary.

3.3   Context-Dependency Generalisation and Alignment

Using the context-independent alignment result from the previous section, we propose and apply a new context-dependency generalisation mechanism. Refer to the hypothesis section, since we deal with the extreme low-resource scenario, no parallel corpus or dictionary is assumed. There are three unsupervised alignment methods we have applied to context-dependency generalisation and alignment; the first two methods are the baselines, and the third one is our proposed generalisation method.

Context-Based Alignment. Instead of using any condition or constraint, the alignment would be learned from the contextual shared space. After conducting MUSE, each word aligns with multiple embeddings with different contexts. It allows to directly handle homonyms during the training process.

Anchored Alignment. This approach also can be done with the adversarial MUSE, and then extended to a context-independent alignment procedure to the contextual space by applying the anchor space of certain tokens [26]. The anchor can be calculated as the average over a subset of the available unlabelled data by using given a context and a token.

Centroid-Based Alignment. The final approach for cross-lingual space construction mechanism for contextual embedding is our proposal, where it integrates with the context-dependent clusters. Like the above two alignment approaches, we firstly apply MUSE to make a context-independent shared space. With context-independent alignment, we extend the space with the context-dependent aspect by integrating with k-means clustering. This is mainly because direct lexical mapping would not align well when raw source language data is scarce. As can be seen in Fig. 2, the proposed centroid-based alignment would work in the following process: (1) We first check the dictionary of the source language and decide the number of clusters (k) to divide the contextual embeddings of each specific word, (2) Using k-means clustering, we group the word vectors in different context with k topics/meanings (the number of k can be estimated based on the number of meanings of the specific word in the document), (3) We calculate the centroid of each cluster by using different distance measure, including euclidean, jaccard, and cosine distance, (4) We conduct discrete word translations by looking for nearest clusters centroid in the projected space.

With this alignment and translation, the proposed mechanism improves transfer by context-aware embeddings. All three above methods, we perform the refinement process in MUSE [4].

3.4 Transformer-Based Named Entity Recognition Model

In this section, we describe the NER model, which is integrated with the proposed multilingual contextual embedding alignment. We firstly translate the entire English NER training data into the target language by taking English sentences $S = s_1, s_2, s_3, ..., s_n$ and translating them into target language sentences $T = t_1, t_2, t_3, ..., t_n$. The translation mechanism is really simple; the label of each words in the English NER is directly copied to be the label of the target words. We can then train an NER model using the translated data. To build the NER model, we applied transformer [29], which learns global-level information on all the inputs and identifies the most important information. Instead of using any recurrent layers, we closely follow the Transformer framework in order to handle the word order difference issue in the extreme unsupervised cross-lingual transfer. In this paper, our goal is to generate a language model to predict the NE so we adopt only the encoder mechanism of the transformer model in order to predict the NER tag. We take the contextual word embedding with the translated data as a sequence of translated words embeddings $(w_1, w_2, ..., w_n)$ and also the corresponding context-independent embedding $(i_1, i_2, ..., i_n)$ for each word. [26] justified that neural models work better when the contextual embedding integrates with context-independent embeddings. Without any recurrent layer, it is difficult to encode the token order within a sentence. The transformer includes a positional encoding to determine the position of each token. Then, the list of embeddings will be passed to the encoder layer, which contains two sub-layers, multi-head self-attention and pairwise feed forward neural network. Both sub layers have a residual connection around it, and are followed by a layer-normalization process. The multi-headed self-attention computes attention weights for each word within a sentence. We use the default attention matrix, dot-product attention [17]. Multi-headed attention mechanism improves the performance of the simple attention layer in two ways: (1) improving the focus on different positions, (2) providing the attention layer multiple representation subspaces [16]. The same FFNN is independently applied to each position. The output of the encoder are fed to the dense layer in order to convert the dimension to the original input/output dimension. The output will be a NE tag for each input token.

4 Experiments

We conducted three sets of experiments: (1) evaluated word translation precision using different context-dependent alignment. (2) compared our methods against state-of-the-art results with a benchmark NER dataset, CoNLL 2002 and 2003 [25,27]. (3) applied our methods to Uyghur, an extreme low-resource scenario.

4.1 Experimental Settings

We limited ourselves where we had the following resources, including monolingual corpora in both source and target language, and an annotated NE training dataset in the high-resource source language. For all experiments, we used

Table 2. Alignment accuracy (in percentages) of word translation to English precision@5 using CSLS [5] with German and Spanish.

Alignment model	Spanish	German
Context-based	68	57
Schuster et al. (2019) [26] without refinement	61	63
Schuster et al. (2019) [26] with refinement	74	72
Context-based Alignment with refinement	82	73
Our model (with euclidean distance)	77	74
Our model (with jaccard distance)	79	71
Our model (with cosine distance)	**84**	**76**

English as the high-resource source language and translate into the target languages, and assumed that we have only English NER dataset.

Word Embeddings. For all source and target languages, we used the pretrained ELMo embeddings [2]. They trained their parameters same as the original ELMo implementation and training [24] for bi-directional Language Model (biLM) and the character Convolutional Neural Networks (CNN). [14] and [26] justified that using the output of the first LSTM layer from ELMo is as good as learning a combination. Hence, we use the first layer output directly to the input of the alignment. [30] justified that neural models work better when the contextual embeddings integrate with context-independent embeddings. Hence, we applied the pre-trained Glove, same as the baseline approach.

Network Parameters. For our experiments, we set the max length of input sequence as 256, the contextual and context-independent embedding size as 512, the encoder stack layer size as 6, the number of heads used in multi-headed attention as 8, and inner layer size in the feedforward network as 2048.

Network Training. We used Adam with the parameters beta1 (0.9), beta2 (0.997) and epsilon (1e−09) to train the NER model for 10 epochs. We chose the initial learning rate to be 2.0 and learning rate decay rate to be 1.0 with learning rate warm up steps to be 16000. We used a batch size of 2048 and evaluated the model per 100 batches within each epoch. We applied dropouts on the attention layer and ReLu layer during training with dropout rate 0.1.

4.2 Experiment 1: Cross-Lingual Word Translation and Alignment

We tested our alignment model in cross-lingual word translation and alignment with a direct context-based alignment and the anchor-based alignment proposed by [26]. We applied MUSE framework with their dictionary tables [5]. Our model, the centroid-based alignment, was tested with several common distance measures, including euclidean, jaccard, and cosine distance. We used the 50k most common words in each language same as the baseline [26]. The MUSE dictionary

Table 3. NER F1 scores of Spanish and Dutch. [19,22,28] use more resources than our proposed model. (The "Wikipedia" in the extra resources column represents not the one used for the monolingual corpus, but for the external knowledge).

Alignment model	Spanish	Dutch	German	Extra resources
Tsai et al. (2016) [28]	60.55	61.60	48.10	Wikipedia
Ni et al. (2017) [22]	65.10	65.40	58.50	Wikipedia, parallel corpus, 5k dict.
Mayhew et al. (2017) [19] - (only English data)	51.82	53.94	50.96	IM dict.
Xie et al. (2018) [30] - (identical character matching)	72.37	70.40	57.76	–
Xie et al. (2018) [30] - (adversarial training)	71.03	71.25	56.90	–
Our model	**75.34**	**75.10**	**58.63**	–

was used for checking the number of meaning of the specific word w. We present the alignment accuracy for those models in Table 2, summarising the precision@5 word-translation from two languages to English. For checking the performance of the word translation, we applied cross-domain similarity local scaling (CSLS) [12], which focus on measuring the distance.

Among all unsupervised methods, our model achieved slightly better than other results in both Spanish and German. As expected, the context-based alignment without refinement produced lowest accuracy for both languages, compared to other models. In addition to this, we can justify that the precision of word translation for all languages is significantly affected by the inclusion of the refinement progress. For all experiments, we included the refinement process and it improved slightly than the context-based alignment with refinement. For experiment 2 and 3, we decided to test our model with cosine distance measure.

4.3   Experiment 2: CoNLL NER Data

In the second experiment, we compared our methods against previous state-of-the-art performance in low-resource NER. As mentioned earlier, we used benchmark NER dataset, CoNLL 2002 and 2003 dataset [25,27], which includes 4 western languages. In this experiment, we used English as a source language and translate its NER dataset into each target language, Spanish, German and Dutch. Then, we trained our transformer-based model with the translated NER dataset.

Table 3 shows the evaluation results on transferring from English to three other languages, alongside results from previous researches [19,22,28,30]. The first three approaches used more than just a monolingual corpus (see column 'Extra Resources' of the table). [30] proposed an unsupervised NER model that does not use any extract resource than the monolingual corpus, and applied

Table 4. NER F1 scores on Uyghur. Approaches using language-specific features and resources.

Alignment model	Uyghur unsequestered set	Extra resources
Mayhew et al. (2017) [19]	27.20	Wikipedia, 100K dict.
Xie et al. (2018) [30]; BWET + self-att	26.38	5K dict.
Combined Mayhew et al. (2017) [19] and Xie et al. (2018) [30]	32.09	Wikipedia, 100K dict., 5K dict.
Our model	42.88	–

identical character matching or adversarial training. The model, however, did not produce high accuracy because it just used only context-independent alignment. The results produced by our transformer-based NER model indicate that our approach was effective, since we managed to improve the performance for all three languages with no parallel and no bilingual dictionary. Hence, we found that identifying the proper alignment position using contextual embeddings is the key of unsupervised NER task.

4.4   Experiment 3: The Extreme Low-Source Scenario: Uyghur

In this section, we conducted an evaluation in the extreme low-resource scenario by choosing Uyghur. Uyghur is an official language of the Xinjiang Uyghur Region in Western China. Uyghur is not supported by Google Translate, and there are less 5000 wikipedia articles in Uyghur. As a result, Uyghur can be considered as a severe low-resource language example for evaluating our hypothesis, 'the extreme low source scenario'.

In this section, we conducted an evaluation in the extreme low-resource scenario by choosing Uyghur. For a fair comparison, we used the same evaluation setting as was used by previous models [19,30] for each scenario. We tested our proposed model on 199 of the annotated evaluation documents, the unsequestered dataset, from the DARPA LORELEI program and compared the result with previous researches [19,30]. Table 4 shows the different model performance of NER F1 score on Uyghur. Compared to others, our model performs extremely well, considering that we use no dictionary; Hence, the results indicate that our approach was better and effective in terms of the performance and the amount of resources.

5   Conclusion

In this paper, we proposed a new and effective unsupervised cross-lingual NER model by integrating with contextual embeddings and the transformer. We focused on the extreme low-resource NER scenario, where no labelled training data or parallel corpus or abundant dictionary is available in the target language. We firstly evaluated word translation precision using different context-dependent alignment. Then, we compared our methods against previous state-of-the-art results in low-resource NER with a benchmark NER dataset, CoNLL 2002 and 2003 dataset. We finally evaluated the challenge of applying the proposed model to the extremely low-resource language, Uyghur. Most of all evaluation results improved the performance of the previous SOTA models. Therefore, the results indicate that our approach was better and effective in terms of the performance and the amount of resources.

References

1. Adams, O., Makarucha, A., Neubig, G., Bird, S., Cohn, T.: Cross-lingual word embeddings for low-resource language modeling. In: Proceedings of the 15th Conference of the European Chapter of the Association for Computational Linguistics: Volume 1, Long Papers, pp. 937–947 (2017)
2. Che, W., Liu, Y., Wang, Y., Zheng, B., Liu, T.: Towards better UD parsing: deep contextualized word embeddings, ensemble, and treebank concatenation. In: CoNLL 2018, p. 55 (2018)
3. Chiu, J.P., Nichols, E.: Named entity recognition with bidirectional LSTM-CNNs. Trans. Assoc. Comput. Linguist. 4, 357–370 (2016)
4. Conneau, A., Lample, G., Ranzato, M., Denoyer, L., Jégou, H.: Word translation without parallel data. In: ICLR 2018 (2018)
5. Conneau, A., et al.: XNLI: evaluating cross-lingual sentence representations. In: Proceedings of the 2018 Conference on Empirical Methods in Natural Language Processing, pp. 2475–2485 (2018)
6. Devlin, J., Chang, M.W., Lee, K., Toutanova, K.: BERT: pre-training of deep bidirectional transformers for language understanding. In: Proceedings of the 2019 Conference of the North American Chapter of the Association for Computational Linguistics: Human Language Technologies, vol. 1, pp. 4171–4186 (2019)
7. Florian, R., Ittycheriah, A., Jing, H., Zhang, T.: Named entity recognition through classifier combination. In: Proceedings of the Seventh Conference on Natural Language Learning at HLT-NAACL 2003, vol. 4, pp. 168–171. Association for Computational Linguistics (2003)
8. Grave, E., Joulin, A., Berthet, Q.: Unsupervised alignment of embeddings with Wasserstein procrustes. In: The 22nd International Conference on Artificial Intelligence and Statistics, pp. 1880–1890 (2019)
9. Joulin, A., Bojanowski, P., Mikolov, T., Jégou, H., Grave, E.: Loss in translation: learning bilingual word mapping with a retrieval criterion. In: Proceedings of the 2018 Conference on Empirical Methods in Natural Language Processing, pp. 2979–2984 (2018)
10. Kim, S., Toutanova, K., Yu, H.: Multilingual named entity recognition using parallel data and metadata from wikipedia. In: Proceedings of the 50th Annual Meeting of the Association for Computational Linguistics: Long Papers, vol. 1, pp. 694–702. Association for Computational Linguistics (2012)
11. Lafferty, J., McCallum, A., Pereira, F.C.: Conditional random fields: probabilistic models for segmenting and labeling sequence data (2001)
12. Lample, G., Conneau, A., Denoyer, L., Jégou, H., et al.: Word translation without parallel data (2018)

13. Li, Q., Li, H., Ji, H., Wang, W., Zheng, J., Huang, F.: Joint bilingual name tagging for parallel corpora. In: Proceedings of the 21st ACM International Conference on Information and Knowledge Management, pp. 1727–1731. ACM (2012)
14. Liu, L., et al.: Empower sequence labeling with task-aware neural language model. In: Thirty-Second AAAI Conference on Artificial Intelligence (2018)
15. Liu, T., Wang, K., Sha, L., Chang, B., Sui, Z.: Table-to-text generation by structure-aware seq2seq learning. In: 32nd AAAI Conference on Artificial Intelligence (2018)
16. Liu, Y., Lapata, M.: Hierarchical transformers for multi-document summarization. In: Proceedings of the 57th Annual Meeting of the Association for Computational Linguistics (2019)
17. Luong, T., Pham, H., Manning, C.D.: Effective approaches to attention-based neural machine translation. In: Proceedings of the 2015 Conference on Empirical Methods in Natural Language Processing, pp. 1412–1421 (2015)
18. Ma, X., Hovy, E.: End-to-end sequence labeling via bi-directional LSTM-CNNs-CRF. In: Proceedings of the 54th Annual Meeting of the Association for Computational Linguistics (Volume 1: Long Papers), pp. 1064–1074 (2016)
19. Mayhew, S., Tsai, C.T., Roth, D.: Cheap translation for cross-lingual named entity recognition. In: Proceedings of the 2017 Conference on Empirical Methods in Natural Language Processing, pp. 2536–2545 (2017)
20. Mikolov, T., Chen, K., Corrado, G.S., Dean, J.: Efficient estimation of word representations in vector space. CoRR abs/1301.3781 (2013)
21. Mikolov, T., Le, Q.V., Sutskever, I.: Exploiting similarities among languages for machine translation. CoRR 1309.4168 (2013)
22. Ni, J., Dinu, G., Florian, R.: Weakly supervised cross-lingual named entity recognition via effective annotation and representation projection. In: Proceedings of the 55th Annual Meeting of the Association for Computational Linguistics (Volume 1: Long Papers), pp. 1470–1480 (2017)
23. Ni, J., Florian, R.: Improving multilingual named entity recognition with wikipedia entity type mapping. In: Proceedings of the 2016 Conference on Empirical Methods in Natural Language Processing, pp. 1275–1284 (2016)
24. Peters, M.E., et al.: Deep contextualized word representations. In: Proceedings of NAACL-HLT, pp. 2227–2237 (2018)
25. Sang, T.K., Erik, F.: Memory-based named entity recognition. In: proceedings of the 6th Conference on Natural Language Learning, vol. 20, pp. 1–4. Association for Computational Linguistics (2002)
26. Schuster, T., Ram, O., Barzilay, R., Globerson, A.: Cross-lingual alignment of contextual word embeddings, with applications to zero-shot dependency parsing. In: Proceedings of the 2019 Conference of the North American Chapter of the Association for Computational Linguistics: Human Language Technologies, Volume 1 (Long and Short Papers), pp. 1599–1613 (2019)
27. Tjong Kim Sang, E.F., De Meulder, F.: Introduction to the CoNLL-2003 shared task: language-independent named entity recognition. In: Proceedings of the Seventh Conference on Natural Language Learning at HLT-NAACL 2003, vol. 4, pp. 142–147. Association for Computational Linguistics (2003)
28. Tsai, C.T., Mayhew, S., Roth, D.: Cross-lingual named entity recognition via wikification. In: Proceedings of The 20th SIGNLL Conference on Computational Natural Language Learning, pp. 219–228 (2016)
29. Vaswani, A., et al.: Attention is all you need. In: Advances in Neural Information Processing Systems, pp. 5998–6008 (2017)

30. Xie, J., Yang, Z., Neubig, G., Smith, N.A., Carbonell, J.: Neural cross-lingual named entity recognition with minimal resources. In: Proceedings of the 2018 Conference on Empirical Methods in Natural Language Processing, pp. 369–379 (2018)
31. Yang, Z., Salakhutdinov, R., Cohen, W.W.: Transfer learning for sequence tagging with hierarchical recurrent networks. In: ICLR 2017 (2017)
32. Zhang, B., et al.: Name tagging for low-resource incident languages based on expectation-driven learning. In: Proceedings of the 2016 Conference of the North American Chapter of the Association for Computational Linguistics: Human Language Technologies, pp. 249–259 (2016)

An Analysis of the Interaction Between Transfer Learning Protocols in Deep Neural Networks

Jo Plested[(✉)] and Tom Gedeon

Research School of Computer Science, Australian National University,
Canberra, Australia
jo.plested@anu.edu.au

Abstract. We extend work on the transferability of features in deep neural networks to explore the interaction between training hyperparameters, optimal number of layers to transfer and the size of a target dataset. We show that using the commonly adopted transfer learning protocols results in increased overfitting and significantly decreased accuracy compared to optimal protocols, particularly for very small target datasets. We demonstrate that there is a relationship between fine-tuning hyperparameters used and the optimal number of layers to transfer. Our research shows that if this relationship is not taken into account, the optimal number of layers to transfer to the target dataset will likely be estimated incorrectly. Best practice transfer learning protocols cannot be predicted from existing research that has analysed transfer learning under very specific conditions that are not universally applicable. Extrapolating transfer learning training settings from previous findings can in fact be counterintuitive, particularly in the case of smaller datasets. We present optimal transfer learning protocols for various target dataset sizes from very small to large when source and target datasets and tasks are similar. Our results show that using these settings results in a large increase in accuracy when compared to commonly used transfer learning protocols. These results are most significant with very small target datasets. We observed an increase in accuracy of 47.8% on our smallest dataset which comprised of only 10 training examples per class. These findings are important as they are likely to improve outcomes from past, current and future research in transfer learning. We expect that researchers will want to re-examine their experiments to incorporate our findings and to check the robustness of their existing results.

Keywords: Transfer learning · Convolutional neural networks

1 Introduction

Transfer learning in neural networks generally involves pre-training weights on a large source dataset then applying these weights to a problem on a related target dataset. In this paradigm either:

© Springer Nature Switzerland AG 2019
T. Gedeon et al. (Eds.): ICONIP 2019, LNCS 11953, pp. 312–323, 2019.
https://doi.org/10.1007/978-3-030-36708-4_26

- all but the last layer of weights are frozen, essentially using these weights as a feature detector for another classification algorithm [2,4,15], or
- fine-tuning is performed where all or some of the weights are retrained to fit the target dataset and the original pre-trained weights act as a regularizer to prevent overfitting [1,5,8,9,12,17].

The former is generally used when the target dataset is small and the latter when it is larger.

Deep convolutional neural networks (CNNs) have revolutionized computer vision [10]. Since then a large body of research has shown that performing transfer learning by pre-training a CNN on a large dataset like ILSVRC2012 [3], and fine-tuning the pre-trained weights on a related target dataset, can improve results on a wide range of target tasks [5,7–9,11,12,16,17].

The most systematic and thorough analysis of transfer learning on CNNs to date is the work of Yosinski et al. [19]. They showed that transferring weights pretrained on a related dataset and then fine-tuning them, results in networks that generalize better than those trained directly on a large target dataset. They also showed that when fine tuning is done with standard hyperparameters, routinely used for training from scratch (initial learning rate of 0.01, decay 0.1 every 30 epochs), accuracy on the target dataset increases as the number of layers transferred also increases.

The results of Yosinski et al. have been regularly adopted as an accepted best practice paradigm for transfer learning with CNNs, notwithstanding differences from Yosinski et al.'s target dataset size. There are many examples in the literature that have adopted this practice of all but the final classification layer being transferred with training settings identical or similar to those outlined above [6,9,12,14,17,18]. These settings have been used to:

- show when transfer learning is effective [6],
- compare transfer learning with other methods for small target datasets [14], and
- question whether transfer learning is useful at all [6,14].

Other works ostensibly appear to back up the conclusions adopted by the community from Yosinski et al.'s results. However, the results were only demonstrated to apply under very specific experiment conditions. For example Azizpour et al. [2] used transferred layers of weights as a feature detector with a linear Support Vector Machine (SVM). They showed that in similar tasks all except the final layer of a CNN should be transferred and for even the least related image tasks all but the final two or three layers should be transferred. Their protocol differs from current standard transfer learning practices in that they performed no fine tuning on the transferred weights, and they did not replace and reinitialize the layers not transferred. Replacing more layers with an SVM results in fewer parameters. This likely biases the experiments towards reporting higher accuracy with more layers transferred, particularly with larger target datasets.

Recent work drives this transfer learning paradigm further by pre-training on datasets that are 6× [7], 300× [16], and even 3000× [11] larger than ILSVRC2012. While this body of work demonstrates significant improvements on image classification transfer learning tasks with large target datasets the opposite has often been shown for less related tasks or smaller target datasets [6,14]. This led us to question whether transfer learning protocols developed in [19] and widely adopted by the community are actually best practice for target datasets that are smaller than those used for the experiments performed by Yosinski et al. To answer the above question this paper explores the relationship between:

- the optimal number of pre-trained layers to transfer to a target task,
- fine-tuning hyperparameteres including initial learning rate for each, and layer and learning rate decay settings
- the size of the target dataset.

We show that the interaction between these settings results in the optimal number of layers to transfer being overestimated or underestimated, depending on the size of the target dataset, if transferred weights are trained for too many epochs at too high a learning rate on the target dataset. This relationship is accentuated for smaller datasets and can result in transfer learning showing no improvement or even a negative effect when performed with the protocols adopted from [19] as was shown in [14].

In this paper we make several contributions. We show:

1. There is an interaction between optimal number of layers to transfer and fine-tuning hyperparameters.
2. Freezing layers of pre-trained weights after transferring them rarely produces the best results.
3. Using optimal transfer learning protocols we developed, based on the outcomes of our experiments, produces large changes in results compared to the commonly adopted existing protocols. This particularly applies when working with smaller target datasets. This is likely to impact results that have compared transfer learning, using commonly adopted protocols, with other methods.
4. Optimal transfer learning protocols cannot be predicted from existing research.

We also provide optimal transfer learning protocols for use with a range of target dataset sizes from very small to large where the source and target datasets are similar.

2   Experiments

Our goal is to extend existing work on transfer learning in particular the seminal work of [19] and to identify limitations of its application. We aim to develop transfer learning and fine-tuning protocols based on the size of the target dataset. Given our intention is to compare transfer learning paradigms only we have used a standard Pytorch [13] implementation of the model Alexnet [10] with no modern architectural improvements. This model is widely used in existing works, allowing our results to be more universally comparable and applicable.

We followed the same experiment protocols as [19]. We split the 1000 object classes in ILSVRC2012 randomly into 500 classes for pre-training with the remaining 500 classes acting as the target dataset. We repeated this process four times for each experiment to create four separate splits of 500 classes for pre-training and 500 classes for the target dataset. We refer to the target dataset that includes all training examples available for each of the 500 random classes as full. The full target datasets have around 645,000 training examples and a minimum of 1,000 per class. We then created different sized target datasets by drawing the first x number of training examples per class to create datasets of size 500x. We selected the first x per class to ensure the same training examples were used across different target dataset sizes and class splits. The other target dataset training set sizes have 500, 250, 100, 50, 25 and 10 training examples per class. We use all the standard ILSVRC2012 validation examples from each random set of 500 target dataset classes for testing. This means there are 50 test examples per class.

3 Results and Discussion

We performed six sets of experiments. The first experiments varied the number of layers transferred for each of a standard set of target dataset sizes and is discussed in Sect. 3.1. Experiments where we varied the number of layers trained at an initial high learning rate are presented in Sect. 3.2. Section 3.3 revisits the experiments varying the number of layers transferred incorporating the best settings from the experiments in Sect. 3.2. Results from experiments varying the number of epochs before the initial high learning rate is decayed are discussed in Sect. 3.4. Experiments to determine the optimal number of layers to freeze are presented in Sect. 3.5. Finally the results using the optimal transfer learning protocols derived from all previous experiments are compared to results using commonly adopted protocols from [19] as well as training from scratch with no transfer learning in Sect. 3.6.

3.1 Vary Number of Layers Transferred for Different Sized Target Datasets

Figure 1 shows the results of all our transfer learning experiments varying the number of layers transferred for our standard set of target dataset sizes while keeping the training hyperparameters constant. The training hyperparameters used were as per [19] with an initial learning rate of 0.01 for all layers reducing by 0.1 every 30 epochs. These results show that for the full target dataset size the accuracy increases slightly with the number of layers transferred. This is in keeping with the outcomes of [19]. However, as soon as the size of the dataset is halved this result no longer holds. It is better to transfer only five layers rather

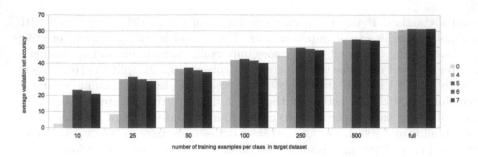

Fig. 1. Number of layers transferred vs dataset size. Each bar represents the average accuracy over the validation set for a model fine-tuned on one size of target training dataset with a particular number of layers of pre-trained weights transferred.

Table 1. Overfitting on small target datasets

Layers	Training examples per class				Average training and validation loss difference
	Loss	10	25	50	
4	Training	1.55	1.22	1.35	2.91
	Validation	5.07	4.27	3.51	
5	Training	0.71	0.82	1.06	3.63
	Validation	5.38	4.43	3.67	
6	Training	0.49	0.60	0.83	3.90
	Validation	5.34	4.48	3.81	
7	Training	0.39	0.48	0.71	4.72
	Validation	6.26	5.18	4.29	

than all seven as per standard practice. This result is most pronounced for the smallest dataset where accuracy increases from 20.9% when transferring all seven layers to 23.4% when only transferring five layers. This is an increase of 12.2% compared to the original accuracy. These results show that for smaller datasets:

- transferring the correct number of layers has an increasing impact on accuracy, and
- transfer learning in general increases in importance as training from scratch is no longer viable.

Another surprising result is that for smaller target datasets overfitting is much more pronounced when more layers are transferred to the target task. This is shown in Table 1. The aim of pre-training is to act as a regularizer and reduce overfitting. Contrary to this, on a small dataset transferring more layers of pre-trained weights exacerbates the overfitting problem compared to transferring less layers. This finding is more intuitive than it sounds. With smaller target datasets the model does not see enough training examples in the fine-tuning stages to make significant changes to the large pre-trained weights. This leaves

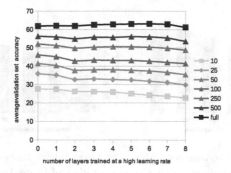

Fig. 2. Number of layers trained at a high learning rate. The degradation in performance, across all target dataset sizes, as more layers are trained with a high initial learning rate is shown.

it with features that are not well suited to the target task, so when aggressive training hyperparameters are used the model overfits to the small training set.

3.2 Vary Number of Layers Trained at a High Learning Rate Initially

Starting from the final classification layer, this experiment varied the number of layers trained at an initial high learning rate of 0.01 for 30 epochs before decaying it by 0.1. The remaining layers were trained with the same regime but using an initial learning rate of 0.001. The number of layers transferred was set at 6 as it produced either the top or comparable to the top accuracy across all target dataset sizes in our other experiments. Figure 2 shows the results of this experiment across the full set of target dataset sizes. It demonstrates that accuracy increases as the number of layers trained at a high learning rate decreases, for all target dataset sizes. This indicates that the fine-tuning hyperparameters used in [19] and in much of the literature since, are too aggressive for the cases examined in our work where source and target datasets and tasks are similar. Another point to note about the results shown in Fig. 2 is that there is a noticeable drop in accuracy when the final two layers are trained with a high learning rate compared to either one or three layers. This is interesting, as it coincides with the number of layers reinitialized. This again highlights overfitting due to aggressively training with features that are not well suited to the target task.

3.3 Compare Number of Layers to Transfer with Low and High Initial Decay epochs

We replicated experiment 3.1 examining the number of layers to transfer, this time only the final layer was trained at a high learning rate initially. We performed the experiment with a high setting of 30 epochs before the initial high learning rate was decayed. We then repeated this with a low setting of five epochs

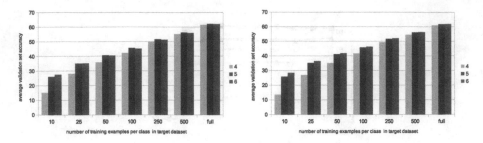

Fig. 3. Number of layers to transfer with low and high initial decay epochs. Comparison of the change in the average accuracies across number of layers transferred with a low (5) left and high (30) right initial number of epochs before decay. All experiments are performed with only the final classification layer trained at a high learning rate initially.

The chart on the left in Fig. 3 shows that with a high setting for initial decay epochs the optimal number of layers to transfer is five, for all but the two smallest target datasets. However, when a low setting for the initial decay epochs is used the optimal number of layers to transfer is six, for all target dataset sizes except the largest. The lower initial decay setting also results in higher accuracies for all but the largest dataset size. The biggest increase in accuracy is 3.5% on the smallest dataset. Whereas the increase on the second largest dataset is only 0.07% and the accuracy on the largest dataset is lower when a small number of epochs before decay are used.

The findings from this experiment are significant as they show the interaction between number of layers to transfer and fine-tuning hyperparameters when pinpointing the optimal transfer learning protocols. This result can also be observed by comparing Figs. 1, 2 and 3. When all layers are trained with an initial high learning rate of 0.01 for 30 epochs, transferring four layers rather than five or six produces only marginally lower results. However, when just the final classification layer is trained with a high learning rate initially, transferring only four layers produces significantly lower results. Both these observations show that if initial learning rates and decay epochs are set too high the optimal number of layers to transfer will be overestimated or underestimated depending on the size of the target dataset.

3.4   Vary Initial Decay Epochs

Our hypothesis was that training for 30 epochs initially at a high learning rate of 0.01 is too aggressive for fine tuning. To test this, we varied the initial decay epochs between 0 and 30 while fixing the number of layers transferred at six. The results of these experiments are shown in Fig. 4. Confirming this hypothesis our results show that training for 30 epochs initially at a high learning rate of 0.01 is too aggressive when fine-tuning on a target dataset and task that is very similar to the pre-training dataset. This continues the pattern noted in the previous experiments that an aggressive training scheme causes overfitting.

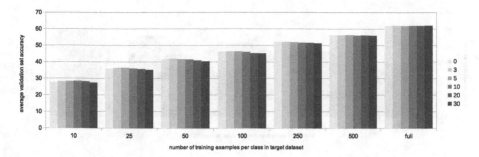

Fig. 4. Initial decay epochs. Changes in the average validation set accuracy are plotted, across all target dataset sizes, as the number of epochs before decay are varied for the high learning rate on the final classification layer.

This experiment shows that the pattern is evident even when only training the final classification layer heavily. A surprising result in these experiments is that as the size of the target dataset decreases the number of epochs to train the classification layer at a high learning rate increases. An unexpected curve can be seen in the optimal number of epochs to train at a high learning rate before decay for each target dataset size. These epochs are as follows:

- for the smallest dataset 10 epochs,
- for medium sized datasets with 50, 100 and 250 training examples per class 0 to 3 epochs, and
  for the largest dataset 30 epochs is optimal.

This may seem counterintuitive, however, the very small number of training examples per epoch for the smallest datasets needs to be considered. When this is taken into account these results once again show the effects of overfitting when fine-tuning transferred weights on smaller target datasets. Our smallest target dataset of 10 training examples per class has 5, 10 and 25 fewer batches per epoch than our target datasets with 50, 100 and 250 training examples respectively. Because of this the weights are changed far fewer times during each training epoch. This means that training for 10 epochs on our smallest dataset results in the same number of weight updates as training for only 1 epoch on a dataset with 100 training examples. This further extends our findings that the fine-tuning hyperparameters commonly adopted from [19] are too aggressive to produce the optimal results, particularly for smaller datasets. The weights for smaller datasets should be updated less times at a high learning rate to achieve the best accuracy.

The optimal number of epochs, to train the final classification layer at a high learning rate, increases significantly when fine-tuning with the full set of target dataset training examples. This is in keeping with the discussion above. With a large dataset there are enough training examples to ensure that:

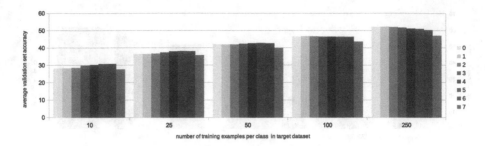

Fig. 5. Number of frozen pre-trained layers. The effect on performance of the number of pre-trained layers of weights frozen during fine-tuning are shown across various target dataset sizes.

- fine tuning the transferred weights at lower learning rates changes the features used for classification enough, and
- performing classification with features that are not optimal for the task does not result in as much overfitting as for smaller datasets.

For this reason, it is not possible to use optimal settings for transfer learning with very large target datasets to perform transfer learning with smaller target datasets or predict the latter from the former.

3.5 Vary Number of Frozen Layers

Current practice for transfer learning with CNNs generally involves locking or freezing the weights of some of the lower layers of a pre-trained CNN while fine-tuning on the target task to prevent overfitting. We tested the assumption that this practice improves performance in transfer learning on CNNs, particularly for small datasets, by varying the number of layers frozen during fine-tuning while keeping the number of layers transferred and hyperparameters constant. The results of the experiments in Fig. 5 show that freezing a high number of layers results in a significant increase in accuracy for very small target datasets of 10 and 25 training examples per class. However, once the target dataset increases to 50 training examples per class, freezing layers has very little effect and freezing more than one layer quickly becomes detrimental as the size of the target dataset continues to grow. When considering these results for freezing layers it should be kept in mind that the source and target datasets for these experiments are as similar as possible, both being drawn from ILSVRC2012, and the tasks, image classification, are identical. We expect that freezing layers will be less useful for very small target datasets and more detrimental for anything larger, for less related source and target datasets and/or tasks. We conclude that freezing layers has very limited scope to improve results on transfer learning.

3.6 Optimal Results

Figure 6 shows the results of using optimal number of layers to transfer and hyperparameters for fine-tuning when performing transfer learning. These results show that while using the optimal transfer learning protocols improves results for all dataset sizes it becomes particularly important as the size of the dataset decreases. For smaller datasets:

- transferring the optimal number of layers and using the best hyperparameters has an increasing impact on accuracy, and
- the importance of transfer learning increases because training from scratch is no longer viable.

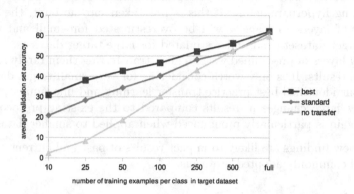

Fig. 6. Optimal transfer learning protocol vs commonly used vs no transfer learning. The final results of using the optimal transfer learning protocols we developed compared to those commonly used in previous research and no transfer learning

Table 2. Optimal transfer learning settings

	Training examples per class						
	10	25	50	100	250	500	Full
Layers to transfer	6	6	6	6	6	6	5
Initial decay epochs	10	5	3	3	3	0	30
Layers to freeze	6	5	5	1	1	0	0
Average validation set accuracy	30.8	38.1	42.7	46.6	52.2	56.3	62.1

For our smallest sized dataset using the best transfer learning settings compared to those often adopted from [19] results in a 47.88% increase in accuracy. The settings used to produce the best accuracy for each target dataset size are shown in Table 2.

4 Discussion

To our knowledge we have performed the most thorough analysis of transfer learning using CNNs to date. Based on this research we identified optimal transfer learning protocols for target dataset sizes from very small to large, when source and target datasets and tasks are similar. Our results show:

1. Using the commonly adopted transfer learning practice of transferring all but the final classification layer and training for 30 epochs at a learning rate of 0.01 causes a significant increase in overfitting compared to using optimal transfer learning protocols, particularly as the size of the target dataset decreases.
2. Best practice transfer learning and fine-tuning protocols for smaller target datasets cannot be derived using the results of the commonly adopted protocols used in performing transfer learning with a large target dataset.
3. There is an interaction between the optimal number of layers to transfer and fine-tuning hyperparameters. If this is not taken into account, the optimal number of layers to transfer will be overestimated for small and medium sized target datasets and underestimated for large target datasets.
4. Freezing layers of pre-trained weights after transferring them rarely results in the best results. It is only worth considering for very small target datasets.
5. Using our identified best practice transfer learning and fine-tuning protocols produces large changes in results compared to the existing protocols. This result again is particularly pronounced when applied to smaller datasets.

These new findings are likely to impact results of past and current research, which used commonly adopted protocols.

5   Conclusion

We have shown that using our identified optimal protocols when performing transfer learning results in a significant increase in accuracy when compared to the commonly adopted protocols. This is particularly evident for small target dataset sizes where we observed a 47.88% increase in accuracy compared to using the more standard protocols. Best practice transfer learning protocols for small target datasets cannot be predicted from previous research that has analysed transfer learning under very specific conditions that are not universally applicable. We have presented optimal transfer learning protocols for various target dataset sizes, from very small to large, when source and target datasets and tasks are similar. We intend to extend our work to analyse more diverse datasets and tasks, along with looking at ways to predict optimal transfer learning protocols. This paper and our ongoing research are significant as it is likely to improve outcomes from past, current and future research in transfer learning.

Acknowledgement. We thank Dawn Olley for her invaluable editing advice.

This work was supported by computational resources provided by the Australian Government through the National Computational Infrastructure (NCI) facility under the ANU Merit Allocation Scheme.

References

1. Agrawal, P., Girshick, R., Malik, J.: Analyzing the performance of multilayer neural networks for object recognition. In: Fleet, D., Pajdla, T., Schiele, B., Tuytelaars, T. (eds.) ECCV 2014. LNCS, vol. 8695, pp. 329–344. Springer, Cham (2014). https:// doi.org/10.1007/978-3-319-10584-0_22

2. Azizpour, H., Razavian, A.S., Sullivan, J., Maki, A., Carlsson, S.: Factors of transferability for a generic convnet representation. IEEE Trans. Pattern Anal. Mach. Intell. **38**(9), 1790–1802 (2016)

3. Deng, J., Dong, W., Socher, R., Li, L.J., Li, K., Fei-Fei, L.: ImageNet: a large-scale hierarchical image database. In: CVPR09 (2009)

4. Donahue, J., et al.: Decaf: a deep convolutional activation feature for generic visual recognition. In: International Conference on Machine Learning, pp. 647–655 (2014)

5. Girshick, R., Donahue, J., Darrell, T., Malik, J.: Rich feature hierarchies for accurate object detection and semantic segmentation. In: Proceedings of the IEEE Conference on Computer Vision and Pattern Recognition, pp. 580–587 (2014)

6. He, K., Girshick, R., Dollár, P.: Rethinking imagenet pre-training. arXiv preprint arXiv:1811.08883 (2018)

7. He, K., Gkioxari, G., Dollár, P., Girshick, R.: Mask R-CNN. In: Proceedings of the IEEE International Conference on Computer Vision, pp. 2961–2969 (2017)

8. Huh, M., Agrawal, P., Efros, A.A.: What makes ImageNet good for transfer learning? arXiv preprint arXiv:1608.08614 (2016)

9. Kornblith, S., Shlens, J., Le, Q.V.: Do better ImageNet models transfer better? In: Proceedings of the IEEE Conference on Computer Vision and Pattern Recognition, pp. 2661–2671 (2019)

10. Krizhevsky, A., Sutskever, I., Hinton, G.E.: Imagenet classification with deep convolutional neural networks. In: Advances in Neural Information Processing Systems, pp. 1097–1105 (2012)

11. Mahajan, D., et al.: Exploring the limits of weakly supervised pretraining. In: Proceedings of the European Conference on Computer Vision (ECCV), pp. 181–196 (2018)

12. Mormont, R., Geurts, P., Marée, R.: Comparison of deep transfer learning strategies for digital pathology. In: Proceedings of the IEEE Conference on Computer Vision and Pattern Recognition Workshops, pp. 2262–2271 (2018)

13. Paszke, A., et al.: Automatic differentiation in PyTorch. In: NIPS Autodiff Workshop (2017)

14. Scott, T., Ridgeway, K., Mozer, M.C.: Adapted deep embeddings: a synthesis of methods for k-shot inductive transfer learning. In: Advances in Neural Information Processing Systems, pp. 76–85 (2018)

15. Sharif Razavian, A., Azizpour, H., Sullivan, J., Carlsson, S.: CNN features off-the-shelf: an astounding baseline for recognition. In: Proceedings of the IEEE Conference on Computer Vision and Pattern Recognition Workshops, pp. 806–813 (2014)

16. Sun, C., Shrivastava, A., Singh, S., Gupta, A.: Revisiting unreasonable effectiveness of data in deep learning era. In: Proceedings of the IEEE International Conference on Computer Vision, pp. 843–852 (2017)

17. Tan, M., Le, Q.V.: Efficientnet: Rethinking model scaling for convolutional neural networks. arXiv preprint arXiv:1905.11946 (2019)

18. Wu, Y., Hassner, T., Kim, K., Medioni, G., Natarajan, P.: Facial landmark detection with tweaked convolutional neural networks. IEEE Trans. Pattern Anal. Mach. Intell. **40**(12), 3067–3074 (2018)

19. Yosinski, J., Clune, J., Bengio, Y., Lipson, H.: How transferable are features in deep neural networks? In: Advances in Neural Information Processing Systems, pp. 3320–3328 (2014)

Feature Learning and Representation

Representation Learning
for Heterogeneous Information Networks
via Embedding Events

Guoji Fu, Bo Yuan, Qiqi Duan, and Xin Yao[✉]

University Key Laboratory of Evolving Intelligent Systems of Guangdong Province,
Department of Computer Science and Engineering, Southern University of Science
and Technology, Shenzhen 518055, People's Republic of China
fuguoji1995@gmail.com, {yuanb,xiny}@sustech.edu.cn, daunqq257@qq.com

Abstract. Network Representation Learning (NRL) has been widely
used to analyze networks by mapping original networks into a low-
dimensional vector space. However, existing NRL methods ignore the
impact of properties of relations on the object relevance in heterogeneous information networks (HINs). To tackle this issue, this paper proposes a new NRL framework, called Event2vec, for HINs to consider
both quantities and properties of relations during the representation
learning process. Specifically, an event (i.e., a complete semantic unit) is
used to represent the relation among multiple objects, and both event-
driven first-order and second-order proximities are defined to measure the
object relevance according to the quantities and properties of relations.
We theoretically prove how event-driven proximities can be preserved in
the embedding space by Event2vec, which utilizes event embeddings to
facilitate learning the object embeddings. Experimental studies demonstrate its advantages over state-of-the-art algorithms on four real-world
datasets and two network analysis tasks (i.e., link prediction and node
classification).

Keywords: Network embedding · Heterogeneous information
networks · Network analysis

1 Introduction

Heterogeneous information networks (HINs), which contain multiple types of
objects and links, are ubiquitous in a variety of real-world scenarios such as
social networks [13], bibliographic networks [19], and user interest networks [5].
Recently, Network Representation Learning (NRL) is widely used to analyze
HINs, which maps original networks into a low-dimensional vector space while
preserving as much of the original network information as possible. Generally,
using the low-dimensional vector representations of objects as input features, the
performance of downstream network analysis can be improved [3]. Due to the
heterogeneities of both objects and relations, the primary challenge of NRL for

© Springer Nature Switzerland AG 2019
T. Gedeon et al. (Eds.): ICONIP 2019, LNCS 11953, pp. 327–339, 2019.
https://doi.org/10.1007/978-3-030-36708-4_27

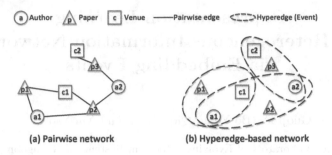

Fig. 1. Example of pairwise-based and hyperedge-based bibliographic networks.

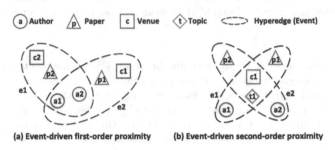

Fig. 2. Examples of event-driven proximities of bibliographic networks.

HINs is that the representation learning process should effectively capture the original network structural and semantic information. To this end, this paper proposes a new NRL framework to learn object embeddings for HINs.

In real-world networks, there may exist some relations among multiple objects. Taking Fig. 1 as an example, the relation among authors, a paper, and a venue is an indecomposable unit. Decomposing it into pairwise object relations will lose some semantic information [21]. Recently, *hyperedge* has been used to represent the relation among multiple objects [11,21], which can be regarded as a complete semantic unit called *event* [11]. These hyperedge-based methods measure the relation among multiple objects as a whole. However, they consider only the quantities of events and ignore their properties during the representation learning process.

Intuitively, objects involved in the same event should be relevant. Meanwhile, objects involved in similar events should be relevant as well. Take two bibliographic networks illustrated in Fig. 2 as examples. In Fig. 2(a), author a_1 and a_2 published two papers together, they are both involved in event e_1 and e_2. Therefore, they are relevant. Figure 2(b) shows author a_1 and a_2 published papers with the same topic in the same venue. They are involved in two similar events e_1 and e_2, respectively. Hence, they should be relevant as well. The properties of events can facilitate capturing the semantic relevance among objects. The relevance among objects in HINs should be driven by both the number of their intersectional events (event-driven first-order proximity) and the similarity between their non-intersectional events (event-driven second-order proximity).

In this paper, events are used to represent the relations among objects, and both event-driven first-order and second-order proximities are used to measure the object relevance according to the quantities and properties of relations. We propose a new NRL framework, called Event2vec, to learn the object embeddings of HINs via two learning steps. The first step intends to learn the event embeddings. Based on the event embeddings learned by the previous step, the second step obtains the object embeddings by preserving the event-driven proximities. We theoretically prove the leaning process which utilizes event embeddings to facilitate learning object embeddings is capable to preserve the event-driven proximities in the embedding space.

The contributions of this paper are summarised as follows:

- We investigate the significance of properties of relations among multiple objects for learning HIN representations.
- We define the event-driven first-order and second-order proximities to measure object relevance driven by quantities and properties of relations, respectively.
- We propose a new NRL framework called Event2vec to learn the object embeddings of HINs and theoretically prove Event2vec can preserve the event-driven first-order and second-order proximities in the embedding space.
- Experiments on four real-world datasets and two network analysis tasks are conducted to demonstrate the effectiveness of Event2vec.

The rest of this paper is organized as follows. Section 2 reviews the related work. In Sect. 3, we give the definition of the problem. The details of the proposed framework are described in Sect. 4. Section 5 presents the experimental results. Finally, we conclude in Sect. 6.

2   Related Work

The related work is in the area of network representation learning. Early works in NRL community were mainly designed for homogeneous information networks, which contain only a single type of objects and links. However, HINs are more ubiquitous in most complex real-world scenarios. Recently, representation learning for HINs has attracted increasing interest in the NRL community.

Many works have been proposed to learn representations of homogeneous information networks. They can be classified into matrix factorization-based methods, probability-based methods, and deep learning-based methods. Matrix factorization-based methods [1,2,17] represent relations between pairwise objects in the form of a matrix, e.g., adjacent matrix, Laplacian matrix, and factorize the matrix to obtain object embeddings using eigen-decomposition. Probability-based methods such as DeepWalk [16] and node2vec [10] use random walks to sample paths from the network and calculate object co-occurrence probabilities which are used to learn object embeddings via the Skip-gram model [15]. LINE [20] preserves both first-order and second-order proximities of networks by minimizing the Kullback-Leibler divergence of two joint probability distributions for each node-pair. Deep learning-based methods [4,14,22] use adjacent matrix, or object co-occurrence probability matrix, or graph convolution as input, and learn object embeddings via a deep neural network.

Those methods are effective to capture the structural and semantic information of homogeneous information networks. However, they fail to capture the complete semantic information of HINs since they ignore the different semantics of relations among different types of objects.

Recently, researchers in NRL field have increasingly engaged in HIN representation learning. The success of applying metapath [19] in HIN analysis has motivated some researchers to propose metapath-based methods to learn representations of HINs. Metapath2vec [7] and HIN2Vec [8] extend the Skip-gram model to learn the embeddings of HINs by employing the metapath-based random walks. HINE [12] optimizes the specific objective function which aims to preserve the metapath-based proximities. However, they only consider the relations between pairwise objects. In order to capture the complete semantics of relations among multiple objects, hyperedges have been used to represent the relations among objects. HEBE [11] preserves the proximities of the objects by modeling the relations among objects as hyperedges. DHNE [21] is a hyperedge-based method that preserves both first-order and second-order hypergraph structural information through a semi-supervised neural network model.

The aforementioned methods consider only the number of relations among objects while overlooking the impact of their properties. However, the properties of relations are important for NRL to capture the semantic information of HINs. On the contrary, Event2vec is able to consider both quantities and properties of relations.

3   Problem Definition

In this section, we formally define the problem of representation learning for HINs. First, we give the definition of HIN as presented below.

Definition 1 *(Heterogeneous Information Network* [18]*). Given an information network $\mathcal{G} = (V, E, T)$, where V is a set of vertexes, E is a set of links, and T is a set of object types and link types. Let $\varphi(v) : V \to T_V \subset T$ be an object type mapping function and $\psi(r) : E \to T_E \subset T$ be a link type mapping function. If $|T_V| + |T_E| > 2$, we say that $\mathcal{G}$ is a heterogeneous information network. Note that if $|T_V| + |T_E| = 2$, it is degraded to a homogeneous information network.*

Figure 1(a) gives an example of HINs, i.e., a tiny bibliographic network containing three types of objects (*author, paper,* and *venue*).

Definition 2 *(Events* [11]*). An event $e \in \Omega$ is an indecomposable unit formed by a set of objects, representing the consistent and complete semantic information of relation among multiple objects. Ω_i denotes the set of events that contain object v_i.*

As shown in Fig. 2(a), the relation among a_1, a_2, p_1, and c_1 is a complete semantic unit, denoted as an event e_2.

Definition 3 (Incident Matrix). *An incident matrix $\mathcal{H}_{|V| \times |\Omega|}$ is a matrix that shows the relationship between objects V and events Ω in which each row represents an object and each column represents an event. If object v_i belongs to event e_j, then $\mathcal{H}_{i,j} = 1$, otherwise $\mathcal{H}_{i,j} = 0$. Given an HIN with $|T_V|$ types of objects, there are $|T_V|$ incident matrices $\{\mathcal{H}^t\}_{t=1}^{|T_V|}$ in which each $\mathcal{H}_t$ represents the relationship among t-th type of objects and all events.*

Definition 4 (Event-driven First-order Proximity (EFP)). *The event-driven first-order proximity of object v_i and v_j is defined to be the ratio of the number of their intersectional events and the number of their unioned events:*

$$s_{i,j}^1 = \frac{|\Omega_i \cap \Omega_j|}{|\Omega_i \cup \Omega_j|}. \tag{1}$$

In Fig. 2(a), a_1 and a_2 have the EFP since they are contained in two same events e_1 and e_2, $s_{1,2}^1 = 2/2 = 1$. EFP considers the relevance among objects driven by the quantities of their relations. Larger $s_{i,j}^1$ of object v_i and object v_j indicates their stronger EFP. As a result, v_i and v_j should be closer in the embedding space.

Definition 5 (Event-driven Second-order Proximity (ESP)). *The event-driven second-order proximity of object v_i and v_j is defined to be the average cosine similarity of their non-intersectional events:*

$$s_{i,j}^2 = sim(\Omega_i, \Omega_j) = \frac{1}{|\Omega_i \cup \Omega_j|} \sum_{e \in \Omega_i, k \in \Omega_j, e \neq k} sim(e, k), \tag{2}$$

where $sim(e, k)$ denotes the cosine similarity between e and k.

In Fig. 2(b), a_1 and a_2 have the ESP since e_1 and e_2 are similar, $s_{1,2}^2 = \frac{1}{2}sim(e_1, e_2)$. ESP considers the relevance among objects driven by the properties of relations. Larger $s_{i,j}^2$ of object v_i and object v_j indicates their stronger ESP. Therefore, v_i and v_j should be closer in the embedding space.

Definition 6 (Heterogeneous Information Network Representation Learning). *Given a HIN $\mathcal{G} = (V, E, T)$, HIN representation learning aims to learn a mapping function $f : V \rightarrow Z \in \mathbb{R}^d$ where $d \ll |V|$, and preserve both event-driven first-order and second-order proximities of objects in the embedding space $\mathbb{R}^d$.*

4   Event2vec

In this section, we introduce the proposed Event2vec to learn the object embeddings of HINs. As shown in Fig. 3, after generating events from the input pairwise-based HIN, the representation learning process of Event2vec consists of two steps. The first step tries to learn the event embeddings. The second step obtains the object embeddings based on the learned event embeddings.

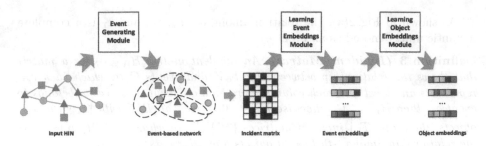

Fig. 3. The framework of Event2vec.

4.1 Event Generating

In this section, we introduce the event generating algorithm. We first define the event identifier q for each link r of the original HIN by defining the mapping function $\Theta(r) : r \to q$. Then the links with the same event identifier are merged into an event e.

The event identifier q for event e can be defined as a subset of objects of e. The choices of those objects are based on the characteristics of the network in question. For example, for a bibliographic network that contains three types of objects (*author, paper,* and *venue*), an incident that authors published a paper in a venue is an indecomposable semantic unit. Therefore, the relation among authors, a paper, and a venue should be regarded as an event. Then the event identifier can be defined as every paper since one event just corresponds to one paper.

Once the event identifiers are defined, events can be generated using Algorithm 1.

Algorithm 1: Event Generating

Input: HIN $\mathcal{G} = (V, E, T)$, event identifier mapping function Θ
Output: Event set Ω
begin

    $\Omega \longleftarrow \emptyset$;
    for $r \in E$ **do**
        $q \longleftarrow \Theta(r)$;
        for $e \in \Omega$ **do**
            if $\Theta(e) = q$ **then**
                $e \longleftarrow e \cup r$;
                update Ω using e;
                break;

        if Ω *is* $\emptyset$ *or* $\Theta(e) \neq q, \forall e \in \Omega$ **then**
            $\Omega \longleftarrow \Omega \cup r$;

4.2   Learning Event Embeddings

Taking the incident matrix as the input, which can be obtained based on the generated events, this module intends to learn the event embeddings. In this paper, we use an autoencoder to learn the event embeddings owing to its simplicity and efficiency of capturing non-linear object relationships [6]. It is worthy to note that other methods, e.g., singular value decomposition [9], can also be adapted to learn event embeddings in our framework.

4.3   Learning Object Embeddings

The object embeddings are obtained based on the event embeddings learned from the above sub-section. As previously discussed, both large $s_{i,j}^1$ and $s_{i,j}^2$ deduce that object v_i and v_j are relevant. To capture the relevance of objects, we need to preserve both their EFP and ESP. Based on this motivation, we obtain the object embedding y_i by taking the average of event embeddings $\{z_e\}, e \in \Omega_i$ as below.

$$y_i = \frac{1}{|\Omega_i|} \sum_{e \in \Omega_i} z_e. \tag{3}$$

Rewriting the above equation into matrix form as below, which we obtain

$$\mathbf{Y}^t = (\mathbf{D}_v^t)^{-1} \mathcal{H}^t \mathbf{Z}^t, \tag{4}$$

where $\mathbf{D}_v^t$ is the diagonal matrix that contains the t-th type of object degrees.

Through the above learning process, the learned object embeddings satisfy the following theorem,

Proposition 1. *The similarity between embedding y_i of object v_i and y_j of v_j is proportional to the sum of their event-driven first- and second-order proximity $s_{i,j}^1$, $s_{i,j}^2$.*

Proof. Given object v_i and v_j, the cosine similarity between their embeddings y_i and y_j is shown as below.

$$sim(y_i, y_j) = sim(\frac{1}{|\Omega_i|} \sum_{e \in \Omega_i} z_e, \frac{1}{|\Omega_j|} \sum_{k \in \Omega_j} z_k)$$

$$\propto \sum_{e \in \Omega_i, k \in \Omega_j} sim(z_e, z_k)$$

$$\propto \frac{1}{|\Omega_i \cup \Omega_j|} \left(\sum_{e \in \Omega_i, k \in \Omega_j, e=k} sim(z_e, z_k) + \sum_{e \in \Omega_i, k \in \Omega_j, e \neq k} sim(z_e, z_k) \right)$$

$$= \frac{|\Omega_i \cap \Omega_j|}{|\Omega_i \cup \Omega_j|} + sim(\Omega_i, \Omega_j)$$

$$= s_{i,j}^1 + s_{i,j}^2.$$

Table 1. Description of four datasets.

Datasets	Object types				#(V)				#(E)
DBLP	Author	Paper	Venue	Term	14475	14376	20	8920	170794
Douban	User	Movie	Actor	Director	3022	6977	3004	789	214392
IMDB	User	Movie	Actor	Director	943	1360	42275	918	136093
Yelp	User	Business	Location	Category	14085	14037	62	575	247698

Hence, objects that have many intersectional events and/or similar events will obtain similar embeddings. Specifically, the larger $s_{i,j}^1$ and/or $s_{i,j}^2$ of objects v_i and v_j, the more similar embeddings they have. Therefore, Event2vec is able to preserve both EFP and ESP of objects in the embedding space.

4.4 Time Complexity Analysis

The computational complexity of event generating is $O(|E||\Omega|)$, where $|E|$ is the number of links in HIN and $|\Omega|$ is the number of generated events. The computational complexity of training autoencoder is $O(|V|dbI)$, where $|V|$ is the number of objects in HIN, d is the representation size, b is the batch size and I is the number of iterations. The computational complexity of generating object embeddings is $O(|V||\Omega|d)$. Hence, the total computational complexity of Event2vec is $O(|E||\Omega|) + O(|V|dbI) + (|V||\Omega|d)$.

5 Experiments

This section reports the experimental results of Event2vec. We use four real-world datasets to evaluate our method on link prediction and node classification tasks.

5.1 Datasets

We evaluate our method on four real-world datasets, including DBLP [19], Douban [23], IMDB[1] and Yelp[2]. DBLP is a bibliographic network in computer science collected from four research areas: database, data mining, machine learning, and information retrieval. In DBLP network, 4057 authors, 20 venues and 100 papers were labeled with one of the four research areas. Douban was collected from a user review website Douban in China. IMDB is a link dataset collected from the Internet Movie Data with 1357 movies were labeled with at least one of the 23 labels. Yelp was extracted from a user review website in America, Yelp, containing four types of objects.

All four datasets are used in link prediction tasks, but only DBLP and IMDB are used in node classification tasks since they provide the ground truth of object labels. The detailed statistics of datasets are shown in Table 1.

---

[1] http://komarix.org/ac/ds/.
[2] https://www.yelp.com/.

5.2 Baseline Algorithms

We compare our method with five state-of-the-art methods, including DeepWalk [16], node2vec [10], LINE [20], metapath2vec [7], and DHNE [21]. The first three are homogeneous NRL methods. They are widely used in learning representations of homogeneous information networks. Metapath2vec is a metapath-based method designed for learning representations of HINs. DHNE is a recent NRL method using hyperedges to model the relations among multiple objects.

5.3 Parameter Settings

In the experiments, the representation size is uniformly set as 64 for all methods. As same as the setting in the previous paper [21], for Deepwalk and node2vec, we set the window size, the walk length and the number of walks on each vertex as 10, 40, and 10, respectively. For LINE, the number of negative samples is set as 5 and the learning rate is set as 0.025. For metapath2vec, we follow the suggestions from the papers [7,23], the metapaths we chose for DBLP are "APA" and "APCPA", for Douban and IMBD are "MUM", "MAM" and "MDM", for Yelp are "BUB", "BLB" and "BCB". For DHNE, following the setting on paper [21] we use one-layer full connection layer to learn tuplewise similarity function. The size of the hidden layer is set as 64 and the size of the fully connected layer is set as the sum of the embedding length from all types, 256. The parameter α in DHNE is tuned by grid search from {0.01, 0.1, 1, 2, 5, 10} and the learning rate is set as 0.025.

For the Event2vec, we use an autoencoder with one hidden layer. The size of the hidden layer is 64 which equals the representation size. The learning rate is set as 0.025 for all experiments. The event identifier for DBLP, Douban, IMDB, and Yelp are set as paper, movie, movie, and business, respectively.

Table 2. AUC of link prediction.

Methods	DBLP	Douban	IMDB	Yelp
Event2vec	**0.901**	**0.823**	0.894	**0.862**
DeepWalk	0.794	0.677	0.839	0.841
node2vec	0.709	0.618	0.652	0.783
LINE	0.697	0.710	0.748	0.531
metapath2vec	0.551	0.589	**0.909**	0.616
DHNE	0.632	0.761	0.811	0.546

5.4 Link Prediction

Link prediction can be used to evaluate the performance of NRL algorithms on capturing the implicit relevance of objects. The better performance on link prediction, the more effective the NRL algorithm is. We present the link prediction task on object embeddings obtained on four datasets by all NRL algorithms. Specifically, we predict the links among objects based on the cosine similarity of their embeddings. The evaluation metrics used in this task is AUC.

We randomly split the edges of the original HIN for training and testing. The training set contains 80% edges of the original network and the testing set contains the left 20%. Each experiment is independently run 10 times and the average performances on the testing set are shown in Table 2. The standard deviation is less than 0.015 for all experiments. From the results, we have the following observations:

- Event2vec significantly outperforms all baselines on DBLP, Douban, and Yelp, and obtains competitive performance against metapath2vec on IMDB. Event2vec is effective to capture the implicit object relevance.
- Both DHNE and Event2vec consider the relationships among multiple objects as a whole. The difference between them is that Event2vec considers both the quantities and properties of relations during the representation learning process, while DHNE considers only the former. However, Event2vec significantly outperforms DHNE on all four datasets. It demonstrates the properties of relations can facilitate capturing the implicit semantic information.

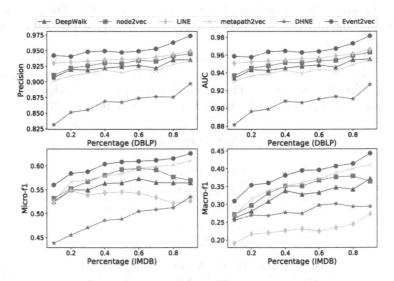

Fig. 4. Top: node classification results on DBLP using Precision and AUC as evaluation metrics; bottom: node classification results on IMDB using Micro-f1 and Macro-f1 as evaluation metrics.

5.5   Node Classification

Node classification in network analysis is an important task in many applications such as user classification in social networks, movie classification in movie-user networks, and so on. Here, we conduct the node classification tasks on DBLP and IMDB to evaluate the effectiveness of NRL algorithms on preserving original HIN information. The better the node classification performance NRL algorithm obtains, the better it works.

The embeddings of objects generated from different methods are used as input features to classify the objects, and the classifier used in our experiments is logistic regression. We randomly sample 10% to 90% of the labeled objects with a step 10% as the training set and use the rest labeled objects as the testing set. For DBLP, since each labeled object only receives one label, we use the precision and AUC as evaluation metrics. For IMDB, each labeled movie has at least one label. Therefore, Micro-f1 and Macro-f1 are used as evaluation metrics. Each experiment is conducted 10 times and the average performance is reported in Fig. 4. The standard deviation is less than 0.015 for all experiments. From the experimental results, we can observe that:

- Event2vec performs better than all baselines for node classification tasks on DBLP and IMDB. It demonstrates that Event2vec is effective to preserve the original structural and semantic information of the original HINs.
- Event2vec achieves good performance when there are few labeled objects, even outperforming the performance of some baselines obtained on the cases of vast labeled objects. It demonstrates the predictability and applicability of object embeddings obtained by Event2vec.

6   Conclusion

In this paper, we showed the relevance among multiple objects in HINs should be considered as a whole and such relevance is driven by both the quantities and properties of relations. However, the existing NRL methods consider only the quantities of relations and ignore the impact of their properties. To tackle this issue, we defined the EFP and ESP to measure the object relevance according to the quantities and properties of relations, respectively. A new NRL framework called Event2vec which can preserve both EFP and ESP was proposed to learn the object embeddings for HINs. The results of link prediction and node classification on four real-world networks demonstrated its effectiveness in preserving the original structural and semantic information of HINs.

Acknowledgments. This work was supported by National Key R&D Program of China (Grant No. 2017YF-C0804003), National Natural Science Foundation of China (Grant No. 61976111), Shenzhen Peacock Plan (Grant No. KQTD2016112514355531), the Science and Technology Innovation Committee Foundation of Shenzhen (Grant Nos. JCYJ20170817112421757 and JCYJ20180504165652917) and the Program for University Key Laboratory of Guangdong Province (Grant No. 2017KSYS008).

References

1. Ahmed, A., Shervashidze, N., Narayanamurthy, S., Josifovski, V., Smola, A.J.: Distributed large-scale natural graph factorization. In: Proceedings of the 22nd International Conference on World Wide Web, pp. 37–48. ACM (2013)

2. Belkin, M., Niyogi, P.: Laplacian eigenmaps and spectral techniques for embedding and clustering. In: Advances in Neural Information Processing Systems, pp. 585–591 (2002)
3. Cai, H., Zheng, V.W., Chang, K.: A comprehensive survey of graph embedding: problems, techniques and applications. IEEE Trans. Knowl. Data Eng. **30**(9), 1616–1637 (2018)
4. Cao, S., Lu, W., Xu, Q.: Deep neural networks for learning graph representations. In: Association for the Advancement of Artificial Intelligence, pp. 1145–1152 (2016)
5. Chen, L., Liu, Y., Zheng, Z., Yu, P.: Heterogeneous neural attentive factorization machine for rating prediction. In: Proceedings of the 27th ACM International Conference on Information and Knowledge Management, pp. 833–842. ACM (2018)
6. Doersch, C.: Tutorial on variational autoencoders. arXiv preprint arXiv:1606.05908 (2016)
7. Dong, Y., Chawla, N.V., Swami, A.: metapath2vec: scalable representation learning for heterogeneous networks. In: Proceedings of the 23rd ACM SIGKDD International Conference on Knowledge Discovery and Data Mining, pp. 135–144. ACM (2017)
8. Fu, T.y., Lee, W.C., Lei, Z.: Hin2vec: explore meta-paths in heterogeneous information networks for representation learning. In: Proceedings of the 2017 ACM on Conference on Information and Knowledge Management, pp. 1797–1806. ACM (2017)
9. Golub, G.H., Reinsch, C.: Singular value decomposition and least squares solutions. Numerische mathematik **14**(5), 403–420 (1970)
10. Grover, A., Leskovec, J.: node2vec: scalable feature learning for networks. In: Proceedings of the 22nd ACM SIGKDD International Conference on Knowledge Discovery and Data Mining, pp. 855–864. ACM (2016)
11. Gui, H., et al.: Embedding learning with events in heterogeneous information networks. IEEE Trans. Knowl. Data Eng. **29**(11), 2428–2441 (2017)
12. Huang, Z., Mamoulis, N.: Heterogeneous information network embedding for meta path based proximity. arXiv preprint arXiv:1701.05291 (2017)
13. Jiang, H., Song, Y., Wang, C., Zhang, M., Sun, Y.: Semi-supervised learning over heterogeneous information networks by ensemble of meta-graph guided random walks. In: Proceedings of the 26th International Joint Conference on Artificial Intelligence, pp. 1944–1950. AAAI Press (2017)
14. Kipf, T.N., Welling, M.: Semi-supervised classification with graph convolutional networks. arXiv preprint arXiv:1609.02907 (2016)
15. Mikolov, T., Sutskever, I., Chen, K., Corrado, G.S., Dean, J.: Distributed representations of words and phrases and their compositionality. In: Advances in Neural Information Processing Systems, pp. 3111–3119 (2013)
16. Perozzi, B., Al-Rfou, R., Skiena, S.: DeepWalk: online learning of social representations. In: Proceedings of the 20th ACM SIGKDD International Conference on Knowledge Discovery and Data Mining, pp. 701–710. ACM (2014)
17. Roweis, S.T., Saul, L.K.: Nonlinear dimensionality reduction by locally linear embedding. Science **290**(5500), 2323–2326 (2000)
18. Shi, C., Li, Y., Zhang, J., Sun, Y., Yu, P.S.: A survey of heterogeneous information network analysis. IEEE Trans. Knowl. Data Eng. **29**(1), 17–37 (2017)
19. Sun, Y., Han, J., Yan, X., Yu, P.S., Wu, T.: PathSim: meta path-based top-k similarity search in heterogeneous information networks. Proc. VLDB Endow. **4**(11), 992–1003 (2011)

20. Tang, J., Qu, M., Wang, M., Zhang, M., Yan, J., Mei, Q.: Line: large-scale information network embedding. In: Proceedings of the 24th International Conference on World Wide Web, pp. 1067–1077. International World Wide Web Conferences Steering Committee (2015)
21. Tu, K., Cui, P., Wang, X., Wang, F., Zhu, W.: Structural deep embedding for hyper-networks. arXiv preprint arXiv:1711.10146 (2017)
22. Wang, D., Cui, P., Zhu, W.: Structural deep network embedding. In: Proceedings of the 22nd ACM SIGKDD International Conference on Knowledge Discovery and Data Mining, pp. 1225–1234. ACM (2016)
23. Zheng, J., Liu, J., Shi, C., Zhuang, F., Li, J., Wu, B.: Recommendation in heterogeneous information network via dual similarity regularization. Int. J. Data Sci. Anal. 3(1), 35–48 (2017)

Unified Framework for Visual Domain Adaptation Using Globality-Locality Preserving Projections

Rakesh Kumar Sanodiya[1(✉)], Chinmay Sharma[2], and Jimson Mathew[1]

[1] Indian Institute of Technology Patna, Patna, India
rakesh.pcs16@iitp.ac.in
[2] Birla Institute of Technology Mesra, Ranchi, India
chinmaysharmacs10@gmail.com

Abstract. Domain Adaptation is a segment of machine learning that allows us to learn from a labelled source data distribution to classify different but related unlabelled target data distribution. In this paper, we propose a novel framework called Unified Framework for Visual Domain Adaptation using Globality-Locality Preserving Projections (UFVDA) that reduces the divergence between source and target domain both statistically and geometrically. In this framework, we use Globality-Locality Preserving Projections (GLPP) instead of primitive methods such as Principal Component Analysis (PCA) or Linear Discriminant Analysis (LDA) for dimensionality reduction and two projection vectors to project the source and the target domain data onto a common subspace. The better performance of our proposed framework than other state-of-the-art visual domain adaptation and the primitive dimensional reduction methods on real-world domain adaptation data-sets has been verified by extensive experiments. Our proposed approach UFVDA achieved a mean accuracy of 84.09% and 79.35% for all tasks of Office-Caltech data-set with VGG-Net features and PIE Face Recognition data-set respectively.

Keywords: Domain Adaptation · Transfer learning · Dimensionality reduction · Manifolds · Unsupervised learning · Classification

1 Introduction

The primitive machine learning techniques are based on the assumption that the training and testing data are subsets of the same data distribution [1,2]. This assumption, however, fails to hold in numerous real-life scenarios. For instance, training a classifier to recognize objects in images taken from different sources. Assume that a classifier was trained using images shot by an old mobile phone camera. This classifier will be able to identify the images shot in the same surroundings with good accuracy, however if we test it using pictures shot by a better camera, say a DSLR, which produces images with better resolution and exposure than those of the initial training images, the classifier will have a tough

© Springer Nature Switzerland AG 2019
T. Gedeon et al. (Eds.): ICONIP 2019, LNCS 11953, pp. 340–351, 2019.
https://doi.org/10.1007/978-3-030-36708-4_28

time recognizing them and will give irregular and unreliable results. This is because the distributions of the new images (captured from a DSLR camera) and old images (captured from an old mobile phone camera) are different. The traditional approaches will not be suitable for such cases. It has been proven that the performance of primitive machine learning methods falls when tested against a target distribution with considerable distinction from the source distribution.

Domain Adaptation (DA) [3, 4] is used to formulate an effective classifier by making use of a large amount of labelled source domain data and unlabelled target domain data. It aims to reduce the discrepancy between the source and target domain data. Based on the literature survey, DA methods can be classified into two methods: (a) semi-supervised DA and (b) unsupervised DA. In the case of semi-supervised DA methods, the target domain contains partially labeled data, but in unsupervised DA methods, the target domain contains completely unlabeled data. However, the source domain contain abundant labelled data samples. In this paper, we focus on unsupervised DA.

We use Globality-Locality Preserving Projections (GLPP) [5] instead of primitive methods such as Linear Discriminant Analysis (LDA) or Principal Component Analysis (PCA), which are widely used by many existing Domain Adaptation methods, to keep intact the discriminative information of source domain. He et al. [6] proposed Locality Preserving Projections (LPP), which is a dimensionality reduction algorithm that uses manifold of data. It had flaws that was later rectified by GLPP.

The proposed framework aims to:

1. Present a novel method called UFVDA that aims to overcome the shortcomings that are present in all other existing transfer learning and non-transfer learning algorithms. This is achieved by incorporating the necessary objectives such as maximization of target domain variance, source domain preservation with GLPP, minimizing marginal and conditional distribution divergence and amalgamating the geometric properties of target and source data into a unified framework.
2. Instead of using the traditional PCA or LDA, we use the GLPP algorithm in our model. This enables the model to jointly learn static (texture and shape) and dynamic part (pose and view) and thus perform better than other existing algorithms.
3. We have evaluated our proposed approach UFVDA on all possible tasks of two widely used real world data-sets: PIE Face Recognition and Office-Caltech data-set. The results obtained by the experiments were compared against results of other existing approaches and it was concluded that UFVDA outperforms all of them.

2   Related Work

Researchers have put a lot of effort in the past few years to optimize Domain Adaptation approaches, in search of new methods to generalize the training model across all types of data. We review some of the existing methods that have contributed to the ideology of our proposed approach.

In the first category, Domain Adaptation methods aim to reduce the discrepancy between both the domains as much as possible using subspace learning or feature learning. Subspace Alignment (SA) [8] generates a function that bring the source domain and target domain in alignment, but feature distribution is not implemented. This was rectified by Subspace Distribution Alignment (SDA) [9] which consists of both distribution alignment and subspace alignment. Transfer Component Analysis (TCA) [10] learns a new transfer subspace and projects data samples onto it to minimize distance between domains. Joint Distribution Adaptation (JDA) [11] considers the conditional distribution shift by producing pseudo labels of the target data. The TCA method is improved by Transfer Joint Matching (TJM) [12] as it jointly re-weights the samples and seeks a common subspace. Joint Geometrical and Statistical Alignment (JGSA) [13] is a framework the simultaneously reduces distribution and geometrical shifts by projecting data onto a subspace of lower dimension. In the second category, instance weighting methods minimize the divergence between domains. Re-weighting is done such that target domain samples look like they are draw from source domain. There are plenty of existing conventional dimensionality reduction algorithms such as Principal Component Analysis (PCA) and Linear Discriminant Analysis (LDA), Regularized Co-planar Discriminant Analysis (RCDA) [14], etc. which are unable to retain the local structure of the manifold but keep the global structure.

A new dimensionality reduction mechanism, Locality Preserving Projections (LPP) [6] has been proven to produce better results than the above-mentioned methods as it can handle non-linear case and doesn't assume anything about the sample distribution. In LLP a matrix of weights is generated which learns a new subspace by measuring similarity between data points. The new subspace can retain local structure of the manifold of data. The Laplacian of the graph gives the transformation matrix which projects data points onto a subspace. In the graph generated by the LLP, static part (subject-invariant factors) of subject is kept constant and geometry of dynamic part (subject-variant part) is captured. However, in many applications, the subjects share a lot of features. So, the static part of the data, such as texture and shape, should also be considered while capturing the manifold of the data. So, Huang et al. [5] proposed an approach in which the interaction between the manifolds of dynamic and static part results in the manifold of the data. It also learns the graphs of static and dynamic factors jointly. Therefore, we adopt the Globality-Locality Preserving Projection (GLPP) method in our proposed Domain Adaptation framework.

3 Unified Framework for Visual Domain Adaptation

To address the drawbacks of the existing approaches we propose a Unified Framework for Visual Domain Adaptation using Globality-Locality Preserving Projections (UFVDA) algorithm.

3.1   Formulation of the Model

Our proposed framework uses Globality-Locality Preserving Projections (GLPP) which prevents distortion of the original relationship between data samples and projects to lower dimension while preserving discriminative information. In the GLPP method, the proper understanding of data is obtained by dividing source domain data into static and dynamic part. This is followed by the Joint Statistical and Geometrical Alignment (JGSA) algorithm that used the common and domain-specific features of both domains to geometrically and statistically reduces the divergence between domains. The JGSA algorithm finds two coupled projections in order to obtain new representations of both the domains.

The proposed model builds upon JGSA to which Globality-Locality Preserving Projections (GLPP) is incorporated. A Laplacian term to account for the manipulation of the geometry of the manifold is also introduced.

Globality-Locality Preserving Projections for Source Domain. As discussed earlier, the GLPP method divides the source domain into dynamic and static parts. The class mean sample defines the static factors. In low-dimensional subspace, they can be represented by:

$$F_s = \sum_{i,j \in C} (\mu_i - \mu_j)^2 S_{ij}^s \tag{1}$$

where C is the number of classes, S^s is the static part similarity matrix and μ_i is the mean of the ith class. Whereas, the dynamic part is described as:

$$F_d = \sum_{c \in C} \sum_{i,j \in c} (\Delta d_i - \Delta d_j)^2 S_{ij}^d \tag{2}$$

where S^d is the dynamic part similarity matrix, $\Delta d_i = x_i - \mu_c, i \in c$, and $\Delta d_j = x_j - \mu_c, j \in c$.

Combining the above equations of the static and dynamic part we obtain the total equation as:

$$F_t = F_s + \lambda F_d \tag{3}$$

Minimization of Distribution Divergence. To minimize the marginal distribution variance between the target and source domain, the Maximum Mean Discrepancy (MMD) criterion is applied. The MMD method calculates the separation between the two domains in d-dimensional subspace as:

$$\underset{P,Q}{\text{Min}} \left\| \frac{1}{n_s} \sum_{x_i \in X_s} P^T x_i - \frac{1}{n_t} \sum_{x_j \in X_t} Q^T x_j \right\|_F^2 \tag{4}$$

where P is the projection for source domain and Q is the projection for the target domain.

When data is distributed in classes, minimizing marginal distribution is not enough. As proposed by Long et al. [11], we predict pseudo labels for the target domain data using source domain classifiers and utilize them to represent class based conditional distribution in the target domain. We follow this approach so that the conditional distribution shift between the domains is minimized:

$$\underset{P,Q}{\text{Min}} \sum_{i=1}^{C} \left\| \frac{1}{n_s^i} \sum_{x_i \in X_s^i} P^T x_i - \frac{1}{n_t^i} \sum_{x_j \in X_t^i} Q^T x_j \right\|_F^2 \tag{5}$$

By combining the marginal and conditional distribution shift minimization terms, we generate the final distribution divergence minimization term:

$$\underset{P,Q}{\min} Tr \left([P^T \ Q^T] \begin{bmatrix} T_s & T_{st} \\ T_{ts} & T_t \end{bmatrix} \begin{bmatrix} P \\ Q \end{bmatrix} \right) \tag{6}$$

The values of T_s, T_t, T_{st} and T_{ts} can be calculated in similar fashion as proposed by Zhang et al. [13]

Maximization of Target Domain Variance. The maximum variance of target domain data is obtained by projecting its features onto a subspace. Thus, maximization of the variance is done as follows:

$$\underset{A}{\text{Max}} \ A^T J_t A \tag{7}$$

where $J_t = (X_t)^T H_t X_t$ and $H_t = I_t - \frac{1}{n_t} 1_t (1_t)^T$ is the target domain centring matrix.

Geometrical Diffusion on Manifolds. A Laplacian regularization term R is incorporated to consider the correct geometry of the manifolds of both the domains. In the lower dimensional subspace, due to similar embedding, similar samples will have the same label.

We can join two data samples x_i and x_j with an edge if they are similar. The K-Nearest Neighbor (K-NN) algorithm with the weight-mode as cosine is used, which calculates the cosine between the two data samples, to assess the similarity between them. Therefore, the weight matrix W is evaluated as:

$$W_{ij} = \begin{cases} 1, & \text{if } x_i \in N_k(x_j) \mid x_j \in N_k(x_i) \\ 0, & \text{otherwise} \end{cases}$$

where, $N_k(x_j)$ and $N_k(x_i)$ represents the set of K nearest neighbours of x_j and x_i respectively. Now, we use the weight matrix to generate a graph. The Laplacian matrix is obtained as $L = (D - W)$, where D is a diagonal matrix with entries as the sum of columns of the weight matrix W i.e. $D_{ii} = \sum_j W_{ij}$. Finally, we can derive the regularization term as:

$$R = \sum_{i,j} (x_i - x_j)^2 W_{ij} = 2XLX^T \tag{8}$$

Here, X represents the set of all data samples of both the source domain and target domain.

Minimization of Subspace Divergence. The divergence of the subspaces can be reduced by bringing the source and target subspaces closer to each other. We optimize P and Q simultaneously, rather than projecting the two subspaces onto another matrix. The following expression is obtained:

$$\min_{P,Q} \|P - Q\|_F^2 \tag{9}$$

As proposed in the JGSA approach, we combine the common features and the domain-specific features so that the two domains become well-aligned.

3.2 Objective Function

In this section, we formulate the objective function for the UFVDA proposed framework by consolidating the objectives described by the Eqs. (3), (6), (8), (7) and (9) into a single model. The overall objective function comes out as:

$$\max \frac{\mu \{\text{Target Domain Var.}\}}{(\alpha\{\text{Sub. shift}\} + \beta\{\text{Total-class Var.}\} + \eta\{\text{Laplacian}\} + \{\text{Dist. shift}\})}$$

where α, β, η, and μ are the trade-off parameters that balance the importance of each term. Sub., Dist, and Var. stand for Subspace, Distribution and Variance respectively. The objective function can be written as:

$$\max_{P,Q} \frac{\mathrm{Tr}\left([P^T\ Q^T] \begin{bmatrix} I & 0 \\ 0 & \mu J_t \end{bmatrix} \begin{bmatrix} P \\ Q \end{bmatrix}\right)}{\mathrm{Tr}\left([P^T\ Q^T] \begin{bmatrix} T_s + \alpha I + \beta F_t + \eta R & T_{st} - \alpha I + \eta R \\ T_{ts} - \alpha I + \eta R & T_t + (\alpha + \mu)I + \eta R \end{bmatrix} \begin{bmatrix} P \\ Q \end{bmatrix}\right)}$$

3.3 Optimization of Objective Function

In order to optimize our objective function, we rewrite $[P^T\ Q^T]$ as U^T. Now, the objective function is written as:

$$\max_U \frac{\mathrm{Tr}\left(U^T \begin{bmatrix} I & 0 \\ 0 & \mu J_t \end{bmatrix} U\right)}{\mathrm{Tr}\left(U^T \begin{bmatrix} T_s + \alpha I + \beta F_t + \eta R & T_{st} - \alpha I + \eta R \\ T_{ts} - \alpha I + \eta R & T_t + (\alpha + \mu)I + \eta R \end{bmatrix} U\right)} \tag{10}$$

This is equivalent to

$$\mathrm{Tr}\left(U^T \begin{bmatrix} I & 0 \\ 0 & \mu J_t \end{bmatrix} U\right)$$

s.t.

$$\mathrm{Tr}\left(U^T \begin{bmatrix} T_s + \alpha I + \beta F_t + \eta R & T_{st} - \alpha I + \eta R \\ T_{ts} - \alpha I + \eta R & T_t + (\alpha + \mu)I + \eta R \end{bmatrix} U\right) = 1 \tag{11}$$

The calculation of the optimal solution of the above objective function is a demanding task. So, we first calculate U, until a certain predefined condition is satisfied. The Lagrange function of the equation comes out to be

$$Z = \mathrm{Tr}\left(U^T \begin{bmatrix} I & 0 \\ 0 & \mu J_t \end{bmatrix} U\right) + \delta\left(\mathrm{Tr}\left(U^T \begin{bmatrix} T_s + \alpha I + \beta F_t + \eta R & T_{st} - \alpha I + \eta R \\ T_{ts} - \alpha I + \eta R & T_t + (\alpha + \mu)I + \eta R \end{bmatrix} U\right) - 1\right) \tag{12}$$

Further, we get a generalized eigenvalue decomposition problem, which on solving gives the matrices δ and U. The top k eigenvalues are contained in the diagonal matrix δ and U contains the corresponding eigenvectors. Thus, P and Q can be calculated from U.

Table 1. Accuracy (%) on PIE Face Recognition data-set

Tasks	Non-DA algorithms				DA algorithms													
	SDA	LDA	PCA	NN	LTSL	GFK	RTML	TSL	JDA	LRSR	TDA-AL	TCA	DGA-DA	CDDA	GA-DA	JGSA	TJM	UFVDA
PIE 15 → 7	27.69	40.64	24.80	26.09	22.96	26.15	60.12	44.08	58.81	65.87	35.97	40.76	65.32	60.22	57.40	68.07	29.52	83.42
PIE 25 → 9	28.55	34.13	25.18	26.59	20.65	27.27	55.21	47.49	54.23	64.09	32.97	41.79	62.81	58.70	60.54	67.52	33.76	76.22
PIE 35 → 27	41.00	49.35	29.26	30.67	31.81	31.15	85.19	62.78	84.50	82.03	35.24	59.63	83.54	83.48	84.05	82.87	59.20	93.03
PIE 45 → 29	15.38	28.00	16.30	16.67	12.07	17.59	52.98	36.15	49.75	54.90	28.43	29.35	56.07	54.17	52.21	46.50	26.96	68.75
PIE 57 → 5	31.78	32.14	24.22	24.49	18.25	25.24	58.13	46.28	57.62	45.04	38.90	41.81	63.69	62.33	57.89	25.21	39.40	74.72
PIE 67 → 9	51.41	37.19	45.53	46.63	16.05	47.37	63.92	57.60	62.93	53.49	49.39	51.47	61.27	64.64	61.58	54.77	37.74	78.67
PIE 77 → 27	77.05	63.47	53.35	54.07	45.15	54.25	76.16	71.43	75.82	71.43	53.26	64.73	82.37	79.90	82.34	58.96	49.80	85.94
PIE 87 → 29	33.21	25.92	25.43	26.53	17.52	27.08	40.38	35.66	39.89	47.97	36.95	33.70	46.63	44.00	41.42	35.41	17.09	73.10
PIE 99 → 5	24.37	37.64	20.95	21.37	22.36	21.82	53.12	36.94	50.96	52.49	34.03	34.69	56.72	58.46	54.14	22.81	37.39	70.46
PIE 109 → 7	46.59	33.27	40.45	41.01	20.26	43.16	58.67	47.02	57.95	55.56	49.54	47.70	61.26	59.73	60.77	44.19	35.29	81.33
PIE 119 → 27	77.20	69.39	46.14	46.53	57.34	46.41	69.81	59.45	68.45	77.50	48.99	56.23	77.83	77.20	77.23	56.86	44.03	84.80
PIE 129 → 29	41.18	39.64	25.31	26.23	24.57	26.78	42.13	36.34	39.95	54.11	39.34	33.15	44.24	47.24	43.50	41.36	17.03	76.16
PIE 1327 → 5	46.49	75.21	31.96	32.95	51.20	34.24	81.12	63.66	80.58	81.54	42.20	55.64	81.84	83.10	79.83	72.14	59.51	94.11
PIE 1427 → 7	80.91	77.90	60.96	62.68	70.10	62.92	8.92	72.68	82.63	85.39	63.90	67.83	85.27	82.26	84.71	88.27	60.58	92.51
PIE 1527 → 9	86.27	80.51	72.18	73.22	72.00	73.35	89.51	83.52	87.25	82.23	61.64	75.86	90.95	86.64	89.17	86.09	64.88	88.60
PIE 1627 → 29	56.31	60.11	35.11	37.19	48.28	37.38	56.26	44.79	54.66	72.61	46.32	40.26	53.80	58.33	53.62	74.32	25.06	84.31
PIE 1729 → 5	25.09	43.82	18.85	18.49	13.06	20.35	29.11	33.28	46.46	52.19	32.92	26.98	57.44	48.02	52.73	17.52	32.86	54.02
PIE 1829 → 7	43.95	39.35	23.39	24.19	21.61	24.62	33.28	34.13	42.05	49.41	37.26	29.90	53.84	45.61	47.64	41.06	22.89	74.46
PIE 1929 → 9	53.00	46.08	27.21	28.31	17.03	28.49	39.85	36.58	53.31	58.45	36.64	29.90	55.27	52.02	51.66	49.20	22.24	77.87
PIE 2029 → 27	55.69	58.52	30.34	31.24	29.59	31.33	47.13	38.75	57.01	64.31	38.96	33.64	61.82	55.99	58.82	34.75	30.72	74.43
Average	46.49	48.72	33.85	34.76	31.59	35.35	58.80	49.43	60.24	63.53	42.14	44.75	65.09	63.10	62.56	53.39	37.29	79.35

Table 2. Accuracy (%) on Office-Caltech data-set using VGG-Net features.

Tasks	Non-DA algorithms			DA algorithms								
	SVM	PCA	NN	JDA	GFK	GFK-PLS	TJM	SA	TCA	ILS	CORAL	UFVDA
A → C	74.2	76.49	70.1	82.01	77.73	77.7	**82.45**	77.1	80.14	78.9	79.0	81.12
A → D	51.7	59.87	52.3	70.06	59.23	63.5	72.61	64.9	65.60	72.5	67.1	**76.43**
A → W	63.1	69.15	69.9	83.72	73.89	74.1	82.71	76.0	76.94	82.4	74.8	**86.77**
C → A	86.7	86.43	81.9	88.10	86.01	86.2	85.80	83.9	86.63	87.6	89.4	**91.02**
C → D	61.5	61.14	55.6	72.61	62.42	66.5	75.79	66.2	69.42	73.0	67.6	**76.43**
C → W	74.8	74.23	65.9	80.67	74.91	76.5	77.96	76.0	74.91	84.4	77.6	**91.18**
D → A	58.7	67.43	57.0	77.13	68.58	69.9	**80.79**	69.0	75.15	79.2	75.6	76.09
D → C	55.5	58.50	48.0	70.52	59.59	64.0	**74.44**	62.3	69.18	66.5	64.7	69.36
D → W	91.8	95.59	86.7	97.62	95.93	92.4	96.94	90.5	96.61	94.2	94.6	**98.98**
W → A	69.8	75.15	62.4	84.2	79.01	77.9	82.25	76.6	80.27	85.9	81.2	**87.16**
W → C	64.7	69.01	57.5	74.21	70.16	71.3	**78.45**	70.7	75.24	77.0	75.2	74.53
W → D	89.4	94.90	83.9	96.81	94.90	92.6	94.90	90.4	93.63	87.4	92.6	**100**
Average	70.15	73.9	65.93	81.52	82.09	76.05	82.09	75.3	78.64	80.7	78.2	**84.09**

4 Experiments

We conducted experiments with our proposed algorithm on two real-life data-sets: Office Caltech data-set with VGG-Net features and PIE Face Recognition data sets. The results were entered into a comparison table to compare the accuracies obtained by our algorithm with other state-of-the-art methods. It can be seen that the proposed method outperforms other state-of-the-art methods in the majority of the tasks.

A. Features and Benchmarks
The PIE Face Recognition data-set [11] contains images of 68 subjects under 21 different lighting conditions. The images have been grouped into 5 groups each containing a different pose, that are PIE (C09), PIE (C05), PIE (C29), PIE (C07), PIE (C27) where C09, C05, C29, C07, and C27 indicate downward pose, left pose, right pose, upward pose and frontal pose respectively. We form 20 different source-target pairs by taking one of the poses as the source domain and one of the others as the target domain.

We also ran tests using the Office-Caltech data-set [7] which has a total of 2533 images from four different distributions: Amazon, DSLR, Webcam, and Caltech256. The Amazon images contain images that were taken under constrained lighting conditions, while the DSLR images are of high resolution and clarity. The images in the Webcam distribution are of low resolution and the Caltech256 set contains the images downloaded from Google. We use the VGG-Net features of the Office-Caltech data-set which have 4096 available features.

B. Comparison with Other Methods
Our proposed approach was compared with other methods like: Nearest Neighbour (NN) Classifier, PCA, LDA, Geodesic Flow Kernel (GFK) [7], Subspace Distribution Alignment (SDA), Robust Transfer Metric Learning (RTML) [15],

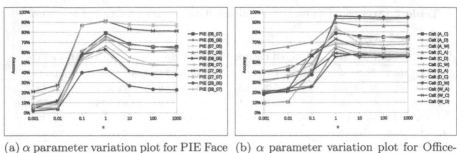

(a) α parameter variation plot for PIE Face data-set

(b) α parameter variation plot for Office-Caltech data-set

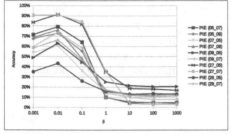

(c) β parameter variation plot for PIE Face data-set

(d) β parameter variation plot for Office-Caltech data-set

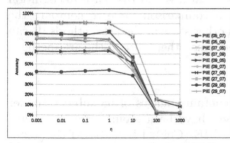

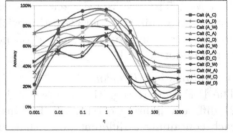

(e) η parameter variation plot for PIE Face data-set

(f) η parameter variation plot for Office-Caltech data-set

Fig. 1. Effect of trade-off parameters on the accuracy of the model for the PIE Face Recognition data-set and Office-Caltech data-set with VGG-Net features

Low-Rank Transfer Subspace Learning (LTSL) [16], Subspace Alignment (SA) [8], Low-Rank Sparse Representation (LRSR) [17], Joint Distribution Adaptation (JDA), Transfer Component Analysis (TCA), Discriminative and Geometry Aware DA (DGA-DA), Close yet Discriminative DA (CDDA), Geometry Aware DA (GA-DA) [18], Joint Geometrical and Statistical Alignment (JGSA), Transfer Joint Matching (TJM), CORrelation ALignment (CORAL) [19], Transductive Domain Adaptation with Affinity Learning (TDA-AL) [20], and ILS [21] (Tables 1 and 2).

C. Parameter Sensitivity Test

We conducted experiments on the two data-sets using our proposed approach for different values of the trade-off parameters. We observe that the there is variation because of the values of these parameters in the accuracy of each data-set task. The proposed model produces best possible results for each data-set task with ideal values of these parameters. Therefore, to determine the ideal values of these parameters, a parameter sensitivity test is conducted.

We use PCA as a prepossessing tool to reduce the dimensionality of the data and reduce computation time. We find the value of d, which represents the dimensionality of the data subspace, at which optimal results can be achieved. The value of d is varied from 150 to 240 for the PIE Face Recognition data-set and from 50 to 500 for the Office-Caltech data-set.

For obtaining the optimal values of α, β, η, λ and μ we vary their values between 10^{-3} and 10^3 one parameter at a time while keeping the values of other parameters fixed. The values of α, β, η, λ, and μ at which highest accuracy is produced by our algorithm for the PIE Face data-set are 1, 10^{-2}, 1,1 and 10^{-1} respectively. Whereas for the Office-Caltech data-set the overall best results were obtained by setting the values of α, β, η, λ, and μ as 1, 10^{-3}, 1, 1 and 10^{-1} respectively. This can be verified by observing the graphs in Fig. 1. k represents the number of topmost eigenvalues. To determine the appropriate value of k for which all the tasks give good output, its values is varied from 60 to 150 in case of PIE Face Recognition data-set and 10 to 150 for Office-Caltech data-set. Highest mean accuracy for all the tasks of PIE Face Recognition data-set is obtained when the value of k is 130 and for the tasks of Office-Caltech data-set when k is 50. The value of the number of nearest neighbours (K), is varied from 1 to 10 for both the data-sets. Highest mean accuracy is achieved by our proposed algorithm when the value of K is 8 for the Office-Caltech data-set and 1 for the PIE Face Recognition data-set.

5 Results and Discussion

Tests were conducted on 2 different data-sets, the Office-Caltech data-set and PIE Face recognition data-set. It is observed that almost all the results obtained by UFVDA were better than the other existing Domain Adaptation approaches. We provide a summary of the obtained results below.

Our proposed algorithm UFVDA produces a mean accuracy of 79.35% with all the combinations of the PIE Face Recognition data-set. An average accuracy of 84.09% is produced by UFVDA for all tasks Office-Caltech data-set. Both these results are better than all other existing algorithms.

6 Conclusion

In this paper, we presented a novel framework, called the Unified Framework for Visual Domain Adaptation using Globality-Locality Preserving Projections (UFVDA), designed for Domain Adaptation. We have provided experimental data and in-depth analysis of the proposed framework. Extensive experiments have verified the effectiveness of our approach and it is proven that it delivers better accuracy than existing Domain Adaptation and primitive approaches. In future we would work on formulating the kernel version of this framework.

References

1. Pan, S.J., Yang, Q.: A survey on transfer learning. IEEE Trans. Knowl. Data Eng. **22**(10), 1345–1359 (2010)
2. Sanodiya, R.K., Mathew, J., Saha, S., Thalakottur, M.D.: A new transfer learning algorithm in semi-supervised setting. IEEE Access **7**, 42956–42967 (2019)
3. Sanodiya, R.K., Mathew, J.: A novel unsupervised globality-locality preserving projections in transfer learning. Image Vis. Comput. **90**, 103802 (2019)
4. Sanodiya, R.K., Mathew, J.: A framework for semi-supervised metric transfer learning on manifolds. Knowl. Based Syst. **176**, 1–14 (2019)
5. Huang, S., Elgammal, A., Huangfu, L., Yang, D., Zhang, X.: Globality-locality preserving projections for biometric data dimensionality reduction. In: Proceedings of the IEEE Conference on Computer Vision and Pattern Recognition Workshops, pp. 15–20 (2014)
6. He, X., Niyogi, P.: Locality preserving projections. In: Advances in Neural Information Processing Systems, pp. 153–160 (2004)
7. Gong, B., Shi, Y., Sha, F., Grauman, K.: Geodesic flow kernel for unsupervised domain adaptation. In: 2012 IEEE Conference on Computer Vision and Pattern Recognition, pp. 2066–2073. IEEE (2012)
8. Fernando, B., Habrard, A., Sebban, M., Tuytelaars, T.: Unsupervised visual domain adaptation using subspace alignment. In: Proceedings of the IEEE International Conference on Computer Vision, pp. 2960–2967 (2013)
9. Sun, B., Saenko, K.: Subspace distribution alignment for unsupervised domain adaptation. In: BMVC, 4, pp. 24.1–24.10 (2015)
10. Pan, S.J., Tsang, I.W., Kwok, J.T., Yang, Q.: Domain adaptation via transfer component analysis. IEEE Trans. Neural Netw. **22**(2), 199–210 (2011)
11. Long, M., Wang, J., Ding, G., Sun, J., Yu, P.S.: Transfer feature learning with joint distribution adaptation. In: Proceedings of the IEEE International Conference on Computer Vision, pp. 2200–2207 (2013)
12. Long, M., Wang, J., Ding, G., Sun, J., Yu, P.S.: Transfer joint matching for unsupervised domain adaptation. In: Proceedings of the IEEE Conference on Computer Vision and Pattern Recognition, pp. 1410–1417 (2014)
13. Zhang, J., Li, W., Ogunbona, P.: Joint geometrical and statistical alignment for visual domain adaptation. In: Proceedings of the IEEE Conference on Computer Vision and Pattern Recognition, pp. 1859–1867 (2017)
14. Huang, K.K., Dai, D.Q., Ren, C.X.: Regularized coplanar discriminant analysis for dimensionality reduction. Pattern Recognit. **62**, 87–98 (2017)
15. Ding, Z., Fu, Y.: Robust transfer metric learning for image classification. IEEE Trans. Image Process. **26**(2), 660–670 (2017)
16. Shao, M., Kit, D., Fu, Y.: Generalized transfer subspace learning through low-rank constraint. Int. J. Comput. Vis. **109**(1–2), 74–93 (2014)
17. Xu, Y., Fang, X., Wu, J., Li, X., Zhang, D.: Discriminative transfer subspace learning via low-rank and sparse representation. IEEE Trans. Image Process. **25**(2), 850–863 (2016)

18. Luo, L., Chen, L., Hu, S., Lu, Y., Wang, X.: Discriminative and geometry aware unsupervised domain adaptation. arXiv preprint arXiv:1712.10042 (2017)
19. Sun, B., Feng, J., Saenko, K.: Return of frustratingly easy domain adaptation. In: Thirtieth AAAI Conference on Artificial Intelligence (2016)
20. Shu, L., Latecki, L.J.: Transductive domain adaptation with affinity learning. In: Proceedings of the 24th ACM International on Conference on Information and Knowledge Management, pp. 1903–1906. ACM (2015)
21. Herath, S., Harandi, M., Porikli, F.: Learning an invariant hilbert space for domain adaptation. In: Proceedings of the IEEE Conference on Computer Vision and Pattern Recognition, pp. 3845–3854 (2017)

Zero-Shot Learning for Intrusion Detection via Attribute Representation

Zhipeng Li, Zheng Qin[✉], Pengbo Shen, and Liu Jiang

School of Software, Tsinghua University, Beijing 100084, China
{lizp14,spb17,jiangl16}@mails.tsinghua.edu.cn,
qingzh@mail.tsinghua.edu.cn

Abstract. Network intrusion detection is an important network security infrastructure. Although numerous studies based on machine learning have explored how to enable intrusion detection to detect unknown novel attack types, so called anomaly detection, little work focuses on using attribute learning methods. An important application of attribute learning is zero-shot learning, which can be used to solve the anomaly detection problem. In this paper, we propose an attribute learning method. A pipeline framework using random forest feature selection and DBSCAN clustering attribute conversion is introduced to convert raw network data into attributes. A comprehensive empirical evaluation demonstrates that our proposed framework sustains the data information effectively and outperforms the state-of-the-art approaches. An extra zero-shot learning experiment show that our attribute approach works well in zero-shot learning scenario.

Keywords: Zero-shot learning · Intrusion detection · Attribute learning

1 Introduction

Network Intrusion Detection System (NIDS) is a specialized network security system which is used to monitor the network state of a designated network. NIDS is one of the two deploying scenario modes of Intrusion Detection System (IDS). Another mode of IDS is based on the host system. IDS also can be categorized as anomaly detection mode and misuse detection mode. Anomaly detection approaches can detect novel attack types with artificial intelligent algorithms, probability inference models, etc. On the contrary, misused detection approaches detect abnormal behavior by rules which are coded by security experts. Each of these methods has its merits and shortcomings. IDS was first proposed as a theoretical framework by Denning in 1986 [5]. Stanford Research Institute realized a true prototype of IDS. The prototype system is a real time system which can work on both the anomaly mode and the detection rules mode. UCDavis developed Network Security Monitor (NSM) as the first network IDS [10]. Snort has attracted a lot of deploy usages and improvement researches since 1998 [18].

© Springer Nature Switzerland AG 2019
T. Gedeon et al. (Eds.): ICONIP 2019, LNCS 11953, pp. 352–364, 2019.
https://doi.org/10.1007/978-3-030-36708-4_29

With the fast growth of Internet of Things, Cloud Computing, AI, how to integrate into the new scenario and combine with new technologies become the major research trend.

Attribute learning was first proposed in computer vision area. In the real world, many categories have very few samples in each for human to collect. In some situations, it is too hard to label annotations for every class or too expensive to form a complete dataset. In other words, lots of objects follow a long tail distribution in an actual environment. There are always test samples that train dataset do not include. Attributes or semantic words are thought to be a media that can transfer information across a specific kind species. Attributes learning or zero-shot learning (ZSL) is being comprehensive recognized as a way to solve the labeled data lack problem. ZSL uses attributes as a middle media to transfer the model's ability to recognize objects [7,11,15,19].

In this work, we are inspired by the idea of attribute learning. One of the major problems of IDS is that the artificial system cannot recognize the rapidly changing new attack forms. We want to solve this problem from the perspective of attribute learning rather than only a matter of anomaly detection. We propose an attribute learning method for intrusion detection to transfer attribute learning conception from image recognition to intrusion detection application. And we introduce the specific feature selection and attribute extraction method which converts features of the KDD99/NSL_KDD dataset into attributes. We conduct experiments to show the sustaining information ability of attributes on a popular NSL_KDD dataset. And we also give a performance test on zero-shot issue to show our method can work well in detecting novel attack species.

The remainder of this paper is organized as follows. In Sect. 2, the related work of attribute learning and intrusion detection systems is reviewed. In Sect. 3, we elaborate the KDD99/NSL_KDD dataset feature format to attribute format conversion procedure and a full connected neural network module for intrusion detection classification. Section 4 illustrates our approach's performance tested by NSL_KDD dataset and performance of zero-shot issue. Finally, Sect. 5 concludes our work and gives a prospect of future work.

2   Related Work

There are many approaches to achieve zero-shot learning, in which the most used attributes are semantic words of object descriptions. Some work considers the semantic words constructing a vector space which has relation with the image feature vector space and tries to learn some linear projection functions of the two vector spaces [1,2,9]. And some other work uses a nonlinear compatible function to relate the feature space and the attribute space [20,24]. There is also some other work expressing the problem as a mixture of seen class proportions [4,14,25], some work further uses relative attributes component comparison [21]. Direct Attribute Prediction (DAP) model is proposed by Lampert and has been considered as a fundamental base line method of zero-shot learning [11]. The DAP model uses attributes as a middle media to transfer the recognition abilities of attributes across classes. The work uses 85 attributes which are not only visual features or specific image processing filter to learn senior knowledge across the train classes. An instant in that work is 'smelly' attribute can be learned by the visual features. Then a new type can be identified under the condition than the relationship between classes and attributes are known. That is to say by using feature to attributes conversion the model gets the abilities to transfer class species knowledge from seen to unseen ones.

Since the advent of intrusion detection, one of the primal problems to be solved has been how to make IDS recognize constantly emerging new attack forms. Scholars strive to try artificial intelligence methods in IDS. In recent years, varieties of methods based on deep learning has been proposed. Deep neural network variants, recursive neural network and convolutional neural network are improved for IDS trial [6,8,12,13]. Attribute learning or zero-shot learning is proposed to solve the problems of identifying data without labels i.e. new species that do not exist in training image dataset. The core concept of attribute learning is very compatible for requirement of anomaly detection scenario. However, there is little work focuses on attribute learning or zero-shot learning on IDS topic. To best of our knowledge, only Rivero proposes a two-stage zero-shot learning method for NIDS [16,17]. The attribute conversion uses a modified tree classification which indicators are entropy and information gain. We think the conversion stage from feature space to attribute space still stay on feature level. And the attribute conversion results are rough and not satisfactory. The Grassmannian inference stage which maps attributes to a specific space and measure distance between each two different classes is not reasonable enough.

3   Proposed Method

In this work, the feature space to attribute space pipeline conversion is introduced. The classification module is inspired by DAP model. Unlike the AwA dataset created in DAP work, whose attributes are manually labeled, we give a feature engineering procedure that contains a conversion stage, which can be understood as a projection from feature space to attribute space. DAP model is one of the prototypes of zero-shot learning. We also use an attributes layer to predict the novel classes. Then a fully connected network is used to verify the attribute's recognizing different classes abilities. The overview of our attribute learning approach is shown in Fig. 1.

3.1   Feature Selection for Attribute Conversion

Feature Engineering is one step of machine learning for cleaning and selecting data. The data preprocess procedure has an important impact on the result of machine learning. Feature engineering includes the following three main areas: feature construction, feature extraction and feature selection. Feature construction uses attribute segmentation and combination to find physical or statistical features. Feature extraction emphasizes the use of some transformation or projection methods to obtain new low-dimensional vectors or more meaningful potential variables, e.g. PCA and LDA. Feature selection is to eliminate irrelevant

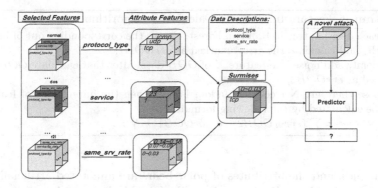

Fig. 1. Proposed attribute learning approach for intrusion detection

and redundant features. By reducing the number of features, feature selection can improve the model accuracy while reducing the model training time. Some statistical methods known as Pearson Correlation and MIC measures the relationship between feature variables. Some methods based on machine learning models are also used for feature selection. For example, by adding regularization items to the linear model to make characteristic coefficients of inefficient features small enough to be closed to zero. Random forest can use some special indicators to select features directly.

Breiman [3] proposed Random Forest in 2001. Random Forest is one of the bagging methods of ensemble learning. As a bagging method, Random Forest performs better than individual decision tree in most datasets. At the same time, Random Forest can be used as a feature selection method. The construction process of Random Forest bases on bagging sampling method is shown in Algorithm 1:

Algorithm 1. Random Forest Algorithm

1: Using bootstrapping method to get m samples with replacement, repeat n_tree times and obtain n_tree sub datasets;

2: Training n_tree decision tree classifier based on the former n_tree sub datasets, the tree uses information gain/information gain rate/gini coefficient as the split indicator;

3: The sub datasets generating trees vote for classification;

The constructed Random Forest can be used for feature selection. The feature importance can be calculated with Algorithm 2:

3.2   Clustering Attribute Conversion

In zero-shot learning problem, attributes are introduced to be a media that can be used to describe objects. The attributes are annotated manually. Some datasets are specially created for zero-shot tasks [7,11,23]. Attributes are given by human semantic describing. E.g., the raw polar bear images are the feature

Algorithm 2. Feature Importance Calculation Algorithm

1: For each decision tree in Random Forest, choose the corresponding out of bag data
    (OOB) and calculate the error, marked as $errOOB1$;
2: Randomly add noise into feature X of OOB data, after that calculate OOB again,
    marked as $errOOB2$;
3: Suppose there are N trees in Random Forest, then the importance of feature X
    can be calculated by the following formula:
    $Importance = \sum (errorOOB2 - errorOOB1) \setminus N$;

---

input samples, and the attributes of polar bears are annotated artificially. The
attributes maybe binary Boolean values, like false black, true white, false brown,
false stripe, true water, true eats fish and so on.

In intrusion detection there is no such dataset with annotated attributes. It is
also difficult to describe a network flow data by natural language words. Semantic words cannot describe the state of a network data properly and accurately.
The raw network must be parsed by the network protocols to produce some
elementary data information. The most famous dataset in intrusion detection
is KDD'99 dataset, which is abstracted from DARPA'98 dataset. DARPA'98 is
a raw network dataset. KDD'99 get 41 abstract meaningful network features
from the raw data form. The successor NSL_KDD dataset reserves the whole 41
abstract features as a guarantee of continuity. The NSL_KDD dataset is popular
in intrusion detection, because it reduces redundant data from KDD'99 dataset
and improves the inter class equilibrium. The KDD'99 and NSL_KDD datasets
do have domain expert features information. However, there is no more "detailed
features" or called attributes dataset, like the semantic descriptions in zero-shot
learning for image recognition. A lot of work attempts to find combination of
features rather than the internal composition of each feature.

We are inspired by the spirit of attribute learning method. For the sake of
finding a more internal detailed partition method of each feature, we introduce
the clustering method. Cluster analysis is one of important techniques in data
mining. Clustering process makes the similar objects into a cluster structure
and the samples between cluster be different. There are many clustering algorithms e.g. partitioning based method K-MEANS, hierarchical based method
BIRCH, density-based methods DBSCAN and so on. Considering the feature
internal constitutive structure (cannot specify a specific clustering number) and
the computational complexity, we choose DBSCAN, a density-based clustering,
as our clustering method.

DBSCAN (Density-Based Spatial Clustering of Applications with Noise) is
a typical density clustering algorithm. DBSCAN can be applied to both convex and non-convex samples. DBSCAN is a density-based clustering algorithm,
which generally assumes that categories can be determined by the compactness
of sample distribution. Samples of the same category are closely related to each
other, that is to say, there must be samples of the same category not far from
any sample of the same category. By grouping closely connected samples into one
group, a clustering category is obtained. By dividing all the closely connected
samples into different categories, we can get the final clustering results.

DBSCAN is based on a set of neighborhoods to describe the compactness of the sample set. Parameters $(\epsilon, MinPts)$ are used to describe the compactness of the sample distribution in neighborhood. Where ϵ describe the neighborhood distance threshold of a sample, and $MinPts$ describes the threshold of samples number in distant of ϵ.

Assuming that a sample set is $D = (x_1, x_2, ..., x_m)$, the specific density description of DBSCAN is defined as follows:

1. ϵ-neighborhood: For $x_j \in D$, its ϵ-neighborhood contains a subset of sample set D whose distance form x_j is not greater than ϵ, i.e. $N_\epsilon(x_j) = \{x_i \in D \mid distance(x_i, x_j) \leq \epsilon\}$, the number of the sub sample is denoted as $|N_\epsilon(x_j)|$.
2. Core object: For any sample $x_j \in D$, if its ϵ-neighborhood corresponding $N_\epsilon(x_j)$ contains $MinPts$ samples at least, i.e. if $|N_\epsilon(x_j)| \geq MinPts$, then x_j is the core object.
3. Density direct: If x_i is located in the ϵ-neighborhood of x_j and x_j is core object, then x_i is "density direct". Note that it is may be not true x_j is also density direct from x_i, unless x_i is core object.
4. Density reachable: For x_i and x_j, if there are sample sequence $p_1, p_2, ..., p_t$, satisfying $p_1 = x_i$, $p_t = x_j$, and each p_{t+1} is density direct from p_t, x_j is "density reachable" from x_i, that is to say density reachable can satisfy transitivity.
5. Density connected: For x_i and x_j, if there is core object sample x_k, so that x_i and x_j are both density reachable from x_k, then x_i and x_j are density connected.

The DBSCAN clustering definition is simple: The maximum density connected sample set, which is derived from the density reachable relationship, is a category or a cluster. The DBSCAN cluster can have one or more core objects. If there is only one core object, the samples of other non-core objects are in the ϵ-neighborhood of the core object. If there are multiple core objects, there must be another core object in the ϵ-neighborhood of anyone core object. Otherwise the two core objects cannot be density reachable. These core objects and samples in their ϵ-neighborhood compose one DBSCAN cluster.

3.3   Classification Module

Inspired by the DAP model [11], we use a simple one-layer neural network to testify the attributes' classification performance. We conduct several classification comparison experiments to demonstrate the presentation ability of attributes. Due to the lack of annotated attribute information of unknown network attack types, we cannot use the measurement of distance between leaned definition of known types and the definition of unknown types (manual annotation). We use the learned attribute model to give the deduction of the major types of novel network attack data. By deducing novel attack types of data, we can prove the feature to attribute conversion is a useful description of abstract feature and can be used for zero-shot learning issue. The classification part is shown in Fig. 2.

We think the attribute presentation is a finely grained representation of input data, one-layer neural network can achieve a good representation effect. Experiments also show that in most cases, one-layer network can obtain the best classification accuracy.

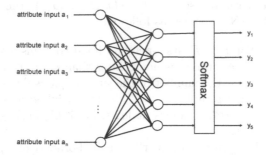

Fig. 2. Attribute classification part of proposed method

4   Experiments and Results

In this section, we conduct experiments to evaluate the efficacy of our proposed attribute learning intrusion detection framework using NSL_KDD dataset. First, we use Random Forest to select important features. Then, we use DBSCAN clustering to convert the features into a more specific attribute description. Finally, we use a neural network to testify the performance of the attribute conversion method.

4.1   Feature Selection on NSL_KDD

In the field of intrusion detection, NSL_KDD is a popular dataset used for anomaly detection test. Because the very versatile usage of network, there is no such an intrusion detection dataset can represent a common standard network. NSL_KDD is proposed as an improved successive version that eliminate some redundant data of KDD'99 dataset [22]. And KDD'99 is derived from the famous 1998 DARPA intrusion detection evaluation dataset. NSL_KDD is still very popular based on the continuity of dataset evaluation criteria.

NSL_KDD Dataset. NSL_KDD dataset keep the feature style of KDD'99 dataset. By eliminating the redundant records both in train and test dataset of KDD'99. NLS_KDD mainly forms a train dataset containing 125973 records and a test dataset containing 22544 records. There are 41 features inherited form KDD'99. The 41 features can be grouped into 4 categories that have some specific physical significance which is shown in Table 1.

Table 1. Features & data types of NSL_KDD

Feature groups	Feature name & data types
Basic features	duration(numeric) protocol_type(categorical) service(categorical) flag(categorical) src_bytes(numeric) dst_bytes(numeric) land(bool) wrong_fragment(numeric) urgent(numeric)
Domain knowledge features	hot(numeric) num_failed_logins(numeric) logged_in(bool) num_compromised(numeric) root_shell(bool) su_attempted(bool) num_root(numeric) num_file_creations(numeric) num_shells(numeric) num_accesses_files(numeric) num_outbound_cmds(numeric) is_host_login(bool) is_guest_login(bool)
2s-window features	count(numeric) srv_count(numeric) serror_rate(numeric) srv_serror_rate(numeric) rerror_rate(numeric) srv_rerror_rate(numeric) same_srv_rate(numeric) diff_srv_rate(numeric) srv_diff_host_rate(numeric)
100-connections features	dst_host_count(numeric) dst_host_srv_count(numeric) dst_host_diff_srv_rate(numeric) dst_host_same_srv_rate(numeric) dst_host_diff_srv_rate(numeric) dst_host_same_src_port_rate(numeric) dst_host_srv_diff_host_rate(numeric) dst_host_srv_serror_rate(numeric) dst_host_srv_serror_rate(numeric) dst_host_rerror_rate(numeric) dst_host_srv_rerror_rate(numeric)

Random Forest Feature Selection. We use Random Forest (the hyper parameters: n_estimators = 20, criterion = 'gini') to select 8 important features from the all features. We use 8 features because we test the accuracy of models using different number of features. Results show that 8 selected features already have certain classification ability. Although more features can improve some accuracy, in order to simplify the feature conversion processing, we select 8 representative features. The selected features with importance are shown in Fig. 3.

4.2 Attributes Conversion on Selected Features

A main contribution of zero-shot learning is the attributes description introduced as side information. By using the attributes, the model gets the ability of recognizing samples that have never been 'seen'. The attributes used in most zero-shot learning is given by human annotation. There is some works using feature engineering methods to select different features for optimal feature combination. Either KDD'99 or NSL_KDD uses the 41 features that have specific networking physical meaning with different types. For continuous features, it is hard to describe them with semantic words. We use DBSCAN clustering to convert the continuous features into cluster groups and use the cluster numbers as semantic attribute descriptions. The conversion results of the selected eight features are shown in Table 2. For category type of features, (e.g. 'protocol_type', 'service') we use a definite number to replace the specific category. For continuous type of features, (e.g. 'same_srv_rate', 'dst_host_same_src_port_rate', 'dst_host_same_srv_rate') we use DBSCAN clustering ($\epsilon = 0.01, MinPts = 50$)

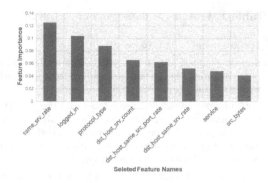

Fig. 3. Feature with importance selected by random forest

on these features and get the cluster number to replace the clustered intervals and points. For integer features, (e.g. 'dst_host_srv_count', 'src_bytes'), we use DBSCAN clustering ($\epsilon = 1, MinPts = 50$) and use the cluster numbers to replace the definite clustered points.

Table 2. Results of selected feature clustering

Feature name	Clusters info
same_srv_rate	[0,0.03] 0.04 [0.05,0.06] [0.07,0.09] [0.1,0.12] 0.13 [0.14,0.15] [0.17,0.18] 0.5 1 noises
logged_in	0 1
protocol_type	tcp udp icmp
dst_host_srv_count	[0,27] [252,255] noises
dst_host_same_src_port_rate	[0,0.03] 0.04 [0.05,0.06] [0.07,0.09] [0.1,0.12] [0.17,0.18] 0.33 0.5 1 noises
dst_host_same_srv_rate	[0,0.03] 0.04 [0.05,0.06] [0.07,0.09] [0.23,0.24] 1 noises
service	1 2 3 4 8 10 11 12 16 23 26 noises
src_bytes	0 1 8 43 44 45 46 147 1032 noises

4.3 Performance on Intrusion Detection Classification

To evaluate the proposed attribute learning method, we conduct several experiments to demonstrate the ability of attributes in describing network data. We use a 1-layer neural network as a classifier to test the effectiveness of feature to attribute conversion. We use Keras to implement the 1-layer fully connected neural network on a DELL PC with a i7-4790 processor and 16 GB RAM. We use the attributes clustered from selected feature in the full training dataset (KDDTrain+) with an ADAM optimization (batch_size = 100, epochs = 300) to train the neural network. And we test the model performance by using the attributes data conversion from KDDTest+. For a fair comparison, we also test a 1-layer neural network using the selected features (with no conversion) from train and test dataset. We get the C4.5 (J48) algorithm as a base line method [22]. The results are shown in Table 3 From the test results, our attribute learning method has exceeded the performance of decision tree in classification missions which is the state-of-the-art [22]. That demonstrate our attribute conversion representation can retain the information which is useful for classification.

Table 3. Results of attack classification test

Model & model input	Acc (5 classes)	Acc (2 classes)
NN with attributes	**73.79%**	**78.40%**
NN with selected features	68.46%	74.43%
NN with selected features & attributes	67.44%	73.24%
C4.5 (J48) with attribute	67.56%	73.39%
C4.5 (J48) with selected features	**72.72%**	**77.38%**
C4.5 (J48) with selected features & attributes	69.47%	75.28%

4.4 Performance on Zero-Shot Learning

And we design a zero-shot shot learning scenario to test the performance of attributes learning as a knowledge transfer media. By selecting data that exists in test dataset but not in train set, we show that the model can recognize some attack types that are 'novel' in train dataset. The NSL_KDD dataset has new attack types in test data. Introducing some new attack forms is an important emulating condition. In a real open network environment, there are novel attack forms every day. Detection of novel attack types is critical for intrusion detection. There are 22 types of attacks in train dataset and 17 types of new attacks in test data as shown in Table 4.

Table 4. NSL_KDD data types statics

	Train+	Test+
Normal	Normal(67343)	Normal(9710)
DOS	back(956) land(18) neptune(41214) pod(201) smurf(2646) teardrop(892)	processtable(685) mailbomb(293) udpstorm(2) apache2(737)
U2R	buffer_overflow(30) loadmodule(9) perl(3) rootkit(10)	httptunnel(133) xtem(13) sqlattack(2) ps(15)
R2L	ftp_write(8) guess_passwd(53) imap(11) multihop(7) phf(4) spy(2) warezclient(890) warezmaster(20)	snmpgetattack(178) snmpguess(331) Named(17) Sendmail(14) Worm(2) Xlock(9) Xsnoop(4)
Probe	ipsweep(3599) nmap(1493) portsweep(2931) satan(3633)	saint(319) mscan(996)

Although new attack data exists in the test dataset. NSL_KDD dataset is not a dataset specially designed for zero-shot learning. There is imbalance among the major five categories and definite attack species, as shown in Table 4. U2R and R2L attacks are lack of efficient training data. The five major categories are defined by human, there is no enough data to test one kind of specific attack. We think there are common attributes features shared among various species of one major attack type. And we test our proposed method the detection performance of five classification. We use the attack types that do not appear in train data as test data, that is to say, the data has never been trained for the model. We find that our method can do recognize some DOS attacks 'apache2' and Probe attacks 'saint'. The accuracy is 34.71%, which is higher than a random 20.00% classification probability. For comparison, we also test the decision tree method with selected features, the state-of-art classifier with features, which only can get a 13.59% accuracy. That is to say our proposed attribute learning method has better generalization ability than classifier with features in recognize new attack types. The attribute learning frame work can be used in zero-shot learning issues.

5 Conclusion

We proposed a general attribute learning framework for intrusion detection, converting raw network data into unsupervised cluster attributes. Several effective strategies have been introduced, random forest based feature selection, DBSCAN cluster attributes conversion and neural network classification module. The effectiveness of the framework has been experimentally demonstrated by comparing it with the same model with different inputs combination including the state-of-the-art feature representation approaches on a popular NSL_KDD dataset. Furthermore, our proposed attribute learning method, being a fundamental attribute labeling method to zero-shot learning, has been demonstrated by a zero-shot learning experiment.

In the future, we plan to extend our model by jointly learning deep feature representation of network data and attack semantic rule definitions. Furthermore, dataset labeled by attributes or semantic words for zero-shot learning can be introduced to achieve more rigorous testing.

References

1. Akata, Z., Perronnin, F., Harchaoui, Z., Schmid, C.: Label-embedding for image classification. IEEE Trans. Pattern Anal. Mach. Intell. **38**(7), 1425–1438 (2016)
2. Akata, Z., Reed, S., Walter, D., Lee, H., Schiele, B.: Evaluation of output embeddings for fine-grained image classification. In: Proceedings of the IEEE Conference on Computer Vision and Pattern Recognition, pp. 2927–2936 (2015)
3. Breiman, L.: Random forests. Mach. Learn. **45**(1), 5–32 (2001)
4. Changpinyo, S., Chao, W.L., Gong, B., Sha, F.: Synthesized classifiers for zero-shot learning. In: Proceedings of the IEEE Conference on Computer Vision and Pattern Recognition, pp. 5327–5336 (2016)

5. Denning, D.E.: An intrusion-detection model. IEEE Trans. Softw. Eng. **2**, 222–232 (1987)
6. Erfani, S.M., Rajasegarar, S., Karunasekera, S., Leckie, C.: High-dimensional and large-scale anomaly detection using a linear one-class SVM with deep learning. Pattern Recogn. **58**, 121–134 (2016)
7. Farhadi, A., Endres, I., Hoiem, D., Forsyth, D.: Describing objects by their attributes. In: 2009 IEEE Conference on Computer Vision and Pattern Recognition, CVPR 2009, pp. 1778–1785. IEEE (2009)
8. Fiore, U., Palmieri, F., Castiglione, A., De Santis, A.: Network anomaly detection with the restricted Boltzmann machine. Neurocomputing **122**, 13–23 (2013)
9. Frome, A., Corrado, G.S., Shlens, J., Bengio, S., Dean, J., Mikolov, T., et al.: Devise: a deep visual-semantic embedding model. In: Advances in Neural Information Processing Systems, pp. 2121–2129 (2013)
10. Heberlein, T.: Network Security Monitor (NSM)-final Report. UC Davis, Davis (1995)
11. Lampert, C.H., Nickisch, H., Harmeling, S.: Attribute-based classification for zero-shot visual object categorization. IEEE Trans. Pattern Anal. Mach. Intell. **36**(3), 453–465 (2014)
12. Li, Z., Qin, Z.: A semantic parsing based LSTM model for intrusion detection. In: Cheng, L., Leung, A.C.S., Ozawa, S. (eds.) ICONIP 2018. LNCS, vol. 11304, pp. 600–609. Springer, Cham (2018). https://doi.org/10.1007/978-3-030-04212-7_53
13. Li, Z., Qin, Z., Huang, K., Yang, X., Ye, S.: Intrusion detection using convolutional neural networks for representation learning. In: Liu, D., Xie, S., Li, Y., Zhao, D., El-Alfy, E.-S.M. (eds.) ICONIP 2017. LNCS, vol. 10638, pp. 858–866. Springer, Cham (2017). https://doi.org/10.1007/978-3-319-70139-4_87
14. Norouzi, M., et al.: Zero-shot learning by convex combination of semantic embeddings. arXiv preprint. arXiv:1312.5650 (2013)
15. Parikh, D., Grauman, K.: Interactively building a discriminative vocabulary of nameable attributes. In: 2011 IEEE Conference on Computer Vision and Pattern Recognition (CVPR), pp. 1681–1688. IEEE (2011)
16. Pérez, J.L.R., Ribeiro, B.: Attribute learning for network intrusion detection. In: Angelov, P., Manolopoulos, Y., Iliadis, L., Roy, A., Vellasco, M. (eds.) INNS 2016. AISC, vol. 529, pp. 39–49. Springer, Cham (2017). https://doi.org/10.1007/978-3-319-47898-2_5
17. Rivero, J., Ribeiro, B., Chen, N., Leite, F.S.: A Grassmannian approach to zero-shot learning for network intrusion detection. In: International Conference on Neural Information Processing, pp. 565–575. Springer, Cham (2017). https://doi.org/10.1007/978-3-319-70087-8_59
18. Roesch, M., et al.: Snort: lightweight intrusion detection for networks. In: Lisa, vol. 99, pp. 229–238 (1999)
19. Rohrbach, M., Stark, M., Schiele, B.: Evaluating knowledge transfer and zero-shot learning in a large-scale setting. In: 2011 IEEE Conference on Computer Vision and Pattern Recognition (CVPR), pp. 1641–1648. IEEE (2011)
20. Socher, R., Ganjoo, M., Manning, C.D., Ng, A.: Zero-shot learning through cross-modal transfer. In: Advances in Neural Information Processing Systems, pp. 935–943 (2013)
21. Souri, Y., Noury, E., Adeli, E.: Deep relative attributes. In: Lai, S.-H., Lepetit, V., Nishino, K., Sato, Y. (eds.) ACCV 2016. LNCS, vol. 10115, pp. 118–133. Springer, Cham (2017). https://doi.org/10.1007/978-3-319-54193-8_8

22. Tavallaee, M., Bagheri, E., Lu, W., Ghorbani, A.A.: A detailed analysis of the KDD CUP 99 data set. In: 2009 IEEE Symposium on Computational Intelligence for Security and Defense Applications, pp. 1–6. IEEE (2009)
23. Welinder, P., et al.: Caltech-UCSD birds 200 (2010)
24. Xian, Y., Akata, Z., Sharma, G., Nguyen, Q., Hein, M., Schiele, B.: Latent embeddings for zero-shot classification. In: Proceedings of the IEEE Conference on Computer Vision and Pattern Recognition, pp. 69–77 (2016)
25. Zhang, Z., Saligrama, V.: Zero-shot learning via semantic similarity embedding. In: Proceedings of the IEEE International Conference on Computer Vision, pp. 4166–4174 (2015)

Region Selection Model with Saliency Constraint for Fine-Grained Recognition

Shaoxiong Zhou[1], Shengrong Gong[1,2(✉)], Shan Zhong[2], Wei Pan[2],
and Wenhao Ying[2]

[1] Department of Computer Science and Technology, Soochow University,
Suzhou 215006, China
20175227098@stu.suda.edu.cn
[2] Department of Computer Science and Engineering,
Changshu Institute of Technology, Suzhou 215500, China
{shrgong,pvv1224}@cslg.edu.cn, sunshine-620@163.com, cslgywh@163.com

Abstract. Learning discriminative local features is the key to improving the accuracy of fine-grained recognition. Methods based on local area labeling are very labor intensive and time costly. Existing weakly supervised methods decide the discriminative areas according to the response of the advanced feature maps. However, the details of the many small objects, which are vital for the region localization, were lost. We propose a region selection model with saliency constraint to capture the details, where the feature pyramid network is used to obtain higher resolution features with stronger semantics, and then the regions on different level feature maps that are consistently to be most informative are selected. This process enhances the model's ability to represent details and capture small but discriminative local regions. Furthermore, a saliency extractor which shares convolutional layers with the backbone network is built to locate the object in an image, which will help to locate the discriminative regions and improve the training efficiency. We use a ranking loss function to optimize the multi-scale and multi-ratio regions which are selected by our model. Experimentally, the proposed method is implemented in datasets CUB-200-2011 and Stanford Cars and it is achieved the state-of-the-art results.

Keywords: Fine-grained recognition · Feature pyramid network · Saliency extraction · Convolutional neural network

1 Introduction

In the past decade, many novel convolutional neural networks (CNNs) [1–3] have emerged. They generally had deeper convolutional layers and stronger feature representation capabilities, which made significant progress in generic object recognition. Fine-grained visual categorization (FGVC) aims to distinguish hundreds of similar subcategories such as bird species [4] and car models [5]. Compared with generic object recognition, FGVC is still very challenging due to

© Springer Nature Switzerland AG 2019
T. Gedeon et al. (Eds.): ICONIP 2019, LNCS 11953, pp. 365–376, 2019.
https://doi.org/10.1007/978-3-030-36708-4_30

the large variance in the same subcategory and small variance among different subcategories.

Learning discriminative local features for FGVC is essential for fine-grained image classification. Existing methods based on CNNs can be easily divided into two kinds. One classifies the discriminative regions by first locating objects and discriminative parts. The two-step process [6–9] demands labor-intensive annotations, which hinders its practical application. The other automatically locates the discriminative parts in a weakly supervised manner. This can be achieved through attention mechanism which infers the attention area based on the response of the convolutional feature maps. However, these methods [10–13] always decide discriminative regions according to the response of advanced convolutional feature maps, resulting in an inaccurate region localization. The discriminative differences normally exists in subtle areas, but the feature maps with high semantic usually lose most of the details. Furthermore, their models usually locate discriminative regions in the whole image which contain much background noise. Therefore, the process of locating discriminative regions is always with much background noise, which makes the object not focused.

In this paper, a region selection model with saliency constraint is proposed for FGVC to address the above problems. In our model, the attention mechanism is used to generate a saliency map for each image. Such a map can be further used to generate a bounding box of the object by using all the convolutional layers of the backbone network followed by a global average pooling layer. Then the bounding box is regarded as a spatial constraint for selecting discriminative regions, as is shown in Fig. 1. In order to improve the model's performance on detecting small but discriminative objects, the pyramid network (FPN) [14] is adopted to fuse the features generated from the backbone network, so as to enhance the ability to capture details in the image. To select the most discriminative regions, the ranking loss function is designed to optimize our model. The final prediction is a combination of the classification results of multiple regions and the whole image.

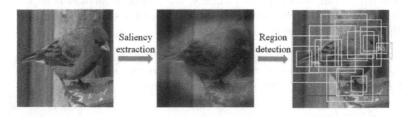

Fig. 1. Visualization of the saliency map of an input image. We use the saliency map to further generate a bounding box as a spatial constraint for region selection.

The rest of this paper is organized as follows. Section 2 presents related works. In Sect. 3, we introduce our approach in detail. In Sect. 4, we show our experimental results on CUB-200-2011 and Stanford Cars, which demonstrate the effectiveness of proposed method. Finally, Sect. 5 is the conclusion of our work.

2   Related Work

2.1   Fine-Grained Image Recognition

Traditional methods [15–18] for fine-grained recognition are mainly based on hand-designed features, which firstly extract local features (e.g., SIFT or HOG features) from the image and then encode them to obtain required feature representation. But the discriminative information has to be captured in these features, resulting in a poor adaptability of the model.

As the deep learning becomes popular, researches on FGVC based on deep learning techniques have evolved from the early multi-stage methods [6,7] that rely heavily on human annotations to the currently popular weakly supervised classification methods [8–12]. The latter only use the image-level labels and many of them can implement end-to-end model training. Zhang et al. [6] proposed a Part R-CNN algorithm based on R-CNN [19] algorithm, where R-CNN is first trained to detect the foreground object and two parts by using annotations. As a result, the spatial and geometric constraints cooperate to correct the region location. Finally, the features of all regions are extracted to train the SVM classifier. Peng et al. [9] proposed an object-part attention model to solve the problems of inaccurate positioning of objects and parts in the case of lacking part annotation information, where a saliency map for object is firstly generated and then used as a constraint on the selection of parts. Though finally it can get comparable performance, the right regions can not be guaranteed to be selected. As a result, the accuracy degrades heavily.

In order to enhance the intermediate learning ability of convolutional neural networks, Wang et al. [10] proposed a method named DFL-CNN, which utilized a self-supervising mechanism using a novel asymmetric multi-stream structure and a non-random layer initialization method. Thus, a set of convolution filters are learned for capturing discriminative regions for specific categories without additional annotation information. Yang et al. [13] proposed a multi-agent cooperation model which consists of a Navigator agent, a Teacher agent and a Scrutinizer agent. They assumed that areas with high informativeness are also highly discriminative, and use pairwise ranking loss to optimize model learning to find more discriminative local regions. Although their model has achieved a comparable good result, the selected regions still have a lot of background noise.

2.2   Weakly Supervised Object Localization

Weakly supervised localization skills play an important role in various visual analysis tasks because they can remove background noise and pay more attention to the object. More importantly, the emergence of these technologies enables researchers not to rely on human experts to tag the information, thus making these techniques easier to be applied to practice. Zhou et al. [20] proposed a method named CAM that has a remarkable localization ability despite the fact that their model was trained only with image-level labels. A fully convolutional network with a global average pooling layer is used for generating class-specific activation maps which reflect the location of objects in an image. Zhang et al. [21] firstly picked discriminative filters which can respond to specific patterns signif-icantly and consistently. Based on the selected filters, the positive samples were iteratively used to train a set of discriminative detectors. In this paper, we fol-low the CAM method to get a saliency map. Figure 2 shows the overview of the saliency extractor.

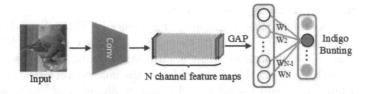

Fig. 2. Overall of the saliency extractor. An image is input into the fully convolutional neural network followed by a global average pooling layer. After training, we can get the weights of the feature maps of the image corresponding to each category. The feature maps are multiplied by their weights for a certain category and then add them together to obtain the saliency map of the image.

2.3   Object Detection

Object detection is a very important research topic in the field of computer vision. The task of object detection is to find all the objects of interest in the image, and also determine their positions and their categories. The famous R-CNN algorithm [19] was proposed in 2014. As an inefficient method, it used the selective search method to generate candidate regions. On the basis of the former works [22,23], Faster R-CNN [24] proposed a network named Region Proposal Network (RPN) which slides on the convolutional feature maps to gen-erate regions with a consequence that the model training was greatly accelerated and the detection accuracy was improved. Feature pyramid network (FPN) [14] proposed in 2017 has an advantage in capturing small objects. The features of low-resolution and high-semantic information are connected with the features of high-resolution and low-semantic information from top to bottom so that the fusion features of all scales have rich semantic information. In this paper, we use the idea of anchors to generate candidate regions and FPN architecture for feature extraction and region selection respectively.

3   Approach

In this section, we introduce the proposed method for FGVC. Since our method does not rely on object or part annotations, we use a saliency extractor to gen-erate saliency map and locate the object in an image. Considering that discrim-inative differences between fine-grained categories exist in subtle areas, we use

FPN to improve the model's detection performance for small targets, so as to enhance the ability to capture detailed information in the image. Inspired by RPN [24], predefined regions are of multi-scale and multi-ratio. The selected K regions are most confident to be discriminative, and the ranking loss is calculated to optimize the selection of more discriminative local regions. Final prediction is the combination of K local regions and the overall image classification results. The framework of our model is shown in Fig. 3.

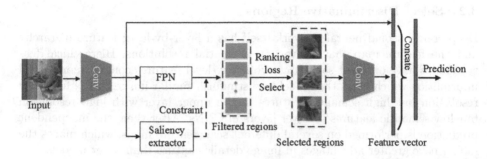

Fig. 3. Overview of proposed method. First, an image is input into a backbone network to extract features. FPN then fuses features and output confidence of candidate regions filtered by saliency constraint. Ranking loss is used for optimizing the selection of most discriminative regions. Finally, K regions and the whole image are combined by model to make a prediction. $K = 3$ there for ease of explanation.

3.1 Saliency Extraction Network

In the absence of object and part annotations, we use a weakly supervised method that makes an image input into a saliency exaction network to obtain a saliency map, then we choose an appropriate threshold to filter the entire image area to get the bounding box of the object. The saliency extractor includes all the convolutional layers of the backbone network and a global average pooling (GAP) layer, and then a soft-max layer is connected for classification. The weights of the GAP layer corresponding to a specific class are multiplied respectively by the feature maps output by the last convolutional layer, and then add them up to produce a saliency map for an input image.

Given an image I and its class label c, the activation value of spatial location (x, y) in the saliency map is defined as follows:

$$M_c(x, y) = \sum_K w_k^c f_k(x, y), \tag{1}$$

where M_c is the saliency map which is upsampled to the input image size. k denotes the number of channels in GAP, w_k^c is the weight of the k-th channel corresponding to the particular subcategory c, c is the label predicted by this saliency extraction network as an image label and $f_k(x, y)$ is the activation of neuron k in the last convolutional layer at spatial location (x, y).

In order to reduce background interference and improve localization efficiency and accuracy, we add a spatial constraint to the region selection. That is, we set an appropriate threshold θ on the saliency map M_c to generate a bounding box as the object region. And then, the proportion of Intersection-over-Union (IoU) overlap of candidate regions and object bounding box must be greater than value ρ which makes the model has a better ability in capturing the image details.

3.2   Select Discriminative Regions

Deep convolutional neural network itself has a layer-by-layer feature hierarchy and the feature maps have a variety of spatial resolutions. Hierarchical feature maps have different semantics, while low-level features contain more detail information which helps the model to distinguish similar images. FPN fuses low resolution but high semantic features in the upper layer with high resolution but low semantic features in lower layers in CNNs. After then, the independent prediction is performed on several different scale feature maps, which makes the model have greater advantages in image details capture than other models.

Specifically, the input images are preprocessed to a fixed size of 448×448, and they are fed into the CNNs with output feature maps with multi-scales. These features are fused to generate multi-scale features. The sliding window slides on these feature maps and then generates anchors with three scales and five aspect ratios, corresponding to the scale of 48×48, 96×96, 192×192 with ratios of 1:2, 2:1, 2:3, 3:2, and 1:1 on the input image.

The regions have scores predicted by FPN as a confidence of discrimination. Then we filter these anchors by the bounding box obtained by the saliency map. In order to select discriminative regions and reduce information redundancy, the NMS algorithm is used to remove regions that have higher overlap with other regions but have lower confidence. Select K regions that have the highest scores and scaled to 224×224 and input them into the ResNet-50 network for classification. Similar to the treatment of Yang et al. [13], we use the ranking loss to optimize the selection of regions. But different from them, we only select K regions, forcing them to have the same order of informativeness as their confidences, without further selection.

Denote the K regions that have the highest score predicted by FPN as $R = \{R_1, R_2, \ldots, R_K\}$, their scores as $S = \{S_1, S_2, \ldots, S_K\}$ which are sorted well, their probabilities belong to ground-truth class predicted by ResNet-50 as $P = \{P_1, P_2, \ldots, P_K\}$. The hinge loss function requires elements S_i and S_j with sequential order in S, suppose that $S_i > S_j$, should have the same order as $P_i > P_j$ in P. Otherwise, it will be punished. The definition of ranking loss in this method is as follows:

$$L(S, P) = \sum_{(i,j):S_i > S_j} f(S_i - S_j), \tag{2}$$

where the hinge loss function $f(x)$ is defined as:

$$f(x) = max\{1 - x, 0\}. \tag{3}$$

In the training of the model, we use the sum of the ranking loss of K regions and its classification loss on the backbone network, and classification loss of input image as the total loss to optimize the model's parameters. The weights of the convolutional layers of the backbone network are always shared. When tested, the final result of each image is determined by the combined prediction of the input image and its K local regions on the backbone network.

4 Experiments

We present the implementation details of the proposed method in Sect. 4.1. In Sect. 4.2, we briefly introduce two datasets, CUB-200-2011 [4] and Stanford Cars [5], and then explain the relevant experiments conducted on the datasets. In Sect. 4.3, we do some qualitative analysis on the proposed method, verified the influence of the hyperparameter K on the classification performance, and prove that the proposed method can improve the training efficiency of the model.

4.1 Implementation Details

All experiments were conducted on 4 NVIDIA TESLA P100 GPUs with 16 GB memory using Pytorch-0.4.1. The images in two datasets are preprocessed to a fixed size of 448×448. When we get a saliency map of an image, a threshold of $\rho = 0.8$ is set for determining a bounding box. In addition, we test several K values to find the best model performance, and results showed that the model can get the highest classification accuracy when $K = 6$. If there is no special explanation, the K is 6. The pre-trained ResNet-50 [3] is used as the backbone network. When it is used for saliency extraction, we only use the fully convolutional layers. In the training phrase, SGD is used as an optimizer with a learning rate set to 0.001 and momentum set to 0.9 and weight decay set to 0.0001.

4.2 Datasets and Experimental Results

Datasets: The CUB-200-2011 dataset [4] and Stanford Cars dataset [5] are the most widely used datasets for fine-grained image classification. The detailed statistics with category numbers and the standard training/testing splits can be found in Table 1.

Experimental Results on CUB-200-2011. Table 2 shows the experimental results of our proposed method on CUB-200-2011 [4]. Our method achieves a classification accuracy of 88.0%. Compared with the early methods based on deep learning, which rely heavily on human annotations, our method is far ahead in classification accuracy. The reason is that these methods mostly uses the AlexNet

Table 1. Detailed statistics of the two datasets used in this paper.

Dataset	#Class	#Train	#Test
CUB-200-2011	200	5,994	5,794
Stanford Cars	196	8,144	8,041

or the VGGNet model as a feature extractor that is somewhat inferior in feature representing. More importantly, the manual annotations only indicate the location of target objects and their parts in the image, such as the scorpion, wings, claws of a bird, but they do not necessarily contain discriminative information. Under the weakly supervised conditions, the trained deep neural network has stronger learning ability to find local areas with discrimination, thus it can achieve a better performance, which benefits from the ingenious design of the model.

Table 2. Experimental results on dataset CUB-200-2011.

Methods	Annotation	Accuracy (%)	Backbone
Part R-CNN [6]	√	76.4	AlexNet
Mask CNN [7]	√	85.4	VGGNet
Two-level [8]	×	77.9	VGGNet
FCAN [27]	×	82.0	VGGNet
B-CNN [12]	×	84.1	VGGNet
PDFR [21]	×	84.5	VGGNet
RACNN [26]	×	85.3	VGGNet
OPAM [9]	×	85.8	VGGNet
MAMC [25]	×	86.5	ResNet
DFL [10]	×	87.4	VGGNet
NTS [13]	×	87.5	ResNet
Ours (without SC)	×	87.7	ResNet
Ours	×	**88.0**	ResNet

Our method uses the feature pyramid network to learn local features, which makes our model have a stronger detection ability for small but discriminative targets. So it is very effective for fine-grained image classification tasks. Without the saliency constraint, we have achieved a comparative result of 87.7% top-1 classification accuracy on dataset CUB-200-2011 (without SC means we do not use saliency constraint). And when we further use the saliency constraint, the model's classification accuracy has an improvement of 3.4%. Compared with other methods, the regions extracted from our model have less background inference, which makes the model focus more on the characteristic of the object itself.

Experimental Results on Stanford Cars. We also carry out experiments on the vehicle dataset Stanford Cars [5], and our model achieved state-of-the-art results of 94.0% top-1 accuracy when we set $K = 4$. And without saliency constraint, we also have achieved a comparative result of 93.8% classification accuracy. Table 3 shows our results on Stanford Cars.

Table 3. Experimental results on dataset Stanford Cars.

Methods	Annotation	Accuracy (%)	Backbone
Two-level [8]	×	88.6	VGGNet
FCAN [27]	×	89.1	VGGNet
B-CNN [12]	×	91.3	VGGNet
RACNN [26]	×	92.5	VGGNet
OPAM [9]	×	92.2	VGGNet
MAMC [25]	×	93.0	ResNet
DFL [10]	×	93.8	VGGNet
NTS [13]	×	93.9	ResNet
Ours (without SC)	×	93.8	ResNet
Ours	×	**94.0**	ResNet

4.3 Qualitative Analysis

The Importance of the Number of Selected Regions. In order to test the influence of the number of selected local regions on the performance of the model, we did several sets of different K value comparison experiments on the CUB-200-2011 under the condition of a fixed threshold $\rho = 0.8$. The experimental results are shown in Fig. 4.

When the value of K is 6, the model can achieve the best performance. As it becomes smaller ($K <= 4$), the classification accuracy of the model drops rapidly. We analyzed that the reason is too few local areas are selected. Only combining few local regions is not enough to distinguish highly similar categories. With the increase of K value, the prediction results of multiple distinguishing regions can complete the recognition task better. However, when the K value is too large, the classification accuracy decreases. The possible reason is that the model is forced to select more local regions, thus introducing more noise regions.

Comparison of Training Efficiency. We also did comparative experiments with and without a saliency constraint. The experimental results are shown in Fig. 5. When a saliency extractor is used, the model is more efficient to train. One reason may be that the spatial constraint filters out a large number of invalid background regions without discriminative information. The other reason is mainly that the interface to fine-grained classification is reduced to make the model training more efficient.

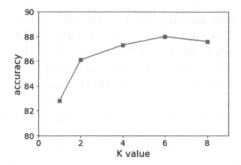

Fig. 4. The influence of K value on dataset CUB-200-2011. When K is small, the classification accuracy drops rapidly. When K exceeds the appropriate value, the accuracy also decreases. When $K = 6$, we get the best performance.

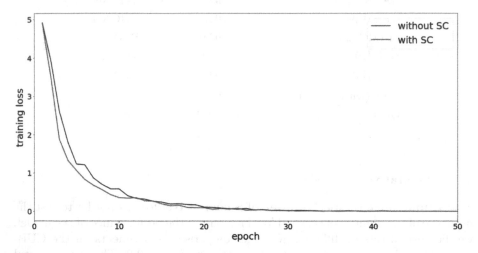

Fig. 5. Comparison of training efficiency. When the saliency map is used as a spatial constraint for region selection, the model's training loss drops faster.

5   Conclusion

In this paper, we present a new approach for fine-grained classification without the help of human annotations. Based on object detection techniques and weakly supervised localization methods, we build a region selection model with saliency constraint which not only improves the fine-grained classification accuracy but also speeds up the training. Compared with other state-of-the-art methods, our method, which is trained in an end-to end manner, achieves comparable performance on datasets CUB-200-2011 and Stanford Cars.

Acknowledgements. The authors would like to thank the anonymous reviewers for their helpful and constructive comments. This work was partially supported by the National Natural Science Foundation of China (NSFC Grant No. 61972059, 61702055,

61773272, 61272059), Natural Science Foundation of Jiangsu Province under Grant (BK20191474, BK20161268). Research and Innovation Fund of the Science and Technology Development Center of the Ministry of Education (2018A01007), and Ministry of Education Science and Technology Development Center Industry-University Research Innovation Fund (2018A02003), and Humanities and Social Sciences Foundation of the Ministry of Education under Grant 18YJCZH229.

References

1. Krizhevsky, A., Sutskever, I., Hinton, G.E.: ImageNet classification with deep convolutional neural networks. In: Advances in Neural Information Processing Systems, pp. 1097–1105 (2012)
2. Simonyan, K., Zisserman, A.: Very deep convolutional networks for large-scale image recognition. arXiv preprint arXiv:1409.1556 (2014)
3. He, K., Zhang, X., Ren, S., Sun, J.: Deep residual learning for image recognition. In: Proceedings of the IEEE Conference on Computer Vision and Pattern Recognition, pp. 770–778 (2016)
4. Wah, C., Branson, S., Welinder, P., Perona, P., Belongie, S.: The Caltech-UCSD birds-200-2011 dataset (2011)
5. Krause, J., Stark, M., Deng, J., Fei-Fei, L.: 3D object representations for fine-grained categorization. In: Proceedings of the IEEE International Conference on Computer Vision Workshops, pp. 554–561 (2013)
6. Zhang, N., Donahue, J., Girshick, R., Darrell, T.: Part-based R-CNNs for fine-grained category detection. In: Fleet, D., Pajdla, T., Schiele, B., Tuytelaars, T. (eds.) ECCV 2014. LNCS, vol. 8689, pp. 834–849. Springer, Cham (2014). https://doi.org/10.1007/978-3-319-10590-1_54
7. Wei, X.S., Xie, C.W., Wu, J.: Mask-CNN: localizing parts and selecting descriptors for fine-grained image recognition. arXiv preprint arXiv:1605.06878 (2016)
8. Xiao, T., Xu, Y., Yang, K., Zhang, J., Peng, Y., Zhang, Z.: The application of two-level attention models in deep convolutional neural network for fine-grained image classification. In: Proceedings of the IEEE Conference on Computer Vision and Pattern Recognition, pp. 842–850 (2015)
9. Peng, Y., He, X., Zhao, J.: Object-part attention model for fine-grained image classification. IEEE Trans. Image Process. **27**(3), 1487–1500 (2017)
10. Wang, Y., Morariu, V.I., Davis, L.S.: Learning a discriminative filter bank within a CNN for fine-grained recognition. In: Proceedings of the IEEE Conference on Computer Vision and Pattern Recognition, pp. 4148–4157 (2018)
11. Zheng, H., Fu, J., Mei, T., Luo, J.: Learning multi-attention convolutional neural network for fine-grained image recognition. In: Proceedings of the IEEE International Conference on Computer Vision, pp. 5209–5217 (2017)
12. Lin, T.Y., RoyChowdhury, A., Maji, S.: Bilinear CNN models for fine-grained visual recognition. In: Proceedings of the IEEE International Conference on Computer Vision, pp. 1449–1457 (2015)
13. Yang, Z., Luo, T., Wang, D., Hu, Z., Gao, J., Wang, L.: Learning to navigate for fine-grained classification. In: Proceedings of the European Conference on Computer Vision (ECCV), pp. 420–435 (2018)
14. Lin, T.Y., Dollár, P., Girshick, R., He, K., Hariharan, B., Belongie, S.: Feature pyramid networks for object detection. In: Proceedings of the IEEE Conference on Computer Vision and Pattern Recognition, pp. 2117–2125 (2017)

15. Lowe, D.G., et al.: Object recognition from local scale-invariant features. In: ICCV, vol. 99, pp. 1150–1157 (1999)
16. Dalal, N., Triggs, B.: Histograms of oriented gradients for human detection. In: international Conference on Computer Vision and Pattern Recognition (CVPR 2005), vol. 1, pp. 886–893. IEEE Computer Society (2005)
17. Jégou, H., Douze, M., Schmid, C., Pérez, P.: Aggregating local descriptors into a compact image representation. In: CVPR 2010–23rd IEEE Conference on Computer Vision and Pattern Recognition, pp. 3304–3311. IEEE Computer Society (2010)
18. Perronnin, F., Dance, C.: Fisher kernels on visual vocabularies for image categorization. In: 2007 IEEE Conference on Computer Vision and Pattern Recognition, pp. 1–8. IEEE (2007)
19. Girshick, R., Donahue, J., Darrell, T., Malik, J.: Rich feature hierarchies for accurate object detection and semantic segmentation. In: Proceedings of the IEEE Conference on Computer Vision and Pattern Recognition, pp. 580–587 (2014)
20. Zhou, B., Khosla, A., Lapedriza, A., Oliva, A., Torralba, A.: Learning deep features for discriminative localization. In: Proceedings of the IEEE Conference on Computer Vision and Pattern Recognition, pp. 2921–2929 (2016)
21. Zhang, X., Xiong, H., Zhou, W., Lin, W., Tian, Q.: Picking deep filter responses for fine-grained image recognition. In: Proceedings of the IEEE Conference on Computer Vision and Pattern Recognition, pp. 1134–1142 (2016)
22. Girshick, R.: Fast R-CNN. In: Proceedings of the IEEE International Conference on Computer Vision, pp. 1440–1448 (2015)
23. He, K., Zhang, X., Ren, S., Sun, J.: Spatial pyramid pooling in deep convolutional networks for visual recognition. IEEE Trans. Pattern Anal. Mach. Intell. $37(9)$, 1904–1916 (2015)
24. Ren, S., He, K., Girshick, R., Sun, J.: Faster R-CNN: towards real-time object detection with region proposal networks. In: Advances in Neural Information Processing Systems, pp. 91–99 (2015)
25. Sun, M., Yuan, Y., Zhou, F., Ding, E.: Multi-attention multi-class constraint for fine-grained image recognition. In: Proceedings of the European Conference on Computer Vision (ECCV), pp. 805–821 (2018)
26. Fu, J., Zheng, H., Mei, T.: Look closer to see better: recurrent attention convolutional neural network for fine-grained image recognition. In: Proceedings of the IEEE Conference on Computer Vision and Pattern Recognition, pp. 4438–4446 (2017)
27. Liu, X., Xia, T., Wang, J., Yang, Y., Zhou, F., Lin, Y.: Fully convolutional attention networks for fine-grained recognition. arXiv preprint arXiv:1603.06765 (2016)

Siamese Network Based Feature Learning
for Improved Intrusion Detection

Houda Jmila[1]([⊠]), Mohamed Ibn Khedher[2], Gregory Blanc[1],
and Mounim A. El Yacoubi[1]

[1] Samovar, CNRS, Télécom SudParis, Institut Polytechnique de Paris,
9 rue Charles Fourier, 91011 Evry Cedex, France
{houda.jmila,gregory.blanc,mounim.el_yacoubi}@telecom-sudparis.eu
[2] IRT - SystemX, 8 Avenue de la Vauve, 91120 Palaiseau, France
mohamed.ibn-khedher@irt-systemx.fr

Abstract. Intrusion detection is a critical Cyber Security subject. Different Machine Learning (ML) approaches have been proposed for Intrusion Detection Systems (IDS). However, their application to real-life scenarios remains challenging due to high data dimensionality. *Representation learning* (RL) allows discriminative feature representation in a low dimensionality space. The application of this technique in IDS requires more investigation. This paper examines and discusses the contribution of *Siamese network* based representation learning in improving the IDS performance. Extensive experimental results under different evaluation scenarios show different improvement rates depending on the scenario.

Keywords: IDS · Anomaly detection · Representation learning ·
Feature extraction · Siamese · UNSW15 data-set

1 Introduction

Intrusion detection is a nearly 40-year old field of cybersecurity that enables a network operator to detect computer and network security violations such as external attacks against internal systems, external attackers masquerading as internal users to gain access to unauthorized resources, compromised internal systems attacking external targets [3]. Intrusion detection systems (IDSs) are usually distributed in the form of network-based or host-based monitoring systems, contributing to a defense-in-depth framework along with perimetric solutions such as firewalls, or endpoint security solutions such as antiviruses. An IDS usually raises alerts when it detects an intrusion and does not actively seek to block it, whereas firewalls filter the boundaries of a network based on specified traffic rules.

IDSs can be also divided into two main categories with respect to their detection ability: *misuse detection* and *anomaly detection*. Signature-based IDSs use misuse detection to detect *known attacks* based on signatures of these intrusions.

© Springer Nature Switzerland AG 2019
T. Gedeon et al. (Eds.): ICONIP 2019, LNCS 11953, pp. 377–389, 2019.
https://doi.org/10.1007/978-3-030-36708-4_31

The list of signatures needs to be regularly updated though, as the attack land-scape evolves quickly. Anomaly detectors, on the other hand, are able to model the *normal behaviour* of the system, and hence detect any deviations from this model. These deviations, called *anomalies*, can be further analyzed to qualify whether the anomaly is an incident, a rare event or an intrusion. This analysis enables to assess the quality of the detection contrary to signature-based detection which can not inform on missed detections. As the number of false positives may be high with anomaly detection, analysis allows the update of the *normal behaviour patterns* to better focus on real anomalies. For these reasons, anomaly detection is often considered more promising by the community.

Although it is not new, the application of Machine Learning (ML) approaches to intrusion detection has seen a recent resurgence due to the combined increase in volume and sophistication of cyber attacks and the decrease in the human workforce able to analyze and respond to these intrusions. Its ability to treat large volumes of data, to find patterns automatically, and to automate the classi-fication of samples have made ML techniques practical tools to support decision in IDSs. A recent survey [17] investigated the use of ML techniques for anomaly detection and classified them into four categories depending on the use of a *single* or *multiple* classifiers, and the classification of *selected* or *all* features of data-sets.

Broadly, the used classifiers can be categorized into three groups: *supervised, semi-supervised,* and *unsupervised* depending on whether the learning data-sets are respectively labeled, partly labeled, or not labeled at all. The most popular ML techniques used for detecting intrusions include Decision Tree, Artificial Neural Networks (ANN), Support Vector Machine (SVM), k-Nearest Neighbors (KNN), Hidden Markov Models (HMM) and Ensemble Learning.

In network anomaly detection, the observed packets partially represent the whole network traffic as the vantage points are often broadly distributed. Chal-lenges posed by network data like sparsity, high dimension and the presence of irrelevant data, can severely damage the performance of these classifiers. In par-ticular, it is not trivial to find the right set of features that appropriately capture the behaviour of the network traffic. The performance of classifiers is then heav-ily dependent on the choice of *data representation* on which they are applied. Learning data representation facilitates the extraction of useful information and improves the work of Network Anomaly Detection Systems (NADS).

Representation learning [4] is a powerful ML approach to learn the best rep-resentation of data to suit a specific space. It consists on training neural networks to *embed* the input features to a *lower and more discriminating space*. In this paper, we investigate the role of *learning feature representation* in improving the performance of IDSs. More specifically, we design a NADS based on *Siamese Network (SN)* to learn the best representation of features prior to attack classifi-cation. Siamese network [13] is a learning algorithm used for learning similarities. It has been successfully used for metric learning in different domains and scenar-ios like person identification [24], image retrieval [21] and drug discovery [23] etc. However, to our best knowledge, there is no work focusing on NADS based on

Siamese network. To the best of our knowledge, this is the first research paper examining *the contribution of representation learning based on Siamese network* in NADS.

This paper is organized as follows. Section 2 sheds light on the state of the art. Section 3 describes our approach (the anomaly detection problem, an introduction to Siamese network and the *Siamese Network based NADS*). Section 4 shows the experimental results and Sect. 5 draws the conclusions.

2   State of the Art

Paper	RL	Classifiers	Evaluation			Main results
			Scenario	Datasets	Metrics	
[26]	AE	- Gaussian - Nave Bayes - KNN - SVM - Xgboost	Binary	NSL-KDD	-Accuracy	- Slight improvement of KNN and SVM performance when preceded by RL (+2%) - Performance degradation for Gradient Boosting (-3%) - Significant improvement of Naïve Bayes when preceded by RL (+20 %)
[18]	-Denoising AE -Variational AE - An enhanced AE designed by the authors	- Centroid Mean distance - Kernel Density estimation - Local Outlier Factor (LOF) - One class SVM	Binary	- 8 most known Network security datasets - 6 non network datasets	-Area under ROC curve (AUC)	Slight improve in high-dimensional and sparse network-related datasets. Results varying between performance degradation and 20% of improve depending on the database and classifier. to perform efficiently and consistently on high-dimensional and sparse network data, even with relatively few training.
[19]	AE, PCA	- LOF - One class SVM - Isolation Forest (IF) - Robust Covariance (RC)	Binary	-UNSW-NB15 -NSL-KDD - CIC-IDS-2017 - Kyoto	-Accuracy -Precision -Recall -F1 score -AUC	- Significant improvement of OC SVM after AE RL (+20%) - Small enhancement for AE RL with other classifiers (+2%) - - Some performance degradation in Kyoto datasets for IF (-3%) and RC (-9%) -PCA RL did not produce significant improvement of classifiers performance

Fig. 1. Summary of existing RL approaches for NADS

Machine learning techniques have been widely used for intrusion detection on computer networks to deal with the dynamic and complex nature of cyber attacks [17]. To face the continuous increase of data dimensionality and to design *real time* IDS, *dimensionality reduction* techniques were applied [14]. We can distinguish two categories of dimensionality reduction techniques: *feature selection* and *feature extraction* [9].

Generally, the feature selection process selects from the *original features*, the best *subset* of features that are adapted to solve a particular problem. Differently, the feature extraction is a more general process where the features are "projected" to a *lower dimensional* subspace to extract a *new set* of features.

Representation Learning [4] is a feature extraction method used to learn *automatic extraction* of discriminative features that suits the most a specific task. Few research papers investigated the use of RL to improve the performance of IDSs. The *Auto Encoders* based RL is the most explored technique. Auto Encoders learn a mapping from high-dimensional observations to a lower-dimensional representation space such that the original observation can be reconstructed from

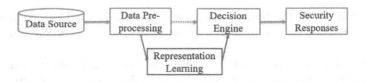

Fig. 2. Components of NADS [18]

the lower-dimensional representation [26]. Thus, it can be used as a dimensionality reduction technique to provide a rich low-dimension feature representation.

In [27], the authors evaluated the performance of Auto Encoders (AE) based RL for anomaly detection and malware classification. The evaluation were conducted using the old NSL-KDD [2] data-set and different classifiers. In [19], the authors proposed an AE based RL for IDS. They designed an enhanced version of AEs and evaluated them in combination with different One Class classifiers (OCC) and using different data-sets. The authors of [20] compared the linear Principle Component Analysis (PCA) and AE for RL in IDS. Results showed better results for AE and no significant improvement for PCA. Figure 1 gives a summary of existing approaches. Note that other interesting research works [15,16] used the AE and other deep learning methods to resolve the intrusion detection task but did not focus on evaluating the contribution of the representation learning step. Different from the state of the art, which focuses on supervised approaches like AE and PCA, we explore a supervised representation learning approach that has demonstrated its effectiveness in different domains. Siamese networks were first introduced in [6] to solve signature verification as an image matching problem. It has since been successively applied to different tasks like person identification [24], image retrieval [21], drug discovery [23], speech representation [22] and protein structure prediction [11], etc. Section 3.2 gives deeper information on this technique.

In this paper, we use the Siamese network to learn feature representation in intrusion detection systems. Moreover, unlike current research that evaluates RL by varying the classifiers and data-sets, we focus on one classifier and one data-set and examine Siamese network based RL in different scenarios depending on classification goal and data-set composition and deduce the most suitable scenario where Siamese network based RL can significantly improve the IDS performance.

3 Our Approach

3.1 The Intrusion Detection Problem

This paper focuses on Network Anomaly Detection Systems (NADSs) which build a model of the system's normal behavior to detect deviations, i.e., abnormal behaviors, that may be caused by unknown attacks. The classical architecture of a NADS contains four components [18] as depicted in the upper part of Fig. 2:

a *data source* from which raw network traffic is collected, a *data pre-processing* module where features are created, encoded and normalized, a *decision engine* module where classification techniques are applied to detect anomalies and the *security responses* taken against malicious events.

A representation learning step can be seen as an additional module introduced between the pre-processing and the decision engine modules to facilitate the latter work. It helps in representing the collected data in the most discriminative way by learning features representation *that suits the most the intrusion detection task*. In this paper, we investigate the potential of Siamese network to achieve this goal.

3.2 The Siamese Network in a Nutshell

A Siamese network is a type of neural network architecture that is used for representation learning. The main idea is to learn a mapping f from the data samples space $\mathbb{R}^p$ to a lower $\mathbb{R}^q$ space where distances between samples of the same class are *small*, and distances between samples of distinct classes are *large*. The created space will facilitate the classification and clustering tasks over the produced data.

More formally, given a training data S, containing n data samples $\{x_i\}_{1 \leqslant i \leqslant n}$, each x_i is a p dimensional vector of the data sample space, i.e. $x_i \in \mathbb{R}^p$. The aim is to find an embedding function $f(x) \in \mathbb{R}^q$ that embeds the vector x into a q-dimensional Euclidean space $(q \leqslant p)$ such that:

- If x_i and x_j belong to the same class, $||f(x_i) - f(x_j)||_2^2$ is small
- If x_i and x_j belong to different classes, $||f(x_i) - f(x_j)||_2^2$ is large

where $||.||_2^2$ is the Euclidean distance. Hence, let D denote the distance between a pair of samples and Y a binary variable indicating if the sample pair belongs to the same class $(Y = 0)$ or not $(Y = 1)$. The loss function that should be minimized is: $Loss(D, Y) = Y \times max(\alpha - D, 0) + (1 - Y) \times D$ where α is a tuning variable quantifying the minimum distance that should be enforced between dissimilar pairs. The first term tries to maximize the distance between dissimilar pairs by reducing their contribution to the loss function to zero if the distance is greater than α. The second term tries to minimize the distance between similar image pairs.

To train the model efficiently, a data-set of positive and negative pairs of samples should be generated. The number of pairs that can be generated can be determined as follows. Let $Class = \{c_1, c_2, ..., c_n\}$ denote the list of existing classes. For each class c_i, a positive pair can be generated by selecting two samples from c_i. There is then a total of $\binom{|c_i|}{2}$ pairs where $|c_i|$ is the number of samples in c_i and $\binom{\cdot}{\cdot}$ denotes the binomial coefficients. A negative pair can be generated by selecting each time a sample of c_i and another from a different class $\bar{c}_i$. There are $|c_i| \times |\bar{c}_i|$ negative pairs, where $\times$ denotes the Cartesian product.

For a total of N generated training pairs, the goal is to minimize the total loss function defined as:

$$\mathcal{L} = \sum_{i=1}^{N}(Loss(D_i, Y_i)) \tag{1}$$

3.3   Siamese Network Based NADS

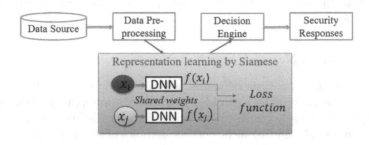

Fig. 3. Overview of our Siamese network based NADS

Based on the general NADS structure described in Sect. 3.1, Fig. 3 illustrates our Siamese network based NADS. The aim is to facilitate the work of the *decision engine* module by performing a RL step where a better feature representation is learned.

To do so, we use a ML network architecture composed of two Deep Neural Networks (DNNs) sharing the same architecture and weights. The DNNs will be trained (i.e., adjusting the weights) to produce a feature representation that minimizes the loss function (Eq. 1) in the embedded Euclidean space. Each DNN consists of 5 fully-connected layers, each of them is followed by an activation function – here, we use Rectified Linear Units (ReLU) – a dropout layer and a batch normalization layer, the final layer is followed by a sigmoid activation function.

The input of each DNN is a data sample x_i describing the traffic. x_i is a p-dimensional column vector, where p is the number of features created, encoded and normalized in the pre-processing step. The output is an embedded vector $f(x_i) \in \mathbb{R}^q$ having the dimension of the embedding space.

Note that the data samples can be classified in two manners: a **binary classification** and a **multi-class classification**. Binary classification classifies the traffic as normal or anomalous (attack). Multi-class classification classifies the anomalous traffic depending on the attack type. As an example of attack type, we can cite the *Denial of Service* (DoS) used to deny legitimate users access to a resource by flooding the target machine with superfluous requests, and *Backdoor* where an attacker bypasses the normal authentication and obtains remote access to a system.

4   Experimental Results

In the following, we assess the performance of a Siamese network based NADS under different scenarios. We will first present the used database and the evaluation settings and then discuss the results.

Category	Training dataset		Test dataset		Extracted dataset (10 %)	
	Size	%	Size	%	Size	%
Normal	37.000	44.93	56.000	31.94	3746	45.49
Generic	18.871	22.92	40.000	22.81	1864	22.64
Exploits	11.132	13.52	33.393	19.04	1132	13.74
Fuzzers	6.062	7.36	18.184	10.37	586	7.11
DoS	4.089	4.96	12.264	6.99	382	4.63
Reconnaissance	3.496	4.24	10.491	5.98	354	4.29
Analysis	677	0.82	2.000	1.14	75	0.91
Backdoor	583	0.70	1.746	1	54	0.65
Shellcode	378	0.45	1.133	0.65	34	0.41
Worms	44	0.05	130	0.07	6	0.07
Total	82332	100	175.341	100	8233	100

Fig. 4. Distribution of records in the training and test UNSW-NB15 data-sets and in the extracted data-set (Color figure online)

4.1   Data-Set Description

Different publicly available data-sets have been generated to evaluate the performance of any IDS approach. Although KDD99 data-set [25] and a refined version NLS-KDD [2] are the most used, they are relatively old and do not contain any contemporary normal and attack behaviours which bias any IDS evaluation. In this paper, we use the UNSW-NB15 data-set [1] which is a more recent data-set. It was created by the cyber security research group at the Australian Centre of Cyber Security (ACCS) in 2015. Approximately 100 GB of raw data representing authentic contemporary normal and attack records was generated. Different network extractor tools were used to generate 49 features. The data-set contains 9 different types of attacks, namely, *Fuzzers*, *Analysis*, *Backdoors*, *DoS*, *Exploits*, *Generic*, *Reconnaissance*, *Shellcode* and *Worms*. UNSW-NB15 comes along with predefined splits for training and test. The first two tables of Fig. 4 show the distribution of records between the different classes in training and test data-sets.

4.2   Experimental Settings

Evaluation Metrics. In the literature, most of research works in the field of intrusion detection focused on the Accuracy, Precision, Recall and F1-score. In this work, we have adopted the same metrics. The definition of these metrics is detailed below.

The metrics definition based on the True Positives (TP), True Negatives (TN), False Positives (FP) and False Negatives (FN). TP (resp. FP) are the correctly (resp. incorrectly) predicted *positive* samples, whereas TN (resp. FN) are the correctly (resp. incorrectly) predicted *false* samples.

- **Accuracy** is the most intuitive performance measure and it is a ratio of correctly predicted observations to the total observations:
  $Accuracy = \frac{TP+TN}{(TP+FP+TN+FN)}$
- **Precision** indicates what percentage of positive predictions were correct:
  $Precision = \frac{TP}{(TP+FP)}$
- **Recall** defines what percentage of positive cases did a classifier catch:
  $Recall = \frac{TP}{(TP+FN)}$
- F_1 **score** is the weighted average of Precision and Recall:
  $F_1 = 2 * \frac{Recall*Precision}{(Recall+Precision)}$

Data-Set Preprocessing. The original size of the IDS data-sets is generally large, therefore, it is common to use only a part of the data to evaluate supervised approach. This will avoid spending too much time in the training stage [7,12]. We randomly extracted 10% of records from the UNSW-NB15 training data-set. The third table in Fig. 4 illustrates the distribution of the extracted samples. Furthermore, to provide more suitable data for the classifier, *Label Encoding* and *Data Normalization* steps are performed. Label Encoding consists in encoding the categorical attributes, such as protocol, service, and state, into numerical values. We used an Ordinal Encoder [5]. This data is then normalized between zero and one to produce more homogeneous values.

Evaluation Protocol. The aim of this paper is to evaluate the performance of *Siamese network based representation learning* to improve network anomaly detection under different scenarios. To do so, we design a NADS using the KNN classifier in the *decision engine* module, and evaluate its performance when preceded or not by a Siamese network RL step. We refer to the algorithm variants by *S-KNN* and *KNN* respectively. For each scenario, the performance is evaluated by computing a weighted average of the different metrics.

Furthermore, to obtain high performance and reduce the bias of machine learning techniques, k-fold cross-validation (10-fold in our experiments) is used. All experiments are implemented in Python 2.7 and the Keras [10] and sklearn [8] libraries were used to implement the DNN and classifier models respectively. The best KNN tuning parameters are selected using gridSearchCV of the sklearn library for each k-fold iteration.

4.3   Results and Discussion

To evaluate the contribution of Siamese network based representation learning to the NADS, different evaluation scenarios were investigated. In addition to classification type (binary or multi-class), the impact of data size (small or big) and composition (balanced or not) were also examined.

Scenario	Binary classification		Majority class classification		Minority class classification	
Metrics	KNN	S-KNN	KNN	S-KNN	KNN	S-KNN
Accuracy	92.64	**95.76**	82.28	**86.34**	51.39	**58.90**
Precision	92.75	**95.41**	83.59	**86.54**	52.16	**59.20**
Recall	92.63	**95.39**	82.59	**86.40**	51.39	**58.90**
F1 Score	92.54	**95.40**	83.59	**86.54**	47.02	**56.37**

Fig. 5. Evaluation of Siamese Network based NADS under different scenarios

Binary Classification. The aim of binary classification is to classify each packet traffic as normal or anomalous (regardless of the attack type). In this scenario, the label indicating the attack type was ignored. The *first* table of Fig. 5 depicts the obtained results and shows that the KNN classifies more efficiently the traffic when it is preceded by a Siamese network based RL step. We can see an increase of 3 percentage points or more for all the metrics.

Multi-class Classification. For the multi-class classification, there are 10 classes representing either normal traffic or one of the 9 attack types. Figure 6 shows the results for each class for both *KNN* and *S-KNN*. Note that the average accuracy (bottom row of the table) has decreased compared to the binary sce-nario for both algorithms, which is expected as the multi-class classification task is more challenging. Moreover, as in the previous scenario, the Siamese network based RL step has increased the average performance of *KNN* (3 percentage points better).

Now looking at the accuracy rates of each class, notice that for the well detected classes, i.e., having high metric rates (Normal and Generic attacks), the performance of *KNN* and *S-KNN* are similar. However, for the classes where KNN has low detection performance, the contribution of Siamese network based RL is more significant (especially for Fuzzers, Reconnaissance and Shellcode where the gain is higher than 6 percentage points. In fact, by embedding the features to the learned representation space where the samples of different classes are distant and those of the same class are close, the samples of "minority" classes are *better isolated* and then more easily detected by *KNN*. Thus, the Siamese net-work based RL could be a promising approach for detecting infrequent attacks.

Category	Nb of samples	Accuracy		Precision		Recall		F1-Score	
		KNN	S-KNN	KNN	S-KNN	KNN	S-KNN	KNN	S-KNN
Normal	3746	96.35	96.71	95.47	94.42	96.35	96.71	91.69	95.54
Generic	1864	97.05	96.69	98.63	98.54	97.05	96.69	97.83	97.60
Exploits	1132	66.17	69.71	68.95	68.72	66.17	70.73	67.51	69.62
Fuzzers	586	34.74	64.97	53.39	63.46	34.74	65.81	41.86	64.33
DoS	382	38.22	36.48	33.36	43.95	38.22	37.35	40.38	39.96
Reconnaissance	354	53.77	63.09	56.64	63.84	53.76	62.15	54.81	62.90
Analysis	75	19.34	21.42	16.78	17.77	19.34	17.26	17.42	17.30
Backdoor	54	11.11	11.11	11.30	12.41	11.11	11.11	11.02	10.47
Shellcode	34	24.99	31.94	38.21	44.28	26.38	22.57	38.33	55.3
Worms	6	3.3	66	3.1	6.7	2.8	6.2	3.2	6.7
Average		82.56	85.06	80.97	84.77	80.97	84.77	80.97	84.77

Fig. 6. Evaluation of Siamese network based NADS for multi-class classification

Majority Classes Classification. The aim of this scenario is to assess the performance of the NADS using the Siamese network based RL when *both the training and test data-sets* are more or less balanced. As shown in Fig. 4, the samples distribution between classes is unbalanced. We can namely identify classes that are "majority", having more than 350 samples, and colored in orange in Fig. 4, and other classes that are "minority", having less than 75 samples and colored in blue. In this scenario, we focus on the detection of the attacks of majority classes. The second table of Fig. 5 shows the results and confirms the superiority of $S - KNN$ (up to 4 percentage points of increase).

Minority Classes Classification. The aim of this scenario is the evaluate the contribution of the Siamese network based RL for small data-sets. We focus on detecting *minority attacks*. As shown in Fig. 4, the 10% extracted from the UNSW-NB15 training data-set contain very few samples of minority classes (169 in total) which is excessively insufficient to train the DNN. To construct a small but realistic data-set, we decided to take into account all the samples of minority classes present in the UNSW-NB15 training data-set (1682 samples). For testing, 10% of the UNSW-NB15 test data-set were extracted (500 samples). The tests were performed 100 times, as cross validation can not be performed because training and test data-sets are separated.

In the third table of Fig. 5, we first notice a significant drop in KNN's performance compared to previous scenarios. This can be explained by the small learning data-set size. However, note that the contribution of Siamese network RL is the most significant in this scenario (+8 percentage points for all the metrics). This can be explained by the fact that Siamese network benefits from a much larger data-set after generating positive and negative pairs. Figure 7 shows the number of pairs that can be generated from the 1682 samples in this data-set. The number of pairs is calculated as explained in Sect. 3.2. In small data-sets,

Class	Analysis	Backdoor	Shellcode	Worms
Nb of samples	677	583	378	44
Nb of Positive pairs	228826	169653	71253	946
Nb of Negative pairs	680385	640717	492912	72072
Total	909211	810370	564165	73018
Total for all classes	2356764			

Fig. 7. Pairs generation statistics

the Siamese network can provide a better data representation for the KNN to improve its performance.

Discussion. The extensive evaluation results demonstrated the contribution of the Siamese network based Representation Learning. The approach improved the NADS performance for both binary and multi-class classifications, as well as for unbalanced data-sets. Moreover, the approach is promising for detecting infrequent attacks. *Data augmentation techniques* [28] may be explored to produce a balanced training data-set, thus enabling the Siamese network to learn a feature representation space where scarce attacks are better represented.

5 Conclusions and Perspectives

This paper investigated to use of the Siamese network to learn feature representation for better intrusion detection. A Siamese network based RL for NADS was designed and evaluated under different scenarios. The results showed the effectiveness of the approach for binary and multi-class classification, and for unbalanced and small data-sets. Data augmentation techniques will be explored to improve the detection of infrequent attacks. Moreover, we plan to compare our approach with unsupervised approaches like the Auto Encoders.

References

1. UNSW-NB15, May 2015. https://www.unsw.adfa.edu.au/unsw-canberra-cyber/cybersecurity/ADFA-NB15-Datasets/
2. Aljawarneh, S., Aldwairi, M., Yassein, M.B.: Anomaly-based intrusion detection system through feature selection analysis and building hybrid efficient model. J. Comput. Sci. **25**, 152–160 (2018)
3. Axelsson, S.: The base-rate fallacy and the difficulty of intrusion detection. ACM Trans. Inf. Syst. Secur. (TISSEC) **3**(3), 186–205 (2000)
4. Bengio, Y., Courville, A., Vincent, P.: Representation learning: a review and new perspectives. IEEE Trans. Pattern Anal. Mach. Intell. **35**(8), 1798–1828 (2013)
5. Botes, F., Leenen, L., De La Harpe, R.: Ant colony induced decision trees for intrusion detection (2017)
6. Bromley, J., Guyon, I., LeCun, Y., Säckinger, E., Shah, R.: Signature verification using a "Siamese" time delay neural network. In: Advances in Neural Information Processing Systems, pp. 737–744 (1994)

7. Elhag, S., Fernández, A., Bawakid, A., Alshomrani, S., Herrera, F.: On the combination of genetic fuzzy systems and pairwise learning for improving detection rates on intrusion detection systems. Expert. Syst. Appl. **42**(1), 193–202 (2015)

8. Feurer, M., Klein, A., Eggensperger, K., Springenberg, J.T., Blum, M., Hutter, F.: Auto-sklearn: efficient and robust automated machine learning. In: Hutter, F., Kotthoff, L., Vanschoren, J. (eds.) Automated Machine Learning, pp. 113–134. Springer, Cham (2019). https://doi.org/10.1007/978-3-030-05318-5_6

9. Ghojogh, B., et al.: Feature selection and feature extraction in pattern analysis: a literature review. arXiv preprint arXiv:1905.02845 (2019)

10. Gulli, A., Pal, S.: Deep Learning with Keras. Packt Publishing Ltd. (2017)

11. Hou, J., Wu, T., Cao, R., Cheng, J.: Protein tertiary structure modeling driven by deep learning and contact distance prediction in CASP13. bioRxiv, p. 552422 (2019)

12. Khammassi, C., Krichen, S.: A GA-LR wrapper approach for feature selection in network intrusion detection. Comput. Secur. **70**, 255–277 (2017)

13. Koch, G., Zemel, R., Salakhutdinov, R.: Siamese neural networks for one-shot image recognition. In: ICML Deep Learning Workshop, vol. 2 (2015)

14. Kwon, D., Kim, H., Kim, J., Suh, S.C., Kim, I., Kim, K.J.: A survey of deep learning-based network anomaly detection. Cluster Comput. **22**, 949–961 (2017)

15. Li, Z., Qin, Z., Huang, K., Yang, X., Ye, S.: Intrusion detection using convolutional neural networks for representation learning. In: Liu, D., Xie, S., Li, Y., Zhao, D., El-Alfy, E.-S.M. (eds.) ICONIP 2017. LNCS, vol. 10638, pp. 858–866. Springer, Cham (2017). https://doi.org/10.1007/978-3-319-70139-4_87

16. Marir, N., Wang, H., Feng, G., Li, B., Jia, M.: Distributed abnormal behavior detection approach based on deep belief network and ensemble SVM using Spark. IEEE Access **6**, 59657–59671 (2018)

17. Mishra, P., Varadharajan, V., Tupakula, U., Pilli, E.S.: A detailed investigation and analysis of using machine learning techniques for intrusion detection. IEEE Commun. Surv. Tutor. **21**(1), 686–728 (2019)

18. Moustafa, N., Hu, J., Slay, J.: A holistic review of network anomaly detection systems: a comprehensive survey. J. Netw. Comput. Appl. **128**, 33–55 (2019)

19. Nicolau, M., McDermott, J., et al.: Learning neural representations for network anomaly detection. IEEE Trans. Cybern. **99**, 1–14 (2018)

20. Pérez, D., Alonso, S., Morán, A., Prada, M.A., Fuertes, J.J., Domínguez, M.: Comparison of network intrusion detection performance using feature representation. In: Macintyre, J., Iliadis, L., Maglogiannis, I., Jayne, C. (eds.) EANN 2019. CCIS, vol. 1000, pp. 463–475. Springer, Cham (2019). https://doi.org/10.1007/978-3-030-20257-6_40

21. Qi, Y., Song, Y.Z., Zhang, H., Liu, J.: Sketch-based image retrieval via Siamese convolutional neural network. In: 2016 IEEE International Conference on Image Processing (ICIP), pp. 2460–2464. IEEE (2016)

22. Riad, R., Dancette, C., Karadayi, J., Zeghidour, N., Schatz, T., Dupoux, E.: Sampling strategies in Siamese networks for unsupervised speech representation learning. arXiv preprint arXiv:1804.11297 (2018)

23. Stephenson, N., Shane, E., Chase, J., Rowland, J., Ries, D., Justice, N., Zhang, J., Chan, L., Cao, R.: Survey of machine learning techniques in drug discovery. Curr. Drug Metab. **20**(3), 185–193 (2019)

24. Taigman, Y., Yang, M., Ranzato, M., Wolf, L.: DeepFace: closing the gap to human-level performance in face verification. In: Proceedings of the IEEE Conference on Computer Vision and Pattern Recognition, pp. 1701–1708 (2014)

25. Tavallaee, M., Bagheri, E., Lu, W., Ghorbani, A.A.: A detailed analysis of the KDD CUP 99 data set. In: 2009 IEEE Symposium on Computational Intelligence for Security and Defense Applications, pp. 1–6. IEEE (2009)
26. Tschannen, M., Bachem, O., Lucic, M.: Recent advances in autoencoder-based representation learning. arXiv preprint arXiv:1812.05069 (2018)
27. Yousefi-Azar, M., Varadharajan, V., Hamey, L., Tupakula, U.: Autoencoder-based feature learning for cyber security applications. In: 2017 International Joint Conference on Neural Networks (IJCNN), pp. 3854–3861. IEEE (2017)
28. Zhou, B., Buyya, R.: Augmentation techniques for mobile cloud computing: a taxonomy, survey, and future directions. ACM Comput. Surv. (CSUR) **51**(1), 13 (2018)

Self-attentive Pyramid Network
for Single Image De-raining

Taian Guo[1], Tao Dai[1,2(✉)], Jiawei Li[1], and Shu-Tao Xia[1,2]

[1] Graduate School at Shenzhen, Tsinghua University, Shenzhen 518055, Guangdong,
People's Republic of China
gta17@mails.tsinghua.edu.cn, daitao.edu@gmail.com
[2] PCL Research Center of Networks and Communications, Peng Cheng Laboratory,
Shenzhen 518055, Guangdong, People's Republic of China

Abstract. Rain Streaks in a single image can severely damage the visual
quality, and thus degrade the performance of current computer vision
algorithms. To remove the rain streaks effectively, plenty of CNN-based
methods have recently been developed, and obtained impressive performance. However, most existing CNN-based methods focus on network design, while rarely exploits spatial correlations of feature. In this
paper, we propose a deep self-attentive pyramid network (SAPN) for
more powerful feature expression for single image de-raining. Specifically, we propose a self-attentive pyramid module (SAM), which consists of convolutional layers enhanced by self-attention calculation units
(SACUs) to capture the abstraction of image contents, and deconvolutional layers to upsample the feature maps and recover image details.
Besides, we propose self-attention based skip connections to symmet-
rically link convolutional and deconvolutional layers to exploit spatial
contextual information better. To model rain streaks with various scales
and shapes, a multi-scale pooling (MSP) module is also introduced to
efficiently leverage features from different scales. Extensive experiments
on both synthetic and real-world datasets demonstrate the effectiveness
of our proposed method in terms of both quantitative and visual quality.

Keywords: Rain streak removal · Encoder-decoder network ·
Self-attention

1 Introduction

Images captured in rain weather are common in real life, thus resulting in images
with rain streaks. Such rain streaks would not only affect the visual quality

This work is supported in part by the National Key Research and Development Program of China under Grant 2018YFB1800204, the National Natural Science Foundation of China under Grant 61771273, the R&D Program of Shenzhen under Grant
JCYJ20180508152204044, and the research fund of PCL Future Regional Network
Facilities for Large-scale Experiments and Applications (PCL2018KP001). We also
gratefully acknowledge the support of NVIDIA Corporation with the donation of Titan
X GPUs for this research.

© Springer Nature Switzerland AG 2019
T. Gedeon et al. (Eds.): ICONIP 2019, LNCS 11953, pp. 390–401, 2019.
https://doi.org/10.1007/978-3-030-36708-4_32

(a) Input   (b) DDN   (c) DID-MDN   (d) PReNet   (e) Ours

Fig. 1. Sample de-raining results on real-world rainy scenes with long heavy rain streaks. The details in the enlarged regions shows that our SAPN removes long heavy rain streaks in the input rainy images more cleanly, while keeps the sharp details of the background objects. The two rows demonstrate that our self-attentive network produces better de-raining results on image regions with long heavy rain streaks.

of images, but also degrade performance of existing computer vision systems, such as self-driving, video surveillance, and object detection. Therefore, it is of crucial importance to remove rain streaks while recovering image details. Image de-raining has received much attention in recent years, and can be generally divided into video-based [1–4] and single image based methods [5–10]. Most video based methods focus on utilizing the temporal correlations in successive frames, which provide extra temporal information of the rainy scene. In contrast, it is more challenging to perform single image de-raining due to the very limited information from a single image (Fig. 1).

In recent years, many single image de-raining methods [5–8,10] have been proposed. Most traditional image de-raining methods focus on exploiting powerful image prior of the rainy images, including sparse prior [7], low rank prior [11] and Gaussian mixture model (GMM) prior [6]. Among them, Luo et al. [5] proposed a dictionary learning based method, which sparsely approximates the patches of the rain layer and the de-rained layer by discriminative sparse codes with a learned dictionary. Li et al. [6] further introduced patch-based Gaussian mixture model (GMM) priors for both the background layer and the rain layer. Zhu et al. [7] introduced three types of priors, and proposed a joint optimization process to alternately remove rain-streak details. However, since such methods rely heavily on the handcrafted feature and the fixed priors, they are limited in practice due to the diversity of rain streaks (e.g., various shapes, scales and density levels).

Due to the powerful feature representation capability, convolutional neural networks have been widely used in image de-raining, and obtained remarkable performance. For example, Fu et al. [8] proposed a deep detail network to learn the high frequency details during the training process, since most rain streaks belong to high-frequency information. To consider various shapes and density of rain drops, Zhang et al. [10] proposed a densely connected network with learned rain streak density information to assist the rain streak removal process.

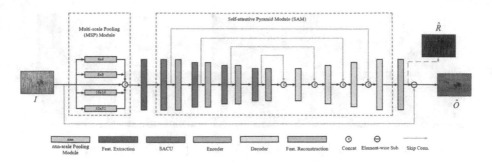

Fig. 2. Framework of our self-attentive pyramid network (SAPN)

Since spatial contextual information is important for rain streaks removal, some methods [12, 13] have been developed. Specifically, Li et al. [12] proposed a multi-stage dilated CNN network to obtain a large receptive field size. Recently, Ren et al. [14] proposed a progressive recurrent network (PReNet) to better take advantage of the recursive computation and exploit the dependencies of deep features across stages.

Although significant progress has been achieved for single image de-raining, most of existing CNN-based methods focus on the network design, while rarely considering the inherent spatial correlations in feature maps. Meanwhile, self-attention [15] exploits the spatial correlations of features by using the attention scores to weight all features to obtain the salient features. To make full use of the spatial correlations of features, we propose a deep self-attentive pyramid network (SAPN) for single image de-raining, which mainly consists of self-attentive pyramid module (SAM) and multi-scale pooling (MSP) module. Specifically, to efficiently exploit the spatial contextual information, we propose the self-attention calculation units (SACUs) based encoding layers to enhance the encoding process, and SACUs based skip connections to enhance the symmetrical decoding process. With the assistance of SACUs, the encoding layers can better utilize the spatial correlations from the input features. Besides, our SACUs based skip connections can not only contribute to the propagation of gradient flows, but also pass the enhanced original feature signal from convolutional layers to symmetrical deconvolutional layers directly, which is helpful for recovering image details. Furthermore, since feature pyramid is helpful for multi-resolution feature representation, we apply multi-scale pooling in the shallow layers of our network. Extensive experiments on synthetic and real-world datasets demonstrate the superiority of our proposed method in terms of both quantitative and visual quality.

2   Self-attentive Pyramid Network (SAPN)

2.1   Network Architecture

As shown in Fig. 2, our SAPN consists of four main parts: multi-scale pooling module, shallow feature extraction, self-attentive pyramid module (SAM) and feature reconstruction.

Multi-scale Pooling Module. Given I as input rainy image and $\hat{R}$ as estimated rain streak image, then the output of SAPN is represented as follows:

$$\hat{O} = I - \hat{R}, \tag{1}$$

where $\hat{O}$ denotes the estimated de-rained image. To model rain streaks with various scales and shapes from the input image I, we firstly introduce a multi-scale pooling operation $H_{msp}(\cdot)$ to get the multi-scale feature F_{msp} from I:

$$\begin{aligned} F_{msp} &= H_{msp}(I) \\ &= [S_1^{32 \times 32}(I), S_2^{16 \times 16}(I), S_3^{8 \times 8}(I), S_4^{4 \times 4}(I), I], \end{aligned} \tag{2}$$

where $[\cdot, \cdot, ..., \cdot]$ denotes channel-wise concatenation and $S_i^{k \times k}(\cdot)$ represents the i-th $k \times k$-scale pooling operation which is defined as:

$$S_i^{k \times k}(I) = U^{k \times k}(ReLU(Conv^{1 \times 1}(D^{k \times k}(I)))), \tag{3}$$

where $D^{k \times k}(\cdot)$ and $U^{k \times k}(\cdot)$ denote $k \times k$-scale downsampling and upsampling respectively. $Conv^{1 \times 1}(\cdot)$ denotes a 1×1 convolutional layer.

Shallow Feature Extraction. After we get multi-scale feature concatenation F_{msp} from Eq. (3), the shallow feature representation F_{fr} can be obtained by

$$F_{fr} = H_{ex}(F_{msp}), \tag{4}$$

where $H_{ex}(\cdot)$ represents two 3×3 convolutional layers with 64 filters respectively, which are designed to extract the shallow feature representation F_{fr} from F_{msp}.

Self-attentive Pyramid Module (SAM). Given the shallow feature representation F_{fr} obtained from the above step, the self-attentive pyramid module (SAM), denoted as $H_{sam}(\cdot)$, adopts a pyramid encoder-decoder structure with Self-attention Calculation Units (SACU) embedded in it, and produce a rain streak layer feature representation F_{rs}:

$$F_{rs} = H_{sam}(F_{fr}). \tag{5}$$

The detailed description of SAM is given in Sect. 2.2.

Feature Reconstruction Part. After obtaining the rain streak layer feature representation F_{rs}, we can reconstruct the estimated rain streak $\hat{R}$ using the feature reconstruction part $H_{rc}(\cdot)$, which is actually a 3×3 convolutional layer:

$$\hat{R} = H_{rc}(F_{rs}) = H_{sapn}(I), \tag{6}$$

where $H_{sapn}(\cdot)$ represents the function of our proposed SAPN.

Loss Function. During the training process, our SAPN is optimized with loss function. To improve not only the pixel-wise reconstruction but the high-level semantic representation, we add perceptual loss to pixel-level L1 loss to get the combined loss L_C:

$$L_C = L_{L1} + \lambda L_P, \tag{7}$$

where λ denotes the trade-off coefficient between the two losses, and the L1 loss L_{L1} and the perceptual loss L_P are defined as:

$$L_{L1} = \frac{1}{CWH} \sum_{c=1}^{C} \sum_{w=1}^{W} \sum_{h=1}^{H} \|\hat{O}^{c,w,h} - O^{c,w,h}\|_1, \tag{8}$$

$$L_P = \frac{1}{CWH} \sum_{c=1}^{C} \sum_{w=1}^{W} \sum_{h=1}^{H} \|(V(\hat{O}))^{c,w,h} - (V(O))^{c,w,h}\|_2^2, \tag{9}$$

where C, W and H denote the channel, width and height dimension of the estimated de-rained image $\hat{O}$ and the ground truth clean image O. $V(\cdot)$ represents the front layers of a pretrained VGG model which is regarded as the high-level feature extractor. The loss function is optimized by Adam optimizer.

After a full glance at the framework of the proposed SAPN, we can conclude that the deep feature representation in our SAPN heavily relies on the self-attentive pyramid module (SAM), which will be shown in the next section.

2.2   Self-attentive Pyramid Module (SAM)

Our SAM is based on encoder-decoder networks [16], which are widely used in image-to-image tasks. However, most existing encoder-decoder based networks focus on network design, while rarely exploits spatial correlations of features and thus limits representation capability of the network. To exploit such correlations inherent in features, we propose a novel self-attentive pyramid module (SAM).

As shown in Fig. 2, the core component of SAPN is self-attentive Pyramid Module (SAM), which is further composed of four Self-attention Calculation Units (SACUs), four encoders and four decoders. The detailed description of SACU will be given in the next section.

Given the feature representation F_{fr} obtained from shallow feature extraction step $H_{ex}(\cdot)$, the original U-net [16] simply encodes the features iteratively and feeds the encoded features to symmetrical decoder. However, the single encoding layer, which consists of several convolutional layers, can not fully utilize the spatial correlations of the features, thus leading to poor ability of modeling the long-range dependency inherent in the features. Given this, we embed self-attention calculation unit (SACU) $H_{sa,i}(\cdot)$ in each encoder $H_{en,i}(\cdot)$ to model the long-range spatial correlations, and thus the encoded features are enhanced before passing through the decoding layer. i-th encoder $H_{en,i}(\cdot)$ is composed of a 3×3 convolutional layer with stride 2 and doubled channels from input, and two

3×3 layers with ReLU activation, which keeps input channels. We can formulate the self-attentive encoding part of the SAM component $H_{sam}(\cdot)$ as:

$$
\begin{aligned}
F_{sa,i} &= H_{sa,i-1}(F_{en,i-1}), \\
F_{en,i} &= H_{en,i}(F_{sa,i}), \quad i = 1, 2, 3, 4,
\end{aligned}
\tag{10}
$$

where $F_{sa,i}$ denotes the output of i-th SACU and $F_{en,i}$ denotes the output of i-th encoder. $F_{en,0}$ denotes F_{fr} for convenience. With the help of self-attention information obtained from the SACU, the encoding process can be enhanced to get more spatial correlation into consideration.

After the self-attentive encoding part, we obtain $F_{sa,i}$ plus the final output (i.e. $F_{en,4}$) of encoders as the input of following decoding part. Unlike the pyramid network and U-net, which directly utilize the symmetrical encoded features $F_{en,4-i}$ from skip connection as the extra information:

$$
F_{de,i} = H_{de,i}([F_{de,i-1}, F_{en,4-i}]),
\tag{11}
$$

we adopt the extra self-attention information besides the original encoded features $F_{en,4-i}$, which is integrated in features $F_{sa,4-(i-1)}$, to decoder $H_{de,i}(\cdot)$ to get output features $F_{de,i}$. Similar with the encoder design, i-th decoder $H_{de,i}(\cdot)$ starts with a 3×3 deconvolutional layer with stride 2 and keeps the channels, followed by two consecutive 3×3 layers with ReLU activation which halves the channels in the former layer. Specifically, we utilize the obtained self-attention $F_{sa,i}$ to enhance the decoding process, which can be formulated as:

$$
F_{de,i} = H_{de,i}([F_{de,i-1}, F_{sa,4-(i-1)}]),
\tag{12}
$$

where $F_{de,4}$, the output features of the last decoder, is also the final output of SAM and input of feature reconstruction layer, which is also denoted as F_{rs}. $F_{de,0}$, or $F_{en,4}$, is the output features of the last encoding layer and also the input of the first decoding layer. Through the skip connection which delivers the output self-attention $F_{sa,4-(i-1)}$ of $(4-i)$-th SACU (i.e. $H_{sa,4-(i-1)}(\cdot)$), the i-th decoder $H_{de,i}(\cdot)$ can get not only the symmetrical features but their self-attention information directly since the skip connection structure in SACU. With the help of the extra self-attention information of features, the decoding process can be further enhanced with the spatial correlation provided by the self-attention information, which makes the representation of long-range dependency possible. The experiments in Sect. 3 demonstrate the performance gain of the utilization of the extra self-attention information. We will give a further explanation to the self-attention calculation unit (SACU) in the next section.

2.3 Self-attention Calculation Unit (SACU)

Self-attention focuses on the attention of feature maps towards themselves, which has been widely researched by previous works [15,17]. The information provided by self-attention properly handles the problem that long-range feature dependency can not be efficiently convolved by the convolutional layers.

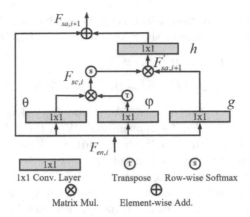

Fig. 3. Self-attention Calculation Unit (SACU)

As shown in Fig. 3, given the output features $F_{en,i}$ of i-th encoder $H_{en,i}(\cdot)$, we firstly obtain three embedding representation $\theta(F_{en,i})$, $\phi(F_{en,i})$, $g(F_{en,i})$ from three different 1×1 convolutional layers $\theta(\cdot)$, $\phi(\cdot)$ and $g(\cdot)$. Then the self-correlation $F_{sc,i}$ of feature map $F_{en,i}$ can be obtained via

$$F_{sc,i} = \theta(F_{en,i})\phi(F_{en,i})^{\mathrm{T}}. \tag{13}$$

Then, we can get the self-weights $F'_{sc,i}$ by softmaxing each row of $F_{sc,i}$, and use it to weight the embedding representation $\theta(F_{en,i})$ by:

$$F'_{sa,i+1} = F'_{sc,i}g(F_{en,i}). \tag{14}$$

After that, the self-attention map $F''_{sa,i+1}$ is obtained via a further 1×1 convolutional layer $h(\cdot)$.

Furthermore, to boost the gradient transmission and avoid the gradient vanishing problem, we add skip connection from the input $F_{en,i}$ to the calculated self-attention map $F''_{sa,i+1}$. To better calibrate the influence between them, unlike the original non-local implementation [17], which regards the balance between the two terms as a hyper-parameter, we bring in a learnable parameter α as a trade-off weight. The final output $F_{sa,i+1}$ of SACU can be formulated as:

$$F_{sa,i+1} = F_{en,i} + \alpha F''_{sa,i+1}. \tag{15}$$

With the learnable parameter α, the weighting of the self-attention information becomes more flexible and thus leads to better utilization of self-attention.

3   Experiments

To validate the advantage of our method, we conduct tremendous experiments on various synthetic datasets and natural rainy images. Since the ground truth images are available in synthetic datasets, PSNR and SSIM are adopted as the evaluation criterion of the de-raining results. We calculate PSNR/SSIM in luminance channel of YCbCr space. Additionally, we compare our proposed SAPN with state-of-the-art de-raining methods, including Deep Detailed Network (DDN) [8], Joing Rain Detection and Removal (JORDER) [9], Density-aware Single Image De-raining using a Multi-stream Dense Network (DID-MDN) [10] and Progressive Recurrent Network (PReNet) [14].

3.1 Datasets

Synthetic Datasets. To make a comparison with previous state-of-the-art de-raining approaches, we adopt three public benchmark synthetic datasets to train and evaluate our SAPN, including DDN-Dataset [8], DID-MDN-Dataset [10] and Rain100H [9]. Specifically, DDN-Dataset contains 14,000 rainy-clean image pairs which is synthesized by 1000 clean images. We randomly select 9100 image pairs as training dataset and use the left 4900 image pairs as the testing dataset. DID-MDN-Dataset is composed of 12000 training rainy-clean image pairs and 1201 testing image pairs. Rain100H contains 100 testing images and there are 1800 training image pairs in the corresponding training dataset (i.e. RainTrainH).

Real-World Images. To validate the effectiveness of the proposed network in real world rainy scenes, we randomly select some images from the previous de-raining works [8,9,18,19] and the internet.

3.2 Training Details

For each of the three datasets, we train our SAPN on a 1080 ti GPU on the training dataset, and evaluate the model on corresponding testing dataset. We train our model for 300, 350 and 50 epochs for DID-MDN-Train, DDN-Train, and RainTrainH respectively. The initial learning rate is set to $2 \cdot 10^{-4}$ and decreased linearly at the end of every epoch. To avoid the problem of over-fitting, we use a weight decay of 10^{-5} and Adam optimizer with betas 0.5 and 0.999. The model is trained on the Pytorch framework.

Table 1. Quantitative results of average PSNR (dB)/SSIM compared with state-of-the-art de-raining works. The two best-performing methods are marked in **bold** and underlined respectively.

Dataset	Matric	Input	DDN [8] (CVPR'17)	JORDER [9] (CVPR'17)	DID-MDN [10] (CVPR'18)	Our SAPN
DID-MDN-Dataset	PSNR (dB)	23.63	<u>30.08</u>	26.80	29.36	**30.86**
	SSIM	.7313	.8788	.8361	<u>.9002</u>	**.9230**
DDN-Dataset	PSNR (dB)	23.74	<u>30.00</u>	26.47	28.00	**30.26**
	SSIM	.7499	<u>.8932</u>	.8276	.8776	**.9110**
Rain100H	PSNR (dB)	13.56	22.26	26.10	<u>26.35</u>	**27.06**
	SSIM	.3800	.6928	.7971	<u>.8287</u>	**.8474**

3.3   Results on Synthetic Datasets

The details of evaluation results on synthetic datasets are shown in Table 1. Note that the pretrained model of PResNet [14] is trained from other datasets, thus we did not report the quantitative results for fair comparison. Results show that our method outperforms other state-of-the-arts consistently. This is mainly because our SAPN utilizes both multi-scale information and spatial correlations of features, which enhances the feature representation capability of the network. In contrast, DDN [8] learns the mapping from high-frequency details of rainy

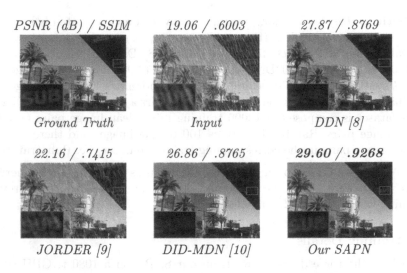

Fig. 4. De-raining results on sample image from DDN-Testset.

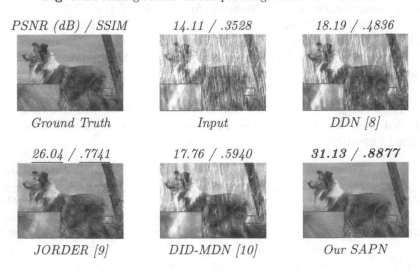

Fig. 5. De-raining results on sample image from Rain100H.

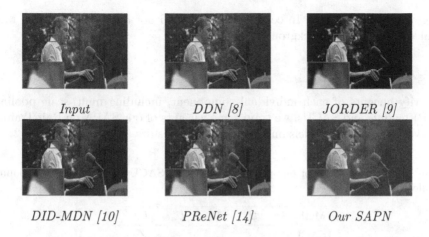

Input   *DDN [8]*   *JORDER [9]*

DID-MDN [10]   *PReNet [14]*   *Our SAPN*

Fig. 6. De-raining results on sample real-world image.

images to clean ones with ResNet [20], while DID-MDN [10] utilize multi-scale features and multi-stream DenseNet [18] architecture, both of which do not take spatial correlations inherent in features into consideration.

Besides the quantitative evaluation on synthetic datasets, we also randomly select several images from the testing datasets to validate the visual effect. As shown in Figs. 4 and 5, our method obtains better visual results. For example, the alphabets in enlarged region in Fig. 4 are clearly recovered by our SAPN, while other methods fail to remove long heavy rain streaks or bring in unpleasant artifacts. Another sample in Fig. 5 also show that our SAPN keeps the background scenes better and removes the rain streaks more cleanly, especially when the image has some long rain streaks or other objects with long shapes, since the adoption of self-attention mechanism enhances the capability of the network to capture long-range dependency and non-local similarity.

3.4 Qualitative Evaluation on Real-World Images

To verify the performance gain of SAPN over previous methods on rainy scenes in real world, we also test our SAPN and other methods on real-world images. The de-raining results on a randomly selected real world image sample is shown in Fig. 6. Noticeably, our method achieves extremely better results when the rain streaks in rainy image are longer than average, just because we adopt self-attention mechanism in our network design, which can better leverage non-local similarity of input rainy image and attain long-range dependency more effectively and more efficiently. This specialty of our SAPN helps locate rainy areas in input rainy images, leading to better final de-raining results. It is clearly shown in Fig. 6 that our SAPN produces preferable results compared with other methods, which tend to either under de-rain or over de-rain the natural rainy images. Specifically, all other four methods fail to remove all long rain streaks, while JORDER even brings in severe artifacts. In contrast, our method not only removes more rain streaks, but preserves background details better.

3.5   Ablation Study

To verify benefits of each individual component, including multi-scale pooling (MSP) module and SACUs, we train some variants of our SAPN on RainTrainH and evaluate trained models on Rain100H. The results are shown in Table 2.

Table 2. Ablation study of our proposed SAPN on SACUs and multi-scale pooling module on Rain100H.

Methods	U_a	U_b	U_c	U_d
SACUs?		✓		✓
MSP?			✓	✓
PSNR (dB)	26.78	26.95	26.89	27.06

We can conclude that the adoption of SACUs effectively promotes the de-raining results of the basic pyramid encoder-decoder network (U_a), while MSP also improves the performance of the network effectively. The combination of SACUs and MSP leads to our final SAPN architecture (U_d).

4   Conclusion

In this paper, we propose a pyramid encoder-decoder network with self-attention calculation units for single image de-raining. Compared with previous methods which does not exploit spatial correlations of features, our method explicitly learns the self-correlation inherent in output features of each encoder layer, making the encoding and symmetrical decoding process more self-attentive and better resolve the long-range dependency problem in images, leading to better eventual de-raining results, especially in long rain streaks conditions. In order to further improve the de-raining results, we add a multi-scale pooling module before feature extraction, which leads to even higher quantitative performance and much better visual experience. Tremendous experiments on various datasets validate that our network outperforms the state-of-the-art methods.

References

1. Bossu, J., Hautière, N., Tarel, J.-P.: Rain or snow detection in image sequences through use of a histogram of orientation of streaks. IJCV **93**, 348–367 (2011)
2. Ren, W., Tian, J., Han, Z., Chan, A., Tang, Y.: Video desnowing and deraining based on matrix decomposition. In: CVPR (2017)

3. Wei, W., Yi, L., Xie, Q., Zhao, Q., Meng, D., Xu, Z.: Should we encode rain streaks in video as deterministic or stochastic. In: CVPR (2017)
4. Garg, K., Nayar, S.K.: Detection and removal of rain from videos. In: CVPR (2004)
5. Luo, Y., Xu, Y., Ji, H.: Removing rain from a single image via discriminative sparse coding. In: ICCV (2015)
6. Li, Y., Tan, R.T., Guo, X., Lu, J., Brown, M.S.: Rain streak removal using layer priors. In: CVPR (2016)
7. Zhu, L., Fu, C.-W., Lischinski, D., Heng, P.-A.: Joint bilayer optimization for single-image rain streak removal. In: ICCV (2017)
8. Fu, X., Huang, J., Zeng, D., Huang, Y., Ding, X., Paisley, J.: Removing rain from single images via a deep detail network. In: CVPR (2017)
9. Yang, W., Tan, R.T., Feng, J., Liu, J., Guo, Z., Yan, S.: Deep joint rain detection and removal from a single image. In: CVPR (2017)
10. Zhang, H., Patel, V.M.: Density-aware single image de-raining using a multi-stream dense network. In: CVPR (2018)
11. Chang, Y., Yan, L., Zhong, S.: Transformed low-rank model for line pattern noise removal. In: ICCV (2017)
12. Li, X., Wu, J., Lin, Z., Liu, H., Zha, H.: Recurrent squeeze-and-excitation context aggregation net for single image deraining. In: ECCV (2018)
13. Li, G., He, X., Zhang, W., Chang, H., Dong, L., Lin, L.: Non-locally enhanced encoder-decoder network for single image de-raining. In: MM (2018)
14. Ren, D., Zuo, W., Hu, Q., Zhu, P., Meng, D.: Progressive image deraining networks: a better and simpler baseline. In: CVPR (2019)
15. Vaswani, A., et al.: Attention is all you need. In: NIPS (2017)
16. Ronneberger, O., Fischer, P., Brox, T.: U-net: convolutional networks for biomedical image segmentation. In: Navab, N., Hornegger, J., Wells, W.M., Frangi, A.F. (eds.) MICCAI 2015. LNCS, vol. 9351, pp. 234–241. Springer, Cham (2015). https://doi.org/10.1007/978-3-319-24574-4_28
17. Wang, X. Girshick, R., Gupta, A., He, K.: Non-local neural networks. In: CVPR (2018)
18. Huang, G., Liu, Z., Van Der Maaten, L., Weinberger, K.Q.: Densely connected convolutional networks. In: CVPR (2017)
19. Zhang, H., Sindagi, V., Patel, V.M.: Image de-raining using a conditional generative adversarial network. arXiv (2017)
20. He, K., Zhang, X., Ren, S., Sun, J.: Deep residual learning for image recognition. In: CVPR (2016)

Human Centred Computing

Feature Fusion Based Deep Spatiotemporal Model for Violence Detection in Videos

Mujtaba Asad[1]($\boxtimes$) (iD), Zuopeng Yang[1], Zubair Khan[1], Jie Yang[1]($\boxtimes$), and Xiangjian He[2]

[1] Institute of Image Processing and Pattern Recognition,
Shanghai Jiao Tong University, Shanghai, China
{asadmujtaba,yzpeng,zubairkhan,jieyang}@sjtu.edu.cn
[2] School of Electrical and Data Engineering, University of Technology Sydney,
Ultimo, Australia
xiangjian.he@uts.edu.au

Abstract. It is essential for public monitoring and security to detect violent behavior in surveillance videos. However, it requires constant human observation and attention, which is a challenging task. Autonomous detection of violent activities is essential for continuous, uninterrupted video surveillance systems. This paper proposed a novel method to detect violent activities in videos, using fused spatial feature maps, based on Convolutional Neural Networks (CNN) and Long Short-Term Memory (LSTM) units. The spatial features are extracted through CNN, and multi-level spatial features fusion method is used to combine the spatial features maps from two equally spaced sequential input video frames to incorporate motion characteristics. The additional residual layer blocks are used to further learn these fused spatial features to increase the classification accuracy of the network. The combined spatial features of input frames are then fed to LSTM units to learn the global temporal information. The output of this network classifies the violent or non-violent category present in the input video frame. Experimental results on three different standard benchmark datasets: Hockey Fight, Crowd Violence and BEHAVE show that the proposed algorithm provides better ability to recognize violent actions in different scenarios and results in improved performance compared to the state-of-the-art methods.

Keywords: Violence detection · CNN · LSTM · Autonomous video · Surveillance spatiotemporal features

1 Introduction

The use of surveillance cameras is essential nowadays, as the rate of public violence has increased in the recent era. To make cities safe from undesirable events, it is important to continuously monitor for detrimental events before subsequent

© Springer Nature Switzerland AG 2019
T. Gedeon et al. (Eds.): ICONIP 2019, LNCS 11953, pp. 405–417, 2019.
https://doi.org/10.1007/978-3-030-36708-4_33

disorder, as violent behavior or criminal activity may occur. As the probability of occurrence of these types of events is diminutive and manually identifying abnormal behavior is a difficult task. Observing the surveillance footage requires constant attention and human resources, so it is a primarily infeasible and tiresome task for a human to monitor a surveillance video uninterruptedly. It is necessary to have a system that can monitor a video feed incessantly and has the ability to automatically detect violent activities without the supervision of a human. Violent behavior detection relies on techniques that are used in related fields of computer vision for action recognition, object detection, tracking, and video classification [8,29]. Compared to action recognition and other computer vision applications, there is not much work for violence detection. There are difficulties in detecting the violent action of a person. For example, some actions may look aggressive or violent, but they may actually be normal. Detection of abnormal behavior is somewhat of a subjective nature, so it may somehow be misclassified. The CCTV cameras, through which the surveillance videos are acquired, are mostly of low resolution and occasionally miss the minor details that might be useful for detecting a particular action. There are some methods such as [3,4,27] which used both the visual and audio features for detection of violent actions. However, most of the CCTV surveillance cameras have only visual information and do not include any audio information, although the latter might be valuable for identifying a specific action related to violence. The presented work in this paper uses only visual features for detection of violent behavior.

Most of the existing techniques, for action recognition, used handcrafted based features, which takes a considerable amount of computational resources and are application specific, so they are not generalized to work on different datasets. The rapid progress in deep learning has also helped to achieve many tasks related to computer vision, such as image classification and object detection [22], video classification [21] action recognition [32] and image fusion [28] etc. A deep-learning architecture can well extract features on unseen data. Furthermore, it does not need a complex prior pre-processing on the data. Contrary to hand-crafted features, a deep-learning architecture can learn features in the form of raw-pixels, so it can be applied to various other related tasks without too much altering the architecture.

In this paper, we proposed a novel end-to-end trainable architecture to learn both spatial and temporal features to efficiently detect violent behavior in videos. Our contributions are as follow:

- Instead of using optical flow as motion characteristics, the proposed method used multi-level spatial feature fusion of two sequential frames to incorporate motion information.
- Additional residual layer blocks are added to the pre-trained CNN to learn multi-level fused spatial feature maps that generate a combined feature vector of two sequential frames which incorporates both local and global motion patterns.

The remaining organization of the paper is in following order. Section 2 discusses the related work in the field. Section 3 explains the proposed architecture and implementation details. Section 4 describes the experimental details and a comparison of the proposed scheme with the existing methods. The conclusion of the paper is presented in Sect. 5.

2   Related Work

Many methods for violence detection have been proposed using visual features [8,29] audio features [14], or both audio and visual features [3,4,15]. As most of the surveillance videos do not have audio information, so our work in this paper considers only the visual features. The existing violence detection architectures can be grouped into two categories: the first ones using handcrafted based features and the latter ones using features learned by an end-to-end deep-learning based model. Before the deep-learning era, most state-of-the-art approaches were based on handcrafted features, which were extracted manually, and used a learning model to learn local features, where the outliers are considered as abnormal events. Local features were first introduced for action recognition and most of the techniques were based on these features, including Space-Time Interest Points (STIP) [23], Histogram of Oriented Flows (HOFs) [7], Histogram of Oriented Gradient (HOGs) [6], Bag of Words(BoW) [5] and Motion Scale-Invariant Feature Transform (MoSIFT) [2]. Bermejo et al. [29] proposed a method for detecting violent behavior by combining the Scale Invariant Feature Transform (SIFT) and MoSIFT feature descriptors with (BoW) features. In [9] de Souza et al. compared both (SIFT) [24] and STIP features and presented that having both spatial and temporal features increase the accuracy compared with the approaches using only scale-invariant features. In [18] Hassner et al. introduced a new feature descriptor named Violent Flow (ViF) to classify violent and non-violent videos. To learn the feature descriptor this technique used a simple liner Support Vector Machine (SVM). Datta et al. in [8] used a trajectory-based method to extract motion information and the directions of moving of human limbs to detect violent activities. Several other techniques also used similar motion patterns to extract the spatiotemporal features. Xu et al. in [38] proposed a method using sparse coding by combining the MoSIFT and (BoW) descriptors for feature extraction and used kernel density estimation for selecting low noise features.

Recently, with the development of deep-learning architectures particularly for image classification, a convolutional neural network (CNN) can effectively learn spatial features from images [22]. Following the exceptional capability of CNN for extracting both high-level and low-level image features, Karpahty et al. [21] proposed a method for action recognition by exploiting CNNs to learn spatiotemporal features from videos using the fusion information of multiple frames across time. Simonyan and Zisserman [32] used two separate CNNs, one for learning spatial features and the other for learning temporal features. They used optical flow frames as input and used an SVM for classification by combining the scores from the two networks. Following the work of [21],

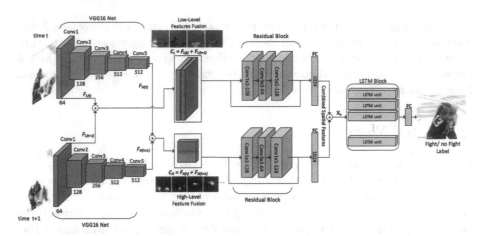

Fig. 1. The architecture of propose violence detection network. The models take two sequential input frames from the video and combine the low and high-level features maps of both frames whereas the additional residual layers are used to learn these fused features of two frames, then the LSTM units learn the temporal patterns in the sequence of two frames to effectively classify the violent actions.

Tran et al. proposed a 3D convolutional network to learn both spatial and temporal information from a video volume but they were unable to learn long temporal dependencies. Donahue et al. [11] provided a full end-to-end trainable model in the form of a Long-term Recurrent Convolutional Network (LRCN), which combined CNN and Recurrent Neural Network (RNN) and used Long Short-Term Memory (LSTM) for temporal feature learning at the end of convolution blocks. Similar to this technique Xinjian et al. [36] proposed a convLSTM architecture for precipitation nowcast by replacing the Fully Connected (FC) layer of the convolutional network with both FC layers and LSTMs or (FC-LSTM). In [25] Medel and Savakis used convLSTMs for the purpose of detecting anomalies in videos. Recently Sultani et al. [35] used a 3D-CNN to extract features from videos, labeled them as positive and negative bags and then incorporated multiple instance rankings to classify videos into abnormal or normal events. In [34], Sudhakaran and Lanz use LSTM along with CNN for detection of violent actions. Similarly, Hanson et al. [17] used bi-directional LSTM instead of simple LSTMs for the same purpose while giving good results.

Based on these above-discussed techniques, this proposed work exploits fusion of spatial feature maps from different layers of CNNs along with LSTM network to efficiently detect violent actions in videos at the frame level. Our method has an ability to run on variable length videos resulting in improved accuracy compared to the existing methods.

3   Proposed Network Architecture

This paper proposes a novel method to detect violent activities in videos using an end-to-end trainable model as shown in Fig. 1, which uses a combination of convolutional neural networks, residual layer blocks and long short-term memory (LSTM) network to learn both spatial and temporal features from the sequence of input frames to classify the videos into violent or non-violent categories. The spatial features from two convective frames are combined using the fusion of low and high-level feature maps to incorporate motion characteristics in the spatial features whereas the LSTM units are used to learn the temporal dependencies between the sequential frames.

3.1   Spatial Feature Learning Through Fusion

In order to extract spatial feature maps from the input video frames, the network takes advantage of transfer learning by using pre-trained VGG-16 [33] network on ImageNet datasets which extracts both low-level and high-level feature maps from input frames. To learn the local and global motion patterns, it is important to include, change of motion information across multiple frames, in this paper instead of using optical flow as motion feature which is computationally complex and results in slow training, spatial feature fusion of sequential video frames is used to assimilate the motion information. The two sequential video frames are used as input to the network. In order to incorporate local motion patterns the low-level features of the frame at time t are combined with low-level features of the frame at time $t + 1$. Similarly, for global motion changes, the high-level features of frame t are combined with the high-level features of the frame at time $t + 1$. Where t is the current timestamp of the input video frame.

Let $F_{L(t)}, F_{L(t+1)} \in \mathbf{R}^{h \times w \times d}$ denote the low-level feature maps of frames at time t and $t + 1$ and $F_{H(t)}, F_{H(t+1)} \in \mathbf{R}^{h \times w \times d}$ represents high-level feature maps of frames at time t and $t + 1$ respectively. Where h, w represents the height and width, and d is the channel depth. The low-level feature concatenation is described by the Eq. (1) whereas high-level features are concatenated by using Eq. (2)

$$C_L = F_{L(t)} + F_{L(t+1)} \tag{1}$$

$$C_H = F_{H(t)} + F_{H(t+1)} \tag{2}$$

Here C_L and C_H represents the combined low-level and high-level features of two sequential input frames, respectively. To further improve the classification accuracy and to add more depth to the network, the fully connected layers of the pre-trained network are replaced by residual layer blocks [19] which are used to learn the fused low-level (C_L) and high-level (C_H) features maps. Separate residual layer blocks are incorporated to learn C_L and C_H as shown in Fig. 1. The output from each residual layer block can be represented by Eqs. 3 and 4.

$$R_1 = f(C_L, \{W_{C_L}\}) + C_L \tag{3}$$

$$R_2 = f(C_H, \{W_{C_H}\}) + C_H \qquad (4)$$

where f is the identity function learned by residual block and W_{C_L} and W_{C_H} are the respective weights of each residual block. The output from fully connected layers of residual layer blocks is then fused together to form a combined spatial feature vector X_s for two sequential input frames. This combined feature vector X_s is then fed to the LSTM unit to learn temporal dependencies.

3.2   Temporal Feature Learning Based on LSTMs

To learn long term temporal dependencies in the input sequences, LSTMs provide very promising results, specially, in the field of natural language processing (NLP), machine translation, image captioning, and other problems involving sequence learning. As videos consist of sequences of image frames, so to successfully classify the videos into violent or non-violent categories, it is important to capture the temporal information by incorporating LSTM units. Unlike simple RNN, LSTM has memory cells and gated inputs through which it selects which input to pass through and which one to forget. This addition of memory cells and gates provided LSTM the ability to overcome the exploding and vanishing gradients problem [20] and made it well suited for the applications of sequence learning. The following Eqs. (5) to (10) shows the working of an LSTM cell unit.

$$f_t = \sigma_g(W_f.[h_{t-1}, x_t] + b_f) \qquad (5)$$

$$i_t = \sigma_g(W_i.[h_{t-1}, x_t] + b_i) \qquad (6)$$

$$\tilde{C} = tanh(W_c.[h_{t-1}, x_t] + b_c) \qquad (7)$$

$$C_t = (f_t \times C_{t-1} + i_t \times \tilde{C}) \qquad (8)$$

$$o_t = \sigma_g(W_o.[h_{t-1}, x_t] + b_o) \qquad (9)$$

$$h_t = o_t \times tanh(C_t) \qquad (10)$$

Where the Eqs. (5), (6) and (9) represent the forgot, input and output gate operations receptively. These gates operations use sigmoid function σ_g to generate their output between 0 and 1. Where the value 0 means the gate is blocking the information and 1 means all information is passing through the gate. Where the parameters W and b are the weights and bias of the respective gates. h_{t-1} is the previous output at timestamp $t-1$ and x_t is the current input at time t. Whereas the Eqs. (7), (8) and (10) describes the cell states and hidden state of LSTM where C_t is memory state of cell and $\tilde{C}$ cell state candidate at time t.

To learn the temporal dependencies between the sequence of video frames, the combined spatial feature vector X_s is then passed to LSTM units to learn global motion changes. The LSTM layer makes a final prediction by averaging label probabilities $Y_t' \in \theta$, for each pair of input frame sequence using a softmax classifier, where θ is a finite set of outcomes. The prediction distribution $P(Y_t)$ is defined as the following Eq. (11).

$$P(Y_t' = j|X_s) = softmax(Y_t') = \frac{e^{Y_t',\theta}}{\sum\limits_{j=0}^{k} e^{Y'^j_t,\theta}} \qquad (11)$$

Here $Y_t' = W_t h_t + b_h$ is the linear prediction layer, W (weight) and b (bias) are trainable parameters and t is current timestamp. The output of LSTM through a softmax layer classifies each frame into violent or non-violent categories. As the model is classifying each frame of the videos as a violent or non-violent frame, so to classify the whole videos, the prediction form each frame is accumulated and used as a threshold to classify at the video level. Figure 1 shows the proposed network model architecture.

3.3 Implementation Details

For the network training, the dataset is first divided into two categories of violent and non-violent videos, and equally spaced frames from each video are extracted and resized to 224×224 pixels. The number of frames in each training video is fixed to 30 frames. If a given video is longer than 30 frames then the intermediate frames are skipped at regular intervals to avoid redundant computation. All the training frames are normalized in the binary range $[0, 1]$. For spatial feature extraction pre-trained weights are used for VGG16 and only the additional residual layer blocks and the LSTM layers are trained on input data whereas the pre-trained model is not trained during the training phase. The residual layer block contains the stack of three convolution layers with a filter size of (1×1), (3×3) and (1×1) where each layer has total of 128, 64 and 128 filters respectively as shown in Fig. 1. The recurrent neural networks take more time to converge because of the sequential inputs and accumulation of gradients [30]. This causes the loss to propagate between the intermediate states, and because of this, the gradient starts to fluctuate and can result in exploding gradient problem, so gradient clipping method [30] is used to solve this problem. Also, dropout and regularization [39] is used between the LSTM cells. The batch size of 5 videos is selected and the shape of the batch data is (b, f, w, h, d) where b is batch size, f is number of frames in a video and w, h and d is the width, height, and depth of input respectively. The initial learning rate of 10^{-5} is used, and the network is trained for 50 epochs. The network is trained using ADAM optimizer to minimize the cross-entropy loss. The LSTM layer has a total number of 1024 units, and it outputs, through a softmax, one of the two classes of videos, i.e., violence or non-violence. As the network is trained using sequential pair of input frames of a video so the final prediction is made at the frame-level and the prediction at video level is calculated by accumulating frame-level predictions using a threshold value which gives maximum accuracy.

4 Experimental Results

In order to check the effectiveness of the proposed network to classify the fight and non-fight videos in different situations, it has been tested on three different popular datasets: Hockey Fights, Crowd Violence and BEHAVE. The network is implemented in Python programming language with the tensorflow framework. The training and testing of the proposed model are done using Nvidia GTX Titan X graphics processing unit. The results of the proposed method are compared with several state-of-the-art violence detection techniques which are based on both hand-crafted features and deep neural network (DNN) based methods. Table 1 shows the testing accuracies of proposed methods and comparison with the existing methods.

Fig. 2. Different samples of violent and non-violent scenes from three datasets. Hockey Fight (1st row), Crowd violence (2nd row) and BEHAVE (3rd row). (a) shows sample frames which do not contain any violent activities whereas (b) corresponds to actions that contain violent actions.

4.1 Datasets

Three popular benchmark datasets are used for testing the effectiveness of proposed model. The first is Hockey Fight dataset [29] which contains violent activities from ice hockey matches of similar context. This dataset contains a total of 1000 videos with an equal number of fight and non-fight videos. The duration of each video is 50 frames. The second dataset "Violent-Flows" introduced in [18] is based on real-world crowd violent activities, e.g. fights in protests or in football matches. This dataset consists of a total of 246 videos each with a duration of 1 to 6 s. The third dataset BEHAVE [1] contains ten different activities performed by a group of people with a static background and no camera movements, similar to fixed CCTV surveillance footages. The activities include meeting in a group, running, fighting, chasing, following, and some other group activities. Each of the four clips has a frame size of 640 × 480 and have different length and contains multiple activities in a single video. However, for the purpose of violence detection, only the video portions which contain fight scenes are taken and labeled as "fights" whereas the rest of the clips are labeled as "non-fights". For the experiments, 20 clips involving fights and 50 clips without

Table 1. The accuracy evaluation of the proposed model and a comparison with the existing methods.

Method	Datasets		
	Hockey Fight	Crowd Violence	BEHAVE
ViF [18]	82.9 ± 0.14%	81.3 ± 0.21%	83.62 ± 0.19%
OViF [13]	87.5 ± 1.7%	88 ± 2.45%	-
MoSIFT+BoW [29]	88.8 ± 0.75%	83.42 ± 8.0%	81.65 ± 0.23 %
MoSIFT+HIK [29]	90.9%	-	-
Mohammadi et al. [26]	-	85.43 ± 0.21%	-
HOG+BoW [29]	88.77 ± 0.73%	57.43 ± 0.37	58.97 ± 0.34
MoSIFT+KDE+SC [38]	94.3 ± 1.68%	89.05 ± 3.26%	87.07 ± 0.13%
Gracia et al. [16]	82.4 ± 0.4%	-	-
Deniz et al. [10]	90.1 ± 0%	-	-
MoI-WLD [40]	96.8 ± 1.04%	93.19 ± 0.12%	88.83 ± 0.11%
LaSIFT+BoW [31]	94.42 ± 2.82%	93.12 ± 8.77%	-
AMDN [37]	89.7 ± 1.13%	84.72 ± 0.17%	84.22 ± 0.17%
Three streams+LSTM [12]	93.9%	-	-
ConvLSTM [34]	97.1 ± 0.55%	94.57 ± 2.34%	-
BiConvLSTM [17] (Spatiotemporal model)	97.9 ± 0.55%	96.32 ± 1.52%	-
Proposed Method	**98.8 ± 0.5%**	**97.3 ± 1.7%**	**94.8 ± 2.3%**

fighting scenes are used from each of the four clips, each with a duration of 2 to 5 s. Figure 2 shows some sample frames from three datasets used.

4.2   Results and Discussion

The 5-fold cross validation method is used to evaluate accuracy of the proposed algorithm where the dataset is divided into five equal size partitions, and four folds are used for training, and one is used for testing. For each test fold, maximum accuracies of each epoch are collected and overall model accuracy is obtained by calculating mean and standard deviation. The cross validation is used to tune the network hyper-parameters. The network model parameters are selected based on maximum accuracy on the validation dataset. Figure 3 shows the graph of testing performance accuracies on three different datasets. For each dataset, the network is run for a total of 50 epochs. In Fig. 3(a) the maximum performance accuracy of the proposed model on Hockey Fight dataset is 98.8%, which occurs first on the 18th epoch. In Fig. 3(b)the test accuracy on Crowd Violence dataset is 97.3% which is occurred first at 25th epoch whereas for the BEHAVE dataset, for which only fighting category is used in this proposed methods, gives the test accuracy of 94.8% as shown in Fig. 3(c). The proposed method provides significant improvement in performance accuracies when compared to existing state-of-the-art methods. Table 1 lists the experimental results and shows extensive comparison with the existing techniques for the detection of violence and demonstrates the superiority of the proposed compared to existing state-of-the-art methods.

The use of feature fusion method and additional residual layer block have significantly improved the performance accuracy of the network architecture. The additional residual layers learn the features of both input frames, which contain combined high-level and combined low-level feature maps of two frames. The recurrent networks with the help of LSTMs then learn the temporal dependencies from combined feature map from two sequential frames whereas the pre-trained VGG16 model helps to extract spatial features and significantly reduce the training times effectively.

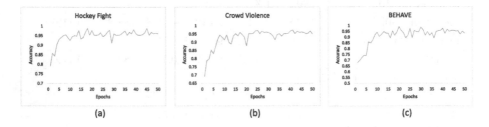

Fig. 3. Test accuracy graphs for three datasets. For (a) Hockey Fight (b) Crowd violence (c) BEHAVE.

5   Conclusion

This paper proposed a novel method for detecting the violent activities in videos by using multi-level spatial feature fusion instead of the optical flow for motion information. The spatial features fusion combined the multi-frame features to provide local and global motion changes pattern between the frames. Additional residual layer blocks, apart from the pre-trained network, that are used to learn these combined spatial features have significantly improved the performance. The LSTM layer block learned the temporal dependencies in the input frame sequence from fused spatial features of two input frames. The proposed method is tested on three standard datasets hockey fight, crowd violence and BEHAVE where the experimental results show significant improvement in performance compared to state-of-the-art violence detection methods

References

1. Blunsden, S., Fisher, R.: The behave video dataset: ground truthed video for multi-person behavior classification. Ann. BMVA **4**(1–12), 4 (2010)

2. Chen, M., Hauptmann, A.: MoSIFT: recognizing human actions in surveillance videos. Research showcase. Computer Science Department, School of Computer Science, Carnegie Mellon University (2009)
3. Cheng, W.H., Chu, W.T., Wu, J.L.: Semantic context detection based on hierarchical audio models. In: Proceedings of the 5th ACM SIGMM International Workshop on Multimedia Information Retrieval, pp. 109–115. ACM (2003)
4. Cristani, M., Bicego, M., Murino, V.: Audio-visual event recognition in surveillance video sequences. IEEE Trans. Multimedia **9**(2), 257–267 (2007)
5. Csurka, G., Dance, C., Fan, L., Willamowski, J., Bray, C.: Visual categorization with bags of keypoints. In: Workshop on Statistical Learning in Computer Vision, ECCV, Prague, vol. 1, pp. 1–2 (2004)
6. Dalal, N., Triggs, B.: Histograms of oriented gradients for human detection. In: International Conference on Computer Vision & Pattern Recognition (CVPR 2005), vol. 1, pp. 886–893. IEEE Computer Society (2005)
7. Dalal, N., Triggs, B., Schmid, C.: Human detection using oriented histograms of flow and appearance. In: Leonardis, A., Bischof, H., Pinz, A. (eds.) ECCV 2006. LNCS, vol. 3952, pp. 428–441. Springer, Heidelberg (2006). https://doi.org/10.1007/11744047_33
8. Datta, A., Shah, M., Lobo, N.D.V.: Person-on-person violence detection in video data. In: Object Recognition Supported by User Interaction for Service Robots. vol. 1, pp. 433–438. IEEE (2002)
9. De Souza, F.D., Chavez, G.C., do Valle Jr, E.A., Araújo, A.D.A.: Violence detection in video using spatio-temporal features. In: 2010 23rd SIBGRAPI Conference on Graphics, Patterns and Images, pp. 224–230. IEEE (2010)
10. Deniz, O., Serrano, I., Bueno, G., Kim, T.K.: Fast violence detection in video. In: 2014 International Conference on Computer Vision Theory and Applications (VISAPP), vol. 2, pp. 478–485. IEEE (2014)
11. Donahue, J., et al.: Long-term recurrent convolutional networks for visual recognition and description. In: Proceedings of the IEEE Conference on Computer Vision and Pattern Recognition, pp. 2625–2634 (2015)
12. Dong, Z., Qin, J., Wang, Y.: Multi-stream deep networks for person to person violence detection in videos. In: Tan, T., Li, X., Chen, X., Zhou, J., Yang, J., Cheng, H. (eds.) CCPR 2016. CCIS, vol. 662, pp. 517–531. Springer, Singapore (2016). https://doi.org/10.1007/978-981-10-3002-4_43
13. Gao, Y., Liu, H., Sun, X., Wang, C., Liu, Y.: Violence detection using oriented violent flows. Image Vis. Comput. **48**, 37–41 (2016)
14. Giannakopoulos, T., Pikrakis, A., Theodoridis, S.: A multi-class audio classification method with respect to violent content in movies using Bayesian networks. In: 2007 IEEE 9th Workshop on Multimedia Signal Processing, pp. 90–93. IEEE (2007)
15. Giannakopoulos, T., Pikrakis, A., Theodoridis, S.: A multimodal approach to violence detection in video sharing sites. In: 2010 20th International Conference on Pattern Recognition, pp. 3244–3247. IEEE (2010)
16. Gracia, I.S., Suarez, O.D., Garcia, G.B., Kim, T.K.: Fast fight detection. PloS One **10**(4), e0120448 (2015)
17. Hanson, A., Pnvr, K., Krishnagopal, S., Davis, L.: Bidirectional convolutional LSTM for the detection of violence in videos. In: Proceedings of the European Conference on Computer Vision (ECCV) (2018)
18. Hassner, T., Itcher, Y., Kliper-Gross, O.: Violent flows: real-time detection of violent crowd behavior. In: 2012 IEEE Computer Society Conference on Computer Vision and Pattern Recognition Workshops, pp. 1–6. IEEE (2012)

19. He, K., Zhang, X., Ren, S., Sun, J.: Deep residual learning for image recognition. In: Proceedings of the IEEE Conference on Computer Vision and Pattern Recognition, pp. 770–778 (2016)
20. Hochreiter, S., Schmidhuber, J.: Long short-term memory. Neural Comput. 9(8), 1735–1780 (1997)
21. Karpathy, A., Toderici, G., Shetty, S., Leung, T., Sukthankar, R., Fei-Fei, L.: Large-scale video classification with convolutional neural networks. In: Proceedings of the IEEE Conference on Computer Vision and Pattern Recognition, pp. 1725–1732 (2014)
22. Krizhevsky, A., Sutskever, I., Hinton, G.E.: ImageNet classification with deep convolutional neural networks. In: Advances in Neural Information Processing Systems, pp. 1097–1105 (2012)
23. Laptev, I.: On space-time interest points. Int. J. Comput. Vis. 64(2–3), 107–123 (2005)
24. Lowe, D.G.: Distinctive image features from scale-invariant keypoints. Int. J. Comput. Vis. 60(2), 91–110 (2004)
25. Medel, J.R., Savakis, A.: Anomaly detection in video using predictive convolutional long short-term memory networks. arXiv preprint. arXiv:1612.00390 (2016)
26. Mohammadi, S., Kiani, H., Perina, A., Murino, V.: Violence detection in crowded scenes using substantial derivative. In: 2015 12th IEEE International Conference on Advanced Video and Signal Based Surveillance (AVSS), pp. 1–6. IEEE (2015)
27. Mu, G., Cao, H., Jin, Q.: Violent scene detection using convolutional neural networks and deep audio features. In: Tan, T., Li, X., Chen, X., Zhou, J., Yang, J., Cheng, H. (eds.) CCPR 2016. CCIS, vol. 663, pp. 451–463. Springer, Singapore (2016). https://doi.org/10.1007/978-981-10-3005-5_37
28. Mustafa, H.T., Yang, J., Zareapoor, M.: Multi-scale convolutional neural network for multi-focus image fusion. Image Vis. Comput. 85, 26–35 (2019)
29. Bermejo Nievas, E., Deniz Suarez, O., Bueno García, G., Sukthankar, R.: Violence detection in video using computer vision techniques. In: Real, P., Diaz-Pernil, D., Molina-Abril, H., Berciano, A., Kropatsch, W. (eds.) CAIP 2011. LNCS, vol. 6855, pp. 332–339. Springer, Heidelberg (2011). https://doi.org/10.1007/978-3-642-23678-5_39
30. Pascanu, R., Mikolov, T., Bengio, Y.: On the difficulty of training recurrent neural networks. In: International Conference on Machine Learning, pp. 1310–1318 (2013)
31. Senst, T., Eiselein, V., Kuhn, A., Sikora, T.: Crowd violence detection using global motion-compensated lagrangian features and scale-sensitive video-level representation. IEEE Trans. Inf. Forensics Secur. 12(12), 2945–2956 (2017)
32. Simonyan, K., Zisserman, A.: Two-stream convolutional networks for action recognition in videos. In: Advances in Neural Information Processing Systems, pp. 568–576 (2014)
33. Simonyan, K., Zisserman, A.: Very deep convolutional networks for large-scale image recognition. arXiv preprint. arXiv:1409.1556 (2014)
34. Sudhakaran, S., Lanz, O.: Learning to detect violent videos using convolutional long short-term memory. In: 2017 14th IEEE International Conference on Advanced Video and Signal Based Surveillance (AVSS), pp. 1–6. IEEE (2017)
35. Sultani, W., Chen, C., Shah, M.: Real-world anomaly detection in surveillance videos. In: Proceedings of the IEEE Conference on Computer Vision and Pattern Recognition, pp. 6479–6488 (2018)
36. Xingjian, S., Chen, Z., Wang, H., Yeung, D.Y., Wong, W.K., Woo, W.C.: Convolutional LSTM network: a machine learning approach for precipitation nowcasting. In: Advances in Neural Information Processing Systems, pp. 802–810 (2015)

37. Xu, D., Yan, Y., Ricci, E., Sebe, N.: Detecting anomalous events in videos by learning deep representations of appearance and motion. Comput. Vis. Image Underst. **156**, 117–127 (2017)
38. Xu, L., Gong, C., Yang, J., Wu, Q., Yao, L.: Violent video detection based on MoSIFT feature and sparse coding. In: 2014 IEEE International Conference on Acoustics, Speech and Signal Processing (ICASSP), pp. 3538–3542. IEEE (2014)
39. Zaremba, W., Sutskever, I., Vinyals, O.: Recurrent neural network regularization. arXiv preprint. arXiv:1409.2329 (2014)
40. Zhang, T., Jia, W., He, X., Yang, J.: Discriminative dictionary learning with motion weber local descriptor for violence detection. IEEE Trans. Circuits Syst. Video Technol. **27**(3), 696–709 (2016)

Learning to Navigate in Human Environments via Deep Reinforcement Learning

Xingyuan Gao[1,2], Shiying Sun[1(✉)], Xiaoguang Zhao[1], and Min Tan[1]

[1] The State Key Laboratory of Management and Control for Complex Systems, Institute of Automation, Chinese Academy of Sciences, Beijing, China
{gaoxingyuan2016,sunshiying2013,xiaoguang.zhao,min.tan}@ia.ac.cn
[2] University of Chinese Academy of Sciences, Beijing, China

Abstract. Mobile robots have been widely applied in human populated environments. To interact with humans, the robots require the capacity to navigate safely and efficiently in complex environments. Recent works have successfully applied reinforcement learning to learn socially normative navigation behaviors. However, they mostly focus on modeling human-robot cooperations and neglect complex interactions between pedestrians. In addition, these methods are implemented using assumptions of perfect sensing about the states of pedestrians, which makes the model less robust to the perception uncertainty. This work presents a novel algorithm to learn an efficient navigation policy that exhibits socially normative navigation behaviors. We propose to employ convolutional social pooling to jointly capture human-robot cooperations and inter-human interactions in an actor-critic reinforcement learning framework. In addition, we propose to focus on partial observability in socially normative navigation. Our model is capable to learn the representation of unobservable states with recurrent neural networks and further improves the stability of the algorithm. Experimental results show that the proposed learning algorithm enables robots to learn socially normative navigation behaviors and achieves a better performance than state-of-the-art methods.

Keywords: Socially normative navigation · Reinforcement learning

1 Introduction

In recent years, mobile robots have been developed to provide mobile services in human populated environments, such as shopping malls and subway stations. The task requires the robot not only to be socially normative with respect to person's space but also to navigate efficiently in crowded environments.

This work is partially supported by the National Natural Science Foundation of China under Grants 61673378 and 61421004.

Different from traditional navigation methods, in "socially normative naviga-tion", pedestrians are considered as more than dynamic obstacles, but rather as rational agents which maintain social relations and comply with social norms.

A usual method [1,2] on socially normative navigation treats pedestrians as dynamic obstacles and uses hand-crafted rules for collision avoidance. However, it is infeasible to program the complex behaviors manually and these methods do not consider human behaviors. To this end, some works [3,4] try to find a collision-free path by forecasting the future states of pedestrians according to pedestrians' motion. Nevertheless, in dense crowds, the set of potential paths may occupy most of the space, which causes the freezing robot problem [5]. A lot of works [6,7] are presented to capture the interdependencies of the trajectories and learn human navigation behaviors. However, these methods suffer from high computational cost. Thus, recent works have applied reinforcement learning (RL) to solve the above issues.

Although several works [8–11] successfully apply RL to the task of socially normative navigation and present good performance, there are some issues to address. First, existing methods [8–10] focus on modeling the effect of pedestrian motion on robot, but neglect complex interactions between pedestrians. Jointly capturing human-robot cooperations and inter-human interactions is essential for the robot to navigate safely and efficiently in complex environments. To this end, Chen et al. [11] propose to learn the collective importance of neighboring humans with a self-attention mechanism. However, the method relies on predicting the future states of pedestrians to find an action form the state-value function, which becomes infeasible in complex environments where the behaviors of pedestrians are difficult to predict. What's more, the methods [8–11] rely on perfect sensors to obtain the states of pedestrians. However, the assumption does not hold in real world. Many sources can lead to pedestrian tracking failures, such as sen-sor limitations, occlusions and perception uncertainty, which results in partial observability. What's more, pedestrians' intended goal position, preferred speed is unobservable. Existing methods [8–11] are unable to infer unobservable states since inferring the unobservable states often relies on history information, which makes the algorithm less robust to the partial observability.

Inspired by the existing methods [8–11], in this work, we present a novel framework to address the above issues of socially normative navigation using RL. The contributions of this work are as follows: (1) We propose to use convolutional social pooling [12] to encode the states of pedestrians and robot. Our model can handle an arbitrary number of pedestrians while jointly capturing human-robot cooperations and inter-human relations. (2) We propose to focus on partial observability in socially normative navigation and employ a recurrent neural network (RNN) architecture called gated recurrent unit (GRU) [13] to infer the unobservable states and further improve the robustness of algorithm. (3) The simulation results show that our proposed model achieves a better performance than state-of-the-art methods.

The paper is organized as follows: In Sect. 2, we introduce the problem for-mulation. In Sect. 3, we present the details of our approach. In Sect. 4, we detail our experiments and discuss the experiment results. Finally, the conclusions are drawn in Sect. 5.

2 Problem Formulation

2.1 Problem Formulation

The task of socially normative navigation is to steer the robot from current position to a desired goal in pedestrian-rich environments, which can be formulated as a sequential decision making problem in a RL framework [8–11]. Let s_t, a_t denote robot's state and action at timestep t. Denote b_t^i the observed state of a nearby pedestrian i. For each agent (including robot and pedestrian) i, the position and velocity can be described by $p^i = [p_x^i, p_y^i]$ and $v^i = [v_x^i, v_y^i]$ in 2D. The joint observation states s_t^{jn} can be divided into two parts: $s_t^{jn} = [s_t, b_t]$, where $s = [p^0, p_g^0, v^0, v_{pref}^0, r^0]$ denotes robot's current position, goal position, velocity, preferred speed and radius; $b = [b^1, ..., b^n]$ refers to the observed state of n pedestrians in the field-of-view, where $b^i = [p^i, v^i, r^i]$. The action a_t is robot's velocity.

The goal of RL is to learn a policy $\pi_\theta : s_t^{jn} \mapsto a_t$ which maximizes the expected discounted reward:

$$J = \mathbb{E}_\tau \left[\sum_{t=1}^\infty \gamma^{t-1} R(s_t^{jn}, a_t) \right] \tag{1}$$

where $\tau = (s_1^{jn}, a_1, ...)$ denotes the whole trajectory and $a_t \sim \pi_\theta(\cdot|s_t^{jn})$. $R(s_t^{jn}, a_t)$ is the reward received. $\gamma \in (0, 1)$ is a discount factor.

As mentioned in [10], previous algorithms [8,9,11] employ a state-value function $V(s_t^{jn})$ to estimate the expected reward at state s_t^{jn}. However, the optimal policy $\pi^*(s_t^{jn})$ can only be extracted indirectly from value function $V^*(s_t^{jn})$:

$$\pi^*(s_t^{jn}) = \arg\max_{a_t} R(s_t^{jn}, a_t) + \gamma \int_{s_{t+1}^{jn}} P(s_{t+1}^{jn}|s_t^{jn}, a_t)V^*(s_{t+1}^{jn})ds_{t+1}^{jn} \tag{2}$$

A major challenge in finding the optimal policy is that the state-transition probability $P(s_{t+1}^{jn}|s_t^{jn}, a_t)$ is unknown. In order to avoid computing integrals in (2), previous algorithms estimate the next state s_{t+1}^{jn} by assuming that pedestrians continue their current velocities for a sufficiently large duration. However, the assumption of constant velocity neglects the effects of inter-human relations, which is not valid in dense crowds [10].

2.2 Policy-Based Learning

To overcome the shortcomings of the assumption of constant velocity, we consider a recently proposed actor-critic framework called Proximal Policy Optimization (PPO) [14,15] instead of using a state-value function. What's more, our model contains a RNN architecture, which will be detailed in Sect. 3. PPO has two improvements which make it convenient to facilitate the use of RNN. First, PPO algorithm relies only on first order gradients. Second, PPO uses a truncated version of generalized advantage estimation with K-steps returns to support variable length episodes:

$$\hat{A}_t = \delta_t + (\gamma\lambda)\delta_{t+1} + ... + ... + (\gamma\lambda)^{K-t+1}\delta_{K-1} \tag{3}$$

where

$$\delta_t = r_t + \gamma V(s_{t+1}^{jn}) - V(s_t^{jn}) \tag{4}$$

where K varies from episode to episode. t specifies the timestep index in $[0, K]$.

Given a current policy $\pi_{\theta_{old}}$, let the probability ratio $r_t(\theta) = \frac{\pi_\theta(a_t|s_t^{jn})}{\pi_{\theta_{old}}(a_t|s_t^{jn})}$, PPO optimizes the policy by maximizing the following surrogate loss function:

$$L_t^{clip}(\theta) = \hat{\mathbb{E}}_t\big[\min(r_t(\theta)\hat{A}_t, \text{clip}(r_t(\theta), 1-\epsilon, 1+\epsilon)\hat{A}_t)\big] \tag{5}$$

where the first term inside the min is an approximation of the expected advantages, and the second term removes the incentive for moving r_t outside of the interval $[1-\epsilon, 1+\epsilon]$ by clipping the probability ratio.

To approximate policy and value function with a neural network architecture, the objective function is formulated to combine the policy surrogate loss and a value function error term, which is maximized:

$$L_t^{clip+vs+s}(\theta) = \hat{\mathbb{E}}_t\big[L_t^{clip}(\theta) - c_1 L_t^{vf}(\theta) + c_2 S[\pi_\theta](s_t^{jn})\big] \tag{6}$$

where S denotes an entropy bonus added to ensure sufficient exploration, and L_t^{vf} is a squared-error loss $(V_\theta(s_t^{jn}) - V_t^{targ})^2$, and c_1, c_2 are hyper-parameters.

3   Approach

In this section, first, we introduce the basic concepts in our RL framework. Second, we describe the architecture of our model. Finally, we describe the training framework and detail the training setup.

3.1   Basic Concepts

We introduce the basic concepts in our RL framework, including state space, action space and reward function.

(1) State Space: Different from the coordinate frame in [8–11], this work uses a robot-centric coordinate frame with the origin at current robot position, and the x-axis points in the direction of linear velocity of the robot. The states of the robot and per pedestrian i through coordinate transformation are parameterized:

$$\tilde{s} = [\tilde{p}_{gx}^0, \tilde{p}_{gy}^0, v_{pref}^0, \tilde{v}^0, r^0] \tag{7}$$

$$\tilde{b}^i = [\tilde{p}_x^i, \tilde{p}_y^i, \tilde{v}_x^i, \tilde{v}_y^i, r^i] \tag{8}$$

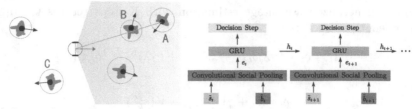

(a) Sensor limitations and occlusion- (b) GRU unrolled for 2 timesteps
s in our simulation

Fig. 1. (a): Sensor limitations and occlusions in our simulation. It is assumed that only the pedestrians in front of the robot can be detected, which simulates the restricted field-of-view of sensors. The pedestrian A is regarded as occluded and can not be detected if the line connecting pedestrian A and robot intersects the circle which is centered at pedestrian B with its radius. (b): GRU unrolled for 2 timesteps. At each time, GRU accepts the final encodings e_t and stores the important information in h_t for next action. So the decision step can utilize information about past.

where $[\tilde{p}^0_{gx}, \tilde{p}^0_{gy}]$ is the goal position of robot in robot-centric coordinate frame, $\tilde{v}^0$ is the translational velocity of the robot.

The previous works [8–11] are based on the assumption of perfect sensing about the states of pedestrians, which is not valid in in reality. In our simulation, we consider the sensor limitations and occlusions which widely exist in real world, as illustrated in Fig. 1(a).

(2) Action Space: The robot's action consists of a translational velocity and change in heading angle. Similarly to [10], the action space is discretized into 11 permissible discrete velocity vectors: with a translational velocity of v_{pref}, there are 5 headings evenly spaced between $\pm\pi/6$, for translational velocity of $0.5v_{pref}$ and 0 the heading choices are $[-\pi/6, 0, \pi/6]$. Although discretizing the action space may lose some information about the structure of the action domain, it makes the algorithm convenient to combine with other obstacle avoidance algorithms in the future work, such as [16].

(3) Reward Function: Inspired by [8], a reward function is designed to guide the robot to achieve the goal without collisions, which awards the robot for reaching its goal and penalizes the robot for colliding with pedestrians or intruding pedestrians' intimate space.

$$R_t(s_t^{jn}, a_t) = \begin{cases} -0.25 & if \quad d_t^{cp} \leqslant 0 \\ -0.1 + 0.5 \cdot d_t^{cp} & if \quad d_t^{cp} < 0.2 \\ 1 & if \quad p^0 = p_g^0 \\ 0 & otherwise \end{cases} \tag{9}$$

where d_t^{cp} is the minimum distance between robot and the closest pedestrian.

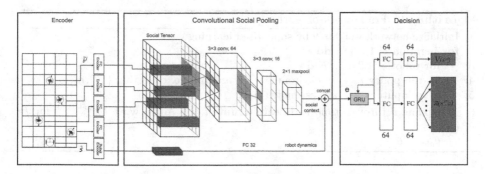

Fig. 2. The total architecture of our model. The pedestrian encoder (FC encoder) is a fully connected layer with shared weights. The convolutional social pooling layers model the human-robot cooperations and inter-human interactions. In decision step, the final encodings are fed into the GRU layer, as unrolled for 2 timesteps in Fig. 1(b).

3.2   Network Architecture

The total architecture of our model is shown in Fig. 2. We introduce our network from the following three aspects:

(1) Convolutional Social Pooling Module: The number of surrounding pedestrians can vary dramatically in different scenes, which certainly brings a great challenge to many learning-based planning methods that require a fixed-size input [10]. Everett et al. [10] propose to feed the states of surrounding pedestrians into LSTMs and take the LSTM's final hidden state as a fixed-length, encoded state of the pedestrians. Although the LSTM encoder can handle an arbitrary number of agent inputs, it fails to capture the inter-human interactions in the scene. Chen et al. [11] propose to aggregate the states into a fixed-length embedding vector by a self-attention mechanism.

Inspired by [12], we propose to extend convolutional social pooling for robustly learning inter-human interactions. We set up our social tensor by defining a grid based on the sensor bandwidth. As shown in Fig. 2, a 9×5 spatial grid is defined in front of the robot, where the grids are separated by a distance of 1 m which approximately equals the diameter (size) of a pedestrian. The state of each pedestrian $\tilde{b}^i$ is fed into a fully connected layer with a hidden layer of 64 units and Leaky ReLU nonlinearity to capture the dynamics of pedestrian. The social tensor is formed by populating this grid with the feature vector according to the location of pedestrians. By defining the social tensor, the model can encode the states of a variable number of pedestrians into a fixed-length vector. Aiming to obtain local features within the spatial grid of the social tensor, two 3×3 convolutional layers are applied to the social tensor. The output of the convolutional layer is fed into a 2×1 max-pooling layer to add local translational invariance. The output of max-pooling layer is denoted as social context encoding which captures inter-human interactions. In addition, the state of the robot $\tilde{s}$ is passed through a fully connected layer with a hidden layer of 32 units and Leaky ReLU nonlinearity to capture the dynamics encoding of robot.

Algorithm 1. Framework of learning

1: Initialize network weights θ by supervised learning
2: **for** iteration = 1,2,3... **do**
3:     **for** robot = 1,2,3,..., N **do**
4:         run policy $\pi_{\theta_{old}}$ in environment for an episode, collecting $\{s_t^{jn}, a_t, r_t\}$
5:         compute advantage estimates $\hat{A}_1...$
6:     Update θ through time with learning rate l_r by Adam w.r.t $L^{clip+vs+s}$ for F epochs
7:     $\theta_{old} \leftarrow \theta$

To jointly model human-robot cooperations and inter-human interactions, the two encodings are concatenated to form the final encoding for the decision step.

(2) Recurrent Module: Due to the existence of sensor limitations, occlusions and perception uncertainty, it seems difficult to perfectly obtain the states of surrounding pedestrians. What's more, the pedestrians' intended goal position, preferred speed is unobservable. The reasons stated above model the task as a partially-observable sequential decision making problem. It is challenging for the models in [8–11] to infer the unobservable states since inferring the unobservable states often relies on history.

Inspired by recent works [14, 17, 18], we add a GRU layer before the final fully connected layers, as shown in Fig. 2. The GRU unrolled is shown in Fig. 1(b). The GRU layer stores important information in its hidden states for making decision on the next action, which helps to infer unobservable state and capture long-term dependency on history.

(3) Decision Module: In decision step, the final encodings are fed into the GRU. The final hidden state is passed through two parallel fully connected layers with two hidden layers of 64 units and tanh nonlinearities. The outputs are policy $\pi(s_t^{jn})$ represented as discrete probability distribution across actions and a state-value function $V(s_t^{jn})$.

3.3   Training Details

(1) Training Scheme: The learning scheme is described in Algorithm 1 (adapted from [14]). Inspired by [8–11], the network is first initialized by supervised learning on a set of state-action-value pairs generated by GA3C-CADRL [10]. The loss of supervised learning phase consists of square-error loss on the value output and cross-entropy loss on the policy output. The initialization step enables the robot to reach the goal in the scenarios with few pedestrians while obtaining positive reward, which improves the convergence ability of the algorithm. The second training step improves the solution with PPO [14, 15]. In each iteration, each of N robots simultaneously follows the same policy $\pi_{\theta_{old}}$ to complete an episode. Then the advantages $\hat{A}_1...$ are estimated using Eq. (3) with state-value function $V(s_t^{jn})$. The collected episodes are used to construct the surrogate loss and the updates begin at the beginning of the episode and proceed forward

through time to the end of the episode for training GRU. The loss is optimized with the Adam [19] optimizer for F epochs.

(2) Training Scenarios: To improve the generalization ability of the model, experiences are generated from simulations of randomly-generated scenarios. In each episode, the robot is generated with fixed initial position, but randomly selected orientation within a 10.0×10.0 square domain. Following current learned policy, the robot tries to navigate to a randomly-sampled goal. The simulated pedestrians are controlled by a random assortment of policies such as ORCA [20] and Social Force [21] to reach the randomly-generated goals. The radius of pedestrians $r \in [0.2, 0.5]m$. The number of the pedestrians in scenarios varies from 2 to 8. In addition, to avoid the simple cases where the robot easily reaches the goal without encountering with pedestrians, the goals are sampled randomly at a distance of more than 5 m to the initial position. The complex training scenarios lead the robot to explore the high-dimensional observation space and improve the robustness of the model.

4   Experiment

This section is organized as follows: First, the details of computation are provided. Second, qualitative experiments are carried out in simulation. Third, experiment metrics and quantitative experiment results are discussed. We refer to our whole model as SNNRL-GRU. To demonstrate the benefit of GRU layer, a copy of our model without GRU (SNNRL) is trained for comparison.

4.1   Computational Details

We implement the model with Tensorflow [22] and train it on a computer with an NVIDIA GTX 1080 graphics card. The offline training takes about 28 h to complete $2.2 \cdot 10^7$ timesteps for the policy to converge. A query of trained model only takes 1.8 ms on an i7-7700K CPU.

4.2   Qualitative Experiments

Qualitative experiments are carried out to evaluate the performance of the algorithm. The trajectories obtained by different algorithms are compared in the same crossing scenario, as illustrated in Fig. 3. In qualitative experiments, aiming to generate the same pedestrian trajectories for comparison, we set the robot invisible to the pedestrians. That means the pedestrians will not cooperate with the robot.

The performance of each algorithm can be roughly evaluated by navigation time and clearance between robot and pedestrians. As shown in Fig. 3, CADRL [8] only considers one neighbor pedestrian, which leads the robot to take longer path for passing on the right side of crowds. The robot controlled by GA3C-CADRL [10] slows down in 6.0 s–9.0 s, hesitating about which side to pass the crowds, which makes the robot maintain smaller clearance to the pedestrians. While, our SNNRL-GRU recognizes the inter-human interactions and finds an efficient and safe path to navigate to the goal with the shortest time.

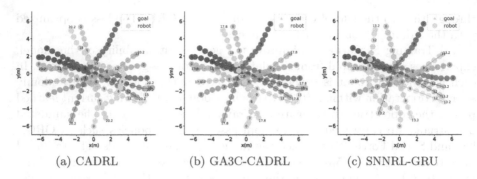

(a) CADRL   (b) GA3C-CADRL   (c) SNNRL-GRU

Fig. 3. The trajectories obtained by different algorithms. The goal of robot is indicated by a yellow triangle. The trajectory of robot is visualized with a pink circle. The circles of other colors represent the trajectories of pedestrians and lighten as time increases. The numbers indicate the time at agent's position. In addiction, the trajectories are recorded until the robot reaches the goal. (a): trajectories of using policy CADRL with navigation time 20.2 s. (b): trajectories of using GA3C-CADRL with navigation time 17.8 s (c): trajectories of using our SNNRL-GRU with navigation time 13.2 s. (Color figure online)

4.3 Experiment Metrics

In order to evaluate quantitatively the performance of our algorithm and compare the different algorithms, the following evaluation metrics are defined:

(1) Success rates: The percentage of cases where the robot reaches their goals within a certain time limit without colliding with pedestrians.
(2) Extra time to goal: The difference between the travel time that robot spends to reach the goal and the lower bound of the travel time (going straight toward the goal at preferred speed [8]).
(3) Proxemic intrusions (PI): According to the distance between robot and the closest pedestrian, a percentage of time spent in pedestrian's intimate zone for a complete trajectory is defined by:

$$PI = \frac{1}{M} \sum_{t=1}^{M} \mathbb{1}(\|p_t^0 - p_t^{cp}\|_2 - r^0 - r^{cp} < 0.2) \tag{10}$$

where M represents the total timesteps in a complete trajectory. p_t^{cp}, r^{cp} denote the position of the closest pedestrian to the robot and its radius at timestep t. $\mathbb{1}(\cdot)$ is the indicator function.

4.4 Quantitative Experiments

We implement three state-of-the-art methods, ORCA [20], CADRL [8] and GA3C-CADRL [10] as baseline method to present a comparison with our algorithm. The training process of the two learning-based algorithms (CADRL and

Table 1. Results of different algorithms in different scenes.

Num[a]	Method	Success (%)	Collision (%)	Stuck (%)	Extra time to goal (s)[b] [Avg / 75th / 90th pctl]	PI(%)
2	ORCA	75.0	25.0	0.0	0.684 / 0.789 / 1.383	12.476
	CADRL	97.6	2.2	0.2	1.031 / 1.549 / 2.182	3.509
	GA3C-CADRL	98.4	1.6	0.0	0.915 / 1.415 / 1.981	5.387
	SNNRL-GRU	97.8	2.2	0.0	1.259 / 1.746 / 2.259	1.450
	SNNRL	97.4	2.4	0.2	1.331 / 1.944 / 2.403	1.631
5	ORCA	61.2	38.8	0.0	0.878 / 1.079 / 1.846	11.593
	CADRL	84.4	11.2	4.4	2.168 / 2.937 / 4.827	3.599
	GA3C-CADRL	90.2	7.6	2.2	2.042 / 2.984 / 4.133	4.274
	SNNRL-GRU	96.0	3.8	0.2	2.373 / 3.375 / 4.435	1.537
	SNNRL	93.4	6.2	0.4	2.614 / 3.611 / 4.834	1.416
8	ORCA	49.8	50.2	0.0	1.135 / 1.420 / 2.027	12.352
	CADRL	76.4	12.4	11.2	3.234 / 4.618 / 6.357	4.173
	GA3C-CADRL	86.4	8.2	5.4	3.338 / 4.622 / 6.561	3.713
	SNNRL-GRU	95.0	4.8	0.2	3.473 / 4.745 / 6.835	1.807
	SNNRL	91.0	8.6	0.4	3.621 / 5.038 / 7.184	1.914

[a] Num represents the number of pedestrians in different scenes.
[b] pctl is the abbreviation of percentile which is used to measure the dispersion degree of experiment results.

GA3C-CADRL) is conducted under the same simulation setup, except that CADRL is trained in a two-agent environment since it does not support multi-agent training.

For the sake of comparing the performances of different algorithms, we define 3 different test scenes with different numbers of pedestrians, as illustrated in Table 1. Each pedestrian is controlled by a randomly selected policy such as ORCA, Social Force and zero velocity. The experiments of each algorithm are conducted under the same 500 test cases.

The test results obtained by different algorithms are listed in Table 1. As can be seen, compared to ORCA [20], three learning-based algorithms take more time to reach the goal as the algorithms try to adapt their pathes to people. However, ORCA achieves a very low success rate due to the short-sighted and conservative behaviors. In $n = 2$ pedestrians, our algorithm gets a similar performance with other learning-based algorithms. GA3C-CADRL is slightly better. However, with the increase of number of pedestrians, the advantages of our proposed algorithm become more obvious. The success rate of CARDL drops to 84.4% when $n = 5$. As described in [8], its minimax implementation is limited in that it only considers one neighbor at a time. The lower success rate shows the importance of considering all the pedestrians simultaneously. When $n = 8$, our model significantly outperforms the other algorithms. The success rate of GA3C-CADRL drops to 86.4%, while our SNNRL-GRU remains 95%. What's more, our algorithm maintains less proxemic intrusions (PI) across all the test cases. The results demonstrate that our proposed algorithm is more applicable to learn a policy that exhibits socially normative navigation behaviors. By comparing the experiment results of two copies of our model, it can be concluded that the GRU layer makes the model more robust.

5   Conclusions

In this paper, we propose a novel algorithm to learn a policy that exhibits socially normative navigation behaviors. Our model uses a convolutional social pooling layer that robustly models human-robot cooperations and complex interactions between pedestrians. Moreover, we focus on partial observability in socially normative navigation. We employ a recurrent policy that infers unobservable states from the history information and further improves the robustness of algorithm. The experiment results show that our approach outperforms the state-of-the-art methods in complex scenarios.

References

1. Kirby, R., Simmons, R., Forlizzi, J.: COMPANION: a constraint-optimizing method for person-acceptable navigation. In: IEEE International Symposium on Robot and Human Interactive Communication, Toyama, pp. 607–612 (2009)
2. Phillips, M., Likhachev, M.: SIPP: safe interval path planning for dynamic environments. In: IEEE International Conference on Robotics and Automation, Shanghai, pp. 5628–5635 (2011)
3. Unhelkar, V.V., Pérez-D'Arpino, C., Stirling, L., Shah, J.A.: Human-robot co-navigation using anticipatory indicators of human walking motion. In: IEEE International Conference on Robotics and Automation, Seattle, pp. 6183–6190 (2015)
4. Aoude, G.S., et al.: Probabilistically safe motion planning to avoid dynamic obstacles with uncertain motion patterns. Auton. Robots 35(1), 51–76 (2013)
5. Trautman, P., Krause, A.: Unfreezing the robot: navigation in dense, interacting crowds. In: IEEE International Conference on Intelligent Robots and Systems, Taipei, pp. 797–803 (2010)
6. Kuderer, M., Kretzschmar, H., Sprunk, C., Burgard, W.: Feature based prediction of trajectories for socially compliant navigation. In: Robotics: Science and Systems (2012)
7. Kretzschmar, H., Spies, M., Sprunk, C., Burgard, W.: Socially compliant mobile robot navigation via inverse reinforcement learning. Int. J. Robot. Res. 35(4), 1289–1307 (2016)
8. Chen, Y.F., Liu, M., Everett, M., How, J.P.: Decentralized non-communicating multiagent collision avoidance with deep reinforcement learning. In: IEEE International Conference on Robotics and Automation, Singapore, pp. 285–292 (2017)
9. Chen, Y.F., Everett, M., Liu, M., How, J.P.: Socially aware motion planning with deep reinforcement learning. In: IEEE International Conference on Intelligent Robots and Systems, Vancouver, BC, pp. 1343–1350 (2017)
10. Everett, M., Chen Y.F., How, J.P.: Motion planning among dynamic, decision-making agents with deep reinforcement learning. In: IEEE International Conference on Intelligent Robots and Systems, Madrid, pp. 3052–3059 (2018)

11. Chen, C., Liu, Y., Kreiss, S., Alahi, A.: Crowd-robot interaction: crowd-aware robot navigation with attention-based deep reinforcement learning. In: IEEE International Conference on Robotics and Automation, Montreal, pp. 6015–6022 (2019)
12. Deo, N., Trivedi, M.M.: Convolutional social pooling for vehicle trajectory prediction. In: IEEE Conference on Computer Vision and Pattern Recognition. pp. 1468–1476 (2018)
13. Cho, K., Van Merrienboer, B., Gulcehre, C.: Learning phrase representations using RNN encoder-decoder for statistical machine translation. arXiv preprint (2014). arXiv:1406.1078
14. Schulman, J., Wolski, F., Dhariwal, P., Radford, A., Klimov, O.: Proximal policy optimization algorithms. arXiv preprint (2017). arXiv:1707.06347
15. Heess, N., et al.: Emergence of locomotion behaviours in rich environments. arXiv preprint (2017). arXiv:1707.02286
16. Lu, D.V., Hershberger D., Smart, W.D.: Layered costmaps for context-sensitive navigation. In: IEEE International Conference on Intelligent Robots and Systems, Chicago, IL, pp. 709–715 (2014)
17. Heess, N., Hunt, J.J., Lillicrap, T.P., Silver, D.: Memory-based control with recurrent neural networks. arXiv preprint (2015). arXiv:1512.04455
18. Mnih, V., Badia, A.P., Lillicrap, T.P., et al.: Asynchronous methods for deep reinforcement learning. In: International Conference on Machine Learning, pp. 1928–1937 (2016)
19. Kingma, D., Ba, J.: Adam: a method for stochastic optimization. arXiv preprint (2014). arXiv:1412.6980
20. van den Berg, J., Guy, S.J., Lin, M., Manocha, D.: Reciprocal n-body collision avoidance. In: Pradalier, C., Siegwart, R., Hirzinger, G. (eds.) Robotics Research, vol. 70, pp. 3–19. Springer, Berlin (2011). https://doi.org/10.1007/978-3-642-19457-3_1
21. Helbing, D., Molnr, P.: Social force model for pedestrian dynamics. Phys. Rev. E. **51**(5), 4282–4286 (1995)
22. Abadi, M., et al.: Tensorflow: a system for large-scale machine learning. OSDI **16**, 265–283 (2016)

An Effective Yawn Behavior Detection Method in Classroom

Zexian Wang, Fei Jiang$^{(\boxtimes)}$, and Ruimin Shen

Department of Computer Science and Engineering,
Shanghai Jiao Tong University, Shanghai, China
{shuimuth,jiangf,rmshen}@sjtu.edu.cn

Abstract. This paper proposes a novel method to detect students' yawn behavior in real classroom scenes, which is beneficial to analyze learning states of students. The challenges of yawn behavior detection include occlusion, low resolution faces, varied face orientation and interference terms with similar feature like talking. To solve the above mentioned challenges, we first build up a yawn gesture dataset from hundreds of real class videos among primary and middle schools. Then we propose an improved R-FCN and mouth fitting method to efficiently detect yawn behavior. Specifically, we firstly integrate feature pyramid into R-FCN to address small yawn gesture detection. Secondly, we refine detection results according to level of mouth opening by fitting mouth with ellipse. Moreover, to reduce the computational resources of inference, we utilize channel pruning method to reduce the amount of parameters and accelerate the speed of detection by 2 times without hurting performances. Combining these strategies with basic R-FCN, we achieve impressive results in our classroom dataset. The yawn detection reaches 0.90 mAP, which meets the requirements of the real applications.

Keywords: Yawn gesture detection · Feature pyramid · Mouth fitting · Channel pruning

1   Introduction

Human behavior analysis is of great importance and has numerous applications, such as human-machine interaction [1], driver behavior analysis for save driving [2] and pedestrian behavior analysis [3]. Among these behavior analyses, student behavior analysis in real classrooms, such as hand-raising detection [4], stand-up detection and sleep detection [5], which faithfully reflects the teaching atmosphere and learning state, has received increasing attentions. In this paper, we focus on detecting yawn gestures of students in real classrooms, which indicates

The work was supported by NSFC (No. 61671290), National Key R&D Program of China (No. 2016YFE0129500), China Postdoctoral Science Foundation (No. 2018M642019), and Shanghai Municipal Commission of Economy and Information (No. 2018-RGZN-02052).

T. Gedeon et al. (Eds.): ICONIP 2019, LNCS 11953, pp. 430–441, 2019.
https://doi.org/10.1007/978-3-030-36708-4_35

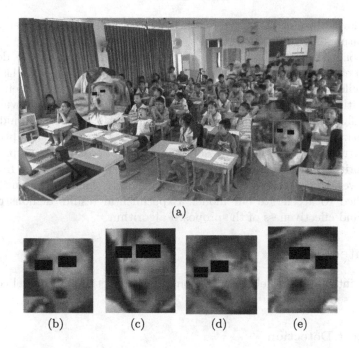

(a)

(b)   (c)   (d)   (e)

Fig. 1. Yawn gesture dataset. (a) Yawn gesture dataset in a real classroom scene. (b)–(e) Varied yawn gestures.

their learning states and interests to the teaching contents. Several challenges exist for yawn gesture detection, including occlusion, various face orientation and interference terms with similar feature like talking, as shown in Fig. 1.

Motivated by researches on other gesture detections [4–6], there are mainly two types of algorithms: pose estimation based algorithms and object detection based algorithms. For the pose-based algorithms [6], the gestures are determined by human key points like heads, shoulders and knees. However, in real classrooms, the bodies of students are often occluded resulting in many key points missing [6]. For object-based algorithms, two-stage methods with impressive performances are frequently utilized for behavior analyses of students in classrooms, such as hand-raising detection [4] and sleep detection [5]. By testing several existing two-stage algorithms on our dataset, R-FCN [7] is chosen as our backbone network architecture.

However, yawn gesture detection is quite different from other behavior analyses of students, which faces several unique challenges, including various face orientation and talking interferences. Specifically, for various face orientation, it is hard to detect yawn gestures from non-frontal faces. While, students spontaneously look up and shake their heads from side to side in real classrooms. For talking interferences, the features like the shapes of mouths are quite similar between talking and yawn, which makes it hard to distinguish these two gestures by object detection methods. Besides, the resolution of faces in real classrooms are quite low. Most of them are between 60 and 100 pixels. Therefore, fine-grained features are difficult to capture.

Based on the above analysis, we propose a novel yawn gesture detection method to effectively solve the above-mentioned challenges in real classrooms. We first build a yawn gesture dataset from real class videos with labeling yawn gestures with bounding boxes. Then, we propose a coarse-to-fine yawn gesture detection algorithm. Firstly, a modified R-FCN with feature pyramid is utilized for coarsely yawn gesture detection. The feature pyramid can capture fine-grained features for detecting low-resolution objects. Secondly, an ellipse mouth fitting algorithm is presented to further distinguish the yawn gesture from talking. Moreover, to detect yawn gesture more efficiently, channel pruning method [8] is applied to accelerate our model. Experimental results demonstrate the efficiency and effectiveness of the proposed algorithm.

2   Related Work

We briefly introduce the related works on object detection and model compression in this section.

2.1   Object Detection

For deep learning object detection algorithms, there are two different approaches—making a fixed number of predictions on grid (one-stage methods) and leverage a region proposal network to find objects and then use a second network to fine-tune the proposals and output final predictions (two-stage methods).

One-stage methods regard detection task as a regression and classification problem, straightly mapping image to bounding box and object category probabilities. The classical models are YOLO [9] and SSD [10]. YOLO divides image into $S \times S$ grid and associates each cell with class probabilities. It is an end-to-end single pipeline network that directly detects object and processes images in real time. But it has difficulty to detect small object. SSD utilizes a set of default boxes with different aspect ratios to handle objects with various sizes. Based on YOLO and SSD, there are several improvement iterations, such as YOLOv2 [11] and DSSD [12].

Two-stage methods generate region proposal first and then classify each proposal into different class, which mainly include R-CNN [13], Fast R-CNN [14], Faster R-CNN [15] and R-FCN [7]. The mainly drawback of R-CNN is slow. Fast R-CNN [14] alleviate this issue and reduce running time. Region proposal computation become a new bottleneck of these networks. Then Faster R-CNN [15] introduce a region proposal network sharing feature map, so the cost of region proposal phase almost can be ignored. In order to avoid using costly per-region subnetwork too frequently, R-FCN introduces a fully convolution network shared computation on the whole image. Position-sensitive score maps of R-FCN solves the problem of translation variance in object detection and translation invariance in image classification.

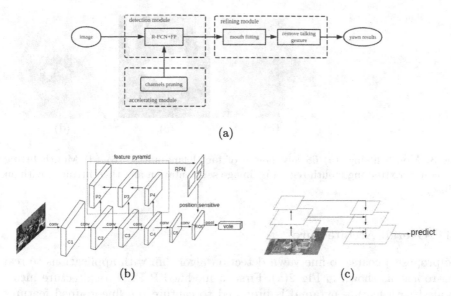

Fig. 2. Overall architecture. (a) The architecture consists of three components, which are detection module, refining module and accelerating module. (b) Modified R-FCN. (c) A top-down feature pyramid.

2.2 Model Compression

Misha [16] argued deep learning neural networks have many redundant weights, thus they are over-parameterized. These redundant weights cause much CPU and GPU resources wasting. Several methods have been proposed to reduce this redundancy.

So as to accelerate convolution layer's computation, sparse connection methods prune unimportant connections between neurons according to weights magnitude [17]. Some optimized implementation approaches reduce convolution overheads using special convolution algorithms like FFT [18]. Several works exploit redundant information of feature maps [19]. Polyak [19] selectively remove input channels by evaluate the less frequently activated feature maps. Channel pruning [20,21] has already been proved effective to achieve high compression ratio. In this paper, we choose channel pruning method to accelerate our model.

3 Method

The proposed algorithm for yawn detection in classrooms has three main parts: a modified R-FCN for coarse yawn detection, a mouth fitting to remove talking behaviors, and a channel pruning method to accelerate the inference. More details are introduced in this section.

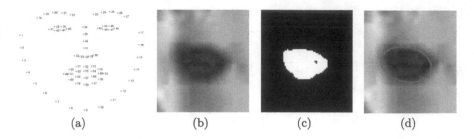

(a)   (b)   (c)   (d)

Fig. 3. Mouth fitting. (a) 68 key points of facial landmarks. (b)–(d) Mouth fitting procedure. Extracting mouth region by image segmentation and then fitting it with an ellipse.

3.1   Overall Architecture

We propose a coarse-to-fine yawn detection algorithm with applications to real classrooms, as shown in Fig. 2(a). First, a modified R-FCN architecture incorporated with feature pyramid is proposed to capture the fine-grained features aiming to overcome the low-resolution of mouths. Due to the similarity between yawn and talking, the modified R-FCN cannot distinguish yawn and talking behaviors. Then, a fine yawn recognition algorithm based on mouth fitting is proposed to remove talking behaviors from the detection results of the R-FCN by considering the differences of mouth opening. After that, a channel pruning method is utilized to compress the trained R-FCN, and accelerate the inference with fewer computational resources.

3.2   R-FCN with Feature Pyramid

As we can see in Fig. 1, most yawn gestures in real classrooms are low resolution. Moreover, different face orientation increase the difficulty of yawn detection. To address these problems, we integrate feature pyramid into R-FCN by taking advantages of multi-scale features, which simultaneously captures the high-level semantic information in high layer feature maps and fine-grained features in low layer feature maps.

The overall architecture of the modified R-FCN is shown in Fig. 2(b). ResNet-101 is used to extract features, which has 5 residual blocks, marked as $\{C_1, C_2, C_3, C_4, C_5\}$. The combined feature pyramid is shown in Fig. 2(c). Different from FPN [22], we use deconvolution [23] instead of bilinear interpolation to upsample, since the straightforward unpsampling may not accurately express the spatial relations between different levels of features. Specifically, the feature pyramid implementation includes bottom-up and top-down pathway. In bottom-up pathway, backbone network outputs hierarchy feature maps at several scales, i.e. $\{C_1, C_2, C_3, C_4, C_5\}$. In top-down pathway, only C_2–C_4 are used to build feature pyramid due to memory and performance compromise.

3.3   Mouth Fitting

Sometimes, yawn gesture detection approach describing above does not work when students are talking. In order to reduce the ratio of wrong results, we make second stage decision by the level of mouth opening. We propose fitting mouth with ellipse method to achieve this goal. As depicted in Fig. 3, firstly, we extract mouth region based on facial landmarks which are computed through ERT (ensemble of regression trees) method [24]. Secondly, we transform RGB image to gray image and then segment it to binary by setting a threshold value. Finally, we fit it with ellipse according to binary image. The general form of ellipse equation is described in Eq. (1).

$$F(\mathbf{a}, \mathbf{x}) = \mathbf{a}^T \mathbf{x} = ax^2 + by^2 + cxy + dx + ey + f = 0 \tag{1}$$

Direct least square fitting of ellipse method is propose by Fitzgibbon [25]. We solve the following constrained minimization problem:

$$\arg \min_{\mathbf{a}} \|\mathbf{Da}\|^2$$
$$\text{subject to } \mathbf{a}^T C \mathbf{a} = 1 \tag{2}$$

where $\mathbf{D} = [\mathbf{x}_1, \mathbf{x}_2, \ldots, \mathbf{x}_n]^T$, and

$$C = \begin{bmatrix} 0 & 0 & 2 & 0 & 0 & 0 \\ 0 & -1 & 0 & 0 & 0 & 0 \\ 2 & 0 & 0 & 0 & 0 & 0 \\ 0 & 0 & 0 & 0 & 0 & 0 \\ 0 & 0 & 0 & 0 & 0 & 0 \\ 0 & 0 & 0 & 0 & 0 & 0 \end{bmatrix}.$$

Once solving the optimization problem, ellipse general form can be transformed to standard form.

$$\frac{x^2}{a^2} + \frac{y^2}{b^2} = 1 \tag{3}$$

We define level of mouth opening as

$$\epsilon = \frac{b}{a} \tag{4}$$

Setting a threshold ϵ', we reject the candidate yawn gesture detection if $\epsilon < \epsilon'$.

3.4   Channel Pruning

Channel pruning method can reduce inference time of detection model and is friendly to implementation comparing to other model compression methods [26,27]. So we choose it as our accelerating approach. Single layer channel pruning method is illustrated in Fig. 4. The aim of channel pruning is to reduce the number of channels of feature maps. Once we determine which channels to

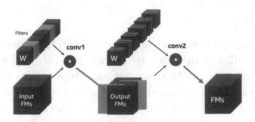

Fig. 4. Channel pruning. If we have two channels to reduce, we can remove corresponding filters which output those channels. Then we also reconfigure the immediate convolution layer, since the input of next layer has less channels. We should shrink the following layer's weights corresponding to the channels we pruned.

Fig. 5. Pruning residual block. A sampler is used to select channels which are not pruned.

prune, the corresponding filters taking these channels as input can be removed. Moreover, the previous filters that output these channels can also be removed.

For a single convolution layer, its input feature map and kernel are denoted as $\mathbf{X}$ and $\mathbf{W}$ respectively. The output feature map $\mathbf{Y}$ can be represented as:

$$\mathbf{Y} = \sum_{i=1}^{c} \mathbf{X}_i \mathbf{W}_i \tag{5}$$

c is the numbers of input channels. $\mathbf{X}_i$ is sub-matrix sliced from ith channel of $\mathbf{X}$. $\mathbf{W}_i$ is sliced from ith channel of $\mathbf{W}$ correspondingly. In order to prune input channels from c to c', Yihui [8] minimized output feature map's reconstruction error as Eq. (6).

$$\arg\min_{\beta, \mathbf{W}} \frac{1}{2N} \left\| \mathbf{Y} - \sum_{i=1}^{c} \beta_i \mathbf{X}_i \mathbf{W}_i \right\|_F^2 \tag{6}$$
$$\text{subject to } \|\boldsymbol{\beta}\|_0 \leq c'$$

c' is the number of kept channels. β is a coefficient vector using to select the desire channels, and β_i is a scalar indicating whether a channel is pruned or not. That is, if $\beta_i = 0$, $\mathbf{X}_i$ does not provide useful information, then can be safely pruned. Correspondingly, $\mathbf{W}_i$ can be removed too.

The minimization problem Eq. (6) can be tackled by firstly solving β via LASSO regression [28], then solving $\mathbf{W}$ by least square regression.

Fig. 6. Detection result. Left and right columns are yawn gesture detection results of baseline and ours, respectively.

It is sufficient to prune single branch networks using the above method. But we could not directly prune residual block because it is shared with shortcut connection. For the first layer, Yihui [8] performs feature map channel sampling before the later convolution layer, as shown in Fig. 5. The last layer of residual block consists of Y_1, Y_2 two inputs. The reconstruction is changed to $Y_1 - Y'_1 + Y_2$, where Y'_1 is the previous output feature map after channel pruning.

4 Experiment

In order to verify the effectiveness of our method, we built up our own yawn dataset which was extracted from 25 different primary and middle schools classrooms videos. The classroom scene yawn dataset is shown in the Fig. 1. We used 8k samples as training set and 4k samples as testing set to verify the performance of the algorithm. We carried out our experiment on Nvidia GeForce GTX 1070 Ti GPU. We evaluated performance of yawn gesture detection by calculating mean average precision (mAP).

Table 1. Comparison baseline with our method.

	Baseline	Ablations	Ours
Feature pyramid?		✓	✓
Mouth fitting?		✓	✓
mAP(%)	87.2	89.6 88.5	90.7

Table 2. Pruning configuration of 5 blocks of backbone network ResNet-101. The last column shows the reduce percentage of FLOPs from the original model. The middle two column shows FLOPs and the number of parameters.

Block	FLOPs	Parameters	Pruned %
Res1	7.53×10^9	9.4×10^3	80%
Res2	1.04×10^9	1.7×10^5	75%
Res3	1.39×10^{10}	1.1×10^6	75%
Res4	8.20×10^{10}	2.6×10^7	50%
Res5	1.07×10^{10}	1.3×10^7	50%
Total	1.15×10^{11}	4.03×10^7	55%

Table 3. Accelerating R-FCN model [7] by ratio of $2\times, 4\times, 5\times$. Smaller value indicates better result.

Decreace of mAP (baseline 87.2%)			
Method	$2\times$	$4\times$	$5\times$
Weight pruning [27]	1.6	9.2	13.7
Filter pruning [26] (fine-tuned)	1.2	5.3	10.4
Channel pruning (without fine-tune)	2.9	12.4	17.6
Channel pruning (fine-tuned)	0	2.3	3.1

4.1 Yawn Gesture Detection

To compare our proposed method with baseline, we conducted experiment on the same training and testing set. We used 8 as mini-batch size, set the learning rate to 0.001 for the first 10k iterations and then set to 0.001 for the next 10k iterations.

The result is shown in Table 1. Our method performs better than baseline. The ablations column of Table 1 shows our different improvements. With feature pyramid, the mAP increases to 89.6%. And our mouth fitting method improves mAP to 88.5%. Combining two improvements with original R-FCN, our method increases mAP by 3.5%.

Figure 6 depicts detection results of baseline and our methods. Comparing with two methods, ours can detect more low resolution yawn gesture and filter wrong results.

4.2 Channel Pruning for Model

We implemented channel pruning method in pytorch. We set learning rate as 0.001 and trained 20 epochs for our dataset, with mini-batch size of 2. The performance can be promoted with fine-tuning.

The ResNet-101, backbone network of R-FCN, consists of 5 blocks, which we denote as $\{C_1, C_2, C_3, C_4, C_5\}$. Figure 7 illustrates the sensitivity of each block

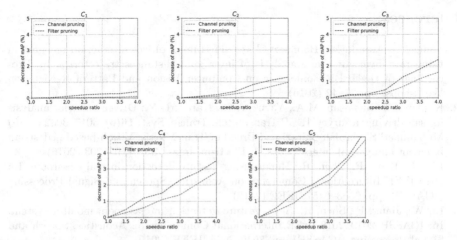

Fig. 7. Sensitivity analysis for the 5 blocks of backbone ResNet-101, measured by decrease of mAP error. Our approach performs better than pruning filter method.

to channel pruning. The first block is lest sensitive to pruning for the reason that it directly interacts with input image, which means they carry less abstract semantic information. So there is more redundancy. The higher layer blocks are more sensitive for the contrary reason. We used sensitivity analysis results to determine threshold of each block. The more sensitive the block is, the smaller threshold we set. Guiding by sensitivity analysis (shown in Fig. 7), we pruned more aggressive for shallow block, since shallow block is less sensitive to pruning. The overall pruning configuration for the 5 blocks is shown in Table 2. Using this configuration, we reached 2 times speedup without hurting performance.

To compare our method with filter pruning [26] and weight pruning [27], we trained each model with the same initialized weights and hyper-parameters. As shown in Table 3, with the same pruning rate, channel pruning method outperforms weight pruning and filter pruning method. With only losing 2.3% mAP, we can accelerate yawn detection model by 4 times, which means there is much redundancy in convolution neural networks. Even for optimized ResNet, it's worth accelerating it to save memory and GPU resources.

5   Conclusion

We propose an effective and efficient yawn behavior detection method in real classroom environment, which can be used to analyze learning states of students. Due to low resolution and varied orientation of face as well as interference terms like talking, we introduce feature pyramid to simultaneously capture semantic and fine-grained features. Then fitting mouth with ellipse so as to refine detection results. Moreover, we accelerates detection model by 2 times without hurting performance. Our method achieves an impressive result in real classroom yawn gesture detection.

References

1. Meng M., Daoudi, M., Boonaert, J., et al.: Human object interaction recognition using rate-invariant shape analysis of inter joint distances trajectories. In: Proceedings of the IEEE Conference on Computer Vision and Pattern Recognition Workshops, pp. 37–42 (2016)
2. Kaplan, S., Guvensan, M.A., Yavuz, A.G., Karalurt, Y.: Driver behavior analysis for safe driving: a survey. IEEE Trans. Intell. Transp. Syst. **16**(6), 3017–3032 (2015)
3. Mohammad Shokrolah Shirazi and Brendan Tran Morris: Vision-based pedestrian behavior analysis at intersections. J. Electron. Imag. **25**(5), 051203 (2016)
4. Lin, J., Jiang, F., Shen, R.: Hand-raising gesture detection in real classroom. In: 2018 IEEE International Conference on Acoustics, Speech and Signal Processing (ICASSP), pp. 6453–6457. IEEE (2018)
5. Li, W., Jiang, F., Shen, R.: Sleep gesture detection in classroom monitor system. In: ICASSP 2019–2019 IEEE International Conference on Acoustics, Speech and Signal Processing (ICASSP), pp. 7640–7644. IEEE (2019)
6. Zhou, H., Jiang, F., Shen, R.: Who are raising their hands? hand-raiser seeking based on object detection and pose estimation. In: Asian Conference on Machine Learning, pp. 470–485 (2018)
7. Dai, J., Li, Y., He, K., Sun, J.: R-fcn: object detection via region-based fully convolutional networks. In: Advances in Neural Information Processing Systems, pp. 379–387 (2016)
8. He, Y., Zhang, X., Sun, J.: Channel pruning for accelerating very deep neural networks. In: Proceedings of the IEEE International Conference on Computer Vision, pp. 1389–1397 (2017)
9. Redmon, J., Divvala, S., Girshick, R., Farhadi, A.: You only look once: unified, real-time object detection. In: Proceedings of the IEEE Conference on Computer Vision and Pattern Recognition, pp. 779–788 (2016)
10. Liu, W., et al.: SSD: single shot multibox detector. In: Leibe, B., Matas, J., Sebe, N., Welling, M. (eds.) ECCV 2016. LNCS, vol. 9905, pp. 21–37. Springer, Cham (2016). https://doi.org/10.1007/978-3-319-46448-0_2
11. Redmon, J., Farhadi, A.: Yolo9000: better, faster, stronger. In: Proceedings of the IEEE Conference on Computer Vision and Pattern Recognition, pp. 7263–7271 (2017)
12. Fu, C.-Y., Liu, W., Ranga, A., Tyagi, A., Berg, A.C.: DSSD: deconvolutional single shot detector. arXiv preprint (2017) arXiv:1701.06659
13. Girshick, R., Donahue, J., Darrell, T., Malik, J.: Rich feature hierarchies for accurate object detection and semantic segmentation. In: Proceedings of the IEEE Conference on Computer Vision and Pattern Recognition, pp. 580–587 (2014)
14. Girshick, R.: Fast r-cnn. In: Proceedings of the IEEE International Conference on Computer Vision, pp. 1440–1448 (2015)
15. Ren, S., He, K., Girshick, R., Sun, J.: Faster r-cnn: towards real-time object detection with region proposal networks. In: Advances in Neural Information Processing Systems, pp. 91–99 (2015)
16. Denil, M., Shakibi, B., Dinh, L., de Freitas, N., et al.: Predicting parameters in deep learning. In: Advances in Neural Information Processing Systems, pp. 2148–2156 (2013)
17. Yang, T.-J., Chen, Y.-H., Sze, V.: Designing energy-efficient convolutional neural networks using energy-aware pruning. In: Proceedings of the IEEE Conference on Computer Vision and Pattern Recognition, pp. 5687–5695 (2017)

18. Vasilache, N., Johnson, J., Mathieu, M., Chintala, S., Piantino, S., LeCun, Y.: Fast convolutional nets with fbfft: a GPU performance evaluation. arXiv preprint (2014) arXiv:1412.7580
19. Polyak, A., Wolf, L.: Channel-level acceleration of deep face representations. IEEE Access **3**, 2163–2175 (2015)
20. Wen, W., Wu, C., Wang, Y., Chen, Y., Li, H.: Learning structured sparsity in deep neural networks. In: Advances in Neural Information Processing Systems, pp. 2074–2082 (2016)
21. Zhou, H., Alvarez, J.M., Porikli, F.: Less is more: towards compact CNNs. In: Leibe, B., Matas, J., Sebe, N., Welling, M. (eds.) ECCV 2016. LNCS, vol. 9908, pp. 662–677. Springer, Cham (2016). https://doi.org/10.1007/978-3-319-46493-0_40
22. Lin, T.-Y., Dollár, P., Girshick, R., Kaiming H., Hariharan, B., Belongie, S.: Feature pyramid networks for object detection. In: Proceedings of the IEEE Conference on Computer Vision and Pattern Recognition, pp. 2117–2125 (2017)
23. Zeiler, M.D., Fergus, R.: Visualizing and understanding convolutional networks. In: Fleet, D., Pajdla, T., Schiele, B., Tuytelaars, T. (eds.) ECCV 2014. LNCS, vol. 8689, pp. 818–833. Springer, Cham (2014). https://doi.org/10.1007/978-3-319-10590-1_53
24. Kazemi, V., Sullivan, J.: One millisecond face alignment with an ensemble of regression trees. In: Proceedings of the IEEE Conference on Computer Vision and Pattern Recognition, pp. 1867–1874 (2014)
25. Fitzgibbon, A., Pilu, M., Fisher, R.B.: Direct least square fitting of ellipses. IEEE Trans. Pattern Anal. Mach. Intell. **21**(5), 476–480 (1999)
26. Li, H., Kadav, A., Durdanovic, I., Samet, H., Graf, H.P.: Pruning filters for efficient convnets. arXiv preprint (2016). arXiv:1608.08710
27. Han, S., Pool, J., Tran, J., Dally, W.: Learning both weights and connections for efficient neural network. In: Advances in Neural Information Processing Systems, pp. 1135–1143 (2015)
28. Tibshirani, R.: Regression shrinkage and selection via the lasso. J. Royal Stat. Soc.: Ser. B (Methodological) **58**(1), 267–288 (1996)

Bidirectional LSTM with MFCC Feature Extraction for Sleep Arousal Detection in Multi-channel Signal Data

Hyunseob Kim, Tae Joon Jun, Giang Nguyen, and Daeyoung Kim$^{(\boxtimes)}$

School of Computing, Korea Advanced Institute of Science and Technology, Daejeon, Republic of Korea
{hskim411,taejoon89,dexter.nguyen7,kimd}@kaist.ac.kr

Abstract. The polysomnography (PSG) can be used as a basis for judging various disorders that occur during sleep such as arousal. Arousal which means wakefulness is the common phenomena disturbing deep sleep. Since arousal appears in various forms, there are areas where research has been less advanced such as Respiratory effort-related arousal (RERA). We develop bidirectional Long Short-Term Memory (LSTM) which used Mel-frequency cepstral coefficient (MFCC) for feature extraction and trained using 13 multi-channel signals from Physionet Challenge 2018. The training model predicts arousal probability on every input data. Signals are processed with MFCC and we test a various combination of features such as the number of features and additional delta feature. Finally, top 3 models are used to construct an ensemble model which shows the best performance in our experiments. We obtain 0.898 AUC-ROC and 0.458 AUC-PR on the test data which is split from 994 training data. Performance of our model is competitive to other methods proposed in the Physionet Challenge 2018. Bidirectional LSTM makes a sequential prediction on arousal and MFCC can be applied uniformly on the signal data regardless of signal type. Therefore, we can process feature extraction efficiently without any manual approaches.

Keywords: Sleep arousal · MFCC · Deep learning · LSTM

1 Introduction

The bio-signal based sleep pattern analysis is a field that has been continuously advanced since it shows a close relationship with human health. Typically, methods [1,2,14] for determining the depth of sleep and detecting sleep disorders such as sleep arousal using machine learning have been developed. However, the cause

This work was supported by the International Research & Development Program of the National Research Foundation of Korea (NRF) funded by the Ministry of Science, ICT & Future Planning of Korea (2016K1A3A7A03952054) and Energy Cloud Technology Development Project through the Ministry of Science and ICT(MSIT) and National Research Foundation of Korea (NRF-2019M3F2A1073036).

T. Gedeon et al. (Eds.): ICONIP 2019, LNCS 11953, pp. 442–453, 2019.
https://doi.org/10.1007/978-3-030-36708-4_36

of sleep disturbance is diverse and investigating only a few phenomena is not enough to clearly judge sleep disorders. Therefore, there is a need for extensive research on arousal status including representative phenomena. An arousal state refers to a phenomenon that is temporarily incomplete awake during sleep and can occur in various types such as snoring, bruxism, respiratory disorders and etc. Especially, respiratory disorders are divided into apnea, hypopnea, RERA and etc. Therefore, detecting arousal can help to identify the cause of disorders and to understand the phenomenon.

In previous works, sleep apnea is the main target of arousal detection. Various deep learning architecture [2–4] such as convolutional neural networks (CNN) and recurrent neural networks (RNN) detect apnea successfully using single-channel signal data. However, there is a need to construct models using the multi-channel signal since PSG is based on multi-channel signal data. By analyzing multi-channel signal, the range of detecting various arousal status can be expanded.

In the Physionet Challenge 2018 [5], various methods are introduced for detecting arousal status using multi-channel bio-signals. Most of the entries that showed high performance use deep neural networks. Howe-Patterson [8] proposes dense convolutional neural networks with transposed filters and auxiliary loss for classification. They use the non-target area as additional data for training and sleep stages as additional label. The approach achieves a first place in the competition.

Þráinsson [17] uses RNN which learns a combination of hand-crafted features. They apply feature extraction techniques to each signal. QRS complex and Heart Rate Variability (HRV) are extracted from ECG. Wavelet packet decomposition is applied on EEG and other statistical features are extracted from rest signals. After that, collected features are aggregated for creating inputs and fed in RNN.

He [6] constructs sequence to sequence deep neural networks which deploy convolutional layer, LSTM, and fully-connected layer. Convolutional layer and LSTM are used for feature learning from the input signal and fully-connected layer classifies the arousal based on extracted features. Also, they propose a segmentation process which can solve training difficulty from the imbalanced large dataset.

Hand-crafted features and convolutional filters are used for constructing the learning model [15]. EEG signals are analyzed in the frequency domain and approximate entropy was additionally applied. For each of the remaining signals, statistical extracting methods are applied. In addition, they use sleep stages as guidance for auxiliary loss.

Patane [12] proposes an ensemble deep learning model using multi-modal CNN for each signal. They extract features on signals with CNN models. The model is the Siamese model which share the parameters between models. Finally, fully-connected layer predicts arousal area based on features from each signal.

Most deep learning architectures in Physionet Challenge 2018 use manual preprocessing for input data such as hand-crafted feature extraction [15,17] and segmentation [6]. Especially, many techniques [6,17] for efficiently compressing long-length signals are proposed. However, those proposed approaches [6,15] are inefficient in the multi-signal domain since each signal requires a different extraction process. Some entries [8,15] that used CNN for feature extraction propose models combined with auxiliary loss. They use additional data and labeling information, making it difficult to consider as a pure performance of a proposed learning model.

Therefore, we propose an automatic and efficient deep RNN model which use MFCC as a feature vector. MFCC is a collection of coefficients from the short-term power spectrum of a sound and is broadly used in speech recognition and music classification. MFCC can represent frequency energy regardless of input signal sources. Therefore, we can use MFCC effectively when we need complex feature extraction from multi-channel signal data. The model applies MFCC processing equally to all signals which can reduce the number of input features and conserve the characteristics of signals. We conduct various experiments on feature extraction part to search proper parameter combination. Using MFCC feature vectors, RNN makes possible to detect arousal sequentially in a single learning model. We use bidirectional LSTM as RNN model and evaluate Many to One and Many to Many approaches in our model. The best performance of our model is 0.898 AUC-ROC and 0.458 AUC-PR. Considering that Howe-Patterson [8] has the best performance using additional data and labeling, our model is superior and competitive to other proposed models in the challenge.

We introduce our deep learning architecture and detail process in Sect. 2. Results are showed in Sect. 3 and compared with other approaches including discussion in Sect. 4. Finally, Sect. 5 concludes the paper.

2   Methods

Figure 1 shows the proposed architecture to detect arousal using multi-channel signals. In data preprocessing, feature vectors are created via MFCC. The RNN model learns the pattern based on the generated input features. We use the sigmoid function on the last layer of RNN for computing the arousal probability. The output shows the arousal state probability according to the continuous-time. Finally, the arousal state is determined based on the obtained probability.

2.1   Data

The dataset released by Physionet is a result of PSG for 1983 people, and the dataset used in this paper is public training data which is composed of 994 subjects. Data are provided by the Massachusetts General Hospital's Computational Clinical Neurophysiology Laboratory and the Clinical Data Animation Laboratory. The sleep stages, arousal status, and etc. are recorded according to the American Academy of Sleep Medicine manual. The average recording length is about 7.7 h and the data is composed of 13 time-series bio-signals. The sampling rate is 200 Hz, and signals such as electroencephalogram (EEG), electrocardiogram (ECG), electromyography (EMG), and airflow are collected. In the case of SaO2, the collected data are resampled to 200 Hz and in the case

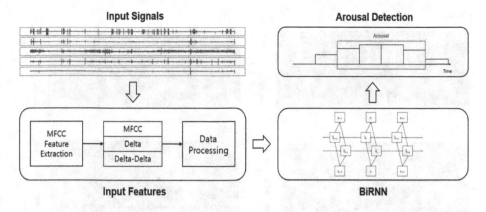

Fig. 1. Overall architecture of the proposed method

of electrooculography (EOG), the left eye is recorded with reference to the right ear EEG (M2). The target arousal is composed of RERA, bruxism, snoring and etc. except apnea and hypopnea which are researched actively compared to other sleep arousals.

2.2 Feature Extraction

MFCC [11] which is widely used in speech recognition is a spectral-based feature extraction method based on a range of frequencies that a human ear can perceive. MFCC extraction starts from the Short-Time Fourier Transform. We can set the window size and hop size to adjust the length of the target range. The sound signal is filtered by Mel filters which reflect the human auditory characteristics after Short-Time Fourier Transform. Filters are sensitive to small changes at low frequencies, but the sensitivity decreases as the frequency increases. The characteristic of filters makes better performance than Fourier Transform in the speech recognition field. Finally, applying logarithm and discrete cosine transform makes the coefficients which are used as MFCC. We can adjust the number of coefficients. Figure 2 shows a detail process of extracting features.

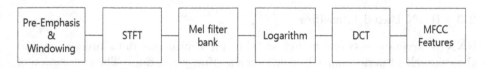

Fig. 2. A detail process of MFCC extraction

MFCC is applied on 13 signals for feature extraction with 50% overlap. Fourier Transform is the traditional approach in signal processing. However, it

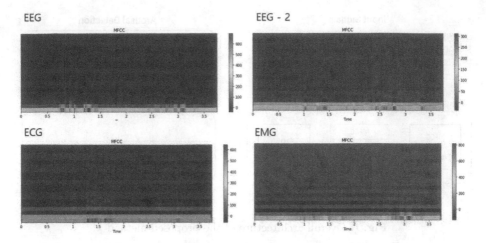

Fig. 3. Some parts of MFCC extraction from EEG, ECG and EMG signal. X-axis represents time and Y-axis means each coefficient from MFCC. Changes in energy over time can be identified with variation of color on each coefficient. (Color figure online)

occurs high dimensional problem in creating feature vectors since we use multi-channel signals. It causes lower performance in the evaluation step. To solve this problem, we apply MFCC which has advantages in reducing the number of features and preserve the characteristics. Delta energy which is the derivative value of MFCC shows better performance and noise-robust [9] in the speech recognition field. Expecting a similar effect on bio-signals, we extract delta and delta-delta energy as additional features. After feature extraction, we apply feature scaling using standardization and concatenate features of 13 signals. We process feature scaling on all signals since the domain of signals is quite different. Obtained input data is split with the fixed length for training. Figure 3 shows results of MFCC extraction on each signal. The value of coefficients corresponding to the number of MFCC is represented with color in each signal.

In MFCC feature extraction, the window size is 512 and hop size is 256. This value is set considering that sampling rate is 200 Hz. The number of MFCC is varied with 13, 20, 40 and 60.

2.3   RNN Based Classifier

RNN is a neural network model suitable for continuous data processing and shows excellent performance in fields such as time-series data. The connection of the hidden state forms a cyclic structure, which can deviate from the input data length constraint. We construct LSTM [7] for handling long sequential input signal data. First and the second layer use bidirectional LSTM [13] and the last layer uses normal LSTM. Combinations of MFCC, delta, and delta-delta are used as feature vectors. Dropout which can solve the over-fitting problem is applied on all recurrent layers. The final prediction probability is restored to the

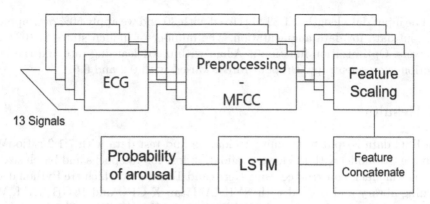

Fig. 4. Feature extraction from multi-channel signals and creating feature vectors for LSTM

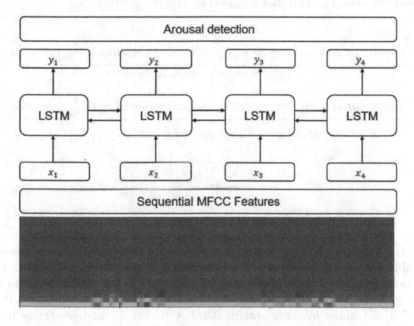

Fig. 5. The training model of the proposed method. Input data is sequential MFCC feature vectors. Output computed by sigmoid function is a probability of arousal over time.

same length as original input signals. The detail process is represented in Figs. 4 and 5.

We construct two different types of RNN models. One is Many to One and the other is Many to Many. Many to One approach uses only final hidden states for output probability. The model predicts arousal based on all sequential input. Whereas, Many to Many approach predicts arousal status on every hidden state.

The input data length of LSTM is fixed with 30 and we apply 50% overlapping on input data for data augmentation. The number of hidden states is 1024 on all layers. Optimization function is Adam with 0.001 learning rate and the loss function is cross-entropy. Dropout rate is varied with 0.2 and 0.5.

3   Results

The PSG data is split to training, validation and test data with 7:1:2 ratio. We evaluate the model with the lowest validation loss for 10 epochs and batch size is 100. The model is constructed using Keras and Tensorflow which are Python deep learning library and trained with NVIDIA Titan X GPU and 16 GB RAM. We evaluate our models in terms of AUC-ROC and AUC-PR. The official metric of the challenge is AUC-PR which applied gross computation instead of an average between subjects. Figure 6 shows the detail process of evaluation.

$$R_j = \frac{Number\ of\ arousal\ samples\ with\ predicted\ probability\ \left(\frac{j}{1000}\right)\ or\ greater}{Total\ number\ of\ arousal\ samples}$$

$$P_j = \frac{Number\ of\ arousal\ samples\ with\ predicted\ probability\ \left(\frac{j}{1000}\right)\ or\ greater}{Total\ number\ of\ samples\ with\ predicted\ probability\ \left(\frac{j}{1000}\right)\ or\ greater}$$

$$AUC - PR = \sum_j P_j(R_j - R_{j+1})$$

Fig. 6. *gross* AUC-PR

Table 1 shows the result of our experiments. We conduct experiments with various kinds of parameters. First, we compare two kinds of RNN models to find appropriate input length for classifying correctly. Many to one achieves 0.286 AUC-PR and Many to many obtains 0.371 AUC-PR. Second, we try to find a proper combination of MFCC and delta features and the number of features. Number of features in Table 1 means the number of features per signal. In the case of delta and delta-delta, the same number of features are extracted. 0.429 and 0.422 AUC-PR are the best score in MFCC + Delta and MFCC + Delta + Delta2. Finally, we conduct additional experiments with varying dropout rate and an ensemble method for improving performance. The ensemble model averages the outputs of models which applied 0.5 dropout rate. The ensemble method shows the best performance on both AUC-ROC and AUC-PR. We compare our model with proposed models in Physionet Challenge. Our model obtains 0.458 AUC-PR and it was higher than the second rank of the challenge as shown in Table 2.

Table 1. Evaluation of proposed model

Model type	Dropout	Feature	Number of features	AUC-ROC	AUC-PR
Many to one	0.2	MFCC	20	0.844	0.286
Many to many	0.2	MFCC	13	0.854	0.356
Many to many	0.2	MFCC	20	0.858	0.371
Many to many	0.2	MFCC	40	0.858	0.342
Many to many	0.2	MFCC + Delta	13	0.876	0.402
Many to many	0.2	MFCC + Delta	20	0.883	0.429
Many to many	0.2	MFCC + Delta	40	0.885	0.418
Many to many	0.2	MFCC + Delta + Delta2	13	0.877	0.406
Many to many	0.2	MFCC + Delta + Delta2	20	0.880	0.407
Many to many	0.2	MFCC + Delta + Delta2	40	0.886	0.422
Many to many	0.5	MFCC + Delta + Delta2	20	0.887	0.430
Many to many	0.5	MFCC + Delta + Delta2	40	0.893	0.446
Many to many	0.5	MFCC + Delta + Delta2	60	0.893	0.438
Ensemble	-	-	-	**0.898**	**0.458**

Table 2. Comparison of our model and proposed models in Physionet Challenge 2018

Rank	Entries	AUC-PR
1	Howe-Patterson [8]	0.54
-	Our model	0.458
2	Þráinsson [17]	0.45
3	He [6]	0.43
4	Varga [15]	0.42
5	Patane [12]	0.40
6	Miller [10]	0.36
6	Warrick [16]	0.36

The Figs. 7 and 8 shows the distribution of subjects about six of the models that have been experimented via box plot. Distributions consist of the score of each subject. Here we list the models selected in our experiments.

- Many2one: Model type - Many to one, Dropout - 0.2, Feature - MFCC, Number of features - 20
- MFCC-20: Model type - Many to many, Dropout - 0.2, Feature - MFCC, Number of features - 20
- Delta2-20-0.5: Model type - Many to many, Dropout - 0.5, Feature - MFCC + Delta + Delta2, Number of features - 20
- Delta2-40-0.5: Model type - Many to many, Dropout - 0.5, Feature - MFCC + Delta + Delta2, Number of features - 40
- Delta2-60-0.5: Model type - Many to many, Dropout - 0.5, Feature - MFCC + Delta + Delta2, Number of features - 60
- Ensemble: Average of Delta2-20-0.5, Delta2-40-0.5 and Delta2-60-0.5.

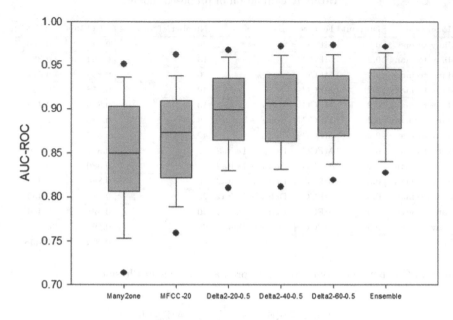

Fig. 7. AUC-ROC box plot

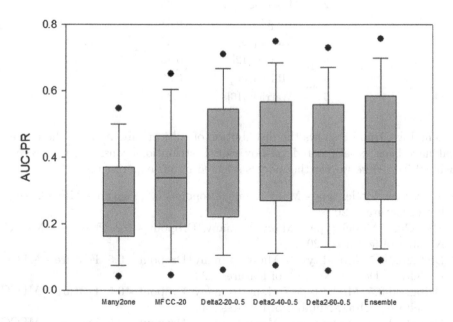

Fig. 8. AUC-PR box plot

In the case of AUC-ROC, the standard deviation decreases in a higher average performance model, indicating that the distribution density around the average increases. In the case of AUC-PR, the increase in performance is greater than AUC-ROC.

4   Discussion

Table 1 shows the improvement of performance according to the change of experiments setup. We design Many to one and Many to many to find a proper input length for classification using the characteristic of RNN that can handle variable input data. As a result, Many to many approach shows better performance than Many to one. Many to many is a proper model type detecting arousal more precisely and sequentially. Performance is also improved when additional delta and delta-delta features are used rather than using MFCC alone. The proper number of features is 20 when used only MFCC. However, 40 is more suitable numbers when the additional features used. When dropout rate is 0.5, overall performance improves and an excessive number of MFCC extraction shows disturbing the learning process.

Howe-Patterson [8] which achieves 0.54 AUC-PR reconstructs arousal area using transposed CNN with auxiliary loss. A transposed convolutional filter is effective in recovering precise arousal area and auxiliary loss helps the converge of the training model with additional data.

CNN is widely used in signal processing for feature extraction and many entries [6,12,15] deploy it in this challenge. They do not use CNN alone but combine LSTM, auxiliary loss, and other techniques. However, they do not show better performance than Þráinsson [17] using feature engineering steps and RNN. Therefore, extracting features by CNN is not always powerful than well-extracted hand-crafted features on the multi-channel domain.

It is remarkable that many methods which use CNN for feature extraction stack RNN at the last stage. CNN is not enough to cover characteristics of signal data which needs continuous prediction. Especially, evaluation of this challenge is performed on every sample of signals. Therefore, to solve that issue, deconvolutional filters [10] and RNN are deployed on the training model.

Þráinsson [17] uses RNN as a learning architecture with manually extracted features. However, our model obtains a better score on AUC-PR even though we use RNN. Therefore, MFCC is more efficient and effective than traditional feature extracting process. Warrick [16] is similar to our training model in that it combines signal processing with RNN. They use scattering transform on each signal for extracting features. However, the performance shows MFCC is better than scattering transform in preserving the characteristics.

5   Conclusion

Detection of awakening during sleep is a necessary field of research since it can serve as a reference to determine the cause of sleep disorders. Among them, breathing-related disorders occur most frequently. However, it is difficult obtaining a large data set and the type of signals is also limited. Recently, dataset published by Physionet is meaningful as public data supplementing these limitations.

We propose a bidirectional LSTM model with MFCC feature vectors that can be continuously discriminated on various sleep signal data. By using MFCC, there is no hand-crafted feature extraction process on preparing input features. MFCC helps to develop efficient learning process compared to other proposed methods in the challenge. In addition, MFCC is able to solve the high dimensional problem of input data generated in Fourier Transform and it is competitive even though our model does not use any information except signal data. We confirm the performance improvement by finding the optimal number of MFCC features and using additional delta and delta-delta feature vectors. Future works will be using additional data and labeling for improving the overall performance.

References

1. Aggarwal, K., Khadanga, S., Joty, S.R., Kazaglis, L., Srivastava, J.: Sleep staging by modeling sleep stage transitions using deep crf. arXiv preprint (2018). arXiv:1807.09119
2. Cen, L., Yu, Z.L., Kluge, T., Ser, W.: Automatic system for obstructive sleep apnea events detection using convolutional neural network. In: 2018 40th Annual International Conference of the IEEE Engineering in Medicine and Biology Society (EMBC), pp. 3975–3978. IEEE (2018)
3. Cheng, M., Sori, W.J., Jiang, F., Khan, A., Liu, S.: Recurrent neural network based classification of ecg signal features for obstruction of sleep apnea detection. In: 2017 IEEE International Conference on Computational Science and Engineering (CSE) and Embedded and Ubiquitous Computing (EUC), vol. 2, pp. 199–202. IEEE (2017)
4. Dey, D., Chaudhuri, S., Munshi, S.: Obstructive sleep apnoea detection using convolutional neural network based deep learning framework. Biomed. Eng. Lett. 8(1), 95–100 (2018)
5. Ghassemi, M.M., et al.: You snooze, you win: the physionet/computing in cardiology challenge 2018. Hypertension 40(41.0), 40–46 (2018)
6. He, R., Wang, K., Liu, Y., Zhao, N., Yuan, Y., Li, Q., Zhang, H.: Identification of arousals with deep neural networks using different physiological signals (2018). https://doi.org/10.22489/CinC.2018.060
7. Hochreiter, S., Schmidhuber, J.: Long short-term memory. Neural Comput. 9(8), 1735–1780 (1997)
8. Howe-Patterson, M., Pourbabaee, B., Benard, F.: Automated detection of sleep arousals from polysomnography data using a dense convolutional neural network. Signal 1, 2 (2018)
9. Kumar, K., Kim, C., Stern, R.M.: Delta-spectral cepstral coefficients for robust speech recognition. In: 2011 IEEE International Conference on Acoustics, Speech and Signal Processing (ICASSP), pp. 4784–4787. IEEE (2011)
10. Miller, D., Ward, A., Bambos, N.: Automatic sleep arousal identification from physiological waveforms using deep learning (2018)

11. Muda, L., Begam, M., Elamvazuthi, I.: Voice recognition algorithms using mel frequency cepstral coefficient (mfcc) and dynamic time warping (dtw) techniques. arXiv preprint (2010). arXiv:1003.4083
12. Patane, A., Ghiasi, S., Scilingo, E.P., Kwiatkowska, M.: Automated recognition of sleep arousal using multimodal and personalized deep ensembles of neural networks (2018)
13. Schuster, M., Paliwal, K.K.: Bidirectional recurrent neural networks. IEEE Trans. Signal Process. **45**(11), 2673–2681 (1997)
14. Tsinalis, O., Matthews, P.M., Guo, Y., Zafeiriou, S.: Automatic sleep stage scoring with single-channel EEG using convolutional neural networks. arXiv preprint (2016). arXiv:1610.01683
15. Varga, B., Görög, M., Hajas, P.: Using auxiliary loss to improve sleep arousal detection with neural network. Sleep **68**(1), 32 (2018)
16. Warrick, P., Nabhan Homsi, M.: Sleep arousal detection from polysomnography using the scattering transform and recurrent neural networks. arXiv preprint (2018). arXiv:1810.08875
17. Þráinsson, H., et al.: Automatic detection of target regions of respiratory effort-related arousals using recurrent neural networks (2018). https://doi.org/10.22489/CinC.2018.126

Development of Biomedical Corpus Enlargement Platform Using BERT for Bio-entity Recognition

Thiptanawat Phongwattana and Jonathan H. Chan[✉]

King Mongkut's University of Technology Thonburi, 126 Pracha Uthit Rd., Bang Mod,
Thung Khru, Bangkok 10140, Thailand
thiptanawat.p@mail.kmutt.ac.th, jonathan@sit.kmutt.ac.th

Abstract. As the volume and availability of textual data dramatically increase in the current digital age, a major challenge is how to properly extract useful information online. A key component of the text mining pipeline is named entity recognition (NER) for extracting knowledge. Currently, there are many publicly available NER tools such as Stanford NLP, NLTK or Spacy python library. However, there is a problem of accurate unknown entity recognition. We focus on using deep learning for recognizing entities, as it has been shown to outperform traditional algorithms for big data in part of its ability for feature extraction and dealing with multi-dimensionality. In this paper, we applied the state-of-the-art language representation model termed BERT (Bidirectional Encoder Representations from Transformers) for NER classification, in order to enlarge the existing biomedical corpus for further machine learning processing. We used additional biomedical corpora for training, and then compared the results to a recent prior work. The end result is precision improvement of 2.24%, recall improvement of 3.55%, and F1-score improvement of 2.98%, in protein recognition of super-pathway of leucine, valine, and isoleucine biosynthesis. We also developed a prototype, in form of an internal web platform, for supporting bio-annotators and corpus enlargement purpose.

Keywords: BERT · Named Entity Recognition (NER) · Part-of-speech tagging · Sentence tagging · Text mining · Corpus enlargement platform

1 Introduction

At present, internet is becoming increasingly accessible to everyone, causing the amount of data to increase dramatically, thus posing challenges in processing and analysis of the data. There are many types of data on the internet, and we found that the majority of the data (over 90%) currently originates from text through Facebook, LinkedIn, Google, and many other web portals. The challenge, therefore, is to extract useful information from the overwhelming amount of data, which can then be used for further analyses. In the biological domain, the use of biomedical text mining has been well documented [1]. Recently, there has been a novel work on biological event extraction from abstracts [2]. They used the existing tool named TEES and applied vector machine (SVM) algorithm for extracting the events. However, there are many text-mining algorithms and tools that

© Springer Nature Switzerland AG 2019
T. Gedeon et al. (Eds.): ICONIP 2019, LNCS 11953, pp. 454–463, 2019.
https://doi.org/10.1007/978-3-030-36708-4_37

can handle this task, and their correctness in entity recognition for new words that are not in the training set could be improved.

In the past few years, deep learning algorithms have continually been gaining popularity over traditional machine learning models, as advancements in hardware make training complex models easier, and availability of libraries that allow the building of deep learning models easier emerges, such as TensorFlow, Theano, and PyTorch.

Deep learning algorithms have been used in many fields, especially in image recognition, where convolutional neural nets are the state-of-the-art. In the field of natural language processing, there are still many challenges to be solved with deep learning techniques such as extracting useful information from sentences, paragraphs, or even from whole documents. In this paper, we propose a deep learning technique based on BERT, which utilizes the bidirectional training of Transformer [3] to handle the entity recognition task. There has been increasing number of scientific works that showed that BERT outperforms the rest of deep learning algorithms in national language processing. For example, BERT is implemented for recognizing people's names, locations and organizations within sentences by using masked and unmasked words for training and evaluation.

Recently, we found that BERT was implemented in the biomedical domain and the pipeline is called BioBERT [4] that is pre-trained by using biomedical data such as genes, proteins, diseases, and so on. Therefore, we utilized BioBERT in our proposed framework and compared the results to the prior works in biomedical entity recognition, in form of protein recognition of the super-pathway of leucine, valine, and isoleucine biosynthesis.

2   Related Work

In the biological field, text mining can be utilized as a routine task for supporting researchers in part of knowledge extraction. Since many biological research papers have been dramatically published over a decade, without a text mining task, bio-curators have had to put much effort in extracting biological entities (e.g. genes, proteins, metabolites) and relationships. In 2016, text mining was implemented for extracting complex relationships (e.g. metabolic interactions) [2].

The authors proposed an integrated text mining framework that contains metabolic event extraction and metabolic interaction network reconstruction module for extracting novel knowledge from complex relationships in research papers. Text mining was also applied in text corpus construction [5] that the authors applied a named entity recognition task for constructing a thyroid cancer intervention corpus from biomedical abstracts. By doing so, they used a gold standard corpus for training, and overfitting avoidance was also concerned in their experiment.

In 2019, the prior work [2] was cited for extending the research by using multitask learning concept [6]. The authors found that an available corpus of the domain of interest may be insufficient in practice, because it needs to be curated by domain experts for annotating. Consequently, they proposed a development of an event extraction system for metabolic interactions from research literature. Thereafter, domain experts can bring the extracted events to fill in metabolic pathways. With the proposed multitask-learning, it could improve the overall performance of the event extraction system.

Since general text mining has been developed over a decade, the state-of-the-art technique has been based on recurrent neural network (e.g. LSTM, GRU). In 2018, Bidirectional Encoder Representations from Transformers (BERT) was introduced by Devlin et al. [3, 7], and it has become the state of the art in text mining field. BERT is used in a variety of machine-learning tasks, such as question answering, language inference and text summarization.

As in the research paper [3], the author described that "the model is designed to pre-train deep bidirectional representations from unlabeled text by jointly conditioning on both left and right context in all layers". Consequently, computational consumption can be a key benefit and outperform the existing text mining algorithms. With this advantage and the exceptional performance, BioBERT was developed by Lee et al. [4].

One of the deep-learning drawbacks is it requires a large amount of training data, and we recognize that the means of data enlargement in this research area is still limit. Therefore, the authors proposed BERT for biomedical text mining that effectively utilizes a transfer-learning technique from biomedical texts to biomedical text mining models.

With the combination of biomedical texts and BERT, the authors showed that the model outperformed all previous state-of-the-art models in the domain specific task.

3 Methodology

In our methodology, we used PyTorch with GPU acceleration as a deep learning platform. BioBERT was used for our training and the word embedding architecture is described as in Fig. 1.

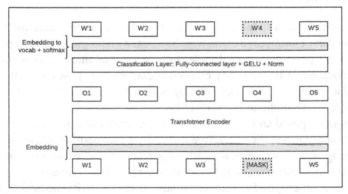

Fig. 1. Bidirectional Encoder Representations from Transformers (BERT) in a masked-word prediction.

As shown in Fig. 1, which represents a high-level architecture of the BERT masking process for predicting a sequence of tokens. The size of input and output is equivalent. The loss function comprises of only the computation of the masked values prediction and ignores the non-masked words.

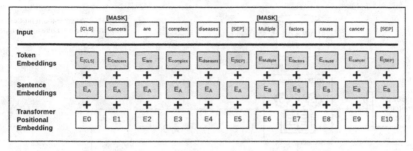

Fig. 2. Modified BERT with multiple biomedical sentences representation.

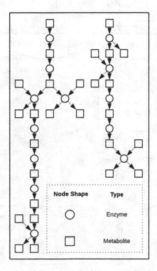

Fig. 3. Super-pathway of leucine, valine, and isoleucine biosynthesis.

In the proposed experiment, as shown in Fig. 2, we use a pair of sentences as an input. All sentences will be divided into two sets, each being 50%. The first half includes pairs of one sentence and its subsequent sentence within the original document; the second half includes pairs of a sentence and a random sentence that is disconnected from the first sentence, within the original document.

To recognize the first sentence in each input, a [CLS] token is inserted at the first position of the sentence. To recognize the end of each sentence, a [SEP] token inserted at the end. A sentence embedding is also added to each token. That means all tokens in one sentence will have the same sentence embedding.

A positional embedding is also needed within the architecture for defining the position of each token within the sequence. This technique is the main part of the Transformer model.

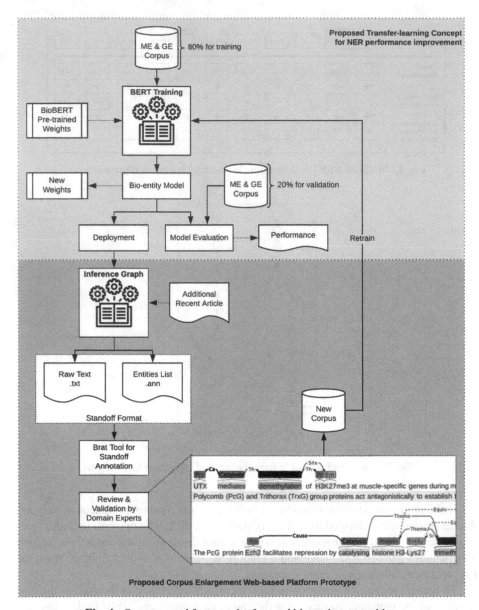

Fig. 4. Our proposed framework of named bio-entity recognition.

As shown in Fig. 4, we use ME and GE corpus, which we obtained from the prior work [2] for our experiment. There are 2 entities consisting of metabolites and proteins that we use for the named entity recognition task [8]. In the task, we used the proposed framework to identify all potential entities, and the identified tokens were then used for filling into a metabolic pathway, which is shown the example in Fig. 3.

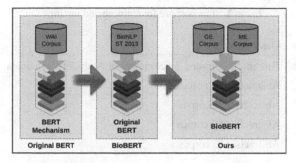

Fig. 5. Our proposed BioBERT with the new corpora.

Figure 5 shows that the original BERT was trained by using Wiki corpus [10]. And the authors in [4] used the original BERT with its pre-trained weights for training BioNLP-ST 2013 corpus. The BioNLP-ST corpus information is summarized in Table 1. As a result, the original BERT became BioBERT that was mainly implemented in biomedical field. In our work, we proposed the use of BioBERT with the pre-trained weights for training GE (GENIA) and ME (metabolic entities) corpora [2, 6]. Finally, we used the outputted classifier for recognizing bio-entities within a published article.

Table 1. 16 entities in the BioNLP-ST corpus.

Group			Entity	Example
Molecule		DNA	Gene	"LEC1" "APETALA2"
			Gene_Family	"LEC AP2-like"
			Box	"5'-GCATCG-3'"
			Promoter	"BCCP2"
	DNA Product		RNA	"FUS3 transcript"
		Amino acid sequence	Protein	"WRI1"
			Protein_Family	"SSPs"
			Protein_Complex	"SIN3/HDAC"
			Protein_Domain	"MADS-domain"
			Hormone	"ABA"
Dynamic Process			Regulatory_Network	"embryonic process"
			Metabolic pathway	"FA biosynthesis"
Context		Biological context	Genotype	"fus3 mutant"
			Tissue	"embryo"
			Development_Phase	"meristem formation"
			Environmental_Factor	"in vitro"

Table 2. The corpora for training and testing.

Corpus Type	Description	Amount
Training set	Full articles on seed development of Arabidopsis thaliana	20
	Abstracts: ME corpus	217
	Abstracts: GE corpus	120
Test set	Abstracts: ME corpus	54
	Abstracts: GE corpus	30

Table 2 shows the number of articles and abstracts that we used for training and testing in the experiment and the source. The training set consists of pairs of sentences with features including token embedding, sentence embedding, and positional embedding. And we also utilized the GE and ME corpus from the relevant paper for our training and testing [6].

The Softmax probability scores generated during training used at the end of the classification layer. The token with highest probability score was converted from numeric embedding into a word. In this experiment, it was necessary to have experts in the biomedical domain validating the predicted results. Then, we improved the existing training corpus by using the validated results. After obtaining the optimized training corpus, the existing model was retrained for optimization.

BERT algorithm utilizes attention mechanism [9] with the following formula

$$Attention(Q, K, V) = softmax\left(\frac{QK^T}{\sqrt{d_k}}\right)V \tag{1}$$

Q is a matrix that represents a dimensional vector of each word in the sequence.
K is a key that represents dimensional vectors of all the words in the sequence.
V is a value that represents dimensional vectors, which are matched to K's keys.
As in the abovementioned, we can simplify formula (1) as below,

$$a = softmax\left(\frac{QK^T}{\sqrt{d_k}}\right) \tag{2}$$

Table 3. BERT model parameters configuration.

Model	Description	Amount
BioBERT	Layer	24
	Hidden	1024
	Heads	16
	Parameters	340M

Table 3 describes BERT's architecture that we used in the experiment for training. The pre-trained weights that we used were the pre-trained weights from BioBERT, which was trained 200,000 steps with PubMed corpus.

In this experiment, we used precision (P), recall (R), and F1 score for evaluating and comparing with other techniques. The formulas can be described as below.

$$P = \frac{TruePositive}{TruePositive + FalsePositive} \tag{3}$$

$$R = \frac{TruePositive}{TruePositive + FalseNegative} \tag{4}$$

$$F1 = 2 \times \frac{Precision(P) \times Recall(R)}{Precision(P) + Recall(R)} \tag{5}$$

Table 4. The confusion matrix for demonstrating the abovementioned formulas.

Confusion matrix table		Predicted	
		Negative	Positive
Actual	Negative	True negative	False positive
	Positive	False negative	True positive

As shown in Table 4, we used a standard confusion matrix for evaluating precision (P), recall (R), and F1 score as shown in the formula (3), (4), and (5).

In our framework, we used the BioBERT pipeline for the bio-entity classification because the algorithm is state-of-the-art currently. And we would like to ensure that the classifier can predict bio-entities precisely as much as possible. The algorithm can be directly implemented for corpus enlargement purpose. However, domain experts are still needed to verify the predicted entities. We found that our entire framework can be utilized for enlarging the existing biomedical corpus by using as a supplementary research tool for researchers in part of corpus annotation.

4 Results and Discussion

As shown in Table 5, it can be seen that GENIA and BANNER, which are traditional algorithms, outperformed LSTM. We found that the dataset was insufficient and not suitable for deep learning training. This was the reason why the traditional algorithm has more efficiency than LSTM. Nonetheless, based on the results summarized, it is evident that, BioBERT has become the state-of-the-art deep learning algorithm in natural language processing. Within the training process, the algorithm takes advantage of LSTM, which reliant on size of available memory to facilitate convergence to the optimum loss computation, whereas the BERT algorithm focuses on pairs of sentences training.

Table 5. The comparison of named entity recognition algorithms based on super-pathway of leucine, valine, and isoleucine biosynthesis.

Super-pathway of leucine, valine, and isoleucine biosynthesis								
Evaluation	Metabolite				Protein			
	GENIA + BANNER	LSTM + SpaCy	LSTM + Standford NLP	BioBERT + Retraining	GENIA + BANNER	LSTM + SpaCy	LSTM + Standford NLP	BioBERT + Retraining
P	91.77	82.93	89.17	**92.52**	92.88	77.49	71.67	**95.12**
R	85.51	78.25	79.10	**88.76**	81.79	76.59	76.56	**85.34**
F1	88.53	80.52	83.83	**90.60**	86.98	77.03	74.03	**89.96**

Table 6. The comparison of named entity recognition algorithms based on super-pathway of pyridoxal 50-phosphate biosynthesis and salvage.

Super-pathway of pyridoxal 50-phosphate biosynthesis and salvage								
Evaluation	Metabolite				Protein			
	GENIA + BANNER	LSTM + SpaCy	LSTM + Standford NLP	BioBERT + Retraining	GENIA + BANNER	LSTM + SpaCy	LSTM + Standford NLP	BioBERT + Retraining
P	87.81	85.49	90.58	**91.63**	83.90	83.62	73.68	**88.26**
R	65.16	76.55	78.81	**80.64**	84.62	70.81	70.62	**83.91**
F1	74.81	80.77	84.29	**85.78**	84.26	76.68	72.12	**86.03**

In our experiment, we also applied the trained model on another super pathway named Pyridoxal 50-phosphate biosynthesis and salvage. As shown in Table 6, only one result, the recall of BERT, was worse than the traditional algorithm, by 0.71%. However, the F1-score outperformed the traditional algorithm by 1.77%.

5   Conclusions

Our experiment proved that BERT algorithm can outperform the existing deep learning algorithm such as LSTM, and also the traditional machine learning algorithm, such as SVM, in the named bio-entity recognition task. One of the major issues in deep learning model training was that, the dataset must be large enough. Therefore, if we need to generalize the model, the size of dataset should be a concern. BERT algorithm's computation consumes very low resources since has a Big-O computational time of $O(n)$.

We used 2 super metabolic pathways consisting of "leucine, valine, and isoleucine biosynthesis" and "pyridoxal 50-phosphate biosynthesis and salvage", which were used in the published paper [2], for bio-entity classification. We used the published paper's results as our baseline for comparing the entity recognition performance. We found that

BioBERT outperformed the baseline in F1 score, and it led us to enlarge the existing corpus with less bio-entity validation time by domain experts.

In the biomedical field, we would like to extract biological events by using BioBERT algorithm, which is one of the most difficult tasks in bioinformatics. After the improvement, we would like to find out a suitable way for reconstructing the existing metabolic networks after retrieving new biological entities or events from published papers.

Acknowledgement. The authors would like to thank Royal Golden Jubilee (RGJ) scholarship for funding the first author's PhD study. Also, we would like to thank Rena Lu, Helen Wang, and Louis Primeau for useful comments and careful proof-reading of this manuscript.

References

1. Zhu, F., et al.: Biomedical text mining and its applications in cancer research. J. Biomed. Inform. **46**(2), 200–211 (2013)
2. Patumcharoenpol, P., Doungpan, N., Meechai, A., Shen, B., Chan, J.H., Vongsangnak, W.: An integrated text mining framework for metabolic interaction network reconstruction. PubMed 27019783 (2016)
3. Devlin, J., Chang, M.W., Lee, K., Toutanova, K.: BERT: pre-training of deep bidirectional transformers for language understanding version 2. arXiv preprint arXiv:1810.04805v2 (2019)
4. Lee, J., et al.: BioBERT: a pre-trained biomedical language representation model for biomedical text mining. Bioinformatics btz682. https://doi.org/10.1093/bioinformatics/btz682
5. Kongburan, W., Padungweang, P., Krathu, W., Chan, J.H.: Semi-automatic construction of thyroid cancer intervention corpus from biomedical abstracts. In: 8th International Conference on Advanced Computational Intelligence (2016)
6. Kongburan, W., Padungweang, P., Krathu, W., Chan, J.H.: Enhancing metabolic event extraction performance with multitask learning concept. J. Biomed. Inform. (2019). https://doi.org/10.1016/j.jbi.2019.103156
7. Devlin, J., Chang, M.W., Lee, K., Toutanova, K.: BERT: pre-training of deep bidirectional transformers for language understanding version 1. arXiv preprint arXiv:1810.04805 (2018)
8. Björne, J., Salakoski, T.: Biomedical event extraction using convolutional neural networks and dependency parsing. In: Proceedings of the BioNLP 2018 Workshop, pp. 98–108, July 2018
9. Vaswani, A., et al.: Attention is all you need. In: Advances in Neural Information Processing Systems, pp. 5998–6008 (2017)
10. Nothman, J., Ringland, N., Radford, W., Murphy, T., Curran, J.R.: Learning multilingual named entity recognition from Wikipedia. Artif. Intell. **194**, 151–175 (2013)

A Generative Face Completion Method Based on Associative Memory

Gang Yang[1,2], Lei Zhang[1,2], and Jieping Xu[1,2(✉)]

[1] Key Lab of Data Engineering and Knowledge Engineering,
Renmin University of China, Beijing, China
{yanggang,xjp}@ruc.edu.cn
[2] School of Information, Renmin University of China, Beijing, China

Abstract. Associative memory is an important brain function human being owns, which could realize storage and cognition of information. Recurrent neural networks possess the function of associative memory, and they can realize image storage and generation basically. Based on stacked recurrent neural networks, a generative face completion method is proposed to utilize their associative memory function to realize face completion. According to different masked regions, the stacked recurrent neural network can memorize the relationship among row pixels from four directions of images, and associate lost pixels of the masked region in face images. In our method, a parallel multi-streams recurrent architecture with context constraints consider both global and local context information to associate the memorized images efficiently. Moreover, we propose an image hybrid strategy to optimize face images, which merges the associated pixels generated from different angles. Experiments on the Wild Face data set (CelebA) reveal that our generative face completion method can get the state-of-the-art results on the face completion problem.

Keywords: Generative face completion · RNN · Masked face

1 Introduction

Image completion aims to fill the missing or masked regions with plausible contents, which is widely used in photo editor. The performance of image completion is evaluated either by matching the original image accurately or by judging reasonability and realizability of the completed images. In application, image completion can be used as a special way of image generation for data augmentation and algorithm optimization.

This work was supported by the Beijing Natural Science Foundation (No. 4192029), and the National Natural Science Foundation of China (61773385, 61672523). We gratefully acknowledge the support of NVIDIA Corporation with the donation of the Titan Xp used for this research.

T. Gedeon et al. (Eds.): ICONIP 2019, LNCS 11953, pp. 464–475, 2019.
https://doi.org/10.1007/978-3-030-36708-4_38

There are two kinds of traditional methods to realize face completion, which are diffusion-based and patch-synthesis-based. Diffusion-based methods mainly fit for filling small missing regions. Provided that the surrounding of a missing region is continuous, these methods take advantage of the surrounding pixels to complete the missing region. Naturally, the methods are not effective to complete large missing regions. Because they are not involving the semantic textures or structures. The other methods are based on texture synthesis. These methods extract the match patches to fill missing regions. They are suitable for filling background (e.g., beach, sky and mountain) or other kind of large missing regions. However, they rely on semantic guidance and are constrained to the assumption that there exist similar patches. Considering object images such as face images for example, according to patch-synthesis-based methods, models need extra semantic guidance for face. Besides, there can be many unique contents or patterns, which may lead to the failure of matching patch. For instance, to recover the missing mouth under the sunglasses rather than eyes, a method need to be well designed to cover every pattern that it may encounter. Generative models based on deep learning offer new solution ideas for object completion. Some realize face completion well but still rely on prior conditions [17].

Fig. 1. Face completion. For each pair, the left is the image with some missing regions, the right is the completion result of our method. These scenes are difficult for other methods to complete.

In this paper, we proposed an associative memory net to effectively realize generative face image completion. Some results are shown in Fig. 1. The input is an image masked with noise and a same size image as labels of the mask position. In the first stage, we rotate the masked images and label images with 0, 90, 180, 270°. Along with the label images, we feed four masked images into associative memory net respectively. The associative memory net will generate four completion images of different directions. In the second stage, we propose a hybrid strategy to make full use of different direction images. Four images are merged with the strategy into a sensitive image, which increases the reasonability of the generated images. Experiments show that our method can handle image completion tasks that are difficult or impossible for traditional methods. Notably, the associative memory net is a generic method for image completion. More importantly, this generative net does not rely on any extra prior conditions.

There are two main contributions of this work: 1. We propose an associative memory net based on a basic recurrent neural network that generates effective missing contents without any prior conditions. 2. The associative memory ability of recurrent neural network is validated definitely to reveal the possibility of image generation by recurrent neural networks.

2 Related Work

2.1 Traditional Methods

One category of traditional image completion methods is diffusion-based. Bertalmio et al. [4] first proposed the method which was extended in various ways [1,5,16,22]. Diffusion-based methods perform well in inpainting small holes. However, owing to the assuming of local continuity, these methods are only suitable for the homogeneous content. And they can hardly handle image with large missing regions. Therefore, patch-synthesis-based methods are proposed.

There are two keys in these methods: extracting patches and synthesizing them. The latter mainly derives from texture synthesis algorithms [8,9,14]. For the former, Criminisi et al. [6] matched patches in the unknown region with content in the known region based on a priority function. This strategy is in greedy fashion, while Wexler et al. [25] proposed an algorithm for finding a global best match between image patches in terms of measuring the global cost. A fast PatchMatch [2] implements dense matching by proposing a randomized nearest neighbor matches algorithm. However, these methods may fail when it comes to filling semantically meaningful holes. Thus, additional semantic guidance is introduced for structured scenes. For example, lines drawn manually [23] are introduced to label the structure association between known and unknown regions. He et al. [12] estimated image structure automatically through the statistics of patch offsets. These methods complete the structure under the semantic guidance first, and then synthesize textures.

However, they perform well by the premise that there are similar patches of the image. Therefore, data-driven methods that use external reference dataset to search matching patches are proposed. Hays and Efros [11] used this strategy first. They proposed an algorithm to complete images using a dataset composed of Internet images. Barnes et al. [3] improved the patch queries by indexing dataset at the pre-computation stage. But it is still a difficulty for these methods to complete object images, especially when there are unique patterns. Because depending on low-level clues is the bottleneck of traditional methods.

2.2 Deep Learning Methods

Recently, deep generative models are applied to image completion. Initial methods [13,27] are also suitable to fill small holes only. Context Encoders [21] is proposed soon which can generate plausible contents in 128 * 128 image with a centered 64 * 64 hole. It uses an adversarial loss [10] and a standard pixel-wise reconstruction loss. Introducing parsing network for semantic regularization, Li et al. [17] proposed a GAN-Like Net [10] for face image completion. Wu et al. [26] improved and extended it to portrait image completion.

Through an additional parsing network trained on labeled dataset, these methods provide a promising direction for object image completion. However, GAN suffers from drawbacks such as mode collapse [19] that only produces similar samples owing to the failure of capturing diversity samples in the training data-set. For instance, Li et al.'s work [17] can fail in covering particular attribution like lip color. That motivates the emerging of distinct methods permits capturing the full diversity of training data-set. A pixel recursive model called PixelRNN [20] achieves that by modeling the distribution of natural images. Dahl et al. [7] extended this probabilistic network derived from two-dimensional RNN to produce plausible super resolution images. However, due to its complicated architecture, it is a problem to train this network. To achieve face completion without the help of additional network using labeled data-set, and keep both effectiveness as well as efficiency, we propose an associative memory net as well as an image hybrid strategy.

3   A Generative Face Completion Method

Inspired by associative memory function of recurrent neural network, we stack many basic recurrent neural networks to memorize rows of pixels and their relationship. When an image loses some regions, these recurrent neural networks can recall pixels of the region to complete the image through their stored relationship and pixels. According to the above work, we propose a generative face completion (GFC) method, consisting of an associative memory net (AMNet) and a hybrid strategy, as shown in Fig. 2.

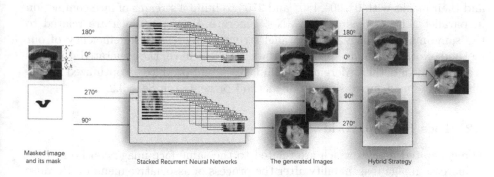

Fig. 2. The Generative Face Completion Method. Taking masked image labeled by its mask as input, it uses the associative memory net to learn the association between the missing regions and the normal regions, which build 4 streams to generate plausible completion images with four directions. Weighted by a hybrid strategy which emphasizes the association, completion images are merged into a realistic output.

3.1 Associative Memory Net

As shown in Fig. 2, the associative memory net (AMNet) contains stacked recurrent neural networks to generate face images, which is the key part of our method. AMNet uses $(l + h)$ simple recurrent neural networks connected sequentially to memorize their related rows of image. l is row number from image top to the first row of mask, and h is the height of mask. Every recurrent neural network has w neurons corresponding to w pixels of one row of the image. For example, there are l rows of pixels from the row 0 of the image to the first row of mask, i.e., the $(l-1)_{th}$ row of image. Then AMNet constructs $(1 + h)$ simple recurrent neural networks to remember these pixels of images. Based on the $0\sim(l-1)_{th}$ (row 0 to row $(l-1)$) rows' information, AMNet can generate a new l_{th} row which contains the first row of missing pixels labeled by mask. AMNet uses these generated pixels corresponding to the missing region and the original unmasked pixels to construct a new row to replace the l_{th} row. Then feed $1\sim l_{th}$ rows to AMNet. Repeat this process recurrently. Finally, a completed image with the same size of the masked image is generated, which is assembled by those new rows orderly. At training stage, mean square error (MSE) is used as fitness function to supervise AMNet. Image similarity between the generated face and its original face are computed on pixel-level.

AMNet takes a masked face image and its mask image which labels the missing regions as input. Regarding probability distribution of the pixel value as the feature, it learns the association between missing regions and normal regions. As AMNet uses side information of the missing region to build information relationship, borders of the masked region can also be associated effectively. Therefore, narrow masked regions are easily completed in images, to some extent. To take advantage of the property of AMNet efficiently, we rotate the face images and their masks with $0°, 90°, 180°$ and $270°$ to build 4 streams of face completion in parallel. The 4 streams of AMNet generate 4 images which are related to the same masked image. The parallel structure increases the efficiency of our method. Notably, due to different l rows AMNets have, the generated 4 images are different in details. Merging the 4 images would produce an optimized image, which is the next processing of our method presented in Sect. 3.2.

3.2 Face Image Hybrid

The generated images which are related to the same face image can be merged to increase image reasonability after the process of associative memory. Because AMNet learns the association among facial features, it successfully fills the missing regions with plausible contents. However, there are flaws like scratch in the generative region. That is because predicted pixels of each row are based on previous rows. And there is inevitable deviation between predicted pixels and original pixels. As the prediction progresses, predicted pixels are increasingly based on generated contents and the deviation getting bigger and bigger. Therefore, the later predicted pixels are less accurate and less realistic than the early predicted pixels. Taking Fig. 3 (2) for example, "scratch" in the eyes is more obvious than mouth. However, for generated image rotated by 180°, condition is opposite, where "scratch" in the eyes is less obvious. Because pixels in the eyes are generated earlier.

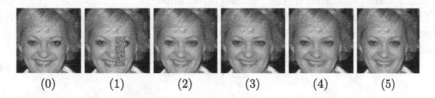

$$\begin{matrix} (0) & (1) & (2) & (3) & (4) & (5) \end{matrix}$$

Fig. 3. Completion results in different stage of our GFC method. (0): Original image. (1): Masked image. (2): Generated image of single stream of AMNet. (3) Result of Eq. 1. (4): Result of average strategy. (5): Result of hybrid strategy.

According to this characteristic of AMNet, we propose a hybrid strategy. It aims to improve the results by merging image with different angles. The design principle is to emphasize the association between the normal region and the missing region. Firstly, as shown in Fig. 2, we merge one pair of generated images each time. Pixel values P in the missing region are defined as:

$$P_{ij} = (1 - \frac{i}{h}) \times p_{ij}^r + \frac{i}{h} \times p_{ij}^{r+\pi} \tag{1}$$

p_{ij} denotes the pixel value at the i_{th} row and the j_{th} column. r and $r + \pi$ are the rotation degree of two images which differ by 180°. h is the height of mask, marked in masked image of Fig. 2. By giving a higher weight to the upper part of both generated images, we emphasize the association between the normal region and the missing region. As for the normal region, we replace it with the original pixels, and then obtain the merged image. Compared to Fig. 3 (2) representing the generated image of AMNet's one stream, completion results are more accurate.

However, this strategy may fail when it comes to the condition shown in Fig. 3. Because taking the AMNet's generating stream of 180° for instance, the reference region consisting of l rows above the mask is too small to learn the association adequately. The upper part of this completion images is worse, leading to a worse result.

Therefore, considering that the larger the reference region, the more accurate the prediction, we further adjust the weights of the two images, which is defined as:

$$W_r = l_r \times (1 - \frac{i}{h}) + l_{r+\pi} \times \frac{i}{h} \tag{2}$$

$$P_{ij} = \frac{l_r \times (1 - \frac{i}{h})}{W_r} \times p_{ij}^r + \frac{l_{r+\pi} \times \frac{i}{h}}{W_r} \times p_{ij}^{r+\pi} \tag{3}$$

For the two images rotated by r and $r + \pi$ degree, W_r denotes the weight of them, and l_r and $l_{r+\pi}$ are the number of rows from image top to the first row of mask separately. The image with a larger l has a higher weight. Merged result is shown in Fig. 3 (3). However, there still exist "scratch" because these two images are generated in the parallel directions.

Therefore, suppose that there are k pairs of merged images Eq. 3, continue to merge them, result of which R is defined as:

$$R_{ij} = \sum_k \frac{h_k}{\sum h_k} \times P_{ij}^k \tag{4}$$

P_{ij}^k denotes pixel value of the image merged according to Eq. 3. h_k is the mask height of the k_{th} pair of merged images. For concreteness, we merge two pairs of merged images, $0°$ with $180°$, and $90°$ with $270°$. That further refines the whole image and eventually eliminates the "scratch". This result is the output of our method, as shown in Fig. 3 (5).

Shown in Fig. 3 (4), result of average strategy R' (Eq. 5) that is also merged by four generated images is introduced to compare with hybrid strategy:

$$R'_{ij} = \frac{1}{2k} \sum_{n=1}^{2k} p_{ij}^n \tag{5}$$

Table 1. Evaluation results on PSNR and MS-SSIM of Fig. 3, where I1–I5 represent the different stage in our method. I1: Generated images of AMNet's stream in $0°$. I2: Generated images of AMNet's stream in $180°$. I3: Result of Eq. 3. I4: Result of average strategy. I5: Result of hybrid strategy. Higher values are better.

Metrics	I1	I2	I3	I4	I5
PSNR	33.3719	33.4049	33.8253	33.6999	33.9571
MS-SSIM	0.9800	0.9793	0.9814	0.9801	0.9817

4   Experiments

In this section, we conduct experiments to demonstrate the ability of our method for face completion. We evaluate our method on CelebA [18] dataset. CelebA consists of 202,599 face images. We process the dataset as [17]. Image is cropped, roughly aligned by the position of two eyes, and re-scaled to 128×128 pixels (Width × Height). We split the dataset following the standard split with 162,770 images for training, 19,867 for validation, and 19,962 for testing. We prepare many kinds of mask images used to occlude different facial components, such as eyes, nose, mouth, or several of them. In our GFC method, we build four streams of AMNet. Therefore, each mask corresponds to four models. We train the AMNet for 20 epochs to get one model, which takes about 10 h. Training in parallel, it spends about 20 h for 4 models corresponding to four directions to nearly get convergence. We evaluate AMNet on a Linux server with 4 Nvidia GTX Titan Xp GPUs.

4.1 Qualitative Results

Figure 4 shows some results of our method in different conditions, which verifies the performance of face completion. In each condition, we mask at least one facial component.

In the first row, we set a big mask to test the performance in extreme situations. The second row is a scene that face with glasses is masked, which tests the scenario with the unique pattern that is hard for traditional methods to recover [12] while it can be completed by our method successfully. In the third row, we present an example with a mask drawn randomly, where the eyes and nose are occluded. That is the simulation of practical application, such as removing the graffiti, which also shows that our method performs well in the common condition.

Overall, these visually realistic and satisfactory results demonstrate that our method is effective.

4.2 Quantitative Results

We also evaluate the performance of our method quantitatively according to two metrics on CelebA [18] test set (19,962 images). The first one is Peak Signal to Noise Ratio (PSNR). It measures the difference of pixel value between images. The second one is Multi-Scale Structure Similarity (MS-SSIM) [24]. It measures the differences of structure between natural images in terms of luminance, contrast and structure. Both metrics compare the result with the original image. We report the evaluation results of Fig. 3 in Table 1. That clearly shows the improvement of each stage step by step.

What's more, using mask in Fig. 5, we compare our method with Context Encoders [21] and Li et al. [17] on CelebA, result of which is shown in Tables 2 and 3. Both of their methods are GAN-Like Net can be used for semantic inpainting. The former is noted as CE. The latter additionally introduces a semantic parsing network for face completion. They train their networks in three stages. The first stage is training with a reconstruction loss on CelebA. Second, they fine-tune the networks using local loss. Then, a global adversarial loss and semantic regularization are used to train the face parsing network on Helen face dataset [15] in the last stage. Their approach is denoted as Li. For the same mask, the mean PSNR of our method is 59.8% higher than that of Li et al. [17], and the mean MS-SSIM is 20.8% higher. In addition, our method do not draw support from semantic guidance in terms of other datasets or object parsing networks. Thus, these comparisons suggest that our method is better at face completion.

Table 2. Evaluation results of PSNR for four different masks M1–M4.

Mask	Method				
	CE [21]	Li [17]	I1	I4	I5
M1	18.6	20.0	28.6238	29.5042	**29.5642**
M2	17.9	18.8	28.8958	30.5357	**30.6471**
M3	19.3	19.5	33.3508	**34.3295**	34.2357
M4	19.3	20.2	29.7280	**30.8983**	30.8518
Mean	18.8	19.6	30.1496	31.3169	**31.3247**

Table 3. Evaluation results of MS-SSIM for four different masks M1–M4.

Mask	Method				
	CE [21]	Li [17]	I1	I4	I5
M1	0.772	0.824	0.9514	0.9562	**0.9576**
M2	0.719	0.759	0.9501	0.9661	**0.9678**
M3	0.757	0.784	0.9798	**0.9841**	0.9840
M4	0.818	0.841	0.9630	0.9687	**0.9690**
Mean	0.767	0.802	0.9611	0.9688	**0.9696**

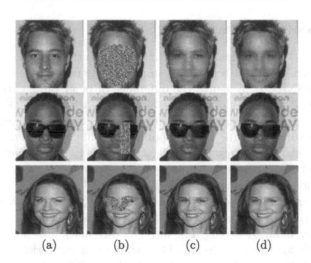

(a)   (b)   (c)   (d)

Fig. 4. Some results by using our GFC method on CelebA [18]. (a): Original image. (b): Masked image. (c): Generated image of single stream of AMNet. (d): Completion result of our method. From top to bottom, the first row is an example with big mask. The second one is a scene that face with glasses is masked. The third one is an example with a random shape mask.

Besides, considering that single stream of AMNet is difficult to get satisfactory result due to its complication and limitation, and to illustrate the efficiency of our method further, we compare the single AMNet's being trained for

M1   M2   M3   M4

Fig. 5. Face images with different masks M1–M4, which are the same as those Li et al. [17] used. These missing regions simulate some real scenes.

Table 4. Evaluation results on PSNR and MS-SSIM of Fig. 6.

Training type	PSNR	MS-SSIM
20 epochs	28.6238	0.9514
80 epochs	28.7277	0.9522
GFC	29.5642	0.9576

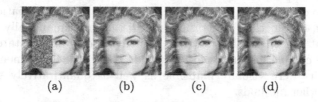

(a)   (b)   (c)   (d)

Fig. 6. Completion results of different training types. (a): Masked image. (b): Single stream of AMNet for 20 epochs. (c): Single stream of AMNet for 80 epochs. (d): Whole method of GFC for 20 epochs.

80 epochs with the whole method of GFC of which each stream is trained for 20 epochs. The result is shown in Table 4. Moreover, metrics on Fig. 6 (d) is better than that on Fig. 6 (c), showing that the whole method is more efficient than the normal single AMNet.

4.3 Analysis and Problems

As the AMNet learns associations between facial features at pixel level, and generates contents based on a region consisting of l rows. It performs well in generating semantic parts, even in scenario with special attributes. Taking the image with red lipsticks in Fig. 1 for instance, for the stream of AMNet with an angle of $270°$, it generates the right half of the lip at pixel level according to the left part that contains information of red lipstick. Similarly, AMNet is capable of generating symmetrical components that are semantically valid, such as unaligned face in Fig. 1. And there are 4 streams in 4 directions that are good at generating different semantic parts respectively. Through the hybrid strategy which makes full use of these generated images, we obtain a visually realistic completion image with plausible contents.

However, there are some problems as well. Firstly, one model only corresponds to one mask because the input shape of recurrent neural networks is fixed, which leads to low versatility and indirectly increases the amount of training. That can be addressed by training a model using a relatively large mask. When a small mask is included by a large one, we can use the weights of the large mask corresponding to the small one. What's more, in the future work, we intend to append AMNet with a GAN [10], to sharp the result and alleviate the inconsistency.

5   Conclusion

We proposed a generative face completion method consisting of an associative memory net and a hybrid strategy. The associative memory net was constructed by stacking recurrent neural networks, which globally utilized their associative memory ability to store and recall images. It was an effective way that the face hybrid strategy applied the specialty of row-level relationship of our association memory net to optimize the generated image. Aware of the association between facial features, our method can produce realistic and semantically reasonable results without special labeled datasets. Our method obtained state-of-the-art results of face completion on experiments. Moreover, the experiments revealed that our results were visually plausible as well as quantitatively satisfactory compared to other methods.

References

1. Ballester, C., Bertalmio, M., Caselles, V., Sapiro, G., Verdera, J.: Filling-in by joint interpolation of vector fields and gray levels (2000)
2. Barnes, C., Shechtman, E., Finkelstein, A., Goldman, D.B.: Patchmatch: a randomized correspondence algorithm for structural image editing. In: ACM Transactions on Graphics (ToG), vol. 28, p. 24. ACM (2009)
3. Barnes, C., Zhang, F.L., Lou, L., Wu, X., Hu, S.M.: Patchtable: efficient patch queries for large datasets and applications. ACM Trans. Graph. (TOG) **34**(4), 97 (2015)
4. Bertalmio, M., Sapiro, G., Caselles, V., Ballester, C.: Image inpainting. In: Proceedings of the 27th Annual Conference on Computer Graphics and Interactive Techniques, pp. 417–424. ACM Press/Addison-Wesley Publishing Co (2000)
5. Bertalmio, M., Vese, L., Sapiro, G., Osher, S.: Simultaneous structure and texture image inpainting. IEEE Trans. Image Process. **12**(8), 882–889 (2003)
6. Criminisi, A., Pérez, P., Toyama, K.: Region filling and object removal by exemplar-based image inpainting. IEEE Trans. Image Process. **13**(9), 1200–1212 (2004)
7. Dahl, R., Norouzi, M., Shlens, J.: Pixel recursive super resolution. In: Proceedings of the IEEE International Conference on Computer Vision, pp. 5439–5448 (2017)
8. Efros, A.A., Freeman, W.T.: Image quilting for texture synthesis and transfer. In: Proceedings of the 28th Annual Conference on Computer Graphics and Interactive Techniques, pp. 341–346. ACM (2001)
9. Efros, A.A., Leung, T.K.: Texture synthesis by non-parametric sampling. In: Proceedings of the Seventh IEEE International Conference on Computer Vision, vol. 2, pp. 1033–1038. IEEE (1999)

10. Goodfellow, I., et al.: Generative adversarial nets. In: Advances in Neural Information Processing Systems, pp. 2672–2680 (2014)
11. Hays, J., Efros, A.A.: Scene completion using millions of photographs. ACM Trans. Graph. (TOG) **26**(3), 4 (2007)
12. He, K., Sun, J.: Statistics of patch offsets for image completion. In: Fitzgibbon, A., Lazebnik, S., Perona, P., Sato, Y., Schmid, C. (eds.) ECCV 2012. LNCS, pp. 16–29. Springer, Heidelberg (2012). https://doi.org/10.1007/978-3-642-33709-3_2
13. Köhler, R., Schuler, C., Schölkopf, B., Harmeling, S.: Mask-specific inpainting with deep neural networks. In: Jiang, X., Hornegger, J., Koch, R. (eds.) GCPR 2014. LNCS, vol. 8753, pp. 523–534. Springer, Cham (2014). https://doi.org/10.1007/978-3-319-11752-2_43
14. Kwatra, V., Schödl, A., Essa, I., Turk, G., Bobick, A.: Graphcut textures: image and video synthesis using graph cuts. ACM Trans. Graph. (ToG) **22**(3), 277–286 (2003)
15. Le, V., Brandt, J., Lin, Z., Bourdev, L., Huang, T.S.: Interactive facial feature localization. In: Fitzgibbon, A., Lazebnik, S., Perona, P., Sato, Y., Schmid, C. (eds.) ECCV 2012. LNCS, vol. 7574, pp. 679–692. Springer, Heidelberg (2012). https://doi.org/10.1007/978-3-642-33712-3_49
16. Levin, A., Zomet, A., Weiss, Y.: Learning how to inpaint from global image statistics. In: Null, p. 305. IEEE (2003)
17. Li, Y., Liu, S., Yang, J., Yang, M.H.: Generative face completion. In: Proceedings of the IEEE Conference on Computer Vision and Pattern Recognition, pp. 3911–3919 (2017)
18. Liu, Z., Luo, P., Wang, X., Tang, X.: Deep learning face attributes in the wild. In: Proceedings of the IEEE International Conference on Computer Vision, pp. 3730–3738 (2015)
19. Metz, L., Poole, B., Pfau, D., Sohl-Dickstein, J.: Unrolled generative adversarial networks. arXiv preprint (2016). arXiv:1611.02163
20. Oord, A.v.d., Kalchbrenner, N., Kavukcuoglu, K.: Pixel recurrent neural networks. arXiv preprint (2016) arXiv:1601.06759
21. Pathak, D., Krahenbuhl, P., Donahue, J., Darrell, T., Efros, A.A.: Context encoders: feature learning by inpainting. In: Proceedings of the IEEE Conference on Computer Vision and Pattern Recognition, pp. 2536–2544 (2016)
22. Roth, S., Black, M.J.: Fields of experts: a framework for learning image priors. In: 2005 IEEE Computer Society Conference on Computer Vision and Pattern Recognition (CVPR 2005), vol. 2, pp. 860–867. Citeseer (2005)
23. Sun, J., Yuan, L., Jia, J., Shum, H.Y.: Image completion with structure propagation. In: ACM Transactions on Graphics (ToG). vol. 24, pp. 861–868. ACM (2005)
24. Wang, Z., Simoncelli, E.P., Bovik, A.C.: Multiscale structural similarity for image quality assessment. In: The Thrity-Seventh Asilomar Conference on Signals, Systems & Computers, 2003, vol. 2, pp. 1398–1402, IEEE (2003)
25. Wexler, Y., Shechtman, E., Irani, M.: Space-time video completion. In: Proceedings of the 2004 IEEE Computer Society Conference on Computer Vision and Pattern Recognition, 2004, CVPR 2004, vol. 1, pp. I-I. IEEE (2004)
26. Wu, X., et al.: Deep portrait image completion and extrapolation. arXiv preprint (2018). arXiv:1808.07757
27. Xie, J., Xu, L., Chen, E.: Image denoising and inpainting with deep neural networks. In: Advances in Neural Information Processing Systems, pp. 341–349 (2012)

White-Box Target Attack for EEG-Based BCI Regression Problems

Lubin Meng[1], Chin-Teng Lin[2], Tzyy-Ping Jung[3], and Dongrui Wu[1(✉)]

[1] School of Artificial Intelligence and Automation,
Huazhong University of Science and Technology, Wuhan, Hubei, China
drwu@hust.edu.cn
[2] Centre of Artificial Intelligence, Faculty of Engineering and Information
Technology, University of Technology, Sydney, Australia
[3] Swartz Center for Computational Neuroscience, Institute for Neural Computation,
University of California San Diego (UCSD), La Jolla, CA, USA

Abstract. Machine learning has achieved great success in many applications, including electroencephalogram (EEG) based brain-computer interfaces (BCIs). Unfortunately, many machine learning models are vulnerable to adversarial examples, which are crafted by adding deliberately designed perturbations to the original inputs. Many adversarial attack approaches for classification problems have been proposed, but few have considered target adversarial attacks for regression problems. This paper proposes two such approaches. More specifically, we consider white-box target attacks for regression problems, where we know all information about the regression model to be attacked, and want to design small perturbations to change the regression output by a predetermined amount. Experiments on two BCI regression problems verified that both approaches are effective. Moreover, adversarial examples generated from both approaches are also transferable, which means that we can use adversarial examples generated from one known regression model to attack an unknown regression model, i.e., to perform black-box attacks. To our knowledge, this is the first study on adversarial attacks for EEG-based BCI regression problems, which calls for more attention on the security of BCI systems.

Keywords: Adversarial attack · Brain-computer interfaces ·
Regression · Target attack · White-box attack

1 Introduction

Machine learning has been widely used to solve many difficult tasks. One of them is brain-computer interfaces (BCIs). BCIs enable a user to directly communicate with a computer via brain signals [18], and have attracted lots of research interest recently [10,11]. Electroencephalogram (EEG) is the most frequently used input signal in BCIs, because of its low-cost and non-invasive nature. Three commonly used BCI paradigms are motor imagery (MI) [15], event-related potentials

© Springer Nature Switzerland AG 2019
T. Gedeon et al. (Eds.): ICONIP 2019, LNCS 11953, pp. 476–488, 2019.
https://doi.org/10.1007/978-3-030-36708-4_39

(ERP) [16,20], and steady-state visual evoked potentials (SSVEP) [12]. Machine learning can be used to extract more generalizable features [23] and construct more accurate models [22], and hence makes BCIs more robust and user-friendly.

Recent research has shown that many machine learning models are vulnerable to adversarial examples. By adding deliberately designed perturbations to legitimate data, adversarial examples can cause large changes in the model outputs. The perturbations are usually so small that they are hardly noticeable by a human or a computer program, but can dramatically degrade the model performance. For example, in image recognition, adversarial examples can easily mislead a classifier to give a wrong output [6]. In speech recognition, adversarial examples can generate audio that sounds meaningless to a human, but be understood as a meaningful voice command by a smart phone [2]. Our recent work [24] also showed that adversarial examples can dramatically degrade the classification accuracy of EEG-based BCIs.

There are many different approaches for crafting adversarial examples. Szegedy et al. [17] first discovered the existence of adversarial examples in 2014, and proposed an optimization-based approach, L-BFGS, to find them. Goodfellow et al. [6] proposed a fast gradient sign method (FGSM) in 2014, which can rapidly find adversarial examples by searching for perturbations in the direction the loss has the fastest change. Carlini and Wagner [3] proposed the CW method in 2017, which can find adversarial examples with very small distortions.

All above approaches focused on classification problems, which find perturbations that can push the original examples cross the decision boundary. Jagielski et al. [7] conducted the first *non-target* adversarial attacks for linear regression models. This paper considers *target* adversarial attacks for regression problems, which change the model output by a pre-determined amount. Our contributions are:

1. We propose two approaches, based on optimization and gradient, respectively, to perform white-box target attack for regression problems.
2. We validate the effectiveness of our proposed approaches in two EEG-based BCI regression problems (drowsiness estimation and reaction time estimation). They can craft adversarial EEG trials that a human cannot distinguish from the original EEG trials, but can dramatically change the outputs of the BCI regression model.
3. We show that adversarial examples crafted by our approaches are transferable: adversarial examples crafted from a ridge regression model can also successfully attack a neural network model, and vice versa. This makes black-box attacks possible.

The attacks proposed in this paper may pose serious security and safety problems in real-world BCI applications. For example, an EEG-based BCI system may be used to monitor the driver's drowsiness level and urge him/her to take breaks accordingly. An attack that deliberately changes the estimated drowsiness level from a high value to a low value may overload the driver, and hence cause accidents.

The remainder of this paper is organized as follows: Sect. 2 introduces several typical adversarial attack approaches for classification problems. Section 3 proposes two white-box target attack approaches for regression problems. Section 4 evaluates the performances of our proposed approaches in two EEG-based BCI regression problems. Section 5 draws conclusion.

2   Adversarial Attacks for Classification Problems

This section introduces two typical adversarial attack approaches for classification problems, which are extended to regression problems in the next section.

2.1   Adversarial Attack Types

Assume a valid benign example $\mathbf{x} \in [0, 1]^k$ (k is the dimensionality of $\mathbf{x}$) is classified into Class y by a classifier $f(\mathbf{x})$. It is possible to find an adversarial example $\mathbf{x}' \in [0, 1]^k$, which is very similar to the original sample $\mathbf{x}$ according to some distance metric d, but is misclassified to $f(\mathbf{x}') \neq y$. According to how $f(\mathbf{x}')$ is different from y, there can be two types of attacks:

1. *Target attack*, in which all adversarial examples are classified into a predetermined class $y' \neq y$.
2. *Non-target attack*, whose goal is to construct adversarial examples that will be misclassified, but does not require them to be misclassified into a particular class.

According to how much knowledge the attacker can obtain about the target model (the model to be attacked), adversarial attacks can also be categorized into:

1. *White-box attack*, in which the attacker knows all information about the target model, such as its architecture and all parameter values.
2. *Black-box attack*, in which the attacker does not know the architecture and parameters of the target model; instead, he/she can feed some inputs to it and observe its outputs. In this way, he/she can obtain some training examples, and train a substitute model to craft adversarial examples to attack the target model. This approach makes use of the transferability of the adversarial examples [13].

2.2   White-Box Target Attack Approaches

This paper considers white-box target attacks only. Assume we know the architecture and all parameters of the classifier $f(\mathbf{x})$. We want to craft an adversarial example $\mathbf{x}'$ from an input $\mathbf{x}$ so that $f(\mathbf{x}') = y_t$, where y_t is a fixed class for all $\mathbf{x}'$.

Two representative target attack approaches for classification problems are:

1. *Carlini and Wagner (CW)* [3], which improves L-BFGS [17]. It introduces a new variable $\boldsymbol{\omega}$ so that

$$\delta = \frac{1}{2}(\tanh(\boldsymbol{\omega}) + 1) - \mathbf{x} \tag{1}$$

automatically satisfies the constraint $\mathbf{x}' = \mathbf{x} + \boldsymbol{\delta} = \frac{1}{2}(\tanh(\boldsymbol{\omega}) + 1) \in [0, 1]^k$. $\boldsymbol{\omega}$ in (1) is the variable to be optimized, which can assume any value in $(-\infty, \infty)$. Given $\mathbf{x}$, $\mathbf{w}$ is found through:

$$\min \left\| \frac{1}{2}(\tanh(\boldsymbol{\omega}) + 1) - \mathbf{x} \right\|_2 + c \cdot \ell \left(\frac{1}{2}(\tanh(\boldsymbol{\omega}) + 1) \right) = \min \| \boldsymbol{\delta} \|_2 + c \cdot \ell(\mathbf{x}') \tag{2}$$

where c is a trade-off parameter, and

$$\ell(\mathbf{x}') = \max \left(\max_{i \neq y_t} Z(\mathbf{x}')_i - Z(\mathbf{x}')_{y_t}, -\lambda \right), \tag{3}$$

in which $Z(\mathbf{x}')_i$ is the logits of the target model in Class i, and λ controls the confidence of the adversarial example. A large λ forces the adversarial example to be classified into the target class y_t with high confidence.

2. *Iterative Target Class Method (ITCM)*[1] [9], which modifies FGSM [6], an efficient approach for non-target attacks:

$$\mathbf{x}' = \mathbf{x} + \epsilon \cdot \text{sign}(\nabla_{\mathbf{x}} J(\mathbf{x}, y_{true})), \tag{4}$$

where ϵ controls the amplitude of the perturbation, J is a loss function, and y_{true} is the true label of $\mathbf{x}$.

ITCM performs target attack by replacing y_{true} in (4) by the target class y_t. It also improves the attack performance by taking multiple small steps of α in the gradient direction and clipping the maximum perturbation to ϵ, instead of taking a single large step of ϵ in (4):

$$\mathbf{x}'_0 = \mathbf{x}, \tag{5}$$

$$\mathbf{x}'_{m+1} = \text{Clip}_{\mathbf{x}, \epsilon} \{ \mathbf{x}'_m - \alpha \cdot \text{sign}(\nabla_{\mathbf{x}'_m} J(\mathbf{x}'_m, y_t)) \}, \tag{6}$$

where $\text{Clip}_{\mathbf{x}, \epsilon}(\mathbf{x}')$ ensures the difference between each dimension of $\mathbf{x}'$ and the corresponding dimension of $\mathbf{x}$ does not exceed ϵ.

3   White-Box Target Attack for Regression Problems

The section proposes two white-box target attack approaches for regression problems.

Let $\mathbf{x}$ be an input, y the groundtruth output, and $g(\mathbf{x})$ the regression model. Target attack aims to generate a small perturbation $\boldsymbol{\delta}$ such that the adversarial example $\mathbf{x}' = \mathbf{x} + \boldsymbol{\delta}$ can change the regression output to $g(\mathbf{x}') \geq y + t$, where $t > 0$ is a predefined target[2]:

$$\min_{\mathbf{x}'} \quad \| \mathbf{x}' - \mathbf{x} \|_2, \quad \text{s.t.} \quad g(\mathbf{x}') - y \geq t \tag{7}$$

---

[1] It is also called the iterative least-likely class method in [9].

[2] The regression output can also be changed to $g(\mathbf{x}') \leq y - t$. Without loss of generality, $g(\mathbf{x}') \geq y + t$ is considered in this paper.

3.1   CW for Regression (CW-R)

To extend the CW target attack approach from classification to regression, we optimize the following loss function:

$$\min_{\omega} \left\| \frac{1}{2}(\tanh(\omega) + 1) - \mathbf{x} \right\|_2 + c \cdot \ell(\mathbf{x}, \omega, t), \tag{8}$$

where

$$\ell(\mathbf{x}, \omega, t) = \max\left\{ g(\mathbf{x}) + t - g\left(\mathbf{x} + \frac{1}{2}(\tanh(\omega) + 1)\right), 0 \right\} \tag{9}$$

$$= \max\{g(\mathbf{x}) + t - g(\mathbf{x}'), 0\}. \tag{10}$$

The constructed adversarial example is then $\mathbf{x}' = \mathbf{x} + \frac{1}{2}(\tanh(\omega) + 1)$.

The pseudocode of the proposed CW method for regression (CW-R) is shown in Algorithm 1. It uses iterative binary search to find the optimal trade-off parameter c.

Algorithm 1. CW for regression (CW-R).

Input: $\mathbf{x}$, the original example;
        $g(\mathbf{x})$, the target regression model;
        t, the minimum change of the output;
        M, the number of the iterations;
        c_0, initialization of the trade-off parameter;
        N, the number of binary search steps for the optimal trade-off parameter.
Output: $\mathbf{x}'$, the adversarial example.
Initialize $c \leftarrow c_0$, $\omega_1 \leftarrow random$, $d_{\min} \leftarrow \infty$, $\bar{c} \leftarrow 1e4$, $\underline{c} \leftarrow 0$
for $n = 1 : N$ **do**
    for $m = 1 : M$ **do**
        $\mathbf{x}'_m \leftarrow \frac{1}{2}(\tanh(\omega_m) + 1)$;
        $\ell \leftarrow \|\mathbf{x}'_m - \mathbf{x}\|_2 + c \cdot \max\{g(\mathbf{x}) + t - g(\mathbf{x}'_m), 0\}$;
        $\omega_{m+1} \leftarrow \omega_m - \alpha \cdot \frac{\partial \ell}{\partial \omega_m}$;
        if $g(\mathbf{x}'_m) \geq g(\mathbf{x}) + t$ and $\|\mathbf{x}'_m - \mathbf{x}\|_2 \leq d_{\min}$ **then**
            $\mathbf{x}' \leftarrow \mathbf{x}'_m$;
            $d_{\min} \leftarrow \|\mathbf{x}'_m - \mathbf{x}\|_2$;
    end
    // Update c using binary search
    $c \leftarrow (\bar{c} + \underline{c})/2$;
    if $g(\mathbf{x}') \geq g(\mathbf{x}) + t$ **then**
        $\bar{c} \leftarrow c$;
    else
        $\underline{c} \leftarrow c$;
    end
end
return $\mathbf{x}'$

3.2   Iterative Fast Gradient Sign Method for Regression (IFGSM-R)

Iterative fast gradient sign method for regression (IFGSM-R) extends ITCM from classification to regression.

Define the loss function

$$\ell(\mathbf{x}, \mathbf{x}'_m, t) = \max\{g(\mathbf{x}) + t - g(\mathbf{x}'_m), 0\}, \tag{11}$$

which is essentially the same as (9), except that a change of variable is not used here. Then, the adversarial example can be iteratively calculated as:

$$\mathbf{x}'_0 = \mathbf{x}, \tag{12}$$
$$\mathbf{x}'_{m+1} = \text{Clip}_{\mathbf{x},\epsilon}\{\mathbf{x}'_m - \alpha \cdot \text{sign}(\nabla_{\mathbf{x}'_m}\ell(\mathbf{x}, \mathbf{x}'_m, t))\}. \tag{13}$$

The pseudocode of the proposed IFGSM-R is shown in Algorithm 2.

Algorithm 2. Iterative fast gradient sign method for regression (IFGSM-R).

Input: $\mathbf{x}$, the original example;
   $g(\mathbf{x})$, the target regression model;
   t, the minimum change of the output;
   M, the number of iterations;
   ϵ, the upper bound of the perturbation;
   α, the step size.
Output: $\mathbf{x}'$, the adversarial example.
$\mathbf{x}'_0 = \mathbf{x}$;
for $m = 0 : M$ **do**
   $\mid \quad \mathbf{x}'_{m+1} \leftarrow \text{Clip}_{\mathbf{x},\epsilon}(\mathbf{x}'_m - \alpha \cdot \text{sign}(\nabla_{\mathbf{x}'_m}\ell(\mathbf{x}, \mathbf{x}'_m, t)))$, using $\ell(\mathbf{x}, \mathbf{x}'_m, t)$ in (11);
end
return $\mathbf{x}'_{M+1}$

---

4   Experiments and Results

This section evaluates the performances of the two proposed white-box target attack approaches in two BCI regression problems.

4.1   The Two BCI Regression Problems

We used the following two BCI regression datasets in our experiments:

1. *Driving.* The driving dataset was collected from 16 subjects (ten males, six females; age 24.2 ± 3.7), who participated in a sustained-attention driving experiment [4,22]. Our task was to predict the drowsiness index from the EEG signals, which were recorded using 32 channels with a sampling rate of 500 Hz. Our preprocessing and feature extraction procedures were identical to those in [19]. We applied a [1,50] Hz band-pass filter to remove artifacts and noise,

and then downsampled the EEG signals from 500 Hz to 250 Hz. Next, we computed the average power spectral density in the theta band (4–7 Hz) and alpha band (7–13 Hz) for each channel, and used them as our features, after removing abnormal channels. Since data from one subject were not recorded correctly, we only used 15 subjects in our paper. Each subject had about 1000 samples. More details about this dataset can be found in [4,19].

2. *PVT.* A psychomotor vigilance task (PVT) [5] uses reaction time (RT) to measure a subject's response speed to a visual stimulus. Our dataset [21] consisted of 17 subjects (13 males, four females; age 22.4 ± 1.6), each with 465–843 trials. The 64-channel EEG signals were preprocessed using the standardized early-stage EEG processing pipeline (PREP) [1]. Then, they were downsampled from 1000 Hz to 256 Hz, and passed through a [1,20] Hz band-pass filter. Similar to the driving dataset, we also computed the average power spectral density in the theta band (4–7 Hz) and alpha band (7–13 Hz) for each channel as our features. The goal was to predict a user's RT from the EEG signals. More details about this dataset can be found in [20,21].

4.2   Experimental Settings and Performance Measures

We performed white-box target attack on the two BCI regression datasets. Assume the attacker knows all information about the regression model, i.e., its architecture and parameters. We crafted adversarial examples that can change the regression model output by a pre-determined amount.

Two regression models were considered. The first was ridge regression (RR) with ridge parameter 0.1. The second was a multi-layer perceptron (MLP) neural network with two hidden layers and 50 nodes in each layer. We used the Adam optimizer [8] and the root mean squared error (RMSE) as the loss function. Early stopping was used to reduce over-fitting.

Two attack scenarios were considered:

1. *Within-subject attack.* For each individual subject, we randomly chose 90% data for training the RR model and the rest 10% for testing. For the MLP, we further randomly set apart 10% of the training set as the validation set in early stopping. We computed the test RMSE for each subject, and also their average across all subjects.
2. *Cross-subject attack.* Each time we picked one subject as the test subject, and concatenated data from all remaining subjects together to train the RR model. For the MLP, 90% of these data were randomly selected for training, and the remaining 10% for validation in early stopping. RMSEs were computed on the test subject.

Attack success rate (ASR) and distortion were used to evaluate the attack performance. The ASR was defined as the percentage of adversarial examples whose prediction satisfied $g(\mathbf{x}') \geq g(\mathbf{x}) + t$, where $t > 0$ was our targeted change. The distortion was computed as the L_2 distance between the adversarial example and the original example.

Table 1. Baseline regression performances on the original EEG data, and the attack performances by CW-P, IFGSM-P, and random noise. $t = 0.2$ was used.

Scenario		Within-subject				Cross-subject			
Dataset		Driving		PVT		Driving		PVT	
Model		RR	MLP	RR	MLP	RR	MLP	RR	MLP
Baseline	RMSE	.1766	.1355	.1293	.1445	.2207	.2124	.2255	.2433
	MO	.3805	.3715	.5262	.5318	.2499	.2371	.5384	.5333
CW-P	RMSE	.2732	.2368	.2569	.2693	.2976	.2753	.3349	.3405
	MO	.5805	.5717	.7262	.7319	.4499	.4374	.7385	.7337
	ASR	99.59%	99.94%	99.68%	100%	99.97%	100%	99.81%	99.91%
	Distortion	2.5835	.5858	6.7537	3.7048	.8687	.4008	.4678	.5333
IFGSM-P	RMSE	.2858	.2788	.2719	.2828	.3176	.3193	.3553	.3857
	MO	.5967	.6168	.7478	.7515	.4790	.4967	.7657	.7884
	ASR	96.88%	99.54%	92.29%	99.19%	98.97%	99.97%	99.94%	99.56%
	Distortion	6.9672	1.7338	14.3129	7.8370	2.6852	1.3415	1.5272	2.3071
Random noise	RMSE	.1766	.1355	.1293	.1445	.2207	.2124	.2255	.2433
	MO	.3805	.3715	.5262	.5318	.2499	.2371	.5384	.5333
	ASR	0.00%	0.00%	0.00%	0.00%	0.00%	0.00%	0.00%	0.00%
	Distortion	7.1023	1.8663	14.5002	8.0664	2.8018	1.4866	1.6348	2.4029

4.3 Experimental Results

The baseline regression performances on the original (unperturbed) EEG data are shown in the first panel of Table 1, where "mean output (MO)" is the mean of the regression outputs for all EEG trials. For each regression model on each dataset, the cross-subject RMSE was always larger than the corresponding within-subject RMSE, which is intuitive, because individual differences make it difficult to develop a model that generalizes well across subjects.

We set $t = 0.2$ in both CW-P and IFGSM-P, and called the attack a success if $g(\mathbf{x}') \geq g(\mathbf{x}) + t$. $N = 9$ and $c_0 = 0.01$ were used in CW-P. $M = 25$, $\alpha = 0.001$, and grid search for $\epsilon \in \{0.001, 0.002, ..., 0.03\}$ were used in IFGSM-P. We used L_2 distance to measure the distortion of the adversarial examples. The attack performances are shown in the second and third panels of Table 1:

1. The RMSEs after CW-P and IFGSM-P attacks were always much larger than those before the attacks, indicating that the attacks dramatically changed the characteristics of the model output.
2. For each regression model on each dataset, the mean output of the adversarial examples was always larger than that of the original examples by at least t, which was our target. This suggests that both CW-P and IFGSM-P were effective.
3. The ASRs of both CW-P and IFGSM-P were always close to 100%, indicating that almost all attacks were successful. A closer look revealed that the ASR of CW-P was always slightly larger than the corresponding ASR of IFGSM-P,

and the RMSE, mean output, and distortion of CW-P were always smaller than the corresponding quantities of IFGSM-P, i.e., CW-P was generally more effective than IFGSM-P. However, the computational cost of CW-P was much higher than IFGSM-P.

It's also interesting to check if adding random noise can significantly degrade the regression performance; if so, then no deliberate adversarial example crafting is needed. To this end, we performed attacks by adding random Gaussian noise $\mathcal{N}(0, \sigma)$ to the original examples, where σ was chosen so that the resulted distortion approximately equaled the maximum distortion introduced by CW-P and IFGSM-P. The corresponding attack performances are shown in the last panel of Table 1. Though the distortion was large, random Gaussian noise almost did not change the regression RMSE and the mean output, and its ASR was always 0.00%, suggesting that sophisticated attack approaches like CW-P and IFGSM-P are indeed needed.

Some examples of the original EEG trials and those after adding adversarial perturbations are shown in Fig. 1. The differences between the original and adversarial trials were too small to be distinguished by a human, which should also be very difficult to be detected by a computer algorithm.

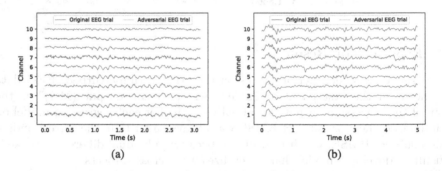

Fig. 1. Examples of the original EEG trials (blue) and the adversarial trials (red), generated by CW-P. (a) driving; (b) PVT. The blue and red curves almost completely overlap. (Color figure online)

4.4   Spectrogram Analysis

This section utilizes spectrogram analysis to further understand the characteristics of the adversarial examples. We computed the mean spectrogram of all EEG trials, the mean spectrogram of all successful adversarial examples, and the mean spectrogram of the corresponding perturbations, using wavelet decomposition. Figure 2 shows the results, where the adversarial examples were designed for MLP on the PVT dataset. There is no noticeable difference between the mean spectrograms of the original EEG trials and the adversarial examples crafted by our two approaches. This suggests that adversarial examples are difficult to distinguish from spectrogram analysis.

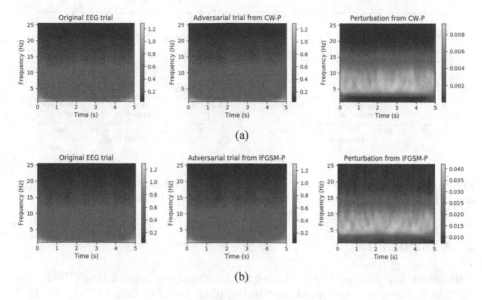

(a)

(b)

Fig. 2. Mean spectrogram of all original EEG trials (first column), mean spectrogram of all successful adversarial examples (second column), and mean spectrogram of the perturbations (third column), from MLP on the PVT dataset. Channel C_z was used. (a) CW-P; (b) IFGSM-P.

The third column of Fig. 2 shows the difference between the mean spectrograms in the first two columns. Note that the amplitudes were much smaller than those in the first two columns. The patterns of those two perturbations are similar. The energy of those perturbations was concentrated in [3,10] Hz, and was almost uniformly distributed in the entire time domain.

4.5   Transferability of Adversarial Examples Between Different Regression Models

The transferability of adversarial examples means that adversarial examples designed to attack one model may also be used to attack a different model. This property makes black-box attacks possible, where we have no information about the target regression model at all [13,14].

Figure 3 shows the mean output, when adversarial examples designed from MLP were used to attack the RR model [Fig. 3(a)], and vice versa [Fig. 3(b)], in within-subject attacks on the PVT dataset. In Fig. 3(a), although the attack performance on RR degraded compared with the attack performance on MLP, the adversarial examples still dramatically changed the outputs of RR. Figure 3(b) is similar. These demonstrate that adversarial examples generated by CW-P and IFGSM-P are also transferrable, and hence may be used in black-box attacks.

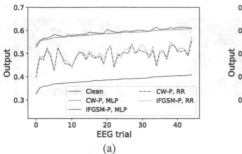 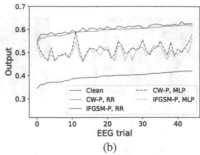

(a)   (b)

Fig. 3. Outputs of the adversarial examples, when transferred from (a) MLP to RR, and (b) RR to MLP, in within-subject attacks on the PVT dataset.

5   Conclusions

This paper has proposed two white-box target attack approaches, CW-P and IFGSM-P, for regression problems, and applied them to two EEG-based BCI regression problems. Both approaches can successfully change the model output by a pre-determined amount. Generally, CW-P achieved better attack performance than IFGSM-P, in terms of a larger ASR and a smaller distortion; however, its computational cost is higher than IFGSM-P. We also verified that the adversarial examples crafted from both CW-P and IFGSM-P are transferrable, and hence adversarial examples generated from a known regression model can also be used to attack an unknown regression model, i.e., to perform black-box attacks.

To our knowledge, this is the first study on adversarial attacks for EEG-based BCI regression problems, which calls for more attention on the security of BCI systems. Our future research will study how to defend such attacks.

Acknowledgement. This research was supported by the National Natural Science Foundation of China Grant 61873321.

References

1. Bigdely-Shamlo, N., Mullen, T., Kothe, C., Su, K.M., Robbins, K.A.: The PREP pipeline: standardized preprocessing for large-scale EEG analysis. Front. Neuroinform. **9**, 16 (2015)
2. Carlini, N., et al.: Hidden voice commands. In: Proceedings of the 25th USENIX Security Symposium, Austin, TX, August 2016
3. Carlini, N., Wagner, D.: Towards evaluating the robustness of neural networks. In: Proceedings of the IEEE Symposium on Security and Privacy, San Jose, CA, May 2017
4. Chuang, C.H., Ko, L.W., Jung, T.P., Lin, C.T.: Kinesthesia in a sustained-attention driving task. Neuroimage **91**, 187–202 (2014)

5. Dinges, D.F., Powell, J.W.: Microcomputer analyses of performance on a portable, simple visual RT task during sustained operations. Behav. Res. Methods Instrum. Comput. **17**(6), 652–655 (1985)

6. Goodfellow, I.J., Shlens, J., Szegedy, C.: Explaining and harnessing adversarial examples. In: Proceedings of the International Conference on Learning Representations, San Diego, CA, December 2014

7. Jagielski, M., Oprea, A., Biggio, B., Liu, C., Nita-Rotaru, C., Li, B.: Manipulating machine learning: poisoning attacks and countermeasures for regression learning. In: Proceedings of the IEEE Symposium on Security and Privacy, San Francisco, CA, May 2018

8. Kingma, D.P., Ba, J.: Adam: a method for stochastic optimization. In: Proceedings of the International Conference on Learning Representations, Banff, Canada, April 2014

9. Kurakin, A., Goodfellow, I.J., Bengio, S.: Adversarial examples in the physical world. In: Proceedings of the International Conference on Learning Representations, Toulon, France, April 2017

10. Lance, B.J., Kerick, S.E., Ries, A.J., Oie, K.S., McDowell, K.: Brain-computer interface technologies in the coming decades. Proc. IEEE **100**(Special Centennial Issue), 1585–1599 (2012)

11. Makeig, S., Kothe, C., Mullen, T., Bigdely-Shamlo, N., Zhang, Z., Kreutz-Delgado, K.: Evolving signal processing for brain-computer interfaces. Proc. IEEE **100**(Special Centennial Issue), 1567–1584 (2012)

12. Middendorf, M., McMillan, G., Calhoun, G., Jones, K.: Brain-computer interfaces based on the steady-state visual-evoked response. IEEE Trans. Rehabil. Eng. **8**(2), 211–214 (2000)

13. Papernot, N., McDaniel, P.D., Goodfellow, I.J.: Transferability in machine learning: from phenomena to black-box attacks using adversarial samples. CoRR abs/1605.07277 (2016). http://arxiv.org/abs/1605.07277

14. Papernot, N., McDaniel, P.D., Goodfellow, I.J., Jha, S., Celik, Z.B., Swami, A.: Practical black-box attacks against machine learning. In: Proceedings of the ACM Asia Conference on Computer and Communications Security, Abu Dhabi, UAE, April 2017

15. Pfurtscheller, G., Neuper, C.: Motor imagery and direct brain-computer communication. Proc. IEEE **89**(7), 1123–1134 (2001)

16. Sutton, S., Braren, M., Zubin, J., John, E.R.: Evoked-potential correlates of stimulus uncertainty. Science **150**(3700), 1187–1188 (1965)

17. Szegedy, C., et al.: Intriguing properties of neural networks. In: Proceedings of the International Conference on Learning Representations, Banff, Canada, April 2014

18. Wolpaw, J.R., Birbaumer, N., McFarland, D.J., Pfurtscheller, G., Vaughan, T.M.: Brain-computer interfaces for communication and control. Clin. Neurophysiol. **113**(6), 767–91 (2002)

19. Wu, D., Chuang, C.H., Lin, C.T.: Online driver's drowsiness estimation using domain adaptation with model fusion. In: Proceedings of the International Conference on Affective Computing and Intelligent Interaction, Xi'an, China, September 2015

20. Wu, D., King, J.T., Chuang, C.H., Lin, C.T., Jung, T.P.: Spatial filtering for EEG-based regression problems in brain-computer interface (BCI). IEEE Trans. Fuzzy Syst. **26**(2), 771–781 (2018)

21. Wu, D., Lance, B.J., Lawhern, V.J., Gordon, S., Jung, T.P., Lin, C.T.: EEG-based user reaction time estimation using Riemannian geometry features. IEEE Trans. Neural Syst. Rehabil. Eng. **25**(11), 2157–2168 (2017)

22. Wu, D., Lawhern, V.J., Gordon, S., Lance, B.J., Lin, C.T.: Driver drowsiness estimation from EEG signals using online weighted adaptation regularization for regression (OwARR). IEEE Trans. Fuzzy Syst. 25(6), 1522–1535 (2017)
23. Zander, T.O., Kothe, C.: Towards passive brain-computer interfaces: applying brain-computer interface technology to human-machine systems in general. J. Neural Eng. 8(2), 025005 (2011)
24. Zhang, X., Wu, D.: On the vulnerability of CNN classifiers in EEG-based BCIs. IEEE Trans. Neural Syst. Rehabil. Eng. 27(5), 814–825 (2019)

Human Centred Computing and Medicine

Real-Time Guidewire Segmentation and Tracking in Endovascular Aneurysm Repair

Yan-Jie Zhou[1,3], Xiao-Liang Xie[1], Gui-Bin Bian[1], Zeng-Guang Hou[1,2,3(✉)],
Bao Liu[4], Zhi-Chao Lai[4], Xin-Kai Qu[5], Shi-Qi Liu[1], and Xiao-Hu Zhou[1]

[1] State Key Laboratory of Management and Control for Complex Systems,
Institute of Automation, Chinese Academy of Sciences, Beijing 100190, China
{zhouyanjie2017,zengguang.hou}@ia.ac.cn
[2] CAS Center for Excellence in Brain Science and Intelligence Technology,
Beijing 100190, China
[3] University of Chinese Academy of Sciences, Beijing 100049, China
[4] Department of Vascular Surgery, Peking Union Medical College Hospital,
Beijing 100032, China
[5] Department of Cardiology, Huadong Hospital Affiliated to Fudan University,
Shanghai 200040, China

Abstract. Endovascular aneurysm repair (EVAR) is currently the treatment of choice for most patients with an abdominal aortic aneurysm (AAA). Real-time guidewire tracking in 2D X-ray fluoroscopy can greatly assist physician in EVAR treatment. Nevertheless, this task is often accompanied by the challenges of the noisy background of X-ray fluoroscopy and the elongated deformable structure of the guidewire. In this work, a novel lightweight network architecture called Fast Attention Segmentation Network is proposed for real-time guidewire tracking. The novel network combines the advantages of attention mechanism, the pre-trained lightweight components and reinforced focal loss to effectively address the problem of extreme foreground-background class imbalance and misclassified examples. Experiment results on clinical 2D X-ray image sequences of 30 patients demonstrate that the proposed approach can achieve the state-of-the-art performance. To the best of our knowledge, this is the first approach capable of real-time segmenting and tracking guidewire in EVAR treatment.

Keywords: Guidewire · Segmentation · Tracking · X-ray fluoroscopy

1 Introduction

Abdominal aortic aneurysm (AAA) has been the most common aneurysm. AAAs are usually asymptomatic until they rupture, with an ensuring mortality 85% to 90% [1]. Hence, AAA has become an important disease threatening human health. Clinical evidence-based research shows a lower perioperative morbidity

© Springer Nature Switzerland AG 2019
T. Gedeon et al. (Eds.): ICONIP 2019, LNCS 11953, pp. 491–500, 2019.
https://doi.org/10.1007/978-3-030-36708-4_40

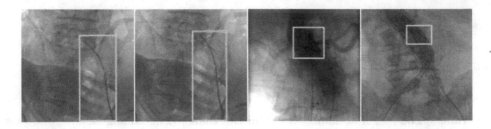

Fig. 1. Low SNR 2D X-ray fluoroscopy of guidewire in EVAR treatment.

and mortality, and similar long-term survival, for EVAR compared with open repair of suitable AAAs. Meanwhile, recent technological advances in EVAR have made it an option for a larger proportion of patients undergoing surgical intervention for AAA. The critical procedure of EVAR treatment is to deliver the guidewire to the lesion through a complex interventional pathway [2]. Thus, real-time and accurate guidewire segmentation and tracking in EVAR is imperative. Nevertheless, segmentation and tracking of guidewire is tough for the following reasons: (1) The X-ray images have low signal-to-noise ratio (SNR) and background noise greatly interferes with the segmentation of guidewire. (2) The extreme foreground-background class imbalance is produced by the low ratio of guidewire pixels to the pixels of the background. (3) The edge pixels of the guidewire turn into misclassified examples due to the contrast agents and wire-like structures such as vertebrae and pelvis contour [3], as shown in Fig. 1.

Research on guidewire tracking in EVAR treatment is less frequent [4]. Traditional tracking methods of interventional instruments are based on spline fitting [5,6], which is difficult in noisy background. And in these methods, the first frame of the fluoroscopy sequence needs to be initialized manually and the instruments between two consecutive frames cannot be significantly deformed. A recent approach based on cascaded convolutional neural network (CNN) in [7] was designed for segmenting the guidewire, using Faster R-CNN to detect the target region where the guidewire is located firstly, and then using Deep-Lab network to achieve the segmentation of guidewire in the cropped region. Whereas cascaded frameworks lead to excessive and redundant use of computational resources and model parameters, which results in slow processing speed at 0.25 s per frame.

In this work, the fast attention segmentation network is proposed for real-time guidewire segmentation and tracking in EVAR. The proposed network has a novel encoder-decoder architecture, which utilizes the power of attention mechanism, pre-trained components of MobileNetV2 as well as reinforced focal loss. The improvements between the proposed model with respect to the regular U-Net model are threefold. First, using attention gate (AG) improves the sensitivity and accuracy of the model for dense label prediction with minimal computational cost. Second, the pre-trained components of MobileNetV2 in encoder can reduce network parameters and improve model processing speed while ensuring performance. Last but not least, we reinforce the Focal Loss [8] as the loss function to

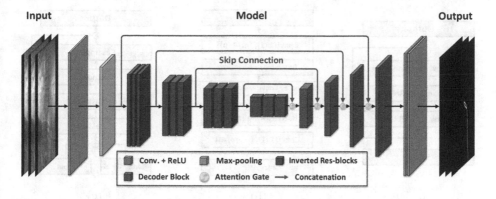

Fig. 2. The architecture of fast attention segmentation network. The pre-trained components of MobileNetV2 are utilized in encoder. The AGs filter the features propagated through the skip connections.

effectively address the problem of extreme foreground-background class imbalance and misclassified examples.

Contributions and Novelties. (1) To the best of our knowledge, this is the first fully automatic approach that achieves real-time guidewire segmentation and tracking in EVAR treatment. (2) A new annotation tool is designed specifically for guidewire labeling and the first 2D X-ray guidewire dataset named GWSeg is established. (3) The proposed novel model not only addresses the problem of misclassified examples, but also alleviates the extreme class imbalance, which is faster and more accurate than the state-of-the-art approach in 2D X-ray fluoroscopy.

2   Proposed Network Architecture

The architecture of the proposed fast attention segmentation network is shown in Fig. 2. The novel network has a encoder-decoder architecture. The encoder starts with a convolution on 512×512 input grayscale images with a kernel of size 7×7 and a stride of 2. The spatial max-pooling is then performed in the area of 3×3 with a stride of 2. The latter part of the encoder consists of the components of MobileNetV2 pre-trained on ImageNet. The key building components in the MobileNetV2 network are inverted residual block [9], which is illustrated in Fig. 3(a). The depthwise separable convolutions replace the standard convolutional layers in the residual block, thereby reducing considerable computational cost. Compared with the pre-trained backbones ResNet-101 (45M), ResNet-50 (24M) and VGG-16 (34M) [10], MobileNetV2 (2.4M) greatly reduces the parameters of the network and improves the processing speed while ensuring performance.

The decoder of the network consists of several decoder blocks. Each decoder block includes 1×1 convolution operation that reduces the number of filters by

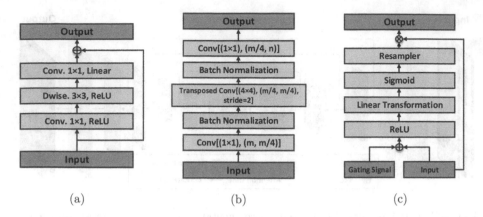

Fig. 3. The major components of the proposed network: (a) Inverted residual block (b) Decoder block (c) Attention gate (AG).

the factor of 4, followed by transposed convolution, which aims to recover the resolution of the feature map from 16×16 to 512×512 through up-sampling [11]. The details of the decoder block are shown in Fig. 3(b). In addition, the decoder blocks are connected to the corresponding encoder blocks through the skip connections, and the AGs in decoder highlight salient features useful for the guidewire which are passed through the skip connections. After decoder block, we obtain the final binary segmentation mask (1 for guidewire, 0 for others).

2.1   Attention Gate

Compared with two-stage methods, the AGs progressively suppress the feature responses of irrelevant background regions, eliminating the need for region of interest (ROI) [12]. As shown in Fig. 3(c), the gating vector g_i is utilized for the ith pixel to determine the attention regions. The attention coefficient $\alpha_i \in [0, 1]$ identifies image salient regions to maintain the activation relevant to the guidewire. Additive attention [13] is utilized to obtain the gating coefficient, which is formulated as follows:

$$\alpha_i^l = \sigma_2(\psi^T(\sigma_1(W_x^T x_i^l + W_g^T g_i + b_g)) + b_\psi) \tag{1}$$

where σ_1 and σ_2 correspond to the ReLU and sigmoid activation respectively. The W_x and W_g are the weights of linear transformation, and b_g, b_ψ are the bias. For the input tensor, use the channel-wise $1 \times 1 \times 1$ convolution ψ to compute the linear transformation. Trilinear interpolation is utilized to resampling the attention coefficients to avoid the region aliasing effect. The information extracted from coarse scale is utilized in gating to disambiguate irrelevant and noisy responses in skip connections. The AGs are merged into our model to implicitly learn to suppress irrelevant regions while highlighting salient features useful for the guidewire, which increase the model sensitivity and prediction accuracy with minimal computational cost.

2.2   Reinforced Focal Loss

In the task of guidewire segmentation and tracking, the elongated guidewire structure triggers extremely imbalanced foreground-background ratio (1 : 1000). Meanwhile, due to the interference of guidewire-like structures and contrast agents, the edge pixels of the guidewire become misclassified examples. The huge number of easy and background examples tend to overwhelm the training. In this work, the reinforced focal loss is utilized to address the problem of extreme class imbalance and misclassified examples. Our reinforced focal loss is represented as follows:

$$Loss = \begin{cases} -\alpha(1 - p_i)^\gamma \log p_i & y_i = 1 \\ -p_i^\gamma \log(1 - p_i) & y_i = 0 \end{cases} \tag{2}$$

where y_i is the label of the ith pixel, 1 for guidewire, 0 for background and p_i is the final mask probability of the ith pixel. The weighting factor α and the modulating factor γ are tunable within the range of $\alpha, \gamma \geq 0$. Whether it is the foreground class or the background class, the loss contribution from easy examples can be decreased by γ. Moreover, we have strengthened the role of the weighting factor α, so that it can increase the weight contribution of the guidewire more effectively, thus addressing the extreme class imbalance.

3   Materials and Implementation

3.1   Data Acquisition

There are no public datasets for the guidewire currently. Hence, we establish a new dataset named GWSeg based on 2D X-ray images, which are provided by Peking Union Medical College Hospital and Shanghai Huadong Hospital. The Innova 3100-IQ digital flat-panel angiography instrument (GE Healthcare) was utilized to acquire clinical sequences of the most representative 30 patients (180 X-ray Sequences). Among them, 144 sequences from 24 patients are training sets and 36 sequences from 6 patients are test sets. To show the generality of our approach, the patient data of the test set is independent of the training set.

In the process of data annotation, a new annotation tool has been designed specifically for labeling the guidewire. We first determine the area where the guidewire is located and enlarge the image of the area through the bounding box. Then we mark some points on the guidewire and fit a spline by these points. For each image frame, it is annotated by two people respectively. When the average error distance of the center line of the guidewire labelled by the two is less than 0.5 pixels, the label is considered valid, and the labeling result of any one of them is taken as the final label, otherwise it needs to be re-labeled. After annotation, each 2D X-ray image in sequences is binary images with size of 512 × 512. In binary images, the pixel value of the guidewire is 1, or else 0.

Table 1. Analysis of AG and pre-trained MobileNetV2.

Methods	F_1-Score	Time (ms)
Ours	**0.946 ± 0.009**	**58.4 ± 1.7**
without AG	0.916 ± 0.005	56.6 ± 1.6
ResNet-50	0.948 ± 0.016	130.5 ± 1.1
ResNet-101	0.953 ± 0.013	168.1 ± 3.9
VGG-16	0.942 ± 0.014	145.6 ± 2.5

3.2 Implementation Details

The proposed network architecture was implemented in PyTorch library (version 0.4.1) with one NVIDIA TITAN Xp GPU with 12 GB memory. In the training phase, two independent sequences in the training set were split as validation set to prevent over-fitting due to insufficient samples. To shorten the training cycle, transfer learning was used as the backbone architecture instead of learning from scratch [14]. Stochastic gradient descent (SGD) was used as optimizer (initial learning rate = 0.001, weight decay = 0.0005, momentum = 0.9). To find the optimal performance, we reduced the learning rate by the factor of 2 when the validation accuracy was saturated. Moreover, we set the batch size of 32, and 300 epochs was utilized for each model training. To tackle the issues of limited guidewire samples, data augmentation algorithm (i.e., rotation with $0° < \alpha < 360°$, flipping along the x and y direction) was applied for our network.

4   Experiments and Results

4.1   Impact of AG and Pre-trained MobileNetV2

To evaluate the contribution of the AG on our approach, we remove the AG from the original network and train it. The results is shown in Table 1. To verify the improvement in processing speed brought by the pre-trained MobileNetV2, we replace the encoder part of the original network with ResNet-50, ResNet-101 and VGG-16. As shown in Table 1, the pretrained MobileNetV2 as the encoder processes one image much faster than other heavy encoders. In summary, it

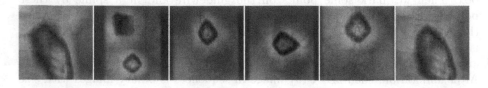

Fig. 4. The class activation maps (CAMs) of typical test frames. The maps highlight the discriminative regions of the guidewire.

Table 2. Comparison of varying α and γ for reinforced focal loss.

Methods		Precision	Sensitivity	F_1-Score
Weighted BCE		0.823 ± 0.016	0.849 ± 0.032	0.830 ± 0.014
GHM-C		$\mathbf{0.958 \pm 0.011}$	0.912 ± 0.028	0.937 ± 0.013
$\alpha = 50$	$\gamma = 1.5$	0.903 ± 0.035	0.934 ± 0.012	0.923 ± 0.009
$\alpha = 50$	$\gamma = 2$	0.949 ± 0.013	0.920 ± 0.018	0.933 ± 0.005
$\alpha = 75$	$\gamma = 2$	0.922 ± 0.007	0.939 ± 0.011	0.930 ± 0.005
$\alpha = 75$	$\gamma = 2.5$	0.940 ± 0.008	0.929 ± 0.010	0.934 ± 0.006
$\alpha = 100$	$\gamma = 2.5$	0.939 ± 0.009	$\mathbf{0.956 \pm 0.020}$	$\mathbf{0.946 \pm 0.009}$
$\alpha = 100$	$\gamma = 3$	0.950 ± 0.014	0.918 ± 0.017	0.934 ± 0.015
$\alpha = 125$	$\gamma = 3$	0.948 ± 0.010	0.897 ± 0.028	0.921 ± 0.009

clearly demonstrates the improvement in accuracy brought by the AG and the promotion in processing speed brought by the pre-trained MobileNetV2.

To further verify the robustness of our proposed framework, the class activation map (CAM) is utilized to visualize the discriminative region of the network for the test frames. The global average pooling outputs the spatial average of the feature map. The predicted class scores are mapped back to the previous convolutional layer to generate the CAMs [15]. The CAM highlights the discriminative regions of the specific class. As shown in Fig. 4, most of the discriminative regions are concentrated around the guidewire, indicating that the network has learned robust discriminative ability.

4.2 Impact of Reinforced Focal Loss

To evaluate the effectiveness of the reinforced focal loss on our approach, we train the network with two other different loss functions. The first is the weighted binary cross entropy (BCE) loss function, which is a commonly used method to address class imbalance in binary image segmentation task. The second is the gradient harmonizing mechanism (GHM), which is currently the state-of-the-art method of solving class imbalance. The GHM is to make a balanced cumulative contribution of samples of various difficulty types by weighting the gradients, which are generated by different samples and changing their contribution [16]. Therefore, we utilize the weighted BCE loss and GHM classification loss (GHM-C) as the experimental baselines.

The reinforced focal loss has two hyperparameters α and γ. The alternative value of α is set around the optimal value of the weighted BCE weighting factor. [8] verified that the optimal value of γ is 2, hence we set the alternative values of γ to 1.5, 2, 2.5 and 3. The experimental results indicate when weighing factor α and modulating factor γ are 100 and 2.5 respectively (as shown in Table 2), the model has the optimal performance. The mean F_1-score, precision and sensitivity are respectively 0.946, 0.939 and 0.956, wherein the F_1-score

Table 3. Comparison with state-of-the-art methods.

Methods	F_1-Score	Time (ms)
Ours	**0.946 ± 0.009**	**58.4 ± 1.7**
U-Net	0.907 ± 0.012	101.3 ± 1.8
ITT [6]	0.857	59.7
DT [17]	0.875	111.1
GE [18]	0.911	\

is improved by 12.26% and 0.95% over baselines respectively. The segmentation and tracking results of typical test frames are shown in Fig. 5. Some of the background pixels in the segmentation and tracking results of weighted BCE are misclassified as the guidewire due to the influence of the vertebrae. The influence of extreme class imbalances and contrast agents results in the misclassification of background pixels and the missing of guidewire pixels in the segmentation and tracking results of GHM-C. In contrast, the segmentation and tracking results of the reinforced focal loss are more smooth and accurate.

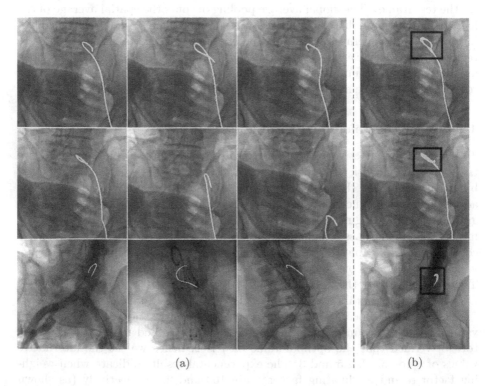

(a) (b)

Fig. 5. Guidewire segmentation and tracking results of typical test frames by different approaches. (a) Reinforced focal loss. (b) Weighted BCE (top, mid), GHMC (bottom).

4.3   Comparison with State-of-the-Art Methods

To further validate the performance of our proposed model, we compare it with widely-used deep learning method (U-Net) [19] and three other previously proposed methods. The quantitative comparison in terms of F_1-score and processing time is shown in Table 3. It clearly demonstrates the advantage of our proposed approach in terms of segmentation accuracy and processing speed. Compared with these methods, our approach can achieve the state-of-the-art performance.

In addition, Heidbuchel *et al.* mentioned that to reduce the radiation intake of physicians, the C-arm system operates at a low frame rate (≤ 6 frames per second (FPS)) [20]. The average processing time per image of our proposed network is about 58.4 ms, which enables accurate real-time tracking. The segmentation and tracking results of typical test frames are shown in Fig. 5(a). As can be seen from the results, this approach is robust to all kinds of guidewires in EVAR treatment, and the segmentation and tracking results of the guidewire are accurate in consecutive frames without any post-processing.

5   Conclusions and Future Work

In this paper, we proposed a novel network, Fast Attention Segmentation Network, to address the challenging task of guidewire segmentation and tracking for EVAR treatment in 2D X-ray fluoroscopy. Experiment results based on clinical sequences of 30 patients demonstrate that our approach completely address extreme class imbalance generated by the elongated guidewire structure and misclassified examples caused by guidewire-like structures and contrast agents. Compared to other approaches, the mean F_1-score of our approach is 0.946, achieving the state-of-the-art performance. In addition, our processing speed is about 17 FPS, which is promising for real-time assisting the physician in completing the EVAR treatment. As future work, we will concentrate on applying the approach proposed in this paper to the vascular interventional surgery robot to achieve the computer-assisted treatment of EVAR.

Acknowledgments. This work is partially supported by the National Natural Science Foundation of China (Grants 61533016, U1613210, 61421004), the National Key Research and Development Plan of China (Grant 2017YFE0112200).

References

1. Kent, K.C.: Abdominal aortic aneurysms. N. Engl. J. Med. **371**(22), 2101–2108 (2014)
2. Buck, D.B., Van Herwaarden, J.A., Schermerhorn, M.L., Moll, F.L.: Endovascular treatment of abdominal aortic aneurysms. Nat. Rev. Cardiol. **11**(2), 112 (2014)
3. Wu, W., et al.: Learning-based hypothesis fusion for robust catheter tracking in 2D X-ray fluoroscopy. In: Conference on Computer Vision and Pattern Recognition (CVPR), pp. 1097–1104. IEEE (2011)

4. Ambrosini, P., Ruijters, D., Niessen, W.J., Moelker, A., van Walsum, T.: Fully automatic and real-time catheter segmentation in X-Ray fluoroscopy. In: Descoteaux, M., Maier-Hein, L., Franz, A., Jannin, P., Collins, D.L., Duchesne, S. (eds.) MICCAI 2017, Part II. LNCS, vol. 10434, pp. 577–585. Springer, Cham (2017). https://doi.org/10.1007/978-3-319-66185-8_65
5. Baert, S.A., Viergever, M.A., Niessen, W.J.: Guide-wire tracking during endovascular interventions. IEEE Trans. Med. Imaging **22**(8), 965–972 (2003)
6. Heibel, H., Glocker, B., Groher, M., Pfister, M., Navab, N.: Interventional tool tracking using discrete optimization. IEEE Trans. Med. Imaging **32**(3), 544–555 (2013)
7. Wu, Y.D., et al.: Automatic guidewire tip segmentation in 2D X-ray fluoroscopy using convolution neural networks. In: International Joint Conference on Neural Networks (IJCNN), pp. 1–7. IEEE (2018)
8. Lin, T., Goyal, P., Girshick, R., He, K., Dollr, P.: Focal loss for dense object detection. In: International Conference on Computer Vision (ICCV), pp. 2999–3007. IEEE (2017)
9. Sandler, M., Howard, A., Zhu, M., Zhmoginov, A., Chen, L.C.: MobileNetV2: inverted residuals and linear bottlenecks. In: Conference on Computer Vision and Pattern Recognition (CVPR), pp. 4510–4520. IEEE (2018)
10. He, K., Zhang, X., Ren, S., Sun, J.: Deep residual learning for image recognition. In: Conference on Computer Vision and Pattern Recognition (CVPR), pp. 770–778. IEEE (2016)
11. Zeiler, M.D., Taylor, G.W., Fergus, R.: Adaptive deconvolutional networks for mid and high level feature learning. In: International Conference on Computer Vision (ICCV), pp. 2018–2025. IEEE (2011)
12. Oktay, O., Schlemper, J., Folgoc, L.L., Lee, M.: Attention U-Net: learning where to look for the pancreas. arXiv preprint: arXiv:1804.03999 (2018)
13. Bahdanau, D., Cho, K., Bengio, Y.: Neural machine translation by jointly learning to align and translate. arXiv preprint: arXiv:1409.0473 (2014)
14. Oquab, M., Bottou, L., Laptev, I., Sivic, J.: Learning and transferring mid-level image representations using convolutional neural networks. In: Conference on Computer Vision and Pattern Recognition (CVPR), pp. 1717–1724. IEEE (2014)
15. Zhou, B., Khosla, A., Lapedriza, A., Oliva, A., Torralba, A.: Learning deep features for discriminative localization. In: Conference on Computer Vision and Pattern Recognition (CVPR), pp. 2921–2929. IEEE (2016)
16. Li, B., Liu, Y., Wang, X.: Gradient harmonized single-stage detector. arXiv preprint: arXiv:1811.05181 (2018)
17. Heibela, T.H., Glockera, B., Grohera, M., Paragios, N., Komodakis, N., Navaba, N.: Discrete tracking of parametrized curves. In: Conference on Computer Vision and Pattern Recognition (CVPR), pp. 1754–1761. IEEE (2009)
18. Honnorat, N., Vaillant, R., Paragios, N.: Guide-wire extraction through perceptual organization of local segments in fluoroscopic images. In: Jiang, T., Navab, N., Pluim, J.P.W., Viergever, M.A. (eds.) MICCAI 2010, Part III. LNCS, vol. 6363, pp. 440–448. Springer, Heidelberg (2010). https://doi.org/10.1007/978-3-642-15711-0_55
19. Ronneberger, O., Fischer, P., Brox, T.: U-Net: convolutional networks for biomedical image segmentation. In: Navab, N., Hornegger, J., Wells, W.M., Frangi, A.F. (eds.) MICCAI 2015, Part III. LNCS, vol. 9351, pp. 234–241. Springer, Cham (2015). https://doi.org/10.1007/978-3-319-24574-4_28
20. Heidbuchel, H., Wittkampf, F.H., Vano, E., Ernst, S., Schilling, R.: Practical ways to reduce radiation dose for patients and staff during device implantations and electrophysiological procedures. Europace **16**(7), 946–964 (2014)

Infra-Slow Electroencephalogram Power Associates with Reaction Time in Simple Discrimination Tasks

Naoyuki Sato[1(✉)] and Yuichi Katori[1,2]

[1] Department of Complex and Intelligent Systems, School of Systems
Information Science, Future University Hakodate, 116-2 Kamedanakano,
Hakodate, Hokkaido 041-8655, Japan
satonao@fun.ac.jp
[2] Institute of Industrial Science, The University of Tokyo,
Bunkyo City, Tokyo 153-8505, Japan

Abstract. Infra-slow (<0.1 Hz) electroencephalography (EEG) activity is recently thought to be an important clue for the elucidation of the default mode network (DMN), one of large-scale brain networks, which is known to activate during relaxed non-task state. On the other hand, the dynamics of the infra-slow EEG during performing cognitive tasks has not been well evaluated, because it has been excluded in the conventional EEG analysis. In this study, we evaluated infra-slow EEG during visual and auditory discrimination and found that the increase in the infra-slow EEG power distributed widely over scalp region was significantly correlated with the increase of reaction time of both tasks. Importantly, this result is consistent with the interpretation that the infra-slow EEG activation reflects DMN activation. It is suggested that the infra-slow EEG power is available for an index for the DMN activation during performing cognitive tasks.

Keywords: Neuroscience · Humans · Neural oscillation · Functional brain network · Cognition

1 Introduction

Functional magnetic resonance imaging (fMRI) studies demonstrated that the large-scale brain networks is essential for the understanding of the cognitive functions [1]. One of major component of the large-scale network is default mode network (DMN) which is known to be activated during relaxed non-task states and self-oriented cognition (i.e., mind wandering or autobiographical memory retrieval) and is deactivated during performing cognitive task [2,3]. During performing tasks with high cognitive demands, such as memory encoding from reading of literatures [4] and complex scenes [5], deactivation of individual functional brain networks are often observed, and it is thought to reflect an effective allocation of cortical resources [6]. These dynamics are an important clue for the understanding of the higher-level cognitive functions.

© Springer Nature Switzerland AG 2019
T. Gedeon et al. (Eds.): ICONIP 2019, LNCS 11953, pp. 501–511, 2019.
https://doi.org/10.1007/978-3-030-36708-4_41

Recent simultaneous electroencephalography (EEG)-fMRI measurement studies have demonstrated that infra-slow (<0.1 Hz) scalp EEG activity is correlated with the DMN activity during sleep [7] and resting [8,9], in line with result shown by a combined electrocorticography (ECoG)-fMRI study [10]. These evidences importantly suggested that the infra-slow EEG may be also available for an index of the DMN activation. However, the infra-slow EEG components have been excluded in the conventional EEG analysis (i.e., event-related potentials (ERPs)) that focused on relatively fast change in electrical potential ranged from ∼0.01 s to ∼1 s. One of reasons is that the infra-slow EEG signals easily contaminated by various kinds of artifices related to body motion, eye movement, respiration, heart rate, skin potentials (or sweat), brain-blood potential difference [11], etc. Therefore, there are few studies evaluating the infra-slow EEG during performing cognitive tasks [12], except for a report by Monto et al. [13], in which the infra-slow EEG phase, but not power, was shown to be correlated with somatosensory detection performance.

In this article, we evaluated the infra-slow EEG while performing simple visual and auditory discrimination tasks (or "oddball tasks"), which are standard tasks in ERP studies. Such an evaluation is important for the development of ERP analyses, as it is expected to combine local activity analyses with large-scale brain network estimates. In the current analysis, the artifact-related EEG components in the measured signals were strictly eliminated using independent component analysis (ICA).

2   Methods

2.1   Participants

Fourteen volunteers (one female, one left-handed; 19–24 years old; mean ± SD: 20.7 ± 1.3 years old) were recruited via poster advertisement at Future University Hakodate. They showed no signs of neurological or psychiatric disorders and gave informed consent. The protocol was approved by the Ethics Committee in Future University Hakodate. Data from the one left handed volunteers and one volunteer with poor recording condition were ultimately excluded from the analysis.

2.2   Stimuli and Procedure

Each participant performed two sessions of visual discrimination task and two sessions of auditory discrimination task, of which order was counter-balanced. Each session of a discrimination task consists of 165 trials, where 50% "left" cue or 50% "right" cue were presented to participants. The participants were instructed to press a key with their left thumb finger, or another key with their right thumb finger, to match with the cue instruction. Stimulus onset asynchrony varied randomly between 1.1–2.2 s in steps of 0.1 s.

In the visual discrimination task, cue stimuli were presented on a LCD monitor (EIZO, FORIS FG2421) with a refresh rate of 60 Hz. Distance between display and participants was ~70 cm. Stimuli were given by single Japanese/Chinese kanji characters representing "left" or "right" and were presented in white (2.2° × 2.2°) on a black background.

In the auditory discrimination task, stimuli were presented by two speakers set on both side of the monitor. Participants were asked to close their eyes. Auditory stimuli representing "left" and "right" in Japanese words were given by artificial voice (Koden-sha, WorldVoice 2) of which pronunciation were "mi-gi" (duration: 0.30 s) and "hi-da-ri" (duration: 0.37 s), respectively. Both sound were presented ~54 dB in the environmental noise of ~32 dB. Rise and fall time were 0.05 s.

2.3   EEG Data Acquisition and Preprocessing

EEG and electrooculography (EOG) data were acquired using Ag/AgCl electrodes with a BrainAmp amplifier (Brain Products GmbH). Twenty seven electrodes were mounted on the scalp according to the standard 10–20 system. Three EOG electrodes were affixed above the nasion, and below the outer canthi of the eyes. EEG data (0.016–100 Hz (time constant, 10 s), 500 Hz sampling rate, impedance of the electrode 5.6 ± 4.1 kΩ; mean $\pm$ SD) were referenced to the FCz electrode during measurements and re-referenced to the average signal recorded at electrodes placed on the two earlobes for analysis. Data from the Fp1, Fp2, O1, and O2 electrodes were ultimately excluded from the analysis, because of their poor recording condition.

Artifacts in measured EEG signals were reduced using ICA. First, raw EEG and EOG signals were low-pass filtered to 0.1 Hz (using a zero-lag Butterworth filter with −12 dB/octave roll-off). Second, independent components (calculated by FastICA [14]) highly correlated to either horizontal, vertical, or radial EOGs [15] (correlation coefficient of the entire time course across sessions >0.2) were discarded. By this procedure, 6.9 ± 3.5 components (mean $\pm$ SD) were discarded and corrected infra-slow EEG signals were calculated. Additionally, in order to evaluate standard ERPs, corrected EEG signals in a spectral range between 1 to 30 Hz were calculated with the similar procedures, except for that the separation matrix was calculated using a data set dominantly including ocular artifacts (see [4] for more details).

2.4   EEG Data Analysis

The corrected infra-slow EEG signals were analyzed in terms of reaction time (RT) in the discrimination tasks. Fist, the EEG amplitude and phase at stimulus onset time were calculated by the Hilbert transform and their correlation with RT was analyzed. Correlation coefficients were calculated for each electrode and their significant levels were defined by 4000 shuffled data sets. The correlation coefficient between phase and RT, r, were given by

$$r = \sqrt{\frac{r_{CR}^2 + r_{SR}^2 - 2r_{CR}r_{SR}r_{CS}}{1 - r_{CR}^2}},$$

where r_{CR}, r_{SR}, and r_{CS} denote Pearson correlation coefficients between $\cos\theta$ and RT, between $\sin\theta$ and RT, and between $\cos\theta$ and $\sin\theta$, respectively. Finally, multiple comparisons among the number of electrodes were corrected using the false discovery rate (FDR) control (q = 0.05). The EEG amplitudes were analyses in the same procedure, except for the correlation coefficient between amplitude and RT was simply given by Pearson coefficient between them.

3   Results

3.1   Task Performance

Hit rates of visual and auditory discriminations were 0.92 ± 0.07 and 0.97 ± 0.04, respectively, where the hit rate of the auditory discrimination was significantly higher than those of the visual discrimination ($t(11) = 3.15$, $p = 0.01$). RT for visual and auditory discriminations were 0.49 ± 0.05 and 0.44 ± 0.04 (mean $\pm$ SD), respectively. Reaction to the auditory stimuli was significantly faster than those to the visual stimuli ($t(11) = 3.47$, $p = 5 \times 10^{-4}$). These results indicate that the auditory discrimination task was easier than the visual discrimination task.

3.2   Relationship Between Infra-slow EEG and Reaction Time

Figure 1a shows a temporal evolution of raw EEG signal and corrected infra-slow EEG signal at central region (at the Cz electrode) during the auditory discrimination. Both plots appear to be well overlapped. Figure 1b and c show spectral power of raw signals at the central and frontal regions (at the Cz and Fz electrodes, respectively) and infra-slow EEG at the central region (at the Cz electrode) during the auditory and visual discriminations. Difference in EEG power between the Fz and Cz electrode in the spectral range from 0.1 to 10 Hz is thought to be ocular artifacts. During the auditory discrimination, alpha power at 10 Hz appeared obvious in relationship to eye closing. In total, these raw data appeared approximately log-log linear including the infra-slow band.

Figure 2 shows a temporal evolution of infra-slow EEG amplitude, power and phase and corresponded time series of RT during the auditory discrimination (participant ID: 5365). Time course of RT appeared similarly to that of the infra-slow EEG. Figure 3a shows correlation between infra-slow power at parietal region (at the Pz electrode) and RT ($r = 0.15$). Figure 3b and c show topographical maps of statistical values of the correlation coefficients integrated across participants during the auditory and visual discriminations, respectively. In both tasks, the infra-slow power widely distributed over scalp region appeared

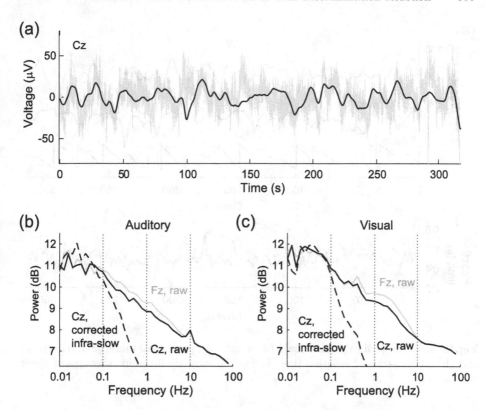

Fig. 1. Infra-slow EEG signals (participant ID: 2337). (a) Raw data and corrected infra-slow EEG signals at the central region (at the Cz electrode) during the auditory discrimination. The former and the latter are plotted in gray and black lines, respectively. (b and c) Spectral power of the raw data at the central and frontal regions (at the Cz and Fz electrodes) during the auditory and visual discriminations. Black and gray solid lines indicate the former and latter plots, respectively. Dashed line denotes the corrected infra-slow EEG signal at the central region (at the Cz electrode).

to be significantly correlate with RT ($p < 0.05$, FDR controlled), where the infra-slow power was higher for the slower RT.

Figure 4a shows an example of infra-slow EEG phase and RT correlation during auditory discrimination ($r = 0.14$). Figure 4b and c show topographical maps of statistical values of the correlation coefficients integrated across participants during the auditory and visual discriminations, respectively. In both tasks, the infra-slow EEG phase in the left temporal region appeared to be weakly correlated with RT ($p < 0.05$, uncorrected).

3.3 Influence of Infra-slow EEG Power on Event-Related Potentials

In the previous report by Monto et al. [13], infra-slow EEG phase was associated with EEG activity in higher spectral range (>1 Hz). In the above results, how-

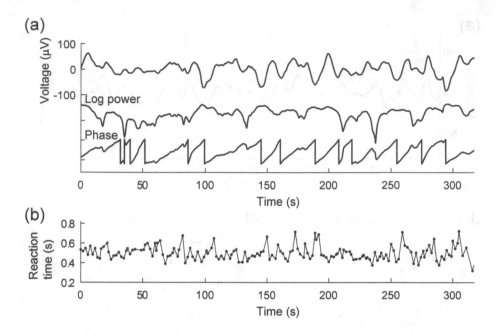

Fig. 2. An example of (a) infra-show EEG amplitude, power and phase (grand average) and (b) a time series of reaction time during the auditory discrimination (participant ID: 2337).

ever, the infra-slow power is more strongly correlated with RT, rather than the infra-slow EEG phase. Therefore, in the following, the influence of the infra-slow power on EEG at the higher spectral bands is evaluated using ERP (1–30 Hz) analysis. Figure 5a and b show ERPs related to the higher and lower infra-slow EEG power during the auditory and visual discriminations, respectively. Only during the auditory discrimination, the left temporal -parietal region in a period from 0.1 to 0.15 s showed a significant difference between them ($p < 0.05$, uncorrected), which is thought to be P1 component. The P1 is known to appear typically as a response to visual stimuli and known to be larger during the higher attention to the stimuli. Thus, the result suggests that the lower infra-slow power is associated with the higher attention.

The ERP difference during the higher and lower infra-slow power is also influenced by RT, which is significantly correlated with the infra-slow power (Fig. 4b). Thus, ERPs related to the longer and shorter RT were additionally evaluated (Fig. 4c and d). In the result, the left temporal-parietal region in a period from 0.1 to 0.15 s showed significant difference of the ERPs ($p < 0.05$, uncorrected). This result appeared similar to the result using the infra-slow power (Fig. 4c), while the period showing the effect is differently appeared from 0.175 s to 0.225 s, which is thought to be associated with N1 component. The N1 component is known to be associated with discrimination process. Thus, the result would suggest that the shorter RT is primarily associated with the

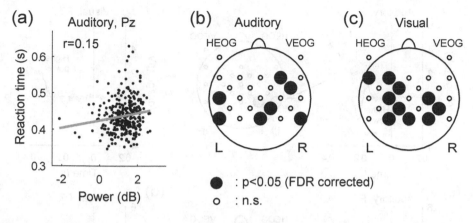

Fig. 3. Correlation between infra-slow EEG power and reaction time. (a) An example of the correlation between infra-slow EEG power at the parietal region (at the Pz electrode) and reaction time during the auditory discrimination (participant ID: 5365). Gray line denotes regression line. (b and c) Topographical map of p-value for the correlation coefficient integrated across participants (N = 12) during the auditory and visual discriminations. Circles represent the electrode locations (nose at the top), where filled circles represent significant correlations ($p < 0.05$, Multiple comparisons were corrected by FDR). HEOG and VEOG denotes horizontal and vertical EOGs and their correlation coefficients to reaction time were not significant (plotted outside of the head maps).

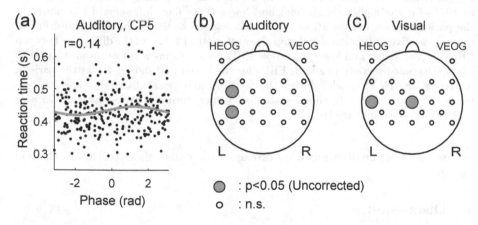

Fig. 4. Correlation between infra-slow EEG phase and reaction time. (a) An example of the relationship between infra-slow EEG power at the left central-parietal region (at the CP5 electrode) and reaction time during the auditory discrimination (participant ID: 1899). Gray line denotes regression line. (b and c) Topographical map of p-value for the correlation coefficient integrated across over participants (N = 12) during the auditory and visual discriminations. Filled gray circle represents significant correlation ($p < 0.05$, uncorrected).

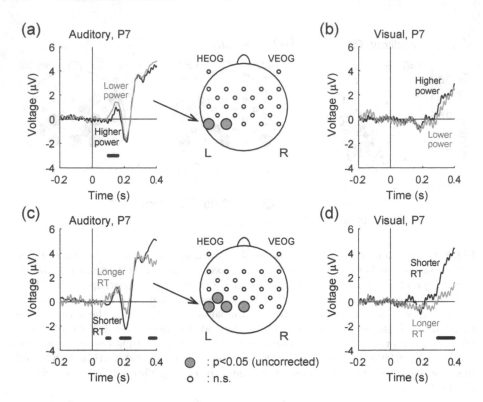

Fig. 5. Event-related potentials (ERPs) averaged across participants (N = 12). (a and b) ERPs for the higher (black line) and lower (gray line) infra-slow EEG power at the parietal region (at the P7 electrode) during the auditory and visual discriminations, respectively. Topographical map shows statistical values of the difference between ERPs for the higher and lower infra-slow EEG power during a period from 0.1 to 0.15 s ($p < 0.05$, uncorrected). (c and d) ERPs for the longer and shorter RT at the parietal region (at the P7 electrode) during the auditory and visual discriminations, respectively. Topographical map shows statistical values during a period from 0.175 s to 0.225 s ($p < 0.05$, uncorrected).

enhancement of the discrimination process, rather than the attention as show in the above.

4   Discussion

In the present article, we examined the relationship between infra-slow EEG and RT during the auditory and visual discriminations. Infra-slow EEG power widely distributed scalp regions were positively correlated with RT of both tasks (Fig. 3). On the other hand, the correlation between infra-slow EEG phase and RT was weak, where the significant correlation appeared in the left temporal region (Fig. 4). In following sections, relationship to previous findings and a possible concern of the current results are discussed.

4.1   Relationship to Previous Findings

Our current results are not in complete agreement with previous findings [13] in which the infra-slow EEG phase, but not the power, was correlated with stimulus detection performance. This difference is thought to be derived from different task types; the current study employed visual and auditory discrimination tasks, whereas the previous study employed a somatosensory detection task. In the current discrimination task, the "left" and "right" stimuli were linguistically presented, thus, certain linguistic processes were included while performing the task. The left temporal region dominance in correlation with the infra-slow EEG phase and RT (Fig. 4) agrees with this idea. In the somatosensory discrimination task [13], the right index finger was stimulated, and thus, left hemisphere dominance in the infra-slow EEG and hit rate would be expected. However, such topographical patterns were not evaluated in their study.

In contrast, the positive correlation between infra-slow power and RT observed in this study (Fig. 3) is consistent with the positive correlation between infra-slow power and DMN activation during resting observed in a previous study [7]; the coupling between larger infra-slow power and slower RT in the current study is likely to be associated with DMN activation. Our additional ERP results regarding the influence of infra-slow power also support the same interpretation that larger infra-slow power is associated with lower attention (Fig. 4).

4.2   Possible Influence of Artefacts on the Results

In the current analysis, the influence of the EOG-related artifacts on the infra-slow EEG data was found to be non-negligible. This is not pointed out by previous studies, in which no ocular artifact correction was applied in their EEG preprocessing [7,8,13]. Figure 6a and b show the EOG signals in the infra-slow band (<0.1 Hz) and those in higher spectral bands (1–30 Hz) during the visual and auditory discriminations. The EOG amplitudes in the infra-slow band were obviously large, and it appeared more critical during the auditory discrimination with eye closing. In the current study, to reduce these artifacts, relatively large number of artifact-related components (30% of all components, on the average, with a criterion; correlation coefficient between EOG and ICA component >0.2) were discarded in the preprocessing. On the other hand, the source of EOG-related artifact is not quite obvious, because topographical map of the correlation coefficients between EOG and ICA components didn't sometimes appear typical as ocular artifacts (i.e., it distributed rather widely beyond the frontal region). It might be possible to be influenced by non-ocular factors, such as skin potential (sweat), brain-blood potential difference [11], and these influences on the reference electrodes (earlobes). In future study, it is essential to construct a reliable protocol to analyze infra-slow EEG during cognition for the understanding of the higher cognitive function processed in the large-scale brain network.

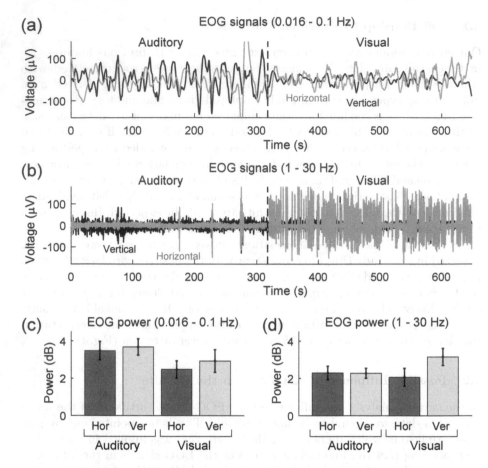

Fig. 6. Horizontal and vertical EOG signals during auditory and discrimination (a and b) Example of time series of horizontal and vertical EOGs in spectral range in <0.1 Hz and 1–30 Hz, respectively (participant ID: 9130). Left and right parts of the plot are signals during auditory and visual discrimination, respectively. Black and gray lines indicate horizontal and vertical EOG signals respectively. (c and d) EOG power averaged across participants in the spectral range in <0.1 Hz and 1–30 Hz, respectively. Dark and light gray bars represent horizontal and vertical EOG power, respectively. Error bars indicate SD among participants (N = 12).

Acknowledgements. This work was supported by MEXT KAKENHI Grant Number 18H04950 (Non-linear Neuro-oscillology) and JSPS KAKENHI Grant Numbers 16K12448, 18H03502, and 18H02709. The authors would like to thank N. Sasamori for her assistance in data collection.

References

1. Bressler, S.L., Menon, V.: Large-scale brain networks in cognition: emerging methods and principles. Trends. Cogn. Sci. **14**(6), 277–290 (2010)
2. Buckner, R.L., Andrews-Hanna, J.R., Schacter, D.L.: The brain's default network: anatomy, function, and relevance to disease. Ann. N. Y. Acad. Sci. **1124**, 1–38 (2008)
3. Raichle, M.E.: The brain's default mode network. Annu. Rev. Neurosci. **38**, 433–447 (2015)
4. Sato, N., Mizuhara, H. : Successful encoding during natural reading is associated with fixation-related potentials and large-scale network deactivation. eNeuro **5**(5) (2018) https://doi.org/10.1523/ENEURO.0122-18
5. Sato, N., et al.: Subsequent memory-dependent EEG theta correlates to parahippocampal blood oxygenation level-dependent response. Neuroreport **21**(3), 168–172 (2010)
6. Hasson, U., Nusbaum, H.C., Small, S.L.: Brain networks subserving the extraction of sentence information and its encoding to memory. Cereb. Cortex **17**, 2899–2913 (2007)
7. Picchioni, D., et al.: Infraslow EEG oscillations organize large-scale cortical-subcortical interactions during sleep: a combined EEG/fMRI study. Brain Res. **1374**, 63–72 (2011)
8. Hiltunen, T., et al.: Infra-slow EEG fluctuations are correlated with resting-state network dynamics in FMRI. J. Neurosci. **34**(2), 356–362 (2014)
9. Grooms, J.K., et al.: Infraslow electroencephalographic and dynamic resting state network activity. Brain Connect. **7**(5), 265–280 (2017)
10. He, B.J., Snyder, A.Z., Zempel, J.M., Smyth, M.D., Raichle, M.E.: Electrophysiological correlates of the brain's intrinsic large-scale functional architecture. Proc. Natl. Acad. Sci. U.S.A. **105**(41), 16039–16044 (2008)
11. Voipio, J., Tallgren, P., Heinonen, E., Vanhatalo, S., Kaila, K.: Millivolt-scale DC shifts in the human scalp EEG: evidence for a nonneuronal generator. J. Neurophysiol. **89**(4), 2208–2214 (2003)
12. Palva, J.M., Palva, S.: Infra-slow fluctuations in electrophysiological recordings, blood-oxygenation-level-dependent signals, and psychophysical time series. Neuroimage **62**(4), 2201–2211 (2012)
13. Monto, S., Palva, S., Voipio, J., Palva, J.M.: Very slow EEG fluctuations predict the dynamics of stimulus detection and oscillation amplitudes in humans. J. Neurosci. **28**(33), 8268–8272 (2008)
14. Hyvärinen, A., Oja, E.: Independent component analysis: algorithms and applications. Neural Netw. **13**(4), 411–430 (2000)
15. Croft, R.J., Barry, R.J.: Removal of ocular artifact from the EEG: a review. Neurophysiol. Clin. **30**(1), 5–19 (2000)

Classifying Speech Data in Parkinson's Disease Based on Class Probability Output Networks

Ye Jin Lee, Dae Hyeon Kim, Rhee Man Kil$^{(\boxtimes)}$, and Hee Yong Youn

College of Computing, Sungkyunkwan University,
2066, Seobu-ro, Jangan-gu, Suwon, Gyeonggi-do 16419, Korea
{yejini824,kdh92,rmkil,youn7147}@skku.edu

Abstract. This paper presents a new method of classifying speech data in Parkinson's disease using the class probability output network (CPON) in which the conditional class probabilities are estimated using Beta distributions. In the proposed CPON, the uncertainty measure describing the uncertainty in the decision of classification is also calculated. If the given input pattern of speech features falls in the uncertain region of classification, the decision network as the second layer is activated and the decision is made from the conditional class probabilities and also the selected reference patterns. Otherwise, the decision is made just using the CPON as the first layer. As a result, the proposed method provides consistently improved classification performances. Through the simulation for classifying speech data in Parkinson's disease using the UCI data set, the effectiveness of the proposed method is demonstrated.

Keywords: Parkinson's disease · Speech data · Conditional class probability · Uncertainty measure

1 Introduction

Parkinson's disease is the second most common neurodegenerative disorder of the central nervous system following Alzheimer's disease, caused by the loss of neurons in the brain [1,2], called the substantia nigra. Dopamine is used in the body to control motion, and loss of nerve cells causes less circulating dopamine [3], making it difficult to control movement and resulting in tremors and anesthesia of the limbs. In 1817, Parkinson's disease was described by Dr. Parkinson [4] as "shaking palsy". Parkinson's disease is generally observed in the elderly [5] and partially or totally loses the motor nervous system, speech, behavior, mind, and other important functions. In particular, 90% of patients with Parkinson's disease show language and motor impairment [6], and generally this disease appears in 1 in 100 people over the age of 65. As the global population ages, the number of Parkinson's patients is expected to increase [7]. Although drug treatment can be used to alleviate the symptoms early in Parkinson's disease,

© Springer Nature Switzerland AG 2019
T. Gedeon et al. (Eds.): ICONIP 2019, LNCS 11953, pp. 512–523, 2019.
https://doi.org/10.1007/978-3-030-36708-4_42

there is no fundamental treatment [8,9]. Therefore, early diagnosis is important for the quality of life and longevity of patients. The disease is generally diagnosed in an invasive manner [10], which complicates the process of diagnosis and treatment of the patient. Because it relies largely on clinical experience, patients with Parkinson's disease require an integrated physical visit for diagnosis and treatment. However, most patients are often inconvenient to move, making it difficult to visit a clinic for diagnosis and treatment.

There are many symptoms of Parkinson's disease, but research shows that about 90% of Parkinson's patients have a speech impairment [11]. Thus, speech disorders can be used as an early indicator of onset, and voice measurements are attracting attention as effective diagnostic methods because they are simple and do not require physical movement. It also reduces the cost of physical visits, speeds the early diagnosis of diseases, and reduces the workload of medical personnel [8,12].

In the diagnosis of Parkinson's disease, studies on the use of speech have been conducted several times. Little et al. [8] created a Parkinson database and proposed a new feature, and proceeded to select a feature to get the best feature set in the entire feature space. It diagnosed the PD using Support Vector Machine (SVM) classifier using the Gaussian Radial Basis Function (RBF) kernel. Sakar et al. [13] selected the features using the mutual information measure and classified them through the SVM classifier. Astrom et al. [3] proposed a parallel feed-forward neural network structure and used it to predict Parkinson's patients. Parallel networks had improved performance and predictive robustness when using a single neural network. However, as the number of parallel networks increased training time and complexity increased. Chen et al. [14] showed better performance through comparison with the SVM model using a combination of principal component analysis (PCA) and fuzzy k-nearest neighbor (FkNN) method. Zuo et al. [15] performed parameter optimization and feature selection using particle swarm optimization (PSO) and used the FkNN model. However, these models do not provide the degree of confidence for the decision as the normalized measure. Furthermore, these models usually have complicated structure to obtain the improved classification performances.

In this context, this paper presents a classification model composed of two layers of decision networks: in the first layer, the conditional class probabilities are estimated for the given speech features using the class probability output network (CPON) [16–18] in which the uncertainty measure representing the degree of uncertainty in the decision of classification is also calculated. If the given speech features lie in the uncertain region in which the uncertainty measure is greater than or equal to θ (in our case, $\theta = 0.05$), the decision is made in the second layer of decision network using the selected reference patterns and also the p-values calculated from the first layer. Otherwise, the decision is made just using the CPON in the first layer. As a result, the proposed method provides consistently improved classification performances. Through the simulation for classifying speech data in Parkinson's disease using UCI data set [19], the effectiveness of the proposed method is demonstrated.

2   Classification System of Speech Data in Parkinson's Disease

In the proposed method of classifying speech data in Parkinson's disease, the overall algorithmic structure of the proposed method is illustrated in Fig. 1. The first layer goes through the CPON process. The decision procedure using the CPON in the first layer is described as follows: (1) for the given speech data, speech features [8] are extracted and normalized between 0 and 1, (2) in the normalized feature space, the proper Gaussian kernels are located and combined linearly in such a way of minimizing classification errors, (3) the linearly combined output of kernel functions is normalized between 0 and 1, (4) the Beta parameters in the normalized output distributions for the Parkinson's disease (PD) and normal (NR) data are determined, respectively, (5) the p-values for testing the PD and NR classes are determined and compared, (6) the uncertainty measure is also calculated using the Beta parameters for the PD and NR data distributions, and (7) if the uncertainty measure is less than or equal to θ (in our case, $\theta = 0.05$), the decision of classification is made using the p-values; that is,

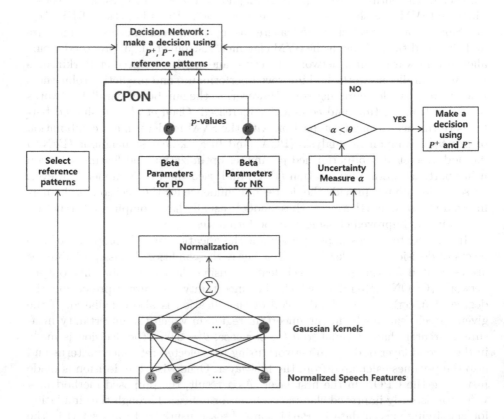

Fig. 1. The CPON with decision network for classifying speech data in Parkinson's disease

if the p-value for the PD class $>$ the p-value for the NR class, then the decision is the PD class; otherwise, the decision is the NR class.

In the case that the uncertainty measure is greater than θ, the decision is made using the decision network in the second layer. The decision procedure for the given speech data is described as follows: (1) among the normalized speech data, the reference patterns are selected as the normalized speech data with the uncertainty measure greater than equal to θ, (2) the p-value ratio defined by the p-value for the PD class over the sum of p-values for the PD and NR classes is calculated, and (3) if the p-value ratio is between 0.05 and 0.95 inclusive, the decision is made using the label of the closest reference pattern; otherwise, the decision is made using the p-value ratio. This implies that the decision for the uncertain pattern is made using the p-values when the difference between two p-values for the PD and NR classes is significant. On the other hand, the reference patterns are used for the decision of classification.

3   Class Probability Output Networks

In many classification problems, it is desirable that the output of a classifier represents the conditional class probability. For the conditional class probability, the distribution of classifier's output can be well approximated by the beta distribution under the assumption that the output of classifier lies within a finite range and the distribution of classifier's output is unimodal; that is, the distribution has one modal value with the greatest frequency. This assumption is quite reasonable for many cases of classification problems with the proper selection of kernel parameters of a classifier. Here, the discriminant function y as the classifier's output for the input pattern $\mathbf{x}$ is given by

$$\hat{y}(\mathbf{x}) = \sum_{i=1}^{m} w_i \phi_i(\mathbf{x}), \tag{1}$$

where m represents the number of kernels and w_i, ϕ_i represent the ith weight and the ith kernel function, respectively. In the above equation, the kernel function is described by the Gaussian function as

$$\phi_i(\mathbf{x}) = e^{-\gamma \|\mathbf{x} - \boldsymbol{\mu}_i\|^2}, \tag{2}$$

where γ and $\boldsymbol{\mu}_i$ represent the kernel width and the ith kernel center, respectively.

In the proposed CPON, the probability model represents the conjugate prior of the binomial distribution; that is, in our case, the conditional class probability in binary classification problems. In this context, the following Beta probability density function (PDF) of a random variable Y as the normalized classifier's output is described by

$$f_Y(y|a, b) = \frac{1}{B(a, b)} y^{a-1} (1 - y)^{b-1}, \quad 0 \le y \le 1, \tag{3}$$

where a and b represent the parameters of beta distribution, and $B(a,b)$ represents a Beta function defined by

$$B(a,b) = \int_0^1 y^{a-1}(1-y)^{b-1}dy. \tag{4}$$

Here, we assume that the classifier's output value; that is, $\hat{y}$ is normalized between 0 and 1. One of features in the Beta distribution is that the distribution parameters can be easily guessed from the mean $E[Y]$ and variance $Var(Y)$ as follows:

$$a = E[Y]\left(\frac{E[Y](1-E[Y])}{Var(Y)} - 1\right) \tag{5}$$

and

$$b = (1 - E[Y])\left(\frac{E[Y](1-E[Y])}{Var(Y)} - 1\right). \tag{6}$$

Although this moment matching (MM) method is simple, these estimators usually don't provide accurate estimations especially for smaller number of data. In such cases, the maximum likelihood estimation (MLE) or the simplex method for searching parameters [20] can be used for more accurate estimation of Beta parameters.

In the construction of CPON for classifying speech data in Parkinson's disease, the output of (1) is normalized between 0 and 1 by using the linear scale and the normalized classifier's output distribution is approximated by the Beta distribution parameters. The algorithm of constructing the CPON for classifying speech data in Parkinson's disease is described as follows:

Step 1. For $i = -3, -2, \cdots, 3$,
- Set $\gamma = 2^i$ in the function $\phi_i(\mathbf{x})$ of (2).
- Apply the SVM algorithm [21] with $\gamma = 2^i$
- Calculate the Kullback-Leibler (K-L) divergence as

$$D_{KL}(P_+||P_-) = -\sum_{x \in X} P_+(x)\log\left(\frac{P_-(x)}{P_+(x)}\right), \tag{7}$$

where $P_+(x)$ and $P_-(x)$ represent the distributions in the output space X of SVM for the PD and NR data, respectively.

Step 2. Select γ with the maximum $D_{KL}(P_{PD}||P_{NR})$ and determine the discriminant function y of (1) using the SVM algorithm.

Step 3. Normalize the output value of (1) between 0 and 1 using the linear scale.

Step 4. The distributions of classifier's normalized output for the PD and NR data are identified by Beta distribution parameters.

After the training of CPON, the classification for an unknown pattern can be determined according to the beta distribution for each class. First, for the unknown pattern, the normalized output y for the classifier is calculated. Here, if the normalized value is greater than 1, we set that value as 1; on the other hand, if the value is less than 0, we set that value as 0. Then, the conditional class probabilities are determined by the CDF values for the classifier's normalized output y: they are,

$$\hat{F}_{Y^+}(y) = P(+|Y^+ \leq y) \text{ and} \tag{8}$$
$$\hat{F}_{Y^-}(y) = P(-|Y^- \leq y), \tag{9}$$

where Y^+ and Y^- represent the Beta random variables for the PD and NR classes, respectively.

Here, the p-values for testing the PD and NR classes are determined by

$$p\text{-value for testing the PD class} = \hat{F}_{Y^+}(y) \text{ and} \tag{10}$$
$$p\text{-value for testing the NR class} = 1 - \hat{F}_{Y^-}(y). \tag{11}$$

From the above equation, the final decision of classifying speech data is made; that is, the final decision can be made by selecting the class with the maximum p-value: if the p-value for testing the PD class is greater than or equal to the p-value for testing the NR class, the decision is the PD class; otherwise, the decision is the NR class. As a result, the proposed CPON provides an effective way of estimating conditional probabilities for pattern classification problems.

4   The CPON with Decision Network

In the proposed method of CPON, the degree of uncertainty for the decision of classification is provided by estimating the confidence intervals for the conditional class probabilities. These confidence intervals can be determined by the K-S statistic [22]:

- First, find the distance measures $D_{n,\alpha}^{\pm}$ for the positive and negative classes; they are

$$D_{n,\alpha}^+ = \frac{K_\alpha}{\sqrt{n^+}} \text{ and } D_{n,\alpha}^- = \frac{K_\alpha}{\sqrt{n^-}}, \tag{12}$$

where K_α represents the value that satisfies $H(K_\alpha) = 1 - \alpha$, and n^+ and n^- represent the sample size of the positive and negative classes, respectively.
- Setting the variables $u^{\pm}$ as follows:

$$u^+ = \hat{F}_{Y^+}(y) \text{ and } u^- = \hat{F}_{Y^-}(y). \tag{13}$$

- Determine the $100(1 - \alpha)$ percent confidence intervals for the CDFs of the positive and negative classes:

$$F_{U^+}^*(u^+) - D_{n,\alpha}^+ \leq F_{Y^+}(y) \leq F_{U^+}^*(u^+) + D_{n,\alpha}^+ \tag{14}$$

and

$$1 - F_{U^-}^*(u^-) - D_{n,\alpha}^- \leq 1 - F_{Y^-}(y)$$
$$\leq 1 - F_{U^-}^*(u^-) + D_{n,\alpha}^-, \tag{15}$$

where $F_{U^+}^*(u^+)$ and $F_{U^-}^*(u^-)$ represent the empirical CDFs of the uniform distribution for the positive and negative classes, respectively.

The two-sided confidence intervals of (14) and (15) can be described by one-sided confidence intervals as follows:

– For the positive class, with a probability of $1 - \alpha/2$,

$$F_{Y^+}(y) \leq F_{U^+}^*(u^+) + D_{n,\alpha}^+ \quad \text{or} \tag{16}$$

$$F_{Y^+}(y) \geq F_{U^+}^*(u^+) - D_{n,\alpha}^+. \tag{17}$$

– For the negative class, with a probability of $1 - \alpha/2$,

$$1 - F_{Y^-}(y) \leq 1 - F_{U^-}^*(u^-) + D_{n,\alpha}^- \quad \text{or} \tag{18}$$

$$1 - F_{Y^-}(y) \geq 1 - F_{U^-}^*(u^-) - D_{n,\alpha}^-. \tag{19}$$

Let $F_{U^+}^*(u^+) \geq 1 - F_{U^-}^*(u^-)$. Then, from (17) and (18), we can find the value of α_0 that these two boundaries are met; that is,

$$F_{U^+}^*(u^+) - D_{n,\alpha_0}^+ = 1 - F_{U^-}^*(u^-) + D_{n,\alpha_0}^- = x_0. \tag{20}$$

With the above condition,

$$F_{Y^+}(y) \geq x_0 \geq 1 - F_{Y^-}(y). \tag{21}$$

This implies that with a probability of $(1 - \alpha_0/2)^2 \approx 1 - \alpha_0$,

$$F_{Y^+}(y) \geq 1 - F_{Y^-}(y). \tag{22}$$

That is, with a probability of $1-\alpha_0$, the true CDF for the positive class is greater than or equal to the true CDF for the negative class. From this description of confidence level $1 - \alpha_0$, the uncertainty measure α_0 is determined as follows:

Step 1. From the output of CPON for the positive and negative classes, determined the empirical CDFs. After the CPON is trained enough for the given patterns,

$$F_{U^+}^*(u^+) \approx \hat{F}_{Y^+}(y) \quad \text{and} \tag{23}$$

$$1 - F_{U^-}^*(u^-) \approx 1 - \hat{F}_{Y^-}(y). \tag{24}$$

Step 2. From the boundary condition x_0, determine the value of K_{α_0}:
  – If $F_{U^+}^*(u^+) \geq 1 - F_{U^-}^*(u^-)$,

$$K_{\alpha_0} = \frac{F_{U^+}^*(u^+) + F_{U^-}^*(u^-) - 1}{1/\sqrt{n^+} + 1/\sqrt{n^-}}. \tag{25}$$

  – Otherwise,

$$K_{\alpha_0} = \frac{1 - F_{U^+}^*(u^+) - F_{U^-}^*(u^-)}{1/\sqrt{n^+} + 1/\sqrt{n^-}}. \tag{26}$$

Step 3. From the value of K_{α_0}, determine the uncertainty measure α_0 as

$$\alpha_0 = 1 - H(K_{\alpha_0}). \tag{27}$$

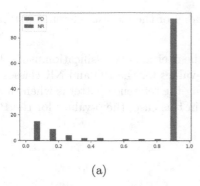
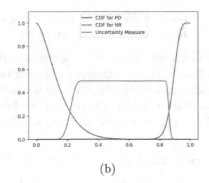

(a)   (b)

Fig. 2. An example of uncertainty measure: (a) represents the histogram of the normalized output of CPON and (b) represents the CDFs for the PD and NR classes, and the corresponding uncertainty measure.

This uncertainty measure α_0 represents how well the CDF values of the positive and negative classes are separated. For example, if the value of α_0 is 0.05, it represents that with a probability of $1 - 0.05$ ($=0.95$), one CDF value is greater than or equal to another CDF value. In this case, the decision of classification is quite certain. Usually, the values of α_0 lie between 0 and 0.5. In this range, if the value of α_0 is near 0.5, the decision of classification is not quite clear so that we may think that the given pattern is uncertain. As an example of uncertainty measure, the CPON is trained using the UCI data set [19] and the output distribution of normalized output and uncertainty measure are obtained as illustrated in Fig. 2. This example shows the uncertain region (uncertainty measure $\alpha_0 \approx 0.5$) in the middle range of output distribution in which both CDF values are very small; that is, smaller p-values.

To construct the decision network, the uncertain patterns are selected using the uncertainty measure α_0 of (27); that is, the given pattern is decided as the uncertain pattern if $\alpha_0 \geq \theta$ (in our case, $\theta = 0.05$). This implies that the probability of correct decision is 0.95 if the given pattern does not belongs to the uncertain region. In the case that the uncertainty measure α_0 for the given input pattern x of normalized speech features is greater than θ, the decision is made using the decision network using the following procedure:

Step 1. Select reference patterns as the normalized speech data with the uncertainty measure $\alpha_0 \geq \theta$.

Step 2. Calculate the p-value ratio p_r as

$$p_r = \frac{p\text{-value for the PD class}}{p\text{-value for the PD class} + p\text{-value for the NR class}}. \quad (28)$$

Step 3. Make a decision using the p-value ratio p_r:
 - if p-value < 0.05, the decision is the NR class,
 - else if p-value > 0.95, the decision is the PD class,

- else the decision is made using the label of the closest reference pattern to the given input pattern x.

As a result, the decision network makes the decision of classification using the p-values when the difference between two p-values for the PD and NR classes is significant, whereas the decision is made using the reference patterns when there is no clear distinction between two classes; in this case, the p-values for the PD and NR classes are usually very small.

5   Simulation

For the evaluation of the proposed method, the voice file feature values [19] obtained from a pool of 31 people were used. Among them, 23 people were Parkinson's disease patients. The diagnosis period for Parkinson's disease patients was between 0 and 28 years, ages from 46 to 85, with an average of 65.8, standard deviation of 9.8. Six syllables between 1 and 36 s in length per person were recorded on the average. The total number of data is 195, NR data is 48, and the rest is PD data. The speech signals were sampled at 44.1 kHz, using 22 speech features. For a detailed description of the data set and a description of the feature, refer to the references [8,12,19].

The proposed CPON with decision network (CPONwD) was compared with the support vector machine (SVM), and CPON models. First, the SVM was trained by the Scikit-learn SVC package [23] with the gamma parameter γ values of 1/8, 1/4, 1/2, 1, 2, 4, and 8. The best classification performance was obtained when $\gamma = 8$. In the case of CPON, the gamma parameter γ was determined when the K-L divergence has the maximum value. As a result, the gamma parameter was selected as $\gamma = 8$ which was same as the gamma parameter of SVM. For the evaluation of the proposed method, 3-fold evaluation method was used due to the limited number of speech data set (in this simulation, the number of patterns were 195); that is, the whole data were divided into 3 disjoint sets in which 2 sets were used as training data and the remaining 1 set used as test data. This evaluation was repeated three times for three different groups of training and test data sets, and the average performances of classification were evaluated using four standard performance measures: the accuracy, precision, recall, and F_1 measures.

The accuracy measure represents one minus the ratio of the wrong assignments over the total number of assignments; that is,

$$Accuracy = 1 - \frac{|FP| + |FN|}{|TP| + |FP| + |TN| + |FN|}, \tag{29}$$

where TP, TN, FP, and FN represents the true positives, true negatives, false positives, and false negatives, respectively.

The precision measure p represents the ratio of true positives over the total of positive assignments:

$$p = \frac{|TP|}{|TP| + |FP|}. \tag{30}$$

The recall measure r is defined as the ratio of true positives over the total of correct assignments:

$$r = \frac{|TP|}{|TP| + |FN|}. \tag{31}$$

Finally, the F_1 measure, a trade-off between the precision and recall, is defined by

$$F_1 = \frac{2pr}{p + r}. \tag{32}$$

Table 1. Simulation results for classifying speech data when the positive class is PD.

Performance measures	Algorithm		
	SVM	CPON	CPONwD
Accuracy	0.923	0.943	**0.954**
Precision	0.908	**0.990**	0.955
Recall	**1.000**	**1.000**	0.986
F_1	0.952	**0.995**	0.970

Table 2. Simulation results for classifying speech data when the positive class is NR.

Performance measures	Algorithm		
	SVM	CPON	CPONwD
Accuracy	0.923	0.943	**0.954**
Precision	**1.000**	0.900	0.957
Recall	0.658	**0.875**	0.854
F_1	0.812	0.883	**0.898**

The simulation results of SVM, CPON, and CPONwD are summarized in Tables 1 and 2. These results showed that (1) the proposed CPONwD provided the best performance of classification accuracy, (2) the CPON made the good performance of F_1 measure for the PD data, whereas the CPONwD made the good performance of F_1 measure for the NR data, and (3) the SVM made the good performance of a recall measure for the PD data. These simulation results demonstrated that the CPON-based methods provided the improved performance by estimating the output distribution of classifier using the Beta parameters and the additional decision network was helpful to improve the decision of CPON using the reference patterns and also p-values. Furthermore, the proposed method provides the uncertainty measure in the decision of classification.

6   Conclusion

There is no fundamental treatment in Parkinson's disease. In this respect, early diagnosis is important because it can improve the quality of life. One of important symptoms is that about 90% of Parkinson's patients have a speech impairment. Thus, speech disorders can be used as an early indicator of onset, and voice measurements are attracting attention as effective diagnostic methods. From this point of view, this paper proposes a new method of classifying speech data in Parkinson's disease using the class probability output network (CPON) in which the conditional class probabilities are estimated using Beta distributions. In the proposed CPON, the uncertainty measure describing the uncertainty in the decision of classification is also calculated. If the given input pattern of speech features falls in the uncertain region of classification, the decision network as the second layer is activated and the decision is made from the log-scaled conditional class probabilities and also the selected feature. Otherwise, the decision is made just using the CPON in the first layer. As a result, the proposed method provides consistently improved classification performances. Through the simulation for classifying speech data in Parkinson's disease using the UCI data set, it has been demonstrated that the proposed method of CPON with decision network improve the classification performance of the existing CPON and also SVM classifiers.

The contributions of the proposed method are summarized as follows: (1) the conditional class probability for the given speech data is calculated to represent the degree of confidence in the PD or NR class, (2) uncertainty measure is also calculated as the degree of uncertainty in the decision, (3) the decision network is introduced to make the better decision of classification for the uncertain data, and (4) the proposed method can be applied for unbalanced data since the decision is made using the Beta distribution parameters which are estimated separately for the PD and NR data distributions. This structure of the CPON with the decision network can be applied to a wide range of classification problems.

Acknowledgment. This work was partly supported by Institute for Information & communications Technology Promotion (IITP) grant funded by the Korea government (MSIT) (No. 2016-0-00133, Research on Edge computing via collective intelligence of hyperconnection IoT nodes and No. 2019-0-00421, AI Graduate School Support Program).

References

1. Manciocco, A., Chiarotti, F., Vitale, A., Calamandrei, G., Laviola, G., Alleva, E.: The application of Russell and Burch 3R principle in rodent models of neurodegenerative disease: the case of Parkinson's disease. Neurosci. Biobehav. Rev. **33**(1), 18–32 (2009)
2. Beal, M.F.: Experimental models of Parkinson's disease. Nat. Rev. Neurosci. **2**(5), 325 (2001)
3. Åström, F., Koker, R.: A parallel neural network approach to prediction of Parkinson's disease. Expert Syst. Appl. **38**(10), 12470–12474 (2011)

4. Parkinson, J.: An Essay on the Shaking Palsy. Sherwood, Neely and Jones, London (1817)
5. Jankovic, J.: Parkinson's disease: clinical features and diagnosis. J. Neurol. Neurosurg. Psychiatry **79**(4), 368–376 (2008)
6. O'Sullivan, S.B., Schmitz, T.J.: Parkinson disease. In: Physical Rehabilitation, 5th edn, pp. 856–894. F. A. Davis Company, Philadelphia, USA (2007)
7. Van Den Eeden, S.K., et al.: Incidence of Parkinson's disease: variation by age, gender, and race/ethnicity. Am. J. Epidemiol. **157**(11), 1015–1022 (2003)
8. Little, M.A., McSharry, P.E., Hunter, E.J., Spielman, J., Ramig, L.O.: Suitability of dysphonia measurements for telemonitoring of Parkinson's disease. IEEE Trans. Bio-Med. Eng. **56**(4), 1015 (2009)
9. Singh, N., Pillay, V., Choonara, Y.E.: Advances in the treatment of Parkinson's disease. Prog. Neurobiol. **81**(1), 29–44 (2007)
10. National Collaborating Centre for Chronic Conditions (Great Britain): Parkinson's Disease: National Clinical Guideline for Diagnosis and Management in Primary and Secondary Care. Royal College of Physicians, London (2006)
11. Ho, A.K., Iansek, R., Marigliani, C., Bradshaw, J.L., Gates, S.: Speech impairment in a large sample of patients with Parkinson's disease. Behav. Neurol. **11**(3), 131–137 (1999)
12. Little, M.A., McSharry, P.E., Roberts, S.J., Costello, D.A., Moroz, I.M.: Exploiting nonlinear recurrence and fractal scaling properties for voice disorder detection. Biomed. Eng. Online **6**(1), 23 (2007)
13. Sakar, C.O., Kursun, O.: Telediagnosis of Parkinson's disease using measurements of dysphonia. J. Med. Syst. **34**(4), 591–599 (2010)
14. Chen, H.L., et al.: An efficient diagnosis system for detection of Parkinson's disease using fuzzy k-nearest neighbor approach. Expert Syst. Appl. **40**(1), 263–271 (2013)
15. Zuo, W.L., Wang, Z.Y., Liu, T., Chen, H.L.: Effective detection of Parkinson's disease using an adaptive fuzzy k-nearest neighbor approach. Biomed. Sig. Process. Control **8**(4), 364–373 (2013)
16. Park, W., Kil, R.: Pattern classification with class probability output network. IEEE Trans. Neural Netw. **20**(10), 1659–1673 (2009)
17. Rosas, H., Kil, R., Han, S.: Automatic media data rating based on class probability output networks. IEEE Trans. Consum. Electron. **56**(4), 2296–2302 (2010)
18. Kim, S., Yu, Z., Kil, R., Lee, M.: Deep learning of support vector machines with class probability output networks. Neural Netw. **64**, 19–28 (2015)
19. Dua, D., Graff, C.: UCI Machine Learning Repository, University of California, School of Information and Computer Science, Irvine, CA (2019). http://archive.ics.uci.edu/ml
20. AbouRizk, S., Halpin, D., Wilson, J.: Fitting beta distributions based on sample data. J. Constr. Eng. Manag. **120**(2), 288–305 (1994)
21. Vapnik, V.: Statistical Learning Theory. Wiley, Hoboken (1998)
22. Rohatgi, V., Saleh, A.: Nonparametric statistical inference. In: An Introduction to Probability and Statistics, 2nd edn. Wiley, New York (2001)
23. Pedregosa, F., et al.: Scikit-learn: machine learning in Python. J. Mach. Learn. Res. **12**, 2825–2830 (2011)

ConvCaps: Multi-input Capsule Network for Brain Tumor Classification

Yiming Cheng[✉], Guihe Qin[✉], Rui Zhao[✉], Yanhua Liang[✉], and Minghui Sun[✉]

College of Computer Science and Technology, Jilin University, Changchun 130012, China
chengym18@mails.jlu.edu.cn, 997085817@qq.com, {qingh,ruizhao, smh}@jlu.edu.cn

Abstract. Brain tumor is considered one of the most deadly cancer. Determining the type of brain tumor has a significant effect on the choice of treatment and improves the survival rate of the patients. In general, manual diagnosis is time-consuming and error-prone. With the development of deep learning, especially the convolutional neural network (CNN), the process of automatic classification and diagnosis of medical images has been greatly promoted. However, CNN's pooling operation decreases a lot of spatial relationships that play important roles in discriminating tumor types, resulting in inaccurate classification results. Capsule Network (CapsNet) is a novel architecture proposed in recent years to overcome shortcomings of CNN. However, it cannot handle inputs in large size. To tackle this problem, a Convolutional Capsule Network (ConvCaps) architecture for brain tumor classification is proposed which has the following properties: (1) It can accept large-size images as input without scaling them in advance. (2) Preserving the spatial relationships of components in the image. (3) Multiple convolutional layers are added in front of the primary capsule layer so that the network can extract low-level features. (4) Image of brain tumor region is fed into our model as extra input to improve the network's attention to the region of interest. The experimental results on the brain MR dataset show that our model improves significantly compared with the previous work, the classification accuracy increases to 93.5%, and the training speed is also improved.

Keywords: Brain tumor classification · Multi-input capsule network · MaxPooling · Tumor region · Convolutional neural network

1 Introduction

According to research statistics, there were 18.1 million new cancer cases and 9.6 million cancer deaths worldwide in 2018 [1]. Among different types of cancer, brain tumor is considered one of the most deadly cancer [2]. Brain tumor has different types (e.g., meningiomas, pituitary tumors, and gliomas), and different brain tumors generally have different locations and properties [3]. Pituitary tumors are a group of tumors that occur from the anterior, posterior pituitary and residual cells of the cranial pharyngeal epithelium. Meningioma is caused by a series of derivatives between the meninges. Glioma

© Springer Nature Switzerland AG 2019
T. Gedeon et al. (Eds.): ICONIP 2019, LNCS 11953, pp. 524–534, 2019.
https://doi.org/10.1007/978-3-030-36708-4_43

is mainly derived from glial cells, including astrocytoma, oligodendroglioma, glioblastoma, medulloblastoma etc., accounting for about 40% of intracranial tumors. The type of brain tumor can be determined according to the size and location of the tumor and whether there are corresponding symptoms. At present, magnetic resonance (MR) imaging technology is generally used to acquire brain tumor images because it can provide high-resolution images of brain tissue. However, brain tumor classification based on MR images is a challenging, error-prone and time-consuming process that is highly dependent on the experience of the attending physician.

With the rapid development of computer vision, it has become a new trend to determine the tumor type by constructing different CNN architectures. In general, CNN [4] is stacks of convolutional layers, pooling layers, activational layers, and fully connected layers. CNN does not require any prior knowledge of the type of features that to be extracted, which makes it a popular architecture in medical image processing [5]. However, CNN has the following shortcomings: (1) A lot of spatial relationships are dropped during the pooling process. For tasks that require location information, we need to build complex network structures to recover the missing information. However, if the pooling layers are removed, the network will be extremely sensitive to minor changes of the image. (2) CNN generally requires a lot of data even augmented data for training. When the amount of data is relatively small, CNN is not suitable. (3) CNN cannot directly contain hierarchical relationships between various components in the image that facilitate classification and recognition.

In view of the above problems, people start to utilize CapsNet that retains the location information in the image. CapsNet [6] is a newly developed neural network architecture that may have a profound impact on deep learning, especially in the field of computer vision. Compared with CNN, CapsNet has the following advantages: (1) It can be trained and generalized with a relatively small amount of data. (2) Status information of the components in the image can be preserved, including their rotation, tilt, size, etc. (3) A consistent framework can be used in different computer vision tasks. (4) It contains the hierarchical relationships among the components in the image directly. However, CapsNet is not proper for large-size input, we proposed a new architecture called ConvCaps that is able to accept large-size input without increasing the number of parameters. Our contributions can be summarized as follows:

1. MR image in the dataset can be fed into ConvCaps directly. Since MaxPooling operation down-samples the image while preserving the prominent features, we down-sample the input image with a MaxPooling operation, which decreases the number of training parameters and achieves higher accuracy.
2. Except for the MR image, the brain tumor region is fed into the network as an extra input to increase the network's attention to the tumor area, then two continuous convolutional layers are added to the above two inputs respectively to extract low-level features. The two feature maps are then fused so that the network contains both the global information and the details of the tumor.
3. We design a new loss function to replace the reconstruction loss with classification loss, thus the training targets are all concentrated on the classification task.

The rest of the paper is organized as follows: The second part briefly introduces related work for tumor classification. The third part introduces the network architecture we proposed. The fourth part presents the experimental results and analysis, and the fifth part summarizes the whole paper.

2 Related Work

Because manual classification of cancer is time-consuming and error-prone, attempts have been made to develop automated or semi-automated systems for tumor classification [7–10]. According to the traditional methods, we need to segment the image to determine the location of the tumor and then extract quantitative features such as shape, intensity and texture that are useful for classification task [11]. Havaei *et al.* [12] have proposed a CNN architecture for brain tumor segmentation. After the tumor region is segmented, different types of features can be extracted and then fed into the classification model. Aerts *et al.* [13] have extracted 400 features from segmented tumors to investigate the relationship between image-based features and clinical outcomes. However, it was found that the extracted features were dependent on tumor annotation. Besides, this kind of method requires the types of features to be extracted in advance, which has poor generalization ability, reliability and applicability.

In response to the shortcomings of traditional methods, people begin to use CNN to classify brain tumors instead of extracting the features in advance [14]. For example, Li *et al.* [15] have used 6-layer CNN to extract features from brain images to classify brain tumors. CNN does not require any prior knowledge about the features and can be trained in an end-to-end way without segmenting the brain tumor image. Although CNN has strong learning ability, it has some fatal shortcomings [6, 16]. For instance, the spatial relationships between components in the image cannot be considered. In addition, a huge amount of data is required to improve the robustness of CNN, or it is necessary to build a complex architecture to recover the missing information that is dropped during the pooling process. In short, CNN is not suitable for brain tumor classification tasks.

Recently, people start to utilize the newly developed structure named Capsule Network [6, 16]. In work [17], Afser *et al.* have employed the finely segmented tumor image as input to demonstrate that CapsNet outperforms CNN for brain tumor classification task. However, CapsNet is sensitive to miscellaneous background and fine segmentation of tumor images is time-consuming and labor-intensive. In [18], a new model was proposed based on the CapsNet. Instead of fine segmentation of the image, the coarse boundary of the tumor in the image was utilized as an additional input for the network, which improved the classification accuracy of brain tumors. The input image needs to be preprocessed for the mentioned methods, scaling the size from 512×512 to 128×128 or even 64×64, leading to serious loss of detailed information. However, if the image is not scaled in advance, the routing layer of the CapsNet generates a large number of parameters, which decreases the training efficiency. To solve the above problems, we propose a new architecture called Convolutional Capsule Network, referred to as ConvCaps. Next, we will elaborate on the reason why we propose this architecture as well as details of it.

3 Proposed Model

3.1 Improved Motivation and Model Structure

According to the above information about CapsNet and CNN, we know that CapsNet is able to contain hierarchical information in the image directly, so it is more suitable for the classification of small dataset, such as our brain tumor dataset. Previous work [17, 18] has verified that CapsNet is superior to CNN in solving brain tumor classification problem. However, they have one thing in common: scaling the image to 1/8 or 1/4 of the original image before feeding it into the network, which will undoubtedly drop a lot of important information. CapsNet has achieved the best accuracy on the MNIST dataset currently, but it is unclear whether it can classify more complex dataset. We use the brain MR dataset [19] for our experiment. The size of the image is 512×512 which is pretty large for CapsNet and our dataset is obviously more complex than MNIST dataset. Considering that the image can be scaled by MaxPooling operation to reduce the number of parameters and preserve the prominent features in the image, we finally choose to perform MaxPooling operation for the input image instead of scaling it in advance. In order to improve the classification accuracy, we also employ the tumor region as an additional input to the network which can be obtained as follows: First, we get the boundary coordinates $\{x_1, y_1, x_2, y_2, \ldots x_n, y_n\}$ of the tumor from our dataset, and then calculate the coordinates of the center point of the tumor according to the following formula:

$$C^x = \sum_{i=1}^{i=n} x_i/n, \quad C^y = \sum_{i=1}^{i=n} y_i/n \tag{1}$$

Centering on this point (C^x, C^y), 64 pixels are expanded up, down, left, and right respectively to form an image of 128×128, as shown in Fig. 1. It provides detailed information about the brain tumor including its size, orientation and texture that are useful for improving classification accuracy.

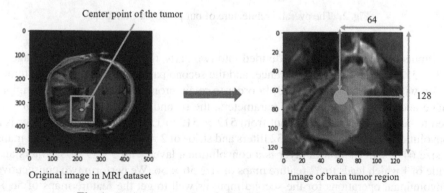

Fig. 1. Brain tumor region obtained from the original image.

In general, the more convolution steps we have, the more complicated features our network will be able to learn to recognize. For example, in image classification tasks,

CNN may learn to detect edges from raw pixels in the first layer, then use the edges to detect simple shapes in the second layer, and next, use these shapes to detect higher-level features, such as facial shapes in higher layers. Inspired by this idea, we design to add two convolutional layers in front of the primary capsule layer of the ConvCaps to extract the low-level features for both inputs. This operation contributes to reduce the number of training parameters as well.

Additionally, in order to focus all our attention on classification task, we try to modify the original defined loss function in the CapsNet, replacing the reconstruction loss function with the cross-entropy loss function for the last layer [18]. In this way, most of parameters in the reconstruction process are dropped.

Motivated by the aforementioned understanding, we design a new network structure named ConvCaps in this paper, which is improved on the basis of CapsNet. The brain tumor classification task can be accomplished better with ConvCaps than the previous models. The structure of the entire network is shown in Fig. 2.

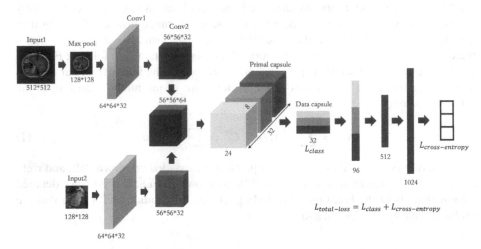

Fig. 2. The overall architecture of our proposed ConvCaps.

Inputs to the network can be divided into two parts, the first part is a MR image of 512×512 without scaling in advance, and the second part is the image of brain tumor region with the size of 128×128. In order to retain prominent features in the original image and reduce the number of parameters, the second layer "MaxPooling layer" is used to down-sample the first input from 512×512 to 128×128. The third layer is a convolutional layer with $7 \times 7 \times 32$ filters and stride of 2 which leads to 32 feature maps of size 64×64. The fourth layer is a convolutional layer with $9 \times 9 \times 32$ filters and stride of 1 which leads to 32 feature maps of size 56×56. We perform two consecutive convolutional operations for the second input as well to get the feature maps of $56 \times 56 \times 32$. Then we merge the two feature maps in the depth direction to get the feature maps of $56 \times 56 \times 64$. The fifth layer is a primary capsule layer resulting from $9 \times 9 \times 256$ filters with stride of 2, as shown in Fig. 2, each location contains 32 capsules of size 8. The primary capsule layer represents low-level features, each capsule reflects the characterization of a particular type of entity. These characterizations include different instantiation parameters such as position, size, orientation, deformation, velocity, reflectivity, color and texture. Then the lower-level capsules predict the high-level capsules with dynamic routing. The sixth layer is the data capsule layer that contains high-level capsules we mentioned before, representing different categories and their instantiation parameters. The number of instantiation parameters in our model corresponding to each capsule is 32. The three data capsules are then elongated to form a long vector of length 96. The vector is connected with 3 fully connected layers having 512, 1024 and 3 neurons. This is the whole details of ConvCaps.

3.2 Loss Function

For CapsNet, the loss function l_j represents the loss for the jth data capsule which is calculated as follows:

$$l_j = T_j \cdot max\left(0, m^+ - \|v_j\|\right)^2 + \lambda(1 - T_j)max(0, \|v_j\| - m^-)^2 \tag{2}$$

Each capsule j ($1 \leq j \leq K$) in the data capsule layer is associated with the loss function l_j, where K is the number of capsules in the data capsule layer. T_j and $\|v_j\|$ represent the label and the modulus of the jth data capsule respectively. m^+, m^-, K and λ are hyperparameters indicated before training.

The total loss of CapsNet is divided into two parts, the first part is the sum over the losses of all the data capsules, the other part is reconstruction loss. CapsNet has a range of fully connected layers called decoder, it takes the instantiation parameters of the corresponding label as input and attempts to reconstruct the original image. The reconstruction loss is defined as a squared error and multiplied by a smaller weight in order to pay more attention on the classification task. Considering that the decoder part introduces a large number of parameters and it has no significant effect on classification. We developed a new loss function, as shown below:

$$total\_loss = \lambda_1 \cdot L_{class} + \lambda_2 \cdot L_{cross-entropy} \tag{3}$$

$$L_{class} = \sum\nolimits_{j=1}^{j=K} l_j \tag{4}$$

$$L_{cross-entropy} = -\sum\nolimits_{i=1}^{i=K} (y^i \log(P(y^i))) \tag{5}$$

Where y^i represents the label for the ith category, and $P(y^i)$ represents the probability that the predicted category is i. L_{class} represents the classification loss of the data capsule, $L_{cross-entropy}$ represents the classification loss of the last layer. λ_1 and λ_2 are their corresponding weights indicated before training. The total loss is propagated back through the entire network, including capsule layers, fully connected layers, and convolutional layers.

The above is an introduction to our proposed multi-input architecture for brain tumor classification. Next, we will present a series of experimental results to evaluate the classification effect of ConvCaps.

4   Experiment and Analysis

4.1   Dataset and Implementation Details

We evaluate our ConvCaps on brain MR dataset [19], which is a widely used dataset for brain tumor classification, including 3,064 T1-weighted contrast-inhanced MR images from 233 patients. The number of meningiomas, gliomas, and pituitary tumors is 708, 1426, and 930, respectively. The size of each image is 512×512. In addition to the MR images, the dataset contains boundary coordinate information of the brain tumor, mask images of the brain tumor, and the label of tumor type corresponding to each image.

We implemented the proposed model based on the Tensorflow framework and a GTX 1080Ti GPU is used for acceleration. In our experiment, we set the value of batch-size to 30, learning-rate to 0.0001, routing-steps to 4, K to 3, m^+ to 0.9, m^- to 0.1, and λ to 0.5.

4.2   Quantitative Results

Overall, the ConvCaps we proposed in this paper outperforms all the other models, achieving the average performance of 93.5%. Table 1 shows the comparison between our results and previous best results. As shown in the table, the classification accuracy of segmented tumor image is better than that of the whole brain image. Besides, it can be known from the experiments [17, 20] that the accuracy of the CapsNet is better than that of the CNN.

We performed five parallel experiments for all experiments in this section to calculate the average classification accuracy and its corresponding error range. Besides, we shuffled the dataset before conducting each parallel experiment.

Table 1. Comparison of experimental results.

Different architecture	Accuracy
CNN that takes brain tumor image as input [20]	0.6197
CNN that takes segmented brain tumor image as input [20]	0.7213
CapsNet that takes brain tumor image as input [17]	0.78
CapsNet that takes finely segmented brain tumor image as input [17]	0.8656
CapsNet that takes rough location of the tumor as extra input [18]	0.9089
ConvCaps	**0.935 ± 0.005**

4.3   Qualitative Results

For previous work, the input image needs to be preprocessed with traditional methods to reduce the size from 512×512 to 128×128 or even smaller. Considering that the traditional method drops a lot of information in the image, we keep the size of input image unchanged before feeding it into our model. Table 2 shows the final classification accuracy of these two manners, and for each case, we conduct five parallel experiments to calculate the average classification accuracy and its corresponding error range. We can see that the accuracy of our method is far more than the previous methods. Besides, we compared the influence of these two manners on classification accuracy and loss during training process. As shown in Fig. 3, the accuracy and loss of the former (a) are basically stable in less than 2000 iterations. In contrast, the latter (b) have not reached stability until 3,000 iterations. This validates our previous ideas and illustrates that downsampling the input image with traditional method indeed ignores many important information which is important for tumor classification.

Table 2. Accuracy of different processing methods for input image.

Two methods to preprocess the input image	Classification accuracy
Keep the original size of 512 × 512	**0.935 ± 0.005**
Reduce the size to 128 × 128 with previous method	0.879 ± 0.007

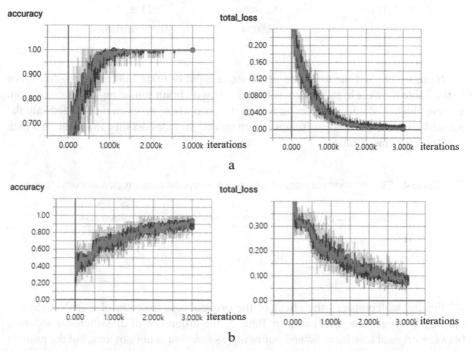

Fig. 3. Accuracy and loss curve during training period of different processing methods for input image. The (a) represents the accuracy and total loss curve of the network which takes the original image of 512 × 512 as input. The (b) represents the accuracy and total loss curve of the network which takes the scaled image of 128 × 128 as input. Curves of different colors represent different parallel experiments.

As mentioned in our previous experiment, we keep the size of input image unchanged. However, large-size input image is not proper for CapsNet. We consider two methods to down-sample the input image while retaining its prominent features, one is to apply MaxPoooling operation, the other is to apply multi-stride convolutional operation. Then, we compared the classification accuracy and parameter quantities with these two methods. As shown in Table 3, for the input image of 512×512, $(3, 3, 1, 16)$ represents a convolutional layer with $3 \times 3 \times 1$ filters and stride of 4 which leads to 16 feature maps of size 128×128. From the table, we know that MaxPooling operation achieves higher accuracy than other convolutional operations. Besides, MaxPooling operation reduces the number of parameters while the convolutional operation introduces new parameters that decreases the training efficiency. In order to balance speed and efficiency, we finally choose the MaxPooling operation as the preferred method for downsampling.

Table 3. Classification accuracy and parameter quantities of different scaling methods.

Different scaling methods	Number of parameters	Classification accuracy
MaxPool	**16230339**	**0.935 ± 0.005**
(3, 3, 1, 16)	16254019	0.915 ± 0.011
(7, 7, 1, 16)	16254659	0.921 ± 0.008
(7, 7, 1, 32)	16280547	0.927 ± 0.006

Next, we studied the influence of the extra input of brain tumor region. As shown in the Table 4, it is obvious that our ConvCaps with brain tumor region as extra input achieves higher accuracy in comparison to the case where no extra input is fed into the network. As explained before, tumor region indeed provides detailed information which is helpful for classification.

Table 4. Classification accuracy of whether to accept the tumor region as extra input.

Whether to Accept the tumor region as extra input	Classification accuracy
Yes	**0.935 ± 0.005**
No	0.917 ± 0.01

Finally, we compared the effect of the original loss function of CapsNet [6] and our new loss function. As shown in Table 5, the difference of classification accuracy between original loss function and our new loss function is not obvious, but the number of parameters of the former is almost twice of the latter which will undoubtedly consume a lot of computer resources. We finally choose to use the new loss function.

Table 5. Analysis of loss function.

Loss function	Number of parameters	Classification accuracy
Original loss function	32324544	0.925 ± 0.006
New loss function	**15566787**	**0.935 $\pm$ 0.005**

After determining the use of our new loss function, we performed a series of experiments on λ_1 and λ_2 to determine the optimal weight setting, as shown in Table 6, the best classification accuracy can be achieved in the case of $\lambda_2 = 0.005(\lambda_1 = 1)$.

Table 6. Analysis of hyperparameter setting.

Value of λ_1 and λ_2	Classification accuracy
$\lambda_1 = 1, \lambda_2 = \mathbf{0.005}$	**0.935 $\pm$ 0.005**
$\lambda_1 = 1, \lambda_2 = 0.05$	0.923 ± 0.003
$\lambda_1 = 1, \lambda_2 = 0.5$	0.915 ± 0.01
$\lambda_1 = 1, \lambda_2 = 1$	0.9 ± 0.007
$\lambda_1 = 0.005, \lambda_2 = 1$	0.916 ± 0.005
$\lambda_1 = 0.05, \lambda_2 = 1$	0.91 ± 0.003
$\lambda_1 = 0.5, \lambda_2 = 1$	0.904 ± 0.012

5 Conclusion

In this paper, we develop a convolutional capsule model called ConvCaps. Firstly, a MaxPooling operation is performed on the MR image to reduce the size of the input image while preserving the salient features. Besides, image of tumor region is also utilized as extra input to improve the classification accuracy. Secondly, in order to extract the low-level features and control the number of parameters during the dynamic routing process, continuous two-layer convolution is employed to obtain the primary capsule. Finally, we use the newly developed loss function to focus all the targets on the classification task and adjust the weight assignment of the two losses to find the most appropriate weight setting. Our model is obviously superior to other models, with an accuracy of 93.5% on the test set. The next step is to optimize the structure and performance of our network, enable ConvCaps to balance both accuracy and speed, and extend its application to more complex dataset.

Acknowledgments. This study has been partially supported by National Natural Science Foundation of China (61872164).

References

1. Bray, F., Ferlay, J., Soerjomataram, I., Siegel, R.L., Torre, L.A., Jemal, A.: Global cancer statistics 2018: GLOBOCAN estimates of incidence and mortality worldwide for 36 cancers in 185 countries. CA Cancer J. Clin. **68**(6), 394–424 (2018)
2. Siegel, R.L., Miller, K.D., Jemal, A.: Cancer statistics, 2016. CA Cancer J. Clin. **60**(5), 277–300 (2010)
3. Cheng, J., et al.: Enhanced performance of brain tumor classification via tumor region augmentation and partition. PLoS ONE **10**(10), e0140381 (2015)
4. Lecun, Y., Bottou, L., Bengio, Y., Haffner, P.: Gradient-based learning applied to document recognition. Proc. IEEE **86**(11), 2278–2324 (1998)
5. Ravi, D., et al.: Deep learning for health informatics. IEEE J. Biomed. Health Inform. **21**(1), 4–21 (2017)
6. Sabour, S., Frosst, N., Hinton, G.E.: Dynamic routing between capsules. In: Advances in Neural Information Processing Systems, pp. 3856–3866 (2017)
7. Usman, K., Rajpoot, K.: Brain tumor classification from multi-modality MRI using wavelets and machine learning. Pattern Anal. Appl. **20**(3), 871–881 (2017)
8. El Abbadi, N.K., Kadhim, N.E.: Brain cancer classification based on features and artificial neural network. Brain **6**(1), 123–134 (2017)
9. Mohsen, H., El-Dahshan, E.S.A., El-Horbaty, E.S.M., Salem, A.B.M.: Classification using deep learning neural networks for brain tumors. Futur. Comput. Inform. J. **3**(1), 68–71 (2018)
10. Mathew, A.R., Anto, P.B.: Tumor detection and classification of MRI brain image using wavelet transform and SVM. In: 2017 International Conference on Signal Processing and Communication (ICSPC), pp. 75–78. IEEE, July 2017
11. Li, X., Plataniotis, K.N.: Color model comparative analysis for breast cancer diagnosis using H and E stained images. In: Medical Imaging 2015: Digital Pathology, vol. 9420, p. 94200L. International Society for Optics and Photonics, March 2015
12. Havaei, M., Davy, A., Warde-Farley, D., Biard, A., Courville, A., Bengio, Y., et al.: Brain tumor segmentation with deep neural networks. Med. Image Anal. **35**, 18–31 (2015)
13. Aerts, H.J., et al.: Decoding tumour phenotype by noninvasive imaging using a quantitative radiomics approach. Nat. Commun. **5**, 4006 (2014)
14. Sutskever, I., Hinton, G.E., Krizhevsky, A.: ImageNet classification with deep convolutional neural networks. In: Advances in Neural Information Processing Systems, pp. 1097–1105 (2012)
15. Li, Z., Wang, Y., Yu, J., Guo, Y., Cao, W.: Deep learning based radiomics (DLR) and its usage in noninvasive IDH1 prediction for low grade glioma. Sci. Rep. **7**(1), 5467 (2017)
16. Sabour, S., Frosst, N., Hinton, G.: Matrix capsules with EM routing. In: 6th International Conference on Learning Representations, ICLR, pp. 1–15, February 2018
17. Afshar, P., Mohammadi, A., Plataniotis, K.N.: Brain tumor type classification via capsule networks. In: 2018 25th IEEE International Conference on Image Processing (ICIP), pp. 3129–3133. IEEE, October 2018
18. Afshar, P., Plataniotis, K.N., Mohammadi, A.: Capsule networks for brain tumor classification based on MRI images and coarse tumor boundaries. In: ICASSP 2019-2019 IEEE International Conference on Acoustics, Speech and Signal Processing (ICASSP), pp. 1368-1372. IEEE, May 2019
19. Cheng, J., Yang, W., Huang, M., Huang, W., Jiang, J., Zhou, Y., et al.: Retrieval of brain tumors by adaptive spatial pooling and fisher vector representation. PLoS ONE **11**(6), e0157112 (2016)
20. Paul, J.S., Plassard, A.J., Landman, B.A., Fabbri, D.: Deep learning for brain tumor classification. In: SPIE Medical Imaging, vol. 10137, pp. 1–16 (2017)

G-ResNet: Improved ResNet for Brain Tumor Classification

Dunsheng Liu[1,2](✉), Yuanning Liu[1,2](✉), and Liyan Dong[1,2](✉)

[1] College of Computer Science and Technology, Jilin University, Changchun 130012, China
ldsscholar@163.com, dongly@jlu.edu.cn
[2] Key Laboratory of Symbolic Computation and Knowledge Engineering
of Ministry of Education, Jilin University, Changchun 130012, China

Abstract. The brain tumors, are the most common and aggressive disease, leading to a short life expectancy and much pain. Timely and accurate diagnosis is the key factor in improving the survival rate of patients. The main method of identifying brain tumors is to analyze MR image that provides detailed information about brain structure and anomaly detection in brain tissue. With the rapid development of deep learning, especially the improvement of computer vision technology, automatic brain tumor detection is proposed by using Convolutional Neural Networks (CNN) classification. In this paper, we propose a new model called Global Average Pooling Residual Network (G-ResNet) to classify brain tumor images. The model has the following characteristics: (1) Applying the well-established CNN architecture in the field of deep learning named ResNet34 for the classification task. (2) To reduce the number of parameters and avoid overfitting, we use the global average pooling layer instead of the flattened layer for classification. (3) In order to be able to fuse the low-level and high-level features of the network to improve the classification accuracy, we concatenate the feature vectors of different layers. (4) We define a loss function, which is sum of the interval loss and the cross entropy loss. The total loss increases the penalty for misclassification. In summary, our model achieves the classification accuracy of 95.00%, which is significantly better than the previous models.

Keywords: Brain tumor classification · ResNet34 (Residual Network) · Global average pooling · Feature fusion · Interval loss

1 Introduction

According to the 2016 World Health Organization, cancer is considered to be the second leading cause of death for human [1]. Brain tumors are also the third most common cancer occurring among adolescents [2]. Brain tumors have different types (e.g., Meningioma, Pituitary, and Glioma) depending on several factors such as the shape, texture, and location of the tumor [3]. Different types of brain tumors require different medical interventions thus the diagnosis of brain tumors plays an important role in treatment planning and patient care. Manual classification is labor-intensive and challenging because

© Springer Nature Switzerland AG 2019
T. Gedeon et al. (Eds.): ICONIP 2019, LNCS 11953, pp. 535–545, 2019.
https://doi.org/10.1007/978-3-030-36708-4_44

brain tumor MR images have similar structures and appearances. Therefore, accurate automatic classification of brain tumors is of great significance.

The traditional machine learning method mainly consists of data preprocessing, feature extraction, feature selection, data dimension reduction and model training. Feature extraction is the most critical step. The quality of the extracted features will directly affect the classification accuracy. Besides, feature extraction relies heavily on the expertise of related fields and it is a challenging, labor-intensive process.

Conventional brain tumor classification methods commonly involve region-based tumor segmentation prior to feature extraction and classification. In this paper, we propose an automatic brain tumor classification method based on CNN. The well-known basic architecture of CNN involves the convolutional layers, the activate layers, the pooling layers and the fully connected layers. Compared with the traditional machine learning methods which require prior segmentation of tumor mass, CNN has the following significant advantages [4]: (1) CNN consists of a convolutional network to perform automatic segmentation and feature extraction, followed by a conventional neural network to perform classification task. (2) CNN takes advantage of the 2D structure of images and the fact that pixels within a neighborhood are usually highly correlated. Therefore, CNN rejects the use of one-to-one connections between all pixel units in favor of using grouped local connections. (3) CNN relies on feature sharing and each channel is thereby generated from convolution with the same filter at all locations. This important characteristic of CNN leads to an architecture that relies on far fewer parameters compared to standard Neural Networks. (4) CNN also introduces a pooling step that provides a degree of translation invariance making the architecture less affected by small variations in position. Each layer of CNN learns the corresponding features, generally, the lower layers of the network extract the low-level features and the subsequent layers extract the higher-level features.

Our contributions are summarized as follows:

1. The flattened layer is replaced with the global average pooling layer to reduce the number of parameters and avoid overfitting. Besides, in order to improve the accuracy of classification, our structure concatenates the low-level feature vectors and the high-level feature vectors.
2. We define a loss function, which is sum of the interval loss and the cross entropy loss. It is verified to improve the classification accuracy of the model.
3. Our model can be trained in an end-to-end manner and the well-established CNN architecture ResNet34 is employed as the fundamental structure of it to improve the performance.

The rest of this paper is organized as follows: Sect. 2 introduces the related work, in Sect. 3, we present our proposed model, and the Sect. 4 shows the experimental results and the corresponding analysis. Finally, Sect. 5 concludes the paper.

2 Related Work

Since manual diagnosis of cancer is time-consuming and error-prone, attempts have been made to develop automated systems for brain tumor classification [5–7]. In general, brain tumor classification divides the image to determine the location of the tumor and extracts quantitative features firstly, but this method requires prior knowledge of the type of features to be extracted. With the development of deep learning and computer vision, people begin to use CNN for cancer diagnosis and classification. CNN does not require any prior knowledge of feature types and can be trained in an end-to-end manner without the need to segment tumor images.

CNN plays an important role in the field of computer vision, especially in image classification [8]. In recent years, many important CNN structures have been developed to solve image classification tasks. LeNet [9] is the pioneer of CNN and solves the task of handwritten digit recognition. It defines the basic components of CNN, namely convolutional layer, pooling layer, and fully connected layer. Krishevsky proposes AlexNet [8], which utilizes Relu activation functions and dropout technology. The use of the ReLU diminishes the problem of vanishing gradient and leads to faster training, dropout contributes to reduce the problem of overfitting. Based on AlexNet, VGGNet [10] stacks more network layers and uses a smaller convolutional kernel to control the number of parameters. Once the number of layers of VGGNet increases to 19, there will be a decline in classification performance. The deeper the network is, the worse the problem of vanishing gradient becomes. Then comes a deeper architecture with 22 layers called GoogLeNet [11], which does not improve the network performance merely by deepening the network like AlexNet or VGG-Nets. It deepens and innovates the network at the same time. GoogLeNet replaces the traditional convolutional layer and activation layer with the Inception structure. Although it is deeper than VGGNet, it requires fewer parameters. GoogLeNet is the first network that no longer merely stacks convolutional and pooling layers, then one of the deepest architectures appears, called ResNet [12]. ResNet introduces the concept of residual modules, which contributes to design deeper network without affecting the classification accuracy, it is the most widely used CNN feature extraction network in nowadays.

At present, some people have tried to employ CNN to solve the classification problem of brain tumors. For example, Paul et al. [13] used 6-layer CNN to classify brain tumor images, which consists of two convolutional layers, two pooling layers and two fully-connected layers, the final classification accuracy is 72.13%. Abiwinanda et al. [14] also built a simple CNN architecture from scratch that consists of one convolutional, max-pooling, and flattened layers, followed by a fully connected layer. The model achieved the classification accuracy of 84.19%. Instead of building the model from scratch, we plan to employ the well-established CNN architecture mentioned earlier to improve the classification accuracy. Because of the small amount of dataset, the network cannot be very deep. Considering that ResNet34 is simple in structure and optimization, and it can deepen the network without affecting the classification effect, this paper built a new structure based on ResNet34 called G-ResNet to solve the problem of brain tumor classification.

3 Proposed Model

3.1 Method Overview

For many well-established CNN architectures, ResNet has achieved state-of-art performance in the ImageNet, CIFAR-10. By using the residual structure, the network gets deeper than before without leading to the problem of vanishing gradient, so we use ResNet34 as the basic model that to be improved.

Traditional convolutional neural networks convolve in the lower layers of the network. For classification, the feature maps of the last convolutional layer are flattened and fed into fully connected layers followed by a softmax logistic regression layer [8, 15, 16]. However, the flattened vector of feature maps is generally so long that the fully connected layer is prone to over-fitting. Dropout is proposed by Hinton *et al.* [17] as a regularizer which improves the generalization ability of the model and prevents overfitting [8]. But in our work, we use another method called global average pooling to replace the traditional flattened layer in CNN. As is shown in Fig. 1, the left graph is CNN with flattened layer while the right shows CNN with global average pooling layer. The resulting vector is directly input to the softmax layer to calculate the probability of each class obtained. In contrast to flattened layer, global average pooling layer has the following advantages [18]: Firstly, it is more native to the convolutional structure by enforcing correspondences between feature maps and feature vectors. Secondly, there are no optimization parameters in the global average pooling layer, thus avoiding over-fitting of this layer. In addition, the global average pooling layer combines spatial information and it's more robust to spatial translation of the input.

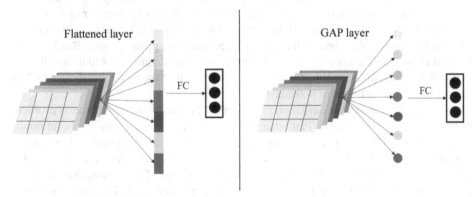

Fig. 1. The contrast between the flattened operation (left) and the global average pooling operation (right).

Deep learning can automatically extract low-level features and high-level features. Moreover, the learning ability of neural network can be extended by integrating the feature maps of different levels through concatenate operation. Considering that the classification accuracy of brain tumor is influenced by both low-level features such as the texture, color of the tumor and high-level features such as contours and shape of the

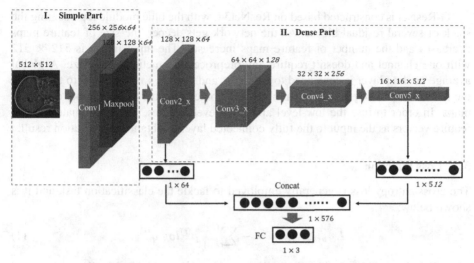

Fig. 2. The overall structure of G-ResNet. (Color figure online)

tumor, we expect to design a network that aggregates features at different levels of the image.

Based on all the above ideas, we proposed the final model, Global Average Pooling Residual Network, referred to as G-ResNet. The overall structure of G-ResNet is shown in Fig. 2, and the detailed information of G-ResNet is shown in Table 1.

Table 1. The detailed information of G-ResNet.

Layer name	Operation	Input	Output
Conv1	7×7, 64, stride2	$512 \times 512 \times 1$	$256 \times 256 \times 64$
Maxpool	3×3, max-pooling, stride2	$256 \times 256 \times 64$	$128 \times 128 \times 64$
Conv2_x	$\begin{bmatrix} 3 \times 3, 64 \\ 3 \times 3, 64 \end{bmatrix} \times 3$	$128 \times 128 \times 64$	$128 \times 128 \times 64$
Conv3_x	$\begin{bmatrix} 3 \times 3, 128 \\ 3 \times 3, 128 \end{bmatrix} \times 4$	$128 \times 128 \times 64$	$64 \times 64 \times 128$
Conv4_x	$\begin{bmatrix} 3 \times 3, 256 \\ 3 \times 3, 256 \end{bmatrix} \times 6$	$64 \times 64 \times 128$	$32 \times 32 \times 256$
Conv5_x	$\begin{bmatrix} 3 \times 3, 512 \\ 3 \times 3, 512 \end{bmatrix} \times 3$	$32 \times 32 \times 256$	$16 \times 16 \times 512$
Concat	–	① 1×64 ② 1×512	1×576
FC	576×3	1×576	1×3

G-ResNet is constructed based on ResNet34, with the blue module representing the stack of several residual blocks. As the network gets deeper, the size of feature maps decreases and the number of feature maps increases. The input image is 512×512 with one channel and doesn't require any preprocessing methods to resize. A global average pooling layer is connected to Conv2_x and Conv5_x respectively to transform the feature maps into pixels. The number of the pixels is equal to the number of feature maps. In order to fuse the low-level and high-level features, we concatenate the two feature vectors as the input to the fully connected layer to obtain the prediction result.

3.2 Loss Function

The cross-entropy loss is generally employed to tackle the classification task and it is shown below:

$$L_{cross-entropy} = -\sum_{i=1}^{C} p^{(i)} \log q^{(i)} \tag{1}$$

where C is the number of categories, $p^{(i)}$ represents the true label of the ith category and $q^{(i)}$ indicates the predicted probability of the ith category. The closer the distribution of true labels and predicted labels is, the smaller the cross entropy loss becomes.

In addition, inspired by the Capsule Network [19], we supplement the interval loss to the total loss to increase the penalty for misclassification.

$$l_k = T_k max\left(0, m^+ - p^{(k)}\right)^2 + \eta(1 - T_k)max\left(0, p^{(k)} - m^-\right)^2 \tag{2}$$

$$L_{margin-loss} = \sum_{k=1}^{C} l_k \tag{3}$$

For the interval loss, C is the number of categories, $p^{(k)}$ represents the probability that the category k exists and is calculated by softmax layer. m^+, m^- and η are hyperparameters indicated before training. In our experiment, m^+, m^- are set to $0.9, 0.1$ respectively, and η is 0.5. T_k represents the true label corresponding to the kth class. If class k exists, T_k is 1, and $(1 - T_k)$ is 0. If the predicted result is accurate, $p^{(k)}$ is close to m^+, then l_k will be equal to a small value close to zero. In contrast, if the predicted result is not accurate, then the difference between $p^{(k)}$ and m^+ is large, then l_k will be larger. Therefore, the closer the distribution of true labels and predicted labels, the smaller the interval loss. As such, we have defined the final loss as:

$$L_{total-loss} = L_{cross-entropy} + L_{margin-loss} \tag{4}$$

We can see that the above two loss functions obey the same rule, which demonstrates that our defined loss function is reasonable.

4 Experimental Framework and Analysis

4.1 Dataset

In this paper, G-ResNet is trained with brain MRI dataset [2]. The dataset is jointly collected by several hospitals and the authority of the data can be guaranteed. This dataset consists of 708 images with glioma, 1426 images with meningioma, and 930 images with pituitary tumors. The dataset was originally provided in .mat format where each file stores a structure containing a label which specifies the type of tumor for a particular brain image, patient ID, image data in 512×512 uint16 format, vector storing the coordinates of discrete points on tumor border, and a binary mask image with the value of one indicating tumor region. In our paper we only make use of the label and image data in the .mat files.

4.2 Implementation Details

We implement the proposed model based on the Pytorch framework and a GTX 1080Ti GPU, which is used for acceleration. During the training process, batch-size is set to 25. The stochastic gradient descent method with momentum is utilized to train the model, where the weight decay is 5×10^{-4}, the initial learning rate is 0.001. If the accuracy of the model has not been improved when the number of epochs exceeds 10, then the learning rate decreases by 0.316 times.

4.3 Result Analysis

First, we compare the classification accuracy between our basic structure ResNet34 and the previous competitive models. As shown in Table 2, ResNet34 achieves similar results to other simple CNN models and traditional methods due to its excellent structural design. It demonstrates that it is reasonable to employ ResNet34 as our basic architecture. Next, we modified the network structure step by step based on ResNet34.

Table 2. The compare between ResNet34 and some other models.

Model	Accuracy
Conventional algorithms [2, 3, 20, 21]	71.39–94.68%
CNN given brain image as input [13]	61.97%
CNN given segmented tumor as input [13]	72.13%
6-layer CNN built from scratch [14]	84.19%
ResNet34	**90.03%**

We then compared another two models, the first one is ResNet34 with flattened layer and the other is ResNet34 with global average pooling layer. During the experiment, we guaranteed that the two contrast models share the same learning rate, batch-size and loss function. Our experimental results on classification accuracy and the number of parameters are shown in Table 3. Under the same conditions, the global average pooling operation can not only improve the accuracy of classification, but also reduce the number of parameters.

Table 3. The effect of global average pooling layer.

Method	Number of parameters	Accuracy
ResNet34 with flattened layer	21432003	90.03%
ResNet34 with global average pooling layer	**21279939**	**94.13%**

Next, we compared the effect of different feature fusion methods of G-ResNet on training accuracy and the number of parameters. We designed four feature-fusion schemes as shown in Fig. 3. The blue rectangle corresponds to the blue block in Fig. 2 with the layer name on it, and the yellow rectangle represents the global average pooling layer. We connect the global average pooling layers to different blue rectangles to form the following four models. G1 means that the global average pooling layers are connected to all the four blue rectangles, G2 removes the second global average pooling layer, G3 removes the third global average pooling layer, and G4 removes both the second and third global average pooling layers. The experimental results are shown in Table 4. It is verified by experiments that among these four models, the model G4 achieves the best performance, with highest accuracy and fewest number of model parameters.

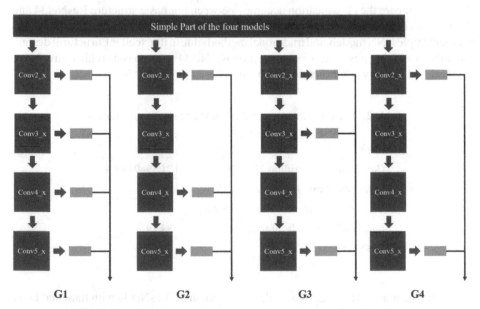

Fig. 3. Several schemes of connecting feature vectors for G-ResNet.

Table 4. The number of parameters and classification accuracy of different schemes in Fig. 3.

Method	Parameter	Accuracy
G1	21281283	93.10%
G2	21280899	93.49%
G3	21280515	94.04%
G4	**21280131**	**94.57%**

Finally, we conducted several experiments to explore the impact of the newly defined loss function on the classification accuracy. We applied the newly defined loss function and cross entropy loss function to the G4 model respectively. As is shown in Table 5, the newly defined loss function increases the accuracy of the model by approximately 0.43%, achieving the classification accuracy of 95.00%.

Table 5. Compare of the classification accuracy of the previous and newly defined loss functions.

Method	Accuracy
G4 with the cross entropy loss function	94.57%
G4 with newly defined loss function	**95.00%**

Figure 4 compares the training process of the models with different loss functions, where Fig. 4(a-1) and (a-2) show the classification accuracy and loss of the model with the cross entropy loss function, Fig. 4(b-1) and (b-2) show the classification accuracy and loss of the model with the newly defined loss function. Solid lines of different colors indicate different experiments and we conducted five experiments for both models. From the graph, we find that the five experiments with the newly defined loss function have almost the same classification accuracy and loss after 40 iterations, while the classification accuracy and loss of the five experiments with the cross entropy loss function is relatively scattered. This demonstrates that our newly defined loss function not only improves the accuracy of classification, but also makes the results of the model more stable.

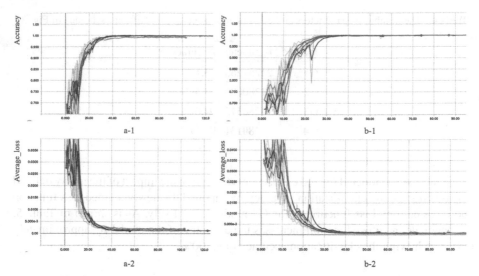

Fig. 4. Training process using different loss functions. (Color figure online)

5 Conclusion

In this paper, we propose an end-to-end network named G-ResNet for tumor classification. Firstly, instead of constructing the model from scratch, we utilize the well-established network ResNet34 as the basic structure. Secondly, in order to reduce the number of parameters and avoid over-fitting, we use the global average pooling layer to replace the flattened layer. This operation integrates spatial information and improves the robustness of the model. Thirdly, in order to integrate the low-level and high-level features of the network to improve the classification accuracy, we concatenate the feature vectors of different layers. Finally, we define a loss function, which is sum of the interval loss and the cross entropy loss. Our model achieves the accuracy of 95.00% on the test set and performs significantly better than the other models.

Acknowledgments. This research is supported by the Jilin Province Key Laboratory of Biometrics New Technology, National Natural Science Foundation (61471181), Jilin Province Industrial Innovation Special Fund Project (2019C053-6, 2019C053-2), Jilin Province Education Department Science and Technology Project (JJKH20180448KJ).

References

1. Siegel, R.L., Miller, K.D., Jemal, A.: Cancer statistics. CA Cancer J. Clin. **60**(5), 277–300 (2010)
2. Cheng, J., et al.: Retrieval of brain tumors by adaptive spatial pooling and fisher vector representation. PLoS ONE **11**(6), e0157112 (2016)
3. Cheng, J., et al.: Enhanced performance of brain tumor classification via tumor region augmentation and partition. PLoS ONE **10**(10), e0140381 (2015)

4. Hadji, I., Wildes, R.P.: What do we understand about convolutional networks? arXiv preprint arXiv:1803.08834 (2018)
5. El Abbadi, N.K., Kadhim, N.E.: Brain cancer classification based on features and artificial neural network. Brain 6(1), 123–134 (2017)
6. Mohsen, H., El-Dahshan, E.S.A., El-Horbaty, E.S.M., Salem, A.B.M.: Classification using deep learning neural networks for brain tumors. Future Comput. Inform. J. 3(1), 68–71 (2018)
7. Mathew, A.R., Anto, P.B.: Tumor detection and classification of MRI brain image using wavelet transform and SVM. In: 2017 International Conference on Signal Processing and Communication (ICSPC), pp. 75–78. IEEE, July 2017
8. Krizhevsky, A., Sutskever, I., Hinton, G.E.: ImageNet classification with deep convolutional neural networks. In: Advances in Neural Information Processing Systems, pp. 1097–1105 (2012)
9. Lecun, Y., Bottou, L., Bengio, Y., Haffner, P.: Gradient-based learning applied to document recognition. Proc. IEEE 86(11), 2278–2324 (1998)
10. Simonyan, K., Zisserman, A.: Very deep convolutional networks for large-scale image recognition. arXiv preprint arXiv:1409.1556 (2014)
11. Szegedy, C., et al.: Going deeper with convolutions. In: Proceedings of the IEEE Conference on Computer Vision and Pattern Recognition, pp. 1–9 (2015)
12. He, K., Zhang, X., Ren, S., Sun, J.: Deep residual learning for image recognition. In: Proceedings of the IEEE Conference on Computer Vision and Pattern Recognition, pp. 770–778 (2016)
13. Paul, J.S., Plassard, A.J., Landman, B.A., Fabbri, D.: Deep learning for brain tumor classification. In: SPIE Medical Imaging, vol. 10137, pp. 1–16 (2017)
14. Abiwinanda, N., Hanif, M., Hesaputra, S.T., Handayani, A., Mengko, T.R.: Brain tumor classification using convolutional neural network. In: Lhotska, L., Sukupova, L., Lacković, I., Ibbott, G.S. (eds.) World Congress on Medical Physics and Biomedical Engineering 2018. IP, vol. 68/1, pp. 183–189. Springer, Singapore (2019). https://doi.org/10.1007/978-981-10-9035-6_33
15. Goodfellow, I.J., Warde-Farley, D., Mirza, M., Courville, A., Bengio, Y.: Maxout networks. arXiv preprint arXiv:1302.4389 (2013)
16. Zeiler, M.D., Fergus, R.: Stochastic pooling for regularization of deep convolutional neural networks. arXiv preprint arXiv:1301.3557 (2013)
17. Hinton, G.E., Srivastava, N., Krizhevsky, A., Sutskever, I., Salakhutdinov, R.R.: Improving neural networks by preventing co-adaptation of feature detectors. arXiv preprint arXiv:1207.0580 (2012)
18. Lin, M., Chen, Q., Yan, S.: Network in network. arXiv preprint arXiv:1312.4400 (2013)
19. Sabour, S., Frosst, N., Hinton, G.E.: Dynamic routing between capsules. In: Advances in Neural Information Processing Systems, pp. 3856–3866 (2017)
20. Usman, K., Rajpoot, K.: Brain tumor classification from multi-modality MRI using wavelets and machine learning. Pattern Anal. Appl. 20(3), 871–881 (2017)
21. Afshar, P., Mohammadi, A., Plataniotis, K.N., Oikonomou, A., Benali, H.: From handcrafted to deep-learning-based cancer radiomics: challenges and opportunities. IEEE Signal Process. Mag. 36(4), 132–160 (2019)

Affinity Graph Based End-to-End Deep Convolutional Networks for CT Hemorrhage Segmentation

Jungrae Cho[1], Inchul Choi[1], Jaeil Kim[2], Sungmoon Jeong[3,4], Young-Sup Lee[5],
Jaechan Park[5], Jungjoon Kim[1], and Minho Lee[1(✉)]

[1] School of Electronics Engineering, Kyungpook National University, Daegu, South Korea
zzemb6@gmail.com, sharpic77@gmail.com, jungkim7@ee.knu.ac.kr,
mholee@gmail.com
[2] School of Computer Science and Engineering,
Kyungpook National University, Daegu, South Korea
threeyears@gmail.com
[3] School of Medicine, Kyungpook National University, Daegu, South Korea
jeongsm00@gmail.com
[4] Bio-Medical Research Institute, Kyungpook National University Hospital, Daegu, South Korea
[5] Department of Neurosurgery, Kyungpook National University, Daegu, South Korea
nsysdoctor@gmail.com, jparkmd@hotmail.com

Abstract. Brain hemorrhage segmentation in Computed Tomography (CT) scan images is challenging, due to low image contrast and large variations of hemorrhages in appearance. Unlike the previous approaches estimating the binary masks of hemorrhages directly, we newly introduce affinity graph, which is a graph representation of adjacent pixel connectivity to a U-Net segmentation network. The affinity graph can encode various regional features of the hemorrhages and backgrounds. Our segmentation network is trained in an end-to-end manner to learn the affinity graph as intermediate features and predict the hemorrhage boundaries from the graph. By learning the pixel connectivity using the affinity graph, we achieve better performance on the hemorrhage segmentation, compared to the conventional U-Net which just learns segmentation masks as targets directly. Experiments in this paper demonstrate that our model can provide higher Dice score and lower Hausdorff distance than the conventional U-Net training only segmentation map, and the model can also improve segmentation at hemorrhagic regions with blurry boundaries.

Keywords: Image segmentation · Brain hemorrhage · CT · Fully convolutional networks · Affinity graph

1 Introduction

Intracranial hemorrhage (ICH) is a type of bleeding within skull, which suffers from rupture or leakage. Due to its association with mortality and fatal after effects, the fast

© Springer Nature Switzerland AG 2019
T. Gedeon et al. (Eds.): ICONIP 2019, LNCS 11953, pp. 546–555, 2019.
https://doi.org/10.1007/978-3-030-36708-4_45

and accurate diagnosis of brain hemorrhage is a crucial task for ICH patients. With this importance, Computed Tomography (CT) images are widely adopted to diagnose brain hemorrhage initially, owing to its relatively rapid scanning speed and cheaper costs [1]. Many researchers have studied automated segmentation of ICH in CT scans to support medical doctor's clinical decision in many different ways. Among them, segmentation of cerebral hemorrhage in CT scans is the most challenging task because of its low contrast of brain hemorrhage and various fluid patterns of bleeding boundaries [2]. There have been several attempts [3] to tackle segmenting hemorrhage in CT (e.g. thresholding [4], range growing [5], fuzzy C-means clustering [1], and level-set algorithm [6]). Recently, with the success of deep learning, fully convolutional networks (FCN) are actively applied for segmenting various types of lesions, such as liver and brain tumor [7, 8]. Brain hemorrhage segmentation in CT scans with FCN-like model has been attempted by many researchers. Kuo et al. [9] has proposed patch-based FCN model for hemorrhage segmentation. Grewal et al. [10] has also introduced segmentation method based on DenseNet [11] for ICH segmentation and classification. However, despite the state-of-the art network structures, FCN-like model has shown its own limitation [12] in recognizing several bleeding patterns such as Subarachnoid Hemorrhage (SAH) which has unclear and complex boundaries with low intensity, compared to intracerebral hemorrhage and intraventricular hemorrhage as shown in Fig. 1.

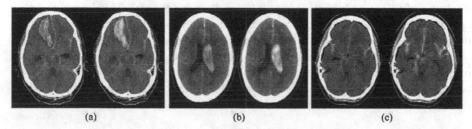

Fig. 1. Example of brain hemorrhages. For each figure, left image is raw CT scan and right image is hemorrhage highlighted CT scan. (a), (b), and (c) indicate Intracerebral Hemorrhage (ICH*), Intraventricular Hemorrhage (IVH), and Subarachnoid Hemorrhage (SAH) respectively.

To overcome such limitation and further enhance the segmentation performance, we propose a novel brain hemorrhage segmentation network based on U-Net [13] with a graph representation, called affinity graph. In our model, U-Net has already shown its accurate segmentation performance on brain tumor and electron microscopic (EM) images of neurons [8, 13, 14]. The affinity graph enables to integrate pixel connectivity information to our network. The affinity graph has been widely used for segmentation of complex patterns such as brain connectomes [15, 16]. However, the segmentation using the affinity map requires a series of post-processing including thresholding and connected components analysis with the empirical settings of hyper-parameters [17]. Unlike these conventional affinity map-based approaches, our segmentation network, denoted as Affinity Graph U-Net (AG U-Net), is trained in an end-to-end manner to learn the affinity graph as intermediate features to predict the hemorrhage boundaries as segmentation output. By learning the pixel connectivity in hemorrhage and background regions, we achieve improved performance on segmentation results than U-Net which only learns segmentation mask as targets directly.

2 Method

2.1 Affinity Graph

Affinity graph is an undirected weighted graph which represents the pixel connectivity with classes (e.g. hemorrhage and backgrounds). All of pixels in a image are regarded as nodes, and connections between adjacent pixels are represented as edges, and a weight of each edge is called as affinity i.e. pixel connectivity. Each affinity is defined with segmentation mask and indicator function δ as shown in Eq. (1), which has been introduced in [16].

$$\delta(s_i, s_j) = \begin{cases} 1 \ if \ s_i = s_j \\ 0 \ otherwise \end{cases} \tag{1}$$

s_i and s_j represents pixel-wise classes of node i and j, respectively. If the classes of two adjacent pixels are same, affinity is assigned as '1' which means they are connected, and '0' for vice versa. In this paper, we only consider affinities along the left-right (x-axis) and anterior-posterior (y-axis) directions for segmentation of hemorrhage, due to larger thickness of CT scans in the superior-inferior direction (z-axis). This larger thickness causes very low resolution in the superior-inferior direction, and it can be challenging to train segmentation model on z-axis features compared to x and y-axes features. Based on Eq. (1), we generate target affinity maps from target segmentation masks for training of our proposed model. Figure 2 describes concepts of affinity graph. In Fig. 2(a) is a part of brain CT slice, (b) is segmentation mask of hemorrhage annotated by medical doctor, and (c) is affinity graph defined by Eq. (1) from segmentation masks (b).

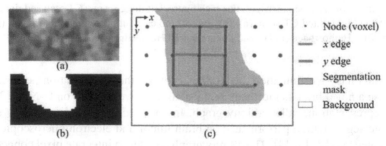

Fig. 2. Concepts of affinity graph. (a) is a part of brain CT slice, (b) is segmentation mask of hemorrhage annotated by medical doctor, and (c) is affinity graph defined by Eq. (1) from segmentation mask (b).

An example of generated affinity graph by Eq. (1) is introduced in Fig. 3. The top-left image is a skull-removed CT slice. From this image, the target segmentation masks of hemorrhage are annotated as shown in top-right image. Bottom-left and bottom-right image are channels of the generated affinity graph for x-axis and y-axis edges respectively. The shape and morphology of target segmentation masks and 2-channel of affinity graph is almost similar because the created affinity graph is just a map of affinities which simply compares adjacent segmentation masks whether they are same or not. However, since one affinity is produced by two nodes (pixels), width and height of affinity graph is smaller than the original segmentation map by 1. For example, for a given $N \times N$ CT slice, dimension of produced affinity graph becomes $(N - 1) \times (N - 1) \times 2$. To provide convenience in dimensionality, an offset row or column filled with zeros is appended in x-axis and y-axis affinity map. We overlay each channel of affinity graph (bottom-left and bottom-right, i.e., the blue area) on the ground truth segmentation map (top-right, i.e., the red area) to visualize the dimensionality explained above.

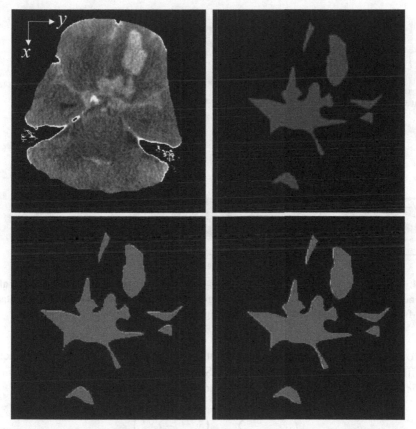

Fig. 3. An example of input CT slice, target segmentation masks, x-axis affinity graph, and y-axis affinity graph (Color figure online)

2.2 Affinity Graph U-Net

Figure 4 shows the structure of the proposed Affinity Graph U-Net (AG U-Net). The proposed model can be divided into 2 parts. The green part in Fig. 4 is conventional

U-Net structure. It has almost same structure as original U-Net [13], which consists of encoding and decoding path. It learns and predicts affinity map for x and y axis edges at the end of U-Net. The predicted affinity graph is fed into the graph-based segmentation network which replaces the post-processing steps of the affinity map, i.e., thresholding and connected components analysis. Our graph-based segmentation network automates the mapping procedures from the affinity graph to the binary mask via an end-to-end training of AG U-Net. Through this approach, we can introduce the pixel connectivity across the hemorrhages and backgrounds to the segmentation process.

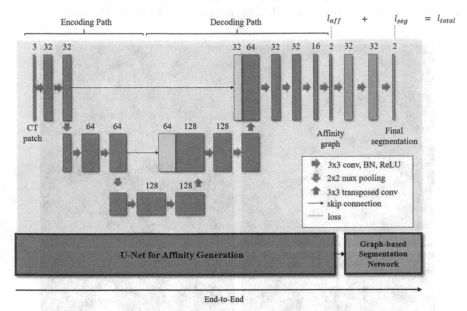

Fig. 4. Structure of Affinity Graph U-Net (AG U-Net). The green part is U-Net structure for affinity generation, and the blue part is graph-based segmentation network which predicts segmentation mask from the generated affinity graph. (Color figure online)

To learn both affinity map and segmentation mask, we define the objective function of affinity map as *mean squared error* (MSE) $\left(l_{aff}\right)$ and segmentation mask as *dice coefficient loss* $\left(l_{seg}\right)$ [18] respectively as shown in Eqs. (2) and (3).

$$l_{aff} = \frac{1}{n} \sum_{i=1}^{n} \left(y_i^{aff} - t_i^{aff}\right)^2 \tag{2}$$

$$l_{seg} = 1 - \frac{2 \sum_i^n y_i^{seg} t_i^{seg}}{\sum_i^n y_i^{seg} + \sum_i^n t_i^{seg}} \tag{3}$$

In Eq. (2), y_i^{aff} is the predicted affinity at i-th pixel, which is activated from sigmoid function, and t_i^{aff} is the target affinity. In Eq. (3), y_i^{seg} indicates predicted segmentation mask for i-th pixel after argmax of pixel-wise softmax. t_i^{seg} is the target mask which consists of background (0) and hemorrhage (1). Finally, total loss l_{total} is calculated with the sum of l_{aff} and l_{seg} as described in Eq. (4).

$$l_{total} = \alpha l_{aff} + \beta l_{seg} \tag{4}$$

For the equal contribution of l_{aff} and l_{seg} to the total loss, I multiply scale parameters α and β. In our approach, we assign those parameters as $\alpha = 1.2$ and $\beta = 1$ empirically. The reason why we put more weight on l_{aff} than l_{seg} is that the input of graph-based segmentation network (the blue part in Fig. 4) is the only predicted affinity graph. It means that the quality of the predicted affinity map highly affects the quality of final segmentation results. Furthermore, the scale of l_{aff} does not correspond to l_{seg}. Due to these reasons, we set weights α and β empirically. Finally, the total loss l_{total} is used to update whole trainable parameters in AG U-Net.

3 Experiments

3.1 Materials

Brain hemorrhage CT scans have been acquired in Kyungpook National Hospital from July 2014–May 2018. The hemorrhage regions are manually delineated by radiologists using the segmentation toolkit of MITK Workbench (Version Nov. 2016). In this paper, among 83 subjects' scans, 60 images are randomly selected as training set, and 10 images are selected as validation set. The rest of 13 scans are used for evaluation of segmentation accuracy. The majority of brain hemorrhage in the dataset is SAH and only few of the hemorrhages are ICH* and IVH. In this work, we regard all kinds of hemorrhage as same 'bleeding' i.e. binary segmentation to simplify the segmentation pattern of brain hemorrhage. Before fed into U-Net, CT scans are preprocessed with skull removing algorithm which reduces the effect of high intensity of skull area. Input of the model is patch image from CT slices in axial plane. The patch size is chosen as 64×64 from original image with size 512×512. For the training set, we sample patches from CT slices depending on the amount of segmentation masks in a patch area [19]. The probability to be chosen as a patch is determined by the ratio of number of segmented pixels to the total number of pixels in a candidate patch area. We extract 100 patches per a CT image in the training set. Finally, we generate 6,000 patches from 60 CT scans for training. To emphasize various levels of brain contrast, we apply multi-intensity windowing method with 3 levels, i.e., tissue level (median of window: 40, range of window: 40), brain level (median of window: 50, range of window: 100), and blood level (median of window: 60, range of window: 40) to give richer information to the model [20].

3.2 Implementation Details

The feature sizes of proposed model are described in Fig. 4. The output size of affinity graph is $64 \times 64 \times 2$. Each channel corresponds to x-axis and y-axis affinities in axial plane. The final output size is $64 \times 64 \times 2$, where first channel is for background, and second channel is for brain hemorrhage segmentation mask. Dataset is split into 60 CT images for training set, 10 images for validation set, and 13 scans for test set.

For training, we choose Adam optimizer with a learning rate of 0.0001 at initial epoch. Every 10 epochs, we gradually drop learning rate by multiplying 0.1. We train with 50 epochs for every model we experimented.

We evaluate our model with conventional U-Net which learns segmentation masks directly for comparison. For evaluation, parameters of baseline U-Net are assigned to the same value as the U-Net part of proposed model. By comparing these two models, we demonstrate the quantitative and qualitative performance of our model. The training is performed on GPU Titan Xp. All models are implemented with Keras.

3.3 Experimental Results

Evaluation of segmentation performance is generally measured with various types of metrics, since every metric has its own limitation [21]. Therefore, we measure Dice score (higher is better) and Hausdorff distance (lower is better) to consider both the extent of overlap and spatial similarity to target masks on 13 test CT images. Table 1 shows mean and standard deviation of Dice score and Hausdorff distance for each model. For both metrics, AG U-Net shows enhanced performances compared to baseline U-Net. The higher Dice score indicates that the predicted area is more overlapped with ground truth. The lower Hausdorff distance suggests that distance of surfaces between predicted segmentation map and ground truth is smaller, i.e., morphology of surfaces between two maps are more similar.

Table 1. Dice score and Hausdorff distance of the conventional U-Net without affinity graph (baseline) and AG U-Net (proposed) on test data. For both metrics, proposed model records improved performance compared to baseline.

Score	Conventional U-Net	AG U-Net
Dice score	0.603 (±0.251)	**0.623 (±0.207)**
Hausdorff distance	88.99 (±54.84)	**74.348 (±47.81)**

We visualize test examples for qualitative evaluation in Fig. 5. The top and second rows in Fig. 5 are test examples including input CT slice, target segmentation mask, prediction of the conventional U-Net without affinity graph (baseline), and AG U-Net (proposed). Figure 5(c) and (d) show local regions of test examples respectively. The zoomed regions in Fig. 5 contain both clear and blurred hemorrhage patterns. The U-Net without learning affinity map shows segmentation mask only for the clear bleeding patterns. On the other hand, AG U-Net that we proposed predicts not only clear bleeding patterns but also blurry hemorrhage compared to baseline model as shown in Fig. 5(c) and (d). These results demonstrate that introducing pixel connectivity to the segmentation process can greatly improve the entire model performance on blurry patterns of brain hemorrhage. In addition, our method also shows enhancement on quantitative performance metrics as in Table 1.

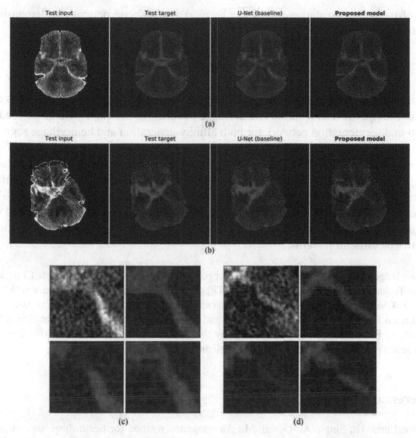

Fig. 5. Visualization of several test input images, target segmentation masks, predicted masks (baseline), and predicted masks (proposed model). (a) and (b) are test examples including input CT, target segmentation mask, prediction masks of baseline and proposed model. (c) and (d) indicate local area (white boxes) of (a) and (b) respectively. In (c) and (d), top left is input region, top right is the ground truth, bottom left is baseline prediction, and bottom right shows prediction of our model.

4 Discussion

From experimental results, we observe that AG U-Net enhances segmentation metrics compared to conventional U-Net structured model. Furthermore, some blurry hemorrhagic regions are predicted by our proposed model. These results suggest that learning multi-objectives including affinity graph and segmentation masks can improve the performance of segmentation of ICH. Those improved segmentation map can be utilized as guideline of segmentation for radiologists. However, since the number of CT scans for training and test is limited, our experiments can be viewed as feasibility check. Therefore, more training and test data can be used to train and evaluated our model. Lastly, this paper chooses U-Net as baseline segmentation model. In the future work, the state-of-the art segmentation model can be used as backbone network to demonstrate our contribution.

5 Conclusion

Segmentation of ICH in non-contrast CT images is challenging problem due to its low contrast, image noise and various hemorrhage patterns. In this paper, we introduced an end-to-end segmentation network for both affinity generation and hemorrhage segmentation which exploits the affinity graph to enhance the segmentation quality of difficult hemorrhage patterns. With this approach, our model showed more improved performance in segmentation of ICH than the baseline U-Net which was trained without the affinity graph for test data. Considering pixel connectivity in training also enabled U-Net to predict segmentation mask for blurry hemorrhage cases. We expect to expand our methods not only to U-Net but also similar structured networks to improve segmentation qualities on difficult patterns.

Acknowledgements. This work was partly supported by Institute of Information & Communications Technology Planning & Evaluation (IITP) grant funded by the Korea government (MSIT) (2016-0-00564, Development of Intelligent Interaction Technology Based on Context Awareness and Human Intention Understanding) (50%) and Institute for Information & communications Technology Promotion (IITP) grant funded by the Korea government (MSIT) (2018-2-00861, Intelligent SW Technology Development for Medical Data Analysis) (50%).

References

1. Bhadauria, H., Singh, A., Dewal, M.: An integrated method for hemorrhage segmentation from brain CT imaging. Comput. Electr. Eng. **39**(5), 1527–1536 (2013)
2. Cohen, W.: Computed tomography of intracranial hemorrhage. Radiol. Clin. N. Am. **2**, 75–87 (1992)
3. Shahangian, B., Pourghassem, H.: Automatic brain hemorrhage segmentation and classification algorithm based on weighted grayscale histogram feature in a hierarchical classification structure. Biocybern. Biomed. Eng. **36**(1), 217–232 (2016)
4. Hu, Q., Qian, G., Aziz, A., Nowinski, W.L.: Segmentation of brain from computed tomography head images. In: 2005 IEEE Engineering in Medicine and Biology 27th Annual Conference, pp. 3375–3378. IEEE (2006)
5. Maksimovic, R., Stankovic, S., Milovanovic, D.: Computed tomography image analyzer: 3D reconstruction and segmentation applying active contour models—'snakes'. Int. J. Med. Inf. **58**, 29–37 (2000)
6. Wasserberg, J., Mitchell, B.: CT scan guideline. Department of Neurosurgery, University of Birmingham (2009)
7. Li, X., Chen, H., Qi, X., Dou, Q., Fu, C.-W., Heng, P.-A.: H-DenseUNet: hybrid densely connected UNet for liver and tumor segmentation from CT volumes. IEEE Trans. Med. Imaging **37**(12), 2663–2674 (2018)
8. Isensee, F., Kickingereder, P., Wick, W., Bendszus, M., Maier-Hein, K.H.: Brain tumor segmentation and radiomics survival prediction: contribution to the BRATS 2017 challenge. In: Crimi, A., Bakas, S., Kuijf, H., Menze, B., Reyes, M. (eds.) BrainLes 2017. LNCS, vol. 10670, pp. 287–297. Springer, Cham (2018). https://doi.org/10.1007/978-3-319-75238-9_25

9. Kuo, W., Häne, C., Yuh, E., Mukherjee, P., Malik, J.: PatchFCN for intracranial hemorrhage detection (2018). arXiv preprint arXiv:180603265

10. Grewal, M., Srivastava, M.M., Kumar, P., Varadarajan, S.: RADNET: radiologist level accuracy using deep learning for hemorrhage detection in CT scans. In: 2018 IEEE 15th International Symposium on Biomedical Imaging (ISBI 2018), pp. 281–284. IEEE (2018)

11. Iandola, F., Moskewicz, M., Karayev, S., Girshick, R., Darrell, T., Keutzer, K.: DenseNet: implementing efficient ConvNet descriptor pyramids (2014). arXiv preprint arXiv:14041869

12. Sales Barros, R., et al.: Abstract WMP29: detection and segmentation of subarachnoid hemorrhages with deep learning, vol. 50 (2019). https://doi.org/10.1161/str.50.suppl_1.wmp29

13. Ronneberger, O., Fischer, P., Brox, T.: U-Net: convolutional networks for biomedical image segmentation. In: Navab, N., Hornegger, J., Wells, W.M., Frangi, A.F. (eds.) MICCAI 2015. LNCS, vol. 9351, pp. 234–241. Springer, Cham (2015). https://doi.org/10.1007/978-3-319-24574-4_28

14. Funke, J., et al.: A deep structured learning approach towards automating connectome reconstruction from 3D electron micrographs (2017). arXiv preprint arXiv:170902974

15. Briggman, K., Denk, W., Seung, S., Helmstaedter, M.N., Turaga, S.C.: Maximin affinity learning of image segmentation. In: Advances in Neural Information Processing Systems, pp. 1865–1873 (2009)

16. Turaga, S.C., et al.: Convolutional networks can learn to generate affinity graphs for image segmentation. Neural Comput. **22**(2), 511–538 (2010)

17. Parag, T., et al.: Anisotropic EM segmentation by 3D affinity learning and agglomeration (2017). arXiv preprint arXiv:170708935

18. Milletari, F., Navab, N., Ahmadi, S.-A.: V-Net: fully convolutional neural networks for volumetric medical image segmentation. In: 2016 Fourth International Conference on 3D Vision (3DV), pp. 565–571. IEEE (2016)

19. Feng, X., Meyer, C.: Patch-based 3D U-Net for brain tumor segmentation. In: International Conference on Medical Image Computing and Computer-Assisted Intervention (MICCAI) (2017)

20. Lee, H., et al.: An explainable deep-learning algorithm for the detection of acute intracranial haemorrhage from small datasets. Nat. Biomed. Eng. **3**(3), 173 (2019)

21. Kim, J.W., Kim, J.H.: Review of evaluation metrics for 3D medical image segmentation. J. Korean Soc. Imaging Inf. Med. **23**, 14–20 (2017)

On the Stability of a Pass-Thought Security System in Different Brain States

Nga Tran, Dat Tran$^{(\boxtimes)}$, Shuangzhe Liu, and Tien Pham

Faculty of Science and Technology, University of Canberra,
Canberra, ACT 2601, Australia
{nga.tran,dat.tran}@canberra.edu.au

Abstract. Using electroencephalogram (EEG) signals for person authentication purpose so that people can access a security system by just thinking a pass-thought instead of typing a password is an interesting research topic. However, many factors can impact on the stability of an EEG-based person authentication system, as they may create instability in the pass-thought, yet the issue has not been comprehensively researched. In this paper, we focus on that gap by investigating the performance variations of an EEG-based person authentication system when users are in different brain states, caused by having different emotional states and users' different experiences toward stimuli while performing mental tasks for pass-thought. Also, we speculate on whether human characteristics such as gender and age have an impact on the performance of EBPA system while users are in different brain states. The experimental results revealed that user changing emotions when logging into the system differ with that when they enroll have a negative impact on the performance of a security system. Further, the young and female groups always give higher accuracy compared to older and male groups regardless of brain state. The results encourage careful consideration of different brain states in order to build a higher security and more stable person authentication system for real world applications.

Keywords: EEG · Authentication · Security · Biometrics · Pattern recognition

1 Introduction

With the increase of advanced techniques, conventional biometrics have been revealed to be vulnerable and have some limitations in preventing unauthorised people from accessing important data and resources. Leaking sensitive information to malicious people can often cause serious problems, especially in important areas such as military and intelligence. Addressing this problem requires better modalities for person authentication. Recently, the substantial research results in the brain-wave area have led electroencephalogram (EEG) signals to become a potential new type of biometric. Moreover, EEG patterns correspond to particular mental tasks, and they are considered to be individualized passwords or

T. Gedeon et al. (Eds.): ICONIP 2019, LNCS 11953, pp. 556–567, 2019.
https://doi.org/10.1007/978-3-030-36708-4_46

pass-thoughts. Having both advantages of biometric-based and password-based authentication, using EEG signals to verify if the user is who he or she claims to be, has been extensively published. A variety of EEG modalities, different features and many classifiers have been introduced to ensure the best performance of EEG-based person authentication (EBPA) systems in [1, 2] and [3].

However, unlike conventional biometrics such as fingerprint, iris, and face, EEG signals have a large variation within subjects, depending upon the subject's different brain states. This raises concerns in real-world applications where a user may have different brain states during the performance of tasks to elicit EEG credentials to login to the security system. How accurate can an EEG-based person authentication system be when users are in different brain states? Are any specific brain states the best for an EBPA system, and within brain states, how is the performance impacted by some factors such as age and gender? How can the impact of different brain states be mitigated to ensure the stability of the EBPA system?

The different brain states could be elicited in many situations such as when people are in different emotional states, when they have different experiences toward stimuli or have different human characteristics. While stability is a fundamental requirement for a person authentication system, the impact of EEG signal changes which are caused by those different brain states have not received necessary attention [4]. In [5], only 3 discrete emotions of stress, calm, and excitement have been investigated to observe the variation of the authentication system. The experiments were conducted using EEG signals from the same emotion for both training and testing phases. The results interestingly showed that stress emotions gave better accuracy compared to other emotions. In addition, the authors in [6] have speculated on the system performance with different affective states, that were presented by a 2D emotional model. The authors ran experiments on various scenarios using different EEG signals from different emotional states to find out which feature and channels have the most stability regardless of emotional states. Their findings revealed that there is a close relationship between emotional states and the performance of biometric systems. One of their striking outcomes is that regardless of emotional states, the gamma band in left-posterior quarter provides more stable features for person identification. However, this study only focused on an EEG-based person identification system, not an EEG-based person authentication system. Moreover, using the 2D emotional model seems to be not thorough compared to the 3D emotional model of valence-arousal-dominance, which is the "framework for a comprehensive description and measurement of emotional states" [7]. The accuracy and sufficiency of the 3D continuous framework to represent a large range of emotions is also proved in [8] in which the authors validated the model using an affect recognition technique that analysed spontaneous EEG signals and frontal face. The comparison and discussion with other 2D emotional models in this paper confirmed the effectiveness of the 3D emotional model in the ability of presenting more complicated emotions.

The influence of some other factors, such as age, gender and pathology, were also mentioned in literature but just in a few publications. The significant issue of ignoring stability of EEG biometric features was emphasized in [9] in which the authors indicated the heavy impact of factors including gender, pathology and age on EEG pattern. They found that there were obvious differences between pathological groups in which patients with temporal lobe epilepsy gave better accuracy than the healthy group. Substantial variety was also found between sex groups, in which the female group performed better than the male group, especially in full frequency range. The accuracies of age groups though does not appear to be significant, but the experimental results showed that the youngest group has the largest confidence interval for both the area under the curve (AUC) and Equal Error Rate (EER). Though the sample of 60 people in this study is not very small, only eight participants were categorised as 'young', which is inequitable compared with the number of 27 samples for both other two older groups. The effect of age on EEG biometric systems was also mentioned in [10], in which the authors tested the person identification accuracy on a small sample of 10 participants in different sections over a time span of just 6 months. The outcomes revealed a substantial amount of difference across sections, which meant that the state of mind was affected by temporal distance. Combined, these interesting findings encouraged the research community to investigate further the influence of not only these aforementioned factors but also other factors on the stability of EBPA system.

In this paper, we are going to speculate on the aforementioned questions by exploring the impact of different brain states caused by different emotional states, which are measured and presented using 3D emotional model, on the performance of an EBPA system. Inspired by the interesting results of the impact of users experience toward stimuli in our previous publication [11], we continue to investigate whether human characteristics such as age and gender influence the system while users are in different brain states, which are caused by both different emotional states and different experience toward stimuli.

The proposed methodology will be introduced in Sect. 2. Section 3 will then describe the experiments and the results and discussion will be presented in Sect. 4. We conclude the issue in Sect. 5 and suggest possibilities for future work.

2   The Proposed Method

2.1   EEG-Based Person Authentication System and the Stability in Different Brain States

In order to investigate the impact of aforementioned factors on the stability of EBPA systems, we propose to consecutively input EEG signals when users are in different brain states to the EBPA system as illustrated in Fig. 1.

Different from a general EBPA system, in this model, in the enrollment phase, each user's brain-wave is elicited using different stimuli in which that user has different brain states. We use EEG signals in each brain state for training and consecutively use different brain states for testing and vice versa. EEG data

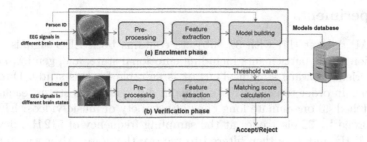

Fig. 1. EEG-based person authentication system in different brain states

corresponding to those states are pre-processed, then features are extracted and put into a classifier to train the models for that person.

In the verification phase, the person is verified using EEG signals when he/she is in each of the aforementioned brain states consecutively. These EEG signals related to each brain state of the claimed user are recorded, pre-processed and features are extracted in the same way as in the enrollment phase. The obtained features in each brain state are then provided to a classifier as different testing dataset to match with the corresponding model of that individual and the matching scores are calculated. Based on that score and a predefine threshold, the EBPA system will decide to accept or reject that person. As usual, Equal Error Rate (EER) values of the system in each scenario are calculated to measure the performance of the system in each different brain state. These values are analyzed and compared to baseline state or to each other to measure how much the system's performance changes when users are in different brain states and with different age and gender. Based on that, the impact of those factors are evaluated and the scenarios which give the most stability and highest accuracy are revealed.

2.2   Feature Extraction and Classification Algorithm

For feature extraction, the Autoregressive (AR) and Power spectral density (PSD) were applied following the recent publications with impressive results in EEG-based person authentication such as [2,3]. The AR model can be implemented for each single channel in which the value of the current sample is formulated by taking into account a number of its previous samples [12] while PSD can be calculated using the discrete time Fourier transform [13].

Regarding classification algorithms, Support Vector Machine (SVM) is deployed since it is a popular classification algorithm which often gives good results in the vast majority of cases, such as in [2,14,15]. The SVM classifier has also been proved to be superior to other well known classifier such as k-Nearest Neighbor and Random Forest [16].

3   Experiments

The DEAP dataset [17] with 32 subjects contains both EEG signals and the information of the participants including emotional state, age, gender, and how they experience toward stimuli. Thus, it is suitable for this study. During the experiment, in order to elicit EEG signals in different brain states, each participant watched 40 one-minute long clips of a variety of music videos. EEG data were recorded by 32 electrodes at the sampling frequency of 512 Hz, downsampled to 128 Hz and were then filtered to remove the noise. After watching each video, subjects self-rated it on scales of valence, arousal, dominance from 1 to 9, a scale of familiarity from 1 to 5, and a scale of liking from 1 to 9.

This study will first investigate how the performance of EBPA system changes when users are in different emotional states. Each emotional state is measured and described using 3D emotional model with 3 dimensions of valence, arousal and dominance as introduced by the authors in [7]. The 3D continuous emotional scale can represent a large range of emotional terms, but it seems impossible to investigate all of them separately. Thus, followed by study in [7], we categorize those terms into eight combinations of two levels each (high (>5) versus low (<5)) of valence, arousal and dominance and investigate these combinations. As a result, there are 8 combinations (or can be called 8 states) including State 1 (high Valence, high Arousal, high Dominance), State 2 (high Valence, high Arousal, low Dominance), State 3 (high Valence, low Arousal, high Dominance), State 4 (high Valence, low Arousal, low Dominance), State 5 (low Valence, high Arousal, high Dominance), State 6 (low Valence, high Arousal, low Dominance), State 7 (low Valence, low Arousal, high Dominance), and State 8 (low Valence, low Arousal, low Dominance). Users often register a system when they are in a comfortable, relax, and secure state, which will be used as a baseline in this study and followed by the classification in [7] listed above, it corresponds to State 3. We run experiments according to the scenarios below:

> **The first scenario: Baseline to Baseline (B2B):** A model for each person is built when he/she is in the baseline state. Then the same baseline state is selected for testing. The EER values of EBPA system in this scenario are used for comparing as a benchmark.
> **The second scenario: Emotions to Baseline (E2B):** A model for each person is built when he/she is in the baseline state. After that the other states consecutively are used for testing.
> **The third scenario: Emotion to Itself (E2I):** A model for each person is built when he/she is in a specific state and then use testing data with that very same state to verify that person in the verification phase.

In order to make a comparison in depth, for each state from 1 to 8, we run the experiment with the same group of people within each scenario by choosing only the people who have both baseline state and the states being tested.

The EEG signals from electrodes F3, F4, C3, C4, P3, P4, O1 and O2 were selected according to studies in [14,18] to obtain good results in person authentication. Aiming to reach a more comprehensive investigation, the selected data were split into epochs of length from 1 s to 5 s. The AR model parameters were estimated with the order 21st while PSD in the band 8–30 Hz was extracted. The feature vectors related to each brain state were divided into 60% for training and 40% for testing. Cross validation 5-fold was applied with the training set of each individual in different brain states, and then the best found parameters γ and ν were used to train models for that user using RBF kernel function. The search ranges were $\{2^k : k = 2l + 1, l = -8, -7, ..., 2\}$ and $\{0.001, 0.01, 0.1\}$ for γ and ν respectively.

4   Results and Discussion

The performance of an EEG-based person authentication system can be evaluated by Detection Error Trade-off (DET) curve, which is presented by False Acceptance Rate (FAR) on y-axis and False Rejection Rate (FRR) on x-axis [19]. FAR occurs when the system accepts an impostor whereas FRR occurs when the system rejects a true client. When the system has multiple DET curves corresponding with different brain states, the value of Equal Error Rate (EER), that is the point on a DET curve where FAR and FRR are equal, is utilized to decide whether the smaller EER value or the lower DET curve both means the better system.

Figure 2 illustrate the EERs of the EBPA system using EEG signals when users are in different emotional states. Some states in 4 or 5 s segments have N/A value in the table because they have too few subjects or have sufficient subjects but the number of features of which are too small. The EER values on three columns at state 3 are the same because this state is chosen to be the baseline state. Overall, there are two striking trends revealed from the experimental results. First, there is a trend that using baseline state for training and other states for testing (E2B) has higher EER values for most states, regardless of data length, compared to other scenarios which use the same state for both training and testing (B2B and E2I). It means that if users' emotional states when logging into the system differ with that when they enroll, this gives a negative impact on the performance of the system. Second, EER values of the EBPA system significantly decrease with data length in most states, with one exception at State 1. It is consistent with the findings from other studies in [20] and [5] in which the accuracy of an authentication system positively correlates with the length of the data segment.

The results also show that the performances of EBPA system differ between different emotional states and data length. Further, the EER values in baseline state does not always give the best performance, for example State 1 when using for both training and testing gives better accuracy. However, State 5 performs worse compared to the baseline state. Data length is also a factor causing the variation in the performance of EBPA systems. Some states or scenarios give good accuracy at long data length but have poorer performance at short ones, and vice versa. For example, at data length of 5 s, when training and testing by the same state (E2I), State 5, 6, and 7 give better performance compared

	State 1			State 2			State 3			State 4		
	B2B	E2B	E2I	B2B	E2B	E2I	B2B	E2B	E2I	B2B	E2B	E2I
1s	0.15383	0.15571	0.1221	0.16064	0.16674	0.14793	0.14991	0.14991	0.14991	0.07191	0.11028	0.09916
2s	0.1478	0.13989	0.11311	0.13698	0.1392	0.11586	0.15334	0.15334	0.15334	0.09944	0.16847	0.13216
3s	0.15933	0.09478	0.11903	0.09831	0.12734	0.08398	0.14573	0.14573	0.14573	0.03669	0.0139	0.00791
4s	0.11693	0.18026	0.1664	N/A	N/A	N/A	0.11665	0.11665	0.11665	0.02371	0.01003	0.00517
5s	0.11058	0.2042	0.13279	N/A	N/A	N/A	0.10734	0.10734	0.10734	N/A	N/A	N/A

	State 5			State 6			State 7			State 8		
	B2B	E2B	E2I	B2B	E2B	E2I	B2B	E2B	E2I	B2B	E2B	E2I
1s	0.1555	0.20386	0.19668	0.16734	0.17876	0.18221	0.14827	0.17011	0.18585	0.14463	0.17585	0.13418
2s	0.12837	0.18178	0.19792	0.1538	0.12069	0.12986	0.1918	0.15875	0.14758	0.17357	0.22407	0.18335
3s	0.06898	0.08745	0.08739	0.15261	0.11855	0.12144	0.16366	0.18805	0.18819	0.1528	0.16977	0.11474
4s	0.0857	0.07975	0.12174	0.08713	0.13932	0.09702	0.09836	0.12663	0.09316	0.08887	0.1511	0.14102
5s	0.0276	0.0649	0.00962	0.0431	0.07003	0.015	0.05536	0.09961	0.04667	0.11641	0.0585	0.03916

Fig. 2. EER values of the EBPA system with different emotional states of three scenarios in the segment data from 1 s to 5 s

to when using baseline state (B2B). However, at 1 s data length, the results are opposite. In addition, the accuracy of EBPA system seems to depend also on the number of population. The result revealed that the states with less samples (State 2 and 4) have lower EER values. It could be explained by the increased population may cause a biometric system more easily to mismatch, which was mentioned in previous study that the accuracy of biometric system based on EEG went down when more subjects were added [21]. This may also be used to support the finding of increasing accuracy with longer data length in this study; although it can not be denied that there may be other factors causing that, such as feature vectors containing more useful information or being more stationary. Thus, in order to make the evaluation more reliable and precise, we only perform the comparison between one certain brain state with baseline state where the same group of people participated.

Regarding the impact of two typical instances of human characteristics namely gender and age when users have different brain states caused by both emotional states and different experience of users toward stimuli. First of all, as can be seen on Fig. 4(a) and (b), which illustrate the EERs of the EBPA system when users were in like and dislike, familiar and unfamiliar brain states, the results is consistent with the previous publication [11]. There is a substantial variation of the performance of the system when user have different experience toward stimuli, in which like and unfamiliar states always give better performance regardless of data segments.

The results in Figs. 3, 5 and 6 all reveal that human characteristics do have an impact on the performance of the EBPA system. The experimental results

	State 1				State 2				State 3				State 4			
	Female	Male	Age>=30	Age<=29	Female	Male	Age>=30	Age<=29	Female	Male	Age>=30	Age<=29	Female	Male	Age>=30	Age<=29
1s	0.1273	0.1819	0.2304	0.1205	0.1318	0.2017	0.1763	0.1615	0.1248	0.175	0.204	0.1259	0.1124	0.1087	0.117	0.1084
2s	0.1255	0.1543	0.2095	0.1138	0.1012	0.162	0.1475	0.1364	0.1449	0.1626	0.1949	0.1387	0.1466	0.1948	0.2255	0.1628
3s	0.0867	0.1037	0.1536	0.0712	0.1616	0.076	0.1377	0.1229	0.1215	0.1748	0.1635	0.1391	0.0038	0.029	0.0026	0.0167
4s	0.1698	0.1919	0.2685	0.1396	N/A	N/A	N/A	N/A	0.1204	0.1121	0.1724	0.0927	0.0026	0.0322	0.0079	0.0107
5s	0.1995	0.2073	0.2307	0.1909	N/A	N/A	N/A	N/A	0.0844	0.1252	0.1118	0.1053	N/A	N/A	N/A	N/A

	State 5				State 6				State 7				State 8			
	Female	Male	Age>=30	Age<=29	Female	Male	Age>=30	Age<=29	Female	Male	Age>=30	Age<=29	Female	Male	Age>=30	Age<=29
1s	0.1946	0.2173	0.2548	0.1848	0.1465	0.2207	0.2441	0.1502	0.1473	0.191	0.2393	0.1398	0.1798	0.1726	0.2104	0.1629
2s	0.1557	0.2153	0.2373	0.1633	0.111	0.136	0.1639	0.1083	0.1158	0.2078	0.1862	0.1488	0.2113	0.2354	0.1999	0.2315
3s	0.1083	0.0632	0.111	0.077	0.1134	0.1326	0.1856	0.1018	0.1423	0.2273	0.1807	0.1913	0.1339	0.2056	0.2225	0.1522
4s	0.087	0.0652	0.0978	0.0707	0.1234	0.2028	0.2783	0.1046	0.0948	0.1585	0.3437	0.0956	0.149	0.1545	0.1889	0.1343
5s	0.0551	0.0796	0.0677	0.063	0.07	N/A	N/A	N/A	0	0.1245	0.1165	0.0954	0.0501	0.0652	0.0852	0.0452

Fig. 3. EERs of the EBPA system using baseline state for training and each emotional state for testing by group of age and gender.

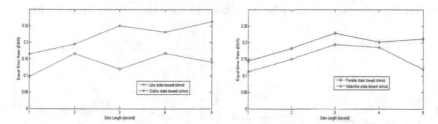

Fig. 4. Equal Error Rates of EBPA system when users have different experiences toward stimuli.

show that regardless of different brain states caused by different emotional states or different experience toward stimuli, the female group and the younger group (age $\leq$ 29) gave a substantially better performance compared to the male and the older group (age $\geq$ 30), respectively. These results are supported by the outcomes from [9] and [10] that indicated the significant impact of gender and age on the performance of EEG based biometric systems. Further, the results regarding sex group are consistent with the findings in [9], in which the authors also found that females gave higher accuracy than males. These findings could be explained by the outcomes from psychological studies where the authors confirm that women have significantly larger occipital beta responses than men [22], and females recognize emotions quicker and more accurately than males [23].

Regarding the lower EER values in younger people compared to the older group, evidence from psychological and neuroscience studies about age-related changes in brain activity can help to clarify. The research in [24] shows a considerable age-related trend for frequency, position, and amplitude of alpha band in which alpha frequency increases in younger people and decreases in the older

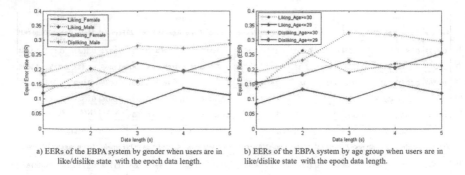

a) EERs of the EBPA system by gender when users are in
like/dislike state with the epoch data length.

b) EERs of the EBPA system by age group when users are in
like/dislike state with the epoch data length.

Fig. 5. EERs of the EBPA system by age and gender when users are in like/dislike
state with the epoch data length.

group. Also, in [25] the authors observed a gradual age-related reduction of
activity in regions with task-related activation. Because alpha band is one of the
primary frequency in our experiments, it could be one of the reasons why the
classification accuracy of the EBPA system in the younger group is higher.

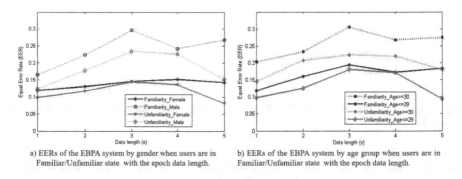

a) EERs of the EBPA system by gender when users are in
Familiar/Unfamiliar state with the epoch data length.

b) EERs of the EBPA system by age group when users are in
Familiar/Unfamiliar state with the epoch data length.

Fig. 6. EERs of the EBPA system by gender and age when users are in Famil-
iar/Unfamiliar state with the epoch data length.

The obtained results suggests some ideas for designing EEG-based person
authentication applications in practice. Firstly, the ideal scenario for the best
accuracy is that users should be trained and tested using the same emotional
state. Thus, in order to enhance the performance as well as the usability of EBPA
systems, users can comfortably choose their preferred emotional state to register
and then try to use that same emotional state to log in. Secondly, choosing a
user-enrolling task should be carefully considered, particularly to older users, to
target both the performance and usability of a person authentication system.
The mental tasks that users like to perform but not too easily to get bored
or too quickly to be familiar with, are encouraged. Thirdly, the older group

and the male group have higher EERs than the younger and the female group respectively, so more training for these users should be considered.

Some other ideas regarding data length are also introduced. The performance of EBPA systems decreases with short data segment regardless of both emotions and other factors, thus in order to have good performance, epoch data length should be long enough. However, long time-consuming for authenticating procedure can be uncomfortable for users who play an important role in the success of the system. Thus, in order to enhance usability of an EBPA system, the accuracy and the duration of producing pass-thoughts should be balanced.

The research obtained interesting results; however, some open questions could be seen. Only data segments from 1 s to 5 s were investigated thoroughly, so would data segments with the length of more than 5 s give the similar results? Are PSD and AR are the best features for investigating the stability of an EBPA system? Similarly, could selected electrodes including F3, F4, C3, C4, P3, P4, O1 and O2 are enough for comprehensive investigation? Which factors else such as alcohol and coffee could impact on user brain states during eliciting EEG signals so that suffering to the stability of the EBPA system? Some factors investigated in this study show a potential influence to the stability of the EBPA system, should the initial results be consistent on other datasets or with longer data segment lengths? Answering these questions requires additional experimentation on more datasets.

5   Conclusion and Future Work

In this study, the effect of users' different brain states, which are caused by different emotional states, and different experience toward stimuli on the stability of EEG-based person authentication system have been speculated. The system's performance variation in the groups of age and gender is also investigated to see whether these human characteristics have an impact on the pattern of EEG signals when people are in different brain states and therefore impact indirectly on the stability of the EBPA system. The experimental results revealed some striking findings involving the variation of the system performance. The results revealed that user changing emotions when logging into the system differ with that when they enroll have a negative impact on the performance of a security system. Further, the young and female groups always give higher accuracy compared to older and male groups regardless of brain state. Based on the outcomes, some ideas to design a real world EBPA system that has a high and stable accuracy are suggested. Our priority in the near future is to carry out more experiments to investigate other factors such as users' health conditions and different stimulant consumption, which may also have an impact on the stability of EBPA systems.

References

1. Piciucco, E., Maiorana, E., Falzon, O., Camilleri, K.P., Campisi, P.: Steady-state visual evoked potentials for EEG-based biometric identification. In: 2017 International Conference of the Biometrics Special Interest Group (BIOSIG), pp. 1–5 (2017)
2. Nakamura, T., Goverdovsky, V., Mandic, D.P.: In-ear EEG biometrics for feasible and readily collectable real-world person authentication. IEEE Trans. Inf. Forensics Secur. **13**(3), 648–661 (2018)
3. Thomas, K.P., Vinod, A.P.: EEG-based biometric authentication using gamma band power during rest state. Circuits Syst. Sig. Process. **37**(1), 277–289 (2018)
4. Campisi, P., La Rocca, D.: Brain waves for automatic biometric-based user recognition. IEEE Trans. Inf. Forensics Secur. **9**(5), 782–800 (2014)
5. Pham, T., Ma, W., Tran, D., Tran, D.S., Phung, D.: A study on the stability of EEG signals for user authentication. In: 2015 7th International IEEE/EMBS Conference on Neural Engineering (NER), pp. 122–125, April 2015
6. Vahid, A., Arbabi, E.: Human identification with EEG signals in different emotional states. In: 2016 23rd Iranian Conference on Biomedical Engineering and 2016 1st International Iranian Conference on Biomedical Engineering (ICBME), pp. 242–246. IEEE (2016)
7. Mehrabian, A.: Framework for a comprehensive description and measurement of emotional states. Genet. Soc. Gen. Psychol. Monogr. **121**, 339–361 (1995)
8. Verma, G., Tiwary, U.S.: Affect representation and recognition in 3D continuous valence-arousal-dominance space. Multimed. Tools Appl. **76**, 11 (2015)
9. Höller, Y., Bathke, A.C., Uhl, A.: Age, sex, and pathology effects on stability of electroencephalographic biometric features based on measures of interaction. IEEE Trans. Inf. Forensics Secur. **14**(2), 459–471 (2018)
10. Kaur, B., Kumar, P., Roy, P.P., Singh, D.: Impact of ageing on EEG based biometric systems. In: 2017 4th IAPR Asian Conference on Pattern Recognition (ACPR), pp. 459–464 (2017)
11. Tran, N., Tran, D., Liu, S., Ma, W., Pham, T.: EEG-based person authentication system in different brain states. In: 2019 9th International IEEE/EMBS Conference on Neural Engineering (NER), pp. 1050–1053. IEEE (2019)
12. Sanei, S., Chambers, J.A.: EEG Signal Processing. Wiley, Hoboken (2008)
13. Stoica, P., Moses, R.L.: Spectral Analysis of Signals. Pearson/Prentice Hall, Upper Saddle River (2005)
14. Nguyen, P., Tran, D., Le, T., Huang, X., Ma, W.: EEG-based person verification using multi-sphere SVDD and UBM. In: Pei, J., Tseng, V.S., Cao, L., Motoda, H., Xu, G. (eds.) PAKDD 2013. LNCS (LNAI), vol. 7818, pp. 289–300. Springer, Heidelberg (2013). https://doi.org/10.1007/978-3-642-37453-1_24
15. Armstrong, B.C., Ruiz-Blondet, M.V., Khalifian, N., Kurtz, K.J., Jin, Z., Laszlo, S.: Brainprint: assessing the uniqueness, collectability, and permanence of a novel method for ERP biometrics. Neurocomputing **166**, 59–67 (2015)
16. Thanh Noi, P., Kappas, M.: Comparison of random forest, k-nearest neighbor, and support vector machine classifiers for land cover classification using sentinel-2 imagery. Sensors **18**(1), 18 (2018)
17. Koelstra, S., et al.: Deap: a database for emotion analysis, using physiological signals. IEEE Trans. Affect. Comput. **3**(1), 18–31 (2012)
18. Nguyen, P., Tran, D., Huang, X., Ma, W.: Age and gender classification using EEG paralinguistic features. In: 2013 6th International IEEE/EMBS Conference on Neural Engineering (NER), pp. 1295–1298. IEEE (2013)

19. Martin, A., Doddington, G., Kamm, T., Ordowski, M., Przybocki, M.: The DET curve in assessment of detection task performance. Technical report, DTIC Document (1997)
20. Lee, H.J., Kim, H.S., Park, K.S.: A study on the reproducibility of biometric authentication based on electroencephalogram (EEG). In: 2013 6th International IEEE/EMBS Conference on Neural Engineering (NER), pp. 13–16. IEEE (2013)
21. Wang, P., Hu, J.: A hybrid model for EEG-based gender recognition. Cogn. Neurodyn. 13, 1–14 (2019)
22. Guntekin, B., Basar, E.: Gender differences influence brain's beta oscillatory responses in recognition of facial expressions. Neurosci. Lett. 424(2), 94–99 (2007)
23. Bilalpur, M., Kia, S.M., Chawla, M., Chua, T.-S., Subramanian, R.: Gender and emotion recognition with implicit user signals. In: Proceedings of the 19th ACM International Conference on Multimodal Interaction, ICMI 2017, pp. 379–387. ACM, New York (2017)
24. Chiang, A.K.I., Rennie, C.J., Robinson, P.A., van Albada, S.J., Kerr, C.C.: Age trends and sex differences of alpha rhythms including split alpha peaks. Clin. Neurophysiol. 122(8), 1505–1517 (2011)
25. Grady, C.L., Springer, M.V., Hongwanishkul, D., McIntosh, A.R., Winocur, G.: Age-related changes in brain activity across the adult lifespan. J. Cogn. Neurosci. 18(2), 227–241 (2006)

Brain Network Decomposition by Auto Encoder (AE) and Graph Auto Encoder (GAE)

Myungwon Choi[1], Pilsub Lee[1], Daegyeom Kim[1], Suji Lee[2], HyunChul Youn[2], Hyun-Ghang Jeong[2], and Cheol E. Han[1(✉)]

[1] Department of Electronics and Information Engineering, Korea University, Sejong, Republic of Korea
{jjchoi0204,teardrizzle,gyeom_91,cheolhan}@korea.ac.kr
[2] Department of Psychiatry, Korea University College of Medicine, Seoul, Republic of Korea
{sujitmp2010,dryounh}@naver.com, jeonghg@korea.ac.kr

Abstract. Brain networks consist of nodes that are anatomically defined brain regions, and edges that connect a pair of brain regions. The diffusion-weighted magnetic resonance images and the advances in computer-aided tractography algorithms showed that human brain networks are strongly associated with cognitive functions. Brain regions dedicated to a specific cognitive function are spatially clustered and efficiently connected each other; this is called local functional segregation. However, it is not well known that such a local segregation is associated with sub-networks which may act as building blocks of brain networks. In this work, we used machine learning techniques to analyze brain networks. Specifically, using an auto-encoder and a graph auto-encoder, we decomposed brain networks into several essential building blocks, and compared their results through various measures of decomposition quality. We observed that the graph auto-encoder out-performed the auto-encoder, and that its results showed significant correlation with cognitive deterioration in Alzheimer's disease.

Keywords: Brain networks · Graph auto-encoder · Graph convolutional neural network · Alzheimer's disease

1 Introduction

Our brain consists of not only neurons but also synapses connecting them. The brain networks consist of nodes, distinct neuronal elements such as a neuron, and edges which connect a pair of them. They can be in a different spatial resolution. In a micro level, the nodes are neurons and the edges are synapses between them. On the contrary, at the macro level, the nodes are anatomically defined brain regions, and the edges are neuronal fiber tracts between them. Advances in neuroimaging techniques enable us to obtain such macro-level brain networks, including diffusion weighted MR imaging, and whole-brain tractography [1]. It has been revealed that the efficient information exchange through the brain network has a strong association with human's cognitive function [2]. For systemic

---

M. Choi and P. Lee—Both authors contribute equally.

© Springer Nature Switzerland AG 2019
T. Gedeon et al. (Eds.): ICONIP 2019, LNCS 11953, pp. 568–579, 2019.
https://doi.org/10.1007/978-3-030-36708-4_47

analysis of such information exchange in the brain network, the graph theory has been massively used in the last two decades.

Recently, deep learning techniques for such a network have been developed [3, 4]. Though the success of the deep learning in the last decade is mostly relied on the convolutional neural network (CNN), since the nature of the network (i.e. graph) is different from images which are best applicable to CNN, it is not appropriate to the brain network. The graph convolutional neural network (GCN) provides a unique framework for extracting sub-graphs of graphs [4]. Extending GCN, the graph auto-encoder (GAE) is also suggested [3], which encodes the in-nature compressed representation from a graph, and reconstructs the original graph. The compressed representation may contain the essential components of the inputs.

Such essential components can be considered as a building block of the brain networks. The building blocks of such graphs can be used to re-construct each person's brain network. Previously, we proposed the method to decompose the brain networks into sub-networks using GAE [5]. In the study, we showed that brain networks can be decomposed into several sub-networks, and their activation levels vary over subjects and over groups.

In this study, extending our previous study, we analyzed the characteristics of such building blocks with respect to the various measures of decomposition quality. To contrast with the traditional machine learning technique, we compared the results of GAE with those of the traditional auto-encoder. One of our main contributions is proposing novel measures of decomposition quality: spatial locality, and sub-network density. We also proposed a novel method for correlation between sub-networks and cognitive measures, showing that distinct sub-networks decomposed by GAE are associated with specific cognitive functions.

2   Method

2.1   Neural Network Models for Subnetwork Extraction

Auto Encoder (AE). The auto-encoder is a simple neural network whose input data and output are identical, and thus can encode the input data as compressed codes and reconstruct the input data by decoding the codes [6].

The network consists of two parts: encoding and decoding. In the encoding part, a hidden layer of AE receives the input data, and converted into compressed expressions. The compressed expressions, codes, are frequently occurred common features that best represent the inputs. This step can be written as the Eq. (1), where X is the input vector, Y is the code, and W and b are learnable weights and bias. We used a rectified linear unit (Relu) as an activation function.

$$Y = Relu(WX + b) \tag{1}$$

In the decoding step, on the other hand, the codes are uncompressed and reconstructed into the input data. Theoretically, the decoding process is the reverse of the encoding process, and the learned weights and bias can be reused as the Eq. (2), that is called as shared weights.

$$Z = Relu\left(W^T(Y - b)\right) \qquad (2)$$

Using the error back-propagation algorithm, we minimize errors between the input data, X and the reconstructed data, Z. In this way, the AE's encoding hidden nodes can have compressed and well-expressed input features. We also imposed the non-negative weight constraints for intuitive and fair comparison with NMF. This constraint also increased interpretability of AE's codes (NCAE) [7].

Graph Auto Encoder (GAE). GAE is recently suggested for a graph structure [3]. Like an auto-encoder, GAE is composed of an encoding layer and a decoding layer. The overall procedure is illustrated in Fig. 1.

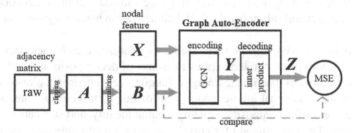

Fig. 1. Overall procedure of a graph auto encoder

The encoding is a process to extract a compressed representation from an input data; GAE used a graph convolutional layer (GCN) [4] as an encoding layer. GCN receives both the nodal feature and an adjacency matrix as its inputs. Though the convolutional operation for graphs is originally based on the spectral graph convolutions, [4] suggested its faster approximation called a layer-wise linear model:

$$Y = Relu(BXW + b) \qquad (3)$$

X is a matrix of nodal features whose size if $N \times D$, where N is the number of nodes, and D is the number of nodal features. When there is no feature for nodes (i.e. featureless), X is the identity matrix [3]. W is a learnable weight vector whose size is $D \times F$, where F is the number of filters. In our case, since X is featureless, D equals to N. b is a bias whose size is $N \times F$. Here, the B is a Laplacian normalized adjacency matrix by (4) where D is a degree matrix whose diagonal elements are the degree of $(I + A)$.

$$B = D^{-1/2}(I + A)D^{-1/2} \qquad (4)$$

On the other hand, the decoding reconstructs the input data, the Laplacian normalized adjacency matrix B, from the results of the encoding layer, Y. Following [3], we used a simple inner product to obtain the output of GAE, Z.

$$Z = YY^T \qquad (5)$$

The major difference of our model compared to the original GAE is the non-negative weight constraints: all weights should not be negative. The previous study showed that the non-negative weight constraints help to extract interpretable representation of the input data [7]. Also, we do not use a sigmoid activation function to the decoder.

We used Keras (v2.2.4) with tensorflow backend for both models. We used an open-source implementation of AE with shared weights (https://gist.github.com/njellinas/ 5f4979a8ff4b231961d8d680d71de427); we additionally imposed non-negative weight constraints on it. We used a GCN implemented by the authors of the original paper (kegra, https://github.com/tkipf/keras-gcn). However, since the implementation does not support the graph auto-encoder, we implemented a decoding layer. The weights and bias of the model were initialized as described in [8]. As the model receives the Laplacian normalized adjacency matrix B, we set B as the target (i.e. output) of the model (See (3) and (4)).

We note that there are neither a test set nor a validation set, since we used deep learning as a tool of analyses, extracting building blocks of given brain networks. The general machine learning model aims to achieve good generalization performance, i.e. the ability to accurately predict on new data samples. The test and validation sets provide data which was not used during training to evaluate generalization performance. The generalization power is not the goal of our model, and thus, we do not require them.

2.2 Sub-network Decomposition

Auto Encoder (AE). The hidden neurons learn the frequently occurred sub-networks, and their activation level capture how strongly (or clearly) the pattern exists in the input. Thus, we reconstruct the output using the activation level of each hidden neurons while all the other hidden neurons are turned off.

Graph Auto Encoder (GAE). To decompose the building blocks from the learned GAE, we used the following procedure [5]. We first define $I(i)$ whose (i, i) element is one otherwise zero. Then, the identity matrix of the size F is:

$$I = \sum_{i=1}^{F} I(i) \tag{6}$$

Inserting the identity matrix between Y and Y^T of (5) would not change Z at all, we can re-write (5) as:

$$Z = \sum_{i=1}^{F} Y I(i) Y^T = \sum_{i=1}^{F} Z(i) \tag{7}$$

where $Z(i) = YI(i)Y^T$. Consequently, $Z(i)$ is the decomposed building blocks in the reconstructed adjacency matrix.

2.3 Quality of Decomposition

Sparsity. Sparsity measures how sparse the extracted pattern is; it considers both the number of non-zero elements in the patterns and their activation levels. We used the formula defined in [9]:

$$sparsity(\mathbf{x}) = \frac{\sqrt{n} - \left(\sum |\mathbf{x}|\right)/\sqrt{\sum \mathbf{x}^2}}{\sqrt{n} - 1} \tag{8}$$

where $\mathbf{x}$ is an adjacency matrix, and n is the number of elements in $\mathbf{x}$ (i.e. the number of elements in the adjacency matrix, 8100). A pattern with high sparsity captures the data using very few non-zero elements, and it can improve the reconstruction performance [7].

Spatial Locality. We suggested a new measure of spatial locality, which measures how much the regional pattern spreads spatially.

$$locality(\mathbf{x}) = \sqrt[3]{\det\left(\mathbf{cov}(coordinates(\mathbf{x}))\right)} \tag{9}$$

where $\mathbf{x}$ represents a sub-network, $\mathbf{cov}$ is the operator for its covariance matrix, $\mathbf{det}$ is the determinant. *coordinates* is the mean coordinates of each brain region in the Euclidean space, which exists in the sub-network, $\mathbf{x}$. Thus, this equation computes the spatial spread of the sub-networks in terms of the covariance matrix of their spatial coordinates in the standard space.

Largest Component (%). Each hidden neuron in AE and each filter in GAE may consist of multiple sub-networks; in this case, the extracted sub-networks is called 'fragmented'. To measure the fragmentness of representation in each hidden neuron or each filter, we measured the portion of the largest component over all non-zero elements. 100% means that there is only one sub-network.

Density. We computed the edge density of the sub-networks. We first collect the number of brain regions connected with the sub-networks, and the number of non-zeros edges for each hidden neuron or each filter. If the value is low, the edges of the sub-networks are rather sporadically located over the brain; if the value is high, the nodes in the extracted sub-network are densely connected. This measure complements the spatial locality; the higher density may be conceptually connected with the low spatial locality.

2.4 Statistical Analysis

The decomposed sub-networks for each subject extracted by AE have the same shape but different overall strength (See the Eq. (2)). Thus, all the statistical analysis can be done over the activation level of the hidden neurons. However, the decomposed sub-networks by GAE does not have the same shape. Thus, traditional statistics cannot be applied. Thus, we employed the similarity-based statistics.

For the group comparison, we first computed the pairwise similarity between all subjects for each decomposed sub-network. Then, following [10], we computed representative statistics for each sub-network, that is, the average intra-group similarity subtracted by the average inter-group similarity. If this value is significantly larger than 0, there exists significant group difference. To estimate its significance level, we used the permutation testing with 5000 permutations. Since we compared multiple times as many as the number of hidden neurons in AE, of filters in GAE, we employed the false discovery rate (FDR) procedure [11].

We performed correlation analysis between behavioral scores with controlling for the effects of gender, age, and the duration of education using the average similarity of the disease group to the normal group. Since the pairwise similarity is based on the relative distance between subjects, the correlation study is not possible. Thus, we suggested a novel approach for correlation analysis using a pairwise similarity matrix [12]. It is based on a simple hypothesis: the symptom of a subject is more severe when her/his decomposed sub-network is farther from that of subjects without the disease. We first computed the average similarity of a subject of the disease group over all of the normal subjects for each extracted sub-network. We called this procedure "anchoring"; the subject with a disease is now anchored to the (standard) normal group, and her/his average similarity captures average distance from the control group. We repeated this for each node ($n \times m$ average similarity, where n is the total number of subjects in the disease group and m is the number of nodes). Similarly, the behavioral scores should be anchored; we computed the average difference of a subject of the disease group over all of the NC subjects' scores. This also generates $n \times m$ average difference matrix. We can now performed the correlation study.

3 Experiments and Results

3.1 Experimental Setup

A total of 54 subjects were recruited from Korea University Guro Hospital. The subjects included 21 normal controls (NC) and 33 subjects with Alzheimer's disease (AD). MRI data of all 54 subjects were acquired on a 3.0-T Siemens Trio Trim scanner and pre-processed to extract the brain networks (See [5] for details). Our brain networks consist of 90 brain regions defined in the automated anatomical labeling [13], and symmetric undirected edges between them. The edge weight represents the number of streamlines quantified by the whole-brain tractography algorithm, as a surrogate of the number of neural fibers connecting them. As a result, we obtained a 90-by-90 connectivity matrix since we used 90 brain regions as nodes (78 cortical and 12 subcortical brain regions). Since the matrix has high peaks in certain edges, we clipped the connectivity that exceeds two standard deviations away from its mean.

We used a single layer AE with 50 hidden neurons and a single layer GAE with 150 filters to match the similar level of sparsity. We vectorized the adjacency matrix for the input of AE; since the adjacency matrix is symmetric, we only used the upper triangle which has 4005 elements. On the contrary, as shown in the Eqs. (3) and (4), we directly fed the adjacency matrix into GAE. We trained the models with all 54 subjects of the data set with the mean square error (MSE) loss function and the Adam optimizer with a learning rate of 0.01 until the learning curve is sufficiently settled.

3.2 Model Performance

Keeping the similar level of sparsity, we decided the number of hidden neurons (in AE) and filters (in GAE). Both models MSE is quite small and good reconstruction performance (Fig. 2). However, the extracted sub-networks looked quite different. We observed that the sub-networks extracted by AE spread over the whole brain, and had disconnected edges. On the contrary, the results of GAE showed connected and spatially clustered which we preferred (see discussion for more details). This non-local and fragmented sub-networks in AE can be the issue of the visualization, since we thresholded in Fig. 3. So, in the next section, we quantified the quality of decomposition in various measures.

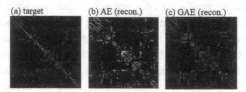

Fig. 2. An example of reconstruction: (a) target adjancency matrix, (b) reconstructed matrix by AE, and (c) by GAE.

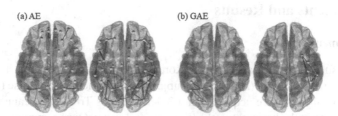

Fig. 3. Example of decomposed sub-networks (a) AE and (b) GAE. The yellow circles represent the connected nodes, and the orange solid lines represent the edges where their strengths are depicted as their thickness. For better visualization, we did not draw the weak connections (weights < 0.01). (Color figure online)

3.3 Quality of Decomposition

GAE out-performed AE in various evaluating measures. Table 1 summarizes the quantitative analyses. With the similar level of sparsity, GAE has lower error (MSE) than AE did. This can be suspected simply because the number of parameters in GAE is larger than AE's, since the number of filters in GAE is larger than the number of hidden neurons in AE. However, it is not the case. The number of weights in GAE is smaller than the one in AE; AE's weight matrix is 4005-by-50 (~200,000) while GAE's weight matrix is 90-by-150 (~13,000).

Table 1. Comparison of decomposition quality between AE and GAE

Measures	AE	GAE
Sparsity[a]	0.935 ± 0.031	0.926 ± 0.032
# of filters	50	150
MSE (loss)	0.0059	0.00023
Spatial Locality[a]	995.005 ± 36.248[b]	549.122 ± 210.577
Largest Component[a]	81.648% ± 28.576	100.000% ± 0.0
# of nodes[a]	70.620 ± 16.481	22.951 ± 10.837
# of edges[a]	130.640 ± 87.733	302.596 ± 270.224
density[a]	0.023 ± 0.008	0.472 ± 0.018

[a]value per filter. [b]mean ± standard deviation

GAE showed smaller spatial locality than AE did. The smaller spatial locality captures that the sub-network is locally clustered, which is preferred (see discussion for more details). It is tightly connected with the sub-network density measure, which is also higher in GAE than in AE. The subnetworks of GAE involves less number of brain regions (more focal) but connected with more edges, leading higher edge density. This means that GAE's sub-networks have more densely connected with focal brain regions. The largest component (%) showed 100% in GAE, that is, each filter of GAE contains a non-fragmented single sub-networks while the hidden neurons of AE captured fragmented sub-networks.

In summary, the sub-networks extracted by GAE are connected (non-fragmented), focal, spatially local, and densely connected within the clustered brain regions.

3.4   Correlation of Sub-networks with Cognitive Scores

The decomposed sub-networks for each subject extracted by AE had the same shape but different overall strength. However, the decomposed sub-networks by GAE did not have the same shape; as average similarity decreases, the shape is farther from the average of the NC group with additional or missing edges.

Figure 4 summarizes correlation results with a few neuropsychological tests. Both models showed significant correlation results. However, GAE showed clear and intuitive association while AE showed mixed results with positive and negative correlation. The spatial locality of each decomposed sub-network has an important role here; since the decomposed sub-networks is less focal in AE, the sub-networks associated with the scores is less specific, too (Fig. 5).

The sub-networks extracted by GAE were generally exclusively associated with the scores, while AE's did not. As an example, the sub-networks extracted by GAE correlated

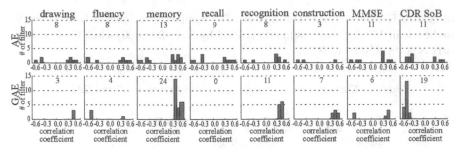

Fig. 4. Correlation with cognitive scores in (upper row) AE and (lower row) GAE sub-networks. The number of each subplot shows the number of filters which have significant correlation with the cognitive score.

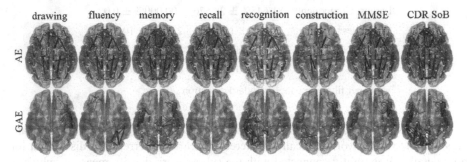

Fig. 5. Sub-networks associated with the cognitive scores in (upper row) AE and (lower row) GAE, where the red solid lines represent positive correlations, and the blue do negative correlations. For better visualization, we did not draw the weak connections. (Color figure online)

with 'drawing' are not associated with any other scores (Table 2 first column, shaded cells); however, the sub-networks extracted by AE correlated with 'drawing' showed significant correlation with other scores too (Table 2, first row, non-shaded cells). This trend can also be found in Fig. 5. The sub-networks with positive correlation with 'drawing' in AE (Fig. 5. left-upper-most, blue lines) are found in 'fluency', 'memory', 'recall', and 'recognition'.

Table 2. Overlap of significantly correlated hidden neurons (AE) and filters (GAE)

Measures	drawing	fluency	memory	recall	recognition	construction	MMSE	CDR SoB
Drawing		5	6	6	4	2	6	5
Fluency	0		6	5	4	3	6	6
Memory	0	0		8	5	3	13	6
Recall	0	0	0		5	2	8	6
Recognition	0	0	2	0		2	5	6
Construction	0	0	6	0	1		3	3
MMSE	0	0	0	0	0	3		8
CDR SoB	0	0	4	0	2	5	4	

The non-shaded cells are the overlaps in AE and the shaded cells are the overlaps in GAE.

Even the sub-networks in GAE correlated with 'Clinical Disease Rating, Sum-of-boxes' (CDR-SoB) and 'memory' showed correlation with multiple scores; it is because CDR-SoB is a collective score to evaluate the overall level of cognitive deterioration, and because the memory function is used in various cognitive task. This implies that sub-network of GAE captures local functional segregation better than those of AE.

4 Discussion

The analysis of whole-brain networks reveals the organization, and information processing of the brain. This has been quantified through the graph theoretical measures of the brain networks including the local efficiency and global efficiency [14]. While the latter represents the information integration over the whole brain, the former captures the information exchange in a relatively shorter range. The brain regions with similar or inter-related functions spatially lay nearby to reduce the connection length and temporal delays of the information. Thus, the higher local efficiency may represent the higher level of local functional segregation.

Both AE and GAE learn the frequently occurred patterns in the input data, and distributed into multiple neurons or filters through unsupervised learning. Each filter represents almost exclusive sub-networks (i.e. building blocks), and thus brain network of each person is linear summation of the learned building blocks owing to non-negative weight constraints.

However, their decomposition quality is quite different. While the subnetworks by AE are fragmented and non-local, those by GAE are spatially and topologically local (Table 1). It is because the graph convolution captures not only frequently occurred patterns but also connected components. This locality has an important role in capturing not only the local segregation of the brain networks, but also the functional segregation which is further investigated by the correlation study. If a certain sub-network includes all edges associated with various cognitive functions, it will be correlated with multiple cognitive scores. However, the sub-networks of GAE are rather exclusive to a specific cognitive score, implying that they capture the functional segregation of brain networks. Though the further in-depth correlation analysis is needed, the analysis at least reveals that the better spatial locality of sub-networks in GAE helps clearer specific association.

The part of the extracted sub-networks responded differently between groups. 40% of filters in GAE showed group difference, while 24% of hidden neurons in AE did. This may imply that GAE will lead to better classification performance. In our previous report, a simple artificial neural network (including AE) may out-perform the traditional CNN for a classification task [15]. It may be because normal convolutional filtering is not optimal for the adjacency matrix since the convolution operator assumes spatial topology of the data. Our results may imply that the GCN and GAE provide a better framework for this purpose.

We note that we do not use the machine learning models for classifying patients with disease from the normal control, but for analyzing the in-nature organization of the brain networks. Thus, the interpretability of sub-networks is most important. We added non-negative weight constraints to GAE and AE, since non-negative weight constraints in an auto-encoder help to extract interpretable representation [7]. Our analysis of decomposition quality is on the same line.

In this study, our contribution is three-folded. First, we extracted building blocks of the brain networks. Second, we defined the decomposition quality, and compared the resultant sub-networks extracted by AE and GAE, showing the feasibility of graph convolution operators on brain networks. Third, we showed that such building blocks capture distinct functional segregation, and thus, changes in filter responses are exclusively correlated with various cognitive functions in GAE.

There are a few limitations. First, it inherits all the limitations of diffusion-weighted imaging. The inability of the current tractography method for crossing fibers has been criticized. Though our MR protocol used relatively large numbers of gradient directions, we may employ a better tractography method in the future. Second, the current models have only a single GCN encoding layer. We are working on extending the model with the hierarchical pooling algorithm [16]. Third, the current GAE has a simple decoding layer using an inner product that could harm the reconstruction performance. A better decoding layer also requires the understanding of extracted representation. This will be further studied in the future.

Acknowledgement. This work was supported by the Korea Health Technology R&D Project through the Korea Health Industry Development Institute (KHIDI) that was funded by the Ministry of Health & Welfare, Republic of Korea (HI19C0645); the Basic Science Research Program through the National Research Foundation of Korea (NRF) funded by the Ministry of Education of the Government of the Republic of Korea (2016R1D1A1B03934990).

References

1. Mori, S., Barker, P.B.: Diffusion magnetic resonance imaging: its principle and applications. Anat. Rec. **257**, 102–109 (1999)
2. van den Heuvel, M.P., Stam, C.J., Kahn, R.S., Hulshoff Pol, H.E.: Efficiency of functional brain networks and intellectual performance. J. Neurosci. **29**, 7619–7624 (2009)
3. Kipf, T.N., Welling, M.: Variational graph auto-encoders. In: NIPS Bayesian Deep Learning Workshop 2016 (2016)
4. Kipf, T.N., Welling, M.: Semi-supervised classification with graph convolutional networks. In: ICLR 2017 (2017)
5. Lee, P., Choi, M., Kim, D., Lee, S., Jeong, H.-G., Han, C.E.: Deep learning based decomposition of brain networks. In: International Conference on Artificial Intelligence in Information and Communication (ICAIIC), pp. 349–354 (2019)
6. Bourlard, H., Kamp, Y.: Auto-association by multilayer perceptrons and singular value decomposition. Biol. Cybern. **59**, 291–294 (1988)
7. Hosseini-Asl, E., Zurada, J.M., Nasraoui, O.: Deep learning of part-based representation of data using sparse autoencoders with nonnegativity constraints. IEEE Trans. Neural Netw. Learn. Syst. **27**, 2486–2498 (2015)
8. Glorot, X., Bengio, Y.: Understanding the difficulty of training deep feedforward neural networks. In: AISTATS, pp. 249–256 (2010)
9. Hoyer, P.O.: Non-negative matrix factorization with sparseness constraints. J. Mach. Learn. Res. **5**, 1457–1469 (2004)
10. Kropf, S., Heuer, H., Gruning, M., Smalla, K.: Significance test for comparing complex microbial community fingerprints using pairwise similarity measures. J. Microbiol. Methods **57**, 187–195 (2004)

11. Benjamini, Y., Hochberg, Y.: Controlling the false discovery rate: a practical and powerful approach to multiple testing. J. R. Stat. Soc. Ser. B. Stat. Methodol. **57**, 289–300 (1995)
12. Han, C.E., Kam, H., Seong, J.-K.: Similarity-based cortical thickness analysis of mild cognitive impairment (MCI). In: Society for Neuroscience, pp. 40.41/H42 (2016)
13. Tzourio-Mazoyer, N., et al.: Automated anatomical labeling of activations in SPM using a macroscopic anatomical parcellation of the MNI MRI single-subject brain. Neuroimage **15**, 273–289 (2002)
14. Latora, V., Marchiori, M.: Efficient behavior of small-world networks. Phys. Rev. Lett. **87**, 198701 (2001)
15. Han, C., Kim, D., Lee, S., Jeong, H.-G.: Deep learning-based brain connectivity analysis. In: 40th Annual International Conference of the IEEE Engineering in Medicine and Biology Society (EMBS) (2018)
16. Ying, Z., You, J., Morris, C., Ren, X., Hamilton, W., Leskovec, J.H.: Hierarchical graph representation learning with differentiable pooling. In: Advances in Neural Information Processing Systems, pp. 4800–4810 (2018)

Hybrid Models

Accelerated Training Algorithms of General Fuzzy Min-Max Neural Network Using GPU for Very High Dimensional Data

Thanh Tung Khuat[✉] [iD] and Bogdan Gabrys [iD]

Advanced Analytics Institute, University of Technology Sydney, Sydney, Australia
thanhtung.khuat@student.uts.edu.au, bogdan.gabrys@uts.edu.au

Abstract. One of the issues of training a general fuzzy min-max neural network (GFMM) on very high dimensional data is a long training
time even if the number of samples is relatively low. This is a quite
common problem shared by many prototype-based methods requiring
frequently repeated distance or similarity calculations. This paper proposes the method of accelerating the learning algorithms of the GFMM
by, first, reformulating and representing them in a format allowing for
their parallel execution and subsequently leveraging the computational
power of the graphics processing unit (GPU). The original implementation of GFMM is modified by matrix computations to be executed on
the GPU for the very high-dimensional datasets. The empirical results
on two very high-dimensional datasets indicated that the training and
testing processes performed on Nvidia Quadro P5000 GPU were from 10
to 35 times faster compared to those running serially on the Xeon CPU
while retaining the same classification accuracy.

Keywords: GPU · Pytorch · General fuzzy min-max neural network

1 Introduction

Pattern classification is one of the critical steps for making data-driven decisions in a plethora of areas such as in economics, engineering, management, and
medicine [5]. Artificial neural networks (ANNs) are one of the most popular
machine learning models deployed for tackling pattern classification problems
[11]. However, one of the shortcomings of many neural networks is their black-
box nature [2], which predictive results are not explained explicitly. Another
main drawback of traditional classifiers in general and the artificial neural networks, in particular, is the stability-plasticity dilemma problem [10], in which
the classifier is unable to retain previously learned instances when new samples
are absorbed into that classifier. This phenomenon gives rise to the obliteration
of learned information in the predictor while learning new knowledge [8]. To cope
with this problem, a classifier has to be flexible enough to gain new information
and simultaneously maintain prior knowledge [8].

© Springer Nature Switzerland AG 2019
T. Gedeon et al. (Eds.): ICONIP 2019, LNCS 11953, pp. 583–595, 2019.
https://doi.org/10.1007/978-3-030-36708-4_48

These problems can be overcome by using a general fuzzy min-max neural network (GFMM) [6]. One of the advantages of this type of neural network is that it combines both supervised and unsupervised learning methods within a single framework. In addition, it may handle the uncertainty of practical problems by accepting the input data in the form of interval values instead of only crisp points. Therefore, the GFMM is subject to be used for the classification problem-solving in our study. The GFMM uses the concept of hyperbox fuzzy sets and several operations between hyperboxes such as expansion, overlap test, and contraction to form the training algorithms for the neural network built by articulating hyperboxes together.

In practical applications, pattern classification of high-dimensional data is a challenging issue. A dataset with N patterns and n features is taken into account as very high dimensional if $n \gg N$, and the value of n is relatively large. The high-dimensional data appear in many real-world applications, especially in genomes data [12] or data sampled from sensor networks as shown in [4] and [13]. In monitoring systems, a network of different sensors is used to supervise the operating statuses. Data of sensor arrays in complex environmental conditions sampled through different time-series exhibit very high dimensionality, even to millions of attributes as in [13]. The similar phenomenon also happen in the gene expression data, where the number of samples for both training and testing sets is regularly less than 100, while the number of attributes ranges from 6000 to 60,000 [12]. High dimensionality imposes high computational cost for the training process. It is needless to say that the long training time is one of the problems hindering machine learning algorithms from applying to real-world applications. Therefore, we propose a method to reduce the training time for the GFMM by taking advantage of the computational capability of the GPU and intrinsic parallelisation characteristics of GFMM.

For leveraging the power of GPU, one has to provide the data in batches so that it is able to perform many operations in parallel at the same time. Therefore, we build the matrix operations for basic calculation steps in the learning algorithms of the GFMM, such as the computation of membership functions, hyperbox expansion conditions, hyperbox overlap checking between two hyperboxes or many pairs of hyperboxes. Coates et al. [3] showed how to build a system to train the deep neural network with 64 Nvidia GPUs on 16 computers executing the learning process more than 6.5 times faster than the system with 1,000 computers using 16,000 CPUs. These results illustrated the power and potential of deploying the training phases on GPUs to significantly lower the training time on large-sized or very high dimensional datasets. Motivated by this study as well as to take advantage of the intrinsic parallelisable features of GFMM, we propose a new method of accelerating the training phase of the GFMM networks by using Pytorch [1] and GPUs for very high dimensional data.

Our main contributions in this study can be summarized as follows:

- Proposing and representing the learning algorithm of GFMM with its various components in a format allowing for parallel execution

- Using matrix computations executed expertly on the GPU to accelerate the training and testing processes of GFMM
- Implementing training algorithms of the GFMM on the GPU using Pytorch framework
- Comparing the training and testing time of the GFMM neural networks implemented by the NumPy library and Pytorch on two very high-dimensional practical datasets.

The rest of this paper is structured as follows. Section 2 briefly describes the architecture of the GFMM as well as its learning algorithms. Some modifications to be suitable for executions on the GPU are presented in Sect. 3. Empirical results and evaluation are shown in Sect. 4. Section 5 concludes the study and discuss several research directions in the future work.

2   Background

2.1   General Fuzzy Min-Max Neural Network

The general fuzzy min-max neural network is constituted by basic components, i.e., hyperbox fuzzy sets. Each hyperbox fuzzy set B_i consists of a minimum point V_i and a maximum point W_i along with a membership function $b_i(X_h, V_i, W_i)$, which shows the degree-of-fit of the input sample X_h with respect to the B_i. The membership function of the GFMM for the ith hyperbox is shown in Eq. 1.

$$b_i(X_h, V_i, W_i) = \min_{j=1}^{n} \left(\min([1 - f(x_{hj}^u - w_{ij}, \gamma_j)], [1 - f(v_{ij} - x_{hj}^l, \gamma_j)]) \right) \quad (1)$$

where $f(\xi, \gamma)$ is two-parameter ramp threshold function shown in Eq. 2, $\gamma = (\gamma_1, \gamma_2, ..., \gamma_n)$ contains the sensitivity parameters related to the pace of decrease of the membership values, and $0 \le b_j(X_h, V_j, W_j) \le 1$.

$$f(\xi, \gamma) = \begin{cases} 1, & \text{if } \xi \cdot \gamma > 1 \\ \xi \cdot \gamma, & \text{if } 0 \le \xi \cdot \gamma \le 1 \\ 0, & \text{if } \xi \cdot \gamma < 0 \end{cases} \quad (2)$$

A general fuzzy min-max neural network consists three layers. The input layer encompasses $2 \cdot n$ nodes, in which each n-dimensional input vector X_h comprises the lower and upper bound vectors X_h^l and X_h^u limited in the n-dimensional unit cube I^n. Each node in the intermediate layer, which contains m nodes, is a hyperbox fuzzy set connected to the first layer by the minimum and maximum vertices, and its activation function is the hyperbox membership function. The connection weights are tuned by utilizing the learning algorithm mentioned in the next subsection. The connections among nodes in the second layer and third layer are binary values stored in the matrix $\mathbf{U}$. The value of each element in $\mathbf{U}$ is computed using Eq. 3. Each output node in the third layer expresses a class and identifies the degree to which the input sample X_h fits within the given class. The activation function for each node in the output layer, containing $p+1$ nodes, is defined in Eq. 4. All unlabeled hyperboxes from the second layer are connected to a special node c_0. The outcomes of the class nodes may be fuzzy if they are directly computed from Eq. 4, or crisp in the case that a value of one is allocated to the node with the largest c_k and zero to the other nodes [6].

$$u_{ik} = \begin{cases} 1, & \text{if } b_i \in c_k \\ 0, & \text{if } b_i \notin c_k \end{cases} \tag{3}$$

$$c_k = \max_{i=1}^{m} b_i \cdot u_{ik} \tag{4}$$

2.2   Learning Algorithms

There are two types of algorithms used to train the general fuzzy min-max neural network, i.e., incremental learning [6] and agglomerative learning [7].

Incremental Learning
This algorithm can build a classifier incrementally with requiring only one pass through the training data. For each input pattern, hyperboxes in the network are adjusted through a four-phase process, i.e., hyperbox initialization, hyperbox expansion, overlap test, and contraction, in which last three steps are repeated many times.

Initialization. Each hyperbox B_i is initialized with the minimum coordinate V_i being one and the maximum coordinate W_i being zero for all dimensions.

Hyperbox Expansion. Assume that the input instance is in the form of $\{X_h = [X_h^l, X_h^u], l_h\}$, where l_h is the label of the input pattern X_h, $X_h^l = (x_{h1}^l, \ldots, x_{hn}^l)$ and $X_h^u = (x_{h1}^u, \ldots, x_{hn}^u)$ are lower and upper bounds of X_h respectively. When the GFMM receives the input X_h, the learning algorithm seeks for the hyperbox B_i with the same class as l_h and having highest membership degree to verify two expansion constraints:

- maximum allowable hyperbox size θ as Eq. 5:

$$\max(w_{ij}, x_{hj}^u) - \min(v_{ij}, x_{hj}^l) \leq \theta, \quad \forall j \in [1, n] \tag{5}$$

- class label compatibility:

$$\text{if } l_h = 0 \text{ then adjust } B_i$$
$$\text{else}$$
$$\text{if } class(B_i) = \begin{cases} 0 \rightarrow & \text{adjust } B_i \text{ and assign } class(B_i) = l_h \\ l_h \rightarrow & \text{adjust } B_i \\ else \rightarrow & \text{find another } B_i \end{cases}$$

where the adjustment procedure of minimum and maximum points of B_i is given as follows:

$$v_{ij}^{new} = \min(v_{ij}^{old}, x_{hj}^l); \quad w_{ij}^{new} = \max(w_{ij}^{old}, x_{hj}^u), \quad \forall j \in [1, n] \qquad (6)$$

If all hyperboxes belonging to the same class with the input instance do not meet the expansion conditions, a new hyperbox is created to cover the input pattern.

Overlap Test. The expanded hyperbox in the previous step is tested for the overlap with hyperboxes belonging to different classes. This operation is done dimension by dimension, and for each dimension, if at least one of four following cases is satisfied, an overlapping region occurs between two hyperboxes. The smallest overlap value δ, ($\delta = 1$ initially), is maintained during the overlap testing phase to support the contraction step. If the expanded hyperbox is B_i, assuming that B_k is the hyperbox of another class being validated the overlap, four cases are examined for each jth dimension as follows:

Case 1: $v_{ij} < v_{kj} < w_{ij} < w_{kj} : \delta^{new} = \min(w_{ij} - v_{kj}, \delta^{old})$

Case 2: $v_{kj} < v_{ij} < w_{kj} < w_{ij} : \delta^{new} = \min(w_{kj} - v_{ij}, \delta^{old})$

Case 3: $v_{ij} < v_{kj} \leq w_{kj} < w_{ij} : \delta^{new} = \min(\min(w_{kj} - v_{ij}, w_{ij} - v_{kj}), \delta^{old})$

Case 4: $v_{kj} < v_{ij} \leq w_{ij} < w_{kj} : \delta^{new} = \min(\min(w_{ij} - v_{kj}, w_{kj} - v_{ij}), \delta^{old})$

If $\delta^{new} < \delta^{old}$, then $\Delta = i$ and $\delta^{old} = \delta^{new}$, showing that there is an overlapping zone for the Δth dimension, and the testing operation will continue with the next dimension. Otherwise, no overlap happens between two hyperboxes, and the contraction process will not been carried out ($\Delta = -1$).

Contraction. The overlapping region between two hyperboxes is removed by adjusting their sizes in only one dimension Δ. The contraction operations can be found in [6].

Agglomerative Learning with Full Similarity Matrix (AGGLO-SM)
Unlike the incremental learning algorithm constructing and adjusting hyperboxes based on coming input patterns, the agglomerative learning algorithm uses all samples in training set for building and merging hyperboxes in a bottom-up approach. The algorithm starts with the initialization of minimum and maximum points of hyperboxes to the values of lower and upper limits of all points in the training set and using the same class labels with these samples. After that, a similarity matrix $\mathbf{S}$ among all pairs of hyperboxes belonging to the same class label is computed using the similarity measures. In [7], Gabrys presented three similarity measures between two hyperboxes. In this work, we only use one of those measures, which is designed to seek for the smallest "gap" between two hyperboxes and defined as Eq. 7 for two hyperboxes B_i and B_k:

$$s_{ik} = s(B_i, B_k) = \min_{j=1}^{n} (\min([1 - f(v_{kj} - w_{ij}, \gamma_j)], [1 - f(v_{ij} - w_{kj}, \gamma_j)])) \quad (7)$$

where f is the ramp function given in Eq. 2. Based on the similarity matrix, a pair of hyperboxes, assuming B_i and B_k, with the largest value of similarity is selected as the subject to the verification process before aggregating. Conditions are checked as follows:

- Overlap test. The newly generated hyperbox from merging B_i and B_k does not overlap with any hyperboxes belonging to different classes.
- The satisfaction of the hyperbox size with predefined maximum hyperbox size parameter θ: $\max(w_{ij}, w_{kj}) - \min(w_{ij}, w_{kj}) \leq \theta \quad \forall j \in [1, n]$
- The minimum similarity threshold (σ): $s_{ik} \geq \sigma$
- The class compatibility verification. The hyperboxes B_i and B_k represent the same class or one or both are unlabelled.

If any of these four constraints is violated, take another pair of hyperboxes with the next highest similarity measure. Otherwise, two selected hyperboxes are aggregated as follows:

- Updating B_i such as new B_i represents the merging results of B_i and B_k:

$$v_{ij}^{new} = \min(v_{ij}^{old}, v_{kj}^{old}); \quad w_{ij}^{new} = \max(w_{ij}^{old}, w_{kj}^{old}), \quad \forall j \in [1, n]$$

- Eliminating the B_k from the current set of hyperboxes
- Updating the similarity matrix $\mathbf{S}$ by removing the kth row and column, and adjusting the ith row and column with the new similarity values between the newly aggregated hyperbox and other hyperboxes.

The above steps are repeated until there are no potential hyperboxes being able to be aggregated.

The Second Agglomerative Learning Algorithm (AGGLO-2)

The computationally expensive parts of the AGGLO-SM include computing and sorting the similarity matrix for all pairs of hyperboxes. These operations can be prohibitively slow for very large-sized datasets. Hence, Gabrys [7] designed the second agglomerative algorithm in an attempt to reduce the computational complexity. Instead of computing the similarity measurements among all possible pairs of hyperboxes, this learning algorithm selects, in turn, a pivotal hyperbox to aggregate with the remaining hyperboxes.

Assuming that the hyperbox B_i is selected in the current iteration, the similarity values between B_i and the remaining hyperboxes are calculated, and then these values are sorted in a descending order. After that, the hyperbox B_k forming the highest similarity value with B_i chosen as a potential candidate for aggregation. Next, four conditions as in the AGGLO-SM are checked for B_i and B_k. If any of the constraints fails, another potential candidate with the second highest similarity value is selected to combine with B_i. This process is repeated until there is no candidate for aggregating with B_i or the aggregation took place. The algorithm continues with subsequently selected hyperboxes, and the training procedure terminates when there is no aggregation realized.

3 Implementation of Learning Algorithms by Matrix Operations

In this study, we reformulate and represent the learning algorithms of GFMM using matrix formats. This representation makes the algorithms execute in parallel effectively. Hence, the GPU can be deployed to accelerate GFMM algorithms. We employ two matrices $\mathbf{V} = \{V_1, \ldots, V_N\}$ and $\mathbf{W} = \{W_1, \ldots, W_N\}$ to contain sets of coordinates of lower and upper bounds of N hyperboxes as well as a vector $L = \{l_1, \ldots, l_N\}$ of hyperbox labels during the training process. Each element V_i of the matrix is an n-dimensional vector $\{v_{i1}, \ldots, v_{in}\}$ maintaining the values of the minimum point of the ith hyperbox. The similar setting is formulated for the maximum point of each hyperbox. These matrices and vector are stored on the GPU and initialized by command $.cuda()$ of Pytorch. The operations of the learning algorithm are performed on these operands.

3.1 Membership Computation

In the incremental learning algorithm, to find the potential expandable hyperbox, we have to compute the membership value between the input pattern $X_h = [X_h^l, X_h^u]$ with all hyperboxes belonging to the same class label or being unlabelled, which are stored in the matrices $\mathbf{V'} \subseteq \mathbf{V}$ and $\mathbf{W'} \subseteq \mathbf{W}$. Assume that N_1 the number of hyperboxes represented by $\mathbf{V'}$ (or $\mathbf{W'}$), vectors X_h^l and X_h^u corresponding to lower and upper bounds of the input sample are replicated N_1 times to form matrices $\mathbf{X}^l$ and $\mathbf{X}^u$. The vector of sensitivity parameters γ is also copied N_1 times to formulate a matrix $\mathbf{G}$. The Eq. 1 is changed to compute the membership degree between the input pattern X_h and all hyperboxes representing the same class as follows:

$$B(X_h, \mathbf{V'}, \mathbf{W'}) = \min(\min([1 - f(\mathbf{X}^u - \mathbf{W'}, \mathbf{G})], [1 - f(\mathbf{V'} - \mathbf{X}^l, \mathbf{G})])) \quad (8)$$

The operation $\min(A, B)$ generates the resulting matrix whose each element is taken from the minimum value of two corresponding elements within two matrices A and B. The procedure $\min(A)$ is used to find the minimum value within each row of the matrix A. The details of the membership computation steps are shown as follows:

function MEMBERSHIP_COMPUTATION($X_h^l, X_h^u, \mathbf{V'}, \mathbf{W'}, \gamma$)
    $N_1 \leftarrow size(\mathbf{V'}, 0)$ ▷ *Compute the number of hyperboxes within* V'
    Replicate γ, X_h^l, and X_h^u N_1 times for each vector to build three matrices $\mathbf{G}$, $\mathbf{X}^l$, and $\mathbf{X}^u$
    $F_1 \leftarrow 1 - $ F_RAMP($\mathbf{X}^u - \mathbf{W'}, \mathbf{G}$); $F_2 \leftarrow 1 - $ F_RAMP($\mathbf{V'} - \mathbf{X}^l, \mathbf{G}$);
    $F \leftarrow \min_{element\text{-}wise}(F_1, F_2)$
    $B \leftarrow \min_{row\text{-}wise}(F)$
    return B
end function
function F_RAMP(Y, G)
    $Z \leftarrow Y \odot G$ ▷ ⊙: *Hadamard product*
    $f \leftarrow [(Z > 0) \odot (Z < 1)] \odot Z + (Z > 1)$
    return f
end function

3.2 Computation of the Similarity Among Hyperboxes in the Agglomerative Learning

In the agglomerative learning algorithm, to find the candidate pair of hyperboxes for aggregation, we need to compute the similarity values among all pairs of hyperboxes representing the same class label in the AGGLO-SM or between currently considered hyperbox and the other hyperboxes representing same class in the AGGLO-2 algorithm. Therefore, the Eq. 7 can be modified as in Eq. 9 to compute the similarity values between the currently considered hyperbox B_i and the other hyperboxes of the same class label shown by matrices $\mathbf{V'}$ and $\mathbf{W'}$.

The $\mathbf{V'}_i$ is the matrix formed by replicating vector V_i of hyperbox B_i N_1 times, assuming that N_1 is the number of hyperboxes represented by $\mathbf{V'}$. Similar method is performed for W_i to generate $\mathbf{W'}_i$. From Eqs. 8 and 9, we can reuse the function MEMBERSHIP_COMPUTATION to compute the similarity measure by replacing the parameters X_h^l and X_h^u with W_i and V_i respectively.

$$s(V_i, W_i, \mathbf{V'}, \mathbf{W'}) = \min(\min([1 - f(\mathbf{V'}_i - \mathbf{W'}, \mathbf{G})], [1 - f(\mathbf{V'} - \mathbf{W'}_i, \mathbf{G})])) \quad (9)$$

After building the similarity matrix, we form a new matrix with three elements in each row, where first two elements are indices of hyperboxes and the last element is the similarity value of those two hyperboxes. It is noted that this matrix only includes pairs of hyperboxes with the similarity values larger than or equal to the predetermined threshold. This matrix is then sorted in descending order according to the values of the last column. All operations are executed on GPU. The sorted matrix is used for further hyperbox aggregation processes.

3.3 Expansion Constraint Checking

Before expanding the selected hyperbox B_i to cover the new input pattern in the incremental learning algorithm, the condition given by Eq. 5 is verified for all dimensions. This operation takes much time to complete in the case that the number of dimensions is very high. The similar phenomenon also occurs when checking the maximum hyperbox size of the aggregated hyperbox in the agglomerative learning algorithms. Fortunately, our data are stored on the GPU, and Pytorch provides us with the functions $torch.max()$, $torch.min()$, and $.all()$ to execute these operations rapidly on the GPU.

3.4 Overlap Testing Between Two Hyperboxes

In the incremental learning algorithm, we need to test overlap in turn between the expanded hyperbox B_i and hyperboxes B_k belonging to other class labels. Four overlap test cases mentioned above are performed for n-dimensional vectors V_i, W_i, V_k, and W_k. Our study is conducted on the very high dimensional datasets, so this operation takes much time during the training process. Therefore, we build the operation among vectors using logical operators to combine four cases aiming to detect whether there is an overlapping region between two hyperboxes, and this task is executed on the GPU.

If the overlap occurs, the second step would determine which dimension needs to be adjusted with the minimum influence and which case detected the overlap. The second step should be run on the CPU because its operations are performed in sequential for each element in vectors. All operations are detailed in the function OVERLAP_TEST. The function returns the special data structure containing the test case detecting overlap and the index of the dimension needing to be adjusted to resolve the overlap.

function OVERLAP_TEST(V_i, W_i, V_k, W_k)
   Step 1: **Detecting the occurrence of overlapping regions**
   $W_i W_k \leftarrow (W_i - W_k) > 0;\quad V_i V_k \leftarrow (V_i - V_k) > 0;$
   $W_k V_i \leftarrow (W_k - V_i) > 0;\quad W_i V_k \leftarrow (W_i - V_k) > 0;$
   $c_1 \leftarrow !W_i W_k\ \&\ !V_i V_k\ \&\ W_i V_k;\quad c_2 \leftarrow W_i W_k\ \&\ V_i V_k\ \&\ W_k V_i;$
   $c_3 \leftarrow W_i W_k\ \&\ !V_i V_k;\quad c_4 \leftarrow !W_i W_k\ \&\ V_i V_k;$
   $c \leftarrow c_1\ |\ c_2\ |\ c_3\ |\ c_4$
   Step 2: **Finding the dimension with minimum influence when doing contraction**
(executed on the CPU)
   $dim \leftarrow \varnothing$
   if $c_j = true,\ \forall c_j \in c$ **then**
     $m \leftarrow 1$
     $p \leftarrow |V_i|$ ▷ The number of dimentions of vector V_i
     for $t = 1 \rightarrow p$ **do**
       if $c_1[t] = true$ and $m > W_i[t] - V_k[t]$ **then**
         $m \leftarrow W_i[t] - V_k[t];\quad dim \leftarrow [1, t]$
       else if $c_2[t] = true$ and $m > W_k[t] - V_i[t]$ **then**
         $m \leftarrow W_k[t] - V_i[t];\quad dim \leftarrow [2, t]$
       else if $c_3[t] = true$ **then**
         if $m > W_k[t] - V_i[t]$ and $W_k[t] - V_i[t] < W_i[t] - V_k[t]$ **then**
           $m \leftarrow W_k[t] - V_i[t];\quad dim \leftarrow [31, t]$
         else if $m > W_i[t] - V_k[t]$ **then**
           $m \leftarrow W_i[t] - V_k[t];\quad dim \leftarrow [32, t]$
         end if
       else if $c_4[t] = true$ **then**
         if $m > W_k[t] - V_i[t]$ and $W_k[t] - V_i[t] < W_i[t] - V_k[t]$ **then**
           $m \leftarrow W_k[t] - V_i[t];\quad dim \leftarrow [41, t]$
         else if $m > W_i[t] - V_k[t]$ **then**
           $m \leftarrow W_i[t] - V_k[t];\quad dim = [42, t]$
         end if
       end if
     end for
   end if
   return dim
end function

3.5   Overlap Testing Between a Hyperbox and a Set of Other Hyperboxes

In the agglomerative learning algorithm, two hyperboxes are merged when the resulting hyperbox after aggregation does not overlap with hyperboxes belonging to other classes. Therefore, we need to verify the occurrence of overlapping regions between the newly aggregated hyperbox B_i and any hyperbox in the set of hyperboxes with other labels represented by two matrices **V'** and **W'**. No hyperbox contraction step is performed in this case, so we only need to detect overlapping regions by using GPU computations. Similar to the overlap detection step between two hyperboxes, logical operators And (&), Or (|), and

Not (!) are deployed on each element of the matrices for the overlap verification process considering four test cases simultaneously. The function OVERLAP_TEST_ONE_MANY describes the computational steps in detail.

```
function OVERLAP_TEST_ONE_MANY($V_i, W_i, \mathbf{V'}, \mathbf{W'}$)
    $N_1 \leftarrow$ the number of hyperboxes represented by $\mathbf{V'}$ (also $\mathbf{W'}$)
    $\mathbf{V'}_i \leftarrow$ Replicate vector $V_i$ $N_1$ times; $\mathbf{W'}_i \leftarrow$ Replicate vector $W_i$ $N_1$ times
    $W_i W_k \leftarrow (\mathbf{W'}_i - \mathbf{W'}) > 0;$   $V_i V_k \leftarrow (\mathbf{V'}_i - \mathbf{V'}) > 0$
    $W_k V_i \leftarrow (\mathbf{W'} - \mathbf{V'}_i) > 0;$   $W_i V_k \leftarrow (\mathbf{W'}_i - \mathbf{V'}) > 0$
    $c_1 \leftarrow \,!W_i W_k \,\&\, !V_i V_k \,\&\, W_i V_k;$   $c_2 \leftarrow W_i W_k \,\&\, V_i V_k \,\&\, W_k V_i;$
    $c_3 \leftarrow W_i W_k \,\&\, !V_i V_k;$   $c_4 \leftarrow \,!W_i W_k \,\&\, V_i V_k;$
    $C \leftarrow c_1 \mid c_2 \mid c_3 \mid c_4$
    if $\exists r \in C : r_j = true, \forall r_j \in r$, then $isOver \leftarrow true$; otherwise, $isOver \leftarrow false$
    return $isOver$
end function
```

4   Experimental Studies

Experiments were conducted on a computer with one Intel Xeon Gold 6150 2.7 GHz processor, running on the Linux operating system and containing one NVIDIA Quadro P5000 GPU. Each GPU has 16 GB of memory and can perform about 8.9 TFLOPS with single-precision of well-optimized code.

Table 1. Summary of datasets

Dataset	#Samples	#Features	#Training	#Testing	#Classes
PEMS database	440	138,672	352	88	7
Complex hydraulic system	2,205	43,680	1764	441	2

Table 2. Training time in seconds of the *PEMS Database* dataset

Algorithm	Mode	$\theta = 0.1$	$\theta = 0.2$	$\theta = 0.3$	$\theta = 0.4$	$\theta = 0.5$	$\theta = 0.6$
Incremental	CPU	32.895	34.891	33.210	33.159	35.095	34.868
	GPU	3.757	3.747	3.744	3.756	3.759	3.753
AGGLO-2	CPU	189.957	191.026	193.133	190.579	191.864	190.441
	GPU	10.203	10.194	10.199	10.213	10.193	10.179
AGGLO-SM	CPU	204.438	202.868	206.134	205.515	203.240	206.418
	GPU	10.658	10.659	10.655	10.661	10.686	10.657

Our experiments were conducted on two very high dimensional datasets. The first dataset is PEMS database taken from [4]. The data values ranging from 0 to 1 show the occupancy rate of various car lanes of San Francisco bay region freeways. Each day in this database is a single time series of 963 sensors sampled every 10 min during the day. Therefore, there are total $963 \times 6 \times 24 = 138{,}672$

Table 3. Training time in seconds of the *Complex Hydraulic System* dataset

Algorithm	Mode	$\theta = 0.1$	$\theta = 0.2$	$\theta = 0.3$	$\theta = 0.4$	$\theta = 0.5$	$\theta = 0.6$
Incremental	CPU	1,386.456	1,382.728	1,387.856	1,380.778	1,229.650	1,069.713
	GPU	144.264	145.787	147.296	148.389	157.143	154.372
AGGLO-2	CPU	2,659.041	2,698.802	2,654.382	4,855.536	4,695.572	6,908.221
	GPU	81.639	81.636	81.633	161.222	161.521	242.325
AGGLO-SM	CPU	2,056.106	2,034.172	1,887.212	16,875.429	91,634.154	170,623.012
	GPU	64.898	64.935	64.905	555.486	2,983.057	5,674.349

features for each record. These data are used to classify each observed day as the correct day of the week. As a result, there are seven labels with integer numbers ranging from one to seven.

The second dataset is obtained from [9], which is measurement data from sensors installed in the hydraulic system. These sensors measure different physical quantities such as pressure, motor power, volume flow, temperature, vibration, efficiency factor, cooling efficiency, and cooling power. Combination of data of all sensors forms a dataset consisting of 2205 patterns with 43,680 features per each sample. This dataset contains many different operational statuses of the complex hydraulic system, but we only consider two basic statuses, those are one meaning that the conditions are stable (1449 samples) and two indicating that the static conditions might not yet be reached (756 patterns).

For each dataset, 80% of the data were used for the training process, and the others were deployed to test the constructed GFMM neural network. The information of datasets is summarized in Table 1. We trained the GFMM neural networks using different learning algorithms implemented by NumPy library and Pytorch framework on these two training datasets and recorded the training time concerning different values of the maximum hyperbox size θ. Table 2 reports the training time in seconds of the algorithms on the *PEMS Database* dataset. Table 3 shows the training time on the *Complex Hydraulic System* dataset.

Table 4. Testing time in seconds of the *Complex Hydraulic System* dataset

Algorithm	Mode	$\theta = 0.1$	$\theta = 0.2$	$\theta = 0.3$	$\theta = 0.4$	$\theta = 0.5$	$\theta = 0.6$
Incremental	CPU	956.687	934.076	942.507	935.316	822.990	679.668
	GPU	28.151	28.141	28.150	28.022	26.215	21.841
AGGLO-2	CPU	939.199	955.927	935.033	870.593	790.102	773.167
	GPU	28.136	28.133	28.133	28.004	26.247	25.266
AGGLO-SM	CPU	957.944	937.624	887.749	841.823	774.469	747.979
	GPU	28.101	28.105	28.101	27.958	26.215	25.389

It is seen that the GPU contributes to reducing the training time of both datasets on all algorithms from 10 to 35 times compared to the CPU-based serial computations. When the value of θ increases, the number of hyperboxes reduces, but the overlapping regions appear more because the expansion or aggregation condition concerning θ is easily met. The number of samples in datasets is quite small, so the number of generated hyperboxes is relatively few. Meanwhile, the number of dimensions is very high, and the overlap test procedure is regularly conducted when the hyperbox expansion or merging process occurs frequently. Hence, the computations for the overlap test on very large dimensional vectors or matrices give rise to increase of the training time. That is the reason why the training time grows when the maximum hyperbox size increases.

Table 4 shows the testing time using the model trained on the *Complex Hydraulic System* dataset through different maximum hyperbox sizes. The most time-consuming computations in the testing process consist the membership computation and finding the maximum membership values. The obtained results indicate that the testing time using GPU is much faster than that employing CPU. These results confirms that our proposed method is very effective for operations of GFMM on high-dimensional datasets.

The use of GPU is only suitable for computations of the matrix with enormous size. In the incremental learning algorithm, we build and adjust hyperboxes gradually based on the input pattern, so the number of hyperboxes is not high. As a result, if the dimensionality of hyperboxes is from tens to hundreds of dimensions, then the usage of GPU computing is regularly ineffective compared to CPU because of interchanging between CPU with the GPU tensor operations and loop instructions being executed on the CPU. These operations cause a lot of overhead and slow down our computations.

5   Conclusion and Future Work

This paper reformulated and represented the GFMM algorithms in a matrix format to facilitate the parallel execution on the GPU. Empirical results indicated the efficiency of the use of GPU computations to accelerate the training and testing processes of the GFMM for very high dimensional data. The GPU implemented by Pytorch framework contributed to reducing the training and testing time of the GFMM from 10 to 35 times in comparison to CPU-based serial execution. These findings advocate a new method to train and expand the GFMM for very high dimensional datasets with minimal software engineering effort.

This study only uses the GPU for some necessary computations of the learning algorithm of the GFMM. The GPU will promote its computation ability highly effectively if the calculations are performed in parallel. Therefore, the future work focuses on forming the parallel training algorithms for the GFMM and running on many GPUs. Research efforts should also be put on constructing strategies to utilize the computational power of the GPUs for datasets with a large number of patterns.

References

1. Pytorch (2019). https://github.com/pytorch/pytorch. Accessed 15 Sept 2019
2. Benitez, J.M., Castro, J.L., Requena, I.: Are artificial neural networks black boxes? IEEE Trans. Neural Netw. **8**(5), 1156–1164 (1997)
3. Coates, A., Huval, B., Wang, T., Wu, D.J., Ng, A.Y., Catanzaro, B.: Deep learning with COTS HPC systems. In: Proceedings of the 30th International Conference on Machine Learning, pp. III-1337–III-1345 (2013)
4. Cuturi, M.: Fast global alignment kernels. In: Proceedings of the 28th International Conference on Machine Learning (ICML), pp. 929–936 (2011)
5. Duda, R.O., Hart, P.E., Stork, D.G.: Pattern Classification, 2nd edn. Wiley, Hoboken (2000)
6. Gabrys, B., Bargiela, A.: General fuzzy min-max neural network for clustering and classification. IEEE Trans. Neural Netw. **11**(3), 769–783 (2000)
7. Gabrys, B.: Agglomerative learning algorithms for general fuzzy min-max neural network. J. VLSI Sig. Process. Syst. Sig. Image Video Technol. **32**(1), 67–82 (2002)
8. Grossberg, S.: Adaptive resonance theory: how a brain learns to consciously attend, learn, and recognize a changing world. Neural Netw. **37**, 1–47 (2013)
9. Helwig, N., Pignanelli, E., Schütze, A.: Condition monitoring of a complex hydraulic system using multivariate statistics. In: The Proceedings of IEEE International Instrumentation and Measurement Technology Conference, pp. 210–215 (2015)
10. McCloskey, M., Cohen, N.J.: Catastrophic interference in connectionist networks: the sequential learning problem. Psychol. Learn. Motiv. **24**, 109–165 (1989)
11. Mukhopadhyay, S., Changhong, T., Huang, J., Mulong, Y., Palakal, M.: A comparative study of genetic sequence classification algorithms. In: Proceedings of the 12th IEEE Workshop on Neural Networks for Signal Processing, pp. 57–66 (2002)
12. Tariq, H., Eldridge, E., Welch, I.: An efficient approach for feature construction of high-dimensional microarray data by random projections. PLoS ONE **13**(4), 1–8 (2018)
13. Vergara, A., Fonollosa, J., Mahiques, J., Trincavelli, M., Rulkov, N., Huerta, R.: On the performance of gas sensor arrays in open sampling systems using inhibitory support vector machines. Sens. Actuators B: Chem. **185**, 462–477 (2013)

Evolving Artificial Neural Networks Using Butterfly Optimization Algorithm for Data Classification

Seyed Mohammad Jafar Jalali[1(✉)], Sajad Ahmadian[2], Parham M. Kebria[1],
Abbas Khosravi[1], Chee Peng Lim[1], and Saeid Nahavandi[1]

[1] Institute for Intelligent Systems Research and Innovation (IISRI),
Deakin University, Geelong, Australia
sjalali@deakin.edu.au
[2] Kermanshah University of Technology, Kermanshah, Iran

Abstract. One of the most difficult challenges in machine learning is the training process of artificial neural networks, which is mainly concerned with determining the best set of weights and biases. Gradient descent techniques are known as the most popular training algorithms. However, they are susceptible to local optima and slow convergence in training. Therefore, several stochastic optimization algorithms have been proposed in the literature to alleviate the shortcomings of gradient descent approaches. The butterfly optimization algorithm (BOA) is a recently proposed meta-heuristic approach. Its inspiration is based on the food foraging behavior of butterflies in the nature. Moreover, it has been shown that BOA is effective in undertaking a wide range of optimization problems and attaining the global optima solutions. In this paper, a new classification method based on the combination of artificial neural networks and BOA algorithm is proposed. To this end, BOA is applied as a new training strategy by optimizing the weights and biases of artificial neural networks. This leads to improving the convergence speed and also reducing the risk of falling into local optima. The proposed classification method is compared with other state-of-the-art methods based on two well-known data sets and different evaluation measures. The experimental results ascertain the superiority of the proposed method in comparison with the other methods.

Keywords: Butterfly optimization algorithm · Artificial neural network · Classification · Meta-heuristic

1 Introduction

Artificial neural networks (ANNs) are commonly applied as intelligent systems for modeling non-parametric and complex problems. In the past couple of decades, ANNs have shown their attractive and distinguishing features in solving classification, function approximation, and prediction problems [1,11,14–16,24,25,27]. As indicated in the literature, the most popular ANN is the

© Springer Nature Switzerland AG 2019
T. Gedeon et al. (Eds.): ICONIP 2019, LNCS 11953, pp. 596–607, 2019.
https://doi.org/10.1007/978-3-030-36708-4_49

multi-layer perceptron (MLP) network, which has been successful in solving a large number of real-world problems [2,4,12,13,21,22]. The performance of the MLP network depends largely on the training procedure. Gradient descent and stochastic techniques are two principal categories of methods for training MLPs. Moreover, the well-known variant of gradient descent, i.e., the back-propagation algorithm, is the most applied approach in training MLPs. However, this technique suffers from two critical drawbacks. Firstly, the MLPs may fall into the local minimum traps instead of attaining the global solution of the search space. Secondly, the MLPs may converge very slowly to the optimal solution.

A reliable preference to gradient-based methods is stochastic algorithms such as meta-heuristic (evolutionary) methods that have been proposed by researchers for MLP optimization [18,19]. The main advantage of these algorithms is to help MLPs to increase their convergence speed and also reduce the probability of falling into the local minimum traps. In other words, the meta-heuristic search algorithms prove their superior efficiency in local minimum avoidance to find the global solutions in a complex search space.

Several meta-heuristic algorithms have been proposed in the literature for training the MLPs [19,20,23]. The genetic algorithm (GA), particle swarm optimization (PSO), and differential evolution (DE) are popular meta-heuristics methods that represent promising results for training the MLPs [6,10]. In spite of competencies of the recent deployed MLP training procedures based on the No-Free-Lunch (NFL) theorem [26], there is no superior optimizer to solve all optimization problems. Therefore, we still need to design new training methods for mitigating the problem of local minimum in training the MLP networks.

In this paper, a novel classification approach is proposed based on a combination of the butterfly optimization algorithm (BOA) [5] and MLP neural network. The inspiration of this meta-heuristic algorithm is from the food foraging behavior of butterflies in the nature. The BOA has shown its superiority in escaping the local optima in several difficult and complex benchmark problems [REF]. To this end, the initial weights and biases of MLP are computed by the BOA, leading to improved convergence in training the MLPs and also avoidance of the local minimum traps. The main contribution and significance of the proposed method are as follows:

1. For the first time, A new hybrid stochastic trainer based on the recently proposed BOA is developed to optimize the weights and biases of MLPs.
2. The proposed hybrid algorithm is effective in tackling two important data sets in the bioinformatics field related to Parkinson and orthopedic patients.
3. The empirical results indicate that the proposed method outperforms other state-of-the-art methods based on various types of evaluation measures.

The rest of this paper is structured as follows. In Sect. 2, we explain the BOA, the MLP network structure, and the proposed classification method. The experimental results and discussion are provided in Sect. 3. Finally, in Sect. 4, the concluding remarks and future research directions are summarized.

2   Methodology

In this section, a general description of the BOA and MLP is provided in the following sub-sections. Then, the proposed method is described in details.

2.1   Butterfly Optimization Algorithm

The BOA is a nature-based inspired optimization algorithm for solving global optimization problems. It is based on food search and mating behavior of butter-flies [5]. The main concept of the BOA is to use the foraging strategy of butterflies in the nature, which relies on their smell sense for determining the nectar location or mating partner. Three important terms, namely stimulus intensity (I), sensory modality (c), and power exponent (a), are used to modeling the concept of sensing and processing of the modality in the foraging behavior of butterflies. Note that sensory refers to measure the energy form and to provide it in similar procedures, while modality refers to the raw input used by the sensors. In the BOA, the modality covers the fragrance (f) is formulated as a function of the physical intensity of stimulus as follows:

$$f = cI^a \tag{1}$$

where f is the perceived magnitude of the fragrance, I is the stimulus intensity, c is the sensory modality, and a is the power exponent dependent on the modality, which accounts for the varying degree of absorption. The values of a and c are in the range $[0, 1]$.

The BOA is based on three main phases, namely the initialization phase, iteration phase, and final phase. In the initialization phase, the algorithm defines the objective function and its solution space. An initial population of butterflies is created, in which their positions are randomly generated in the solution space. In the iteration phase, a number of iterations are performed. All butterflies in the solution space move to new positions, with their fitness values evaluated. Then, the fragrance of butterflies is generated at their positions using Eq. 1. The iteration phase is continued till the stopping criterion is matched. In the final phase, the algorithm outputs the best solution found, which has attained the best fitness value.

Two main strategies are used in the BOA: global search and local search. In global search, the butterfly moves into the fittest butterfly/solution g using the following equation:

$$x_i^{t+1} = x_i^t + (r^2 \times g^* - x_i^t) \times f_i \tag{2}$$

where x_i^t is the vector of solution for the ith butterfly in iteration t, g^* refers to the best solution found in the current iteration, f_i is the fragrance of the ith butterfly and r is a random number in $[0, 1]$.

On the other hand, the local search strategy is modeled by the following equation:

$$x_i^{t+1} = x_i^t + (r^2 \times x_j^t - x_k^t) \times f_i \tag{3}$$

where x_j^t and x_k^t are the jth and kth butterflies from the solution space. The pseudocode of the BOA is presented in Algorithm 1.

Algorithm 1. Pseudocode of the Butterfly Optimization Algorithm

Initialize sensor modality (c), power exponent (a), and switch probability (p)
Define the fitness function $f(x)$, $x = (x_1, x_2, ..., x_{dim})$, dim = number of dimensions
Generate the initial population of n butterflies
while (stopping criteria not met) **do**
    for (each bf in population) **do**
        Calculate fragrance for bf using Eq. 1
    end for
    Find the best bf
    for (each butterfly bf in population) **do**
        Generate a random number r from $[0, 1]$
        if $r < p$ **then**
            Move towards best butterfly using Eq. 2
        else
            Move randomly using Eq. 3
        end if
    end for
    Update the value of a
end while
Output the best solution found

2.2   Multilayer Perceptron Neural Network

Artificial neural networks (ANNs) are non-parametric models which consist of a set of processing elements called neurons. The feed-forward neural networks are a class of supervised ANNs, which normally contain three layers of nodes, namely the input, output, and hidden layers. The MLP is the most popular and common type of feedforward networks. The MLP nodes are hierarchically arranged in multiple fully connected layers. Specifically, the MLP contains an input layer, an output layer, and the hidden layers that reside between the input and output layers. In the MLP, the hidden layers provide the computational and processing power to produce the network outputs. The connections are represented by the network weights, which are real numbers in the interval $[-1, 1]$.

In the MLP, two steps are performed to yield the output value of each node in each layer. In the first step, the weighted summation of the input values is calculated as follows:

$$S_j = \sum_{i=1}^{n} (w_{ij} I_i + \beta_j) \tag{4}$$

where I_i is the ith input variable, n refers to the total number of nodes (neurons) in the input layer, w_{ij} is the connection weight between I_i and the hidden node j, and β_j denotes the bias (threshold) weight of the jth hidden node.

In the second step, the output value of each node in the hidden layer is computed based on a weighted summation. To this end, a special function called activation is used to trigger the output based on the value of the summation function. In the MLP, different types of activation functions can be used. The

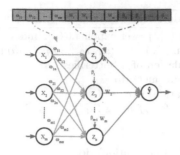

Fig. 1. The representation of each solution in BOAMLP.

sigmoid activation function is commonly used to map the hidden layer output values which can be calculated as follows:

$$f_j(x) = \frac{1}{1 + e^{-S_j}} \tag{5}$$

Finally, the network output can be obtained using Eq. 6 as follows:

$$\hat{y}_k = \sum_{i=1}^{m} (w_{kj} f_i + \beta_k) \tag{6}$$

The MLP performance largely depends on the values of biases and connection weights established in the training phase. Therefore, the main purpose of training the MLP is to find a set of optimal biases and connection weights to minimize the prediction error.

2.3 Proposed Classification Model

This section presents the proposed classification method, known as BOA-MLP, for training the MLP neural network using the BOA. The performance and convergence of the MLP training process depends on the initialization of the connection weights and biases. Therefore, the purpose of the proposed method is to apply the BOA as a meta-heuristic approach on the search space of the initial weights and biases to find their optimal values. It should be noted that, initializing the weights and biases with optimal values leads to improved convergence and also prediction accuracy. Before applying the BOA, two important issues should be considered: the encoding scheme of individuals (butterflies) and the fitness function.

In the proposed method, each butterfly (solution) contains three parts: the connection weights between the input and hidden layers, the connection weights between the hidden and output layers, and the biases. In other words, each solution is encoded as a vector of real numbers in the range $[-1, 1]$, whereby the number of elements in this vector can be calculated as follows:

$$Vector\_length = (n \times m) + (2 \times m) + 1 \tag{7}$$

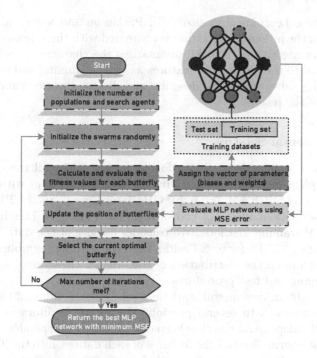

Fig. 2. The overall steps of the proposed classification model.

where n denotes the number of input features in the dataset, and m is the number of nodes in the hidden layer. Figure 1 shows the format of each solution in the proposed method.

The second important issue is to define the fitness function. To this end, the fitness value of each individual is evaluated using the mean square error (MSE). This function calculates the difference between the actual and predicted values generated by the MLP network for all the training samples. Equation 8 is used to compute the MSE score:

$$MSE = \frac{1}{n} \sum_{i=1}^{n} (y_i - \hat{y}_i)^2 \tag{8}$$

where y_i represents the actual output, $\hat{y}_i$ is the predicted output, and n denotes the number of samples in the training dataset.

After determining the representation of solutions and selecting the fitness function, the BOA can be applied to training the MLP based on Algorithm 1. The overall steps of the proposed classification method are shown in Fig. 2.

3 Experiments and Results

In this section, the conducted experiments for evaluating the performance of the proposed BOA-MLP algorithm is benchmarked using three medical data sets in the UCI Machine Learning Repository [7]: Parkinson and Vertebral. Then, the performance of the proposed algorithm is compared with those from other recent and well-known algorithms. Table 1 summarizes the characteristics of the data sets with regard to the numbers of features as well as training and test samples. In the following sub-sections, we describe and discuss the experimental set-up and analysis of the results.

3.1 Experimental Set-Up

In order to compare the optimization algorithm fairly, all the experiments have been implemented on a 64-bit Ubuntu operating system with MATLAB R2019a using a 32 GB RAM and a 1.9 GHz Intel Core i7-8650 CPU. All three medical data sets are divided into two sub-sets for training and testing of the all EA-based MLP training methods. We consider 66.66% of the data for training and the remaining 33.33% for test. Besides that, the stratified sampling technique is utilized to maintain the distribution of the original class samples of the data set in the training and test procedures.

In order to obtain meaningful statistical results, we conduct 30 independent training and test runs. In several previous studies in the literature, the same number (30) of independent runs has been carried out by independent researchers [19,20]. We have normalized all the features of each dataset into the [0, 1] interval by the min-max scaling normalization technique given in following equation: This procedure of normalization is essential before MLP training since it eliminates the influence of one feature having value in a wider range over another.

$$K_i' = \frac{K_i - min_K}{max_K - min_K}, \tag{9}$$

One of the important steps in evaluating the evolutionary algorithms is the selection of other compared metaheuristic algorithms, in order to ensure a fair comparison. Therefore, in this study, in order to ascertain the efficiency of the proposed BOA-MLP algorithm, we use well-established meta-heuristics including the GA, PSO, DE, GOA, and FPA (flower pollination algorithm). There are two main motivations behind choosing these algorithms from a plethora of meta-heuristic algorithms available in the literature. Firstly, the chosen algorithms are popular, and have been widely-used in the machine learning and optimization field. Secondly, they show competitive and stable results and performance in common optimization problems, including single-objective, multi-objective problems.

Table 1. Description of medical classification datasets

No.	Dataset	#Features	#Training samples	#Testing samples
1	Parkinson	22	128	67
2	Vertebral	6	204	106

Table 2. The initial parameter settings of each algorithm

Algorithm	Parameter	Value
GA	Crossover probability	0.9
	Mutation probability	0.1
	Selection mechanism	Roulette wheel
PSO	Acceleration constants	[2.1, 2.1]
	Inertia weights	[0.9, 0.6]
DE	Crossover probability	0.9
	Differential weight	0.5
GOA	Interval	[0, 2.079]
	l	1.5
	f	0.5
FPA	Scaling factor	0.1
	Step size	1.5
	Probability switch	0.8
BOA	c	0.01
	a	[0.1, 0.3]
	p	0.5

In all experiments, the maximum number of iterations and the population size of all algorithms have been set to 100 and 50, as recommended in [9]. The control parameters of other meta heuristic algorithm have been in accordance with those reported in the literature [3,5,8,17,23], as given in Table 2.

In order to determine the number of nodes in hidden layer of the MLP, many different rules have been proposed in the literature. There is not a clear and definite agreement among researchers with respect to the best rule to use. We select a common standard rule used by many researchers in the literature [3,8,9], i.e., the number of hidden nodes is set to *2 × number of features in the dataset + 1*.

3.2 Results and Discussion

In this section, the proposed BOA-MLP algorithm is compared with five optimization methods using the three medicine classification data sets based on different evaluation metrics.

Table 3 summarizes the evaluation results for the Parkinson data set. The BOA-based MLP network is capable of achieving high accuracy and AUC scores. The GOA trainer performs closely to the BOA, and outperforms other models. The advantage of the AUC is the ability to display the relationship between the specificity and sensitivity rates, in order not to over-fit to one single class. As an example, the specificity rate of DE-MLP is the best among those from other networks; however, it performs poorly in terms of sensitivity. By checking the

Table 3. The experimental results of Parkinsons dataset

Algorithms	Accuracy	AUC	Specificity	Sensitivity
BOAMLP	0.88209	0.90276	0.68653	0.95763
GOAMLP	0.86567	0.89313	0.66977	0.95141
FPAMLP	0.87015	0.86822	0.52036	0.93644
GAMLP	0.84478	0.85702	0.48751	0.96841
PSOMLP	0.83198	0.84497	0.56691	0.94229
DEMLP	0.87356	0.85572	0.89544	0.55836

convergence curves in Fig. 3, it is clearly shown that the BOA has the lowest average MSE score, the fastest convergence speed, and a stable performance.

In regards to the Vertebral data set, the evaluation results are presented in Table 4. The BOA-MLP algorithm has the highest rates of accuracy, AUC, and specificity. In terms of sensitivity, most of the competitors and specifically, GA-MLP, yield competitive results as compared with those of BOA-MLP. However, BOA-MLP has highest stability (as can be seen in Fig. 3c) with a slow convergence curve.

Table 4. The experimental results of Vertebral dataset

Algorithms	Accuracy	AUC	Specificity	Sensitivity
BOAMLP	0.87084	0.94877	0.89166	0.83356
GOAMLP	0.86981	0.94117	0.87885	0.82669
FPAMLP	0.86792	0.92885	0.84553	0.86106
GAMLP	0.83208	0.92955	0.84665	0.90156
PSOMLP	0.83962	0.91788	0.80094	0.87933
DEMLP	0.81792	0.89006	0.76636	0.87115

In summary, the BOA-MLP algorithm is competitive in some evaluation metrics such as sensitivity and specificity. In addition, the main drawback of all studied methods is that they are not able to keep a balance between exploitation and exploration in comparison with the BOA-MLP algorithm. Consequently, the problem of trapping into local minima and obtaining immature convergence can be observed in the results of other methods. The main underlying mechanism demonstrating the robust results in escaping from the local minima and avoiding immature convergence is that BOA uses the mating behavior of butterflies for ameliorating the quality of the obtained solutions in the search space. In this algorithm, two key phases including global search and local search allow the BOA to improve the MLP performance in exploration and exploitation of the search space extensively during the course of iterations. These dynamic capabilities of the BOA in both exploration and exploitation operations lead to more robust outcomes in comparison with those from other evolutionary-MLP competitors.

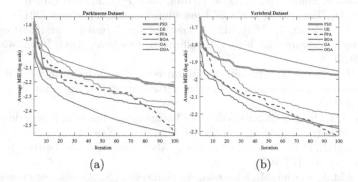

(a)   (b)

Fig. 3. Visual comparison for convergence curves of evolutionary-based MLP trainers in logarithmic scale based on Parkinsons and Vertebral datasets.

4   Conclusion

In this paper, a new neural network training method based on a recent nature-inspired evolutionary algorithm called the butterfly optimization algorithm has been proposed. The new method performs efficiently in a two challenging benchmark medical classification data sets. The results compare favorably with those from a number of well-regarded meta-heuristic training algorithms, including the GOA, FPA, GA, PSO and DE.

For further research, the proposed method will be rigorously evaluated using other classification data sets in different types of classification problems such as one-class classification and multi-class classification. Using the BOA to train other machine learning and neural network models such as the extreme learning machine or the radial basis function network is another research direction.

References

1. Agrawal, S., Agrawal, J.: Neural network techniques for cancer prediction: a survey. Procedia Comput. Sci. **60**, 769–774 (2015)
2. Ahmadian, S., Khanteymoori, A.R.: Training back propagation neural networks using asexual reproduction optimization. In: 2015 7th Conference on Information and Knowledge Technology (IKT), pp. 1–6. IEEE (2015)
3. Aljarah, I., et al.: Optimizing connection weights in neural networks using the whale optimization algorithm. Soft Comput. **22**(1), 1–15 (2016)
4. Amiri, M.J., Abedi-Koupai, J., Jalali, S.M.J., Mousavi, S.F.: Modeling of fixed-bed column system of Hg(II) ions on ostrich bone Ash/nZVI composite by artificial neural network. J. Environ. Eng. **143**(9), 04017061 (2017)

5. Arora, S., Singh, S.: Butterfly optimization algorithm: a novel approach for global optimization. Soft. Comput. **23**(3), 715–734 (2019)
6. Chau, K.W.: Particle swarm optimization training algorithm for ANNs in stage prediction of Shing Mun River. J. Hydrol. **329**(3–4), 363–367 (2006)
7. Dheeru, D., Taniskidou, E.K.: UCI machine learning repository (2017)
8. Faris, H., Aljarah, I., Mirjalili, S.: Training feedforward neural networks using multi-verse optimizer for binary classification problems. Appl. Intell. **45**(2), 322–332 (2016)
9. Faris, H., Aljarah, I., Mirjalili, S.: Improved monarch butterfly optimization for unconstrained global search and neural network training. Appl. Intell. **48**(2), 445–464 (2018)
10. Gupta, J.N., Sexton, R.S.: Comparing backpropagation with a genetic algorithm for neural network training. Omega **27**(6), 679–684 (1999)
11. Jalali, S.M.J., Park, H.W.: Conversations about open data on twitter. Int. J. Contents **13**(1), 31–37 (2017)
12. Jalali, S.M.J., Karimi, M., Khosravi, A., Nahavandi, S.: An efficient neuroevolution approach for heart disease detection. In: 2019 IEEE International Conference on Systems, Man, and Cybernetics (SMC), pp. 1–6 (2019)
13. Jalali, S.M.J., Khosravi, A., Kebria, P.M., Hedjam, R., Nahavandi, S.: Autonomous robot navigation system using the evolutionary multi-verse optimizer algorithm. In: 2019 IEEE International Conference on Systems, Man, and Cybernetics (SMC), pp. 1–6 (2019)
14. Jalali, S.M.J., Mahdizadeh, E., Mahmoudi, M.R., Moro, S.: Analytical assessment process of e-learning domain research between 1980 and 2014. Int. J. Manag. Educ. **12**(1), 43–56 (2018)
15. Jalali, S.M.J., Park, H.W.: State of the art in business analytics: themes and collaborations. Qual. Quant. **52**(2), 627–633 (2018)
16. Jalali, S.M.J., Moro, S., Mahmoudi, M.R., Ghaffary, K.A., Maleki, M., Alidoostan, A.: A comparative analysis of classifiers in cancer prediction using multiple data mining techniques. Int. J. Bus. Intell. Syst. Eng. **1**(2), 166–178 (2017)
17. Mafarja, M., et al.: Binary grasshopper optimisation algorithm approaches for feature selection problems. Expert Syst. Appl. **117**, 267–286 (2019)
18. Mirjalili, S.: How effective is the grey wolf optimizer in training multi-layer perceptrons. Appl. Intell. **43**(1), 150–161 (2015)
19. Mirjalili, S., Hashim, S.Z.M., Sardroudi, H.M.: Training feedforward neural networks using hybrid particle swarm optimization and gravitational search algorithm. Appl. Math. Comput. **218**(22), 11125–11137 (2012)
20. Mirjalili, S., Mirjalili, S.M., Lewis, A.: Let a biogeography-based optimizer train your multi-layer perceptron. Inf. Sci. **269**, 188–209 (2014)
21. Shahzadeh, A., Khosravi, A., Nahavandi, S.: Improving load forecast accuracy by clustering consumers using smart meter data. In: 2015 International Joint Conference on Neural Networks (IJCNN), pp. 1–7. IEEE (2015)
22. She, F.H., Kong, L.X., Nahavandi, S., Kouzani, A.Z.: Intelligent animal fiber classification with artificial neural networks. Text. Res. J. **72**(7), 594–600 (2002)
23. Shehu, G.S., Çetinkaya, N.: Flower pollination-feedforward neural network for load flow forecasting in smart distribution grid. Neural Comput. Appl. **31**(10), 1–12 (2018)
24. Vanani, I.R., Jalali, S.M.J.: Analytical evaluation of emerging scientific trends in business intelligence through the utilisation of burst detection algorithm. Int. J. Bibliometr. Bus. Manag. **1**(1), 70–79 (2017)

25. Vanani, I.R., Jalali, S.M.J.: A comparative analysis of emerging scientific themes in business analytics. Int. J. Bus. Inf. Syst. **29**(2), 183–206 (2018)
26. Wolpert, D.H., Macready, W.G.: No free lunch theorems for optimization. IEEE Trans. Evol. Comput. **1**(1), 67–82 (1997)
27. Zhang, Q., Yang, L.T., Chen, Z., Li, P.: A survey on deep learning for big data. Inf. Fusion **42**, 146–157 (2018)

Evolving an Optimal Decision Template for Combining Classifiers

Tien Thanh Nguyen[1]([⊠]), Anh Vu Luong[2], Manh Truong Dang[1],
Lan Phuong Dao[3], Thi Thu Thuy Nguyen[2], Alan Wee-Chung Liew[2],
and John McCall[1]

[1] School of Computing Science and Digital Media,
Robert Gordon University, Aberdeen, UK
{t.nguyen11,t.dang1,mccall}@rgu.ac.uk
[2] School of Information and Communication Technology,
Griffith University, Gold Coast, Australia
{vu.luong,thithuthuy.nguyen}@griffithuni.edu.au,
a.liew@griffith.edu.au
[3] AN Company, Hanoi, Vietnam
lan.pd@outlook.com

Abstract. In this paper, we aim to develop an effective combining algorithm for ensemble learning systems. The Decision Template method, one of the most popular combining algorithms for ensemble systems, does not perform well when working on certain datasets like those having imbalanced data. Moreover, point estimation by computing the average value on the outputs of base classifiers in the Decision Template method is sometimes not a good representation, especially for skewed datasets. Here we propose to search for an optimal decision template in the combining algorithm for a heterogeneous ensemble. To do this, we first generate the base classifier by training the pre-selected learning algorithms on the given training set. The meta-data of the training set is then generated via cross validation. Using the Artificial Bee Colony algorithm, we search for the optimal template that minimizes the empirical 0–1 loss function on the training set. The class label is assigned to the unlabeled sample based on the maximum of the similarity between the optimal decision template and the sample's meta-data. Experiments conducted on the UCI datasets demonstrated the superiority of the proposed method over several benchmark algorithms.

Keywords: Ensemble method · Combining classifiers · Multiple classifiers · Classifier fusion · Artificial Bee Colony

1 Introduction

In recent years, there has been an intense research activity focusing on ensemble learning [11,13]. The interest emerges from the fact that ensemble methods can achieve higher performance than using single learners in many learning tasks

© Springer Nature Switzerland AG 2019
T. Gedeon et al. (Eds.): ICONIP 2019, LNCS 11953, pp. 608–620, 2019.
https://doi.org/10.1007/978-3-030-36708-4_50

such as supervised (i.e. classification and prediction) and unsupervised learning
(i.e. clustering). Until now, ensemble methods have been applied to many areas
such as bioinformatics, computer vision, and software engineering [18].

In this paper, we focus on the heterogeneous ensemble in which several learning algorithms train base classifiers on a given training set. A combining algorithm is then used to aggregate the output of these base classifiers to obtain the
final prediction. The research here is to develop new combiners to obtain high
accuracy [11–14].

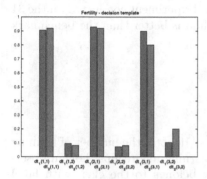 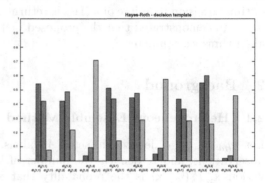

* $dt_j(k, m)$ is defined in Section 2.2

Fig. 1. Decision templates for class labels computed on Fertility and Hayes-Roth
datasets

Among the combining algorithms developed for heterogeneous ensemble systems, Decision Template is one of the most popular methods [11]. In this method,
we group the outputs of base classifiers on the training observations (called meta-
data) based on their class labels. The decision template for each class label is
computed as the mean i.e. average of the meta-data of the observations in the
associated group. It is noted that Decision Template method may perform poorly
if it does not provide a good enough representation for a class. When data distribution is skewed for example, the mean loses its ability to provide the best
central location. Moreover, the base classifiers will tend to predict the dominant class on some imbalanced datasets. Figure 1 shows the decision templates
computed on the outputs of an example of ensemble with 3 base classifiers, i.e.
Linear Discriminative Analysis (denoted by LDA), Naïve Bayes, and k Nearest
Neighbor (k set to 5, denoted by KNN_5), on the two imbalanced datasets: 2-class
Fertility and 3-class Hayes-Roth. In Fertility dataset, 80% of the observations
belongs to the first class label. Clearly, the Decision Templates of the 2 classes
are very similar and consequently have low discriminative ability. On Hayes-Roth
dataset, the decision templates of the first two classes have the same values. This
makes Decision Template method poor on these datasets.

In this paper, we aim to search for the optimal decision template for a heterogeneous ensemble. To do this, we first generate the base classifiers by training

the pre-selected learning algorithms on the given training set. The meta-data of the training set is then generated via a cross validation procedure. By using the Artificial Bee Colony algorithm [4,5], we search for the optimal decision template which minimizes the empirical 0–1 loss on the training set. In detail, for each candidate template, we measure the similarity between it and the meta-data of each training observations. The class label is assigned to the observations based on the maximum similarity. The optimal decision template is the candidate that minimizes the loss function. During classification, the class label that maximizes the similarity between the meta-data of the unlabeled sample and the optimal decision template of a class is returned. Experiment conducted on the 31 datasets demonstrated that the proposed method is better than the benchmark algorithms we compared.

2 Background

2.1 Heterogeneous Ensemble Method

Let $\{y_m\}_{m=1,\dots,M}$ denotes the set of M labels, N denotes the number of training observations, and K denotes the number of learning algorithms. For an observation $\mathbf{x}$, $P_k(y_m|\mathbf{x})$ is the probability that $\mathbf{x}$ belongs to the class with label y_m given by the kth classifier. In this study, we focus on the soft label output: $P_k(y_m|\mathbf{x}) \in [0,1]$ and $\sum_m P_k(y_m|\mathbf{x}) = 1$. In heterogeneous ensemble learning, the soft labels output by the base classifiers for the training set become the *meta-data* of the training set, which is given by the $N \times KM$ matrix:

$$\mathbf{L} = \begin{bmatrix} P_1(y_1|\mathbf{x}_1) & \dots & P_K(y_1|\mathbf{x}_1) & \dots & P_K(y_M|\mathbf{x}_1) \\ \vdots & \ddots & & & \vdots \\ P_1(y_1|\mathbf{x}_N) & \dots & P_K(y_1|\mathbf{x}_N) & \dots & P_K(y_M|\mathbf{x}_N) \end{bmatrix} \tag{1}$$

Meanwhile, the meta-data of an observation $\mathbf{x}_i$ is given by:

$$\mathbf{L}(\mathbf{x}_i) = \begin{bmatrix} P_1(y_1|\mathbf{x}_i) & \dots & P_1(y_M|\mathbf{x}_i) \\ & \dots & \\ P_K(y_1|\mathbf{x}_i) & \dots & P_K(y_M|\mathbf{x}_i) \end{bmatrix} \tag{2}$$

There are two combining approaches for the heterogeneous ensemble: fixed combining method and trainable combining method [13]. For fixed combining method, the combiner works directly on the meta-data of a test sample to assign the class label and does not exploit the meta-data of the training set. It therefore has fast training time. There are some popular fixed combining methods such as fixed combining rules [6,14] and fixed combining based on Ordered Weighted Averaging operator (OWA) [7]. Among these methods, the Sum Rule is the most popular [6].

For the trainable combining method, two well-known strategies to obtain the discriminative decision model are weighted classifiers combining methods and methods based on meta-data representation. In weighted classifiers combining methods, each classifier is assumed to differently contribute to the combining result i.e. putting a different weight on each class. The combining algorithm is based on the M linear combinations of posterior probabilities and the associated weights for the M classes. There are several approaches in this category such as the Multi-Response Linear Regression (MLR) method [17] and MLR with hinge loss [15]. On the other hand, the meta-data representation approach aims to find the representation for the meta-data associated with each class label. The class label is assigned to a test sample based on the similarity between its meta-data and the representation. Some examples of meta-data representation methods are the Decision Template method [8], the Bayesian-based method [13], and granular-based prototype [12].

Heuristic search based approaches have also been proposed to enhance the heterogeneous ensemble. These approaches aim to search for the optimal sub-set of base classifiers, of meta-classifier, the input features, and the meta-data features, to boost the performance of the ensemble system. In detail, Nguyen et al. [10] encoded the base classifiers and the features in a single chromosome and used Genetic Algorithm to simultaneously search for the optimal set of classifiers and associated features. Nguyen et al. [9] also proposed a new encoding for meta-data feature and used Genetic Algorithm to search for the optimal set of meta-data features for the Decision Tree meta-classifiers. Shunmugapriya and Kanmani [16] used Artificial Bee Colony (ABC) to find the optimal set of base classifiers and the meta-classifiers. Chen et al. [2] used Ant Colony Optimization (ACO) to find the optimal set of base classifiers in an ensemble system with the Decision Tree as the meta-classifier.

2.2   Decision Template Method

In this section, we briefly introduce the Decision Template method [8] which is the basis for our approach. In this method, after obtaining the base classifiers by learning the learning algorithms on the training set, the meta-data $\mathbf{L}$ is obtained via a cross validation procedure. The decision template $\boldsymbol{\mathcal{DT}} = \{\mathbf{DT}_j\}$ where $\mathbf{DT}_j$ is the decision template for j^{th} class, computed on the meta-data is given by:

$$\mathbf{DT}_j = \begin{bmatrix} dt_j(1,1) & \dots & dt_j(1,M) \\ \dots & \ddots & \dots \\ dt_j(K,1) & \dots & dt_j(K,M) \end{bmatrix} \tag{3}$$

where each element is computed by:

$$dt_j(k,m) = \frac{\sum_{i=1}^{N} \mathbb{I}[y_j = \hat{y}_i] P_k(y_m|\mathbf{x}_i)}{\sum_{i=1}^{N} \mathbb{I}[y_j = \hat{y}_i]} \tag{4}$$

for $k = 1, ..., K$; $m = 1, ..., M$; $j = 1, ..., M$ in which $\hat{y}_i$ is the true class label of $\mathbf{x}_i$, $\mathbb{I}[\cdot]$ is the indicator function which returns 1 if the condition is true and 0 otherwise. In (4), the $dt_j(k,m)$ is the average value of the meta-data of the observations belonging to the jth class (the condition $y_j = \hat{y}_i$ is true for observations that belong to class y_j) associated with the kth classifier and class label y_m.

In the classification stage, the distance between the meta-data of a test sample $\mathbf{x}$ and $\mathbf{DT}_j (j = 1, ..., M)$ are computed. The class label is assigned to $\mathbf{x}|$ based on the maximum similarity or the minimum dissimilarity between $\mathbf{L}(\mathbf{x})$ and $\mathbf{DT}_j$.

As mentioned in Sect. 1, the Decision Template method has some limitations when modelling skewed data or working with imbalance datasets. We address these disadvantages in our proposed method.

3   Proposed Method

3.1   Problem Formulation

In this study, we focus on searching for the optimal decision template on the meta-data of the training observations for the combining classifiers. For an observation $\mathbf{x}$ and an arbitrary decision template $\mathcal{DT} = \{\mathbf{DT}_j\}$, we compute the similarity between its meta-data $\mathbf{L}(\mathbf{x})$ and $\mathbf{DT}_j$ as:

$$S(\mathbf{L}(\mathbf{x}), \mathbf{DT}_j) = \frac{C\{\mathbf{L}(\mathbf{x}) \cap \mathbf{DT}_j\}}{C\{\mathbf{L}(\mathbf{x}) \cup \mathbf{DT}_j\}} \tag{5}$$

where the relative cardinality $C\{\cdot\}$ is given by:

$$C\{\mathbf{L}(\mathbf{x}) \cap \mathbf{DT}_j\} = \frac{1}{MK} \sum_{k=1}^{K} \sum_{m=1}^{M} \min\left(P_k(y_m|\mathbf{x}), dt_j(k, m)\right) \tag{6}$$

and

$$C\{\mathbf{L}(\mathbf{x}) \cup \mathbf{DT}_j\} = \frac{1}{MK} \sum_{k=1}^{K} \sum_{m=1}^{M} \max\left(P_k(y_m|\mathbf{x}), dt_j(k, m)\right) \tag{7}$$

The class label is assigned to $\mathbf{x}$ by selecting the one that has the maximum similarity among the M decision templates:

$$\mathbf{x} \in y_t \ if \ y_t = \mathrm{argmax}_{y_j, j=1,...,m} S\{\mathbf{L}(\mathbf{x}), \mathbf{DT}_j\} \tag{8}$$

The empirical loss function $\mathcal{L}_{0-1}$ computed on the training set is given by:

$$\mathcal{L}_{0-1}(\mathcal{DT}) = \frac{1}{N} \sum_{i=1}^{N} \mathbb{I}\left[\mathrm{argmax}_{y_j, j=1,...,M} S\{\mathbf{L}(\mathbf{x}_i), \mathbf{DT}_j\} \neq \hat{y}_i \right] \tag{9}$$

where $\mathbf{x}_i$ is the training observation with true label $\hat{y}_i$.

We can simply show that $0 \leq dt_j(k, m) \leq 1$. It is straightforward that: $0 \leq P_k(y_m|\mathbf{x}_i) \leq 1.$. For each $\mathbf{x}_i \in \mathcal{D}$, we have: $0 \leq \mathbb{I}[y_j = \hat{y}_i] P_k(y_m|\mathbf{x}_i) \leq \mathbb{I}[y_j = \hat{y}_i]$. Hence:

$$0 \leq \sum_{i=1}^{N} \mathbb{I}[y_i = \hat{y}_i] P_k(y_m|\mathbf{x}_i) \leq \sum_{i=1}^{N} \mathbb{I}[y_j = \hat{y}_i]$$

Therefore:

$$0 \leq dt_j(k,m) \leq 1 \quad \square \tag{10}$$

To find the optimal decision template for the ensemble, we minimize the loss function (9) subject to the constraints (10).

3.2   The Algorithm

The training phase of the proposed method is given in Algorithms 1 and 2. We first generate the base classifiers $\{BC_k\}$ by learning K learning algorithms on the training set $\mathcal{D}$. The meta-data from the training set is then obtained by the cross validation procedure in the form of matrix $\mathbf{L}$ (1) [13]. Meanwhile, the meta-data of $\mathbf{x}_i \in \mathcal{D}, \mathbf{L}(\mathbf{x}_i)$ is obtained from $\mathbf{L}$ in form of (2).

In this study, we applied the Artificial Bee Colony (ABC) algorithm [4] to find the optimal decision template $\mathcal{ODT}$ that minimize $\mathcal{L}_{0-1}$ on the training set $\mathcal{D}$. The ABC algorithm, proposed by Karaboga [4], is a meta-heuristic search algorithm inspired by the intelligent foraging behavior of honey bee swarms. This algorithm provides a simple but powerful tool to search for the optimal solution with fewer control parameters [16]. In ABC, there are three types of bees in the swarm: employed bee, onlooker bee, and scout. The number of employed bee and onlooker bee is equal to the number of solution in the swarm (denoted by $nPop$). Employed bees exploit the food sources and share the information of nectar amount (the fitness of the solutions) to the onlooker bees. The onlooker bees tend to select good food sources. A food source becomes exhausted if it does not improve through a predetermined number of cycles (denoted by $maxC$). The employed bees of exhausted food sources then become scouts, which start to search for new food sources.

For the candidate generated by the ABC algorithm, $\mathcal{DT} = \{\mathbf{DT}_j = \{dt_j(1,1), dt_j(1,2), ..., dt_j(K,M)\}\}$, we compute the fitness associated with $\mathcal{DT}$ and the probabilistic selection for the candidate by (11) and (12)

$$fitness(\mathcal{DT}) = exp\left(\frac{-\mathcal{L}_{0-1}(\mathcal{DT})}{(\sum \mathcal{L}_{0-1}(\mathcal{DT}))/nPop}\right) \tag{11}$$

$$P(\mathcal{DT}) = \frac{fitness}{\sum_j fitness_j} \tag{12}$$

The value of the loss function $\mathcal{L}_{0-1}(\mathcal{DT})$ associated with the candidate $\mathcal{DT}$ is computed in Algorithm 2. It is the average of the 0–1 loss function of all training observations $\mathbf{x}_i \in \mathcal{D}$

$$\mathcal{L}_{0-1}(\mathcal{DT}) = \frac{1}{N} \sum_{i=1}^{N} \mathcal{L}_{0-1}(\mathbf{x}_i) \tag{13}$$

In the ABC algorithm, the new candidate solution is generated from $\mathcal{DT}$ by searching for its neighborhood. If the solution cannot be improved over the pre-defined number of cycles $maxC$, the food source is abandoned and the employed

Algorithm 1. Training phase

Input: Training set $\mathcal{D}$, K learning algorithms $\{\mathcal{K}_k\}$, maximum number of iteration: $maxT$, population size: $nPop$, abandonment limit parameter: $maxC$
Output: The optimal Decision Template of $\boldsymbol{ODT}$ and $\{BC_k\}$

    (Generate the base classifier)
1: Learn K classifiers $\{BC_k\}$ on $\mathcal{D}$ using $\mathcal{K}_k$, $k = 1, ..., K$
    (Generate the meta-data)
2: Meta-data $\mathbf{L} = \emptyset$
3: **for each** $\mathcal{D}_i$ **do**
4:    $\mathcal{D}^{-i} = \mathcal{D} - \mathcal{D}_i$
5:    Learn ensemble of classifiers on $\mathcal{D}^{-i}$ using $\{\mathcal{K}_k\}$
6:    Classify samples of $\mathcal{D}_i$ by these classifiers
7:    Add outputs on samples in $\mathcal{D}_i$ to $\mathbf{L}$ (1)
8: **end for**
9: Use ABC method: for each $\boldsymbol{DT}$, compute the loss value using Algorithm 2
10: Select the optimal $\boldsymbol{ODT}$ with the smallest loss at the end of ABC
11: Return $\boldsymbol{ODT}$ and $\{BC_k\}$

Algorithm 2. Compute the loss value for each candidate generated in ABC algorithm

Input: Candidate $\boldsymbol{DT}$
Output: The loss value for $\boldsymbol{DT}$

1: **for each** $\mathbf{x}_i \in \mathcal{D}$ **do**
2:    **for each** $\mathbf{DT}_j$ in $\boldsymbol{DT}$ **do**
3:        Compute cardinality between $\mathbf{L}(\mathbf{x}_i)$ and $\mathbf{DT}_j$ (6) (7)
4:        Compute the similarity $S(\mathbf{L}(\mathbf{x}_i), \mathbf{DT}_j)$ (5)
5:    **end for**
6:    Assign the class label y for $\mathbf{x}_i$ by using (8)
7:    $\mathcal{L}_{0-1}(\mathbf{x}_i) = \mathbb{I}[y \neq \hat{y}_i]$
8: **end for**
9: Compute $\mathcal{L}_{0-1}(\boldsymbol{DT})$ by (13)
10: Return $\mathcal{L}_{0-1}(\boldsymbol{DT})$

---

bee of the abandoned food source becomes a scout. We also follow the original ABC algorithm [4,5] to find the new food source with the note that $dt_j(k, m)$ is bounded in $[0, 1]$.

4   Experimental Studies

4.1   Datasets and Experimental Settings

We conducted experiments on 31 datasets selected from the UCI data depository to compare the performance of the proposed method and the benchmark algorithms (Table 1). We chose 3 learning algorithms: LDA, Naïve Bayes, and KNN$_5$ to construct the ensemble system [13]. These algorithms were chosen because they perform significantly different strategies to train the base classifier therefore they ensure the generation of diverse outputs. For the ABC algorithm, we set the

Algorithm 3.   Classification phase

Input: Unlabeled sample **x**, the optimal Decision Template $\{\mathcal{ODT}_j\}$ and $\{BC_k\}$

Output: Predicted class label for **x**

1: Obtain the meta-data $\mathbf{L}(\mathbf{x})$ by using BC_k (2)
2: **for each** $\mathcal{ODT}_j$ **do**
3:    Compute cardinality between $\mathbf{L}(\mathbf{x})$ and $\mathcal{ODT}_j$ (6) (7)
4:    Compute the similarity $S(\mathbf{L}(\mathbf{x}), \mathcal{ODT}_j)$ (5)
5: **end for**
6: Assign the class label by using (8)

maximum number of iterations $maxT$ to 100, the number of food source $nPop$ to 50, and the abandonment limit parameter $maxC$ to $round(0.6 \times K \times nPop)$.

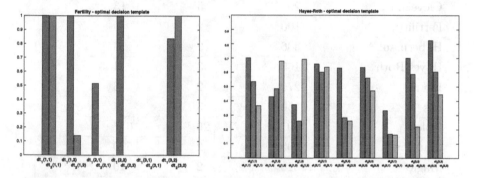

Fig. 2. The Optimal Decision Templates of Fertility and Hayes-Roth datasets

The benchmark algorithms we used are:

- Decision Template [8] and Sum Rule [6]: We used similar settings as in the proposed method.
- ACO1 and ACO2 [2]: The methods aim to search for optimal subset of base classifiers with Decision Tree as meta-classifier (ACO1) or with the optimal meta-classifier (ACO2) for the heterogeneous ensemble. We used the same three learning algorithms as in the proposed method. For ACO2, one of the three learning algorithms was randomly chosen to train the meta-classifier according to the uniform distribution like in [2].
- Random Subspace [1]: We used Decision Tree as the learning algorithm to train 200 base classifiers.
- GA Meta-data [9]: The method searches for the optimal subset of meta-data for heterogeneous ensemble.

We performed 10-fold cross validation and run the test 3 times to obtain 30 test results for each dataset. We used the Wilcoxon signed rank test [3] to compare the

Table 1. Datasets in the experimental studies

Dataset name	# of observations	# of classes	# of dimensions
Abalone	4174	3	8
Appendicitis	106	2	7
Australian	690	2	14
Balance	625	3	4
Banana	5300	2	2
Biodeg	1055	2	41
Breast-Cancer	683	2	9
Bupa	345	2	6
Cleveland	297	5	13
Fertility	100	2	9
Haberman	306	2	3
Hayes-Roth	160	3	4
Heart	270	2	13
Iris	150	3	4
Isolet	7797	26	617
Madelon	2000	2	500
Magic	19020	2	10
Musk1	476	2	166
Musk2	6598	2	166
Newthyroid	215	3	5
Page-Blocks	5472	5	10
Phoneme	5404	2	5
Pima	768	2	8
Ring	7400	2	20
Skin_NonSkin	245057	2	3
Spambase	4601	2	57
Vehicle	846	4	18
Vertebral	310	3	6
Waveform_w_Noise	5000	3	40
Waveform_wo_Noise	5000	3	21
Wdbc	569	2	30

classification results of the proposed method and each benchmark algorithm on each dataset. The performance scores of two methods are treated as significantly different if the p-value of the test is smaller than a given significance level. For all tests, the level of significance was set to 0.05. The details of these tests can be found in [3].

4.2 Results and Discussions

Comparison of Benchmark Algorithms: Table 2 shows the mean and standard deviation of classification error rate computed on 30 runs on each experimental dataset. Because of the singularity property of the covariance matrix of the meta-data [13], some learning methods such as LDA cannot be used as a meta-classifier. This explains why ACO2 cannot be run on the Iris dataset in the experiment. Therefore ACO2 and the proposed method were compared on 30 datasets. The proposed method is developed to work on diverse datasets, not only handling imbalanced ones. Therefore we did not use an appropriate metric to evaluate imbalanced data.

From the Wilcoxon test results in Table 2, we can see that the proposed method is better than the benchmark algorithms on the experimental datasets. Compared to Random Subspace, the proposed method wins on 14 datasets and loses on 6 datasets. Our method also performs better than Sum Rule (the proposed method wins in 21 cases and loses in only 1 case) and Decision Template (the proposed method wins in 21 cases).

In comparison to GA Meta-data, the proposed method wins on 14 datasets while does not lose on any dataset. The pattern is nearly similar when comparing to ACO1 as ours wins on 18 datasets. The proposed method meanwhile performs slightly better compared to ACO2 as ours wins in 5 cases and loses in 2 cases.

Discussion: We explain some reasons why the proposed method is better than the benchmark algorithms. Random Subspace generates the new training sets by choosing observations with a random subset of features from the original feature set. On datasets with high dimension like Musk1 and Musk2 (166 features), Random Subspace can generate the new diverse training sets, resulting in high classification accuracy. Obviously, the proposed method is significantly better than Sum Rule because Sum Rule do not train the combiner on the meta-data of the training set.

GA Meta-data meanwhile uses GA to learn the optimal subset of meta-data from the training set. Since the dimension of the meta-data depends on the number of class labels and the number of learning algorithms, for datasets with a small number of class labels, the subset of meta-data is not diverse enough to enhance the ensemble performance. ACO1 searches for the optimal subset of base classifiers for the training set. The limitation of not searching for meta-classifier makes ACO1 ineffective on many datasets. ACO2 meanwhile performs well since it searches for not only the base classifiers but also the meta-classifier for the optimal solution.

Table 2. Classification error rates of the benchmark algorithms and the proposed method

Dataset	Sum Rule	Random Subspace	Decision Template	GA Meta-data	ACO1	ACO2	Proposed Method
Abalone	0.4681±0.0183	0.4679±0.0255	0.4867±0.0197	0.4736±0.0233	0.4720±0.0283	0.4531±0.0178	0.4553±0.0198
Appendicitis	0.1197±0.0940	0.1385±0.0861	0.1173±0.0846	0.1600±0.1018	0.1877±0.1229	0.1488±0.0940	0.1358±0.0934
Australian	0.1411±0.0355	0.1522±0.0330	0.1382±0.0317	0.1807±0.0360	0.1816±0.0488	0.1280±0.0367	0.1314±0.0339
Balance	0.1099±0.0221	0.2129±0.0355	0.0976±0.0312	0.0852±0.0331	0.0960±0.0285	0.0959±0.0577	0.0853±0.0325
Banana	0.1098±0.0097	0.3746±0.0469	0.1117±0.0117	0.1116±0.0111	0.1129±0.0152	0.1122±0.0117	0.1093±0.0109
Biodeg	0.1425±0.0313	0.1352±0.0251	0.1387±0.0303	0.1836±0.0350	0.1800±0.0348	0.1368±0.0386	0.1286±0.0230
Breast-Cancer	0.0464±0.0260	0.0283±0.0220	0.0459±0.0267	0.0420±0.0285	0.0405±0.0264	0.0347±0.0240	0.0361±0.0248
Bupa	0.2899±0.0532	0.3420±0.0762	0.3324±0.0790	0.3804±0.0925	0.3548±0.0737	0.3209±0.0743	0.2967±0.0625
Cleveland	0.4218±0.0561	0.4184±0.0380	0.4454±0.0615	0.4433±0.0637	0.4642±0.0781	0.4041±0.0706	0.4141±0.0688
Fertility	0.1333±0.0537	0.1200±0.0400	0.4167±0.1655	0.1900±0.1136	0.1467±0.0562	0.1300±0.0526	0.1533±0.0670
Haberman	0.2595±0.0470	0.2961±0.0548	0.3103±0.0574	0.2964±0.0476	0.2984±0.0415	0.2801±0.0507	0.2822±0.0518
Hayes-Roth	0.3417±0.1450	0.3458±0.1395	0.4292±0.1278	0.2917±0.0959	0.2708±0.1145	0.2833±0.1079	0.3000±0.0919
Heart	0.1704±0.0609	0.1877±0.0765	0.1741±0.0559	0.2395±0.0832	0.2185±0.0909	0.1815±0.0692	0.1691±0.0639
Iris	0.0333±0.0375	0.0511±0.0536	0.0333±0.0375	0.0333±0.0413	0.0400±0.0442	-	0.0289±0.0330
Isolet	0.0656±0.0097	0.0588±0.0078	0.0583±0.0093	0.0623±0.0081	0.0650±0.0081	0.0491±0.0076	0.0561±0.0085
Madelon	0.3680±0.0331	0.3800±0.0325	0.2868±0.0290	0.2870±0.0264	0.2870±0.0264	0.2882±0.0254	0.2832±0.0232
Magic	0.1909±0.0061	0.1730±0.0068	0.1901±0.0079	0.1920±0.0117	0.1902±0.0069	0.1918±0.0302	0.1852±0.0068
Musk1	0.1471±0.0426	0.0805±0.0356	0.1308±0.0452	0.1344±0.0401	0.1245±0.0420	0.1205±0.0470	0.1092±0.0406
Musk2	0.0497±0.0078	0.0209±0.0035	0.0463±0.0068	0.0350±0.0059	0.0355±0.0059	0.0399±0.0226	0.0349±0.0055
Newthyroid	0.0948±0.0507	0.0420±0.0390	0.0684±0.0492	0.0371±0.0350	0.0418±0.0369	0.0668±0.0465	0.0573±0.0444
Page-Blocks	0.0497±0.0069	0.0319±0.0055	0.0504±0.0082	0.0420±0.0066	0.0462±0.0085	0.0422±0.0077	0.0431±0.0071
Phoneme	0.1747±0.0173	0.1627±0.0183	0.1780±0.0278	0.1149±0.0145	0.1149±0.0145	0.1163±0.0161	0.1153±0.0137
Pima	0.2465±0.0437	0.2570±0.0477	0.2465±0.0427	0.3056±0.0484	0.3078±0.0485	0.2309±0.0490	0.2288±0.0477
Ring	0.2088±0.0110	0.0298±0.0051	0.1930±0.0128	0.1231±0.0135	0.1211±0.0114	0.1140±0.0126	0.1068±0.0125
Skin_NonSkin	4.12E-02±1.10E-03	2.62E-03±2.74E-04	3.30E-02±1.07E-03	4.31E-04±1.19E-04	4.34E-04±1.13E-04	4.39E-04±1.09E-04	4.15E-04±1.20E-04
Spambase	0.0969±0.0116	0.0960±0.0135	0.0920±0.0109	0.1185±0.0140	0.1224±0.0172	0.0942±0.0131	0.0909±0.0116
Vehicle	0.2605±0.0427	0.2600±0.0361	0.2151±0.0337	0.2627±0.0435	0.2597±0.0379	0.2187±0.0362	0.2186±0.0360
Vertebral	0.2054±0.0603	0.2893±0.0568	0.1925±0.0648	0.1893±0.0581	0.1527±0.0589	0.1516±0.0501	0.1785±0.0605
Waveform_w_Noise	0.1671±0.0127	0.1755±0.0171	0.1634±0.0140	0.1787±0.0143	0.1770±0.0149	0.1457±0.0136	0.1459±0.0163
Waveform_wo_Noise	0.1646±0.0186	0.1498±0.0191	0.1562±0.0181	0.1738±0.0211	0.1705±0.0166	0.1389±0.0188	0.1389±0.0168
Wdbc	0.0352±0.0188	0.0381±0.0187	0.0346±0.0190	0.0352±0.0249	0.0457±0.0292	0.0305±0.0197	0.0305±0.0175
	Win: 21	Win: 14	Win: 21	Win: 14	Win: 18	Win: 5	
	Equal: 9	Equal: 11	Equal: 10	Equal: 17	Equal: 13	Equal: 23	
	Loss: 1	Loss: 6	Loss: 0	Loss: 0	Loss: 0	Loss: 2	

Finally, the proposed method is significantly better than the Decision Template method. Figure 2 illustrates the optimal decision templates on the Fertility and Hayes-Roth datasets. It is clear that for imbalanced datasets like Fertility, while the decision template is nearly identical among the two class labels, the optimal decision template from our algorithm can clearly distinguish between the two class labels. In proposed method, we search for the optimal decision template that maximizes the discrimination between the different classes and that strategy does not take into account by the Decision Template method.

5   Conclusions

In summary, we proposed a combining algorithm for heterogeneous ensemble systems. Our method is motivated by the observation that Decision Template method, a popular combining algorithm for heterogeneous ensemble, underperforms on imbalanced datasets because of the similar representations for the class labels. In addition, the average value-based meta-data representation in this method is not good for data with a skewed distribution. To overcome these limitations, we proposed the method to search for a decision template yielding an optimal representation for the meta-data. We used ABC algorithm to minimize the empirical 0–1 loss function on the training set to obtain the optimal solution. For the classification process, we assigned the label for a sample based on the maximization of similarity between the optimal templates and the sample's meta-data. Experiments on 31 UCI datasets showed that the proposed method is better than the selected benchmark algorithms.

References

1. Barandiaran, I.: The random subspace method for constructing decision forests. IEEE Trans. Pattern Anal. Mach. Intell. **20**(8), 1–22 (1998)
2. Chen, Y., Wong, M.L., Li, H.: Applying ant colony optimization to configuring stacking ensembles for data mining. Expert Syst. Appl. **41**(6), 2688–2702 (2014)
3. Demšar, J.: Statistical comparisons of classifiers over multiple data sets. J. Mach. Learn. Res. **7**(Jan), 1–30 (2006)
4. Karaboga, D.: An idea based on honey bee swarm for numerical optimization. Technical report, Technical report-tr06, Erciyes University, Engineering Faculty, Computer Engineering Department (2005)
5. Karaboga, D., Akay, B.: A comparative study of artificial bee colony algorithm. Appl. Math. Comput. **214**(1), 108–132 (2009)
6. Kittler, J., Hatef, M., Duin, R.P., Matas, J.: On combining classifiers. IEEE Trans. Pattern Anal. Mach. Intell. **20**(3), 226–239 (1998)
7. Kuncheva, L.I.: Combining Pattern Classifiers: Methods and Algorithms. Wiley, Hoboken (2004)
8. Kuncheva, L.I., Bezdek, J.C., Duin, R.P.: Decision templates for multiple classifier fusion: an experimental comparison. Pattern Recogn. **34**(2), 299–314 (2001)
9. Nguyen, T.T., Liew, A.W.-C., Pham, X.C., Nguyen, M.P.: A novel 2-stage combining classifier model with stacking and genetic algorithm based feature selection. In: Huang, D.-S., Jo, K.-H., Wang, L. (eds.) ICIC 2014. LNCS (LNAI), vol. 8589, pp. 33–43. Springer, Cham (2014). https://doi.org/10.1007/978-3-319-09339-0_4

10. Nguyen, T.T., Liew, A.W.C., Tran, M.T., Pham, X.C., Nguyen, M.P.: A novel genetic algorithm approach for simultaneous feature and classifier selection in multi classifier system. In: 2014 IEEE Congress on Evolutionary Computation (CEC), pp. 1698–1705. IEEE (2014)
11. Nguyen, T.T., Nguyen, M.P., Pham, X.C., Liew, A.W.C.: Heterogeneous classifier ensemble with fuzzy rule-based meta learner. Inf. Sci. **422**, 144–160 (2018)
12. Nguyen, T.T., Nguyen, M.P., Pham, X.C., Liew, A.W.C., Pedrycz, W.: Combining heterogeneous classifiers via granular prototypes. Appl. Soft Comput. **73**, 795–815 (2018)
13. Nguyen, T.T., Nguyen, T.T.T., Pham, X.C., Liew, A.W.C.: A novel combining classifier method based on variational inference. Pattern Recogn. **49**, 198–212 (2016)
14. Nguyen, T.T., Pham, X.C., Liew, A.W.C., Pedrycz, W.: Aggregation of classifiers: a justifiable information granularity approach. IEEE Trans. Cybern. **49**, 2168–2177 (2018)
15. Şen, M.U., Erdogan, H.: Linear classifier combination and selection using group sparse regularization and hinge loss. Pattern Recogn. Lett. **34**(3), 265–274 (2013)
16. Shunmugapriya, P., Kanmani, S.: Optimization of stacking ensemble configurations through artificial bee colony algorithm. Swarm Evol. Comput. **12**, 24–32 (2013)
17. Ting, K.M., Witten, I.H.: Issues in stacked generalization. J. Artif. Intell. Res. **10**, 271–289 (1999)
18. Zhou, Z.H.: Ensemble Methods: Foundations and Algorithms. Chapman and Hall/CRC, Boca Raton (2012)

Performance Comparison of Type-1 and Type-2 Neuro-Fuzzy Controllers for a Flexible Joint Manipulator

Afshar Shamsi Jokandan[1(✉)], Abbas Khosravi[2(✉)], and Saeid Nahavandi[2(✉)]

[1] University of Tabriz, Tabriz, East Azerbaijan, Iran
afshar.shamsi.j@gmail.com
[2] Institute for Intelligent Systems Research and Innovation,
Deakin University, Geelong, Australia
{abbas.khosravi,saeid.nahavandi}@deakin.edu.au

Abstract. Flexible joint manipulators are extensively used in several industries and precise control of their nonlinear dynamics has proven to be a challenging task. In this work, we want to compare two intelligent controllers by proposing two Takagi-Sugeno-Kang Neuro-Fuzzy Approaches (Type-1 and Type-2) to control a flexible joint. For both controllers, The inverse models are found using identification techniques, then they are put in series as inverse controllers to control the flexible joint in an online structure. Interval weights are trained by gradient descent approaches using backpropagation algorithms. Results reveal that, without any knowledge about the dynamic of the robot, the methods can control the flexible joint which is highly unstable. As illustrated in result section, One level more fuzziness of Type-2 in compare to type-1 fuzzy controllers helps this controller to more effectively deals with information from a knowledge base. The proposed models can effectively handle uncertainties arising from friction and other structural nonlinearities.

Keywords: Type-2 neuro-fuzzy · Type-1 neuro-fuzzy · Gradient descent

In recent years, Flexible Joint Robots (FJR)s with their nonlinear dynamics have been used for different purposes to perform commands with high sensitivity and accuracy [1]. For nonlinear dynamics, traditional controllers have low stability as they are sensitive to internal and external disturbance. These difficulties lead to the emergence of new controllers such as adaptive, robust and intelligent controllers [2]. Fuzzy controllers were widely used in control systems due to their ability to approximate the mapping from input to output with preferred accuracy [3]. In this regard, Takagi-Sugeno-Kang (TSK) [4] fuzzy model is a powerful tool to control complex systems by using different linear control laws. Zadeh proposed type-2 (T2) fuzzy logic to preclude some drawbacks of type-1 (T1) fuzzy logic [5]. The membership function of a T2 fuzzy set is uncertain

© Springer Nature Switzerland AG 2019
T. Gedeon et al. (Eds.): ICONIP 2019, LNCS 11953, pp. 621–632, 2019.
https://doi.org/10.1007/978-3-030-36708-4_51

(footprint of uncertainty) which enable the model to handle the uncertainties more easily than T1 fuzzy sets [6].

Mendel revealed that T2 fuzzy logic has one level more fuzziness which can be useful for inexact and uncertain variables [7]. In that article the foot print of uncertainty (FOU) consists of three dimensional membership functions adding computational complexities to T2 fuzzy systems. To overcome this difficulty, interval T2 fuzzy logic (T2FL) is emerged which is consists of membershib functions that have the value of one. Karnik and Mendel [8] showed that interval T2FL can be resembled as a combination of many different T1FL.

Researchers often use a combination of both neural networks and T2 fuzzy logic [9]. In [10] the structure of the T2 TSK neuro-fuzzy system was proposed. Updating rules for parameters are based on fuzzy clustering for antecedent and gradient descent learning algorithm. Extracting fuzzy rules for interval T2 neuro-fuzzy is proposed in [11]; In that study for learning the parameters, the antecedent parts and regulation parameters are trained using the error back-propagation learning; Kalman filter also helps to improve accuracy by adjusting the consequent part parameters.

Castro presented three different structures for interval T2 neuro-fuzzy networks and two ways for fuzzification (T2 fuzzy neuron and adaptive nodes) [12]. He also used two type reduction algorithms (Karnik-Mendel algorithm and adaptive layers). There are several methods to train T2 fuzzy neural networks such as genetic algorithm [13] and particle swarm optimization [14]. In order to reduce the rules in a fuzzy system, Farrokhi and Moodi used T-norms and S-norms [15]. In recent years, T2 neuro-fuzzy approach has been using for different purposes such as load forecasting [16], robot control [17] and sliding mode control [18]. Over the past years, researchers have grown a preference for adaptive inverse controllers. In this technique, the inverse model of the system is identified and can be used as a controller [19]. Li et al. suggested an inverse controller based on least squares methods to control a cable-driven parallel mechanism [20]. In [21], adaptive neuro-fuzzy inverse control is used to control the level of the water and compare this method with fuzzy control method.

T2 fuzzy logic has become more popular in recent years due to their flexibility in approximating the nonlinear dynamics [22]. FJRs have high level of nonlinearity in their dynamics. The FJR considered in this study has several sources of uncertainties which are listed below:

- Uncertainty in shaft encoders may change the dynamic of the model by generating additional terms which should be added to the mathematical model of the robot.
- Link flexibility which has tolerance.
- The exact model of motor cannot be obtained.
- The experimental samples for the training part are extracted by manually adjusting the FJR which may lead to noisy data.

For handling these uncertainties, we use two intelligent controllers which do not need any information about the dynamic of the model. In this paper, we design

Fig. 1. A single link FJR

T2 neuro-fuzzy (T2NF) and T1 neuro-fuzzy (T1NF) controllers for a flexible joint. We use both T1NF and T2NF structures trained using backpropagation algorithm to control an uncertain FJR. Performances of T1 and T2 controllers implemented on a simulated FJR are compared and discussed in details. T2NF is also applied to the real world FJR to check its real world performance.

This paper is organized as follows: Sect. 1 introduces the model of FJR used in this research. In Sect. 2, T1NF and T2NF structures are explained in details. The design of online inverse controllers is described in Sect. 3. Section 4 discusses obtained results and performance comparison of T1NF and T2NF controllers. Finally, the study is summarized in Sect. 5.

1   Modeling of the Flexible Joint

A single FJR used for experiments in this study is shown in Fig. 1. Several fixed ball-rings on parallel bases are used to fix shafts [23]. Dynamic equations of the robot are obtained by Lagrange equations as:

$$\left(I_L + m_p(l)^2\right)\frac{d^2}{dt}\theta_1 + \left(\frac{1}{2}m_l + m_p\right)gl\sin\theta_1 = U_c - U_{FL} - U_{EI} \tag{1}$$

$$J\frac{d^2}{dt}\theta_2 + B\frac{d}{dt}\theta_2 = U_{in} - U_{Fa} - U_{E2} \tag{2}$$

where U_{E1}, U_{E2} are axles position shaft-encoders torques. U_{Fa} and U_{FL} are friction torques in the link and actuator which are generated by viscous and coulomb frictions and can be written as:

$$U_{FL} = F_{VL}\frac{d}{dt}\theta_1 + U_{CL} \tag{3}$$

$$U_{ca} = C_f\left(\tan(C\frac{d}{dt}\theta_2) + \frac{A\frac{d}{dt}\theta_2}{1 + B\frac{d^2}{dt}\theta_2^2}\right); \frac{d}{dt}\theta_2 \in \Re \tag{4}$$

$$S_f = Max\left(C_f\left(\tan(C\frac{d}{dt}\theta_2) + \frac{A\frac{d}{dt}\theta_2}{1 + B\frac{d^2}{dt}\theta_2^2}\right)\right) \tag{5}$$

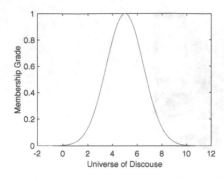

Fig. 2. T1 membership function   Fig. 3. Uncertainty in mean

here C_f is the coefficient of kinetic. S_f can be used instead of C_f as its upper limit. Saturated motor modeling can be written as [24]:

$$u_{motor} = \frac{K_m \left(V_m - K_b \frac{d}{dt}\theta_m\right)}{L_s + R} \tanh \left(\frac{\left(V_m - K_B \frac{d}{dt}\theta_2\right)}{(L_S + R)\, i_{a(Max)}}\right) \qquad (6)$$

In FJRs, gearbox has following equations [24]:

$$U_c = \hat{a}_1\varphi + \hat{a}_3\varphi^3 + \hat{a}_5\varphi^5 \qquad (7)$$

where $\hat{a}_i$ can be obtained as:

$$\hat{a}_i = a_i\left(1 + w_{ai}\right) \qquad (8)$$

$$a_i = \left(\frac{a_i^- - a_i^+}{2} \in \Re^+\right) \text{ or } \left(a_i^- \text{ and } a_i^+ \in \Re^-\right) \qquad (9)$$

$$w_{ai} \;<\; \left\|\; \frac{\mid a_i^- - a_i^+ \mid}{a_i^- + a_i^+} \;\right\| \qquad (10)$$

The equation of the FJR can be obtained by substituting the parameters in (1) and (2). As discussed above, the approximations are used to obtain some parameters such as friction. These approximations add some uncertainties.

2   T1 and T2 Neuro Fuzzy Systems

A T1 fuzzy set A in X is defined in X by $A = (x, \mu_A(x)) \mid \forall x \in X$ where μ_A is the membership function of A $\mu_A : X \to [0, 1]$. Figure 2 shows a typical T1 fuzzy set with Gaussian distribution. The TSK-style fuzzy rules can be written as:

$$IF\ x_1 is\ A_{1n}\ and \cdots and\ x_m\ is\ A_{mn}, THEN\ y = \beta_{0n}+\beta_{1n}x_1+\cdots+\beta_{mn}x_m \qquad (11)$$

which shows that output (y) is a linear combination of inputs as been illustrated in Fig. 4.

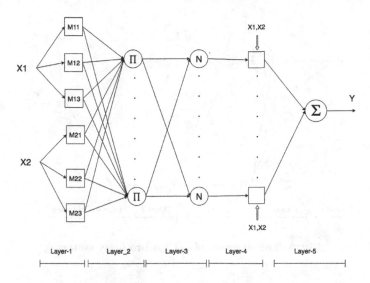

Fig. 4. The structure of a T1 neuro fuzzy system

For doing a compare between two class of Neuro-Fuzzy systems. We also design a T2NF which is very similar in structure to T2NF. The only difference is that T2 structures are using one level more fuzziness than T1 structures. The membership degree of T1 is a crisp number. However when it fixed, It cannot deal with extra uncertainty. Thus T2 fuzzy sets are emerged. The membership degree of a T2 fuzzy set is a T1 fuzzy number (T2 fuzzy sets can be resembled as several T1 fuzzy sets packed together). The typical gaussian T2 membership function is shown in Fig. 3, which shows a fixed standard deviation σ and uncertain means that are in $[m_1, m_2]$. The colored part of the figure is called foot print of uncertainty.

In T2 TSK fuzzy system, the output is T1 fuzzy sets. The suggested T2 TSK fuzzy system has 6 layers. Which is shown in Fig. 5. An example of fuzzy rules for this structure can be written as:

$$R^k \ : \ if \ X_1 \ is \ \hat{A}_n^k \ then \ \hat{y}_k \ = \ C_{k,0} + C_{k,1}x_1 + \cdots + C_{k,n}x_n \qquad (12)$$

In the above equation $X = \{x_1, x_2, \cdots, x_n\}$ is input of the system, $\{\hat{A}_1^k, \hat{A}_2^k, \ldots, \hat{A}_k^k\}$ are T2 membership functions, $\hat{y}_k$ is the system output which has a fuzzy value and $C_{k,i} \in [c_{k,i} - s_{k,i}, c_{k,i} + s_{k,i}]$ are coefficients of the consequent part and are T1 fuzzy sets. $c_{k,i}$ and $s_{k,i}$ are means and widths of Gaussian membership function. For better understanding the structure of T2 neuro-fuzzy, each layer is explained as follows:

Layer 0: This layer has two nodes. The number of nodes are equal to the number of inputs. This layer is also called input layer.

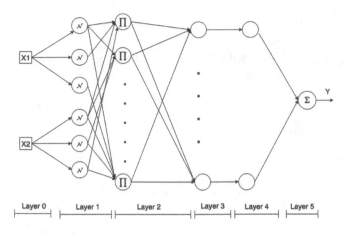

Layer 0   Layer 1   Layer 2   Layer 3   Layer 4   Layer 5

Fig. 5. The structure of a T2 neuro fuzzy system

Layer 1: In this layer, inputs are become fuzzy. The output of this layer is as:

$$^1\mu_{k,i}(x_i, [\sigma_{k,i}, {}^1m_{k,i}]) = e^{-0.5\left(\frac{x_i - {}^1m_{k,i}}{\sigma_{k,i}}\right)^2} \tag{13}$$

$$^2\mu_{k,i}(x_i, [\sigma_{k,i}, {}^2m_{k,i}]) = e^{-0.5\left(\frac{x_i - {}^2m_{k,i}}{\sigma_{k,i}}\right)^2} \tag{14}$$

Based on the T-norm and S-norm, the output of a T2 fuzzy neuron is produced by calculating the upper and lower bounds of membership function.

$$\underline{\mu}_{k,i}(x_i) = {}^1\mu_{k,i}(x_i) \times^2 \mu_{k,i}(x_i) \tag{15}$$

$$\bar{\mu}_{k,i}(x_i) = {}^1\mu_{k,i}(x_i) +^2 \mu_{k,i}(x_i) - \underline{\mu}_{k,i}(x_i) \tag{16}$$

Layer 2: This layer is called rule layer. In this layer AND operation is done as bellow:

$$\underline{f}^k = \prod_{i=1}^{n} \underline{\mu}_{k,i} \; ; \; \bar{f}^k = \prod_{i=1}^{n} \bar{\mu}_{k,i} \tag{17}$$

Layer 3: This layer is called result layer. A linear combination of inputs are produced here:

$$y_l^k = \sum_{i=1}^{n} c_{k,i}x_i + c_{k,0} - \sum_{i=1}^{n} s_{k,i} \mid x_i \mid -s_{k,0} \tag{18}$$

$$y_r^k = \sum_{i=1}^{n} c_{k,i}x_i + c_{k,0} + \sum_{i=1}^{n} s_{k,i} \mid x_i \mid +s_{k,0} \tag{19}$$

Layer 4: This layer is called type reduction layer which is done by Karnik-Mendel algorithms where the centroid of the whole result rules is calculated:

$$\hat{y}_l = \frac{\sum_{k=1}^{M} f_l^k y_l^k}{\sum_{k=1}^{M} f_l} \; ; \; \hat{y}_r = \frac{\sum_{k=1}^{M} f_r^k y_r^k}{\sum_{k=1}^{M} f_r} \tag{20}$$

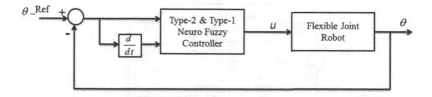

Fig. 6. T2 TSK neuro-fuzzy network structure

Layer 5: The final output of the network is calculated:

$$\hat{y} = \frac{\hat{y}_l + \hat{y}_r}{2} \tag{21}$$

3   Controller Design

The structure of our proposed T1NF and T2NF controllers are shown in Fig. 6. Note that two controllers are acting separately (although the figure shows two controllers in a single box, for a given input-output pair we use each controller separately). In this architecture, T2NF inverse model is placed in series with the flexible joint. In order to obtain the inverse model of FJR, training process is shown in Fig. 7. The data are acquired from real experiments to reflect input-output characteristics of the FJR. The inputs and the outputs of the training data are the values of $(\theta, \frac{d}{dt}\theta)$ (θ is the angle of the FJR) and the corresponding control signal u. Using 320 training samples $((\theta_1, \frac{d}{dt}\theta_1, u_1), (\theta_2, \frac{d}{dt}\theta_2, u_2), \cdots, (\theta_{320}, \frac{d}{dt}\theta_{320}, u_{320}))$, T2NF is trained using the gradient descent algorithm to minimize the error function. The same process is also applied for finding the inverse model of FJR and using it as a controller to control the robot by T1NF network. For both controllers the same data is used to identify the inverse dynamic.

In order to accelerate the training part of T2NF, it is better to find the minimum and the maximum of the input signal. Thus input can be divided into equal sections each corresponding to a fuzzy membership function. For example, if the desired point is $\theta = 90$, we could use 5 membership functions. Membership functions can be written as: $(mean = 0, d = 20)$, $(m = 20, d = 20)$, $(m = 40, d = 20)$, $(m = 60, d = 20)$, and $(m = 80, d = 20)$. Please note that these numbers are not optimal and just mentioned as an example. The above algorithm could be done automatically as well, in a way that the maximum of the input can be calculated, then the input space could be divided into equal membership functions.

After training the controllers based on Fig. 7, they are put in series with the FJR as shown in Fig. 6. It is note that for each controller, the inverse of the model is found by identification techniques in an offline process then it is used as a controller in an online process. For the robot to follow θ_{Ref}, the trained controllers produce a correspondent control signal for the robot. Now the robot

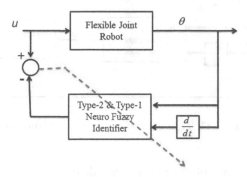

Fig. 7. Training section of T2NF (identification of the inverse model)

has its input and goes to θ_{out}. The difference between $\theta_{Ref} - \theta_{out}$ is called error term. The controllers try to minimize the error term by adjusting the parameters by backpropagating the error using gradient descent algorithm. This process will continue until the differences are near to zero. In our application of controlling the FJR, we tune both parameters of the antecedent part and the consequent part of the T2NF inverse structure to approximate the characteristics of the robot.

4   Experimental Results and Discussion

In this section, experimental results for implementation of T2NF on a real FJR are demonstrated. For T2NF, the real experiments are compare with the simulated ones. Also, the simulation of the robot is used to give a comparison between our two controllers (T2NF & T1NF) on some desired points. The robots coefficients are shown in Table 1. It is obvious that some parameters have tolerances which add some level of uncertainties to the robot.

The root mean square error (RMSE) is defined as:

$$RMSE = (\frac{1}{n}\Sigma_{i=1}^{n}(y - \hat{y}_i)^2)^{\frac{1}{2}} \tag{22}$$

where y is the desired output and $\hat{y}_i$ is output of the system in the ith iteration. n is the number of iterations which ensures that the robot goes to desired point. The initial values for W, S, and C are set to one. The initial values for inputs are shown in Tables 2 and 3 for both controllers. Three gaussian membership functions for each input (6 membership functions totally) which leads to 9 rules per controller. In order to have a good comparison, equal number of rules are selected.

Figure 8 shows the RMSE for $\theta = 90$ (training data) for both controllers for 500 epochs. $\theta = 90$ is one of the critical points for this robot since the flexibility easily disturbs its equilibrium. Figure 8 shows that RMSE is sharps drop up to epoch 100. Then it is gradually reduced until full convergence by epoch 400.

Table 1. FJR properties.

Parameters	Nominal values	Tolerance
Joint stifness	$a_1 = 3.35$	1.5%
Joint stifness	$a_3 = -0.16$	97%
Link length	$L = 0.53$	6%
Link mass	$M = 0.12$	9%
Gravity coefficient	$g = 9.8$	1%
Inertia	$I = 0.083$	4%
Coil inductance	$l = 0.1\text{H}$	5%
Torque constant	$K_m = 3.3$	3%
Back emf constant	$K_b = 5.62$	3%
Gearbox ratio	$N = 100:1$	—
Motor inertia	$J = 2.15$	3%
Operating maximum voltage	$V = 36$	—
Max. armature current	$i_a(Max) = 4A$	—

Table 2. The initial values of the first and second inputs of T2

$M_{11} = 20$	$m_{11} = 10$	$z_{11} = 10$	$M_{12} = 7$	$m_{12} = 3$	$z_{12} = 10$
$M_{21} = 50$	$m_{21} = 40$	$z_{21} = 10$	$M_{22} = 1$	$m_{22} = -4$	$z_{22} = 10$
$M_{31} = 90$	$m_{31} = 70$	$z_{31} = 10$	$M_{32} = -7$	$m_{32} = -9$	$z_{32} = 10$

(T2 converges faster to optimal minimum during training). The responses to $\theta = 90$ are shown in Fig. 9 as well. It is obvious that both controllers can control the robot effectively. Accordingly, although T2NF controller has a bigger overshoot, it is more quickly converges to the desired point in comparison to T1NF controller. This clearly highlights the advantage of using T2NF. This is mainly due to the promising ability of T2 fuzzy sets to handle uncertainty in an efficient way. The bigger overshoot for T2NF is caused by transforming the T1 fuzzy set to the T2 fuzzy set.

$\theta = 74$ cannot be achieved during the identification process (when we manually adjust the FJR to extract the input-output pairs). Thus it can be used for testing controllers. Figure 10 shows the responses to unseen data in simulations. Table 4 also shows some quantitative metrics for results of both controllers.

Table 3. The initial values of the first and second inputs of T1

$m_{11} = 10$	$z_{11} = 10$	$m_{12} = 3$	$z_{12} = 10$
$m_{21} = 40$	$z_{21} = 10$	$m_{22} = -4$	$z_{22} = 10$
$m_{31} = 70$	$z_{31} = 10$	$m_{32} = -9$	$z_{32} = 10$

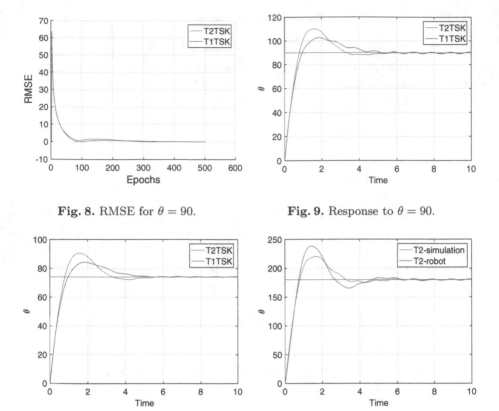

Fig. 8. RMSE for $\theta = 90$.

Fig. 9. Response to $\theta = 90$.

Fig. 10. Response to $\theta = 74$.

Fig. 11. Response to $\theta = 180$.

Due to computational complexity of T2NF (T2 fuzzy membership functions) the overshoot for T2 controller is larger than T1 controller which leads to higher settling time. The RMSE calculated for 500 epochs shows that T2 has lower RMSE than T1. RMSE is also called fit function. Thus T2 is fitter than T1 in approximating the model. 0.9% improvement is achieved, when T2 is used instead of T1.

Figure 11 illustrates the response of real FJR and simulated one for T2 controller. By saving the output response of the robot at $\theta = 180$, we can compare our controller with simulation. $\theta = 180$ is also a critical point since it can be easily unstable. Experimental results reveal that T2NF could conduct the robot to the desired point. However overshoot and settling time is increased in real experience. There is also an undershoot is seen in the real experience which may because of time consuming computations of T2 fuzzy sets. The state-of-the-art T2NF is a powerful controller which has the potential of handling uncertainties with acceptable accuracy.

Table 4. Quantitative comparison

Type	Overshoot	Settling time	Peak	RMSE
$T2$	22.30	4.443	90.50	2.5%
$T1$	13.85	4.288	84.25	3.4%

5 Conclusion

In this paper, T2NF and T1NF are applied to control a flexible joint. The equation of FJR shows that it has uncertainty in its dynamic. The controllers are first trained offline with training data in order to find the inverse model of FJR. Then the trained T2NF is placed in series with the FJR in order to control that in an online structure. We use nonlinear rules and to reduce them, T-norm and S-norm are used to calculate the approximations of Gaussian function. Karnik-Mendel algorithm is used for defuzzification. These Controllers do not need any background knowledge about the dynamic of the system. This approach could be applied to more challenging systems with unstable dynamics. In this regard, future works and studies could be divided into one of the following parts:

- T2 fuzzy controllers are slow in nature. There are some techniques which increase their computational speed such as normalization techniques or using different optimization algorithms such as mean least square.
- Both training and control process could applied online (the training process is offline in this article), but it may be expensive.
- Try to reduce the nonlinear rules by different methods which will increase the speed of the controller.

References

1. Siciliano, B.: Control in robotics: open problems and future directions. In: IEEE International Conference on Control Applications, vol. 1, no. 1, pp. 81–85 (1998)
2. Khorasani, K.: Adaptive control of FJR. IEEE J. Robot. Autom. **8**(2), 250–267 (1992)
3. Long, Z., Yuan, Y., Xu, Y., Du, S.: High-accuracy positioning of lathe servo system using fuzzy controllers based on variable universe of discourse. Int. J. Smart Sens. Intell. Syst. **7**(3), 1114–1133 (2014)
4. Ho, W.H., Chou, J.H.: Design of optimal controllers for Takagi-Sugeno fuzzy-model-based systems. IEEE Trans. Syst. Man Cybern. A **37**(3), 329–339 (2007)
5. Zadeh, L.A.: The concept of a linguistic variable and its application to approximate reasoning. Inf. Sci. **8**(3), 199–249 (1975)
6. Hagras, H.: A hierarchical type-2 fuzzy logic control architecture for autonomous mobile robots. IEEE Trans. Fuzzy Syst. **12**(4), 524–539 (2004)
7. Liang, Q., Mendel, J.M.: Interval T2 fuzzy logic systems: theory and design. IEEE Trans. Fuzzy Syst. **8**(5), 535–550 (2000)
8. Karnik, N.N., Mendel, J.M., Liang, Q.: Type-2 fuzzy logic systems. IEEE Trans. Fuzzy Syst. **7**(6), 643–658 (1999)

9. Wang, C.H., Cheng, C.S., Lee, T.T.: Dynamical optimal training for interval T2 fuzzy neural network (T2NFN). IEEE Trans. Syst. Man Cybern. 1462–1477 (2004)
10. Abiyev, R.H., Kaynak, O., Alshanableh, T., Mamedov, M.: A T2 neuro-fuzzy system based on clustering and gradient techniques applied to system identification and channel equalization. Appl. Soft Comput. **11**, 1396–1406 (2011)
11. Lin, C.T., Pal, N.R., Wu, S.L., Liu, Y.T., Lin, Y.Y.: An interval T2 neural fuzzy system for online system identification and feature elimination. IEEE Trans. Neural Netw. Learn. Syst. **26**(7), 1442–1455 (2015)
12. Castro, J.R., Castillo, O., Melin, P., Rodriguez-Diaz, A.: A hybrid learning algorithm for a class of interval T2 fuzzy neural networks. J. Inf. Sci. **179**, 2175–2193 (2009)
13. Martinez, R., Castillo, O., Aguilar, L.T.: Optimization of interval T2 fuzzy logic controllers for a perturbed autonomous wheeled mobile robot using genetic algorithms. J. Inf. Sci. **179**, 2158–2174 (2009)
14. Olivas, F., Valdez, F., Castillo, O., Melin, P.: Dynamic parameter adaptation in particle swarm optimization using interval T2 fuzzy logic. J. Soft Comput. **20**(3), 1057–1070 (2016)
15. Moodi, H., Farrokhi, M.: Robust observer design for Sugeno systems with incremental quadratic nonlinearity in the consequent. Int. J. Appl. Math. Comput. Sci. **23**(4), 711–723 (2013)
16. Khosravi, A., Nahavandi, S., Creighton, D., Srinivasan, D.: Interval Type-2 fuzzy logic systems for load forecasting. IEEE Trans. Power Syst. **27**(3), 1274–1282 (2012)
17. Hagras, H.A.: A hierarchical T2 fuzzy logic control architecture for autonomous mobile robots. IEEE Trans. Fuzzy Syst. **12**(4), 524–539 (2014)
18. Lin, T.C.: Based on interval T2 fuzzy-neural network direct adaptive sliding mode control for SISO nonlinear systems. Commun. Nonlinear Sci. Numer. Simul. **15**(12), 4084–4099 (2010)
19. Clavo-Rolle, J.L., Fontelna-Romero, O., Perez-Sanchez, B., Guijarro-Berdinas, B.: Adaptive inverse control using an online learning algorithm for neural networks. Informatica **25**(3), 401–414 (2014)
20. Li, C.H.D., Yi, J.Q., Yu, Y., Zhao, D.B.: Inverse control of cable-driven parallel mechanism using T2 fuzzy neural network. Acta Automatica Sinica **36**(3), 459–464 (2010)
21. Kadhim, H.H.: Self-learning of ANFIS inverse control using iterative learning technique. Int. J. Comput. Appl. **21**(8), 24–29 (2011)
22. Sang, X., Liu, X.: An analytical solution to the TOPSIS model with interval T2 fuzzy sets. Soft Comput. **20**, 1213–1230 (2015)
23. Akbari, M.E., Badamchizadeh, M.A., Poor, M.A.: Implementation of a fuzzy TSK controller for a flexible joint robot. J. Discret. Dyn. Nat. Soc. **2012** (2012)
24. Akbari, M.E., Alizadeh, G., Khanmohammadi, S., Hassanzadeh, I., Mirzaei, M., Badamchizadeh, M.A.: Design and implementation of a nonlinear H_∞ tracking controller for high elastic joint robot with compensated friction. Int. J. Eng. Sci. Technol. **2**, 7691–7702 (2010)

Fuzzy Deep Neural Network for Classification of Overlapped Data

Rukshima Dabare[1,2]($\boxtimes$), Kok Wai Wong[1]($\boxtimes$), Mohd Fairuz Shiratuddin[1], and Polychronis Koutsakis[1]

[1] Discipline of Information Technology, Mathematics and Statistics, Murdoch University, Perth, WA, Australia
{rukshima.dabare,K.Wong,F.Shiratuddin, p.koutsakis}@murdoch.edu.au
[2] Faculty of Engineering Technology, The Open University of Sri Lanka, Nawala, Nugegoda, Sri Lanka

Abstract. Deep Learning is a popular and promising technique for classification problems. This paper proposes the use of fuzzy deep learning to improve the classification capability when dealing with overlapped data. Most of the research focuses on classification and uses traditional truth and false criteria. However, in reality, a data item may belong to different classes at different degrees. Therefore, the degree of belonging of each data item to a class needs to be considered for classification purposes in some cases. When a data item belongs to different classes with different degrees, then there exists an overlap between the classes. For this reason, this paper proposes a Fuzzy Deep Neural Network based on Fuzzy C-means clustering, fuzzy membership grades and Deep Neural Networks to address the over-lapping issue focused on binary classes and multi-classes. The proposed method converts the original attribute values to relevant cluster centres using the proposed Fuzzy Deep Neural Network. It then trains them with the original output class values. Thereafter, the test data is checked with the Fuzzy Deep Neural Network model for its performance. Using three popular datasets in overlapped and fuzzy data literature, the method presented in this paper outperforms the other methods compared in this study, which are Deep Neural Networks and Fuzzy classification.

Keywords: Classification · Deep learning · Fuzzy · Fuzzy C-means clustering · Overlapped data

1 Introduction

Class overlap occurs when data with similar characteristics appear in the feature space with different degree of belongings [1]. In ideal situations, the feature space should be well separated, and one should be able to identify the class it belongs to. However, this is not the case because real-world data may have overlapping regions which makes it hard for a traditional classifier to classify them into different classes [2] or distinguish between the different classes [3]. Recently, Deep Neural Network (DNN) technique has

© Springer Nature Switzerland AG 2019
T. Gedeon et al. (Eds.): ICONIP 2019, LNCS 11953, pp. 633–643, 2019.
https://doi.org/10.1007/978-3-030-36708-4_52

become popular in solving classification tasks. However, the work done is minimal on handling overlapped data. Therefore, in this paper, we propose an approach to handle overlapped data, which is different from most of the related literature (see Sect. 2).

When a data item belongs to two or more clusters, it is said to be overlapped, and its degree of belonging can be identified through Fuzzy C-means clustering [4]. This is something that hard clustering techniques are not able to address [5]. Therefore, when overlapped data is clustered, it may belong to two or more clusters [6]. Each data item will have a membership to every cluster it belongs to. In our approach, we identify the features which will have an overlapping behaviour and address them separately. The features which are non-categorical will be fuzzified, and the relevant cluster centre will be identified for the training of the DNN along with the categorical features. DNN was selected as the classifier because of its proven efficiency in recent years [7, 8] due to its multiple processing layers which will allow systems to abstract more and learn a representation of data better than with shallow networks [9]. Therefore, in order to deal with the class overlapping issue, in our study, we propose a Fuzzy Deep Neural Network (FuzzyDNN) based on Fuzzy C-means clustering, fuzzy membership grades, and DNN (Deep Neural Network).

The performance of our proposed method is validated using three datasets, Heart, Wisconsin and Wavform from UCI data repository that is commonly used in overlapped data and fuzzy literature [3, 10] with the use of the accuracy metric. In order to demonstrate the proposed method, we compare our results with two other classifiers, which are a DNN and a fuzzy classifier.

This paper is organized as follows. Section 2 gives an overview of related work carried out by other researchers related to fuzzy deep learning and overlapped data classification. Section 3 presents the novel FuzzyDNN model. In Sect. 4, the experimental setup, datasets and the results of our study are presented and analyzed. The final section concludes the paper.

2   Related Work

Deep Neural Networks (DNN) have shown excellent results across different domains, including but not limited to pharmacological science [11], emotion predictions [12], speech enhancement [13] and medical [14]. The excellent results of DNN across these different domains are the reason that we have selected DNN as the classifier along with the fuzzy approach in our study. However, the DNN has problems handling the overlap uncertainties appears in some datasets [15]. On the other hand, fuzzy sets can be used to represent the uncertainties and impreciseness of data [16]. This is addressed by assigning a membership grade ranging from 0 to 1 for each object (or data item) to the different sets or clusters [16, 17]. The fuzzy concept has been widely used in domains ranging from manufacturing [17] to the medical field [18] and network security [19]. In the following section, we briefly discuss some of the related work on Fuzzy Deep Learning on overlapped data and clustering.

In recent years, few studies have been carried out by combining the fuzzy concept with deep learning. The work of [20–25] and [26] have successfully used the fuzzy concept in different formats with deep learning. Most of the work mentioned have used fuzzy concept in order to improve the representational ability of the classifiers as well as to ensure the interpretability of the whole system. However, only the work of [15] concentrates on handling overlapped data with the use of fuzzy logic concept and DNN. In [15], the fuzzy C-means is used to handle the overlapping uncertainties by implementing fuzzy inference rules, apply them on the previously clustered data and generate corresponding membership values. Thus their method required the steps of implementing fuzzy inference rules which in some cases could be difficult and complex than our proposed method.

In order to address the overlapping issue in classification, there are various methods adopted by researchers. The work in [27] introduces a novel method based on Fuzzy Adaptive Resonance Theory (ART) which can be used for clustering. However, this work is only applicable to unsupervised learning, whereas our work concentrates on supervised learning. The work of [3, 28, 29] and [30] have concentrated more on the imbalanced data set with overlapped data, and therefore, the focus is different from our work. Therefore, in order to handle the overlapping issue in classification, in our work, the fuzzy and deep learning concepts are combined with the use of Fuzzy C-means clustering, fuzzy membership grades, and a DNN. With the adoption of deep learning, we expect the system to learn a better representation of data [9] and with the use of the fuzzy approach that it will address the overlapping problem [15].

3 Proposed FuzzyDNN Model

The proposed FuzzyDNN comprises of three main phases. The first phase is the fuzzification of each attribute by clustering and identifying the membership grade for each input attribute. The second phase is the identification of the new input attribute values by using different α-cuts and cluster centre identification. The third phase is the learning phase with the use of a DNN with the cluster centres as the input to the DNN. The description of each phase is given below, and the overall proposed method, if the attribute values were only non-categorical values, are shown in Fig. 1. All the phases presented in this proposed model are applicable only for training the model; therefore, only for the training dataset.

3.1 Phase 1:- Fuzzification of Each Attribute

In this phase, the attributes which are not categorical are given a fuzzy value. By doing so, we are trying to solve the overlapping issue of non-categorical features. Here the non-categorical features will be fuzzified in order to check their belongings to each class and thereby identifying the degree of overlapping. This process is explained under step 1 of this phase. In this paper, we refer to this as fuzzification. Each attribute of the dataset is clustered with the use of Fuzzy C-Means clustering. The reason for the selection of this clustering method is its capability of identifying the membership grade for each cluster [4]. The three steps of the first phase are given below in detail.

Step 1. Use Fuzzy C-means to cluster each attribute in the training dataset with continuous values. Here we used three clusters for all three (3) datasets. Experiments were also carried out with different numbers of clusters, but we got the best result from three (3) clusters. The attributes with categorical values were not clustered.

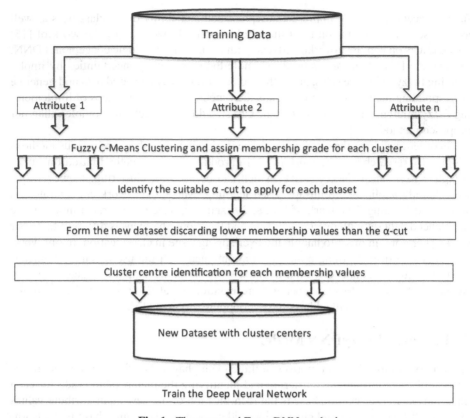

Fig. 1. The proposed FuzzyDNN method

Step 2. Identify the degree of membership of each attribute value to each cluster. By doing so, an attribute will have three (3) membership values relevant to the three (3) clusters it belongs to.

Step 3. When forming the new training dataset, the descending order of the membership grade to each attribute was taken into consideration. Here, for each attribute value considered, the membership grades with the highest values are used to form the new record of data. Then after the first set is formed the second-highest membership grades are considered to form the next set of records. Therefore, after forming the whole dataset, the number of records is increased by the number of clusters. For example, in our experiments for Heart, Wisconsin and Waveform datasets, the number of records increased by three (3) as we used three (3) clusters for each attribute. Thereafter, for all the attributes that were not fuzzified (because of the categorical nature of the attributes), then their original values were used in forming the new dataset. When forming the new input dataset, the original values of the labels will be used as they are not fuzzified.

Phase 1 is explained using the matrix format below: -

Assuming there are n input records (patterns) and k number of attributes for each record (each pattern) in the dataset. The input space and the output space can be represented in a matrix form as X and Y, respectively.

$$X = \begin{bmatrix} x_{11} & x_{12} & x_{13} & \cdots\cdots & x_{1k} \\ x_{21} & x_{22} & x_{23} & \cdots\cdots & x_{2k} \\ x_{31} & x_{32} & x_{33} & \cdots\cdots & x_{3k} \\ \cdots & \cdots & \cdots\cdots\cdots\cdots \\ x_{n1} & x_{n2} & x_{n3} & \cdots\cdots & x_{nk} \end{bmatrix} \tag{1}$$

and,

$$Y = y_1 \ y_2 \ y_3 \ \cdots \ y_n \tag{2}$$

Therefore,

$$y_i = x_{i1} \ x_{i2} \ x_{i3} \cdots\cdots x_{ik} \tag{3}$$

where i is a record of the dataset.

The Fuzzy C-Means clustering will consider each column at a time for clustering of matrix X, which is an attribute value of the dataset. Therefore, Fuzzy C-Means clustering will be performed on each column of the X matrix, and the membership grade relevant to each cluster along with the input attributes will form the new matrix W_i that is:

$$W_n = \begin{bmatrix} \mu_{11}(x_{i1}) & \mu_{11}(x_{i2}) & \mu_{11}(x_{i3}) & \cdots\cdots & \mu_{11}(x_{ik}) \\ \mu_{12}(x_{i1}) & \mu_{12}(x_{i2}) & \mu_{12}(x_{i3}) & \cdots\cdots & \mu_{12}(x_{ik}) \\ \mu_{13}(x_{i1}) & \mu_{13}(x_{i2}) & \mu_{13}(x_{i2}) & \cdots\cdots & \mu_{13}(x_{ik}) \\ \mu_{21}(x_{i1}) & \mu_{21}(x_{i2}) & \mu_{21}(x_{i3}) & \cdots\cdots & \mu_{21}(x_{ik}) \\ \mu_{22}(x_{i1}) & \mu_{22}(x_{i2}) & \mu_{22}(x_{i3}) & \cdots\cdots & \mu_{22}(x_{ik}) \\ \mu_{23}(x_{i1}) & \mu_{23}(x_{i1}) & \mu_{23}(x_{i1}) & \cdots\cdots & \mu_{22}(x_{ik}) \\ \cdots & \cdots & \cdots & \cdots\cdots \\ \mu_{n3}(x_{i1}) & \mu_{n3}(x_{i2}) & \mu_{n3}(x_{i4}) & \cdots\cdots & \mu_{n3}(x_{ik}) \end{bmatrix} \tag{4}$$

where μ_{ik} is the fuzzy membership grade. Therefore, for example, μ_{12} is the fuzzy membership grade for the 1st attribute for the 2nd cluster which belongs to the 1st record of the original dataset. Now the X matrix is converted into W which also can be represented as

$$W_n = \begin{bmatrix} w_1 \\ w_2 \\ w_3 \\ \cdots \\ w_n \end{bmatrix} \tag{5}$$

Where W_i is the memberships grade details of the record i.

For example, the W_1 will represent the membership grades of the 1st record when three (3) clusters are used.

$$W_1 = \begin{bmatrix} \mu_{11}(x_{i1}) & \mu_{11}(x_{i2}) & \mu_{11}(x_{i3}) & \cdots\cdots & \mu_{11}(x_{ik}) \\ \mu_{12}(x_{i1}) & \mu_{12}(x_{i2}) & \mu_{12}(x_{i3}) & \cdots\cdots & \mu_{12}(x_{ik}) \\ \mu_{13}(x_{i1}) & \mu_{13}(x_{i2}) & \mu_{13}(x_{i3}) & \cdots\cdots & \mu_{13}(x_{ik}) \end{bmatrix} \tag{6}$$

The final step of this phase is to combine all the W_i to form the inputs of the dataset, which is explained under **Step 3** of **phase 1.**

3.2 Phase 2:- Identification of the New Attribute Values

This phase is only applicable to the input attributes that were given a fuzzy value. Identification of the new input attribute values is achieved by identifying the cluster centre and α-cut assignment to the fuzzified input attributes. Below are the three steps required for phase 2.

Step 1. Identify the best α-cut for each dataset and apply it in order to address the overlapping.
Step 2. If the membership degree is less than the identified α-cut value, then that fuzzified attribute is discarded from the newly formed training dataset.
Step 3. Identify the associated cluster centre for each attribute.

Phase 2 is explained in detail below: -
A threshold for W_n is then identified considering the dataset. Here the threshold value is fuzzy α-cut performed on W_n:

$$W_\alpha = \{u \in U/\mu_{ik} \geq \alpha\} \tag{7}$$

where U is the universe of discourse, μ_{ik} is the membership grade, which takes the values between in interval [0, 1] and α takes values in the interval [0, 1] [31]. After applying the fuzzy α-cut for W_n, the number of rows of W_n will be reduced according to the fuzzy α-cut value. The reason is that if the membership value of any item is less than the α-cut value, then the relevant record is discarded from the dataset. By doing so, we expect our proposed method will respond differently to different fuzziness that is available on the dataset.

Finally, for each element of W_n, the cluster centre for each cluster is assigned instead of the membership grade values. So, if n is the number of records the cluster centre matrix would be,

$$C_n = \begin{bmatrix} C_1 \ C_2 \ C_3 \ \dots \ C_n \end{bmatrix}^T \tag{8}$$

Therefore, for an example in the case where no records were discarded from W_n, meaning $\alpha = 0$, then the cluster centre matrix C_i would be:

$$C_i = \begin{bmatrix} C_{11} \ C_{12} \ C_{13} \ \dots \ C_{1k} \\ C_{21} \ C_{22} \ C_{23} \ \dots \ C_{2k} \\ C_{31} \ C_{32} \ C_{33} \ \dots \ C_{3k} \\ \dots \ \dots \ \dots \ \dots \ \dots \\ C_{j1} \ C_{j2} \ C_{j3} \ \dots \ C_{jk} \end{bmatrix} \tag{9}$$

Where k is the number of attributes and j is the number of clusters.

Phase 3:- Training of the DNN Using the New Input Attributes
The input for the DNN will be the output of the 2nd Phase. The fuzzified input dataset will then be fed to the DNN, and the DNN will learn according to the new cluster centre values (assigned to the continuous attributes) and the original data for the non-continuous attributes which are also known as categorical attributes.

4   Experimental Procedure and Evaluation of Results

4.1   Experimental Procedure

In our study, we used the Heart, Wisconsin and Waveform datasets from the UCI repository [32]. All three datasets are popular in overlapped and fuzzy data literature and are used for performance evaluation in recent studies such as in [3, 10, 33, 34]. In our study, the dataset was divided into 5-folds for each experiment, and the average of the 5 experiments is used for evaluation. For both datasets, 80% was used for training, and the rest was used for testing. The Heart dataset consists of 13 attributes, and out of those 13 attributes, only 5 attributes were fuzzified by the FuzzyDNN as the others were categorical values. The Wisconsin dataset contains 9 attributes, and for the FuzzyDNN all 9 attributes were fuzzified. Waveform dataset contained 21 attributes as all of them are non-categorical, and we fuzzified all attributes according to the proposed method.

The DNN architecture was decided by trial and error, considering the number of input attributes to the model. The DNN architecture and the relevant details are given in Table 1.

Table 1. DNN architecture and relevant details

Dataset	Number of hidden layers	Type	Number of hidden nodes	Number of epoch	Batch size
Heart	4	Binary	20, 20, 20, 20	500	100
Wisconsin	4	Binary	50, 100, 100, 40	1500	100
Waveform	3	Multi	20, 10, 50	500	1

The activation function used in the nodes of the hidden layers are Rectified Linear Unit (relu) as recommended by many studies [35], and the nodes of the last layer use the sigmoid activation function for the Heart and Wisconsin datasets as they are binary classification problems [36]. The activation function used for the Waveform dataset is relu for the hidden layers and softmax for output layer as the classification task is a multi-class classification problem [36]. The DNN model used the loss function binary cross entropy and used a batch size of 100 for the binary classes and for the Waveform class used a sparse_categorical_crossentropy function while the batch size was 1 for each training phase. Dropout technique [37], which is a popular regularization technique, is used to avoid overfitting when training our model. Table 2 presents the classification performance in terms of accuracy of the trained FuzzyDNN model, DNN and fuzzy classification for the Heart, Wisconsin and Waveform datasets.

4.2   Evaluation of Result

As shown in Table 2, the FuzzyDNN model outperforms the other approaches in terms of accuracy for the Heart, Wisconsin and Waveform datasets. FuzzyDNN improves the classification accuracy by 8.89%, 0.88% and 1.24% for the Heart, Wisconsin and Waveform datasets, respectively, when compared with DNN and by 9.63%, 2.48%, 3.57% when compared with Fuzzy Classification. The FuzzyDNN achieved higher accuracy in all cases as it was able to address the overlapped data issue separately for each attribute and use that knowledge to train the data.

Table 2. The best accuracies of the Heart, Wisconsin, and Waveform datasets

Dataset	Best α-cut	FuzzyDNN	DNN	Fuzzy classification
Heart	0.05	0.8407	0.7518	0.7444
Wisconsin	0.01	0.9739	0.9651	0.9491
Waveform	0.05	0.8332	0.8208	0.7975

It can be observed from the results provided in Table 2 that the use of FuzzyDNN model provides better results for the three datasets considered. Here as mentioned earlier, the threshold value is the α-cut value applied to the fuzzy set identified by the clustering. According to the fuzzy theory, low α-cut values means lesser overlapping between classes. Therefore, the threshold value selected for the α-cut is important for accurate classification.

As we wanted to investigate the most suitable threshold value for each dataset, we carried out experiments for different threshold values, which in our model are the α-cut values. Tables 3, 4 and 5 show the accuracy of the classification task for the Heart, Wisconsin and Waveform datasets, respectively, with the application of different α-cut values. As shown in Tables 3, 4 and 5 by choosing the appropriate α-cut value according to the dataset, we can adjust how much overlap is handled by the proposed model.

Table 3. The accuracy of the Heart dataset for different threshold values

Threshold value	Number of training data	Accuracy
0.05	**229**	**0.8407**
0.1	222	0.8111
0.2	218	0.8148
0.3	216	0.7888

Table 4. The accuracy of the Wisconsin dataset for different threshold values

Threshold value	Number of training data	Fuzzy DNN
0.01	**554**	**0.9739**
0.05	545	0.9710
0.1	545	0.9681
0.2	545	0.9710

Table 5. The accuracy of the Waveform dataset for different threshold values

Threshold value	Number of training data	Fuzzy DNN
0.05	**4001**	**0.8332**
0.1	4000	0.8204
0.2	4000	0.8208
0.3	4000	0.8202

5 Conclusion

In this work, we proposed a novel method to handle overlap between classes using fuzzy concept with the use of a DNN, Fuzzy C-means clustering and fuzzy membership grades. The features or the attributes that had continuous values were fuzzified by first clustering them using Fuzzy C-means clustering and identifying a membership grade for each attribute to the cluster it belongs to. After the identification of the membership values, according to the dataset, fuzzy α-cut was used to select the data which has more belongings or higher membership. Thereafter, this information was used to assign new values to the attribute values, which are the cluster centre of each cluster in order to handle the overlap. This approach was shown to improve deep learning performance in terms of the performance metric, accuracy and thereby improve the accuracy of the classifier. After carrying out experiments on three popular datasets in overlapped and fuzzy literature, our proposed FuzzyDNN approach was shown to perform better than the DNN classifier and a traditional fuzzy classifier.

References

1. Xiong, H., et al.: Classification algorithm based on NB for class overlapping problem. Appl. Math. Inf. Sci. **7**(2L), 409–415 (2013)
2. Tang, W., et al.: Classification for overlapping classes using optimized overlapping region detection and soft decision. In: 13th Conference on Information Fusion (FUSION). IEEE (2010)
3. Lee, H.K., Kim, S.B.: An overlap-sensitive margin classifier for imbalanced and overlapping data. Expert Syst. Appl. **98**, 72–83 (2018)

4. Bezdek, J.C., Ehrlich, R., Full, W.: FCM: the fuzzy c-means clustering algorithm. Comput. Geosci. **10**(2–3), 191–203 (1984)
5. Setyohadi, D.B., Bakar, A.A., Othman, Z.A.: Optimization overlap clustering based on the hybrid rough discernibility concept and rough K-Means. Intell. Data Anal. **19**(4), 795–823 (2015)
6. Banerjee, A., et al.: Model-based overlapping clustering. In: Proceedings of the Eleventh ACM SIGKDD International Conference on Knowledge Discovery in Data Mining. ACM (2005)
7. Faust, O., et al.: Deep learning for healthcare applications based on physiological signals: a review. Comput. Methods Programs Biomed. **161**, 1–13 (2018)
8. Young, T., et al.: Recent trends in deep learning based natural language processing. IEEE Comput. Intell. Mag. **13**(3), 55–75 (2018)
9. LeCun, Y., Bengio, Y., Hinton, G.: Deep. Learn. Nat. **521**(7553), 436 (2015)
10. Patwary, M.J., Wang, X.-Z.: Sensitivity analysis on initial classifier accuracy in fuzziness based semi-supervised learning. Inf. Sci. **490**, 93–112 (2019)
11. Wang, C.-S., et al.: Detecting potential adverse drug reactions using a deep neural network model. J. Med. Internet Res. **21**(2), e11016 (2019)
12. Kim, H.-C., Bandettini, P.A., Lee, J.-H.: Deep neural network predicts emotional responses of the human brain from functional magnetic resonance imaging. NeuroImage **186**, 607–627 (2019)
13. Saleem, N., et al.: deep neural network for supervised single-channel speech enhancement. Arch. Acoust. **44**(1), 3–12 (2019)
14. Katzman, J.L., et al.: DeepSurv: personalized treatment recommender system using a Cox proportional hazards deep neural network. BMC Med. Res. Methodol. **18**(1), 24 (2018)
15. Sumit, S.H., Akhter, S.: C-means clustering and deep-neuro-fuzzy classification for road weight measurement in traffic management system. Soft Comput. **23**, 4329–4340 (2019). https://doi.org/10.1007/s00500-018-3086-0
16. Zadeh, L.A.: Fuzzy sets. Inf. Control **8**(3), 338–353 (1965)
17. De Silva, C.W.: Intelligent Control: Fuzzy Logic Applications. CRC Press, Boca Raton (2018)
18. Korenevskiy, N.: Application of fuzzy logic for decision-making in medical expert systems. Biomed. Eng. **49**(1), 46–49 (2015)
19. Dotcenko, S., Vladyko, A., Letenko, I.: A fuzzy logic-based information security management for software-defined networks. In: 16th International Conference on Advanced Communication Technology (ICACT), 2014. IEEE (2014)
20. Park, S., et al.: Intra-and inter-fractional variation prediction of lung tumors using fuzzy deep learning. IEEE J. Transl. Eng. Health Med. **4**, 1–12 (2016)
21. El Hatri, C., Boumhidi, J.: Fuzzy deep learning based urban traffic incident detection. Cogn. Syst. Res. **50**, 206–213 (2018)
22. Davoodi, R., Moradi, M.H.: Mortality prediction in intensive care units (ICUs) using a deep rule-based fuzzy classifier. J. Biomed. Inform. **79**, 48–59 (2018)
23. Zheng, Y.-J., et al.: Airline passenger profiling based on fuzzy deep machine learning. IEEE Trans. Neural Netw. Learn. Syst. **28**(12), 2911–2923 (2017)
24. Deng, Y., et al.: A hierarchical fused fuzzy deep neural network for data classification. IEEE Trans. Fuzzy Syst. **25**(4), 1006–1012 (2017)
25. Chen, C.P., et al.: Fuzzy restricted Boltzmann machine for the enhancement of deep learning. IEEE Trans. Fuzzy Syst. **23**(6), 2163–2173 (2015)
26. Nugaliyadde, A., Pruengkarn, R., Wong, K.W.: The fuzzy misclassification analysis with deep neural network for handling class noise problem. In: Cheng, L., Leung, A.C.S., Ozawa, S. (eds.) ICONIP 2018. LNCS, vol. 11304, pp. 326–335. Springer, Cham (2018). https://doi.org/10.1007/978-3-030-04212-7_28

27. Mak, L.O., et al.: A merging Fuzzy ART clustering algorithm for overlapping data. In: 2011 IEEE Symposium on Foundations of Computational Intelligence (FOCI). IEEE (2011)
28. Xiong, H., Wu, J., Liu, L.: Classification with class overlapping: a systematic study. In: The 2010 International Conference on E-Business Intelligence (2010)
29. Vorraboot, P., et al.: Improving classification rate constrained to imbalanced data between overlapped and non-overlapped regions by hybrid algorithms. Neurocomputing **152**, 429–443 (2015)
30. Das, B., Krishnan, N.C., Cook, D.J.: Handling class overlap and imbalance to detect prompt situations in smart homes. In: 2013 IEEE 13th International Conference on Data Mining Workshops. IEEE (2013)
31. Harris, C.J., Moore, C.G., Brown, M.: Intelligent Control: Aspects of Fuzzy Logic and Neural Nets, vol. 6. World Scientific (1993)
32. Dua, D., Taniskidou, E.K.: UCI Machine Learning Repository (2017). http://archive.ics.uci.edu/ml
33. Singh, H.R., Biswas, S.K., Purkayastha, B.: A neuro-fuzzy classification technique using dynamic clustering and GSS rule generation. J. Comput. Appl. Math. **309**, 683–694 (2017)
34. Liu, X., et al.: A hybrid classification system for heart disease diagnosis based on the RFRS method. Comput. Math. Methods Med. **2017** (2017). 11 pages, Article ID 8272091. https://doi.org/10.1155/2017/8272091
35. Goodfellow, I., Bengio, Y., Courville, A.: Deep Learning. MIT Press, Cambridge (2016)
36. Géron, A.: Hands-On Machine Learning with Scikit-Learn and TensorFlow: Concepts, Tools, and Techniques to Build Intelligent Systems. O'Reilly Media Inc, Sebastopol (2017)
37. Srivastava, N., Hinton, G., Krizhevsky, A., Sutskever, I., Salakhutdinov, R.: Dropout: a simple way to prevent neural networks from ovrfitting. J. Mach. Learn. Res. **15**, 1929–1958 (2014)

On the Use of Diversity Mechanisms in Dynamic Constrained Continuous Optimization

Maryam Hasani-Shoreh[✉] and Frank Neumann

Optimisation and Logistics, School of Computer Science,
The University of Adelaide, Adelaide, SA, Australia
{maryam.hasanishoreh,frank.neumann}@adelaide.edu.au

Abstract. Population diversity plays a key role in evolutionary algorithms that enables global exploration and avoids premature convergence. This is especially more crucial in dynamic optimization in which diversity can ensure that the population keeps track of the global optimum by adapting to the changing environment. Dynamic constrained optimization problems (DCOPs) have been the target for many researchers in recent years as they comprehend many of the current real-world problems. Regardless of the importance of diversity in dynamic optimization, there is not an extensive study investigating the effects of diversity promotion techniques in DCOPs so far. To address this gap, this paper aims to investigate how the use of different diversity mechanisms may influence the behavior of algorithms in DCOPs. To achieve this goal, we apply and adapt the most common diversity promotion mechanisms for dynamic environments using differential evolution (DE) as our base algorithm. The results show that applying diversity techniques to solve DCOPs in most test cases lead to significant enhancement in the baseline algorithm in terms of modified offline error values.

Keywords: Dynamic constrained optimization · Diversity mechanisms · Differential evolution · Continuous optimization

1 Introduction

Dynamic constrained optimization problems (DCOPs), in which the objective function or/and the constraints change over time, comprehend a variety of real world problems. An example of such problems is hydro-thermal scheduling [1], in which the dynamism arises as the available resources or demand vary over time, or source identification problem [2], in which the information about the problem reveals gradually. In these (so-called time-dependant or dynamic) optimization problems, the goal is to find and track the optimal solution of each instance of the dynamic problem given a limited computational budget. Another approach is to apply an independent optimization method to each problem instance, however, a more efficient approach tackles them in a dynamic manner, in which the

© Springer Nature Switzerland AG 2019
T. Gedeon et al. (Eds.): ICONIP 2019, LNCS 11953, pp. 644–657, 2019.
https://doi.org/10.1007/978-3-030-36708-4_53

algorithm detects and responds to the changes on-the-fly [3]. Mathematically, the objective is to find a solution vector $(x \in \mathbb{R}^D)$ at each time period t such that: $\min_{x \in F_t} f(x,t)$, where $f : S \rightarrow \mathbb{R}$ is a single objective function, and $t \in N^+$ is the current time period. $F_t = \{x \mid x \in [L,U], g_i(x,t) \leq 0, h_j(x,t) = 0\}$, is the feasible region at time t, where L and U are the boundaries of the search space; $g_i(x,t)$ and $h_j(x,t)$ are the linear ith inequality and jth equality constraints at time t, respectively. To solve these problems, evolutionary algorithms (EAs) are commonly used as they have the ability to easily adapt to changing environments [3,4]. In addition, they often provide good solutions to complex problems without a large design effort.

For avoiding premature convergence that is a common problem in EAs a diverse population is needed. Otherwise there is no benefit of having a population; lack of diversity in population in the worst case, may lead the EA to behave like a local search algorithm, but with an additional overhead from maintaining many similar solutions [5]. Premature convergence in dynamic environments pose more serious challenges to EAs as when they are converged, they cannot adapt well to the changes. Indeed, having a diverse set of solutions in population helps to ensure the algorithm caters for changes in a dynamic environment. In the literature of EAs, diversity has been found to have manifold positive effects. To name a few, it is highly beneficial for enhancing the global exploration capabilities of EAs. It enables crossover to work effectively, improves performance and robustness in dynamic optimization, and helps to search for the whole Pareto front for evolutionary multiobjective optimization [6]. In the related studies of runtime analysis [5], diversity mechanisms proved to be highly effective for the considered problems, speeding up the optimization time by constant factors, polynomial factors, or even exponential factors.

Diversity in EAs has been promoted through different approaches. A comprehensive classification is given in [7] that overally divides them into niching and non-niching approaches. Moreover, another classification is given based on the affected section of the algorithm: population-based, selection-based, crossover/mutation-based, fitness-based, and replacement-based. These approaches have been applied in many different classes of optimization problem so far including multi-objective [6], multi-modal [8], constrained optimization [9]. To name a few of them in DCOPs based on the aforementioned classification include: mutation-based [10], replacement-based [11] or population-based diversity mechanisms [12,13].

However, regardless of the manifold benefits of diversity in EAs and in particular in dynamic optimization, there is not an extensive study so far in DCOPs. What makes study of diversity in this problem class important is that as diversity mechanisms spread the solutions over the search space, the constraint handling technique has tendency to guide the search toward feasible areas. The results of such study gives insight into the role of these opposing forces and their overall effect on algorithm's performance. What we aim is to carry a survey study over commonly used explicit diversity promotion methods (we exclude implicit methods that are via parameter tuning or selection mechanisms) investigating their effects in DCOPs. Our comparison aims to reveal which diversity promotion technique work better in each specific problem characteristic and why. Our investigations help to develop a better understanding of diversity role in DCOPs.

We choose differential evolution (DE) as our baseline algorithm which has showed competitive results in dynamic and constrained optimization problems [14]. The presented results reveal applying the diversity promotion techniques enhanced algorithm performance significantly based on statistical test applied in modified offline error values.

The outline of the paper is as follows. Section 1, gives an introduction and motivation to our work. Section 2 introduces DE algorithm and diversity mechanisms. Experimental setup will be presented in Sect. 3. Results and discussion are reviewed in Sect. 4 and finally in Sect. 5 conclusions and future work are summarized.

2   Preliminaries

In this section, an overview of adapted differential evolution (DE) algorithm to solve DCOPs and diversity handling mechanisms are presented.

2.1   DE Algorithm for Solving DCOPs

DE is a stochastic search algorithm that is simple, reliable and fast which showed competitive results in constrained and dynamic optimization [14]. Each vector $x_{i,G}$ in the current population (called at the moment of the reproduction as target vector) generates one trial vector $u_{i,G}$ by using a mutant vector $v_{i,G}$. The mutant vector is created applying $v_{i,G} = x_{r0,G} + F(x_{r1,G} - x_{r2,G})$, where $x_{r0,G}$, $x_{r1,G}$, and $x_{r2,G}$ are vectors chosen at random from the current population ($r0 \neq r1 \neq r2 \neq i$); $x_{r0,G}$ is known as the base vector and $x_{r1,G}$, and $x_{r2,G}$ are the difference vectors and $F > 0$ is a parameter called scale factor. The trial vector is created by the recombination of the target vector and mutant vector using a crossover probability $CR \in [0, 1]$. For the constraint handling technique feasibility rules [15] is applied. In addition to constraint handling techniques, the algorithms in DCOPs need a mechanism to detect the environment changes. In the related literature, re-evaluation of the solutions is the most common change-detection approach [3]. The algorithm regularly re-evaluates specific solutions (for us the first and the middle individual of the population) to detect changes in their function values or/and constraints. If a change is detected, then all the population is re-evaluated to avoid obsolete information.

2.2   Diversity Maintenance Techniques

In this section diversity handling mechanisms are reviewed. Among the many popular niching methods like fitness sharing, clearing and species-based, we used standard crowding in this work. The reason for excluding other niching methods is that they are originally designed and applied in multi-modal functions. An extensive separate study is needed to apply these methods with moving peak benchmark (that is designed for testing multi-modal optimization in DCOPs) to investigate the methods thoroughly.

Chaos Local Search: Chaos is a nature phenomenon characterized by randomness and sensibility to initial conditions. Due to those attributes, chaos has been implemented with success in local searches [16], which is the case for this mechanism for promoting diversity. In our case the chaos only affects the best solution at each iteration. We applied an adaptive dynamic search length that is triggered with change detection.

Crowding: Among the many niching methods in literature, we choose the standard crowding method [17]. In this method, similar individuals in the population are avoided, creating genotypic diversity. Instead of competition between the offspring and the parents, the offspring competes with the individual with lowest Euclidean distance.

Fitness Diversity: While the other methods focus is on creating genotypic diversity, this method creates phenotypic diversity by avoiding individuals with close fitness values. The offspring in this method competes with the individual with closest fitness value [18].

No Diversity Mechanism: This method is a base DE algorithm with feasibility rules [15] used as its constraint handling technique and no explicit method is used as its diversity promotion technique. Note that all the other methods use feasibility rules as their constraint handling mechanism.

Opposition: This mechanism is based in the estimation of the symmetric opposites of individuals in the population, since it leads to find new positions closer to the problem optimum [19]. The authors claim that evaluating opposites, when solving a problem without a priori knowledge with several dimensions, helps in finding fitter individuals. Purely random re-sampling or selection of solutions from a given population has the chance of visiting or even revisiting unproductive regions of the search space.

Random Immigrants: This infusion technique replaces certain number of individuals (defined by a parameter called replacement rate) with random solutions in the population, so as to assure continuous exploration [11].

3   Experimental Setup

In this section, the applied performance measures and the test problems are reviewed.

3.1   Performance Measures

The first two performance measures calculate the precision of solutions compared to optimal values. The third and fourth measures represent speed of convergence and the success rate for each algorithm to reach to a precision from the optimum. Finally, the last measure calculates diversity of solutions in population.

Modified offline error (MOF) is defined as: $\frac{1}{G_{max}} \sum_{G=1}^{G_{max}} (|f(\boldsymbol{x}^*, t) - f(\boldsymbol{x}_{best,G}, t)|)$ that represents the average of the sum of errors in each generation divided by the total number of generations [20]. Where G_{max} is the maximum generation, $f(\boldsymbol{x}^*, t)$ is the global optimum at current time t, and $f(\boldsymbol{x}_{best,G}, t)$ represents the best solution found so far at generation G at current time t.

Tracking error (TE) is defined as: $\frac{1}{t_{end}-t_0} \sum_{t=t_0}^{t_{end}} |f(\boldsymbol{x}^*, t) - f(\boldsymbol{x}_{best}, t)|$ and reflects the overall error at the end of each change period.

Number of fitness evaluations (NFE) needed at each time to reach to an ϵ-precision from the global optimum are averaged over all the times for this measure. The termination criteria is to find a value smaller than the ϵ-level from the global optimum (value to reach (VTR)) before reaching to the next change.

$$NFE = \frac{1}{t_{end}-t_0} \sum_{t=t_0}^{t_{end}} NFE_t$$

$$VTR = \frac{|f(\boldsymbol{x}^*, t) - f(\boldsymbol{x}_{best,G}, t)|}{|f(\boldsymbol{x}^*, t)|}$$

(1)

Success rate (SR) calculates the percentage of the number of times each algorithm is successful to reach to ϵ-precision from the global optimum (VTR) over all time scale.

Diversity: Diversity measures differences among individuals at distinct levels; genotypic: considers individuals position within the search space or phenotypic: evaluate populations fitness distribution. We choose a genotypic measure as its more common in the literature. For this purpose we measure relative standard deviation of the population (known as coefficient of variation): $CV = \frac{\sigma}{\mu}$ at each generation, where σ is the standard deviation and μ is the mean of the population.

3.2   Test Problems

Our algorithms were tested on two benchmarks for DCOPs [12,21], which contains 22 problems in total. The first 18 test cases are from [21] that captures different characteristics of DCOPs like multiple disconnected feasible regions, gradually moving feasible regions and global optimum switching between different feasible regions. The last 4 test cases are from [12] in which Bu used a parameter in the original test cases in [21] that controls the size and the number of disconnected feasible regions. In the experiments, medium severity is chosen for the objective function ($k = 0.5$) and the constraints ($S = 20$). The other parameters are: frequency of change (f_c) = 1000, runs = 30 and the number of considered times for dynamic perspective of the algorithm $5/k$ ($k = 0.5$). Parameters of DE are chosen as $n_p = 20$, $CR = 0.2$, F is a random number in $[0.2, 0.8]$, and rand/1/bin is the chosen variant of DE [14].

4   Results and Discussion

In this section first the results for diversity measure is reviewed and then the results for MOF, TE, SR, and NFE values will be discussed.

4.1   Diversity Results

Figure 1 illustrates the results for coefficient of variation of population (a measure for considering diversity explained in Sect. 3.1) for different methods per generation. Three functions have been opted for plots considering a range of different characteristics. Notice that the generations are not equal for all methods as the frequency of changes is mapped with the number of fitness evaluations, and some methods like Opp and RI use different number of fitness evaluations per generations compared to the other methods. Opp has almost half the number of generations when a change happens and RI is different from the other methods within a range (based on what the replacement rate is).

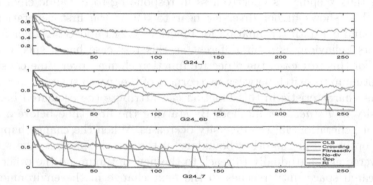

Fig. 1. Y-axis: Diversity score (coefficient of variation of population), X-axis: Generations

In general RI shows almost the same trajectory regardless of the test case. It starts with maximum diversity around 0.6 and remains with a minor drop through the last generations. The lack of convergence in this method is due to random individuals inserted in the population at each iteration keeping diversity at a consistent level. For $No-div$ and CLS also an identical behaviour is observed regardless of the test case. They both start with a high value for diversity measure equal to 1 and converge to near zero after 45 generations which represents the number of generations in which the first change happens. Thus as diversity measure shows these two methods are not able to promote any diversity in population after they converge in the first change. As explained in Sect. 2.1, the way the tested algorithms react to changes is through re-evaluation of the solutions. For the other methods due to the applied diversity promotion technique, they can diverge faster leading to higher MOF values overall (is discussed in next section). But for these two methods finding new optimum after a change is very slow. This is because DE relies on differential vectors to maintain diversity, which are dependent on the population's diversity itself. So without increasing diversity extrinsically, diversity will remain low in them leading their inability to track new optimum.

For Opp the diversity depends weather the opposite individual is accepted in the population or not. For test cases with smaller feasible regions, the diversity is low as the opposite individual is infeasible and hence it is rejected. As if it is accepted there is more diversity in the population otherwise this method behaves like No-div technique. For G24_7, the feasible area shrinks from 44.61% to 7.29% over time. This explains the behavior of Opp in which at each change, the diversity increases sharply and then reduces gradually until next change happens. This pattern is repeated until around generation 160. From this generation afterwards, it loses its diversity as all of the opposite individuals fail to be chosen in the selection process (due to small feasible region).

$Crowding$ in all test cases is able to maintain high diversity over many generations, thus keeping its effectiveness in responding to dynamic environment. This method shows higher diversity near to 0.9 at the first generations and linger around o.4 until termination for functions G24_f and G24_7. For function G24_6b its behaviour is a bit different as this test case has a special characteristic. For this test case, the objective function changes over time causing the global optimum to switch between two corners of the search space at each change step. This characteristic in this function can attribute the oscillated behaviour of diversity in $Fitnessdiv$ method. By starting the first time before a change happen at generation 45, the diversity decreases. When the change happens as the new optima is in the other boundary of the search space, so the solutions must diverge again gradually to reach to the new optimum on the other corner of the search space until reaches to the next change in the environment and the same pattern repeats. For the other two test cases, $Fitnessdiv$ showed a similar trend to $Crowding$ but with lower diversity. Another difference is after 150 generations it looses its diversity. However, $Crowding$ still keeps its diversity at around 0.4 until the end of generations. In general, as our selected measure of diversity is based on genotypic level, $Crowding$ that is based of promoting diversity in genotypic level has got higher scores.

4.2 Statistical Results

The results obtained for the compared algorithms using MOF values are summarized in Table 1. Furthermore, for the statistical validation, the 95%-confidence Kruskal-Wallis (KW) test and the Bonferroni post-hoc test, as suggested in [22] are presented (see Table 2). Based on Tables 1 and 2, MOF shows significantly superior results for almost all of the methods compared to the base algorithm, $No - div$, for most of the test cases. Among them, $Crowding$ has the highest frequencies of wins over the base algorithm compared to other methods. The difference of outperformance of $Crowding$ compared to other methods is more significant in test cases by dynamic objective functions. This shows the other methods decrease in their performance dealing with dynamic objective functions compared to static ones, leading to bigger difference in dynamic cases.

Table 1. Average and standard deviation of MOF values over 30 runs. Best results are remarked in boldface.

Algorithms	Functions					
	G24_u	G24_1	G24_f	G24_uf	G24_2	G24_2u
CLS	0.4331(±0.022)	0.5658(±0.014)	**0.0294(±0.012)**	0.0027(±0.002)	0.7965(±0.085)	0.3125(±0.058)
Crowding	0.0576(±0.027)	**0.0823(±0.025)**	0.0698(±0.029)	0.0033(±0.004)	0.2030(±0.049)	0.2488(±0.247)
Fitnessdiv	0.2084(±0.161)	0.5804(±0.014)	0.0394(±0.014)	0.0046(±0.004)	0.9292(±0.202)	0.8327(±0.293)
No-div	0.6215(±0.002)	0.5737(±0.014)	0.0332(±0.014)	0.0026(±0.002)	1.5727(±0.091)	1.5208(±0.002)
Opp	0.6118(±0.013)	0.5364(±0.080)	0.0446(±0.019)	**0.0020(±0.002)**	1.3765(±0.076)	0.0299(±0.015)
RI	**0.0344(±0.017)**	0.5183(±0.044)	0.4356(±0.040)	0.0031(±0.003)	**0.1935(±0.029)**	**0.0292(±0.011)**
	G24_3	G24_3b	G24_3f	G24_4	G24_5	G24_6a
CLS	0.2433(±0.058)	0.7861(±0.108)	**0.0263(±0.014)**	0.8449(±0.109)	0.7077(±0.099)	1.9470(±0.146)
Crowding	0.1618(±0.039)	**0.1556(±0.023)**	0.0471(±0.017)	**0.1204(±0.017)**	**0.1628(±0.033)**	**0.0734(±0.022)**
Fitnessdiv	**0.0745(±0.013)**	0.5126(±0.112)	0.0314(±0.009)	0.6216(±0.052)	0.8183(±0.134)	1.8504(±0.131)
No-div	0.3619(±0.152)	0.9496(±0.192)	0.0269(±0.011)	0.6756(±0.073)	1.2418(±0.094)	2.1163(±0.434)
Opp	0.3036(±0.117)	0.6724(±0.180)	0.0460(±0.020)	0.3271(±0.070)	0.9553(±0.041)	1.5525(±0.546)
RI	0.4339(±0.038)	0.5102(±0.037)	0.4079(±0.040)	0.5129(±0.043)	0.2170(±0.034)	0.2753(±0.075)
	G24_6b	G24_6c	G24_6d	G24_7	G24_8a	G24_8b
CLS	0.9702(±0.397)	1.7536(±0.458)	0.6860(±0.013)	0.3440(±0.094)	0.7243(±0.031)	0.6747(±0.028)
Crowding	0.2554(±0.064)	**0.0993(±0.050)**	0.0775(±0.015)	**0.1475(±0.026)**	0.5850(±0.030)	**0.1864(±0.039)**
Fitnessdiv	1.1505(±0.377)	0.9252(±0.523)	0.5438(±0.061)	0.1614(±0.032)	0.5200(±0.056)	0.7040(±0.069)
No-div	1.7479(±0.789)	1.9300(±0.646)	0.7887(±0.010)	0.3442(±0.162)	1.1064(±0.013)	0.7265(±0.007)
Opp	0.8291(±0.624)	0.8088(±0.696)	0.7756(±0.012)	0.2025(±0.148)	1.1914(±0.050)	0.7510(±0.032)
RI	**0.1876(±0.023)**	0.1882(±0.025)	0.2320(±0.039)	0.3904(±0.044)	**0.4755(±0.031)**	0.5557(±0.041)
	G24v_3	G24v_3b	G24w_3	G24w_3b		
CLS	0.5923(±0.507)	0.6941(±0.205)	1.0406(±0.503)	1.2456(±0.161)		
Crowding	**0.2529(±0.081)**	0.2214(±0.057)	0.5503(±0.198)	**0.6458(±0.141)**		
Fitnessdiv	0.2943(±0.147)	0.4219(±0.051)	**0.4784(±0.161)**	0.6905(±0.186)		
No-div	0.8776(±0.701)	0.9734(±0.222)	1.1860(±0.467)	1.2710(±0.215)		
Opp	0.7725(±0.719)	0.6778(±0.132)	1.1778(±0.371)	1.1999(±0.213)		
RI	1.4512(±0.101)	0.8169(±0.097)	1.2991(±0.091)	1.2263(±0.085)		

On the contrary the method that is very similar to $No-div$ method is CLS. As diversity results showed, this method is not increasing diversity that much, as it is more like a local search. This explains its superior performance compared to other methods in fixed test cases (G24_3f, G24_f). But it can not promote diversity that much (as only best solution at each iteration changes) and its inability to react to changes explains its higher MOF values.

RI preformed worse than the base algorithm for the problems with small feasible area (like G24_3f, G24_f, G24v_3, G24w_3) as there is a high probability that the inserted solutions are infeasible and hence they can not compete with the current best solution based on the applied constraint handling technique. On the contrary, for unconstrained ones and the ones with large feasible areas showed the best results (like G24_u, G24_2, G24_2u, G24_6b, G24_8a). So generally, although the diversity of population is increased by inserting new solutions to the population, but because they are not feasible solutions they are not that effective. In addition, in this method the algorithm spends some more fitness evaluations (to the extent of replacement rate) compared to the base algorithm at each generation. Thus the algorithm will have less computation budget for the evolution process itself as the changes happen after known

Table 2. The 95%-confidence Kruskal-Wallis (KW) test and the Bonferroni post-hoc test on the MOF values in Table 1. The compared variants are denoted as: $1 = CLS$, $2 = Crowding$, $3 = Fitnessdiv$, $4 = No - div$, $5 = Opp$, and $6 = RI$.

Functions	Statistical test
G24_u	$1 > 2, 4 > 1, 1 > 6, 4 > 2, 5 > 2, 4 > 3, 5 > 3, 3 > 6, 4 > 6, 5 > 6$
G24_1	$1 > 2, 3 > 2, 4 > 2, 5 > 2, 6 > 2, 3 > 6, 4 > 6, 5 > 6$
G24_f	$2 > 1, 6 > 1, 2 > 3, 2 > 4, 6 > 2, 6 > 3, 6 > 4, 6 > 5$
G24_uf	
G24_2	$1 > 2, 4 > 1, 5 > 1, 1 > 6, 3 > 2, 4 > 2, 5 > 2, 4 > 3, 3 > 6, 4 > 6, 5 > 6$
G24_2u	$4 > 1, 1 > 5, 1 > 6, 3 > 2, 4 > 2, 2 > 5, 2 > 6, 3 > 5, 3 > 6, 4 > 5, 4 > 6$
G24_3	$1 > 3, 6 > 1, 2 > 3, 4 > 2, 5 > 2, 6 > 2, 4 > 3, 5 > 3, 6 > 3, 6 > 5$
G24_3b	$1 > 2, 1 > 3, 1 > 6, 3 > 2, 4 > 2, 5 > 2, 6 > 2, 4 > 3, 4 > 5, 4 > 6, 5 > 6$
G24_3f	$2 > 1, 5 > 1, 6 > 1, 2 > 4, 6 > 2, 6 > 3, 5 > 4, 6 > 4, 6 > 5$
G24_4	$1 > 2, 1 > 3, 1 > 5, 1 > 6, 3 > 2, 4 > 2, 6 > 2, 3 > 5, 4 > 5, 4 > 6$
G24_5	$1 > 2, 4 > 1, 5 > 1, 1 > 6, 3 > 2, 4 > 2, 5 > 2, 4 > 3, 3 > 6, 4 > 6, 5 > 6$
G24_6a	$1 > 2, 1 > 6, 3 > 2, 4 > 2, 5 > 2, 3 > 6, 4 > 5, 4 > 6, 5 > 6$
G24_6b	$1 > 2, 1 > 6, 3 > 2, 4 > 2, 5 > 2, 3 > 6, 4 > 5, 4 > 6, 5 > 6$
G24_6c	$1 > 2, 1 > 5, 1 > 6, 3 > 2, 4 > 2, 5 > 2, 4 > 3, 3 > 6, 4 > 5, 4 > 6, 5 > 6$
G24_6d	$1 > 2, 4 > 1, 1 > 6, 3 > 2, 4 > 2, 5 > 2, 4 > 3, 5 > 3, 4 > 6, 5 > 6$
G24_7	$1 > 2, 1 > 3, 1 > 5, 4 > 2, 6 > 2, 4 > 3, 6 > 3, 4 > 5, 6 > 5$
G24_8a	$1 > 3, 5 > 1, 1 > 6, 4 > 2, 5 > 2, 2 > 6, 4 > 3, 5 > 3, 4 > 6, 5 > 6$
G24_8b	$1 > 2, 4 > 1, 5 > 1, 3 > 2, 4 > 2, 5 > 2, 5 > 3, 3 > 6, 4 > 6, 5 > 6$
G24v_3	$1 > 2, 6 > 1, 4 > 2, 5 > 2, 6 > 2, 4 > 3, 6 > 3, 6 > 5$
G24v_3b	$1 > 2, 1 > 3, 4 > 1, 4 > 2, 5 > 2, 6 > 2, 4 > 3, 5 > 3, 6 > 3, 4 > 5$
G24w_3	$1 > 2, 1 > 3, 4 > 2, 5 > 2, 6 > 2, 4 > 3, 5 > 3, 6 > 3$
G24w_3b	$1 > 2, 1 > 3, 4 > 2, 5 > 2, 6 > 2, 4 > 3, 5 > 3, 6 > 3$

number of fitness evaluations. In this benchmark there are some pairs of test cases that are used to test one behaviour of the algorithms like their abilities to handle constraints in the boundaries or the cases with disconnected feasible regions versus non-disconnected feasible area. Comparing the pairs of test cases with optima in constraint or search boundary over optima not in constraint or search boundary, with $No - div$ the optima in constraint boundary has got better results (G24_1, G24_2), (G24_4, G24_5), (G24_8b, G24_8a). While for other methods the trend is similar, for RI the trend is the other way, meaning with increasing diversity by inserting random solutions in RI, algorithm enhances its ability for finding optima which is not in constraint boundary. The pairs of fixed constraints versus dynamic constraints (G24_f, G24_7), (G24_3f, G24_3) show significant decrease in MOF values for dynamic constraints as it gets harder for the methods to deal with dynamism. The only exception is the behaviour of RI method in which MOF values are almost the same in these two cases and this is attributed with stochastic nature of this method. The pairs of test cases for observing the effect of connected feasible region versus disconnected feasible region (G24_6b, G24_6a), (G24_6b, G24_6d) do not show any trend in the results. As this behaviour depends to the constraint handling technique of algorithms to a greater extent, that is similar in our case. Opp showed similar performance to the base algorithm in most of the cases with some exceptions. As the authors claim this method is to enhance convergence speed compared to base DE algorithm and is more effective in higher dimension problems. Our case is a two dimension, it is recommended to test this algorithm with higher dimension to see its effects in DCOPs.

Due to space limitation, we discarded to bring the results of TE values. But the results of this measure also proof $Crowding$ has the best performance over the other methods in most of the test cases. In addition for two test cases (G24_2, G24_8a) that RI showed better results in MOF values, based on TE values $Crowding$ has better performance meaning $Crowding$ end-up to closer values to optimum at the end of the change periods. For G24_uf all the methods except RI reach to optimum values as the TE values are zero. Also for G24_u, $Crowding$ and RI reach to optimum at all times. Figure 2 shows the distribution of NFE values in box-plots. Boxes represent the values obtained in the central 25%–75%, while the line inside the box shows the median values. Whiskers depicts highest and lowest values within interquartile range and dots show outliers. The figure is color-coded based on SR values. The dark-red color shows SR values lower than 20%, the purple color belongs to $SR \in [20\%-50\%]$, the blue color is for $SR \in [50\%-80\%]$, and finally the dark-green belongs to SR values above 80%. In general for the test cases with fixed characteristics (G24_f, G24_uf, G24_3f) or unconstrained cases (G24_u, G24_2u) in most cases the algorithms manage to reach to VTR values in lower NFE and higher SR values. For the rest of the test cases, there is this general observation that shows regardless of the test case, $Crowding$ and $Fitnessdiv$ are more successful based on SR values that is easily observable based on stages that we defined and color-coded. Based on the colors, these two methods are usually one stage higher than the other methods in SR values.

Based on the characteristics of some functions, the distribution of NFE show quiet a high standard deviation in results. These cases show less reliability in algorithms behaviour as in each run they achieve the VTR in different NFE values. Those belong to test cases with either smaller feasible areas or the test cases with specific characteristics (G24_2, G24_5). In these two test cases in some change periods the landscape is either a plateau or contains infinite number of optimum. In some cases the algorithms are almost unable to reach VTR in the given number of evaluations. The cases are colored with dark-red based of SR values. Figure 2 for RI shows in unconstrained cases it reaches to 10% VTR values with 100% of SR in almost of the cases but with high NFE values. In addition, for the functions with small feasible areas the results show a high number of standard deviation. Indeed, this was expected based on the random

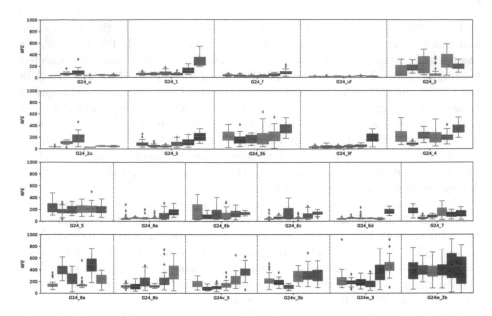

Fig. 2. Boxplot of NFE values for $\epsilon = 10\%$ VTR, color-coded with SR values: dark-red: $SR < 20\%$, purple: $SR \in [20\%-50\%]$, blue: $SR \in [50\%-80\%]$, dark-green: $SR > 80\%$. From left to right $1 = CLS$, $2 = Crowding$, $3 = Fitnessdiv$, $4 = No - div$, $5 = Opp$, and $6 = RI$. (Color figure online)

nature of this method. So depending on the random solutions inserted, in some cases they can manage to track the optima and in the others they are unable to do so. In general RI is the most different method that has different trend compared to other methods in almost all the functions.

4.3   Discussions

Overall, results show *Crowding* that has higher diversity in population could reach to better MOF values. It also shows higher speed and frequency of reaching to 10% VTR values due to the results of SR and NFE values. Statistical test shows (Table 2) this method not only have significantly better results compared to base algorithm ($No - div$), but also compared to other methods in most of the test cases. While this method shows competitive results regardless of the test case, success of some methods highly depend on the tested problem. In this method high diversity in population is created by avoiding genotypic similar individuals and without the need for extra fitness evaluations. While for some other methods like RI high diversity in population is achieved with the need for extra evaluations and the new solutions are inserted randomly. While the random insertion of solutions is often successful in unconstrained problems, in constrained problems it is dependant to the feasibility status of the new solutions and the applied constraint handling method. Indeed the constraint handling technique forces the solutions toward feasible areas avoiding infeasible areas while diversity mechanisms tend to have solutions spread over the search space. Of course the severity of the competition depends to both opposing forces: diversity promotion technique and constraint handling technique applied. So depending to the methods applied, the created solution may not be accepted (rejected by constraint handling method) to be inserted to the population like in Opp, leading to low diversity in constrained problems; Or the solutions are inserted in the population increasing diversity (like in RI) but unable to compete with the best solution. Thus one solution is applying adaptive constraint handling mechanisms. They can be designed in a way that at the first generations after a change, they increase their threshold (more relaxed with constraint violation) in order to allow diversity mechanisms explore the whole search space and then decrease to conduct the search toward feasible areas. The other suggestion is to use repair methods [23] as constraint handling technique, in which if the created solution by diversity handling mechanism is infeasible but a good solution (in terms of fitness function), preserve it in the population by repairing it. For more elaborate investigations on the roles of these two forces over each other and the overal algorithm performance, a measure that shows percentages of feasible and infeasible solutions that are selected for next generation can be helpful. As this measure can imply diversity handling mechanism ability to how it will balance exploiting feasible regions while exploring infeasible regions.

As the results of $Fitnessdiv$ are not as promising as $Crowding$ in the problem types in this benchmark, this can be concluded as phynotypic diversity has less effectiveness as gynotypic diversity. For CLS, although an adaptive approach is used in such a way that at the first generations after a change, the local scarch length is large and gradually reduces; But as this local search is only applied to best solution at each generation, it is not enough to promote diversity as the results show. One solution is to do chaos local search randomly for some other individuals of the population besides to the best solution to increase diversity more. RI showed less reliability in NFE and SR values (based on high standard deviation in results) and its worse performance for MOF values for problems with small feasible area. Conversely, this method is highly suggested to be used for unconstrained problems as it showed best results for these cases.

5   Conclusions and Future Works

Maintaining and promoting diversity in EAs is crucial to enable them adapt to dynamic environments in DCOPs. We have surveyed analysis of the diversity mechanisms, ranging from chaos local search, crowding, fitness diversity, opposition and random immigrants with a base DE algorithm for solving DCOPs. We have seen that diversity can be highly beneficial for enhancing the capabilities of DE for solving DCOPs. We found that diversity mechanisms that are effective for one problem may be ineffective for other problems, and vice versa. We observed that in some cases, the diversity mechanisms tend to have an opposing force toward the constraint handling technique. To gain more insights, comparing combination of diversity promoting mechanisms with different constraint handling techniques is worth to be more investigated. Another future study is the application of popular niching methods like clearing, fitness sharing and others with a moving peak benchmark in DCOPs. As these methods show their best effectiveness in multi-modal optimization, comparing them in the current work over our applied benchmark was not fair.

Acknowledgment. This work has been supported through Australian Research Council (ARC) grant DP160102401.

References

1. De Prada, C., Sarabia, D., Cristea, S., Mazaeda, R.: Plant-wide control of a hybrid process. Int. J. Adapt. Control Signal Process. **22**(2), 124–141 (2008)
2. Liu, L., Zechman, E.M., Brill Jr., E.D., Mahinthakumar, G., Ranjithan, S., Uber, J.: Adaptive contamination source identification in water distribution systems using an evolutionary algorithm-based dynamic optimization procedure. In: Water Distribution Systems Analysis Symposium 2006, pp. 1–9 (2006)
3. Nguyen, T., Yang, S., Branke, J.: Evolutionary dynamic optimization: a survey of the state of the art. Swarm Evol. Comput. **6**, 1–24 (2012)
4. Hasani-Shoreh, M., Ameca-Alducin, M.Y., Blaikie, W., Neumann, F., Schoenauer, M.: On the behaviour of differential evolution for problems with dynamic linear constraints. In: IEEE Congress on Evolutionary Computation, CEC 2019, Wellington, New Zealand, 10–13 June 2019, pp. 3045–3052 (2019)
5. Sudholt, D.: The benefits of population diversity in evolutionary algorithms: a survey of rigorous runtime analyses. CoRR, vol. abs/1801.10087 (2018)
6. Ishibuchi, H., Tsukamoto, N., Nojima, Y.: Diversity improvement by non-geometric binary crossover in evolutionary multiobjective optimization. IEEE Trans. Evol. Comput. **14**(6), 985–998 (2010)
7. Črepinšek, M., Liu, S.-H., Mernik, M.: Exploration and exploitation in evolutionary algorithms: a survey. ACM Comput. Surv. (CSUR) **45**(3), 35 (2013)
8. Yin, X., Germay, N.: A fast genetic algorithm with sharing scheme using cluster analysis methods in multimodal function optimization. In: Albrecht, R.F., Reeves, C.R., Steele, N.C. (eds.) Artificial Neural Nets and Genetic Algorithms, pp. 450–457. Springer, Vienna (1993). https://doi.org/10.1007/978-3-7091-7533-0_65
9. Contreras-Varela, L., Mezura-Montes, E.: A diversity promotion study in constrained optimizations. In: 2018 IEEE Congress on Evolutionary Computation (CEC), pp. 1–8, July 2018
10. Cobb, H.G.: An investigation into the use of hypermutation as an adaptive operator in genetic algorithms having continuous, time-dependent nonstationary environments. Naval Research lab Washington DC, Technical report (1990)
11. Grefenstette, J.J., et al.: Genetic algorithms for changing environments. In: PPSN, vol. 2, pp. 137–144 (1992)
12. Bu, C., Luo, W., Yue, L.: Continuous dynamic constrained optimization with ensemble of locating and tracking feasible regions strategies. IEEE Trans. Evol. Comput. **PP**(99), 1 (2016)
13. Goh, C.K., Tan, K.C.: A competitive-cooperative coevolutionary paradigm for dynamic multiobjective optimization. IEEE Trans. Evol. Comput. **13**(1), 103–127 (2009)

14. Ameca-Alducin, M.Y., Hasani-Shoreh, M., Blaikie, W., Neumann, F., Mezura-Montes, E.: A comparison of constraint handling techniques for dynamic constrained optimization problems. In: 2018 IEEE Congress on Evolutionary Computation, CEC 2018, Rio de Janeiro, Brazil, 8–13 July 2018, pp. 1–8 (2018)
15. Deb, K.: An efficient constraint handling method for genetic algorithms. Comput. Methods Appl. Mech. Eng. **186**(2), 311–338 (2000)
16. Jia, D., Zheng, G., Khan, M.K.: An effective memetic differential evolution algorithm based on chaotic local search. Inf. Sci. **181**(15), 3175–3187 (2011)
17. Sareni, B., Krahenbuhl, L.: Fitness sharing and niching methods revisited. IEEE Trans. Evol. Comput. **2**(3), 97–106 (1998)
18. Hutter, M., Legg, S.: Fitness uniform optimization. IEEE Trans. Evol. Comput. **10**(5), 568–589 (2006)
19. Rahnamayan, S., Tizhoosh, H.R., Salama, M.M.: Opposition-based differential evolution. IEEE Trans. Evol. Comput. **12**(1), 64–79 (2008)
20. Nguyen, T.T., Yao, X.: Continuous dynamic constrained optimization—the challenges. IEEE Trans. Evol. Comput. **16**(6), 769–786 (2012)
21. Nguyen, T.: A proposed real-valued dynamic constrained benchmark set. School Computer Science, University Birmingham, Birmingham, U.K., Technical report (2008)
22. Derrac, J., García, S., Molina, D., Herrera, F.: A practical tutorial on the use of nonparametric statistical tests as a methodology for comparing evolutionary and swarm intelligence algorithms. Swarm Evol. Comput. **1**(1), 3–18 (2011)
23. Ameca-Alducin, M.-Y., Hasani-Shoreh, M., Neumann, F.: On the use of repair methods in differential evolution for dynamic constrained optimization. In: Sim, K., Kaufmann, P. (eds.) EvoApplications 2018. LNCS, vol. 10784, pp. 832–847. Springer, Cham (2018). https://doi.org/10.1007/978-3-319-77538-8_55

A Deep Hierarchical Reinforcement Learner for Aerial Shepherding of Ground Swarms

Hung T. Nguyen$^{(\boxtimes)}$, Tung D. Nguyen , Matthew Garratt ,
Kathryn Kasmarik , Sreenatha Anavatti , Michael Barlow ,
and Hussein A. Abbass

School of Engineering and Information Technology,
University of New South Wales, Canberra, Australia
{hung.nguyen,tung.nguyen}@student.adfa.edu.au,
{m.garratt,k.merrick,s.anavatti,m.barlow,h.abbass}@adfa.edu.au

Abstract. This paper introduces a deep reinforcement learning method to train an autonomous aerial agent acting as a shepherd to provide guidance for a swarm of ground vehicles. The learner is situated within a high-fidelity robotic-operating-system (ROS)-based simulation environment consisting of an Unmanned Aerial Vehicle (UAV) learning to guide a swarm of Unmanned Ground Vehicles (UGVs) to a target location. Our approach uses a combination of machine education, apprenticeship bootstrapping, and deep-learning-based methodologies to decompose the complex shepherding strategy into sub-problems requiring simpler skills that get fused to form the overall skills required for shepherding. The proposed methodology is effective in training the UAV agent with multiple reward designing schemes.

Keywords: Apprenticeship bootstrapping · Swarm guidance · Deep hierarchical reinforcement learning · Shepherding · UAV · UGVs

1 Introduction

The bio-inspired swarm control problem brings novel perspectives from a variety of fields including control theory and computational intelligence [10]. Studies in multi-agent systems and swarm robotics attempt to address the question of how groups of simple agents/robots can be designed such that their collective behavior emerges from their interaction with themselves and their environment [2,16]. Approaches to control a swarm of agents can be divided into two categories: rule-based algorithms, and learning-based algorithms [1,17]. The former introduces a set of fixed rules or predefined equations to compute the dynamics of the system based on global or local states of agents in the swarm [7,23]. While they achieve simple design, fast implementation, and scalability in relation with the number of agents, they often suffer from a lack of adaptability and generalizability to different contexts.

© Springer Nature Switzerland AG 2019
T. Gedeon et al. (Eds.): ICONIP 2019, LNCS 11953, pp. 658–669, 2019.
https://doi.org/10.1007/978-3-030-36708-4_54

The latter approach is based on machine learning, offers flexibility, and eliminates the need for a large amount of knowledge about the model being used for swarm dynamics, or the need to validate the rules. Various methods applying reinforcement learning or deep reinforcement learning combined with team communication or a shared mental model have been proposed to learn decentralized policies for swarm control [15, 18, 19]. Nevertheless, these approaches do not scale up with an increasing number of swarm members due to the significant increase in the computational resources required to train multiple agents simultaneously.

The shepherding problem is inspired by the real behaviour of herding sheep using a sheepdog in agriculture. Strömbom et al. [20] developed a heuristic model to explain the interaction between one intelligent individual, the sheepdog, and a swarm of agents/sheep, which can be extended to many other problems in human-swarm interaction. Shepherding-inspired methods for swarm control might employ one learning agent to influence a larger swarm of rule-based entities.

The coordination between unmanned aerial vehicles (UAVs) and unmanned ground vehicles (UGVs) is an active area of research [14] due to the significant benefits of this coordination wherein UAVs have a wide field of view (FoV) allowing it to guide ground vehicles effectively. This support enables the ground vehicles to better plan in complex scenarios. The coordination can be useful in crowd control operations, rescue missions in disasters, or in surveillance, reconnaissance, and intelligence (SRI) missions. Solutions to the shepherding problem show promise for the robust coordination of autonomous air-ground vehicles [3]. In this case, the problem of coordinating autonomous air-ground vehicles will simply focus on how to develop an effective agent for the aerial vehicles while the ground vehicles will be controlled by the rules of Strömbom et al. [20].

Recent successes in deep reinforcement learning models, which even surpass top human competitors in some particular tasks such as playing Atari games or developing autonomous robots [11, 24], have attracted researchers and technologists. More autonomous systems with deep reinforcement learning algorithms are investigated in an effort to address various practical problems.

Therefore, it is promising to approach the deep reinforcement learning method to develop an agent for the UAV acting as an aerial shepherd guiding the group of UGVs. However, designing the deep reinforcement learning agent for this task is not trivial because of the complexity of the task described in [20] and the dynamic environment [14]. To address this problem, we adopt successful ideas of our previous research: machine education [4, 6] and apprenticeship bootstrapping deep-learning-based method [13]. These approaches effectively address the complexity of both the task and the environment as they decompose the task into simpler sub-skills in order to also reduce the search space of the environment.

In this paper, we propose deep hierarchical reinforcement learning (DHRL) to address the problem of the aerial shepherding of ground vehicles. We decompose the task into sub-skills including learning to collect and learning to drive behaviors, and individually train these two sub-skills by a deep reinforcement learning algorithm with a designed reward function. Results show that our DHRL agent is able to perform competitively with the heuristic approach of Strömbom, and is scalable when its performance is independent of the number of UGVs.

2 Background

2.1 Shepherding: A Problem Formulation for Effective Swarm Control

The shepherding model proposed by Strömbom et al. [20] introduces a heuristically comprehensive fusion function to compute the displacement of sheep, and from there introduces an effective control strategy for the shepherd. In this paper, we describe the Strömbom et al. [20] model by presenting the notations and mechanism that are utilized later in our experimental design.

The environment for shepherding is a square paddock with length of L. There are two types of agents initialized in this environment belonging to a set of sheep (influenced agents) $\Pi = \{\pi_1, \ldots, \pi_i, \ldots, \pi_N\}$, or a set of shepherds (influencing agents) $B = \{\beta_1, \ldots, \beta_j, \ldots, \beta_M\}$. Three behaviors of each shepherd and four behaviors of each sheep at a time step t are denoted as below.

1. For shepherd β_j:
   - *Driving* behaviour σ_1: If all sheep have been collected in a group, i.e. all distances of observed sheep to their center of mass is lower the threshold $f(N)$ in Eq. 1, the shepherd moves towards a driving point located behind the sheep's group on the line formed between the center of mass of the sheep and the target position by using a normalized force vector, $F^t_{\beta_j cd}$.

$$f(N) = R_{\pi\pi}N^{\frac{2}{3}} \tag{1}$$

   - *Collecting* behaviour σ_2: If there is an outlier sheep whose distance to sheep center of mass is greater than $f(N)$, the shepherd switches to collecting behaviour and computes its normalized force vector, $F^t_{\beta_j cd}$, towards a collecting position located behind the furthest sheep on the line formed between the center of mass of the sheep and the furthest sheep.
   - *Jittering* behaviour σ_3: To avoid a moving impasse, a random noise is presented $F^t_{\beta_j \epsilon}$ with weight $W_{e\beta_j}$ and summed into the total force.

   Shepherd β_j total force $F^t_{\beta_j}$ (total force behaviour σ_8) is a weighted summation of the forces generated by driving/collecting behaviour and jittering behaviour.

$$F^t_{\beta_j} = F^t_{\beta_j cd} + W_{e\beta_j}F^t_{\beta_j \epsilon} \tag{2}$$

2. For sheep π_i:
   - *Escaping* behaviour σ_4: This behaviour is represented by a repulsive force $F^t_{\pi_i \beta_j}$ if the distance between sheep π_i at position $P^t_{\pi_i}$ and shepherd β_j at position $P^t_{\beta_j}$ is less than $R_{\pi\beta}$; that is,

$$\|P^t_{\pi_i} - P^t_{\beta_j}\| \leq R_{\pi\beta} \tag{3}$$

- *Collision avoidance* σ_5: Repulsion of sheep π_i from other sheep $\pi_{k \neq i}$. The condition for the force to be able to exist between a pair of sheep is that the distance between them is less than $R_{\pi\pi}$; that is,

$$\exists k, \ such \ that \ \|P_{\pi_i}^t - P_{\pi_k}^t\| \leq R_{\pi\pi} \tag{4}$$

We then denote $F_{\pi_i\pi_{-i}}^t$ to represent the summed force vectors from all other sheep within the threshold distance applied onto sheep π_i.
- *Grouping behaviour* σ_6: Sheep π_i is attracted to the center of mass of its neighbors $\Lambda_{\pi_i}^t$ by a force $F_{\pi_i\Lambda_{\pi_i}^t}^t$.
- *Jittering behaviour* σ_7: To avoid moving impasse, a random noise is presented $F_{\pi_i\epsilon}^t$ with weight $W_{e\pi_i}$ and summed into the total force.

Sheep π_i total force behaviour σ_9 is represented by the total force $F_{\pi_i}^t$ which is a weighted sum of force vectors $F_{\pi_i\beta_j}^t$, $F_{\pi_i\pi_{-i}}^t$, $F_{\pi_i\Lambda_{\pi_i}^t}^t$, and $F_{\pi_i\epsilon}^t$; that is,

$$F_{\pi_i}^t = W_{\pi_v}F_{\pi_i}^{t-1} + W_{\pi\Lambda}F_{\pi_i\Lambda_{\pi_i}^t}^t + W_{\pi\beta}F_{\pi_i\beta_j}^t + W_{\pi\pi}F_{\pi_i\pi_{-i}}^t + W_{e\pi_i}F_{\pi_i\epsilon}^t \tag{5}$$

The positions of shepherds and sheep are updated according to Eqs. 6 and 7 given $S_{\beta_j}^t$ and $S_{\pi_i}^t$ be the speed of β_j and the speed of π_i at time t. However, in the original Strömbom model, the speeds of agents are constant.

$$P_{\beta_j}^{t+1} = P_{\beta_j}^t + S_{\beta_j}^t F_{\beta_j}^t \tag{6}$$

$$P_{\pi_i}^{t+1} = P_{\pi_i}^t + S_{\pi_i}^t F_{\pi_i}^t \tag{7}$$

2.2 Double Deep Q-Learning/DDQN

Deep Reinforcement Learning/DRL (DRL) [12] was a recent breakthrough which utilizes the ability of deep neural networks to more effectively learn representations of large and continuous state spaces in a reinforcement learning problem. Deep hierarchical representations of input information can be learned through the depth of the networks with multiple layers and nodes without feature engineering. Thus, this approach is a game-changer that offers robustness and human-level performance for a variety of tasks found in the literature.

We use concepts and notations for a regular Markov Decision Process (MDP) [9], a basic process to formulate a reinforcement learning (RL) problem and from there we discuss the fundamentals of DDQN. A RL problem considers four basic components at a time t including an observed state s_t in a state space $\mathcal{S}$, an action that the agent choose a_t in an action space $\mathcal{A}$, a probabilistic transition model $P(s|s_{t+1}, a)$ and a reward r_t received by the agent according to a reward function $\mathcal{R}$. The optimized policy is found by the model through the reinforce signal (reward) when the interaction between the learner and the environment occurs such that the cumulative reward over time is maximized.

$$R_t = \sum_{t'=t}^{T} \gamma^{t'-t} r_{t'} \tag{8}$$

where T is the number of time steps, and γ is the discount factor.

The Q-learning algorithm [22] tries to approximate each state-action pair's value $Q(s_t, a_t)$ in the absence of the transition model $P(s|s_{t+1}, a)$. Deep Q-learning shows an advance over conventional Q-learning by using deep neural networks to approximate Q-values and be able to generalize for large continuous state spaces that cannot commonly be represented by a look-up table. Van Hasselt et al. [21] introduced Double Deep Q-Network (DDQN) to enhance network performance and avoid over-fitting by using two networks which are responsible for estimating two sets of Q-values for current states and target states (with sets of hyper-parameters θ_t and θ'_t, respectively). The loss function is computed as follows:

$$\mathcal{L}_t(\theta_t) = (y_t - Q(s_t, a_t|\theta_t))^2 \tag{9}$$

where y_t represents the target Q-values yielded from:

$$y_t = r_t + \gamma max_a Q(s_{t+1}, a|\theta'_t) \tag{10}$$

Hence, the updating function is represented as follows:

$$\theta \leftarrow \theta - \alpha \cdot \nabla_\theta \mathcal{L}(\theta) \tag{11}$$

where α is the learning rate and $\nabla_\theta \mathcal{L}(\theta)$ is the loss gradient.

DDQN is frequently practiced with experience replay. A reinforcement learner's experiences of transitions are stored and randomly sampled to perform a batch training process for better data efficiency and to eliminate the effects of correlation in the dataset due to temporal dependencies.

3   Methodology

In this section, we discuss our proposed methodology for shepherding a swarm of agents using one reinforcement learning agent as a shepherd.

3.1   Our Proposed Framework

Figure 1 demonstrates all components of our reinforcement learning framework. As mentioned in Sect. 1, one of the challenges for learning shepherding skills is the complexity of the mission's objectives involving multiple sub-tasks to cover. Therefore, the search space might be too large for guaranteeing convergence of one single deep network. By decomposing the problem space of shepherding task into two sub-spaces corresponding to sheep driving and sheep collecting sub-tasks, the complexity of the problem can be managed.

Two DDQN models are trained to master two primitive skills: collecting outlier sheep to form a cluster of sheep and driving the cluster of sheep to the target. The network for driving skill is fully trained in a scenario where all sheep are already clustered. The agents are guided by a reward function to learn to locate and reach the driving point. On the other hand, the skill network for

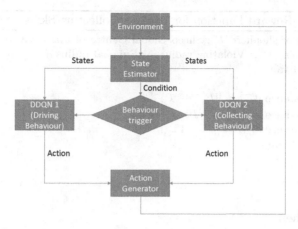

Fig. 1. Deep reinforcement learning framework with task decomposition.

collecting is trained in another scenario where there is one sheep located far away from the sheep center of mass. The positions of the shepherd and the swarm of sheep are initially randomized but complies to the conditions representing such situations as described above.

We then later combine two trained networks in a framework where a behaviour selection component at each time step chooses to trigger one of the networks based on the threshold specified in Eq. 1. We test the performance of the system by continuously activating two deep networks in a full shepherding problem scenario.

3.2 Reward Design

For each training scenario, we design a reward function to aid the learning of each skill. The sub-problems can be generalized in a form of navigation problem with the sub-goal is either the driving point or the collecting point. For our implementation of the shepherding problem, we define a sub-goal radius d_s from the sub-goal location so that if the agent is within this range from sub-goal, it is considered as successfully reaching the sub-goal. This variation makes the sub-goal more achievable due to the dynamics of the agents in the environment as well as the lack of the computed force presented to the shepherd as defined in the original problem. Algorithm 1 illustrates our reward function for training. The agent is presented with a small positive reward if it moves closer to the sub-goal and a small negative reward if it moves further from the sub-goal. One episode of training is a success when the sub-goal is reached and a failure when the formation of the swarm is broken by the acts of the learning/shepherding agent. The deformation of the swarm is assumed to be the violation of the shepherd's position to the cluster of swarm defined by the violating radius d_v.

Algorithm 1. Reward Function for Driving/Collecting Skills

Input: Position of shepherd P_β^t; Sheep Global Centre of Mass (GCM) $\Gamma_{\pi_i}^t$; Position of subgoal point $P_{\beta\sigma}^t$; Violating radius d_v; Subgoal radius d_s;
Output: reward value r^t
1: $r_1^t = 0$; $r_2^t = 0$;
2: Calculate distance $d^{t-1} = ||P_\beta^{t-1} - P_{\beta\sigma}^{t-1}||$
3: Calculate distance $d^t = ||P_\beta^t - P_{\beta\sigma}^t||$
4: Calculate distance $d_{CM}^t = ||P_\beta^t - \Gamma_{\pi_i}^t||$
5: **if** $d^t < d^{t-1}$ **then**
6:    $r_1^t = 0.1$
7: **else**
8:    $r_1^t = $ -0.1
9: **end if**
10: **if** $d^t < d_s$ **then**
11:    $r_2^t = 10$
12: **end if**
13: **if** $d_{CM}^t < d_v$ **then**
14:    $r_2^t = $ -10
15: **end if**
16: $r^t = r_1^t + r_2^t$

3.3 Evaluation Metrics

The performance of each DDQN network representing two skills is assessed through the training phases and the performance for shepherding problem is evaluated in the testing phases when we combine two networks under one architecture. Due to the dynamics of the environment and initialization of training scenarios, we employ the ratio $\frac{total\ reward}{total\ number\ of\ actions}$ in each episode to see if the learned policy is optimized or not.

For testing phases, our proposed methodology is further compared to the influence force vector method introduced by Strömbom et.al [20], as baseline method, in terms of the number of steps/actions to complete the task and success rate. Moreover, we investigate the scalability of our methodology through the independent performance - reward per action errors with the increasing number of the ground vehicles. Finally, we also visualize the footprints of the aerial shepherd and the ground vehicles corresponding to the two methods above to show the learning policy efficiency.

4 Experiments and Results

In this paper, we apply the shepherding context in research [20] for coordinating between UAVs and a swarm of UGVs. In our shepherding context, there is one UAV which acts as a shepherd and four UGVs which act like sheep; and the UAV has global-sensing ability that means the UAV is able to know the positions of the UGVs in the entire environment. The mission of the UAV is to shepherd the swarm of UGVs to a concentrated area. A clear illustration of the UAV-UGVs shepherding mission is shown in Fig. 2.

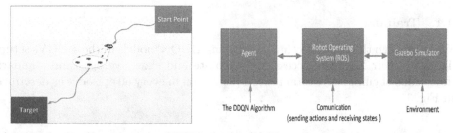

(a) UAV shepherding a swarm of UGVs.   (b) The communication protocol

Fig. 2. UAV shepherding a swarm of UGVs.

Robotic Operating System (ROS) is used as an interface between the agent and the Gazebo simulator environment. Tum-Simulator [8] package is used to simulates the Parrot AR Drone 2's model and its behaviour. The simulator package Husky [5] is used for the UGVs. The communicating protocol among the agent, ROS, and Gazebo simulator is illustrated in Fig. 2b.

The UGVs'action space consists of 2 continuous real-valued actions representing the linear velocity, V, and the angular velocity (yaw rate), ω. The linear velocity of the UGVs is set to 0.5 (m/s), representing the step length allowed for a sheep to move per second. The UAV actions space consists of four discrete actions with each action representing the linear velocity in the longitudinal and lateral directions, and these are denoted using the values (p, r, a), respectively. The speed of the UAV is set at 1 (m/s). For each episode in training or testing, the UAV is automatically taken off to a height of 2 m, and this height is maintained until the end of the episode. The step time of the UAV is set to 0.2 s. We adopt the parameters in the shepherding model of Strömbom et al. [20] except for the environment size, the sheep step, and the shepherd detection radius. In our Gazebo simulation, the size of the paddock is $20 \times 20 (m \times m)$. We conduct three setups representing the increasing number of the UGVs: 4-UGVs (the number of UGVs is 4), 5-UGVs (the number of UGVs is 5), and 6-UGVs (the number of UGVs is 6). The shepherd detection radius for these setups are set to 5 m, 6 m, and 7 m, respectively.

The DDQN algorithm with a deep feedforward architecture is used in this paper. Two hidden layers with 32 and 16 nodes respectively are used. The optimizer method is stochastic gradient descent. The DDQN algorithm is trained with a replay memory size of 100,000 state-action pairs, the discount factor $\gamma = 0.99$, mini-batch size 32, and the learning rate 0.00025. During training, the $\epsilon - greedy$ is decreased linearly from 1 to 0.1, and fixed at 0.1 thereafter. The epsilon decay is 0.999 for every episode. The maximum number of steps for both collecting and driving DDQN models is 1000. The states space includes two vectors: a vector from GCM to the shepherd and a vector from the sub goal to shepherd. They are used as inputs while the outputs, as discussed above, are four discrete actions of the UAV.

4.1 Training

We train both the two collecting and driving DDQN models in the 4-UGVs setup. To show their learning success, we calculate and show averages and standard deviations of cumulative total reward per action in every 50 episodes as described in Fig. 3.

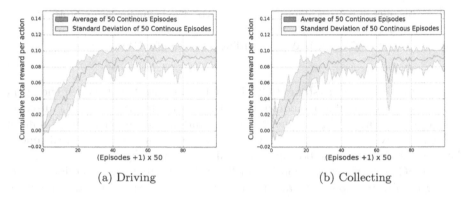

(a) Driving   (b) Collecting

Fig. 3. Learning curves of two driving and collecting DDQN models

It is clear that the cumulative total rewards per action of both the collecting and driving models increase significantly in the first 1000 episodes, and then maintain relatively constant around 0.085 till the end of training. The tendencies demonstrate that these collecting and driving DDQN models are able to learn effectively when they converge at approximately 0.085.

4.2 Testing

After the collecting and driving DDQN models are fully trained, we conduct 30 different testing cases in three setups by our DHRL approach and Strömbom's approach. We calculate average and standard deviations of reward per action, the number of steps, and success rate in these testing cases shown in Table 1 in order to investigate the effectiveness and scalability of the proposed approach. Firstly, the success rate is 100% being similar in both our method and Strömbom's approach. Secondly, regarding the scalability of our approach, the average action reward of the DHRL model is not changed at 0.07 when the number of the UGVs increases. It is essential to note that although the average number of steps generated by DHRL is slightly higher than that of Strömbom's approach in all three setups, their variations are smaller. This show the behaviour of the DHRL is more stable than that produced by Strömbom's approach. Additionally, the action of the UAV in the DHRL is discrete compared to the continuous values of the UAV in Strömbom's approach so that the movement of the DHRL aerial agent is less smooth and take more steps to reach the destination.

Table 1. Averages and standard deviations of reward per action, number of steps, and success rates of the three setups in 30 different testing cases.

Experimental ID	DHRL			Strombom	
	Action reward	# Steps	Success rate (%)	# Steps	Success rate (%)
4 UGVs	0.07 ± 0.01	340 ± 21	100	327 ± 81	100
5 UGVs	0.07 ± 0.01	344 ± 35	100	289 ± 71	100
6 UGVs	0.07 ± 0.01	349 ± 28	100	302 ± 47	100

An another interesting point is that in Strömbom's approach, the aerial agent does not truly reach to collecting and driving sub-goals when herding the UGVS. It can be clearly seen in Fig. 4. Instead of collecting the furthest UGV, the aerial agent of Strömbom's approach visits to a sub-goal located between the furthest and the driving point to herd the entire swarm described in Fig. 4a. It is different from our method when the aerial agent of the DHRL needs to collect the furthest UGV first, and then drive the whole swarm to the target shown in Fig. 4b. Our DHRL agent enables a formation of UGV agents to be established before driving them towards the target. This approach helps maintain the formation more exactly in herding, and then avoid obstacles as illustrated in Fig. 4, where the DHRL agent drives far away from the boundary in contrast to the Strömbom agent hitting into the wall.

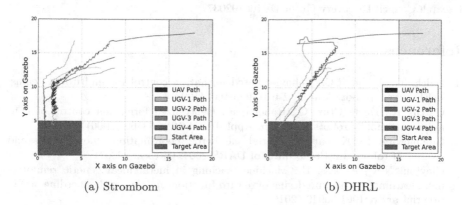

(a) Strombom   (b) DHRL

Fig. 4. Trajectories of the UAV and the four UGVs in a testing case.

5   Conclusion and Future Work

This paper proposes a shepherding-inspired strategy applied to a UAV-UGV swarm control scenario. We introduce a deep reinforcement learning framework which decomposes a complex shepherding strategy involving a UAV controlling a swarm of UGV agents into two smaller search spaces each requiring distinct low-level skills. Two DDQN models have been used with different designed reward functions to fit each sub-problem and to facilitate the learning process. Simulation results show effective learning with stabilized average reward values received per each step of the UAV agent even with dynamic initialization of the UAV and UGVs' positions.

Two fully trained networks are then selected by a rule-based mechanism to generate the actions when testing in full scenarios. The framework offers flexible and effective behaviours of UAV shown by precise movements of the UAV to create a formation/cluster of UGV agents, control the swarm of agents to reach a target location while maintaining the formation on the trajectories. The behaviour generated by DHRL are more stable and requires less prior knowledge compared to the traditional force vector computation implemented in Strömbom's method. The advantages of our proposed approach become necessary when the UAV operates in an environment including obstacles, for which the Strömbom method is not practical.

Future studies will investigate the design of a learning algorithm to replace the rule-based selection of low-level skills. This is particularly important when the number of low-level skills increases. Additionally, a deep reinforcement learning approach for continuous actions will be investigated in order to produce smoother and more practical behaviours of the aerial agent.

Acknowledgement. This material is based upon work supported by the Air Force Office of Scientific Research under award number FA2386-17-1-4054 and an Australian Research Council Discovery Grant DP160102037.

References

1. Balch, T., Arkin, R.C.: Behavior-based formation control for multirobot teams. IEEE Trans. Robot. Autom. **14**(6), 926–939 (1998)
2. Carelli, R., De la Cruz, C., Roberti, F.: Centralized formation control of non-holonomic mobile robots. Lat. Am. Appl. Res. **36**(2), 63–69 (2006)
3. Chaimowicz, L., Kumar, V.: Aerial shepherds: coordination among UAVs and swarms of robots. In: Proceedings of DARS 2004. Citeseer (2004)
4. Clayton, N.R., Abbass, H.: Machine teaching in hierarchical genetic reinforcement learning: curriculum design of reward functions for swarm shepherding. arXiv preprint arXiv:1901.00949 (2019)
5. ClearpathRobotics: ROS husky robot (2017). http://wiki.ros.org/Robots/Husky. Accessed 20 June 2019
6. Gee, A., Abbass, H.: Transparent machine education of neural networks for swarm shepherding using curriculum design. arXiv preprint arXiv:1903.09297 (2019)

7. Guillet, A., Lenain, R., Thuilot, B., Rousseau, V.: Formation control of agricultural mobile robots: a bidirectional weighted constraints approach. J. Field Robot. **34**, 1260–1274 (2017)
8. Huang, H., Sturm, J.: Tum simulator (2014). http://wiki.ros.org/tum_simulator. Accessed 20 June 2019
9. Kaelbling, L.P., Littman, M.L., Moore, A.W.: Reinforcement learning: a survey. J. Artif. Intell. Res. **4**, 237–285 (1996)
10. Martinez, S., Cortes, J., Bullo, F.: Motion coordination with distributed information. IEEE Control Syst. Mag. **27**(4), 75–88 (2007)
11. Mnih, V., et al.: Asynchronous methods for deep reinforcement learning. In: International Conference on Machine Learning, pp. 1928–1937 (2016)
12. Mnih, V., et al.: Human-level control through deep reinforcement learning. Nature **518**(7540), 529 (2015)
13. Nguyen, H., et al.: Apprenticeship bootstrapping via deep learning with a safety net for UAV-UGV interaction. arXiv preprint arXiv:1810.04344 (2018)
14. Nguyen, H.T., Garratt, M., Bui, L.T., Abbass, H.: Supervised deep actor network for imitation learning in a ground-air UAV-UGVs coordination task. In: 2017 IEEE Symposium Series on Computational Intelligence (SSCI), pp. 1–8. IEEE (2017)
15. Nguyen, T., Nguyen, H., Debie, E., Kasmarik, K., Garratt, M., Abbass, H.: Swarm Q-learning with knowledge sharing within environments for formation control. In: 2018 International Joint Conference on Neural Networks (IJCNN), pp. 1–8. IEEE (2018)
16. Oh, H., Shirazi, A.R., Sun, C., Jin, Y.: Bio-inspired self-organising multi-robot pattern formation: a review. Robot. Auton. Syst. **91**, 83–100 (2017)
17. Oh, K.K., Park, M.C., Ahn, H.S.: A survey of multi-agent formation control. Automatica **53**, 424–440 (2015)
18. Palmer, G., Tuyls, K., Bloembergen, D., Savani, R.: Lenient multi-agent deep reinforcement learning. In: Proceedings of the 17th International Conference on Autonomous Agents and MultiAgent Systems, pp. 443–451. International Foundation for Autonomous Agents and Multiagent Systems (2018)
19. Speck, C., Bucci, D.J.: Distributed UAV swarm formation control via object-focused, multi-objective SARSA. In: 2018 Annual American Control Conference (ACC), pp. 6596–6601. IEEE (2018)
20. Strömbom, D., et al.: Solving the shepherding problem: heuristics for herding autonomous, interacting agents. J. R. Soc. Interface **11**(100), 20140719 (2014)
21. Van Hasselt, H., Guez, A., Silver, D.: Deep reinforcement learning with double q-learning. In: AAAI, Phoenix, AZ, vol. 2, p. 5 (2016)
22. Watkins, C.J., Dayan, P.: Q-learning. Mach. Learn. **8**(3), 279–292 (1992)
23. Xu, D., Zhang, X., Zhu, Z., Chen, C., Yang, P.: Behavior-based formation control of swarm robots. Math. Probl. Eng. **2014** (2014)
24. Yang, Z., Merrick, K., Jin, L., Abbass, H.A.: Hierarchical deep reinforcement learning for continuous action control. IEEE Trans. Neural Netw. Learn. Syst. **99**, 1–11 (2018)

Fuzzy Bilinear Latent Canonical Correlation Projection for Feature Learning

Yun-Hao Yuan[1,2]([envelope]), Hui Zhang[1], Yun Li[1], Jipeng Qiang[1], Jianping Gou[3], Guangwei Gao[4], and Bin Li[1]

[1] School of Information Engineering, Yangzhou University, Yangzhou, China
{yhyuan,liyun}@yzu.edu.cn, HuiZhang3212@163.com
[2] School of Computer Science and Technology, Fudan University, Shanghai, China
[3] School of Computer Science, Jiangsu University, Zhenjiang, China
[4] Institute of Advanced Technology,
Nanjing University of Posts and Telecommunications, Nanjing, China

Abstract. Canonical correlation analysis (CCA) is a widely used linear unsupervised subspace learning method. However, standard CCA works with vectorized representation of image matrix, which loses the spatial structure information of image data. In addition, a real-world observation often simultaneously belongs to multiple distinct classes with different degrees of membership, while conventional CCA methods can not deal with this situation. Inspired by aforementioned issues, we in this paper propose a fuzzy bilinear canonical correlation projection (FBCCP) approach. FBCCP not only considers two-dimensional spatial structure of images, but also membership degree of practical observation belonging to different classes at the same time. Experimental results on visual recognition show that the proposed FBCCP approach is more effective than related feature learning approaches.

Keywords: Multi-view learning · Canonical correlation analysis · Two-dimensional feature learning · Fuzzy relation · Feature reduction

1 Introduction

In numerous practical applications in pattern recognition and computer vision, the same objects can usually be represented by diverse representations or modalities due to different feature descriptors or heterogeneous sensors. This kind of

Supported by Undergraduate Education and Teaching Reform Project of Yangzhou University under Grant YZUJX2016-32C; National Natural Science Foundation of China under Grants 61402203, 61703362, and 61611540347; Natural Science Foundation of Jiangsu Province of China under Grants BK20161338 and BK20170513; Yangzhou Science Project Fund of China under Grants YZ2016238 and YZ2017292; Excellent Young Backbone Teacher (Qing Lan) Project and Scientific Innovation Project Fund of Yangzhou University of China under Grant 2017CXJ033.

© Springer Nature Switzerland AG 2019
T. Gedeon et al. (Eds.): ICONIP 2019, LNCS 11953, pp. 670–678, 2019.
https://doi.org/10.1007/978-3-030-36708-4_55

data with multiple representations is referred to as multiple view data in the literature. In contrast with single view data (i.e., only one feature representation), multi-view data usually have different statistical properties and diversity of information, thus being able to more accurately describe the objects. In recent years, analyzing multi-view high dimensional data called multi-view learning has attracted wide attention.

Canonical correlation analysis (CCA), originally presented by Hotelling [1], is a classic but effective multi-view learning method. CCA aims at learning pairs of projection vectors by linearly projecting two views of high dimensional data onto a low dimensional subspace where they are of maximal correlation. Despite the effectiveness of CCA, it is essentially a linear multi-view subspace learning approach, thus failing to uncover the nonlinear relationships between multiple views. To this end, kernel CCA (KCCA) [2] is proposed to solve this problem, where implicit nonlinear mappings are employed to project the original data onto higher-dimensional feature space. Other nonlinear variants of CCA can be found in, for example, [3,4] and [5]. Among those nonlinear improvements, deep CCA (DCCA) [3] is one of the most attractive works in recent years, which makes use of two deep neural networks to project the original observations into new representations.

Standard CCA and its foregoing improvements are based on vector representation of image data. But, vectorized representation has several remarkable shortcomings. First, it breaks image pixels' spatial structure relationship. Second, it leads to high-dimensional small sample problem, thus making intra-set covariance matrix possible to be singular. At last, it makes learning cost expensive due to large amounts of computation. Therefore, it is desirable to learn low-dimensional correlational features directly based on 2-dimensional (2D) image matrix rather than vectorized representation. To this end, a few 2D variants of CCA have been proposed; see, for example, [6–8], and [9]. Note that all the aforementioned 2D improvements are unsupervised. This means that those approaches do not make use of the class label information of multi-view training samples. The extracted 2D features may be not very effective in real-world classification system.

On the other hand, in practice there often exists the situation where an observation simultaneously belongs to multiple distinct classes with different degrees of membership. For instance, a sample point lying on the margin of two classes may belong to one class with degree of membership as x, while to the other class with membership grade as $(1 - x)$. To address this issue, a fuzzy CCA (FCCA) approach [10] was proposed, where the fuzzy class label matrix is regarded as one view. Later, Yang and Sun [11] presented a generalized fuzzy CCA (GFCCA) framework in feature fusion, which makes use of the theory of fuzzy set to construct intraclass and interclass fuzzy scatter matrices. In addition, a nonlinear version of GFCCA was further proposed in [11]. Despite the effectiveness of fuzzy improvements, they are also based on the vectorized representation of image data, which must face the same problems as standard CCA, as mentioned above.

In this paper, we propose a fuzzy bilinear canonical correlation projection (FBCCP) approach, where the fuzzy sample encoding information is embedded into 2D canonical correlation learning. Different from traditional correlation-based projection approaches such as 2DCCA [12] and FCCA, FBCCP not only considers two-dimensional spatial structure of image matrix, but also the membership degree of practical observation belonging to different classes at the same time. Experimental results on visual recognition show that the proposed FBCCP approach is more effective than related feature learning approaches.

2   Background

2.1   Two-Dimensional CCA

Let two random image matrices be $X \in \mathbb{R}^{m \times n_x}$ and $Y \in \mathbb{R}^{m \times n_y}$. Two-dimensional CCA (2DCCA) [12] aims at seeking for pairwise projection directions $w_x \in \mathbb{R}^{n_x}$ and $w_y \in \mathbb{R}^{n_y}$, which maximize the correlation between Xw_x and Yw_y. Directions w_x and w_y can be obtained by the following optimization problem

$$
\begin{aligned}
(w_x^*, w_y^*) = \arg \max_{w_x, w_y} \; \mathrm{cov}(Xw_x, Yw_y) \\
s.t. \; \mathrm{var}(Xw_x) = 1, \; \mathrm{var}(Yw_y) = 1,
\end{aligned}
\tag{1}
$$

where $\mathrm{cov}(\cdot)$ and $\mathrm{var}(\cdot)$ denote covariance operator and variance operator, respectively, and

$$
\mathrm{cov}(Xw_x, Yw_y) = w_x^T [E(X - EX)^T (Y - EY)] w_y = w_x^T \Sigma_{xy} w_y, \tag{2}
$$
$$
\mathrm{var}(Xw_x) = w_x^T [E(X - EX)^T (X - EX)] w_x = w_x^T \Sigma_{xx} w_x, \tag{3}
$$
$$
\mathrm{var}(Yw_y) = w_y^T [E(Y - EY)^T (Y - EY)] w_y = w_y^T \Sigma_{yy} w_y \tag{4}
$$

with $E(\cdot)$ as the expectation operator and Σ_{xy}, Σ_{xx}, and Σ_{yy} as

$$
\Sigma_{xy} = E(X - EX)^T (Y - EY),
$$
$$
\Sigma_{xx} = E(X - EX)^T (X - EX),
$$
$$
\Sigma_{yy} = E(Y - EY)^T (Y - EY).
$$

Via the Lagrange multipliers technique, the optimization problem in (1) can be solved by the next generalized eigenvalue problem.

$$
\begin{bmatrix} & \Sigma_{xy} \\ \Sigma_{xy}^T & \end{bmatrix} \begin{bmatrix} w_x \\ w_y \end{bmatrix} = \lambda \begin{bmatrix} \Sigma_{xx} & \\ & \Sigma_{yy} \end{bmatrix} \begin{bmatrix} w_x \\ w_y \end{bmatrix},
\tag{5}
$$

where λ is the eigenvalue corresponding to the eigenvector $[w_x^T \; w_y^T]^T$.

2.2 Fuzzy K-Nearest Neighbors

Fuzzy K-nearest neighbor (FKNN) algorithm [13] introduces the theory of fuzzy sets into traditional K-nearest neighbor (KNN) algorithm. Different from KNN where one sample point belongs to only one class, FKNN can assign one sample point to multiple distinct classes through fuzzy memberships.

FKNN is able to store the class membership values of all sample points by a membership degree matrix $R = (r_{ij}) \in \mathbb{R}^{n \times c}$, where n is the number of training samples, c is the number of classes, and r_{ij} denotes the membership degree of the ith sample belonging to jth class computed by the next steps.

Step 1. Compute K nearest neighbors of a given sample using KNN algorithm.

Step 2. Calculate all the membership degrees r_{ij} to generate membership degree matrix R, as follows:

$$r_{ij} = \begin{cases} 0.51 + 0.49(n_{ij}/K) & \text{If } i\text{th sample belongs to } j\text{th class,} \\ 0.49(n_{ij}/K) & \text{Otherwise,} \end{cases} \tag{6}$$

where n_{ij} is the number of samples from K nearest neighbors belonging to jth class. Note that all r_{ij}s satisfy $\sum_{j=1}^{c} r_{ij} = 1$ and $0 < \sum_{i=1}^{n} r_{ij} \leq n$.

3 Proposed FBCCP

Let $X = \{X_1, X_2, \cdots, X_n\}$ and $Y = \{Y_1, Y_2, \cdots, Y_n\}$ be two sets of 2-dimensional feature vectors with a total of c classes, where $X_i \in \mathbb{R}^{m \times p}$ and $Y_i \in \mathbb{R}^{m \times q}$. The goal of our FBCCP is to seek pairs of projection directions $\alpha \in \mathbb{R}^p$ and $\beta \in \mathbb{R}^q$ to maximize the correlation between canonical projections $\{X_i \alpha\}_{i=1}^{n}$ and $\{Y_i \beta\}_{i=1}^{n}$.

For X and Y, we employ FKNN to construct membership degree matrices $R_x = (r_{x,ij}) \in \mathbb{R}^{n \times c}$ and $R_y = (r_{y,ij}) \in \mathbb{R}^{n \times c}$, respectively, where $r_{.,ij}$ denotes the membership degree of ith sample belonging to jth class. According to the idea in [11], we use membership degree matrices R_x and R_y to separately define fuzzy jth class mean vectors $\mu_{x,j}$ and $\mu_{y,j}$, total mean vectors μ_x and μ_y, as follows.

$$\mu_{x,j} = \frac{1}{n_{x,j}} \sum_{i=1}^{n} r_{x,ij}^{o} X_i, \text{and } \mu_{y,j} = \frac{1}{n_{y,j}} \sum_{i=1}^{n} r_{y,ij}^{o} Y_i, \tag{7}$$

$$\mu_x = \frac{1}{n_x} \sum_{j=1}^{c} \sum_{i=1}^{n} r_{x,ij}^{o} X_i, \text{and } \mu_y = \frac{1}{n_y} \sum_{j=1}^{c} \sum_{i=1}^{n} r_{y,ij}^{o} Y_i, \tag{8}$$

where o is a parameter that controls the influence of fuzzy membership degree, $n_{x,j} = \sum_{i=1}^{n} r_{x,ij}^{o}$, $n_{y,j} = \sum_{i=1}^{n} r_{y,ij}^{o}$, $n_x = \sum_{j=1}^{c} n_{x,j}$, and $n_y = \sum_{j=1}^{c} n_{y,j}$.

With (7), fuzzy within-set scatter matrices of X and Y can be separately defined as

$$S_{xx} = \sum_{j=1}^{c} \sum_{i=1}^{n} r_{x,ij}^{o}(X_i - \mu_{x,j})^T (X_i - \mu_{x,j}), \tag{9}$$

$$S_{yy} = \sum_{j=1}^{c} \sum_{i=1}^{n} r_{y,ij}^{o}(Y_i - \mu_{y,j})^T (Y_i - \mu_{y,j}). \tag{10}$$

Using (8), we can define fuzzy between-set scatter matrix of X and Y as

$$S_{xy} = \sum_{i=1}^{n} (X_i - \mu_x)^T (Y_i - \mu_y). \tag{11}$$

With (9), (10), and (11), we are able to construct the optimization model of our FBCCP method by the following

$$\max_{\alpha,\beta} \alpha^T S_{xy} \beta \tag{12}$$
$$s.t. \ \alpha^T S_{xx} \alpha = 1, \beta^T S_{yy} \beta = 1.$$

Using the Lagrange multiplier technique, optimization problem in (12) can be solved by the following generalized eigenvalue problem.

$$\begin{bmatrix} & S_{xy} \\ S_{xy}^T & \end{bmatrix} \begin{bmatrix} \alpha \\ \beta \end{bmatrix} = \eta \begin{bmatrix} S_{xx} & \\ & S_{yy} \end{bmatrix} \begin{bmatrix} \alpha \\ \beta \end{bmatrix} \tag{13}$$

where η denotes the eigenvalue associated with the eigenvector $[\alpha^T \ \beta^T]^T$.

Using (13), we select the d eigenvectors corresponding to the first d largest eigenvalues to yield the projection matrices $A = [\alpha_1, \alpha_2, \cdots, \alpha_d] \in \mathbb{R}^{p \times d}$ for X and $B = [\beta_1, \beta_2, \cdots, \beta_d] \in \mathbb{R}^{q \times d}$ for Y. As used in [14], we employ the same feature fusion strategies to combine the 2-dimensional features of given X and Y, i.e.,

$$[XA, YB] \tag{14}$$
$$XA + YB \tag{15}$$

where (14) is referred to as feature fusion strategy 1 (FFS1) and (15) is referred to as feature fusion strategy 2 (FFS2). The fused features are used for classification.

4 Experiment

To test the effectiveness of the proposed FBCCP, we carry out several recognition experiments on the AT&T and AR face databases and compare it with 2DCCA and generalized 2DCCA (G2DCCA). Note that G2DCCA is a two-dimensional variant of generalized CCA [15].

Table 1. Recognition rate with $l = 5$ on the AT&T database.

Method	FBCCP	G2DCCA	2DCCA
FFS1	0.94	0.91	0.86
FFS2	0.93	0.91	0.86

Table 2. Recognition rate with $l = 6$ on the AT&T database.

Method	FBCCP	G2DCCA	2DCCA
FFS1	0.988	0.944	0.913
FFS2	0.988	0.956	0.913

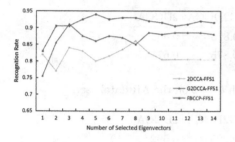 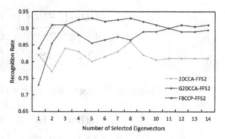

Fig. 1. Recognition rate with $l = 5$ versus the number of selected eigenvectors on the AT&T database.

Our FBCCP has two important parameters, i.e., fuzzy K-Nearest neighbor parameter K and membership control parameter o. In all our experiments, we empirically choose K from 1 to 15 and o from 1 to 5. The nearest neighbor classifier is used for the performance evaluation. In addition, in order to obtain two sets of 2D facial features, we employ the original 2D face images as X view and extract 2D wavelet features of original faces as Y view.

4.1   AT&T Face Database

The AT&T face database[1] contains 400 grayscale images of 40 people, each of which has 10 images with size as 112×92. From some people, the images were taken at different times, varying the lighting, facial expressions and facial details.

In this experiment, the first l ($l = 5$ and 6) images per person are used for training, while the rest for testing. For 2DCCA, G2DCCA, and FBCCP, we explore the performance of each method on all possible eigenvectors and record the best result. Tables 1 and 2 list the recognition accuracy of 2DCCA, G2DCCA, and our proposed FBCCP under both FFS1 and FFS2, respectively. Figures 1 and 2 show the recognition rates of each method with FFS1 and FFS2 versus the top 14 eigenvectors, respectively.

---

[1] https://www.cl.cam.ac.uk/research/dtg/attarchive/facedatabase.html

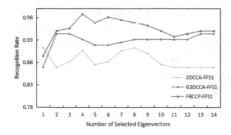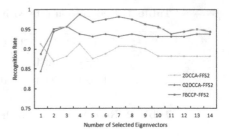

Fig. 2. Recognition rate with $l = 6$ versus the number of selected eigenvectors on the AT&T database.

Table 3. Recognition rate with $l = 10$ on the AR database.

Method	FBCCP	G2DCCA	2DCCA
FFS1	0.896	0.875	0.669
FFS2	0.877	0.875	0.671

Table 4. Recognition rate with $l = 12$ on the AR database.

Method	FBCCP	G2DCCA	2DCCA
FFS1	0.933	0.925	0.592
FFS2	0.888	0.854	0.592

As we can see from Tables 1 and 2, our FBCCP method obviously outperforms other methods, whether feature fusion strategy is FFS1 or FFS2. G2DCCA performs the second best and 2DCCA performs the worst on all cases. From Figs. 1 and 2, we can see that FBCCP performs better than the other two methods with the increasing number of eigenvectors. These results reveal that the extracted 2D features by FBCCP are effective for face recognition tasks.

4.2   AR Face Database

The AR face database[2] includes over 4,000 color face images of 126 people, where there are 70 men and 56 women. Images feature frontal view faces with different facial expressions, illumination conditions, and occlusions. The pictures of most persons are taken in two sessions, separated by two weeks. Each section includes 13 color face images and 120 persons participate in both sessions. In our experiment, the images of 120 people are selected from both sessions and each person has 14 images. We resize these face images to 50×40 and transform them into grayscale images.

In this experiment, the first l ($l = 10$ and 12) images per person are used for training, while the rest for testing. For each method, we explore the result on all

---

[2] http://www2.ece.ohio-state.edu/~aleix/ARdatabase.html

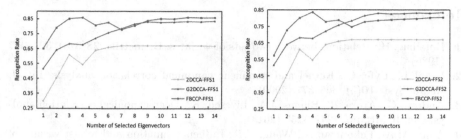

Fig. 3. Recognition rate with $l = 10$ versus the number of selected eigenvectors on the AR database.

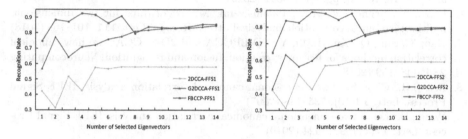

Fig. 4. Recognition rate with $l = 12$ versus the number of selected eigenvectors on the AR database.

possible eigenvectors and record the best result. Tables 3 and 4 summarize the recognition accuracy of 2DCCA, G2DCCA, and FBCCP under both FFS1 and FFS2, respectively. Figures 3 and 4 report the recognition rates of each method with FFS1 and FFS2 versus the top 14 eigenvectors, respectively.

From Tables 3 and 4, we can clearly see that our FBCCP performs better than 2DCCA and G2DCCA, whatever feature fusion strategies are used under $l = 10$ and $l = 12$ cases. Although our FBCCP method achieves the best recognition results, it performs unstably when the number of eigenvectors gradually increases, as can be seen from Figs. 3 and 4.

5 Conclusion

In this paper, we propose a fuzzy bilinear canonical correlation projection (FBCCP) approach, which extracts more discriminative features. FBCCP can effectively reduce computational complexity and minimize the loss of intrinsic spatial structure information, especially enhancing the discriminative 2D representations. Experiments show that our FBCCP method has better recognition performance than other existing multi-view 2D feature extraction methods.

References

1. Hotelling, H.: Relations between two sets of variates. Biometrika **28**(3/4), 321–377 (1936)
2. Lai, P.L., Fyfe, C.: Kernel and nonlinear canonical correlation analysis. Int. J. Neural Syst. **10**(5), 365–377 (2000)
3. Andrew, G., Arora, R., Bilmes, J.A., Livescu, K.: Deep canonical correlation analysis. In: ICML, pp. 1247–1255 (2013)
4. Alam, M.A., Fukumizu, K., Wang, Y.P.: Influence function and robust variant of kernel canonical correlation analysis. Neurocomputing **304**, 12–29 (2018)
5. Uurtio, V., Bhadra, S., Rousu, J.: Large-scale sparse kernel canonical correlation analysis. In: ICML, pp. 6383–6391 (2019)
6. Desai, N., Seghouane, A.K., Palaniswami, M.: Algorithms for two dimensional multi-set canonical correlation analysis. Pattern Recogn. Lett. **111**, 101–108 (2018)
7. Gao, X., Sun, Q., Xu, H., Li, Y.: 2D-LPCCA and 2D-SPCCA: two new canonical correlation methods for feature extraction, fusion and recognition. Neurocomputing **284**, 148–159 (2018)
8. Lee, S.H., Choi, S.: Two-dimensional canonical correlation analysis. IEEE Signal Process. Lett. **14**(10), 735–738 (2007)
9. Wang, H.: Local two-dimensional canonical correlation analysis. IEEE Signal Process. Lett. **17**(11), 921–924 (2010)
10. Liu, Y., Liu, X., Su, Z.: A new fuzzy approach for handling class labels in canonical correlation analysis. Neurocomputing **71**, 1735–1740 (2008)
11. Yang, J.Y., Sun, Q.S.: A novel generalized fuzzy canonical correlation analysis framework for feature fusion and recognition. Neural Process. Lett. **46**(2), 521–536 (2017)
12. Sun, Q.-S.: Research on feature extraction and image recognition based on correlation projection analysis. Ph.D. dissertation. Nanjing University of Science and Technology, Nanjing (2006)
13. Keller, J.M., Gray, M.R., Givens, J.A.: A fuzzy k-nearest neighbor algorithm. IEEE Trans. Syst. Man Cybern. **15**(4), 580–585 (1985)
14. Yuan, Y.-H., Sun, Q.-S., Zhou, Q., Xia, D.-S.: A novel multiset integrated canonical correlation analysis framework and its application in feature fusion. Pattern Recogn. **44**(5), 1031–1040 (2011)
15. Sun, Q.-S., Liu, Z.-D., Heng, P.-A., Xia, D.-S.: A theorem on the generalized canonical projective vectors. Pattern Recogn. **38**(3), 449–452 (2005)

Evolving Pictures in Image Transition Space

Bradley Alexander[(✉)], David Hin, Aneta Neumann, and Safwan Ull-Karim

Optimisation and Logistics Group, School of Computer Science,
The University of Adelaide, Adelaide, Australia
bradley.alexander@adelaide.edu.au

Abstract. Evolutionary art creates novel images through a processes inspired by natural selection. Images are high dimensional objects, which can present challenges for evolutionary processes. Work to date has handled this problem by evolving compressed or encoded forms of images or by starting with prior images and evolving constrained variations of these. In this work we extend the prior-image concept by evolving interesting images in the *transition-space* between two bounding images. We define new feature metrics based on proximity to the two bounding images and show how these metrics, combined with other aesthetic features, can be used to drive the creation of new images incorporating features of both starting images. We extend this work further to evolve sets images that are diverse in one and two feature dimensions. Finally, we accelerate this evolutionary process using an autoencoder to capture the transition space and reduce the dimensionality of the search space.

Keywords: Evolutionary computation · Diversity · Convolutional autoencoder · Features · Computational aesthetics

1 Introduction

The field of evolutionary art aims to create novel artworks through stochastic processes [18]. These processes generate image variants and retain those which are measured to be interesting or aesthetically pleasing for further development. One challenge for this search process is that images have many dimensions – even small images are encoded with several thousand pixel values. High dimensional spaces are not easily searched by evolutionary processes [2].

Research in evolutionary art has addressed this problem with two broad approaches. The first approach is to develop a more compact representation that encodes the image [3,4,12] or encodes a process to generate an image [17]. The second approach is to start with prior images [1,8,20] and constrain search using these images. An interesting sub-case of the second type is where two images are used. Recent work [19,20] has generated art by using evolutionary processes to transition one image to another by changing pixel values from those of a source image S to a target image T. This process is capable of producing a

© Springer Nature Switzerland AG 2019
T. Gedeon et al. (Eds.): ICONIP 2019, LNCS 11953, pp. 679–690, 2019.
https://doi.org/10.1007/978-3-030-36708-4_56

compelling array of image variants. However, to date, the pixel values have been limited to being from either S or T but not between.

This paper presents a preliminary exploration of the effects of removing this pixel constraint. Here, we take two images A and B and evolve interesting variants of both by freely exploring the *transition space* between corresponding pixels. To help structure this process we define a metric for the distance between two images and define new composite features built from these metrics. We combine these metrics with aesthetic features to build fitness functions that drive the production of images. We also apply techniques from recent work in image diversity [1,21] to generate ensembles of images in the transition space. Finally, we speed up the evolutionary process by encoding a distribution of images from the transition space in an autoencoder and searching over the latent vector of the decoder. This improved process makes it possible to generate diverse image populations in multiple feature dimensions and track how features interact.

The remainder of this work is structured as follows. Section 2 briefly outlines related work. Section 3 defines the transition space and describes the methodology for the experiments. Section 4 outlines the experimental results and Sect. 5 presents our conclusions.

2 Related Work

There are a variety of works that generate art through optimisation of image features [1,9,11,12,15,20]. Machado et al. [15] used aesthetic measures to guide the evolution of images in a GP System. Greenfield [9] evolved images based on image features related to colour image segmentation. Den Heijer and Eiben [11, 12] explored the impact of using established aesthetic measures on the production of evolutionary art. Correia et al. [3] evolved images to maximise matching of Haar features of different image classes. Later work by Neumann et al. [20] evolved images using image co-variance features.

Recent work has applied population diversity measures [6] to the evolution of image ensembles [1,21]. Alexander et al. [1] evolved variants of an image for diversity in given feature dimensions. Neumann et al. [21] used an improved discrepancy metric to evolve images for feature diversity. This work has been extended to diversity optimization using popular indicators measures in multi-objective optimisation [22].

The current work extends on ideas used in art generated through image transition [19,20]. Neumann et al. [19] defined evolutionary processes that flipped pixels in box and strip patterns destination image to produce novel artworks. Later work [20] explored how transition processes using random walks interacted with image features. This paper extends these ideas by allowing images to evolve in the transition space between individual image pixels.

Finally, in terms of using neural networks to compress representations for evolution of image variants, Neumann et al. [23] used the latent space of a GAN [7] to evolve images scoring high or low in given feature dimensions.

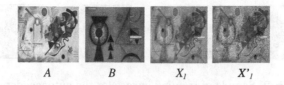

$$A \qquad B \qquad X_1 \qquad X'_1$$

Fig. 1. Image A (Yellow-Red-Blue, 1925 by Wassily Kandinsky) and image B (Soft Hard, 1927 by Wassily Kandinsky). Our framework generates images in the space between two images such as these. Image X_1 halfway between image A and B is randomly mutated to produce an image such as X'_1 which forms the starting point for the evolutionary processes. (Color figure online)

3 Methodology

This paper describes search processes to produce interesting images in the space between two images. The following defines, respectively, image representations and the search space; image feature metrics used in search; and the search operators and frameworks.

3.1 Image Representations and Search Space

We aim to produce new images in the space between two images A and B. The specific images A and B used in this paper to define the space in our experiments are shown in Fig. 1. Every colour image X can be represented as a flattened vector: $\mathbf{x} = [v_{x1}, \ldots, v_{xn}]$ where $n = channels \times rows \times cols$ where $channels = 3$ represent the RGB channels of the image and $rows$ and $cols$ are, respectively, the number of rows and columns in the image. All v_i are pixel colour channel values in the interval: $[0.0, 1.0]$. We assume, without loss of generality, that the v_i are ordered first by channel, then by row and then by column and $rows = cols$. We also assume that the vector representations: $\mathbf{a}$ and $\mathbf{b}$ of the images A and B, and all intermediate images, have the same shape and size.

We define the transition space $\mathbb{TR}^n_{ab}$ between two images $\mathbf{a} = [v_{a1}, \ldots, v_{an}]$ and $\mathbf{b} = [v_{b1}, \ldots, v_{bn}]$ to be the n-dimensional interval:

$$\mathbb{TR}^n_{ab} = \mathbb{V}_1 \times \ldots \times \mathbb{V}_n$$

where each interval $\mathbb{V}_i = [min(v_{ai}, v_{bi}), max(v_{ai}, v_{bi}) + \epsilon]$. The small constant ϵ ensures that all dimensions of $\mathbb{TR}^n_{ab}$ have non-zero extent[1]. To simplify search, we define a bijective mapping function

$$m : \mathbb{I}^n \to \mathbb{TR}^n_{ab} : u_i \mapsto min_i + u_i((max_i - min_i)/1.0)$$

where $min_i = min(v_{ai}, v_{bi})$, $max_i = max(v_{ai}, v_{bi})$, and $\mathbb{I} = [0.0, 1.0]$ (the unit interval). The function application $m(\mathbf{u})$ converts a search vector $\mathbf{u} \in \mathbb{I}^n$ to its

---

[1] In the extreme cases where values start at 0.0 or 1.0 we snap values back to their respective boundaries.

Fig. 2. Sample of training images for the autoencoder.

corresponding image vector $\mathbf{x} \in \mathbb{TR}_{ab}^n$. By using m we can search in a domain where all dimensions are the unit interval and map each dimension to the appropriate interval in the transition space. We also use the inverse m^{-1} to map from $\mathbb{TR}_{ab}^n$ to $\mathbb{I}^n$ when measuring the distance between two images in $\mathbb{TR}_{ab}^n$.

Compressed Representation. Even for small images a vector $\mathbf{u}$, in the search domain will have thousands of elements. Such large representations can sometimes impede search. As a remedy, in our last set of experiments we train a 2D convolutional autoencoder [14] with 10,000 (128×128) images sampled from $\mathbb{TR}_{ab}^n$. The decoder part of this autoencoder can then be used to generate images during the search process. The training images are generated by mapping sine functions with random frequency and amplitude over the transition space: $\mathbb{TR}_{ab}^n$. Some example training images for the autoencoder are shown in Fig. 2. In our experiments the input layer of the decoder has just 64 values. This highly compressed representation greatly improves the speed of search.

3.2   Image Feature Metrics Used in Search

In this work we use search to maximise or minimise one or more feature metrics applied to single and multiple images in $\mathbb{TR}_{ab}^n$. All features are functions from an image X (or its flattened vector representation $\mathbf{x}$) to a scalar score.

The following describes three categories of image features: 1. automatically evaluated aesthetic measures; 2. metrics for *similarity* of an image $\mathbf{x}$ to the bounding images of the transition space $\mathbf{a}$ or $\mathbf{b}$; and 3. multi-image metrics to assess the *diversity* of a population of images in one or more feature dimensions. We describe features from each category in turn.

Standard Aesthetic Features. Aesthetic features are function mapping an image X (or $\mathbf{x}$) to a scalar that representing the score of that image in some aesthetic dimension. We use features that are described in the literature [24], and are empirically obtained from survey studies [11].

In our experiments we use the following features: Mean Saturation, Reflectional Symmetry [11], Mean Hue, Entropy [25], Global Contrast Factor [16], and Benford's Law [13]. The features are defined as follows.

Mean Saturation is the mean value of saturation for all pixels of image $\mathbf{x}$. The range is $[0, 1]$ with 0 representing low saturation and 1 representing high saturation.

Reflectional Symmetry (Sym_R) is a measure introduced in [11] to measure the degree which an image reflects itself. Symmetry divides an image into four quadrants and measures horizontal, vertical, and diagonal symmetry. Note Symmetry is defined for image X as: $Sym_R(X) = S_h(X) + S_v(X) + S_d(X)/3$ where $S_h(X)$, $S_v(X)$, and $S_d(X)$ are, respectively, the horizontal, vertical, and diagonal symmetry of X.

Mean Hue is the mean value of the hue of every pixel in the image $\mathbf{x}$. The range of *Hue* is $[0, 1]$. Note that both 0 and 1 represent the colour red due to the periodic nature of this function.

Entropy estimates the Shannon entropy of the intensity of the pixels. Rigau et al. [25] used physical entropy to quantify the aesthetic experience. We define the Shannon entropy *Ent* for image vector $\mathbf{x}$ as: $Ent(\mathbf{x}) = -\sum_{x=0}^{n} p(\mathbf{x}_i) log \cdot p(\mathbf{x}_i)$, where $p(\mathbf{x}_i)$ is the probability of intensity $\mathbf{x}_i$, scaled to the range $[0, ..., 255]$. If the image $\mathbf{x}$ has a high value $Ent(\mathbf{x})$ this means that the intensity values of image $\mathbf{x}$ are quite uniformly distributed.

Global Contrast Factor (GCF) is a measure of mean contrast between neighbouring pixels at different image resolutions in image X. GCF is determined by calculating the local contrast at each pixel at resolution r:
$lc_r(X_{ij}) = \sum_{X_{kl} \in N(X_{ij})} |lum(X_{kl}) - lum(X_{ij})|$, where $lum(P)$ is the perceptual luminosity of pixel P and $N(X_{ij})$ are the four neighbouring pixels of X_{ij} at resolution r. The mean local contrast at the current resolution is defined as: $C_r = (\sum_{i=1}^{m} \sum_{j=1}^{n} lc_r(X_{ij}))/(mn)$. From these local contrasts, GCF is calculated as: $GCF = \sum_{r=1}^{9} w_r \cdot C_r$.

Here, the pixel resolutions correspond to different *superpixel* sizes of 1, 2, 4, 8, 16, 25, 50, and 100. Each superpixel is set to the average luminosity of the pixels it contains. The w_r are empirically derived weights of resolutions from [16] giving highest weight to moderate resolutions. The maximum attainable value of GCF depends on image resolution and GCF is not bounded by $[0, 1]$.

Benford's Law This feature is a measure of image naturalness. It compares the sorted luminosity histogram of an image $\mathbf{x}$ to the nine-bin distribution, $H_{Benford}$ defined by Benford's law [13]. Here we use the feature metric defined by den Heijer [11]. To evaluate $Ben(\mathbf{x})$, we first calculate the nine-bin histogram $H_{\mathbf{x}}$ of pixel luminosities of $\mathbf{x}$. From this we define $Ben(\mathbf{x}) = 1 - d_{total}/d_{max}$ where $d_{total} = \sum_{i=1}^{9} |H_I(i) - H_{Benford}(i)|$ and d_{max} is the maximum discrepancy between an image histogram and $H_{Benford}$ (which happens when all pixels are in one bin).

Similarity Features. A feature used in this work is the similarity of two flattened images $\mathbf{x}$ and $\mathbf{y}$ to each other within the transition space. The feature metric $Sim_p(\mathbf{x}, \mathbf{y})$ is defined as:

$$Sim_p(\mathbf{x}, \mathbf{y}) = 1.0 - ||m^{-1}(\mathbf{x}) - m^{-1}(\mathbf{y})||_p$$

This calculation first uses m^{-1} to map $\mathbf{x}$ and $\mathbf{y}$ to the unit interval and then finds the p-norm distance between these vectors. This distance is then subtracted from 1.0 to derive a similarity measure. Note that the p-norm of $\mathbf{x} - \mathbf{y}$ is defined: $||\mathbf{x} - \mathbf{y}||_p = (\sum_{i=1}^n |\mathbf{x}_i - \mathbf{y}_i|^p)^{1/p}$. High values of p will make the similarity metric sensitive to the most distant corresponding pixel values in $\mathbf{x}$ and $\mathbf{y}$. For an individual image $\mathbf{x}$ the most interesting similarities are $Sim_p(\mathbf{x}, \mathbf{a}) = SimA_p(\mathbf{x})$ and $Sim_p(\mathbf{x}, \mathbf{b}) = SimB_p(\mathbf{x})$ which represent the similarity of $\mathbf{x}$ to the bounding images ($\mathbf{a}$ and $\mathbf{b}$) of the transition space.

Interesting results can be achieved by creating composite features by combining $SimA_p(\mathbf{x})$ and $SimB_p(\mathbf{x})$ using the scalar operators: $+, \times, \min, -, \max$. Thus, for example, we can create a new feature $\max(SimA_p(\mathbf{x}), SimB_p(\mathbf{x}))$ which scores highly if $\mathbf{x}$ is similar to *either* $\mathbf{a}$ or $\mathbf{b}$.

Diversity Metrics. In our later experiments we aim to evolve a population of images *pop* to be *diverse* in one or more feature dimensions. To measure diversity we use the feature diversity contribution measure: $d(X, pop)$ from [1,6] which returns the contribution of image X with respect to its population *pop*. For the case of a single feature f, which maps an image X to a scalar feature value $f(X)$, the diversity measure $d(I, pop)$ is derived by the following steps. First, we sort the individuals I_i in *pop* according to the feature values $f(I_i)$ to produce a range: $f(I_1) \le f(I_2) \le \dots \le f(I_k)$. Now, where $f(I_i) \ne f(I_1) \ne f(I_k)$ we calculate $d(I_i, pop) = (f(I_i) - f(I_{i-1})) \times (f(I_i) - f(I_{i+1}))$. This means $d(I_i, pop)$ will be large when I_i is far from its neighbours in the feature dimension represented by f. For the extremes: $f(I_i) = f(I_1)$ or $f(I_i) = f(I_k)$ we set $d(I_i, pop) = R^2$ where $R = f(I_1) - f(I_k)$.

To extend $d(I, pop)$ to multiple features $\{f_1, \dots, f_k\}$ we use a population weighted diversity measure d' (from [6]): $d'(I, pop) = \sum_{i=1}^k (w_i \times d_{f_i}(I, pop))$ where w_i is a weighting assigned to each feature dimension bias search toward or away from selected features. In our experiments we use $k \in \{1, 2\}$. In our experiments we set $w_i = 1$.

3.3   Search Operators and Heuristics

We use search heuristics to produce image variants that score highly on fitness functions built using the image feature metrics described below. We run three sets of experiments. Our first *maximisation* experiments run a simple $1 + 1EA$ [5] which successively mutates a single image to produce a new variant and keeps the new variant if it has a higher fitness. The second experiment set are *diversity* experiments using a $\mu + \lambda EA$ [1] to evolve populations of image which are *diverse* in a given feature dimension. The third set of experiments are *autoencoder experiments* using CMA-ES [10] to create individuals encoding 10 diverse images using the latent vector space of an autoencoder trained with images from $\mathbb{TR}_{ab}^n$ (as described in Sect. 3.1 above).

In the first two sets of experiments we initialise the images by first deriving an image X_1 halfway between image A and B. An example of X_1 is shown in Fig. 1. Then we create starting images by a normally distributed random perturbation

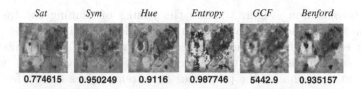

Sat	Sym	Hue	Entropy	GCF	Benford
0.774615	0.950249	0.9116	0.987746	5442.9	0.935157

Fig. 3. Images resulting from $1+1$EA maximising aesthetic features. Feature score is shown below each image.

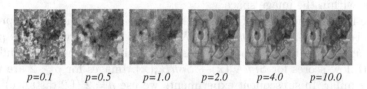

p=0.1	p=0.5	p=1.0	p=2.0	p=4.0	p=10.0

Fig. 4. Images produced by maximising $SimA_p(\mathbf{x}) + SimB_p(\mathbf{x})$ for different values of p

($\sigma = 0.5$ to each pixel of X_1 to produce an image such as X_1', shown in Fig. 1. For the $\mu + \lambda$EA ($\mu = 5, \lambda = 2$) we start with population of such images.

For the *autoencoder experiments* each individual takes the form:
$$[v_{1,1}, v_{1,2}, \ldots, v_{1,64}, v_{2,1}, v_{2,2}, \ldots, v_{2,64}, \ldots, v_{m,1}, v_{2,2}, \ldots, v_{m,64}]$$
where each group of 64 elements is a compressed representation of an individual image. And the whole vector is a set of $m = 10$ images that are optimised for diversity in one or more feature dimensions using CMA-ES. In our autoencoder experiments there is a population of these image sets maintained by CMA-ES.

Experimental Setup. For the *maximisation* experiments we run the $1+1$EA for two million evaluations on 70×70 pixel images. These experiments produce images resulting from maximisation of given aesthetic features. We also assess the impact of p on the results produced by maximising distance metric features such as $\max(SimA_p(\mathbf{x}), SimB_p(\mathbf{x}))$. Finally, we examine the results of combining selected distance and feature metrics.

For the *diversity* experiments we run the $\mu + \lambda$EA for five million iterations on both aesthetic features (except GCF) and distance feature combinations. GCF takes much longer to evaluate and we ran for 1.8 million evaluations.

For the *autoencoder* experiments we run CMA-ES [10] with a population 10 for 100,000 iterations. Each individual itself encodes set of 10 images. For these experiments we traced feature values in two dimensions to observe how they interact.

4 Results

We present results for $1+1$EA maximisation experiments first, followed by the $\mu + \lambda$EA diversity experiments and the autoencoder experiments.

Feature Maximisation. Figure 3 shows the results of running the framework to maximise the standard features described in Sect. 3.2. To produce pleasing images, in each run fitness was multiplied by a metric of image smoothness, where the smoothness metric was capped at 0.985 to preventing it dominating evolution. In each case the properties of extreme values for the feature are clearly visible - especially in the case of the first three features. The Benford feature, which is related purely to image intensity is interesting in that it produces a coherent structure, this may due to an interaction with the smoothness constraint within the image space.

Figure 4 shows the effect of changing the value of p on the images produced by maximising $SimA_p(\mathbf{x}) + SimB_p(\mathbf{x})$. We can see that low values of p produce noisier images - this because low p-norms are relatively insensitive to individual pixels with low scores for $SimA_p(\mathbf{x}) + SimB_p(\mathbf{x})$. Images for $p \geq 2$ are smooth and very similar. In subsequent experiments we use $p = 2$ (L2 distance).

Aesthetic and similarity features can be combined in interesting ways. Figure 5 combines the $SimB_2(\mathbf{x}) - SimA_2(\mathbf{x})$ (favouring similarity to image B) with a linear penalty from deviation from a given target hue value. The first two images, for low hue values, are similar to image A - this is due to image A being a good match for these hue values. For $Hue = 0.5$ image B is produced. The last two images, again, look more like image A.

Diversity Maximisation. Figure 6 shows the images resulting from using the $\mu + \lambda$EA to maximise diversity in an aesthetic feature dimension. The last row, is feature composed of a product of hue and $max(SimB_2(\mathbf{x}), SimA_2(\mathbf{x}))$. The rows for Saturation (Sat), Symmetry (Sym) and the combination feature (last row) are visually interesting. The use of $max(SimB_2(\mathbf{x}), SimA_2(\mathbf{x}))$ produces a set of images resembling either image A or B with different coloration. The Benford feature is omitted and resembles the images for Entropy.

Figure 7 shows images generated by the same process for selected combined distance metrics. The first row shows the results for the $+$ operator ($\times$ is similar) which shows an interesting progression from chaos to order. The *min* operator (second row) progresses from image B on the left a half-way image on the right. The $-$ operator (third row) shows a smooth progression from B to A ($/$ is similar). Finally, the *max* operator (fourth row) flips between B and A as max similarity approaches.

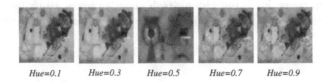

| *Hue=0.1* | *Hue=0.3* | *Hue=0.5* | *Hue=0.7* | *Hue=0.9* |

Fig. 5. Maximising $SimB_2(\mathbf{x}) - SimA_2(\mathbf{x})$ multiplied by a linear penalty for deviation from the hue value shown with each picture.

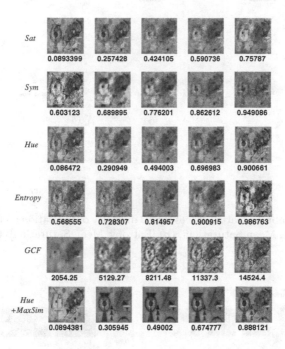

Fig. 6. Image populations evolved for diversity in aesthetic feature dimensions. Feature metric scores are shown below each image. The last row combines a distance metric with mean hue.

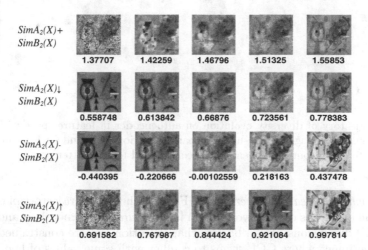

Fig. 7. Image populations evolved for diversity in selected combinations of distance metrics. The metric is given besides each row. The metric values are under each image.

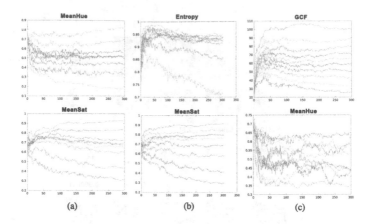

Fig. 8. Plot of combined feature traces for 2D diversity optimisation on the autoencoder for (a) [Mean Hue, Mean Saturation], (b) [Entropy, Mean Saturation], (c) [GCF, Mean Hue].

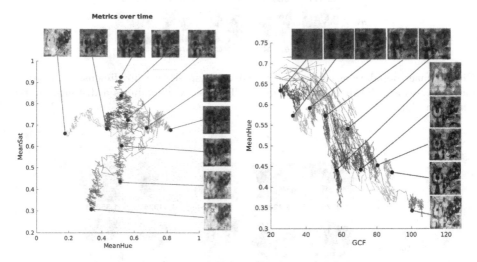

Fig. 9. Trajectory of diversity evolution on autoencoder in feature space with corresponding finishing images. Mean-hue vs. mean-saturation (left) and GCF vs. mean-hue (right). Note that evolution appears more constrained for the latter pair.

Two-Dimensional Feature Experiments. Figure 9 shows the trajectory of the best population of images during evolution in [*hue, saturation*] dimensions and in the [*hue, GCF*] dimensions. It can be seen that evolution is more constrained in the latter experiment where GCF seems to conflict with some values of hue.

Elements of this constrained interaction are seen in Fig. 8(c) where the evolution of hue is quite chaotic compared to part (a). The middle charts (b) in this figure show the traces for a run optimising diversity of [*Entropy, Saturation*]

There is considerable variation in saturation but more constrained behavior from entropy. Figure 10 hints that the spread of saturation is aided by diversity of saturation between A and B (image A less saturated than B).

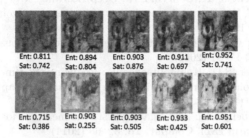

Fig. 10. Images produced by diversity optimisation in hue and entropy. Entropy increases from left to right. Low saturation images are on the bottom row. High saturation images resemble image A.

5   Discussion and Future Work

This work is a preliminary exploration of generating art in the transition space between two images. We have shown that, by using aesthetic features and distance metrics it is possible evolve very interesting image ensembles. Moreover it is possible, using compact encodings, to see how features interact two dimensions and how the bounding images may affect diversity in given feature dimensions.

This work, as a proof-of-concept, is currently limited to exploring two images of similar style. Future work would entail a more systematic study of more image pairs and feature interactions for these. Other directions to explore include use of more robust distance metrics and use of alternative networks to the autoencoder used in this work.

References

1. Alexander, B., Kortman, J., Neumann, A.: Evolution of artistic image variants through feature based diversity optimisation. In: Proceedings of the Genetic and Evolutionary Computation Conference, GECCO 2017, pp. 171–178. ACM (2017)
2. Chu, W., Gao, X., Sorooshian, S.: A new evolutionary search strategy for global optimization of high-dimensional problems. Inf. Sci. **181**(22), 4909–4927 (2011)
3. Correia, J., Machado, P., Romero, J., Carballal, A.: Evolving figurative images using expression-based evolutionary art. In: International Conference on Computational Creativity, ICCC 2013, pp. 24–31 (2013)
4. Dawkins, R.: The Blind Watchmaker: Why the Evidence of Evolution Reveals a Universe Without Design. W. W. Norton & Company (1986)
5. Eiben, A.E., Smith, J.E.: Introduction to Evolutionary Computing. Natural Computing Series. Springer, Heidelberg (2015). https://doi.org/10.1007/978-3-662-05094-1

6. Gao, W., Nallaperuma, S., Neumann, F.: Feature-based diversity optimization for problem instance classification. In: Handl, J., Hart, E., Lewis, P.R., López-Ibáñez, M., Ochoa, G., Paechter, B. (eds.) PPSN 2016. LNCS, vol. 9921, pp. 869–879. Springer, Cham (2016). https://doi.org/10.1007/978-3-319-45823-6_81

7. Goodfellow, I., Bengio, Y., Courville, A.: Deep Learning. MIT press (2016)

8. Graf, J., Banzhaf, W.: Interactive evolution of images. In: Evolutionary Programming, pp. 53–65 (1995)

9. Greenfield, G.R.: On the co-evolution of evolving expressions. Int. J. Comput. Intell. Appl. 2(1), 17–31 (2002)

10. Hansen, N., Müller, S.D., Koumoutsakos, P.: Reducing the time complexity of the derandomized evolution strategy with covariance matrix adaptation (CMA-ES). Evol. Comput. 11(1), 1–18 (2003)

11. den Heijer, E., Eiben, A.E.: Investigating aesthetic measures for unsupervised evolutionary art. Swarm Evol. Comput. 16, 52–68 (2014)

12. den Heijer, E., Eiben, A.: Using aesthetic measures to evolve art. In: IEEE Congress on Evolutionary Computation, pp. 1–8. IEEE (2010)

13. Jolion, J.M.: Images and Benford's law. J. Math. Imaging Vis. 14(1), 73–81 (2001)

14. Keras: Autoencoder. https://github.com/shibuiwilliam/KerasAutoencoder

15. Machado, P., Cardoso, A.: All the truth about NEvAr. Appl. Intell. 16(2), 101–118 (2002)

16. Matkovic, K., Neumann, L., Neumann, A., Psik, T., Purgathofer, W.: Global contrast factor-a new approach to image contrast. Comput. Aesthet. 159–168 (2005)

17. McCormack, J.: Interactive evolution of L-system grammars for computer graphics modelling. In: Complex Systems: From Biology to Computation, vol. 2 (1993)

18. McCormack, J., d'Inverno, M. (eds.): Computers and Creativity. Springer, Heidelberg (2012). https://doi.org/10.1007/978-3-642-31727-9

19. Neumann, A., Alexander, B., Neumann, F.: The evolutionary process of image transition in conjunction with box and strip mutation. In: Hirose, A., Ozawa, S., Doya, K., Ikeda, K., Lee, M., Liu, D. (eds.) ICONIP 2016. LNCS, vol. 9949, pp. 261–268. Springer, Cham (2016). https://doi.org/10.1007/978-3-319-46675-0_29

20. Neumann, A., Alexander, B., Neumann, F.: Evolutionary image transition using random walks. In: Correia, J., Ciesielski, V., Liapis, A. (eds.) EvoMUSART 2017. LNCS, vol. 10198, pp. 230–245. Springer, Cham (2017). https://doi.org/10.1007/978-3-319-55750-2_16

21. Neumann, A., Gao, W., Doerr, C., Neumann, F., Wagner, M.: Discrepancy-based evolutionary diversity optimization. In: Proceedings of the Genetic and Evolutionary Computation Conference, GECCO 2018, pp. 991–998. ACM (2018)

22. Neumann, A., Gao, W., Wagner, M., Neumann, F.: Evolutionary diversity optimization using multi-objective indicators. In: Proceedings of the Genetic and Evolutionary Computation Conference, GECCO 2019, pp. 837–845 (2019)

23. Neumann, A., Pyromallis, C., Alexander, B.: Evolution of images with diversity and constraints using a generative adversarial network. In: Cheng, L., Leung, A.C.S., Ozawa, S. (eds.) ICONIP 2018. LNCS, vol. 11306, pp. 452–465. Springer, Cham (2018). https://doi.org/10.1007/978-3-030-04224-0_39

24. Nixon, M., Aguado, A.S.: Feature Extraction & Image Processing, 2nd edn. Academic Press (2008)

25. Rigau, J., Feixas, M., Sbert, M.: Informational aesthetics measures. IEEE Comput. Graphics Appl. 28(2), 24–34 (2008)

Improved Multi-objective Evolutionary Subspace Clustering

Dipanjyoti Paul[✉], Abhishek Kumar, Sriparna Saha, and Jimson Mathew

Indian Institute of Technology Patna, Patna, India
{dipanjyoti.pcs17,abhishek.cs15,sriparna,jimson}@iitp.ac.in

Abstract. This paper presents a subspace clustering method using an evolutionary-based multi-objective optimization framework. Recently, subspace clustering techniques become popular in solving many clustering problems where the key task is to identify groups of objects where the objects in each group have some similar properties with respect to a subset of features which are relevant to the group. Again, the simultaneous optimization of multiple objective functions helps to identify the subspace clusters effectively. The proposed method optimizes multiple objective functions simultaneously *so* that it *can* generate good quality subspace clusters. Two cluster validity indices namely XB-index and PBM-index are modified to make them applicable for subspace clustering problem. The evolutionary-based technique is used to simultaneously optimize these two validity indices to generate the subspace clusters. Various mutation operators have been used to generate good offsprings and to explore the search space effectively. The proposed approach is tested on 7 real-life data sets and 16 synthetic data sets. The efficacy of the proposed method is shown by comparing the results with many state-of-the-art algorithms.

Keywords: Multi-objective optimization · Subspace clustering · XB-index · PBM-index · Cluster Validity index

1 Introduction

Now a days, a huge amount of data are being generated by different application domains represented by a large number of dimensions. In case of high dimensional data, the similarity measure between two objects using Euclidean distance doesn't perform well as it suffers from the curse of dimensionality problem [1]. Therefore, the Manhattan distance, which doesn't suffer from this effect, can be used. However, all the features that represent data may not be relevant for all the samples. It has been observed that a subset of features may be relevant for a subset of samples. Subspace clustering technique is based on this concept and it divides the data set into groups such that the objects that are similar to each other are placed in the same group and each group is represented by a subset of features that are relevant to the objects in the group. In subspace clustering,

© Springer Nature Switzerland AG 2019
T. Gedeon et al. (Eds.): ICONIP 2019, LNCS 11953, pp. 691–703, 2019.
https://doi.org/10.1007/978-3-030-36708-4_57

the grouping of objects and the selection of feature-space for that group are performed in parallel.

Many algorithms have been developed in the area of subspace clustering which primarily optimize a single objective function. The algorithms, CLIQUE [1], SUBCLU [2], use the density-based approach for clustering of data. SUB-CLU uses the DBSCAN [3] algorithm to find out the dense regions whereas, in CLIQUE, a unit is called dense if the number of objects within that unit is greater than some predetermined threshold value. Both the algorithms use bottom-up approaches to select the subspace feature set, i.e., the algorithm starts searching for dense regions in one-dimensional space. In general, a k-dimensional cluster is detected from (k-1)-dimensional dense regions. The algorithms DOC [4] and MINECLUS [5] also use density based technique for subspace clustering. Both DOC [4] and MINECLUS [5] discover only one cluster at a time. At each step, DOC picks a random point from the data set called medoid and attempts to optimize that medoid. Then it discovers a cluster centered at that medoid. The cluster contains a set of sample points which are at a certain distance from the medoid. After a cluster has been discovered, the records in it are removed from the original data and the process is iteratively applied on the rest of the points. MINECLUS [5] transforms the problem of finding a best-projected cluster for a random medoid to the problem of finding the best itemset. ChameleoClust [6] and KymereoClust [7] are two evolutionary based subspace clustering algorithms which optimize intra-cluster compactness as a fitness function. The difference in the two algorithms lies in the use of mutation operators to explore the search space.

Most of the previous subspace clustering algorithms implicitly or explicitly optimize only a single cluster quality measure which is limited in identifying only a particular shape or property. However, incorporating the concept of multiple objective optimization can overcome these problems. Multi-objective optimization (MOO) techniques optimize more than one objective functions and therefore, are able to optimize different properties of the clusters at the same time. Many multi-objective optimization techniques that have solved the clustering problems [8], illustrate the superiority of optimizing multiple objective functions.

Inspired by the algorithm ChameleoClust [6], in this paper we developed an evolutionary-based multi-objective subspace clustering technique that incorporates a genome having an evolvable structure. Inspired from [9], the genome that is considered is a coarse-grained genome, which is defined as a set of tuples of numbers. Each genome is mapped as a phenotype which provides the core-point locations. A core-point can also be contemplated as center of a subspace cluster. The genome contains a variable proportion of functional as well as non-functional elements as in [10] and the mutation operations that have been used are subjected to point mutation and rearrangements similar to those used in [10]. The mutation operators that have been used in [6] are modified and the modified versions of mutation operators are used in this algorithm. The rearrangements of mutation operators are named as deletions, duplications and translocations.

The rearrangements modify the genome length, and the point mutation modifies the genome elements and changes the proportion of non-functional elements. Therefore, the algorithm can take advantage of such an evolvable structure and is able to detect variable number of clusters in subspaces having variable number of features.

In machine learning problems, to find the subspace clusters, simultaneous optimization of multiple objectives improves the quality of clusters. Inspired by the success of multi-objective based clustering techniques and advantages of evolutionary-based subspace clustering, in the current study a multi-objective optimization based framework is developed for evolutionary subspace clustering. However, the clusters in a solution are said to be optimal, if the objects within the cluster are tightly compact, and the separation between two clusters is high. In this paper also, we optimize compactness within the cluster and separation between two clusters as objective functions in the form of two validity indices such as XB-index and PBM-index. These two validity indices are modified and the modified versions of these two indices are optimized simultaneously in this algorithm. Again, in the evolutionary-based technique, initially solutions are generated from the randomly created genomes and the subsequent solutions are generated by applying mutation operators on the previous solutions. The mutation operators that have been used are point substitution and rearrangements. The developed algorithm is evaluated on 7 real-life data sets and 16 synthetic data sets. Experimentation shows that the proposed algorithm takes the advantages of multiple objective functions and is able to generate good quality clusters.

2   Proposed Algorithm

In the proposed algorithm, the subspace clusters are generated from the variable length genome which comprises of both functional and nonfunctional elements and also includes chromosomal rearrangements. These properties are inspired by the *in silico* experimental evolution formalism of [9] and [10], provide the algorithm a large degree of freedom by making the genome structure evolvable. The concept of MOO is incorporated in order to optimize the subspace clusters and is able to generate good quality subspace clusters.

2.1   Problem Definition

- Given
  - Let the data set be $X = \{x_1, x_2, ..., x_S\}$ of size S represented by a feature set $F = \{f_1, f_2, ..., f_Z\}$ of size Z.
  - A set of m objective functions such as $\{O_1, O_2, ..., O_m\}$ in the form of cluster validity indices which measure the qualities of partitions.
- Find
  - Partition of the data set X into C subspace clusters such as $\{Y_1, Y_2, ..., Y_C\}$, each of the clusters is represented by a subset of features F_i.

- The subspace cluster $Y_i = \{x_1^i, x_2^i, ..., x_{n_i}^i\}$ is represented by a subspace feature $F_i = \{f_1^i, f_2^i, ..., f_Z^i\}$ where n_i: number of data points in cluster i, x_j^i: jth element of cluster i, f_j^i: jth feature of the feature set F in cluster i, either selected (non-zero value) or not selected (zero value).
- Produces disjoint clusters, i.e., $\cup_{i=1}^{C} Y_i = S$ and $Y_i \cap Y_j = \phi$ for all $i \neq j$.

2.2   Phenotype and Genome Representation

A genome is represented by a list of tuples $\Delta = \{\delta_1, \delta_2, ..., \delta_q\}$ where each tuple δ_i is defined as $<t_i, c_i, f_i, x_i>$. The element t_i takes the value either 0, a non-functional element or 1, a functional element. The elements c_i and f_i take the values uniformly from $\{1, 2, ..., SC_{max}\}$ and $\{1, 2, ..., Z\}$, respectively, where SC_{max} denotes the maximum number of clusters and Z is the size of the features. $x \in CoordValue$, with $CoordValue = \{j * \frac{x_{max}}{1000} \mid j \in \{-1000, ..., 1000\}\}$, x_{max} is the maximum value of the normalized data set. The data set is normalized by replacing each feature value x by its z-score value: $z = \frac{x-\theta}{\sigma}$. Where θ is the mean of the data set and σ is the standard deviation for the given feature.

A phenotype P, which can also be called as a solution, contains a set of core points. A core point is considered as a center of the subspace cluster and around a center, a set of points will be grouped together. Each core point, p_c, is represented by a number and the maximum possible core points that can be considered in this algorithm is denoted by SC_{max} i.e., $c \in [1, SC_{max}]$. Phenotype can be represented as a two-dimensional matrix of size $SC_{max} * Z$ and is initialized with zero values. The phenotype is updated to a non-zero matrix by the tuples present in the initial genome. A tuple takes part in the generation of a core point of a phenotype if the tuple is functional, i.e., $t_i = 1$. The values of c_i and f_i in a tuple represent the core point number and the feature number, respectively, and the corresponding position (c_i^{th} row, f_i^{th} column) of the phenotype is updated with the value x_i of that tuple.

2.3   Mutation Operators

Mutation operators are used to generate new genomes from the previous genomes. The previous genome is copied and the new genome is formed by two types of mutation operators: *global rearrangements* and *point substitution*. However, the global rearrangements as in ChameleoClust [6], sometimes may lead to the genome size extremely small or sometimes it may double the size. Such a huge change may not be necessary when the algorithm is near to the optimal solution. The proposed algorithm modifies the rearrangement operations by providing a limitation towards varying size of the genome. For a genome Δ, the point mutation operator is defined as follows:

Point Substitution. Let the value $\delta_i \in \Delta$ and $a \in \{1, 2, 3, 4\}$ be chosen uniformly. The point mutation substitution operator replaces the ath element of the tuple δ_i by a new value drawn uniformly from the associated range of the element.

$$\delta_i \leftarrow \begin{cases} < replace(\{0,1\}), c, f, x >, & \text{if } a = 1 \\ < t, replace(\{1, 2, ..., SC_{max}\}), f, x >, & \text{if } a = 2 \\ < t, c, replace(\{1, 2, ..., Z\}), x >, & \text{if } a = 3 \\ < t, c, f, replace(CoordValue) >, & \text{if } a = 4 \end{cases}$$

The replace function uniformly selects a new element from the set and replaces the old value.

Merge Operator M. Let $\delta = <t, c, f, x>$ and $\delta' = <t', c', f', x'>$ be two tuples and a value $a \in \{1, 2, 3, 4\}$ is chosen uniformly. Therefore, the merge operation can be performed in four possible ways.

$$M(\delta, \delta', a) = \begin{cases} < t, c', f', x' >, & \text{if } a = 1 \\ < t, c, f', x' >, & \text{if } a = 2 \\ < t, c, f, x' >, & \text{if } a = 3 \\ < t, c, f, x >, & \text{if } a = 4 \end{cases}$$

In order to increase or decrease the genome length or to change the positions of the tuples, rearrangements of tuples have been applied. However, the rearrangement breakpoints operate inside the tuples and the rearrangement breakpoints can be recombined for creating new tuples. Three kinds of rearrangement operators have been used which are *deletions*, *duplications* and *translocations*. A number i is drawn uniformly within the range of the genome size and another number j is obtained simply by adding or subtracting the value obtained after applying binomial law $\beta(\eta_r, L)$ on genome size to i. Where η_r is the mutation rate and L is the size of the genome. The value i must be chosen in such a way that it should satisfy $(i - \beta(\eta_r, L)) > 0$ and $(i + \beta(\eta_r, L)) < L$. The portion of the tuple Δ, bounded by $(\delta_i$ and $\delta_j)$ or $(\delta_j$ and $\delta_i)$, is considered for rearrangements. Again a breakpoint index $a \in \{1, 2, 3, 4\}$ is chosen uniformly to specify where the rearrangement limit is located within the bounding tuples. The three kinds of rearrangement operators are defined as follows:

Deletions. The segment between tuples δ_i and δ_j, if $i \leq j$ or δ_j and δ_i, if $j > i$ is simply deleted from the original tuple Δ.

$$\Delta \leftarrow \begin{cases} \Delta_{1,i-1} + M(\delta_i, \delta_j, a) + \Delta_{j+1,q}, & \text{if } i \leq j \\ \Delta_{1,j-1} + M(\delta_j, \delta_i, a) + \Delta_{i+1,q}, & \text{if } i > j \end{cases}$$

Duplications. The segment between tuples δ_i and δ_j, if $i \leq j$ or δ_j and δ_i, if $j > i$, is simply copied from the original tuple Δ and inserted at randomly chosen third position p.

$$\Delta \leftarrow \begin{cases} \Delta_{1,p-1} + M(\delta_p, \delta_i, a) + \Delta_{i+1,j-1} + M(\delta_j, \delta_p, a) + \Delta_{p+1,q}, & \text{if } i \leq j \\ \Delta_{1,p-1} + M(\delta_p, \delta_j, a) + \Delta_{j+1,i-1} + M(\delta_i, \delta_p, a) + \Delta_{p+1,q}, & \text{if } i > j \end{cases}$$

Translocation. The segment between tuples δ_i and δ_j, if $i \leq j$ or δ_j and δ_i, if $j > i$, is cut from the original tuple Δ and inserted at randomly chosen third position p such that $p \notin [i,j]$ if $i \leq j$ and $p \notin [j,i]$ if $i > j$.

During the reproduction of a solution, these three kinds of rearrangement operators have been applied in random order. Once the rearrangement operators have been applied, *point substitution* operator is applied. The number of *point substitution* operators that have to be applied are drawn from the binomial law $\beta(\eta_r, L')$, where L' is the genome size after rearrangements. Again, for the first generation, $\frac{1}{3}$ times of the initial genome size, functional elements (i.e., t = 1) are considered.

2.4   Objective Functions

Two objective functions that have been considered in this method are *compactness* and *separation* which are represented in the form of validity indices such as XB-index [11] and PBM-index [12]. These two validity indices are modified and the modified version of XB-index and modified version of PBM index are optimized simultaneously in this algorithm to generate subspace clusters.

Pakhira Bandyopadhyay Maulik (PBM) Index: In PBM-index [12], the distances between an object to its cluster center and the distance between two centers are computed using Manhattan distance as it is robust to the *concentration effect* [1]. A subspace cluster represented by the phenotype P, contains many centers such that each center $p_c \in P$ is associated to a subspace F_i of F. The index function is mathematically defined as:

$$PBM(X, P) = \left[\frac{1}{C} * \frac{H_\mu}{H_{xC}} * H_{CC} \right]^2$$

Where X is the data set and C is the number of subspace clusters generated from a maximum value of SC_{max}. The term H_μ measures the overall distance of each pattern x_s to the origin of the entire space, μ (the value is zero after standardization of data set). The term is computed as:

$$H_\mu = \sum_{s=1}^{S} \sum_{f=1}^{Z} |x_{s,f} - \mu_f|$$

Where $|\ |$ refers to the absolute value. The term H_{xC} measures the distances of all the objects to their cluster centers and is computed as:

$$H_{xC} = \sum_{s=1}^{S} \sum_{c=1}^{C} min_c \left[dis(x_s, p_c) \right]$$

where $dis(x_s, p_c) = \sum_{f \in F_i} |x_{s,f} - p_{c,f}| + \sum_{f \in F \setminus F_i} |x_{s,f} - \mu_f|$. The factor H_{CC}

measures the maximum distance between any two clusters and is computed as:

$$H_{CC} = max_{1 \leqslant i \leqslant C, 1 \leqslant j \leqslant C} \, dis(p_i, p_j)$$

where $dis(p_i, p_j) = \sum_{f \in F_i \cap F_j} |p_{i,f} - p_{j,f}| + \sum_{f \in F \setminus (F_i \cap F_j)} |p_{i,f} - \mu_f|$. From the definition of PBM-index, PBM (X, P), it is visible that, more the value of this index, better will be the quality of clusters. However, in this paper, we inverse the PBM-index value and therefore the task is to minimize this index.

Xie-Beni (XB) Index: The Xie and Beni index [11], is another validity index which also optimizes the compactness within the clusters and separation between the clusters. The XB-index is computed as:

$$XB(X, P) = \frac{\sum_{s=1}^{S} \sum_{c=1}^{C} min_c \, [dis(x_s, p_c)]^2}{S * min_{1 \leqslant i \leqslant C, 1 \leqslant j \leqslant C} dis(p_i, p_j)^2}$$

The less the value of XB-index, better is the generated subspace clusters. Therefore, the best partitioning of the data set is indicated by the minimum value of XB-index.

2.5 Overview of the Algorithm

The algorithm starts with N uniformly selected model (phenotype or cluster centers) also called as solutions and N new solutions are generated after applying mutation operators. Subspace clusters are generated by assigning each objects to a particular cluster based on the minimum distance. Again, based on the objective values of each solution, non-dominated sorting and crowding distance [13] operators returns top N solutions from $2N$ solutions. The process is repeated *Iter* number of times on a sample data set to get the best N models. Finally the subspace clusters on whole data set is generated and considered for evaluation.

3 Experimental Setup

The algorithm is evaluated on several real-life and synthetic data sets. The various parameters that have been used in this algorithm are explained in this section. The developed algorithm is compared with several state-of-the-art algorithms. The comparison is performed with respect to various evaluation measures presented in [15] that are designed to quantify the quality of subspace clusters.

3.1 Datasets

The proposed algorithm is tested with seven benchmark real-life data sets and 16 synthetic data sets collected from [14]. The real-life data sets are glass, breast, liver, pendigits, diabetes, vowel and shape. The synthetic data sets are D75, D50, D25, D20, D15, D10, D05 (varying in dimensions), S5500, S4500, S3500, S2500,

S1500 (varying in size), N75, N50, N30, N10 (varying in the noise incorporated). Each synthetic data set has 10 hidden subspace clusters. The results obtained by the proposed algorithm are then compared with those obtained by different state-of-the-art algorithms, CLIQUE [1], ChameleoClust [6], KymeroClust [7] to name a few as reported in [7] with respect to different performance metrics.

3.2   Parameter Settings and Evaluation Measures

The parameter, mutation rate η_r, is considered as $\eta_r = 0.05$ and the number of iterations is $Iter = 4000$. The number of solutions $N = 10$ and the initial genome size that have been considered for real-life data sets and synthetic data sets are $q = 200$ and $q = 100$, respectively. In case of real-life data set, the expected number of clusters is considered as three times the number of classes, i.e., $ExpCluster = 3 * NumClasses$. However, the sample data set size that has been considered for temporal subspace cluster generation, must be considered in such a way that it should reflect the impact of the whole data set and is considered as $ExpCluster * 25$ as in [7]. In the case of synthetic data sets, since the number of clusters is fixed to 10, this sample size value becomes $10 * 25$. The maximum possible number of subspace clusters, SC_{max}, is defined such a way that, for each data set, each of the classes with respect to all the features has given a chance either to present in the subspace or not and therefore, $SC_{max} = NumClasses * \lceil \frac{Z}{2} \rceil$. In the case of synthetic data sets, since we know the actual number of clusters, we provide the flexibility as two times the actual number of clusters. Therefore, the value is considered as $SC_{max} = 20$, the same value is also used in [6].

The qualities of the generated subspace clusters have been evaluated using the standard evaluation measures presented in [15]. These evaluation measures comprise of $F\text{-}Measure$ [15], Accuracy [15], Clustering Error (CE) [16], Relative Non-intersecting Area, $\overline{RNIA}$ (1-RNIA) [16] and $\overline{Entropy}$ (1-Entropy) [15]. A few secondary evaluation metrics are also considered for evaluation such as coverage, number of clusters, average number of features and execution time.

4   Experimental Results

The developed algorithm is tested with 7 real-life data sets and 16 synthetic data sets. The results of the algorithm are reported using both the primary as well as secondary evaluation metrics. The algorithm is executed 10 times for all the data sets and both the maximum value and the minimum value corresponding to each evaluation metrics are reported. The comparison shows that different algorithms take advantages over different metrics and it is very difficult to declare a particular algorithm a winner. However, the superiority of the proposed algorithm is justified below.

Table 1. Results for the real-life data sets with respect to primary and secondary evaluation metrics

	F-Measure		Accuracy		CE		RNIA		Entropy		Coverage		NumCluster		AvgDim		RunTime	
Dataset Breast	Max	Min	Max	Min	Max	Min	Max	Min	Max	Min	Max	Min	Max	Min	Max	Min	Max	Min
Proposed	0.69	0.61	**0.81**	**0.78**	0.23	0.16	0.35	0.27	0.33	0.29	1.0	1.0	7	4	10.14	8.92	14977	14574
CHAMELEOCLUST	0.60	0.51	0.76	0.76	0.23	0.11	0.53	0.25	0.25	0.22	1.0	1.0	8	4	16.75	5.75	339	131
CLIQUE	0.67	**0.67**	0.71	0.71	0.02	0.02	0.40	0.40	0.26	0.26	1.0	1.0	107	107	1.7	1.7	453	453
DOC	0.73	0.61	**0.81**	0.76	0.11	0.04	**0.84**	0.07	0.46	0.27	1.0	0.8	60	6	27.2	2.8	1.00E+06	37515
FIRES	0.49	0.03	0.76	0.76	0.03	0.0	0.05	0.0	1.0	0.01	0.76	0.04	11	1	2.5	1	250	31
INSCY	0.74	0.55	0.77	0.76	0.02	0.0	0.24	0.11	0.60	**0.39**	0.97	0.74	2038	167	11	4.4	134373	63484
KYMEROCLUST	0.66	0.57	0.79	0.76	0.18	0.14	0.56	**0.51**	0.31	0.25	1.0	1.0	19	13	12.36	9.26	8	7
MINECLUS	**0.78**	0.69	0.78	0.76	0.19	**0.18**	1.0	1.0	**0.56**	0.37	1.0	1.0	64	32	33	33	40359	29437
P3C	0.63	0.63	0.77	0.77	0.04	0.04	0.19	0.19	0.36	0.36	0.85	0.85	28	28	6.9	6.9	6281	6281
PROCLUS	0.57	0.52	0.80	0.74	**0.51**	0.11	0.65	0.43	0.32	0.23	0.89	0.69	9	2	24	18	703	141
SCHISM	0.67	**0.67**	0.75	0.69	0.01	0.01	0.36	0.34	0.35	0.34	1.0	0.99	248	197	2.3	2.2	158749	114609
STATPC	0.41	0.41	0.78	**0.78**	0.16	0.16	0.33	0.33	0.29	0.29	0.43	0.43	5	5	33	33	5187	4906
SUBCLU	0.68	0.51	0.77	0.67	0.02	0.01	0.54	0.04	0.27	0.24	1.0	0.82	357	5	2	1	5265	16
Dataset Diabetes	Max	Min	Max	Min	Max	Min	Max	Min	Max	Min	Max	Min	Max	Min	Max	Min	Max	Min
Proposed	0.72	0.62	**0.74**	**0.71**	0.37	0.23	0.57	0.49	0.26	0.19	1.0	1.0	7	5	5.71	4.88	12396	11514
CHAMELEOCLUST	0.70	0.62	0.73	0.70	0.17	0.09	0.66	0.47	0.28	0.23	1.0	1.0	29	19	5	2.75	598	438
CLIQUE	0.70	0.39	0.72	0.69	0.03	0.01	0.14	0.01	0.23	0.13	1.0	1.0	349	202	4.2	2.4	11953	203
DOC	0.71	0.71	0.72	0.69	0.31	**0.26**	**0.92**	**0.79**	0.31	0.24	1.0	0.93	67	17	8	5.1	1.00E+06	51640
FIRES	0.52	0.03	0.65	0.64	0.12	0.0	0.27	0.0	0.68	0.0	0.81	0.03	17	1	2.5	1	4234	360
INSCY	0.65	0.39	0.70	0.65	0.37	0.11	0.45	0.42	0.44	0.15	0.83	0.73	132	3	6.7	5.7	112093	33531
KYMEROCLUST	0.69	0.64	0.73	0.70	0.21	0.08	0.55	0.40	0.25	0.21	1.0	1.0	16	13	3.69	2.87	3	3
MINECLUS	0.72	**0.66**	0.71	0.69	**0.63**	0.13	0.89	0.58	0.29	0.17	0.99	0.96	39	3	6	5.2	3578	62
P3C	0.39	0.39	0.66	0.65	0.56	0.11	0.85	0.22	0.09	0.07	0.97	0.88	2	1	7	2	656	141
PROCLUS	0.67	0.61	0.72	**0.71**	0.34	0.21	0.78	0.69	0.23	0.19	0.92	0.78	9	3	8	6	360	109
SCHISM	0.7	0.62	0.73	0.68	0.08	0.01	0.36	0.09	0.34	0.2	1.0	0.79	270	21	4.2	3.9	35468	250
STATPC	0.73	0.59	0.70	0.65	0.06	0.0	0.63	0.17	**0.72**	**0.28**	0.97	0.75	363	27	8	8	27749	4657
SUBCLU	**0.74**	0.45	0.71	0.68	0.01	0.01	0.01	0.01	0.14	0.11	1.0	1.0	1601	325	4.7	4	190122	58718
Dataset Glass	Max	Min	Max	Min	Max	Min	Max	Min	Max	Min	Max	Min	Max	Min	Max	Min	Max	Min
Proposed	0.49	0.39	0.58	**0.5**	0.28	0.24	0.58	0.48	0.46	0.4	1.0	1.0	12	9	5.5	4	7929	7598
CHAMELEOCLUST	0.43	0.28	0.57	0.50	**0.43**	**0.26**	0.88	0.55	0.46	0.36	1.0	1.0	8	4	7.5	4.75	195	95
CLIQUE	0.51	0.31	**0.67**	0.50	0.02	0.0	0.06	0.0	0.39	0.24	1.0	1.0	6169	175	5.4	3.1	411195	1375
DOC	0.74	0.50	0.63	0.50	0.23	0.13	**0.93**	0.33	0.72	0.50	0.93	0.91	64	11	9	3.3	23172	78
FIRES	0.30	0.30	0.49	0.49	0.21	0.21	0.45	0.45	0.40	0.40	0.86	0.86	7	7	2.7	2.7	78	78
INSCY	0.57	0.41	0.65	0.47	0.23	0.09	0.54	0.26	0.67	0.47	0.86	0.79	72	30	5.9	2.7	4703	578
KYMEROCLUST	0.65	0.51	0.71	0.60	0.32	0.24	0.85	**0.76**	0.65	0.55	1.0	1.0	23	19	6.74	5.7	18	16
MINECLUS	**0.76**	0.40	0.52	0.50	0.24	0.19	0.78	0.45	0.72	0.46	1.0	0.87	64	6	7	4.3	907	15
P3C	0.28	0.23	0.47	0.39	0.14	0.13	0.3	0.27	0.43	0.38	0.89	0.81	3	2	3	3	32	31
PROCLUS	0.60	**0.56**	0.60	**0.57**	0.13	0.05	0.51	0.17	0.76	**0.68**	0.79	0.57	29	26	8	2	375	250
SCHISM	0.46	0.39	0.63	0.47	0.11	0.04	0.33	0.20	0.44	0.38	1.0	0.79	158	30	3.9	2.1	313	31
STATPC	0.75	0.40	0.49	0.36	0.19	0.05	0.67	0.37	**0.88**	0.36	0.93	0.8	106	27	9	9	1265	390
SUBCLU	0.50	0.45	0.65	0.46	0.0	0.0	0.01	0.01	0.42	0.39	1.0	1.0	1648	831	4.9	4.3	14410	4250
Dataset Liver	Max	Min	Max	Min	Max	Min	Max	Min	Max	Min	Max	Min	Max	Min	Max	Min	Max	Min
Proposed	0.7	0.64	0.64	0.59	0.46	**0.38**	0.83	**0.7**	0.12	0.08	1.0	1.0	6	4	4.25	3.6	4814	4344
CHAMELEOCLUST	0.65	0.59	**0.68**	0.62	0.20	0.10	0.53	0.41	0.14	0.07	1.0	1.0	27	22	2.48	1.85	202	158
CLIQUE	0.68	0.65	0.67	0.58	0.08	0.02	0.38	0.03	0.10	0.02	1.0	1.0	1922	19	4.1	1.7	38281	15
DOC	0.67	0.64	**0.68**	0.58	0.11	0.07	0.51	0.35	0.18	0.11	0.99	0.9	45	13	3	1.9	625324	1625
FIRES	0.58	0.04	0.58	0.56	0.14	0.0	0.39	0.01	0.37	0.0	0.84	0.03	10	1	3	1	531	46
INSCY	0.66	0.66	0.62	0.61	0.03	0.03	0.42	0.39	0.21	**0.20**	0.85	0.81	166	130	2.1	2.1	407	234
KYMEROCLUST	0.65	0.56	0.67	0.60	0.21	0.09	0.56	0.43	0.12	0.04	1.0	1.0	17	11	2.82	2	2	2
MINECLUS	**0.73**	0.63	0.65	0.58	0.09	0.09	0.68	0.48	0.33	0.16	0.99	0.92	64	32	4	3.7	49563	1954
P3C	0.36	0.35	0.58	0.58	**0.55**	0.27	**0.96**	0.47	0.02	0.01	0.98	0.94	2	1	6	3	172	32
PROCLUS	0.53	0.39	0.63	**0.63**	0.26	0.11	0.66	0.25	0.05	0.05	0.83	0.46	6	2	5	3	78	31
SCHISM	0.69	**0.60**	**0.68**	0.50	0.04	0.00	0.45	0.20	0.10	0.08	0.99	0.99	90	68	2.7	2.1	31	0
STATPC	0.69	0.57	0.65	0.58	0.23	0.01	0.58	0.37	**0.63**	0.05	0.77	0.71	159	4	6	3.3	1890	781
SUBCLU	0.68	0.68	0.64	0.58	0.11	0.02	0.68	0.05	0.07	0.02	1.0	1.0	334	64	3.4	1.3	1422	47
Dataset Pendigits	Max	Min	Max	Min	Max	Min	Max	Min	Max	Min	Max	Min	Max	Min	Max	Min	Max	Min
Proposed	0.67	0.55	0.75	0.68	0.23	0.18	0.34	0.28	0.59	0.55	1.0	1.0	29	25	3.94	2.88	65402	53151
CHAMELEOCLUST	0.71	0.51	0.74	0.59	**0.51**	0.30	0.78	0.49	0.68	0.58	1.0	1.0	14	10	12.4	7.21	4476	4226
CLIQUE	0.30	0.17	**0.96**	0.86	0.06	0.01	0.20	0.06	0.41	0.26	1.0	1.0	1890	36	3.1	1.5	67891	219
DOC	0.52	0.52	0.54	0.54	0.18	0.18	0.35	0.35	0.53	0.53	0.91	0.91	15	15	5.5	5.5	178358	178358
FIRES	0.45	0.45	0.73	0.73	0.09	0.09	0.33	0.33	0.31	0.31	0.94	0.94	27	27	2.5	2.5	169999	169999
INSCY	0.65	0.48	0.78	0.68	0.07	0.07	0.30	0.28	0.77	0.69	0.91	0.82	262	106	5.3	4.6	2.00E+06	1.00E+06
KYMEROCLUST	**0.92**	**0.89**	0.92	**0.89**	0.40	0.34	0.80	0.78	0.89	**0.86**	1.0	1.0	41	34	12.21	10.51	556	523
MINECLUS	0.87	0.87	0.86	0.86	0.48	**0.48**	**0.89**	**0.89**	0.82	0.82	1.0	1.0	64	64	12.1	12.1	780167	692651
P3C	0.74	0.74	0.72	0.72	0.28	0.28	0.58	0.58	0.76	0.76	0.9	0.9	31	31	9	9	2.00E+06	2.00E+06
PROCLUS	0.78	0.73	0.74	0.73	0.31	0.27	0.64	0.45	**0.90**	0.71	0.9	0.74	37	17	14	8	6045	4250
SCHISM	0.45	0.26	0.93	0.71	0.05	0.01	0.30	0.08	0.5	0.45	1.0	0.93	1092	290	10.1	3.4	5.00E+08	21266
STATPC	0.91	0.32	0.92	0.10	0.09	0.0	0.67	0.11	1.0	0.53	0.99	0.84	4109	56	16	16	5.00E+06	3.00E+06
SUBCLU	-	-	-	-	-	-	-	-	-	-	-	-	-	-	-	-	-	-
Dataset Shape	Max	Min	Max	Min	Max	Min	Max	Min	Max	Min	Max	Min	Max	Min	Max	Min	Max	Min
Proposed	0.85	0.8	0.85	**0.81**	0.22	0.19	0.25	0.21	0.86	0.81	1.0	1.0	13	11	3.22	3.08	13913	13772
CHAMELEOCLUST	0.75	0.63	0.80	0.71	0.54	0.49	0.78	0.71	0.77	0.67	1.0	1.0	14	10	12.4	10.79	462	252
CLIQUE	0.31	0.31	0.76	0.76	0.01	0.01	0.07	0.07	0.66	0.66	1.0	1.0	486	486	3.3	3.3	235	235
DOC	0.90	0.83	0.79	0.54	0.56	0.38	**0.90**	**0.82**	0.93	0.86	1.0	1.0	52	29	13.8	12.8	2.00E+06	86500
FIRES	0.36	0.36	0.51	0.44	0.20	0.13	0.25	0.20	0.88	0.82	0.45	0.39	10	5	7.6	5.3	63	47
INSCY	0.84	0.59	0.76	0.48	0.18	0.16	0.37	0.24	**0.94**	0.87	0.88	0.82	185	48	9.8	9.5	22578	11531
KYMEROCLUST	0.82	0.72	**0.86**	0.79	0.57	**0.53**	0.86	0.80	0.83	0.77	1.0	1.0	19	16	13.5	12.56	101	91
MINECLUS	**0.94**	**0.86**	0.79	0.60	**0.58**	0.46	1.0	1.0	0.93	0.82	1.0	1.0	64	32	17	17	46703	3266
P3C	0.51	0.51	0.61	0.61	0.14	0.14	0.17	0.17	0.8	0.8	0.66	0.66	9	9	4.1	4.1	140	140
PROCLUS	0.84	0.81	0.72	0.71	0.25	0.18	0.61	0.37	0.93	**0.91**	0.89	0.79	34	34	13	7	593	469
SCHISM	0.51	0.3	0.74	0.49	0.10	0.0	0.26	0.01	0.85	0.55	1.0	0.92	8835	90	6	3.9	712964	9031
STATPC	0.43	0.43	0.74	0.74	0.45	0.45	0.55	0.55	0.56	0.56	0.92	0.92	9	9	17	17	250	171
SUBCLU	0.36	0.29	0.70	0.64	0.0	0.0	0.05	0.04	0.89	0.88	1.0	1.0	3468	3337	4.5	4.1	4063	1891
Dataset Vowel	Max	Min	Max	Min	Max	Min	Max	Min	Max	Min	Max	Min	Max	Min	Max	Min	Max	Min
Proposed	0.42	0.35	0.44	0.38	**0.19**	**0.14**	0.33	0.27	0.39	0.33	1.0	1.0	19	14	3.39	3.07	34170	28320
CHAMELEOCLUST	0.41	0.37	0.42	0.38	0.17	0.13	0.65	0.54	0.45	0.40	1.0	1.0	33	24	6	4.57	995	787
CLIQUE	0.23	0.17	**0.64**	0.37	0.05	0.0	0.44	0.01	0.10	0.09	1.0	1.0	3062	267	4.9	1.9	523233	1953
DOC	0.49	**0.49**	0.44	0.44	0.14	**0.14**	**0.85**	**0.85**	0.58	0.58	0.86	0.86	64	64	10	10	120015	120015
FIRES	0.16	0.14	0.13	0.11	0.02	0.02	0.14	0.13	0.16	0.13	0.50	0.45	32	24	2.1	1.9	563	250
INSCY	**0.82**	0.33	0.61	0.15	0.09	0.07	0.75	0.26	**0.94**	0.21	0.90	0.81	163	74	9.5	4.3	75706	39390
KYMEROCLUST	0.53	0.48	0.53	0.47	0.16	**0.14**	0.75	0.70	0.56	0.52	1.0	1.0	50	45	6.82	6.3	364	339
MINECLUS	0.48	0.43	0.37	0.37	0.09	0.04	0.62	0.34	0.60	0.46	0.98	0.87	64	64	7.2	3.6	7734	5204
P3C	0.08	0.05	0.17	0.16	0.12	0.08	0.69	0.43	0.13	0.12	0.98	0.95	3	2	7	4.7	1610	625
PROCLUS	0.49	**0.49**	0.44	0.44	0.11	0.11	0.53	0.53	0.65	**0.65**	0.67	0.67	64	64	8	8	766	766
SCHISM	0.37	0.23	0.62	0.52	0.05	0.01	0.43	0.11	0.29	0.21	1.0	0.93	494	121	4.3	2.8	23031	391
STATPC	0.22	0.22	0.56	**0.56**	0.06	0.06	0.12	0.12	0.14	0.14	1.0	1.0	39	39	10	10	18485	16671
SUBCLU	0.24	0.18	0.58	0.38	0.04	0.01	0.39	0.04	0.30	0.13	1.0	1.0	10881	709	3.6	2	26047	2250

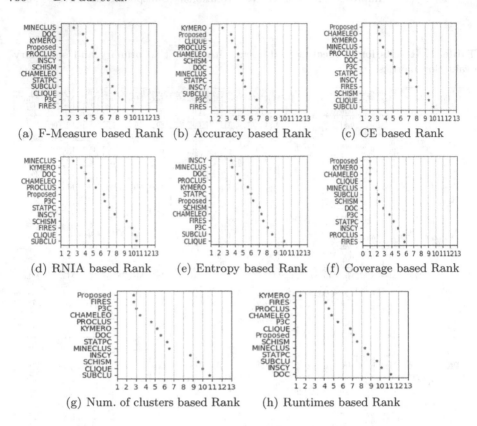

(a) F-Measure based Rank (b) Accuracy based Rank   (c) CE based Rank

(d) RNIA based Rank   (e) Entropy based Rank   (f) Coverage based Rank

(g) Num. of clusters based Rank   (h) Runtimes based Rank

Fig. 1. Rankings of different clustering algorithms with respect to primary metrics

4.1   Comparison with Real-Life Data Sets

Results of the 7 real-life data sets with respect to both primary and secondary
evaluation metrics are shown in Table 1. In order to understand the comparison
more clearly, a rank based comparison approach is made. Rank of an algorithm is
calculated simply by taking the mean of the ranks obtained with respect to both
the minimum and the maximum scores for all the real-life data sets corresponding
to each evaluation metric. The ranks of the various algorithms corresponding to
both primary as well as secondary evaluation metrics are shown in Fig. 1(a)–(h).
The observations that can be made from the comparison are listed below.

- The proposed algorithm provides the best results with respect to metrics CE,
  (Fig. 1(c)), coverage, (Fig. 1(f)) and number of clusters, (Fig. 1(g)). However,
  with respect to accuracy (Fig. 1(b)) also, the proposed algorithm performs
  well as it ranks second in the list.
- With respect to F-measure, (Fig. 1(a)), and RNIA, (Fig. 1(d)), the algorithm
  MINECLUS performs best. However, MINECLUS, doesn't provide the full
  coverage (Fig. 1(f)), and the algorithm is time inefficient (Fig. 1(h)).

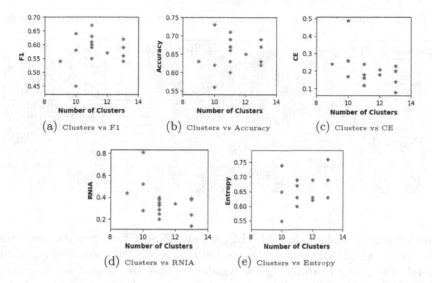

Fig. 2. Values of evaluation metrics vs number of clusters for 16 synthetic data sets

- For metrics, accuracy, (Fig. 1(b)), runtime (Fig. 1(h)) and also for coverage, (Fig. 1(f)), the algorithm Kymeroclust provides the best results. Again, the algorithm INSCY provides the best result for entropy, (Fig. 1(e)), however it doesn't perform well with respect to other metrics.

4.2   Comparison with Synthetic Data Sets

The results obtained for all the synthetic data sets are reported in Table 2. For each of the data sets, we consider that run which produces the best score for a particular metric among 10 runs. Then for each evaluation metric, we plot a graph representing the metric value with respect to the number of clusters obtained for 16 data sets as shown in Fig. 2(a)–(e). However, the following observations can also be made from the number of clusters produced by the proposed algorithm for the synthetic data sets.

- The range of the clusters produced by the proposed algorithm is 9–13. Many a time, the number of clusters generated by this algorithm exactly matches with the actual number of clusters i.e., 10.
- The difference between the maximum and the minimum number of clusters produced by the proposed algorithm is 4 (9–13), which is the minimum, whereas it is 5 (9–14), 7 (9–16) and 10 (6–16) for algorithms, KymereoClust, ChameleoClust and P3C respectively.

Considering real-data sets and all the evaluation metrics, it is observed that, the proposed algorithms and the algorithm KymereoClust rank 1st in three cases, MINECLUS and INSCY rank 1st in two and one case, respectively. The proposed

Table 2. Results of the primary evaluation metrics for the 16 synthetic data sets

Dataset	F-Measure		Accuracy		CE		RNIA		Entropy		NumClusters		AvgDim		RunTime	
	Max	Min	Max	Min	Max	Min	Max	Min	Max	Min	Max	Min	Max	Min	Max	Min
D05	0.64	0.60	0.73	0.68	0.49	0.40	0.81	0.66	0.74	0.65	12	10	3.92	3.73	4221	3600
D10	0.45	0.30	0.56	0.52	0.26	0.21	0.52	0.43	0.55	0.43	12	10	6.55	4.9	4271	4135
D15	0.54	0.36	0.63	0.49	0.24	0.17	0.44	0.32	0.65	0.50	13	9	6.69	5.8	5720	3879
D20	0.54	0.38	0.62	0.54	0.20	0.16	0.39	0.33	0.63	0.48	14	13	8.06	7	6352	6237
D25	0.67	0.62	0.67	0.59	0.24	0.21	0.38	0.29	0.69	0.62	12	10	9.58	7.08	6503	6037
D50	0.55	0.46	0.60	0.55	0.12	0.10	0.25	0.18	0.60	0.56	12	11	11.37	8.59	10779	10627
D75	0.56	0.38	0.63	0.45	0.08	0.05	0.14	0.10	0.62	0.43	15	13	14.5	11.12	15034	14654
S1500	0.59	0.40	0.69	0.59	0.23	0.15	0.38	0.28	0.76	0.68	15	13	8.47	9.95	13112	11015
S2500	0.57	0.37	0.65	0.46	0.18	0.11	0.34	0.21	0.63	0.45	14	12	6.92	5.62	9726	8812
S3500	0.59	0.43	0.71	0.62	0.26	0.20	0.40	0.28	0.74	0.63	13	11	8.47	7.12	11213	10743
S4500	0.63	0.52	0.69	0.55	0.16	0.09	0.29	0.16	0.67	0.55	12	10	6.82	5.92	9417	8787
S5500	0.60	0.54	0.63	0.58	0.18	0.11	0.35	0.23	0.63	0.49	13	11	8.16	6.18	11324	11626
N10	0.63	0.43	0.67	0.51	0.21	0.13	0.33	0.23	0.69	0.50	13	11	7.88	5.57	10360	9105
N30	0.58	0.34	0.62	0.42	0.17	0.10	0.28	0.19	0.63	0.57	12	10	6.82	5.67	8978	8558
N50	0.62	0.41	0.67	0.49	0.14	0.10	0.24	0.15	0.69	0.50	14	13	6.43	4.28	10490	9170
N70	0.61	0.41	0.66	0.47	0.12	0.09	0.20	0.14	0.69	0.49	13	11	7.53	5.07	9720	7995

algorithm beats the algorithms MINECLUS and INSCY for five and seven times, respectively. Again, considering the synthetic data sets, the proposed algorithm performs the best in producing the number of clusters. Therefore, combining both real-life and synthetic data sets, it can be claimed that the proposed algorithm is superior to other algorithms.

5 Conclusions and Future Work

The developed algorithm takes the advantage of its evolvable genome structure and multi-objective optimization in generating subspace clusters. The comparison shows that the proposed algorithm is competitive to the other algorithms, also in many cases it provides superior result. Therefore, from the results and comparison with the state-of-the-art algorithms it can be established that the proposed algorithm can take benefits of the evolutionary-based MOO technique.

The proposed algorithm is developed inspired by the algorithm, Chameleo-Clust. In future, we shall try to develop an algorithm which will take care of all the limitations of the existing techniques. However, we will also try to develop an algorithm for data which arrives in online fashion.

Acknowledgement. Dr. Sriparna Saha would like to acknowledge the support of Early Career Research Award of Science and Engineering Research Board (SERB) of Department of Science and Technology India to carry out this research.

References

1. Agrawal, R., Gehrke, J., Gunopulos, D., Raghavan, P.: Automatic subspace clustering of high dimensional data for data mining applications, vol. 27. ACM (1998)
2. Kailing, K., Kriegel, H.P., Kröger, P.: Density-connected subspace clustering for high-dimensional data. In: Proceedings of the 2004 SIAM International Conference on Data Mining, pp. 246–256. SIAM (2004)
3. Ester, M., Kriegel, H.P., Sander, J., Xu, X., et al.: A density-based algorithm for discovering clusters in large spatial databases with noise. In: Kdd, vol. 96, pp. 226–231 (1996)

4. Procopiuc, C.M., Jones, M., Agarwal, P.K., Murali, T.: A Monte Carlo algorithm for fast projective clustering. In: Proceedings of the 2002 ACM SIGMOD International Conference on Management of Data, pp. 418–427. ACM (2002)
5. Yiu, M.L., Mamoulis, N.: Frequent-pattern based iterative projected clustering. In: Third IEEE International Conference on Data Mining, pp. 689–692. IEEE (2003)
6. Peignier, S., Rigotti, C., Beslon, G.: Subspace clustering using evolvable genome structure. In: Proceedings of the 2015 Annual Conference on Genetic and Evolutionary Computation, pp. 575–582. ACM (2015)
7. Peignier, S.: Subspace clustering on static datasets and dynamic data streams using bio-inspired algorithms. Ph.D. thesis, Université de Lyon; INSA Lyon (2017)
8. Bandyopadhyay, S., Saha, S., Maulik, U., Deb, K.: A simulated annealing-based multiobjective optimization algorithm: AMOSA. IEEE Trans. Evol. Comput. 12(3), 269–283 (2008)
9. Crombach, A., Hogeweg, P.: Chromosome rearrangements and the evolution of genome structuring and adaptability. Mol. Biol. Evol. 24(5), 1130–1139 (2007)
10. Knibbe, C., Coulon, A., Mazet, O., Fayard, J.M., Beslon, G.: A long-term evolutionary pressure on the amount of noncoding dna. Mol. Biol. Evol. 24(10), 2344–2353 (2007)
11. Xie, X.L., Beni, G.: A validity measure for fuzzy clustering. IEEE Trans. Pattern Anal. Mach. Intell. 13(8), 841–847 (1991)
12. Pakhira, M.K., Bandyopadhyay, S., Maulik, U.: Validity index for crisp and fuzzy clusters. Pattern Recognit. 37(3), 487–501 (2004)
13. Deb, K., Pratap, A., Agarwal, S., Meyarivan, T.A.M.: A fast and elitist multiobjective genetic algorithm: NSGA-II. IEEE Trans. Evol. Comput. 6, 182–197 (2002)
14. Lichman, M.: UCI machine learning repository (2013). http://archive.ics.uci.edu/ml
15. Müller, E., Günnemann, S., Assent, I., Seidl, T.: Evaluating clustering in subspace projections of high dimensional data. Proc. VLDB Endow. 2(1), 1270–1281 (2009)
16. Patrikainen, A., Meila, M.: Comparing subspace clusterings. IEEE Trans. Knowl. Data Eng. 18(7), 902–916 (2006)

Network of Experts: Learning from Evolving Data Streams Through Network-Based Ensembles

Heitor Murilo Gomes[1]([✉]) [iD], Albert Bifet[1], Philippe Fournier-Viger[2],
Jones Granatyr[3], and Jesse Read[4]

[1] University of Waikato, Hamilton, New Zealand
{heitor.gomes,albert.bifet}@waikato.ac.nz
[2] Harbin Institute of Technology, Shenzhen, China
philfv8@yahoo.com
[3] University of Lisbon, Lisbon, Portugal
jones.granatyr@gaips-inesc-id.pt
[4] LIX - École Polytechnique, Palaiseau, France
jesse.read@polytechnique.edu

Abstract. Ensemble classifiers are a promising approach for data stream classification. Though, diversity influences the performance of ensemble classifiers, current studies do not take advantage of relations between component classifiers to improve their performance. This paper addresses this issue by proposing a new kind of ensemble learner for data stream classification, which explicitly defines relations between component classifiers. These relations are then used in various ways, e.g., to combine the decisions of component models. The hypothesis is that an ensemble learner can yield accurate predictions in a streaming environment based on a structural analysis of a weighted network of its component models. Implications, limitations and benefits of this assumption, are discussed. A formal description of a network-based ensemble for data streams is presented, and an algorithm that implements it, named Network of Experts (NetEx). Empirical experiments show that NetEx's accuracy and processing time are competitive with state-of-the-art ensembles.

Keywords: Data stream · Classification · Ensemble learning

1 Introduction

High-speed data stream mining has gained in importance in recent years due to the tremendous amount of real-time data generated by networks, mobile phones and sensors. Building predictive models from data streams is of uttermost necessity for many applications such as those related to the Internet of Things [11]. But designing an effective data stream learning algorithm is not easy as it must process a large number of instances at a fast pace. A key challenge is that an

© Springer Nature Switzerland AG 2019
T. Gedeon et al. (Eds.): ICONIP 2019, LNCS 11953, pp. 704–716, 2019.
https://doi.org/10.1007/978-3-030-36708-4_58

algorithm must learn useful models using limited computational resources. A second challenge is that data evolves, i.e., the underlying data distribution may change over time, resulting in the well known problem of concept drifts [15].

An important data stream mining task is classification. In recent years, classifiers have been proposed to cope with different aspects of data stream classification. An emerging approach is to use classifier ensembles [1,4,18,22,28] as they frequently achieve better accuracy than single classifiers. Moreover, ensembles can often deal with concept drifts in a less drastic way than using a single classifier. For example, a single classifier may discard an hypothesis completely when faced with a concept drift, while an ensemble may only replace (or reset) a few of its component classifiers. Some of the first studies on ensemble classifiers for data streams have focused on adapting existing algorithms to handle data streams. This is the case of Online Bagging and Online Boosting [28]. Many ensembles were designed for data stream classification, some dealing with concept drift explicitly [1,4], and others implicitly [18,19,22].

Most ensemble classifiers are based on the intuition that component classifiers must be diverse to allow their combination to achieve higher accuracy than a single classifier [17]. That is true for many successful ensemble methods such as Bagging [6], AdaBoost [13] and Random Forest [7]. The subjective notion of diversity has been well-studied [8,24,25] and yet there is not a "one size fits all" metric for measuring diversity between ensemble members, or any proof that correlates a given diversity measure and its impact on predictive performance. Even though it is difficult to formalize or measure the contribution of "diversity" to an ensemble's overall prediction accuracy, it is intuitively easy to rationalize why combining an homogeneous set of classifiers cannot achieve better (or worse) accuracy than any of its members. A limitation of current ensemble classifiers is that they do not take advantage of the relations between component classifiers to improve their performance.

This paper addresses this issue by proposing a new kind of ensemble learner for data stream classification, called *network-based ensemble*. Such ensemble explicitly defines relations between members. These relations are then used in various ways such as to combine the decisions of similar classifiers. A structure is imposed on components of an ensemble to highlight their diversity, so that it can be better exploited. An algorithm implementing this idea is presented, named Network of Experts (NetEx). Experiments show that NetEx's accuracy and processing time are competitive with state-of-the-art ensembles.

The rest of this paper is organized as follows. Section 2 defines network-based ensembles. Section 3 describes the proposed NetEx algorithm. Finally, Sect. 4 presents experimental results and Sect. 5 draws the conclusion.

2   Network-Based Ensembles

The proposed concept of network-based ensemble is defined as follows. Let $C = \{c_1, c_2, \ldots, c_M\}$ be a diverse set of classifiers, R a **relation** that defines connections $\Phi = \{\phi_1, \phi_2, \ldots, \phi_P\}$ between members of C, β **a combination**

method that takes into account the structure formed by Φ, and f_ψ **an adaptation function** that updates C and Φ according to the current state of a data stream S. Moreover, it is expected that members of C are different from one another (diverse) to be consistent with the intuitive principle that a homogeneous subset of classifiers cannot contribute to the overall decision any better than any of them alone [23]. We note that for the sake of generality the definition is not bound to any specific method to induce diversity into the ensemble.

The connections defined by the relation R are not restricted to be between pairs of classifiers, although using pairs is an intuitive way of grouping elements in a network [30] and of measuring diversity between classifiers [24]. Also, the relation R is not restricted to be a diversity or similarity measure. The combination method β should use the set of connections Φ to group ensemble members in a way that they can be explored to produce accurate predictions. For example, β can be defined such that any pair (c_k, c_l) from C which connection ϕ_{c_k, c_l} is smaller than a given threshold T must be grouped together for voting. The last component of the proposed definition is the adaptation function f_ψ, which updates the ensemble structure, either periodically or incrementally, to allow it to adapt to drifts. These updates may include adding, removing, or replacing classifiers, and refreshing statistics extracted from classifiers, such as similar predictions counters.

3   The Network of Experts Algorithm

This section presents a novel network-based ensemble, named Network of Experts (NetEx). It relies on an active drift detection strategy instead of relying on a fixed period length parameter as previous approaches [18,19]. The main benefit is that NetEx does not require to fine tune the period length, yet it increases the algorithm's complexity as an adaptive window must be considered for each component model. In SAE2 [19] the relation R was defined as the similarity coefficient (Sc) between a pair of classifiers, connections were activated if they surpassed a Sc_{min} threshold, and a network was induced based on the maximal cliques. SAE2 performed predictions by combining the weighted votes (based on current period accuracy) first at the subnetwork level and then at the network level, which contributes to an indirect drift adaptation technique as recently added classifiers, probably better adapted to the current concept, tend to receive higher weights.

Differently, NetEx defines the relation R as either the Kappa statistic between the output of base model pairs or the Jaccard similarity of the features used to induce the model, and the network is build using the k nearest strategy presented in [29]. NetEx uses an adaptation strategy based on one drift/warning detector per base model, training background learners whenever warnings are detected, and weighting votes based on accuracy calculated on adaptive windows. Also, NetEx uses two diversity inducing techniques: vertical (similar to Leveraging Bagging) and horizontal (random subspaces). The rest of this section describes each aspect of NetEx in details.

Two different similarity weighting functions are presented to define the relation R, namely Kappa statistic κ and Jaccard Index. The reason for using Kappa is because it accounts for agreements that might happen by chance, while also precisely measuring divergence votes on multiclass problems.

Jaccard Index is used to estimate the similarity between finite sample sets [26], and is defined as the size of the intersection divided by the size of the union of the sample sets as shown in Eq. 1, where A and B represents subsets of features used to induce models a and b. The intuition behind using Jaccard to measure the similarity among base models is that models induced using approximately the same features might as well generate very similar models even if online bagging is used. There are other set distance metrics that could be used instead of Jaccard, such as Sorensen-Dice index [12]. However, our problem matches the ideal scenario for applying Jaccard, i.e., it is defined in terms of a binary set membership and element identity (features either belong to the subset or not), and two features are either completely equal or not at all.

$$ J(A, B) = \frac{A \cap B}{A \cup B} \tag{1} $$

There are three important factors to take into account when comparing Kappa and Jaccard for measuring similarity in NetEx:

1. Input data to estimate similarity: Kappa is calculated on the output predictions, while Jaccard is calculated on the feature subset;
2. Domain: Kappa ranges from -1 (Inverse dependency) to 1 (Dependency), where 0 represents independency. Jaccard ranges from 0 (No features are shared between models) to 1 (Exactly the same subset or one subset is a superset of the other[1]).
3. Update frequency: To maintain an updated estimation, Kappa must be recalculated after training using each new instance, while Jaccard is updated only when subspaces are defined for each model or when subspaces are reset.

In overall, Kappa provides a more accurate similarity estimation as it is based on the actual outputs. For example, it may happen that a completely different subset of features is used to induce two models, yet the features that compose these subsets may be correlated, thus both models will output very similar predictions. The main concern about using Kappa is that NetEx does not use a fixed update period length to control network updates, thus it is necessary to recalculate Kappa after training using each new instance, which requires a lot of computational resources. Optionally, we could have defined a grace period after which Kappa would be recalculated and the network rebuilt. But we would then be tied to a parameter similar to the period length l of SAE2.

Beyond defining relations, it is also necessary to specify how they will be explored by the ensemble. In this case, how the structure induced by them will be used to boost predictions. In our formal framework this is equivalent

---

[1] In NetEx, the number of subspaces is fixed, the number of features is the same for all classifiers.

to defining the combination method β. In SAE2, classifiers were combined based on dichotomous connections created based on the Sc_{min} parameter. The goal was to first decide within a set of highly similar classifiers a class label, and then use this decision at a secondary level in which all subsets of classifiers decisions were combined to form the overall ensemble decision.

NetEx uses a similar voting strategy, i.e., it first combines votes within subnetworks and then combines subnetwork votes to obtain an overall prediction. Precisely, when an unknown instance x is to be classified each component model yields one vote weighted by its current estimated accuracy. These individual votes are then combined into an overall subnetwork vote, which is weighted by the average accuracy estimation of its members. This final vote per subnetwork is used to define the overall decision.

The network structure is created based on a variation of the k nearest neighbors network construction technique as proposed in [29]. This method must not be confused with the classical k nearest neighbor learner. In [29] authors present a deterministic approach to construct a network given an arbitrary distance function. Basically, once set a reference vertex, the remaining non-reference vertices are ordered according to the their distance to it. Then, the reference vertex creates a connection with the top k vertices, i.e., closest, from the ordered list.

The base algorithm [29] does not specify how the reference vertices are selected. Thus, we have changed it to accommodate a more intuitive network construction approach given our problem. First, we define the k reference vertices, which we name as seed models/nodes, to maximize the overall distance among them. Intuitively, our goal is to create subnetworks as diverse as possible from one another. To do that, we maximize the dissimilarity among seed nodes in an iterative process: first we select the 2 most distant nodes, then the node that is most distant from the previously selected 2, and continue until k is reached. For example, assuming $k = 3$ and that nodes are arranged in Fig. 1 with distance corresponding to their Kappa (or Jaccard) measure, the nodes selected as seeds would be first 14 and 81, and then 12.

There are a multitude of algorithms for finding subgroups on networks [5]. For example, SAE [18] uses weakly connected components to build subnetworks; and [27] which uses a so-called *degeneracy* framework.

This network formation strategy still depends on an hyperparameter (k). However, it is an improvement over SAE2 Sc_{min}'s parameter as it is independent of the connections weight scale. For example, assuming each connection in the example from Fig. 1 were 25% "closer", the resulting subnetworks would be the same.

3.1 The Adaptation Function f_ψ

Following our definition of a network-based ensemble, we have to define the adaptation function f_ψ, responsible for matters such as: how training takes place and when/how the ensemble structure is updated. Our general definition of a network-based ensemble does not explicitly defines a training method, although

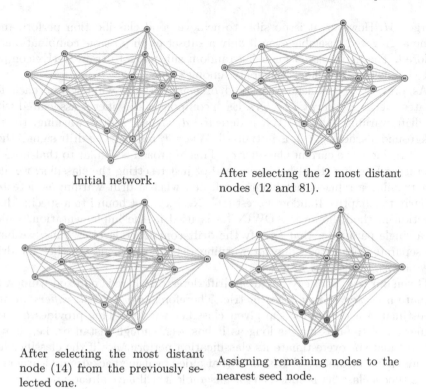

Initial network.

After selecting the 2 most distant nodes (12 and 81).

After selecting the most distant node (14) from the previously selected one.

Assigning remaining nodes to the nearest seed node.

Fig. 1. NetEx network formation example.

the definition specifies that component classifiers must be diverse. Thus, this must be taken into account for implementation.

We decided to simulate Online Bagging [28] using a poisson ($\lambda = 6$) distribution as in Leveraging Bagging [1]. Both methods train each model using a randomly selected subset of instances. These methods simulated bootstrap aggregation in an online setting by using a Poisson distribution. The Online Bagging algorithm uses $Poisson(\lambda = 1)$, which means that around 37% of the values output by the Poisson distribution are 0, another 37% are 1, and 26% are greater than 1. This implies that by using Poison (1), 37% of the instances are not used for training (value 0), 37% are used once (value 1), and 26% are trained with repetition (values greater than 1). Leveraging Bagging uses $Poisson(\lambda = 6)$, which implies that 0.25% of values are 0, 45% are lower than 6, 16% are 6, and 39% are greater than 6. Effectively, base models are trained using more instances in Leveraging Bagging, still more resources are used in comparison to Online Bagging.

Besides training classifiers on different subsets of instances, NetEx also trains them on different *subsets of features*. This strategy is known as the Random Subspace Method (RSM) [20]. There are $2^M - 1$ different non-empty subsets of features, which makes it not practical to try every possible combination given a larger M. However, it is possible to achieve good classification performance in the aggregated ensemble even if only a subset of all possible combinations is explored. The main reason for using random subspaces to train NetEx component classifiers is to enhance diversity among them.

As previously commented, instead of using a fixed window approach for updates, NetEx uses *drift detectors*. Each component classifier is associated with one drift/warning detector. When detector d_j signals a drift warning, then a background learner $c_{bkg}(j)$, is initialized. When d_j outputs the drift signal, then $c_{bkg}(j)$ replaces the current classifier c_j. This approach is similar to that used in Leveraging Bagging [1], although instead of just resetting the classifier, we also start training a replacement beforehand, i.e., when a drift warning is detected similarly to Adaptive Random Forest [16]. NetEx is not bound to a specific drift detection method, however ADWIN [2] is used in the implementation, which has a single parameter that specify the drift confidence level δ. Thus, we have two separate parameters, one for warning detection δ_w and another for drift detection δ_d.

Given our reset strategy based on drift detectors there is no fixed window to estimate accuracy or any other metric. Therefore, to *weight classifiers* we use the estimated accuracy for the given classifier window. This provides a good estimation of the classifier as long as it has seen enough instances, i.e., it will underestimate or overestimate its classification performance if the classifier has seen just a few instances. This is somewhat aided by using background learners as by the time a classifier is added to the ensemble it will have already been trained on a few instances (hundreds or thousands) and will have a good estimation of its accuracy.

It is very difficult to achieve a hyperparameter-free ensemble classifier. For example, we were not able to eliminate the parameter to limit the number of classifiers n and introduced a few other hyperparameters. The following list presents NetEx's hyperparameters accompanied by their short descriptions.

- n defines the total amount of active based models that the ensemble will have at any time. In a stream learning context it is very important to limit the number of classifiers, since memory and processing time are limited assets. n is different from max_c from SAE2, as NetEx starts execution with n component classifiers and maintain it during the whole execution, while in SAE2 max_c defines the maximum number of component classifiers, thus at some point of the execution there might be less than max_c active classifiers.
- k defines the number of seed nodes to build the network. This parameter serves a similar purpose as that from Sc_{min} in SAE2, i.e., it guides connection and subnetwork creation. However, k is easier to set as it is independent from the similarity metric used scale.
- m is the subspace size, which defines the percentage of features randomly assigned to be used for training each base model. A small m increases diversity into the ensemble as it lower the chances that the same subspaces are assigned to the same component classifiers. However, it can decrease performance as low subspace sizes for a high dimensional problem may incur that some important features are never selected.

– δ_d and δ_w represent the ADWIN drift and warning confidence levels. These parameters effectively replace SAE2 l period length, since they define individually the periodicity of when each base model is updated. Effectively, each base model has its own adaptive window.

4 Experiments

We present empirical results comparing ensemble classifiers in both real and synthetic datasets, with and without concept drifts. All experiments were configured and executed using the MOA (Massive On-line Analysis) framework [3]. To evaluate accuracy in all experiments, we applied the Prequential [14] evaluation procedure. The processing time is measured in seconds per MOA CPU time estimation (i.e., it measures the CPU time of the current thread).

The datasets include five real datasets and ten variations of synthetic data streams. The synthetic data contains 1 million instances each, and they simulate either evolving (abrupt, gradual or incremental drifts) or stationary (no drift) streams. Abrupt and gradual drifts are simulate thrice, i.e., one every 250 thousand instances. The data stream configuration is identified by a subscript, e.g., LED_a, such that: {a}brupt, {g}radual, incremental {m}oderate and {f}ast), and {n}o drift (stationary). Table 1 presents a summary of the real datasets used.

Table 1. Real datasets.

ID	# Instances	# Attributes	# Classes
Airlines	539,383	8	2
Electricity	45,312	8	2
Covertype	581,012	54	7
GMSC	150,000	11	2
KDD99	4,898,431	41	23

All experiments in this section use 100 base models[2]; the base learner for all ensembles is the Hoeffding Naive Bayes Tree (HNBT) [21] (grace period = 50 and split confidence = 0.01); specific parameter values for methods other than NetEx were set according to their original publications. Other algorithms used for comparison include the Online Accuracy Updated Ensemble (OAUE) [9], Online Smooth Boosting (OSBoost) [10], Online Bagging (OzaBag) and Online Boosting (OzaBoost) [28], Leveraging Bagging (LevBag) [1] and the Social Adaptive Ensemble algorithm (version 2) (SAE2) [19].

---

[2] DWM [22] is an exception as it does not include a maximum or target number of base models.

4.1   Jaccard and Kappa Networks

We start the experiments comparing the two connection weighting functions described in Sect. 3, i.e. Jaccard and Kappa. Specifically, we present the results for $k = 5, 10, 20, 30$ using Jaccard or Kappa. As previously mentioned, k stands for the number of seed base models used to create subnetworks according to either Kappa or Jaccard measures. Table 2 presents the results for these experiments.

Table 2. Accuracy - NetEx Jaccard and Kappa varying k. KDD99 did not finish for some variations of Kappa versions, thus KDD99 is not used for the average and ranking calculations.

Dataset	$NetEx_{kap5}$	$NetEx_{kap10}$	$NetEx_{kap20}$	$NetEx_{kap30}$	$NetEx_{jac5}$	$NetEx_{jac10}$	$NetEx_{jac20}$	$NetEx_{jac30}$
LED_a	73.77	73.8	**73.8**	73.78	73.73	73.74	73.76	73.76
LED_g	73.1	73.11	73.1	**73.12**	73.06	73.07	73.09	73.11
SEA_a	89.49	89.49	89.49	**89.49**	89.49	89.49	89.49	89.48
SEA_g	**89.08**	89.07	89.07	89.07	89.07	89.07	89.07	89.07
AGR_a	90.16	90.38	90.66	**90.85**	90.71	90.21	90.27	90.33
AGR_g	86.25	86.63	86.99	87.09	**87.24**	86.48	86.55	86.65
RTS	97.33	97.31	97.06	96.94	**97.39**	97.37	97.36	97.32
RBF_m	86.46	86.47	86.47	86.49	86.36	86.5	86.51	**86.52**
RBF_f	77.11	77.16	77.29	**77.34**	76.9	77.14	77.18	77.22
HYPER	85.08	85.05	85.03	85.08	85.18	85.24	85.26	**85.29**
AIRL	64.94	65.04	**65.14**	65.14	65	64.87	64.92	64.96
ELEC	89.66	89.61	89.65	**89.75**	89.58	89.73	89.67	89.67
COVT	95.11	95.12	95.14	95.12	95.1	95.12	95.14	**95.15**
GMSC	93.55	93.55	93.55	93.55	**93.57**	93.55	93.54	93.55
KDD99	99.96	-	-	-	99.96	99.96	**99.96**	99.96
Avg Rank	5.5	4.54	4.19	**3.08**	4.85	4.85	4.88	4.12
Avg Rank Real	5.63	4	3.63	**3**	5.25	5.5	5.13	3.88
Avg Rank Synt.	5.44	4.78	4.44	**3.11**	4.67	4.56	4.78	4.22

The results in Table 2 suggests that $NetEx_{kap30}$ is the most effective, yet the non-parametric Friedman test indicates that there are no differences among the methods.

4.2   NetEx Compared to Other Ensembles

In this section we compare NetEx against state-of-the-art ensemble learners using prequential accuracy [14].

We highlight NetEx stability in comparison to other ensembles. For example, OAUE obtain good results in general, but fails to obtain a reasonable model for KDD99 (2.45% accuracy while others obtain a minimum of 99.93% accuracy). The same happens for OzaBoost, which obtains the best result for the ELEC dataset (90.67% accuracy), yet obtains the worse results for LED_a, LED_g, RBF_m and RBF_f. Using the same parametrization (besides varying the subspace reset strategy) NetEx may obtain the best results for all datasets considered in this experiment. This is interesting, since there is a multitude of different problems represented in this benchmark.

We followed these experiments with a non-parametric Friedman test, which indicate that there are significant differences among the evaluated classifiers for these datasets, both when we evaluate all datasets at once and when we conduct the test separately for synthetic and real datasets. Figures 2 presents the results of applying the nemenyi posthoc test to identify the statistically relevant differences (Table 3).

Table 3. Accuracy - NetEx vs. others.

Dataset	OAUE	OSBoost	OzaBag	OzaBoost	LevBag	DWM	SAE2	$NetEx_{jac30}$
LED_a	73.39	72.47	69.04	68.9	**73.95**	71.69	72.53	73.85
LED_g	72.58	72.12	68.71	68.54	**73.22**	70.72	72.07	73.16
SEA_a	88.8	89.16	87.21	88.25	88.44	86.81	88.94	**89.48**
SEA_g	88.19	88.94	87.11	87.92	**89.09**	86.38	88.72	89.07
AGR_a	90.16	90.37	83.83	88.12	88.72	76.91	88.17	**91.31**
AGR_g	85.24	87.83	79.25	84.66	83.71	76.3	82.4	**87.93**
RTS	96.81	94.78	95.12	96.93	**97.85**	94.76	95.68	97.4
RBF_m	84.26	74.51	73.06	65.23	84.34	73.51	65.43	**86.47**
RBF_f	57.15	48.7	43.54	26.16	76.77	53.88	39.83	**77.15**
HYPER	**87.8**	86.96	79.37	85.3	85.74	81.04	85.11	85.51
AIRL	65.23	64.56	64.89	60.63	62.82	61.67	59.03	**66.3**
ELEC	87.41	89.51	85.08	**90.67**	89.51	82.19	83.66	89.82
COVT	92.86	92.69	91.49	94.82	95.1	90.03	91.98	**95.18**
GMSC	**93.57**	93.05	93.52	92.32	93.54	92.92	93.46	93.55
KDD99	2.45	99.94	99.93	99.49	**99.97**	99.93	99.88	99.96
Avg Rank	3.47	3.83	6.17	5.87	2.63	6.77	5.6	**1.67**
Avg Rank Synt.	3.2	3.6	6.8	6.2	2.5	6.8	5.2	**1.7**
Avg Rank Real	4	4.3	4.9	5.2	2.9	6.7	6.4	**1.6**

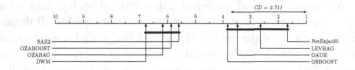

Fig. 2. Nemenyi posthoc with 95% confidence.

Finally, we compare NetEx and the other ensembles in terms of the average CPU time for in Fig. 3. The overall good classification performance of NetEx comes at the expense of a high resources demand. The inefficiency in using computational resources by NetEx is attributable mainly to three aspects of its implementation: (1) it is rare that all base models in the ensemble maintain a background learner at the same time, however in the worst case it is necessary to maintain 2 versions of each base model concomitantly; (2) when a drift is detected it triggers a change in the ensemble, effectively replacing the learner where it was detected by its background learner and causing a recalculation of the

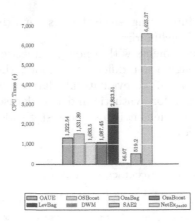

Fig. 3. Average CPU Time for NetEx and others.

network; (3) the subspace reset based on accuracy demands further calculation to estimate each feature probability. For $NetEx_{jac30}$ (2) and (3) are not applicable, since there are no subspace resets in this version and thus it is not necessary to recalculate the network structure, neither perform any estimation on the features.

5   Conclusion

We presented a definition for network-based ensembles for data stream classification and an ensemble learning algorithm based on that definition called the Network of Experts (NetEx). We experimented with NetEx by varying its combination method and including different resetting strategies for the features' subspaces. We compared NetEx against other ensembles for data stream classification and found out that it obtains reasonable results for all datasets. One of the main limitations of the proposed method is the high computational cost, specifically to keep the network structure updated. For future work, we plan to exploit network-based ensembles for semi-supervised learning and other tasks beyond classification problems.

References

1. Bifet, A., Holmes, G., Pfahringer, B.: Leveraging bagging for evolving data streams. In: PKDD, pp. 135–150 (2010)
2. Bifet, A., Gavaldà, R.: Learning from time-changing data with adaptive windowing. In: SIAM (2007)
3. Bifet, A., Holmes, G., Kirkby, R., Pfahringer, B.: MOA data stream mining - a practical approach. Centre for Open Software Innovation (2011). http://heanet.dl. sourceforge.net/project/moa-datastream/documentation/StreamMining.pdf

4. Bifet, A., Holmes, G., Pfahringer, B., Gavaldà, R.: Improving adaptive bagging methods for evolving data streams. In: Zhou, Z.-H., Washio, T. (eds.) ACML 2009. LNCS (LNAI), vol. 5828, pp. 23–37. Springer, Heidelberg (2009). https://doi.org/10.1007/978-3-642-05224-8_4

5. Boccaletti, S., Latora, V., Moreno, Y., Chavez, M., Hwang, D.U.: Complex networks: structure and dynamics. Phys. Rep. **424**(4), 175–308 (2006)

6. Breiman, L.: Bagging predictors. Mach. Learn. **24**(2), 123–140 (1996)

7. Breiman, L.: Random forests. Mach. Learn. **45**(1), 5–32 (2001)

8. Brown, G., Wyatt, J., Harris, R., Yao, X.: Diversity creation methods: a survey and categorisation. J. Inf. Fusion **6**, 5–20 (2005)

9. Brzezinski, D., Stefanowski, J.: Combining block-based and online methods in learning ensembles from concept drifting data streams. Inf. Sci. **265**, 50–67 (2014)

10. Chen, S.T., Lin, H.T., Lu, C.J.: An online boosting algorithm with theoretical justifications. In: ICML, June 2012

11. Da Xu, L., He, W., Li, S.: Internet of Things in industries: a survey. IEEE Trans. Industr. Inf. **10**(4), 2233–2243 (2014)

12. Dalirsefat, S.B., da Silva Meyer, A., Mirhoseini, S.Z.: Comparison of similarity coefficients used for cluster analysis with amplified fragment length polymorphism markers in the silkworm, bombyx mori. J. Insect Sci. **9**(71), 1–8 (2009)

13. Freund, Y., Schapire, R.E., et al.: Experiments with a new boosting algorithm. ICML **96**, 148–156 (1996)

14. Gama, J., Rodrigues, P.: Issues in evaluation of stream learning algorithms. In: 15th ACM SIGKDD, pp. 329–338. ACM SIGKDD, June 2009

15. Gama, J., Zliobaite, I., Bifet, A., Pechenizkiy, M., Bouchachia, A.: A survey on concept drift adaptation. ACM CSUR **46**(4), 44:1–44:37 (2014)

16. Gomes, H.M., et al.: Adaptive random forests for evolving data stream classification. Mach. Learn. **106**, 1–27 (2017)

17. Gomes, H.M., Barddal, J.P., Enembreck, F., Bifet, A.: A survey on ensemble learning for data stream classification. ACM CSUR **50**(2), 23:1–23:36 (2017)

18. Gomes, H.M., Enembreck, F.: SAE: Social adaptive ensemble classifier for data streams. In: CIDM, pp. 199–206 (2013)

19. Gomes, H.M., Enembreck, F.: SAE2: advances on the social adaptive ensemble classifier for data streams. In: SAC. ACM, March 2014

20. Ho, T.K.: The random subspace method for constructing decision forests. IEEE Trans. Pattern Anal. Mach. Intell. **20**(8), 832–844 (1998)

21. Holmes, G., Kirkby, R., Pfahringer, B.: Stress-testing Hoeffding trees. In: PKDD, pp. 495–502 (2005)

22. Kolter, J.Z., Maloof, M.A.: Dynamic weighted majority: an ensemble method for drifting concepts. J. Mach. Learn. Res. **8**, 2755–2790 (2007)

23. Kuncheva, L.I.: Combining Pattern Classifiers: Methods and Algorithms. Wiley, Hoboken (2004)

24. Kuncheva, L.I., Whitaker, C.J.: Measures of diversity in classifier ensembles and their relationship with the ensemble accuracy. Mach. Learn. **51**(2), 181–207 (2003)

25. Kuncheva, L.I., Whitaker, C.J., Shipp, C.A., Duin, R.P.: Limits on the majority vote accuracy in classifier fusion. Pattern Anal. Appl. **6**(1), 22–31 (2003)

26. Levandowsky, M., Winter, D.: Distance between sets. Nature **234**(5323), 34–35 (1971)

27. Nikolentzos, G., Meladianos, P., Limnios, S., Vazirgiannis, M.: A degeneracy framework for graph similarity. In: IJCAI, pp. 2595–2601 (2018)

28. Oza, N.: Online bagging and boosting. In: IEEE SMC, vol. 3, pp. 2340–2345 (2005)

29. Silva, T.C., Zhao, L.: Machine Learning in Complex Networks, vol. 2016. Springer, Cham (2016). https://doi.org/10.1007/978-3-319-17290-3
30. Wasserman, S., Faust, K.: Social Network Analysis: Methods and Applications, vol. 8. Cambridge University Press, Cambridge (1994)

Deep Extremely Randomized Trees

Abdelkader Berrouachedi[✉], Rakia Jaziri[✉], and Gilles Bernard

LIASD research Lab, University of Paris VIII, Paris, France
{aberrouachedi,rjaziri,gb}@ai.univ-paris8.fr

Abstract. In this paper, we propose Deep Extremely Randomized Trees (DET), a deep extension of the extremely randomized trees (Extra-Trees) approach. Our approach unifies classification trees with the layered learning method inspired from deep neural networks. The DET is a deep structure where each layer is a set of Extra-Trees. We look at experimental results on machine learning gold standard datasets and find on-par or superior results when compared to state-of-the-art deep models, with much less parameters to tune. It performs faster than deep neural classifiers, and in most cases even faster than gcForest, without losing accuracy.

Keywords: Machine learning · Extra-Trees · Deep forest · Deep learning

1 Introduction

In recent years, deep artificial neural networks have won numerous clustering and classification contests in pattern recognition and machine learning [9,17, 24,26]. But neural networks, though powerful, are complex to use, with many parameters, need lots of resources, making it hard for researchers outside large firms to make the most of their abilities, and present the risk of overfitting.

The question we address here is: can simpler learning models with less parameters benefit from deep layered structure? We propose here Deep Extremely Randomized Trees (DET), a deep decision tree sets approach, which has been able to obtain results close or sometimes better than deep neural networks, without the risk of overfitting. Next section will present related works. We will next introduce DET, then our experiments, and end with a conclusion.

2 Related Work

In 2015, the Deep Neural Decision Trees, a hybrid architecture, was proposed in [14]. In this model, whose performance is higher than the deep neural network alone, the output of the network is post-processed by a random forest [3]. The process is highly time consuming. More advanced models were proposed in 2017.

GcForest, a deep forest, was proposed as alternative to deep neural networks in [30]. In this multi-layered structure each layer is a set of random forests,

© Springer Nature Switzerland AG 2019
T. Gedeon et al. (Eds.): ICONIP 2019, LNCS 11953, pp. 717–729, 2019.
https://doi.org/10.1007/978-3-030-36708-4_59

without back-propagation. This first answer to the question addressed here was slower than previous approaches due to the high number of random forests on each level.

The Siamese Deep Forest (SDF), an enhancement of gcForest, was proposed in [28]. It integrates into gcForest the metric learning of the Siamese Neural Network [13].

Neural Network with Random Forest (NNRF) was proposed in [29]. This neural network operates like random forests: it only activates one path per input and thus efficiently performs forward and backward propagation. In addition, the single path method, using few parameters, gives the model the ability to deal with small datasets. NNRF learns complex multivariate functions in each node in order to choose between relevant paths, and is able to learn more complex datasets than random forests; NNRF was applied to various datasets.

The Forward Thinking Deep Random Forest (FTDRF), close to gcForest, was proposed in [22]. While gcForest transmits the output of whole random forests, concatenated with the original data, to subsequents layers, FTDRF transmits only the outputs of the individual trees. This diminishes the number of trees needed while yielding a similar performance. The general mathematical formulation of Forward Thinking allows for other types of deep learning models to be considered. FTDRF has been successfully applied on MNIST dataset.

3   The Proposed Approach

This section will present Extra-Trees, the elements of our layers, then the global architecture and operation of our model, ending with its parameters.

3.1   Extra-Trees

The extremely randomized trees (Extra-Trees) was proposed in [7], in the context of numerical input features. Like random forest, Extra-Trees builds multiple trees and splits nodes using random subsets of features, to minimize overlearning and overfitting. But it has two key differences: it does not bootstrap observations and nodes are split on random splits of all observations. In summary:

1. It builds multiple trees without applying the bagging procedure to construct the set of training samples for each tree, which means it samples without replacement; the same input training is used to train all trees;
2. it splits nodes based on random splits (both a variable index and a variable splitting value are chose randomly) among a random subset of the features selected at every node.

A forest of Extra-Trees produces an estimation of class distribution by counting the percentage of different classes of training examples at the leaf node containing the concerned instances, and then averaging across all trees. Extra-Trees are particularly fast due to their extreme randomization, and are particularly attractive in terms of computational efficiency during learning, while being competitive with other set methods in terms of accuracy.

3.2   Deep Extra-Trees Architecture

Learning in deep neural networks mostly relies on the layer-by-layer processing of raw features. Similarly, DET presents a deep architecture, as illustrated in Fig. 1, where each level is a set of forests of Extra-Trees that receives feature information processed by the preceding level, and outputs its result to the next level. All layers have the same number of forests.

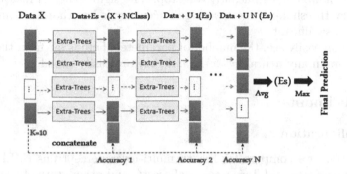

Fig. 1. Deep Extra-Trees architecture

We have used a k-fold cross-validation. This method randomly divides the data into k blocks of roughly equal size. Each of the blocks is left out in turn and the other $k-1$ blocks are used to train the model.

The principle of operation at each level has the following stages:

1. generate k batches of data across the forests;
2. compute the output of each forest;
3. average all the outputs;
4. compute accuracy;
5. if accuracy is worsening by a threshold, terminate;
6. else, update estimate of class distribution,
7. then transmit the output vector to next level and repeat.

The output of each forest is a vector representing the distribution of its batch vectors in classes. For a first level forest, the input simply is its batch of vectors. For every other level forest, the input is its batch of vectors concatenated with the output of the preceeding level (the vector representing the average class distribution of input data).

The number of levels is automatically determined by the data, as a new level is produced only if accuracy is not at its maximum value. In contrast to most deep neural networks whose depth is previously fixed, DET adaptively decides its depth by terminating training when performance cannot be bettered, as is also the case with FTDRF [22]. Thus it can be applied to training data of different scales, not only to large-scale ones.

The parameters of DET are the following, with their default values:

- k for k-fold: as is usual in the literature, we take $k = 10$;
- number of forests: $k - 1$;
- number of extra-trees in forest: 500; with small datasets, 100;
- accuracy threshold: 0.3%.

If accuracy keeps getting higher or if it does not lower significantly, we keep going on. If it lowers significantly, we stop. The significance is measured with the accuracy threshold; if the lowering of accuracy is less than the threshold, it is deemed unsignificant.

As one can easily see, the number of parameters here is far from the number of parameters in any neural network, and they are easily tuned.

4   Experiments

4.1   Configuration

In this section, we compare DET with multi-layer perceptrons (MLP), implemented[1] with Keras and Tensorflow, gcForest[2], and other state-of the art algorithms for which *scikit-learn*[3] library was used, with CART as Decision Tree. We have used 13 popular gold standard datasets for classification problems, publicly available and without missing values or non-numerical attributes. Overall, these datasets cover a wide range of conditions in terms of number of classes (between 2 and 10), learning sample size (between 280 and 60,000), number of attributes. They were divided in 70% for training and 30% for testing. Our experiments use a PC Intel Xeon E5-2686 v4 with 64 vCPUs and 256 GiB of RAM.

Default values for DET are those given above, tuned in our first experiments. Otherwise explicitly indicated, MLP has two fully connected layers with 1024 and 512 units and a sigmoid layer appended. ReLU is used as activation function, categorical cross-entropy as loss function, Adam for optimization. GcForest was used with its own default values. Default values of scikit-learn library was used for the others, but for Random Forest, with the same number of trees as DET.

4.2   Results

We present two types of result: tables of performances and traces of DET growing depth with accuracy values in chosen cases.

ALIO is a collection of images provided by Geusebroek [8], used for outlier detection. The data is represented with 27 numeric attributes (HSB histograms) and consist of 50,000 instances, divided into 1508 outliers (3.04%) and 48492 inliers (96.98%). Table 1 shows DET has best accuracy and F-score.

---

[1] https://github.com/KaderBerrouachedi/Deep-Models/tree/master/
DeepExtraTrees.

[2] https://github.com/kingfengji/gcForest.

[3] https://scikit-learn.org.

Table 1. Performances on ALIO

	Accuracy	Precision	Recall	F1-score
Deep Extra-Trees (DET)	**97.77%**	**98%**	**98%**	**98%**
Extra-Trees	97.32%	97%	97%	97%
MLP	97.19%	/	/	/
Random Forest	97.14%	97%	97%	97%
AdaBoost	97.00%	96%	97%	96%
Decision Tree	95.60%	95%	96%	96%
Gaussian Naive Bayes	76.72%	73%	67%	70%

CTG contains cardiotocography records for the fetal heartbeat and uterine contractions during pregnancy. 1688 fetal cardiotocograms were automatically processed and respective diagnostic features measured. Data was classified by three expert obstetricians, according to a morphological pattern out of 10 (A, B, C...) and to a fetal heart disease state (N for normal, S for suspect, P for pathological). It was used for detection of outliers as in [4], with normal patients treated as inliers and the 34 remaining as outliers. Table 2 shows DET gives the best performances even with this very unbalanced dataset.

Table 2. Performances on CTG

	Accuracy	Precision	Recall	F1-score
Deep Extra-Trees (DET)	**99.1%**	**99%**	**99%**	**99%**
MLP	98.30%	/	/	/
gcForest	97.83%	97%	98%	97%
Extra-Trees	97.63%	98%	98%	98%
Random Forest	97.43%	96%	97%	97%
AdaBoost	97.23%	96%	97%	97%
Decision Tree	96.63%	97%	98%	97%

PageBlocks, from the UCI Machine Learning Repository [6], was designed for the separation of text and picture in document analysis. The 5473 instances are blocks of page layout of 54 documents, detected by a segmentation process [21]. Blocks with textual content are labeled as inlier, else as outlier. Table 3 shows that DET has best accuracy and F-score equal to the others. DET took 33.07 s, while MLP took 18.48 min.

PenDigits contains 10 classes of handwritten digits [5]. It has 16 numeric attributes and 9868 instances, divided into 20 outliers (0.2%) and 9848 inliers (99.8%). It is normalized, i.e., all 16 attributes (spatial coordinates) have the same range [0,100]. It has been used in [15, 25]. Table 4 shows the excellent performances are nearly identical for all models.

Table 3. Performances on PageBlocks

	Accuracy	Precision	Recall	F1-score
Deep Extra-Trees (DET)	**99.09%**	99%	99%	99%
gcForest	98.79%	99%	99%	99%
AdaBoost	98.79%	99%	99%	99%
Decision Tree	98.32%	98%	98%	98%
MLP	98.53%	/	/	/
Extra-Trees	97.06%	99%	99%	99%

Table 4. Performances on PenDigits

	Accuracy	Precision	Recall	F1-score
Deep Extra-Trees (DET)	**99.97%**	100%	100%	100%
Extra-Trees	99.96%	100%	100%	100%
Random Forest	99.93%	100%	100%	100%
AdaBoost	99.93%	100%	100%	100%
MLP	99.91%	/	/	/

SpamBase, created by Blake and Merz [2], contains 4601 instances with 58 attributes, extracted from emails coming from postmasters and individuals who had filed spam [6]. In those emails, 1813 are spam (39.4%), labelled as outliers, the remaining as inliers. Table 5 shows performances nearly identical for all models except Naive Bayes.

Table 5. Performances on SpamBase

	Accuracy	Precision	Recall	F1-score
Deep Extra-Trees (DET)	**95.25%**	95%	95%	95%
Extra-Trees	95.01%	95%	95%	95%
gcForest	94.61%	95%	95%	95%
Random Forest	94.45%	94%	94%	94%
AdaBoost	94.37%	94%	94%	94%
MLP	93.91%	/	/	/
Gaussian Naive Bayes	81.63%	86%	82%	82%

Waveform contains three classes of waves, with 33% of each, 21 numeric attributes and 3443 instances. Class 0 was defined here as outlier and down-sampled to 100 objects (2.9%) [31]. Table 6 shows the results; DET is more than 100 times faster than MLP and 26 times faster than gcForest.

Table 6. Performances on Waveform

	Accuracy	Precision	Recall	F1-score
Deep Extra-Trees (DET)	**98.06%**	**98%**	**98%**	**98%**
gcForest	97.96%	**98%**	**98%**	97%
Random Forest	97.57%	97%	97%	96%
Extra-Trees	97.28%	97%	97%	96%
MLP	97.05%	/	/	/
AdaBoost	96.70%	96%	97%	96%
Decision Tree	96.32%	96%	96%	96%

Wilt consists of 4,819 image segments, generated by segmenting pansharpened images of land cover. They contain spectral information from the QuickBird multispectral image bands and texture information from the panchromatic (Pan) image band. It comes from a remote sensing study [11], that involved detecting diseased trees in QuickBird imagery. Segments with such trees are labelled as outliers. Table 7 shows all models have equivalent performances, except Naive Bayes, with a slight advantage to DET. As for computing time, MLP took 1084 s, gcForest 185 s; in contrast, DET took 8.3 s.

Table 7. Performances on Wilt

	Accuracy	Precision	Recall	F-score
Deep Extra-Trees (DET)	**98.74%**	**99%**	**99%**	**99%**
gcForest	98.20%	98%	98%	98%
Extra-Trees	97.57%	98%	98%	97%
Random Forest	97.23%	97%	97%	97%
Decision Tree	96.68%	96%	97%	97%
MLP	93.91%	/	/	/
Gaussian Naive Bayes	90.52%	93%	91%	92%

HTRU2 describes a sample of pulsar candidates collected during the High Time Resolution Universe Survey (South) [12]. It contains 17,898 spurious examples caused by RFI/noise, checked by human annotators, described by 8 continuous attributes computed from the pulse folded profile, describing a longitude-resolved version of the signal that has been averaged in both time and frequency [20]. It is labelled positive or negative. Table 8 includes the performances of GH-VFDT from [19]. They keep close to each other, Naive Bayes being behind. DET takes 96.21 s, while Deep MLP takes 1062 s and gcForest 123 s, the best accuracy reached in layer 11, Fig. 2.

Table 8. Performances on HTRU2

	Accuracy	Precision	Recall	F1-score
Deep Extra-Trees (DET)	**98.19%**	98%	98%	98%
Extra-Trees	98.06%	98%	98%	98%
gcForest	98.06%	98%	98%	98%
Random Forest	98.10%	98%	98%	98%
GH-VFDT	97.80% [19]	/	/	/
MLP	97.54%	/	/	/
Decision Tree	96.75%	97%	97%	97%
Gaussian Naive Bayes	94.89%	96%	95%	95%

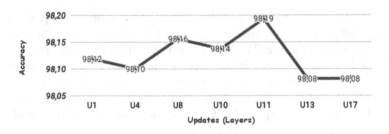

Fig. 2. Accuracy and depth for HTRU2

Table 9. Performances on MNIST

	Accuracy	Precision	Recall	F1-score
Deep Extra-Trees (DET)	**98.38%**	98%	98%	98%
gcForest	98.22%	98%	98%	98%
Extra-Trees	97.17%	97%	97%	97%
Random Forest	96.93%	97%	97%	97%
Decision Tree	87.78%	88%	88%	88%
AdaBoost	72.96%	73%	73%	73%
Gaussian Naive Bayes	55.58%	69%	56%	52%

MNIST [18] consists of handwritten digits, size-normalized and centered in a fixed-size image (28×28 black and white). MNIST predefines training and testing sets (60000 vs 10000). Table 9 shows performances nearly identical for all models except Naive Bayes and Adaboost.

ORL [23] contains 400 gray-scale facial images taken from 40 persons (10 for each), taken at different times against a dark homogeneous background with the subjects in an upright, frontal position (with tolerance for some side movement), varying lighting, facial expressions and facial details (glasses/no glasses).

Table 10. Performances on ORL

	Accuracy	Precision	Recall	F1-score
Deep Extra-Trees (DET)	**97.50%**	**98%**	**97%**	**98%**
gcForest	92.50%	95%	93%	93%
CNN	86.50% [30]	/	/	/
Random Forest	85.00%	91%	85%	85%
Gaussian Naive Bayes	74.16%	90%	74%	76%
Decision Tree	47.50%	56%	47%	47%
MLP	25.00%	/	/	/

Table 10 includes a CNN (2 conv-layers with 32 feature maps of 3×3 kernel) from [30]; DET clearly has the best performances.

CIFAR-10 [16] consists of 60000 32×32 colour images in 10 classes (6000 images per class). CIFAR predefines training and testing sets (50000 vs 10000). Results (Table 11) are bad for all models; only DET is slightly above random result.

Table 11. Performances on CIFAR-10

	Accuracy	Precision	Recall	F1-score
Deep Extra-Trees (DET)	**53.85%**	**54%**	**51%**	**51%**
Extra-Trees	47.32%	47%	47%	47%
Random Forest	46.98%	46%	47%	47%
MLP	42.20% [1]	/	/	/
AdaBoost	33.08%	32%	33%	32%
Gaussian Naive Bayes	29.76%	31%	30%	28%
Decision Tree	26.25%	27%	27%	27%

Table 12. Performances on MAGIC

	Accuracy	Precision	Recall	F1-score
Deep Extra-Trees (DET)	**87.87%**	88%	88%	88%
Extra-Trees	87.64%	88%	88%	87%
AdaBoost	84.08%	84%	84%	87%
MLP	84%	/	/	/
Decision Tree	81.09%	81%	81%	81%
Gaussian Naive Bayes	72.45%	72%	72%	70%

MAGIC is Monte-Carlo generated and approximately triggered and pre-processed for an imaging gamma-ray Cherenkov telescope, originating from a case study comparing different multivariate classifiers [10]. Data belong to two classes, 12,332 originating from incident gamma rays and 6,688 caused by hadronic showers. There is only a weak discrimination between signal (gamma) and background (hadrons), making the data an excellent proving ground for classification techniques. Table 12 gives the results.

Diabetes is from the National Institute of Diabetes and Digestive and Kidney Diseases [27], used for diagnosis prediction, extracted from a larger database, with all patients being females at least 21 years old of Pima Indian heritage. Attributes are several medical predictor variables (number of pregnancies the patient has had, BMI, insulin level, age...) and one target variable. Out of the 768 persons, 500 are labeled as non diabetic and 268 as diabetic, in Fig. 3 shows DET is more efficient; DET is also faster than MLP and gcForest (Table 13).

Table 13. Performances on Diabetes dataset

	Accuracy	Precision	Recall	F1-score
Deep Extra-Trees (DET)	**79.65%**	**79%**	**80%**	**79%**
Random Forest	77.92%	77%	78%	77%
Extra-Trees	77.05%	76%	77%	77%
gcForest	76.62%	76%	77%	76%
AdaBoost	75.32%	74%	75%	74%
Decision Tree	71.42%	72%	71%	72%
MLP	69.80%	/	/	/

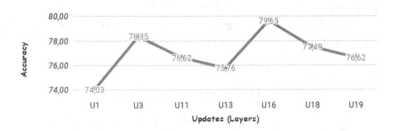

Fig. 3. Accuracy and depth for Diabetes dataset

5   Conclusion

One first observation is that DET, for all datasets, however different, always is at least on par with the best algorithms, often slightly better, specially on accuracy. Except for the ORL dataset, where DET has a clear-cut advantage on all other models, the advantage in performance is not such that it cannot be attributed to bias. The second observation, reflected in Fig. 4, is that, in training, DET is

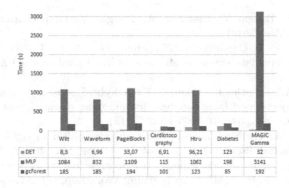

	Wilt	Waveform	PageBlocks	Cardiotoco graphy	Htru	Diabetes	MAGIC Gamma
■ DET	8,3	6,96	33,07	6,91	96,21	123	32
■ MLP	1084	832	1109	115	1062	198	3141
■ gcForest	185	185	194	101	123	85	192

Fig. 4. Running time.

in every case way faster than MLP. It is even, in most cases (with the notable exception of Diabetes), faster than gcForest, which constitutes the second best.

These models have been trained on a representative list of datasets, balanced and unbalanced, small-scale and large-scale, with different contexts of use, in order to limit the effect of data bias on the results. Our experiments definitely show that DET is a good alternative to deep neural networks in classification tasks, all the more so as it is very easy to configure. At the same time, they confirm that deep learning can benefit to non-neural models. We hope these results will entice other researchs on bringing deep-layered architectures to other learning models.

References

1. Ba, J., Caruana, R.: Do deep nets really need to be deep? In: Advances in Neural Information Processing Systems, pp. 2654–2662 (2014)
2. Blake, C., Merz, C.: UCI repository of machine learning databases. Department of Information and Computer Science, University of California, Irvine, CA 55 (1998). http://www.ics.uci.edu/mlearnmlrepository.html
3. Breiman, L.: Random forests. Mach. Learn. **45**(1), 5–32 (2001)
4. Ayres-de Campos, D., Bernardes, J., Garrido, A., Marques-de Sa, J., Pereira-Leite, L.: SisPorto 2.0: a program for automated analysis of cardiotocograms. J. Matern. Fetal Med. **9**(5), 311–318 (2000)
5. Campos, G.O., Zimek, A., Sander, J., Campello, R.J., Micenková, B., Schubert, E., Assent, I., Houle, M.E.: On the evaluation of unsupervised outlier detection: measures, datasets, and an empirical study. Data Min. Knowl. Discov. **30**(4), 891–927 (2016)
6. Dua, D., Taniskidou, E.K.: UCI machine learning repository. School of Information and Computer Science, University of California, Irvine, CA 144 (2017). http://archive.ics.uci.edu/ml
7. Geurts, P., Ernst, D., Wehenkel, L.: Extremely randomized trees. Mach. Learn. **63**(1), 3–42 (2006)
8. Geusebroek, J.M., Burghouts, G.J., Smeulders, A.W.: The Amsterdam library of object images. Int. J. Comput. Vis. **61**(1), 103–112 (2005)

9. Goodfellow, I., Bengio, Y., Courville, A., Bengio, Y.: Deep Learning, vol. 1. MIT Press, Cambridge (2016)
10. Heck, D., Knapp, J., Capdevielle, J.N., Schatz, G., Thouw, T.: CORSIKA: a Monte Carlo code to simulate extensive air showers. Technical report FZKA-6019, Germany (1998)
11. Johnson, B.A., Tateishi, R., Hoan, N.T.: A hybrid pansharpening approach and multiscale object-based image analysis for mapping diseased pine and oak trees. Int. J. Remote Sens. **34**(20), 6969–6982 (2013)
12. Keith, M., et al.: The high time resolution universe pulsar survey-I. System configuration and initial discoveries. Mon. Not. R. Astron. Soc. **409**(2), 619–627 (2010)
13. Koch, G., Zemel, R., Salakhutdinov, R.: Siamese neural networks for one-shot image recognition. In: ICML Deep Learning Workshop, vol. 2 (2015)
14. Kontschieder, P., Fiterau, M., Criminisi, A., Rota Bulo, S.: Deep neural decision forests. In: Proceedings of the IEEE International Conference on Computer Vision, pp. 1467–1475 (2015)
15. Kriegel, H.P., Kroger, P., Schubert, E., Zimek, A.: Interpreting and unifying outlier scores. In: Proceedings of the 2011 SIAM International Conference on Data Mining, pp. 13–24. SIAM (2011)
16. Krizhevsky, A., Hinton, G.: Learning multiple layers of features from tiny images. Technical report, Citeseer (2009)
17. Krizhevsky, A., Sutskever, I., Hinton, G.E.: ImageNet classification with deep convolutional neural networks. In: Advances in Neural Information Processing Systems (2012)
18. LeCun, Y., Bottou, L., Bengio, Y., Haffner, P.: Gradient-based learning applied to document recognition. Proc. IEEE **86**(11), 2278–2324 (1998)
19. Lyon, R.J., Stappers, B., Cooper, S., Brooke, J., Knowles, J.: Fifty years of pulsar candidate selection: from simple filters to a new principled real-time classification approach. Mon. Not. R. Astron. Soc. **459**(1), 1104–1123 (2016)
20. Lyon, R.J.: Why are pulsars hard to find? Ph.D. thesis, The University of Manchester, UK (2016)
21. Malerba, D., Esposito, F., Semeraro, G.: A further comparison of simplification methods for decision-tree induction. In: Fisher, D., Lenz, H.J. (eds.) Learning from Data, pp. 365–374. Springer, New York (1996). https://doi.org/10.1007/978-1-4612-2404-4_35
22. Miller, K., Hettinger, C., Humpherys, J., Jarvis, T., Kartchner, D.: Forward thinking: building deep random forests. arXiv preprint arXiv:1705.07366 (2017)
23. Samaria, F.S., Harter, A.C.: Parameterisation of a stochastic model for human face identification. In: Proceedings of the Second IEEE Workshop on Applications of Computer Vision, pp. 138–142. IEEE (1994)
24. Schmidhuber, J.: Deep learning in neural networks: an overview. Neural Netw. **61**, 85–117 (2015)
25. Schubert, E., Wojdanowski, R., Zimek, A., Kriegel, H.P.: On evaluation of outlier rankings and outlier scores. In: Proceedings of the 2012 SIAM International Conference on Data Mining, pp. 1047–1058. SIAM (2012)
26. Simonyan, K., Zisserman, A.: Very deep convolutional networks for large-scale image recognition. CoRR abs/1409.1556 (2014). http://arxiv.org/abs/1409.1556
27. Smith, J.W., Everhart, J., Dickson, W., Knowler, W., Johannes, R.: Using the ADAP learning algorithm to forecast the onset of diabetes mellitus. In: Proceedings of the Annual Symposium on Computer Application in Medical Care, p. 261. American Medical Informatics Association (1988)

28. Utkin, L.V., Ryabinin, M.A.: A Siamese deep forest. arXiv preprint arXiv:1704.08715 (2017)
29. Wang, S., Aggarwal, C., Liu, H.: Using a random forest to inspire a neural network and improving on it. In: Proceedings of the 2017 SIAM International Conference on Data Mining, pp. 1–9. SIAM (2017)
30. Zhou, Z.H., Feng, J.: Deep forest: towards an alternative to deep neural networks. arXiv preprint arXiv:1702.08835 (2017)
31. Zimek, A., Gaudet, M., Campello, R.J., Sander, J.: Subsampling for efficient and effective unsupervised outlier detection ensembles. In: Proceedings of the 19th ACM SIGKDD International Conference on Knowledge Discovery and Data Mining, pp. 428–436. ACM (2013)

Artificial Intelligence and Cybersecurity

An Advanced Version of MDNet
for Visual Tracking

Junfei Zhuang[1](✉) ⓘ, Yuan Dong[1](✉), Hongliang Bai[2](✉), and Gang Wang[3](✉)

[1] Beijing University of Posts and Telecommunications, Beijing, China
{zjf1,yuandong}@bupt.edu.cn
[2] Beijing Faceall Technology Co., Ltd., Beijing, China
hongliang.bai@faceall.cn
[3] Ricoh Software Research Center (Beijing) Co. Ltd., Beijing, China
gang.wang@srcb.ricoh.com

Abstract. Tracking-by-detection is an effective framework for visual tracking tasks. For example, the Multi-Domain Convolution Neural Network (MDNet) achieves outstanding results in multiple benchmarks. However, the tracking performance of MDNet is restricted by two factors. First, the robustness is hindered by the semantic background since the backbone network is trained for the classification task. Second, MDNet discriminates target and background in individual domains and ignores the relationship between samples during the training process. We present an advanced version of MDNet (MDNet+) to solve the problems with two improvements. First, we propose an attention block that forces the network to focus on the most different features between the target and the semantic backgrounds to achieve higher robustness. Second, we introduce a joint loss consists of a basic classification loss and a triplet-loss. With the use of the triplet-loss, we minimize intra-class inertia and maximize the inter-class inertia between samples from multi-domains. The proposed algorithm outperforms the state-of-the-art tracking methods in multiple benchmarks even without dataset-specific parameter tuning.

Keywords: Visual tracking · Multi-domain learning · Attention mechanism · Joint loss

1 Introduction

Visual object tracking is an important field of computer vision with many applications, such as automated surveillance, traffic monitoring, human-computer interaction, and vehicle navigation. However, there are still many challenging problems in practical applications due to deformation, fast motion, occlusions, and illumination. In recent years, single object tracking consists of two main branches, one is Discriminative Correlation Filter (DCF) based frameworks, and

---

Supported by Beijing Faceall Technology Co., Ltd. & Ricoh software research center (Beijing) Co. Ltd.

the other is Convolution Neural Networks (CNN) based frameworks. Some DCF frameworks [15,26] also benefit from deep features, but they take a few advantages of end-to-end training. Hence, CNN becomes mainstream for visual tracking task.

MDNet [21] is a popular CNN-based tracking algorithm with state-of-the-art accuracy on multiple benchmarks [14,28]. MDNet follows the tracking-by-detection framework, which samples candidate regions and classifies them with a classification CNN pre-trained on a large-scale dataset. Since each candidate is processed independently, MDNet ignores the underlying connections between candidates. As a result, a tremendous appearance change of target leads to model drift. Besides, MDNet recognizes non-semantic background easily but always confuses the target object with a semantic background for the reason that MDNet bases on a pre-trained classification CNN. For example, a target of interest could be one particular person in a crowd, or a specific product (e.g., coke can) in a broader category (e.g., soda cans). Consequently, it is difficult for MDNet to discriminate target objects with similar semantics in test sequences.

In this paper, we tackle the above critical limitations by designing an attention module and a joint loss function. In particular, we integrate a triplet-loss [24] with classification loss as the final loss to mine the potential relationship among candidate regions. We choose the anchors, positive instances, and negative instances from different frames to calculate the triplet-loss that reduces intra-class distance and increases the inter-class distance between samples. The triplet-loss is helpful to recognize targets with dramatic appearance change. Besides, we propose an attention module whose backbone is an Hourglass Convolution Neural Network model [22] to learn contextualized feature representation. The feature maps and attention maps are combined to enhance the ability to discriminate distractors which has the same semantic information with object targets.

To summarize, the main contributions of this work are three-fold.

- We propose a joint loss to mine relationship between samples, and we prove that the joint loss improves tracking performance without additional data.
- We propose an attention mechanism to distribute unequal weights for each feature that helps our tracker to focus on useful deep features. The attention mechanism improves the distinguishing ability between targets and distractors.
- We perform the proposed algorithm on multiple benchmarks and demonstrate outstanding performance without dataset-specific parameter tuning.

2   Related Works

Attention Mechanisms. Attention mechanisms have been wildly used in the deep learning area, such as image classification [12,13], object detection [11], pose estimation [8], *etc.* For visual tracking, DAVT [9] used discriminative spatial attention that identifies some special regions on the target. ACFN [3] developed

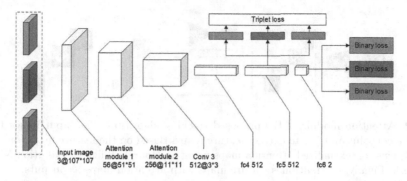

Fig. 1. Overview of the proposed tracking method. The input of the network is three 107×107 images, an anchor image, a positive sample, and a negative sample. We choose anchor images and positive samples from the same domain, and the negative samples are extracted from a different domain. The three images are input to the network and go through multiple layers (*Attention module*1, *Attention module*2, *Conv*3, and $fc4$). From $fc5$ layer, we extract deep features $f \in \mathbb{R}^{1*512}$ that are denote as f_{an}, f_{pos} and f_{neg} separately. After that, we calculate a triplet loss using f_{an}, f_{pos} and f_{neg}. Finally, those features are entered into the last layer $fc6$ to calculate three binary classification losses. The final loss function is composed of three binary classification losses and one triplet loss.

an attentional mechanism that chooses a subset of the associated correlation filters for enhancing the tracking robustness. CSR-DCF [19] introduced the channel and spatial reliability concepts to DCF tracking. In contrast to these attention mechanisms, our proposed attention module is trained through an end-to-end network that benefits from the off-line training dataset.

Joint Loss. Joint loss is a common technique in the computer vision area. For instance, [10] integrates softmax loss with smooth L1 loss as the final loss function, and it accomplishes classification and regression tasks at the same time. [25] employs both face identification and verification signals as supervision. [16] shows the advantages of jointly learning local and global features by aiming to discover correlated local and global features in a different context. For visual tracking, [29] proposes parametric gating functions are trained to control the depth of the convolution feature extractor by minimizing a joint loss of computational cost and tracking error. Different from the above methods, we utilize a joint loss to establish connections between samples from different domains.

3   Approach

To produce effective visual tracking, we propose an advanced version of MDNet (MDNet+). Figure 1 shows the pipeline of our proposed framework. In contrast to the baseline MDNet, the MDNet+ has two enhancements: (1) **Attention Mechanisms**, (2) **Joint Loss**. In the following subsections, we elaborate on the formulation of MDNet+ for tracking and the learning procedure of these networks.

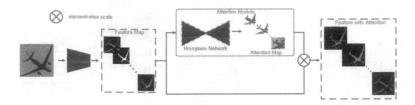

Fig. 2. Attention module of the proposed tracking algorithm. The input image flows into the convolution layer to extract feature maps. Based on the feature maps, our network learns contextualized attention maps using an Hourglass-like Convolution Neural Network. Finally, we multiplies feature maps with attention maps as outputs.

3.1 Attention Mechanisms for Distractor Discriminating

MDNet trains a multi-domain CNN to distinguish targets and backgrounds in an arbitrary domain. Essentially, MDNet is a classification network which can be disturbed by semantic background easily. As we know, convolution features often correspond to a specific type of visual pattern. In certain circumstances, some features are more significant than the others. Motivated by this fact, we develop an attention module for adaptive feature refinement. The attention module forces our network focus on special parts of features that help our framework to distinguish the target from semantic backgrounds. The attention module can be regarded as the process of selecting semantic attributes for different contexts.

The output features from $fc5$ layer can be represented as $\varphi(R) \in \mathbb{R}^{m \times n \times d}$, where R is the input image. We expand the feature more precisely and replenish the target feature maps as shown in Eq. (1)

$$\varphi_{i'j'c'} = \sum_{i=0}^{m} \sum_{j=0}^{n} \sum_{c=0}^{d} \gamma_{i,j,c} \cdot \varphi_{ijc} \tag{1}$$

where $\gamma_{i,j,c}$ is an element-wise attention weight, $i \in (0, m)$ is horizontal coordinates, $j \in (0, n)$ is vertical coordinates, and $c \in (0, d)$ is channel index in the feature map. [27] also proposes an attention mechanism for Siamese tracker, it only provides $m \cdot n + d$ weight parameters. Be different from [27], our attention mechanism provides more accurate attention maps because we distribute attention weight for each element in feature maps. The number of weight parameters in our algorithm is $m \cdot n \cdot d$. Figure 2 illustrates attention mechanism in our framework.

3.2 Joint Loss for Sample Association

To learn an algorithm that trains a discriminative feature embedding applicable to multiple domains. MDNet has separate shared layers and domain-specific layers to learn the representations distinguishing between target and background.

Each domain is trained with positive examples and negative examples deriving from the same sequence. MDNet only attempts to discriminate targets and backgrounds in individual domain, and ignores the relationship between samples resulting in degradation of discriminative ability. Considering the above problem, we propose a new loss term that enforces intra-class distances become closer and inter-class distances get farther away.

Formally, given all training videos $V = \{v_1, v_2, \ldots, v_N\}$, each of videos corresponds a domain for MDNet. $D = \{d_1, d_2, \ldots, d_N\}$ is denoted as domains set, where d_n is the nth domain. We assumes that d_n has I frames and each frame extracts J samples around a bounding box R, the output score of the network for domain d_n, denoted by f_{ij}^d

$$f_{ij}^d = \phi(R_{ij}^d) \tag{2}$$

where ϕ is a 2D binary classification score from the last fully connected layer $fc6^d$ in domain d. The output feature is fed to a softmax function for binary classification

$$\sigma_{ij}^d = \frac{exp(f_{ij}^d)}{\sum_{k=1}^{2} exp(f_{ij}^d)} \tag{3}$$

The binary classification loss with all domains is given by

$$\mathcal{L}_{cls} = -\frac{1}{NIJ} \sum_{d=1}^{N} \sum_{i=1}^{I} \sum_{j=1}^{J} y_{dij} \cdot log(\sigma_{ij}^d) \tag{4}$$

where $y_i \in \{0, 1\}$ is a one-hot encoding of a ground-truth label. y_i is 1 if a bounding box R_{ij} in domain d is the positive sample, otherwise 0. Also, the triplet loss with all domains is represented as

$$\mathcal{L}_{tri} = \frac{1}{NIJ} \sum_{d=1}^{N} \sum_{i=1}^{I} \sum_{j=1}^{J} max(dist(a_i^d, p_{ij}^d) - dist(a_i^d, n_{ij}^d) + margin, 0) \tag{5}$$

where $dist(x, y)$ is pairwise distance between x and y, a_i^d is the anchor feature from frame i in domain d, p_{ij}^d, n_{ij}^d is positive sample and negative sample respectively, margin is a constant value, all features in L_{tri} comes from $fc5$ layer. Our network minimizes a joint loss L which is given by

$$\mathcal{L} = L_{cls} + \alpha \cdot L_{tri} \tag{6}$$

where α is a hyper-parameter that controls balance between the two loss terms. As a result of the proposed loss, the distances between exemplar-positive pairs become closer while the distances between exemplar-negative pairs become larger. The proposed loss leads to a more powerful discriminative ability.

3.3 Online Tracking Algorithm

Our tracking algorithm is almost identical to MDNet [21]. Once the off-line training is completed, the multiple branches of domain-specific layers $fc6$ are

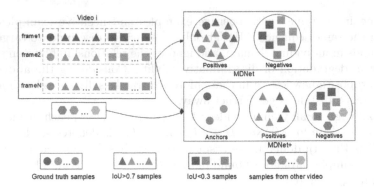

Fig. 3. Sample strategy comparison between MDNet and MDNet+. Intersection-over-union (IoU) is defined as an overlap between ground truth and sample bounding boxes. MDNet extracts positives and negatives from a sole video sequence, $IoU \geq 0.7$ is defined as the positive sample, and $IoU \leq 0.3$ is defined as the negative sample. MDNet+ training samples contain anchors, positives, and negatives. Anchors are drew from different frames according to the ground truths. Positives are extracted in the same way as MDNet. Negatives are composed of negative samples from same video, and samples from other videos whether they are positive samples or negative samples.

replaced with a single branch for a new test sequence. We fine-tune all fully connected layers using the ground-truth of first frame while convolutional layers are fixed. For the rest frames of test sequence, we apply an online updating scheme. We extract N target candidates $x^1, \ldots, x^N$ sampled around the previous target state, and pass them through the network. Finally, we obtain positive scores $f^+(x^i)$. The optimal target state x^* is given by finding the example with the maximum positive score as

$$x^* = \arg\max_{x^i} f^+(x^i) \qquad (7)$$

Besides, we perform two complementary update strategies as in MDNet [21]: long-term and short-term updates to maintain robustness and adaptiveness, respectively.

4   Experiments

4.1   Datasets and Settings

We evaluate our tracker denoted by MDNet+ on three standard benchmarks: OTB-2015 [28], UAV123 [20], and TempleColor-128 [17]. OTB-2015 is a well-known tracking benchmark including 98 videos and 100 tracking sequences with fully annotated ground truth bounding box. UAV123 consists of 123 video sequences with more than 110K frames that are obtained by unmanned aerial vehicles (UAVs). TempleColor-128 contains 128 color sequences. The challenging attributes for visual object tracking on these three datasets include occlusion, illumination variation, rotation, motion blur, fast motion, in-plane rotation, out-of-plane rotation, out-of-view, background clutter, and low resolution. In our experiments, we used the one-pass evaluation (OPE) followed the standard evaluation metrics on these benchmarks. Each tracker was initialized with the ground truth location. Specifically, the overlap success rate measures the overlap between predicted bounding boxes and ground truth bounding boxes. The distance precision metric is the percentage of frames where the estimated location center error from the ground truth is smaller than a given distance threshold 20 (Prec@20).

4.2 Implementation Details

We implemented our tracker in Python using the Pytorch library and runs at around 2 fps with an Intel(R) Xeon(R) 2.60 GHz CPU and a GeForce GTX 1080Ti GPU.

Backbone Network: The backbone network contains two attention modules (*Attention module*1 and *Attention module*2), one convolution layer (*Conv*3), and two fully connected layers (*fc*4 and *fc*5) with ReLUs and dropouts. Additionally, the network has the last fully connected layer corresponding to multi-domains. There are three convolution layers in backbone network, two in *Attention module* and one in *Conv*3. The weights of three convolution layers are initialized by the VGG-M network [2] pretrained on ImageNet [23] while all fully connected layers are initialized randomly.

Attention Modules: There are two attention modules in our proposed algorithm. Each attention module contains a convolution layer and an Hourglass-like network. The Hourglass like network has two convolution layers and two deconvolution layers with *ReLU* activation. The convolution and deconvolution layers have the same input channel with the corresponding convolution layer. The stride of each layer is 2.

Network Training: The training process is divided into online training and off-line training. The off-line training is proceeding on ImageNet VID [23]. We construct a mini-batch with samples collected from multiple domains. Firstly, we randomly select eight frames in a single video and collect 8 anchors, 32 positives and 32 negatives. Figure 3 illustrates the sampling strategy of our proposed method. Next, we combine those samples into 32 triplets as a mini-batch. We accumulate the gradients from backward passes in 50 iterations and use those gradients to update our network. The learning rates of convolution layers and the deconvolution layers are set to 0.0001, the learning rates of fully connected layers are set to 0.001. During the online training process, we draw 200 triplets based on the same IoU criteria with the pre-training stage. After that, we update the model with learning rate 0.0005 and 50 iterations. For subsequent frames, the number of fine-tuning iterations is 15, and the learning rate is set to 0.0005. The long-term interval is every 10 frames. Our network is trained by a Stochastic Gradient Descent (SGD) method.

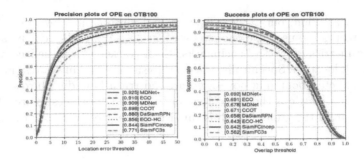

Fig. 4. Overall performance on the OTB-2015 [28].

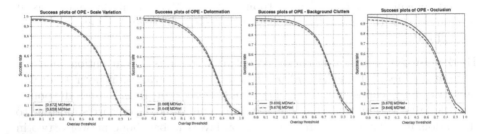

Fig. 5. The success plots over four tracking challenges, including deformation, scale variations, background clutters, and occlusion for MDNet+ and MDNet on OTB-2015.

4.3   Overall Performance

OTB-2015 Dataset. We fairly compare the proposed MDNet+ with state-of-the-art trackers including ECO [4], MDNet [21], CCOT [7], DaSiamRPN [31], ECO-HC [4], SiamFC3s [1], and SiamIncep [30]. Figure 4 shows the performance of different trackers in terms of precision and success rate on OTB-2015. Overall, our tracker outperforms the state-of-the-art trackers on both the precision and the success rate. We also compare our tracker with the original MDNet on four different challenge attributes, including deformation, scale variations, background clutters, and occlusion. Figure 5 demonstrates that our tracker has batter robustness than MDNet on the four kinds of challenging situations that often require more accurate semantic understanding. Remarkably, our MDNet+ is more robust than MDNet on deformation and scale variations attributes.

TempleColor-128 Dataset. The evaluation setting of TempleColor-128 is the same as the OTB-2015 dataset. We compare our tracker with MDNet [21], DSLT [18], ECO [4], ECO-HC [4], DeepSRDCF [5] and SRDCF [6]. Figure 6 shows that the proposed method achieves the best distance precision and ranks second in terms of overlap success. It is observed that TempleColor-128 contains a large number of small target objects. Thus, best precision implies that our tracker performs well in tracking small targets.

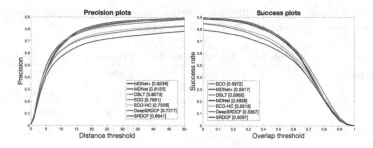

Fig. 6. Overall performance on the TempleColor-128 [17]

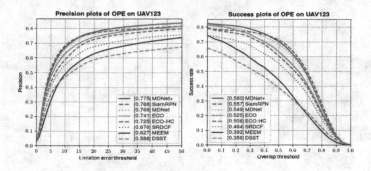

Fig. 7. Overall performance on the UAV123 [20]

UAV123 Dataset. We also evaluate our tracker on the aerial video benchmark, UAV123 whose characteristics inherently differ from other datasets such as OTB-2015 and TempleColor-128. Figure 7 illustrates the precision and success plots of the trackers. Compared with MDNet, our tracker improves dramatically on both precision and success.

4.4   Comparison with Baseline MDNet

As shown in Fig. 8, all compared sequences come from OTB-2015 benchmark, we compare our MDNet+ with baseline MDNet [21] on four challenging series: *DragonBaby* (the first column), *Bolt2* (the second column), *Box* (the third column), and *Couple* (the fourth column). From the first two sequences *DragonBaby* and *Bolt2*, we observe that MDNet and MDNet+ can track the target successfully for the whole video. However, the predicted boxes from MDNet may drift to the background in a particular period (#79 in *DragonBaby* and #20 in *Bolt2*) while our MDNet+ avoids this issue. The phenomenon proves our MDNet+ has more robustness than the MDNet. Snapshots on the last two videos *Box* and *Couple* demonstrate that MDNet fails to predict (#626 in *Box* and #139 in *Couple*) the trajectories while our MDNet+ predicts boxes always successfully. Compared with MDNet, MDNet+ learns more discriminative features by the proposed attention mechanism and triplet-loss.

Table 1. The comparisons of different ablation variants over the distance precision and overlap success plots on the OTB-2015 dataset.

Variants	Joint loss	Attention module	Precision (%)	Success (%)
MDNet			0.909	0.678
MDNet-JL	√		0.913	0.682
MDNet-AM		√	0.919	0.687
MDNet+(Ours)	√	√	0.925	0.692

Ground Truth — MDNet — MDNet+

Fig. 8. Snap shots between MDNet and MDNet+ on the OTB2015.

4.5 Ablation Study

To show the impacts of different components, we perform three variants of our tracker by integrating the different components and evaluate them on the OTB-2015 dataset. In this section, all training parameters are the same for the variants. We first test the impact of the Joint Loss training (MDNet-JL) on the quality of our tracking algorithm. Table 1 summarizes that MDNet-JL outperforms the baseline tracker by 0.4% and 0.6% on the precision and success overlap, respectively. This is a minor improvement because we do not provide extra data for training compared with original MDNet. However, it proves that the joint loss part extracts powerful features for object tracking. Second, we investigate the impact of attention module (MDNet-AM), Table 1 shows that MDNet-AM makes extraordinary progress on the precision 1.1% and success overlap 1.3%. This fact proves that each deep feature has the same weight is not advisable for a visual tracking task. In other words, not all features are helpful. Overall, all results consistently support that each component of our improved methods makes a meaningful contribution to tracking performance improvement.

5   Conclusion and Future Works

In this paper, we proposed a novel visual tracking algorithm named MDNet+. Our algorithm demonstrated that the joint loss improves tracking performance by mining potential relationships among samples. Furthermore, an attention module was constructed to extract more powerful features for visual tracking. The proposed algorithm was evaluated on the public visual tracking benchmark datasets and demonstrated outstanding performance compared to the state-of-the-art techniques. Although our algorithm is successful un terms of accuracy, it suffers from high computational cost mainly due to critical time consuming components within the methods including feature computation of multiple samples, and backpropagation for model updates. We will focus on accelerating the speed of MDNet+.

References

1. Bertinetto, L., Valmadre, J., Henriques, J.F., Vedaldi, A., Torr, P.H.S.: Fully-convolutional Siamese networks for object tracking. In: Hua, G., Jégou, H. (eds.) ECCV 2016. LNCS, vol. 9914, pp. 850–865. Springer, Cham (2016). https://doi.org/10.1007/978-3-319-48881-3_56
2. Chatfield, K., Simonyan, K., Vedaldi, A., Zisserman, A.: Return of the devil in the details: delving deep into convolutional nets. arXiv preprint arXiv:1405.3531 (2014)
3. Choi, J., Chang, H.J., Yun, S., Fischer, T., Demiris, Y., Choi, J.Y.: Attentional correlation filter network for adaptive visual tracking. In: The IEEE Conference on Computer Vision and Pattern Recognition (CVPR), July 2017
4. Danelljan, M., Bhat, G., Shahbaz Khan, F., Felsberg, M.: ECO: efficient convolution operators for tracking. In: Proceedings of the IEEE Conference on Computer Vision and Pattern Recognition, pp. 6638–6646 (2017)
5. Danelljan, M., Hager, G., Shahbaz Khan, F., Felsberg, M.: Convolutional features for correlation filter based visual tracking. In: Proceedings of the IEEE International Conference on Computer Vision Workshops, pp. 58–66 (2015)
6. Danelljan, M., Hager, G., Shahbaz Khan, F., Felsberg, M.: Learning spatially regularized correlation filters for visual tracking. In: Proceedings of the IEEE International Conference on Computer Vision, pp. 4310–4318 (2015)
7. Danelljan, M., Robinson, A., Shahbaz Khan, F., Felsberg, M.: Beyond correlation filters: learning continuous convolution operators for visual tracking. In: Leibe, B., Matas, J., Sebe, N., Welling, M. (eds.) ECCV 2016. LNCS, vol. 9909, pp. 472–488. Springer, Cham (2016). https://doi.org/10.1007/978-3-319-46454-1_29
8. Du, W., Wang, Y., Qiao, Y.: RPAN: an end-to-end recurrent pose-attention network for action recognition in videos. In: Proceedings of the IEEE International Conference on Computer Vision, pp. 3725–3734 (2017)
9. Fan, J., Wu, Y., Dai, S.: Discriminative spatial attention for robust tracking. In: Daniilidis, K., Maragos, P., Paragios, N. (eds.) ECCV 2010. LNCS, vol. 6311, pp. 480–493. Springer, Heidelberg (2010). https://doi.org/10.1007/978-3-642-15549-9_35
10. Ren, S., He, K., Girshick, R. and Sun, J., 2015. Faster R-CNN: towards real-time object detection with region proposal networks (2015)

11. Hara, K., Liu, M.Y., Tuzel, O., Farahmand, A.m.: Attentional network for visual object detection. arXiv preprint arXiv:1702.01478 (2017)
12. Hu, J., Shen, L., Sun, G.: Squeeze-and-excitation networks. In: Proceedings of the IEEE Conference on Computer Vision and Pattern Recognition, pp. 7132–7141 (2018)
13. Jaderberg, M., Simonyan, K., Zisserman, A., et al.: Spatial transformer networks. In: Advances in Neural Information Processing Systems, pp. 2017–2025 (2015)
14. Kristan, M., et al.: The visual object tracking VOT2015 challenge results. In: Proceedings of the IEEE International Conference on Computer Vision Workshops, pp. 1–23 (2015)
15. Li, F., Tian, C., Zuo, W., Zhang, L., Yang, M.H.: Learning spatial-temporal regularized correlation filters for visual tracking. In: Proceedings of the IEEE Conference on Computer Vision and Pattern Recognition, pp. 4904–4913 (2018)
16. Li, W., Zhu, X., Gong, S.: Person re-identification by deep joint learning of multi-loss classification. arXiv preprint arXiv:1705.04724 (2017)
17. Liang, P., Blasch, E., Ling, H.: Encoding color information for visual tracking: algorithms and benchmark. IEEE Trans. Image Process. **24**(12), 5630–5644 (2015)
18. Lu, X., Ma, C., Ni, B., Yang, X., Reid, I., Yang, M.H.: Deep regression tracking with shrinkage loss. In: Proceedings of the European Conference on Computer Vision (ECCV), pp. 353–369 (2018)
19. Lukezic, A., Vojir, T., Cehovin Zajc, L., Matas, J., Kristan, M.: Discriminative correlation filter with channel and spatial reliability. In: Proceedings of the IEEE Conference on Computer Vision and Pattern Recognition, pp. 6309–6318 (2017)
20. Mueller, M., Smith, N., Ghanem, B.: A benchmark and simulator for UAV tracking. In: Leibe, B., Matas, J., Sebe, N., Welling, M. (eds.) ECCV 2016. LNCS, vol. 9905, pp. 445–461. Springer, Cham (2016). https://doi.org/10.1007/978-3-319-46448-0_27
21. Nam, H., Han, B.: Learning multi-domain convolutional neural networks for visual tracking. In: Proceedings of the IEEE Conference on Computer Vision and Pattern Recognition, pp. 4293–4302 (2016)
22. Newell, A., Yang, K., Deng, J.: Stacked hourglass networks for human pose estimation. In: Leibe, B., Matas, J., Sebe, N., Welling, M. (eds.) ECCV 2016. LNCS, vol. 9912, pp. 483–499. Springer, Cham (2016). https://doi.org/10.1007/978-3-319-46484-8_29
23. Russakovsky, O., et al.: ImageNet large scale visual recognition challenge. Int. J. Comput. Vis. **115**(3), 211–252 (2015)
24. Schroff, F., Kalenichenko, D., Philbin, J.: FaceNet: a unified embedding for face recognition and clustering. In: The IEEE Conference on Computer Vision and Pattern Recognition (CVPR), June 2015
25. Sun, Y., Chen, Y., Wang, X., Tang, X.: Deep learning face representation by joint identification-verification. In: Advances in Neural Information Processing Systems, pp. 1988–1996 (2014)
26. Wang, N., Zhou, W., Tian, Q., Hong, R., Wang, M., Li, H.: Multi-cue correlation filters for robust visual tracking. In: Proceedings of the IEEE Conference on Computer Vision and Pattern Recognition, pp. 4844–4853 (2018)
27. Wang, Q., Teng, Z., Xing, J., Gao, J., Hu, W., Maybank, S.: Learning attentions: residual attentional Siamese network for high performance online visual tracking. In: Proceedings of the IEEE Conference on Computer Vision and Pattern Recognition, pp. 4854–4863 (2018)

28. Wu, Y., Lim, J., Yang, M.H.: Online object tracking: a benchmark. In: Proceedings of the IEEE Conference on Computer Vision and Pattern Recognition, pp. 2411–2418 (2013)
29. Ying, C., Fragkiadaki, K.: Depth-adaptive computational policies for efficient visual tracking. In: Pelillo, M., Hancock, E. (eds.) EMMCVPR 2017. LNCS, vol. 10746, pp. 109–122. Springer, Cham (2018). https://doi.org/10.1007/978-3-319-78199-0_8
30. Zhipeng, Z., Houwen, P., Qiang, W.: Deeper and wider Siamese networks for real-time visual tracking. arXiv preprint arXiv:1901.01660 (2019)
31. Zhu, Z., Wang, Q., Li, B., Wu, W., Yan, J., Hu, W.: Distractor-aware Siamese networks for visual object tracking. In: Proceedings of the European Conference on Computer Vision (ECCV), pp. 101–117 (2018)

Enhanced LSTM with Batch Normalization

Li-Na Wang[1], Guoqiang Zhong[1(✉)], Shoujun Yan[1], Junyu Dong[1],
and Kaizhu Huang[2]

[1] Department of Computer Science and Technology, Ocean University of China,
238 Songling Road, Qingdao 266100, China
gqzhong@ouc.edu.cn
[2] Department of Electrical and Electronic Engineering,
Xi'an Jiaotong-Liverpool University, 111 Ren'ai Road, SIP, Suzhou 215123, China

Abstract. Recurrent neural networks (RNNs) are powerful models for
sequence learning. However, the training of RNNs is complicated because
the internal covariate shift problem, where the input distribution at
each iteration changes during the training as the parameters have been
updated. Although some work has applied batch normalization (BN)
to alleviate this problem in long short-term memory (LSTM), unfortunately, BN has not been applied to the update of the LSTM cell. In this
paper, to tackle the internal covariate shift problem of LSTM, we introduce a method to successfully integrate BN into the update of the LSTM
cell. Experimental results on two benchmark data sets, i.e. MNIST and
Fashion-MNIST, show that the proposed method, enhanced LSTM with
BN (eLSTM-BN), has achieved a faster convergence than LSTM and
its variants, while obtained higher classification accuracy on sequence
learning tasks.

Keywords: Recurrent neural networks · Long short-term memory ·
Batch normalization

1 Introduction

Deep neural networks have been successfully applied to many real world tasks,
such as image classification and handwritten digits recognition [6,10,18]. However, training very deep models remains a difficult task. The main difficulty is
the gradient vanishing and exploding problem [3,7]. Particularly, recurrent neural networks (RNNs) are a special type of deep neural networks, which can be
unfolded in term of time steps. As a result, RNNs have also the gradient vanishing and exploding problem. The so-called long short-term memory (LSTM)
network is a well designed RNNs model, which to some extent solves the gradient vanishing and exploding problem of RNNS [8]. Nevertheless, the training of
LSTM is complicated due to the internal covariate shift problem, which means
that the input distribution at each iteration changes during the training as the
parameters have been updated in previous iteration.

© Springer Nature Switzerland AG 2019
T. Gedeon et al. (Eds.): ICONIP 2019, LNCS 11953, pp. 746–755, 2019.
https://doi.org/10.1007/978-3-030-36708-4_61

To tackle the internal covariate shift problem of LSTM [5,11], batch normalization (BN) [9] has been applied to constrain the distribution of the flowing data in LSTM. Unfortunately, BN has not been successfully applied to the update of the LSTM cell. In this paper, to address the internal covariate shift problem of LSTM, we introduce a method to seamlessly integrate BN into the update of the LSTM cell. Experimental results on sequence learning tasks show that the proposed method, enhanced LSTM with BN (eLSTM-BN), has achieved faster convergence and higher classification accuracy than LSTM and related models.

In the following section, we briefly introduce some related work. In Sect. 3, we present the proposed model, enhanced LSTM with BN (eLSTM-BN), in detail, including its parameter initialization method and update formulas. In Sect. 4, we report the experimental results with comparison to related LSTM approaches on two benchmark data sets, i.e. MNIST [16] and Fashion-MNIST [15]. In the final section, we conclude this paper with remarks and future work.

2 Related Work

In recent years, recurrent neural networks (RNNs) and their variants attract much attention in the area of deep learning. To improve the performance of RNNs, progresses are made mainly in two aspects. On the one hand, researchers have modified the internal recurrent structure of the traditional RNNs, and generated some effective models for sequential data processing, such as long short-term memory (LSTM) [8] and gated recurrent units (GRUs) [4]. On the other hand, it has been found that initializing the weight matrix in RNNs with special matrices, such as identity, orthogonal and unitary matrices, can to some extent avoid the gradient vanishing and exploding problem. In the following, we introduce some related work from these two aspects.

With similar structure as GRUs, LSTM is a variant of RNNs. It modifies the internal recurrent module of RNNs. Based on this modification and improvement, LSTM can not only avoid the gradient vanishing problem, but also memorize long term dependencies. However, LSTM is computationally expensive during its training and the problem of gradient exploding is not fundamentally solved. Hence, gradient clipping and the dropout regularization are generally needed.

Dropout is the most successful technique for regularizing neural networks. However, it is generally ineffective for LSTMs. Zaremba, Sutskever and Vinyals [17] presented a simple regularization technique for LSTM. They showed how to correctly apply dropout to LSTMs, which can reduce the overfitting problem on a variety of sequence learning tasks.

In traditional RNNs, to overcome the gradient vanishing and exploding problems in training, some researchers explored the use of orthogonal and unitary matrices for parameter initialization [1,12,14], which have shown effective performance. However, although RNNs have been widely used in many applications, they lack the ability to learn long term dependencies. Hence, most of the research has been focused on the modification of RNNs' internal architecture.

Batch normalization (BN) is a regularization method, which is commonly used in deep neural networks. After batch normalization is successful applied in many deep neural networks, some researchers have tried to utilize it in RNNs for replacing the dropout operation [2]. Recently, Laurent et al. [11] have applied BN to the input-to-hidden transition of recurrent models, and hypothesize that applying BN to the hidden-to-hidden transition may hurt the training of LSTM. However, Liao et al. [13] prove that BN can be applied to the hidden-to-hidden transition of the LSTM unit. Furthermore, Cooijmans et al. [5] demonstrate that BN is beneficial to both the input-to-hidden and hidden-to-hidden transitions. Their experimental results show that BN can lead to faster convergence and improve the generalization performance of LSTM. However, as far as we know, no one has successfully applied BN to the update of the LSTM cell.

3   The Proposed Model

The long short-term memory (LSTM) networks are introduced by Hochreiter and Schmidhuber in 1997 [8]. They are a special type of RNNs, capable of learning long-term dependencies. The LSTM networks perform tremendously well on a large variety of problems, and are now widely used in many pattern recognition applications, such as speech recognition and handwritten character recognition. The LSTM unit is well designed to avoid the gradient vanishing and exploding problem of RNNs. Figure 1 shows the architecture of the LSTM memory cell. With the special architecture design, memorizing information for long periods of time is practically the default behavior of LSTMs, not something they struggle to do.

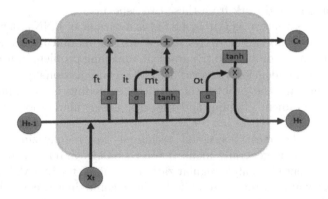

Fig. 1. The memory cell of LSTM.

In LSTM, the architecture of the memory cell is relatively complicated, which includes three gates to control the data flow: The forget gate (f_t) decides what information to remove from the cell state; The input gate (i_t) specifies what information to use for the update of the cell; the output gate (o_t) indicates what information to output. Moreover, the candidate state (m_t) determines what new information to store in the cell (C_t). The whole state update formulas of the LSTM cell are as follows.

$$\hat{i}_t = \mathbf{W_{ih}}h_{t-1} + \mathbf{W_{ix}}x_t + b_i, \tag{1}$$

$$\hat{f}_t = \mathbf{W_{fh}}h_{t-1} + \mathbf{W_{fx}}x_t + b_f, \tag{2}$$

$$\hat{o}_t = \mathbf{W_{oh}}h_{t-1} + \mathbf{W_{ox}}x_t + b_o, \tag{3}$$

$$m_t = \mathbf{W_{ch}}h_{t-1} + \mathbf{W_{cx}}x_t + b_m, \tag{4}$$

$$C_t = sigmoid(\hat{f}_t) \odot C_{t-1} + sigmoid(\hat{i}_t) \odot tanh(m_t), \tag{5}$$

$$h_t = sigmoid(\hat{o}_t) \odot tanh(C_t), \tag{6}$$

where $\hat{i}_t$, $\hat{f}_t$ and $\hat{o}_t$ correspond to the input gate, forget gate and output gate, respectively, $(\mathbf{W_{ih}}, \mathbf{W_{fh}}, \mathbf{W_{oh}}, \mathbf{W_{ch}}) \in R^{d_h \times d_h}$, $(\mathbf{W_{ix}}, \mathbf{W_{fx}}, \mathbf{W_{ox}}, \mathbf{W_{cx}}) \in R^{d_x \times d_h}$, (b_i, b_f, b_o, b_m) are the biases, C_t denotes the state of the memory cell and the $\odot$ operator represents the Hadamard product.

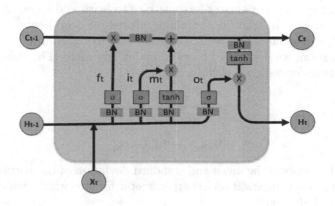

Fig. 2. The architecture of the eLSTM-BN cell.

In the training of a machine learning model, we generally assume that the training and test data are independent and identically distributed (i.i.d). However, there may exist the internal covariate shift problem, which means the distribution of the features is different in the training and test data sets, breaking the i.i.d. assumption. This happens because, as the network learns and the weights are updated, the distribution of outputs of the neurons in the network changes that forces later learning steps to adapt to that drift, which slows down the learning process.

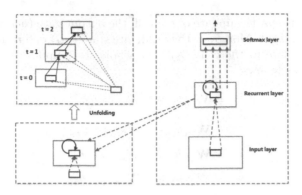

Fig. 3. The eLSTM-BN network.

In [9], the batch normalization (BN) is levaraged to solve the internal covariate shift problem of LSTM. Typically, BN is performed by normalizing the activations using empirical estimates of the mean and standard deviation of features. BN has a wide application in the deep learning area, and achieves good performance in many tasks. Since BN has limited the activations to a standard distribution, we can use a greater learning rate to learn and speed up the training. Simultaneously, in traditional training process of deep neural network, we usually use the dropout regularization to avoid overfitting. However, after adding the BN operation, we don't need to use dropout any more. The standard batch normalized transformation is defined as follows:

$$\hat{\mathbf{x}}_t = \frac{\mathbf{x}_t - E(\hat{\mathbf{x}}_t)}{\sqrt{Var(\hat{\mathbf{x}}_t) + \varepsilon}}, \tag{7}$$

$$BN(\mathbf{x}_t) = \beta + \gamma \odot \hat{\mathbf{x}}_t, \tag{8}$$

where β and γ denotes the mean and standard deviation of the normalized activations, and ε is a regularization hyperparameter for smoothing, which prevents $Var(\hat{\mathbf{x}}_t)$ from being zero.

The work by Laurent et al. [11] has successfully applied BN to the input-to-hidden transition ("vertically data flowing") of LSTM, but it does not apply BN to the more important hidden-to-hidden transition. The authors state that BN is not suitable for the recurrent connection of LSTM, because of the exploding gradients resulted from the repeated rescaling. In contrary, Cooijmans et al. [5] show that the recurrent connection of LSTM can apply BN with proper initialization of the batch normalization parameters. However, no one has successfully applied BN to the update of the LSTM cell.

In this paper, we apply BN to the update of the LSTM cell as well as the input-to-hidden and hidden-to-hidden transitions. The cell of the proposed model eLSTM-BN is shown in Fig. 2. As the forget gate in the memory cell is a very important part, which plays a role in removing the unimportant cell information of previous time step, applying BN to it during the cell update is

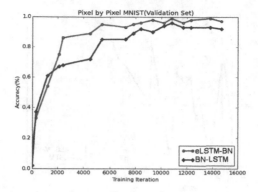

Fig. 4. The Results obtained by the implemented BN-LSTM and eLSTM-BN on the MNIST dataset.

critical and necessary. Here, we initialize the weight matrix in the network as an orthogonal matrix. Because orthogonal matrices have the property that they can preserve norm as shown in Eq. (9),

$$\|\mathbf{W}h\|_2 = \|h\|_2, \tag{9}$$

iterative multiplication of a vector by an orthogonal matrix leaves the norm of the vector unchanged. For concreteness, the state update formulas of eLSTM-BN can be defined with Eqs. (10)–(15):

$$\hat{i}_t = BN(\mathbf{W_{ih}}h_{t-1}) + BN(\mathbf{W_{ix}}x_t) + b_i, \tag{10}$$

$$\hat{f}_t = BN(\mathbf{W_{fh}}h_{t-1}) + BN(\mathbf{W_{fx}}x_t) + b_f, \tag{11}$$

$$\hat{o}_t = BN(\mathbf{W_{oh}}h_{t-1}) + BN(\mathbf{W_{ox}}x_t) + b_o, \tag{12}$$

$$m_t = BN(\mathbf{W_{ch}}h_{t-1}) + BN(\mathbf{W_{cx}}x_t) + b_m, \tag{13}$$

$$C_t = BN(sigmoid(\hat{f}_t) \odot C_{t-1}) + sigmoid(\hat{i}_t) \odot tanh(m_t), \tag{14}$$

$$h_t = sigmoid(\hat{o}_t) \odot tanh(BN(C_t)). \tag{15}$$

Compared to traditional LSTM models, we apply BN not only to the input-to-hidden and hidden-to-hidden translations, as shown in Eqs. (10)–(13), but also to the cell update, as shown in Eq. (14).

In the training process, we initialize $(\mathbf{W_{ih}}, \mathbf{W_{fh}}, \mathbf{W_{oh}}, \mathbf{W_{ch}})$ to an identity matrix and $(\mathbf{W_{ix}}, \mathbf{W_{fx}}, \mathbf{W_{ox}}, \mathbf{W_{cx}})$ to an orthogonal matrix. Due to hidden-to-hidden transition is sensitive to β and γ, we set β and γ as the same way as [5].

Figure 3 shows the whole eLSTM-BN network, in which we apply BN to the cell state update, the input-to-hidden and hidden-to-hidden translations of the unfolded units in the recurrent layer.

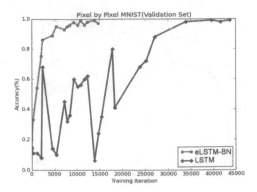

Fig. 5. The Results obtained by the traditional LSTM and eLSTM-BN on the MNIST dataset.

Fig. 6. Example images of the Fashion-MNIST dataset.

4   Experiments

To evaluate the proposed eLSTM-BN model, we have conducted experiments on two benchmark data sets, MNIST [16] and Fashion-MNIST [15]. The experimental code has been implemented using Tensorflow. In the experimental process, due to the source code of BN-LSTM [5] is not written in Python, we implement it by ourselves. In the following, we mainly compare LSTM and the implemented BN-LSTM to the proposed eLSTM-BN model.

4.1   Results on the MNIST Data Set

MNIST (a subset of NIST) is one of the most well known datasets in the machine learning community, which consists of handwriten digits of 0 to 9. There are 60,000 training images and 10,000 testing images. The images are in gray scale with size 28 × 28 pixels and the digits have been size-normalized and centered in a fixed-size image.

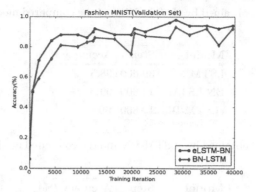

Fig. 7. The results obtained by the implemented BN-LSTM and eLSTM-BN on the Fashion-MNIST dataset.

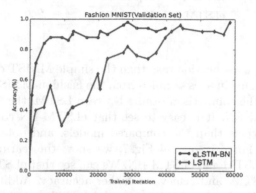

Fig. 8. The results obtained by the implemented LSTM and eLSTM-BN on the Fashion-MNIST dataset.

Figure 4 shows the learning curves of the implemented BN-LSTM and eLSTM-BN. As we can see that, compared to the implemented BN-LSTM, eLSTM-BN converges faster and obtains higher accuracy.

In order to compare eLSTM-BN to traditional LSTM, we have conducted an experiment on the MNIST data set. From the results shown in Fig. 5, we can see that, eLSTM-BN reaches a high accuracy in very short time. However, traditional LSTM has huge shock in the test process. To the end, eLSTM-BN performs much better than to LSTM. Table 1 shows that eLSTM-BN obtains higher classification accuracy than LSTM.

4.2 Results on the Fashion-MNIST Data Set

Fashion-MNIST is a MNIST-like fashion product dataset, consisting of a training set of 60,000 examples and a test set of 10,000 examples. Each example is a 28×28 grayscale image, associated with a label from 10 classes (T-shirt, Trouser, Pullover, Dress, Coat, Sandal, Shirt, Sniaker, Bag, and Ankle boot). Fashion-MNIST poses

Table 1. The results obtained by eLSTM-BN and the compared models on the MNIST data set.

Model	Step	Accuracy (%)
LSTM	39,600	98.5
BN-LSTM	13,800	99
eLSTM-BN	10,800	**99**

Table 2. The results obtained by eLSTM-BN and the compared models on the Fashion-MNIST data set.

Model	Step	Accuracy (%)
LSTM	27,000	90
BN-LSTM	21,000	90
eLSTM-BN	13,200	**91**

a more challenging classification task than the simple MNIST digits data. In the Fig. 6, we display some images sampled from the Fashion-MNIST dataset.

Table 2 shows the comparison results between LSTM, the implemented BN-LSTM and eLSTM-BN. It is easy to see that eLSTM-BN converges fast with less steps of iterations than the compared models, and obtains higher classification accuracy. Furthermore, in Fig. 7, we show the learning curves of the implemented BN-LSTM and eLSTM-BN. We can see that eLSTM-BN converges faster than BN-LSTM, and achieves a higher accuracy. Additionally, in Fig. 8, we show the learning curves of the traditional LSTM and eLSTM-BN. We can basically obtain the same conclusion that eLSTM-BN performs better than the compared method.

5   Conclusion

In this paper, we present a new model, called enhanced long short-term memory with batch normalization (eLSTM-BN). In eLSTM-BN, we apply the batch normalization regularization to the memory cell, input-to-hidden and hidden-to-hidden transitions of LSTM. To some extent, it addresses the internal covariate shift problem of LSTM. Experimental results show that eLSTM-BN has achieved faster convergence and better performance than LSTM and related models. In future work, we plan to add the peephole connection into the memory cell of LSTM, in order to strengthen the sharing of information.

Acknowledgments. This work was supported by the Major Project for New Generation of AI under Grant No. 2018AAA0100400, the National Key R&D Program of China under Grant No. 2016YFC1401004, the National Natural Science Foundation of China (NSFC) under Grant No. 41706010, the Science and Technology Program of Qingdao under Grant No. 17-3-3-20-nsh, the CERNET Innovation Project under

Grant No. NGII20170416, the Joint Fund of the Equipments Pre-Research and Ministry of Education of China under Grand No. 6141A020337, the Open Project Program of Key Laboratory of Research on Marine Hazards Forecasting, National Marine Environmental Forecasting Center, State Oceanic Administration (SOA), under Grand No. LOMF1802, the Graduate Education Reform and Research Project of Ocean University of China under Grand No. HDJG19001, and the Fundamental Research Funds for the Central Universities of China.

References

1. Arjovsky, M., Shah, A., Bengio, Y.: Unitary evolution recurrent neural networks. In: ICML, pp. 1120–1128 (2016)
2. Bayer, J., Osendorfer, C., Chen, N., Urban, S., Smagt, P.: On fast dropout and its applicability to recurrent networks. CoRR abs/1311.0701 (2013)
3. Bengio, Y., Simard, P., Frasconi, P.: Learning long-term dependencies with gradient descent is difficult. IEEE Trans. Neural Netw. **5**(2), 157–166 (1994)
4. Cho, K., van Merrienboer, B., Gülçehre, Ç., Bougares, F., Schwenk, H., Bengio, Y.: Learning phrase representations using RNN encoder-decoder for statistical machine translation. CoRR abs/1406.1078 (2014)
5. Cooijmans, T., Ballas, N., Laurent, C., Courville, A.: Recurrent batch normalization. CoRR abs/1603.09025 (2016)
6. Hinton, G., Salakhutdinov, R.: Reducing the dimensionality of data with neural networks. Science **313**, 504–507 (2006)
7. Hochreiter, S.: Untersuchungen zu Dynamischen Neuronalen Netzen. Master's thesis, Institut Fur Informatik, Technische Universitat, Munchen (1991)
8. Hochreiter, S., Schmidhuber, J.: Long short-term memory. Neural Comput. **9**(8), 1735–1780 (1997)
9. Ioffe, S., Szegedy, C.: Batch normalization: accelerating deep network training by reducing internal covariate shift. In: ICML, pp. 448–456 (2015)
10. Krizhevsky, A., Sutskever, I., Hinton, G.: ImageNet classification with deep convolutional neural networks. In: NIPS, pp. 1106–1114 (2012)
11. Laurent, C., Pereyra, G., Brakel, P., Zhang, Y., Bengio, Y.: Batch normalized recurrent neural networks. In: ICASSP, pp. 2657–2661 (2016)
12. Le, Q., Jaitly, N., Hinton, G.: A simple way to initialize recurrent networks of rectified linear units. CoRR abs/1504.00941 (2015)
13. Liao, Q., Poggio, T.: Bridging the gaps between residual learning, recurrent neural networks and visual cortex. CoRR abs/1604.03640 (2016)
14. Saxe, A., McClelland, J., Ganguli, S.: Exact solutions to the nonlinear dynamics of learning in deep linear neural networks. CoRR abs/1312.6120 (2013)
15. Xiao, H., Rasul, K., Vollgraf, R.: Fashion-MNIST: a novel image dataset for benchmarking machine learning algorithms. CoRR abs/1708.07747 (2017)
16. Yann, L., Lon, B., Yoshua, B., Patrick, H.: Gradient-based learning applied to document recognition, pp. 2278–2324. IEEE (1998)
17. Zaremba, W., Sutskever, I., Vinyals, O.: Recurrent neural network regularization. CoRR abs/1409.2329 (2014)
18. Zheng, Y., Zhong, G., Liu, J., Cai, X., Dong, J.: Visual texture perception with feature learning models and deep architectures. In: Li, S., Liu, C., Wang, Y. (eds.) CCPR 2014. CCIS, vol. 483, pp. 401–410. Springer, Heidelberg (2014). https://doi.org/10.1007/978-3-662-45646-0_41

Combating Threat-Alert Fatigue with Online Anomaly Detection Using Isolation Forest

Muhamad Erza Aminanto[1(✉)], Lei Zhu[1,2], Tao Ban[1], Ryoichi Isawa[1], Takeshi Takahashi[1], and Daisuke Inoue[1]

[1] National Institute of Information and Communications Technology, Tokyo, Japan
aminanto@nict.go.jp
[2] Lingnan Normal University, Zhanjiang, China

Abstract. The threat-alert fatigue problem, which is the inability of security operators to genuinely investigate each alert coming from network-based intrusion detection systems, causes many unexplored alerts and hence a deterioration of the quality of service. Motivated by this pressing need to reduce the number of threat-alerts presented to security operators for manual investigation, we propose a scheme that can triage alerts of significance from massive threat-alert logs. Thanks to the fully unsupervised nature of the adopted isolation forest method, the proposed scheme does not require any prior labeling information and thus is readily adaptable for most enterprise environments. Moreover, by taking advantage of the temporal information in the alerts, it can be used in an online mode that takes in the most recent information from past alerts and predicts the incoming ones. We evaluated the performance of our scheme using a 10-month dataset consisting of more than half a million alerts collected in a real-world enterprise environment and found that it could screen out 87.41% of the alerts without missing any single significant ones. This study demonstrates the efficacy of unsupervised learning in screening minor threat-alerts and is expected to shed light on the threat-alert fatigue problem.

Keywords: Threat-alert fatigue · Intrusion detection system · Stacked autoencoder · Isolation forest

1 Introduction

Intrusion detection systems (IDSs) implemented to monitor enterprise networks for identifying malicious activities and output an enormous number of threat-alerts despite most of the alerts being false positive (non-important) ones. Security operators have to investigate every single alert to verify whether they are critical or not and if further action needs to be taken. These overwatching tactics are impractical when the number of alerts exceeds a certain limit. The enormous number of threat-alerts leads to a severe problem known as threat-alert fatigue [2], which is

© Springer Nature Switzerland AG 2019
T. Gedeon et al. (Eds.): ICONIP 2019, LNCS 11953, pp. 756–765, 2019.
https://doi.org/10.1007/978-3-030-36708-4_62

defined as the inability of the operator to analyze every single alert due to the massive number of them. It may incur human errors, including misjudgments. A recent report by CISCO [10] states that operators entirely ignored about 44% of incoming alerts because they receive too many. To overcome this issue, CISCO [10] suggested developing automated security solutions that can help enterprises understand the threats, thus enabling them to reduce the time cost for detection, investigation, and remediation. Therefore, in this study, we present a technique that resolves threat-alert fatigue by automated alert screening.

Recently, Hassan et al. [2] proposed *NoDoze* to overcome threat-alert fatigue by means of automated provenance triage. Data provenance can provide contextual information of incoming alerts by transforming a chain of alerts into a single event. In other words, the authors considered a group of alerts as a single event for better separability between benign and malicious activities. In this paper, we use network-based IDS data instead of host-based IDS data so as to have wider monitoring capability in the network.

In this paper, we propose a real-time alert screening scheme based on a fully unsupervised isolation forest [4]. The isolation forest is an unsupervised anomaly detection algorithm that can identify anomalies without profiling the normal instances. It creates several decision trees and calculates an anomaly score for each node by considering how deep the tree is and/or how many branches exist on it. The shallower or fewer the branches, the higher the probability for the corresponding node to be an anomaly. Through alert message decoding, we obtain a total of 49 fields containing many categorical fields that are signature-like and have a vast number of unique values. To prevent overfitting, a rule-based field selection is applied, including fields with limited unique values. Temporal pattern variation is also taken into account by predicting the current day alert with the model trained from accumulative data from the past few days.

We evaluate the proposed method on an alert dataset drawn from real-world network traffic at our company. The alert logs are collected from one particular security appliance in Common Event Format (CEF) [3] and labeled manually by our security operators. We include the alert logs from January 2017 to October 2017 (ten months) comprising 564,561 alerts. There are only two classes in the dataset, false positives and true positives, and the proportion is skewed where only 291 true alerts exist. In this paper, our dataset is a threat-alert log that consists of all threat instances. However, among all threat instances, some are critical and the rest are less critical. Therefore, false positive here means true threat-alerts with lesser priority than the true threat-alerts with higher priority. We tested the proposed approach using several schemes and found that the proposed approach achieved 100% recall and a 12.55% false positive rate. This means the operator can focus on the remaining 12.59% of the total alerts in order to obtain the 291 true alerts. We believe this approach will be beneficial to fight the threat-alert fatigue problem.

The main contributions of this study are summarized as follows:

– An automated screening system is proposed, using a machine learning model to reduce the number of threat-alerts that require human investigation, so that the threat-alert fatigue is resolved to a certain extent.
– The proposed model is fully unsupervised, so no prior labeling information is required. Thus, the expense of labeling a training set and the risk of degrading the screening results due to problematic labels can be prevented.
– The proposed model works in real time and takes temporal information into account, since the model for predicting the current day's data is trained with accumulated alerts from previous days.

In Sect. 2 of this paper, we introduce previous work on reducing threat-alerts. We describe our data preparation in Sect. 3. Section 4 explains the proposed methodology and Sect. 5 discusses the experimental results. We conclude in Sect. 6 with a brief summary and overview of future work.

2   Related Work

Valeur et al. [11] developed a comprehensive correlation to reduce the number of IDS alerts. The performance of this approach depends on the characteristics of the dataset; e.g., it reduced 99.20% of a honeypot dataset but only 53% of the MIT/LL 2000 dataset. Despite the excellent performance, some of the correlation components might be impossible to run, such as the alert verification component, which requires the security operator to have access rights to the victim host. More recently, Hassan et al. [2] proposed an automated provenance triage called *NoDoze* to overcome threat-alert fatigue. The main drive behind this approach is adjusting the suspiciousness of every event in the provenance graph on the basis of the suspicious level of neighboring events in the graph. They introduced behavioral execution partitioning by separating benign and malicious behavior and generated the most malicious dependency graph of a true alert in order to prevent dependency explosion caused by previous data provenance.

We also examined two isolation forest implementations in IDS. Sun et al. [6] leveraged isolation forest to detect deviation of employee behaviors. The authors did not examine the temporal factor; rather, they gathered the data for a particular period and then performed anomaly detection. Ding and Fei [1] implemented an isolation forest algorithm for streaming data using a sliding window. Similar to threat-alert reduction, Tuor et al. [9] published an alert reduction but for anomalous employee behaviors. Two deep learning models, the deep neural network (DNN) and the recurrent neural network (RNN), were implemented and trained with employee behavior data gathered for one day.

3   Data Preparation

3.1   Data Collection and Labelling

The original alerts are presented in .tsv files. Each alert consists of an alert message generated by the security appliance that offers the most information, as well as appliance ID, the time the alert was received, alert ID, etc. An example of an alert message is shown in Fig. 1.

Jan 05 03:26:29 previct.lastline.local CEF:0|Lastline|Enterprise|7.10|network-connection|Suspicious Network Connection|7|act=LOG cat=command&control/Locky cn1=70 cn1Label=impact cn2=27866 cn2Label=IncidentId cn3=70 cn3Label=IncidentImpact cnt=1 cs1=54cd2324:30fbe7df:30fbe7df cs1Label=detectionId cs2=https://prm00.cyrec.nict.go.jp//event#/3311502819/1781650753/1345741?event_tim e\\=2017-01-05 cs2Label=EventDetailLink cs3=http://stat.orbitum.ru/installer.php cs3Label=EventUrl deviceExternalId=3311502819:1781650753 dpt=80 dst=193.0.201.36 end=Jan 05 2017 12:25:15 JST externalId=1345741 proto=TCP smac=cc:4e:24:14:c9:1c sourceDnsDomain=proxy1.nict.go.jp src=133.243.18.20 start=Jan 05 2017 12:25:15 JST

Fig. 1. Example of an alert message. (Color figure online)

The messages utilized in this research are in the Common Event Format (CEF), an event interoperability standard introduced by ArcSight [3,5]. A CEF message starts with a common prefix containing the date and hostname (e.g., 'Jan 24 06:26:38 previct.#AppName#.local' in the above example) and is followed by a message with the format 'CEF:Version|Device Vendor|Device Product|Device Version|Signature ID|Name|Severity|Extension'. The Extension part of the message is a placeholder for additional fields that are logged as key-value pairs.

To utilize such an alert message, we developed a parser to extract key-value pairs in accordance with the above message formation. The message is first split into a header (the red part) and a body. The message header consists of a prefix and the first seven fields and is then split into eight fields with '|' as a delimiter, with the content in the second to eighth fields associated with predefined keys (Device Vendor, Device Product, etc.). The first field in the header is further split into five fields with white-space ' ' as a delimiter, corresponding to month, day, time, hostname, and CEF_Version keys.

For the message body (i.e., message extension), we can see that it is mostly organized as 'key1=value1 key2=value2', where the white space ' ' acts as a delimiter between key/value pairs and the '=' acts as a delimiter between key and value. However, there are exceptions, such as 'start=Jan 05 2017 12:25:15 JST', by the end of the example message. To tackle this issue, we examine each element after the key/value pair by splitting (by ' ') in the reverse order to see if there is a '=' delimiter. If not, we merge this string with the former string until it has one. Note that we apply a regular expression check to differentiate '\\=' and '=', as the former apparently does not separate key and value. After parsing, each alert is transformed into a dictionary (a set of key/value pairs) and stored in json files.

4   Methodology

In this section, we describe our proposed approach: automated and real-time threat-alert screening using a fully unsupervised isolation forest. Its stepwise

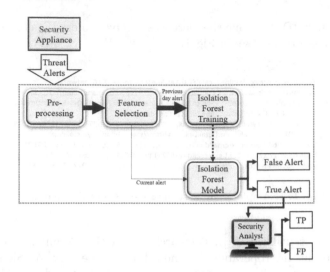

Fig. 2. Stepwise procedure of proposed approach.

procedure is shown in Fig. 2, with dotted lines indicating the model generated by previous training and solid lines indicating the data flow.

4.1 Fields Selection and Digitization

After the message decoding, we obtain a dataset with 49 fields (keys) in total (note that most alerts have around 20–30 fields, and thus empty values appear in most fields). There are two types of fields in our dataset: numerical and categorical. The values in the numerical fields (i.e., Severity, Impact, IncidentImpact) are in the form of integers, where a larger value indicates that the alert is more significant. The values in the categorical fields are strings, and the number of unique values varies from less than ten (e.g., the field protocol has only two values: UDP and unknown) to nearly one million (e.g., the alert receive time).

Intuitively, fields with a large number of unique values are more signature-like, so very limited alerts share the same value and thus have lower generalization capability for classification. Moreover, such fields will lead to dimension explosion in the later digitization step. Here, we implement a rule-based approach to filter fields. For numerical fields, we keep all of them. For categorical fields, we pick fields that have unique values greater than one and smaller than or equal to a pre-defined threshold.

The next step is converting categorical values into numerical values. For simplicity, we use the one-hot-encoding method for this, where the missing values are treated as a new value for each original field. Lastly, we normalize all numerical fields using the min-max method, as shown in Eq. (1), to balance the contribution of all fields during the training phase.

$$z_i = \frac{x_i - min(x)}{max(x) - min(x)} \tag{1}$$

4.2 Anomaly Detection

An anomaly detector detects abnormal behaviors from unusual behaviors, which is of particular interest. In this paper, we leverage an anomaly detector called isolation forest [4], which isolates anomalies instead of profiling benign behaviors by exploiting two properties, sparseness and difference, in a tree structure. Anomaly nodes are located close to the root of the tree, while benign behaviors are located far from the root of the tree. In the isolation forest algorithm, an ensemble of trees is built for a given dataset, and anomalies are nodes that have shallow heights on the trees on average.

Assume an input dataset $X = \{x_1, ..., x_n\}$, where n is the number of alert instances. An isolation tree (i_tree) is built by recursively dividing X, specifically, by randomly selecting a field q and a split value p, until either the i_tree reaches a height limit, $|X| = 1$, or X has uniform values [4]. Isolation forest outputs an anomaly score s for each instance x, as

$$s(x, n) = 2^{-\frac{E(h(x))}{c(n)}}, \tag{2}$$

where $E(h(x))$ denotes the average path length $h(x)$ of i_tree and $c(n)$ is an adjustment factor that considers the cardinality of the sub-sampled dataset [7]. Equation 2 leads to three conditions:

- $E(h(x)) \to 0$, $s \to 1$; in this case, x appears as an outlier.
- $E(h(x)) \to n - 1$, $s \to 0$; in this case, x appears as a normal instance.
- $E(h(x)) \to c(n)$, $s \to 0.5$; in this case, no distinct anomaly exists.

Algorithm 1 describes the anomaly detection process. The isolation forest algorithm is a two-phase process consisting of training and testing. The training phase builds ensemble trees using a subset of the training set with a random selection without replacement. During the training, two important parameters are α and γ, which are defined as the size of the sample and the degree of contamination, respectively. α defines the size of the sub-sample drawn from the training set, while γ defines the percentage of instances that would be considered anomalies. The training is performed once a day with the input X_r, which is the accumulation of the previous day's alerts. At the initialization, the first day of training uses only the first-day logs $X_r = X_{r1}$, while the second-day training uses the first-day alerts as well. The testing phase provides the test set, X_{ti}, to the generated $Model$ to acquire an anomaly score for each instance. The algorithm returns Y_{ti} to show whether the instances are an anomaly or normal. In the proposed approach, we train the isolation forest using accumulated instances from previous days and test the test set by the model built in the training phase. In other words, the test set is unseen during the training phase.

```
     input  : X_{ri}
     output: Y_t
 1  initialize X_{ri} ← X_{r1};
 2  Function Training(X_{ri}):
 3      for i in Day do
 4          X_r ← ∑_{i=1}^{i-1} X_{ri};
 5          Model ← iForestTrain(X_r, α, γ);
 6          return Model
 7      end
 8  End Function;
 9  Function Testing(X_{ti}):
10      for i in Day do
11          Y_{ti} ← Predict(Model, X_{ti});
12          X_r ← X_r + X_{ti} ;
13          return Y_{ti}
14      end
15  End Function;
```

Algorithm 1. Anomaly Detection using Isolation Forest

5   Experimental Analysis

We set up an experiment environment using Python 3.6 running on an Intel(R) Core(TM) i5-6400 CPU @2.70 GHz, RAM 16 GB. As performance metrics, we use Recall, also known as detection rate, which is the number of correctly identified high-priority threat-alerts divided by the total number of high-priority threat-alerts, and the False Positive Rate (FPR), which is defined as the number of less-priority threat-alert instances that are classified incorrectly as high-priority threat-alerts divided by the total number of less-priority threat-alerts. Intuitively, we want Recall to be as high as possible and FPR to be as low as possible. In this study, we aim to not miss any high-priority threat-alerts (100% Recall), while we can relax about false positives since the false positive alerts would be inspected by security operators later. Equations (3) and (4) define the above measures.

$$Recall = \frac{TP}{TP + FN}, \tag{3}$$

$$FPR = \frac{FP}{TN + FP}, \tag{4}$$

where True Positive (TP) is the number of high-priority threat-alerts correctly classified as such, True Negative (TN) is the number of less-priority threat-alerts correctly classified as such, False Negative (FN) is the number of high-priority threat-alerts incorrectly classified as less-priority threat-alerts, and False Positive (FP) is the number of less-priority threat-alerts incorrectly classified as high-priority threat-alerts.

We also evaluate the performance using the Area Under Curve (AUC) in the Receiver Operating Characteristic (ROC). Accuracy and F-score are not used as performance metrics because both are sensitive to imbalanced data [8] and our dataset is extremely imbalanced (564,270 and 291 alerts).

5.1 Experiment Results

We built two models for our experiment: daily and accumulated models. Unlike the accumulated model, which is described in Algorithm 1, the daily model trains and tests using the same daily alerts. In other words, $X_r = X_t$, while in the accumulated model, $X_r \neq X_t$. The daily model aims to validate our hypothesis that a smaller time-window size outputs a better FPR. Table 1 shows the experimental results of both models. We observed that the daily model has a lower FPR than the accumulated model, but it also has a lower Recall. We tuned the contamination degree, γ, to determine the impact of the level of contamination threshold. The γ values defined a trade-off between Recall and FPR. This result demonstrates that, to obtain a better Recall, we need a wider time-window and a higher γ, while in contrast, to reduce the FPR, we need a narrow time-window and a lower γ. By the accumulated model, we expect to achieve a real-time model because only the previous-day alerts are pooled; in other words, there is no delay for the test.

Table 1. Results on both models.

ID	Train	Test	γ (%)	Recall (%)	FPR (%)
daily-a	1 day	1 day	10	95.87	8.21
daily-b	1 day	1 day	5	91.06	4.19
daily-c	1 day	1 day	1	51.21	0.81
acc-a	Accumulated	Each alert	10	100.00	20.13
acc-b	Accumulated	Each alert	5	100.00	12.55
acc-c	Accumulated	Each alert	1	86.94	3.10

We also compare our proposed approach to three other unsupervised clustering algorithms, K-means (k = 2), agglomerative, and DBSCAN, as shown in

Table 2. Results on different algorithms.

Algorithm	Data (%)	Time (s)	FPR (%)	Recall (%)
K-means	100	6.43	51.15	100
Isolation Forest	100	70.41	9.30	100
K-means	10	0.68	48.49	0
Isolation Forest	10	7.48	9.00	100
DBSCAN	10	188.32	1.80	100
Agglomerative	10	420.03	48.49	0

Table 2. We test two schemes, 10% and 100% of the dataset, because DBSCAN and Agglomerative could not be executed at one time due to memory limitation. Despite the DBSCAN best result, the clustering time was much slower than K-means, which means not scalable. Isolation Forest suits the requirements of our alert screening because it can detect all the true positives and minimize the FPR within a reasonable execution time and with less memory.

5.2   Comparison with Security Appliance Reference

The dataset used in this study was released by a security vendor who provides a "threat score" feature called "severity" to denote how severe an alert is. We compared our model, acc-b, against the filtering results using the "severity" values. As shown in Fig. 3, there are eleven different levels, and we plot the ROC for each level to compare with model-acc-b, which outperformed other baselines. We found that our model could reduce the threat-alerts by 87.41% with 100% Recall and 12.55% FPR, thus enabling the security operator to focus on the remaining 12.59%[1] to obtain the true alerts. Although we are using different datasets and thus cannot perform a direct comparison, Hassan et al. [2] achieved a similar performance, detecting 100% of true positives with a 16% FPR. Therefore, we believe that our model is a significant step towards combating the threat-alert fatigue problem.

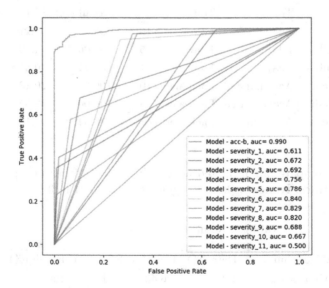

Fig. 3. ROC of acc-b against the 'level' provided by the security appliance.

---

[1] The 0.04% difference here caused by 291 of the true alerts is excluded from the 12.55% FPR.

6   Conclusion

We proposed an unsupervised model using the isolation forest algorithm to reduce threat-alert fatigue. Our approach accumulates the previous day's data for training and screens the incoming alerts simultaneously. Experimental results show that our proposed approach reduced the threat-alert logs by 87.41% without missing any single true alerts. This result implies that the security operator will only need to monitor 12.59% of the 564,561 total alerts received at our enterprise. This model is practical since it requires no prior labeling, and it is lightweight to implement.

In this study, we focused on threat-alerts generated by one security vendor only; thus, we plan to generalize this model to work with multiple log formats from any security vendor in future work. Although the proposed approach outperforms filtering using the vendor severity label, we aim to further reduce the false positive rate by examining reconstruction error values during the decoding step.

References

1. Ding, Z., Fei, M.: An anomaly detection approach based on isolation forest algorithm for streaming data using sliding window. IFAC Proc. Vol. **46**(20), 12–17 (2013)
2. Hassan, W.U., Guo, S., Li, D., Chen, Z., Jee, K., Li, Z., Bates, A.: NoDoze: combatting threat alert fatigue with automated provenance triage. In: Network and Distributed Systems Security (NDSS) Symposium 2019 (2019)
3. ArcSight, Inc.: Common event format (2010). https://kc.mcafee.com/resources/sites/MCAFEE/content/live/CORP-KNOWLEDGEBASE/78000/KB78712/. Accessed 17 Apr 2019
4. Liu, F.T., Ting, K.M., Zhou, Z.H.: Isolation forest. In: 2008 Eighth IEEE International Conference on Data Mining, pp. 413–422. IEEE (2008)
5. Marwaha, N.: System and method for providing common event format using alert index. US Patent 7,139,938, 21 November 2006
6. Sun, L., Versteeg, S., Boztas, S., Rao, A.: Detecting anomalous user behavior using an extended isolation forest algorithm: an enterprise case study. arXiv preprint arXiv:1609.06676 (2016)
7. Susto, G.A., Beghi, A., McLoone, S.: Anomaly detection through on-line isolation forest: an application to plasma etching. In: 2017 28th Annual SEMI Advanced Semiconductor Manufacturing Conference (ASMC), pp. 89–94. IEEE (2017)
8. Tharwat, A.: Classification assessment methods. Appl. Comput. Inform. (2018). https://doi.org/10.1016/j.aci.2018.08.003
9. Tuor, A., Kaplan, S., Hutchinson, B., Nichols, N., Robinson, S.: Deep learning for unsupervised insider threat detection in structured cybersecurity data streams. In: Workshops at the Thirty-First AAAI Conference on Artificial Intelligence (2017)
10. Ulevitch, D.: Cisco 2017 Annual Cybersecurity Report: The Hidden Danger of Uninvestigated Threats (2017). https://blogs.cisco.com/security/cisco-2017-annual-cybersecurity-report-the-hidden-danger-of-uninvestigated-threats. Accessed 17 Apr 2019
11. Valeur, F., Vigna, G., Kruegel, C., Kemmerer, R.A.: Comprehensive approach to intrusion detection alert correlation. IEEE Trans. Dependable Secur. Comput. **1**(3), 146–169 (2004)

A Fast Algorithm for Constructing Phylogenetic Trees with Application to IoT Malware Clustering

Tianxiang He[1]([✉]), Chansu Han[1,2], Ryoichi Isawa[2], Takeshi Takahashi[2], Shuji Kijima[1], Jun'ichi Takeuchi[1,2], and Koji Nakao[2]

[1] Kyushu University, Fukuoka, Japan
he@me.inf.kyushu-u.ac.jp, {kijima,tak}@inf.kyushu-u.ac.jp
[2] National Institute of Information and Communications Technology,
Tokyo, Japan
takeshi_takahashi@ieee.org, {han,isawa,ko-nakao}@nict.go.jp

Abstract. For efficiently handling thousands of malware specimens, we aim to quickly and automatically categorize those into malware families. A solution for this could be the neighbor-joining method using NCD (Normalized Compression Distance) as similarity of malware. It creates a phylogenetic tree of malware based on the NCDs between malware binaries for clustering. However, it is frustratingly slow because it requires $(N^2 + N)/2$ compression attempts for the NCDs, where N is the number of given specimens. For fast clustering, this paper presents an algorithm for efficiently constructing a phylogenetic tree by greatly reducing compression attempts. The key idea to do so is not to construct a tree of N specimens all at once. Instead, it divides N specimens into temporal clusters in advance, constructs a small tree for each temporal cluster, and joins the trees as a united tree. Intuitively, separately constructing small trees requires a much smaller number of compression attempts than $(N^2 + N)/2$. With experiments using 4,109 in-the-wild malware specimens, we confirm that our algorithm achieved clustering 22 times faster than the neighbor-joining method with a good accuracy of 97%.

Keywords: IoT malware · Clustering · Phylogenetic tree · Fast approximation algorithm

1 Introduction

IoT (Internet of Things) malware specimens have rapidly increased on the Internet for the past few years, infecting such IoT devices as web cameras and home routers worldwide. A major reason for this rapid increase is because source programs of IoT malware including *Bashlite* and *Mirai* were leaked on the Internet [3,6]. Thanks to this, malware authors can easily create malware variants customized for their own malicious purposes based on a leaked source program. Even worse, there are automated cross-compiling scripts available online that

© Springer Nature Switzerland AG 2019
T. Gedeon et al. (Eds.): ICONIP 2019, LNCS 11953, pp. 766–778, 2019.
https://doi.org/10.1007/978-3-030-36708-4_63

automatically compile a leaked source program into various malware executables running on different CPU architectures (e.g., Intel x86 and ARM), which also contributes to the rapid increase of malware.

Malware analysts working for an anti-malware institute often receive a set of thousands of IoT malware specimens obtained from various sources like honeypots and anti-malware platforms (e.g., VirusTotal [2] and malware [1]). Due to quite a few number of malware specimens, they are strongly required to efficiently analyze the malware. *Clustering* is a solution for efficient analysis. That is, according to a clustering algorithm, malware specimens can be automatically grouped into several clusters before analysis. The analysts then analyze some specimens in each cluster. At which time, the other specimens in each cluster are similar to the analyzed specimens in the same cluster. This means that the clustering enables the analysts to successfully recognize the entire malware set by just analyzing comparatively a small number of specimens.

Towards efficient malware analysis, our main purpose in this paper is to achieve clustering that quickly and automatically categorizes IoT malware specimens into clusters of malware families, based on their similarity. The similarity we use between two specimens is measured by the NCD (Normalized Compression Distance) [7,8] as: *the similarity is higher as the NCD is smaller.* This is based on the fact that IoT malware specimens categorized into a malware family are often generated from a leaked source program with some modifications [3], which results in generating similar binaries. Thus the NCD represents the similarity well because it is mainly determined by the compressed size of a binary concatenated with the other (i.e., the similarity of the binaries).

There exists a conventional scheme to construct a phylogenetic tree for clustering as follows. Given N specimens ($N = 2, 3, \cdots$), an analyst first computes the NCDs for every pair of N specimens, which requires $(N^2 + N)/2$ compression attempts in total. The analyst then constructs a phylogenetic tree with the neighbor-joining method [16], taking as input the obtained NCDs, and finally the phylogenetic tree is cut into subtrees as clusters. Examples of cut-off methods include a very common method that cuts a tree into clusters at a constant height cutoff value [12]. A major drawback of the conventional scheme is that it requires a large number of compression attempts (i.e., $(N^2 + N)/2$ attempts). This makes clustering very slow, as a result.

This paper presents a fast algorithm[1] to efficiently construct a phylogenetic tree based on the NCDs between malware specimens. It mainly focuses on how it greatly reduces compression attempts overall. The key idea to do so is not to construct a tree of N specimens all at once. Instead, it divides N specimens into temporal clusters in advance, constructs a small tree for each temporal cluster, and joins the trees as a united tree. Intuitively, separately constructing small trees requires a much smaller number of compression attempts than $(N^2 + N)/2$ attempts in total, provided that every small tree contains a much smaller number of specimens than N.

---

[1] A preliminary version of this algorithm was proposed by Takumi Yone in the master's thesis [19] of Kyushu University, who was supervised by some authors of this paper.

With experiments using 4,109 in-the-wild malware specimens including Bash-lite and Mirai, we confirm that our algorithm achieved clustering 22 times faster than the conventional scheme while achieving a good clustering accuracy of 97%. At which time, the runtime of our algorithm and that of the conventional scheme were around 5 h and 240 h, respectively. This runtime was measured from the start of compression attempts for NCDs until the end of clustering, using three cores of a 2.60 GHz Intel-Xeon CPU. In addition, we also confirm that our algorithm caused low approximation errors of a tree against NCDs.

Our contributions in this paper are threefold: (1) we present a fast algorithm to construct a phylogenetic tree, which leads to efficient malware analysis, (2) we evaluated efficiency of our algorithm using in-the-wild malware captured by an IoT honeypot, which reflects the real environment and increases reliability of our algorithm, and (3) we used a large dataset containing 4,109 specimens for the experiments, which shows scalability of our algorithm.

2 Background

2.1 Normalized Compression Distance

The NCD is a way of measuring the similarity between two objects [13]. The advantage of the NCD is that the object being measured can be many things: documents, pictures, programs, music, etc. In this paper, we used it to measure the distance between IoT malware.

Definition 1. *For two objects x and y, the NCD is defined as below:*

$$NCD(x,y) = \frac{C(xy) - \min\{C(x), C(y)\}}{\max\{C(x), C(y)\}}, \tag{1}$$

where $C(x)$ is length of x which be compressed by compression algorithm C. xy is the concatenation of objects x and y.

2.2 Neighbor-Joining Method

The neighbor-joining method [16] is an algorithm to create a tree whose tree distance approximates the given distance matrix over a finite set. Here the tree distance means that a distance between two nodes is defined as total branch length of all branches on the shortest path between the two nodes. Usually the obtained tree is used as a phylogenetic tree. The inputs of the Neighbor-joining method are a finite set L and a distance matrix d defined upon it. The output is a tree with elements of L on its leaves. In the Neighbor-joining method, two nodes i and j that minimize d'_{ij}, defined below, will join to a newly created node p.

$$d'_{ij} = d_{ij} - \frac{\sum_{k \in L}(d_{ik} + d_{jk})}{|L| - 2}, \tag{2}$$

where d_{ij} is the (i,j) entry of the given distance matrix d. Nodes i and j will be deleted from the set L, and add node p instead of it. Repeat this step until all the nodes are linked. An pseudocode of Neighbor-joining method is shown in Algorithm 1, where D is the set of branch length.

Algorithm 1. Neighbor-joining method

Input: finite dataset L with a distance matrix (d_{ij}) over $L \times L$
Output: phylogenetic tree T

1 **while** $|L| \geq 2$ **do**
2   choose (u, v) $(u \neq v)$ which minimizes $d'_{u,v}$
3   create a new node p, $V := V \cup \{u, v, p\}$, $E = E \cup \{\{u, p\}, \{v, p\}\}$
4   branch length of $\{u, p\}$ is defined as: $D_{u,p} = (d_{u,v} + \frac{\sum_{k \in L \setminus \{u,v\}}(d_{uk} - d_{vk})}{|L| - 2})/2$
5   branch length of $\{v, p\}$ is defined as: $D_{v,p} = (d_{u,v} + \frac{\sum_{k \in L \setminus \{u,v\}}(d_{vk} - d_{uk})}{|L| - 2})/2$
     $L := (L \setminus \{u, v\}) \cup \{p\}$
6   for $w \in L \setminus \{p\}$, $d(w, p) := (1/2)(d_{u,w} + d_{v,w} - d_{u,v})$
7 **end**
8 return $T = (V, E), D$

2.3 Related Work

Bailey et al. propose a method for automatically categorizing malware specimens into clusters that reflect their behaviors on Windows OS [4]. Their method, taking as input behavior lists of specimens, computes the NCDs between specimens by compressing every pair of the behavior lists, and constructs a dendrogram of malware for clustering. It is evaluated as effective; however, it should compress every pair of behavior lists, and it should observe malware behaviors, for which Bailey et al. executed every malware binary for five minutes. In contrast, our algorithm greatly reduces compression attempts, and it does not execute malware binaries. Bayer et al. also propose a behavior-based clustering method [5], in which every malware specimen should be also run for a few minutes. In addition, Karim et al. also propose a method for generating phylogenetic trees of malware, using n-perms for measuring the similarity. It, however, still requires every pair of malware similarities [11].

There are existing algorithms to focus on how a phylogenetic tree is efficiently constructed based on a distance matrix between given objects. Examples of such algorithms include Elias et al.'s [10], Simonsen et al.'s [18], and Price et al.'s [15]. Those algorithms greatly improve efficiency of the neighbor-joining itself; however, every pair of the distances between all objects are still required. Since we focus on how to greatly reduce computation attempts (i.e., compression attempts in this paper), our research direction totally differs from theirs.

3 Fast Algorithm for Constructing Phylogenetic Trees

In the neighbor-joining method, the distance matrix needs to be fully calculated and its computational cost is $O(N^2)$, which usually matters in practice. Therefore, we propose a fast approximation algorithm that generates a phylogenetic tree which does not need a full distance matrix. Note that our algorithm is an improvement of the algorithm which was proposed in [19].

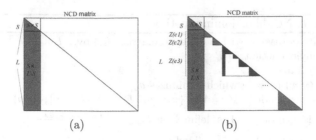

Fig. 1. The schematic diagram of our algorithm.

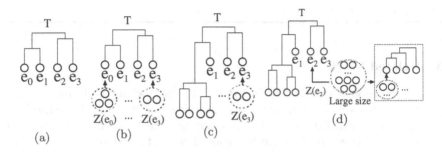

Fig. 2. The phased schematic diagram of our algorithm.

An outline of the algorithm is as follows. First, it selects a seeds set $S \subset L$ ($|S| = k, |L| = N$) with k ($k \ll N$) randomly. Then, it calculates the distance matrix between S and L as in Fig. 1(a), and using the distance matrix over $S \times S$ creates a phylogenetic tree T by the neighbor-joining method as in Fig. 2(a). For each element z in $L \setminus S$, using the distance matrix over $(L \setminus S) \times S$, links it with the leaf e of T, which is nearest to the element z as in Fig. 2(b).

Then, to increase the approximation accuracy of the tree distance between set $L \setminus S$, it recalculates the tree distance recursively for each $Z(e)$ as in Fig. 1(b). If $|Z(e)| < h$, then it calculates the distance matrix over $Z(e) \cup \{e\}$ and creates a phylogenetic tree $T_Z(e)$ with it. Then it combines $T_Z(e)$ and T as in Fig. 2(c). Here, h is a predefined threshold. The reason why e is also included in the recalculation is that we want to know which part of the $T_Z(e)$ is corresponding to the T. If $|Z(e)| > h$, then it recursively uses this algorithm for $Z(e) \cup e$ as in Fig. 2(d). An pseudocode of our algorithm is shown in Algorithm 2, where ∂T denotes a set of all leaves of T.

The schematic diagram is shown in Fig. 1. The grey parts of the distance matrix are calculated, while the white parts are not. The black parts represent recursively using the fast algorithm. Compare to the neighbor-joining method,

---

Algorithm 2. Fast Algorithm for Constructing Phylogenetic Trees

---

    Input: finite dataset L, size k of seeds set, threshold h
    Output: phylogenetic tree T

1 Choose a certain seeds set $S \subset L$ with $|S| = k$
2 Calculate the distances d_{ij} for $(i, j) \in S \times L$
3 Create a phylogenetic tree T for S by the Neighbor-joining method using d_{ij}
4 **for** $e \in \partial T$ **do**
5 | $Z(e) = \emptyset$
6 **end**
7 **for** $z \in L \backslash S$ **do**
8 | $Z(e) = Z(e) \cup \{z\}$ where e is nearest to z
9 **end**
10 **for** $e \in \partial T$ **do**
11   **if** $|Z(e)| > h$ **then**
12 | recursively use Algorithm 2 for $Z(e) \cup \{e\}$
13   **end**
14   **if** $1 < |Z(e)| < h$ **then**
15 | calculate d_{ij} for $(i, j) \in (Z(e) \cup \{e\})^2$ and create a phylogenetic tree $T_Z(e)$ with it.
16 | replace the corresponding parts of T with $T_Z(e)$
17   **end**
18 **end**

---

which needs to calculate the lower triangular of the distance matrix, the fast algorithm significantly reduces the computational cost. In the next section, we show experimental evaluation of our algorithm about the computational cost.

4 Evaluation

This section evaluates efficiency of our algorithm with a dataset of in-the-wild malware, in particular it shows how well our algorithm can reduce compression attempts, comparing our algorithm with a conventional method.

4.1 Dataset

To capture IoT malware specimens, Pa et al. proposed the IoT honeypot system named *IoTPOT* [14]. The IoTPOT deployed by the developer team [14] provided us with a dataset of IoT malware. It contains 55,624 malware specimens captured from September 1st in 2016 to December 31st in 2017. Among these, our algorithm should take as input a set of binaries running on the same CPU architecture. This is because two binaries generated even from the same program source differ from each other in terms of ISA (Instruction Set Architecture) if they are built for different CPU architectures. Fortunately, the CPU architecture is very easily identified with `file` command of Linux.

Table 1. Evaluation results of our algorithm. The 0.16 in column *Ratio (Error/0.16)* means the approximation error caused by conv_scheme, and the runtime of conv_scheme was 243.4 h.

Parameter		RCR (%)	Runtime		Approximation		Clustering
h	k		Runtime (hours)	Runtime reduction (%)	Error	Ratio (Error/0.16)	Overall accuracy (%)
100	20	97.26	4.73	98.06	1.16	7.25	96.67
	30	96.66	5.58	97.71	0.99	6.19	94.40
	50	95.54	7.32	96.99	0.72	4.50	94.43
	100	93.60	10.60	95.65	0.48	3.00	97.79
200	20	96.66	5.90	97.58	1.18	7.38	91.77
	30	95.99	7.53	96.91	0.84	5.25	95.57
	50	94.97	12.75	94.76	0.62	3.88	97.08
	100	93.35	10.85	95.54	0.52	3.25	97.81

We checked the CPU architecture of each specimen to determine the target CPU architecture in the experiments. Among all specimens, 23.23% of the specimens are built for ARM CPU-architecture, 14.57% for Intel x86, 12.76% for MIPS (big-endian), 10.82% for MIPS (little-endian), 8.07% for PowerPC, 7.61% for Intel x86-64, 7.61% for SPARC, 7.85% for Renesas/SuperH SH, 7.38% for Motorola MC68000, and one specimen for ARCompact. Because we sensed that ARM was most targeted by IoT malware through a telescope of the IoTPOT, we focused on specimens running on ARM in the experiments.

Specifically, from the specimens of ARM, we chose 5,198 specimens determined as "ELF 32-bit LSB exec-utable, ARM, EABI4 version 1 (SYSV)" by file command, and checked the malware name by Dr.Web [9], one of the most popular anti-malware software tools. Out of 5,198 specimens, Dr.Web identified 3,114 specimens as *Bashlite*, 919 as *Mirai*, 23 as *Tunami*, 21 as *Packed*, 13 as *Hajime*, 7 as *ProxyM*, 6 as *Remaiten*, 4 as *Trojan*, 2 as *DDoS*, and 1089 as *Unknown*. We then discarded unknown specimens, and categorized all specimens except for Bashlite and Mirai into *Others* category because they were comparatively much smaller families than Bashlite and Mirai. Finally, the *Others* category contained 76 specimens, and our dataset had 4,109 specimens that were divided into three categories: Bashlite, Mirai, and Others.

The average and the standard deviation of the file size of the 4,109 binaries were 57.75 KBytes and 65.35 KBytes, respectively, which affect the time elapsed for compression.

4.2 Experimental Setup

Implementation. We implemented our algorithm using the programming language R, in which xz command (version 5.1.0alpha) of Linux was used to compress malware binaries for computing NCDs. This xz adopted the Lempel-Ziv-Markov chain algorithm (LZMA) [17] as a compression algorithm.

As a benchmark for our algorithm, we used a conventional scheme: it first compressed every pair of 4,109 malware binaries to compute the NCDs between them, and then constructed a phylogenetic tree of malware with the neighbor-joining method described in Sect. 2.2, which is expressed as conv_scheme in this section. We also implemented conv_scheme using R and xz.

Evaluation Metrics. To measure how well compression attempts were reduced by our algorithm, we define RCR (Rate of Compression-attempt Reduction) as follows:

$$RCR = 100 - \frac{\text{\# of compression attempts by ours}}{\text{\# of compression attempts by conv\_scheme}} \times 100 \qquad (3)$$

where # of compression attempts by conv_scheme is $(N^2 + N)/2$ and N is the number of specimens that equals 4,109 in the experiments. The RCR decreases as the compression attempts are more reduced by our algorithm.

We also measured *runtime* and *approximation error* for our algorithm and conv_scheme. The *runtime* means the time measured from the start of compression attempts for computing the NCDs until the end of completing the construction of a phylogenetic tree of 4,109 specimens. The runtime values of our algorithm and conv_scheme were measured on Ubuntu 16.04 Linux running on a 2.6 GHz Intel-Xeon-Gold-6126 machine. The *approximation error* refers to the mean error between every NCD and a corresponding distance of a tree. It is defined as: $\Sigma_{ij}^N |d_{ij} - T_{ij}|/N^2$, where d and T denote a matrix of NCDs and a matrix of tree distances, respectively.

In addition, we measured how well our algorithm conducted clustering. As metrics for this measure, we calculated overall accuracy over the whole dataset as: *Overall Accuracy* = $\#TP/(\#TP + \#FP)$, and also calculated accuracy, precision, recall, and FPR (False Positive Rate) for each category of *Bashlite*, *Mirai*, and *Others* as: *Accuracy* = $\#TP/(\#TP + \#FP)$, *Precision* = $\#TP/(\#TP + \#FP)$, *Recall* = $\#TP/(\#TP + \#FN)$, and *FPR* = $\#FP/(\#FP + \#TN)$, where $\#TP$, $\#FP$, $\#TN$, and $\#FN$ denote the number of true positives, false positives, true negatives, and false negatives, respectively. At this time, the label of each cluster was determined by the greatest number of specimens contained in that cluster.

As a case study for understanding clustering results, suppose that 30 *Bashlite*, 30 *Mirai*, and no *Others* specimens are given and that they are divided into the following three clusters: the first contains 20 Bashlite and 10 Mirai specimens, and the second cluster contains six Bashlite and five Mirai specimens, and the last cluster contains four Bashlite and 15 Mirai specimens. In this case, the label of the first, second, and last clusters are determined as Bashlite, Bashlite, and Mirai, respectively. For Bashlite, $\#TP$, $\#FP$, $\#TN$, $\#FN$ equal 26, 15, 15, and 4, respectively. For Mirai, $\#TP$, $\#FP$, $\#TN$, $\#FN$ equal 15, 4, 26, and 15, respectively. The overall accuracy equals 0.68 (=(26 + 15)/60).

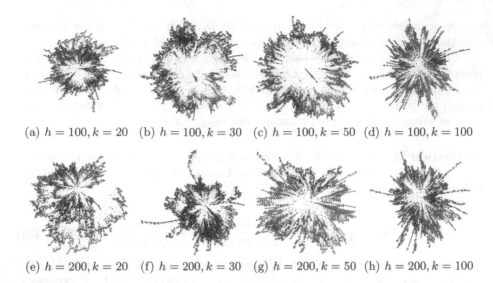

(a) $h = 100, k = 20$ (b) $h = 100, k = 30$ (c) $h = 100, k = 50$ (d) $h = 100, k = 100$

(e) $h = 200, k = 20$ (f) $h = 200, k = 30$ (g) $h = 200, k = 50$ (h) $h = 200, k = 100$

Fig. 3. Results of the phylogenetic tree for each parameter. (Color figure online)

Parameter Tuning. Recall that our algorithm has two parameters k and h, where the k denotes the number of specimens that are chosen at random to construct a primary phylogenetic tree in Fig. 2(a) and the h denotes the threshold representing the maximum size of temporal clusters in Fig. 2(d). For parameter tuning, we used every pair of k and h, taking k from $\{20, 30, 50, 100\}$ and h from $\{100, 200\}$ because these parameters should be determined with a grid search.

4.3   Evaluation Results

RCR and Runtime. Table 1 shows a breakdown of RCR and the runtime of our algorithm for each pair of parameters. Overall, the obtained RCR values confirm that the compression attempts were greatly reduced by our algorithm. In particular, 97.26% of $(N^2 + N)/2$ compression attempts were reduced at best when h and k were set to 100 and 20, respectively, where N equals 4,109.

The runtime of conv_scheme was 243.4 h. In contrast, that of our algorithm worked much faster than it overall. At best, with a h of 100 and a k of 20, it was 4.73 h, which means our algorithm reduced the runtime of covn_scheme by 98.06%. Even in the worst case, with a h of 200 and a k of 100, it was 10.85 h, which means our algorithm reduced the runtime of covn_scheme by 95.54%. At this time, the RCR was a good value of 93.35. This successful reduction could confirm that the key idea of our algorithm worked well, which is not to construct a phylogenetic tree all at once.

Approximation Error. The approximation error of conv_scheme was 0.16, and that of our algorithm is shown in Table 1 for each pair of h and k. Regarding the *ratio (Error/0.16)* in the table, the approximation error values of our

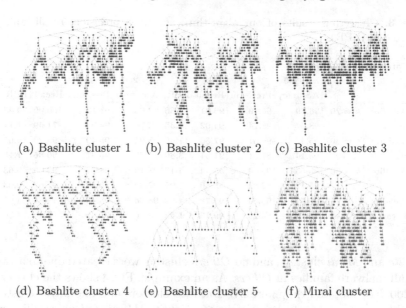

(a) Bashlite cluster 1   (b) Bashlite cluster 2   (c) Bashlite cluster 3

(d) Bashlite cluster 4   (e) Bashlite cluster 5   (f) Mirai cluster

Fig. 4. Clustering results for $h = 200, k = 100$

Table 2. Multiclass confusion matrix by Bashlite, Mirai, Others when $h = 100, k = 100$ and $h = 200, k = 100$.

$h = 100, k = 100$				$h = 200, k = 100$			
Predict	Actual			Predict	Actual		
	Bashlite	Mirai	Others		Bashlite	Mirai	Others
Bashlite	3107	8	38	Bashlite	3108	8	41
Mirai	7	911	38	Mirai	6	911	35
Others	0	0	0	Others	0	0	0

algorithm were comparatively larger than conv_scheme, although the approximation error decreased as k increased. This error increase seems to be caused by our algorithm in exchange for greatly reducing compression attempts. However, how the approximation error could affect clustering was unknown.

Clustering. Figure 3 shows the phylogenetic tree of 4,109 specimens constructed by our algorithm for each parameter pair of h and k. The red and green points denote *Bashlite* and *Mirai* specimens, respectively, and the other color points denote the specimens of *Others*. Considering each phylogenetic tree, the specimens were grouped well, and thus we simply cut the tree at a depth of 2 from the root for clustering. At this time, the specimens were divided into

Table 3. Clustering results of our algorithm: accuracy, precision, recall, and false positive rate (FPR).

Category	k	h							
		$h = 100$				$h = 200$			
		Accuracy	Precision	Recall	FPR	Accuracy	Precision	Recall	FPR
Bashlite	$k = 20$	96.79	96.10	99.81	12.66	92.63	91.13	100.00	30.45
Mirai		98.37	98.74	94.02	0.35	92.70	94.94	71.49	1.11
Bashlite	$k = 30$	95.47	96.51	97.56	11.06	95.91	95.49	99.29	14.67
Mirai		95.14	87.51	91.51	3.80	97.03	95.87	90.86	1.15
Bashlite	$k = 50$	95.55	98.64	95.44	4.12	98.10	98.22	99.29	5.63
Mirai		95.12	82.85	98.80	5.95	97.89	93.34	97.61	2.03
Bashlite	$k = 100$	98.71	98.54	99.78	4.62	98.66	98.45	99.81	4.92
Mirai		98.70	95.29	99.13	1.43	98.80	95.69	99.13	1.30

Bashlite and *Mirai* clusters, and no *Others* clusters were created due to a variety of small malware families in *Others*. As an example, Fig. 4 shows the clusters for $h = 200, k = 100$, and they were five *Bashlite* clusters and one *Mirai* cluster.

Table 2 shows a confusion matrix of *Bashlite, Mirai, Others* families when $(h, k) = (100, 100)$ and $(h, k) = (200, 100)$. As is shown in Table 1 the overall accuracy was 97.79% when $(h, k) = (100, 100)$, which was calculated as $(3107 + 911 + 0)/4109 * 100 = 97.79\%$. Besides, when $(h, k) = (200, 100)$, the overall accuracy was 97.81%, which was calculated as $(3108 + 911 + 0)/4109 * 100$. For any pairs of parameters, the overall accuracy became better as h and k increased, whereas the RCR values decreased as h and k increased.

Table 3 shows the accuracy, precision, recall, and false positive rate (FPR) of *Bashlite* and *Mirai*, while the results of *Others* cluster are excluded because no *Others* clusters were created. Any values improve as h and k also increases. In particular, FPR of *Bashlite* was comparatively improved to 4.62 with $(h, k) = (100, 100)$, whereas it was 12.66 with $(h, k) = (100, 20)$.

Evaluation Summary. We conclude that the best result of our algorithm was obtained at $(h, k) = (200, 100)$, in which a RCR, a runtime reduction, and the overall accuracy were 93.35%, 95.54%, and 97.81%, respectively. And accuracy values for *Bashlite* and *Mirai* families were 98.66% and 98.80%, respectively.

To emphasize the contribution of our algorithm, we give the following case study. If 30,000 specimens were given, `conv_scheme` could spend 12,971 h (540 days) , which is calculated as $((30000^2 + 30000)/2)/((4109^2 + 4109)/2) \times 243.4$ h (24 days). In contrast, our algorithm could achieve it for 578 h, based on the runtime reduction of 95.54% at $(h, k) = (200, 100)$. This can be very efficient in practice with application to clustering IoT malware.

5   Conclusion

In this paper, we proposed a fast algorithm to construct a phylogenetic tree for clustering. The RCR and runtime were reduced by 93.35% and 95.54% from those of the conventional scheme, while achieving a good overall accuracy of 97.81% for clustering. By using our algorithm, malware analysts can efficiently divide malware specimens into malware families, which leads to efficient malware analysis. In our future work, we plan to conduct additional experiments using malware specimens running on various CPU architectures. We also plan to improve our algorithm as follows. Even after a tree of given specimens has been constructed, an improved algorithm can dynamically insert newly-given specimens into that tree online. This functionality will enable our algorithm to expand a tree every time malware specimens are captured, which is more practical.

Acknowledgment. The authors wish to thank the IoTPOT team from Yokohama National University for providing the dataset. This research was partially supported by JSPS KAKENHI Grant Number 18H03291.

References

1. Malwr. https://malwr.com/
2. Virustotal. https://www.virustotal.com/
3. Antonakakis, M., et al.: Understanding the Mirai botnet. In: Proceedings of the 26th USENIX Conference on Security Symposium, SEC 2017, pp. 1093–1110. USENIX Association, Berkeley (2017)
4. Bailey, M., Oberheide, J., Andersen, J., Mao, Z.M., Jahanian, F., Nazario, J.: Automated classification and analysis of internet malware. In: Kruegel, C., Lippmann, R., Clark, A. (eds.) RAID 2007. LNCS, vol. 4637, pp. 178–197. Springer, Heidelberg (2007). https://doi.org/10.1007/978-3-540-74320-0_10
5. Bayer, U., Comparetti, P.M., Hlauschek, C., Krügel, C., Kirda, E.: Scalable, behavior-based malware clustering. In: Proceedings of the Network and Distributed System Security Symposium, NDSS 2009, San Diego, pp. 8–11 (2009)
6. Black Lotus Labs: Attack of things! https://www.netformation.com/our-pov/attack-of-things-2/
7. Cebrian, M., Alfonseca, M., Ortega, A.: The normalized compression distance is resistant to noise. IEEE Trans. Inf. Theory **53**(5), 1895–1900 (2007)
8. Cilibrasi, R., Vitanyi, P.M.B.: Clustering by compression. IEEE Trans. Inf. Theory **51**(4), 1523–1545 (2005)
9. Doctor Web: Dr.Web. https://www.drweb.com
10. Elias, I., Lagergren, J.: Fast neighbor joining. In: Caires, L., Italiano, G.F., Monteiro, L., Palamidessi, C., Yung, M. (eds.) ICALP 2005. LNCS, vol. 3580, pp. 1263–1274. Springer, Heidelberg (2005). https://doi.org/10.1007/11523468_102
11. Karim, M.E., Walenstein, A., Lakhotia, A., Parida, L.: Malware phylogeny generation using permutations of code. J. Comput. Virol. **1**(1–2), 13–23 (2005)
12. Langfelder, P., Zhang, B., Horvath, S.: Defining clusters from a hierarchical cluster tree: the dynamic tree cut package for R. Bioinformatics **24**(5), 719–720 (2007)
13. Li, M., Chen, X., Li, X., Ma, B., Vitányi, P.M.B.: The similarity metric. IEEE Trans. Inf. Theory **50**(12), 3250–3264 (2004)
14. Pa, Y.M.P., Suzuki, S., Yoshioka, K., Matsumoto, T., Kasama, T., Rossow, C.: IoTPOT: analysing the rise of IoT compromises. In: 9th USENIX Workshop on Offensive Technologies, WOOT 2015. USENIX Association, Washington, D.C. (2015)
15. Price, M.N., Dehal, P.S., Arkin, A.P.: Fasttree 2 - approximately maximum-likelihood trees for large alignments. PLOS ONE **5**(3), 1–10 (2010)

16. Saitou, N., Nei, M.: The neighbor-joining method: a new method for reconstructing phylogenetic trees. Mol. Biol. Evol. **4**(4), 406–425 (1987)
17. Salomon, D.: Data Compression - The Complete Reference, 4th edn. Springer, London (2007). https://doi.org/10.1007/978-1-84628-603-2
18. Simonsen, M., Mailund, T., Pedersen, C.N.S.: Rapid neighbour-joining. In: Crandall, K.A., Lagergren, J. (eds.) WABI 2008. LNCS, vol. 5251, pp. 113–122. Springer, Heidelberg (2008). https://doi.org/10.1007/978-3-540-87361-7_10
19. Yone, T.: Phylogenetic tree estimation for large-scale malware datasets. Master's thesis. Kyushu University, Japan (2016). (in Japanese)

Author Index

Printed in the United States
By Bookmasters